T0185760

Lecture Notes in Computer Science 12172

More information about this series at http://www.springer.com/series/7410

Daniele Micciancio · Thomas Ristenpart (Eds.)

Advances in Cryptology – CRYPTO 2020

40th Annual International Cryptology Conference, CRYPTO 2020
Santa Barbara, CA, USA, August 17–21, 2020
Proceedings, Part III

 Springer

Editors
Daniele Micciancio 🆔
UC San Diego
La Jolla, CA, USA

Thomas Ristenpart 🆔
Cornell Tech
New York, NY, USA

ISSN 0302-9743   ISSN 1611-3349   (electronic)
Lecture Notes in Computer Science
ISBN 978-3-030-56876-4   ISBN 978-3-030-56877-1   (eBook)
https://doi.org/10.1007/978-3-030-56877-1

LNCS Sublibrary: SL4 – Security and Cryptology

This Springer imprint is published by the registered company Springer Nature Switzerland AG
The registered company address is: Gewerbestrasse 11, 6330 Cham, Switzerland

Preface

The 40th International Cryptology Conference (Crypto 2020), sponsored by the International Association of Cryptologic Research (IACR), was exceptional in many ways. The COVID-19 pandemic meant that for the first time in the conference's 40-year history, Crypto was not held at the University of California, Santa Barbara. Safety mandated that we shift to an online-only virtual conference.

Crypto 2020 received 371 submissions. Review occurred during what, for many countries, was the height thus far of pandemic spread and lockdowns. We thank the 54 person Program Committee (PC) and the 286 external reviewers for their efforts to ensure that, in the face of challenging work environments, illness, and death, we nevertheless were able to perform a standard double-blind review process in which papers received multiple independent reviews, authors were allowed a rebuttal, and papers were subsequently further reviewed and discussed. The two program chairs were not allowed to submit a paper, and PC members were limited to two submissions each. The PC ultimately selected 85 papers for acceptance, a record number for Crypto.

The PC selected four papers to receive recognition via awards, via a voting-based process that took into account conflicts of interest (including for the program chairs). Three papers were selected to receive a Best Paper award and were invited to the Journal of Cryptology: "Improved Differential-Linear Attacks with Applications to ARX Ciphers" by Christof Beierle, Gregor Leander, and Yosuke Todo; "Breaking the Decisional Diffie-Hellman Problem for Class Group Actions using Genus Theory" by Wouter Castryck, Jana Sotáková, and Frederik Vercauteren; and "Chosen Ciphertext Security from Injective Trapdoor Functions" by Susan Hohenberger, Venkata Koppula, and Brent Waters. One paper was selected to receive the Best Paper by Early Career Researchers award: "Handling Adaptive Compromise for Practical Encryption Schemes" by Joseph Jaeger and Nirvan Tyagi.

In addition to the regular program, Crypto 2020 included the IACR Distinguished Lecture by Silvio Micali on "Our Models and Us" and an invited talk by Seny Kamara on "Crypto for the People". Crypto 2020 carried forward the long-standing tradition of having a rump session, this year organized in a virtual format by Antigoni Polychroniadou, Bertram Poettering, and Martijn Stam.

The chairs would also like to thank the many people whose hard work helped ensure Crypto 2020 was a success:

- Leonid Reyzin (Boston University) – Crypto 2020 general chair.
- Sophia Yakoubov for helping with general chair duties, and Muthuramakrishnan Venkitasubramaniam, Tal Rabin, and Fabrice Benhamouda for providing valuable advice to the general chair.
- Carmit Hazay (Bar Ilan University) – Crypto 2020 workshop chair.
- Antigoni Polychroniadou, Bertram Poettering, and Martijn Stam – Crypto 2020 rump session chairs.

- Chris Peikert for his role in overseeing reviews and the Best Paper by Early Career Researchers award selection for which the program chairs were conflicted.
- Kevin McCurley and Christian Cachin for their critical assistance in setting up and managing a (new for Crypto) paper submission and review system.
- Kevin McCurley, Kay McKelly, and members of the IACR's emergency pandemic team for their work in designing and running the virtual format.
- Whitney Morris and Eriko Macdonald from UCSB event services for their help navigating the COVID-19 shutdown logistics.
- Anna Kramer and her colleagues at Springer.

July 2020

Daniele Micciancio
Thomas Ristenpart

Organization

General Chair

Leonid Reyzin   Boston University, USA

Program Committee Chairs

Daniele Micciancio   UC San Diego, USA
Thomas Ristenpart   Cornell Tech, USA

Program Committee

Adi Akavia   University of Haifa, Israel
Martin Albrecht   Royal Holloway, University of London, UK
Roberto Avanzi   ARM, Germany
Lejla Batina   Radboud University, The Netherlands
Jeremiah Blocki   Purdue University, USA
David Cash   University of Chicago, USA
Melissa Chase   Microsoft Research, USA
Hao Chen   Microsoft Research, USA
Ilaria Chillotti   KU Leuven, Zama, Belgium
Henry Corrigan-Gibbs   EPFL, Switzerland, and MIT CSAIL, USA
Craig Costello   Microsoft Research, USA
Joan Daemen   Radboud University, The Netherlands
Thomas Eisenbarth   University of Lübeck, Germany
Pooya Farshim   University of York, UK
Sanjam Garg   UC Berkeley, USA
Daniel Genkin   University of Michigan, USA
Steven Goldfeder   Cornell Tech, USA
Shay Gueron   University of Haifa, Israel, and AWS, USA
Felix Günther   ETH Zurich, Switzerland
Tetsu Iwata   Nagoya University, Japan
Tibor Jager   Bergische Universitaet, Germany
Antoine Joux   CISPA – Helmholtz Center for Information Security,
                                   Germany
Jonathan Katz   George Mason Univeristy, USA
Eike Kiltz   Ruhr University Bochum, Germany
Elena Kirshanova   I.Kant Baltic Federal University, Russia
Venkata Koppula   Weizmann Institute of Science, Isarel
Anna Lysyanskaya   Brown University, USA
Vadim Lyubashevsky   IBM Research Zurich, Switzerland
Mohammad Mahmoody   University of Virginia, USA

Giulio Malavolta	Carnegie Mellon University and UC Berkeley, USA
Florian Mendel	Infineon Technologies, Germany
María Naya-Plasencia	Inria, France
Adam O'Neill	University of Massachusetts, USA
Olya Ohrimenko	The University of Melbourne, Australia
Claudio Orlandi	Aarhus University, Denmark
Elisabeth Oswald	University of Klagenfurt, Austria
Chris Peikert	University of Michigan, USA
Bertram Poettering	IBM Research Zurich, Switzerland
Antigoni Polychroniadou	JP Morgan AI Research, USA
Ananth Raghunathan	Google, USA
Mariana Raykova	Google, USA
Christian Rechberger	TU Graz, Austria
Alon Rosen	IDC, Israel
Mike Rosulek	Oregon State University, USA
Alessandra Scafuro	NC State University, USA
Dominique Schroeder	Florida Atlantic University, USA
Thomas Shrimpton	University of Florida, USA
Fang Song	Texas A&M University, USA
Marc Stevens	CWI Amsterdam, The Netherlands
Dominique Unruh	University of Tartu, Estonia
Michael Walter	IST, Austria
David Wu	University of Virginia, USA

Additional Reviewers

Masayuki Abe	Fabrice Benhamouda
Shweta Agrawal	Sebastian Berndt
Shashank Agrawal	Ward Beullens
Shweta Agrawal	Ritam Bhaumik
Gorjan Alagic	Nina Bindel
Navid Alamati	Alex Block
Greg Alpar	Xavier Bonnetain
Joel Alwen	Charlotte Bonte
Elena Andreeva	Carl Bootland
Gilad Asharov	Jonathan Bootle
Thomas Attema	Raphael Bost
Saikrishna Badrinarayanan	Christina Boura
Shi Bai	Elette Boyle
Foteini Baldimtsi	Zvika Brakerski
Marshall Ball	Benedikt Bünz
James Bartusek	Matteo Campanelli
Carsten Baum	Anne Canteaut
Asli Bay	André Chailloux
Mihir Bellare	Suvradip Chakraborty

Yilei Chen
Jie Chen
Nai-Hui Chia
Arka Rai Choudhuri
Kai-Min Chung
Michele Ciampi
Carlos Cid
Michael Clear
Ran Cohen
Kelong Cong
Aisling Connolly
Sandro Coretti
Daniele Cozzo
Tingting Cui
Benjamin Curtis
Jan Czajkowski
Dana Dachman-Soled
Alex Davidson
Leo De Castro
Luca De Feo
Thomas Debris
Jean Paul Degabriele
Cyprien Delpech de Saint Guilhem
Patrick Derbez
Apoorvaa Deshpande
Benjamin Diamond
Christoph Dobraunig
Nico Doettling
Benjamin Dowling
Yfke Dulek
Stefan Dziembowski
Christoph Egger
Maria Eichlseder
Daniel Escudero
Saba Eskandarian
Serge Fehr
Rex Fernando
Dario Fiore
Ben Fisch
Wieland Fischer
Nils Fleischhacker
Daniele Friolo
Georg Fuchsbauer
Tommaso Gagliardoni
Juan Garay
Romain Gay

Nicholas Genise
Rosario Gennaro
Marios Georgiou
Riddhi Ghosal
Satrajit Ghosh
Esha Ghosh
Koustabh Ghosh
Irene Giacomelli
Andras Gilyen
S. Dov Gordon
Rishab Goyal
Lorenzo Grassi
Matthew Green
Hannes Gross
Aldo Gunsing
Tim Güneysu
Mohammad Hajiabadi
Shai Halevi
Koki Hamada
Dominik Hartmann
Eduard Hauck
Carmit Hazay
Alexander Helm
Lukas Helminger
Julia Hesse
Dennis Hofheinz
Alex Hoover
Akinori Hosoyamada
Kathrin Hövelmanns
Andreas Hülsing
Ilia Iliashenko
Gorka Irazoqui
Joseph Jaeger
Eli Jaffe
Abhishek Jain
Aayush Jain
Samuel Jaques
Stanislaw Jarecki
Zhengfeng Ji
Zhengzhong Jin
Saqib Kakvi
Daniel Kales
Chethan Kamath
Akinori Kawachi
Mahimna Kelkar
Hamidreza Khoshakhlagh

Dakshita Khurana
Sam Kim
Michael Kim
Susumu Kiyoshima
Karen Klein
Dmitry Kogan
Markulf Kohlweiss
Ilan Komargodski
Daniel Kuijsters
Mukul Kulkarni
Ashutosh Kumar
Stefan Kölbl
Thijs Laarhoven
Russell W. F. Lai
Kim Laine
Virginie Lallemand
Changmin Lee
Tancrede Lepoint
Antonin Leroux
Gaëtan Leurent
Kevin Lewi
Baiyu Li
Xin Li
Xiao Liang
Feng-Hao Liu
Alex Lombardi
Julian Loss
Ji Luo
Fermi Ma
Bernardo Magri
Urmila Mahadev
Christian Majenz
Eleftheria Makri
Nathan Manohar
Sai Krishna Deepak Maram
Daniel Masny
Eleanor McMurtry
Sarah Meiklejohn
Bart Mennink
Peihan Miao
Tarik Moataz
Esfandiar Mohammadi
Hart Montgomery
Tal Moran
Andrew Morgan
Fabrice Mouhartem

Pratyay Mukherjee
Michael Naehrig
Samuel Neves
Ruth Francis Ng
Ngoc Khanh Nguyen
Valeria Nikolaenko
Ryo Nishimaki
Satoshi Obana
Sabine Oechsner
Jiaxin Pan
Omer Paneth
Lorenz Panny
Sunoo Park
Alain Passelègue
Valerio Pastro
Jacques Patarin
Kenneth Paterson
Alice Pellet–Mary
Zack Pepin
Ludovic Perret
Léo Perrin
Peter Pessl
Jeroen Pijnenburg
Benny Pinkas
Rachel Player
Oxana Poburinnaya
Eamonn Postlethwaite
Robert Primas
Willy Quach
Rahul Rachuri
Ahmadreza Rahimi
Divya Ravi
Ling Ren
Joost Renes
M. Sadegh Riazi
João L. Ribeiro
Silas Richelson
Doreen Riepel
Dragos Rotaru
Ron Rothblum
Adeline Roux-Langlois
Arnab Roy
Carla Ràfols
Paul Rösler
Simona Samardjiska
Yu Sasaki

Contents – Part III

Delay Functions

Zero Knowledge

Multi-party Computation

Two-Sided Malicious Security for Private Intersection-Sum with Cardinality

Peihan Miao[2($\boxtimes$)], Sarvar Patel[1], Mariana Raykova[1], Karn Seth[1($\boxtimes$)], and Moti Yung[1]

[1] Google LLC, Mountain View, USA
sarvar@google.com, marianar@google.com,
karn@google.com, moti@google.com
[2] Visa Research, Palo Alto, USA
pemiao@visa.com

Abstract. Private intersection-sum with cardinality allows two parties, where each party holds a private set and one of the parties additionally holds a private integer value associated with each element in her set, to jointly compute the cardinality of the intersection of the two sets as well as the sum of the associated integer values for all the elements in the intersection, and nothing beyond that.

We present a new construction for private intersection sum with cardinality that provides malicious security with abort and guarantees that both parties receive the output upon successful completion of the protocol. A central building block for our constructions is a primitive called *shuffled distributed oblivious PRF (DOPRF)*, which is a PRF that offers oblivious evaluation using a secret key shared between two parties, and in addition to this allows obliviously permuting the PRF outputs of several parallel oblivious evaluations. We present the first construction for shuffled DOPRF with malicious security. We further present several new sigma proof protocols for relations across Pedersen commitments, ElGamal encryptions, and Camenisch-Shoup encryptions that we use in our main construction, for which we develop new batching techniques to reduce communication.

We implement and evaluate the efficiency of our protocol and show that we can achieve communication cost that is only $4-5\times$ greater than the most efficient semi-honest protocol. When measuring monetary cost of executing the protocol in the cloud, our protocol is $25\times$ more expensive than the semi-honest protocol. Our construction also allows for different parameter regimes that enable trade-offs between communication and computation.

1 Introduction

Private Set Intersection. A private set intersection (PSI) protocol enables two parties, each with a private input set, to compute the intersection of the two sets while revealing nothing more than the intersection itself. Despite the

---

P. Miao—Part of work done while interning at Google LLC.

D. Micciancio and T. Ristenpart (Eds.): CRYPTO 2020, LNCS 12172, pp. 3–33, 2020.
https://doi.org/10.1007/978-3-030-56877-1_1

simplicity of the functionality, PSI has found many applications in privacy-preserving location sharing [50], testing of fully sequenced human genomes [3], collaborative botnet detection [48], data mining [2], social networks [45,49], online gaming [10], measuring ads conversion rates [39], and so on. Due to its importance and wide applications, PSI has been extensively studied in a long sequence of works [17,21,22,24,25,27,31,37,38,42,44,54,56,58–62].

Enhanced Functionality. While the PSI functionality models successfully the confidentiality requirements in several application scenarios, there are information-sharing settings where revealing the whole intersection is unacceptable and instead a more fine-grained privacy preserving computation is needed. In particular different aggregated computations over the intersection set model a wide range of applications with restricted privacy leakage. PSI-cardinality is one example of such an aggregated functionality that limits the two parties to learning only the *cardinality* (or size) of the intersection [1,20,31,38,41,51,63].

The private intersection-sum functionality introduced by Ion et al. [39] is another example of an aggregate functionality where one of the input sets has integer values associated with the elements in the set and the two parties compute the cardinality of the intersection as well as the aggregate of the integer values associated with the intersection set. This primitive models many applications in practice. These include settings where one party holds private statistics about a set of people and another party has information about the membership of the people in a particular group, and the two parties want to compute an aggregate of the statistics over the members of the set. A particular instantiation of this scenario was consider by Nagu et al. [49] in the context of social networks where a user has knowledge of weights associated with each of her friends and wants to compute the total (or average) weight of the friends that she has in common with another user. In measuring ads conversion rates [39], an advertiser may know the purchase amount for every customer, and the advertiser and an ads publisher can jointly compute the total number and total purchase amount of the customers who have seen the ads from the publisher and end up buying the product.

Existing solutions for private intersection-sum [39] provide security only in the semi-honest case where each party is assumed to follow the protocol honestly. While this level of security might be sufficient in settings where the interacting parties have external incentives (e.g. legal agreements) to follow the protocol, this level of security is not sufficient for a broad set of scenarios where the adversary could deviate arbitrarily from the protocol. In the setting of malicious security we have protocols that achieve only the PSI functionality, however, constructions with competitive efficiency [30,60,61] have a major shortcoming that they support only one-sided output, where in many settings both parties need to obtains the output of the computation. Upgrading these protocols to achieve two-sided output in a non-trivial task. For example, as explained by Rindal et al. [61], the output recipient from the one-sided protocol will need to prove that it executed the last step of the protocol honestly. We do not have tailored constructions for this task and applying generic approaches comes with a high price.

In this work we consider the problem of private intersection sum with cardinality in the malicious setting which provides protection against such adversaries. We require that either both parties receive the output of the computation or they abort. Our focus is on optimizing the communication efficiency of the protocol since as discussed in the work of Ion et al. [39] this is the most significant cost in practice.

Our Contributions. We present a new protocol for private intersection-sum with cardinality which achieves malicious security with abort, which guarantees that both parties receive the intersection sum if the protocol does not abort. Our protocol provides two-sided output, which is already an improvement even if we restrict our attention only to the PSI functionality since existing malicious PSI protocols [30,60,61] are restricted to a single output recipient.

Our construction is the first construction for private intersection-sum with cardinality with malicious security to achieve linear communication and computation overhead in the size n of the sets. This improves significantly over the only other existing approach [37] that can be used to solve this problem, which uses existing generic MPC techniques with malicious security, and as we discuss in the related work, incurs at least a factor of $\lambda \log n$ multiplicative overhead assuming a security parameter λ. As can be seen in Table 6, these generic techniques incur 250× higher communication and 65× higher monetary cost than our protocol on inputs of size 2^{20}.

Our construction can also be instantiated such that the overhead required to achieve malicious security over the semi-honest version requires sublinear communication $O(\sqrt{n})$ with computation $O(n \log n)$, which would be advantageous in setting where communication is much more expensive that computation.

Our construction adopts the general approach from the work of Ion et al. [39], which leverages an oblivious pseudorandom function (PRF) with a shared key, which can be evaluated in a distributed way to permute and map the input set values to a pseudorandom space that enables the computation of the intersection, and homomorphic encryption, which allows to pair the associated values during the PRF evaluation and then evaluate the intersection sum. In order to upgrade this general approach to malicious security we develop several new techniques, which can be of independent interest.

New Distributed OPRF. A central building block for our solution is a distributed oblivious PRF with malicious security. In order to achieve distributed oblivious evaluation with malicious security we leverage a PRF construction due to Dodis and Yampolskiy [23], for which we can construct proofs for honest evaluation with respect to a committed PRF key. An issue that we need to deal with is the fact that this PRF was proven secure only for polynomial domains. To circumvent this problem we introduce a weaker selective security notion for the PRF, which is satisfied by the construction with exponential domain, and we show that this property suffices for our PSI-sum with cardinality protocol.

Verifiable Parameter Generation. We construct a distributed PRF evaluation protocol, which uses several times evaluations on committed and encrypted values. Thus, in order to achieve malicious security for this protocol we use proofs for relations among encrypted and committed values, which crucially rely on the assumption that the parameters for these schemes were generated honestly. Since we do not want to assume any trusted setup, we present protocols for verifiable generation of parameters for Pedersen commitments, Camenish-Shoup (CS) and ElGamal encryption with shared key.

Range Proofs with Slack. The final extension to the distributed OPRF is to enable a shuffle of the oblivious evaluations on multiple inputs that are executed in parallel, which hides the mapping to the original inputs and is required in order to hide what elements are in the intersection. In order to enable that we develop a proof protocol for shuffle decryption of Camenisch-Shoup encryptions. We leverage the Bayer-Groth shuffle proof [5], which allows to prove that two sets of cipheretexts encrypt the same set of plaintexts up to a permutation. In order to enable proving knowledge of exponents in this step, the prover needs to switch from Camenisch-Shoup encryption to ElGamal encryption, which have different domains. We introduce a proof technique for consistency of values encrypted under CS and ElGamal encryptions that uses range proofs with a slack.

Our construction leverages heavily sigma proof protocols [18] in several places including the proofs for evaluation of the DOPRF, the re-encryption step for shuffling, the re-randomization for intersection-sum.

Batching for Range Proofs. We introduce new batching techniques for range proofs based on sigma protocols. While existing efficient batch proofs that do not work with the bit level representation of the values operate in a group of unknown order [9,13], batching techniques for sigma protocols have been constructed only in the case of a known order group [33]. We show how to batch range proof over groups of unknown order while avoiding a large blowup in the slack of the range proof which is incurred if we adapt directly the batching approach for known group order to hidden order by providing sufficient space to avoid the need for modulus reduction.

Batching Proofs for CS and ElGamal Encryptions. We also use batching techniques for commitments and develop batching approaches for Camenisch-Shoup encryptions. We leverage multi-exponentiation arguments from the work of Bayer and Groth [5] in a new way to batch proofs for relations among ElGamal ciphertexts for which prover does not know the encryption randomness. Since we need an additively homomorphic encryption scheme that has a provable threshold decryption, we use exponential ElGamal to encrypt associated values. This means that our construction supports evaluations for which the final intersection-sum is within a polynomial domain where discrete log can be computed for decryption.

Implementation and Evaluation. We implemented our malicious secure private intersection-sum protocol and evaluated its performance on large-scale datasets. Our experiments show that, when we set parameters to minimize communication overhead, our protocol performs with communication cost approximately $4\times$ greater than the most communication-efficient semi-honest protocol based on DDH. A less aggressive choice of parameters leads to about $7\times$ expansion over the semi-honest DDH-based protocol, with a much improved computational efficiency. We also estimate the monetary cost of running our protocols using the pricing for Google Cloud and obtain that executing our PSI-Sum protocols on inputs of size 2^{20} costs 13 cents. The monetary cost is about $25\times$ more than that of the semihonest protocol, which we believe is a reasonable cost for the much stronger security guarantees. We present our experimental measurements in Sect. 6. Our costs give a large improvement in monetary cost over existing generic approaches for private intersection sum with cardinality. Our monetary costs are also within a factor of 2 of the most efficient protocols for Malicious PSI [61], which we note only provide one-sided output and are not compatible with computing functions on the intersection.

Related Work. Before presenting the technical overview of our construction, we overview existing PSI solutions in the malicious setting [11,15,17,21,30,35, 36,40,41,60,61] and discuss the challenges in extending the approaches from these works to the private intersection-sum problem. We restrict our discussion to constructions that provide linear communication complexity as our major goal is communication efficiency.

The work of De Cristofaro et al. [21] presents a PSI protocol, where only one party (P_2) learns the PSI output and nothing is revealed to the other party (P_1). Our goal is to obtain a protocol where both parties receive the output, and next we explain the challenges for achieving this functionality here. At a high level the protocol works as follows. First, the two parties jointly evaluate an oblivious pseudorandom function (OPRF) on every element of P_2 where P_1 holds the OPRF key k and only P_2 obtains the OPRF values. Second, P_1 computes the OPRF values on its own elements using the key k and sends to P_2. Finally, P_2 computes the intersection of the OPRF values and the corresponding set intersection. The protocol used an OPRF defined as $F_k(x) = H_2(x||H_1(x)||H_1(x)^k)$, where $H_1(\cdot), H_2(\cdot)$ are hash functions modeled as random oracles [7]. In the OPRF protocol, P_2 learns $H_1(x)^k$ without revealing any information about x to P_1, and finally computes $H_2(x||H_1(x)||H_1(x)^k)$. Since we want both parties to learn the PSI output, one natural idea is to let P_2 send back its OPRF values to P_1, but P_2 has to prove that $H_2(\cdot)$ is computed correctly on desired inputs without revealing any information about x, which is a challenge. Another idea is to run the protocol twice with alternative roles, where the parties have to prove input consistency during the two executions. In other words, P_1 should prove in zero knowledge that its inputs to $F_k(\cdot)$ in the first execution are consistent with its inputs to the OPRF in the second execution, which is also challenging. More importantly, it is hard to extend this protocol to PSI-cardinality or private intersection-sum. In the last step of their OPRF protocol, P_2 computes H_2 on $x||H_1(x)||H_1(x)^k$ for each of its element x. It is crucial that P_2 knows the inputs to H_2 to compute the OPRF value. Therefore, the elements in the intersection must be known to P_2, making it hard to extend the protocol to even PSI-cardinality.

The PSI protocol of Jarecki and Liu [40] is also based on an OPRF protocol similarly as above, but the parties can prove consistency of their inputs to the OPRF with previously committed values. Therefore, the two parties can first commit to their inputs and then run the above protocol in both directions so that both parties learn the PSI output. However, the protocol has some limitations. First, their security proof requires the domain of the elements to be restricted to polynomial in the security parameter. Besides, the protocol requires a Common Reference String (CRS), where the CRS includes a safe RSA modulus that must be generated by a trusted third party, which is something we would like to avoid. To extend this protocol to PSI-cardinality, the receiver (P_2) of the OPRF protocol should learn the OPRF values without learning the correspondence between its elements $\{x\}_{x \in X}$ and OPRF values $\{F_k(x)\}_{x \in X}$, which requires shuffling techniques that we develop in this work. More ingredients and techniques are needed for extending the protocol to private intersection-sum as well as removing the above restrictions.

The idea in the protocol of Freedman et al. [30] to achieve malicious security is to require one party (P_1) to redo the other party's (P_2's) computation on the elements in the intersection and verify consistency. This is achieved as follows: P_1 generates a polynomial $Q(\cdot)$ of degree m, with roots set to the m elements of P_1's set, and sends the homomorphically encrypted coefficients of $Q(\cdot)$ to P_2. Then for each element x in P_2's set, P_2 replies with an encryption of $r \cdot Q(x) + s$ for random r and s. Importantly, the randomness used in this computation is taken from $H(s)$ where $H(\cdot)$ is a hash function modeled as a random oracle. If x is in the intersection, then P_1 can learn s and verify P_2's computation on x; otherwise nothing about x is revealed to P_1. This protocol crucially needs P_1 to learn the elements in the intersection, therefore extending the protocol to even PSI-cardinality seems to require innovative ideas. Moreover, the techniques of hashing into bins are leveraged in the protocol for achieving linear computational complexity. Computing PSI for each bin is sufficient for the PSI problem, however revealing intersection-cardinality or intersection-sum for each bin compromises security in the problem of PSI-cardinality or private intersection-sum.

Another option for constructing a private intersection-sum protocol with malicious security is to apply directly malicious two-party computation protocols to our functionality. Such protocols use the circuit representation of the evaluated functionality. The most efficient way to compute the intersection of two sets of size $O(n)$ uses oblivious sorting which reduces the number of needed comparisons from $O(n^2)$ to $O(n \log n)$. In our construction, in contrast, we aim for linear dependence on the number of inputs. Further, circuit solutions are bound to incur additional security factor multiplicative overhead since they need to operate with the bit-level representation of the set values. In the case of garbled circuit-based solutions this is inherent in the constructions, and in the case of solutions using arithmetic circuits the need for using the bit representation comes from the fact that we will be computing comparisons over these values and the most efficient way to do this is using the binary representation of the values. The recent circuit-based PSI protocols [16,28,56,57] only provide security in the semi-honest setting and it is nontrivial to extend them to the malicious setting due to their use of specific primitives such as Cuckoo hashing. Moreover, their protocols require super-linear communication. The work of

Pinkas et al. [57] presents a semi-honest circuit-based PSI construction that achieves linear communication, however, this construction achieves only linear number of comparison in the circuit by using oblivious programmable PRF techniques [43] and Cuckoo hashing [52]. Generalizing these techniques to the malicious setting presents many challenges. Our construction presents an approach to obtain oblivious PRF evaluation in the malicious setting.

2   Technical Overview

In this section we give a technical overview of our malicious secure private intersection-sum protocol. Our starting point is the semi-honest private intersection-sum protocol [39]. We identify the technical challenges to obtain malicious security from the semi-honest version and then present our approach to addressing them.

Semi-honest Private Intersection-Sum. The semi-honest protocol of Ion et al. [39] leverages a cryptographic primitive called distributed oblivious pseudo-random function (DOPRF), which enables the following functionality. The key k of a DOPRF is shared between two parties, where each party can generate independently their share. The DOPRF has an oblivious evaluation functionality, which is a 2-party computation protocol, which the two parties jointly evaluate the PRF F, under key k, on an input x, held by one of the parties who receives the PRF output $F_k(x)$ and nothing more is revealed to either party.

The DOPRF functionality suffices to construct a PSI protocol as follows. First, the two parties generate independently key shares of the DOPRF key. Then, they use the oblivious evaluation protocol to evaluate the DOPRF on each of P_1's input elements x_i, from which P_2 learns $F_k(x_i)$ and then sends it back to P_1. Similarly, they evaluate the DOPRF on P_2's input elements y_j to obtain $F_k(y_j)$. Computing the intersection of the resulting two sets of PRF values enables both parties to compute the PSI since each party has the mapping from the intersecting PRF values to their corresponding input elements.

The above PSI protocol can be extended to obtain PSI-cardinality and private intersection-sum protocols. To achieve PSI-cardinality, it suffices to construct a shuffled DOPRF protocol, which allows n parallel executions of the oblivious PRF evaluation where the PRF value that one of the parties receives are randomly shuffled with a permutation selected by the other party. The party who receives the PRF values can still compute the intersection between the two sets of PRF values but no longer has a mapping between the intersecting PRF values and the inputs to which they correspond. Thus, the only thing this party can learn is the cardinality of the intersection. We can extend this idea to further obtain private intersection-sum in the setting where one party (say P_1) has associated integer values with its set elements. In this setting, the two parties first run the shuffled DOPRF for P_2's input set. For P_1's input set, the two parties evaluate the DOPRF on each of P_1's inputs x_i. In addition, P_1 attaches an encryption of x_i's associated integer v_i under re-randomizable additive-homomorphic encryption for which P_1 holds the secret key. This allows P_2 to learn an $(F_k(x_i), \mathsf{Enc}_{pk}(v_i))$-pair for each x_i, so it can compute the set intersection from the two sets of PRF values and then homomorphically add up the corresponding ciphertexts. The resulting ciphertext is then re-randomized and sent back to P_1, who has the decryption key to recover the intersection-sum.

The primitives and protocols described above are only secure against semi-honest adversaries. In order to construct a private intersection-sum protocol that provides malicious security, we design malicious counterparts of these tools.

Malicious DOPRF. The semi-honest intersection-sum protocol of Ion et al. [39] uses the following Diffie-Hellman-based PRF construction, which is defined as $F_k(x) = H(x)^k$, where the hash function $H(\cdot)$ is modeled as a random oracle [7]. It can be instantiated as a DOPRF by sharing the PRF key as $k = k_1 k_2$. Specifically, the two parties can independently generate key shares k_1 and k_2. To evaluate the DOPRF on P_1's input x, P_1 sends $y = H(x)^{k_1}$ to P_2 and then P_2 can compute the PRF output $z = y^{k_2}$. When we switch to the malicious setting, a malicious P_1 may send $\widetilde{y} = H(x)^{r \cdot k_1}$ to P_2 for an arbitrary r and obtain $\widetilde{z} = H(x)^{r \cdot k_1 k_2}$, from which P_2 can learn the PRF output by raising $\widetilde{z}$ to the power r^{-1}. In order to upgrade this DOPRF protocol to the malicious setting especially with simulation-based security, P_1 needs to prove that the hash function $H(\cdot)$ was properly applied or equivalently prove the knowledge of a preimage for a hash value, which is a challenge.

In view of the above difficulties associated with the use of the DH-based DOPRF in the malicious setting, we choose to use a different PRF as a starting point for a new DOPRF construction, for which correct evaluation can be proven. We use the function $F_k(x) = g^{\frac{1}{k+x}}$, which is defined on a group $\langle g \rangle$ of prime order. This function was originally introduced as a weak signature in the work of Boneh-Boyen [8], and subsequently was proven to be a pseudorandom function under the decisional q-Diffie Hellman Inversion (q-DHI) assumption [47] by Dodis-Yampolskiy [23]. We combine ideas from Belenkiy et al. [6] and Jarecki-Liu [40] to construct a distributed oblivious evaluation protocol for this PRF and prove its security in the malicious setting.

We start with a description of a distributed evaluation protocol for the above PRF that provides semi-honest security. We refer to the two parties as a sender and a receiver, where the party holding the input x is called the sender and the party obtaining the PRF output is called the receiver. For the distributed key generation the two parties randomly pick secret key shares k_s and k_r such that the PRF key k is set as $k = k_s + k_r$. The starting point for our distributed evaluation protocol is the following idea. The receiver encrypts its key share k_r using an additive-homomorphic public-key encryption scheme for which it holds the secret key, and sends the encryption $\mathsf{Enc}_{pk}(k_r)$ to the sender. The sender then homomorphically computes $\mathsf{Enc}_{pk}(k_s + k_r + x)$ and sends it back to the receiver. The receiver can decrypt the ciphertext to obtain $k_s + k_r + x$ and compute the PRF output $g^{\frac{1}{k_s + k_r + x}}$.

In the above protocol the receiver learns information beyond the PRF output, which consists of the value $k_s + k_r + x$. To remove this leakage we introduce a random multiplicative mask a on the sender's side. That is, the encrypted value that the receiver obtains is $a(k_s + k_r + x)$. We remove this mask during exponentiation by having the sender also send g^a to the receiver and letting the receiver compute $(g^a)^{\frac{1}{a(k_s+k_r+x)}}$. In fact, this randomization does not suffice for a simulation proof. Since $a(k_s+k_r+x)$ is homomorphically computed by the sender who cannot take modulo operation under the homomorphic encryption, the value $a(k_s+k_r+x)$ learned by the receiver may still leak information about k_s+k_r+x. That is why we further modify the randomization to $a(k_s+k_r+x)+bq$ where b is random and q is the order of the group $\langle g \rangle$. This randomization guarantees that the value obtained by the receiver is simulatable and at the same time correct since the order of the group is q.

To obtain malicious security in the above protocol, the sender needs to prove the correctness of the homomorphic encryption and the consistency of a in the new ciphertext and in g^a. To achieve this we use Camenisch-Shoup encryption [13], for which we can use sigma protocols to provide zero-knowledge proofs for these operations.

Exponential Domain for Dodis-Yampolskiy PRF. The work of Dodis and Yampolsky [23] proved adaptive security for the PRF construction that we discussed above but only in the setting of polynomial size domains. However, this is not true for the inputs used in many real-world applications. Therefore, we revisit the security proof for this construction and show that for exponential size domains the PRF satisfies a weaker notion of selective security, where the inputs to the PRF are chosen by the adversary in advance in the security game, under the q-DHI assumption. Furthermore, this level of security for the PRF is sufficient for the security of our private intersection-sum protocol for the following reason. At a high level, we make the two parties first commit to their own input along with a zero-knowledge proof of knowledge and then jointly decide the PRF parameters. In the simulation-based proof, the simulator can first extract the adversary's input and then reduce to the security game of the PRF, where selective security suffices for our purpose.

Malicious PSI. As we discussed for the semi-honest setting, a secure DOPRF protocol suffices for a PSI protocol. In the malicious setting, to construct a malicious PSI protocol from the above malicious DOPRF protocol, the receiver should send back the PRF values to the sender and prove correctness of its computation $(g^a)^{\frac{1}{a(k_s+k_r+x)+bq}}$ with respect to g^a and the ciphertext $\mathsf{Enc}_{pk}(a(k_s+ k_r + x) + bq)$, in a zero-knowledge fashion. This can also be achieved by sigma protocols.

Malicious Shuffled DOPRF. To extend the malicious PSI protocol to malicious PSI-cardinality, we need to additionally enable the shuffled DOPRF functionality that provides all the PRF outputs to the sender in a randomly shuffled (permuted) order determined by the receiver. While our malicious DOPRF protocol provides the receiver with the leverage to shuffle the PRF outputs before sending back to the sender, we still need a way to prove the correctness of the shuffle.

While it is possible to try to leverage generic zero-knowledge protocols to prove directly the correctness of the shuffled outputs, we choose to use a shuffle-and-decrypt protocol by Bayer-Groth [5], which can efficiently prove in zero-knowledge that given a set of ciphertexts and a set of plaintexts, the plaintexts correspond to the decryption of some permutation of the ciphertexts. To incorporate this shuffle proof in our protocol, the receiver no longer just sends the PRF outputs back to the sender after the DOPRF evaluation, but rather sends encryptions of these outputs together with proofs that each of them encrypts the correctly computed value $(g^a)^{\frac{1}{a(k_s+k_r+x)+bq}}$. In addition to this the receiver sends the PRF outputs in the clear in a shuffled order together with a Bayer-Groth shuffle proof that they are consistent with the decryption of the above ciphertexts in some permuted order.

In the above construction which we design in order to leverage an efficient shuffle proof, let $\beta := a(k_s + k_r + x) + bq$. The prover needs to switch from Camenisch-Shoup encryption to ElGaml encryption because β was encrypted in Camenisch-Shoup encryption while the value to encrypt in this step is $\sigma = (g^a)^{\beta^{-1}}$ and what the prover needs to prove knowledge about is β_i^{-1} instead of σ. Encrypting σ using ElGamal in the group $\langle g \rangle$ enables proof of knowledge in the exponent. However, the prover needs to provide a proof that the Camenish-Shoup ciphertext, which has plaintext domain $\mathbb{Z}_N$, and the ElGamal cipheretext, which has plaintext domain $\mathbb{Z}_q$ where $q \ll N$, encrypt consistent values β and β^{-1}. To achieve this we observe that it suffices to prove the consistency of the two encrypted values in their respective domains (i.e., $x \mod N = x' \mod q$) and in addition to this prove that $x' < q$. For the later since $q \ll N$, it suffices to use range proofs that have slack for sigma protocols, which can only guarantee that $x' < q \cdot r$. This completes a malicious DOPRF protocol with randomly shuffled PRF outputs.

From Shuffled DOPRF to Intersection-Sum. The shuffled DOPRF protocol suffices to obtain PSI-cardinality in the semi-honest setting by running two shuffled DOPRF with the same key, where in one protocol P_1 holds the input and acts as the sender while in the other protocol their roles are reversed. In the malicious setting when the two protocols are executed in parallel, we have to additionally make sure the two parties are using consistent DOPRF key shares. Each party will first commit to their DOPRF key shares and then prove consistency of their key shares used in the two protocols, which can be done using sigma protocols.

To further achieve private intersection-sum, similar to the semi-honest setting, we encrypt the integer values associated with one of the sets using additive homomorphic encryption. The secret key for this encryption is now shared between the two parties, which will be important for preserving the secrecy guarantees of the shuffle proof. The sender appends these encryptions to the corresponding inputs in the malicious shuffled DOPRF evaluation. Now the receiver that applies the shuffle in this protocol additionally needs to re-randomize the encryptions of the associated values and provides a proof that the shuffle applied to these encryptions is the same as the shuffle on the PRF values. This can be achieved in the Bayer-Groth shuffle proof because in their protocol the prover commits to the permutation and we can use the same commitment through the two shuffle proofs. Different from the semi-honest setting, now both parties can compute the intersection of the two sets of PRF values and homomorphically add up the corresponding re-randomized ciphertexts. To jointly decrypt the resulting ciphertext, each party partially decrypts the ciphertext using their own key share and sends to the other party. They also have to prove the correctness of their partial decryption, again by sigma protocols.

Batching Protocol Components. In our construction outlined above we use sigma style protocols to provide proofs for the correctness of DOPRF evaluation, re-encryption for shuffling, and re-randomization for intersection-sum. In order to optimize the communication efficiency of such protocols, we utilize various techniques to batch components of the protocol. At a high level there are three types of batching we use: batching Pedersen commitments, batching Camenisch-Shoup encryptions, and batching sigma protocols.

These batching techniques are described in Sect. 5. Further care needs to be taken to ensure the compatibility between different batching techniques. We describe the detailed composition of these techniques in the full version of our paper.

We believe that these batching techniques may be of independent interest. For example, our batched sigma protocols include tighter bounds on proofs of ranges than known techniques, and our batched Camenisch-Shoup encryption enables batched proofs of decryption, which brings asymptotic efficiency gains.

Organization. We introduce our notations, security assumptions, important definitions and cryptographic schemes in Sect. 3 and present our private intersection-sum protocol in Sect. 4. Our batching techniques are described in Sect. 5. For the detailed malicious security proof of our protocol, concrete sigma protocols, and the selective security proof of the PRF used in our protocol, refer to the full version of our paper [46].

3   Preliminaries

3.1   Notation

We use λ to denote the security parameter. Let $\mathbb{Z}_n$ be the set $\{0, 1, 2, \ldots, n-1\}$. $\mathbb{Z}_n^*$ is defined as $\mathbb{Z}_n^* := \{x \in \mathbb{Z}_n \mid \gcd(x, n) = 1\}$. We use $[n]$ to denote the set $\{1, 2, \ldots, n\}$. We use $\mathsf{ord}(\mathbb{G})$ to denote the order of a group $\mathbb{G}$. By $\mathsf{negl}(\lambda)$ we denote a negligible function, i.e., a function f such that $f(\lambda) < 1/p(\lambda)$ holds for any polynomial $p(\cdot)$ and sufficiently large λ.

3.2 Computational Assumptions

Decisional q-Diffie-Hellman Inversion (q-DHI) Assumption [47]. The computational q-DHI problem in a group $\mathbb{G}$ with generator g and order p is to compute $g^{1/\alpha}$ given the tuple $(g, g^{\alpha}, \ldots, g^{\alpha^q})$ for random α in $\mathbb{Z}_p^*$. We define the hardness of the *decisional* version of this problem for any fixed constant q as follows. Let gGen be an algorithm which on input a security parameter 1^λ picks a modulus p and a generator g of a multiplicative group $\mathbb{G}$ of order p. We say that the *Decisional q-DHI Assumption* holds on group (family) $\mathbb{G}$ if for every efficient algorithm $\mathcal{A}$,

$$\left| \Pr\left[\mathcal{A}(g, g^{\alpha}, \ldots, g^{\alpha^q}, g^{1/\alpha}) = 1 \middle| (g, p) \leftarrow \mathsf{gGen}(1^\lambda); \alpha \leftarrow \mathbb{Z}_p^* \right] \right.$$

$$\left. - \Pr\left[\mathcal{A}(g, g^{\alpha}, \ldots, g^{\alpha^q}, h) = 1 \middle| (g, p) \leftarrow \mathsf{gGen}(1^\lambda); \alpha \leftarrow \mathbb{Z}_p^*; h \leftarrow \mathbb{G} \right] \right| \leq \mathsf{negl}(\lambda).$$

Strong RSA Assumption [4,32]. The strong RSA assumption states that given an RSA modulus N of unknown factorization and a random element $g \in \mathbb{Z}_N^*$, it is computationally hard to find any pair of $h \in \mathbb{Z}_N^*$ and $e > 1$ such that $h^e = g \mod N$.

3.3 Cryptographic Tools

We introduce some cryptographic tools in this section. See the full version of the paper for descriptions of Pedersen commitment [53], Camenisch-Shoup encryption [13], ElGamal encryption [26], and 2-out-of-2 threshold encryption.

Zero-Knowledge Argument of Knowledge. We use the notation introduced in [14] for the various zero-knowledge argument of knowledge of discrete logarithms and arguments of the validity of statements about discrete logarithms. The following example is taken verbatim from [13].

$$\mathsf{ZK\text{-}AoK}\{(a, b, c) : y = g^a h^b \wedge \mathfrak{y} = \mathfrak{g}^a \mathfrak{h}^c \wedge (v < a < u)\}$$

denotes a *"zero-knowledge argument of knowledge of integers a, b, and c such that $y = g^a h^b$ and $\mathfrak{y} = \mathfrak{g}^a \mathfrak{h}^c$ hold, where $v < a < u$,"* in which $y, g, h, \mathfrak{y}, \mathfrak{g}, \mathfrak{h}$ are elements of some groups $\mathbb{G} = \langle g \rangle = \langle h \rangle$ and $\mathfrak{G} = \langle \mathfrak{g} \rangle = \langle \mathfrak{h} \rangle$. The convention is that the elements listed in the round brackets denote quantities the knowledge of which is being proved (and are in general not known to the verifier), while all other parameters are known to the verifier. Using this notation, a proof-protocol can be described by just pointing out its aim while hiding all details.

We use similar notations for zero-knowledge proofs. As an example,

$$\mathsf{ZK}\{\exists x : h = g^x\}$$

denotes a zero-knowledge proof that there exists x such that $h = g^x$.

In our protocol we instantiate this form of zero-knowledge arguments of knowledge and zero-knowledge proofs by sigma protocols. We elaborate how this can be done and how batching techniques work for sigma protocols in Sect. 5. The concrete sigma protocols used in our construction are presented in our full version.

Fiat-Shamir Heuristic. All the sigma protocols are interactive and public-coin, where the messages from the verifier are all chosen uniformly at random and independently of the messages sent by the prover. We only prove they are honest-verifier zero-knowledge. By the Fiat-Shamir heuristic [29], these protocols can be turned into a non-interactive proof or argument where the prover computes the public-coin challenges with a cryptographic hash function instead of interacting with a verifier, which reduces rounds of communication as well as total communication cost. Furthermore, the resulting non-interactive protocol can be proved malicious secure in the random oracle model.

Shuffle Proof. Bayer-Groth [5] proposed a zero-knowledge argument of knowledge for the correctness of re-randomized and shuffled of homomorphic encryptions, which achieves sublinear communication complexity. More specifically, given the public key pk of the homomorphic encryption, original ciphertexts $\{\mathsf{ct}_i\}_{i\in[n]}$, a permutation π over $[n]$, re-randomized and shuffled ciphertexts $\{\mathsf{ct}'_{\pi(i)}\}_{i\in[n]}$ where $\mathsf{ct}'_{\pi(i)} = \mathsf{ct}_i \cdot \mathsf{Enc}_{\mathsf{pk}}(1; r_i)$. The following ZK-AOK

$$\mathsf{ZK\text{-}AoK}\left\{(\pi, \{r_i\}_{i\in[n]}) : \mathsf{ct}_i \cdot \mathsf{Enc}_{\mathsf{pk}}(1; r_i) \quad \forall i \in [n]\right\}$$

can be prove with communication complexity $O(\sqrt{n})$. In addition, two statements can be proved to use the same permutation π. The protocol is interactive with public-coins, hence it can be turned into a non-interactive malicious secure one using the Fiat-Shamir heuristic.

3.4 Security Model

We define security of a private intersection-sum protocol against malicious adversaries in the ideal/real world paradigm. The definition compares the output of a real-world execution to the output of an ideal-world execution involving a trusted third party, which we call an ideal functionality. The ideal functionality $\mathcal{F}$, defined in Fig. 1, receives the two parties' inputs, computes the intersection-sum and returns the output to both parties. Loosely speaking, the protocol Π is secure if the output of the adversary in the real-world execution is computationally indistinguishable from the output of the adversary in the ideal-world execution, which means that a real-world execution of the protocol does not leak any more information than the ideal-world execution. Hence, the parties can only learn what they can infer from their inputs and the output.

Formally, we say a private intersection-sum protocol is secure against malicious adversaries if for every PPT adversary $\mathcal{A}$ in the real world, there exists a PPT adversary $\mathcal{S}$ in the ideal world such that for any input (X, V) and Y,

$$\mathsf{Real}_{\Pi, \mathcal{A}}((X, V), Y) \overset{c}{\approx} \mathsf{Ideal}_{\mathcal{F}, \mathcal{S}}((X, V), Y),$$

Public Parameters: P_1's set size n_1 and P_2's set size n_2.

Inputs: Party P_1 inputs a set of identifiers along with associated integer values $(X, V) = \{(x_i, v_i)\}_{i \in [n_1]}$, Party P_2 inputs a set of identifiers $Y = \{y_i\}_{i \in [n_2]}$.

Output: Upon receiving the inputs from both parties, the ideal functionality $\mathcal{F}$ computes the intersection $I = X \cap Y$ and intersection-sum $S = \sum_{i:x_i \in I} v_i$ and outputs the intersection-cardinality $|I|$ and intersection-sum S first to the corrupted party, then to the honest party.

Corrupted Party: The corrupted party may deviate from its input, may abort the procedure at any time by sending **abort** to the ideal functionality, and may decide the time of message delivery.

Fig. 1. Ideal functionality of malicious secure private intersection-sum.

where $\mathsf{Real}_{\Pi, \mathcal{A}}((X, V), Y)$ denotes the output of $\mathcal{A}$ in the real-world execution of protocol Π, and $\mathsf{Ideal}_{\mathcal{F}, \mathcal{S}}((X, V), Y)$ denotes the output of $\mathcal{S}$ in the ideal-world execution.

4   Protocol Description

Our constructions consists of two phases. The first one is an offline setup where the two parties jointly decide parameters for the cryptographic primitives, which will be used in the online computation. Note that we do not assume trusted setup for any of the primitives and provide secure two party computation protocols for those. The second phase is the online computation that is dependent on the input sets and uses the parameters from the setup. The main building block for our online phase is a shuffled distributed oblivious PRF (DOPRF) construction, which is a primitive of independent interest and other potential applications. Thus, we present the shuffled DOPRF construction separately.

Offline Setup. In our malicious secure private intersection-sum protocol, the two parties first run a (one-time) offline setup to generate the parameters for encryption and commitment schemes. The two parties first agree on a group $\mathbb{G}$ where $\max(n_1, n_2)$-DHI assumption holds. This group will be the group where they compute DOPRF on. Each party generates parameters for Camenisch-Shoup encryption, ElGamal encryption and Pedersen commitments, and sends the public parts to the other party with corresponding proofs for correct generation (which is discussed in our full version). The two parties generate parameters for the 2-out-of-2 threshold ElGamal encryption, which can be done by each party generating locally ElGamal parameters and setting the shared secret key to be the sum of the two local secret keys, and computing the corresponding public key. The detailed protocol is described in Fig. 2.

Online Phase. After the one-time offline setup, for each private intersection-sum instance, the two parties run an online protocol described in Fig. 3.

---

0. P_1 and P_2 agree on a group $\mathbb{G}$ of order q with a generator $\widetilde{g}$ for which the $\max(n_1, n_2)$-DHI assumption holds.

1. Each party P_b generates $(\mathsf{pk}_b, \mathsf{sk}_b) \leftarrow \mathsf{CS\_Gen}(1^\lambda)$ where $g_b = (r_b)^{2N}$ for a random element $r_b \in \mathbb{Z}_{N^2}$, $\mathsf{pk}_b = (N_b, r_b, g_b, y_b)$ and $N_b \geq 2^{3\lambda} q^2$, $\mathsf{sk}_b = x_b$. Party P_b sends pk_b to the other party along with a ZK-proof that N_b is a product of two large safe primes and that y_b is correctly formed:

$$\mathsf{ZK}\left\{ \exists x_b : y_b = (g_b)^{x_b} \bmod N_b^2 \right\}.$$

2. Each party P_b generates Pedersen commitment parameters $(\mathfrak{g}_b, \mathfrak{h}_b)$ for the large subgroup of $\mathbb{Z}_{N_b}^*$ and sends $(\mathfrak{g}_b, \mathfrak{h}_b)$ to the other party together with a zero-knowledge proof that $\mathfrak{g}_b \in \langle \mathfrak{h}_b \rangle$:

$$\mathsf{ZK\text{-}AoK}\left\{ \exists r_b : \mathfrak{g}_b = (\mathfrak{h}_b)^{r_b} \right\}.$$

3. Each party P_b generates $(\mathsf{tpk}_b, \mathsf{tsk}_b) \leftarrow \mathsf{EG\_Gen}(1^\lambda)$ for the 2-out-of-2 threshold encryption scheme on the group $\mathbb{G}$ with generator $\widetilde{g}$ and sends tpk_b to the other party along with a ZK-AOK of tsk_b:

$$\mathsf{ZK\text{-}AoK}\{\mathsf{tsk}_b : \mathsf{tpk}_b = (\widetilde{g})^{\mathsf{tsk}_b}\}.$$

Both parties compute the public key $\mathsf{tpk} = \mathsf{tpk}_1 \cdot \mathsf{tpk}_2$.

4. Each party P_b generates an ElGamal key pair $(\mathfrak{pk}_b, \mathfrak{sk}_b)$ for the group $\mathbb{G}$ with generator $\widetilde{g}$ and sends $\mathfrak{pk}_b$ to the other party with a proof:

Fig. 2. One-time offline setup of the malicious secure private intersection-sum protocol.

The inputs for the two parties are as follows: P_1 has an input set of elements $X = \{x_i\}_{i \in [n_1]}$ with associated integer values $V = \{v_i\}_{i \in [n_1]}$, while P_2 has only a set of elements $Y = \{y_i\}_{i \in [n_2]}$. The output of the protocol is that either both parties abort, or both parties obtain the intersection sum $\sum_{i:x_i \in Y} v_i$.

At a high level this protocol uses the shuffled DOPRF to enable both parties to obtain shuffled PRF evaluations for the values in X and Y, where the PRF values from X are paired with ElGamal encryptions of the corresponding integer values from V, which are encrypted under the 2-out-of-2 threshold ElGamal. Afterwards, the two parties compute independently the ElGamal encryption of the intersection sum since they can compute the intersection on the PRF values and then sum the encryptions of the integer values. At that point, the two ciphertexts held by the parties should be identical. Now each party verifiably half-decrypts the ciphertexts it has obtained and sends the resulting verifiable partial decryption to the other party. Then both parties can half-decrypt the partial decryption they received to obtain the output.

Shuffled DOPRF Protocol. We describe our malicious secure shuffled DOPRF construction as a stand-alone primitive in Fig. 4. For the purposes of the following discussion P_1 is the party that holds input elements $\{x_i\}_{i \in [n_1]}$, and P_1 and P_2 jointly evaluate the shuffled DOPRF on these elements. First,

1. Each party P_b samples a random PRF key share $k_b \xleftarrow{\$} [q]$.
2. P_1 computes $\mathsf{C}_{x_i} \leftarrow \mathsf{com}_{\mathfrak{g}_2,\mathfrak{h}_2}(x_i)$ for all $i \in [n_1]$, sends C_{x_i} with ZK-AOK to P_2:

$$\text{ZK-AoK}\left\{(x_i, r_i) : \mathsf{C}_{x_i} = (\mathfrak{g}_2)^{x_i} \cdot (\mathfrak{h}_2)^{r_i}\right\}.$$

   P_2 computes $\mathsf{C}_{y_i} \leftarrow \mathsf{com}_{\mathfrak{g}_1,\mathfrak{h}_1}(y_i)$ for all $i \in [n_2]$, sends C_{y_i} with ZK-AOK to P_1:

$$\text{ZK-AoK}\left\{(y_i, s_i) : \mathsf{C}_{y_i} = (\mathfrak{g}_1)^{y_i} \cdot (\mathfrak{h}_1)^{s_i}\right\}.$$

3. P_1 and P_2 jointly decide on a random generator g for the group $\mathbb{G}$.
4. P_1 and P_2 run two shuffled DOPRF protocols described in Figure 4 in parallel, one with P_1 holding the input and the other with P_2 holding the input:
   - **Shuffled DOPRF 1**: P_1 and P_2 perform the shuffled DOPRF protocol on P_1's input $X = \{x_i\}_{i \in [n_1]}$. The output PRF values are denoted as $\{\sigma_{\pi(i)}\}_{i \in [n_1]}$. In parallel to this protocol, they do the following:
     - **Round 2**: P_1 computes $\mathsf{ct}_{v_i} \leftarrow \mathsf{Exp\_EG\_Enc}_{\mathsf{tpk}}(v_i)$ for each $i \in [n_1]$ and sends $\{\mathsf{ct}_{v_i}\}_{i \in [n_1]}$ to P_2.
     - **Round 3**: P_2 re-randomizes $\{\mathsf{ct}_{v_i}\}_{i \in [n_1]}$ to obtain $\{\mathsf{ct}'_{v_i}\}_{i \in [n_1]}$, and then uses the permutation π (same as in the shuffled DOPRF protocol) to shuffle the re-randomized ciphertexts to obtain $\left\{\mathsf{ct}'_{v_{\pi(i)}}\right\}_{i \in [n_1]}$. P_2 sends $\left\{\mathsf{ct}'_{v_{\pi(i)}}\right\}_{i \in [n_1]}$ to P_1 along with a ZK-AOK:

$$\text{ZK-AoK}\left\{(\pi, \{r_i\}_{i \in [n_1]}) : \mathsf{ct}'_{v_{\pi(i)}} = \mathsf{ct}_{v_i} \cdot \mathsf{Exp\_EG\_Enc}_{\mathsf{tpk}}(1; r_i) \quad \forall i \in [n_1]\right\}$$

   - **Shuffled DOPRF 2**: P_1 and P_2 perform the shuffled DOPRF protocol, with roles reversed, on P_2's input $Y = \{y_i\}_{i \in [n_2]}$. We denote the set of PRF values as $F_k(Y)$.
5. Each party P_b determines the intersection set $I := \{t : \sigma_t \in F_k(Y)\}$ and computes $\mathsf{ct}_S = \prod_{t \in I} \mathsf{ct}'_{v_t}$. P_b verifiably half-decrypts ct_S using tsk_b and sends to the other party.
6. Each party half-decrypts the ciphertext half-decrypted by the other party, and outputs the intersection sum S.

Fig. 3. Online phase of the malicious secure private intersection-sum protocol.

P_2 commits to its PRF key share k_2 and also sends a Camenisch-Shoup encryption of it under its own key to P_1 together with a proof that the encrypted and the committed values are the same. P_1 can then homomorphically compute $\mathsf{CS\_Enc}_{\mathsf{pk}_2}(k_1 + k_2 + x_i)$ for each of its element x_i. To mask the value $k_1 + k_2 + x_i$, P_1 chooses randomizing values a_i and b_i and compute $\mathsf{ct}_{\beta_i} = \mathsf{CS\_Enc}_{\mathsf{pk}_2}(a_i \cdot (k_1 + k_2 + x_i) + b_i \cdot q)$ and $g_i = g^{a_i}$. P_1 also commits to the values $a_i, b_i, \alpha_i = a_i \cdot (k_1 + x_i)$ together with proofs that these commitments and encryptions use consistent values. P_2 verifies the correctness of the proofs, decrypts ct_{β_i} to obtain $\beta_i = a_i \cdot (k_1 + k_2 + x_i) + b_i \cdot q$ and computes the PRF evaluation $\sigma_i = g_i^{\beta_i^{-1}} = g^{\frac{1}{k_1+k_2+x_i}}$. Then, P_2 computes an ElGamal encryption

---

Round 1. Party P_2 computes $\mathsf{ct}_{k_2} \leftarrow \mathsf{CS\_Enc}_{\mathsf{pk}_2}(k_2)$ and $\mathsf{C}_{k_2} \leftarrow \mathsf{com}_{\mathfrak{g}_1,\mathfrak{h}_1}(k_2)$. Recall that $\mathsf{pk}_2 = (N_2, g_2, y_2)$. P_2 sends $\mathsf{ct}_{k_2} = (u, e)$ and C_{k_2} to P_1 along with a ZK-AOK

$$\mathsf{ZK\text{-}AoK}\Big\{(k_2, r_1, r_2) : u = g_2^{r_1} \ \wedge \ e = (1 + N_2)^{k_2} \cdot y_2^{r_1} \ \wedge$$
$$\mathsf{C}_{k_2} = (\mathfrak{g}_1)^{k_2} \cdot (\mathfrak{h}_1)^{r_2} \ \wedge \ k_2 \le q \cdot 2^{2\lambda+1}\Big\}.$$

Round 2. For each input x_i where $i \in [n_1]$, party P_1 does the following:

(a) Choose a random $a_i \xleftarrow{\$} [q]$ and $b_i \xleftarrow{\$} [q \cdot 2^\lambda]$. Compute $\mathfrak{g}_i = g^{a_i}$.

(b) Compute $\alpha_i = a_i \cdot (k_1 + x_i)$ and commitments $\mathsf{C}_{a_i} \leftarrow \mathsf{com}_{\mathfrak{g}_2,\mathfrak{h}_2}(a_i)$, $\mathsf{C}_{b_i} \leftarrow \mathsf{com}_{\mathfrak{g}_2,\mathfrak{h}_2}(b_i)$, $\mathsf{C}_{\alpha_i} = \mathsf{com}_{\mathfrak{g}_2,\mathfrak{h}_2}(\alpha_i)$.

(c) Let $\beta_i = a_i \cdot (k_1 + k_2 + x_i) + b_i \cdot q = a_i \cdot k_2 + \alpha_i + b_i \cdot q$ and compute $\mathsf{ct}_{\beta_i} \leftarrow (\mathsf{ct}_{k_2})^{a_i} \cdot \mathsf{CS\_Enc}_{\mathsf{pk}_2}(\alpha_i) \cdot (\mathsf{CS\_Enc}_{\mathsf{pk}_2}(b_i))^q$.

(d) Send $(\mathsf{C}_{a_i}, \mathsf{C}_{b_i}, \mathsf{C}_{\alpha_i}, \mathsf{ct}_{\beta_i}, \mathfrak{g}_i)$ to P_2, together with a ZK-AOK

$$\mathsf{ZK\text{-}AoK}\Big\{(a_i, b_i, \alpha_i, r_1, r_2, r_3, r_4, r_5, r_6):$$
$$\mathsf{C}_{a_i} = (\mathfrak{g}_2)^{a_i} \cdot (\mathfrak{h}_2)^{r_1} \ \wedge \ a_i \le q \cdot 2^{2\lambda+1} \ \wedge$$
$$\mathsf{C}_{b_i} = (\mathfrak{g}_2)^{b_i} \cdot (\mathfrak{h}_2)^{r_2} \ \wedge \ b_i \le q \cdot 2^{3\lambda+1} \ \wedge$$
$$\mathsf{C}_{\alpha_i} = (\mathfrak{g}_2)^{\alpha_i} \cdot (\mathfrak{h}_2)^{r_3} \ \wedge \ \mathsf{C}_{\alpha_i} = (\mathsf{C}_{k_1} \cdot \mathsf{C}_{x_i})^{a_i} \cdot (\mathfrak{h}_2)^{r_4} \ \wedge \ \alpha_i \le q \cdot 2^{2\lambda+1} \ \wedge$$
$$\mathsf{ct}_{\beta_i} = (\mathsf{ct}_{k_2})^{a_i} \cdot \mathsf{CS\_Enc}_{\mathsf{pk}_2}(\alpha_i; r_5) \cdot (\mathsf{CS\_Enc}_{\mathsf{pk}_2}(b_i; r_6))^q \wedge$$
$$\mathfrak{g}_i = g^{a_i}\Big\}.$$

Note that C_{x_i} was sent by P_1 in Step 2 of the online phase, and C_{k_1} was sent by P_1 in Round 1 of the other shuffled DOPRF protocol where P_2 holds the input.

Round 3. Party P_2 does the following:

(a) Verify all the ZK-AOKs received from P_1; otherwise abort.

(b) For each $i \in [n_1]$, compute $\beta_i \leftarrow \mathsf{CS\_Dec}_{\mathsf{sk}_2}(\mathsf{ct}_{\beta_i})$ and $\mathsf{C}_{\beta_i} \leftarrow \mathsf{com}_{\mathfrak{g}_1,\mathfrak{h}_1}(\beta_i)$. Compute $\gamma_i = \beta_i^{-1} \bmod q$ and $\sigma_i = \mathfrak{g}_i^{\gamma_i}$. Compute $\mathsf{ct}_{\sigma_i} \leftarrow \mathsf{EG\_Enc}_{\mathsf{pk}_2}(\sigma_i)$.

(c) Verify that $\{\sigma_i\}_{i \in [n_1]}$ are all distinct; otherwise abort.

(d) For each $i \in [n_1]$, send $(\mathsf{C}_{\beta_i}, \mathfrak{ct}_{\sigma_i})$ to P_2 together with a ZK-AOK

$$\mathsf{ZK\text{-}AoK}\Big\{(\mathsf{sk}_2, \beta_i, r_1, r_2) : \beta_i = \mathsf{CS\_Dec}_{\mathsf{sk}_2}(\mathsf{ct}_{\beta_i}) \ \wedge$$
$$\mathsf{C}_{\beta_i} = (\mathfrak{g}_1)^{\beta_i} \cdot (\mathfrak{h}_1)^{r_1} \ \wedge \ \beta_i \le q^2 \cdot 2^{3\lambda+1} \ \wedge$$
$$\mathfrak{ct}_{\sigma_i} = \mathsf{EG\_Enc}_{\mathsf{pk}_2}\Big((g_i)^{\beta_i^{-1}}; r_2\Big)\Big\}.$$

(e) Re-randomize $\{\mathfrak{ct}_{\sigma_i}\}_{i \in [n_1]}$ to obtain $\{\mathfrak{ct}'_{\sigma_i}\}_{i \in [n_1]}$ with randomness 0. Pick a random permutation π over $[n_1]$ and send $\left\{\mathfrak{ct}'_{\sigma_{\pi(i)}}\right\}_{i \in [n_1]}$ to P_1 together with a ZK-AOK:

$$\mathsf{ZK\text{-}AoK}\left\{(\pi, \{r_i\}_{i \in [n_1]}) : \mathfrak{ct}'_{\sigma_{\pi(i)}} = \mathfrak{ct}_{\sigma_i} \cdot \mathsf{EG\_Enc}_{\mathsf{pk}_2}(1; r_i) \quad \forall i \in [n_1]\right\}.$$

As $\left\{\mathfrak{ct}'_{\sigma_{\pi(i)}}\right\}_{i \in [n_1]}$ has randomness 0, P_1 obtains $\{\sigma_{\pi(i)}\}_{i \in [n_1]}$.

Output. P_1 verifies all the ZK-AOKs received from P_2 and aborts otherwise. Both parties obtain $\{\sigma_{\pi(i)}\}_{i \in [n_1]}$.

Fig. 4. Malicious secure shuffled DOPRF protocol where P_1 holds the input.

$\mathsf{EG\_Enc}_{\mathsf{pk}_2}(\sigma_i)$ and a commitment C_{β_i} and sends them to P_1 together with a proof that these values encrypt and commit to the decryption of ct_{β_i}, which P_1 verifies. In addition P_2 re-randomizes and shuffles values ct_{σ_i} with output $\{\mathsf{ct}'_{\sigma_{\pi(i)}}\}_{i\in[n_1]}$, and sends these values together with a proof of shuffling. Finally, $\sigma_{\pi(i)}$ are revealed to P_1 if P_2 re-randomizes the ciphertexts using randomness 0. P_1 verifies the proofs and accepts the values $\sigma_{\pi(i)}$ as its output PRF values. In this step, P_2 switches from Camenisch-Shoup encryption to ElGaml encryption because the value to encrypt is $\sigma_i = g_i^{\beta_i^{-1}}$ and what P_2 needs to prove knowledge about is β_i^{-1} instead of σ_i. Encrypting σ_i using ElGamal in the group $\mathbb{G}$ enables this proof of knowledge. If the verification of any of the proofs during the execution so the protocol fails, then the parties abort.

Additionally, during the execution of the DOPRF on the inputs of P_1, the parties run the following additional steps in parallel with the DOPRF evaluation in order to facilitate keeping the values v_i paired with the appropriate PRF evaluations. In Round 2 of the DOPRF protocol, P_1 encrypts the v_i values using the ElGamal encryption parameters where the secret key is shared between the two parties. P_1 sends these encryptions paired with the partial PRF evaluations on its elements x_i. When P_2 returns the completed DOPRF evaluations in a permuted order, it also sends the re-randomized encryptions of the values v_i permuted in the same order along with a proof that these two sets were shuffled with the same permutation.

Enabling Batching. So far we described our shuffled DOPRF construction for each element x_i and the ZK-AOKs in the protocol are all sigma protocols for single statements. To reduce communication of the protocol we utilize various batching techniques which we describe in Sect. 5. The concrete instantiation of our private intersection-sum protocol does not use the shuffled DOPRF in a completely non-black box way, which we discuss in the following.

In Step 2 of the online phase, P_1 will commit implicitly to its inputs by committing to the values a_i and $\alpha_i = a_i(k_1 + x_i)$ and P_2 will implicitly commit to its inputs similarly. These values can be batched and the sigma protocols for the batched commitments can also be batched. In addition each party will commit to their DOPRF key share in this step. This change does not affect our security guarantee because the commitments of a_i and α_i suffice to extract the set elements in the simulation proofs before the PRF parameters are generated and hence security can still be reduced to the weaker selective security notion for the underlying PRF. Looking ahead, the commitments of a_i, α_i and k_b will be used directly later in Round 2 of the DOPRF protocol for further computation avoiding the need to prove the consistency of x_i, a_i and α_i in batched C_{x_i} and batched C_{α_i}, which would have been the case if the parties commit only to their elements before the PRF parameter generation.

To enable batching the first component of the Camenisch-Shoup ciphertexts, every batched Camenisch-Shoup ciphertext has t slots. In Round 1 of the DOPRF protocol, P_2 will encrypt t copies of k_2, where the i-th copy of k_2 is encrypted in the i-th slot and the other slots are all 0. These encryptions will be used later in Round 2 of the shuffled DOPRF protocol to enable batching Camenisch-Shoup encryptions of β_i.

Finally, in Round 2 of the DOPRF protocol, P_1 can make use of previously committed a_i, α_i, k_1 along with encryption of k_2 to batch Camenisch-Shoup encryptions and Pedersen commitments of β_i. The sigma protocols in this step can also be batched. The details of batching each sigma protocol are presented in the full version of the paper.

5   Batching Techniques

In this section we discuss batching techniques in various parts of our protocol. These techniques have a significant effect on our protocol's communication cost and may be of independent interest.

5.1   Batching Pedersen Commitments

As mentioned in Sect. 3.3, Pedersen commitments can be genenralized to allow committing to *vectors* of values. For batched commitments of vectors of length t, the parameters are group generators $g_1, \ldots, g_t, h \in \mathbb{G}$ such that $\log_{g_i} h$ is hard to compute for each i, and $\log_{g_i} g_j$ is hard to compute for any pair i, j. The commitment to a vector $\boldsymbol{x} = (x_1, \ldots, x_t)$ is $c = \prod_{i=1}^{t} g_i^{x_i} \cdot h^r$ where r is selected at random $r \xleftarrow{\$} \mathsf{ord}(\mathbb{G})$.

Batched Pedersen commitments are also compatible with sigma protocols of the knowledge and equality of exponents. To do so, the prover simply proves knowledge of all exponents simultneously. Furthermore, if the group $\mathbb{G}$ is one in which the Strong RSA assumption holds, then the following generalization of Theorem 3 from [13] holds: given randomly chosen $g_1, \ldots, g_t, h \in \mathbb{G}$, it is hard to find $w \in \mathbb{G}$ and $(a_1, ..., a_t, b, c)$ such that

$$w^c = \prod_{i=1}^{t} g_i^{a_i} \cdot h^b$$

Unless $c \mid a_i$ for all $i \in [t]$, and also $c \mid b$. The proof of this generalization closely follows from the proofs of Theorems 2 and 3 from [13].

Given these properties, we can replace most commitments in our protocols with batched commitments, that is, we commit to t values together. To enable this, each of our sigma protocols will commit to and prove statements about t messages simultaneously. Note that this reduces the number of commitments we send by a factor of t, but we still need to send one element per committed value in the last step of each sigma protocol. At first this does not seem to lead to a significant gain in efficiency. However, sigma protocols for batched commitments can also be batched, enabling the prover to send a single set of t elements in the last step to verify ℓ sigma protocols simultaneously. Combining the two forms of batching by setting t and ℓ to approximately $\sqrt{n}$, we can reduce the overall communication cost of the sigma protocols to be sublinear. We will discuss how to batch sigma protocols in Sect. 5.3, and we refer the reader to the full version of the our paper for a concrete example of batching sigma protocols for batched commitments.

5.2 Batching Camenisch-Shoup Encryption

We notice that Camenisch Shoup encryption introduces a $4\times$ expansion in the ciphertext as compared to the plaintext. This is due to the fact that a ciphertext contains 2 elements mod N^2 of total length $4n$ bits (where $n = \log N$), while the ciphertext can only hold a message of $|n|$ bits. This causes a significant constant expansion to our protocol messages.

We describe various types of batching that enable reducing the expansion of Camenisch-Shoup encryption to be as close to $1\times$ as desired.

5.2.1 Computing Mod N^{s+1}

Analogous to the Damgård-Jurik extension to the Paillier cryptosystem [19], one can generalize the Camenisch-Shoup cryptosystem to compute modulo N^{s+1}. In more detail, the public key in this generalization consists of (N, g, y, s) where N is generated same as before, g is a random $2N^s$-th residue modulo N^{s+1}, and $y = g^x \mod N^{s+1}$ for a random $x \in \mathbb{Z}_{\lfloor N/4 \rfloor}$, and x is the secret key.

Similarly to the Damgård-Jurik extension, this generalization of Camenisch-Shoup encryption enables encrypting messages of size up to N^s. Concretely, given $m \in \mathbb{Z}_{N^s}$, it would be encrypted as $\mathsf{ct} = (g^r \mod N^{s+1}, (1+N)^m y^r \mod N^{s+1})$, where $r \xleftarrow{\$} \mathbb{Z}_{\lfloor N/4 \rfloor}$. Decryption is slightly more involved. To decrypt $\mathsf{ct} = (u, e)$, one must compute $e/(u^x) \mod N^{s+1}$ and then perform a recursive decoding to recover m, exactly as described in Sect. 3 of [19].

Additionally, similar to the proof of Theorem 1 in [19], the security of the generalized Camenisch-Shoup scheme follows from the Decisional Composite Residuousity Assumption.

We note that, with this generalization, one can encrypt a message of length $n \cdot s$ using a ciphertext of size $2 \cdot n \cdot (s+1)$, meaning that the expansion factor is reduced from $4\times$ to $\frac{2(s+1)}{s}\times$, which becomes arbitrarily close to $2\times$ as s grows.

5.2.2 Sharing the First Ciphertext Component

A remaining source of ciphertext expansion is that each ciphertext has 2 components, (u, e). One way to reduce this type of expansion is to have multiple components e that all share the first component u.

More concretely, we modify the scheme so that the public key consists of $(N, g, \{y_i\}_{i=1}^t)$, where $y_i = g^{x_i} \mod N^2$ for random $x_i \in \mathbb{Z}_{\lfloor N/4 \rfloor}$. The secret key becomes $\{x_i\}_{i=1}^t$.

This scheme allows encrypting t messages by $t+1$ components. Specifically, to encrypt messages $\{m_i\}_{i=1}^t$, one computes $u = g^r \mod N^2$ for $r \xleftarrow{\$} \mathbb{Z}_{\lfloor N/4 \rfloor}$, and $e_i = (1 + N)^{m_i} \cdot y_i^r \mod N^2$ for each $i \in [t]$, and sets $\mathsf{ct} = (u, \{e_i\}_{i=1}^t)$. To decrypt a particular ciphertext, one simply decrypts each piece, computing $m_i = \frac{\left(\frac{e_i}{u^{x_i}} - 1\right) \mod N^2}{N}$.

This scheme is also entry-wise additively homomorphic. Given $\mathsf{ct} = (u, \{e_i\}_{i=1}^t)$ encrypting $\{m_i\}_{i=1}^t$ and $\mathsf{ct}' = (u', \{e_i'\}_{i=1}^t)$ encrypting $\{m_i'\}_{i=1}^t$, the ciphertext $\mathsf{ct}_{\mathsf{sum}} = (u \cdot u' \mod N^2, \{e \cdot e_i' \mod N^2\}_{i=1}^t)$ is an encryption of $\{m_i + m_i' \mod N\}_{i=1}^t$. One can also homomorphically multiply each underlying m_i with a single scalar a by computing $\mathsf{ct}^a = (u^a \mod N^2, \{(e_i)^a \mod N^2\}_{i=1}^t)$, which is an encryption of $\{a \cdot m_i \mod N\}_{i=1}^t$.

This optimization enables t messages of size n bits to be encrypted using a ciphertext of size $(t + 1) \cdot 2n$ bits, which corresponds to an expansion factor of $\frac{2(t+1)}{t}$.

The two optimizations can be combined, meaning that for any choice s and t, we can encrypt t messages each of size $n \cdot s$ bits using a ciphertext of size $(s+1) \cdot (t+1) \cdot n$ bits. This means the ciphertext has an expansion of $\frac{(s+1) \cdot (t+1)}{s \cdot t} \times$. As t and s grow, this means we can make the ciphertext expansion as close to 1 as we like.

5.2.3   Encrypting Multiple Messages in a Single Ciphertext

Utilizing the batching techniques in the previous two subsections, one can reduce the ciphertext expansion of the Camenisch-Shoup encryption scheme, but the plaintext space becomes as large as N^s. We now describe how the plaintext space can be decomposed into slots of size B each. More concretely, each ciphertext can be viewed as having $t \cdot s'$ "slots" of messages $\leq B$, where $s' = \lfloor \frac{N^s}{B} \rfloor$. Recall that t comes from the fact that we encrypt t messages each of size up to N^s with shared first component. The s' component comes from the fact that the message space N^s is now divided into s' slots of size B each. Specifically, given $t \cdot s'$ messages $\{m_{i,j}\}_{i\in[t], j\in[s']}$ in $\mathbb{Z}_B$, we compute $m_i = \sum_{j=1}^{s'} m_{i,j} \cdot B^{j-1}$ for each $i \in [t]$ and then encrypt the t messages $\{m_i\}_{i=1}^t$. (Note that each $m_i \leq N^s$.) Given a public key $(g, \{y_i\}_{i\in[t]})$ the ciphertext is computed as follows:

$$
\mathsf{ct} = \begin{cases}
u = (g)^r \\
e_1 = (1+N)^{\sum_{j=1}^{s'} m_{1,j} \cdot B^{j-1}} \cdot (h_1)^r \\
\quad \vdots \\
e_i = (1+N)^{\sum_{j=1}^{s'} m_{i,j} \cdot B^{j-1}} \cdot (h_i)^r \\
\quad \vdots \\
e_t = (1+N)^{\sum_{j=1}^{s'} m_{t,j} \cdot B^{j-1}} \cdot (h_t)^r
\end{cases}
$$

We observe that the resulting encryption is slot-wise additively homomorphic as long as the sum in each slot never exceeds B. In addition, all the slots can be homomorphically multiplied by a single scalar simultaneously as long as the resulting value in each slot does not exceed B.

These slotted encryptions are compatible with all the other pieces of our protocol. In particular the following needed properties of the Camenisch-Shoup encryption scheme can be extended to the slotted encryptions (including in combination):

1. Proof that the value encrypted in a ciphertext is identical to the value underlying another commitment.
2. Proof that a ciphertext decrypts to a value underlying another commitment.
3. Proof that a ciphertext was produced by homomorphically adding a committed value to another ciphertext, and rerandomizing.
4. Proof that a ciphertext was produced by homomorphically scalar-multiplying a committed value to another ciphertext and rerandomizing.

5.2.4   Batching Commitments of Decrypted Values

In our protocol, we need to commit to a set of values $\{\beta_i\}$ that are decrypted from the batched Camenisch-Shoup ciphertexts and prove consistency between the committed values and decrypted values. We can batch the commitments as described in Sect. 5.1, and prove consistency between batched commitments with batched decryption. The high-level idea is the following. Given a set of commitments and ciphertexts, the verifier first picks a set of random coefficients $\{c_i\}$. Then both parties can compute a single commitment and a single encryption of a random linear combination of the underlying values, namely $\sum c_i \beta_i$. After that, the prover simply proves consistency between the resulting commitment and encryption. Our batched proof for this step has sublinear communication complexity.

5.3   Batching Sigma Protocols

In certain circumstances, it is possible to batch a set of ℓ sigma protocols that prove similar statements, such that the batched protocol has communication cost similar to a single sigma protocol. Batching sigma protocols is well-known in the literature [33,34]. In this section we describe a variant that is compatible with range proofs, and in particular, induces much less slack in the range-proof bound.

We describe the technique by an example. Let g be a generator of a group $\mathbb{G}$ of order q, and let $\{y_i = g^{x_i}\}_{i \in [\ell]}$, where each $x_i \in [q]$. We give a batched sigma protocol in Fig. 5 for the following ZK-AOK:

$$\mathsf{ZK\text{-}AoK}\left\{\{x_i\}_{i \in [\ell]} : y_i = g^{x_i} \quad \forall i \in [\ell]\right\}.$$

We can see in the figure that the prover sends a single group element in its first message (as opposed to ℓ group elements in an unbatched execution) and a single element in its response to the verifier (as opposed to ℓ elements in an unbatched execution). The verifier sends ℓ challenges instead of one, but the communication cost of these can be ignored if we use the Fiat-Shamir heuristic to make the protocol non-interactive. This means that the communication cost is essentially

1. Prover samples $\widetilde{x} \xleftarrow{\$} [q]$ and sends $\widetilde{y} = g^{\widetilde{x}}$ to Verifier.
2. Verifier chooses random challenges $c_i \xleftarrow{\$} \{0,1\}^{\lambda}$ for $i \in [\ell]$, and sends to Prover.
3. Prover computes $\widehat{x} = \widetilde{x} + \sum_{i=1}^{\ell} c_i \cdot x_i \bmod q$, and sends $\widehat{x}$ to Verifier.
4. Verifier verifies that $g^{\widehat{x}} = \widetilde{y} \cdot \prod_{i=1}^{\ell}(y_i)^{c_i}$.

Fig. 5. Example for batching sigma protocols.

the same as a single unbatched sigma-protocol execution. Completeness of the protocol is straightforward. Next we prove its soundness and zero-knowledge property.

Soundness and Extraction. We construct a PPT extractor that interacts with a cheating prover and extracts valid witnesses $\{x_i\}_{i \in [\ell]}$. The extractor first executes the protocol honestly with the prover and obtains a transcript $(\widetilde{y}, \{c_i\}_{i \in [\ell]}, \widehat{x})$ such that $g^{\widehat{x}} = \widetilde{y} \cdot \prod_{i=1}^{\ell} y_i^{c_i}$.

Now the extractor rewinds the protocol to Step 2 and sends a different random challenge c_1' while keeping all the other challenges the same, and obtains $\widehat{x}'$ such that $g^{\widehat{x}'} = \widetilde{y} \cdot (y_1)^{c_1'} \prod_{i=2}^{\ell}(y_i)^{c_i}$. Combining the two equations, the extractor gets $g^{\Delta\widehat{x}} = y_1^{\Delta c}$ where $\Delta\widehat{x} = \widehat{x} - \widehat{x}'$ and $\Delta c = c_1 - c_1'$. Now the extractor can compute $x_1 = \Delta\widehat{x} \cdot (\Delta c)^{-1} \bmod q$. This process can be repeated for all $i \in [\ell]$ to extract all x_i.

Zero-Knowledge. We prove this protocol is honest-verifier zero-knowledge by constructing a PPT simulator that does the following. First it samples $c_i \xleftarrow{\$} \{0,1\}^{\lambda}$ for all $i \in [\ell]$ and $\widehat{x} \xleftarrow{\$} [q]$, and then computes $\widetilde{y} = g^{\widehat{x}} / \prod_{i=1}^{\ell}(y_i)^{c_i}$. Finally it outputs the transcript $(\widetilde{x}, \{c_i\}_{i \in [\ell]}, \widehat{x})$. The simulated transcript is statistically identical to the real protocol.

This batching technique extends naturally to more complex sigma protocols that prove relations between multiple elements and consistency between exponents. Concrete examples of the batched sigma protocols we use in our protocol can be found in our full version.

Effect of Batching on Range Proofs. Batching has a small effect on the slack of range proofs that we consider. Recall that the size bound on a particular exponent x is related to the size of $\widehat{x}$, that is, the part of the prover's response related to that element. Batching ℓ sigma protocols increases the size of each element of the prover's response by a factor of ℓ. This is because the value needs to be big enough to statistically mask $\sum_{i=1}^{\ell} c_i \cdot x_i$, which is ℓ times larger than the unbatched case. Therefore, batching introduces an additional factor of ℓ to the proved range.

5.4   Multi-exponentiation Argument

In our protocol, we will need to batch a set of arguments that an ElGamal ciphertext ct_i' is a re-randomization of another ciphertext ct_i raised to a hidden committed value β_i. Our idea is to first take a random linear combination of these equations and then prove an ElGamal ciphertext $\widetilde{\mathsf{ct}}$ is the product of a set of known ciphertexts $\{\widetilde{\mathsf{ct}}_i\}$ raised to a set of hidden committed values $\{\beta_i\}$, where the commitments are batched as described in Sect. 5.1. We notice that this can be achieved by a multi-exponentiation argument from the work of Bayer and Groth [5], which has sublinear communication complexity. One subtlety is that the values $\{\beta_i\}$ are committed in the group of the Camenisch-Shoup encryption for proving consistency with the decrypted values, but to the apply multi-exponentiation argument, they must be committed in the group of the ElGamal encryption. Therefore, we commit to $\{\beta_i\}$ in both groups and prove consistency between the commitments. Since all the commitments and sigma protocols can be batched, the overall communication complexity is sublinear.

6   Communication, Computation and Monetary Costs

In this section, we present the communication, computation and monetary costs of our protocol. The offline phase for generating parameters for the different primitive we will use has a fixed cost, which includes four ZK-AoK of exponent per party plus one proof that a modulus N is a product of safe primes [12], which requires $O(\kappa^2 \log N)$ communication and computation where κ is the security parameter for the soundness of the last proof.

For our online phase, we have several batching optimizations described in Sect. 5 that allow us to achieve different trade-offs between communication and computation. Thus, we state our efficiency estimates parameterized with the different batching parameters presented in Table 1 that we apply for the commitments and encryptions. Our shuffled DOPRF has 3 rounds, each of which has an associated sigma protocol. Wherever the sigma protocols can be batched, we batch them into a single execution, and this is reflected in the costs. The specifics of the batching can be found in our the version of the paper.

In Table 2 we present the computation and communication cost estimates for the different phases of out protocol. There are three different types of computational operations we perform in the protocol, namely group operations in $\mathbb{G}$, exponentiations mod N (for commitments), and exponentiations mod $N^{s_{cam}+1}$ for Camenisch-Shoup encryption. There are also 4 types of elements we communicate: group elements in $\mathbb{G}$, elements modulo N, elements modulo N^{s+1}, and sigma protocol response messages from the prover. The entries of Table 2 reflect counts of each of these types of operations and elements transferred.

We will compare our protocol's cost against the baseline, namely the semi-honest Diffie-Hellman based intersection-sum protocol [39]. In our concerete instantiation, we use safe RSA moduli of length 1536 bits. We use NIST curve prime256v1 as our group $\mathbb{G}$.

Table 1. Parameter notation

Notation	Parameter Meaning
n	number of inputs in each set
$\mathbb{G}$	group for OPRF
$size_{\mathbb{G}}$	size of elements in $\mathbb{G}$
N	RSA modulus
λ	security parameter for sigma protocol soundness and hiding
s_{cam}	modulus parameter for CS encryptions, their modulus will be $N^{s_{cam}+1}$
s'_{cam}	number of plaintexts that fit in the message space $N^{s_{cam}+1}$
t_{cam}	number of components e_i per CS encryption that share the first component u
N_{cam}	total number of CS ciphertexts ($\lceil n/(s'_{cam} \cdot t_{cam}) \rceil$)
s_{ped}	number of values committed in a Pedersen vector commitment in DOPRF round 2
n_{ped}	number of Pedersen vector commitments in DOPRF round 2 ($\lceil n/s_{ped} \rceil$)
n'_{cam}	number of batched CS ciphertexts per batched Pedersen commitment $\lceil s_{ped}/(s'_{cam} \cdot t_{cam}) \rceil$
$m_{multiexp}$	dimension m to use in the multiexponentiation proof from Bayer et al. [5] in DOPRF Round 3.

Table 2. Counts of various operations performed in each step of the DOPRF protocol, and corresponding communication cost.

	Computation	Communication
DOPRF Round 1		
Messages	2 exp mod N $+t_{cam} \cdot (t_{cam}+1)$ exp mod $N^{s_{cam}+1}$	$|N| \cdot (1 + t_{cam} \cdot (t_{cam}+1) \cdot (s_{cam}+1))$
Sigma Protocol	5 exp mod N $+3t_{cam} \cdot (t_{cam}+1)$ exp mod $N^{s_{cam}+1}$	$|N| \cdot (t_{cam}+3+t_{cam} \cdot (t_{cam}+1) \cdot (s_{cam}+1))$
DOPRF Round 2		
Messages	$(n+n_{cam}) \cdot (t_{cam}+1)$ exp mod $N^{s_{cam}+1}$ $+(3n+3n_{ped})$ exp mod N + n exp in $\mathbb{G}$	$(n_{cam} \cdot (t_{cam}+1)(s_{cam}+1) \cdot |N|))$ $+n \cdot size_{\mathbb{G}} + 3n_{ped} \cdot |N|$
Sigma Protocol	$2 \cdot (n_{cam}+s_{ped}) \cdot n_{sig}(t_{cam}+1)$ exp mod $N^{s_{cam}+1}$ $(10s_{ped}+10)+5n_{ped}$ exp mod N + $(2s_{ped}+n)$ exp in $\mathbb{G}$	$|N| \cdot n'_{cam}((s_{cam}+1) \cdot (t_{cam}+1)+\log n_{ped}+k)$ $+(5s_{ped}+8) \cdot |N| + s_{ped} \cdot size_{\mathbb{G}}$
DOPRF Round 3		
Messages	n/s'_{cam} exp mod $N^{s_{cam}+1}$ + $(n+n_{ped})$ exp mod N $+4n+n_{ped}$ exp in $\mathbb{G}$	$(3n+n_{ped}) \cdot size_{\mathbb{G}} + n_{ped}|N|$
Sigma Protocol 1	$(2+n_{ped}) \cdot (n_{cam}+1) \cdot (t_{cam}+1)$ exp mod $N^{s_{cam}+1}$ $+2(s_{ped}+1)+n_{ped}$ exp mod N $+2(s_{ped}+1)+n_{ped}$ exp in $\mathbb{G}$	$(n_{cam}+1) \cdot (s_{cam}+1) \cdot (t_{cam}+1)|N|$ $+(|N|+k)t_{cam}$ $+s_{ped} \cdot (3k+2size_{\mathbb{G}})$
Sigma Protocol 2	$2n(m_{multiexp}+6 \cdot \lceil n \, m_{multiexp} \rceil$ + exp in $\mathbb{G}$	$(5m_{multiexp}+\lceil n \, m_{multiexp} \rceil+10) \cdot size_{\mathbb{G}}$

To minimize communication costs, in the first and seconds rounds of the shuffled DOPRF protocol, we set $s_{ped} = \sqrt{n}$ and batch $\sqrt{n}$ sigma protocols together. We further set $t_{cam} = 8$. $s_{cam} = 4$, $s'_{cam} = 8$ and $m_{multiexp} = 8$. We compare costs with the DDH-based shuffled DOPRF with semi-honest security. The measurements appear in Table 3.

We briefly discuss how we choose our parameters. First we discuss our choice of s_{ped}. In Round 2 of the DOPRF, batching Pedersen commitments allows us to send 1 element mod N instead of s_{ped} elements in the Round 2 messages. However, each sigma protocol statement in this round now also grows to be of length s_{ped}, since we must prove knowledge of all values contained in a commitment together. Since each sigma protocol is of size s_{ped} individually, the batched sigma protocol is also be of length s_{ped}. In order to minimize both the number of commitments sent and the size of the batched sigma protocol, we set $s_{ped} = \sqrt{n}$, and $b_{sig} = \sqrt{n}$.

We note that generating the messages of the DOPRF Round 2 constitutes the computation bottleneck of the protocol. In this round, for each entry in the Receiver's set, the Receiver has to perform a homomorphic Camenisch-Shoup

Table 3. Comparison of communication and computation costs between our shuffled DOPRF protocol with parameters set to minimize communication, and the baseline protocol, namely the semi-honest DDH-based shuffled DOPRF.

	Our Protocol		DDH-based		
Input size	Comm. (KB)	Comp. (s)	Comm. (KB)	Comp. (s)	Comm. Expansion
2^{12}	1,287	1,150	256	0.71	5.03 $\times$
2^{16}	17,716	17,865	4,096	11.39	4.325 $\times$
2^{20}	275,675	284,075	65,536	182.29	4.21 $\times$

scalar multiplication with the encrypted key, and homomorphically add it to its encrypted and masked entry. In fact, the overall computation scales with t_{cam}, the number of components in the Camenisch-Shoup ciphertext. This means that if we increase the number of components of the Camenisch-Shoup ciphertexts, we end up greatly increasing the computation. Furthermore, when we increase the parameter s_{cam}, we are performing operations in the substantially larger group $n^{s_{cam}+1}$, which induces non-linearly increasing computation cost. In Table 4, we attempt to minimize computation, by reducing t_{cam} to 2, s_{cam} to 1 and s'_{cam} to 2. In this case, communication cost increases by about 60%, but computation cost drops by about 90%.

Table 4. Comparison of communication and computation costs between our shuffled DOPRF protocol when we set parameters to minimize computational cost. These parameters also minimize monetary cost.

	Our Protocol			DDH-based			
Input size	Comm(KB)	Comp(s)	Cost(c)	Comm(KB)	Comp(s)	Cost(c)	Cost Increase
2^{12}	1,893	141	0.053	256	0.71	0.002	24.9$\times$
2^{16}	28,289	2,215	0.831	4,096	11.39	0.034	24.2$\times$
2^{20}	436,719	35,583	13.1	65,536	182.29	0.551	24.00$\times$

To compare monetary costs, we use the costs from Google Cloud Platform.[1] The costs are given in Table 5. For computation, we use the price for pre-emptible virtual CPUs, which correspond to machines with an Intel Xeon E5 processor and 3.75 GB of memory, which matches the machines we used for benchmarking. We consider pre-emptible computation to capture the offline batch-processing scenario described by works that deploy PSI in practice [39]. We also use the cheapest tier of network cost, considering the cost for internet egress, since that captures the scenario of the two parties being in different datacenters or clouds. We note that, at the time of publication, all the major cloud providers have costs that are within a tight range.

---

[1] See https://cloud.google.com/compute/network-pricing/ for the network cost and https://cloud.google.com/compute/vm-instance-pricing for the computation cost.

Table 5. Costs for network and computation on Google Cloud Platform.

Network cost(USD per GB)	Computational cost (USD per CPU-hour)
$0.08	0.01

Table 6. Comparison of computation, communication and monetary costs of our protocols compared to related works. Monetary costs use the values in Table 5. Communication cost is in KB, Time is in seconds, and Cost is in cents (USD).

	Input size 2^{12}			Input size 2^{16}			Input size 2^{20}		
	Comm	Comp	Cost	Comm	Comp	Cost	Comm	Comp	Cost
DDH-DOPRF (semihonest)	256	0.71	0.002	4096	11.39	0.034	65536	182.29	0.55
Sort-Compare-Shuffle [37]	209920	0.61	1.60	4941824	12.65	37.7	108691456	235.3	829.3
EC-ROM (one-sided PSI) [61]	4915.2	0.19	0.037	80896	0.94	0.61	1353728	12.6	10.3
DE-ROM (one-sided PSI) [61]	3584	0.23	0.027	62464	1.3	0.47	1118208	18	8.53
Our SDOPRF (low comm.)	1287	1150	0.329	17716	17865	5.09	275675	284075	81.01
Our SDOPRF (low comp.)	1893	141	0.05	28289	2215	0.83	436719	35583	13.21

Comparison with Existing Works. In Table 6, we compare concrete costs of our protocol against existing works that achieve security against malicious adversaries. The key comparison is against the Sort-Compare-Shuffle (SCS) approach of Huang et al [37], which is the only existing work that is compatible with malicious security, two sided output, and computing a function on associated values in the intersection. We note that both our SDOPRFs have significantly lower communication, and crucially, lower concrete monetary cost. In particular, the "Low Computation" variant of our SDOPRF has monetary cost $30\times$ less for 2^{12} entries, and $64\times$ less for 2^{20} entries. We note that the SCS approach has lower computation costs and end-to-end running time, but that in the batch-processing setting, the computation cost is less of a factor than concrete monetary costs, since responses are not needed in real time.

We also compare against the most efficient one-sided malicious PSI works of Rindal et al. [61], and show that our protocols are in the same ballpark of total monetary cost. In particular, the "Low Computation" variant of our SDOPRF has monetary cost about $1.5\times$ that of the DE-ROM variant of [61]. We note that [61] do not easily support two sided output or computing over the intersection. We believe the modest increased cost of our protocol is reasonable in order to support these additional functionalities.[2]

References

1. Agrawal, R., Evfimievski, A., Srikant, R.: Information sharing across private databases. In: Proceedings of the 2003 ACM SIGMOD International Conference on Management of Data (2003)

---

[2] Concurrent to our work, Pinkas at el. [55] present a new one-sided malicious PSI that achieves better efficiency than [61], but we note that their protocol also does not easily support our two-sided functionality.

2. Applebaum, B., Ringberg, H., Freedman, M.J., Caesar, M., Rexford, J.: Collaborative, privacy-preserving data aggregation at scale. In: Atallah, M.J., Hopper, N.J. (eds.) PETS 2010. LNCS, vol. 6205, pp. 56–74. Springer, Heidelberg (2010). https://doi.org/10.1007/978-3-642-14527-8_4

3. Baldi, P., Baronio, R., De Cristofaro, E., Gasti, P., Tsudik, G.: Countering GATTACA: efficient and secure testing of fully-sequenced human genomes. In: ACM CCS (2011)

4. Barić, N., Pfitzmann, B.: Collision-free accumulators and fail-stop signature schemes without trees. In: Fumy, W. (ed.) EUROCRYPT 1997. LNCS, vol. 1233, pp. 480–494. Springer, Heidelberg (1997). https://doi.org/10.1007/3-540-69053-0_33

5. Bayer, S., Groth, J.: Efficient zero-knowledge argument for correctness of a shuffle. In: Pointcheval, D., Johansson, T. (eds.) EUROCRYPT 2012. LNCS, vol. 7237, pp. 263–280. Springer, Heidelberg (2012). https://doi.org/10.1007/978-3-642-29011-4_17

6. Belenkiy, M., Camenisch, J., Chase, M., Kohlweiss, M., Lysyanskaya, A., Shacham, H.: Randomizable proofs and delegatable anonymous credentials. In: Halevi, S. (ed.) CRYPTO 2009. LNCS, vol. 5677, pp. 108–125. Springer, Heidelberg (2009). https://doi.org/10.1007/978-3-642-03356-8_7

7. Bellare, M., Rogaway, P.: Random oracles are practical: a paradigm for designing efficient protocols. In: ACM CCS (1993)

8. Boneh, D., Boyen, X.: Short signatures without random oracles. In: Cachin, C., Camenisch, J.L. (eds.) EUROCRYPT 2004. LNCS, vol. 3027, pp. 56–73. Springer, Heidelberg (2004). https://doi.org/10.1007/978-3-540-24676-3_4

9. Boudot, F.: Efficient proofs that a committed number lies in an interval. In: Preneel, B. (ed.) EUROCRYPT 2000. LNCS, vol. 1807, pp. 431–444. Springer, Heidelberg (2000). https://doi.org/10.1007/3-540-45539-6_31

10. Bursztein, E., Hamburg, M., Lagarenne, J., Boneh, D.: OpenConflict: preventing real time map hacks in online games. In: IEEE Symposium on Security and Privacy (2011)

11. Camenisch, J., Kohlweiss, M., Rial, A., Sheedy, C.: Blind and anonymous identity-based encryption and authorised private searches on public key encrypted data. In: Jarecki, S., Tsudik, G. (eds.) PKC 2009. LNCS, vol. 5443, pp. 196–214. Springer, Heidelberg (2009). https://doi.org/10.1007/978-3-642-00468-1_12

12. Camenisch, J., Michels, M.: Proving in zero-knowledge that a number is the product of two safe primes. In: Stern, J. (ed.) EUROCRYPT 1999. LNCS, vol. 1592, pp. 107–122. Springer, Heidelberg (1999). https://doi.org/10.1007/3-540-48910-X_8

13. Camenisch, J., Shoup, V.: Practical verifiable encryption and decryption of discrete logarithms. In: Boneh, D. (ed.) CRYPTO 2003. LNCS, vol. 2729, pp. 126–144. Springer, Heidelberg (2003). https://doi.org/10.1007/978-3-540-45146-4_8

14. Camenisch, J., Stadler, M.: Efficient group signature schemes for large groups. In: Kaliski, B.S. (ed.) CRYPTO 1997. LNCS, vol. 1294, pp. 410–424. Springer, Heidelberg (1997). https://doi.org/10.1007/BFb0052252

15. Camenisch, J., Zaverucha, G.M.: Private intersection of certified sets. In: Dingledine, R., Golle, P. (eds.) FC 2009. LNCS, vol. 5628, pp. 108–127. Springer, Heidelberg (2009). https://doi.org/10.1007/978-3-642-03549-4_7

16. Ciampi, M., Orlandi, C.: Combining private set-intersection with secure two-party computation. In: Catalano, D., De Prisco, R. (eds.) SCN 2018. LNCS, vol. 11035, pp. 464–482. Springer, Cham (2018). https://doi.org/10.1007/978-3-319-98113-0_25

17. Dachman-Soled, D., Malkin, T., Raykova, M., Yung, M.: Efficient robust private set intersection. In: Abdalla, M., Pointcheval, D., Fouque, P.-A., Vergnaud, D. (eds.) ACNS 2009. LNCS, vol. 5536, pp. 125–142. Springer, Heidelberg (2009). https://doi.org/10.1007/978-3-642-01957-9_8

18. Damgard, I.: On Σ-protocols (2002). http://www.cs.au.dk/~ivan/Sigma.pdf

19. Damgård, I., Jurik, M.: A generalisation, a simplification and some applications of Paillier's probabilistic public-key system. In: Kim, K. (ed.) PKC 2001. LNCS, vol. 1992, pp. 119–136. Springer, Heidelberg (2001). https://doi.org/10.1007/3-540-44586-2_9

20. De Cristofaro, E., Gasti, P., Tsudik, G.: Fast and private computation of cardinality of set intersection and union. In: Pieprzyk, J., Sadeghi, A.-R., Manulis, M. (eds.) CANS 2012. LNCS, vol. 7712, pp. 218–231. Springer, Heidelberg (2012). https://doi.org/10.1007/978-3-642-35404-5_17

21. De Cristofaro, E., Kim, J., Tsudik, G.: Linear-complexity private set intersection protocols secure in malicious model. In: Abe, M. (ed.) ASIACRYPT 2010. LNCS, vol. 6477, pp. 213–231. Springer, Heidelberg (2010). https://doi.org/10.1007/978-3-642-17373-8_13

22. Debnath, S.K., Dutta, R.: Secure and efficient private set intersection cardinality using bloom filter. In: Lopez, J., Mitchell, C.J. (eds.) ISC 2015. LNCS, vol. 9290, pp. 209–226. Springer, Cham (2015). https://doi.org/10.1007/978-3-319-23318-5_12

23. Dodis, Y., Yampolskiy, A.: A verifiable random function with short proofs and keys. In: Vaudenay, S. (ed.) PKC 2005. LNCS, vol. 3386, pp. 416–431. Springer, Heidelberg (2005). https://doi.org/10.1007/978-3-540-30580-4_28

24. Dong, C., Chen, L., Wen, Z.: When private set intersection meets big data: an efficient and scalable protocol. In: ACM CCS (2013)

25. Egert, R., Fischlin, M., Gens, D., Jacob, S., Senker, M., Tillmanns, J.: Privately computing set-union and set-intersection cardinality via bloom filters. In: Foo, E., Stebila, D. (eds.) ACISP 2015. LNCS, vol. 9144, pp. 413–430. Springer, Cham (2015). https://doi.org/10.1007/978-3-319-19962-7_24

26. ElGamal, T.: A public key cryptosystem and a signature scheme based on discrete logarithms. IEEE Trans. Inf. Theory **31**, 469–472 (1985)

27. Falk, B.H., Noble, D., Ostrovsky, R.: Private set intersection with linear communication from general assumptions (2018)

28. Falk, B.H., Noble, D., Ostrovsky, R.: Private set intersection with linear communication from general assumptions. In: WPES@CCS (2019)

29. Fiat, A., Shamir, A.: How to prove yourself: practical solutions to identification and signature problems. In: Odlyzko, A.M. (ed.) CRYPTO 1986. LNCS, vol. 263, pp. 186–194. Springer, Heidelberg (1987). https://doi.org/10.1007/3-540-47721-7_12

30. Freedman, M.J., Hazay, C., Nissim, K., Pinkas, B.: Efficient set intersection with simulation-based security. J. Cryptol. **29**, 115–155 (2016)

31. Freedman, M.J., Nissim, K., Pinkas, B.: Efficient private matching and set intersection. In: Cachin, C., Camenisch, J.L. (eds.) EUROCRYPT 2004. LNCS, vol. 3027, pp. 1–19. Springer, Heidelberg (2004). https://doi.org/10.1007/978-3-540-24676-3_1

32. Fujisaki, E., Okamoto, T.: Statistical zero knowledge protocols to prove modular polynomial relations. In: Kaliski, B.S. (ed.) CRYPTO 1997. LNCS, vol. 1294, pp. 16–30. Springer, Heidelberg (1997). https://doi.org/10.1007/BFb0052225

33. Gennaro, R., Leigh, D., Sundaram, R., Yerazunis, W.: Batching schnorr identification scheme with applications to privacy-preserving authorization and low-bandwidth communication devices. In: Lee, P.J. (ed.) ASIACRYPT 2004. LNCS, vol. 3329, pp. 276–292. Springer, Heidelberg (2004). https://doi.org/10.1007/978-3-540-30539-2_20

34. Groth, J.: Linear algebra with sub-linear zero-knowledge arguments. In: Halevi, S. (ed.) CRYPTO 2009. LNCS, vol. 5677, pp. 192–208. Springer, Heidelberg (2009). https://doi.org/10.1007/978-3-642-03356-8_12

35. Hazay, C., Lindell, Y.: Efficient protocols for set intersection and pattern matching with security against malicious and covert adversaries. In: Canetti, R. (ed.) TCC 2008. LNCS, vol. 4948, pp. 155–175. Springer, Heidelberg (2008). https://doi.org/10.1007/978-3-540-78524-8_10

36. Hazay, C., Nissim, K.: Efficient set operations in the presence of malicious adversaries. In: Nguyen, P.Q., Pointcheval, D. (eds.) PKC 2010. LNCS, vol. 6056, pp. 312–331. Springer, Heidelberg (2010). https://doi.org/10.1007/978-3-642-13013-7_19

37. Huang, Y., Evans, D., Katz, J.: Private set intersection: are garbled circuits better than custom protocols? In: NDSS (2012)

38. Huberman, B.A., Franklin, M., Hogg, T.: Enhancing privacy and trust in electronic communities. In: ACM Conference on Electronic Commerce (1999)

39. Ion, M., et al.: Private intersection-sum protocol with applications to attributing aggregate ad conversions. Cryptology ePrint Archive, Report 2017/738 (2017). https://eprint.iacr.org/2017/738

40. Jarecki, S., Liu, X.: Efficient oblivious pseudorandom function with applications to adaptive OT and secure computation of set intersection. In: Reingold, O. (ed.) TCC 2009. LNCS, vol. 5444, pp. 577–594. Springer, Heidelberg (2009). https://doi.org/10.1007/978-3-642-00457-5_34

41. Kissner, L., Song, D.: Privacy-preserving set operations. In: Shoup, V. (ed.) CRYPTO 2005. LNCS, vol. 3621, pp. 241–257. Springer, Heidelberg (2005). https://doi.org/10.1007/11535218_15

42. Kolesnikov, V., Kumaresan, R., Rosulek, M., Trieu, N.: Efficient batched oblivious PRF with applications to private set intersection. In: ACM CCS (2016)

43. Kolesnikov, V., Matania, N., Pinkas, B., Rosulek, M., Trieu, N.: Practical multi-party private set intersection from symmetric-key techniques. In: ACM CCS (2017)

44. Lambæk, M.: Breaking and fixing private set intersection protocols. Cryptology ePrint Archive, Report 2016/665 (2016). https://eprint.iacr.org/2016/665

45. Li, M., Cao, N., Yu, S., Lou, W.: FindU: privacy-preserving personal profile matching in mobile social networks. In: IEEE INFOCOM (2011)

46. Miao, P., Patel, S., Raykova, M., Seth, K., Yung, M.: Two-sided malicious security for private intersection-sum with cardinality. Cryptology ePrint Archive, Report 2020/385 (2020). https://eprint.iacr.org/2020/385

47. Mitsunari, S., Sakai, R., Kasahara, M.: A new traitor tracing. IEICE Trans. Fundam. Electron. Commun. Comput. Sci. **85**, 481–484 (2002)

48. Nagaraja, S., Mittal, P., Hong, C.Y., Caesar, M., Borisov, N.: BotGrep: finding P2P bots with structured graph analysis. In: USENIX Security (2010)

49. Nagy, M., De Cristofaro, E., Dmitrienko, A., Asokan, N., Sadeghi, A.R.: Do i know you?: efficient and privacy-preserving common friend-finder protocols and applications. In: ACSAC (2013)

50. Narayanan, A., Thiagarajan, N., Lakhani, M., Hamburg, M., Boneh, D., et al.: Location privacy via private proximity testing. In: NDSS, vol. 11 (2011)

51. Narayanan, G.S., Aishwarya, T., Agrawal, A., Patra, A., Choudhary, A., Rangan, C.P.: Multi party distributed private matching, set disjointness and cardinality of set intersection with information theoretic security. In: Garay, J.A., Miyaji, A., Otsuka, A. (eds.) CANS 2009. LNCS, vol. 5888, pp. 21–40. Springer, Heidelberg (2009). https://doi.org/10.1007/978-3-642-10433-6_2
52. Pagh, R., Rodler, F.F.: Cuckoo hashing. J. Algorithms (2004)
53. Pedersen, T.P.: Non-interactive and information-theoretic secure verifiable secret sharing. In: Feigenbaum, J. (ed.) CRYPTO 1991. LNCS, vol. 576, pp. 129–140. Springer, Heidelberg (1992). https://doi.org/10.1007/3-540-46766-1_9
54. Pinkas, B., Rosulek, M., Trieu, N., Yanai, A.: SpOT-light: lightweight private set intersection from sparse OT extension. In: Boldyreva, A., Micciancio, D. (eds.) CRYPTO 2019. LNCS, vol. 11694, pp. 401–431. Springer, Cham (2019). https://doi.org/10.1007/978-3-030-26954-8_13
55. Pinkas, B., Rosulek, M., Trieu, N., Yanai, A.: PSI from PaXoS: fast, malicious private set intersection. In: Canteaut, A., Ishai, Y. (eds.) EUROCRYPT 2020. LNCS, vol. 12106, pp. 739–767. Springer, Cham (2020). https://doi.org/10.1007/978-3-030-45724-2_25
56. Pinkas, B., Schneider, T., Segev, G., Zohner, M.: Phasing: private set intersection using permutation-based hashing. In: USENIX Security (2015)
57. Pinkas, B., Schneider, T., Tkachenko, O., Yanai, A.: Efficient circuit-based PSI with linear communication. In: Ishai, Y., Rijmen, V. (eds.) EUROCRYPT 2019. LNCS, vol. 11478, pp. 122–153. Springer, Cham (2019). https://doi.org/10.1007/978-3-030-17659-4_5
58. Pinkas, B., Schneider, T., Weinert, C., Wieder, U.: Efficient circuit-based PSI via cuckoo hashing. In: Nielsen, J.B., Rijmen, V. (eds.) EUROCRYPT 2018. LNCS, vol. 10822, pp. 125–157. Springer, Cham (2018). https://doi.org/10.1007/978-3-319-78372-7_5
59. Pinkas, B., Schneider, T., Zohner, M.: Faster private set intersection based on OT extension. In: USENIX Security (2014)
60. Rindal, P., Rosulek, M.: Improved private set intersection against malicious adversaries. In: Coron, J.-S., Nielsen, J.B. (eds.) EUROCRYPT 2017. LNCS, vol. 10210, pp. 235–259. Springer, Cham (2017). https://doi.org/10.1007/978-3-319-56620-7_9
61. Rindal, P., Rosulek, M.: Malicious-secure private set intersection via dual execution. In: ACM CCS (2017)
62. Segal, A., Ford, B., Feigenbaum, J.: Catching bandits and only bandits: privacy-preserving intersection warrants for lawful surveillance. In: FOCI (2014)
63. Vaidya, J., Clifton, C.: Secure set intersection cardinality with application to association rule mining. J. Comput. Secur. **13**, 593–622 (2005)

Private Set Intersection in the Internet Setting from Lightweight Oblivious PRF

Melissa Chase[1(⊠)] and Peihan Miao[2(⊠)]

[1] Microsoft Research, Redmond, USA
melissac@microsoft.com
[2] Visa Research, Palo Alto, USA
pemiao@visa.com

Abstract. We present a new protocol for two-party private set intersection (PSI) with semi-honest security in the plain model and one-sided malicious security in the random oracle model. Our protocol achieves a better balance between computation and communication than existing PSI protocols. Specifically, our protocol is the fastest in networks with moderate bandwidth (e.g., 30–100 Mbps). Considering the monetary cost (proposed by Pinkas et al. in CRYPTO 2019) to run the protocol on a cloud computing service, our protocol also compares favorably.

Underlying our PSI protocol is a new lightweight multi-point oblivious pseudorandom function (OPRF) protocol based on oblivious transfer (OT) extension. We believe this new protocol may be of independent interest.

1 Introduction

Private set intersection (PSI) enables two parties, each holding a private set of elements, to compute the intersection of the two sets while revealing nothing more than the intersection itself. PSI has found many applications including privacy-preserving location sharing [NTL+11], private contact discovery [CLR17, RA17, DRRT18], DNA testing and pattern matching [TPKC07], testing of fully sequenced human genomes [BBDC+11], collaborative botnet detection [NMH+10], and measuring the effectiveness of online advertising [IKN+17]. In the past several years PSI has been extensively studied and has become truly practical with extremely fast implementations [HFH99, FNP04, DSMRY09, DCKT10, ADCT11, DCGT12, HEK12, DCW13, PSZ14, PSSZ15, KKRT16, RR17a, RR17b, CLR17, RA17, DRRT18, FNO18, PSWW18, GN19, PRTY19, PRTY20].

When measuring the efficiency of a PSI protocol, there are two major aspects usually considered. First, the *computation cost*, which is the amount of computing time necessary to run the protocol. Optimizing the computation cost is especially important in practice because of limited computational resources. The state-of-the-art computationally efficient semi-honest PSI protocol [KKRT16] uses only oblivious transfer (OT) [Rab05], a cryptographic hash

---

P. Miao—Part of the work done while visiting Microsoft Research.

D. Micciancio and T. Ristenpart (Eds.): CRYPTO 2020, LNCS 12172, pp. 34–63, 2020.
https://doi.org/10.1007/978-3-030-56877-1_2

function, symmetric-key cryptographic operations, and bitwise operations. It can privately compute the intersection of two million-size sets in about 4 s. This is because OT itself has been heavily optimized, and in particular because of work on OT extension [IKNP03, ALSZ13], which allows many oblivious transfers to be performed using only a small number of public key operations and a combination of symmetric primitives (hash functions/AES) and bitwise operations.

The second aspect in the measurement is the *communication cost*, which refers to the total amount of communication in the protocol. Minimizing the communication cost is also crucial in practice due to limited network bandwidth, which is often a shared resource for multiple applications. The communication-optimal PSI protocol [ADCT11] requires communication that is only marginally more than a naïve and insecure protocol (where one party simply sends hash of its elements to the other party), but the protocol is computationally too expensive to be adopted in practice.

On the more practical side, Pinkas et al. [PRTY19] achieve communication that is half that of [KKRT16] and roughly 8 times the naïve approach at the cost of more expensive operations based on finite field arithmetic.[1] The result is roughly a 6–7 times overhead compared to [KKRT16]. This leaves open the question of whether reducing the communication cost of [KKRT16] requires more expensive computational tools, or whether it could be achieved with significantly lower computational overhead.

Can we achieve the best of both computation and communication?

When we look at tradeoffs between communication and computation, one valuable metric is the total running time of the protocol, which includes both the computation time and the time to transmit and receive the necessary messages. Of course this time will vary depending on the network bandwidth, and different protocols may perform better in different network settings. Viewed in this light, [KKRT16] can be viewed as a protocol optimized for the LAN setting, where bandwidth is not a bottleneck, while [PRTY19] is targeted at very low bandwidth settings. However, we argue that it is valuable to design optimized protocols for the full range of settings, and that the middle range (e.g. 30–100 Mbps) is in fact very important. During Q2–Q3 2018, the average download speed over fixed broadband in the U.S. was 95.25 Mbps and average upload speed was 32.88 Mbps [LLC18]. For example, the Comcast Standard business internet package includes 75 Mbps; larger businesses might have higher bandwidth but would not want to devote all of it to a single protocol. Thus, this seems like a very valuable range to consider.

In the work of Pinkas et al. [PRTY19], they propose an alternative efficiency metric—the *monetary cost* to run the protocol on a cloud computing service. This new metric takes both computation cost and communication cost into

---

[1] The work [PRTY19] describes two protocols, one optimized for speed (spot-fast) and one optimized for communication cost (spot-low). Here the comparison is for their fast protocol because the communication optimized one is significantly slower.

consideration. The PSI protocols proposed in [PRTY19] have much less communication compared to the computation-optimized protocol [KKRT16] and much faster running time compared to the communication-optimized protocol [ADCT11]. As a result, they achieve a better balance between computation and communication and have the least monetary cost. We can ask though, whether they achieve the *best* balance.

1.1   Our Contribution

In this work, we make positive progress on the aforementioned questions by presenting a new PSI protocol that achieves a better balance between computation and communication.

A New PSI. We present a new PSI construction which we believe achieves better computation/communication tradeoffs. This protocol is based only on oblivious transfer, hashing, symmetric-key and bitwise operations, and as such it has favorable computation; at the same time its communication is almost as small as [PRTY19]. In particular, our protocol is 2.53–$3.65\times$ faster than spot-fast and 19.4–$28.7\times$ faster than spot-low [PRTY19] in computation and requires 1.46–$1.69\times$ lower communication than [KKRT16]. Overall, our protocol is the fastest in a network with moderate bandwidth (e.g., 30–100 Mbps). In addition, we theoretically and experimentally analyze the monetary cost according to the metric from [PRTY19] and show that it compares very favorably.

Efficient Multi-point OPRF. The PSI protocol of [PRTY19] is based on a multi-point oblivious PRF (OPRF) protocol that requires polynomial interpolation over a large field, which is computationally significantly more expensive than the symmetric-key and bitwise operations in the single-point OPRF of [KKRT16]. We propose a new multi-point OPRF protocol that is based on OT extension that again relies only on symmetric-key and bitwise operations and hashing. It is conceptually very simple to understand and easy to implement. Additionally, our protocol is more flexible in that it allows for tuning parameters to achieve better computation or better communication. We believe this protocol may be of independent interest.

Security Against Malicious Sender. In most of this work, we focus on the *semi-honest* security model, where both parties follow the PSI protocol description honestly while trying to extract more information about the other party's input set, and aim to achieve the optimal practical efficiency. However, we can show that our protocol also achieves security in the random oracle model when one of the parties is malicious, in particular if we refer to the parties as sender and receiver where the receiver is the party who receives the output, then we protect against the malicious sender. In the previous work [KKRT16,PRTY19], only the spot-low variant of [PRTY19] achieves one-sided malicious security. As will be shown in Sect. 5, our protocol is much more efficient in running time and cheaper in monetary cost than spot-low.

We note that this sort of asymmetric guarantee is very appropriate in settings where the computation is between a large established company and a small business or a consumer. A large company may have a reputation to maintain and more policies and procedures in place to protect against misbehaviour, so assuming semi-honest security may be more reasonable. On the other hand, if the protocol is run with many different consumers or small businesses it may be hard to ensure that all of them are sufficiently trustworthy to assume semi-honest security.

In light of this, when we consider our efficiency metrics we also consider an asymmetric setting where the sender runs on a cloud service like AWS while the receiver has its own internet service; this should capture the example of a small business who does not have its own dedicated servers but would instead outsource its computations to the cloud. We see that in this setting our protocol is even more advantageous, achieving 5.01–$6.48\times$ lower monetary cost than spot-low [PRTY19] in all of the settings we consider.

1.2 Technical Overview

Conceptually speaking, our PSI protocol leverages a primitive called an oblivious pseudorandom function (OPRF) [FIPR05], which allows a sender to learn a PRF key k and a receiver to learn the PRF output $\mathsf{OPRF}_k(y_1), \ldots, \mathsf{OPRF}_k(y_n)$ on its inputs $y_1, \ldots, y_n \in Y$. Nothing about the receiver's inputs is revealed to the sender and nothing more about the key k is revealed to the receiver. If the sender additionally computes $\mathsf{OPRF}_k(x_1), \ldots, \mathsf{OPRF}_k(x_n)$ on its inputs $x_1, \ldots, x_n \in X$ and sends them to the receiver, then the receiver can identify the intersecting PRF values and the corresponding set intersection. In this section we describe how to construct an efficient OPRF protocol based on OT extension.

Our starting point is the computationally most efficient PSI proto-col [KKRT16], which can be conceptually viewed as evaluating n single-point OPRFs, where the sender learns a PRF key k while the receiver can only obliviously evaluate on a single input y. We first describe their protocol at a high level and then elaborate how to extend the single-point OPRF to a multi-point OPRF while still only using the efficient OT extension and symmetric-key operations.

Single-Point OPRF. The single-point OPRF realized in [KKRT16] is evaluated as follows. Let the PRF key k consist of two bit-strings $q, s \in \{0, 1\}^\lambda$. Let $F(\cdot)$ be a *pseudorandom code* that produces a pseudorandom string and let H be a hash function. The pseudorandom function is computed as

$$\mathsf{OPRF}_k(x) = H(q \oplus [F(x) \cdot s]),$$

where $\cdot$ denotes bitwise-AND and $\oplus$ denotes bitwise-XOR. For a randomly generated s, if $F(x)$ has enough Hamming weight then the function $\mathsf{OPRF}_k(x)$ is pseudorandom assuming the hash function H is *correlation robust*.

To evaluate this single-point OPRF on the receiver's input y, the receiver first samples a random string $r_0 \xleftarrow{\$} \{0, 1\}^\lambda$ and computes $r_1 = r_0 \oplus F(y)$. The sender also samples a random string $s \xleftarrow{\$} \{0,1\}^\lambda$. Then the two parties execute λ oblivious transfers where the sender acts as a receiver in the OT and inputs λ choice bits $s[1], s[2], \ldots, s[\lambda]$ while the receiver acts as a sender in the OT and inputs λ pairs of messages $\{r_0[i], r_1[i]\}_{i \in [\lambda]}$ (each message is a single bit). At the end of the OT, the sender receives λ bits $\{r_{s[i]}[i]\}_{i \in \lambda}$. Now the sender simply sets $q = r_{s[1]}[1] \| \ldots \| r_{s[\lambda]}[\lambda]$ and lets the PRF key be $k = (q, s)$. The PRF value on y learned by the receiver is $H(r_0)$. Correctness can easily be checked, namely $q \oplus [F(x) \cdot s] = r_0$ if $x = y$.

PSI From Single-Point OPRF. Given the above construction of single-point OPRF, [KKRT16] built a PSI protocol as follows. They first use Cuckoo hashing [PR04] to assign the receiver's elements into b bins such that each bin contains at most one element. Then the sender and receiver run the single-point OPRF for each bin so that the sender obtains b PRF keys and the receiver learns b PRF values. Now for each bin, the sender computes the PRF for that bin on all the possible elements in that bin, and sends all the PRF values to the receiver.

In the above single-point OPRF, the only heavy cryptographic tool needed is OT, which requires public-key operations. Since the same choice bits can be used for all the n instances of OPRF, all the OTs can be done via λ instances of string OTs, which can be efficiently instantiated by OT extension.

In this protocol, each element on the sender's side is evaluated on multiple PRFs (the number of hash functions plus the stash size in Cuckoo hashing), which incurs a constant overhead in communication from the sender to the receiver. We get rid of this overhead by constructing a multi-point ORPF so that every element is only evaluated once.

Extending to Multi-point OPRF. In the single-point OPRF construction, there are 2^λ possible choices of s and different resulting PRF keys k that the sender will receive. However, no matter which s is chosen, $\mathsf{OPRF}_k(y) = r_0$. We extend this idea to multi-point OPRF.

Our new PRF key contains a matrix M of size $m \times w$. To evaluate the PRF on input x, we again need a hash function H, and we evaluate a pseudorandom code $F(x)$ which produces a vector in $v \in [m]^w$. Let M_i denote the i-th column of M. The pseudorandom function is computed as

$$\mathsf{OPRF}_M(x) = H\left(M_1[v[1]] \| \ldots \| M_w[v[w]]\right).$$

The sender picks a random string $s \in \{0,1\}^w$. The receiver prepares two sets of column vectors $A_1, \ldots, A_w \in \{0,1\}^m$ and $B_1, \ldots, B_w \in \{0,1\}^m$. The two parties run w number of OTs where the sender behaves as a receiver and the receiver behaves as the sender. At the end of the protocol, the sender obtains w column vectors, which will form the PRF key M. On the other hand, the receiver forms an $m \times w$ matrix $A = [A_1 \ldots A_w]$ and computes the OPRF on its values by $\mathsf{OPRF}_A(y)$. At a high level, the receiver prepares the two sets of column vectors $\{A_1, \ldots, A_w\}$ and $\{B_1, \ldots, B_w\}$ such that no matter what s is chosen, $\mathsf{OPRF}_M(x) = \mathsf{OPRF}_A(x)$ for every $x \in Y$. The parameters m, w are carefully chosen such that $\mathsf{OPRF}_M(x)$ is pseudorandom to the receiver for every $x \notin Y$.

Preparing the column vectors takes the receiver linear time in n and only involves cheap symmetric-key and bitwise operations. The OTs can be instantiated by the efficient OT extension.

Multi-point OPRF From [PRTY19]. We note that [PRTY19] takes a different approach to achieving multi-point OPRF by high-degree polynomial interpolation and evaluation over a large field. Their computation complexity is asymptotically $\mathcal{O}(n \log^2 n)$ while ours is $\mathcal{O}(n)$. For concrete efficiency, our protocol only relies on efficient OT extension and AES operations. More details on performance comparison can be found in Sect. 5.

One-Sided Malicious Security. We further prove our protocol is secure against a malicious sender. We note that [PRTY19] also proves one-sided malicious security for spot-low. In their security proof, a pseudorandom function used in their protocol is modeled as a random oracle. Since the malicious party knows the PRF key, the PRF cannot be instantiated by efficient block ciphers like AES. Instantiating it using a hash function makes the protocol much less efficient than the semi-honest secure protocol. In our protocol, the pseudorandom code $F(\cdot)$ is instantiated by a pseudorandom function $F_k(\cdot)$ and both parties know the PRF key, hence the same problem arises. In order to achieve the best efficiency, we only model hash functions as random oracles and assume F is a PRF, which makes our security proof more involved.

1.3   Related Work

In this work we primarily compare with [KKRT16] and [PRTY19] since as discussed above they currently provide the best tradeoffs between computation and communication. [PSZ14,PSSZ15] provide a good overview and performance comparison of a variety of approaches to PSI. To briefly mention a few, generic MPC based PSI [HEK12] incurs higher communication and computation costs, and Diffie-Hellman based PSI (e.g. [IKN+17]) has relatively small communication (comparable to [PRTY19]) but incurs significantly higher computation costs. There are protocols based on garbled circuit-based OPRFs which can be competitive when the set sizes are very unequal [KRS+19]. There have also been other works based on OT extension [PSSZ15,PSZ18], which can achieves the best performance for very short elements and small set sizes.

There have also been several other works which followed up on the [KKRT16] approach, notably [FNO18]. They describe a scheme which replaces the Cuckoo hash table with another algorithm for assigning elements to table rows which is more complex to compute but allows for a slightly smaller table and removes the stash. They do not provide an implementation, but they claim that for most set sizes their scheme achieves a 10–15% improvement in communication costs over [KKRT16] whereas we achieve a 30–40% improvement in communication with what we would expect to be much lighter computational overhead.

2   Preliminaries

2.1   Notation

We use λ, σ to denote the computational and statistical security parameters, respectively. We use $[n]$ to denote the set $\{1, 2, \ldots, n\}$. For a vector v of length ℓ, we use $v[i]$ to denote the i-th element of the vector. For a matrix M of dimension $n \times m$, we use M_i to denote its i-th column vector ($i \in [n]$). We use $\|x\|_{\mathsf{H}}$ to denote the hamming weight of a binary string x. By $\mathsf{negl}(\lambda)$ we denote a negligible function, i.e., a function f such that $f(\lambda) < 1/p(\lambda)$ holds for any polynomial $p(\cdot)$ and sufficiently large λ.

2.2   Security Model

Private Set Intersection (PSI) is a special case of secure two-party computation. We follow the standard security definitions for secure two-party computation in this work. The ideal functionality of PSI is defined in Fig. 1.

Parameters: P_1's input set size n_1 and P_2's input set size n_2.

Inputs: Party P_1 inputs a set of elements $X = \{x_1, \ldots, x_{n_1}\}$ where $x_i \in \{0,1\}^*$. Party P_2 inputs a set of elements $Y = \{y_1, \ldots, y_{n_2}\}$ where $y_i \in \{0,1\}^*$.

Output: Party P_2 receives the set intersection $I = X \cap Y$.

Fig. 1. Ideal functionality for PSI $\mathcal{F}_{\mathsf{PSI}}$.

Semi-honest Security. Let $\mathsf{view}_1^{\varPi}(X, Y)$ and $\mathsf{view}_2^{\varPi}(X, Y)$ be the view of P_1 and P_2 in the protocol $\varPi$, respectively. Let $\mathsf{out}^{\varPi}(X, Y)$ be the output of P_2 in the protocol. Let $f(X, Y)$ be the output of P_2 in the ideal functionality. The protocol $\varPi$ is semi-honest secure if there exists PPT simulators $\mathcal{S}_1$ and $\mathcal{S}_2$ such that for all inputs X, Y,

$$\left(\mathsf{view}_1^{\varPi}(X, Y), \mathsf{out}^{\varPi}(X, Y)\right) \overset{c}{\approx} \left(\mathcal{S}_1(1^n, X, n_2), f(X, Y)\right);$$

$$\mathsf{view}_2^{\varPi}(X, Y) \overset{c}{\approx} \mathcal{S}_2(1^n, Y, n_1, f(X, Y)).$$

Malicious Security Against P_1. The protocol $\varPi$ is secure against a malicious P_1 if for any PPT adversary $\mathcal{A}$ in the real world (acting as P_1) that could arbitrarily deviate from the protocol, there exists a PPT adversary $\mathcal{S}$ in the ideal world (acting as P_1) that could change its input to the ideal functionality and abort the output, such that for all inputs X, Y,

$$\mathsf{Real}_{\mathcal{A}}^{\varPi}(X, Y) \overset{c}{\approx} \mathsf{Ideal}_{\mathcal{S}}^{\mathcal{F}}(X, Y),$$

where $\mathsf{Real}_{\mathcal{A}}^{\varPi}(X, Y)$ is the output of $\mathcal{A}$ and P_2 in the real world, $\mathsf{Ideal}_{\mathcal{S}}^{\mathcal{F}}(X, Y)$ is the output of $\mathcal{S}$ and P_2 in the ideal world.

2.3 Oblivious Transfer

Oblivious Transfer (OT), introduced by Rabin [Rab05], is a central cryptographic primitive in the area of secure computation. 1-out-of-2 OT refers to the setting where a sender has two input strings (m_0, m_1) and a receiver has an input choice bit $b \in \{0, 1\}$. As the result of the OT protocol, the receiver learns m_b without learning anything about m_{1-b} while the sender learns nothing about b. This primitive requires expensive public-key operations. Ishai et al. [IKNP03] introduced a technique called OT extension that allows for a large number of OT executions at the cost of computing a small number of public-key operations. In Random OT (ROT), the sender's OT inputs (m_0, m_1) are randomly chosen, which allows the protocol itself to produce these random values. Hence a random OT protocol requires much less communication especially from the sender to the receiver. In this work we only need the weaker primitive of random OT, whose functionality is defined in Fig. 2.

Parameters: Message length L.

Inputs: The receiver inputs a choice bit $b \in \{0, 1\}$ and the sender inputs nothing.

Output: Sample $m_0, m_1 \overset{\$}{\leftarrow} \{0, 1\}^L$. Output (m_0, m_1) to the sender and m_b to the receiver.

Fig. 2. Ideal functionality for Random Oblivious Transfer $\mathcal{F}_{\mathsf{ROT}}$.

2.4 Correlation Robustness

Our PSI construction is proven secure under a *correlation robustness* assumption on the on the underlying hash function, which was introduced for OT extension [IKNP03] and later generalized in [KK13, KKRT16, PRTY19] to the version we use in this work.

Definition 1 (Hamming Correlation Robustness). *Let H be a hash function with input length n. Then H is d-Hamming correlation robust if, for any $a_1, \ldots, a_m, b_1, \ldots, b_m \in \{0, 1\}^n$ with $\|b_i\|_{\mathsf{H}} \geq d$ for each $i \in [m]$, the following distribution, induced by random sampling of $s \overset{\$}{\leftarrow} \{0, 1\}^n$, is pseudorandom. Namely,*

$$\left(H(a_1 \oplus [b_1 \cdot s]), \ldots, H(a_m \oplus [b_m \cdot s]) \right) \overset{c}{\approx} \left(F(a_1 \oplus [b_1 \cdot s]), \ldots, F(a_m \oplus [b_m \cdot s]) \right),$$

where $\cdot$ denotes bitwise-AND and $\oplus$ denotes bitwise-XOR, F is a random function.

The IKNP protocol uses this assumption with $n = d = \lambda$. In that case, the only valid choice for b_i is 1^λ and the distribution simplifies to $H(a_1 \oplus s), \ldots, H(a_m \oplus s)$. In our case, we use $n > d = \lambda$, so other choices for the b_i values are possible.

3   Our PSI Protocol

In this section we describe our protocol and prove its semi-honest security in the plain model and malicious security against P_1 in the random oracle model.

3.1   Construction

We describe our PSI protocol in Fig. 3. During the protocol in Step 2 the two parties need to run an OT protocol. Since the matrix A is randomly sampled by P_2, this step can be instantiated efficiently using random OT as shown in Fig. 4.

   At a high level, P_2 constructs two matrices A and B of special form from its input elements. Note that for each $y \in Y$, let $v = F_k(H_1(y))$, the matrices A and B are constructed such that $D_i[v[i]] = 0$ for all $i \in [w]$, and hence $A_i[v[i]] = B_i[v[i]] = C_i[v[i]]$ for all $i \in [w]$. That means, if P_1's element $x = y$ for some $y \in Y$ (i.e., x is in the intersection), then its input to the hash function in Step 3 will be the same as y's input to the hash function. On the other hand, if x is not in the intersection, then its input to the hash function would be significantly different from any y's input to the hash function, and the PRF output would be pseudorandom to P_2. Note that the hash function $H_1(\cdot)$ is not necessary for semi-honest security, but is applied for extracting P_1's inputs in the malicious case.

   The parameters m, w in our protocol are chosen such that if F is a random function and $H_1(x)$ is different for each $x \in X \cup Y$, then for each $x \in X \setminus I$ and $v = F(H_1(x))$, there are at least d 1's in $D_1[v[1]], \ldots, D_w[v[w]]$ with all but negligible probability. We discuss how to choose these parameters in Sect. 3.3.

3.2   Security Proof

Theorem 1. *If F is a PRF, H_1 is a collision resistant hash function, and H_2 is a d-Hamming correlation robust hash function, then the protocol in Fig. 3 securely realizes $\mathcal{F}_{\mathsf{PSI}}$ in the semi-honest model when parameters m, w, ℓ_1, ℓ_2 are chosen as described in Sect. 3.3.*

Security Against Corrupt P_1. We construct $\mathcal{S}_1$ as follows. It is given P_1's input set X. $\mathcal{S}_1$ runs the honest P_1 protocol to generate its view with the following exceptions: For the oblivious transfer, $\mathcal{S}_1$ generates P_1's random string $s \xleftarrow{\$} \{0,1\}^w$ honestly and chooses a random matrix $C \in \{0,1\}^{m \times w}$, and runs the OT simulator to simulate the view for an OT receiver with inputs $s[1], \ldots, s[w]$ and outputs $C_1, \ldots, C_w$. In Step 3a $\mathcal{S}_1$ sends a uniformly random PRF key k to P_1. Finally $\mathcal{S}_1$ outputs P_1's view. We prove $\left(\mathsf{view}_1^{\Pi}(X,Y), \mathsf{out}^{\Pi}(X,Y)\right) \overset{c}{\approx} (\mathcal{S}_1(1^n, X, n_2), f(X,Y))$ via the following hybrid argument:

Hyb_0 P_1's view and P_2's output in the real protocol.

0. P_1 and P_2 agree on security parameters λ, σ, protocol parameters m, w, ℓ_1, ℓ_2, two hash functions $H_1 : \{0,1\}^* \to \{0,1\}^{\ell_1}$ and $H_2 : \{0,1\}^w \to \{0,1\}^{\ell_2}$, pseudorandom function $F : \{0,1\}^\lambda \times \{0,1\}^{\ell_1} \to [m]^w$.

1. **Precomputation**
   - P_1 samples a random string $s \xleftarrow{\$} \{0,1\}^w$.
   - P_2 does the following:
     (a) Initialize an $m \times w$ binary matrix D to all 1's. Denote its column vectors by $D_1, \ldots, D_w$. Then $D_1 = \cdots = D_w = 1^m$.
     (b) Sample a uniformly random PRF key $k \xleftarrow{\$} \{0,1\}^\lambda$.
     (c) For each $y \in Y$, compute $v = F_k(H_1(y))$. Set $D_i[v[i]] = 0$ for all $i \in [w]$.

2. **Oblivious Transfer**
   (a) P_2 randomly samples an $m \times w$ binary matrix $A \xleftarrow{\$} \{0,1\}^{m \times w}$. Compute matrix $B = A \oplus D$.
   (b) P_1 and P_2 run w oblivious transfers where P_2 is the sender with inputs $\{A_i, B_i\}_{i \in [w]}$ and P_1 is the receiver with inputs $s[1], \ldots, s[w]$. As a result P_1 obtains w number of m-bit strings as the column vectors of matrix C (with dimension $m \times w$).

3. **OPRF Evaluation**
   (a) P_2 sends the PRF key k to P_1.
   (b) For each $x \in X$, P_1 computes $v = F_k(H_1(x))$ and its OPRF value $\psi = H_2(C_1[v[1]]\| \ldots \|C_w[v[w]])$ and sends ψ to P_2.
   (c) Let Ψ be the set of OPRF values received from P_1. For each $y \in Y$, P_2 computes $v = F_k(y)$ and its OPRF value $\psi = H_2(A_1[v[1]]\| \ldots \|A_w[v[w]])$ and outputs y iff $\psi \in \Psi$.

Fig. 3. Our private set intersection protocol.

Hyb_1 Same as Hyb_0 except that on P_2's side, for each $i \in [w]$, if $s[i] = 0$, then sample $A_i \xleftarrow{\$} \{0,1\}^m$ and compute $B_i = A_i \oplus D_i$; otherwise sample $B_i \xleftarrow{\$} \{0,1\}^m$ and compute $A_i = B_i \oplus D_i$. This hybrid is identical to Hyb_0.

Hyb_2 Same as Hyb_1 except that $\mathcal{S}_1$ (instead of P_2) chooses the random PRF key k. This hybrid is statistically identical to Hyb_1.

Hyb_3 Same as Hyb_2 but the protocol aborts if there exists $x, y \in X \cup Y, x \neq y$ such that $H_1(x) = H_1(y)$. The aborting probability is negligible because H_1 is collision resistant.

Hyb_4 Same as Hyb_3 but the protocol also aborts if there exists $x \in X \setminus I$ such that, for $v = F_k(H_1(x))$, there are fewer than d 1's in $D_1[v[1]], \ldots, D_w[v[w]]$. The parameters m, w are chosen such that if F is a random function and $H_1(x)$ is different for each $x \in X \cup Y$, then the aborting probability is negligible. If the aborting probability in Hyb_4 is non-negligible, then we can construct a PPT adversary $\mathcal{A}$ to break the security of PRF. In particular, given the sets X and Y, $\mathcal{A}$ constructs the matrix D as in Hyb_4 except that

1. P_1 and P_2 perform w random OTs with message length m, where P_1 is the receiver with inputs choice bits $s[1], \ldots, s[w]$. As a result, P_2 gets w pairs of random messages $\{r_i^{(0)}, r_i^{(1)}\}_{i \in [w]}$ and P_1 gets w messages $\{r_i\}_{i \in [w]}$ where $r_i = r_i^{(s[i])}$.

2. P_2 does the following:
   (a) Let $\{r_i^{(0)}\}_{i \in [w]}$ form the column vectors of the matrix A and compute the matrix $B = A \oplus D$.
   (b) Compute $\Delta_i = B_i \oplus r_i^{(1)}$ for all $i \in [w]$ and send to P_1.

3. P_1 computes the matrix C as follows: if $s[i] = 0$ then set $C_i = r_i$; otherwise set $C_i = r_i \oplus \Delta_i$.

Fig. 4. Step 2 of our PSI protocol instantiated using random OT.

whenever it needs to compute F_k, $\mathcal{A}$ queries the PRF challenger for the output. Finally, if there exists $x \in X \backslash I$ such that, for $v = F_k(H_1(x))$, there are fewer than d 1's in $D_1[v[1]], \ldots, D_w[v[w]]$, namely the protocol aborts, then $\mathcal{A}$ guesses PRF, otherwise $\mathcal{A}$ guesses random function. $\mathcal{A}$ guesses correctly with probability $\frac{1}{2} +$ non-negl. Therefore, the protocol aborts with negligible probability in Hyb_4.

Hyb_5 Same as Hyb_4 but party P_2's output is replaced by $f(X, Y)$ (i.e., the intersection $I = X \cap Y$). This hybrid changes P_2's output if and only if there exists $x \in X, y \in Y, x \neq y$ such that, for $v = F_k(H_1(x)), u = F_k(H_1(y))$, $H_2(C_1[v[1]] \| \ldots \| C_w[v[w]]) = H_2(A_1[u[1]] \| \ldots \| A_w[u[w]])$. This happens with negligible probability as $H_2(C_1[v[1]] \| \ldots \| C_w[v[w]])$ is pseudorandom by the correlation robustness of H_2, so for sufficiently large ℓ_2 this probability will be negligible.

Specifically, for each $x_i \in X \setminus I$, let $v_i = F_k(H_1(x))$, $a_i = A_1[v_i[1]] \| \ldots \| A_w[v_i[w]]$, and $b_i = D_1[v_i[1]] \| \ldots \| D_w[v_i[w]]$. Then x_i's input to the hash function H_2 is $C_1[v_i[1]] \| \ldots \| C_w[v_i[w]]$, which is $a_i \oplus [b_i \cdot s]$. Additionally we have the guarantee that $\|b_i\|_{\mathsf{H}} \geq d$. Since s is randomly sampled, by the d-Hamming correlation robustness of H_2, the outputs of $H_2(C_1[v_i[1]] \| \ldots \| C_w[v_i[w]])$ are pseudorandom.

If the outputs of $H_2(C_1[v_i[1]] \| \ldots \| C_w[v_i[w]])$ are truly random, then a collision of $H_2(C_1[v[1]] \| \ldots \| C_w[v[w]]) = H_2(A_1[u[1]] \| \ldots \| A_w[u[w]])$ happens with negligible probability. If the collision in this hybrid happens with non-negligible probability, then we can construct a PPT adversary $\mathcal{A}$ to break the correlation robustness of H_2. In particular, given the sets X and Y, $\mathcal{A}$ constructs the matrix A as in this hybrid and $H_2(A_1[u_i[1]] \| \ldots \| A_w[u_i[w]])$ for each $y_i \in Y$. $\mathcal{A}$ can also compute the matrix D as in this hybrid and (a_i, b_i) for each $x_i \in X \setminus I$. As we explained above, $H_2(C_1[v_i[1]] \| \ldots \| C_w[v_i[w]]) = H_2(a_i \oplus [b_i \cdot s])$. $\mathcal{A}$ queries the oracle for the outputs of $H_2(a_i \oplus [b_i \cdot s])$. If a collision happens, then $\mathcal{A}$ guesses the hash function; otherwise $\mathcal{A}$ guesses random function. $\mathcal{A}$ guesses correctly with probability $\frac{1}{2} +$ non-negl. Therefore, the probability of collision is negligible by our choice of ℓ_2 for semi-honest security in Sect. 3.3.

Hyb_6 Same as Hyb_5 but the protocol does not abort. The indistinguishability of Hyb_6 and Hyb_5 follows from the collision resistance of H_1 and the pseudorandomness of F_k by the same arguments as above.

Hyb_7 The simulated view of $\mathcal{S}_1$ and $f(X,Y)$. The only difference from Hyb_6 is that $\mathcal{S}_1$ samples the matrix C and runs the OT simulator to simulate the view of an OT receiver for P_1. This hybrid is computationally indistinguishable from Hyb_6 by security of the OT protocol.

Security Against Corrupt P_2. We construct $\mathcal{S}_2$ as follows. It is given as input P_2's set Y, the size of P_1's set n_1, and the intersection $I = f(X,Y)$. $\mathcal{S}_2$ runs the honest P_2 protocol with the following exceptions: For the oblivious transfer, $\mathcal{S}_2$ computes the matrices A and B honestly and run the OT simulator to produce a simulated view for the OT sender. For each $x \in I$, it computes $v = F_k(H_1(x))$ and the OPRF value $\psi = H_2(A_1[v[1]]\|\dots\|A_w[v[w]])$. Let this set of OPRF values be Ψ_I. Choose $n_1 - |I|$ random ℓ_2-bit strings and let this set be Ψ_{rand}. Send $\Psi = \Psi_I \cup \Psi_{\mathsf{rand}}$ to P_2 in Step 3b. Finally $\mathcal{S}_2$ outputs P_2's view in this invocation. We argue $\mathsf{view}_2^{\Pi}(X,Y) \overset{c}{\approx} \mathcal{S}_2(1^n, Y, n_1, f(X,Y))$ through the following hybrids:

Hyb_0 P_2's view in the real protocol.

Hyb_1 Same as Hyb_0 but the protocol aborts if there exists $x, y \in X \cup Y, x \neq y$ such that $H_1(x) = H_1(y)$. The aborting probability is negligible because H_1 is collision resistant for sufficiently large ℓ_1 chosen in Sect. 3.3.

Hyb_2 Same as Hyb_1 except that the protocol aborts if there exists $x \in X \setminus I$ such that, for $v = F_k(H_1(x))$, there are fewer than d 1's in $D_1[v[1]], \dots, D_w[v[w]]$. The parameters m, w are chosen such that if F is a random function and $H_1(x)$ is different for each $x \in X \cup Y$, then the aborting probability is negligible. If the aborting probability in Hyb_2 is non-negligible, then we can construct a PPT adversary $\mathcal{A}$ to break the security of PRF. In particular, given the sets X and Y, $\mathcal{A}$ constructs the matrix D as in Hyb_2 except that whenever it needs to compute F_k, $\mathcal{A}$ queries the PRF challenger for the output. Finally, if there exists $x \in X \setminus I$ such that, for $v = F_k(H_1(x))$, there are fewer than d 1's in $D_1[v[1]], \dots, D_w[v[w]]$, namely the protocol aborts, then $\mathcal{A}$ guesses PRF, otherwise $\mathcal{A}$ guesses random function. $\mathcal{A}$ guesses correctly with probability $\frac{1}{2} + \mathsf{non\text{-}negl}$. Therefore, the protocol aborts with negligible probability in Hyb_2.

Hyb_3 Same as Hyb_2 except that $\mathcal{S}_2$ runs the OT simulator to produce a simulated view of an OT sender for P_2. This hybrid is computationally indistinguishable to Hyb_2 by security of the OT protocol.

Hyb_4 Same as Hyb_3 except that we replace the OPRF values for $x \in X \setminus I$ by random ℓ_2-bit strings. Hyb_4 is computationally indistinguishable from Hyb_3 because of the d-Hamming correlation robustness of H_2. Specifically, for each $x_i \in X \setminus I$, let $v_i = F_k(H_1(x))$, $a_i = A_1[v_i[1]]\|\dots\|A_w[v_i[w]]$, and $b_i = D_1[v_i[1]]\|\dots\|D_w[v_i[w]]$. Then x_i's input to the hash function H_2 is $C_1[v_i[1]]\|\dots\|C_w[v_i[w]]$, which is $a_i \oplus [b_i \cdot s]$. Additionally we have the guarantee that $\|b_i\|_H \geq d$. Since s is randomly sampled and unknown to the P_2, by the d-Hamming correlation robustness of H_2, the outputs of $H_2(C_1[v_i[1]] \| \ldots \| C_w[v_i[w]])$, i.e., the OPRF values for $x_i \in X \setminus I$, are pseudorandom by the choice of ℓ_2 for semi-honest security in Sect. 3.3.

Hyb_5 Same as Hyb_4 except that the protocol does not abort. The indistinguishability of Hyb_4 and Hyb_5 follows from the collision resistance of H_1 and the pseudorandomness of F by the same arguments as above. The hybrid is the view output by $\mathcal{S}_2$.

Theorem 2. *If F is a PRF, H_1 and H_2 are modeled as random oracles, and the underlying OT protocol is secure against a malicious receiver, then the protocol in Fig. 3 is secure against malicious P_1 when parameters m, w, ℓ_1, ℓ_2 are chosen as described in Sect. 3.3.*

We construct $\mathcal{S}$ that interacts with the malicious P_1 as follows. $\mathcal{S}$ samples a random matrix $C \in \{0,1\}^{m \times w}$, and runs the malicious OT simulator on P_1 with output $C_1, \ldots, C_w$. $\mathcal{S}$ honestly chooses the random PRF key k and sends k to P_1 in Step 3a. On P_1's query x to the random oracle H_1, $\mathcal{S}$ records the pair $(x, H_1(x))$ in a table T_1, which was initialized empty. On P_1's query z to the random oracle H_2, $\mathcal{S}$ records the pair $(z, H_2(z))$ in a table T_2, which was initialized empty. In Step 3b when P_1 sends OPRF values Ψ, $\mathcal{S}$ finds all the values $\psi \in \Psi$ such that $\psi = H_2(z)$ for some z in T_2, and $z = C_1[v[1]] \| \ldots \| C_w[v[w]]$ where $v = F_k(H_1(x))$ for some x in T_1. Then $\mathcal{S}$ sends these x's to the ideal functionality. Finally $\mathcal{S}$ outputs whatever P_1 outputs.

Let $\mathcal{Q}_1, \mathcal{Q}_2$ be the set of queries P_1 makes to H_1, H_2 respectively, and let $Q_1 = |\mathcal{Q}_1|, Q_2 = |\mathcal{Q}_2|$. We will abuse notation, and for $m \times w$ bit-matrix C and vector $u \in [m]^w$, we write $C[v]$ to mean $C_1[v[1]] \| \ldots \| C_w[v[w]]$. Similarly, for a set V of vectors in $[m]^w$, we use $C[V]$ to denote the set $\{C[v] | v \in V\}$.

We prove $\mathsf{Real}_{\mathcal{A}}^{\Pi}(X,Y) \overset{c}{\approx} \mathsf{Ideal}_{\mathcal{S}}^{\mathcal{F}}(X,Y)$ via the following hybrid argument:

Hyb_0 The outputs of P_1 and P_2 in the real world.

Hyb_1 Same as Hyb_0 except that $\mathcal{S}$ runs the OT simulator on P_1 to extract s, lets $C_i = A_i$ if $s[i] = 0$ and $C_i = B_i$ otherwise, gives $C_1, \ldots, C_w$ to the OT simulator as output. This hybrid is computationally indistinguishable from Hyb_0 because of OT security against a malicious receiver.

Hyb_2 Same as Hyb_1 but the protocol aborts if there exists $x, y \in \mathcal{Q}_1 \cup Y, x \neq y$ such that $H_1(x) = H_1(y)$. The aborting probability is negligible because H_1 is a random oracle, hence also collision resistant for sufficiently large ℓ_1 chosen in Sect. 3.3.

Hyb_3 Same as Hyb_2 but in Step 3c, for each OPRF value ψ sent by P_1, if $\psi \notin H_2(\mathcal{Q}_2)$, then P_2 ignores ψ when computing the set intersection. This hybrid changes P_2's output with negligible probability because H_2 is a random oracle with output length at least ℓ_2 (see Sect. 3.3 for the choice of ℓ_2 in the malicious case). Specifically, the probability that ψ equals the output of H_2 on one of P_2's elements is negligible.

Hyb_4 Same as Hyb_3 but the protocol aborts if in Step 3c, there exists $z \in \mathcal{Q}_2, z' \in A[F_k(H_1(Y))]$ with $z \neq z'$ and $H_2(z) = H_2(z')$. If this happens, then we find a collision of H_2, which happens with negligible probability because H_2 is a random oracle with sufficiently large output length ℓ_2 chosen in Sect. 3.3 for malicious security.

Hyb_5 Same as Hyb_4 but in Step 3c, for each OPRF value ψ sent by P_1, P_2 ignores ψ when computing the set intersection if $\psi = H_2(z)$ for some $z \in \mathcal{Q}_2$ where $z \notin C[F_k(H_1(\mathcal{Q}_1))]$.

This hybrid changes P_2's output only if there exists $y \in Y$ such that $\psi = H_2(A[F_k(H_1(y))])$, which implies $z = A[F_k(H_1(y))]$ by the abort condition added in Hyb_4.

First, note that if $y \in \mathcal{Q}_1$, then we have $z = A[F_k(H_1(y))] = C[F_k(H_1(y))] \in C[F_k(H_1(\mathcal{Q}_1))]$ where the second equality follows from construction of the matrix D. Thus, we need only consider $y \in Y \setminus \mathcal{Q}_1$. Also note that for all $y \in Y$, $A[F_k(H_1(y))] = C[F_k(H_1(y))]$, so we can say that the hybrid output changes only if there exists $y \in Y \setminus \mathcal{Q}_1, z \in \mathcal{Q}_2$ such that $z = C[F_k(H_1(y))]$. Suppose there is a PPT adversary $\mathcal{A}$ that with non-negligible probability produces $\mathcal{Q}_1, \mathcal{Q}_2, Y$ such that there exist $z \in \mathcal{Q}_2, y \in Y \setminus \mathcal{Q}_1$ such that $z = C[F_k(H_1(y))]$. Then we show we can break security of the PRF.

To see this, consider the following experiment:

1. Pick random outputs to be used for $H_1(\mathcal{Q}_1)$.
2. Pick random C, simulate the OTs with $\mathcal{A}$, responding to its H_1 queries using the pre-chosen outputs, and responding to its H_2 queries using random function table T_2 filled in on demand, and abort if any of the abort conditions are triggered.
3. Send a random k to $\mathcal{A}$ in Step 3a and continue to respond to oracle queries the same way.
4. $\mathcal{A}$ sends Ψ.
5. Pick random outputs to be used for $H_1(Y \setminus \mathcal{Q}_1)$, and output 1 if there exist $z \in \mathcal{Q}_2, y \in Y \setminus \mathcal{Q}_1$ such that $z = C[F_k(H_1(y))]$.

Observe that if $\mathcal{A}$ succeeds in distinguishing the two hybrids, then this experiment outputs 1 with non-negligible probability. The intuition is that $\mathcal{A}$ fixes $\mathcal{Q}_2$ before we choose $H_1(Y \setminus \mathcal{Q}_1)$, so if the game succeeds then the PRF must be very biased, to the point where it is straightforwardly detectable.

To make this more formal, consider the following PRF adversary $\mathcal{B}$. $\mathcal{B}$ will choose random C, then sample 2 sets of $|Y|$ random values each, $\mathcal{L}, \mathcal{L}'$. Call the PRF challenger to obtain $F(\mathcal{L}), F(\mathcal{L}')$. Output PRF if $C[F(\mathcal{L})] \cap C[F(\mathcal{L}')]$ is non-empty.

If F is a PRF: Define $P_{C,k}$ as the probability of the above experiment outputting 1 conditioned on (C, k). Note that we are assuming for the sake of contradiction that the experiment outputs 1 with non-negligible probability ϵ. Hence there must exist at least ϵ fraction of (C, k) pairs such that $P_{C,k} > \epsilon$. Conditioned on (C, k), let $\mathcal{W}_{C,k}$ be the set of H_2 queries that maximizes the probability that the experiment outputs 1. Then we know that if $P_{C,k} > \epsilon$, then the probability that for random choice of $\mathcal{L}$ we get

$\mathcal{W}_{C,k} \cap C[F_k(\mathcal{L})] \neq \emptyset$ is at least ϵ. That means that there exists $z_{C,k} \in \mathcal{W}_{C,k}$ such that the probability over random choice of $\mathcal{L}$ that $z \in C[F_k(\mathcal{L})]$ is at least ϵ/Q_2. And for such $z_{C,k}$, if we pick 2 random sets $\mathcal{L}, \mathcal{L}'$, the probability that we get $z_{C,k} \in C[F_k(\mathcal{L})]$ and $z_{C,k} \in C[F_k(\mathcal{L}')]$ and therefore $C[F_k(\mathcal{L})] \cap C[F_k(\mathcal{L}')] \neq \emptyset$ is at least ϵ^2/Q_2^2. Thus, the overall probability that $\mathcal{B}$ outputs PRF is at least ϵ^3/Q_2^2, which is non-negligible.

If F is random function: First, note that with all but negligible probability, $\mathcal{L}, \mathcal{L}'$ are disjoint sets with no repeated elements, so computing $F(\mathcal{L}), F(\mathcal{L}')$ is equivalent to choosing $2|Y \setminus \mathcal{Q}_1|$ random values $\mathcal{W}, \mathcal{W}'$. Now, for any pair of j, j' and any column i, the probability that $C_i[\mathcal{W}_j[i]] = C_i[\mathcal{W}_{j'}[i]]$, taken over the choice of $\mathcal{W}, \mathcal{W}', C$ is: $\Pr[\mathcal{W}_j[i] = \mathcal{W}_{j'}[i]] + \Pr[\mathcal{W}_j[i] \neq \mathcal{W}_{j'}[i]] \cdot \frac{1}{2} = \frac{1}{2} + \frac{1}{2m}$, and these probabilities are independent across columns. Thus, the probability that $C[\mathcal{W}_j] = C[\mathcal{W}_{j'}]$ is $\left(\frac{1}{2} + \frac{1}{2m}\right)^w$, which is negligible by our choice of parameters m, w in Sect. 3.3.

Hyb_6 Same as Hyb_5 but the protocol also aborts if there exists $x \in \mathcal{Q}_1, y \in Y$ such that, $z = C[F_k(H_1(x))] = A[F_k(H_1(y))]$ but $x \neq y$. We argue that this abort happens with negligible probability by security of the PRF.

Suppose that there exists a PPT adversary $\mathcal{A}$ who can cause this abort to happen with non-negligible probability. Let Q be a polynomial upper bound on the number of H_1 queries made by the adversary. Then we build the following algorithm $\mathcal{B}$ to break security of the PRF. $\mathcal{B}$ will first choose $Q + |Y|$ random outputs to H_1. $\mathcal{B}$ will then choose random C and use the OT simulator to extract s from the OTs. If $\mathcal{A}$ makes H_1 queries during this process it will use the pre-chosen outputs. Then $\mathcal{B}$ computes the matrix D using the appropriate H_1 outputs and using its oracle to compute F. From C, D and s it will compute the matrix A. Finally, it will output PRF if there exist a pair of outputs h, h' in its pre-chosen random H_1 output set for which $C[F(h)] = A[F(h')]$.

Clearly this game outputs PRF with non-negligible probability in the PRF case if the abort in Hyb_6 happens with non-negligible probability. Now we will argue that in the random function case it outputs PRF with only negligible probability.

Consider the following game, which produces outputs identical to the above experiment with $\mathcal{B}$ in random function case: We first pick the random function F and the H_1 outputs. Then compute D. Then extract s from the OTs and choose random C. Finally, compute the corresponding A, and output PRF as above if there exist a pair of outputs h_1, h_2 in its pre-chosen random H_1 output set for which $C[F(h_1)] = A[F(h_2)]$.

Now we evaluate the probability of producing PRF in this game. First consider the probability that for a particular pair of H_1 outputs h, h' we obtain $C[F(h)] = A[F(h')]$. Consider the step where we choose random C and compute A. Let $u = F(h)$ and $v = F(h')$. Since C is chosen at random, if $s_i \wedge D_i[v_i] = 0$, then we have $\Pr[C_i[u_i] = A_i[v_i]] = \Pr[C_i[u_i] = C_i[v_i]] = \frac{1}{2} + \frac{1}{2m}$ and if $s_i \wedge D_i[v_i] = 1$, then $\Pr[C_i[u_i] = A_i[v_i]] = \Pr[C_i[u_i] \neq C_i[v_i]] = \frac{1}{2} - \frac{1}{2m}$, and these probabilities are independent for different i's. Thus even in the worst case we have that the probability that $C[F(h)] = A[F(h')]$ is at most $\left(\frac{1}{2} + \frac{1}{2m}\right)^w$, which for our choice of parameters in Sect. 3.3 is negligible.

Hyb_7 Same as Hyb_6 except that party P_2's output is replaced by its output in the ideal world. This hybrid changes P_2's output if and only if there exists an OPRF value ψ sent by P_1 and considered by P_2 such that, $\psi = H_2(C[F_k(H_1(x))])$ for some $x \in \mathcal{Q}_1$, and $\psi = H_2(A[F_k(H_1(y))])$ for some $y \in Y, y \neq x$. We already know that $C[F_k(H_1(x))] \neq A[F_k(H_1(y))]$ by the abort condition introduced in Hyb_6, hence we find a collision of H_2, which happens with negligible probability because H_2 is a random oracle with sufficiently large output length ℓ_2 chosen in Sect. 3.3 for malicious security.

Hyb_8 Same as Hyb_7 but the protocol does not abort. Hyb_8 and Hyb_7 are computationally indistinguishable because H_1 and H_2 are random oracles and F_k is a PRF by the same arguments as above.

Hyb_9 The outputs of $\mathcal{S}$ and P_2 in the ideal world. The only difference of this hybrid from Hyb_8 is that $\mathcal{S}$ (instead of P_2) samples the random matrix C, which is identically distributed.

3.3 Parameter Analysis

Choice of m, w. The parameters m, w in our PSI protocol are chosen such that if F is a random function and $H_1(x)$ is different for each $x \in X \cup Y$, then for each $x \in X \setminus I$ and $v = F(H_1(x))$, there are at least d 1's in $D_1[v[1]], \ldots, D_w[v[w]]$ with all but negligible probability. We now discuss how to choose the parameters. We first fix m and then decide on w as follows.

Consider each column D_i, initialized as 1^m. Then for each $y \in Y$, P_2 computes $v = F(H_1(y))$ and sets $D_i[v[i]] = 0$. Since $H_1(y)$ is different for each $y \in Y$ and F is a random function, v is random and independent for each $y \in Y$. The probability $\Pr[D_i[j] = 1]$ is the same for all $j \in [m]$. In particular,

$$\Pr[D_i[j] = 1] = \left(1 - \frac{1}{m}\right)^{n_2}.$$

Let $p = \left(1 - \frac{1}{m}\right)^{n_2}$. For any $x \in X \setminus I$, let $v = F(H_1(x))$, then $\Pr[D_i[v[i]] = 1] = p$ and the probability is independent for all $i \in [w]$. Hence the probability that there are k 1's in $D_1[v[1]], \ldots, D_w[v[w]]$ is

$$\binom{w}{k} p^k (1-p)^{w-k}.$$

We want there to be at least d 1's for each $x \in X \setminus I$ with all but negligible probability. By the union bound, it is sufficient for the following probability to be negligible:

$$n_1 \cdot \sum_{k=0}^{d-1} \binom{w}{k} p^k (1-p)^{w-k} \leq \mathsf{negl}(\sigma).$$

From this we can derive a proper w.

In our security proof against malicious P_1, we further require that $\left(\frac{1}{2} + \frac{1}{2m}\right)^w \leq \mathsf{negl}(\lambda)$. For all the concrete parameters we choose in Sect. 4.1, this requirement is also satisfied.

Choice of ℓ_1. The parameter ℓ_1 is the output length of the hash function H_1. For security parameter λ, we need to set $\ell_1 = 2\lambda$ to guarantee collision resistance against the birthday attack.

Choice of ℓ_2. The parameter ℓ_2 is the output length of the hash function H_2, which controls the collision probability of the PSI protocol. For semi-honest security, it can be computed as $\ell_2 = \sigma + \log(n_1 n_2)$, similarly as in [KKRT16, PRTY19]. For security against malicious P_2, it can be computed similarly as $\ell_2 = \sigma + \log(Q_2 \cdot n_2)$ where Q_2 is the maximum number of queries the adversary can make to H_2.

4   Implementation Details

We implement our PSI protocol in C++. In this section we discuss the concrete parameters used in our implementation and how we instantiate all the cryptographic primitives. Our implementation is available on GitHub: https://github.com/peihanmiao/OPRF-PSI.

4.1   Parameters

Our computational security parameter is set to $\lambda = 128$ and statistical security parameter is $\sigma = 40$. We also set d to be 128. We focus on the setting where $n_1 = n_2 = n$, i.e., the two parties have sets of equal size. The other parameters are

- m: the number of rows (or height) of the matrix D.
- w: the number of columns (or width) of the matrix D.
- ℓ_1: the output length in bits of the hash function H_1, set as 256.
- ℓ_2: the output length in bits of the hash function H_2.

Our protocol is flexible in that we can set these parameters differently to trade-off between computation and communication. Specifically, once we fix n and m, we can compute w as in Sect. 3.3. Intuitively, for a fixed set size n, if we set a bigger m, then we will get a bigger fraction of 1's in each column of the matrix D, which leads to a smaller w and requires less computation of the pseudorandom function F in the PSI protocol. To guarantee collision resistance of H_1, the parameter ℓ_1 is set to be 256. For security against malicious P_1, we assume the maximum number of queries the adversary can make to H_2 is 2^{64}. We list different choices of the other parameters in Table 1. In our experiment, we will set $m = n$ for all settings as it achieves nearly optimal communication among all choices of m and allows for optimal computation.

Table 1. Parameters for set size n, matrix height m, matrix width w, and output length ℓ_2 in bits of the hash function H_2 for semi-honest and malicious security.

n	m	w	ℓ_2 (semi-honest)	ℓ_2 (malicious)
2^{16}	n	609	72	120
2^{18}	n	615	76	122
2^{20}	n	621	80	124
2^{22}	n	627	84	126
2^{24}	n	633	88	128
2^{24}	$0.9n$	717	88	128
2^{24}	$1.1n$	571	88	128
2^{24}	$2n$	349	88	128

4.2   Instantiation of Cryptographic Primitives

Our PSI protocol requires the following cryptographic primitives:

- F: a pseudorandom function.
- H_1: a collision-resistant hash function.
- H_2: a Hamming correlation robust hash function.
- Base OTs for OT extension.

In our implementation, H_1 and H_2 are instantiated using BLAKE2 [BLA]. Base OTs are instantiated using Naor-Pinkas OT [NP99]. We use the implementation of base OTs from the libOTe library [Rin].

Instantiation of F. We would like to instantiate F using AES, but note that the input and output length of AES is 128 bits. Recall that in our protocol, we require $F : \{0,1\}^\lambda \times \{0,1\}^{\ell_1} \to [m]^w$, where the input length is $\ell_1 = 256$ and output length is $w \cdot \log m$.

One way to instantiate F is to apply a pseudorandom generator (PRG) on top of cipher block chaining message authentication code (CBC-MAC). In particular, let $G : \{0,1\}^\lambda \times \{0,1\}^\lambda \to \{0,1\}^\lambda$ be a pseudorandom function (instantiated by AES) and $\mathsf{PRG} : \{0,1\}^\lambda \to \{0,1\}^{t \cdot \lambda}$ be a PRG (instantiated by AES CTR mode), where $t = \lceil \frac{w \cdot \log m}{\lambda} \rceil$. Let $x = x_0 \| x_1$ be the input where $x_0, x_1 \in \{0,1\}^\lambda$. Then we instantiate F by

$$F_k(x) := \mathsf{PRG}(G_k(G_k(x_0) \oplus x_1)).$$

By the security of CBC-MAC [BKR00] and PRG, F is still a PRF. In this construction, $G_k(\cdot)$ is parallelizable for multiple inputs and can be efficiently instantiated by AES ECB mode. However, PRG has to be computed on each element and cannot be parallelized for multiple elements.

To achieve better concrete efficiency, we try to parallelize the computation over multiple elements as much as possible so as to make best use of the hardware optimized AES ECB mode implementation. In particular, let $G : \{0,1\}^\lambda \times \{0,1\}^\lambda \to \{0,1\}^\lambda$ be a pseudorandom function and $\mathsf{PRG} : \{0,1\}^\lambda \to \{0,1\}^{(t+1)\cdot\lambda}$ be a PRG where $t = \lceil \frac{w \cdot \log m}{\lambda} \rceil$. On a key k and input $x = x_0 \| x_1$, we construct F as

$$F_k(x) = G_{k_1}(G_{k_0}(x_0) \oplus x_1) \| G_{k_2}(G_{k_0}(x_0) \oplus x_1) \| \ldots \| G_{k_t}(G_{k_0}(x_0) \oplus x_1),$$

where $k_0 \| k_1 \| \ldots \| k_t \leftarrow \mathsf{PRG}(k)$. Now PRG (instantiated by AES CTR mode) is only applied once on the key k, and $G_{k_i}(\cdot)$ are all parallelizable by AES ECB mode. The security proof of F is deferred to Appendix A.

In our implementation, the PRF key k is sent right after the base OT instead of after the entire OT extension. This allows both parties to run PRF evaluations in parallel and does not hurt malicious security because P_1 does not send any message in the OT extension after the base OT.

5 Performance Evaluation

We implement our PSI protocol and report on its performance in comparison with the state-of-the-art OT-extension-based protocols:

– KKRT: the computation-optimized protocol [KKRT16].
– SpOT-Light: the communication-optimized protocol [PRTY19]. They have two variants of the protocol, a speed-optimized variant (spot-fast) and a communication-optimized variant (spot-low). We compare our protocol with both variants.

In this section, we only report the performance with semi-honest security for comparison with KKRT and SpOT-Light. To achieve security against malicious P_1, our protocol requires the same amount of computation cost and 5–7% more communication cost (because ℓ_2 is bigger as shown in Table 1).

5.1 Benchmark Comparison

Our benchmarks are implemented on two Microsoft Azure virtual machines with Intel(R) Xeon(R) 2.40 GHz CPU and 140 GB RAM. The two machines are connected in a LAN network with 20 Gbps bandwidth and 0.1 ms RTT latency. We simulate the WAN connection between the two machines using the Linux tc command. In the WAN setting, the average RTT is set to be 80 ms and we test on various network bandwidths. All of our experiments use a single thread for each party. A detailed benchmark for set sizes $2^{16} - 2^{24}$ and controlled network configurations is presented in Table 2.

Table 2. Communication cost (in MB) and running time (in seconds) comparing our protocol to [KKRT16], spot-fast and spot-low [PRTY19]. Each party holds n elements. The LAN network has 20 Gbps bandwidth and 0.1 ms RTT latency. All the other network settings have 80 ms RTT. Communication cost of P_b ($b = 1, 2$) indicates the outgoing communication from P_b to the other party. Cells with "–" denote settings where the programs run out of memory.

n	Protocol	Comm. (MB)			Total running time (s)							
		P_1	P_2	Total	LAN	150Mbps	100Mbps	80Mbps	50Mbps	30Mbps	10Mbps	1Mbps
2^{16}	KKRT	3.95	4.82	8.77	0.34	1.94	2.01	2.22	2.62	3.54	8.41	77.4
	spot-fast	1.14	3.47	4.61	2.08	2.97	2.99	2.99	3.03	3.12	4.86	40.9
	spot-low	0.53	3.38	3.91	12.2	13.5	13.6	13.6	13.6	13.7	14.5	41.2
	Ours	0.58	4.76	5.34	0.63	1.71	1.78	1.87	2.14	2.66	5.53	47.4
2^{18}	KKRT	17.5	19.2	36.7	1.08	3.98	4.71	5.44	7.79	12.0	33.2	323
	spot-fast	5.02	13.9	18.9	8.24	9.45	9.49	9.51	9.84	10.6	17.5	166
	spot-low	2.06	13.5	15.6	57.1	58.8	59.2	59.4	59.7	60.3	64.9	167
	Ours	2.52	19.2	21.7	2.26	3.01	3.34	3.77	5.08	7.53	20.0	192
2^{20}	KKRT	60.0	76.8	137	4.58	10.8	14.7	17.5	26.5	42.5	122	1,204
	spot-fast	20.0	56.4	76.4	28.9	30.9	31.5	31.6	33.1	35.8	69.3	676
	spot-low	8.18	55.0	63.2	271	276	275	277	279	282	301	731
	Ours	10.0	77.6	87.6	9.44	10.4	10.8	11.5	16.9	27.1	78.2	772
2^{22}	KKRT	264	307	571	18.4	42.3	58.8	71.2	108	175	509	5,027
	spot-fast	88.0	226	314	117	123	125	126	133	146	283	2,773
	spot-low	32.7	220	253	1,291	1,303	1,305	1,311	1,315	1,331	1,406	3,311
	Ours	44.1	314	358	46.3	49.2	50.6	51.1	65.5	107	317	3,152
2^{24}	KKRT	880	1,229	2,109	67.9	157	219	264	403	648	1,882	18,562
	spot-fast	352	919	1,271	537	559	567	566	598	647	1,149	11,231
	spot-low	–	–	–	–	–	–	–	–	–	–	–
	Ours	176	1,266	1,442	190	200	216	234	289	431	1,277	12,717

Communication Improvement. The total communication cost of our protocol is 1.46–1.69× smaller than that of KKRT. For example, to compute the set intersection of size $n = 2^{20}$, our protocol requires 87.6 MB communication, which is a 1.56× improvement of KKRT that requires 137 MB communication.

Computation Improvement. In the LAN network where the running time is dominated by computation, our protocol achieves a 2.53–3.65× speedup comparing to spot-fast and a 19.4–28.7× speedup comparing to spot-low. For example, to compute the set intersection of size $n = 2^{20}$, our protocol runs in 9.44 s, which is 3.06× faster than spot-fast that runs in 28.9 s and 28.7× faster than spot-low that runs in 271 s.

Overall Improvement. In the WAN setting, we plot in Fig. 5 the running time growth with decreasing network bandwidth for our protocol comparing to KKRT, spot-fast, and spot-low for set sizes $n = 2^{20}$ and $n = 2^{24}$. Note that spot-low runs out of memory for set size $n = 2^{24}$, so we do not include it in the comparison for $n = 2^{24}$. As shown in the figure, with moderate bandwidth (in particular, 30–100 Mbps), our protocol is faster than all the other protocols because we have lower communication than KKRT and faster computation than spot-fast and spot-low. For example, in the 50 Mpbs network, for set size $n = 2^{20}$,

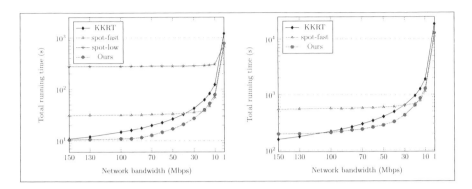

Fig. 5. Growth of total running time (in seconds) on decreasing network bandwidth for our protocol compared with [KKRT16], spot-fast and spot-low [PRTY19]. The y-axis is in log scale. The network latency is 80 ms RTT for all settings. The figure on the left is for set size $n = 2^{20}$ and the figure on the right is for set size $n = 2^{24}$. Note that since spot-low runs out of memory for $n = 2^{24}$, it is not included in the right figure.

our protocols takes 16.9 s to run, which is a 1.57× speedup to KKRT that takes 26.5 s, a 1.96× speedup to spot-fast that takes 33.1 s, and a 16.5× speedup to spot-low that takes 279 s.

5.2   Monetary Cost

We follow the same method as [PRTY19] to evaluate the real-world monetary cost of running our protocol on the Amazon Web Services (AWS) Elastic Compute Cloud (EC2). In this section we give both theoretical analysis and experimental comparison in various settings.

5.2.1   Pricing Scheme

The price for a protocol consists of two parts—machine cost and communication cost.[2] We elaborate each cost in the following.

Machine Cost. The machine cost is charged proportional to the total time an instance is launched. The unit machine cost varies for different types of instances and also depends on the specific region. Generally speaking, an instance with more computation power and more memory would have higher cost per hour. The same type of instance costs in the Asia Pacific than in the US and Europe.

In our experiment we choose the general purpose virtual machine type m5.large with Intel(R) Xeon(R) 2.50 GHz CPU and 8 GB RAM, which is the same as in [PRTY19]. The machine cost per hour (in USD) for m5.large is 0.096 (US), 0.112 (Paris), 0.12 (Sydney). For example, if we choose the machine type

---

[2] The pricing scheme can be found here: https://aws.amazon.com/ec2/pricing/on-demand/.

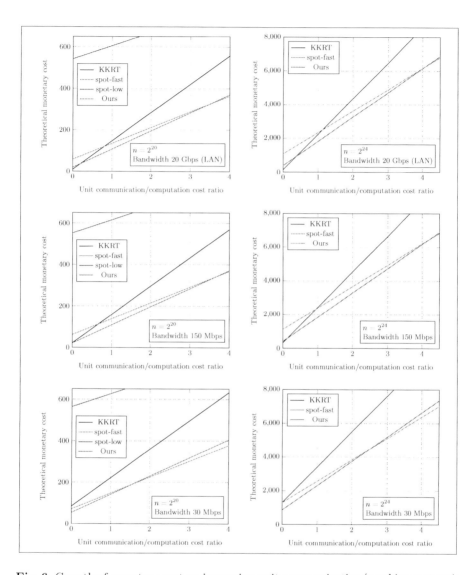

Fig. 6. Growth of monetary cost on increasing unit communication/machine cost ratio (namely y/x – communication cost per MB/computation cost per second) for our protocol compared with [KKRT16], spot-fast and spot-low [PRTY19]. (For some real world y/x values, see Table 3.) The network latency is 80 ms RTT for all settings. The figures on the left are for set size $n = 2^{20}$ and the ones on the right are for set size $n = 2^{24}$. The network bandwidth is indicated in each individual figure. Note that since spot-low runs out of memory for $n = 2^{24}$, it is not included in the right figures.

m5.4xlarge with 64 GB RAM, then the cost per hour (in USD) is 0.768 (US), 0.896 (Paris), 0.96 (Sydney).

Communication Cost. The communication cost is charged proportional to the amount of data transfer. The unit data transfer cost varies depending on whether both endpoints are within AWS or only one party is in AWS. It also depends on the specific region of the endpoints. Generally speaking, data transfer from AWS to the Internet is more expensive than data transfer within AWS; data transfer from the Asia Pacific costs more than from the US or Europe. Specially:

- Data transfer in from the Internet to EC2 is free.
- Data transfer out from EC2 to the Internet is charged depending on the region of the EC2 instance. Cost per GB (in USD) is 0.09 (US), 0.09 (Paris), 0.114 (Sydney).
- Data transfer from one EC2 instance to another EC2 instance is charged depending on both endpoints' regions. Cost per GB (in USD) is 0.01 (Virginia-to-Ohio), 0.02 (US-to-Paris), 0.02 (US-to-Sydney), 0.02 (Paris-to-US), 0.02 (Paris-to-Sydney), 0.14 (Sydney-to-US), 0.14 (Sydney-to-Paris).
- Additionally, using a public IP address costs 0.01 USD/GB for all regions.

Network Settings. We consider the two network settings proposed in [PRTY19]. In a business-to-business (B2B) setting, two organizations want to regularly perform PSI on their dynamic data, where both endpoints may be within the AWS network. In an Internet setting, one organization wants to regularly perform PSI with a dynamically changing partner, where only one party may be within the AWS network. As the communication cost from P_1 to P_2 is much less than the cost from P_2 to P_1 for all the PSI protocols we consider, in our experiment we let P_1 be the party within the AWS network.

5.2.2   Theoretical Analysis

Internet Setting. In the Internet setting where only one party (P_1) runs on an AWS EC2 instance, our protocol costs the least compared to all the other three protocols. At a high level, since our protocol takes less time to run on networks with moderate bandwidth (see Table 2), the machine cost for our protocol is the lowest among the three protocols. In addition, the communication from P_1 to P_2 in our protocol is lower than KKRT and spot-fast and almost the same as spot-low. Therefore, overall our protocol is the cheapest to run in all the settings, as we will see in the experimental results.

B2B Setting. In the B2B setting where we run each party of the PSI protocol on an AWS EC2 instance, there is a trade-off between computation and communication. At a high level, since spot-fast and spot-low have lower communication than KKRT and our protocol, the communication cost for them is lower. However, the total running time of our protocol is the shortest among all the protocols on networks with moderate bandwidth (see Table 2), hence the machine cost for our protocol is the lowest among all the protocols. The total monetary cost is a combination of the machine and communication costs, and which protocol costs the least depends on the ratio of unit communication cost to unit machine cost.

More specifically, suppose the total running time is T seconds and the total data transfer between them is C MB. Assume the machine cost of an AWS EC2 instance is x per second and the communication cost is y per MB in both directions. Then the total cost in this setting is $2 \cdot T \cdot x + C \cdot y$. For a fixed set size n and fixed network setting, the running time T and communication complexity C for each protocol is fixed, hence which protocol costs the least only depends on the ratio of y/x.

In Fig. 6 we plot the theoretical monetary cost of our protocol compared with KKRT, spot-fast, and spot-low in various network settings and for set sizes $n = 2^{20}$ and $n = 2^{24}$. As we can see in all the figures, our protocol costs the least when the ratio of unit communication cost to unit machine cost (namely, y/x) is within a certain range. More concretely, for set size $n = 2^{20}$, our protocol costs the least when $0.20 \leq y/x \leq 3.48$ for LAN networks, when $y/x \leq 3.66$ for networks with bandwidth 150 Mbps, and when $y/x \leq 1.55$ for networks with bandwidth 30 Mbps. On the other hand, if y/x is sufficiently large, meaning that the unit communication cost is much higher than unit machine cost, then spot-fast achieves the lowest cost for all settings because of their lower communication.

5.2.3   Experimental Results

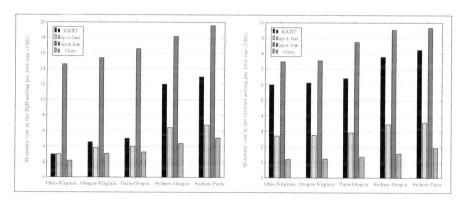

Fig. 7. Monetary cost per 1000 runs in the B2B setting (left) and Internet setting (right) comparing our protocol to [KKRT16], spot-fast and spot-low [PRTY19]. Each party holds $n = 2^{20}$ elements and locates in different regions.

We plot the experimental monetary cost of our protocol compared with KKRT, spot-fast, and spot-low in both B2B and Internet settings in Fig. 7.

Table 3. Total monetary cost (in USD) per 1000 runs in the B2B and Internet settings comparing our protocol to [KKRT16], spot-fast and spot-low [PRTY19]. Each party holds $n = 2^{20}$ elements and locates in different regions. The network bandwidth, RTT latency, and y/x ratio (communication cost per MB/computation cost per second) for each setting are indicated in the table.

Regions	Bandwidth	Latency	y/x	Protocol	Runtime	B2B Cost	Internet Cost
				KKRT	**5.15**	2.95	6.00
Ohio-Virginia	1.09 Gbps	12 ms	0.73	spot-fast	27.9	2.98	2.70
				spot-low	251	14.6	7.50
				Ours	8.17	**2.15**	**1.20**
				KKRT	10.1	4.55	6.13
Oregon-Virginia	170 Mbps	74 ms	1.10	spot-fast	29.9	3.83	2.75
				spot-low	254	15.4	7.57
				Ours	**9.23**	**3.06**	**1.23**
				KKRT	17.7	5.03	6.41
Paris-Oregon	75.6 Mbps	167 ms	1.01	spot-fast	31.0	4.03	2.92
				spot-low	256	16.6	8.75
				Ours	**12.0**	**3.26**	**1.35**
				KKRT	16.3	12.0	7.81
Sydney-Oregon	85.0 Mbps	143 ms	2.69	spot-fast	30.7	6.43	3.45
				spot-low	257	18.2	9.55
				Ours	**10.8**	**4.39**	**1.57**
				KKRT	29.9	13.0	8.26
Sydney-Paris	40.5 Mbps	286 ms	2.50	spot-fast	34.2	6.79	3.57
				spot-low	261	19.6	9.68
				Ours	**21.3**	**5.12**	**1.93**

The concrete running time and network bandwidth and latency are presented in Table 3. We also list the y/x ratio (communication cost per MB/computation cost per second) for each setting in the table. We see that our protocol is the cheapest in all the settings we consider. This result aligns with our theoretical analysis in Sect. 5.2.2. We only show the results for set size $n = 2^{20}$ while our protocol is the cheapest for other set sizes as well. In the B2B setting, our protocol is 1.37–2.73× cheaper than KKRT, 1.24–1.46× cheaper than spot-fast, and 3.75–6.80× cheaper than spot-low. In the Internet setting, our protocol is 4.28–5.00× cheaper than KKRT, 1.85–2.25× cheaper than spot-fast, and 5.01–6.48× cheaper than spot-low.

A   Security Proof of PRF F

Theorem 3. *Let $G : \{0,1\}^\lambda \times \{0,1\}^\lambda \to \{0,1\}^\lambda$ be a pseudorandom function. Let $\mathsf{PRG} : \{0,1\}^\lambda \to \{0,1\}^{(t+1)\cdot\lambda}$ be a pseudorandom generator. Define $F : \{0,1\}^\lambda \times \{0,1\}^{2\lambda} \to \{0,1\}^{t\cdot\lambda}$ as follows. On a key k and input $x = x_0\|x_1$ where $k, x_0, x_1 \in \{0,1\}^\lambda$,*

$$F_k(x) = G_{k_1}(G_{k_0}(x_0) \oplus x_1)\|G_{k_2}(G_{k_0}(x_0) \oplus x_1)\| \ldots \|G_{k_t}(G_{k_0}(x_0) \oplus x_1),$$

where $k_0\|k_1\|\ldots\|k_t \leftarrow \mathsf{PRG}(k)$. Then F is also a pseudorandom function.

Proof. We show that any PPT adversary $\mathcal{A}$ cannot distinguish F from a random function via a sequence of hybrids:

Hyb_0 The adversary $\mathcal{A}$ has access to F.

Hyb_1 The adversary $\mathcal{A}$ has access to the following function

$$G_{k_1}(G_{k_0}(x_0) \oplus x_1)\|G_{k_2}(G_{k_0}(x_0) \oplus x_1)\| \ldots \|G_{k_t}(G_{k_0}(x_0) \oplus x_1),$$

where $k_0, k_1, \ldots, k_t \xleftarrow{\$} \{0,1\}^\lambda$ are sampled uniformly at random.
If $\mathcal{A}$ can distinguish between Hyb_0 and Hyb_1, then we can construct another PPT adversary $\mathcal{B}$ that breaks the security of PRG. In particular, $\mathcal{B}$ first gets $k_0\|k_1\|\ldots\|k_t$ from the PRG challenger. On query $x = x_0\|x_1$ from $\mathcal{A}$, $\mathcal{B}$ responds with $G_{k_1}(G_{k_0}(x_0) \oplus x_1)\|\ldots\|G_{k_t}(G_{k_0}(x_0) \oplus x_1)$. Finally $\mathcal{B}$ outputs whatever $\mathcal{A}$ outputs.
If the PRG challenger generates $k_0\|k_1\|\ldots\|k_t$ from PRG, then $\mathcal{A}$ is accessing Hyb_0; otherwise, the challenger generates $k_0\|k_1\|\ldots\|k_t$ uniformly at random, then $\mathcal{A}$ is accessing Hyb_1. Hence, if $\mathcal{A}$ can distinguish between Hyb_0 and Hyb_1, then $\mathcal{B}$ can break the PRG security.

Hyb_2 The adversary $\mathcal{A}$ has access to the following function

$$G_1(G_{k_0}(x_0) \oplus x_1)\| \ldots \|G_t(G_{k_0}(x_0) \oplus x_1),$$

where $k_0 \xleftarrow{\$} \{0,1\}^\lambda$ is sampled uniformly at random, and $G_1, \ldots, G_t$ are all independent random functions. We argue that Hyb_2 is computationally indistinguishable from Hyb_1 via a sequence of hybrids, where $\mathsf{Hyb}_{2,0} = \mathsf{Hyb}_1$ and $\mathsf{Hyb}_{2,t} = \mathsf{Hyb}_2$:

$\mathsf{Hyb}_{2,i}$ The adversary $\mathcal{A}$ has access to the following function

$$G_1(G_{k_0}(x_0) \oplus x_1)\| \ldots \|G_i(G_{k_0}(x_0) \oplus x_1)\|G_{k_{i+1}}(G_{k_0}(x_0) \oplus x_1)\| \ldots \|G_{k_t}(G_{k_0}(x_0) \oplus x_1),$$

where $k_0, k_{i+1}, \ldots, k_t \xleftarrow{\$} \{0,1\}^\lambda$ are sampled uniformly at random, and $G_1, \ldots, G_i$ are independent random functions. Note that $\mathsf{Hyb}_{2,0} = \mathsf{Hyb}_1$. If $\mathcal{A}$ can distinguish between $\mathsf{Hyb}_{2,i-1}$ and $\mathsf{Hyb}_{2,i}$ for any $1 \leq i \leq t$, then we can construct another PPT adversary $\mathcal{B}$ that breaks the PRF security of G_i. In particular, $\mathcal{B}$ first randomly samples $k_0, k_{i+1}, \ldots, k_t \xleftarrow{\$} \{0,1\}^\lambda$, and then starts the experiment with $\mathcal{A}$. On query $x_0\|x_1$ from $\mathcal{A}$, $\mathcal{B}$ computes $z = G_{k_0}(x_0) \oplus x_1$ and $G_{k_{i+1}}(z)\| \ldots \|G_{k_t}(z)$. $\mathcal{B}$ also randomly samples the outputs of $G_1(z), \ldots, G_{i-1}(z)$. Note that if z already appears as an input to $G_1, \ldots, G_{i-1}$ before, $\mathcal{B}$ uses the previous outputs. Then $\mathcal{B}$ queries the PRF challenger on input z for an output t, and sends the following back to $\mathcal{A}$:

$$G_1(z)\| \ldots \|G_{i-1}(z)\|t\|G_{k_{i+1}}(z)\| \ldots \|G_{k_t}(z).$$

Finally $\mathcal{B}$ outputs whatever $\mathcal{A}$ outputs.

If the PRF challenger chooses a PRF, then $\mathcal{A}$ is accessing $\mathsf{Hyb}_{2,i-1}$; otherwise $\mathcal{A}$ is accessing $\mathsf{Hyb}_{2,i}$. Hence, if $\mathcal{A}$ can distinguish between $\mathsf{Hyb}_{2,i-1}$ and $\mathsf{Hyb}_{2,i}$, then $\mathcal{B}$ can distinguish PRF from a random function.

Hyb_3 The adversary $\mathcal{A}$ has access to the following function

$$G_1(G_0(x_0) \oplus x_1)\| \ldots \|G_t(G_0(x_0) \oplus x_1),$$

where $G_0, \ldots, G_t$ are all independent random functions.

If $\mathcal{A}$ can distinguish between Hyb_2 and Hyb_3, then we can construct another PPT adversary $\mathcal{B}$ that breaks the PRF security of G_{k_0}. $\mathcal{B}$ first starts the experiment with $\mathcal{A}$. On query $x_0\|x_1$ from $\mathcal{A}$, $\mathcal{B}$ queries the PRF challenger on x_0 for an output y. Then $\mathcal{B}$ computes $z = y \oplus x_1$ and randomly samples the outputs of $G_1(z), \ldots, G_t(z)$. Note that if z already appears as an input to $G_1, \ldots, G_t$ before, $\mathcal{B}$ uses the previous outputs. Afterwards $\mathcal{B}$ sends $G_1(z)\| \ldots \|G_{k_t}(z)$ back to $\mathcal{A}$. Finally $\mathcal{B}$ outputs whatever $\mathcal{A}$ outputs.

If the PRF challenger chooses a PRF, then $\mathcal{A}$ is accessing Hyb_2; otherwise $\mathcal{A}$ is accessing Hyb_3. Hence, if $\mathcal{A}$ can distinguish between Hyb_2 and Hyb_3, then $\mathcal{B}$ can distinguish PRF from a random function.

Hyb_4 The adversary $\mathcal{A}$ has access to a random function $F(x_0\|x_1)$. Let the queries from $\mathcal{A}$ be $x_0^1\|x_1^1, \ldots, x_0^n\|x_1^n$, and assume WLOG that they are all distinct queries. We argue that Hyb_3 is computationally indistinguishable from Hyb_4 via a sequence of hybrids, where $\mathsf{Hyb}_{4,0} = \mathsf{Hyb}_3$ and $\mathsf{Hyb}_{4,n} = \mathsf{Hyb}_4$:

$\mathsf{Hyb}_{4,i}$ For the first i queries $x_0^1\|x_1^1, \ldots, x_0^i\|x_1^i$ from $\mathcal{A}$, choose the outputs $r^1, \ldots, r^i$ independently at random. For each $j \in [i]$, internally also choose a random $G_0(x_0^j)$. Let $z^j = G_0(x_0^j) \oplus x_1^j$, then also store the implied table for $G_1, \ldots, G_t$, namely store $G_1(z^j)\| \ldots \|G_t(z^j) = r^j$. If there is any collision in this table (i.e. $G_0(x_0^{j_1}) \oplus x_1^{j_1} = G_0(x_0^{j_2}) \oplus x_1^{j_2}$ within the first i queries), record $G_1(z^j)\| \ldots \|G_t(z^j) = r^j$ for the first queried $x_0^j\|x_1^j$. After the first i queries, compute the output according to this $G_0, \ldots, G_t$.

The hybrid $\mathsf{Hyb}_{4,i}$ is identical to $\mathsf{Hyb}_{4,i-1}$ unless the i-th query from $\mathcal{A}$ collides with $G_0(x_0^j) \oplus x_1^j$ for a previous query $x_0^j\|x_1^j$. However, note that when $\mathcal{A}$ makes the i-th query, it has seen no information on G_0. So the probability that $\mathcal{A}$ can find such a collision is negligible (in particular, $i/2^\lambda$).

References

[ADCT11]   Ateniese, G., De Cristofaro, E., Tsudik, G.: (If) size matters: size-hiding private set intersection. In: Catalano, D., Fazio, N., Gennaro, R., Nicolosi, A. (eds.) PKC 2011. LNCS, vol. 6571, pp. 156–173. Springer, Heidelberg (2011). https://doi.org/10.1007/978-3-642-19379-8_10

[ALSZ13]   Asharov, G., Lindell, Y., Schneider, T., Zohner, M.: More efficient oblivious transfer and extensions for faster secure computation. In: 2013 ACM SIGSAC Conference on Computer and Communications Security, CCS 2013, Berlin, Germany, 4–8 November 2013, pp. 535–548 (2013)

[BBDC+11] Baldi, P., Baronio, R., De Cristofaro, E., Gasti, P., Tsudik, G.: Countering GATTACA: efficient and secure testing of fully-sequenced human genomes. In: Proceedings of the 18th ACM Conference on Computer and Communications Security, pp. 691–702. ACM (2011)

[BKR00]   Bellare, M., Kilian, J., Rogaway, P.: The security of the cipher block chaining message authentication code. J. Comput. Syst. Sci. **61**, 362–399 (2000)

[BLA]   BLAKE2 - fast secure hashing. https://blake2.net/. Accessed 24 Jan 2020

[CLR17]   Chen, H., Laine, K., Rindal, P.: Fast private set intersection from homomorphic encryption. In: Proceedings of the 2017 ACM SIGSAC Conference on Computer and Communications Security, pp. 1243–1255. ACM (2017)

[DCGT12]   De Cristofaro, E., Gasti, P., Tsudik, G.: Fast and private computation of cardinality of set intersection and union. In: Pieprzyk, J., Sadeghi, A.-R., Manulis, M. (eds.) CANS 2012. LNCS, vol. 7712, pp. 218–231. Springer, Heidelberg (2012). https://doi.org/10.1007/978-3-642-35404-5_17

[DCKT10]   De Cristofaro, E., Kim, J., Tsudik, G.: Linear-complexity private set intersection protocols secure in malicious model. In: Abe, M. (ed.) ASIACRYPT 2010. LNCS, vol. 6477, pp. 213–231. Springer, Heidelberg (2010). https://doi.org/10.1007/978-3-642-17373-8_13

[DCW13]   Dong, C., Chen, L., Wen, Z.: When private set intersection meets big data: an efficient and scalable protocol. In: Proceedings of the 2013 ACM SIGSAC Conference on Computer & Communications Security, pp. 789–800. ACM (2013)

[DRRT18]   Demmler, D., Rindal, P., Rosulek, M., Trieu, N.: PIR-PSI: scaling private contact discovery. Proc. Priv. Enhanc. Technol. **2018**(4), 159–178 (2018)

[DSMRY09] Dachman-Soled, D., Malkin, T., Raykova, M., Yung, M.: Efficient robust private set intersection. In: Abdalla, M., Pointcheval, D., Fouque, P.-A., Vergnaud, D. (eds.) ACNS 2009. LNCS, vol. 5536, pp. 125–142. Springer, Heidelberg (2009). https://doi.org/10.1007/978-3-642-01957-9_8

[FIPR05]   Freedman, M.J., Ishai, Y., Pinkas, B., Reingold, O.: Keyword search and oblivious pseudorandom functions. In: Kilian, J. (ed.) TCC 2005. LNCS, vol. 3378, pp. 303–324. Springer, Heidelberg (2005). https://doi.org/10.1007/978-3-540-30576-7_17

[FNO18]   Falk, B.H., Noble, D., Ostrovsky, R.: Private set intersection with linear communication from general assumptions. IACR Cryptology ePrint Archive, 2018:238 (2018)

[FNP04]   Freedman, M.J., Nissim, K., Pinkas, B.: Efficient private matching and set intersection. In: Cachin, C., Camenisch, J.L. (eds.) EUROCRYPT 2004. LNCS, vol. 3027, pp. 1–19. Springer, Heidelberg (2004). https://doi.org/10.1007/978-3-540-24676-3_1

[GN19]   Ghosh, S., Nilges, T.: An algebraic approach to maliciously secure private set intersection. In: Ishai, Y., Rijmen, V. (eds.) EUROCRYPT 2019. LNCS, vol. 11478, pp. 154–185. Springer, Cham (2019). https://doi.org/10.1007/978-3-030-17659-4_6

[HEK12]   Huang, Y., Evans, D., Katz, J.: Private set intersection: are garbled circuits better than custom protocols? In: NDSS (2012)

[HFH99]   Huberman, B.A., Franklin, M., Hogg, T.: Enhancing privacy and trust in electronic communities. In: EC 1999, pp. 78–86 (1999)

[IKN+17]   Ion, M., et al.: Private intersection-sum protocol with applications to attributing aggregate ad conversions. IACR Cryptology ePrint Archive, 2017:738 (2017)

[IKNP03]   Ishai, Y., Kilian, J., Nissim, K., Petrank, E.: Extending oblivious transfers efficiently. In: Boneh, D. (ed.) CRYPTO 2003. LNCS, vol. 2729, pp. 145–161. Springer, Heidelberg (2003). https://doi.org/10.1007/978-3-540-45146-4_9

[KK13]   Kolesnikov, V., Kumaresan, R.: Improved OT extension for transferring short secrets. In: Canetti, R., Garay, J.A. (eds.) CRYPTO 2013. LNCS, vol. 8043, pp. 54–70. Springer, Heidelberg (2013). https://doi.org/10.1007/978-3-642-40084-1_4

[KKRT16]   Kolesnikov, V., Kumaresan, R., Rosulek, M., Trieu, N.: Efficient batched oblivious PRF with applications to private set intersection. In: Proceedings of the 2016 ACM SIGSAC Conference on Computer and Communications Security, pp. 818–829. ACM (2016)

[KRS+19]   Kales, D., Rechberger, C., Schneider, T., Senker, M., Weinert, C.: Mobile private contact discovery at scale. In: 28th USENIX Security Symposium, USENIX Security 2019, Santa Clara, CA, USA, 14–16 August 2019, pp. 1447–1464 (2019)

[LLC18]   Ookla LLC. 2018 United States speedtest market report (2018). https://www.speedtest.net/reports/united-states/2018/#fixed

[NMH+10]   Nagaraja, S., Mittal, P., Hong, C.-Y., Caesar, M., Borisov, N.: BotGrep: finding P2P bots with structured graph analysis. In: USENIX Security Symposium 2010, pp. 95–110 (2010)

[NP99]   Naor, M., Pinkas, B.: Oblivious transfer and polynomial evaluation. In: Proceedings of the Thirty-First Annual ACM Symposium on Theory of Computing, pp. 245–254. ACM (1999)

[NTL+11]   Narayanan, A., Thiagarajan, N., Lakhani, M., Hamburg, M., Boneh, D., et al.: Location privacy via private proximity testing. In: NDSS, vol. 11 (2011)

[PR04]   Pagh, R., Rodler, F.F.: Cuckoo hashing. J. Algorithms **51**(2), 122–144 (2004)

[PRTY19]   Pinkas, B., Rosulek, M., Trieu, N., Yanai, A.: SpOT-light: lightweight private set intersection from sparse OT extension. In: Boldyreva, A., Micciancio, D. (eds.) CRYPTO 2019. LNCS, vol. 11694, pp. 401–431. Springer, Cham (2019). https://doi.org/10.1007/978-3-030-26954-8_13

[PRTY20]   Pinkas, B., Rosulek, M., Trieu, N., Yanai, A.: PSI from PaXoS: fast, malicious private set intersection. In: Canteaut, A., Ishai, Y. (eds.) EUROCRYPT 2020. LNCS, vol. 12106, pp. 739–767. Springer, Cham (2020). https://doi.org/10.1007/978-3-030-45724-2_25

[PSSZ15]   Pinkas, B., Schneider, T., Segev, G., Zohner, M.: Phasing: private set intersection using permutation-based hashing. In: 24th USENIX Security Symposium, pp. 515–530 (2015)

[PSWW18] Pinkas, B., Schneider, T., Weinert, C., Wieder, U.: Efficient circuit-based PSI via cuckoo hashing. In: Nielsen, J.B., Rijmen, V. (eds.) EUROCRYPT 2018. LNCS, vol. 10822, pp. 125–157. Springer, Cham (2018). https://doi.org/10.1007/978-3-319-78372-7_5

[PSZ14] Pinkas, B., Schneider, T., Zohner, M.: Faster private set intersection based on OT extension. In: Fu, K., Jung, J. (eds.) Proceedings of the 23rd USENIX Security Symposium, pp. 797–812 (2014)

[PSZ18] Pinkas, B., Schneider, T., Zohner, M.: Scalable private set intersection based on OT extension. ACM Trans. Priv. Secur. **21**(2), 7:1–7:35 (2018)

[RA17] Resende, A.C.D., Aranha, D.F.: Unbalanced approximate private set intersection. IACR Cryptology ePrint Archive, 2017:677 (2017)

[Rab05] Rabin, M.O.: How to exchange secrets with oblivious transfer. IACR Cryptology ePrint Archive, 2005:187 (2005)

[Rin] Rindal, P.: libOTe: an efficient, portable, and easy to use Oblivious Transfer Library. https://github.com/osu-crypto/libOTe

[RR17a] Rindal, P., Rosulek, M.: Improved private set intersection against malicious adversaries. In: Coron, J.-S., Nielsen, J.B. (eds.) EUROCRYPT 2017. LNCS, vol. 10210, pp. 235–259. Springer, Cham (2017). https://doi.org/10.1007/978-3-319-56620-7_9

[RR17b] Rindal, P., Rosulek, M.: Malicious-secure private set intersection via dual execution. In: Proceedings of the 2017 ACM SIGSAC Conference on Computer and Communications Security, pp. 1229–1242. ACM (2017)

[TPKC07] Troncoso-Pastoriza, J.R., Katzenbeisser, S., Celik, M.: Privacy preserving error resilient DNA searching through oblivious automata. In: Proceedings of the 14th ACM Conference on Computer and Communications Security, pp. 519–528. ACM (2007)

Multiparty Generation of an RSA Modulus

Megan Chen[✉], Ran Cohen, Jack Doerner, Yashvanth Kondi, Eysa Lee,
Schuyler Rosefield, and Abhi Shelat

Northeastern University, Boston, MA, USA
meganchen@gmail.com

Abstract. We present a new multiparty protocol for the distributed
generation of biprime RSA moduli, with security against any subset of
maliciously colluding parties assuming oblivious transfer and the hardness of factoring.

Our protocol is highly modular, and its uppermost layer can be viewed
as a template that generalizes the structure of prior works and leads to a
simpler security proof. We introduce a combined sampling-and-sieving
technique that eliminates both the inherent leakage in the approach
of Frederiksen et al. (Crypto'18), and the dependence upon additively
homomorphic encryption in the approach of Hazay et al. (JCrypt'19). We
combine this technique with an efficient, privacy-free check to detect malicious behavior retroactively when a sampled candidate is not a biprime,
and thereby overcome covert rejection-sampling attacks and achieve both
asymptotic and concrete efficiency improvements over the previous state
of the art.

1 Introduction

A *biprime* is a number N of the form $N = p \cdot q$ where p and q are primes.
Such numbers are used as a component of the public key (i.e., the *modulus*)
in the RSA cryptosystem [33], with the factorization being a component of the
secret key. A long line of research has studied methods for sampling biprimes
efficiently; in the early days, the task required specialized hardware and was not
considered generally practical [31,32]. In subsequent years, advances in computational power brought RSA into the realm of practicality, and then ubiquity.
Given a security parameter κ, the de facto standard method for sampling RSA
biprimes involves choosing random κ-bit numbers and subjecting them to the
Miller-Rabin primality test [27,30] until two primes are found; these primes are
then multiplied to form a 2κ-bit modulus. This method suffices when a single
party wishes to generate a modulus, and is permitted to know the associated
factorization.

The full version [7] of this work is available at http://ia.cr/2020/370.

D. Micciancio and T. Ristenpart (Eds.): CRYPTO 2020, LNCS 12172, pp. 64–93, 2020.
https://doi.org/10.1007/978-3-030-56877-1_3

Boneh and Franklin [3,4] initiated the study of *distributed* RSA modulus generation.[1] This problem involves a set of parties who wish to jointly sample a biprime in such a way that no corrupt and colluding subset (below some defined threshold size) can learn the biprime's factorization.

It is clear that applying generic multiparty computation (MPC) techniques to the standard sampling algorithm yields an impractical solution: implementing the Miller-Rabin primality test requires repeatedly computing $a^{p-1} \bmod p$, where p is (in this case) secret, and so such an approach would require the generic protocol to evaluate a circuit containing many modular exponentiations over κ bits each. Instead, Boneh and Franklin [3,4] constructed a new biprimality test that generalizes Miller-Rabin and avoids computing modular exponentiations with secret moduli. Their test carries out all exponentiations modulo the public biprime N, and this allows the exponentiations to be performed locally by the parties. Furthermore, they introduced a three-phase structure for the overall sampling protocol, which subsequent works have embraced:

1. **Prime Candidate Sieving**: candidate values for p and q are sampled jointly in secret-shared form, and a weak-but-cheap form of trial division sieves them, culling candidates with small factors.
2. **Modulus Reconstruction**: $N := p \cdot q$ is securely computed and revealed.
3. **Biprimality Testing**: using a distributed protocol, N is tested for biprimality. If N is not a biprime, then the process is repeated.

The seminal work of Boneh and Franklin considered the semi-honest n-party setting with an honest majority of participants. Many extensions and improvements followed (as detailed in Sect. 1.3), the most notable of which (for our purposes) are two recent works that achieve malicious security against a dishonest majority. In the first, Hazay et al. [19,20] proposed an n-party protocol in which both sieving and modulus reconstruction are achieved via additively homomorphic encryption. Specifically, they rely upon both ElGamal and Paillier encryption, and in order to achieve malicious security, they use zero-knowledge proofs for a variety of relations over the ciphertexts. Thus, their protocol represents a substantial advancement in terms of its security guarantee, but this comes at the cost of additional complexity assumptions and an intricate proof, and also at substantial concrete cost, due to the use of many custom zero-knowledge proofs.

The subsequent protocol of Frederiksen et al. [16] (the second recent work of note) relies mainly on oblivious transfer (OT), which they use to perform both sieving and, via Gilboa's classic multiplication protocol [17], modulus reconstruction. They achieved malicious security using the folklore technique in which a "Proof of Honesty" is evaluated as the last step and demonstrated practicality

---

[1] Prior works generally consider RSA *key generation* and include steps for generating shares of e and d such that $e \cdot d \equiv 1 \pmod{\varphi(N)}$. This work focuses only on the task of sampling the RSA modulus N. Prior techniques can be applied to sample (e, d) after sampling N, and the distributed generation of an RSA modulus has standalone applications, such as for generating the trusted setup required by verifiable delay functions [28,35]; consequently, we omit further discussion of e and d.

by implementing their protocol; however, it is not clear how to extend their approach to more than two parties in a straightforward way. Moreover, their approach to sieving admits selective-failure attacks, for which they account by including some leakage in the functionality. It also permits a malicious adversary to selectively and *covertly* induce false negatives (i.e., force the rejection of true biprimes after the sieving stage), a property that is again modeled in their functionality. In conjunction, these attributes degrade *security*, because the adversary can rejection-sample biprimes based on the additional leaked information, and *efficiency*, because ruling out malicious false-negatives involves running sufficiently many instances to make the probability of statistical failure in all instances negligible.

Thus, given the current state of the art, it remains unclear whether one can sample an RSA modulus among two parties (one being malicious) without leaking additional information or permitting covert rejection sampling, or whether one can sample an RSA modulus among many parties (all but one being malicious) without involving heavy cryptographic primitives such as additively homomorphic encryption, and their associated performance penalties. In this work, we present a protocol which efficiently achieves both tasks.

1.1   Results and Contributions

A Clean Functionality. We define $\mathcal{F}_{\mathsf{RSAGen}}$, a simple, natural functionality for sampling biprimes from the same well-known distribution used by prior works [4,16,20], with no leakage or conflation of sampling failures with adversarial behavior.

A Modular Protocol, with Natural Assumptions. We present a protocol π_{RSAGen} in the $(\mathcal{F}_{\mathsf{AugMul}}, \mathcal{F}_{\mathsf{Biprime}})$-hybrid model, where $\mathcal{F}_{\mathsf{AugMul}}$ is an augmented multiplier functionality and $\mathcal{F}_{\mathsf{Biprime}}$ is a biprimality-testing functionality, and prove that it UC-realizes $\mathcal{F}_{\mathsf{RSAGen}}$ in the malicious setting, assuming the hardness of factoring. More specifically, we prove:

Theorem 1.1. (Main Security Theorem, Informal). In the presence of a PPT malicious adversary corrupting any subset of parties, $\mathcal{F}_{\mathsf{RSAGen}}$ can be securely computed with abort in the $(\mathcal{F}_{\mathsf{AugMul}}, \mathcal{F}_{\mathsf{Biprime}})$-hybrid model, assuming the hardness of factoring.

Additionally, because our security proof relies upon the hardness of factoring only when the adversary cheats, we find to our surprise that our protocol achieves *perfect* security against semi-honest adversaries.

Theorem 1.2. (Semi-Honest Security Theorem, Informal). In the presence of a computationally unbounded semi-honest adversary corrupting any subset of parties, $\mathcal{F}_{\mathsf{RSAGen}}$ can be computed with perfect security in the $(\mathcal{F}_{\mathsf{AugMul}}, \mathcal{F}_{\mathsf{Biprime}})$-hybrid model.

Supporting Functionalities and Protocols. We define $\mathcal{F}_{\mathsf{Biprime}}$, a simple, natural functionality for biprimality testing, and show that it is UC-realized in the semi-honest setting by a well known protocol of Boneh and Franklin [4], and in the malicious setting by a derivative of the protocol of Frederiksen et al. [16]. We believe this dramatically simplifies the composition of these two protocols, and as a consequence, leads to a simpler analysis. Either protocol can be based exclusively upon oblivious transfer.

We also define $\mathcal{F}_{\mathsf{AugMul}}$, a functionality for sampling and multiplying secret-shared values in a special form derived from the Chinese Remainder Theorem. In the context of π_{RSAGen}, this functionality allows us to efficiently sample numbers in a specific range, with no small factors, and then compute their product. We prove that it can be UC-realized exclusively from oblivious transfer, using derivatives of well-known multiplication protocols [13,14].

Asymptotic Efficiency. We perform an asymptotic analysis of our composed protocols and find that our semi-honest protocol is a factor of $\kappa/\log \kappa$ more bandwidth-efficient than that of Frederiksen et al. [16]. Our malicious protocol is a factor of κ/s more efficient than theirs in the optimistic case (when parties follow the protocol), and a factor of κ more efficient when parties deviate from the protocol. Recall that κ is the bit-length of the primes p and q, and s is a statistical security parameter. Frederiksen et al. claim in turn that their protocol is strictly superior to the protocol of Hazay et al. [20] with respect to asymptotic bandwidth performance.

Concrete Efficiency. We perform a closed-form concrete analysis of our protocol (with some optimizations, including the use of random oracles), and find that in terms of communication, it outperforms the protocol of Frederiksen et al. (the most efficient prior work) by a factor of roughly five in the presence of worst-case malicious adversaries, and by a factor of eighty or more in the semi-honest setting.

1.2   Overview of Techniques

Constructive Sampling and Efficient Modulus Reconstruction. Most prior works use rejection sampling to generate a pair of candidate primes, and then multiply those primes together in a separate step. Specifically, they sample a shared value $p \leftarrow [0, 2^\kappa)$ uniformly, and then run a trial-division protocol repeatedly, discarding both the value and the work that has gone into testing it if trial division fails. This represents a substantial amount of wasted work in expectation. Furthermore, Frederiksen et al. [16] report that multiplication of candidates after sieving accounts for two thirds of their concrete cost.

We propose a different approach that leverages the Chinese Remainder Theorem (CRT) to *constructively* sample a pair of candidate primes and multiply them together efficiently. A similar sieving approach (in spirit) was initially formulated as an optimization in a different setting by Malkin et al. [26]. The CRT implies an isomorphism between a set of values, each in a field modulo a distinct prime, and a single value in a ring modulo the product of those primes (i.e., $\mathbb{Z}_{m_1} \times \ldots \times \mathbb{Z}_{m_\ell} \simeq \mathbb{Z}_{m_1 \cdot \ldots \cdot m_\ell}$). We refer to the set of values as the *CRT form* or *CRT representation* of the single value to which they are isomorphic. We formulate a sampling mechanism based on this isomorphism as follows: for each of the first $O(\kappa/\log\kappa)$ odd primes, the parties jointly (and efficiently) sample shares of a value that is nonzero modulo that prime. These values are the shared CRT form of a single κ-bit value that is guaranteed to be indivisible by any prime in the set sampled against. For technical reasons, we sample two such candidates simultaneously.

Rather than converting pairs of candidate primes from CRT form to standard form, and then multiplying them, we instead multiply them component-wise in CRT form, and then convert the product to standard form to complete the protocol. This effectively replaces a single "full-width" multiplication of size κ with $O(\kappa/\log\kappa)$ individual multiplications, each of size $O(\log\kappa)$. We intend to perform multiplication via an OT-based protocol, and the computation and communication complexity of such protocols grows at least with the square of their input length, even in the semi-honest case [17]. Thus in the semi-honest case, our approach yields an overall complexity of $O(\kappa\log\kappa)$, as compared to $O(\kappa^2)$ for a single full-width multiplication. In the malicious case, combining the best known multiplier construction [13,14] with the most efficient known OT extension scheme [5] yields a complexity that also grows with the product of the input length and a statistical parameter s, and so our approach achieves an overall complexity of $O(\kappa\log\kappa + \kappa \cdot s)$, as compared to $O(\kappa^2 + \kappa \cdot s)$ for a single full-width malicious multiplication. Via closed-form analysis, we show that this asymptotic improvement is also reflected concretely.

Achieving Security with Abort Efficiently. The fact that we sample primes in CRT form also plays a crucial role in our security analysis. Unlike the work of Frederiksen et al. [16], our protocol achieves the *standard*, intuitive notion of security with abort: the adversary can instruct the functionality to abort regardless of whether a biprime is successfully sampled, and the honest parties are always made aware of such adversarial aborts. There is, in other words, absolutely no conflation of sampling failures with adversarial behavior. For the sake of efficiency, our protocol permits the adversary to cheat prior to biprimality testing, and then rules out such cheats retroactively using one of two strategies. In the case that a biprime is successfully sampled, adversarial behavior is ruled out retroactively in a privacy-preserving fashion using well-known but moderately expensive techniques, which is tolerable only because it need not be done more than once. In the case that a sampled value is not a biprime, however, the inputs to the sampling protocol are revealed to all parties, and the retroactive check is carried out in the clear. Proving the latter approach secure turns out to be surprisingly subtle.

The challenge arises from the fact that the simulator must simulate the protocol transcript for the OT-multipliers on behalf of the honest parties without knowing their inputs. Later, if the sampling-protocol inputs are revealed, the simulator must "explain" how the simulated transcript is consistent with the true inputs of the honest parties. Specifically, in maliciously secure OT-multipliers of the sort we use [13,14], the OT receiver (Bob) uses a high-entropy encoding of his input, and the sender (Alice) can, by cheating, learn a one-bit predicate of this encoding. Before Bob's true input is known to the simulator, it must pick an encoding at random. When Bob's input is revealed, the simulator must find an encoding of his input which is consistent with the predicate on the random encoding that Alice has learned. This task closely resembles solving a random instance of subset sum.

We are able to overcome this difficulty because our multiplications are performed component-wise over CRT-form representations of their operands. Because each component is of size $O(\log \kappa)$ bits, the simulator can simply guess random encodings until it finds one that matches the required constraints. We show that this strategy succeeds in strict polynomial time, and that it induces a distribution statistically close to that of the real execution.

This form of "privacy-free" malicious security (wherein honest behavior is verified at the cost of sacrificing privacy) leads to considerable efficiency gains in our case: it is up to a multiplicative factor of s (the statistical parameter) cheaper than the privacy-preserving check used in the case that a candidate passes the biprimality test (and the one used in prior OT-multipliers [13,14]). Since most candidates fail the biprimality test, using the privacy-free check to verify that they were generated honestly results in substantial savings.

Biprimality Testing as a Black Box. We specify a functionality for biprimality testing, and prove that it can be realized by a maliciously secure version of the Boneh-Franklin biprimality test. Our functionality has a clean interface and does not, for example, require its inputs to be authenticated to ensure that they were actually generated by the sampling phase of the protocol. The key insight that allows us to achieve this level of modularity is a reduction to factoring: if an adversary is able to cheat by supplying incorrect inputs to the biprimality test, relative to a candidate biprime N, and the biprimality test succeeds, then we show that the adversary can be used to factor biprimes. We are careful to rely on this reduction only in the case that N is actually a biprime, and to prevent the adversary from influencing the distribution of candidates.

The Benefits of Modularity. We claim as a contribution the fact that modularity has yielded both a simpler protocol description and a reasonably simple proof of security. We believe that this approach will lead to derivatives of our work with stronger security properties or with security against stronger adversaries. As a first example, we prove that a semi-honest version of our protocol (differing only in that it omits the retroactive consistency check in the protocol's final step) achieves *perfect* security. We furthermore observe that in the malicious setting, instantiating $\mathcal{F}_{\mathsf{Biprime}}$ and $\mathcal{F}_{\mathsf{AugMul}}$ with security against *adaptive* adversaries yields an RSA modulus sampling protocol that is adaptively secure.

Similarly, only minor adjustments to the main protocol are required to achieve security with *identifiable abort* [11,22]. If we assume that the underlying functionalities $\mathcal{F}_{\mathsf{AugMul}}$ and $\mathcal{F}_{\mathsf{Biprime}}$ are instantiated with identifiable abort, then it remains only to ensure the use of consistent inputs across these functionalities, and to detect which party has provided inconsistent inputs if an abort occurs. This can be accomplished by augmenting $\mathcal{F}_{\mathsf{Biprime}}$ with an additional interface for revealing the input values provided by all the parties upon global request (e.g., when the candidate N is not a biprime). Given identifiable abort, it is possible to guarantee output delivery in the presence of up to $n-1$ corruptions via standard techniques, although the functionality must be weakened to allow the adversary to reject one biprime per corrupt party.[2] A proof of this extension is beyond the scope of this work; we focus instead on the advancements our framework yields in the setting of security with abort.

1.3 Additional Related Work

Frankel, MacKenzie, and Yung [15] adjusted the protocol of Boneh and Franklin [3] to achieve security against malicious adversaries in the honest-majority setting. Their main contribution was the introduction of a method for robust distributed multiplication over the integers. Cocks [8] proposed a method for multiparty RSA key generation under heuristic assumptions, and later attacks by Coppersmith (see [9]) and Joye and Pinch [23] suggest this method may be insecure. Poupard and Stern [29] presented a maliciously secure two-party protocol based on oblivious transfer. Gilboa [17] achieved improved efficiency in the semi-honest two-party model, and introduced a novel method for multiplication from oblivious transfer, from which our own multipliers ultimately derive.

Malkin, Wu, and Boneh [26] implemented the protocol of Boneh and Franklin and introduced an optimized sieving method similar in spirit to ours. In particular, their protocol generates sharings of random values in $\mathbb{Z}_M^*$ (where M is a primorial modulus) during the sieving phase, instead of naïve random candidates for primes p and q. However, their method produces *multiplicative* sharings of p and q, which are converted into additive sharings for biprimality testing via an honest-majority, semi-honest protocol. This conversion requires rounds linear in the party count, and it is unclear how to adapt it to tolerate a malicious majority of parties without a significant performance penalty.

Algesheimer, Camenish, and Shoup [1] described a method to compute a distributed version of the Miller-Rabin test: they used secret-sharing conversion techniques reliant on approximations of $1/p$ to compute exponentiations modulo a shared p. However, each invocation of their Miller-Rabin test still has complexity in $O(\kappa^3)$ per party, and their overall protocol has communication complexity in $O(\kappa^5/\log^2\kappa)$, with $\Theta(\kappa)$ rounds of interaction. Concretely, Damgård and Mikkelsen [12] estimate that 10000 rounds are required to sample a 2000-bit biprime using this method. Damgård and Mikkelsen also extended their work to

---

[2] The folklore technique involves invoking the protocol iteratively, each iteration eliminating one corrupt party until a success occurs. For a constant fraction of corruptions, the implied linear round complexity overhead can be reduced to super-constant (e.g., $\log^* n$) [10].

improve both its communication and round complexity by several orders of magnitude, and to achieve malicious security in the honest-majority setting. Their protocol is at least a factor of $O(\kappa)$ better than that of Algesheimer, Camenish, and Shoup, but it still requires *hundreds* of rounds. We were not able to compute an explicit complexity analysis of their approach.

1.4 Organization

Basic notation and background information are given in Sect. 2. Our ideal biprime-sampling functionality is defined in Sect. 3, and we give a protocol that realizes it in Sect. 4. In Sect. 5, we present our biprimality-testing protocol. In the full version [7] of this work, we give an efficiency analysis, full proofs of security, and the details of our multiplication protocol.

2 Preliminaries

Notation. We use $=$ for equality, $:=$ for assignment, $\leftarrow$ for sampling from a distribution, $\equiv$ for congruence, $\approx_c$ for computational indistinguishability, and $\approx_s$ for statistical indistinguishability. In general, single-letter variables are set in *italic* font, multi-letter variables and function names are set in sans-serif font, and string literals are set in slab-serif font. We use mod to indicate the modulus operator, while $(\bmod\ m)$ at the end of a line indicates that all equivalence relations on that line are to be taken over the integers modulo m. By convention, we parameterize computational security by the bit-length of each prime in an RSA biprime; we denote this length by κ throughout. We use s to represent the statistical parameter. Where concrete efficiency is concerned, we introduce a second computational security parameter, λ, which represents the length of a symmetric key of equivalent strength to a biprime of length 2κ.[3] κ and λ must vary together, and a recommendation for the relationship between them has been laid down by NIST [2].

Vectors and arrays are given in bold and indexed by subscripts; thus $\mathbf{x}_i$ is the ith element of the vector $\mathbf{x}$, which is distinct from the scalar variable x. When we wish to select a row or column from a two-dimensional array, we place a $*$ in the dimension along which we are not selecting. Thus $\mathbf{y}_{*,j}$ is the jth column of matrix $\mathbf{y}$, and $\mathbf{y}_{j,*}$ is the jth row. We use $\mathcal{P}_i$ to denote the party with index i, and when only two parties are present, we refer to them as Alice and Bob. Variables may often be subscripted with an index to indicate that they belong to a particular party. When arrays are owned by a party, the party index always comes first. We use $|x|$ to denote the bit-length of x, and $|\mathbf{y}|$ to denote the number of elements in the vector $\mathbf{y}$.

---

[3] In other words, a biprime of length 2κ provides λ bits of security.

Universal Composability. We prove our protocols secure in the Universal Composability (UC) framework, and use standard UC notation. We refer the reader to Canetti [6] for further details. In functionality descriptions, we leave some standard bookkeeping elements implicit. For example, we assume that the functionality aborts if a party tries to reuse a session identifier inappropriately, send messages out of order, etc. For convenience, we provide a function GenSID, which takes *any* number of arguments and deterministically derives a unique Session ID from those arguments.

Chinese Remainder Theorem. The Chinese Remainder Theorem (CRT) defines an isomorphism between a set of residues modulo a set of respective coprime values and a single value modulo the product of the same set of coprime values. This forms the basis of our sampling procedure.

Theorem 2.1. (CRT). Let $\mathbf{m}$ be a vector of coprime positive integers and let $\mathbf{x}$ be a vector of numbers such that $|\mathbf{m}| = |\mathbf{x}| = \ell$ and $0 \leq \mathbf{x}_j < \mathbf{m}_j$ for all $j \in [\ell]$, and finally let $M := \prod_{j \in [\ell]} \mathbf{m}_j$. Under these conditions there exists a unique value y such that $0 \leq y < M$ and $y \equiv \mathbf{x}_j \pmod{\mathbf{m}_j}$ for every $j \in [\ell]$.

We refer to $\mathbf{x}$ as the *CRT form* of y with respect to $\mathbf{m}$. For completeness, we give the CRTRecon algorithm, which finds the unique y given $\mathbf{m}$ and $\mathbf{x}$.

Algorithm 2.2. CRTRecon$(\mathbf{m}, \mathbf{x})$

1. With $\ell := |\mathbf{m}|$, compute $M = \prod_{j \in [\ell]} \mathbf{m}_j$.
2. For $j \in [\ell]$, compute $\mathbf{a}_j := M/\mathbf{m}_j$ and find $\mathbf{b}_j$ satisfying $\mathbf{a}_j \cdot \mathbf{b}_j \equiv 1 \pmod{\mathbf{m}_j}$ using the Extended Euclidean Algorithm (see Knuth [25]).
3. Output $y := \sum_{j \in [\ell]} \mathbf{a}_j \cdot \mathbf{b}_j \cdot \mathbf{x}_j \bmod M$.

---

3   Assumptions and Ideal Functionality

We begin this section by discussing the distribution of biprimes from which we sample, and thus the precise factoring assumption that we make, and then we give an efficient sampling algorithm and an ideal functionality that computes it.

3.1   Factoring Assumptions

The standard factoring experiment (Experiment 3.1) as formalized by Katz and Lindell [24] is parametrized by an adversary $\mathcal{A}$ and a biprime-sampling algorithm GenModulus. On input 1^κ, this algorithm returns (N, p, q), where $N = p \cdot q$, and p and q are κ-bit primes.[4]

---

[4] Technically, Katz and Lindell specify that sampling failures are permitted with negligible probability, and require GenModulus to run in strict polynomial time. We elide this detail.

Experiment 3.1 $\mathsf{Factor}_{\mathcal{A},\mathsf{GenModulus}}(\kappa)$

1. Run $(N, p, q) \leftarrow \mathsf{GenModulus}(1^\kappa)$.
2. Send N to $\mathcal{A}$, and receive $p', q' > 1$ in return.
3. Output 1 if and only if $p' \cdot q' = N$.

In many cryptographic applications, $\mathsf{GenModulus}(1^\kappa)$ is defined to sample p and q *uniformly* from the set of primes in the range $[2^{\kappa-1}, 2^\kappa)$ [18], and the factoring assumption with respect to this common $\mathsf{GenModulus}$ function states that for every PPT adversary $\mathcal{A}$ there exists a negligible function negl such that

$$\Pr\left[\mathsf{Factor}_{\mathcal{A},\mathsf{GenModulus}}(\kappa) = 1\right] \leq \mathsf{negl}(\kappa).$$

Because *efficiently* sampling according to this uniform biprime distribution is difficult in a multiparty context, most prior works sample according to a different distribution, and thus using the moduli they produce requires a slightly different factoring assumption than the traditional one. In particular, several recent works use a distribution originally proposed by Boneh and Franklin [4], which is well-adapted to multiparty sampling. Our work follows this pattern.

Boneh and Franklin's distribution is defined by the sampling algorithm BFGM, which takes as an additional parameter the number of parties n. The algorithm samples n integer shares, each in the range $[0, 2^{\kappa-\log n})$, and sums these shares to arrive at a candidate prime. This does *not* induce a uniform distribution on the set of κ-bit primes. Furthermore, BFGM only samples individual primes p or q that have $p \equiv q \equiv 3 \pmod 4$, in order to facilitate efficient distributed primality testing, and it filters out the subset of otherwise-valid moduli $N = p \cdot q$ that have $p \equiv 1 \pmod q$ or $q \equiv 1 \pmod p$.[5]

Algorithm 3.2. $\mathsf{BFGM}(\kappa, n)$

1. For $i \in [n]$, sample $p_i \leftarrow [0, 2^{\kappa-\log n})$ and $q_i \leftarrow [0, 2^{\kappa-\log n})$ subject to $p_1 \equiv q_1 \equiv 3 \pmod 4$ and $p_j \equiv q_j \equiv 0 \pmod 4$ for $j \in [2, n]$.
2. Compute

$$p := \sum_{i \in [n]} p_i \quad \text{and} \quad q := \sum_{i \in [n]} q_i \quad \text{and} \quad N := p \cdot q$$

3. If $\gcd(N, p + q - 1) = 1$, and both p and q are primes, then output $(N, \{(p_i, q_i)\}_{i \in [n]})$. Otherwise, repeat this procedure from Step 1.

Any protocol whose security depends upon the hardness of factoring moduli output by our protocol (including our protocol itself) must rely upon the assumption that for every PPT adversary $\mathcal{A}$,

$$\Pr\left[\mathsf{Factor}_{\mathcal{A},\mathsf{BFGM}}(\kappa, n) = 1\right] \leq \mathsf{negl}(\kappa)$$

---

[5] Boneh and Franklin actually propose two variations, one of which has no false negatives; we choose the other variation, as it leads to a more efficient sampling protocol.

3.2   The Distributed Biprime-Sampling Functionality

Unfortunately, our ideal modulus-sampling functionality cannot merely call BFGM; we wish our functionality to run in *strict* polynomial time, whereas the running time of BFGM is only *expected* polynomial. Thus, we define a new sampling algorithm, CRTSample, which might fail, but conditioned on success outputs samples statistically close to BFGM.[6] Furthermore, we give CRTSample a specific distribution of failures that is tied to the design of our protocol. As a second concession to our protocol design (and following Hazay et al. [20]), CRTSample takes as input up to $n-1$ integer shares of p and q, arbitrarily determined by the adversary, while the remaining shares are sampled randomly. We begin with a few useful notions.

Definition 3.3. (Primorial Number). The ith *primorial number* is defined to be the product of the first i prime numbers.

Definition 3.4. ((κ, n)-Near-Primorial Vector). Let ℓ be the largest number such that the ℓth primorial number is less than $2^{\kappa - \log n - 1}$, and let $\mathbf{m}$ be a vector of length ℓ such that $\mathbf{m}_1 = 4$ and $\mathbf{m}_2, \ldots, \mathbf{m}_\ell$ are the odd factors of the ℓth primorial number, in ascending order. $\mathbf{m}$ is the unique (κ, n)-*near-primorial vector*.

Definition 3.5. (m-Coprimality). Let $\mathbf{m}$ be a vector of integers. An integer x is $\mathbf{m}$-*coprime* if and only if it is not divisible by any $\mathbf{m}_i$ for $i \in [\|\mathbf{m}\|]$.

Algorithm 3.6. CRTSample($\kappa, n, \{(p_i, q_i)\}_{i \in \mathbf{P}^*}$)

1. Let $\mathbf{m}$ be the (κ, n)-near-primorial vector, with length ℓ, and let M be the product of $\mathbf{m}$.
2. For $i \in [n] \setminus \mathbf{P}^*$, sample $p_i \leftarrow [0, M)$ and $q_i \leftarrow [0, M)$ subject to

$$p_i \equiv q_i \equiv \begin{cases} 3 \pmod{4} & \text{if } i = 1 \\ 0 \pmod{4} & \text{if } i \neq 1 \end{cases}$$

   and subject to p and q being $\mathbf{m}$-coprime, where

$$p := \sum_{i \in [n]} p_i \quad \text{and} \quad q := \sum_{i \in [n]} q_i$$

   are computed over the integers.
3. If $\gcd(p \cdot q, p + q - 1) = 1$, and if both p and q are primes, and if $p \equiv q \equiv 3 \pmod{4}$, then output $(\text{success}, p, q)$; otherwise, output $(\text{failure}, p, q)$.

---

[6] CRTSample never outputs biprimes with factors smaller than κ, whereas BFGM outputs such biprimes with negligible probability. The discrepancy of share ranges can be remedied by using non-integer values of κ with BFGM.

Boneh and Franklin [4, Lemma 2.1] showed that knowledge of $n - 1$ integer shares of the factors p and q does not give the adversary any meaningful advantage in factoring biprimes from the distribution produced by BFGM and, by extension, CRTSample. Hazay et al. [20, Lemma 4.1] extended this argument to the malicious setting, wherein the adversary is allowed to choose its own shares.

Lemma 3.7. ([4,20]). *Let* $n < \kappa$ *and let* $(\mathcal{A}_1, \mathcal{A}_2)$ *be a pair of PPT algorithms. For* (state, $\{(p_i, q_i)\}_{i \in [n-1]}$) $\leftarrow \mathcal{A}_1(1^\kappa, 1^n)$, *let* N *be a biprime sampled by running* CRTSample($\kappa, n, \{(p_i, q_i)\}_{i \in [n-1]}$). *If* $\mathcal{A}_2(\text{state}, N)$ *outputs the factors of* N *with probability at least* $1/\kappa^d$, *then there exists an expected-polynomial-time algorithm* $\mathcal{B}$ *that succeeds with probability* $1/2^4 n^3 \kappa^d$ *in the experiment* $\text{Factor}_{\mathcal{B}, \text{BFGM}(\kappa, n)}$.

Multiparty Functionality. Our ideal functionality $\mathcal{F}_{\text{RSAGen}}$ is a natural embedding of CRTSample in a multiparty functionality: it receives inputs $\{(p_i, q_i)\}_{i \in \mathbf{P}^*}$ from the adversary and runs a single iteration of CRTSample with these inputs when invoked. It either outputs the corresponding modulus $N := p \cdot q$ if it is valid, or indicates that a sampling failure has occurred. Running a single iteration of CRTSample per invocation of $\mathcal{F}_{\text{RSAGen}}$ enables significant freedom in the use of $\mathcal{F}_{\text{RSAGen}}$, because it can be composed in different ways to tune the trade-off between resource usage and execution time. It also simplifies the analysis of the protocol π_{RSAGen} that realizes $\mathcal{F}_{\text{RSAGen}}$, because the analysis is made independent of the success rate of the sampling procedure.

The functionality may not deliver N to the honest parties for one of two reasons: either CRTSample failed to sample a biprime, or the adversary caused the computation to abort. In either case, the honest parties are informed of the cause of the failure, and consequently the adversary is unable to conflate the two cases. This is essentially the standard notion of security with abort, applied to the multiparty computation of the CRTSample algorithm. In both cases, the p and q output by CRTSample are given to the adversary. This leakage simplifies our proof considerably, and we consider it benign, since the honest parties never receive (and therefore cannot possibly use) N.

Functionality 3.8. $\mathcal{F}_{\text{RSAGen}}(\kappa, n)$. **Distributed Biprime Sampling**

This n-party functionality attempts to sample an RSA modulus with prime length κ, and interacts directly with an ideal adversary $\mathcal{S}$ who corrupts the parties indexed by $\mathbf{P}^*$. Let M be the largest number such that $M/2$ is a primorial number and $M < 2^{\kappa - \log n}$.

Sampling: On receiving (sample, sid) from each party $\mathcal{P}_i$ for $i \in [n] \setminus \mathbf{P}^*$ and (adv-sample, sid, i, p_i, q_i) from $\mathcal{S}$ for $i \in \mathbf{P}^*$, if $0 \leq p_i < M$ and $0 \leq q_i < M$ for all $i \in \mathbf{P}^*$, then run CRTSample($\kappa, n, \{(p_i, q_i)\}_{i \in \mathbf{P}^*}$), and receive as a result either (success, p, q) or (failure, p, q).
- If $p \not\equiv 3 \pmod 4$ or $q \not\equiv 3 \pmod 4$, then send (factors, sid, p, q) to $\mathcal{S}$ and abort, informing all parties in an adversarially delayed fashion.
- If $p \equiv q \equiv 3 \pmod 4$, and the result was failure, then store (non-biprime, sid, p, q) in memory and send (factors, sid, p, q) to $\mathcal{S}$.

- If $p \equiv q \equiv 3 \pmod{4}$, and the result was `success`, then compute $N := p \cdot q$, store $(\text{biprime}, \text{sid}, N, p, q)$ in memory, and send $(\text{biprime}, \text{sid}, N)$ to $\mathcal{S}$.

Output: On receiving either $(\text{proceed}, \text{sid})$ or $(\text{cheat}, \text{sid})$ from $\mathcal{S}$, if $(\text{biprime}, \text{sid}, N, p, q)$ or $(\text{non-biprime}, \text{sid}, p, q)$ exists in memory,

- If `proceed` was received, then send either $(\text{biprime}, \text{sid}, N)$ or $(\text{non-biprime}, \text{sid})$ to all parties as adversarially delayed output, as appropriate. Terminate successfully.
- If `cheat` was received, then abort, notifying all parties in an adversarially delayed fashion, and send $(\text{factors}, \text{sid}, p, q)$ directly to $\mathcal{S}$.

Regardless, ignore all further instructions with this sid.

4   The Distributed Biprime-Sampling Protocol

In this section, we present the distributed biprime-sampling protocol π_{RSAGen}, with which we realize $\mathcal{F}_{\mathsf{RSAGen}}$. We begin with a high-level overview, and then in Sect. 4.2, we formally define the two ideal functionalities on which our protocol relies, after which in Sect. 4.3 we give the protocol itself. In Sect. 4.4, we present proof sketches of semi-honest and malicious security.

4.1   High-Level Overview

As described in the Introduction, our protocol derives from that of Boneh and Franklin [4], the main technical differences relative to other recent Boneh-Franklin derivatives [16,20] being the modularity with which it is described and proven, and the use of CRT-based sampling. Our protocol has three main phases, which we now describe in sequence.

Candidate Sieving. In the first phase of our protocol, the parties jointly sample two κ-bit candidate primes p and q without any small factors, and multiply them to learn their product N. Our protocol achieves these tasks in a unified, integrated way, thanks to the Chinese Remainder Theorem.

Consider a prime m and a set of shares x_i for $i \in [n]$ over the field $\mathbb{Z}_m$. As in the description of CRTRecon, let a and b be defined such that $a \cdot b \equiv 1 \pmod{m}$, and let M be an integer. Observe that if m divides M, then

$$\sum_{i \in [n]} x_i \not\equiv 0 \pmod{m} \quad \Longrightarrow \quad \sum_{i \in [n]} a \cdot b \cdot x_i \bmod M \not\equiv 0 \pmod{m} \quad (1)$$

Now consider a vector of coprime integers $\mathbf{m}$ of length ℓ, and let M be their product. Let $\mathbf{x}$ be a vector, each element secret shared over the fields defined by the corresponding element of $\mathbf{m}$, and let $\mathbf{a}$ and $\mathbf{b}$ be defined as in CRTRecon (i.e., $\mathbf{a}_j := M/\mathbf{m}_j$ and $\mathbf{a}_j \cdot \mathbf{b}_j \equiv 1 \pmod{\mathbf{m}_j}$). We can see that for any $k, j \in [\ell]$ such that $k \neq j$,

$$\mathbf{a}_j \equiv 0 \pmod{\mathbf{m}_k} \quad \Longrightarrow \quad \sum_{i \in [n]} \mathbf{a}_j \cdot \mathbf{b}_j \cdot \mathbf{x}_{i,j} \bmod M \equiv 0 \pmod{\mathbf{m}_k} \quad (2)$$

and the conjunction of Eqs. 1 and 2 gives us

$$\sum_{j \in [\ell]} \sum_{i \in [n]} \mathbf{a}_j \cdot \mathbf{b}_j \cdot \mathbf{x}_{i,j} \bmod M \equiv \sum_{i \in [n]} \mathbf{x}_{i,k} \pmod{\mathbf{m}_k}$$

for all $k \in [\ell]$. Observe that this holds regardless of which order we perform the sums in, and regardless of whether the mod M operation is done at the end, or between the two sums, or not at all.

It follows then that we can sample n shares for an additive secret sharing over the integers of a κ-bit value x (distributed between 0 and $n \cdot M$) by choosing $\mathbf{m}$ to be the (κ, n)-near-primorial vector (per Definition 3.4), instructing each party $\mathcal{P}_i$ for $i \in [n]$ to pick $\mathbf{x}_{i,j}$ locally for $j \in [\ell]$ such that $0 \leq \mathbf{x}_{i,j} < \mathbf{m}_j$, and then instructing each party to *locally* reconstruct $x_i := \mathsf{CRTRecon}(\mathbf{m}, \mathbf{x}_{i,*})$, its share of x. It furthermore follows that if the parties can contrive to ensure that

$$\sum_{i \in [n]} \mathbf{x}_{i,j} \not\equiv 0 \pmod{\mathbf{m}_j} \quad (3)$$

for $j \in [\ell]$, then x will not be divisible by any prime in $\mathbf{m}$.

Observe next that if the parties sample two shared vectors $\mathbf{p}$ and $\mathbf{q}$ as above (corresponding to the candidate primes p and q) and compute a shared vector $\mathbf{N}$ of identical dimension such that

$$\sum_{i \in [n]} \mathbf{p}_{i,j} \cdot \sum_{i \in [n]} \mathbf{q}_{i,j} \equiv \sum_{i \in [n]} \mathbf{N}_{i,j} \pmod{\mathbf{m}_j} \quad (4)$$

for all $j \in [\ell]$, then it follows that

$$\sum_{i \in [n]} \mathsf{CRTRecon}(\mathbf{m}, \mathbf{p}_{i,*}) \cdot \sum_{i \in [n]} \mathsf{CRTRecon}(\mathbf{m}, \mathbf{q}_{i,*}) = \sum_{i \in [n]} \mathsf{CRTRecon}(\mathbf{m}, \mathbf{N}_{i,*})$$

and from this it follows that the parties can calculate integer shares of $N = p \cdot q$ by multiplying $\mathbf{p}$ and $\mathbf{q}$ together element-wise using a modular-multiplication protocol for linear secret shares, and then locally running $\mathsf{CRTRecon}$ on the output to reconstruct N. In fact, our sampling protocol makes use of a special functionality $\mathcal{F}_{\mathsf{AugMul}}$, which samples $\mathbf{p}$, $\mathbf{q}$, and $\mathbf{N}$ simultaneously such that the conditions in Eqs. 3 and 4 hold.

There remains one problem: our vector $\mathbf{m}$ was chosen for sampling integer-shared values between 0 and $n \cdot M$ (with each share no larger than M), but N might be as large as $n^2 \cdot M^2$. In order to avoid wrapping during reconstruction of N, we must reconstruct with respect to a *larger* vector of primes (while continuing to sample with respect to a smaller one). Let $\mathbf{m}$ now be of length ℓ', and let ℓ continue to denote the length of the prefix of $\mathbf{m}$ with respect to which sampling is performed. After sampling the initial vectors $\mathbf{p}$, $\mathbf{q}$, and $\mathbf{N}$, each party $\mathcal{P}_i$ for $i \in [n]$ must extend $\mathbf{p}_{i,*}$ locally to ℓ' elements, by computing

$$\mathbf{p}_{i,j} := \mathsf{CRTRecon}\left(\{\mathbf{m}_{j'}\}_{j' \in [\ell]}, \{\mathbf{p}_{j'}\}_{j' \in [\ell]}\right) \bmod \mathbf{m}_j$$

for $j \in [\ell + 1, \ell']$, and then likewise for $\mathbf{q}_{i,*}$. Finally, the parties must use a modular-multiplication protocol to compute the appropriate extension of $\mathbf{N}$; from this extended $\mathbf{N}$, they can reconstruct shares of $N = p \cdot q$. They swap these shares, and thus each party ends the Sieving phase of our protocol with a candidate biprime N and an integer share of each of its factors, p_i and q_i.

Each party completes the first phase by performing a local trial division to check if N is divisible by any prime smaller than some bound B (which is a parameter of the protocol). The purpose of this step is to reduce the number of calls to $\mathcal{F}_{\mathsf{Biprime}}$ and thus improve efficiency.

Biprimality Test. The parties jointly execute a biprimality test, where every party inputs the candidate N and its shares p_i and q_i, and receives back a biprimality indicator. This phase essentially comprises a single call to a functionality $\mathcal{F}_{\mathsf{Biprime}}$, which allows an adversary to force spurious negative results, but never returns false positive results. Though this phase is simple, much of the subtlety of our proof concentrates here: we show via a reduction to factoring that cheating parties have a negligible chance to pass the biprimality test if they provide wrong inputs. This eliminates the need to authenticate the inputs in any way.

Consistency Check. To achieve malicious security, the parties must ensure that none among them cheated during the previous stages in a way that might influence the result of the computation. This is what we have previously termed the retroactive consistency check. If the biprimality test indicated that N is *not* a biprime, then the parties use a special interface of $\mathcal{F}_{\mathsf{AugMul}}$ to reveal the shares they used during the protocol, and then they verify locally and independently that p and q are not both primes. If the biprimality test indicated that N is a biprime, then the parties run a secure test (again via a special interface of $\mathcal{F}_{\mathsf{AugMul}}$) to ensure that length extensions of $\mathbf{p}$ and $\mathbf{q}$ were performed honestly. To achieve semi-honest security, this phase is unnecessary, and the protocol can end with the biprimality test.

4.2   Ideal Functionalities Used in the Protocol

Augmented Multiparty Multiplier. The augmented multiplier functionality $\mathcal{F}_{\mathsf{AugMul}}$ (Functionality 4.1) is a reactive functionality that operates in multiple phases and stores an internal state across calls. It is meant to help in manipulating CRT-form secret shares. It contains five basic interfaces.

– The `sample` interface allows the parties to sample shares of non-zero multiplication triplets over small primes. That is, given a prime m, the functionality receives a triplet (x_i, y_i, z_i) from every corrupted party $\mathcal{P}_i$, and then samples a triplet $(x_j, y_j, z_j) \leftarrow \mathbb{Z}_m^3$ for every honest $\mathcal{P}_j$ conditioned on

$$\sum_{i \in [n]} z_i \equiv \sum_{i \in [n]} x_i \cdot \sum_{i \in [n]} y_i \not\equiv 0 \pmod{m}$$

In the context of π_{RSAGen}, this is used to sample CRT-shares of p and q.

- The input and multiply interfaces, taken together, allow the parties to load shares (with respect to some small prime modulus m) into the functionality's memory, and later perform modular multiplication on two sets of shares that are associated with the same modulus. That is, given a prime m, each party $\mathcal{P}_i$ inputs x_i and, independently, y_i, and when the parties request a product, with each corrupt party $\mathcal{P}_j$ also supplying its own an output share z_j, the functionality samples a share of z from $\mathbb{Z}_m$ for each honest party subject to

$$\sum_{i \in [n]} z_i \equiv \sum_{i \in [n]} x_i \cdot \sum_{i \in [n]} y_i \pmod{m}$$

In the context of π_{RSAGen}, this interface is used to perform length-extension on CRT-shares of p and q.

- The check interface allows the parties to securely compute a predicate over the set of stored values. In the context of π_{RSAGen}, this is used to check that the CRT-share extension of p and q has been performed correctly, when N is a biprime.

- The open interface allows the parties to retroactively reveal their inputs to one another. In the context of π_{RSAGen}, this is used to verify the sampling procedure and biprimality test when N is not a biprime.

These five interfaces suffice for the malicious version of the protocol, and the first three alone suffice for the semi-honest version. We make a final adjustment, which leads to a substantial efficiency improvement in the protocol with which we realize $\mathcal{F}_{\mathsf{AugMul}}$ (which we describe in the full version of this paper [7]). Specifically, we give the adversary an interface by which it can request that any stored value be leaked to itself, and by which it can (arbitrarily) determine the output of any call to the sample or multiply interfaces. However, if the adversary uses this interface, the functionality remembers, and informs the honest parties by aborting when the check or open interfaces is used.

Functionality 4.1. $\mathcal{F}_{\mathsf{AugMul}}(n)$. **Augmented n-Party Multiplication**

This functionality is parametrized by the party count n. In addition to the parties it interacts with an ideal adversary $\mathcal{S}$ who corrupts the parties indexed by $\mathbf{P}^*$. The remaining honest parties are indexed by $\overline{\mathbf{P}^*} := [n] \setminus \mathbf{P}^*$.

Cheater Activation: Upon receiving (cheat, sid) from $\mathcal{S}$, store (cheater, sid) in memory and send every record of the form (value, sid, i, x_i, m) to $\mathcal{S}$. For the purposes of this functionality, we will consider session IDs to be fresh even when a cheater record already exists in memory.

Sampling: Upon receiving $(\mathtt{sample}, \mathsf{sid}_1, \mathsf{sid}_2, m)$ from each party $\mathcal{P}_i$ for $i \in \overline{\mathbf{P}^*}$ and $(\mathtt{adv\text{-}sample}, \mathsf{sid}_1, \mathsf{sid}_2, x_i, y_i, z_i, m)$ from $\mathcal{S}$ for $i \in \mathbf{P}^*,^a$ if sid_1 and sid_2 are fresh, agreed-upon values and if m is an agreed-upon prime, and if neither $(\mathtt{cheater}, \mathsf{sid}_1)$ nor $(\mathtt{cheater}, \mathsf{sid}_2)$ exists in memory, then sample $(x_i, y_i, z_i) \leftarrow \mathbb{Z}_m^3$ uniformly for each $i \in \overline{\mathbf{P}^*}$ subject to

$$\sum_{i \in [n]} z_i \equiv \sum_{i \in [n]} x_i \cdot \sum_{i \in [n]} y_i \not\equiv 0 \pmod{m}$$

If the previous conditions hold, but $(\mathtt{cheater}, \mathsf{sid}_1)$ or $(\mathtt{cheater}, \mathsf{sid}_2)$ exists in memory, then send $(\mathtt{cheat\text{-}sample}, \mathsf{sid}_1, \mathsf{sid}_2)$ to $\mathcal{S}$ and in response receive $(\mathtt{cheat\text{-}samples}, \mathsf{sid}_1, \mathsf{sid}_2, \{(x_i, y_i, z_i)\}_{i \in \overline{\mathbf{P}^*}})$ where $0 \leq x_i, y_i, z_i < m$ for all i and where

$$\sum_{i \in [n]} z_i \not\equiv 0 \pmod{m}$$

(if these conditions are violated, then ignore the response from $\mathcal{S}$). Regardless, store $(\mathtt{value}, \mathsf{sid}_1, i, x_i, m)$ and $(\mathtt{value}, \mathsf{sid}_2, i, y_i, m)$ in memory for $i \in [n]$, and then send $(\mathtt{sampled\text{-}product}, \mathsf{sid}_1, \mathsf{sid}_2, x_i, y_i, z_i)$ to each party $\mathcal{P}_i$ as adversarially delayed private output.

Input: Upon receiving $(\mathtt{input}, \mathsf{sid}, x_i, m)$ from each party $\mathcal{P}_i$, where $i \in [n]$: if sid is a fresh, agreed-upon value and if m is an agreed-upon prime, and if $0 \leq x_i < m$ for all $i \in [n]$, then store $(\mathtt{value}, \mathsf{sid}, i, x_i, m)$ in memory for each $i \in [n]$ and send $(\mathtt{value\text{-}loaded}, \mathsf{sid})$ to all parties. If $(\mathtt{cheater}, \mathsf{sid})$ exists in memory, then send $(\mathtt{value}, \mathsf{sid}, i, x_i, m)$ to $\mathcal{S}$ for each $i \in [n]$.

Multiplication: Upon receiving $(\mathtt{multiply}, \mathsf{sid}_1, \mathsf{sid}_2, \mathsf{sid}_3)$ from each party $\mathcal{P}_i$ for $i \in \overline{\mathbf{P}^*}$ and $(\mathtt{adv\text{-}multiply}, \mathsf{sid}_1, \mathsf{sid}_2, \mathsf{sid}_3, i, z_i)$ from $\mathcal{S}$ for each $i \in \mathbf{P}^*,^a$ if all three session IDs are agreed upon and sid_3 is fresh, and if no record of the form $(\mathtt{cheater}, \mathsf{sid}_1)$ or $(\mathtt{cheater}, \mathsf{sid}_2)$ exists in memory, and if records of the form $(\mathtt{value}, \mathsf{sid}_1, i, x_i, m_1)$ and $(\mathtt{value}, \mathsf{sid}_2, i, y_i, m_2)$ exist in memory for all $i \in [n]$ such that $m_1 = m_2$, then sample $z_i \leftarrow \mathbb{Z}_{m_1}$ for $i \in \overline{\mathbf{P}^*}$ subject to

$$\sum_{i \in [n]} z_i \equiv \sum_{i \in [n]} x_i \cdot \sum_{i \in [n]} y_i \pmod{m_1}$$

If the previous conditions hold, but $(\mathtt{cheater}, \mathsf{sid}_1)$ or $(\mathtt{cheater}, \mathsf{sid}_2)$ exists in memory, then send $(\mathtt{cheat\text{-}multiply}, \mathsf{sid}_1, \mathsf{sid}_2, \mathsf{sid}_3)$ to $\mathcal{S}$ and in response receive $(\mathtt{cheat\text{-}product}, \mathsf{sid}_3, \{z_i\}_{i \in \overline{\mathbf{P}^*}})$ where $0 \leq z_i < m_1$ for all i. Regardless, send $(\mathtt{product}, \mathsf{sid}_3, z_i)$ to each party $\mathcal{P}_i$ for $i \in [n]$ as adversarially delayed private output. Note that this procedure only permits multiplications of values associated with the *same* modulus.

Predicate Cheater Check: Upon receiving $(\mathtt{check}, \mathbf{sids}, f)$ from all parties, where f is the description of a predicate over the set of stored values associated with the vector of session IDs $\mathbf{sids}$, if f is not agreed upon, or if any record (cheater, sid) exists in memory such that sid ∈ **sids**, then abort, informing all parties in an adversarially delayed fashion. Otherwise, let **x** be the vector of stored values associated with **sids**, or in other words, let it be a vector such that for all $j \in [\|\mathbf{x}\|]$ and $i \in [n]$, records of the form (value, $\mathbf{sids}_j, i, y_i, m$) exist in memory such that

$$0 \leq \mathbf{x}_j < m \qquad \text{and} \qquad \mathbf{x}_j \equiv \sum_{i \in [n]} y_i \pmod{m}$$

Send (predicate-result, **sids**, $f(\mathbf{x})$) to all parties as adversarially delayed private output, and refuse all future messages with any session ID in **sids**.

Input Revelation: Upon receiving (open, sid) from all parties, if a record of the form (cheater, sid) exists in memory, then abort, informing all parties in an adversarially delayed fashion. Otherwise, for each record of the form (value, sid, i, x_i) in memory, send (opening, sid, i, x_i) to all parties as adversarially delayed output. Refuse all future messages with this sid.

---

[a]In the semi-honest setting, the adversary does not send these values to the functionality; instead the functionality samples the shares for corrupt parties just as it does for honest parties.

Biprimality Test. The biprimality-test functionality $\mathcal{F}_{\mathsf{Biprime}}$ (Functionality 4.2) abstracts the behavior of the biprimality test of Boneh and Franklin [4]. The functionality receives from each party a candidate biprime N, along with shares of its factors p and q. It checks whether p and q are primes and whether $N = p \cdot q$. The adversary is given an additional interface, by which it can ask the functionality to leak the honest parties' inputs, but when this interface is used then the functionality reports to the honest parties that N is not a biprime, even if it is one.

Functionality 4.2. $\mathcal{F}_{\mathsf{Biprime}}(M, n)$. Distributed Biprimality Test

This functionality is parametrized by the integer M and the party-count n. In addition to the parties it interacts with an ideal adversary $\mathcal{S}$.

Biprimality Test:

1. Wait to receive (check-biprimality, sid, N, p_i, q_i) from each party $\mathcal{P}_i$ for $i \in [n]$, where sid is a fresh, agreed-upon value.
2. Over the integers, compute

$$p := \sum_{i \in [n]} p_i \qquad \text{and} \qquad q := \sum_{i \in [n]} q_i \qquad \text{and} \qquad N' := p \cdot q$$

3. If all parties agreed on the value of N in Step 1, and $N = N'$, and both p and q are primes, and $p \not\equiv 1 \pmod{q}$, and $q \not\equiv 1 \pmod{p}$, and $0 \leq p < M$ and $0 \leq q < M$, then send a message (biprime, sid) to $\mathcal{S}$. If $\mathcal{S}$ responds with (proceed, sid), then output (biprime, sid) to all parties as adversar-

ially delayed output. If $\mathcal{S}$ responds with $(\texttt{cheat}, \texttt{sid})^a$, or if any of the previous predicates is false, then output $(\texttt{leaked-shares}, \texttt{sid}, \{(p_i, q_i)\}_{i \in [n]})$ directly to $\mathcal{S}$, and output $(\texttt{not-biprime}, \texttt{sid})$ to all parties as adversarially delayed output.

---

[a] Semi-honest adversaries are forbidden to send the $\texttt{cheat}$ instruction.

Realizations. In the full version of this paper [7], we discuss a protocol to realize $\mathcal{F}_{\mathsf{AugMul}}$, and in Sect. 5, we propose a protocol to realize $\mathcal{F}_{\mathsf{Biprime}}$. Both make use of generic MPC, but in such a way that no generic MPC is required unless N is a biprime.

4.3   The Protocol Itself

We refer the reader back to Sect. 4.1 for an overview of our protocol. We have mentioned that it requires a vector of coprime values, which is prefixed by the (κ, n)-near-primorial vector. We now give this vector a precise definition. Note that the efficiency of our protocol relies upon this vector, because we use its contents to sieve candidate primes. Since smaller numbers are more likely to be factors for the candidate primes, we choose the largest allowable set of the smallest sequential primes.

Definition 4.3. $((\kappa, n)$-*Compatible Parameter Set*). Let ℓ' be the smallest number such that the ℓ'^{th} primorial number is greater than $2^{2\kappa - 1}$, and let $\mathbf{m}$ be a vector of length ℓ' such that $\mathbf{m}_1 = 4$ and $\mathbf{m}_2, \dots, \mathbf{m}_{\ell'}$ are the odd factors of the ℓ'^{th} primorial number, in ascending order. $(\mathbf{m}, \ell', \ell, M)$ is the (κ, n)-*compatible parameter set* if $\ell < \ell'$ and the prefix of $\mathbf{m}$ of length ℓ is the (κ, n)-near-primorial vector per Definition 3.4, and if M is the product of this prefix.

Protocol 4.4. $\pi_{\mathsf{RSAGen}}(\kappa, n, B)$. **Distributed Biprime Sampling**

This protocol is parametrized by the RSA prime length κ, the number of parties n, and the trial-division bound B. Let $(\mathbf{m}, \ell', \ell, M)$ be the (κ, n)-compatible parameter set, per Definition 4.3. In this protocol the parties have access to the functionalities $\mathcal{F}_{\mathsf{AugMul}}$ and $\mathcal{F}_{\mathsf{Biprime}}$.

Candidate Sieving:
1. Upon receiving input $(\texttt{sample}, \texttt{sid})$ from the environment, the parties begin the protocol. Every party $\mathcal{P}_i$ for $i \in [n]$ computes three vectors of session IDs

$$\mathbf{psids} := \{\mathsf{GenSID}(\texttt{sid}, j, \mathsf{p})\}_{j \in [\ell']}$$
$$\mathbf{qsids} := \{\mathsf{GenSID}(\texttt{sid}, j, \mathsf{q})\}_{j \in [\ell']}$$
$$\mathbf{Nsids} := \{\mathsf{GenSID}(\texttt{sid}, j, \mathsf{N})\}_{j \in [\ell']}$$

and sends $(\texttt{sample}, \mathbf{psids}_j, \mathbf{qsids}_j, \mathbf{m}_j)$ to $\mathcal{F}_{\mathsf{AugMul}}(n)$ for every $j \in [2, \ell]$, and receives $(\texttt{sampled-product}, \mathbf{psids}_j, \mathbf{qsids}_j, \mathrm{p}_{i,j}, \mathrm{q}_{i,j}, \mathrm{N}_{i,j})$ in response. The parties also set $\mathbf{p}_{1,1} := \mathbf{q}_{1,1} := 3$ and $\mathbf{p}_{i',1} := \mathbf{q}_{i',1} := 0$ for $i' \in [2, n]$.

2. Each party $\mathcal{P}_i$ for $i \in [n]$ computes

$$p_i := \mathsf{CRTRecon}\left(\{\mathbf{m}_j\}_{j\in[\ell]}, \{\mathbf{p}_{i,j}\}_{j\in[\ell]}\right)$$

$$q_i := \mathsf{CRTRecon}\left(\{\mathbf{m}_j\}_{j\in[\ell]}, \{\mathbf{q}_{i,j}\}_{j\in[\ell]}\right)$$

and then, for $j \in [\ell + 1, \ell']$, $\mathcal{P}_i$ computes

$$\mathbf{p}_{i,j} := p_i \bmod \mathbf{m}_j \qquad \text{and} \qquad \mathbf{q}_{i,j} := q_i \bmod \mathbf{m}_j$$

Note that each party $\mathcal{P}_i$ is now in possession of a pair of vectors

$$\mathbf{p}_{i,*} \in \mathbb{Z}_{\mathbf{m}_1} \times \ldots \times \mathbb{Z}_{\mathbf{m}_{\ell'}} \qquad \text{and} \qquad \mathbf{q}_{i,*} \in \mathbb{Z}_{\mathbf{m}_1} \times \ldots \times \mathbb{Z}_{\mathbf{m}_{\ell'}}$$

3. For $j \in [\ell + 1, \ell']$, every party $\mathcal{P}_i$ for $i \in [n]$ sends the following sequence of messages to $\mathcal{F}_{\mathsf{AugMul}}(n)$, waiting for confirmation after each:
   (a) $(\mathtt{input}, \mathbf{psids}_j, \mathbf{p}_{i,j}, \mathbf{m}_j)$
   (b) $(\mathtt{input}, \mathbf{qsids}_j, \mathbf{q}_{i,j}, \mathbf{m}_j)$
   (c) $(\mathtt{multiply}, \mathbf{psids}_j, \mathbf{qsids}_j, \mathbf{Nsids}_j)$
   and at the end of this sequence, each party $\mathcal{P}_i$ receives $(\mathtt{product}, \mathbf{Nsids}_j, \mathbf{N}_{i,j})$ from $\mathcal{F}_{\mathsf{AugMul}}(n)$ in response. Note that each party $\mathcal{P}_i$ is now in possession of a vector $\mathbf{N}_{i,*} \in \mathbb{Z}_{\mathbf{m}_1} \times \ldots \times \mathbb{Z}_{\mathbf{m}_{\ell'}}$.

4. For $j \in [2, \ell']$, each party $\mathcal{P}_i$ for $i \in [n]$ broadcasts $\mathbf{N}_{i,j}$. Once all parties have received shares from all other parties, they compute

$$N := \mathsf{CRTRecon}\left(\mathbf{m}, \left\{\sum_{i'\in[n]} \mathbf{N}_{i',j} \bmod \mathbf{m}_j\right\}_{j\in[\ell']}\right)$$

5. Each party $\mathcal{P}_i$ performs a local trial division on N by all primes less than B. If N is divisible by some prime, then the parties skip directly to Step 7, and take the privacy-free branch.

Biprimality Test:

6. Each party $\mathcal{P}_i$ for $i \in [n]$ sends $(\mathtt{check\text{-}biprimality}, \mathsf{sid}, N, p_i, q_i)$ to $\mathcal{F}_{\mathsf{Biprime}}(M, n)$ and waits for either $(\mathtt{biprime}, \mathsf{sid})$ or $(\mathtt{not\text{-}biprime}, \mathsf{sid})$ in response.

Consistency Check: [a]

7. Let f be the predicate that is defined to compute

$$p_{i'} := \mathsf{CRTRecon}\left(\mathbf{m}, \mathbf{p}_{i',*}\right) \qquad \text{and} \qquad q_{i'} := \mathsf{CRTRecon}\left(\mathbf{m}, \mathbf{q}_{i',*}\right)$$

for all $i' \in [n]$ and to return 1 if and only if

$$N = \sum_{i' \in [n]} p_{i'} \cdot \sum_{i' \in [n]} q_{i'}$$

$$\wedge \quad 0 \le p_{i'} < M \quad \wedge \quad 0 \le q_{i'} < M \qquad \text{for all } i' \in [n]$$

where the sums and product are taken over the integers.

- If biprime is received from $\mathcal{F}_{\mathsf{Biprime}}(M, n)$, then N is a biprime, and a privacy-preserving check must be performed. Each party sends $(\mathsf{check}, \mathbf{psids} \| \mathbf{qsids}, f)$ to $\mathcal{F}_{\mathsf{AugMul}}(n)$. If $\mathcal{F}_{\mathsf{AugMul}}$ returns $(\mathsf{predicate\text{-}result}, \mathbf{psids} \| \mathbf{qsids}, 1)$ then the parties halt successfully and output $(\mathsf{biprime}, \mathsf{sid}, N)$ to the environment; otherwise, they abort.
- If not-biprime is received from $\mathcal{F}_{\mathsf{Biprime}}(M, n)$, then either N is not a biprime or some party has cheated; consequently, a privacy-free check is performed.
  (a) For $j \in [2, \ell']$, each party $\mathcal{P}_i$ for $i \in [n]$ sends $(\mathsf{open}, \mathbf{psids}_j)$ and $(\mathsf{open}, \mathbf{qsids}_j)$ to $\mathcal{F}_{\mathsf{AugMul}}(n)$. If $\mathcal{P}_i$ observes $\mathcal{F}_{\mathsf{AugMul}}(n)$ to abort in response to any of these queries, then $\mathcal{P}_i$ itself aborts. Otherwise, $\mathcal{P}_i$ receives $(\mathsf{opening}, \mathbf{psids}_j, \mathbf{p}_{i',j})$ and $(\mathsf{opening}, \mathbf{qsids}_j, \mathbf{q}_{i',j})$ for each $i' \in [n]$ and $j \in [2, \ell']$.
  (b) The parties individually check that the predicate f holds over the vectors of shares which they now all possess. If this predicate holds and p and q are not both prime, then all parties halt successfully and output $(\mathsf{non\text{-}biprime}, \mathsf{sid})$ to the environment. Otherwise, a party has cheated, and they abort.

---

[a]If only security against semi-honest adversaries is required, the protocol can terminate after the Biprimality-Test phase, and these checks are unnecessary.

4.4   Security Sketches

We now informally argue that π_{RSAGen} realizes $\mathcal{F}_{\mathsf{RSAGen}}$ in the semi-honest and malicious settings. We give a full proof for the malicious setting in the full version of this paper [7].

Theorem 4.5. π_{RSAGen} UC-realizes $\mathcal{F}_{\mathsf{RSAGen}}$ with perfect security in the $(\mathcal{F}_{\mathsf{AugMul}}, \mathcal{F}_{\mathsf{Biprime}})$-hybrid model against a static, semi-honest adversary that corrupts up to $n - 1$ parties.

Proof Sketch. In lieu of arguing for the correctness of our protocol, we refer the reader to the explanation in Sect. 4.1, and focus here on the strategy of a simulator $\mathcal{S}$ against a semi-honest adversary $\mathcal{A}$ who corrupts the parties indexed by $\mathbf{P}^*$. $\mathcal{S}$ forwards all messages between $\mathcal{A}$ and the environment faithfully.

In Step 1 of π_{RSAGen}, for each $j \in [2, \ell]$, $\mathcal{S}$ receives the sample instruction with modulus $\mathbf{m}_j$ on behalf of $\mathcal{F}_{\mathsf{AugMul}}$ from all parties indexed by $\mathbf{P}^*$. For each j it then samples $(\mathbf{p}_{i,j}, \mathbf{q}_{i,j}, \mathbf{N}_{i,j}) \leftarrow \mathbb{Z}_{\mathbf{m}_j}^3$ uniformly for $i \in \mathbf{P}^*$, and returns each triple to the appropriate party.

Step 2 involves no interaction on the part of the parties, but it is at this point that $\mathcal{S}$ computes p_i and q_i for $i \in \mathbf{P}^*$, in the same way that the parties themselves do. Note that since $\mathbf{p}_{*,1}$ and $\mathbf{q}_{*,1}$ are deterministically chosen, they are known to $\mathcal{S}$. The simulator then sends these shares to $\mathcal{F}_{\mathsf{RSAGen}}$ via the functionality's adv-input interface, and receives in return either a biprime N, or two factors p and q such that $N := p \cdot q$ is not a biprime. Regardless, it instructs $\mathcal{F}_{\mathsf{RSAGen}}$ to proceed.

In Step 3 of π_{RSAGen}, $\mathcal{S}$ receives two input instructions from each corrupted party for each $j \in [\ell+1, \ell']$ on behalf of $\mathcal{F}_{\mathsf{AugMul}}$, and confirms receipt as $\mathcal{F}_{\mathsf{AugMul}}$ would. Subsequently, for each $j \in [\ell+1, \ell']$, the corrupt parties all send a multiply instruction, and then $\mathcal{S}$ samples $\mathbf{N}_{i,j} \leftarrow \mathbb{Z}_{\mathbf{m}_j}$ for $i \in [n]$ subject to

$$\sum_{i \in [n]} \mathbf{N}_{i,j} \equiv N \pmod{\mathbf{m}_j}$$

and returns each share to the matching corrupt party.

In Step 4 of π_{RSAGen}, for every $j \in [\ell']$, every corrupt party $\mathcal{P}_{i'}$ for $i' \in \mathbf{P}^*$, and every honest party $\mathcal{P}_i$ for $i \in [n] \setminus \mathbf{P}^*$, $\mathcal{S}$ sends $\mathbf{N}_{i,j}$ to $\mathcal{P}_{i'}$ on behalf of $\mathcal{P}_i$, and receives $\mathbf{N}_{i',j}$ (which it already knows) in reply.

To simulate the final steps of π_{RSAGen}, $\mathcal{S}$ tries to divide N by all primes smaller than B. If it succeeds, then the protocol is complete. Otherwise, it receives check-biprimality from all of the corrupt parties on behalf of $\mathcal{F}_{\mathsf{Biprime}}$, and replies with biprime or not-biprime as appropriate. It can be verified by inspection that the view of the environment is identically distributed in the ideal-world experiment containing $\mathcal{S}$ and honest parties that interact with $\mathcal{F}_{\mathsf{RSAGen}}$, and the real-world experiment containing $\mathcal{A}$ and parties running π_{RSAGen}.   □

Theorem 4.6. If factoring biprimes sampled by BFGM is hard, then π_{RSAGen} UC-realizes $\mathcal{F}_{\mathsf{RSAGen}}$ in the $(\mathcal{F}_{\mathsf{AugMul}}, \mathcal{F}_{\mathsf{Biprime}})$-hybrid model against a static, malicious PPT adversary that corrupts up to $n-1$ parties.

Proof Sketch. We observe that if the adversary simply follows the specification of the protocol and does not cheat in its inputs to $\mathcal{F}_{\mathsf{AugMul}}$ or $\mathcal{F}_{\mathsf{Biprime}}$, then the simulator can follow the same strategy as in the semi-honest case. At any point if the adversary deviates from the protocol, the simulator requests $\mathcal{F}_{\mathsf{RSAGen}}$ to reveal all honest parties' shares, and thereafter the simulator uses them by effectively running the code of the honest parties. This matches the adversary's view in the real protocol as far as the distribution of the honest parties' shares is concerned.

It remains to be argued that any deviation from the protocol specification will also result in an abort in the real world with honest parties, and will additionally be recognized by the honest parties as an adversarially induced cheat (as opposed to a statistical sampling failure). Note that the honest parties must only detect cheating when N is truly a biprime and the adversary has sabotaged a successful candidate; if N is not a biprime and would have been rejected anyway, then cheat-detection is unimportant. We analyze all possible cases where the adversary deviates from the protocol below. Let N be defined as the value implied by parties' sampled shares in Step 1 of π_{RSAGen}.

Case 1: N is a non-biprime and reconstructed correctly. In this case, $\mathcal{F}_{\mathsf{Biprime}}$ will always reject N as there exist no satisfying inputs (i.e., there are no two prime factors p, q such that $p \cdot q = N$).

Case 2: N is a non-biprime and reconstructed incorrectly as N'. If by fluke N' happens to be a biprime then the incorrect reconstruction will be caught by the explicit secure predicate check during the consistency-check phase. If N' is a non-biprime then the argument from the previous case applies.

Case 3: N is a biprime and reconstructed correctly. If consistent inputs are used for the biprimality test and nobody cheats, the candidate N is successfully accepted (this case essentially corresponds to the semi-honest case). Otherwise, if inconsistent inputs are used for the biprimality test, one of the following events will occur:

– $\mathcal{F}_{\mathsf{Biprime}}$ rejects this candidate. In this case, all parties reveal their shares of p and q to one another (with guaranteed correctness via $\mathcal{F}_{\mathsf{AugMul}}$) and locally test their primality. This will reveal that N was a biprime, and that $\mathcal{F}_{\mathsf{Biprime}}$ must have been supplied with inconsistent inputs, implying that some party has cheated.
– $\mathcal{F}_{\mathsf{Biprime}}$ accepts this candidate. This case occurs with negligible probability (assuming factoring is hard). Because N only has two factors, there is exactly one pair of inputs that the adversary can supply to $\mathcal{F}_{\mathsf{Biprime}}$ to induce this scenario, apart from the pair specified by the protocol. In our full proof (see the full version [7] of this paper) we show that finding this alternative pair of satisfying inputs implies factoring N. We are careful to rely on the hardness of factoring only in this case, where by premise N is a biprime with κ-bit factors (i.e., an instance of the factoring problem).

Case 4: N is a biprime and reconstructed incorrectly as N'. If N' is a biprime then the incorrect reconstruction will be caught during the consistency-check phase, just as when N is a biprime. If N' is a non-biprime then it will by rejected by $\mathcal{F}_{\mathsf{Biprime}}$, inducing all parties to reveal their shares and find that their shares do not in fact reconstruct to N', with the implication that some party has cheated.

Thus the adversary is always caught when trying to sabotage a true biprime, and it can never sneak a non-biprime past the consistency check. Because the real-world protocol always aborts in the case of cheating, it is indistinguishable from the simulation described above, assuming that factoring is hard.   □

5   Distributed Biprimality Testing

In the semi-honest setting, $\mathcal{F}_{\mathsf{Biprime}}$ can be realized by the biprimality-testing protocol of Boneh and Franklin [4]. We discuss this in the full version [7] of this paper. The following lemma follows immediately from their work.

Lemma 5.1. The biprimality-testing protocol described by Boneh and Franklin [4] UC-realizes $\mathcal{F}_{\mathsf{Biprime}}$ with statistical security in the $\mathcal{F}_{\mathsf{ComCompute}}$-hybrid model against a static, semi-honest adversary who corrupts up to $n - 1$ parties.

5.1   The Malicious Setting

Unlike a semi-honest adversary, we permit a malicious adversary to force a true biprime to fail our biprimality test, and detect such behavior using independent mechanisms in the π_{RSAGen} protocol. However, we must ensure that a non-biprime can never pass the test with more than negligible probability. To achieve this, we use a derivative of the biprimality-testing protocol of Frederiksen et al. [16]; relative to their protocol, ours is simpler, and we prove that it UC-realizes $\mathcal{F}_{\mathsf{Biprime}}$.

The protocol essentially comprises a randomized version of the semi-honest Boneh-Franklin test described previously, followed by a Schnorr-like protocol to verify that the test was performed correctly. The soundness error of the underlying biprimality test is compounded by the Schnorr-like protocol's soundness error to yield a combined error of $3/4$; this necessitates an increase in the number of iterations by a factor of $\log_{4/3}(2) < 2.5$. While this is sufficient to ensure the test itself is carried out honestly, it does not ensure the correct inputs are used. Consequently, generic MPC is used to verify the relationship between the messages involved in the Schnorr-like protocol and the true candidate given by N and shares of its factors. As a side effect, this generic computation samples $r \leftarrow \mathbb{Z}_N$ and outputs $z = r \cdot (p + q - 1) \bmod N$ so that the GCD test can afterward be run locally by each party.

Our protocol makes use of a number of subfunctionalities, all of which are standard and described in the full version of this paper [7]. Namely, we use a coin-tossing functionality $\mathcal{F}_{\mathsf{CT}}$ to uniformly sample an element from some set, the one-to-many commitment functionality $\mathcal{F}_{\mathsf{Com}}$, the generic MPC functionality over committed inputs $\mathcal{F}_{\mathsf{ComCompute}}$, and the integer-sharing-of-zero functionality $\mathcal{F}_{\mathsf{Zero}}$. In addition, the protocol uses the algorithm VerifyBiprime (Algorithm 5.3).

Protocol 5.2. $\pi_{\mathsf{Biprime}}(M, n)$. **Distributed Biprimality Testing**

This protocol is parametrized by an integer M and the number of parties n. In addition, there is a statistical parameter s. The parties have access to the $\mathcal{F}_{\mathsf{CT}}$, $\mathcal{F}_{\mathsf{Com}}$, $\mathcal{F}_{\mathsf{ComCompute}}$, and $\mathcal{F}_{\mathsf{Zero}}$ functionalities.

Input Commitment:

1. Upon receiving input $(\mathtt{check\text{-}biprimality}, sid, N, p_i, q_i)$ from the environment, each party $\mathcal{P}_i$ for $i \in [n]$ samples $\tau_{i,j} \leftarrow \mathbb{Z}_{M \cdot 2^{s+1}}$ for $j \in [2.5s]$

and commits to these values, along with its shares of p and q, by sending $(\texttt{commit}, \textsf{GenSID}(\textsf{sid}, i), (p_i, q_i, \tau_{i,*}))$ to $\mathcal{F}_{\textsf{ComCompute}}(n)$.

Boneh-Franklin Test:

2. Each party $\mathcal{P}_i$ for $i \in [n]$ sends $(\texttt{sample}, \textsf{sid})$ to $\mathcal{F}_{\textsf{Zero}}(n, 2^{2\kappa+s})$ and receives $(\texttt{zero-share}, \textsf{sid}, r_i)$ in response.

3. For $j \in [2.5s]$, the parties invoke $\mathcal{F}_{\textsf{CT}}(n, \mathbb{J}_N)$, where $\mathbb{J}_N$ is the subdomain of $\mathbb{Z}_N^*$ that contains only values with Jacobi symbol 1. The parties define vector γ that contains the $2.5s$ sampled values.

4. For every $j \in [2.5s]$, party $\mathcal{P}_1$ computes[a]

$$\chi_{1,j} := \gamma_j^{r_1 - (p_1 + q_1 - 6)/4} \quad \bmod\ N$$

and every other party $\mathcal{P}_i$ for $i \in [2, n]$ computes

$$\chi_{i,j} := \gamma_j^{r_i - (p_i + q_i)/4} \quad \bmod\ N$$

5. Every $\mathcal{P}_i$ for $i \in [n]$ sends $(\texttt{commit}, \textsf{GenSID}(\textsf{sid}, i), \chi_{i,*}, [n])$ to $\mathcal{F}_{\textsf{Com}}(n)$.

6. After being notified that all other parties are committed, each party $\mathcal{P}_i$ for $i \in [n]$ sends $(\texttt{decommit}, \textsf{GenSID}(\textsf{sid}, i))$ to $\mathcal{F}_{\textsf{Com}}(n)$, and in response receives $\chi_{i',*}$ from $\mathcal{F}_{\textsf{Com}}(n)$ for $i' \in [n] \setminus \{i\}$.

7. The parties output $(\texttt{not-biprime}, \textsf{sid})$ to the environment and halt if there exists $j \in [2.5s]$ such that

$$\gamma_j^{(N-5)/4} \cdot \prod_{i \in [n]} \chi_{i,j} \not\equiv \pm 1 \pmod{N}$$

Consistency Check and GCD Test:

8. For $j \in [2.5s]$, each party $\mathcal{P}_i$ for $i \in [n]$ computes $\alpha_{i,j} := \gamma_j^{\tau_{i,j}} \bmod N$. The parties all broadcast the values they have computed to one another.

9. The parties all send $(\texttt{flip}, \textsf{sid})$ to $\mathcal{F}_{\textsf{CT}}(n, \{0,1\}^{2.5s})$ to obtain an agreed-upon random bit vector $\mathbf{c}$ of length $2.5s$.

10. For $j \in [2.5s]$, party $\mathcal{P}_1$ computes $\zeta_{1,j} := \tau_{1,j} - \mathbf{c}_j \cdot (p_1 + q_1)/4$, and every other party $\mathcal{P}_i$ for $i \in [2, n]$ computes $\zeta_{i,j} := \tau_{i,j} - \mathbf{c}_j \cdot (p_i + q_i - 6)/4$. They all broadcast the values they have computed to one another.

11. The parties halt and output $(\texttt{not-biprime}, \textsf{sid})$ if there exists any $j \in [2.5s]$ such that

$$\prod_{i \in [n]} \gamma_j^{\zeta_{i,j}} \not\equiv \prod_{i \in [n]} \alpha_{i,j} \cdot \chi_{i,j}^{\mathbf{c}_j} \pmod{N}$$

12. Let C be a circuit computing $\textsf{VerifyBiprime}(N, M, \mathbf{c}, \{\cdot, \cdot, \cdot, \zeta_{i,*}\}_{i \in [n]})$; that is, let it be a circuit representation of Algorithm 5.3 with

the public values N, M, $\mathbf{c}$, and ζ hardcoded. The parties send $(\texttt{compute}, \texttt{sid}, \{\texttt{GenSID}(\texttt{sid}, i)\}_{i \in [n]}, C)$ to $\mathcal{F}_{\mathsf{ComCompute}}(n)$, and in response they all receive $(\texttt{result}, \texttt{sid}, z)$. If $z = \perp$, or if $\mathcal{F}_{\mathsf{ComCompute}}(n)$ aborts, then the parties halt and output $(\texttt{not-biprime}, \texttt{sid})$.

13. The parties halt and output $(\texttt{biprime}, \texttt{sid})$ to the environment if $\gcd(z, N) = 1$, or halt and output $(\texttt{not-biprime}, \texttt{sid})$ otherwise.

---

[a]Recall that $p_1 \equiv q_1 \equiv 3 \pmod 4$, and so subtracting 6 from their sum ensures that division by 4 can be performed without computing a modular multiplicative inverse in $\mathbb{Z}_N^*$. We compensate for this offset using another offset in Step 7.

Below we present the algorithm VerifyBiprime that is used for the GCD test. The inputs are the candidate biprime N, an integer M (the bound on the shares' size), a bit-vector $\mathbf{c}$ of length $2.5s$, and for each $i \in [n]$ a tuple consisting of the shares p_i and q_i with the Schnorr-like messages $\tau_{i,*}$ and $\zeta_{i,*}$ generated by $\mathcal{P}_i$. The algorithm verifies that all input values are compatible, and returns $z = r \cdot (p + q - 1) \bmod N$ for a random r.

Algorithm 5.3. $\mathsf{VerifyBiprime}(N, M, \mathbf{c}, \{(p_i, q_i, \tau_{i,*}, \zeta_{i,*})\}_{i \in [n]})$

1. Sample $r \leftarrow \mathbb{Z}_N$ and compute

$$z := r \cdot \left(-1 + \sum_{i \in [n]} (p_i + q_i) \right) \bmod N$$

2. Return z if and only if it holds that

$$N = \sum_{i \in [n]} p_i \cdot \sum_{i \in [n]} q_i$$

$$\wedge \quad 0 \leq p_i < M \quad \wedge \quad 0 \leq q_i < M \qquad \text{for all } i \in [n]$$

$$\wedge \quad \tau_{1,j} = \zeta_{1,j} + \mathbf{c}_j \cdot (p_1 + q_1 - 6)/4 \qquad \text{for all } j \in [2.5s]$$

$$\wedge \quad \tau_{i,j} = \zeta_{i,j} + \mathbf{c}_j \cdot (p_i + q_i)/4 \qquad \text{for all } i \in [2, n] \text{ and } j \in [2.5s]$$

If any part of the above predicate does not hold, output $\perp$.

Theorem 5.4. π_{Biprime} UC-realizes $\mathcal{F}_{\mathsf{Biprime}}$ in the $(\mathcal{F}_{\mathsf{Com}}, \mathcal{F}_{\mathsf{ComCompute}}, \mathcal{F}_{\mathsf{CT}}, \mathcal{F}_{\mathsf{Zero}})$-hybrid model with statistical security against a static, malicious adversary that corrupts up to $n - 1$ parties.

Proof Sketch. Our simulator $\mathcal{S}$ for $\mathcal{F}_{\mathsf{Biprime}}$ receives N as common input. Let $\mathbf{P}^*$ and $\overline{\mathbf{P}}^*$ be vectors indexing the corrupt and honest parties, respectively. To simulate Steps 1 through 3 of π_{Biprime}, $\mathcal{S}$ simply behaves as $\mathcal{F}_{\mathsf{CT}}$, $\mathcal{F}_{\mathsf{Zero}}$, and $\mathcal{F}_{\mathsf{ComCompute}}$ would in its interactions with the corrupt parties on their behalf, remembering the values received and transmitted. Before continuing, $\mathcal{S}$ submits the corrupted parties' shares of p and q to $\mathcal{F}_{\mathsf{Biprime}}$ on their behalf. In response, $\mathcal{F}_{\mathsf{Biprime}}$ either informs $\mathcal{S}$ that N is a biprime, or leaks the honest parties' shares.

In Step 4, $\mathcal{S}$ again behaves exactly as $\mathcal{F}_{\mathsf{Com}}$ would. During the remainder of the protocol, the simulator must follow one of two different strategies, conditioned on whether or not N is a biprime. We will show that both strategies lead to a simulation that is statistically indistinguishable from the real-world experiment.

- If $\mathcal{F}_{\mathsf{Biprime}}$ reported that N is a biprime, then we know by the specification of $\mathcal{F}_{\mathsf{Biprime}}$ that the corrupt parties committed to correct shares of p and q in Step 1 of π_{Biprime}. Boneh and Franklin [4] showed that the value (i.e., sign) of the right-hand side of the equality in Step 7 is predictable and related to the value of γ_j. We refer to them for a precise description and proof. If without loss of generality we take that value to be 1, then $\mathcal{S}$ can simulate iteration j of Steps 6 and 7 as follows. First, $\mathcal{S}$ computes $\hat{\chi}_{i,j}$ for $i \in \mathbf{P}^*$ to be the corrupt parties' ideal values of $\chi_{i,j}$ as defined in Step 4 of π_{Biprime}. Then, $\mathcal{S}$ samples $\chi_{i,j} \leftarrow \mathbb{Z}_N^*$ uniformly for $i \in \overline{\mathbf{P}^*}$ subject to

$$\prod_{i \in \overline{\mathbf{P}^*}} \chi_{i,j} \equiv \frac{\gamma_j^{(5-N)/4}}{\prod_{i \in \mathbf{P}^*} \hat{\chi}_{i,j}} \pmod{N}$$

and simulates Step 6 by releasing $\chi_{i,j}$ for $i \in \overline{\mathbf{P}^*}$ to the corrupt parties on behalf of $\mathcal{F}_{\mathsf{Com}}$. These values are statistically close to their counterparts in the real protocol. Finally, $\mathcal{S}$ simulates Step 7 by running the test for itself and sending the cheat command to $\mathcal{F}_{\mathsf{Biprime}}$ on failure.

Given the information now known to $\mathcal{S}$, Steps 8 through 11 of π_{Biprime} can be simulated in a manner similar to the simulation of a common Schnorr protocol: $\mathcal{S}$ simply chooses $\zeta_{i,*} \leftarrow \mathbb{Z}_{M \cdot 2^{s+1}}^{2.5s}$ uniformly for $i \in \overline{\mathbf{P}^*}$, fixes $\mathbf{c} \leftarrow \{0,1\}^{2.5s}$ ahead of time, and then works backwards via the equation in Step 11 to compute the values of $\alpha_{i,*}$ for $i \in \overline{\mathbf{P}^*}$ that it must send on behalf of the honest parties in Step 8. These values are statistically close to their counterparts in the real protocol.

$\mathcal{S}$ finally simulates the remaining steps of π_{Biprime} by checking the VerifyBiprime predicate itself (since the final GCD test is purely local, no action need be taken by $\mathcal{S}$). If at any point after Step 4 the corrupt parties have cheated (i.e., sent an unexpected value or violated the VerifyBiprime predicate), then $\mathcal{S}$ sends the cheat command to $\mathcal{F}_{\mathsf{Biprime}}$. Otherwise, it sends the proceed command to $\mathcal{F}_{\mathsf{Biprime}}$, completing the simulation.

- If $\mathcal{F}_{\mathsf{Biprime}}$ reported that N is *not* a biprime (which may indicate that the corrupt parties supplied incorrect shares of p or q), then it also leaked the honest parties' shares of p and q to $\mathcal{S}$. Thus, $\mathcal{S}$ can simulate Steps 4 through 13 of π_{Biprime} by running the honest parties' code on their behalf. In all instances of the ideal-world experiment, the honest parties report to the environment that N is a non-biprime. Thus, we need only prove that there is no strategy by which the corrupt parties can successfully convince the honest parties that N is a biprime in the real world.

In order to get away with such a real-world cheat, the adversary must cheat in every iteration j of Steps 4 through 6 for which

$$\gamma_j^{(N-p-q)/4} \not\equiv \pm 1 \pmod{N}$$

Specifically, in every such iteration j, the corrupt parties must contrive to send values $\chi_{i,j}$ for $i \in \mathbf{P}^*$ such that

$$\gamma_j^{(N-5)/4} \cdot \prod_{i \in [n]} \chi_{i,j} \equiv \gamma_j^{(N-p-q)/4+\mathbf{\Delta}_{1,j}} \equiv \pm 1 \pmod{N}$$

for some nonzero offset value $\mathbf{\Delta}_{1,j}$. We can define a similar offset $\mathbf{\Delta}_{2,j}$ for the corrupt parties' transmitted values of $\alpha_{i,j}$, relative to the values of $\tau_{i,j}$ committed in Step 1:

$$\gamma_j^{\mathbf{\Delta}_{2,j}} \cdot \prod_{i \in [n]} \alpha_{i,j} \equiv \prod_{i \in [n]} \gamma_j^{\tau_{i,j}} \pmod{N}$$

Since we have presupposed that the protocol outputs `biprime`, we know that the corrupt parties *must* transmit correctly calculated values of $\zeta_{i,*}$ in Step 10 of π_{Biprime}, or else Step 12 would output `non-biprime` when these values are checked by the VerifyBiprime predicate. It follows from this fact and from the equation in Step 11 that $\mathbf{\Delta}_{2,j} \equiv \mathbf{c}_j \cdot \mathbf{\Delta}_{1,j} \pmod{\varphi(N)}$, where $\varphi(\cdot)$ is Euler's totient function. However, both $\mathbf{\Delta}_{1,*}$ and $\mathbf{\Delta}_{2,*}$ are fixed before $\mathbf{c}$ is revealed to the corrupt parties, and so the adversary can succeed in this cheat with probability at most $1/2$ for any individual iteration j.

Per Boneh and Franklin [4, Lemma 4.1], a particular iteration j of Steps 4 through 6 of π_{Biprime} produces a false positive result with probability at most $1/2$ if the adversary behaves honestly. If we assume that the adversary cheats always and only when a false positive would not have been produced by honest behavior, then the total probability of an adversary producing a positive outcome in the jth iteration of Steps 4 through 6 is upper-bounded by $3/4$. The probability that an adversary succeeds over all $2.5s$ iterations is therefore at most $(3/4)^{2.5s} < 2^{-s}$. Thus, the adversary has a negligible chance to force the acceptance of a non-biprime in the real world, and the distribution of outcomes produced by $\mathcal{S}$ is statistically indistinguishable from the real-world distribution. □

Acknowledgements. The authors thank Muthuramakrishnan Venkitasubramaniam for the useful conversations and insights he provided, Tore Frederiksen for reviewing and confirming our cost analysis of his protocol [16], and Xiao Wang and Peter Scholl for providing detailed cost analyses of their respective protocols [21,34].

This research was supported in part by the Office of the Director of National Intelligence (ODNI), Intelligence Advanced Research Project Activity (IARPA) under contract number 2019-19-020700009 (ACHILLES).

The views and conclusions contained herein are those of the authors and should not be interpreted as necessarily representing the official policies or endorsements, either expressed or implied, of ODNI, IARPA, DoI/NBC, or the U.S. Government. The U.S. Government is authorized to reproduce and distribute reprints for Governmental purposes notwithstanding any copyright annotation thereon.

References

1. Algesheimer, J., Camenisch, J., Shoup, V.: Efficient computation modulo a shared secret with application to the generation of shared safe-prime products. In: Yung, M. (ed.) CRYPTO 2002. LNCS, vol. 2442, pp. 417–432. Springer, Heidelberg (2002). https://doi.org/10.1007/3-540-45708-9_27

2. Barker, E.: NIST special publication 800–57, part 1, revision 4 (2016). https://doi.org/10.6028/NIST.SP.800-57pt1r4

3. Boneh, D., Franklin, M.K.: Efficient generation of shared RSA keys. In: Kaliski, B.S. (ed.) CRYPTO 1997. LNCS, vol. 1294, pp. 425–439. Springer, Heidelberg (1997). https://doi.org/10.1007/BFb0052253

4. Boneh, D., Franklin, M.K.: Efficient generation of shared RSA keys. J. ACM **48**(4), 702–722 (2001)

5. Boyle, E., et al.: Efficient two-round OT extension and silent non-interactive secure computation. In: ACM CCS, pp. 291–308 (2019)

6. Canetti, R.: Universally composable security: a new paradigm for cryptographic protocols. In: FOCS, pp. 136–145 (2001)

7. Chen, M., et al.: Muliparty generation of an RSA modulus (2020). http://eprint.iacr.org/2020/370

8. Cocks, C.: Split knowledge generation of RSA parameters. In: Darnell, M. (ed.) Cryptography and Coding 1997. LNCS, vol. 1355, pp. 89–95. Springer, Heidelberg (1997). https://doi.org/10.1007/BFb0024452

9. Cocks, C.: Split generation of RSA parameters with multiple participants (1998). http://citeseerx.ist.psu.edu/viewdoc/summary?doi=10.1.1.177.2600

10. Cohen, R., Haitner, I., Omri, E., Rotem, L.: From fairness to full security in multiparty computation. In: Catalano, D., De Prisco, R. (eds.) SCN 2018. LNCS, vol. 11035, pp. 216–234. Springer, Cham (2018). https://doi.org/10.1007/978-3-319-98113-0_12

11. Cohen, R., Lindell, Y.: Fairness versus guaranteed output delivery in secure multiparty computation. JCRYPT **30**(4), 1157–1186 (2017)

12. Damgård, I., Mikkelsen, G.L.: Efficient, robust and constant-round distributed RSA key generation. In: Micciancio, D. (ed.) TCC 2010. LNCS, vol. 5978, pp. 183–200. Springer, Heidelberg (2010). https://doi.org/10.1007/978-3-642-11799-2_12

13. Doerner, J., Kondi, Y., Lee, E., Shelat, A.: Secure two-party threshold ECDSA from ECDSA assumptions. In: S&P, pp. 980–997 (2018)

14. Doerner, J., Kondi, Y., Lee, E., Shelat, A.: Threshold ECDSA from ECDSA assumptions: the multiparty case. In: S&P (2019)

15. Frankel, Y., MacKenzie, P.D., Yung, M.: Robust efficient distributed RSA-key generation. In: PODC, p. 320 (1998)

16. Frederiksen, T.K., Lindell, Y., Osheter, V., Pinkas, B.: Fast distributed RSA key generation for semi-honest and malicious adversaries. In: Shacham, H., Boldyreva, A. (eds.) CRYPTO 2018. LNCS, vol. 10992, pp. 331–361. Springer, Cham (2018). https://doi.org/10.1007/978-3-319-96881-0_12

17. Gilboa, N.: Two party RSA key generation. In: Wiener, M. (ed.) CRYPTO 1999. LNCS, vol. 1666, pp. 116–129. Springer, Heidelberg (1999). https://doi.org/10.1007/3-540-48405-1_8

18. Goldreich, O.: The Foundations of Cryptography - Volume 1: Basic Techniques. Cambridge University Press (2001)

19. Hazay, C., Mikkelsen, G.L., Rabin, T., Toft, T.: Efficient RSA key generation and threshold paillier in the two-party setting. In: Dunkelman, O. (ed.) CT-RSA 2012. LNCS, vol. 7178, pp. 313–331. Springer, Heidelberg (2012). https://doi.org/10.1007/978-3-642-27954-6_20

20. Hazay, C., Mikkelsen, G.L., Rabin, T., Toft, T., Nicolosi, A.A.: Efficient RSA key generation and threshold paillier in the two-party setting. JCRYPT **32**(2), 265–323 (2019)

21. Hazay, C., Scholl, P., Soria-Vazquez, E.: Low cost constant round MPC combining BMR and oblivious transfer. In: Takagi, T., Peyrin, T. (eds.) ASIACRYPT 2017. LNCS, vol. 10624, pp. 598–628. Springer, Cham (2017). https://doi.org/10.1007/978-3-319-70694-8_21

22. Ishai, Y., Ostrovsky, R., Zikas, V.: Secure multi-party computation with identifiable abort. In: Garay, J.A., Gennaro, R. (eds.) CRYPTO 2014. LNCS, vol. 8617, pp. 369–386. Springer, Heidelberg (2014). https://doi.org/10.1007/978-3-662-44381-1_21

23. Joye, M., Pinch, R.: Cheating in split-knowledge RSA parameter generation. In: Workshop on Coding and Cryptography, pp. 157–163 (1999)

24. Katz, J., Lindell, Y.: Digital signature schemes. In: Introduction to Modern Cryptography, 2nd edn, pp. 443–486. Chapman & Hall/CRC (2015)

25. Knuth, D.E.: The Art of Computer Programming, Volume II: Seminumerical Algorithms (1969)

26. Malkin, M., Wu, T., Boneh, D.: Experimenting with shared RSA key generation. In: NDSS, pp. 43–56 (1999)

27. Miller, G.L.: Riemann's hypothesis and tests for primality. J. Comput. Syst. Sci. **13**(3), 300–317 (1976)

28. Pietrzak, K.: Simple verifiable delay functions. In: ITCS, pp. 60:1–60:15 (2019)

29. Poupard, G., Stern, J.: Generation of shared RSA keys by two parties. In: Ohta, K., Pei, D. (eds.) ASIACRYPT 1998. LNCS, vol. 1514, pp. 11–24. Springer, Heidelberg (1998). https://doi.org/10.1007/3-540-49649-1_2

30. Rabin, M.O.: Probabilistic algorithm for testing primality. J. Number Theory **12**(1), 128–138 (1980)

31. Rivest, R.L.: A description of a single-chip implementation of the RSA cipher (1980)

32. Rivest, R.L.: RSA chips (past/present/future). In: Beth, T., Cot, N., Ingemarsson, I. (eds.) EUROCRYPT 1984. LNCS, vol. 209, pp. 159–165. Springer, Heidelberg (1985). https://doi.org/10.1007/3-540-39757-4_16

33. Rivest, R.L., Shamir, A., Adleman, L.M.: A method for obtaining digital signatures and public-key cryptosystems. Commun. ACM **21**(2), 120–126 (1978)

34. Wang, X., Ranellucci, S., Katz, J.: Global-scale secure multiparty computation. In: ACM CCS, pp. 39–56 (2017)

35. Wesolowski, B.: Efficient verifiable delay functions. In: Ishai, Y., Rijmen, V. (eds.) EUROCRYPT 2019. LNCS, vol. 11478, pp. 379–407. Springer, Cham (2019). https://doi.org/10.1007/978-3-030-17659-4_13

Secret Sharing

Non-malleability Against Polynomial Tampering

Marshall Ball[1](✉), Eshan Chattopadhyay[2], Jyun-Jie Liao[2], Tal Malkin[1], and Li-Yang Tan[3]

[1] Columbia University, New York, USA
{marshall,tal}@cs.columbia.edu
[2] Cornell University, Ithaca, USA
{eshanc,jl3825}@cornell.edu
[3] Stanford University, Stanford, USA
liyang@cs.stanford.edu

Abstract. We present the first explicit construction of a *non-malleable code* that can handle tampering functions that are *bounded-degree polynomials*. Prior to our work, this was only known for degree-1 polynomials (affine tampering functions), due to Chattopadhyay and Li (STOC 2017). As a direct corollary, we obtain an explicit non-malleable code that is secure against tampering by bounded-size arithmetic circuits.

We show applications of our non-malleable code in constructing *non-malleable secret sharing schemes* that are robust against bounded-degree polynomial tampering. In fact our result is stronger: we can handle adversaries that can adaptively choose the polynomial tampering function based on initial leakage of a bounded number of shares.

Our results are derived from explicit constructions of *seedless non-malleable extractors* that can handle bounded-degree polynomial tampering functions. Prior to our work, no such result was known even for degree-2 (quadratic) polynomials.

1 Introduction

1.1 Non-malleable Codes

Non-malleable codes were introduced by Dziembowski, Pietrzak, and Wichs [33] as a natural and useful modification of error correcting codes, which can handle stronger forms of adversarial tampering attacks (including ones that can change all symbols of the codeword), while still providing meaningful guarantees. Informally, a non-malleable code is a pair of algorithms $(\mathrm{Enc}, \mathrm{Dec})$, and it is secure against a tampering function family $\mathcal{F}$ if for every tampering function $f \in \mathcal{F}$, the decoding of a tampered codeword, namely $\mathrm{Dec}(f(\mathrm{Enc}(s)))$ for an arbitrary message s, will either be the original message s, or a value completely unrelated to s. (See Sect. 3.3 for a formal definition).

As an example of an application of non-malleable codes, one can consider s as being the signing key of a digital signature scheme, and is stored as $\mathrm{Enc}(s)$ in

© International Association for Cryptologic Research 2020
D. Micciancio and T. Ristenpart (Eds.): CRYPTO 2020, LNCS 12172, pp. 97–126, 2020.
https://doi.org/10.1007/978-3-030-56877-1_4

memory. The non-malleability guarantee ensures that for any tampering attack which turns $\mathrm{Enc}(s)$ into $f(\mathrm{Enc}(s))$, the tampered signature is signed under either s or a completely unrelated key. In both cases the tampered signature does not help the adversary learn how to forge a valid signatures on its own.

Non-malleable codes have also found other useful applications in cryptography, such as in constructing non-malleable commitments [37], public-key encryption systems [25], and, as we discuss in Sect. 1.2, non-malleable secret sharing [1,6,35,36].

Dziembowski et al. [33] observed that some restrictions on the tampering function family is necessary. Indeed, it is impossible to achieve non-malleability if the adversary is able to decode the codeword, tamper the message, and then re-encode the tampered message. In the last 10 years, non-malleable codes have been shown to exist for numerous rich tampering function families and in various settings. In this work we focus on *explicit, information-theoretic* constructions.

A successful line of work focused on *split-state* tampering functions, where the codeword is broken into several disjoint parts and the adversary can tamper each part arbitrarily but independently [2–4,16,19,21,32,38,41,42,44,45]. This line of work has culminated in the construction of near-optimal codes in this setting.

Recently there has been significant interest and progress on constructing non-malleable codes in a more general setting, where the tampering functions are not restricted to fixed partitions, and can act *globally* on the codeword. Global tampering classes that have been studied include permutations and bit flipping [5], local functions [9], affine functions over $\mathbb{F}_2$ [17], small-depth circuits [8,17], and small-depth decision trees [10]. Our work fits into this line of research.

Our Results. We consider the tampering class of *bounded-degree polynomials*. This is a natural class of tampering functions, and significantly generalizes the class of affine tampering functions (i.e. degree-1 polynomials) studied in [17]. We define the setting more precisely as follows. Let q be a prime, and $\mathrm{Poly}_{n,q,d}$ denote the family of n-variate polynomials over $\mathbb{F}_q$ of degree at most d. We are interested in the following family of tampering functions:

$$\mathcal{F}_{n,q,d} := \{(p_1,\ldots,p_n) : \forall i \in [n], p_i \in \mathrm{Poly}_{n,q,d}\}.$$

For $P = (p_1,\ldots,p_n) \in \mathcal{F}_{n,q,d}$, and $x \in \mathbb{F}_q^n$, define $P(x) := (p_1(x),\ldots,p_n(x))$.

The following is our main result.

Theorem 1 (NMCs for bounded-degree polynomials).   *There exists a constant $C > 0$ such that for all integers n, d, m, any $\varepsilon > 0$ and any prime $q > (Cn^2 d^4 m 2^{2m}/\varepsilon^2) \cdot \log(nd/\varepsilon)$, there exists a non-malleable code on alphabet $[q]$, with block length n, message length m, relative rate $\Omega(m/n \log q)$ and error ε, with respect to the family $\mathcal{F}_{n,q,d}$.*

Prior to our work, no explicit construction of a non-malleable code was known even for quadratic polynomials $(d = 2)$.

To prove Theorem 1, we construct new explicit seedless non-malleable extractors that can handle the tampering class $\mathcal{F}_{n,q,d}$. A similar strategy was adopted in [17], where they constructed seedless non-malleable extractors against affine tampering functions (i.e, $\mathcal{F}_{n,q,1}$). However, their construction of such extractors heavily exploit the linearity of the tampering functions and explicit constructions of extractors that are linear, and their techniques seem to break down even against quadratic tampering functions. We introduce a completely different approach to construct seedless non-malleable extractors against higher degree polynomial tampering. We discuss this in detail in Sect. 1.3.

We use Theorem 1 to derive a non-malleable code that is secure against tampering by arithmetic circuits. Consider the following family of tampering functions:

$$\mathcal{E}_{n,q,s} := \{(e_1, \ldots, e_n) : e_i \text{ is an } n\text{-variate size-}s \text{ arithmetic circuit over } \mathbb{F}_q\}.$$

For $E = (e_1, \ldots, e_n) \in \mathcal{E}_{n,q,s}$ and $x \in \mathbb{F}_q^n$, we define $E(x) := (e_1(x), \ldots, e_n(x))$.

Corollary 1 (NMCs for arithmetic circuits). *There exists a constant $C > 0$ such that for all integers n, s, m, any $\varepsilon > 0$ and any prime $q > (Cn^2sm2^{4s+2m}/\varepsilon^2) \cdot \log(n/\varepsilon)$, there exists a non-malleable code on alphabet $[q]$, with block length n, message length m, relative rate $\Omega(m/n\log q)$ and error ε, with respect to the family $\mathcal{E}_{n,q,s}$.*

To our knowledge, this is the first explicit construction of a non-malleable code that can handle tampering by arithmetic circuits.

Corollary 1 follows as a straightfoward consequence of Theorem 1, using the fact that a size-s arithmetic circuit computes a polynomial of degree at most 2^s.

1.2 Non-malleable Secret Sharing

A t-out-of-n secret sharing scheme [13,55] allows a dealer to share a secret $s \in \{0,1\}^m$ among n parties such that any t parties can collectively recover the secret, and yet any colluding $(t-1)$ parties learn nothing about the secret. Recently, Goyal and Kumar [35] initiated the study of the more robust notion of *non-malleable secret sharing*. A non-malleable secret sharing scheme further requires the shares to be non-malleable against a family of tampering functions $\mathcal{F}$. That is, when the shares are tampered by any function $f \in \mathcal{F}$, for any t parties the reconstructed secret should be either s or a value completely unrelated to s.

Similar to non-malleable codes, non-malleable secret sharing schemes aim to provide protection against tampering attacks, and there are strong connections between non-malleable secret sharing schemes and non-malleable codes. In fact, it can be shown that non-malleable codes in the 2-split-state model are 2-out-of-2 secret sharing schemes. In [35], the authors constructed t-out-of-n non-malleable secret sharing schemes in different tampering models. A detailed comparison of these models and references to other related work can be found in [1]. These models have in common that the tampering functions are "compartmentalized", applying the function independently to different disjoint parts.

A natural direction of investigation is to construct non-malleable secret sharing against tampering functions that are *not* compartmentalized. Recently,

Lin et al. [46] construct a t-out-of-n secret sharing against affine tampering for every t and large enough n, and Chattopadhyay and Li [18] construct a non-malleable ramp secret sharing against affine tampering composed with joint tampering.

Our Results. We construct a non-malleable secret sharing scheme that is secure against the class of polynomial tampering functions. Prior to our work, no such explicit construction was known even against the tampering class of quadratic polynomials. The following is an informal version of our result:

Theorem 2 (NM secret sharing for polynomial tampering). *For all integers n, d, r, any prime $q > poly(2^m, n, d)$ and $1 \le r \le n$, there exists an r-out-of-n non-malleable secret sharing scheme with respect to polynomial tampering $\mathcal{F}_{n,q,d}$ for m-bit secrets.*
In fact our construction is stronger and can handle an adaptive tampering adversary who chooses the polynomial tampering function $f \in \mathcal{F}_{n,q,d}$ depending on any $r - 1$ of the shares.

As in the case of non-malleable codes, the above theorem directly yields explicit non-malleable secret sharing schemes that are secure against the tampering class of bounded-size arithmetic circuits.

1.3   Seedless Non-malleable Extractors

Informally, a *randomness extractor* is a deterministic algorithm that produces nearly uniform bits of randomness from defective sources of randomness. The study of randomness extractors is motivated by the fact that many applications in computer science require high-quality random bits, whereas most naturally occurring sources of randomness are of much lower quality. Before defining a randomness extractor formally, we first define the notion of min-entropy that is typically used as a measure of the quality of a source:

Definition 1 (Min-entropy and (n, k)-sources). *Let X be a distribution on $\{0, 1\}^n$. The min-entropy of X, denoted by $H_\infty(X)$, is defined as $\min_x(\log(1/\Pr[X = x]))$.*
An (n, k)-source is a distribution on $\{0, 1\}^n$ with min-entropy at least k.

For two distributions D_1 and D_2 on the same universe Ω, we use $|D_1 - D_2|$ to denote the statistical distance between them. We are now ready to define a randomness extractor for a class of sources.

Definition 2 (Extractor). *Let $\mathcal{X}$ be a family of sources on $\{0, 1\}^n$. A function* $\text{Ext} : \{0, 1\}^n \to \{0, 1\}^m$ *is called an extractor for the family $\mathcal{X}$ with error ε if for any $X \in \mathcal{X}$,*

$$|\text{Ext}(X) - U_m| \le \varepsilon,$$

where U_m is the uniform distribution over $\{0, 1\}^m$.

It turns out that there cannot exist an extractor that works for the family of distributions on $\{0,1\}^n$ with min-entropy at least $n-1$. To circumvent this difficulty, a long line of work has focused on extracting from a weak source X assuming access to a short independent seed Y. Such extractors are called *seeded extractors* [48] and we now have almost optimal constructions of such extractors [31,39]. Another successful line of research focused on extracting random bits assuming more structure on the source X. Such extractors are called as *seedless extractors*. Examples include assuming that the weak source consists of multiple independent sources [11,14,20,23], assuming that the source is supported on an affine subspace [15,34] or an algebraic variety [29], or even simply assuming that there are some unknown coordinates of the source that are uniform and independent [24]. Explicit constructions of seeded and seedless extractors have found numerous applications in complexity theory [60], coding theory [57] and cryptography [12,47].

Recently, several works studied a more robust notion of a randomness extractor called *non-malleable extractor*. The main motivations for studying this stronger variant is from applications in cryptography. Surprisingly, explicit constructions of non-malleable extractors have led to improved constructions of standard extractors. As in the case of standard extractors, there are *seeded non-malleable extractors* and *seedless non-malleable extractors*. The seeded variant was introduced by Dodis and Wichs [27] with applications to the problem of privacy application [12]. The seedless variant of non-malleable extractors was introduced by Cheraghchi and Guruswami [21] with applications to constructions of non-malleable codes.

We focus on the seedless variant of non-malleable extractors. For the sake of simplicity, we define seedless non-malleable extractors in slightly less generality and refer the reader to Sect. 3.3 for the more general definition.

Definition 3 (Seedless non-malleable extractor). *Let $\mathcal{X}$ be a family of sources on $\{0,1\}^n$ and $\mathcal{F}$ be a class of tampering functions acting on $\{0,1\}^n$. Further assume that all $f \in \mathcal{F}$ does not have any fixed points. A function $\mathrm{nmExt} : \{0,1\}^n \to \{0,1\}^m$ is defined to be a non-malleable extractor with respect to $\mathcal{X}$ and $\mathcal{F}$ with error ε if the following hold: for any $X \in \mathcal{X}$ and $f \in \mathcal{F}$, we have*

$$|(\mathrm{nmExt}(X), \mathrm{nmExt}(f(X))) - (\mathrm{U}_m, \mathrm{nmExt}(f(X)))| \leq \varepsilon.$$

An informal way of interpreting the above definition is as follows. Let X be a source from the family $\mathcal{X}$. The distribution $X' = f(X)$ represents the tampered distribution, where $f \in \mathcal{F}$ (note that $X' \neq X$). The task of the non-malleable extractor nmExt is to remove the correlation between the random variables X and X' (which are clearly dependent).

Chattopadhyay and Zuckerman [19] gave explicit constructions of seedless non-malleable extractors assuming X consists of 10 independent sources, and each source is arbitrarily tampered. This was improved by Chattopadhyay, Goyal and Li [16] to construct seedless non-malleable extractors for 2 independent sources. Chattopadhyay and Li [17] constructed a seedless non-malleable extractor against the class of affine functions. In another work, Chattopadhyay and

Li [18] constructed seedless non-malleable extractors when the source X consists of 2 independent sources that are interleaved in an unknown way. They also consider some generalizations such as composition of linear tampering and partitioned tampering.

Our Results. We give a seedless non-malleable extractor that can handle polynomial tampering. Prior to our work, Chattopadhyay and Li [17] handled the special case of affine tampering. Their construction heavily relied on linearity of the tampering functions and linearity properties of extractors, and their techniques do not seem to extend even to the case tampering functions that are quadratic polynomials. While a seedless non-malleable extractor for uniform source is sufficient for the reduction in [21], we show that our non-malleable extractor in fact works for *skew affine source* defined below. This generality is useful in our construction of non-malleable secret sharing schemes that are robust to polynomial tampering.

Definition 4. *Let $\mathbb{F}_q$ be a finite field, and let $X = (X_1, \ldots, X_n)$ be a distribution on $\mathbb{F}_q^n$. We say X is an* affine source *if X is uniform over an affine subspace $W \subseteq \mathbb{F}_q^n$. We define the dimension of X to be the dimension of W. We say X is a* skew affine source *if X is an affine source and for every $i \in [n]$, X_i has support size greater than 1.*

We are now ready to state our result on explicit non-malleable extractors against polynomial tampering.

Theorem 3. *There exists a constant $C > 0$ such that for all integers n, d, m, any prime q and any $\varepsilon > 0$ such that $q > (Cn^2 d^4 m 2^{2m}/\varepsilon^2) \cdot \log(nd/\varepsilon)$, there exists an explicit function $\mathrm{nmExt} : \mathbb{F}_q^n \to \{0,1\}^m$, that is a seedless non-malleable extractor with respect to the family of sources*

$$\mathcal{X} = \{X : X \text{ is a skew affine source on } \mathbb{F}_q^n \text{ of dimension } \geq 1\}$$

and the tampering family $\mathcal{F}_{n,q,d}$.

Prior to our work, no explicit construction of a seedless non-malleable extractor was known against even quadratic polynomials ($d = 2$).

We use the above theorem to derive a non-malleable extractor against arithmetic circuits.

Corollary 2. *There exists a constant $C > 0$ such that for all integers n, s, m, any prime q and any $\varepsilon > 0$ such that $q > (Cn^2 s m 2^{4s+2m}/\varepsilon^2) \cdot \log(n/\varepsilon)$, there exists an explicit function $\mathrm{nmExt} : \mathbb{F}_q^n \to \{0,1\}^m$, that is a seedless non-malleable extractor with respect to the*

$$\mathcal{X} = \{X : X \text{ is a skew affine source on } \mathbb{F}_q^n \text{ of dimension } \geq 1\}$$

and the tampering family $\mathcal{E}_{n,q,s}$.

To the best of our knowledge, this is the first explicit construction of a non-malleable extractor that can handle tampering by arithmetic circuits.

We in fact show that the non-malleable extractors constructed are efficiently invertible, i.e, given any output z, there exists an efficient sampling algorithm that produces a sample from a distribution that is close to uniform on the set nmExt$^{-1}(z)$. We discuss the sampling algorithm in Sect. 5. We then use the connection established in [21] (see Sect. 3.4) to derive the explicit non-malleable codes with respect to polynomials (Theorem 1) and arithmetic circuits (Corollary 2).

Organization. We give an overview of our techniques in Sect. 2. We discuss some preliminaries in Sect. 3. In Sect. 4, we explicitly construct a non-malleable extractor against polynomial tampering functions. In Sect. 5, we present efficient sampling algorithms necessary to construct efficient non-malleable codes. We use Sect. 6 to construct a non-malleable secret sharing scheme that can handle polynomial tampering.

2   Overview of Techniques

In this section we discuss the main ideas that are used in our explicit constructions of non-malleable codes, non-malleable extractors, and non-malleable secret sharing schemes. We start by discussing the explicit non-malleable extractor against polynomial tampering (Theorem 3). We then discuss ideas that go into using this construction to construct efficient non-malleable codes and non-malleable secret sharing schemes that are robust to polynomial tampering.

Seedless Non-malleable Extractors Against Polynomials. We discuss the main ideas behind the construction of the non-malleable extractor from Theorem 3. We consider the simpler setting and assume the source is uniform (instead of being a skew affine source as in Theorem 3). This setting cleanly captures our main ideas. The setup is as follows:

Let n, d be arbitrary integers, and fix any $\varepsilon > 0$. Let $q = \text{poly}(n, d, 1/\varepsilon)$ be a large enough prime (for exact details, see the statement of Theorem 3). Let X be the uniform distribution on $\mathbb{F}_q^n$. Our goal is to construct a polynomial time function nmExt : $\mathbb{F}_q^n \to \{0,1\}^m$ such that for any tampering function $P = (p_1, \ldots, p_n)$ from the class $\mathcal{F}_{n,q,d}$, such that there exits $i \in [n]$ for which $p_i(x) \neq x_i$, we have

$$|(\text{nmExt}(X), \text{nmExt}(P(X))) - (\text{U}_m, \text{nmExt}(P(X)))| \leq \varepsilon.$$

The high level idea of our construction is to observe that we can express X as a convex combination of distributions that are flat[1] on lines in $\mathbb{F}_q^n$, and then design a non-malleable extractor for such line sources. We note that Gabizon

---

[1] We say a distribution is *flat* if it is uniformly distributed on its support.

and Raz [34] used such an approach for constructing affine extractors on large fields.

We now describe our approach more precisely. Our plan is to construct a low-degree multivariate polynomial $h : \mathbb{F}_q^n \to \mathbb{F}_q$ such that the following hold: for all $\beta \in \mathbb{F}_q$, the polynomial

$$g_\beta = h(x) + \beta h(P(x))$$

is non-constant. (We stress that the choice of h cannot depend on P.) Now, for a suitable choice of m (we pick $m = \nu \log q$ for some small enough ν), we claim that for such an h, defining

$$\mathrm{nmExt}(x) = h(x) \pmod{2^m}$$

would satisfy the conclusion of Theorem 3.

Before constructing such an h, we first discuss why this is indeed enough. For any $a \in \mathbb{F}_q^n$, $b \in \mathbb{F}_q^n \setminus \{0^n\}$, define the line $L_{a,b} = \{(a_1 + tb_1, \ldots, a_n + tb_n) : t \in \mathbb{F}_q\}$. We abuse notation, also use $L_{a,b}$ to denote the flat distribution on $L_{a,b}$. Then clearly, X can be sampled by first uniformly sampling a, b (from their respective domains), and then sampling from $L_{a,b}$.

The first observation is the following: let $D = deg(g_\beta)$, and let $g_{\beta,a,b}(t)$ be the univariate restriction of g_β to the line $L_{a,b}$. We note that the coefficient of t^D is $g_\beta(b)$. Appealing to the fact that a low degree polynomial has few roots (Lemma 4), it follows that with high probability (over sampling a, b), the univariate polynomial $g_{\beta,a,b}(t)$ is a non-constant polynomial of degree D. Fix such vectors a, b so that $g_{\beta,a,b}$ is a non-constant polynomial. We now use a deep result from algebraic geometry known as the Weil bound (see Theorem 4) to conclude that for any non-trivial character[2] χ of $\mathbb{F}_q$, we have

$$|\mathbb{E}_{t \sim \mathbb{F}_q}[\chi(g_{\beta,a,b}(t))]| \le D/\sqrt{q}.$$

Roughly, this asserts the fact that the non-trivial Fourier coefficients of the distribution $g_{\beta,a,b}(U_{\mathbb{F}_q})$ are bounded, where $U_{\mathbb{F}_q}$ denotes the uniform distribution on $\mathbb{F}_q$. Such a bound can be now be translated into statistical closeness of the distribution $(\mathrm{nmExt}(L_{a,b}), \mathrm{nmExt}(P(L_{a,b})))$ to $(U_m, \mathrm{nmExt}(P(L_{a,b})))$ using known XOR lemmas (see Lemma 1, Lemma 2). To conclude that $(\mathrm{nmExt}(X), \mathrm{nmExt}(P(X)))$ is close to $(U_m, \mathrm{nmExt}(P(X)))$, we combine the fact that X is a convex combination of the flat sources $L_{a,b}$, and that for most a, b, we have $(\mathrm{nmExt}(L_{a,b}), \mathrm{nmExt}(P(L_{a,b})))$ is close to $(U_m, \mathrm{nmExt}(P(L_{a,b})))$.

Given the above discussion, all that remains to construct the required non-malleable extractor is to find such an h. We recall the guarantee we need from h for convenience of the reader:

- for all $\beta \in \mathbb{F}_q$ and $P = (p_1, \ldots, p_n) \in \mathcal{F}_{n,q,d}$ satisfying that for some $i \in [n]$ $p_i(x) \ne x_i$, the polynomial $g_\beta(x) = h(x) + \beta h(P(x))$ is a non-constant polynomial.

---

[2] See Sect. 3 for a quick recap of characters of finite fields.

– h must a low degree polynomial. In particular, we require $deg(h) \ll q^{1/2}$.

An initial attempt to construct such an h could be to use a polynomial similar to the one used by Gabizon and Raz [34] in their affine extractor construction and define

$$h(x_1, x_2, \ldots, x_n) = x_1^{c_1} + x_2^{c_2} + \ldots + x_n^{c_n},$$

where $c_1, c_2, \ldots, c_n$ are arbitrary distinct positive integer. It is not hard to see that this does not work as follows. It is always possible to find $\beta, \gamma_1, \gamma_2, \ldots, \gamma_n \in \mathbb{F}_q^*$ such that $\gamma_i^{c_i} = -\beta^{-1}$ for every i and $\gamma_i \neq 1$ for at least one i. Now defining $P = (\gamma_1 x_1, \ldots, \gamma_n x_n)$ gives the desired counterexample since for this choice of β and P, $h(x) + \beta h(P(x))$ is identically the zero polynomial.

We avoid the above counterexample as follows: Pick $c_1, c_2, \ldots, c_{2n}$ from an arithmetic progression such that the common difference is co-prime with $q - 1$, and define

$$h(x_1, x_2, \ldots, x_n) = \sum_{i=1}^{n} \left(x_i^{c_{2i-1}} + x_i^{c_{2i}} \right).$$

For this choice of h, it is not hard to prove that if each $p_i(x) = \gamma_i x_i$ (for some $\gamma_i \in \mathbb{F}_q$), and $g(x)$ is a constant polynomial, it must be that each γ_i is 1, and $\beta = -1$. However this contradicts our assumption on P that for some i, $p_i(x) \neq x_i$. Thus we avoid the counterexample discussed above.

We in fact prove that this choice of h works for all $P \in \mathcal{F}_{n,q,d} \setminus \{(x_1, \ldots, x_n)\}$. To prove this, we rely on a result (Lemma 3) which shows that for such a choice of c_i's, for any distinct $i_1, i_2 \in [n]$, $deg(p_{i_1}^{c_{i_1}})$ is well separated from $deg(p_{i_2}^{c_{i_2}})$. With a careful case analysis, we use this to show that some monomial (of degree at least 1) in $g(x)$ survives. We provide the details in Sect. 4.

Non-malleable Extractors for Skew Affine Sources Against Polynomial Tampering. In the previous paragraph we sketched how to construct a non-malleable extractor against polynomial tampering assuming access to a uniform source on $\mathbb{F}_q^n$. In Sect. 4, we actually show that the non-malleable extractor works for any affine source which is non-constant on every coordinate. We call such source a *skew affine source*. In other words, our non-malleable extractor is resilient to affine leakage which does not reveal any single coordinate in the source. We will see the application of this property in non-malleable secret sharing.

To prove this stronger property of the non-malleable extractor, recall that in previous section we defined a polynomial $g_\beta(x) = h(x) + \beta h(P(x))$, and its restriction to the line $L_{a,b}$, denoted by $g_{\beta,a,b}(t)$. We then sketched a proof that $g_{\beta,a,b}$ is non-constant if $g_\beta(b) \neq 0$, which happens with high probability over b. In Sect. 4, we actually show the following stronger result: $\forall i, b_i \neq 0$ is a sufficient condition for $g_{\beta,a,b}$ to be non-constant. In fact, it is also a necessary condition. If there exists i such that $b_i = 0$, the adversary can set $p_j(x) = x_j$ for every $j \neq i$ and $p_i(x) = c$ for a constant $c \neq a_i$. One can verify that $g_{-1,a,b}$ is a constant in this case.

The proof idea is that a similar case analysis as sketched in the previous section also works for $g_{\beta,a,b}$ if $b_i \neq 0$ for every i. We then show that every skew affine source is a convex combination of line source $L_{a,b}$ where $b_i \neq 0$ for every i (Lemma 7) to finish the proof.

Non-malleable Codes Against Polynomial Tampering. We now turn to cryptographic applications of our non-malleable extractors. To build a non-malleable code against polynomial tampering, we use the connection between non-malleable code and non-malleable extractor established in [21]. To apply the reduction in [21], we need an efficient algorithm which samples almost uniformly from a pre-image of our non-malleable extractor on any output.

Recall that our non-malleable extractor is of the form $\mathrm{nmExt}(x) = \sigma(h(x))$, where σ is modulo 2^m and h is a bounded-degree polynomial. Inverting σ is easy, and there exists an algorithm by Cheraghchi and Shokrollahi [22] which almost-uniformly samples a pre-image of bounded-degree polynomial (over any large enough prime field). An initial attempt to sample from $\mathrm{nmExt}^{-1}(z)$ would be first sample $y \in \sigma^{-1}(z)$ and then sample from $h^{-1}(y)$. However this does not work since $h^{-1}(y)$ might have different size for different $y \in \mathbb{F}_q$. So we need to sample $y \in \sigma^{-1}(z)$ with probability proportional to $|h^{-1}(y)|$. A possible way to perform such weighted sampling from $\sigma^{-1}(z)$ is to do a rejection sampling which samples $y \in \sigma^{-1}(z)$ uniformly in each round and accept with probability proportional to $|h^{-1}(y)|$. However, we need to (approximately) count $|h^{-1}(y)|$ in this approach, which is difficult in general.

Chattopadhyay and Zuckerman [19] handled a similar sampling task while constructing efficient non-malleable codes in the split-state model, with the crucial difference being that they were dealing with polynomials on a constant number of variables. In [19], they adopted a similar sampling strategy as the one sketched above, and they count $|h^{-1}(y)|$ with an algorithm from [40], which has running time doubly exponential in the number of variables (which, in their case, still takes constant time).

To get around this difficulty, we observe that the algorithm in [22] is actually a rejection sampling which has accepting probability proportional to $|h^{-1}(y)|$ in each round. Therefore, we can embed an uniform sampling of y in each round of [22] and bypass the computation of $|h^{-1}(y)|$. We provide the details of our sampling algorithm in Sect. 5.

Non-malleable Secret Sharing Against Polynomial Tampering. As another application of our non-malleable extractor, we build a non-malleable secret sharing that can handle polynomial tampering. We obtain this by plugging in our extractor into a scheme by Lin, Cheraghchi, Guruswami, Safavi-Naini and Wang [46]. In this scheme, they take an efficiently invertible non-malleable extractor nmExt and a linear erasure code $(\mathrm{Enc}, \mathrm{Dec})$, then define the sharing function to be $\mathrm{Enc} \circ \mathrm{nmExt}^{-1}$ and the reconstruction function to be $\mathrm{nmExt} \circ \mathrm{Dec}$. If in the erasure code $(\mathrm{Enc}, \mathrm{Dec})$, Dec only needs r symbols in the codeword to reconstruct the original message, then so does $\mathrm{nmExt} \circ \mathrm{Dec}$ in the secret sharing scheme. Therefore the correctness holds as long as there is an efficient inverter for nmExt which succeeds with high probability.

To prove privacy and non-malleability we need the following guarantee on nmExt. To guarantee non-malleability, for every tampering function f, nmExt should be non-malleable against the composed tampering function $\text{Dec} \circ f \circ \text{Enc}$. For polynomial tampering, taking the erasure code to be a linear code over $\mathbb{F}_q$ naturally satisfies this requirement. To guarantee privacy, given a uniform source X, $\text{nmExt}(X)$ should be uniform conditioned on that some symbols of $\text{Enc}(X)$ is leaked to the adversary. When (Enc, Dec) is a linear code, this means nmExt should be an affine extractor. This is also true for our extractor (see Appendix A in the online version of this paper [7]).

We in fact achieve a stronger result and construct a non-malleable secret sharing scheme where the adversary can choose the polynomial tampering function based on some of the shares. If given a secret the adversary can learn a symbol of $\text{nmExt}^{-1}(s)$ from their shares, the secret sharing scheme sketched above will become malleable. We show that we can avoid this problem by taking Enc to be a "truncated systematic MDS code". That is, we take a MDS (maximum distance separable) code for which the encoding is in the form $f(x) = (x, f'(x))$,[3] then we discard x and only keep $f'(x)$. For $x \in \mathbb{F}_q^r$, we can prove that given any $r - 1$ symbols in $f'(x)$, it is not possible to recover any symbol in x. Roughly speaking, if given $r - 1$ symbols in $f'(x)$ it is possible to recover a symbol x_i, then these symbols together with x_i form a collection of r symbols which contain "redundant information". This violates the property of MDS codes that the original message can be recovered with any r symbols in the codeword. This is conceptually similar to Shamir's secret sharing scheme, and the only difference is we want to hide every single symbol in the message while Shamir's secret sharing is only hiding the first symbol because the others are random. Because our extractor is non-malleable given any other form of affine leakage (using the fact that our non-malleable extractor works for any skew affine source of dimension at least 1), we can conclude that the corresponding r-out-of-n secret sharing is non-malleable even if the adversary choose their tampering function based on $r - 1$ shares. We provide more details of our non-malleable secret sharing scheme in Sect. 6.

3 Preliminaries

Define $e(x) = e^{2\pi i x}$, where $i = \sqrt{-1}$.

For any distribution D, let $D(x)$ denote $\Pr[D = x]$, and let $\text{Supp}(D)$ denote the support of D.

Let U_m denote the uniform distribution over m bits. Let U_Σ denote the uniform distribution over the finite set Σ.

For two distributions D_1 and D_2 on the same universe, we use $|D_1 - D_2|$ to denote the statistical distance. We use $D_1 \approx_\varepsilon D_2$ to denote the fact that D_1 and D_2 are ε-close in statistical distance.

---

[3] The definition of MDS codes and the construction of systematic MDS codes can be found in Sect. 3.5.

For non-negative integers $\lambda_1, \ldots, \lambda_n$ that sum to 1, and arbitrary distributions $D_1, \ldots, D_n$, we use $\sum_i \lambda_i D_i$ to denote the distribution that places weight $\sum_i \lambda_i D_i(x)$ at the point x.

For $n \in \mathbb{N}$, we use $[n]$ to denote the set $\{1, 2, \ldots, n\}$. For non-negative integer k, we use $\binom{[n]}{k}$ denote the set of all subsets of $[n]$ of size k. Let Σ be a set of symbol. For sequence $X = (x_1, \ldots, x_n) \in \Sigma^n$ and $S = \{i_1, \ldots, i_k\} \subseteq [n]$ such that $i_1 < i_2 < \ldots < i_k$, we use X_S to denote the sequence $(x_{i_1}, x_{i_2}, \ldots, x_{i_k})$.

3.1   Characters Sums over Finite Fields

Let q be a prime. The additive characters of $\mathbb{F}_q$ are of the form $\chi_j(x) = e(xj/q)$, for $j = 0, 1, \ldots, q - 1$. χ_0 is called the trivial character, and the others are called as non-trivial characters of $\mathbb{F}_q$. We now recall a deep result from algebraic geometry that has found various applications in pseudorandomness.

Theorem 4 (Weil bound [58]**).** *Let p be a non-constant univariate polynomial of degree $d < q$ over $\mathbb{F}_q$. For any non-trivial additive character χ of $\mathbb{F}_q$, we have*

$$\left| \sum_{y \in \mathbb{F}_q} \chi(p(y)) \right| \leq d\sqrt{q}.$$

We record a couple of XOR lemmas that lets us translate bounds on expectations of characters under a distribution D, to the closeness of D in statistical distance to the uniform distribution.

Lemma 1 ([50]**).** *For every prime q, there exists an efficiently computable map $\sigma : \mathbb{F}_q \to \{0, 1\}^m$ such that if Y is a distribution on $\mathbb{F}_q$ such that for every non-trivial additive character χ of $\mathbb{F}_q$,*

$$\mathbb{E}[\chi(Y)] \leq \delta,$$

then it is the case that

$$|\sigma(Y) - U_m| \leq \varepsilon,$$

where $\varepsilon = \delta 2^{m/2} + O(2^m/q)$.

Lemma 2 ([26,50]**).** *For every prime q, there exists an efficiently computable map $\sigma : \mathbb{F}_q \to \{0, 1\}^m$ such that if (Y, Y') is a distribution on $\mathbb{F}_q \times \mathbb{F}_q$ where for all additive characters χ, ϕ of $\mathbb{F}_q$, where χ is non-trivial,*

$$\mathbb{E}[\chi(Y)\phi(Y')] \leq \delta,$$

then it is the case that

$$|(\sigma(Y), \sigma(Y')) - (U_m, \sigma(Y'))| \leq \varepsilon,$$

where $\varepsilon = \delta 2^m + O(2^m/q)$.

3.2   Useful Lemmas About Polynomials

We recall a useful result from [30] (Lemma 4.2).

Lemma 3. *Let n, r, d, λ be arbitrary positive integers, and q be a prime. Let $p_1(x), \ldots, p_r(x) \in Poly_{n,q,d}$ be non-constant polynomials. Suppose that $d_i = deg(p_i)$. Define $c_i = \lambda(2dr + 1) + \lambda i$. Then, for all $1 \leq i < j \leq r$, we have*

$$|deg(p_i^{c_i}) - deg(p_j^{c_j})| = |c_i \cdot d_i - c_j \cdot d_j| \geq \lambda.$$

We also record the Schwartz-Zippel Lemma.

Lemma 4 ([54,59]). *Let $p(x) \in Poly_{n,q,d}$ be a non-zero polynomial. Then,*

$$\Pr_{x \in \mathbb{F}_q^n} [p(x) = 0] \leq d/q.$$

3.3   Non-malleable Codes and Seedless Non-malleable Extractors

Definition 5 (Coding schemes). *Let Σ be a finite alphabet set. A pair of functions $(\mathrm{Enc}, \mathrm{Dec})$, where $\mathrm{Enc} : \{0,1\}^k \to \Sigma^n$ is a randomized function and $\mathrm{Dec} : \Sigma \to \{0,1\}^k \cup \{\bot\}$ is a deterministic function, is defined to be a coding scheme with block length n and message length k if for all $z \in \{0,1\}^k$, $\Pr[\mathrm{Dec}(Enc(s)) = s] = 1$.*

Definition 6 (Tampering functions). *Let Σ be a finite alphabet set. For any $n > 0$, let $\mathcal{H}_{\Sigma,n}$ denote the set of all functions $h : \Sigma^n \to \Sigma^n$. Any subset $\mathcal{G} \subseteq \mathcal{H}_{\Sigma,n}$ is a family of tampering functions.*

For simplicity, we sometimes do not specify the domain of tampering functions when it is clear from the context. We define a function that will be useful in defining non-malleable codes:

$$\mathrm{copy}(x,y) = \begin{cases} x & \text{if } x \neq \text{same} \\ y & \text{if } x = \text{same.} \end{cases}$$

Definition 7 (Non-malleable codes). *Let Σ be a finite alphabet set. A coding scheme $(\mathrm{Enc}, \mathrm{Dec})$ on alphabet Σ with block length n and message length k is a non-malleable code with respect to a tampering family $\mathcal{G} \subset \mathcal{H}_{\Sigma,n}$ and error ε if for every $g \in \mathcal{G}$ there is a random variable D_g supported on $\{0,1\}^k \cup \{\text{same}\}$ that is independent of the randomness in Enc, and any message $z \in \{0,1\}^k$, we have*

$$|\mathrm{Dec}(f(\mathrm{Enc}(z))) - \mathrm{copy}(D_g, z)| \leq \varepsilon$$

We define the rate of a non-malleable code $\mathcal{C}$ to be the quantity $\frac{k}{n \log(|\Sigma|)}$.

Definition 8 (Seedless non-malleable extractors). *Let Σ be a finite alphabet set, $\mathcal{G}$ be a class of tampering functions $\Sigma^n \to \Sigma^n$ and $\mathcal{X}$ be a class of distribution over Σ^n. A function $\mathrm{nmExt} : \Sigma^n \to \{0,1\}^m$ is called a seedless non-malleable extractor that works for $\mathcal{X}$ with respect to $\mathcal{G}$ with error ε if for every distribution $X \in \mathcal{X}$ and every tampering function $g \in \mathcal{G}$, there exists a random variable D_g on $\{0,1\}^m \cup \{\mathrm{same}\}$ that is independent of X, such that*

$$|(\mathrm{nmExt}(X), \mathrm{nmExt}(g(X))) - (\mathrm{U}_m, \mathrm{copy}(D_g, \mathrm{U}_m))| \leq \varepsilon.$$

3.4   Non-malleable Codes via Seedless Non-malleable Extractors

Cheraghchi and Guruswami [21] established the following connection between non-malleable codes and seedless non-malleable extractors.

Theorem 5. *Let Σ be some finite alphabet set. Let $\mathrm{nmExt} : \Sigma^n \to \{0,1\}^m$ be a polynomial time computable seedless non-malleable extractor that works for uniform distribution with respect to a class of tampering functions $\mathcal{G}$ acting on Σ^n. Suppose there is a sampling algorithm Samp that on any input $z \in \{0,1\}^m$ runs in time $\mathrm{poly}(n, \log|\Sigma|)$ and samples from a distribution that is δ-close to uniform on the pre-image set $\mathrm{nmExt}^{-1}(s)$.*

Then there exists an efficient construction of a non-malleable code on alphabet Σ with block length n, relative rate $\frac{m}{n}$, error $2^m\varepsilon + \delta$ with respect to the tampering family $\mathcal{G}$.

Given such an invertible non-malleable extractor, the non-malleable code for $\mathcal{G}$ is defined as follows: Any message $v \in \{0,1\}^m$ is encoded as $\mathrm{Samp}(v)$. The decoding of a codeword $c \in \Sigma^n$ is $\mathrm{nmExt}(c) \in \{0,1\}^m$.

3.5   MDS Code

Definition 9. *Let $C \subseteq \mathbb{F}_q^n$ be a linear subspace of dimension k where $\mathbb{F}_q$ is the finite field with q elements. We say C is a $[n,k,d]_q$ code if every two distinct codewords $c_1, c_2 \in C$ coincide in at most $n - d$ coordinates. We say C is a $[n,k]_q$ MDS (maximum distance separable) code if C is a $[n,k,n-k+1]$ code, i.e. C matches Singleton bound [56].*

Definition 10. *Let C be a $[n,k,d]_q$ code and Enc be a bijective linear mapping from $\mathbb{F}_q^k$ to C. We say Enc is systematic encoding of C if there exists a function $\mathrm{Enc}' : \mathbb{F}_q^k \to \mathbb{F}_q^{n-k}$ such that for every $x \in \mathbb{F}_q^k$, $\mathrm{Enc}(x) = (x, \mathrm{Enc}'(x))$.*

The distance property of a $[n,k]_q$ MDS code guarantees that the codewords remain distinct even when restricted to only k out of n symbols. Moreover, it is well-known that Reed-Solomon code [51] is a MDS code, and every linear code has a systematic encoding. (For example, see [43] for a systematic encoding of Reed-Solomon code.) Therefore we have the following lemma.

Lemma 5. *For every finite field $\mathbb{F}_q$ of q element, and every integer k, n such that $k \leq n \leq q$, there exists a $[n, k]_q$ MDS code $C \subseteq \mathbb{F}_q^n$ and an efficient systematic encoding $\mathrm{Enc} : \mathbb{F}_q^k \to C$. Moreover, for every $R \subseteq [n]$ of size $|R| = k$, there exists an efficient decoding algorithm $\mathrm{Dec}_R : \mathbb{F}_q^k \to \mathbb{F}_q^k$ such that for every $x \in \mathbb{F}_q^k$, $\mathrm{Dec}_R(\mathrm{Enc}(x)_R) = x$, where $\mathrm{Enc}(x)_R$ denote the restriction of $\mathrm{Enc}(x)$ on the coordinates specified by R.*

3.6   Other Useful Lemmas

We will also use the following lemma for statistical distance in [46] (Lemma 13).

Lemma 6. *Let $\mathcal{V}, \mathcal{W}$ be finite sets, and let $(V, W), (V', W')$ be joint distribution on $\mathcal{V} \times \mathcal{W}$. Let $\varepsilon > 0$ be real number such that*

$$(V, W) \approx_\varepsilon (V', W').$$

Then for every event $\mathcal{E} \subseteq \mathrm{Supp}(W) \cap \mathrm{Supp}(W')$,

$$|(V \mid W \in \mathcal{E}) - (V' \mid W' \in \mathcal{E})| \leq \frac{\varepsilon}{\Pr[W \in \mathcal{E}]}.$$

4   Non-malleable Extractors Against Polynomials

We present the proof of Theorem 3 in this section. On a high level, our idea is to express X as a convex combination of sources on lines in $\mathbb{F}_q^n$, and design a non-malleable extractor for such line sources. We note that Gabizon and Raz [34] adopted such an approach for constructing affine extractors over large fields. First we show that a skew affine source is a convex combination of skew line source.

Lemma 7. *Let q be a prime, $n < q$ be a integer and $X \in \mathbb{F}_q^n$ be a skew affine source of dimension k. Then there exists a distribution $A \in \mathbb{F}_q^n$ and a vector $b \in (\mathbb{F}_q \backslash \{0\})^n$ such that $X \equiv A + Tb$, where T is uniform over $\mathbb{F}_q$. In other word,*

$$X = \sum_{a \in \mathbb{F}_q^n} \Pr[A = a] \cdot L_{a,b},$$

where $L_{a,b}$ is the uniform distribution over the line $\{a + tb : t \in \mathbb{F}_q\}$.

Proof. Suppose X is uniform over the affine subspace $W + z$ where W is a linear subspace of $\mathbb{F}_q^n$ and $z \in \mathbb{F}_q^n$ is a fixed vector. Our goal is to find a vector $b \in W$ s.t. $b_i \neq 0$ for every $i \in [n]$. Given such b we can set $A \equiv X$, and the lemma holds because $tb \in W$ for every $t \in \mathbb{F}_q$, and $X + w \equiv X$ for every $w \in W$.

Fix a basis $\{w_1, \ldots, w_k\}$ of the linear subspace W. For every $i \in [k]$, define $S_i = \{j \in [n] : (w_i)_j \neq 0\}$ (i.e. the indices of the non-zero coordinates of w_i) and $\overline{S}_i = \bigcup_{j=1}^i S_j$. Note that $\overline{S}_k = [n]$ because $W + z$ does not have any constant coordinate. We will prove by induction that for every $i \in [k]$ there exists $v_i \in$ span$(w_1, \ldots, w_i)$ s.t. $(v_i)_j \neq 0$ for every $j \in S_i$. Assume that there exists v_{i-1} which satisfies the induction hypothesis. (Note that $v_0 = 0$.) Consider the set of q distinct vectors $L_i = \{v_{i-1} + tw_i : t \in \mathbb{F}_q\} \subseteq$ span$(w_1, \ldots, w_i)$. Observe that for every $j \in S_i$, there exists at most one vector $u_j \in L_i$ satisfying that $(u_j)_j = 0$. Since $n < q$, there must exist $u^* \in L_i$ s.t. $(u^*)_j \neq 0$ for every $j \in S_i$. Moreover, for every $j \in \overline{S_i} \setminus S_i \subseteq \overline{S_{i-1}}$, $(u^*)_j = (v_{i-1})_j \neq 0$. Therefore $(u^*)_j \neq 0$ for every $j \in \overline{S_i}$. By mathematical induction theorem, our claim is true for every $i \in [k]$. Finally observe that v_k is a valid choice of b because $\overline{S_k} = [n]$ and span$(w_1, \ldots, w_k) = W$.

Next we present the extractor construction and prove correctness. Let B be the smallest integer greater than 3 such that $\gcd(B, q - 1) = 1$. Note that B must be a prime. We can deduce an upper bound on B as follows. Define the primorial function $\nu(\ell)$ as the product of the first ℓ primes. It is known that $\nu(\ell) = e^{(1+o(1))\ell \log(\ell)}$ [28]. Further, it is known that the ℓ'th smallest prime number is at most $O(\ell \log(\ell))$ [52,53]. Hence, it must be that $B \leq \mu \log q$, for some large enough constant μ. We can thus find such a B efficiently.

For $i \in [2n]$, define $c_i = B(4dn + 1) + Bi$. Define the function $h : \mathbb{F}_q^n \to \mathbb{F}_q$ as

$$h(x_1, \ldots, x_n) = \sum_{i=1}^{n}(x_i^{c_{2i-1}} + x_i^{c_{2i}}).$$

Let $\sigma : \mathbb{F}_q \to \{0,1\}^m$ be the mapping from Lemma 2. We now define the non-malleable extractor:

$$\mathrm{nmExt}(x) = \sigma(h(x)).$$

For any $a \in \mathbb{F}_q^n$ and $b \in \mathbb{F}_q^n \setminus \{0^n\}$, define the line $L_{a,b} = \{a + tb : t \in \mathbb{F}_q\}$. We overload notation, and also use $L_{a,b}$ to denote the flat source on this line. We will show that nmExt is a non-malleable extractor against $\mathrm{Poly}_{n,q,d}$ for every skew line source. Theorem 3 then follows using Lemma 7.

Lemma 8. Let $a \in \mathbb{F}_q^n, b \in (\mathbb{F}_q \setminus \{0\})^n$. For every tampering function $P \in \mathrm{Poly}_{n,q,d}$ which is not identity on $L_{a,b}$,[4]

$$(\mathrm{nmExt}(L_{a,b}), \mathrm{nmExt}(P(L_{a,b}))) \approx_\varepsilon (\mathrm{U}_m, \mathrm{nmExt}(P(L_{a,b}))),$$

where $\varepsilon = O\left(\frac{2^m d^2 n \log q}{\sqrt{q}}\right)$

The following bound is the key ingredient. Indeed, Lemma 8 then follows using Lemma 2.

Lemma 9. Let χ, ϕ be additive characters of $\mathbb{F}_q$ such that χ is non-trivial. Then,

$$|\mathbb{E}[\chi(h(L_{a,b}))\phi(h(P(L_{a,b})))]| \leq O((d^2 n \log q)/\sqrt{q}).$$

---

[4] That is, there exists $x \in L_{a,b}$ s.t. $P(x) \neq x$.

Let $\chi(y) = e^{2\pi\alpha y/q}$ and $\phi(y) = e^{2\pi\alpha' y/q}$. Since χ is non-trivial, we know that $\alpha \neq 0$. Let $\beta = \alpha'/\alpha$. Define the polynomial

$$g_\beta(x) = h(x) + \beta h(P(x)).$$

We note that

$$|\mathbb{E}[\chi(h(X))\phi(h(P(X)))]| \leq \left|\mathbb{E}\left[e\left(\frac{\alpha g_\beta(X)}{q}\right)\right]\right|.$$

Let $g_{\beta,a,b}(t)$ be the univariate polynomial obtained by restricting $g(x)$ to the line $L_{a,b}$. The following two claims directly yields Lemma 9.

Lemma 10. *Suppose for some $a, b \in \mathbb{F}_q^n$, $g_{\beta,a,b}$ is a non-constant polynomial. Then,*

$$\left|\mathbb{E}_{t\sim\mathbb{F}_q}\left[e\left(\frac{\alpha \cdot g_{\beta,a,b}(t)}{q}\right)\right]\right| \leq O((d^2 n \log q)/\sqrt{q}).$$

Lemma 11. *For every $a \in \mathbb{F}_q^n$, $b \in (\mathbb{F}_q\backslash\{0\})^n$, $g_{\beta,a,b}$ is a constant polynomial only if P is identity on $L_{a,b}$.*

Lemma 10 is indeed simple to obtain using the Weil bound.

Proof (Proof of Lemma 10). Follows directly from Theorem 4 using the fact that $deg(g_{\beta,a,b}(t)) \leq O(d^2 n \log q)$.

Now we prove Lemma 11.

Proof (Proof of Lemma 11). For every $i \in [n]$, define the polynomial $q_i(t) = p_i(a + tb)$. Since $a + tb$ is an affine function, $deg(q_i) \leq deg(p_i) \leq d$. Let $d_i = deg(q_i)$. For every $i \in [n]$, define

$$w_i(t) = (a_i + tb_i)^{c_{2i-1}} + (a_i + tb_i)^{c_{2i}} + \beta q_i(t)^{c_{2i-1}} + \beta q_i(t)^{c_{2i}}.$$

Recall that

$$g_{\beta,a,b}(t) = \sum_i w_i(t).$$

First we prove that $deg(w_i) \in \{0, c_{2i}d_i, c_{2i}, c_{2i-1}, c_{2i} - 1\}$. Moreover, $deg(w_i) = 0$ if and only if $\beta = -1$ and $q_i(t) = a_i + tb_i$. (In other word, w_i is constant if and only if $\beta = -1$ and $p_i(x) = x_i$ for every $x \in L_{a,b}$.) To prove this statement, first we consider the case $deg(q_i) \geq 2$. Suppose that the leading coefficient in q_i is $s_i \neq 0$. If $\beta \neq 0$, the coefficient of $t^{c_{2i}d_i}$ in w_i is $\beta s_i^{c_{2i}} \neq 0$. Therefore $deg(w_i) = c_{2i}d_i$. If $\beta = 0$, the coefficient of $t^{c_{2i}}$ in w_i is $b_i^{c_{2i}} \neq 0$. Therefore $deg(w_i) = c_{2i}$. Next consider the case $deg(q_i) = 0$. With an argument similar to the case $\beta = 0$, we also have $deg(w_i) = c_{2i}$. Finally consider the case $deg(q_i) = 1$. Suppose $q_i(t) = r_i + ts_i$. Observe that the coefficient of $t^{c_{2i}}$ in w_i is $b_i^{c_{2i}} + \beta s_i^{c_{2i}}$ and the coefficient of $t^{c_{2i}-1}$ in w_i is $c_{2i}(a_i b_i^{c_{2i}-1} + \beta r_i s_i^{c_{2i}-1})$. In this case either $deg(w_i) \in \{c_{2i}, c_{2i} - 1\}$ or

$$b_i^{c_{2i}} = -\beta s_i^{c_{2i}} \text{ and } a_i b_i^{c_{2i}-1} = -\beta r_i s_i^{c_{2i}-1}.$$

The equations hold only when there exists $k \in \mathbb{F}_q$ s.t.

$$r_i = ka_i, s_i = kb_i \text{ and } k^{c_{2i}} = -\beta^{-1}.$$

If such k exists, we can write $w_i(t) = (1 - k^{-B}(a_i + tb_i)^{c_{2i}-1}$. If $\beta = -1$, we have $k = 1$, $w_i(t) = 0$ and $q_i(t) = a_i + tb_i$. If $\beta \neq -1$, then $k \neq 1$, which implies $(1 - k^{-B}) \neq 0$ because $\gcd(B, q - 1) = 1$. Therefore w_i contains a monomial of degree c_{2i-1} with coefficient $(1 - k^{-B})b_i^{c_{2i}-1} \neq 0$, and hence $deg(w_i) = c_{2i-1}$.

Now we show that $g_{\beta,a,b}(t)$ is a constant polynomial only if $\beta = -1$ and $q_i(t) = a_i + tb_i$ for every $i \in [n]$. Consider the set of index $I = \{i \in [n] : deg(w_i) > 0\}$. Then for every $i \in I$, $deg(w_i) \in \{d_i c_{2i}, c_{2i}, c_{2i-1}, c_{2i} - 1\}$ if $d_i > 0$, or $deg(w_i) \in \{c_{2i}, c_{2i-1}, c_{2i} - 1\}$ if $d_i = 0$. By Lemma 3, for every pair $i, j \in I$ s.t. $i \neq j$, we have $deg(w_i) \neq deg(w_j)$. Therefore $deg(g_{\beta,a,b}) > 0$ if I is non-empty. If $g_{\beta,a,b}$ is a constant polynomial, it must be the case that $deg(w_i) = 0$ for every $i \in [n]$. This only happens when $\beta = -1$ and $q_i(t) = a_i + tb_i$ for every $i \in [n]$, i.e. $\beta = -1$ and $P(x) = x$ for every $x \in L_{a,b}$. Lemma 11 then follows directly.

Finally we prove Theorem 3 formally.

Theorem 6 (Theorem 3, restated). *There exists a constant $C > 0$ such that for every integers n, m, d, any $\varepsilon > 0$, any prime q such that $q > Cn^2 d^4 m 2^{2m} \cdot \log(nd/\varepsilon)$, any skew affine source $X \in \mathbb{F}_q^n$ of dimension ≥ 1 and any tampering function $f \in Poly_{n,q,d}$, there exists a distribution D_f on $\{0,1\}^m \cup \{same\}$ that is independent of X, such that*

$$|(\mathrm{nmExt}(X), \mathrm{nmExt}(f(X))) - (\mathrm{U}_m, \mathrm{copy}(D_f, \mathrm{U}_m))| \leq \varepsilon.$$

Proof. By Lemma 7, there exists a distribution A on $\mathbb{F}_q^n$ and vector b such that $X = \sum_a \Pr[A = a] \cdot L_{a,b}$. Define $I = \{a \in \mathbb{F}_q^n : f \text{ is identity on } L_{a,b}\}$. For every $a \in I$, define $(D_f)_a = $ same. For every $a \notin I$ define $(D_f)_a = \mathrm{nmExt}(f(L_{a,b}))$. Then we claim that $D_f = \sum_a \Pr[A = a] \cdot (D_f)_a$ satisfies the requirement:

$$|\mathrm{nmExt}(X), \mathrm{nmExt}(f(X)) - \mathrm{U}_m, \mathrm{copy}(D_f, \mathrm{U}_m)|$$

$$\leq \sum_a \Pr[A = a] \cdot |\mathrm{nmExt}(L_{a,b}), \mathrm{nmExt}(f(L_{a,b})) - \mathrm{U}_m, \mathrm{copy}((D_f)_a, \mathrm{U}_m)|$$

$$= \sum_{a \in I} \Pr[A = a] \cdot |\mathrm{nmExt}(L_{a,b}), \mathrm{nmExt}(L_{a,b}) - \mathrm{U}_m, \mathrm{U}_m|$$

$$+ \sum_{a \notin I} \Pr[A = a] \cdot |\mathrm{nmExt}(L_{a,b}), \mathrm{nmExt}(f(L_{a,b})) - \mathrm{U}_m, \mathrm{nmExt}(f(L_{a,b}))|$$

$$\leq \sum_{a \in I} \Pr[A = a] \cdot \varepsilon + \sum_{a \notin I} \Pr[A = a] \cdot \varepsilon$$

$$= \varepsilon$$

The first inequality is by the convexity of statistical distance, and the second inequality is by Lemma 8.

5 Efficient Sampling

Recall that to construct efficient non-malleable codes using the connection established in [21], we need to efficiently sample from the pre-image of any given output of the non-malleable extractor constructed in the previous section. (We discuss this connection in Sect. 3.4.) In this section we show how to construct such a sampler for the non-malleable extractor constructed in Theorem 3. Note that Theorem 2 uses the same non-malleable extractors.

Theorem 7. *Let* $\mathrm{nmExt} : \mathbb{F}_q^n \to \{0,1\}^m$ *be the non-malleable extractor against* $\mathcal{F}_{n,q,d}$ *tampering in Theorem 3. Then there exists a randomized algorithm* $\overline{\mathrm{nmExt}^{-1}}$ *such that for every* $z \in \{0,1\}^m$ *the distribution of* $\overline{\mathrm{nmExt}^{-1}}(z)$ *is* ε-*close to uniform distribution on* $\mathrm{nmExt}^{-1}(z)$. *The running time of* $\overline{\mathrm{nmExt}^{-1}}$ *is bounded by* $\mathrm{poly}(n, d, \log q, \log(1/\varepsilon))$.

Our starting point to prove Theorem 7 is a sampling algorithm from [19], which has running time $O(d^{n^{O(n)}}(\log q)^{O(1)})$ and error $O(d^{O(n^n)}/\sqrt{q})$. We will show how to modify this algorithm and get an improved running time of $\mathrm{poly}(n, d, \log q, \log(1/\varepsilon))$ for arbitrarily small error ε.

Let nmExt be the non-malleable extractor from Theorem 3. Recall that $\mathrm{nmExt} = \sigma \circ h$ where $\sigma : \mathbb{F}_q \to \{0,1\}^m$ is defined as $\sigma(x) = x \pmod{2^m}$ and $h : \mathbb{F}_q^n \to \mathbb{F}_q$ is a multivariate polynomial of degree d over $\mathbb{F}_q$. Given $z \in \{0,1\}^m$, the pre-image of z under nmExt is

$$\mathrm{nmExt}^{-1}(z) = \bigcup_{y \in \sigma^{-1}(z)} h^{-1}(y),$$

and our goal is to sample from $\mathrm{nmExt}^{-1}(z)$ almost uniformly. The sampling algorithm in [19] is based on the following rejection sampling strategy.

Let $M \geq \max_y |h^{-1}(y)|$.

1. Sample $y \in \sigma^{-1}(z)$ uniformly at random.
2. Compute $|h^{-1}(y)|$ (approximately), and accept y with probability $|h^{-1}(y)|/M$. If y is rejected, go back to step 1.
3. Output an (almost) uniform sample from $h^{-1}(y)$.

In [19], the second step is achieved by an algorithm from [40] that has running time $O(d^{n^{O(n)}}(k \log q)^{O(1)})$.

The third step is based on the following algorithm in [22].

Lemma 12 ([22]). *Let* q *be a sufficiently large prime,* $f \in \mathbb{F}_q[x_1, \ldots, x_n]$ *be polynomials of total degree bounded by* d, *and each polynomial has at most* ℓ *monomials. Let* $S \subseteq \mathbb{F}_q^n$ *be the set of common zeroes of* f. *There exists a randomized algorithm which takes* f *as input (as a list of monomials) and outputs a random value* $X \in \mathbb{F}_q^n$ *such that the distribution of* X *is* $O(d^{O(1)}/q)$-*close to uniform distribution on* S. *The worst-case running time of this algorithm is* $\mathrm{poly}(\log q, d, n, \ell)$.

Thus the bottleneck in achieving a polynomial time sampling algorithm is Step (2) which takes time that is doubly exponential in n. We get around this difficulty as follows: first note that the rejection sampling in Step (2) is to ensure that the subset $h^{-1}(y)$ is selected with probability proportional to $|h^{-1}(y)|$. Our crucial observation is that the algorithm in Lemma 12 is actually a rejection sampling which accepts an output with probability proportional to $|h^{-1}(y)|$ in each round. Therefore we can actually combine the rejection sampling in Step 2 and 3, and bypass the computation of $|h^{-1}(y)|$.

First we explain the relation between the algorithm in Lemma 12 and rejection sampling. A naive way to sample from the variety $h^{-1}(y)$ is to repeatedly sample a point $x \in \mathbb{F}_q^n$ and verify if $h(x) = y$. However, the success probability of the naive rejection sampling is only $|h^{-1}(y)|/q^n$, which is too small. The idea in [22] is that the space $\mathbb{F}_q^n$ can be split into lines, and the variety S is split into many "slices" by these lines. The naive rejection sampling is equivalent to first sampling a line and then sampling a point from this line. Since each line has q points, the probability of a certain point in the variety being chosen is still $1/q^{n-1} \cdot 1/q$. However, if we choose a *good direction* to split the space, each slice of the variety only has at most d points where $d \ll q$, and these points can be enumerated efficiently. Therefore instead of sampling every point in this subspace with equal probability we can sample only from the *slice of variety* instead. This allows us to increase the accepting probability in each round to $|h^{-1}(y)|/dq^{n-1}$, which is high enough and still proportional to $|h^{-1}(y)|$. With the ideas above we get the following lemma.

Lemma 13. *Let $h : \mathbb{F}_q^n \to \mathbb{F}_q$ be a n-variate polynomial of degree $d < q/2$ with ℓ monomials, and $\sigma : \mathbb{F}_q \to \{0,1\}^m$ be any function. Suppose we have access to an oracle Samp_σ which takes input z and outputs a sample from $\sigma^{-1}(z)$ uniformly at random. Then for every $\varepsilon > 0$, there exists a randomized algorithm A such that for every $z \in \{0,1\}^m$, the algorithm either outputs a uniformly random sample from $(\sigma \circ h)^{-1}(z)$ or output $\perp$. The probability that the algorithm outputs $\perp$ is at most ε.*

Moreover, the expected running time of A on z is $T \cdot \mathrm{poly}(\log q, n, d, \ell)$ plus T oracle calls to Samp_σ, where

$$T = O\left(\frac{q^{n-1} \cdot d \cdot |\sigma^{-1}(z)|}{|(\sigma \circ h)^{-1}(z)|} \log(1/\varepsilon)\right).$$

Before we formally prove Lemma 13, first we show how to prove Theorem 7 based on Lemma 13. The following corollary shows that the algorithm in Lemma 13 is efficient when $\sigma \circ h$ is an "extractor for uniform distribution" and σ does not concentrate on certain output.

Corollary 3. *Suppose that $\sigma(h(U_{\mathbb{F}_q^n})) \approx_{1/2^{m+1}} U_m$, and $|\sigma^{-1}(z)| \le Cq/2^m$ for every z. Then the running time of the algorithm in Lemma 13 is $C\log(1/\varepsilon)\mathrm{poly}(n, \ell, \log q, d)$.*

Proof. The number of rounds of rejection sampling in the algorithm from Lemma 13 is $T = O\left(\frac{q^{n-1} \cdot d \cdot |\sigma^{-1}(z)|}{|(\sigma \circ h)^{-1}(z)|} \log(1/\varepsilon)\right)$.

Observe that

$$\left|(\sigma \circ h)^{-1}(z)\right| = q^n \cdot \Pr[\sigma(h(U_{\mathbb{F}_q^n})) = z] \geq q^n \cdot (1/2^m - 1/2^{m+1}) = q^n/2^{m+1}.$$

Plugging this in, and the upper on $\sigma^{-1}(z)$, we have $T = O(d \log(1/\varepsilon))$. The corollary now follows directly from Lemma 13.

Proof (Proof of Theorem 7). To prove Theorem 7 we only need to show that our non-malleable extractor satisfies the condition in Corollary 3. The fact that $\sigma(h(U_{\mathbb{F}_q^n}))$ is close to U_m follows from Theorem 3, and the second condition is also true because $\sigma(x) = x \mod 2^m$, which satisfies $|\sigma^{-1}(z)| \leq \lceil q/2^m \rceil$ for every $z \in \{0,1\}^m$.

We now prove Lemma 13. First we need the following lemma which is analogous to Proposition 4.3 in [22]. Note that we slightly tweak the lemma to make the sampling algorithm able to handle arbitrarily small error. The lemma says a random direction is a good direction to split the space with high probability.

Lemma 14. *Let* $h : \mathbb{F}_q^n \to \mathbb{F}_q$ *be a n-variate polynomial of degree at most d, and let $b = (b_1, \ldots, b_n)$ be uniformly random samples from $\mathbb{F}_q$. Then with probability at least $1 - d/q$, $h_{a,b}(t) = h(a_1 + b_1 t, \ldots, a_n + b_n t)$ is a non-constant polynomial of t for every $a = (a_1, \ldots, a_n) \in \mathbb{F}_q^n$.*

Proof. Let g be the highest-degree homogeneous part of h. Then observe that $h_{a,b}(t)$ has degree at most d, and its coefficient of t^d equals to $g(b_1, \ldots, b_n)$. By Lemma 4, the probability that $g(b_1, \ldots, b_n)$ is non-zero is at least $1 - d/q$. Therefore with probability $1 - d/q$ over b, $h_{a,b}(t)$ has degree exactly d for every $a \in \mathbb{F}_q^n$.

Proof (Proof of Lemma 13). In algorithm A, first we repeatedly sample $b \in \mathbb{F}_q^n$ uniformly at random until we find b which satisfies the condition in Lemma 14. If we fail to find such b in $\log(1/\varepsilon) + 1$ rounds, abort and output $\perp$. Then repeat the following steps for at most T rounds:

Sample $y \in \sigma^{-1}(z)$ with oracle Samp_σ, and sample $a = (a_1, \ldots, a_n)$ uniformly at random. Compute the restriction of $h(x) = y$ on the line $L_{a,b} = \{(a_1 + b_1 t, \ldots, a_n + b_n t) : b \in \mathbb{F}_q\}$, i.e. $h_{a,b}(t) = y$ where $h_{a,b}(t) = h(a_1 + b_1 t, \ldots, a_n + b_n t)$. Note that $h_{a,b}$ is a non-constant polynomial of degree at most d. Then we run Berlekamp-Rabin algorithm [49] to enumerate all the roots of $h_{a,b}$ in $\mathbb{F}_q$, denoted by $t_1, \ldots, t_k$ where $k \leq d$. Now pick a number $i \in [d]$ uniformly at random. If $i \leq k$, the algorithm succeeds, and we will return $(a_1 + b_1 t_i, \ldots, a_n + b_n t_i)$. Otherwise sample y and a again and repeat. If no value is returned after all T rounds, return $\perp$.

To prove the correctness of A, first we compute the distribution $A(z)$ conditioned on that the algorithm succeeds. Observe that $A(z)$ never returns an element which is not in $(\sigma \circ h)^{-1}(z)$. Moreover, for every $v \in (\sigma \circ h)^{-1}(z)$, in each round the probability that $A(z)$ outputs v is

$$\frac{1}{|\sigma^{-1}(z)|} \cdot \frac{1}{q^{n-1}} \cdot \frac{1}{d}.$$

The first factor is the probability that $y = h(v)$, the second factor is the probability that $L_{a,b} \ni v$, and the third factor is the probability that v is chosen from the list of roots of $h_{a,b}$. Since this formula does not depend on v, we can conclude that $A(z)$ is a uniform distribution on $(\sigma \circ h)^{-1}(z)$, conditioned on $A(z) \neq \bot$.

Now we compute the probability that A fails. Assuming $q \geq 2d$, the probability that we fail to find a b satisfying the condition in Lemma 14 in $log(1/\varepsilon)+1$ rounds is at most $(d/q)^{\log(1/\varepsilon)+1} \leq \varepsilon/2$. If we find such b successfully, observe that A successfully returns a sample with probability

$$p = \frac{|(\sigma \circ h)^{-1}(z)|}{|\sigma^{-1}(z)| \cdot q^{n-1} \cdot d}$$

in one round. Now define

$$T = \frac{C \log(1/\varepsilon)}{p},$$

for a large enough constant C. Then the probability that A does not output any element after T rounds is at most $(1-p)^T < \varepsilon/2$. Therefore $\Pr_A[A(z) = \bot] \leq \varepsilon$.

Finally we analyze the running time of A. Finding a vector b which satisfies Lemma 14 (or abort and output $\bot$) takes at most $\log(1/\varepsilon)\mathrm{poly}(n, \ell, \log q, d)$ steps. After finding b, we run at most T rounds of rejection sampling, where in each round we first make an oracle call to Samp_σ, sample a and compute the polynomial $h_{a,b}$ which takes $\mathrm{poly}(n, \ell, \log q, d)$ steps, and run Berlekamp-Rabin which takes expected $\mathrm{poly}(n, \ell, \log q, d)$ steps. Therefore the total expected running time is as claimed.

Remark 1. While we only show the expected running time in Lemma 13, it is possible to bound the worst-case running time by introducing a small error to the output distribution. That is, we can let the algorithm "time out" and output $\bot$ when the running time is too long. A full explanation can be found in the online version [7, Remark 1].

6   Non-malleable Secret Sharing

In this section we construct a non-malleable secret sharing scheme that is non-malleable against polynomial tampering. This extends a recent work of Lin et al. [46] where they could handle affine tampering functions. We use the framework that was introduced in [46] to derive our secret sharing scheme. In short, the framework in [46] takes a linear erasure code $(\mathrm{Enc}, \mathrm{Dec})$ and an invertible affine extractor Ext, and define the share function to be $\mathrm{Enc}(\mathrm{Ext}^{-1})$. If Ext is non-malleable against a class of tampering function $\mathcal{F}$ which is closed under composition with linear function, the non-malleability will be inherited by the secret sharing scheme. We show that the non-malleable extractor in Theorem 3 is also an extractor for arbitrary affine source (see Appendix A in the online version [7]). Thus the framework in [46] directly gives a non-malleable secret sharing against polynomial tampering.

Besides the direct application, we further show how to construct a r-out-of-n secret sharing which is non-malleable against adversaries who can (adaptively) corrupt $(r-1)$ shares and choose the polynomial tampering functions based on the corrupted shares. To handle such adaptive adversary, we cannot directly plug our extractor into the framework in [46] because our extractor is non-malleable only for skew affine source. Nevertheless, we will show that non-malleablility for skew affine source is sufficient if we choose a proper erasure code in the [46] scheme. In short, the erasure code we choose has the property that no single symbol in the message can be determined by $(r-1)$ symbols in the codeword. The property above ensures that when a uniformly random secret S is distributed using the scheme $\mathrm{Enc}(\mathrm{Ext}^{-1}(S))$ and $(r-1)$ shares are revealed to the adversary, none of the symbol in $\mathrm{Ext}^{-1}(S)$ is constant in the adversary's view, which means $\mathrm{Ext}^{-1}(S)$ is a skew affine source in the adversary's view. Since our extractor is non-malleable for skew affine source, we can prove our claim above following a similar path to the proof in [46].

Before we state our theorem and proof, first we formally define the non-malleable secret sharing.

Definition 11 (Adaptive adversary). *Let Σ denote a set of symbols. We say $\mathcal{A} : \Sigma^n \to \Sigma^k$ is a (n, k)-adaptive adversary if $\mathcal{A}(x_1, \ldots, x_n) = (x_{s_1}, \ldots, x_{s_k})$ for indices $s_1, \ldots, s_k$ defined as follows.*

- *s_1 is fixed.*
- *For every i, there exists a function $f_i : \Sigma^i \to [n]$ such that $s_{i+1} = f_i(x_{s_1}, \ldots, x_{s_i})$.*

Definition 12 (Non-malleable secret sharing). *Let Σ be a finite alphabet set. Let $\mathrm{Share} : \{0, 1\}^m \to \Sigma^n$ be a randomized algorithm mapping m bits to into n shares, each being an alphabet from Σ. Let $\mathcal{F} : \Sigma^n \to \Sigma^n$ be a family of tampering function. We say Share is a r-out-of-n ε-non-malleable secret sharing with respect to $\mathcal{F}$ if the following properties hold.*

- ***Correctness.*** *For every authorized set $R \subseteq [n]$ of size $|R| = r$, there exists a deterministic algorithm $\mathrm{Rec}_R : \Sigma^r \to \{0, 1\}^m$ such that for every secret $s \in \{0, 1\}^m$,*
$$\Pr[\mathrm{Rec}_R(\mathrm{Share}(s)_R) = s] \geq 1 - \varepsilon,$$
  where $\mathrm{Share}(s)_R$ denotes the r shares in $\mathrm{Share}(s)$ identified by the set R.
- ***Privacy.*** *For every $(n, r-1)$-adaptive adversary $\mathcal{A}$ and every pair of secret $a, b \in \{0, 1\}^m$,*
$$\mathcal{A}(\mathrm{Share}(a)) \approx_\varepsilon \mathcal{A}(\mathrm{Share}(b)).$$

– **Non-malleability.** *For every $(n, r-1)$-adaptive adversary $\mathcal{A}$, every reconstruction strategy $\mathcal{R} : \Sigma^{r-1} \rightarrow \binom{[n]}{r}$, every secret $s \in \{0,1\}^m$ and every tampering strategy $\mu : \Sigma^{r-1} \rightarrow \mathcal{F}$, define the tampering experiment*

$$\tilde{S} = \left\{ \begin{array}{c} share \leftarrow \mathrm{Share}(s) \\ v \leftarrow \mathcal{A}(share) \\ f \leftarrow \mu(v) \\ R \leftarrow \mathcal{R}(v) \\ \widetilde{share} \leftarrow f(share) \\ Output : \mathrm{Rec}_R(\widetilde{share}_R) \end{array} \right\}$$

which is a random variable over the randomness of Share. *Then there exists a distribution $D_{\mathcal{A},\mathcal{R},\mu}$ on $\{0,1\}^m \cup \{same\}$ which does not depend on s such that*

$$\tilde{S} \approx_\varepsilon \mathrm{copy}(D_{\mathcal{A},\mathcal{R},\mu}, s).$$

As observed in [46], since the tampering function f can be based on the view of adversary, the adversary can jointly tamper $(r-1)$ adaptively chosen shares arbitrarily. The tampering on shares which the adversary cannot see depends on how strong $\mathcal{F}$ is. In our construction $\mathcal{F}$ would be bounded-degree polynomials. With the non-malleable extractor in Theorem 3, we show the following.

Theorem 8. *There exists a constant $C > 0$ such that for all integers n, d, r, any prime q and any $\varepsilon > 0$ such that $q > (C2^m n^2 d^4 / \varepsilon^2) \cdot \log(nd/\varepsilon)$ and $1 \leq r \leq n$, there exists a r-out-of-n ε-non-malleable secret sharing scheme with respect to polynomial tampering $\mathcal{F}_{n,q,d}$ for m-bit secret.*

Proof. First we specify the construction. Let $\mathrm{nmExt} : \mathbb{F}_q^r \rightarrow \{0,1\}^m$ be the non-malleable extractor with respect to $\mathcal{F}_{r,q,d}$ with error $\varepsilon/2^{m+2}$ in *Theorem 3*. Let $\mathrm{Enc}(x) = (x, \mathrm{Enc}'(x))$ be the systematic encoding of a $[n+r, r]_q$ MDS code in Lemma 5. Let $\overline{\mathrm{nmExt}^{-1}}$ be the sampling algorithm in Theorem 7 with error $\varepsilon/2^{m+2}$. Then we define

$$\mathrm{Share}(s) = \mathrm{Enc}'(\overline{\mathrm{nmExt}^{-1}}(m)),$$

where $\overline{\mathrm{nmExt}^{-1}}$ is the almost-uniform inverter of nmExt in Sect. 4. Next we prove the three properties in Definition 12. The proof basically follows [46], but additionally we need to show that the decoded shares is a skew affine source conditioned on adversary view.

– **Correctness.** For every authorized set $R \subseteq [n]$ of size $|R| = r$, let Dec_R denote the decoding function of Enc' specified by R in Lemma 5. Then we define

$$\mathrm{Rec}_R(v) = \mathrm{nmExt}(\mathrm{Dec}_R(v)).$$

Rec is a correct reconstruction because for every secret s,

$$\Pr[\mathrm{Rec}_R(\mathrm{Share}(s)_R) = s] = \Pr[\mathrm{nmExt}\left(\mathrm{Dec}_R\left(\mathrm{Enc}(\overline{\mathrm{nmExt}^{-1}}(s))_R\right)\right) = s] \geq 1 - \varepsilon.$$

Note that the correctness is not perfect because $\overline{\mathrm{nmExt}^{-1}}(x)$ does not always output a pre-image of x.

– **Privacy.** Let $S = \mathrm{nmExt}(\mathrm{U}_{\mathbb{F}_q^r})$, and define $X = \overline{\mathrm{nmExt}^{-1}}(S)$. Fix any $(n, r-1)$-adaptive adversary $\mathcal{A} : \mathbb{F}_q^n \to \mathbb{F}_q^{r-1}$. Since $\overline{\mathrm{nmExt}^{-1}}$ is an inverter of nmExt with error $\varepsilon/2^{m+2}$, we have $(X, S) \approx_{\varepsilon/2^{m+2}} (\mathrm{U}_{\mathbb{F}_q^r}, S)$, which implies

$$\left(\mathcal{A}\left(\mathrm{Enc}'(X)\right), S\right) \approx_{\varepsilon/2^{m+2}} \left(\mathcal{A}\left(\mathrm{Enc}'(\mathrm{U}_{\mathbb{F}_q^r})\right), \mathrm{nmExt}(\mathrm{U}_{\mathbb{F}_q^r})\right).$$

Define $V = \mathcal{A}\left(\mathrm{Enc}'(\mathrm{U}_{\mathbb{F}_q^r})\right)$. We claim that for every $v \in \mathbb{F}_q^{r-1}$, $Y_v = (\mathrm{U}_{\mathbb{F}_q^r} \mid V = v)$ is a skew affine source with positive min-entropy. Observe that there exists a set $T_v \in \binom{[n]}{r-1}$ uniquely determined by v such that $\mathcal{A}\left(\mathrm{Enc}'(\mathrm{U}_{\mathbb{F}_q^r})\right) = \mathrm{Enc}'(\mathrm{U}_{\mathbb{F}_q^r})_{T_v}$. Since Enc' is a linear mapping, $V = v$ corresponds to $r-1$ linear constraints for Y_v. Therefore Y_v is an affine source with positive min-entropy. Now assume for contradiction that Y_v is not skew. Then there exists $i \in [r]$ such that $(Y_v)_i$ is a constant. Since Y_v is not a constant, there exist two distinct value $y_1, y_2 \in \mathrm{Supp}(Y_v)$. Observe that $\mathrm{Enc}'(y_1)_{T_v} = v = \mathrm{Enc}'(y_2)_{T_v}$ and $(y_1)_i = (y_2)_i$. Then $\mathrm{Enc}(y_1) := (y_1, \mathrm{Enc}'(y_1))$ and $\mathrm{Enc}(y_2) := (y_2, \mathrm{Enc}'(y_2))$ coincide on $(r-1) + 1$ coordinates, which contradicts to the fact that Enc is a MDS code. Therefore Y_v is skew. By Theorem 3,

$$\left(\mathcal{A}\left(\mathrm{Enc}'(\mathrm{U}_{\mathbb{F}_q^r})\right), \mathrm{nmExt}(\mathrm{U}_{\mathbb{F}_q^r})\right) \approx_{\varepsilon/2^{m+2}} \left(\mathcal{A}\left(\mathrm{Enc}'(\mathrm{U}_{\mathbb{F}_q^r})\right), \mathrm{U}_m\right).$$

By triangle inequality we have

$$\left(\mathcal{A}\left(\mathrm{Enc}'(X)\right), S\right) \approx_{\varepsilon/2^{m+1}} \left(\mathcal{A}\left(\mathrm{Enc}'(\mathrm{U}_{\mathbb{F}_q^r})\right), \mathrm{U}_m\right),$$

which by Lemma 6 implies

$$\left(\mathcal{A}\left(\mathrm{Enc}'(X)\right) \mid S = a\right) \approx_{\varepsilon/2} \left(\mathcal{A}\left(\mathrm{Enc}'(\mathrm{U}_{\mathbb{F}_q^r})\right)\right) \approx_{\varepsilon/2} \left(\mathcal{A}\left(\mathrm{Enc}'(X)\right) \mid S = b\right)$$

for every $a, b \in \mathrm{Supp}(S)$. Finally, observe that $\mathrm{Supp}(S) = \{0, 1\}^m$ because S is $\varepsilon/2^{m+2} < 1/2^m$ close to uniform. Therefore for every $a, b \in \{0, 1\}^m$,

$$\mathcal{A}\left(\mathrm{Enc}'\left(\overline{\mathrm{nmExt}^{-1}}(a)\right)\right) \approx_{\varepsilon} \mathcal{A}\left(\mathrm{Enc}'\left(\overline{\mathrm{nmExt}^{-1}}(b)\right)\right).$$

– **Non-malleability.** Let $S = \mathrm{nmExt}(\mathrm{U}_{\mathbb{F}_q^r})$, and define $X = \overline{\mathrm{nmExt}^{-1}}(S)$. Fix any $(n, r-1)$-adaptive adversary $\mathcal{A} : \mathbb{F}_q^n \to \mathbb{F}_q^{r-1}$, any reconstruction strategy $\mathcal{R} : \mathbb{F}_q^{r-1} \to \binom{[n]}{r}$ and any tampering strategy $\mu : \mathbb{F}_q^{r-1} \to \mathcal{F}_{n,q,d}$. Recall the tampering experiment

$$\widetilde{S} = \left\{ \begin{array}{c} share \leftarrow \mathrm{Enc}'(X) \\ V \leftarrow \mathcal{A}(share) \\ f \leftarrow \mu(V) \\ R \leftarrow \mathcal{R}(V) \\ \widetilde{share} \leftarrow f(share) \\ Output : \mathrm{Rec}_R(\widetilde{share}_R) \end{array} \right\}$$

Note that this tampering experiment is equivalent to applying the tampering experiment in Definition 12 on S. Now define

$$\widetilde{S'} = \left\{ \begin{array}{c} share' \leftarrow \mathrm{Enc}(\mathrm{U}_{\mathbb{F}_q^n}) \\ V' \leftarrow \mathcal{A}(share') \\ f \leftarrow \mu(V') \\ R \leftarrow \mathcal{R}(V') \\ \widetilde{share'} \leftarrow f(share') \\ Output : \mathrm{Rec}_R(\widetilde{share}_R) \end{array} \right\}$$

Since $\overline{\mathrm{nmExt}^{-1}}$ is an inverter of nmExt with error $\varepsilon/2^{m+2}$, we have $(S, X) \approx_{\varepsilon/2^{m+2}} (S, \mathrm{U}_{\mathbb{F}_q^n})$ which implies

$$(S, \widetilde{S}) \approx_{\varepsilon/2^{m+2}} (S, \widetilde{S'}).$$

For every $v \in \mathbb{F}_q^{r-1}$, define $Y_v = (\mathrm{U}_{\mathbb{F}_q^r} \mid V' = v)$. With the same proof in the privacy part, we can show that Y_v is a skew affine source with positive min-entropy. Now define $f_v = \mu(v)$, $R_v = \mathcal{R}(v)$ and $g_v : \mathbb{F}_q^r \rightarrow \mathbb{F}_q^r$ to be $g_v(x) := \mathrm{Dec}_{R_v}(f_v(\mathrm{Enc}'(x))_{R_v})$. Since both Enc' and Dec_{R_v} are linear and $f_v \in \mathcal{F}_{n,q,d}$, we have $g_v \in \mathcal{F}_{r,q,d}$. By Theorem 3, there exists a distribution D_{g_v} on $\{0,1\}^m \cup \{\mathrm{same}\}$ such that

$$(\mathrm{nmExt}(\mathrm{U}_{\mathbb{F}_q^r}), \mathrm{nmExt}(g_v(\mathrm{U}_{\mathbb{F}_q^r})) \mid V' = v) \approx_{\varepsilon/2^{m+2}} (\mathrm{U}_m, \mathrm{copy}(D_{g_v}, \mathrm{U}_m)).$$

Define $D_{\mathcal{A},\mathcal{R},\mu} = \sum_v \Pr[V' = v] \cdot D_{g_v}$. By convexity of statistical distance,

$$(S, \widetilde{S'}) = (\mathrm{nmExt}(\mathrm{U}_{\mathbb{F}_q^r}), \widetilde{S'}) \approx_{\varepsilon/2^{m+2}} (\mathrm{U}_m, \mathrm{copy}(D_{\mathcal{A},\mathcal{R},\mu}, \mathrm{U}_m)),$$

which by triangle inequality implies

$$(S, \widetilde{S}) \approx_{\varepsilon/2^{m+1}} (\mathrm{U}_m, \mathrm{copy}(D_{\mathcal{A},\mathcal{R},\mu}, \mathrm{U}_m))).$$

Finally by Lemma 6 and the fact that $\mathrm{Supp}(S) = \{0,1\}^m$ we can conclude that for every $s \in \{0,1\}^m$,

$$(\widetilde{S} \mid S = s) \approx_\varepsilon \mathrm{copy}(D_{\mathcal{A},\mathcal{R},\mu}, s).$$

7   Open Questions

Obvious questions that arise from our work include improving the parameters (such as rate and error) of our non-malleable code against polynomials, and similarly obtaining seedless non-malleable extractors against polynomials with smaller error.

Another interesting direction is to construct such non-malleable codes and extractors against polynomials over smaller fields. In particular, over $\mathbb{F}_2$ would be the most interesting. We expect this to require significantly different ideas from our construction: we crucially rely on exponential sum estimates for our non-malleable extractor construction, and such estimates are not available over smaller fields.

More broadly, we believe it to be a very interesting question to construct non-malleable codes against other natural complexity classes (e.g., small-width branching programs, AC^0 with PARITY gates, etc.).

Acknowledgements. Marshall Ball is supported by an IBM Research PhD Fellowship. Tal Malkin and Marshall Ball: This work is based upon work supported in part by the Office of the Director of National Intelligence (ODNI), Intelligence Advanced Research Projects Activity (IARPA) via Contract No. 2019-1902070006. The views and conclusions contained herein are those of the authors and should not be interpreted as necessarily representing the official policies, either express or implied, of ODNI, IARPA, or the U.S. Government. The U.S. Government is authorized to reproduce and distribute reprints for governmental purposes notwithstanding any copyright annotation therein.

Eshan Chattopadhyay and Jyun-Jie Liao are supported by NSF grant CCF-1849899. Li-Yang Tan is supported by NSF grant CCF-1921795.

References

1. Aggarwal, D., et al.: Stronger leakage-resilient and non-malleable secret-sharing schemes for general access structures. IACR Cryptology ePrint Archive 2018, 1147 (2018)
2. Aggarwal, D., Dodis, Y., Kazana, T., Obremski, M.: Non-malleable reductions and applications. In: Proceedings of the Forty-Seventh Annual ACM Symposium on Theory of Computing, pp. 459–468. ACM (2015)
3. Aggarwal, D., Dodis, Y., Lovett, S.: Non-malleable codes from additive combinatorics. SIAM J. Comput. **47**(2), 524–546 (2018)
4. Aggarwal, D., Obremski, M.: A constant-rate non-malleable code in the split-state model. IACR Cryptology ePrint Archive 2019, 1299 (2019)
5. Agrawal, S., Gupta, D., Maji, H.K., Pandey, O., Prabhakaran, M.: A rate-optimizing compiler for non-malleable codes against bit-wise tampering and permutations. In: Dodis, Y., Nielsen, J.B. (eds.) TCC 2015, Part I. LNCS, vol. 9014, pp. 375–397. Springer, Heidelberg (2015). https://doi.org/10.1007/978-3-662-46494-6_16
6. Badrinarayanan, S., Srinivasan, A.: Revisiting non-malleable secret sharing. IACR Cryptology ePrint Archive 2018, 1144 (2018)
7. Ball, M., Chattopadhyay, E., Liao, J., Malkin, T., Tan, L.: Non-malleability against polynomial tampering. IACR Cryptology ePrint Archive 2020, 147 (2020). https://eprint.iacr.org/2020/147
8. Ball, M., Dachman-Soled, D., Guo, S., Malkin, T., Tan, L.Y.: Non-malleable codes for small-depth circuits. In: 2018 IEEE 59th Annual Symposium on Foundations of Computer Science (FOCS), pp. 826–837. IEEE (2018)
9. Ball, M., Dachman-Soled, D., Kulkarni, M., Malkin, T.: Non-malleable codes for bounded depth, bounded fan-in circuits. In: Fischlin, M., Coron, J.-S. (eds.) EUROCRYPT 2016. LNCS, vol. 9666, pp. 881–908. Springer, Heidelberg (2016). https://doi.org/10.1007/978-3-662-49896-5_31

10. Ball, M., Guo, S., Wichs, D.: Non-malleable codes for decision trees. IACR Cryptology ePrint Archive 2019, 379 (2019)
11. Barak, B., Impagliazzo, R., Wigderson, A.: Extracting randomness using few independent sources. SIAM J. Comput. **36**(4), 1095–1118 (2006). https://doi.org/10.1137/S0097539705447141
12. Bennett, C., Brassard, G., Robert, J.M.: Privacy amplification by public discussion. SIAM J. Comput. **17**, 210–229 (1988)
13. Blakley, G.R.: Safeguarding cryptographic keys. In: Proceedings of the 1979 AFIPS National Computer Conference, pp. 313–317 (1979)
14. Bourgain, J.: More on the sum-product phenomenon in prime fields and its applications. Int. J. Number Theory **01**(01), 1–32 (2005). https://doi.org/10.1142/S1793042105000108
15. Bourgain, J.: On the construction of affine extractors. GAFA Geom. Funct. Anal. **17**(1), 33–57 (2007)
16. Chattopadhyay, E., Goyal, V., Li, X.: Non-malleable extractors and codes, with their many tampered extensions. In: STOC (2016)
17. Chattopadhyay, E., Li, X.: Non-malleable codes and extractors for small-depth circuits, and affine functions. In: Proceedings of the 49th Annual ACM SIGACT Symposium on Theory of Computing, pp. 1171–1184. ACM (2017)
18. Chattopadhyay, E., Li, X.: Non-malleable codes, extractors and secret sharing for interleaved tampering and composition of tampering. Technical report, Cryptology ePrint Archive, Report 2018/1069, 2018 (2019)
19. Chattopadhyay, E., Zuckerman, D.: Non-malleable codes against constant split-state tampering. In: Proceedings of the 55th Annual IEEE Symposium on Foundations of Computer Science, pp. 306–315 (2014)
20. Chattopadhyay, E., Zuckerman, D.: Explicit two-source extractors and resilient functions. Ann. Math. **189**(3), 653–705 (2019). https://doi.org/10.4007/annals.2019.189.3.1
21. Cheraghchi, M., Guruswami, V.: Non-malleable coding against bit-wise and split-state tampering. In: Lindell, Y. (ed.) TCC 2014. LNCS, vol. 8349, pp. 440–464. Springer, Heidelberg (2014). https://doi.org/10.1007/978-3-642-54242-8_19
22. Cheraghchi, M., Shokrollahi, A.: Almost-uniform sampling of points on high-dimensional algebraic varieties. In: 26th International Symposium on Theoretical Aspects of Computer Science, STACS 2009, Freiburg, Germany, 26–28 February 2009, Proceedings, pp. 277–288 (2009)
23. Chor, B., Goldreich, O.: Unbiased bits from sources of weak randomness and probabilistic communication complexity. SIAM J. Comput. **17**(2), 230–261 (1988)
24. Chor, B., Goldreich, O., Hasted, J., Freidmann, J., Rudich, S., Smolensky, R.: The bit extraction problem or t-resilient functions. In: IEEE Symposium on Foundations of Computer Science, pp. 396–407 (1985). https://doi.org/10.1109/SFCS.1985.55
25. Coretti, S., Maurer, U., Tackmann, B., Venturi, D.: From single-bit to multi-bit public-key encryption via non-malleable codes. In: Dodis, Y., Nielsen, J.B. (eds.) TCC 2015. LNCS, vol. 9014, pp. 532–560. Springer, Heidelberg (2015). https://doi.org/10.1007/978-3-662-46494-6_22
26. Dodis, Y., Li, X., Wooley, T.D., Zuckerman, D.: Privacy amplification and non-malleable extractors via character sums. SIAM J. Comput. **43**(2), 800–830 (2014)
27. Dodis, Y., Wichs, D.: Non-malleable extractors and symmetric key cryptography from weak secrets. In: STOC, pp. 601–610 (2009)
28. Dusart, P.: Estimates of some functions over primes without RH. arXiv preprint arXiv:1002.0442 (2010)

29. Dvir, Z.: Extractors for varieties. Comput. Complex. **21**(4), 515–572 (2012)
30. Dvir, Z., Gabizon, A., Wigderson, A.: Extractors and rank extractors for polynomial sources. Comput. Complex. **18**(1), 1–58 (2009)
31. Dvir, Z., Kopparty, S., Saraf, S., Sudan, M.: Extensions to the method of multiplicities, with applications to Kakeya sets and mergers. In: Proceedings of the 50th Annual IEEE Symposium on Foundations of Computer Science, pp. 181–190 (2009)
32. Dziembowski, S., Kazana, T., Obremski, M.: Non-malleable codes from two-source extractors. In: Canetti, R., Garay, J.A. (eds.) CRYPTO 2013. LNCS, vol. 8043, pp. 239–257. Springer, Heidelberg (2013). https://doi.org/10.1007/978-3-642-40084-1_14
33. Dziembowski, S., Pietrzak, K., Wichs, D.: Non-malleable codes. J. ACM **65**(4), 20:1–20:32 (2018). https://doi.org/10.1145/3178432
34. Gabizon, A., Raz, R.: Deterministic extractors for affine sources over large fields. Combinatorica **28**(4), 415–440 (2008)
35. Goyal, V., Kumar, A.: Non-malleable secret sharing. In: Proceedings of the 50th Annual ACM SIGACT Symposium on Theory of Computing, pp. 685–698. ACM (2018)
36. Goyal, V., Kumar, A.: Non-malleable secret sharing for general access structures. In: Shacham, H., Boldyreva, A. (eds.) CRYPTO 2018, Part I. LNCS, vol. 10991, pp. 501–530. Springer, Cham (2018). https://doi.org/10.1007/978-3-319-96884-1_17
37. Goyal, V., Pandey, O., Richelson, S.: Textbook non-malleable commitments. In: Proceedings of the Forty-Eighth Annual ACM Symposium on Theory of Computing, pp. 1128–1141. ACM (2016)
38. Gupta, D., Maji, H.K., Wang, M.: Constant-rate non-malleable codes in the split-state model. Technical report, Technical Report Report 2017/1048, Cryptology ePrint Archive (2018)
39. Guruswami, V., Umans, C., Vadhan, S.P.: Unbalanced expanders and randomness extractors from Parvaresh-Vardy codes. J. ACM **56**(4), 1–34 (2009)
40. Huang, M.-D., Wong, Y.-C.: An algorithm for approximate counting of points on algebraic sets over finite fields. In: Buhler, J.P. (ed.) ANTS 1998. LNCS, vol. 1423, pp. 514–527. Springer, Heidelberg (1998). https://doi.org/10.1007/BFb0054889
41. Kanukurthi, B., Obbattu, S.L.B., Sekar, S.: Four-state non-malleable codes with explicit constant rate. In: Kalai, Y., Reyzin, L. (eds.) TCC 2017. LNCS, vol. 10678, pp. 344–375. Springer, Cham (2017). https://doi.org/10.1007/978-3-319-70503-3_11
42. Kanukurthi, B., Obbattu, S.L.B., Sekar, S.: Non-malleable randomness encoders and their applications. In: Nielsen, J.B., Rijmen, V. (eds.) EUROCRYPT 2018. LNCS, vol. 10822, pp. 589–617. Springer, Cham (2018). https://doi.org/10.1007/978-3-319-78372-7_19
43. Lacan, J., Fimes, J.: Systematic MDS erasure codes based on vandermonde matrices. IEEE Commun. Lett. **8**(9), 570–572 (2004). https://doi.org/10.1109/LCOMM.2004.833807
44. Li, X.: Improved non-malleable extractors, non-malleable codes and independent source extractors. In: Proceedings of the 49th Annual ACM SIGACT Symposium on Theory of Computing, STOC 2017, pp. 1144–1156 (2017)
45. Li, X.: Non-malleable extractors and non-malleable codes: partially optimal constructions. In: 34th Computational Complexity Conference, CCC 2019, New Brunswick, NJ, USA, 18–20 July 2019, pp. 28:1–28:49 (2019)
46. Lin, F., Cheraghchi, M., Guruswami, V., Safavi-Naini, R., Wang, H.: Non-malleable secret sharing against affine tampering. arXiv preprint arXiv:1902.06195 (2019)

47. Lu, C.-J.: Hyper-encryption against space-bounded adversaries from on-line strong extractors. In: Yung, M. (ed.) CRYPTO 2002. LNCS, vol. 2442, pp. 257–271. Springer, Heidelberg (2002). https://doi.org/10.1007/3-540-45708-9_17
48. Nisan, N., Zuckerman, D.: Randomness is linear in space. J. Comput. Syst. Sci. **52**(1), 43–52 (1996). https://doi.org/10.1006/jcss.1996.0004
49. Rabin, M.O.: Probabilistic algorithms in finite fields. SIAM J. Comput. **9**(2), 273–280 (1980). https://doi.org/10.1137/0209024
50. Rao, A.: An exposition of Bourgain's 2-source extractor. In: Electronic Colloquium on Computational Complexity (ECCC), vol. 14 (2007)
51. Reed, I.S., Solomon, G.: Polynomial codes over certain finite fields. J. Soc. Ind. Appl. Math. **8**(2), 300–304 (1960)
52. Robin, G.: Permanence de relations de récurrence dans certains développements asymptotiques. Pub. Inst. Math. Beograd **43**(57), 17–25 (1988)
53. Rosser, B.: The n-th prime is greater than nlogn. Proc. Lond. Math. Soc. **2**(1), 21–44 (1939)
54. Schwartz, J.T.: Probabilistic algorithms for verification of polynomial identities. In: Ng, E.W. (ed.) Symbolic and Algebraic Computation. LNCS, vol. 72, pp. 200–215. Springer, Heidelberg (1979). https://doi.org/10.1007/3-540-09519-5_72
55. Shamir, A.: How to share a secret. Commun. ACM **22**(11), 612–613 (1979)
56. Singleton, R.C.: Maximum distance q-nary codes. IEEE Trans. Inf. Theory **10**(2), 116–118 (1964). https://doi.org/10.1109/TIT.1964.1053661
57. Ta-Shma, A., Zuckerman, D.: Extractor codes. IEEE Trans. Inf. Theory **50**(12), 3015–3025 (2004)
58. Weil, A.: On some exponential sums. Proc. Natl. Acad. Sci. U.S.A. **34**(5), 204 (1948)
59. Zippel, R.: Probabilistic algorithms for sparse polynomials. In: Ng, E.W. (ed.) Symbolic and Algebraic Computation. LNCS, vol. 72, pp. 216–226. Springer, Heidelberg (1979). https://doi.org/10.1007/3-540-09519-5_73
60. Zuckerman, D.: Linear degree extractors and the inapproximability of max clique and chromatic number. In: Proceedings of the Thirty-Eighth Annual ACM Symposium on Theory of Computing, pp. 681–690 (2006)

Non-malleable Secret Sharing Against Bounded Joint-Tampering Attacks in the Plain Model

Gianluca Brian[1]([⊠]), Antonio Faonio[2], Maciej Obremski[3], Mark Simkin[4], and Daniele Venturi[1]

[1] Sapienza University of Rome, Rome, Italy
brian@di.uniroma1.it
[2] IMDEA Software Institute, Madrid, Spain
[3] National University of Singapore, Singapore, Singapore
[4] Aarhus University, Aarhus, Denmark

Abstract. Secret sharing enables a dealer to split a secret into a set of shares, in such a way that certain authorized subsets of share holders can reconstruct the secret, whereas all unauthorized subsets cannot. Non-malleable secret sharing (Goyal and Kumar, STOC 2018) additionally requires that, even if the shares have been tampered with, the reconstructed secret is either the original or a completely unrelated one.

In this work, we construct non-malleable secret sharing tolerating p-time *joint-tampering* attacks in the plain model (in the computational setting), where the latter means that, for any $p > 0$ fixed *a priori*, the attacker can tamper with the same target secret sharing up to p times. In particular, assuming one-to-one one-way functions, we obtain:

- A secret sharing scheme for threshold access structures which tolerates joint p-time tampering with subsets of the shares of maximal size (*i.e.*, matching the privacy threshold of the scheme). This holds in a model where the attacker commits to a partition of the shares into non-overlapping subsets, and keeps tampering jointly with the shares within such a partition (so-called *selective partitioning*).
- A secret sharing scheme for general access structures which tolerates joint p-time tampering with subsets of the shares of size $O(\sqrt{\log n})$, where n is the number of parties. This holds in a stronger model where the attacker is allowed to adaptively change the partition

A. Faonio—Supported by the Spanish Government under projects SCUM (ref. RTI2018-102043-B-I00), CRYPTOEPIC (ref. EUR2019-103816), and SECURITAS (ref. RED2018-102321-T), by the Madrid Regional Government under project BLOQUES (ref. S2018/TCS-4339).

M. Obremski—Supported by MOE2019-T2-1-145 Foundations of quantum-safe cryptography.

M. Simkin—Supported by the European Research Council (ERC) under the European Unions's Horizon 2020 research and innovation programme under grant agreement No 669255 (MPCPRO), grant agreement No 803096 (SPEC), Danish Independent Research Council under Grant-ID DFF-6108-00169 (FoCC), and the Concordium Blockhain Research Center.

D. Micciancio and T. Ristenpart (Eds.): CRYPTO 2020, LNCS 12172, pp. 127–155, 2020.
https://doi.org/10.1007/978-3-030-56877-1_5

within each tampering query, under the restriction that once a subset of the shares has been tampered with jointly, that subset is always either tampered jointly or not modified by other tampering queries (so-called *semi-adaptive partitioning*).

At the heart of our result for selective partitioning lies a new technique showing that every one-time *statistically* non-malleable secret sharing against joint tampering is in fact *leakage-resilient* non-malleable (*i.e.*, the attacker can leak jointly from the shares prior to tampering). We believe this may be of independent interest, and in fact we show it implies lower bounds on the share size and randomness complexity of statistically non-malleable secret sharing against *independent* tampering.

Keywords: Secret sharing · Non-malleability · Joint tampering

1   Introduction

In the past 40 years, secret sharing [9,32] became one of the most fundamental cryptographic primitives. Secret sharing schemes allow a trusted dealer to split a message m into shares $s_1, \ldots, s_n$ and distribute them among n participants, such that only certain authorized subsets of share holders are allowed to recover m. The collection $\mathcal{A}$ of authorized subsets is called the *access structure*. The most basic security guarantee is that any *unauthorized* subset outside $\mathcal{A}$ collectively has no information about the shared message. Shamir [32] and Blakley [9] showed how to construct secret sharing schemes with information-theoretic security, and Krawczyk [25] presented the first computationally-secure construction with improved efficiency parameters.

Non-malleable Secret Sharing. A long line of research [2,8,11,12,14,21,23,24,26, 31,33] has focused on different settings with active adversaries that were allowed to tamper with the shares in one or another way. In verifiable secret sharing [31] the dealer is considered to be untrusted and the share holders want to ensure they hold shares of a consistent secret. In robust secret sharing [12] some parties may act maliciously and try to prevent the correct reconstruction of the shared secret by providing incorrect shares. It is well known that robust secret sharing is impossible when more than half of the parties are malicious.

A recent line of works considers an adversary that has some form of restricted access to *all* shares. In non-malleable secret sharing [23] the adversary can partition the shares in disjoint sets and can then independently tamper with each set of shares. Security guarantees that whatever is reconstructed from the tampered shares is either the original secret, or a completely unrelated value. Most previous works have focused on the setting of independent tampering [2,8,11,21,23,24,26,33], where the adversary is only allowed to tamper with each share *independently*. Only a few papers [11,14,23,24] have considered the stronger setting where the adversary is allowed to tamper with subsets of shares *jointly*.

Continuous Non-malleability. The first notions of non-malleability only focused on security against a *single* round of tampering. A natural extension of this setting is to consider adversaries that may perform several rounds of tampering attacks on a secret sharing scheme. Badrinarayanan and Srinivasan [8] and Aggarwal *et al.* [2] considered p-time tampering attacks in the information-theoretic setting, where p must be *a-priori* bounded. The works of Faonio and Venturi [21] and Brian, Faonio and Venturi [11] considered *continuous*, i.e., poly-many tampering attacks in the computational setting. It is well known that cryptographic assumptions are inherent in the latter case [8,21,22].

An important limitation of all works mentioned above is that, with the exception of [11], they only consider the setting of independent tampering. Brian Faonio, and Venturi [11] achieve continuous non-malleability against joint tampering, where each tampering function can tamper with $O(\log n)$-large sets of shares assuming a trusted setup in the form of a common reference string. This leads to the following question:

Can we obtain continuously non-malleable secret sharing against joint tampering in the plain model?

1.1   Our Contributions

In this work, we make progress towards answering the above question. Our main contribution is a general framework for reducing *computational* p-time non-malleability against joint tampering to *statistical* one-time non-malleability against joint tampering. Our framework encompasses the following models:

– **Selective partitioning.** Here, the adversary has to initially fix any k-sized partition[1] of the n shares, at the beginning of the experiment. Afterwards, the adversary can tamper p times with the shares within each subset in a joint manner. We call this notion k-joint p-time non-malleability under *selective partitioning.*
– **Semi-adaptive partitioning.** In this setting, the adversary can adaptively choose different k-sized partitions for each tampering query. However, once a subset of the shares has been tampered with jointly, that subset is always either tampered jointly or not modified by other tampering queries. We call this notion k-joint p-time non-malleability under *semi-adaptive partitioning.*

Combining known constructions of one-time statistically non-malleable secret sharing schemes against joint tampering [14,23,24] with a new secret sharing scheme that we present in this work, we obtain the following result:

Theorem 1 (Main Theorem, Informal). *Assuming the existence of one-to-one one-way functions, there exist:*

---

[1] This a sequence of non-overlapping subsets $\mathcal{B}_1, \ldots, \mathcal{B}_t$ covering $[n]$, such that each $\mathcal{B}_i$ has size at most k.

(i) *A τ-out-of-n secret sharing scheme satisfying k-joint p-time non-malleability under selective partitioning,[2] for any $\tau \le n$, $k \le \tau - 1$, and $p > 0$.*

(ii) *An (n, τ)-ramp[3] secret sharing scheme with binary shares satisfying k-joint p-time non-malleability under selective partitioning, for $\tau = n - n^\beta$, $k \le \tau - 1$, $\beta < 1$, and $p \in O(\sqrt{n})$.*

(iii) *A secret sharing scheme satisfying k-joint p-time non-malleability under semi-adaptive partitioning, for $k \in O(\sqrt{\log n})$ and $p > 0$, and for any access structure that can be described by a polynomial-size monotone span program for which authorized sets have size greater than k.*

1.2   Technical Overview

Our initial observation is that a slight variant of a transformation by Ostrovsky *et al.* [30] allows to turn a *bounded leakage-resilient*, statistically one-time non-malleable secret sharing Σ into a *bounded-time* non-malleable secret sharing Σ^* against joint tampering. Bounded leakage resilience here means that, prior to tampering, the attacker may also repeatedly leak information jointly from the shares of Σ, as long as the overall leakage is bounded.

In the setting of joint tampering under selective partitioning, the leakage resilience property of Σ has to hold w.r.t. the same partition used for tampering. For joint tampering under semi-adaptive partitioning, we need Σ to be leakage-resilient under a semi-adaptive choice of the partitions too. A nice feature of this transformation is that it only requires perfectly binding commitments, which can be built from injective one-way functions. Moreover, it preserves the access structure of the underlying secret sharing scheme Σ.

Given the above result, we can focus on the simpler task of constructing bounded leakage-resilient, statistically one-time non-malleable secret sharing, instead of directly attempting to construct their multi-time counterparts. We show different ways of doing that for both settings of selective and semi-adaptive partitioning.

Selective Partitioning. First, we show that every statistically one-time non-malleable secret sharing scheme Σ is also resilient to *bounded leakage* under selective partitioning. Let ℓ be an upper bound on the total bit-length of the leakage over all shares. We use an argument reminiscent to standard complexity leveraging to prove that every one-time non-malleable secret sharing scheme with statistical security $\epsilon \in [0, 1)$ is also ℓ-bounded leakage-resilient one-time non-malleable under selective partitioning with statistical security $\epsilon/2^\ell$. The proof roughly works as follows. Given an unbounded attacker A breaking the leakage-resilient one-time non-malleability of Σ, we construct an unbounded attacker Â against one-time non-malleability of Σ (without leakage). The challenge is how

---

[2] Here, we inherit a few restrictions from [23]. Namely, the attacker is allowed to tamper jointly using a partition of a minimal reconstruction set in subsets of different sizes. We can remove these restrictions relying on the scheme from [24], which however only works for the n-out-of-n access structure.

[3] This means privacy holds with threshold τ, but all of the n shares are required to reconstruct the message.

$\hat{A}$ can answer the leakage queries done by A. Our strategy is to simply guess the overall leakage Λ by sampling it uniformly at random, and use this guess to answer all of A's leakage queries.

The problem with this approach is that, whenever our guess was incorrect, the attacker A may notice that it is being used in a simulation and start behaving arbitrarily. We solve this issue with the help of $\hat{A}$'s final tampering query. Recall that in the model of selective partitioning, all leakage queries and the tampering query, act on the same arbitrary but fixed subsets $\mathcal{B}_1, \ldots, \mathcal{B}_t$ of a k-sized partition of the shares. Hence, when A outputs its tampering query $(f_1, \ldots, f_t)$, the reduction $\hat{A}$ defines a modified tampering query $(\hat{f}_1, \ldots, \hat{f}_t)$ that first checks whether the guessed leakage from each subset $\mathcal{B}_i$ was correct; if not, the tampering function sets[4] the modified shares within $\mathcal{B}_i$ to $\perp$, else it acts identically to f_i. This strategy ensures that our reduction either performs a correct simulation or destroys the secret. In turn, destroying the secret whenever we guessed incorrectly implies that the success probability of $\hat{A}$ is exactly that of A times the probability of guessing the leakage correctly, which is $2^{-\ell}$.

By plugging the schemes from [23, Thm. 2], [24, Thm. 6], and [14, Thm. 3], together with our refined analysis of the transformation by Ostrovsky *et al.* [30], the above insights directly imply items i and ii of Theorem 1.

Semi-adaptive Partitioning. Unfortunately, the argument for showing that one-time non-malleability implies bounded leakage resilience breaks in the setting of adaptive (or even semi-adaptive) partitioning. Intuitively, the problem is that the adversary can leak jointly from adaptively chosen partitions, and thus it is unclear how the reduction can check whether the simulated leakage was correct using a single tampering query.

Hence, we take a different approach. We directly construct a bounded leakage-resilient, statistically one-time non-malleable secret sharing scheme for general access structures. Our construction Σ combines a 2-out-of-2 non-malleable secret sharing scheme Σ_2 with two auxiliary leakage-resilient secret sharing schemes Σ_0 and Σ_1 realizing different access structures. When taking Σ_0 to be the secret sharing scheme from [26, Thm. 1], our construction achieves k-joint bounded leakage-resilient statistical one-time non-malleability under semi-adaptive partitioning for $k \in O(\sqrt{\log n})$. This implies item iii of Theorem 1. We refer the reader directly to Sect. 5 for a thorough description of our new secret sharing scheme and its security analysis.

Lower Bounds. Our complexity leveraging argument implies that every statistically one-time non-malleable secret sharing scheme against *independent* tampering with the shares is also statistically bounded leakage resilient against independent leakage (and no tampering).

By invoking a recent result of Nielsen and Simkin [29], we immediately obtain lower bounds on the share size and randomness complexity of any statistically one-time non-malleable secret sharing scheme against *independent* tampering.

---

[4] We assume that the reconstruction algorithm outputs $\perp$ whenever one of the input shares is set to $\perp$. As we will see later, this is without loss of generality.

1.3 Related Works

Non-malleable secret sharing is intimately related to non-malleable codes [19]. The difference between the two lies in the privacy property: While any non-malleable code in the split-state model [1,3,5–7,13,15–17,19,20,22,27,28,30] is also a 2-out-of-2 secret sharing [17], for any $n \geq 3$ there are n-split-state non-malleable codes that are not private.

Continuously non-malleable codes in the n-split-state model are currently known for $n = 8$ [4] (with statistical security), and for $n = 2$ [16,20,22,30] (with computational security).

Non-malleable secret sharing schemes have useful cryptographic applications, such as non-malleable message transmission [23] and continuously non-malleable threshold signatures [2,21].

1.4 Paper Organization

The rest of this paper is organized as follows. In Sect. 2, we recall a few standard definitions. In Sect. 3, we define our model of k-joint non-malleability under selective and semi-adaptive partitioning.

In Sect. 4 and Sect. 5, we describe our constructions of bounded leakage-resilient statistically one-time non-malleable secret sharing schemes under selective and semi-adaptive partitioning. The lower bounds for non-malleable secret sharing, and the compiler for achieving p-time non-malleability against joint tampering are presented in Sect. 6. Finally, in Sect. 7, we conclude the paper with a list of open problems for further research.

2 Preliminaries

2.1 Standard Notation

For a string $x \in \{0,1\}^*$, we denote its length by $|x|$; if $\mathcal{X}$ is a set, $|\mathcal{X}|$ represents the number of elements in $\mathcal{X}$. We denote by $[n]$ the set $\{1, \ldots, n\}$. For a set of indices $\mathcal{I} = (i_1, \ldots, i_t)$ and a vector $x = (x_1, \ldots, x_n)$, we write $x_{\mathcal{I}}$ to denote the vector $(x_{i_1}, \ldots, x_{i_t})$. When x is chosen randomly in $\mathcal{X}$, we write $x \leftarrow_\$ \mathcal{X}$. When A is a randomized algorithm, we write $y \leftarrow_\$ \mathsf{A}(x)$ to denote a run of A on input x (and implicit random coins r) and output y; the value y is a random variable and $\mathsf{A}(x; r)$ denotes a run of A on input x and randomness r. An algorithm A is *probabilistic polynomial-time* (PPT for short) if A is randomized and for any input $x, r \in \{0,1\}^*$, the computation of $\mathsf{A}(x; r)$ terminates in a polynomial number of steps (in the size of the input).

Negligible Functions. We denote with $\lambda \in \mathbb{N}$ the security parameter. A function p is *polynomial* (in the security parameter), denoted $p \in \mathsf{poly}(\lambda)$, if $p(\lambda) \in O(\lambda^c)$ for some constant $c > 0$. A function $\nu : \mathbb{N} \to [0,1]$ is *negligible* (in the security parameter) if it vanishes faster than the inverse of any polynomial in λ, *i.e.* $\nu(\lambda) \in O(1/p(\lambda))$ for all positive polynomials $p(\lambda)$. We often write $\nu(\lambda) \in$

$\mathsf{negl}(\lambda)$ to denote that $\nu(\lambda)$ is negligible. Unless stated otherwise, throughout the paper, we implicitly assume that the security parameter is given as input (in unary) to all algorithms.

Random Variables. For a random variable $\mathbf{X}$, we write $\mathbb{P}[\mathbf{X} = x]$ for the probability that $\mathbf{X}$ takes on a particular value $x \in \mathcal{X}$, with $\mathcal{X}$ being the set where $\mathbf{X}$ is defined. The statistical distance between two random variables $\mathbf{X}$ and $\mathbf{Y}$ over the same set $\mathcal{X}$ is defined as

$$\Delta(\mathbf{X}, \mathbf{Y}) := \frac{1}{2} \sum_{x \in \mathcal{X}} |\mathbb{P}[\mathbf{X} = x] - \mathbb{P}[\mathbf{Y} = x]|.$$

Given two ensembles $\mathbf{X} = \{\mathbf{X}_\lambda\}_{\lambda \in \mathbb{N}}$ and $\mathbf{Y} = \{\mathbf{Y}_\lambda\}_{\lambda \in \mathbb{N}}$, we write $\mathbf{X} \equiv \mathbf{Y}$ to denote that they are identically distributed, $\mathbf{X} \overset{s}{\approx} \mathbf{Y}$ to denote that they are *statistically close*, i.e. $\Delta(\mathbf{X}_\lambda, \mathbf{Y}_\lambda) \in \mathsf{negl}(\lambda)$, and $\mathbf{X} \overset{c}{\approx} \mathbf{Y}$ to denote that they are *computationally indistinguishable, i.e.* for all PPT distinguishers D:

$$|\mathbb{P}[\mathsf{D}(\mathbf{X}_\lambda) = 1] - \mathbb{P}[\mathsf{D}(\mathbf{Y}_\lambda) = 1]| \in \mathsf{negl}(\lambda).$$

Sometimes we explicitly denote by $\mathbf{X} \overset{s}{\approx}_\epsilon \mathbf{Y}$ the fact that $\Delta(\mathbf{X}_\lambda, \mathbf{Y}_\lambda) \leq \epsilon$ for a parameter $\epsilon = \epsilon(\lambda)$. We also extend the notion of computational indistinguishability to the case of interactive experiments (a.k.a. games) featuring an adversary A. In particular, let $\mathbf{G}_\mathsf{A}(\lambda)$ be the random variable corresponding to the output of A at the end of the experiment, where wlog. we may assume A outputs a decision bit. Given two experiments $\mathbf{G}_\mathsf{A}(\lambda, 0)$ and $\mathbf{G}_\mathsf{A}(\lambda, 1)$, we write $\{\mathbf{G}_\mathsf{A}(\lambda, 0)\}_{\lambda \in \mathbb{N}} \overset{c}{\approx} \{\mathbf{G}_\mathsf{A}(\lambda, 1)\}_{\lambda \in \mathbb{N}}$ as a shorthand for

$$|\mathbb{P}[\mathbf{G}_\mathsf{A}(\lambda, 0) = 1] - \mathbb{P}[\mathbf{G}_\mathsf{A}(\lambda, 1) = 1]| \in \mathsf{negl}(\lambda).$$

The above naturally generalizes to statistical distance, which we denote by $\Delta(\mathbf{G}_\mathsf{A}(\lambda, 0), \mathbf{G}_\mathsf{A}(\lambda, 1))$, in case of *unbounded* adversaries.

We recall a lemma from Dziembowski and Pietrzak [18]:

Lemma 1. *Let $\mathbf{X}$ and $\mathbf{Y}$ be two independent random variables, and $\mathcal{O}_{\mathsf{leak}}(\cdot, \cdot)$ be an oracle that upon input arbitrary functions (g_0, g_1) returns $(g_0(\mathbf{X}), g_1(\mathbf{Y}))$. Then, for any adversary A outputting $\mathbf{Z} \leftarrow_\$ \mathsf{A}^{\mathcal{O}_{\mathsf{leak}}(\cdot, \cdot)}$, it holds that the random variables $\mathbf{X}|\mathbf{Z}$ and $\mathbf{Y}|\mathbf{Z}$ are independent.*

2.2 Secret Sharing Schemes

An n-party secret sharing scheme Σ consists of polynomial-time algorithms $(\mathsf{Share}, \mathsf{Rec})$ specified as follows. The randomized sharing algorithm Share takes a message $m \in \mathcal{M}$ as input and outputs n shares $s_1, \ldots, s_n$, where each $s_i \in \mathcal{S}_i$. The deterministic algorithm Rec takes some number of shares as input and outputs a value in $\mathcal{M} \cup \{\bot\}$. We define $\mu := \log |\mathcal{M}|$ and $\sigma_i := \log |\mathcal{S}_i|$ respectively, to be the bit length of the message and of the ith share.

Which subsets of shares are authorized to reconstruct the secret and which are not is defined via an *access structure*, which is the set of all authorized subsets.

Definition 1 (Access structure). *We say that $\mathcal{A}$ is an access structure for n parties if $\mathcal{A}$ is a monotone class of subsets of $[n]$, i.e., if $\mathcal{I}_1 \in \mathcal{A}$ and $\mathcal{I}_1 \subseteq \mathcal{I}_2$, then $\mathcal{I}_2 \in \mathcal{A}$. We call authorized or qualified any set $\mathcal{I} \in \mathcal{A}$, and unauthorized or unqualified any other set. We say that an authorized set $\mathcal{I} \in \mathcal{A}$ is minimal if any proper subset of $\mathcal{I}$ is unauthorized, i.e., if $\mathcal{U} \subsetneq \mathcal{I}$, then $\mathcal{U} \notin \mathcal{A}$.*

Intuitively, a perfectly secure secret sharing scheme must be such that all qualified subsets of players can efficiently reconstruct the secret, whereas all unqualified subsets have no information (possibly in a computational sense) about the secret.

Definition 2 (Secret sharing scheme). *Let $n \in \mathbb{N}$ and $\mathcal{A}$ be an access structure for n parties. We say that $\Sigma = (\mathsf{Share}, \mathsf{Rec})$ is a secret sharing scheme realizing access structure $\mathcal{A}$ with message space $\mathcal{M}$ and share space $\mathcal{S} = \mathcal{S}_1 \times \ldots \times \mathcal{S}_n$ if it is an n-party secret sharing with the following properties.*

(i) ***Correctness:*** *For all $\lambda \in \mathbb{N}$, all messages $m \in \mathcal{M}$ and all authorized subsets $\mathcal{I} \in \mathcal{A}$, we have that $\mathsf{Rec}((\mathsf{Share}(m))_\mathcal{I}) = m$ with overwhelming probability over the randomness of the sharing algorithm.*

(ii) ***Privacy:*** *For all PPT adversaries A, all pairs of messages $m_0, m_1 \in \mathcal{M}$ and all unauthorized subsets $\mathcal{U} \notin \mathcal{A}$, we have that*

$$\{(\mathsf{Share}(1^\lambda, m_0))_\mathcal{U}\}_{\lambda \in \mathbb{N}} \stackrel{c}{\approx} \{(\mathsf{Share}(1^\lambda, m_1))_\mathcal{U}\}_{\lambda \in \mathbb{N}}.$$

If the above ensembles are statistically close (resp. identically distributed), we speak of statistical *(resp.* perfect*) privacy.*

2.3   Non-interactive Commitments

A non-interactive commitment scheme Commit is a randomized algorithm taking as input a message $m \in \mathcal{M}$ and outputting a value $c = \mathsf{Commit}(m; r)$ called commitment, using random coins $r \in \mathcal{R}$. The pair (m, r) is called the opening.

Intuitively, a secure commitment satisfies two properties called binding and hiding. The first property says that it is hard to open a commitment in two different ways. The second property says that a commitment hides the underlying message. The formal definition follows.

Definition 3 (Binding). *We say that a non-interactive commitment scheme Commit is computationally binding if for all PPT adversaries A, all messages $m \in \mathcal{M}$, and all random coins $r \in \mathcal{R}$, the following probability is negligible:*

$$\mathbb{P}\left[m' \neq m \wedge \mathsf{Commit}(m'; r') = \mathsf{Commit}(m; r) : (m', r') \leftarrow_\$ \mathsf{A}(m, r)\right].$$

If the above holds even in the case of unbounded adversaries, we say that Commit is statistically binding. Finally, if the above probability is exactly 0 for all adversaries (i.e., each commitment can be opened to at most a single message), then we say that Commit is perfectly binding.

Definition 4 (Hiding). *We say that a non-interactive commitment scheme* Commit *is computationally hiding if, for all* $m_0, m_1 \in \mathcal{M}$, *it holds that*

$$\big\{ \mathsf{Commit}(1^\lambda; m_0) \big\}_{\lambda \in \mathbb{N}} \overset{c}{\approx} \big\{ \mathsf{Commit}(1^\lambda; m_1) \big\}_{\lambda \in \mathbb{N}}.$$

In case the above ensembles are statistically close (resp. identically distributed), we say that Commit *is statistically (resp. perfectly) hiding.*

3   Our Leakage and Tampering Model

In this section we define various notions of non-malleability against joint tampering and leakage for secret sharing. Very roughly, in our model the attacker is allowed to partition the set of share holders into t (non-overlapping) blocks with size at most k, covering the entire set $[n]$. This is formalized through the notion of a k-sized partition.

Definition 5 (k-sized partition). *Let* $n, k, t \in \mathbb{N}$. *We call* $\mathcal{B} = (\mathcal{B}_1, \ldots, \mathcal{B}_t)$ *a* k-sized partition of $[n]$ when: (i) $\bigcup_{i=1}^{t} \mathcal{B}_i = [n]$; (ii) $\forall i_1, i_2 \in [t]$ such that $i_1 \neq i_2$, $\mathcal{B}_{i_1} \cap \mathcal{B}_{i_2} = \emptyset$; (iii) $\forall i \in [t]$, $|\mathcal{B}_i| \leq k$.

Let $\mathcal{B} = (\mathcal{B}_1, \ldots, \mathcal{B}_t)$ be a k-sized partition of $[n]$. To define non-malleability, we consider an adversary A interacting with a target secret sharing $s = (s_1, \ldots, s_n)$ via the following queries:

- **Leakage queries.** For each $i \in [t]$, the attacker can leak jointly from the shares $s_{\mathcal{B}_i}$. This can be done repeatedly and in an adaptive[5] fashion, as long as the total number of bits that the adversary leaks from each share does not exceed $\ell \in \mathbb{N}$.
- **Tampering queries.** For each $i \in [t]$, the attacker can tamper jointly with the shares $s_{\mathcal{B}_i}$. Each such query yields mauled shares $(\tilde{s}_1, \ldots, \tilde{s}_n)$, for which the adversary is allowed to see the corresponding reconstructed message w.r.t. a reconstruction set $\mathcal{T} \in \mathcal{A}$ of his choice. This can be done for at most $p \in \mathbb{N}$ times, and in an adaptive fashion.

Depending on the partition $\mathcal{B}$ being fixed, or chosen adaptively with each leakage/tampering query, we obtain two different flavors of non-malleability, as defined in the following subsections.

3.1   Selective Partitioning

Here, we restrict the adversary to jointly leak from and tamper with subsets of shares belonging to a fixed partition of $[n]$.

---

[5] This means that the choice of the next leakage query depends on the overall leakage so far.

Definition 6 (Selective bounded-leakage and tampering admissible adversary). *Let $n, k, t, \ell, p \in \mathbb{N}$, and fix an arbitrary message space $\mathcal{M}$, sharing space $\mathcal{S} = \mathcal{S}_1 \times \cdots \times \mathcal{S}_n$, and access structure $\mathcal{A}$ for n parties. We say that a (possibly unbounded) adversary A is selective k-joint ℓ-bounded leakage p-tampering admissible (selective (k, ℓ, p)-BLTA for short) if, for every fixed k-sized partition $(\mathcal{B}_1, \ldots, \mathcal{B}_t)$ of $[n]$, A satisfies the following conditions:*

- A *outputs a sequence of poly-many leakage queries $(g_1^{(q)}, \ldots, g_t^{(q)})$, such that for all $q \in \mathsf{poly}(\lambda)$ and all $i \in [t]$,*

$$g_i^{(q)} : \bigtimes_{j \in \mathcal{B}_i} \mathcal{S}_j \to \{0, 1\}^{\ell_i^{(q)}},$$

  where $\ell_i^{(q)}$ is the length of the output $\Lambda_i^{(q)}$ of $g_i^{(q)}$. The only restriction is that $|\Lambda| \leq \ell$, where Λ is the string containing the total leakage performed (over all queries).
- A *outputs a sequence of tampering queries $(\mathcal{T}^{(q)}, (f_1^{(q)}, \ldots, f_t^{(q)}))$, such that, for all $q \in [p]$, and for all $i \in [t]$, it holds that*

$$f_i^{(q)} : \bigtimes_{j \in \mathcal{B}_i} \mathcal{S}_j \to \bigtimes_{j \in \mathcal{B}_i} \mathcal{S}_j \qquad and \qquad \mathcal{T}^{(q)} \cap \mathcal{B}_i \neq \emptyset,$$

  and moreover $\mathcal{T}^{(q)} \in \mathcal{A}$ is a minimal authorized subset.
- *All queries performed by A are chosen adaptively, i.e. each query may depend on the information obtained from all the previous queries.*
- *If $p > 0$, the last query performed by A is a tampering query.*

Note that A can choose a different reconstruction set $\mathcal{T}^{(q)}$ with each tampering query, in a fully adaptive manner. This feature is known as *adaptive reconstruction* [21]. However, we consider the following two restrictions (that were not present in previous works): (i) Each set $\mathcal{T}^{(q)}$ must be minimal and contain at least one mauled share from each subset $\mathcal{B}_i$; (ii) The last query asked by A is a tampering query. Looking ahead, these technical conditions are needed for the complexity leveraging argument used in Theorem 3. Note that the above restrictions are still meaningful, as they allow, *e.g.*, to capture the setting in which the attacker first leaks from all the shares and then tampers with the shares in a minimal authorized subset.

3.2   Semi-adaptive Partitioning

Next, we generalize the above definition to the stronger setting in which the adversary is allowed to change the k-sized partition with each leakage and tampering query. Here, we do not consider the restriction (i) mentioned above as it is not needed for the analysis of our secret sharing scheme in Sect. 5; yet we still consider the restriction (ii), and we will need to restrict the way in which the attacker specifies the partitions corresponding to each leakage and tampering query. For this reason, we refer to our model as *semi-adaptive* partitioning.

Definition 7 (Semi-adaptive bounded-leakage and tampering admissible adversary). *Let $n, k, \ell, p \in \mathbb{N}$ and $\mathcal{M}, \mathcal{S}, \mathcal{A}$ as in Definition 6. We say that a (possibly unbounded) adversary A is semi-adaptive k-joint ℓ-bounded leakage p-tampering admissible (semi-adaptive (k, ℓ, p)-BLTA for short) if it satisfies the following conditions:*

- *A outputs a sequence of poly-many leakage queries $(\mathcal{B}^{(q)}, (g_1^{(q)}, \ldots, g_{t^{(q)}}^{(q)}))$, chosen adaptively, such that, for all $q \in \mathsf{poly}(\lambda)$, and for all $i \in [t^{(q)}]$, it holds that $\mathcal{B}^{(q)} = (\mathcal{B}_1^{(q)}, \ldots, \mathcal{B}_{t^{(q)}}^{(q)})$ is a k-sized partition of $[n]$ and*

$$g_i^{(q)} : \bigtimes_{j \in \mathcal{B}_i^{(q)}} \mathcal{S}_j \to \{0,1\}^{\ell_i^{(q)}},$$

  where $\ell_i^{(q)}$ is the length of the output. The only restriction is that $|\Lambda| \leq \ell$, where $\Lambda = (\Lambda^{(1)}, \Lambda^{(2)}, \ldots)$ is the total leakage (over all queries).
- *A outputs a sequence of p tampering queries $(\mathcal{B}^{(q)}, \mathcal{T}^{(q)}, (f_1^{(q)}, \ldots, f_t^{(q)}))$, chosen adaptively, such that, for all $q \in [p]$, and for all $i \in [t^{(q)}]$, it holds that $\mathcal{B}^{(q)}$ is a k-sized partition of $[n]$ and*

$$f_i^{(q)} : \bigtimes_{j \in \mathcal{B}_i^{(q)}} \mathcal{S}_j \to \bigtimes_{j \in \mathcal{B}_i^{(q)}} \mathcal{S}_j.$$

- *All queries performed by A are chosen adaptively, i.e. each query may depend on the information obtained from all the previous queries.*
- *If $p > 0$, the last query performed by A is a tampering query.*
- *Given a tampering query $(\mathcal{B}, \mathcal{T}, f)$, let $\mathcal{T} = \{\beta_1, \ldots, \beta_\tau\}$ for $\tau \in \mathbb{N}$. We write $\xi(i)$ for the index such that $\beta_i \in \mathcal{B}_{\xi(i)}$; namely, the i-th share used in the reconstruction is tampered by the $\xi(i)$-th tampering function. Then:*
  (i) For all leakage queries $(\mathcal{B}, g)$ and all tampering queries $(\mathcal{B}', \mathcal{T}', f')$, where $\mathcal{B} = (\mathcal{B}_1, \ldots, \mathcal{B}_t)$ and $\mathcal{B}' = (\mathcal{B}_1', \ldots, \mathcal{B}_{t'}')$, the following holds: for all indices $i \in [t]$, either there exists $j \in \mathcal{T}'$ such that $\mathcal{B}_i \subseteq \mathcal{B}_{\xi(j)}'$, or for all $j \in \mathcal{T}'$ we have $\mathcal{B}_i \cap \mathcal{B}_{\xi(j)}' = \emptyset$.
  (ii) For any pair of tampering queries $(\mathcal{B}', \mathcal{T}', f')$ and $(\mathcal{B}'', \mathcal{T}'', f'')$, where $\mathcal{B}' = \{\mathcal{B}_1', \ldots, \mathcal{B}_{t'}'\}$ and $\mathcal{B}'' = \{\mathcal{B}_1'', \ldots, \mathcal{B}_{t''}''\}$, the following holds: for all $i \in \mathcal{T}'$, either there exists $j \in \mathcal{T}''$ such that $\mathcal{B}_{\xi(i)}' \subseteq \mathcal{B}_{\xi(j)}''$, or for all $j \in \mathcal{T}''$ we have $\mathcal{B}_{\xi(i)}' \cap \mathcal{B}_{\xi(j)}'' = \emptyset$.

Intuitively, condition (i) means that whenever the attacker leaks jointly from the shares within a subset $\mathcal{B}_i$, then for any tampering query the adversary must either tamper jointly with the shares within $\mathcal{B}_i$, or do not modify those shares at all. Condition (ii) is the same translated to the partitions corresponding to different tampering queries. Looking ahead, condition (i) is needed for the proof in Sect. 5.3, whereas condition (ii) is needed for the proof in Sect. 6.2. Note that the above restrictions are still meaningful, as they allow, *e.g.*, to capture the setting

$\mathbf{JSTamper}_{\Sigma,\mathsf{A}}^{\mathcal{B},m_0,m_1}(\lambda,b)$:

$s := (s_1,\ldots,s_n) \leftarrow\!\!{\scriptstyle\$}\ \mathsf{Share}(m_b)$
$\mathsf{stop} \leftarrow \mathsf{false}$
Return $\mathsf{A}^{\mathcal{O}_{\mathsf{nmss}}(s,\mathcal{B},\cdot,\cdot),\mathcal{O}_{\mathsf{leak}}(s,\mathcal{B},\cdot)}(1^\lambda)$

$\mathbf{JATamper}_{\Sigma,\mathsf{A}}^{m_0,m_1}(\lambda,b)$:

$s := (s_1,\ldots,s_n) \leftarrow\!\!{\scriptstyle\$}\ \mathsf{Share}(m_b)$
$\mathsf{stop} \leftarrow \mathsf{false}$
Return $\mathsf{A}^{\mathcal{O}_{\mathsf{nmss}}(s,\cdot,\cdot,\cdot),\mathcal{O}_{\mathsf{leak}}(s,\cdot,\cdot)}(1^\lambda)$

Oracle $\mathcal{O}_{\mathsf{leak}}(s,\mathcal{B},(g_1,\ldots,g_t))$:

Return $g_1(s_{\mathcal{B}_1}),\ldots,g_t(s_{\mathcal{B}_t})$

Oracle $\mathcal{O}_{\mathsf{nmss}}(s,\mathcal{B},\mathcal{T},(f_1,\ldots,f_t))$:

If $\mathsf{stop} = \mathsf{true}$
    Return $\bot$
Else
    $\forall i \in [t] : \tilde{s}_{\mathcal{B}_i} := f_i(s_{\mathcal{B}_i})$
    $\tilde{s} = (\tilde{s}_1,\ldots,\tilde{s}_n)$
    $\tilde{m} = \mathsf{Rec}(\tilde{s}_{\mathcal{T}})$
    If $\tilde{m} \in \{m_0,m_1\}$
        Return $\diamond$
    If $\tilde{m} = \bot$
        Return $\bot$
        $\mathsf{stop} \leftarrow \mathsf{true}$
    Else return $\tilde{m}$

Fig. 1. Experiments defining selective (**JSTamper**) and adaptive (**JATamper**) joint leakage-resilient (continuously) non-malleable secret sharing. The oracle $\mathcal{O}_{\mathsf{nmss}}$ is implicitly parameterized by the flag stop.

in which the attacker defines two non-overlapping[6] subsets of $[n]$ and then performs joint leakage under adaptive partitioning within the first subset and joint leakage/tampering under selective partitioning within the second subset.

3.3 The Definition

Very roughly, leakage-resilient non-malleability states that no admissible adversary, as defined above, can distinguish whether it is interacting with a secret sharing of m_0 or of m_1.

Definition 8 (Leakage-resilient non-malleability). *Let $n,k,\ell,p \in \mathbb{N}$ and $\epsilon \in [0,1]$ be parameters, and $\mathcal{A}$ be an access structure for n parties. We say that $\Sigma = (\mathsf{Share},\mathsf{Rec})$ is a k-joint ℓ-bounded leakage-resilient p-time ϵ-non-malleable secret sharing scheme realizing $\mathcal{A}$, shortened (k,ℓ,p,ϵ)-BLR-NMSS, if it is an n-party secret sharing scheme realizing $\mathcal{A}$, and additionally, for all pairs of messages $m_0,m_1 \in \mathcal{M}$, we have one of the following:*

– *For all selective (k,ℓ,p)-BLTA adversaries A, and for all k-sized partitions $\mathcal{B}$ of $[n]$,*

$$\left\{\mathbf{JSTamper}_{\Sigma,\mathsf{A}}^{\mathcal{B},m_0,m_1}(\lambda,0)\right\}_{\lambda\in\mathbb{N}} \overset{\mathsf{s}}{\approx}_\epsilon \left\{\mathbf{JSTamper}_{\Sigma,\mathsf{A}}^{\mathcal{B},m_0,m_1}(\lambda,1)\right\}_{\lambda\in\mathbb{N}}. \quad (1)$$

In this case, we speak of (k,ℓ,p,ϵ)-BLR-NMSS under selective *partitioning.*
– *For all semi-adaptive (k,ℓ,p)-BLTA adversaries A,*

$$\left\{\mathbf{JATamper}_{\Sigma,\mathsf{A}}^{m_0,m_1}(\lambda,0)\right\}_{\lambda\in\mathbb{N}} \overset{\mathsf{s}}{\approx}_\epsilon \left\{\mathbf{JATamper}_{\Sigma,\mathsf{A}}^{m_0,m_1}(\lambda,1)\right\}_{\lambda\in\mathbb{N}}. \quad (2)$$

---

[6] In fact, the two subsets do not need to be fixed a priori.

In this case, we speak of (k, ℓ, p, ϵ)-BLR-NMSS under semi-adaptive partitioning.

Experiments $\mathbf{JSTamper}_{\Sigma,\mathsf{A}}^{\mathcal{B},m_0,m_1}(\lambda, b)$ *and* $\mathbf{JATamper}_{\Sigma,\mathsf{A}}^{m_0,m_1}(\lambda, b)$*, for* $b \in \{0,1\}$*, are depicted in Fig. 1.*

In case there exists $\epsilon = \epsilon(\lambda) \in \mathsf{negl}(\lambda)$ such that indistinguishability still holds computationally in the above definitions for any $p = p(\lambda) \in \mathsf{poly}(\lambda)$, and any PPT adversaries A, we call Σ bounded leakage-resilient continuously non-malleable, shortened (k, ℓ)-BLR-CNMSS, under selective/semi-adaptive partitioning.

Non-malleable Secret Sharing. When no leakage is allowed (*i.e.*, $\ell = 0$), we obtain the notion of non-malleable secret sharing as a special case. In particular, an adversary is k-joint p-time tampering admissible, shortened (k, p)-TA, if it is $(k, 0, p)$-BLTA. Furthermore, we say that Σ is a k-joint p-time ϵ-non-malleable secret sharing, shortened (k, p, ϵ)-NMSS, if Σ is a $(k, 0, p, \epsilon)$-BLR-NMSS scheme.

Leakage-Resilient Secret Sharing. When no tampering is allowed (*i.e.*, $p = 0$), we obtain the notion of leakage-resilient secret sharing as a special case. In particular, an adversary is k-joint ℓ-bounded leakage admissible, shortened (k, ℓ)-BLA, if it is $(k, \ell, 0)$-BLTA. Furthermore, we say that Σ is a k-joint ℓ-bounded ϵ-leakage-resilient secret sharing, shortened (k, ℓ, ϵ)-BLRSS, if Σ is a $(k, \ell, 0, \epsilon)$-BLR-NMSS scheme.

Finally, we denote by $\mathbf{JSLeak}_{\Sigma,\mathsf{A}}^{\mathcal{B},m_0,m_1}(\lambda, b)$ and $\mathbf{JALeak}_{\Sigma,\mathsf{A}}^{m_0,m_1}(\lambda, b)$ the experiments in Definition 8 defining leakage resilience against selective and semi-adaptive partitioning respectively. However, note that when no tampering happens the conditions (i) and (ii) of Definition 7 are irrelevant, and thus we simply speak of (k, ℓ, ϵ)-BLRSS under adaptive partitioning.

Augmented Leakage Resilience. We also define a seemingly stronger variant of leakage-resilient secret sharing, in which A is allowed to obtain the shares within a subset of the partition $\mathcal{B}$ (in the case of selective partitioning, or any unauthorized subset of at most k shares in the case of adaptive partitioning) at the end of the experiment. In particular, in the case of selective partitioning, an *augmented* admissible adversary is an attacker $\mathsf{A}^+ = (\mathsf{A}_1^+, \mathsf{A}_2^+)$ such that:

- A_1^+ is an admissible adversary in the sense of Definition 6, the only difference being that A_1^+ outputs a tuple (α, i^*), where α is an auxiliary state, and $i^* \in [t]$;
- A_2^+ takes as input α and all the shares $s_{\mathcal{B}_{i^*}}$, and outputs a decision bit.

In case of adaptive partitioning, the definition changes as follows: the adversary A_1^+ is admissible in the sense of Definition 7 and outputs an unauthorized subset $\mathcal{U} \notin \mathcal{A}$ of size at most k instead of the index i^*, and A_2^+ takes as input the shares $s_\mathcal{U}$ instead of the shares $s_{\mathcal{B}_{i^*}}$.

This flavor of security is called *augmented leakage resilience*. The theorem below, which was established by [11,26] for the case of independent leakage, shows that any joint LRSS is also an augmented LRSS at the cost of an extra bit of leakage.

Theorem 2. *Let Σ be a $(k, \ell + 1, \epsilon)$-BLRSS realizing access structure $\mathcal{A}$ under selective/adaptive partitioning. Then, Σ is an augmented (k, ℓ, ϵ)-BLRSS realizing $\mathcal{A}$ under selective/adaptive partitioning.*

Proof. By reduction to non-augmented leakage resilience. Let $\mathsf{A}^+ = (\mathsf{A}_1^+, \mathsf{A}_2^+)$ be a (k, ℓ, ϵ)-BLA adversary violating augmented leakage-resilience; we construct an adversary A breaking the non-augmented variant of leakage resilience. Fix $m_0, m_1 \in \mathcal{M}$ and a k-sized partition $\mathcal{B} = (\mathcal{B}_1, \ldots, \mathcal{B}_t)$. Attacker A works as follows.

- Run A_1^+ and, upon input a leakage query $(g_1, \ldots, g_t)$, forward the same query to the target leakage oracle and return the answer to A_1^+.
- Let (α, i^*) be the final output of A_1^+. Define the leakage function $\hat{g}_{i^*}^{\alpha, \mathsf{A}_2^+}$ which hard-wires α and a description of A_2^+, takes as input the shares $s_{\mathcal{B}_{i^*}}$ and returns the decision bit $b' \leftarrow_{\$} \mathsf{A}_2^+(\alpha, s_{\mathcal{B}_{i^*}})$.
- Forward $(\varepsilon, \ldots, \varepsilon, \hat{g}_{i^*}^{\alpha, \mathsf{A}_2^+}, \varepsilon, \ldots, \varepsilon)$ to the target leakage oracle, obtaining a bit b'.
- Output b'.

The statement follows by observing that A's simulation to A^+'s leakage queries is perfect, thus A and A^+ have the same advantage, and moreover A leaks a total of at most $\ell + 1$ bits. $\qquad\square$

4   Selective Partitioning

In this section, we construct bounded leakage-resilient, statistically one-time non-malleable secret sharing under selective partitioning. We achieve this in two steps. First, in Sect. 4.1, we prove that every statistically one-time non-malleable secret sharing is in fact bounded leakage-resilient, statistically one-time non-malleable under selective partitioning at the price of a security loss exponential in the size of the leakage. Then, in Sect. 4.2, we provide concrete instantiations using known results from the literature.

4.1   Non-malleability Implies Bounded Leakage Resilience

Theorem 3. *Let $\Sigma = (\mathsf{Share}, \mathsf{Rec})$ be a $(k, 1, \epsilon/2^\ell)$-NMSS realizing $\mathcal{A}$. Then, Σ is also a $(k, \ell, 1, \epsilon)$-BLR-NMSS realizing $\mathcal{A}$ under selective partitioning.*

Proof. By contradiction, assume that there exist a pair of messages $m_0, m_1 \in \mathcal{M}$, a k-partition $\mathcal{B} = (\mathcal{B}_1, \ldots, \mathcal{B}_t)$ of $[n]$, and a $(k, \ell, 1)$-BLTA unbounded adversary A such that

$$\left| \mathbb{P}\left[\mathbf{JSTamper}_{\Sigma, \mathsf{A}}^{\mathcal{B}, m_0, m_1}(\lambda, 0) = 1\right] - \mathbb{P}\left[\mathbf{JSTamper}_{\Sigma, \mathsf{A}}^{\mathcal{B}, m_0, m_1}(\lambda, 1) = 1\right]\right| > \epsilon.$$

Consider the following unbounded reduction $\hat{\mathsf{A}}$ trying to break $(k, 0, 1, \epsilon/2^\ell)$-non-malleability using the same partition $\mathcal{B}$, and the same messages m_0, m_1.

1. Run $A(1^\lambda)$.
2. Upon input the q-th leakage query $g^{(q)} = (g_1^{(q)}, \ldots, g_t^{(q)})$, generate a uniformly random string $\Lambda^{(q)} = (\Lambda_1^{(q)}, \ldots, \Lambda_t^{(q)})$ compatible with the range of $g^{(q)}$, and output $\Lambda^{(q)}$ to A.
3. Upon input the final tampering query $f = (f_1, \ldots, f_t)$, construct the following tampering function $\hat{f} = (\hat{f}_1, \ldots, \hat{f}_t)$:
   - The function hard-wires (a description of) all the leakage functions $g^{(q)}$, the tampering query f, and the guess on the leakage $\Lambda = \Lambda^{(1)} || \Lambda^{(2)} || \cdots$.
   - Upon input the shares $(s_j)_{j \in \mathcal{B}_i}$, the function $\hat{f}_i$ checks that the guess on the leakage was correct, i.e. $g_i^{(q)}((s_j)_{j \in \mathcal{B}_i}) = \Lambda_i^{(q)}$ for all q. If the guess was correct, compute and output $f_i((s_j)_{j \in \mathcal{B}_i})$; else, output $\bot$.
4. Send $\hat{f}$ to the tampering oracle and pass the answer $\tilde{m} \in \mathcal{M} \cup \{\diamond, \bot\}$ to A.
5. Output the same guessing bit as A.

For the analysis, we now compute the distinguishing advantage of $\hat{A}$. In particular, call $\mathbf{Miss}_b$ the event in which the guess on the leakage was wrong in experiment $\mathbf{JSTamper}_{\Sigma, A}^{\mathcal{B}, m_0, m_1}(\lambda, b)$, i.e. there exists $i \in [t]$ such that $\hat{f}_i$ outputs $\bot$ in step 3, and call $\mathbf{Hit}_b$ its complementary event. We notice that the probability of $\mathbf{Hit}_0$ is equal to the probability of $\mathbf{Hit}_1$, since the strings $\Lambda^{(q)}$ are sampled uniformly at random:

$$\mathbb{P}[\mathbf{Hit}_b] = \sum_{\Lambda \in \{0,1\}^\ell} \mathbb{P}[\mathbf{U}_\ell = \Lambda \wedge g(\mathbf{S}^b) = \Lambda] = 2^{-\ell} \sum_{\Lambda \in \{0,1\}^\ell} \mathbb{P}[g(\mathbf{S}^b) = \Lambda] = 2^{-\ell},$$

where $\mathbf{S}^b$ is the random variable corresponding to $\mathsf{Share}(m_b)$, $\mathbf{U}_\ell$ is the uniform distribution over $\{0,1\}^\ell$, and g is the concatenation of all the leakage functions. Then, we can write:

$$\left| \mathbb{P}\left[\mathbf{JSTamper}_{\Sigma, \hat{A}}^{\mathcal{B}, m_0, m_1}(\lambda, 0) = 1 \right] - \mathbb{P}\left[\mathbf{JSTamper}_{\Sigma, \hat{A}}^{\mathcal{B}, m_0, m_1}(\lambda, 1) = 1 \right] \right|$$

$$= \left| \mathbb{P}[\mathbf{Hit}_0] \, \mathbb{P}\left[\mathbf{JSTamper}_{\Sigma, \hat{A}}^{\mathcal{B}, m_0, m_1}(\lambda, 0) = 1 \middle| \mathbf{Hit}_0 \right] \right. \tag{3}$$

$$- \mathbb{P}[\mathbf{Hit}_1] \, \mathbb{P}\left[\mathbf{JSTamper}_{\Sigma, \hat{A}}^{\mathcal{B}, m_0, m_1}(\lambda, 1) = 1 \middle| \mathbf{Hit}_1 \right]$$

$$+ \mathbb{P}[\mathbf{Miss}_0] \, \mathbb{P}\left[\mathbf{JSTamper}_{\Sigma, \hat{A}}^{\mathcal{B}, m_0, m_1}(\lambda, 0) = 1 \middle| \mathbf{Miss}_0 \right]$$

$$\left. - \mathbb{P}[\mathbf{Miss}_1] \, \mathbb{P}\left[\mathbf{JSTamper}_{\Sigma, \hat{A}}^{\mathcal{B}, m_0, m_1}(\lambda, 1) = 1 \middle| \mathbf{Miss}_1 \right] \right|$$

$$= 2^{-\ell} \left| \mathbb{P}\left[\mathbf{JSTamper}_{\Sigma, \hat{A}}^{\mathcal{B}, m_0, m_1}(\lambda, 0) = 1 \middle| \mathbf{Hit}_0 \right] \right. \tag{4}$$

$$\left. - \mathbb{P}\left[\mathbf{JSTamper}_{\Sigma, \hat{A}}^{\mathcal{B}, m_0, m_1}(\lambda, 1) = 1 \middle| \mathbf{Hit}_1 \right] \right|$$

$$= 2^{-\ell} \left| \mathbb{P}\left[\mathbf{JSTamper}_{\Sigma, A}^{\mathcal{B}, m_0, m_1}(\lambda, 0) = 1 \right] \right. \tag{5}$$

$$\left. - \mathbb{P}\left[\mathbf{JSTamper}_{\Sigma, A}^{\mathcal{B}, m_0, m_1}(\lambda, 1) = 1 \right] \right| > \frac{\epsilon}{2^\ell}, \tag{6}$$

In the above derivation, Eq. (3) follows from the law of total probability, Eq. (4) comes from the fact that, when $\mathbf{Miss}$ happens, the view of A (i.e. the leakage

Λ and the output of the tampering query) is independent[7] of the target secret sharing, and thus its distinguishing advantage is zero, and Eq. (5) follows because $\mathbb{P}[\mathbf{Hit}] = 2^{-\ell}$ and moreover, when $\mathbf{Hit}$ happens, the view of A is perfectly simulated and thus $\hat{\mathsf{A}}$ has the same distinguishing advantage of A, which is at least ϵ by assumption.

Therefore, $\hat{\mathsf{A}}$ has a distinguishing advantage of at least $\epsilon/2^\ell$. Finally, note that $\hat{\mathsf{A}}$ performs no leakage and uses only one tampering query, and thus $\hat{\mathsf{A}}$ is $(k, 1)$-TA. The lemma follows.   □

4.2   Instantiations

Using known constructions of one-time non-malleable secret sharing schemes against joint tampering, we obtain the following:

Corollary 1. *For every $\lambda, \ell, n \geq 0$, and every $k, \tau \geq 0$ such that $k < \tau \leq n$, there exists a τ-out-of-n secret sharing Σ that is a $(k, \ell, 1, 2^{-\lambda})$-BLR-NMSS under selective partitioning.*

Proof. Follows by combining Theorem 3 with the secret sharing scheme[8] of [23, Thm. 4], using security parameter $\lambda' + \ell$ and choosing $\lambda \geq (\lambda' + \ell)^{\Omega(1)} - \ell$ in order to obtain

$$\epsilon = 2^\ell \cdot 2^{-(\lambda'+\ell)^{\Omega(1)}} \leq 2^{-\lambda}.$$

□

Corollary 2. *For every $\ell, n \geq 0$, any $\beta < 1$, and every $k, \tau \geq 0$ such that $k < \tau \leq n$, there exists an (n, τ)-ramp secret sharing Σ that is a $(k, \ell, 1, 2^\ell \cdot 2^{-n^{\Omega(1)}})$-BLR-NMSS under selective partitioning with binary shares.*

Proof. Follows by combining Theorem 3 with the secret sharing scheme of [14, Thm. 4.1].

5   Semi-adaptive Partitioning

As mentioned in the introduction, the proof of Theorem 3 breaks in the setting of semi-adaptive partitioning. To overcome this issue, in Sect. 5.1, we give a direct construction of a bounded leakage-resilient, one-time statistically non-malleable secret sharing (for general access structures) under semi-adaptive partitioning. We explain the main intuition behind our design in Sect. 5.2, and formally prove security in Sect. 5.3. Finally, in Sect. 5.4, we explain how to instantiate our construction using known results from the literature.

---

[7] Here is where we use the restriction that the reconstruction set $\mathcal{T}$ must be minimal and contain at least one share from each subset $\mathcal{B}_i$; otherwise, we cannot argue that the output of the tampering query is $\bot$, and thus independent of the target.

[8] The construction in [23, Thm. 4] actually only achieves security against joint tampering within a partition $\mathcal{B}$ of the reconstruction set $\mathcal{T}$ (rather than the entire set $[n]$). Accordingly, in this case we can only tolerate joint leakage from the shares within the same partition $\mathcal{B}$.

5.1   Our New Secret Sharing Scheme

Let Σ_0 be a secret sharing realizing access structure $\mathcal{A}$, let Σ_1 be a k_1-out-of-n secret sharing, and let Σ_2 be a 2-out-of-2 secret sharing. Consider the following scheme $\Sigma = (\mathsf{Share}, \mathsf{Rec})$:

- **Algorithm** Share: Upon input m, first compute $(s_0, s_1) \leftarrow_\$ \mathsf{Share}_2(m)$, $(s_{0,1}, \ldots, s_{0,n}) \leftarrow_\$ \mathsf{Share}_0(s_0)$, and $(s_{1,1}, \ldots, s_{1,n}) \leftarrow_\$ \mathsf{Share}_1(s_1)$. Then set $s_i := (s_{0,i}, s_{1,i})$ for all $i \in [n]$, and output $(s_1, \ldots, s_n)$.
- **Algorithm** Rec: Upon input $(s_i)_{i \in \mathcal{I}}$, parse $s_i = (s_{0,i}, s_{1,i})$ and $\mathcal{I} = \{i_1, \ldots, i_{|\mathcal{I}|}\}$, and define $\mathcal{I}_{|k_1} := \{i_1, \ldots, i_{k_1}\}$; compute $s_1 = \mathsf{Rec}_1((s_{1,i})_{i \in \mathcal{I}_{|k_1}})$ and $s_0 = \mathsf{Rec}_0((s_{0,i})_{i \in \mathcal{I}})$, and finally output $m' = \mathsf{Rec}_2((s_0, s_1))$.

With the above defined scheme, we achieve the following:

Theorem 4. *Let $n, k(\lambda), \ell(\lambda), \sigma_0(\lambda) \in \mathbb{N}$ and $\epsilon_0, \epsilon_1, \epsilon_2 \in [0, 1]$ be parameters, and set $k_1 := \sqrt{k}$, $\ell_0 := \ell + 1$ and $\ell_1 := \ell + n \cdot \sigma_0$. Let $\mathcal{A}$ be an arbitrary access structure for n parties, where for any $\mathcal{I} \in \mathcal{A}$ we have $|\mathcal{I}| > k_1$. Assume that:*

1. *Σ_0 is a (k, ℓ_0, ϵ_0)-BLRSS realizing $\mathcal{A}$ under adaptive partitioning, with share space such that $\log|\mathcal{S}_{0,i}| \le \sigma_0$ (for any $i \in [n]$);*
2. *Σ_1 is a $(k_1 - 1, \ell_1, \epsilon_1)$-BLRSS realizing the k_1-out-of-n threshold access structure under adaptive partitioning;*
3. *Σ_2 is a one-time ϵ_2-non-malleable 2-out-of-2 secret sharing (i.e. a $(1, 1, \epsilon_2)$-NMSS).*

Then, the above defined Σ is a $(k_1 - 1, \ell, 1, 2(\epsilon_0 + \epsilon_1) + \epsilon_2)$-BLR-NMSS realizing $\mathcal{A}$ under semi-adaptive partitioning.

5.2   Proof Overview

In order to prove Theorem 4, we first make some considerations on the tampering query $(\mathcal{T}, \mathcal{B}, f)$. In particular, we construct two disjoint sets $\mathcal{T}_0^*$ and $\mathcal{T}_1^*$ that are the union of subsets from the partition $\mathcal{B}$, in such a way that (i) $\mathcal{T}_0^* \cap \mathcal{T}$ contains at least k_1 elements (so that it can be used as a reconstruction set for Rec_1); and (ii) each subset $\mathcal{B}_i$ of the partition $\mathcal{B}$ intersects at most one of $\mathcal{T}_0^*, \mathcal{T}_1^*$ (so that both leakage and tampering queries can be computed on $\mathcal{T}_0^*$ and on $\mathcal{T}_1^*$ independently). Hence, we define four hybrid experiments as described below.

First Hybrid: In the first hybrid experiment, we change how the tampering query is answered. Namely, after the last leakage query, we replace all the left shares $(s_{0,\beta})_{\beta \in \mathcal{T}_1^*}$ with new shares $(s_{0,\beta}^*)_{\beta \in \mathcal{T}_1^*}$ that are valid shares of s_0 and consistent with the leakage obtained by the adversary and with the shares $(s_{0,\beta})_{\beta \in \mathcal{T}_0^*}$. Here, we note that due to the fact that we only consider *semi-adaptive* partitioning,[9] the shares $(s_{0,\beta})_{\beta \in \mathcal{T}_1^*}$ and $(s_{1,\beta})_{\beta \in \mathcal{T}_0^*}$ are independent

---

[9] We thank Ashutosh Kumar for pointing out to us that independence given the leakage does not necessarily hold in the case of fully adaptive (rather than semi-adaptive) partitioning.

even given the leakage. In particular, the above shares are independent before the leakage occurs, and furthermore condition (i) in Definition 7 ensures that the adversary never leaks jointly from shares in $\mathcal{T}_0^*$ and in $\mathcal{T}_1^*$. Thus, since the old and the new shares are sampled from the same distribution, this change does not affect the view of the adversary and does not modify its advantage.

Second Hybrid: In the second hybrid experiment, we change the distribution of the left shares. Namely, we discard the original ones and we replace them with left shares of some unrelated message $\hat{s}_0$, where $(\hat{s}_0, \hat{s}_1) \leftarrow_\$ \mathsf{Share}_2(0)$. In order to prove that this hybrid experiment is ϵ_0-close to the previous one, we construct an admissible reduction to leakage resilience of Σ_0, thus proving that, if some admissible adversary is able to notice the difference between the old and the new experiment with advantage more than ϵ_0, then our reduction can distinguish between a secret sharing of s_0 and a secret sharing of $\hat{s}_0$ with exactly the same advantage.

The key idea here is to forward leakage queries to the target oracle and, once the adversary outputs its tampering query, obtain all the shares in $\mathcal{T}_0^*$ from the challenger, using the augmented property ensured by Theorem 2; the reduction remains admissible because Σ_0 has security against adaptive k-partitioning and $|\mathcal{T}_0^*| \leq k$. After receiving such shares, the reduction can sample the shares $(s_{0,\beta}^*)_{\mathcal{T}_1^*}$ as in the first hybrid experiment and compute the tampering on both s_0 (using the shares in $\mathcal{T}_0^*$ and the sampled shares in $\mathcal{T}_1^*$) and s_1 (only using the shares in $\mathcal{T}_0^*$), which allows to simulate the tampering query.

Third Hybrid: In the third hybrid experiment, we change how the tampering query is answered. Similarly to the modification introduced in the first hybrid experiment, after the last leakage query, we replace all the right shares $(s_{1,\beta})_{\beta \in \mathcal{T}_0^*}$ with new shares $(s_{1,\beta}^*)_{\beta \in \mathcal{T}_0^*}$ that are valid shares of s_1 and consistent with the leakage obtained by the adversary. However, we now further require that this change does not affect the outcome of the tampering query on the left shares; in particular, if the tampering function applied to $(\hat{s}_{0,\beta}, s_{1,\beta})$ leads to $(\tilde{s}_{0,\beta}, *)$, the same tampering function applied to $(\hat{s}_{0,\beta}, s_{1,\beta}^*)$ must lead to $(\tilde{s}_{0,\beta}, *)$. This is required in order to keep consistency with the modifications introduced in the second hybrid experiment. As before, since the old and the new shares are sampled from the same distribution, this change does not modify the advantage of the adversary.

Fourth Hybrid: In the fourth hybrid experiment, we change the distribution of the right shares. Similarly to the modification introduced in the third hybrid experiment, we discard the original shares and replace them with the right shares of the previously computed unrelated message, i.e. $\hat{s}_1$. In order to prove that this hybrid experiment is ϵ_1-close to the previous one, we construct an admissible reduction to leakage resilience of Σ_1.

The key idea here is to simulate the tampering query with a leakage query that yields the result of the tampering on all the left shares $(\tilde{s}_{0,\beta})_{\beta \in \mathcal{T}^*}$, where $\mathcal{T}^* = \mathcal{T}_0^* \cup \mathcal{T}_1^*$. This is allowed because of the restriction on the shares of Σ_0 being at most σ_0 bits long, so that the total performed leakage is bounded by $\ell + n\sigma_0$. In particular, after sampling the fake shares

$(\hat{s}_{0,1}, \dots, \hat{s}_{0,n})$, forwarding the leakage queries to the target oracle and receiving the tampering query, the reduction samples the shares $(s^*_{0,\beta})_{\beta \in \mathcal{T}^*_1}$ as in the second hybrid experiment and hard-wires them, along with the shares $(\hat{s}_{0,1}, \dots, \hat{s}_{0,n})$, inside a leakage function that computes $(\tilde{s}_{0,\beta}, \tilde{s}_{1,\beta})_{\beta \in \mathcal{T}^*}$ and outputs $(\tilde{s}_{0,\beta})_{\beta \in \mathcal{T}^*}$. After receiving the mauled shares, the reduction samples the shares $(s^*_{1,\beta})_{\beta \in \mathcal{T}^*_0}$ as in the third hybrid and computes the corresponding tampered shares $(\tilde{s}_{1,\beta})_{\beta \in \mathcal{T}^*_0}$. Given the mauled shares $(\tilde{s}_{0,\beta})_{\beta \in \mathcal{T}^*}$ and $(\tilde{s}_{1,\beta})_{\beta \in \mathcal{T}^*_0}$, the reduction can then simulate the tampering query correctly.

Since the above defined hybrid experiments are all statistically close, it only remains to show that no adversary can distinguish between the last hybrid experiment with bit $b = 0$ and the same experiment with $b = 1$ with an advantage more than ϵ_2, thus proving the security of our scheme. Here, we once again construct a reduction, this time to one-time ϵ_2-non-malleability, that achieves the same advantage of an adversary distinguishing between the two experiments.

The key idea is to use s_0 to sample the shares $(s^*_{0,\beta})_{\beta \in \mathcal{T}^*_1}$ and s_1 to sample the shares $(s^*_{1,\beta})_{\beta \in \mathcal{T}^*_0}$. In particular, all the missing shares needed for the computation are the one sampled from $(\hat{s}_0, \hat{s}_1)$ and, since $\mathcal{T}^*_0 \cap \mathcal{T}^*_1 = \emptyset$, there is no overlap and the tampering can be split between two functions f_0, f_1 that hard-wire the sampled values. These two functions take as input s_0 and s_1, respectively, and can thus compute the mauled values $\tilde{s}_0$ and $\tilde{s}_1$, which in turn allows the reduction to simulate the tampering query.

5.3   Security Analysis

Before proceeding with the analysis, we introduce some useful notation. We will define a sequence of hybrid experiments $\mathbf{H}_i(\lambda, b)$ for $i \in \mathbb{N}$ and $b \in \{0, 1\}$, starting with $\mathbf{H}_0(\lambda, b)$ which is identical to the $\mathbf{JATamper}_{\Sigma, \mathsf{A}}(\lambda, b)$ experiment. Recall that, after the leakage phase, the adversary sends a single tampering query $(\mathcal{T}, \mathcal{B}, f)$.

– Let $\tau \in \mathbb{N}$ and $\mathcal{T} = \{\beta_1, \dots, \beta_\tau\}$, and write $\xi(i)$ for the index such that $\beta_i \in \mathcal{B}_{\xi(i)}$ (*i.e.*, the i-th share of the reconstruction is tampered by the $\xi(i)$-th tampering function).
– We define some subsets starting from $\mathcal{T}$. Call

$$\mathcal{T}^*_0 = \bigcup_{\beta \in \mathcal{T}_{|k_1}} \mathcal{B}_{\xi(\beta)} \qquad \text{and} \qquad \mathcal{T}_0 = \mathcal{T}^*_0 \cap \mathcal{T}.$$

Then, use the above to define

$$\mathcal{T}_1 = \mathcal{T} \setminus \mathcal{T}_0 \qquad \text{and} \qquad \mathcal{T}^*_1 = \bigcup_{\beta \in \mathcal{T}_1} \mathcal{B}_{\xi(\beta)}.$$

and let $\mathcal{T}^* = \mathcal{T}^*_0 \cup \mathcal{T}^*_1$.

Note that, with the above notation, we can write:

$$\bigcup_{\beta \in \mathcal{T}_{|k_1}} \mathcal{B}_{\xi(\beta)} = \bigcup_{\beta \in \mathcal{T}_0} \mathcal{B}_{\xi(\beta)}.$$

Moreover, $\mathcal{T}_0$ and $\mathcal{T}_1$ are defined in such a way that $|\mathcal{T}_0| \geq k_1$ and, if $\mathcal{B}_i \cap \mathcal{T} \neq \emptyset$, then either $\mathcal{B}_i \cap \mathcal{T}_0 \neq \emptyset$ or $\mathcal{B}_i \cap \mathcal{T}_1 \neq \emptyset$, but not both. In this way, we also obtain that $\mathcal{T}_0^* \cap \mathcal{T}_1^* = \emptyset$.

Finally recall that the adversary sends leakage queries $(\mathcal{B}^{(1)}, g^{(1)}), \ldots, (\mathcal{B}^{(q)}, g^{(q)})$, for $q \in \mathsf{poly}(\lambda)$, and by condition (i) in the definition of semi-adaptive admissibility (cf. Definition 7) we have that for all $\mathcal{B}^* \in \bigcup_{i \in [q]} \mathcal{B}^{(i)}$ either (1) $\exists j \in \mathcal{T} : \mathcal{B}^* \subseteq \mathcal{B}_{\xi(j)}$, or (2) $\forall j \in \mathcal{T} : \mathcal{B}^* \cap \mathcal{B}_{\xi(j)} = \emptyset$.

Hybrid 1. Let $\mathbf{H}_1(\lambda, b)$ be the same as $\mathbf{H}_0(\lambda, b)$ except for the shares of s_0 being re-sampled at the end of the leakage phase. Namely, in $\mathbf{H}_1(\lambda, b)$ we sample $(s_{0,\beta}^*)_{\beta \in \mathcal{T}_1^*}$ such that $(s_{0,\beta})_{\beta \in \mathcal{T}_0^*}, (s_{0,\beta}^*)_{\beta \in \mathcal{T}_1^*}$ are valid shares of s_0 and consistent with the leakage. Then, we answer to A's queries as follows:

- upon receiving a leakage query, use $(s_{0,1}, s_{1,1}), \ldots, (s_{0,n}, s_{1,n})$ to compute the answer;
- upon receiving the tampering query, use $(s_{0,\beta}, s_{1,\beta})_{\beta \in \mathcal{T}_0^*}, (s_{0,\beta}^*, s_{1,\beta})_{\beta \in \mathcal{T}_1^*}$ to compute the answer.

Lemma 2. *For $b \in \{0,1\}$, $\Delta(\mathbf{H}_0(\lambda, b), \mathbf{H}_1(\lambda, b)) = 0$.*

Proof. Let $(\mathbf{S}_{0,\beta})_{\beta \in \mathcal{T}_1^*}$ and $(\mathbf{S}_{0,\beta}^*)_{\beta \in \mathcal{T}_1^*}$ be the random variables for the values $(s_{0,\beta})_{\beta \in \mathcal{T}_1^*}$ and $(s_{0,\beta}^*)_{\beta \in \mathcal{T}_1^*}$ in experiments $\mathbf{H}_0$ and $\mathbf{H}_1$. More in details, the random variable $(\mathbf{S}_{0,\beta}^*)_{\beta \in \mathcal{T}_1^*}$ comes from the distribution of the shares $(s_{0,\beta})_{\beta \in \mathcal{T}_1^*}$ conditioned on the fixed values $(s_{0,\beta})_{\beta \in \mathcal{T}_0^*}$ and the overall leakage Λ. We claim that $(\mathbf{S}_{0,\beta}^*)_{\beta \in \mathcal{T}_1^*}$ and $(\mathbf{S}_{1,\beta})_{\beta \in \mathcal{T}_0^*}$ are independent conditioned on the leakage $\mathbf{\Lambda}$. This is because the random variables $(\mathbf{S}_{0,\beta})_{\beta \in \mathcal{T}_1^*}$ and $(\mathbf{S}_{1,\beta})_{\beta \in \mathcal{T}_0^*}$ are independent in isolation, and, by condition (i) in the definition of semi-adaptive admissibility, none of the leakage functions leaks simultaneously from a share in $\mathcal{T}_0^*$ and a share in $\mathcal{T}_1^*$. The latter holds as otherwise there would exist $\mathcal{B}^* \in \bigcup_{i \in [q]} \mathcal{B}^{(i)}$ such that $\mathcal{T}_1^* \cap \mathcal{B}^* \neq \emptyset$ and $\mathcal{T}_0^* \cap \mathcal{B}^* \neq \emptyset$, and therefore: (1) $\forall j \in \mathcal{T} : \mathcal{B}^* \not\subseteq \mathcal{B}_{\xi(j)}$, and (2) $\exists j \in \mathcal{T} : \mathcal{B}^* \cap \mathcal{B}_{\xi(j)} \neq \emptyset$. Finally, by Lemma 1, we can conclude that the two random variables are independent even conditioned on the leakage.

For any string $\bar{s}$, let $\mathbf{B}_0^{\bar{s}}$ and $\mathbf{B}_1^{\bar{s}}$ be, respectively, the event that $(\mathbf{S}_{0,\beta})_{\beta \in \mathcal{T}_1^*} = \bar{s}$ and $(\mathbf{S}_{0,\beta}^*)_{\beta \in \mathcal{T}_1^*} = \bar{s}$. Then:

$$\mathbb{P}\left[\mathbf{H}_0(\lambda, b) = 1\right] - \mathbb{P}\left[\mathbf{H}_1(\lambda, b) = 1\right]$$
$$= \sum_{\bar{s}} \mathbb{P}\left[\mathbf{B}_0^{\bar{s}}\right] \mathbb{P}\left[\mathbf{H}_0(\lambda, b) = 1 \big| \mathbf{B}_0^{\bar{s}}\right] - \sum_{\bar{s}} \mathbb{P}\left[\mathbf{B}_1^{\bar{s}}\right] \mathbb{P}\left[\mathbf{H}_1(\lambda, b) = 1 \big| \mathbf{B}_1^{\bar{s}}\right]$$
$$= \sum_{\bar{s}} \mathbb{P}\left[\mathbf{B}_0^{\bar{s}}\right] \left(\mathbb{P}\left[\mathbf{H}_0(\lambda, b) = 1 \big| \mathbf{B}_0^{\bar{s}}\right] - \mathbb{P}\left[\mathbf{H}_1(\lambda, b) = 1 \big| \mathbf{B}_1^{\bar{s}}\right]\right) \tag{7}$$
$$= 0, \tag{8}$$

where Eq. (7) holds because of $(\mathbf{S}^*_{0,\beta})_{\beta \in \mathcal{T}^*_1}$ is re-sampled from the distribution of the $(s_{0,\beta})_{\beta \in \mathcal{T}^*_1}$ conditioned on the measured leakage Λ and fixed $(s_{0,\beta})_{\beta \in \mathcal{T}^*_0}$ and moreover it is independent of $(s_{1,\beta})_{\beta \in \mathcal{T}^*_0}$ thus is distributed exactly as the conditional distribution of the $(\mathbf{S}_{0,\beta})_{\beta \in \mathcal{T}^*_1}$. The Eq. (8) holds because, once fixed the value of $\bar{s}$, if both $\mathbf{B}^{\bar{s}}_0$ and $\mathbf{B}^{\bar{s}}_1$ happen, then $(\mathbf{S}_{0,\beta})_{\beta \in \mathcal{T}^*_1} = \bar{s} = (\mathbf{S}^*_{0,\beta})_{\beta \in \mathcal{T}^*_1}$ and the two hybrids are the same.   □

Hybrid 2. Let $\mathbf{H}_2(\lambda, b)$ be the same as $\mathbf{H}_1(\lambda, b)$ except for the leakage being performed on fake shares of s_0. Namely, compute $(\hat{s}_0, \hat{s}_1) \leftarrow_\$ \mathsf{Share}_2(0)$, let $\hat{s}_i = (\hat{s}_{0,i}, s_{1,i})$ where $(\hat{s}_{0,1}, \ldots, \hat{s}_{0,n}) \leftarrow_\$ \mathsf{Share}_0(\hat{s}_0)$, and sample the shares $(s^*_{0,\beta})_{\beta \in \mathcal{T}^*_1}$ of $\mathbf{H}_1$ such that $(\hat{s}_{0,\beta})_{\beta \in \mathcal{T}^*_0}, (s^*_{0,\beta})_{\beta \in \mathcal{T}^*_1}$ are valid shares of s_0 and consistent with the leakage. Then:

- upon receiving a leakage query, use $(\hat{s}_{0,1}, s_{1,1}), \ldots, (\hat{s}_{0,n}, s_{1,n})$ to compute the answer;
- upon receiving the tampering query, use $(\hat{s}_{0,\beta}, s_{1,\beta})_{\beta \in \mathcal{T}^*_0}, (s^*_{0,\beta}, s_{1,\beta})_{\beta \in \mathcal{T}^*_1}$ to compute the answer.

Lemma 3. *For $b \in \{0, 1\}$, $\Delta((\mathbf{H}_1(\lambda, b), \mathbf{H}_2(\lambda, b))) \leq \epsilon_0(\lambda)$.*

Proof. By reduction to leakage resilience of Σ_0. Suppose towards contradiction that there exist $b \in \{0, 1\}$, messages m_0, m_1, and an adversary A able to tell apart $\mathbf{H}_1(\lambda, b)$ and $\mathbf{H}_2(\lambda, b)$ with advantage more than $\epsilon_0(\lambda)$. Let (s_0, s_1) and $(\hat{s}_0, \hat{s}_1)$ be, respectively, a secret sharing of m_b and of the all-zero string under Σ_2. Consider the following reduction trying to distinguish a secret sharing of s_0 and a secret sharing of $\hat{s}_0$ under Σ_0, where we call s^{target}_0 the target secret sharing in the leakage oracle.

Adversary $\hat{\mathsf{A}}^{\mathcal{O}_{\mathsf{leak}}((s^{\mathsf{target}}_{0,i})_{i \in [n]}, \cdot, \cdot)}(1^\lambda)$:
1. Sample $(s_{1,1}, \ldots, s_{1,n}) \leftarrow_\$ \mathsf{Share}_1(s_1)$ and run the experiment as in $\mathbf{H}_1$ with the adversary A; upon receiving each leakage function, hard-code into it the shares of s_1 and forward it to the leakage oracle.
2. Eventually, the adversary sends its tampering query. Obtain from the challenger the shares $(s^{\mathsf{target}}_{0,\beta})_{\beta \in \mathcal{T}^*_0}$ (using the augmented property from Theorem 2).
3. For all $\beta \in \mathcal{T}_0$, compute $(\tilde{s}_{0,j}, \tilde{s}_{1,j})_{j \in \mathcal{B}_{\xi(\beta)}} = f_{\xi(\beta)}((s^{\mathsf{target}}_{0,j}, s_{1,j})_{j \in \mathcal{B}_{\xi(\beta)}})$ and compute $\tilde{s}_1 = \mathsf{Rec}_1((\tilde{s}_{1,\beta})_{\beta \in \mathcal{T}_{|_{k_1}}})$.
4. Sample $(s^*_{0,\beta})_{\beta \in \mathcal{T}^*_1}$ as described in $\mathbf{H}_2$ and compute $\tilde{s}_0$ as follows: for all $\beta \in \mathcal{T}_1$, let $(\tilde{s}_{0,j}, \tilde{s}_{1,j})_{j \in \mathcal{B}_{\xi(\beta)}} = f_{\xi(\beta)}((s^*_{0,j}, s_{1,j})_{j \in \mathcal{B}_{\xi(\beta)}})$ and $\tilde{s}_0 = \mathsf{Rec}_0((\tilde{s}_{0,\beta})_{\beta \in \mathcal{T}})$.
5. Compute the value $\tilde{m} = \mathsf{Rec}_2(\tilde{s}_0, \tilde{s}_1)$. In case $\tilde{m} \in \{m_0, m_1\}$ return $\diamond$ to A, and else return $\tilde{m}$.
6. Output the same as A.

For the analysis, note that the reduction is perfect. In particular, the reduction perfectly simulates $\mathbf{H}_1$ when $(s^{\mathsf{target}}_{0,i})_{i \in [n]}$ is a secret sharing of s_0 and perfectly simulates $\mathbf{H}_2$ when $(s^{\mathsf{target}}_{0,i})_{i \in [n]}$ is a secret sharing of $\hat{s}_0$. Moreover, the leakage requested by A is forwarded to the leakage oracle of $\hat{A}$ and perfectly simulated by it. Finally, the reduction gets in full $(s_{0,\beta}^{\text{target}})_{\beta \in \mathcal{T}_0^*}$, which allows it to compute $\tilde{s}_1$, and computes $\tilde{s}_0$ by sampling the values $(s_{0,\beta}^*)_{\beta \in \mathcal{T}_1^*}$ as in $\mathbf{H}_1$.

Let us now analyze the admissibility of $\hat{A}$. The only leakage performed by $\hat{A}$ is the one requested by A, and augmented leakage resilience can be obtained with 1 extra bit of leakage by Theorem 2. Finally, since $|\mathcal{T}_0^*| \leq k_1(k_1 - 1) \leq k$, it follows that if A is $(k_1 - 1, \ell, 1)$-BLTA, $\hat{A}$ is $(k, \ell + 1)$-BLA.   □

Hybrid 3. Let $\mathbf{H}_3(\lambda, b)$ be the same as $\mathbf{H}_2(\lambda, b)$ except for the shares of s_1 being re-sampled at the end of the leakage phase. Namely, in $\mathbf{H}_3(\lambda, b)$ we sample $(s_{1,\beta}^*)_{\beta \in \mathcal{T}_0^*}$ such that (1) the shares $(s_{1,\beta})_{\beta \in \mathcal{T}_0^*}$ and $(s_{1,\beta}^*)_{\beta \in \mathcal{T}_0^*}$ agree with the same leakage and the same reconstructed secret s_1, and (2) for all $\beta \in \mathcal{T}_0$, applying the tampering function $f_{\xi(\beta)}$ to $(\hat{s}_{0,j}, s_{1,j}^*)_{j \in \mathcal{B}_{\xi(\beta)}}$ or to $(\hat{s}_{0,j}, s_{1,j})_{j \in \mathcal{B}_{\xi(\beta)}}$ leads to the same values $(\tilde{s}_{0,j})_{j \in \mathcal{B}_{\xi(\beta)}}$. Then, we answer to A's queries as follows:

- upon receiving a leakage query, use $(\hat{s}_{0,1}, s_{1,1}), \ldots, (\hat{s}_{0,n}, s_{1,n})$ to compute the answer;
- upon receiving the tampering query, use $(\hat{s}_{0,\beta}, s_{1,\beta}^*)_{\beta \in \mathcal{T}_0^*}, (s_{0,\beta}^*, s_{1,\beta})_{\beta \in \mathcal{T}_1^*}$ to compute the answer.

Lemma 4. *For $b \in \{0, 1\}$, $\Delta(\mathbf{H}_2(\lambda, b), \mathbf{H}_3(\lambda, b)) = 0$.*

Proof. The proof is similar to that of Lemma 2, and thus omitted.

Hybrid 4. Let $\mathbf{H}_4(\lambda, b)$ be the same as $\mathbf{H}_3(\lambda, b)$ except for the leakage being performed on fake shares of s_1. Namely, let $(\hat{s}_{1,i})_{i \in [n]} \leftarrow_{\$} \mathsf{Share}_1(\hat{s}_1)$, where $\hat{s}_1$ comes from $\mathsf{Share}_2(0)$ as in $\mathbf{H}_2$. Then:

- upon receiving a leakage query, use $(\hat{s}_{0,1}, \hat{s}_{1,1}), \ldots, (\hat{s}_{0,n}, \hat{s}_{1,n})$ to compute the answer;
- upon receiving the tampering query, use $(\hat{s}_{0,\beta}, s_{1,\beta}^*)_{\beta \in \mathcal{T}_0^*}, (s_{0,\beta}^*, \hat{s}_{1,\beta})_{\beta \in \mathcal{T}_1^*}$ to compute the answer.

Lemma 5. *For $b \in \{0, 1\}$, $\Delta(\mathbf{H}_3(\lambda, b), \mathbf{H}_4(\lambda, b)) \leq \epsilon_1(\lambda)$.*

Proof. By reduction to the leakage resilience of Σ_1. Suppose towards contradiction that there exist $b \in \{0, 1\}$, messages m_0, m_1, and an adversary A able to tell apart $\mathbf{H}_3(\lambda, b)$ and $\mathbf{H}_4(\lambda, b)$ with advantage more than $\epsilon_1(\lambda)$. Let (s_0, s_1) and $(\hat{s}_0, \hat{s}_1)$ be, respectively, a secret sharing of m_b and of the all-zero string under Σ_2. Consider the following reduction trying to distinguish a secret sharing of s_1 and a secret sharing of $\hat{s}_1$ under Σ_1, where we call s_1^{target} the target secret sharing in the leakage oracle.

Adversary $\hat{A}^{\mathcal{O}_{\text{leak}}((s_{1,i}^{\text{target}})_{i \in [n]}, \cdot, \cdot)}(1^\lambda)$:

1. Sample $(\hat{s}_{0,1}, \ldots, \hat{s}_{0,n}) \leftarrow_{\$} \mathsf{Share}_0(\hat{s}_0)$ and run the experiment as in $\mathbf{H}_3$ with the adversary A; upon receiving each leakage function, hard-code into it the shares of $\hat{s}_0$ and forward it to the leakage oracle.
2. Eventually, the adversary sends its tampering query $(\mathcal{T}, \mathcal{B}, f)$.

3. Sample $(s^*_{0,\beta})_{\beta \in T_1^*}$ as in $\mathbf{H}_2$. In particular, recall that we can sample these share as a function of just the shares $(s_{0,\beta})_{\beta \in T_0^*}$ and the leakage. Then, set

$$s'_{0,\beta} := \begin{cases} \hat{s}_{0,\beta} & \text{if } \beta \in T_0^*, \\ s^*_{0,\beta} & \text{if } \beta \in T_1^*. \end{cases}$$

Note that this is well defined since $T_0^* \cap T_1^* = \emptyset$.

4. For all $i \in [t]$, construct the leakage function g_i that, given as input $(s^{\text{target}}_{1,\beta})_{\beta \in \mathcal{B}_i}$, computes $(\tilde{s}_{0,\beta}, \tilde{s}_{1,\beta})_{\beta \in \mathcal{B}_i} = f_j((s'_{0,\beta}, s^{\text{target}}_{1,\beta})_{\beta \in \mathcal{B}_i})$ and outputs $(\tilde{s}_{0,\beta})_{\beta \in \mathcal{B}_i}$. Send $(\mathcal{B}, (g_1, \ldots, g_t))$ to the leakage oracle obtaining values $(\tilde{s}_{0,\beta})_{\beta \in T^*}$.

5. Sample the values $(s^*_{1,\beta})_{\beta \in T_0^*}$ as in $\mathbf{H}_3$ using $(\tilde{s}_{0,\beta})_{\beta \in T^*}$ and the leakage.

6. For all $j \in T_0$, compute $(\tilde{s}_{0,\beta}, \tilde{s}_{1,\beta})_{\beta \in \mathcal{B}_{\xi(j)}} = f_j((s'_{0,\beta}, s^*_{1,\beta})_{\beta \in \mathcal{B}_{\xi(j)}})$; then, compute $s_0 = \mathsf{Rec}_0((\tilde{s}_{0,\beta})_{\beta \in T})$ and $s_1 = \mathsf{Rec}_1((\tilde{s}_{1,\beta})_{\beta \in T_{|k_1}})$ and let $\tilde{m} = \mathsf{Rec}_2(s_0, s_1)$. In case $\tilde{m} \in \{m_0, m_1\}$ return $\diamond$ to A, and else return $\tilde{m}$ to A.

7. Output the same as A.

For the analysis, note that the reduction is perfect. In particular, the reduction perfectly simulates $\mathbf{H}_3$ when $(s^{\text{target}}_{1,i})_{i \in [n]}$ is a secret sharing of s_1 and perfectly simulates $\mathbf{H}_4$ when $(s^{\text{target}}_{1,i})_{i \in [n]}$ is a secret sharing of $\hat{s}_1$. Moreover, the leakage requested by the adversary A is forwarded to the leakage oracle of $\hat{\mathsf{A}}$ and perfectly simulated by it. Finally, the reduction obtains all the shares $(\tilde{s}_{0,\beta})_{\beta \in T^*}$, and thus it is able to both compute $\tilde{s}_0$ and sample the values $(s^*_{1,\beta})_{\beta \in T_0^*}$.

Let us now analyze the admissibility of $\hat{\mathsf{A}}$. The only leakage performed by $\hat{\mathsf{A}}$ is the one requested by A in step 1 plus the one needed in order to get the values $(\tilde{s}_{0,\beta})_{\beta \in T^*}$ in step 4; summing up, the overall leakage performed by $\hat{\mathsf{A}}$ is:

$$\ell + \sum_{\beta \in T^*} \log |\mathcal{S}_{0,\beta}| \le \ell + \sum_{i \in [n]} \log |\mathcal{S}_{0,i}| \le \ell + n\sigma_0,$$

where the last inequality follows by the fact that $\log |\mathcal{S}_{0,i}| \le \sigma_0$ for all $i \in [n]$. Therefore, we can conclude that $\hat{\mathsf{A}}$ is $(k_1 - 1, \ell + n\sigma_0)$-BLA.   □

Final Step. Finally, we show:

Lemma 6. $\Delta(\mathbf{H}_4(\lambda, 0), \mathbf{H}_4(\lambda, 1)) \le \epsilon_2(\lambda)$.

Proof. By reduction to non-malleability of Σ_2. Suppose by contradiction that there exist messages m_0, m_1 and an adversary A telling apart $\mathbf{H}_4(\lambda, 0)$ and $\mathbf{H}_4(\lambda, 1)$ with advantage more than $\epsilon_2(\lambda)$. Fix values $(\hat{s}_i)_{i \in [n]} = ((\hat{s}_{0,i}, \hat{s}_{1,i})_{i \in [n]})$ and (s_0, s_1) being either a (2-out-of-2) secret sharing of m_0 or of m_1. Consider the following reduction:

Adversary $\hat{\mathsf{A}}^{\mathcal{O}_{\text{nmss}}((s^{\text{target}}_0, s^{\text{target}}_1), \cdot)}(1^\lambda)$:

1. Run the experiment as in $\mathbf{H}_4$ with the adversary A; upon receiving each leakage function, answer using the values $(\hat{s}_i)_{i\in[n]}$.
2. Upon input the tampering query $(\mathcal{T}, \mathcal{B}, f)$, construct the following two tampering functions:
   - Function f_0, upon input s_0, samples $(s_{0,\beta}^*)_{\beta\in\mathcal{T}_1^*}$ as in $\mathbf{H}_2$; notice that the reduction knows all the information needed to re-sample the shares, as in particular it samples $(s_{0,\beta})_{\beta\in[n]}$ and simulates the leakage. Then, f_0 computes $(\tilde{s}_{0,j}, \tilde{s}_{1,j})_{j\in\mathcal{B}_{\xi(\beta)}} = f_{\xi(\beta)}((\hat{s}_{0,j}, \hat{s}_{1,j})_{j\in\mathcal{B}_{\xi(\beta)}})$ for all $\beta \in \mathcal{T}_0$ and $(\tilde{s}_{0,j}, \tilde{s}_{1,j})_{j\in\mathcal{B}_{\xi(\beta)}} = f_{\xi(\beta)}((s_{0,j}^*, \hat{s}_{1,j})_{j\in\mathcal{B}_{\xi(\beta)}})$ for all $\beta \in \mathcal{T}_1$ and outputs $\tilde{s}_0 = \mathsf{Rec}_0((\tilde{s}_{0,\beta})_{\beta\in\mathcal{T}})$.
   - Function f_1, upon input s_1, samples $(s_{1,\beta}^*)_{\beta\in\mathcal{T}_0^*}$ as in $\mathbf{H}_3$. Then, f_1 computes $(\tilde{s}_{0,j}, \tilde{s}_{1,j})_{j\in\mathcal{B}_{\xi(\beta)}} = f_{\xi(\beta)}((\hat{s}_{0,j}, s_{1,j}^*)_{j\in\mathcal{B}_{\xi(\beta)}})$ for all $\beta \in \mathcal{T}_0$ and outputs $\tilde{s}_1 = \mathsf{Rec}_1((\tilde{s}_{1,\beta})_{\beta\in\mathcal{T}})$.
3. Send (f_0, f_1) to the tampering oracle, receiving an answer $\tilde{m}$.
4. Return $\tilde{m}$ to A and output the same as A.

For the analysis, note that the reduction is perfect. In particular, shares $(s_{0,\beta}^*)_{\beta\in\mathcal{T}_1^*}$ and $(s_{1,\beta}^*)_{\beta\in\mathcal{T}_0^*}$ are computed using s_0 and s_1 respectively; more-over, both $\tilde{s}_0$ and $\tilde{s}_1$ are computed as in experiment $\mathbf{H}_4$ and thus the tampering query is perfectly simulated. Finally, the leakage is computed using the fake shares $(\hat{s}_i)_{i\in[n]}$ as in $\mathbf{H}_4$ and thus, once again, perfectly simulated. The lemma follows.

Proof (Theorem 4). Follows by the above lemmas and the triangular inequality:

$$\Delta(\mathbf{H}_0(\lambda, 0), \mathbf{H}_0(\lambda, 1))$$

$$\leq \sum_{b\in\{0,1\}} \sum_{i\in[4]} \Delta(\mathbf{H}_{i-1}(\lambda, b), \mathbf{H}_i(\lambda, b)) + \Delta(\mathbf{H}_4(\lambda, 0), \mathbf{H}_4(\lambda, 1))$$

$$\leq 2\left(\Delta(\mathbf{H}_1(\lambda, b), \mathbf{H}_2(\lambda, b)) + \Delta(\mathbf{H}_3(\lambda, b), \mathbf{H}_4(\lambda, b))\right) + \Delta(\mathbf{H}_4(\lambda, 0), \mathbf{H}_4(\lambda, 1))$$

$$\leq 2(\epsilon_0 + \epsilon_1) + \epsilon_2.$$

$\square$

5.4   Instantiation

Using a previous construction of bounded leakage-resilient secret sharing scheme against joint leakage under adaptive partitioning, we obtain the following:

Corollary 3. *For every $\ell, n, \lambda \geq 0$, every $k \in O(\sqrt{\log n})$, and every access structure $\mathcal{A}$ over n parties that can be described by a polynomial-size monotone span program for which authorized sets have size greater than k, there exists a $(k, \ell, 1, 2^{-\Omega(\lambda/\log(\lambda))})$-BLR-NMSS with message length $\Omega(\lambda/\log(\lambda))$ realizing $\mathcal{A}$ under semi-adaptive partitioning.*

Proof. By Theorem 4, we need to instantiate Σ_0, Σ_1, and Σ_2. Using [26, Thm. 1] and [26, Cor. 2], we can take $\epsilon_0 = \epsilon_1 = 2^{-\Omega(\lambda/\log(\lambda))}$, $k \in O(\log n)$, and thus $k_1 \in O(\sqrt{\log n})$, $\sigma_0 = \mathsf{poly}(\lambda)$ and any $\ell_0, \ell_1 > 0$. As for Σ_2, we can take the split-state non-malleable code in [27, Thm. 1.12], which achieves error $2^{-\Omega(\lambda/\log(\lambda))}$.

$\square$

6   Applications

6.1   Lower Bounds for Non-malleable Secret Sharing

Combining our result from Theorem 3 with the lower bound of Nielsen and Simkin [29], we obtain a lower bound on the share size and randomness complexity of non-malleable secret sharing schemes. In particular, we obtain the following:

Corollary 4. *Any τ-out-of-n $(1, 1, \epsilon)$-NMSS must satisfy*

$$\sigma \geq \frac{(\log(1/\epsilon) - 1)(1 - \tau/n)}{\widehat{\tau}},$$

where $\widehat{\tau}$ is the number of shares needed to reconstruct the full *vector of shares and σ is the bit-length of each share.*

Observe that $\widehat{\tau}$ is a simplified notion of entropy. If $\tau = \widehat{\tau}$, then any authorized set can reconstruct all remaining shares, meaning that those shares have no entropy left.

6.2   Bounded-Time Non-malleability

Here, we revisit the compiler from Ostrovsky *et al.* [30] in the setting of non-malleable secret sharing against joint tampering.

The basic idea is as follows. First, we commit to the message m using random coins r, thus obtaining a cryptographic commitment c. Then, we secret share the string $m\|r$ using an auxiliary secret sharing scheme Σ, thus obtaining shares $s_1, \ldots, s_n$. The final share of the i-th party is set to be $s_i^* = (c, s_i)$. Given an authorized set $\mathcal{I}$, the reconstruction first checks that all commitments in $s_{\mathcal{I}}^*$ are equal, and then uses $s_{\mathcal{I}}$ to recover $m\|r$, and verifies consistency of the commitments. If any of these checks fails, it outputs $\perp$; else, it returns m.

The original analysis by Ostrovsky *et al.* shows that if Σ is a 2-out-of-2 secret sharing that is bounded leakage-resilient, statistically one-time non-malleable, and further satisfies additional non-standard properties, then Σ^* is continuously non-malleable. In a follow up work, Brian *et al.* [11] proved that the additional properties on Σ can be avoided if one assumes that Σ satisfies a stronger form of leakage resilience known as *noisy* leakage resilience, and further extended the original analysis to any value $n \geq 2$ and for arbitrary access structures.

Both the proofs in [11, 30] are for the setting of independent tampering. The theorem below says that the same construction works also in the case of joint p-time tampering under selective/semi-adaptive partitioning as long as Σ tolerates joint bounded leakage resilience, where there is a natural trade off between the leakage bound and the number of tampering queries. The main idea behind the proof is to reduce the security of Σ^* to that of Σ, where the bounded leakage is used to simulate multiple tampering queries. The main difference with the original proof is that we need a small leakage for each tampering query, and thus the analysis only works in case the number of tampering queries is *a priori*

Let Commit be a non-interactive commitment scheme with message space $\mathcal{M}$, randomness space $\mathcal{R}$ and commitment space $\mathcal{C}$. Let $\Sigma = (\mathsf{Share}, \mathsf{Rec})$ be an auxiliary secret sharing scheme realizing access structure $\mathcal{A}$ with message space $\mathcal{M} \times \mathcal{R}$ and share space $\mathcal{S} = \mathcal{S}_1 \times \ldots \times \mathcal{S}_n$. Define the following secret sharing scheme $\Sigma^* = (\mathsf{Share}^*, \mathsf{Rec}^*)$ with message space $\mathcal{M}$ and share space $\mathcal{S}^* = \mathcal{S}_1^* \times \ldots \times \mathcal{S}_n^*$, where, for each $i \in [n]$, we have $\mathcal{S}_i^* = \mathcal{C} \times \mathcal{S}_i$

Sharing algorithm Share^*: Upon input a value $m \in \mathcal{M}$, sample random coins $r \leftarrow_\$ \mathcal{R}$ and compute $c = \mathsf{Commit}(m; r)$ and $(s_1, \ldots, s_n) \leftarrow_\$ \mathsf{Share}(m||r)$. Return the shares $s^* = (s_1^*, \ldots, s_n^*)$ where, for each $i \in [n]$, $s_i^* = (c, s_i)$.

Reconstruction algorithm Rec^*: Upon input shares $(s_i^*)_{i \in \mathcal{I}}$, parse $s_i^* = (c_i, s_i)$ for each $i \in \mathcal{I}$. Hence, proceed as follows.

1. If $\exists i_1, i_2 \in \mathcal{I}$ for which $c_{i_1} \neq c_{i_2}$, return $\perp$; else, let the input shares be $s_i^* = (c, s_i)$.
2. Run $m||r = \mathsf{Rec}((s_i)_{i \in \mathcal{I}})$; if the outcome equals $\perp$, return $\perp$.
3. If $c = \mathsf{Commit}(m; r)$, return m; else, return $\perp$.

Fig. 2. Compiler for obtaining bounded-time non-malleability against joint tampering.

bounded. Moreover, in the case of semi-adaptive partitioning, we need to make sure that the leakage performed by the reduction does not violate condition (i) in the definition of semi-adaptive admissibility (cf. Definition 7); intuitively, the latter holds thanks to the fact that the tampering queries chosen by the attacker must satisfy condition (ii) in Definition 7. We refer to the full version of the paper for the details [10].

Theorem 5. *Let $n \in \mathbb{N}$ and let $\mathcal{A}$ be an arbitrary access structure for n parties without singletons. Assume that:*

1. Commit *is a perfectly binding and computationally hiding non-interactive commitment;*
2. Σ *is a n-party k-joint ℓ-bounded leakage-resilient one-time non-malleable secret sharing scheme realizing access structure $\mathcal{A}$ against joint semi-adaptive (resp., selective) partitioning with information-theoretic security and with message space $\mathcal{M}$ such that $|\mathcal{M}| \in \omega(\log(\lambda))$.*

Then, the secret sharing scheme Σ^* described in Fig. 2 is a n-party k-joint p-time non-malleable secret sharing scheme realizing access structure $\mathcal{A}$ against joint semi-adaptive (resp., selective) partitioning with computational security, as long as $\ell = p \cdot (\gamma + n) + 1$, where $\gamma = \log |\mathcal{C}|$ is the size of a commitment.

7   Conclusions

We presented new constructions of non-malleable secret sharing schemes against joint tampering with the shares, both in the setting of selective and adaptive partitioning.

Our constructions for selective partitioning are for threshold access structures and tolerate joint tampering with maximal subsets of unauthorized parties, *i.e.*, of size equal to the privacy threshold. Our construction for adaptive partitioning is for general access structures, but tolerates joint tampering with much smaller subsets of size $k \in O(\sqrt{\log n})$ (where n is the number of parties) and under some restrictions on the way the partitions are determined by the attacker. Removing the latter limitation is an intriguing open question.

The above results hold for any *a priori* fixed bound $p > 0$ on the number of tampering queries, and under computational assumptions. We leave it as an open problem to design *continuously* non-malleable (*i.e.*, for $p = p(\lambda)$ being an arbitrary polynomial in the security parameter) secret sharing schemes tolerating joint tampering under selective/adaptive partitioning.

Another interesting question would be to improve the rate, *i.e.*, the ratio between message size and maximal size of a share, for non-malleable secret sharing against joint tampering. Note that, in the computational setting, it is always possible to boost the rate as follows: First, share the secret key $\kappa \in \{0,1\}^\lambda$ of an authenticated symmetric encryption using a secret sharing scheme with poor rate, obtaining shares $s_1, \ldots, s_n$; hence, encrypt the message m using κ, obtaining a ciphertext c, and define the final i-th share to be $s_i^* = (c, s_i)$. Such a rate-optimizing compiler was originally analyzed in the setting of non-malleable codes [1,16,19], and more recently in the setting of non-malleable secret sharing against independent tampering [21]. While this transformation may be proven secure even in the setting of joint tampering with the shares, it yields a rate asymptotically approaching one, which is still far from the optimal share size of $O(\mu/n)$ [25] (where μ is the message size).

Acknowledgments. We thank Ashutosh Kumar for clarifications on the tampering model in [23] and for pointing out an issue in a previous version of the proof of Theorem 4 (leading to the restriction of semi-adaptive partitioning).

References

1. Aggarwal, D., Agrawal, S., Gupta, D., Maji, H.K., Pandey, O., Prabhakaran, M.: Optimal computational split-state non-malleable codes. In: Kushilevitz, E., Malkin, T. (eds.) TCC 2016, Part II. LNCS, vol. 9563, pp. 393–417. Springer, Heidelberg (2016). https://doi.org/10.1007/978-3-662-49099-0_15

2. Aggarwal, D., et al.: Stronger leakage-resilient and non-malleable secret sharing schemes for general access structures. In: Boldyreva, A., Micciancio, D. (eds.) CRYPTO 2019, Part II. LNCS, vol. 11693, pp. 510–539. Springer, Cham (2019). https://doi.org/10.1007/978-3-030-26951-7_18

3. Aggarwal, D., Dodis, Y., Kazana, T., Obremski, M.: Non-malleable reductions and applications. In: Servedio, R.A., Rubinfeld, R. (eds.) 47th ACM STOC, pp. 459–468. ACM Press, June 2015

4. Aggarwal, D., Döttling, N., Nielsen, J.B., Obremski, M., Purwanto, E.: Continuous non-malleable codes in the 8-split-state model. In: Ishai, Y., Rijmen, V. (eds.) EUROCRYPT 2019, Part I. LNCS, vol. 11476, pp. 531–561. Springer, Cham (2019). https://doi.org/10.1007/978-3-030-17653-2_18

5. Aggarwal, D., Dziembowski, S., Kazana, T., Obremski, M.: Leakage-resilient non-malleable codes. In: Dodis, Y., Nielsen, J.B. (eds.) TCC 2015, Part I. LNCS, vol. 9014, pp. 398–426. Springer, Heidelberg (2015). https://doi.org/10.1007/978-3-662-46494-6_17

6. Aggarwal, D., Kazana, T., Obremski, M.: Inception makes non-malleable codes stronger. In: Kalai, Y., Reyzin, L. (eds.) TCC 2017, Part II. LNCS, vol. 10678, pp. 319–343. Springer, Cham (2017). https://doi.org/10.1007/978-3-319-70503-3_10

7. Aggarwal, D., Obremski, M.: A constant-rate non-malleable code in the split-state model. Cryptology ePrint Archive, Report 2019/1299 (2019). https://eprint.iacr.org/2019/1299

8. Badrinarayanan, S., Srinivasan, A.: Revisiting non-malleable secret sharing. In: Ishai, Y., Rijmen, V. (eds.) EUROCRYPT 2019, Part I. LNCS, vol. 11476, pp. 593–622. Springer, Cham (2019). https://doi.org/10.1007/978-3-030-17653-2_20

9. Blakley, G.R.: Safeguarding cryptographic keys. In: Proceedings of AFIPS 1979 National Computer Conference, vol. 48, pp. 313–317 (1979)

10. Brian, G., Faonio, A., Obremski, M., Simkin, M., Venturi, D.: Non-malleable secret sharing against bounded joint-tampering attacks in the plain model. Cryptology ePrint Archive, Report 2020/725 (2020). https://eprint.iacr.org/2020/725

11. Brian, G., Faonio, A., Venturi, D.: Continuously non-malleable secret sharing for general access structures. In: Hofheinz, D., Rosen, A. (eds.) TCC 2019, Part II. LNCS, vol. 11892, pp. 211–232. Springer, Cham (2019). https://doi.org/10.1007/978-3-030-36033-7_8

12. Carpentieri, M., De Santis, A., Vaccaro, U.: Size of shares and probability of cheating in threshold schemes. In: Helleseth, T. (ed.) EUROCRYPT 1993. LNCS, vol. 765, pp. 118–125. Springer, Heidelberg (1994). https://doi.org/10.1007/3-540-48285-7_10

13. Chattopadhyay, E., Goyal, V., Li, X.: Non-malleable extractors and codes, with their many tampered extensions. In: Wichs, D., Mansour, Y. (eds.) 48th ACM STOC, pp. 285–298. ACM Press, June 2016

14. Chattopadhyay, E., Li, X.: Non-malleable extractors and codes for composition of tampering, interleaved tampering and more. Cryptology ePrint Archive, Report 2018/1069 (2018). https://eprint.iacr.org/2018/1069

15. Cheraghchi, M., Guruswami, V.: Non-malleable coding against bit-wise and split-state tampering. In: Lindell, Y. (ed.) TCC 2014. LNCS, vol. 8349, pp. 440–464. Springer, Heidelberg (2014). https://doi.org/10.1007/978-3-642-54242-8_19

16. Coretti, S., Faonio, A., Venturi, D.: Rate-optimizing compilers for continuously non-malleable codes. In: Deng, R.H., Gauthier-Umaña, V., Ochoa, M., Yung, M. (eds.) ACNS 2019. LNCS, vol. 11464, pp. 3–23. Springer, Cham (2019). https://doi.org/10.1007/978-3-030-21568-2_1

17. Dziembowski, S., Kazana, T., Obremski, M.: Non-malleable codes from two-source extractors. In: Canetti, R., Garay, J.A. (eds.) CRYPTO 2013, Part II. LNCS, vol. 8043, pp. 239–257. Springer, Heidelberg (2013). https://doi.org/10.1007/978-3-642-40084-1_14

18. Dziembowski, S., Pietrzak, K.: Intrusion-resilient secret sharing. In: 48th FOCS, pp. 227–237. IEEE Computer Society Press, October 2007

19. Dziembowski, S., Pietrzak, K., Wichs, D.: Non-malleable codes. In: Yao, A.C.C. (ed.) ICS 2010, pp. 434–452. Tsinghua University Press, January 2010

20. Faonio, A., Nielsen, J.B., Simkin, M., Venturi, D.: Continuously non-malleable codes with split-state refresh. In: Preneel, B., Vercauteren, F. (eds.) ACNS 2018. LNCS, vol. 10892, pp. 121–139. Springer, Cham (2018). https://doi.org/10.1007/978-3-319-93387-0_7

21. Faonio, A., Venturi, D.: Non-malleable secret sharing in the computational setting: adaptive tampering, noisy-leakage resilience, and improved rate. In: Boldyreva, A., Micciancio, D. (eds.) CRYPTO 2019, Part II. LNCS, vol. 11693, pp. 448–479. Springer, Cham (2019). https://doi.org/10.1007/978-3-030-26951-7_16

22. Faust, S., Mukherjee, P., Nielsen, J.B., Venturi, D.: Continuous non-malleable codes. In: Lindell, Y. (ed.) TCC 2014. LNCS, vol. 8349, pp. 465–488. Springer, Heidelberg (2014). https://doi.org/10.1007/978-3-642-54242-8_20

23. Goyal, V., Kumar, A.: Non-malleable secret sharing. In: Diakonikolas, I., Kempe, D., Henzinger, M. (eds.) 50th ACM STOC, pp. 685–698. ACM Press, June 2018

24. Goyal, V., Kumar, A.: Non-malleable secret sharing for general access structures. In: Shacham, H., Boldyreva, A. (eds.) CRYPTO 2018, Part I. LNCS, vol. 10991, pp. 501–530. Springer, Cham (2018). https://doi.org/10.1007/978-3-319-96884-1_17

25. Krawczyk, H.: Secret sharing made short. In: Stinson, D.R. (ed.) CRYPTO 1993. LNCS, vol. 773, pp. 136–146. Springer, Heidelberg (1994). https://doi.org/10.1007/3-540-48329-2_12

26. Kumar, A., Meka, R., Sahai, A.: Leakage-resilient secret sharing against colluding parties. In: Zuckerman, D. (ed.) 60th FOCS, pp. 636–660. IEEE Computer Society Press, November 2019

27. Li, X.: Improved non-malleable extractors, non-malleable codes and independent source extractors. In: Hatami, H., McKenzie, P., King, V. (eds.) 49th ACM STOC, pp. 1144–1156. ACM Press, June 2017

28. Liu, F.-H., Lysyanskaya, A.: Tamper and leakage resilience in the split-state model. In: Safavi-Naini, R., Canetti, R. (eds.) CRYPTO 2012. LNCS, vol. 7417, pp. 517–532. Springer, Heidelberg (2012). https://doi.org/10.1007/978-3-642-32009-5_30

29. Nielsen, J.B., Simkin, M.: Lower bounds for leakage-resilient secret sharing. In: Canteaut, A., Ishai, Y. (eds.) EUROCRYPT 2020, Part I. LNCS, vol. 12105, pp. 556–577. Springer, Cham (2020). https://doi.org/10.1007/978-3-030-45721-1_20

30. Ostrovsky, R., Persiano, G., Venturi, D., Visconti, I.: Continuously non-malleable codes in the split-state model from minimal assumptions. In: Shacham, H., Boldyreva, A. (eds.) CRYPTO 2018, Part III. LNCS, vol. 10993, pp. 608–639. Springer, Cham (2018). https://doi.org/10.1007/978-3-319-96878-0_21

31. Rabin, T., Ben-Or, M.: Verifiable secret sharing and multiparty protocols with honest majority (extended abstract). In: 21st ACM STOC, pp. 73–85. ACM Press, May 1989

32. Shamir, A.: How to share a secret. Commun. Assoc. Comput. Mach. **22**(11), 612–613 (1979)

33. Srinivasan, A., Vasudevan, P.N.: Leakage resilient secret sharing and applications. In: Boldyreva, A., Micciancio, D. (eds.) CRYPTO 2019, Part II. LNCS, vol. 11693, pp. 480–509. Springer, Cham (2019). https://doi.org/10.1007/978-3-030-26951-7_17

Nearly Optimal Robust Secret Sharing Against Rushing Adversaries

Pasin Manurangsi[1]([⊠]), Akshayaram Srinivasan[2],
and Prashant Nalini Vasudevan[2]

[1] Google Research, Mountain View, USA
pasin@google.com
[2] University of California, Berkeley, USA
{akshayaram,prashvas}@berkeley.edu

Abstract. Robust secret sharing is a strengthening of standard secret sharing that allows the shared secret to be recovered even if some of the shares being used in the reconstruction have been adversarially modified. In this work, we study the setting where out of all the n shares, the adversary is allowed to adaptively corrupt and modify up to t shares, where $n = 2t + 1$ (Note that if the adversary is allowed to modify any more shares, then correct reconstruction would be impossible.). Further, we deal with *rushing* adversaries, meaning that the adversary is allowed to see the honest parties' shares before modifying its own shares.

It is known that when $n = 2t + 1$, to share a secret of length m bits and recover it with error less than $2^{-\lambda}$, shares of size at least $m + \lambda$ bits are needed. Recently, Bishop, Pastro, Rajaraman, and Wichs (EURO-CRYPT 2016) constructed a robust secret sharing scheme with shares of size $m + O(\lambda \cdot \text{polylog}(n, m, \lambda))$ bits that is secure in this setting against non-rushing adversaries. Later, Fehr and Yuan (EUROCRYPT 2019) constructed a scheme that is secure against rushing adversaries, but has shares of size $m + O(\lambda \cdot n^\varepsilon \cdot \text{polylog}(n, m, \lambda))$ bits for an arbitrary constant $\varepsilon > 0$. They also showed a variant of their construction with share size $m + O(\lambda \cdot \text{polylog}(n, m, \lambda))$ bits, but with super-polynomial reconstruction time.

We present a robust secret sharing scheme that is simultaneously close-to-optimal in all of these respects – it is secure against rushing adversaries, has shares of size $m + O(\lambda \log n(\log n + \log m))$ bits, and has polynomial-time sharing and reconstruction. Central to our construction is a polynomial-time algorithm for a problem on semi-random graphs that arises naturally in the paradigm of local authentication of shares used by us and in the aforementioned work.

1 Introduction

Secret sharing, first studied by Shamir [Sha79] and Blakley [Bla79], is a fundamental cryptographic primitive that allows a secret to be shared among several parties in such a way that certain authorized subsets of parties can reconstruct the secret, while unauthorized subsets learn no information about the secret

© International Association for Cryptologic Research 2020
D. Micciancio and T. Ristenpart (Eds.): CRYPTO 2020, LNCS 12172, pp. 156–185, 2020.
https://doi.org/10.1007/978-3-030-56877-1_6

from their shares. Secret sharing has widespread applications across cryptography, ranging from secure multiparty computation [GMW87,BGW88,CCD88] to threshold cryptographic systems [DF90,Fra90,DDFY94].

Typically, threshold secret sharing schemes[1] are required to satisfy two properties: *correctness*, which says that more than a certain number of parties can use their shares to reconstruct the secret, and *privacy*, which says that if there are fewer than this number of parties, then their shares together reveal nothing about the secret. A number of strengthenings of secret sharing have also been studied in the past owing to various applications, such as verifiable secret sharing [CGMA85], robust secret sharing [RB89], leakage-resilient secret sharing [BDIR18,GK18], etc. In this work, we focus on robust secret sharing.

Robust Secret Sharing. In robust secret sharing, in addition to the standard correctness and privacy properties, we require the following robustness property: even if some of the shares are adversarially modified, there is a reconstruction procedure that can recover the original secret given all the shares (among which it does not know which have been modified). In this sense, robust secret sharing is to standard threshold secret sharing as decoding from errors is to decoding from erasures in coding theory.

To be more specific, suppose a secret of length m bits is to be shared among n parties with threshold t – meaning the adversary is allowed to (adaptively) corrupt up to t of the parties. The properties we ask of a robust secret sharing scheme are:

- Correctness – given $(t + 1)$ shares, it is possible to reconstruct the secret,
- Privacy – given t shares, the secret is hidden, and,
- Robustness – even if the adversary arbitrarily modifies up to t shares belonging to the parties it corrupts, the secret should be recoverable given all n shares.

If $t < n/3$, it may be seen that Shamir secret sharing [Sha79] with threshold t satisfies the robustness requirement, owing to the error correcting properties of the Reed-Solomon code. On the other hand, if $t \geqslant n/2$, robustness is impossible as the adversary could modify a majority of the shares. In addition, it is known that for $n/3 \leqslant t < n/2$, it is not possible to achieve perfect robustness, and any construction will necessarily have a small probability of failure of reconstruction [Cev11], which we will call the *robustness error*. Further, any robust secret sharing scheme for $n = 2t + 1$ that has robustness error at most $2^{-\lambda}$ has shares of length at least $(m + \lambda)$ bits [CDV94].

In this work, we are interested in schemes that are robust in this extreme case of $n = 2t + 1$. And the quantity we are most interested in is the size of the shares as a function of the robustness error and the number of parties.

---

[1] Throughout this work, we will be concerned only with threshold secret sharing, and thus we leave out this specification hereafter.

Prior Work. There has been significant past work [RB89, CDV94, CDF01, CDF+08, CFOR12, Che15, BP16, BPRW16, HO18, FY19b] in studying and constructing robust secret sharing schemes, both in the setting where $n = 2t + 1$, and where $t < (1 - \delta)n/2$ for some constant $\delta > 0$. We discuss here only the former line of work, which is what leads up to our own, and refer the reader to the paper by Bishop et al. [BPRW16] for discussions of the rest.

The first construction of robust secret sharing was by Rabin and Ben-Or[RB89], and had a share size of $m + \tilde{O}(n\lambda)$ bits.[2] This was done by giving each party a set of $(n-1)$ keys of a message authentication code (MAC) that it could use to authenticate the shares held by each other party, and a set of $(n-1)$ MAC tags that other parties could use to authenticate its share. This was improved by Cramer, Damgard and Fehr [CDF01] to $m + \tilde{O}(n + \lambda)$ but with inefficient reconstruction, and later Cevallos et al. [CFOR12] achieved the same overhead with efficient reconstruction. The approach of the latter was to reduce the size of the authentication keys used in the MAC at the expense of a more complicated reconstruction procedure.

Recently, Bishop et al. [BPRW16] improved the overhead in the share size to $m + \tilde{O}(\lambda)$. The central idea in their work is to not authenticate each share to every other party, but instead, for each party to have d (roughly $O(\log n)$) authentication keys/tags corresponding to d other randomly chosen parties. They further showed that even though some of the keys/tags themselves could be adversarially modified, enough information can be recovered after such corruptions to reconstruct the secret. However, it was pointed out later by Fehr and Yuan [FY19b] that the proof of robustness of this scheme relies on the adversary being *non-rushing*.

Rushing Adversaries. A rushing adversary, in our context, is one that decides how to change the shares of the parties it has corrupted after seeing the honest parties' shares. In the case of interactive reconstruction (which is what is used in our construction and in prior work), in each round the parties corrupted by the adversary may wait till they see all the honest parties' messages and then decide what to send. Robustness against such adversaries becomes relevant, for instance, if the parties are conducting the reconstruction amongst themselves as happens in multiparty computation protocols.

As mentioned above, Fehr and Yuan [FY19b] noted that the proof of robustness of Bishop et al. [BPRW16] does not work if the adversary is rushing, though it is not known whether their construction is actually non-robust in this case. Fehr and Yuan then presented a construction of robust secret sharing, using the local authentication approach of Bishop et al. that was robust against rushing adversaries, but with a share size of $m + \tilde{O}(\lambda \cdot n^\varepsilon)$ for an arbitrary constant $\varepsilon > 0$. They also showed how to improve this to $m + \tilde{O}(\lambda)$ if the reconstruction procedure was allowed to run in super-polynomial time.

---

[2] Throughout the introduction, we use $\tilde{O}$ to hide polylogarithmic factors in λ, n, and m.

Our Results. We construct robust secret sharing against rushing adversaries in the setting of $n = 2t + 1$, with a share size of $m + O(\lambda \cdot \log n(\log n + \log m))$ for secrets of size m and robustness error $2^{-\lambda}$. (Note that the overhead here is only polylogarithmically larger than in the lower bound of $m + \lambda$ for share size shown in [CDV94].) Our reconstruction procedure is interactive, with two rounds of interaction, and both sharing and reconstruction are polynomial-time. Our approach is similar to those of Bishop et al. [BPRW16] and Fehr and Yuan [FY19b], though our construction is simpler than either and does not use some of the sophisticated tools used there.

1.1   Technical Overview

In this subsection, we give a high-level overview of our construction and the techniques we use. Recall that we wish to share secrets of length m among n parties, with a threshold of t (the adversary is allowed to corrupt up to t parties), with a robustness error smaller than $2^{-\lambda}$, and with $n = 2t + 1$.

Sharing and Reconstruction. We follow the local authentication paradigm used in [BPRW16,FY19b]. In this approach, each party is given authentication information about the shares of a small set of parties, which we will call its "watchlist." We will set the size of the watchlist to be roughly $O(\log n)$, thus this contributes only a polylog(n) factor to the overhead in the size of each share. This is to be contrasted with Rabin and Ben-Or's approach [RB89] where each party stores authentication information about every other party, thus leading to a linear blow-up in the overhead. We now give some more details on how we use the local authentication paradigm.

Sharing. In the sharing phase, we first compute a set of Shamir shares $(\mathsf{Sh}_1, \ldots, \mathsf{Sh}_n)$ for the given secret. Then, for each $i \in [n]$, we pick a random multiset S^i of size d (where d is roughly $O(\log n)$) from $[n] \setminus \{i\}$. S^i will be the set of parties in the watchlist of party i. For every $j \in S^i$, we pick a random MAC key $k_{i \to j}$ and compute the tag $\sigma_{i \to j}$ of the jth Shamir share Sh_j using $k_{i \to j}$. The tuple $(k_{i \to j}, \sigma_{i \to j})$ constitutes authentication information for Sh_j. The share corresponding to the ith party includes the Shamir share Sh_i, the watchlist S^i, and the authentication information $\{k_{i \to j}, \sigma_{i \to j}\}_{j \in S^i}$ of the parties in its watchlist.

There is, however, a concern about privacy as we are storing both the key $k_{i \to j}$ and the tag $\sigma_{i \to j}$ together and this might leak some information about the share Sh_j that is being authenticated. In order to deal with this issue, we use a tool called private (randomized) MAC introduced in [BPRW16]. This private MAC has the property that for any key $k_{i \to j}$, the pair $(k_{i \to j}, \sigma_{i \to j})$ does not reveal any information about Sh_j. This allows us to argue that even when the key is stored together with the tag, the privacy is still preserved.

Reconstruction. Recontruction is performed by a two-round interactive protocol that proceeds as follows.

– In the first round, the i-th party broadcasts its Shamir share Sh_i. The honest
  parties will broadcast the correct shares, whereas for the adversarial parties,
  the broadcasted shares could either be the original share or some modified
  (even empty) share. At this point, we may partition the set of parties into
  three sets – the set H of honest parties, the set P of "passive" corrupted
  parties i that are corrupted but broadcast the correct share Sh_i, and the set
  A of "active" corrupt parties that broadcast a modified share.
  At the end of the first round, all the parties can determine if the shares
  of the parties in its watchlist have been modified or not by checking if the
  corresponding MAC tag verifies under the respective key. Specifically, for
  every $j \in S^i$, such that the $\sigma_{i \to j}$ verifies, party i labels j as "good." Similarly,
  if the tag does not verify, it labels j as "bad." Thus, at the end of the first
  round, the parties can obtain the labels for each $j \in S^i$. Note that the honest
  parties will always label a party $j \in H \cup P$ as "good" and with overwhelming
  probability, will label a party in A as "bad." Furthermore, at the end of the
  first round, the adversarial parties do not learn any information about the
  watchlist of the honest parties. This will be crucially used to argue robustness.
– In the second round, each party i broadcasts S^i along with the labels it
  computed as above for each $j \in S^i$. Again, the honest parties will broadcast
  the correct information whereas the adversarial parties, including the parties
  in P, can broadcast incorrect information. In particular, an adversarial party
  might modify its watchlist, and also incorrectly accuse some honest party as
  being "bad" or label a party in A as "good."
  The action of any adversary in this protocol effectively induces a (labelled
  directed) graph on the vertex set $V = [n]$ (with a vertex representing each
  party) that is generated by the following process:

- The adversary partitions V into sets H, P, and A, where $|H| \geq t + 1$.
- For every $i \in H$, we choose a random multiset S^i of size d from $[n] \setminus \{i\}$.
  For each $j \in S^i$, we add an edge (i, j) to the graph. We label the edge (i, j)
  to be "good" if $j \in H \cup P$, and "bad" if $j \in A$.
- The outgoing edges from $P \cup A$ and their labels are generated adversarially
  after seeing the edges and labels from H.

(In the above process, we sample the watchlists S^i of honest parties *after* the
adversary has partitioned the set into H, P, A. We note that this is fine, in spite
of the fact that the watchlists are actually sampled during the sharing, since the
adversary does not learn any information about the watchlist of honest parties
at the end of the first round of the reconstruction protocol.)

Suppose we have an algorithm that on input the above graph, outputs the
set $S = H \cup P$. In this case, we are done since we can use the shares of these
parties to reconstruct the correct secret by the correctness of Shamir sharing.
We give an algorithm that finds an S that has a large intersection with $H \cup P$
and a small intersection with A. With such an S, we can use the error correction
properties of Shamir secret sharing (a.k.a. Reed-Solomon codes) to recover the
correct secret.

We next briefly describe how the above graph algorithm works.

Vertex Identification Algorithm. Our vertex identification algorithm cru-cially uses the connection between the problem at hand and the *independent set* problem. Recall that a subset of vertices in an *undirected graph* is said to be an independent set if there is no edge between any pair of vertices in the set. While our graph G is a directed graph, there is a natural way to view it as an undi-rected graph: by simply keeping each edge with a "bad" label as an undirected edge and discarding all edges with "good" labels. It is not hard to show that a maximum independent set in this undirected version of G would give the desired set S.

Unfortunately, computing the maximum independent set is NP-hard in the worst case [Kar72]. On the other hand, our graph is not a worst case graph since all edges from H are random, although the edges from $A \cup P$ are worst case (i.e., adversarially generated). Finding independent sets in such "semi-random" graphs has long been a topic of study in literature, starting with the work of Feige and Kilian [FK01] (see also [FK00, CSV17, MMT18]). Unfortunately, these works do not apply to our scenario because of the following two reasons. First, the guarantees from this line of work do not suffice for us; a typical guarantee there is that an independent set found has a large size relative to the maximum independent set, whereas we need the fact that the independent set has a large intersection with $H \cup P$ and a small intersection with A. Second, the distribution of our graph is unlike those considered in [FK01, FK00, CSV17, MMT18]. Specif-ically, the distributions considered in literature are often the following: pick a set I of vertices (i.e., the "planted independent set") and add random edges between I and the remaining vertices. Then, the adversary is allowed to add arbitrary edges that are not within I. However, this is not the case for us since the edges from P to H are not random.

Despite the challenges mentioned in the previous paragraph, several things go in our favor. First, our directed graph G actually contains more information than its undirected variant considered in the previous paragraph. For instance, if we have two vertices u_1, u_2 each having a directed edge pointing to v but with different labels, then we know that either u_1 or u_2 must be corrupted. Such information is not included when we just consider finding an independent set in the trivial undirected version of G. This motivates us to look instead to what we call the *conflict graph* G^{conf}, where we add an edge between every pair of vertices u_1, u_2 that label a common neighbor differently. Clearly, H remains an independent set in G^{conf}. Moreover, from the definition of G^{conf}, any independent set I of G^{conf} has a "consistent opinion" on all vertices in the following sense: every vertex v is labelled with the same label by all its in-neighbors that lie in I. This leads us to the overall structure of our algorithm: (1) find a large independent set I in G^{conf} and (2) output the set of all vertices labelled "good" by (at least one vertex in) I.

Of course, we have not yet specified how we find a large independent set I in G^{conf}. This is indeed where a second advantage of our scenario comes in: we are guaranteed to have an independent set H of size more than half of the graph, unlike previous works that place weaker assumptions on the size of the "planted" independent set. It turns out that this $1/2$ threshold makes the problem "easier." For instance, Nemhauser and Trotter [NT74] show that any extremal solution to the linear program (LP) relaxation of the independent set problem is half integral (i.e., every variable is assigned either 0, $1/2$, or 1), which means that at least one vertex in H is assigned 1 in the solution. In our proof, we use a more specific structural lemma from [ACF+04] (Lemma 3) together with the expansion property of the random part of our graph (Lemma 4) to argue that, if we let I be the set of all vertices assigned 1 by the LP solution, then it contains sufficiently many vertices from H. This in turn implies that I labels most of the vertices in $H \cup P$ as "good" and most of those in A as "bad." A more quantitative version of this argument shows that the output set satisfies the desired properties.

1.2   Comparison with Prior Work

As mentioned earlier, our construction follows the paradigm of local authentication of shares introduced by Bishop et al. [BPRW16] and used also by Fehr and Yuan [FY19b]. There are a number of similarities and differences between how we proceed in this paradigm and how these papers do, and we briefly explain these below.

Bishop et al. [BPRW16]. The authors here use local authentication of shares to reduce the robust reconstruction to a graph theoretic problem called graph bisection, which when solved gives a set S of trustworthy parties whose shares are used to reconstruct the secret.

   Their reduction also involves partitioning the corrupted parties into a set P of "passive" corruptions and a set A of "active" corruptions according to whether a certain part of the shares are reported correctly during reconstruction. But their notion of passive corruption is stronger than the one we use here – they also require that parties in P never falsely label a party in H as being "bad." This required them to store the authentication information in a distributed manner, using a primitive they call robust distributed storage. Additionally, they had to authenticate not only the Shamir shares (as we do), but also the MAC keys themselves. As pointed out by Fehr and Yuan [FY19b], authenticating the keys in this way is what causes their proof of robustness to not include rushing adversaries. In the end, the set S that is the solution to the graph bisection problem instance generated by this reduction is the set $H \cup P$.

   We use a weaker notion of passive corruptions, where parties in P are allowed to label parties in H as "bad." This allows us leave out the distributed storage and the authentication of the MAC keys, enabling proofs of security against rushing adversaries. And solving the graph problem that we reduce to does not require recovering the entire set $H \cup P$, but only a set S that has a large intersection with $H \cup P$ and a small intersection with A. Such a set is easier to find, which is what lets us relax the definition of passive corruptions, and is still sufficient to recover the shared secret due to the error correction properties of Shamir sharing.

Fehr and Yuan [FY19b]. The approach of Fehr and Yuan is more similar to ours. They also partition the parties into sets H, P and A, and their definitions for these sets are the same as ours. However, they still use robust distributed storage to store authentication information. Our construction is simpler, using only private MACs, which both of these papers also use.

Their approach is also to recover a set S of vertices that has a large intersection with $H \cup P$ and a small intersection with A, and then use the error correction properties of Shamir sharing to recover the secret. Further, similarly to us, they do this by reducing robust reconstruction to the vertex identification problem in the model of random graphs that comes up in our work.

But their algorithm to solve this problem over n vertices with out-degree d only works when the number of passive parties ($|P|$) is at most roughly $n \cdot (\log d / \log n)^2$. And so, when they find that $|P|$ is more than this and their algorithm fails, they fall back to list-decoding of all the shares together to recover a list of possible sharings and then iterate over this list to find the actual secret. The size of this list is roughly $(\log n / \log d)^{\tilde{O}((\log n / \log d)^2)}$, leading to the restriction of $d \geqslant n^\varepsilon$ for some constant ε for the list-decoding to run in polynomial-time.

Our algorithm, on the other hand, solves the same graph problem without any such restriction on $|P|$. To be more precise, it first solves the problem when $|P|$ is at most roughly $0.84 \cdot n$, and then observes that if $|P|$ is more than this, then $S = [n]$ is already a solution. As $|P|$ can be efficiently estimated from the graph, this solves the problem. This releases us from their restriction on d, which we can set to be $O(\log n)$, leading to our shares being significantly smaller.

1.3   Concurrent Work

In concurrent and independent work, Fehr and Yuan [FY19a] also give a construction of a robust secret sharing scheme secure against rushing adversaries in the setting of $n = 2t + 1$ with near-optimal parameters. Their construction has shares of size $m + O(\lambda \cdot \log^3 n(\log n + \log m))$ for secrets of size m and robustness error $2^{-\lambda}$, and polynomial-time sharing and reconstruction, where the latter involves five rounds of interaction. We obtain the slightly better share size of $m + O(\lambda \cdot \log n(\log n + \log m))$, and our reconstruction procedure has two rounds of interaction.

In terms of techniques, while both papers have as their starting point the ideas underlying the construction in [FY19b], the papers differ significantly in how they proceed from there. Our improvements come from designing a better algorithm for the vertex identification problem described in Sect. 1.2. [FY19a] use the same algorithm for this problem that [FY19b] did, and develop new techniques to deal with the case where the algorithm fails. Specifically, they add additional instances of the consistency graph that are revealed over the course of the reconstruction, and use this information to do better list-decoding, thus eliminating the restrictions described above that the construction in [FY19b] was subject to.

Outline of paper. In Sect. 2, we define robust secret sharing and private MACs, and state some known facts and theorems that will be useful later. In Sect. 3, we present our vertex identification algorithm that will be used in our reconstruction procedure. For readers who are only interested in our cryptographic constructions, we suggest to look at Theorem 3 in Sect. 3 and skip to Sect. 4, where we present our robust secret sharing scheme.

2   Preliminaries

Notation. We use capital letters to denote distributions and their support, and corresponding lowercase letters to denote a sample from the same. Let $[n]$ denote the set $\{1, 2, \ldots, n\}$ and U_r denote the uniform distribution over $\{0,1\}^r$. For a finite set S, we denote $x \xleftarrow{\$} S$ as sampling x uniformly at random from the set S. For any $i \in [n]$, let x_i denote the symbol at the i-th co-ordinate of x, and for any $T \subseteq [n]$, let $x_T \in \{0,1\}^{|T|}$ denote the projection of x to the co-ordinates indexed by T. We write $\circ$ to denote concatenation.

Multisets. Let S be a multiset and for any element a, we define the multiplicity $m_a(S)$ to be the number of times a occurs in the multiset S. For any two multisets S_1, S_2, we define $S_1 \| S_2$ to be the multiset such that for any element a, $m_a(S_1 \| S_2) = m_a(S_1) + m_a(S_2)$.

We assume the reader's familiarity with the definition of statistical distance.

2.1   Private MAC

In this subsection, we recall the definition of a private message authentication code (MAC) used by Bishop et al. [BPRW16] and Fehr and Yuan [FY19b], but using different terminology. A private MAC for message space $\{0,1\}^\eta$ for some $\eta \in \mathbb{N}$ consists of the following algorithms, all of them running in time $\text{poly}(\eta)$.

- KeyGen : A randomized algorithm that outputs a key k.
- Tag$(k, (m,r))$: A deterministic algorithm that takes a key k, a "message tuple" $(m,r) \in \{0,1\}^\eta \times \{0,1\}^\kappa$ for some $\kappa \in \mathbb{N}$ (called the randomness length), and outputs a tag σ.
- Verify$(k, (m,r), \sigma)$: A deterministic algorithm that takes a key k, a message tuple (m,r), and a tag σ, and outputs 1 or 0.

Definition 1. *For an $\eta, \ell \in \mathbb{N}$ and $\epsilon \in [0,1]$, a triple of algorithms* (KeyGen, Tag, Verify) *is an (ℓ, ϵ)-private MAC for a message space $\{0,1\}^\eta$ if the following properties are satisfied for some $\kappa \in \mathbb{N}$.*

- **Correctness.** *For every message tuple* $(m,r) \in \{0,1\}^\eta \times \{0,1\}^\kappa$, *with* $k \leftarrow$ KeyGen, *and* $\sigma \leftarrow$ Tag$(k, (m,r))$,

$$\Pr[\text{Verify}(k, (m,r), \sigma) = 1] = 1$$

– **Unforgeability.** *For any message tuple* $(m,r) \in \{0,1\}^\eta \times \{0,1\}^\kappa$, *and any adversary* $\mathcal{A}$, *with* $k \leftarrow \mathsf{KeyGen}$, $\sigma \leftarrow \mathsf{Tag}(k,(m,r))$, *and* $(m',r',\sigma') \leftarrow \mathcal{A}(m,r,\sigma)$,

$$\Pr[(m,r) \neq (m',r') \wedge \mathsf{Verify}(k,(m',r'),\sigma') = 1] \leqslant \epsilon.$$

– **Privacy.** *For every* $m_0, m_1 \in \{0,1\}^\eta$, *any arbitrary set of* ℓ *keys* $\{k_1, \ldots, k_\ell\}$, *and any adversary* $\mathcal{A}$, *with* $k \leftarrow \mathsf{KeyGen}$, $r \leftarrow \{0,1\}^\kappa$, *and* $\sigma_i^b \leftarrow \mathsf{Tag}(k_i, (m_b, r))$ *for* $i \in [\ell]$ *and* $b \in \{0,1\}$,

$$\Pr[\mathcal{A}(\sigma_1^0, \sigma_2^0, \ldots, \sigma_\ell^0) = 1] = \Pr[\mathcal{A}(\sigma_1^1, \sigma_2^1, \ldots, \sigma_\ell^1) = 1]$$

– **Uniformity.** *There is an* $s \in \mathbb{N}$ *such that for every* $(m,r) \in \{0,1\}^\eta \times \{0,1\}^\kappa$, *with* $k \leftarrow \mathsf{KeyGen}$, *the distribution of* $\sigma \leftarrow \mathsf{Tag}(k,(m,r))$ *is uniform over* $\{0,1\}^s$.

The following theorem follows from the construction of a private MAC presented in [BPRW16], using $\mathrm{GF}[2^\lambda]$ as the field there.

Theorem 1 ([BPRW16]). *For any* $\eta, \ell \in \mathbb{N}$ *and* $\varepsilon \in [0,1]$, *there exists an* (ℓ, ε)-*private MAC for message space* $\{0,1\}^\eta$, *with randomness length* $\ell\lambda$, *key length* 2λ *and tag length* λ, *where* $\lambda = \lceil \log((\eta + \ell)/\varepsilon) \rceil$.

2.2 Secret Sharing Scheme

We start with the definition of the sharing function and then give the definition of a threshold secret sharing scheme.

Definition 2 (Sharing Function [Bei11]). *Let* $[n] = \{1, 2, \ldots, n\}$ *be a set of identities of* n *parties. Let* $\mathcal{M}$ *be the domain of secrets. A sharing function* Share *is a randomized mapping from* $\mathcal{M}$ *to* $\mathcal{S}_1 \times \mathcal{S}_2 \times \ldots \times \mathcal{S}_n$, *where* $\mathcal{S}_i$ *is called the domain of shares of party with identity* i. *A dealer distributes a secret* $m \in \mathcal{M}$ *by computing the vector* $\mathsf{Share}(m) = (\mathsf{S}_1, \ldots, \mathsf{S}_n)$, *and privately communicating each share* S_i *to the party* i. *For a set* $T \subseteq [n]$, *we denote* $\mathsf{Share}(m)_T$ *to be a restriction of* $\mathsf{Share}(m)$ *to its* T *entries.*

Definition 3 ($(t, n, \epsilon_c, \epsilon_s)$-Secret Sharing Scheme). *Let* $\mathcal{M}$ *be a finite set of secrets, where* $|\mathcal{M}| \geqslant 2$. *Let* $\epsilon_c, \epsilon_s \in [0,1]$, $t, n \in \mathbb{N}$ *such that* $t \leqslant n$, *and* $[n] = \{1, 2, \ldots, n\}$ *be a set of identities (indices) of* n *parties. A sharing function* Share *with domain of secrets* $\mathcal{M}$ *is a* $(t, n, \epsilon_c, \epsilon_s)$-*secret sharing scheme if the following two properties hold :*

– **Correctness:** *The secret can be reconstructed by any* t-*out-of-*n *parties. That is, for any set* $T \subseteq [n]$ *such that* $|T| \geqslant t$, *there exists a deterministic, interactive reconstruction protocol* Rec *between the parties in* T *with the input of* $i \in T$ *being* $\mathsf{Share}(m)_i$ *such that for every* $m \in \mathcal{M}$,

$$\Pr[\mathsf{Rec}(\mathsf{Share}(m)_T) = m] = 1 - \epsilon_c$$

where the probability is over the randomness of the Share *function. We will slightly abuse the notation and denote* Rec *as the reconstruction protocol that takes in* T *and* $\mathsf{Share}(m)_T$ *where* T *is of size at least* t *and outputs the secret.*

– **Statistical Privacy:** *Any collusion of less than t parties should have "almost" no information about the underlying secret. More formally, for any unauthorized set $U \subseteq [n]$ such that $|U| < t$, and for every pair of secrets $m_0, m_1 \in M$, for any distinguisher D with output in $\{0,1\}$, the following holds :*

$$|\Pr[D(\mathsf{Share}(m_0)_U) = 1] - \Pr[D(\mathsf{Share}(m_1)_U) = 1]| \leqslant \epsilon_s$$

We define the rate of the secret sharing scheme as

$$\lim_{|m| \to \infty} \frac{|m|}{\max_{i \in [n]} |\mathsf{Share}(m)_i|}$$

Remark 1. The above definition of privacy considers a weaker notion where the unauthorized set U is specified upfront. We can also consider a stronger variant where the adversary adaptively specifies this set U one party at a time, seeing the share of each party as it is specified. We note that for the case of perfect privacy (i.e., $\epsilon_s = 0$), the above two variants are equivalent.

2.3   Robust Secret Sharing

We now give the definition of robust secret sharing scheme.

Definition 4. *Let $\epsilon_c, \epsilon_s, \delta \in [0,1]$, $t, n, \kappa, \tau \in \mathbb{N}$ such that $t \leqslant n$, and $\tau \leqslant \kappa \leqslant n$. An $(t, n, \epsilon_c, \epsilon_s)$ secret sharing scheme $(\mathsf{Share}, \mathsf{Rec})$ for message space $\mathcal{M}$ is said to be (δ, κ, τ)-robust if for every interactive adversary $\mathcal{A}$ and message $m \in \mathcal{M}$,*

$$\Pr[\mathsf{Expt}_{\mathcal{A}, m, \kappa, \tau} = 1] \leqslant \delta$$

where $\mathsf{Expt}_{\mathcal{A}, m, \kappa, \tau}$ is defined below.

– *$(\mathsf{share}_1, \ldots, \mathsf{share}_n) \leftarrow \mathsf{Share}(m)$.*
– *$\mathcal{A}$ outputs a set $\Gamma \subseteq [n]$ such that $|\Gamma| = \kappa$.*
– *Set $T = \emptyset$. Repeat until $|T| = \tau$:*
   • *$\mathcal{A}$ chooses $i \in \Gamma \setminus T$.*
   • *Update $T = T \cup \{i\}$ and give share_i to $\mathcal{A}$.*
– *Run the reconstruction protocol among the parties in Γ with every party $i \in \Gamma \setminus T$ behaving honestly using its share share_i and the adversary $\mathcal{A}$ taking control the parties in T. $\mathcal{A}$ is allowed to behave maliciously (possibly using a different share) and can deviate arbitrarily from the specification of the reconstruction protocol. Here, we assume that in every round of the reconstruction protocol, $\mathcal{A}$ can send its outgoing messages after seeing all its incoming messages from the honest parties (a.k.a. rushing adversary). For every $i \in \Gamma \setminus T$, let m'_i be the output of the i-th party at the end of the reconstruction algorithm.*
– *Output 1 if and only if there exists an $i \in \Gamma \setminus T$ such that $m \neq m'_i$.*

We call $\log(1/\epsilon_s)$ as the privacy parameter and $\log(1/\delta)$ as the robustness parameter.

Fact 2. *Fix $t \in \mathbb{N}$, $n, \kappa \geqslant t$. There is a robust reconstruction protocol such that Shamir secret sharing is a $(t, n, 0, 0)$ secret sharing scheme that is $(0, \kappa, \lfloor (\kappa - t)/2 \rfloor)$-robust.*

3   Vertex Identification Algorithm

In this section, we give a polynomial time graph algorithm that we call the vertex identification algorithm, which will be used as a building block in the construction of robust secret sharing. We start with the description of the model of semi-random graphs the algorithm works for.

Model. Our (directed) graph[3] G where $|V| = n$ and a labeling $L : E_G \rightarrow$ $\{\text{good}, \text{bad}\}$ is generated as follows:

- First, the adversary partitions V into three parts H, P, A such that $|H| \geqslant \frac{n+1}{2}$.
- For every $u \in H$ and every $i \in \{1, \ldots, d\}$, select a vertex $v_i \in (V \setminus \{u\})$ uniformly at random and add an edge (u, v_i) to the graph. The label for $L(u, v_i)$ of the edge is "good" if v_i lies in $H \cup P$, and is "bad" if $v_i \in A$.
- The outgoing edges of $A \cup P$ and their labels are generated by the adversary after seeing the edges and the labels from H.

For notational convenience, we will always think of each vertex $v \in V$ as having a self-loop with label $L(v, v) = \text{good}$. Our main theorem in this section is the following:

Theorem 3. *There is a polynomial-time (deterministic) algorithm* VertexID *that, given G, L generated as above with $d \geqslant C \log n$, outputs a set $S \subseteq V$ that satisfies*

$$|S \cap (H \cup P)| \geqslant \frac{n+1}{2} + 2 \cdot |S \cap A| \qquad (1)$$

with probability $1 - O(e^{-\beta d})$, where $C > 1$ and $\beta > 0$ are some constants.

The Algorithm. Our algorithm relies on the linear programming (LP) relaxation of the Independent Set problem. To state the LP relaxation for Independent Set, let first recall that we may reformulate Independent Set on an undirected graph $F = (V, E_F)$ as the following *integer* program (IP):

$$\max \sum_{v \in V} x_v$$

$$\text{subject to } x_v \in \{0, 1\} \qquad \qquad \forall v \in V$$

$$x_u + x_v \leqslant 1 \qquad \qquad \forall \{u, v\} \in E_F$$

Notice that a solution $(x_v)_{v \in V}$ to the above IP corresponds to an independent set $\{v \in V \mid x_v = 1\}$. Since solving the above IP is equivalent to finding the maximum indepent set of the graph F, the problem remains NP-hard. As a result, we have to resort to the LP relaxation of the above IP where the condition $x_v \in \{0, 1\}$ is relaxed to $0 \leqslant x_v \leqslant 1$.

---

[3] We note that our graph allows multi-edges and self-loops.

More specifically, the LP relaxation of Independent Set for an undirected graph $F = (V, E_F)$ can be stated as:

$$\max \sum_{v \in V} x_v \tag{2}$$

$$\text{subject to } 0 \leqslant x_v \leqslant 1 \qquad\qquad \forall v \in V \tag{3}$$

$$x_u + x_v \leqslant 1 \qquad\qquad \forall \{u, v\} \in E_F \tag{4}$$

We refer to the above relaxation as LP-IS of F.

As the reader might have noticed, the Independent Set (IS) problem is defined on undirected graphs, whereas our input graph G is a directed graph. To turn this into an instance of Independent Set, we create what we will call the *conflict graph* of G, L:

Definition 4. *Given a directed graph $G = (V, E_G)$ and a labeling $L : E_G \to \{good, bad\}$, their* conflict graph *is denoted[4] by $G^{conf} = (V, E^{conf})$. This is an undirected graph on the same vertex set of G, and there is an edge between two vertices $u, v \in V$ iff there exists a common out-neighbor w of u, v such that $L(u, w) \neq L(v, w)$.*

Recall that we always add a self-loop with "good" label to every vertex in G, which means that $\{u, v\}$ will always be an edge in the conflict graph if $(u, v) \in E_G$ and $L(u, v) = $ bad.

There are a couple (straightforward) observations that will be useful to keep in mind. The first one is that H is an independent set in this conflict graph:

Observation 5. *H is an independent set in the conflict graph of G, L.*

The second is that, for any independent set I of the conflict graph, its vertices never label a vertex inconsistently. This follows from the definition of the conflict graph, as such an inconsistency would create an edge in the graph.

Observation 6. *Let I be any independent set of a conflict graph of G, L. Then, for any $v \in V$, it must fall into one of the following three categories:*

- *v has no in-neighbor (w.r.t. G) in I.*
- *v has at least one in-neighbor (w.r.t. G) in I and each of v's neighbors in I labels it with good.*
- *v has at least one in-neighbor (w.r.t. G) in I and each of v's neighbors in I labels it with bad.*

Moreover, we have to recall the concept of *extreme point solutions* of linear programs. A feasible solution is said to be an extreme point solution if it cannot be written as a convex combination of other feasible solutions[5]. For any LP with

---

[4] Of course, the conflict graph depends on the labeling. However, we choose not to have L in the notation to avoid cumbersomeness.

[5] Equivalently, the solution must be a vertex of the polytope defined by the constraints.

a finite feasible region, it is known that an extreme point optimum solution exists and can be found in polynomial time (see e.g. [Jai98]). Extreme point solutions are widely used in approximation algorithms; interested readers may refer to the survey [LRS11] for more details.

With these ready, we can now describe our algorithm, which we call CONFLICT-LP:

CONFLICT-LP$(G = (V, E_G), L)$

0. For each vertex $v \in V$, let b_v denote the number of vertices labelled bad by it. If the median of b_v's is at most $0.16d$, then output V and terminate.
1. Construct the *conflict graph* G^{conf} of G, L (as in Definition 4).
2. Solve for an extreme point optimum solution $\{x_v^*\}_{v \in V}$ of LP-IS of G^{conf}. Let I denote the set of all vertices $u \in V$ such that $x_u^* = 1$.
3. Let S be the set of all vertices $v \in V$ that has at least one in-neighbor (w.r.t. G) in I and is labelled good by the neighbor(s). Output S.

It is obvious to see that the algorithm runs in polynomial time.

Correctness Intuition. Before we proceed with the formal proof of correctness, let us briefly give an informal intuition behind the proof. First, Step 0 simply helps us deal with the "trivial" case where $|A|$ is less than[6] say $0.15(n-1)$. In this case, we can simply output the whole vertex set V; this is indeed what Step 0 does. Thus, from this point onward, we may assume that $|A| \geqslant 0.15(n-1)$.

Next, a priori, it is not even clear that I must be non-empty. To see this, let us first recall a classic result of Nemhauser and Trotter that an extreme point solution of LP-IS is always *half-integral*, meaning that $x_v \in \{0, 1/2, 1\}$ for every vertex v.

Theorem 7 ([NT74]). *In any extreme point solution of LP-IS, $x_v \in \{0, 1/2, 1\}$ for all $v \in V$.*

Now, if I were empty, then we would have $x_v \in \{0, 1/2\}$, which would imply that the optimum of LP-IS is at most $n/2 < |H|$. This would be a contradiction to Observation 5.

Next, let us consider the set $T = \{v \mid x_v^* = 0\}$. It is well-known that $|I| \geqslant |T|$; this can be easily seen because otherwise we can instead assign 1 to T and 0 to I and obtain a valid LP solution with larger objective value. (In fact, we will use a stronger property between the two sets below.)

For simplicity of exposition, let us assume for now that I only contains honest players, i.e., $I \subseteq H$, and that T only contains active adversary, i.e., $T \subseteq A$. Observe that, due to condition (4) of the relaxation, we must have

---

[6] The constant 0.15 here can be replaced with any constant less than $1/6$. We only use 0.15 to avoid introducing an additional parameter.

$N_{G^{\mathrm{conf}}}(I) \subseteq T$. Notice also that, since every honest player labels its out-neighbor in A as "bad", we must have $N_{G^{\mathrm{conf}}}(I) \supseteq (N_G^{out}(I) \cap A)$. From this and from the bound $|I| \geqslant |T|$ in the previous paragraph, it must be that $|I| \geqslant |N_G^{out}(I) \cap A|$. However, recall that the edges from I to A are ("essentially") random of degree $\Omega(d) \geqslant 100 \log n$. Such a "non-expansion" condition can only hold when $N_G^{out}(I) \cap A$ already contains all but $o(1)$ fraction of A. In other words, we have $|I| \geqslant |N_G^{out}(I) \cap A| \geqslant (1 - o(1))|A| \geqslant (0.15 - o(1))n$, where the last inequality comes from our assumption that $|A| \geqslant 0.15(n-1)$.

Now, note that we never output vertices from $N_G^{out}(I) \cap A$ because they are already labelled as bad by at least one vertex in I. This means that $S \cap A$ is small (i.e. $o(n)$). On the other hand, we always output all vertices in $N_G^{out}(I) \cap (H \cup P)$ because they are labelled good by at least one vertex in I; since we concluded that $|I| \geqslant (0.15 - o(1))n$ in the previous paragraph, it follows from vertex expansion of random graphs that $|N_G^{out}(I) \cap (H \cap P)| \geqslant |H \cup P| - o(n) \geqslant \frac{n+1}{2} + |P| - o(n)$. By a more careful calculation of the terms $o(n)$, it is then possible to show that (1) holds.

To turn the above intuition into a formal proof, we not only have to make the calculations more precise, but we also need to deal with the case where $I \not\subseteq H$ (or $T \not\subseteq A$). Nevertheless, we can still show, using a more general structural result (see Lemma 3), that $I \cap H$ still satisfies "non-expansion". This allows the proof to go through in a similar manner.

3.1   Proof of Correctness of the Algorithm

We now give a formal proof of correctness of our algorithm. We will need several additional notations:

– Once again, let $I = \{v \in V \mid x_v^* = 1\}$ and $T = \{v \in V \mid x_v^* = 0\}$. Moreover , let $R = \{v \in V \mid x_v^* = 1/2\}$.
– Let I_H, T_H and R_H denote $I \cap H, T \cap H$ and $R \cap H$ respectively. Similarly, let $I_{\overline{H}}, T_{\overline{H}}$ and $R_{\overline{H}}$ denote $I \setminus H$, $T \setminus H$ and $R \setminus H$ respectively.

We will prove our main theorem for the constants $C = 10^{10}$ and $\beta = 10^{-10}$. It is henceforth assumed that $d \geqslant C \log n$, and this will not be explicitly stated. We remark that we make no attempt in optimizing these constants and it is likely that they can be reduced substantially.

Step 0: Dealing with the trivial case. As stated earlier, Step 0 in our algorithm helps us take care of the "trivial" case where A is already small. In particular, we can show that, if $|A| \leqslant 0.15(n-1)$, then the algorithm w.h.p. simply outputs V, which is a correct output in this case. Moreover, it is not hard to see that, when A is larger than $(n-1)/6$ and V is the wrong answer, then we do not terminate in this step and proceed to the remaining part of the algorithm. This is encapsulated in the following lemma.

Lemma 1. *When $|A| \leqslant 0.15(n-1)$, our algorithm outputs V and terminates at Step 0 with probability $1 - O(e^{-\beta d})$. On the other hand, when $|A| > (n-1)/6$, our algorithm terminates at Step 0 with probability only $O(e^{-\beta d})$.*

It turns out that the above lemma follows easily from the concentration of the number of bad labels given by each honest vertex. This concentration is stated and proved below.

Observation 8. *With probability* $1 - O(e^{-\beta d})$*, for all vertices* $u \in H$*, we have* $(\mu - 0.001)d \leqslant |N_G^{out}(u) \cap A| \leqslant (\mu + 0.001)d$ *where* $\mu = \frac{|A|}{n-1}$*.*

Proof. We will only prove that $|N_G^{out}(u) \cap A| \geqslant (\mu - 0.001)d$ for every $u \in H$ with high probability. The upper bound can be shown analogously. Note that our desired bound is obvious when $\mu \leqslant 0.001$. Hence, we may assume that $\mu \geqslant 0.001$, or equivalently $|A| \geqslant 0.001(n-1)$.

Let us fix $u \in H$ and a vertex $v \in A$. The probability that v belongs to $N_G^{out}(u)$ is exactly $\frac{d}{n-1}$. Moreover, from how the graph is generated, the events $v \in N_G^{out}(u)$ for different v's are independent. Hence, Chernoff bounds implies that

$$\Pr\left[|N_G^{out}(u) \cap A| < 0.999 \cdot \left(\frac{d}{n-1} \cdot |A|\right)\right]$$
$$\leqslant \exp\left(-\frac{10^{-6}}{2} \cdot \frac{d}{n-1} \cdot |A|\right)$$
$$\leqslant \exp\left(-\frac{10^{-6}}{2} \cdot \frac{d}{n-1} \cdot 0.001(n-1)\right)$$
$$\leqslant n^{-2} \cdot e^{-\beta d},$$

where the second and third inequalities follow from $|A| \geqslant 0.001(n-1)$ and $d \geqslant 10^{10} \log n$ respectively. Furthermore, observe that $0.999 \cdot \left(\frac{d}{n-1} \cdot |A|\right) = 0.999 \mu d \geqslant (\mu - 0.001)d$. Hence, we have $\Pr\left[|N_G^{out}(u) \cap A| < (\mu - 0.001)d\right] \leqslant n^{-2} \cdot e^{-\beta d}$. Using union bound over all $u \in H$ concludes our proof. $\square$

Now that we have proved the concentration, we can prove Lemma 1 simply as follows.

Proof of Lemma 1: Suppose that $|A| \leqslant 0.15(n-1)$. Then, from Observation 8, w.p. $1 - O(e^{-\beta d})$ we have $|N_G^{out}(u) \cap A| \leqslant \left(\frac{|A|}{n-1} + 0.001\right)d < 0.16d$ for all $u \in H$. Notice that $N_G^{out}(u) \cap A$ is exactly the set of vertices for which u labels bad. As a result, for these $|H| \geqslant t+1$ vertices, they label bad to at most $0.16d$ vertices. This means that the condition in Step 0 is satisfied and the algorithm outputs V.

On the other hand, if $|A| > (n-1)/6$, then Observation 8 gives the bound $|N_G^{out}(u) \cap A| \geqslant \left(\frac{|A|}{n-1} - 0.001\right)d > 0.16d$ with probability $1 - O(e^{\beta d})$. When this event occurs, each $u \in H$ labels more than $0.16d$ vertices as bad. Thus, the condition in Step 0 is not satisfied in this case. $\square$

Step I: Non-Expansion of I_H *to* A*.* The first step of the remaining part of the proof is to show that the set I_H does not (vertex-)expand in A (w.r.t out-edges in G), as stated below. We remark here that it also implicitly implies that $I_H \neq \emptyset$.

Lemma 2. $|I_H| > |N_G^{out}(I_H) \cap A|$.

To prove non-expansion of I_H, we will resort to a structural result regarding an extreme point LP solution. It is easiest to state in terms of *crown* as defined below [CFJ04, ACF+04]:

Definition 9. *For any undirected graph $F = (V, E_F)$ and disjoint subsets $I, T \subseteq F$, (I, T) is said to be a* crown *of F if (i) $T = N(I)$ and (ii) there is a matching between T and I such that all vertices in T are matched.*

Lemma 3 ([AFLS07]). *For any undirected graph $F = (V, E_F)$, let $\{x_v^*\}_{v \in V}$ be an extreme point solution, and let $I = \{v \in V \mid x_v^* = 1\}$ and $T = \{v \in V \mid x_v^* = 0\}$. Then, (I, T) forms a crown (w.r.t F).*

Notice that if (I, T) is a crown, then it must be that $|I| \geqslant |T|$ due to (ii). Hence, the above result is stronger than the one we used in the informal exposition. We are now ready to prove Lemma 2.

Proof of Lemma 2: First, we claim that

$$|R_H| \leqslant |R_{\overline{H}}|. \tag{5}$$

This is because otherwise we can instead set $x_v^* = 1$ for $v \in R_H$ and $x_v^* = 0$ for $v \in R_{\overline{H}}$, which would give an LP solution with higher value. (Note that this is a valid LP solution because R_H is an independent set from Observation 5, and all neighbors of I lie in T.)

From Lemma 3, (I, T) forms a crown. Consider a matching from T to I such that all vertices in T are matched (which is guaranteed to exist from the definition of a crown). Notice that there is no edge from T_H to I_H in the graph G^{conf}; hence, all vertices in T_H must be matched to vertices in $I_{\overline{H}}$. In other words, we have

$$|T_H| \leqslant |I_{\overline{H}}|. \tag{6}$$

From (5) and (6), we have

$$|I_H| = |H| - |T_H| - |R_H| > |A \cup P| - |R_{\overline{H}}| - |I_{\overline{H}}| = |T_{\overline{H}}|.$$

Finally, observe that $(N_G^{out}(I_H) \cap A) \subseteq (N_{G^{conf}}(I_H) \cap A) \subseteq T_{\overline{H}}$, which yields the desired bound. $\qquad \square$

Step II: Expansion of Subsets of H in G. Similar to the outline, the second step of the proof is to observe that most subsets $X \subseteq H$ expands very well into A (or V), with respect to out-edges in G. The reason is simply that the graph from H to these sets are (essentially) random bipartite graphs of out-degree $\Omega(d)$. Due to technical reasons, we will also state the vertex expansion properties in terms of the in-degree graphs to V. The formal statement is as follows.

Lemma 4. *Suppose that $|A| \geqslant 0.15(n-1)$. Then, with probability $1 - O(e^{-\beta d})$, the following holds:*

1. For any set $X \subseteq H$ such that $|X| \leqslant 0.05(n-1)$, we have

$$|A \cap N_G^{out}(X)| \geqslant |X|. \tag{7}$$

2. For any set $W \subseteq V$, we have

$$|H \cap N_G^{in}(W)| \geqslant \min\{|H| - 0.05(n-1), 10|W|\}. \tag{8}$$

We remark here that the above lemma is the main place we use $|A| \geqslant \Omega(n)$ as guaranteed from Step 0; otherwise the inequality (7) may not be true (some vertex in H might not even have an outgoing edge to A at all if A is too small).

The proof is via a standard approach to prove vertex/edge expansion of graph: we bound the probability that each neighbor is a subset of a too-small set and then use union bound in the end.

Proof. 1. Let us consider any sets $X \subseteq H$ and $Y \subseteq A$. For any vertex $u \in X$, the probability that $(N_G^{out}(u) \cap A) \subseteq Y$ is exactly $\left(\frac{|H|-1+|Y|}{n-1}\right)^d$. Since the events $N_G^{out}(u) \subseteq Y$ are independent for all $u \in X$, we have

$$\Pr[(N_G^{out}(X) \cap A) \subseteq Y] = \left(\frac{|H|-1+|Y|}{n-1}\right)^{d|X|} \leqslant \left(1 - \frac{|A \setminus Y|}{n-1}\right)^{d|X|}.$$

Hence, the undesired event happens with probability at most

$$\sum_{\substack{X \subseteq H, Y \subseteq A \\ |X| \leqslant 0.05(n-1), |Y|=|X|-1}} \Pr[(N_G^{out}(X) \cap A) \subseteq Y]$$

$$\leqslant \sum_{\substack{X \subseteq H, Y \subseteq A \\ |X| \leqslant 0.05(n-1), |Y|=|X|-1}} \left(1 - \frac{|A \setminus Y|}{n-1}\right)^{d|X|}$$

$$\leqslant \sum_{\substack{X \subseteq H, Y \subseteq A \\ |X| \leqslant 0.05(n-1), |Y|=|X|-1}} (0.9)^{d|X|}$$

$$= \sum_{i=1}^{\lfloor 0.05(n-1) \rfloor} \binom{|H|}{i} (0.9)^{d|X|}$$

$$\leqslant \sum_{i=1}^{\lfloor 0.05(n-1) \rfloor} n^i (0.9)^{di}$$

$$\leqslant \sum_{i=1}^{\lfloor 0.05(n-1) \rfloor} n^{-2} \cdot e^{-\beta d}$$

$$= O(e^{-\beta d}),$$

where the second inequality follows from $|A| \geqslant 0.15(n-1)$ and $|Y| \leqslant 0.05(n-1)$ and we use our choice of $d \geqslant 10^{10} \log n$ in the last inequality.

2. Consider any set $W \subseteq V$ and $X \subseteq H$. We will bound the probability that $(H \cap N_G^{in}(W))$ is a subset of X. Recall from our definition that every vertex has a self-loop. Hence, if $(W \cap H) \not\subseteq X$, it is immediate that $\Pr[(H \cap N_G^{in}(W)) \subseteq X] = 0$.

Now, for the case $(W \cap H) \subseteq X$, we can bound $\Pr[(H \cap N_G^{in}(W)) \subseteq X]$ as follows. First, notice that each vertex $u \in (H \setminus X)$, u does *not* belongs to $N_G^{in}(W)$ (or equivalently $N_G^{out}(u) \cap W = \emptyset$) with probability exactly $\left(1 - \frac{|W|}{n-1}\right)^d$. Since the events $u \notin N_G^{in}(W)$ are independent for all $u \in (H \setminus X)$, we have

$$\Pr[(H \cap N_G^{in}(W)) \subseteq X] = \left(1 - \frac{|W|}{n-1}\right)^{d \cdot |H \setminus X|} \leqslant e^{-\frac{d|W| \cdot (|H| - |X|)}{n-1}}.$$

For convenience, let $\mu(|W|)$ denote $\lceil \min\{|H| - 0.05(n-1), 10|W|\}\rceil - 1$. From union bound and the previous inequality, the probability of the undesired event is at most

$$\sum_{\substack{W \subseteq V, X \subseteq H \\ |X| = \mu(|W|)}} \Pr[(H \cap N_G^{in}(W)) \subseteq X] \leqslant \sum_{\substack{W \subseteq V, X \subseteq H \\ |X| = \mu(|W|)}} e^{-\frac{d \cdot |W| \cdot (|H| - |X|)}{n-1}}$$

$$\leqslant \sum_{\substack{W \subseteq V, X \subseteq H \\ |X| = \mu(|W|)}} e^{-0.05d|W|}$$

$$= \sum_{i=1}^{n} \binom{n}{i} \binom{|H|}{\mu(i)} e^{-0.05di}$$

$$\leqslant \sum_{i=1}^{n} n^{11i} e^{-0.05di}$$

$$\leqslant \sum_{i=1}^{n} n^{-2} \cdot e^{-\beta d}$$

$$= O(e^{-\beta d})$$

where the second inequality is due to $\mu(|W|) \leqslant |H| - 0.05(n-1)$ and the last inequality follows from $d \geqslant 10^{10} \log n$. This completes our proof. $\square$

We can deduce from the above lemma the following corollary, which will be more convenient to use in the main proof.

Corollary 1. *Suppose that $|A| \geqslant 0.15(n - 1)$. Then, with probability $1 - O(e^{-\beta d})$, for any set $X \subseteq H$, at least one of the following must hold: (i) $|X| \leqslant |N_G^{out}(X) \cap A|$ or (ii) $|N_G^{out}(X) \cap (H \cup P)| \geqslant \frac{n+1}{2} + 2 \cdot |A \setminus N_G^{out}(X)|$.*

Proof. Suppose for the sake of contradiction that there exists $X \subseteq H$ that violates both inequalities. Since X violates (i) and from the first item (i.e. (7)) of Lemma 4, we must have $|X| > 0.05(n - 1)$, which means

$$|H \setminus X| < |H| - 0.05(n - 1). \tag{9}$$

Let $Y = (A \setminus N_G^{out}(X))$ and $k = |Y|$. From the violation of (i), we have

$$|X| \geqslant |N_G^{out}(X) \cap A| + 1 = |A| - k + 1 = (n - |H| - |P|) - k + 1$$

From the above, we have

$$|H \setminus X| = |H| - |X| \leqslant |P| + k + 2\left(|H| - \frac{n+1}{2}\right).$$

For convenience, we let $\Gamma = |H| - \frac{n+1}{2}$. We may write the above inequality as

$$|H \setminus X| \leqslant |P| + k + 2\Gamma \tag{10}$$

Now, from (8) in Lemma 4 with $W = Y$, we have

$$|H \setminus X| \geqslant |N_G^{in}(Y) \cap H| \geqslant \min\{|H| - 0.05(n-1), 10k\}.$$

From (9), it cannot be that $|H \setminus X| \geqslant |H| - 0.05(n-1)$. As a result, we have

$$|H \setminus X| \geqslant 10k. \tag{11}$$

Similarly, let $Z = (H \cup P) \setminus N_G^{out}(X)$. From the violation of (ii), we have

$$|Z| = |H| + |P| - |N_G^{out}(X) \cap (H \cup P)| \geqslant |H| + |P| - \frac{n-1}{2} - 2k$$
$$= |P| - 2k + 1 + \Gamma. \tag{12}$$

Moreover, from (8) in Lemma 4 with $W = Z$, we have

$$|H \setminus X| \geqslant |N_G^{in}(Z) \cap H| \geqslant \min\{|H| - 0.05(n-1), 10|Z|\}.$$

Once again, (9) implies that $|H \setminus X|$ cannot be at least $|H| - 0.05(n-1)$. Hence, we have

$$|H \setminus X| \geqslant 10|Z| \overset{(12)}{\geqslant} 10(|P| - 2k + 1 + \Gamma). \tag{13}$$

By combining (10), (11) and (13), we arrive at

$$|P| + k + 2\Gamma \overset{(10)}{\geqslant} |H \setminus X| = 0.8|H \setminus X| + 0.2|H \setminus X|$$
$$\overset{(11),(13)}{\geqslant} 8k + 2(|P| - 2k + 1 + \Gamma)$$
$$= 2|P| + 4k + 1 + 2\Gamma,$$

a contradiction. □

Step III: Putting things together. With the above lemmas ready, we now prove our main theorem by simply plugging them together.

Proof of Theorem 3: From Lemma 1, if $|A| < 0.15(n-1)$, then we output the entire vertex set V and terminates with probability $1 - O(e^{-\beta d})$; this is a correct output. Moreover, Lemma 1 also ensures that we w.p. $1 - O(e^{\beta d})$ do not terminate here with an incorrect output.

We may now assume for the rest of the proof that $|A| \geqslant 0.15(n-1)$. From Lemma 2, we have $|I_H| > |N_G^{out}(I_H) \cap A|$. As a result, from Corollary 1, we with probability $1 - O(e^{-\beta d})$ must have

$$|N_G^{out}(I_H) \cap (H \cup P)| \geqslant \frac{n+1}{2} + 2 \cdot |A \setminus N_G^{out}(I_H)|. \tag{14}$$

Now, observe that, every vertex in $N_G^{out}(I_H) \cap (H \cup P)$ is labelled good by at least one vertex in $I_H \subseteq I$; hence, they will be included in S. In other words, $S \cap (H \cup P) \supseteq N_G^{out}(I_H) \cap (H \cup P)$.

On the other hand, all vertices in $N_G^{out}(I_H) \cap A$ are labelled bad by at least one vertex in $I_H \subseteq I$; hence, they will not be included in S. In other words, we have $S \cap A \subseteq (A \setminus N_G^{out}(I_H))$.

As a result, we arrive at

$$|S \cap (H \cup P)| \geqslant |N_G^{out}(I_H) \cap (H \cup P)| \overset{(14)}{\geqslant} \frac{n+1}{2} + 2 \cdot |A \setminus N_G^{out}(I_H)|$$
$$\geqslant \frac{n+1}{2} + 2 \cdot |S \cap A|,$$

which concludes our proof.   □

4   Construction of Robust Secret Sharing

Let λ be the robustness parameter. In this section, we give a construction of robust secret sharing for messages of length m with share size $m + O(\lambda \log n(\log n + \log m))$. In Sect. 4.1, we first give a construction of a basic robust secret sharing scheme with share size $m + O(\lambda^2 + \lambda(\log n + \log m) + \log^2 n + \log n \log m)$. In the Sect. 4.2, we use parallel repetition (as was done by Bishop et al. [BPRW16]) to improve the share size of our construction to $m + O(\lambda \log n(\log n + \log m))$.

4.1   Basic Scheme

The construction is described in Fig. 1 and we show the following theorem.[7]

Theorem 10. *For some $t, d, \lambda, \rho \in \mathbb{N}$, $\epsilon_2, \epsilon_3 \in [0,1]$, $n \geqslant 2t + 1$, and message space $\mathcal{M}$, assume we have the following:*

---

[7] Recall the definition of multiplicity of a multiset and $\|$ from Sect. 2.

- A $(t + 1, n, 0, 0)$ secret sharing scheme (Share, Rec) for $\mathcal{M}$ that is $(0, s, \lfloor (s - (t+1))/2 \rfloor)$-robust for any $s \geqslant t+1$. Further, the shares are strings in $\{0, 1\}^\rho$.
- A $(2d, \epsilon_2)$-secure private MAC scheme (KeyGen, Tag, Verify) for message space $\{0, 1\}^\rho$ with randomness length ν, key length κ and tag length λ.
- The vertex identification algorithm VertexID from Theorem 3, when run on graphs with out-degree d, has error probability at most ϵ_3.

Then, the construction in Fig. 1 is a $(t + 1, n, ne^{-d/3}, 0)$ secret sharing scheme for $\mathcal{M}$ that is $(nd\epsilon_2 + \epsilon_3 + ne^{-d/3}, n, t)$-robust. The size of each share is $(\rho + \nu + d\lceil \log n \rceil + d(\kappa + \lambda))$ bits.

BasRobShare(m) : To share a secret $m \in \mathcal{M}$:

1. For each $i \in [n]$, select a multiset $S^i \subseteq [n] \setminus \{i\}$ of size d uniformly at random with replacement.
2. If there is an $i' \in [n]$ such that the multiplicity of i' in $(S^1 \| S^2 \| \dots \| S^n)$ is greater than $2d$, select $m^* \leftarrow \mathcal{M}$. Else, set $m^* = m$.
3. Run Share(m^*) to obtain the shares $(\mathsf{Sh}_1, \dots, \mathsf{Sh}_n)$.
4. For each $i \in [n]$, choose $r_i \leftarrow \{0, 1\}^\nu$.
5. For each $i \in [n]$ and each $j \in [d]$ do:
   (a) Let v_j^i be the j-th element in the ordered multiset S^i.
   (b) Choose a private MAC key $k_{i \to v_j^i}^j \leftarrow \mathsf{KeyGen}(1^\lambda)$.
   (c) Compute $\sigma_{i \to v_j^i}^j \leftarrow \mathsf{Tag}(k_{i \to v_j^i}^j, (\mathsf{Sh}_{v_j^i}, r_{v_j^i}))$.
6. Set share$_i = (\mathsf{Sh}_i, r_i, S^i, \{k_{i \to v_j^i}^j, \sigma_{i \to v_j^i}^j\}_{j \in [d]})$.

BasRobRec : The reconstruction algorithm proceeds in two rounds.

- **Round-1:**
  1. For each $i \in [n]$, party i broadcasts (Sh_i, r_i) to every other party and initializes an empty list N_i.
  2. For every $j \in [d]$, party i does:
     (a) Let v_j^i be the j-th element in the ordered multiset S^i.
     (b) Check if $\mathsf{Verify}(k_{i \to v_j^i}^j, (\mathsf{Sh}_{v_j^i}, r_{v_j^i}), \sigma_{i \to v_j^i}^j) = 1$.
     (c) If the verification passes, party i adds $((i, v_j^i), \mathsf{good})$ to N_i. Else, it adds $((i, v_j^i), \mathsf{bad})$ to N_i.
- **Round-2:**
  1. For each $i \in [n]$, party i broadcasts N_i to every other party and initializes an empty graph G and an empty labeling L.
  2. For every $i \in [n]$ and every entry $((i, v), \mathsf{lab}_{i,v}) \in N_i$, the parties add the edge (i, v) in G and set $L(i, v) = \mathsf{lab}_{i,v}$.
  3. The parties (locally) run the algorithm VertexID on G and L to obtain the vertex set S.
  4. The parties then (locally) run $\mathsf{Rec}(\{\mathsf{Sh}_i\}_{i \in S})$ to obtain the secret m.

Fig. 1. Basic construction of robust secret sharing (using terminology from Theorem 10)

Proof of Theorem 10: The share size may be verified by inspection. We first show the correctness and privacy properties of our construction and finally show its robustness.

Correctness. Note that in an honest execution of the sharing and the reconstruction algorithm, in the absence of any corruptions, every edge in the graph G will be labeled as good. Thus, the algorithm VertexID will output $V = [n]$. It now follows from the perfect correctness of Rec that the secret output by BasRobRec will be equal to m^* with probability 1. We will now bound the probability that m^* is not equal to m.

We estimate the probability that the chosen multisets $\{S^i\}_{i\in[n]}$ has the property such that for $v \in [n]$, the multiplicity of v in $S^1\|\ldots\|S^n$ is at most $2d$. Let us fix a party $v \in [n]$, and call the event that its multiplicity is more than $2d$ as Bad_v. For any $i \neq v$, v might get selected (possibly multiple times) in the multiset S^i. Thus, there are totally $d(n-1)$ random draws where v might get selected. For any $i \in [d(n-1)]$, let X_i be the indicator random variable which is 1 if and only if v is selected in the i-th draw. Now, for any $i \in [d(n-1)]$,

$$\Pr[X_i = 1] = \frac{1}{n-1} \tag{15}$$

Then, Bad_v occurs if $\sum_i X_i > 2d$. The variables $\{X_i\}_i$ are independent and hence from Chernoff bounds,

$$\Pr[\mathsf{Bad}_v] = \Pr[\sum_i X_i > 2d] \leqslant e^{-d/3} \tag{16}$$

Let Bad be the event that there exists at least one $v \in [n]$ such that Bad_v happens. By union bound,

$$\Pr[\mathsf{Bad}] \leqslant \sum_v \Pr[\mathsf{Bad}_v] = ne^{-d/3} \tag{17}$$

Thus, with probability at least $1 - ne^{-d/3}$, the chosen multisets $\{S^i\}_{i\in[n]}$ satisfies the property the multiplicity of every $v \in [n]$ in $S^1\|\ldots\|S^n$ is at most $2d$. Notice that when this happens, $m^* = m$. Thus, the correctness error is at most $ne^{-d/3}$. We will call $\{S^i\}_{i\in[n]}$ that satisfies the above property to be *bounded*.

Privacy. To show perfect privacy, we need to argue that for every set U of size at most t, for every pair of secrets $m_0, m_1 \in M$, the distributions of BasRobShare$(m_0)_U$ and BasRobShare$(m_1)_U$ are identical.[8] It is sufficient to show that this is in the case when $\{S^i\}$ is bounded, and when it is not bounded, by design the output of BasRobShare is independent of the message being shared, and so the shares of U are identical.

When $\{S^i\}$ is bounded, we show this by the following hybrid argument. Fix any choice of the multisets $\{S^i\}_{i\in[n]}$ such that it is bounded. For every $i \in [n]$,

---

[8] From Remark 1, we also satisfy the stronger notion of adaptive privacy.

we define T^i to be the sequence of $(v, j) \in [n] \times [d]$ such that the j-th entry of the multiset S^v is equal to i. From the choice of the fixed $\{S^i\}_{i \in [n]}$, each $|T^i| \leqslant 2d$. We first fix all the MAC keys chosen during the share phase, and make the following argument for any such set of keys. We now argue that $\mathsf{BasRobShare}(m_0)_U$ is identical to $\mathsf{BasRobShare}(m_1)_U$, going through the following hybrid distributions over the shares of U:

- Hyb_1 : This is the same as $\mathsf{BasRobShare}(m_0)_U$.
- Hyb_2 : In this hybrid, during the share phase, for every $i \notin U$, we generate $\sigma^j_{v \to i}$ (for any $j \in [d]$ and $v \in [n]$) as $\mathsf{Tag}(k^j_{v \to i}, (0^\rho, r_i))$. We finally output the shares corresponding to U. Note that Hyb_1 is identical to Hyb_2 from the perfect privacy property of the private MAC scheme, which is $(2d, \varepsilon_2)$-secure, since $|T^i| \leqslant 2d$ for every $i \in [n]$.
- Hyb_3 : In this hybrid, during the share phase, instead of running $\mathsf{Share}(m^*)$ to get the Sh_i's, we run $\mathsf{Share}(0)$.[9] We run the rest of the sharing normally and output the shares corresponding to U. Hyb_3 is identical to Hyb_2 by the perfect privacy of the secret sharing scheme $(\mathsf{Share}, \mathsf{Rec})$.

Note that via a similar argument we can show that $\mathsf{BasRobShare}(m_1)_U$ is also identical to Hyb_3, and thus to $\mathsf{BasRobShare}(m_0)_U$, proving perfect privacy.

Robustness. We now argue the robustness of our construction. Consider an interactive adversary $\mathcal{A}$ that adaptively corrupts a set T of parties. We assume without loss of generality that this adversary corrupts $\lfloor (n-1)/2 \rfloor$ number of parties. In the case where the adversary corrupts less than this many parties, we consider another adversary that corrupts all the parties corrupted by the original adversary and corrupts some additional parties such that the total number of corrupted parties is $\lfloor (n-1)/2 \rfloor$. For the parties corrupted by the original adversary, this new adversary behaves exactly as specified by the original adversary. For the additional corrupted parties, this new adversary follows the reconstruction protocol as specified. The adversary is given $\{\mathsf{share}_i\}_{i \in T}$. Let H be the set of honest parties. Consider the interactive reconstruction algorithm.

- In the first round of the reconstruction algorithm, the party i broadcasts (Sh_i, r_i) to every other party. Now, every party $i \in T$ might broadcast the correct (Sh_i, r_i) or a modified (Sh'_i, r'_i). Based on this, we partition T into two sets P and A. P consists of the parties that send the unmodified (Sh_i, r_i) whereas the parties in A modify the shares and send $(\mathsf{Sh}'_i, r'_i) \neq (\mathsf{Sh}_i, r_i)$. Note that at the end of the first round, the adversarial parties learn no information about the multisets S^i of the honest parties and conditioned on the information available to the adversary at the end of the first round, these multisets S^i are still random.
- At the end of the first round, the parties will verify the tags of the MAC. Every $i \in H$ will generate the set N_i as follows:
  - Let $S^i = (v^i_1, \ldots, v^i_d)$.

---

[9] 0 denoting some universally fixed element in $\mathcal{M}$.

- For every $j \in [d]$ such that $v_j^i \in H \cup P$, party i adds $((i, v_j^i), \mathsf{good})$ to N_i.
- For every $j \in [d]$ such that $v_j^i \in A$, party i adds $((i, v_j^i), \mathsf{bad})$ to N_i except with probability at most ϵ_2. The ϵ_2 error probability follows directly from the ε_2-unforgeability of the private MAC.

By standard union bound, the probability that there exists an $i \in H$ such that for some $v \in A$, party i adds $((i, v), \mathsf{good})$ to N_i is at most $nd\epsilon_2$ since each multiset S^i has size d.

– Conditioned on the above event not happening, the graph $G = (V, E)$ with $V = [n]$ and the edge labeling L is effectively generated as follows.

  1. The adversary partitions V into H, P, A where $|H| = n - \lfloor(n-1)/2\rfloor \geqslant (n+1)/2$.
  2. For every $u \in H$, choose a multiset S^u uniformly at random from $[n] \setminus \{u\}$ with replacement and let $S^u = (v_1^u, \ldots, v_d^u)$. For every $j \in [d]$, add an edge (u, v_j^u) and set $L(u, v_j^u) = \mathsf{good}$ if and only if $v_j^u \in H \cup P$. This is identically distributed to the distribution where we choose S^u uniformly at random during the sharing phase since at the end of the first round, the adversary learns no information about the multisets of the honest parties.
  3. The outgoing edges and their labels of $A \cup P$ can be generated adversarially after looking at the outgoing edges and the labels of the vertices in H.

  This is exactly same as the graph generation procedure given in Sect. 3.

– It now follows from the correctness of the VertexID algorithm (Theorem 3) that its output S when run on this graph satisfies the property that $|S \cap (H \cup P)| \geqslant (n+1)/2 + 2 \cdot |S \cap A| \geqslant (t+1) + 2 \cdot |S \cap A|$ except with probability ϵ_3. The fact that $\mathsf{Rec}(\{\mathsf{Sh}_j\}_{j \in S}) = m^*$ follows from robustness of secret sharing (Fact 2).

– Finally, as in the correctness argument, m^* is equal to the actual secret m except with probability $ne^{-d/3}$. Thus, by the union bound, the probability of error of the whole reconstruction procedure is at most $(nd\varepsilon_2 + \varepsilon_3 + ne^{-d/3})$.

This completes the proof of the theorem.   □

Remark 2. While they are not explicitly covered by the discussion so far, our construction extends to the case of aborting adversaries in a straightforward manner. If an adversary does not send a message in the reconstruction phase then it must be a corrupted party. In this case, all the honest parties which have this party in its watchlist will mark the corresponding edge as being bad. Further, the parties will consider some default set of d parties, (say the first d parties) as being part of this corrupted party's watchlist and consider some default labeling of the edges. Notice that our vertex identification algorithm allows the watchlist and the labeling from the malicious parties to be arbitrary.

Instantiation. We now provide the following instantiation of the building blocks of our robust secret sharing scheme. Let us fix the robustness parameter λ, and the length m of the secret to be shared (if $m < \lceil \log n \rceil$, replace it with $\lceil \log n \rceil$ in the following).

- We set $d = 10\lambda/\beta + 3C \log n/\beta$, where C (> 1) and β ($\in (0,1)$) are constants from Theorem 3.
- We instantiate the secret sharing with Shamir secret sharing over $\mathrm{GF}[2^m]$. This gives $\rho = m$.
- We instantiate the private MAC with the (ℓ, ε_2)-secure MAC for message space $\{0,1\}^\rho$ from Theorem 1, with $\ell = 2d$ and $\epsilon_2 = 2^{-\lambda}/(2nd)$. The randomness, tag and key lengths are, respectively, $2d(\lambda + \log(2nd(\rho + 2d)))$, $\lambda + \log(2nd(\rho + 2d))$, and $2(\lambda + \log(2nd(\rho + 2d)))$.
- The VertexID algorithm has error probability $\epsilon_3 < 2^{-10\lambda}$.

The robustness error is $nd\epsilon_2 + \epsilon_3 + ne^{-d/3} < 2^{-\lambda}/2 + 2^{-10\lambda} + n2^{-3\lambda - \log n} \leqslant 2^{-\lambda}$. The correctness error is $ne^{-d/3} \leqslant 2^{-\lambda}$. The size of each share is $\rho + 2d(\lambda + \log(2nd(\rho+2d))) + d\log n + 3d(\lambda + \log(2nd(\rho+2d))) = m + 5d\lambda + O(d\log(2nd(m+2d))) = m + O(\lambda^2) + O(\lambda \log n) + O((\lambda + \log n)(\log n + \log \lambda + \log m)) = m + O(\lambda^2 + \lambda(\log n + \log m) + \log^2 n + \log n \log m)$.

Corollary 2. *For any $\lambda, t, m, n \in \mathbb{N}$ with $n \geqslant 2t + 1$, there exists a $(t + 1, n, 2^{-\lambda}, 0)$-secret sharing scheme that is $(2^{-\lambda}, n, t)$-robust and, for secrets of length m bits, has shares of size $m + O(\lambda^2 + \lambda(\log n + \log m) + \log^2 n + \log n \log m)$ bits.*

4.2   Improved Parameters via Parallel Repetition

In this subsection, we improve the share size of our basic construction to $m + O(\lambda \log n(\log n + \log m))$ to achieve robustness error of $2^{-\lambda}$ via parallel repetition. This is similar to the ideas explained in [BPRW16]. Before we describe the construction, we start with some notation.

Notation. We split BasRobRec into two steps. The first step BasRobRec$_1$ is an interactive protocol comprising of the first two rounds of BasRobRec and the output of the protocol is the set S which is the output of VertexID algorithm on the constructed graph G and the labeling L. The second step consists of running Rec on $\{\mathsf{Sh}_i\}_{i\in S}$ and outputting the message.

Construction. The construction of robust secret sharing (RobShare, RobRec) with improved parameters is described in Fig. 2.

Theorem 11. *For any $\lambda, t, m, n \in \mathbb{N}$, with $n \geqslant 2t+1$, the construction in Fig. 2 is a $(t + 1, n, 0, 0)$ secret sharing scheme (with expected polynomial time sharing algortithm) for secrets of length m that is $(e^{-\lambda/24}, n, t)$-robust. The size of each share is $m + O(\lambda \log n(\log n + \log m))$.*

Due to page limits, we defer the proof of this theorem to the full version of the paper.

Set $\lambda' = 2$, and $d = 10\lambda'/\beta + 3C\log n/\beta$, where C and β are the constants from Theorem 3. In the following, $(\mathsf{Share}, \mathsf{Rec})$ represents $(t + 1, n, 0, 0)$ Shamir secret sharing over $\mathrm{GF}[2^m]$. The private MAC $(\mathsf{KeyGen}, \mathsf{Tag}, \mathsf{Verify})$ used for the message space $\{0, 1\}^m$ is the (ℓ, ε)-secure MAC from Theorem 1 with $\ell = 2d$ and $\varepsilon = 2^{-\lambda'}/2nd$. The protocol $\mathsf{BasRobRec}$ is from the construction in Figure 1.

$\mathsf{RobShare}(m)$: To share a secret $m \in \{0, 1\}^m$:
1. Run $\mathsf{Share}(m)$ to obtain the shares $(\mathsf{Sh}_1, \ldots, \mathsf{Sh}_n)$.
2. For each q in 1 to λ do:
   (a) For each $i \in [n]$, select a multiset $S^{q,i} \subseteq [n] \setminus \{i\}$ of size d uniformly at random with replacement.
   (b) If there is an $i' \in [n]$ such that the multiplicity of i' in $S^{q,1}\|S^{q,2}\|\ldots\|S^{q,n}$ is greater than $2d$, then go back to step (2a).
3. For each $q \in [\lambda]$, $i \in [n]$ and each $j \in [d]$ do:
   (a) For each $i \in [n]$, choose $r_i^q \leftarrow \{0,1\}^\nu$.
   (b) Let $v_j^{q,i}$ be the j-th element in the ordered multiset $S^{q,i}$.
   (c) Choose a private MAC key $k_{i \to v_j^{q,i}}^{q,j} \leftarrow \mathsf{KeyGen}$.
   (d) Compute $\sigma_{i \to v_j^{q,i}}^{q,j} \leftarrow \mathsf{Tag}(k_{i \to v_j^{q,i}}^{q,j}, (\mathsf{Sh}_{v_j^{q,i}}, r_{v_j^{q,i}}^q))$.
4. Set $\mathsf{share}_i = \left(\mathsf{Sh}_i, \{r_i^q\}_{q \in [k]}, \{S^{q,i}\}_{q \in [k]}, \{k_{i \to v_j^{q,i}}^{q,j}, \sigma_{i \to v_j^{q,i}}^{q,j}\}_{j \in [d], q \in [k]} \right)$.

RobRec :
1. For each q in 1 to λ do in parallel:
   (a) Run $\mathsf{BasRobRec}_1 \left(\left\{ \mathsf{Sh}_i, r_i^q, S^{q,i}, \{k_{i \to v_j^{q,i}}^{q,j}, \sigma_{i \to v_j^{q,i}}^{q,j}\}_{j \in [d]} \right\}_{i \in [n]} \right)$ to obtain the set Γ_q.
   (b) Set $m_q := \mathsf{Rec}(\{\mathsf{Sh}_i\}_{i \in \Gamma_q})$.
2. If there is a majority value m in the sequence $(m_1, \ldots, m_\lambda)$ then output m. Else, output $\bot$.

Fig. 2. Improved construction of robust secret sharing

Acknowledgment. Pasin would like to thank Theo McKenzie for useful discussions on the independent set problem on semi-random graphs.

Akshayaram Srinivasan and Prashant Nalini Vasudevan were supported in part by AFOSR Award FA9550-19-1-0200, AFOSR YIP Award, NSF CNS Award 1936826, DARPA and SPAWAR under contract N66001-15-C-4065, a Hellman Award and research grants by the Okawa Foundation, Visa Inc., and Center for Long-Term Cybersecurity (CLTC, UC Berkeley). The views expressed are those of the authors and do not reflect the official policy or position of the funding agencies.

References

[ACF+04] Abu-Khzam, F.N., Collins, R.L., Fellows, M.R., Langston, M.A., Suters, W.H., Symons, C.T.: Kernelization algorithms for the vertex cover problem: Theory and experiments. In: Proceedings of the Sixth Workshop on Algorithm Engineering and Experiments and the First Workshop on Analytic Algorithmics and Combinatorics, New Orleans, LA, USA, 10 January 2004, pp. 62–69 (2004)

[AFLS07] Abu-Khzam, F.N., Fellows, M.R., Langston, M.A., Suters, W.H.: Crown structures for vertex cover kernelization. Theory Comput. Syst. **41**(3), 411–430 (2007)

[BDIR18] Benhamouda, F., Degwekar, A., Ishai, Y., Rabin, T.: On the local leakage resilience of linear secret sharing schemes. In: Shacham, H., Boldyreva, A. (eds.) CRYPTO 2018. LNCS, vol. 10991, pp. 531–561. Springer, Cham (2018). https://doi.org/10.1007/978-3-319-96884-1_18

[Bei11] Beimel, A.: Secret-sharing schemes: a survey. In: Chee, Y.M., Guo, Z., Ling, S., Shao, F., Tang, Y., Wang, H., Xing, C. (eds.) IWCC 2011. LNCS, vol. 6639, pp. 11–46. Springer, Heidelberg (2011). https://doi.org/10.1007/978-3-642-20901-7_2

[BGW88] Ben-Or, M., Goldwasser, S., Wigderson, A.: Completeness theorems for non-cryptographic fault-tolerant distributed computation (extended abstract). In: Proceedings of the 20th Annual ACM Symposium on Theory of Computing, Chicago, Illinois, USA, 2–4 May 1988, pp. 1–10 (1988)

[Bla79] Blakley, G.R.: Safeguarding cryptographic keys. In: Proceedings of AFIPS 1979 National Computer Conference, vol. 48, pp. 313–317 (1979)

[BP16] Bishop, A., Pastro, V.: Robust secret sharing schemes against local adversaries. In: Cheng, C.-M., Chung, K.-M., Persiano, G., Yang, B.-Y. (eds.) PKC 2016. LNCS, vol. 9615, pp. 327–356. Springer, Heidelberg (2016). https://doi.org/10.1007/978-3-662-49387-8_13

[BPRW16] Bishop, A., Pastro, V., Rajaraman, R., Wichs, D.: Essentially optimal robust secret sharing with maximal corruptions. In: Fischlin, M., Coron, J.-S. (eds.) EUROCRYPT 2016. LNCS, vol. 9665, pp. 58–86. Springer, Heidelberg (2016). https://doi.org/10.1007/978-3-662-49890-3_3

[CCD88] Chaum, D., Crepeau, C., Damgaard, I.: Multiparty unconditionally secure protocols (extended abstract). In: Proceedings of the 20th Annual ACM Symposium on Theory of Computing, Chicago, Illinois, USA, 2–4 May 1988, pp. 11–19. ACM (1988)

[CDF01] Cramer, R., Damgard, I., Fehr, S.: On the cost of reconstructing a secret, or VSS with optimal reconstruction phase. In: Kilian, J. (ed.) CRYPTO 2001. LNCS, vol. 2139, pp. 503–523. Springer, Heidelberg (2001). https://doi.org/10.1007/3-540-44647-8_30

[CDF+08] Cramer, R., Dodis, Y., Fehr, S., Padró, C., Wichs, D.: Detection of algebraic manipulation with applications to robust secret sharing and fuzzy extractors. In: Smart, N. (ed.) EUROCRYPT 2008. LNCS, vol. 4965, pp. 471–488. Springer, Heidelberg (2008). https://doi.org/10.1007/978-3-540-78967-3_27

[CDV94] Carpentieri, M., De Santis, A., Vaccaro, U.: Size of shares and probability of cheating in threshold schemes. In: Helleseth, T. (ed.) EUROCRYPT 1993. LNCS, vol. 765, pp. 118–125. Springer, Heidelberg (1994). https://doi.org/10.1007/3-540-48285-7_10

[Cev11] Cevallos, A.: Reducing the share size in robust secret sharing. Universiteit Leiden, Mathematisch Instituut (2011)

[CFJ04] Chor, B., Fellows, M., Juedes, D.: Linear kernels in linear time, or how to save k colors in $O(n^2)$ steps. In: Graph-Theoretic Concepts in Computer Science, 30th International Workshop, WG 2004, Bad Honnef, Germany, 21–23 June 2004, pp. 257–269 (2004). Revised Papers

[CFOR12] Cevallos, A., Fehr, S., Ostrovsky, R., Rabani, Y.: Unconditionally-secure robust secret sharing with compact shares. In: Pointcheval, D., Johansson, T. (eds.) EUROCRYPT 2012. LNCS, vol. 7237, pp. 195–208. Springer, Heidelberg (2012). https://doi.org/10.1007/978-3-642-29011-4_13

[CGMA85] Chor, B., Goldwasser, S., Micali, S., Awerbuch, B.: Verifiable secret sharing and achieving simultaneity in the presence of faults (extended abstract). In: 26th Annual Symposium on Foundations of Computer Science, pp. 383–395. IEEE Computer Society Press, October 1985

[Che15] Cheraghchi, M.: Nearly optimal robust secret sharing. Cryptology ePrint Archive, Report 2015/951 (2015). http://eprint.iacr.org/2015/951

[CSV17] Charikar, M., Steinhardt, J., Valiant, G.: Learning from untrusted data. In: Proceedings of the 49th Annual ACM SIGACT Symposium on Theory of Computing, STOC 2017, Montreal, QC, Canada, 19–23 June 2017, pp. 47–60 (2017)

[DDFY94] De Santis, A., Desmedt, Y., Frankel, Y. , Yung, M.: How to share a function securely. In: 26th Annual ACM Symposium on Theory of Computing, pp. 522–533. ACM Press, May 1994

[DF90] Desmedt, Y., Frankel, Y.: Threshold cryptosystems. In: Brassard, G. (ed.) CRYPTO 1989. LNCS, vol. 435, pp. 307–315. Springer, New York (1990). https://doi.org/10.1007/0-387-34805-0_28

[FK00] Feige, U., Krauthgamer, R.: Finding and certifying a large hidden clique in a semirandom graph. Random Struct. Algorithms **16**(2), 195–208 (2000)

[FK01] Feige, U., Kilian, J.: Heuristics for semirandom graph problems. J. Comput. Syst. Sci. **63**(4), 639–671 (2001)

[Fra90] Frankel, Y.: A practical protocol for large group oriented networks. In: Quisquater, J.-J., Vandewalle, J. (eds.) EUROCRYPT 1989. LNCS, vol. 434, pp. 56–61. Springer, Heidelberg (1990). https://doi.org/10.1007/3-540-46885-4_8

[FY19a] Fehr, S., Yuan, C.: Robust secret sharing with optimal share size and security against rushing adversaries. IACR Cryptology ePrint Archive, 2019:1182 (2019)

[FY19b] Fehr, S., Yuan, C.: Towards optimal robust secret sharing with security against a rushing adversary. In: Ishai, Y., Rijmen, V. (eds.) EUROCRYPT 2019. LNCS, vol. 11478, pp. 472–499. Springer, Cham (2019). https://doi.org/10.1007/978-3-030-17659-4_16

[GK18] Goyal, V., Kumar, A.: Non-malleable secret sharing. In: Diakonikolas, I., Kempe, D., Henzinger, M. (eds.) 50th Annual ACM Symposium on Theory of Computing, pp. 685–698. ACM Press, June 2018

[GMW87] Goldreich, O., Micali, S., Wigderson, A.: How to play any mental game or a completeness theorem for protocols with honest majority. In: Aho, A. (ed.) 19th Annual ACM Symposium on Theory of Computing, pp. 218–229. ACM Press, May 1987

[HO18] Hemenway, B., Ostrovsky, R.: Efficient robust secret sharing from expander graphs. Cryptograph. Commun. **10**(1), 79–99 (2017). https://doi.org/10.1007/s12095-017-0215-z

[Jai98] Jain, K.: Factor 2 approximation algorithm for the generalized Steiner net-work problem. In: 39th Annual Symposium on Foundations of Computer Science, FOCS 1998, Palo Alto, California, USA, 8–11 November 1998, pp. 448–457. IEEE Computer Society (1998)

[Kar72] Karp, R.M.: Reducibility among combinatorial problems. In: Proceedings of a Symposium on the Complexity of Computer Computations, IBM Thomas J. Watson Research Center, Yorktown Heights, New York, USA, 20–22 March 1972, pp. 85–103 (1972). https://doi.org/10.1007/978-1-4684-2001-2_9

[LRS11] Lau, L.C., Ravi, R., Singh, M.: Iterative Methods in Combinatorial Optimization, vol. 46. Cambridge University Press, Cambridge (2011)

[MMT18] McKenzie, T., Mehta, H., Trevisan, L.: A new algorithm for the robust semi-random independent set problem. CoRR, abs/1808.03633 (2018)

[NT74] Nemhauser, G.L., Trotter, L.E.: Properties of vertex packing and independence system polyhedra. Math. Program. 6(1), 48–61 (1974)

[RB89] Rabin, T., Ben-Or, M.: Verifiable secret sharing and multiparty protocols with honest majority (extended abstract). In: 21st Annual ACM Symposium on Theory of Computing, pp. 73–85. ACM Press, May 1989

[Sha79] Shamir, A.: How to share a secret. Commun. Assoc. Comput. Mach. 22(11), 612–613 (1979)

Cryptanalysis

Cryptanalytic Extraction of Neural Network Models

Nicholas Carlini[1]([✉]), Matthew Jagielski[2], and Ilya Mironov[3]

[1] Google, Mountain View, CA, USA
nicholas@carlini.com
[2] Northeastern University, Boston, USA
[3] Facebook, Menlo Park, USA

Abstract. We argue that the machine learning problem of *model extraction* is actually a cryptanalytic problem in disguise, and should be studied as such. Given oracle access to a neural network, we introduce a differential attack that can efficiently steal the parameters of the remote model up to floating point precision. Our attack relies on the fact that ReLU neural networks are piecewise linear functions, and thus queries at the critical points reveal information about the model parameters.

We evaluate our attack on multiple neural network models and extract models that are 2^{20} times more precise and require $100\times$ fewer queries than prior work. For example, we extract a 100,000 parameter neural network trained on the MNIST digit recognition task with $2^{21.5}$ queries in under an hour, such that the extracted model agrees with the oracle on all inputs up to a worst-case error of 2^{-25}, or a model with 4,000 parameters in $2^{18.5}$ queries with worst-case error of $2^{-40.4}$. Code is available at https://github.com/google-research/cryptanalytic-model-extraction.

1 Introduction

The past decade has seen significant advances in machine learning, and deep learning in particular. Tasks viewed as being completely infeasible at the beginning of the decade became almost completely solved by the end. AlphaGo [SHM+16] defeated professional players at Go, a feat in 2014 seen as being at least ten years away [Lev14]. Accuracy on the ImageNet recognition benchmark improved from 73% in 2010 to 98.7% in 2019, a $20\times$ reduction in error rate [XHLL19]. Neural networks can generate photo-realistic high-resolution images that humans find indistinguishable from actual photographs [KLA+19]. Neural network achieve higher accuracy than human doctors in limited settings, such as early cancer detection [EKN+17].

These advances have brought neural networks into production systems. The automatic speech recognition systems on Google's Assistant, Apple's Siri, and Amazon's Alexa are all powered by speech recognition neural networks. Neural

M. Jagielski—Northeastern University, part of work done at Google. I. Mironov—Facebook, part of work done at Google.

D. Micciancio and T. Ristenpart (Eds.): CRYPTO 2020, LNCS 12172, pp. 189–218, 2020.
https://doi.org/10.1007/978-3-030-56877-1_7

Machine Translation [BCB15] is now the technique of choice for production language translation systems [WSC+16]. Autonomous driving is only feasible because of these improved image recognition neural networks.

High-accuracy neural networks are often held secret for at least two reasons. First, they are seen as a competitive advantage and are treated as trade secrets [Wen90]; for example, none of the earlier systems are open-source. Second, is seen as improving both security and privacy to keep these models secret. With full white-box access it is easy to mount evasion attacks and generate *adversarial examples* [SZS+14, BCM+13] against, for instance, abuse- or spam-detection models. Further, white-box access allows *model inversion* attacks [FJR15]: it is possible to reconstruct identifiable images of specific people given a model trained to recognize specific human faces. Similarly, given a language model trained on text containing sensitive data (e.g., credit card numbers), a white-box attacker can pull this sensitive data out of the trained model [CLE+19].

Fortunately for providers of machine learning models, it is often expensive to reproduce a neural network. There are three reasons for this cost: first, most machine learning requires extensive training data that can be expensive to collect; second, neural networks typically need *hyper-parameter tuning* requiring training many models to identify the optimal final model configuration; and third, even performing a final training run given the collected training data and correctly configured model is expensive.

For all of the above reasons, it becomes clear that (a) adversaries are motivated for various reasons to obtain a copy of existing deployed neural network, and (b) preserving the secrecy of models is highly important. In practice companies ensure the secrecy of these models by either releasing only an API allowing query access, or releasing on-device models, but attempting to tamper-proof and obfuscate the source to make it difficult to extract out of the device.

Understandably, the above weak forms of protection are often seen as insufficient. The area of "secure inference" improves on this by bringing tools from Secure Function Evaluation (SFE), which allows mutually distrustful cooperating parties to evaluate $f(x)$ where f is held by one party and x by the other. The various proposals often apply fully homomorphic encryption [Gen09, GBDL+16], garbled circuits [Yao86, RWT+18], or combinations of the two [MLS+20]. Per the standard SFE guarantee, secure inference "does not hide information [about the function f] that is revealed by the result of the prediction" [MLS+20]. However this line of work often implicitly assumes that total leakage from the predictions is small, and that recovering the function from its output would be difficult.

In total, it is clear that protecting the secrecy of neural network models is seen as important both in practice and in the academic research community. This leads to the question that we study in this paper:

> *Is it possible to* extract *an identical copy of a neural network given oracle (black-box) access to the target model?*

While this question is not new [TZJ+16, MSDH19, JCB+19, RK19], we argue that model extraction should be studied as a cryptanalytic problem. To do this, we focus on model extraction in an idealized environment where a machine learning model is made available as an oracle $\mathcal{O}$ that can be queried, but with no timing or other side channels. This setting captures that of obfuscated models made public, prediction APIs, and secure inference.

1.1 Model Extraction as a Cryptanalytic Problem

The key insight of this paper is that model extraction is closely related to an extremely well-studied problem in cryptography: the cryptanalysis of block-ciphers. Informally, a symmetric-key encryption algorithm is a keyed function $E_k \colon \mathcal{X} \to \mathcal{Y}$ that maps inputs (plaintexts) $x \in \mathcal{X}$ to outputs (ciphertexts) $y \in \mathcal{Y}$. We expect all practically important ciphers to be resistant, at the very least, to key recovery under the adaptive chosen-plaintext attack, i.e., given some bounded number of (adaptively chosen) plaintext/ciphertext pairs $\{(x_i, y_i)\}$ an encryption algorithm is designed so that the key k cannot be extracted by a computationally-bounded adversary.

Contrast this to machine learning. A neural network model is (informally) a parameterized function $f_\theta \colon \mathcal{X} \to \mathcal{Y}$ that maps input (e.g., images) $x \in \mathcal{X}$ to outputs (e.g., labels) $y \in \mathcal{Y}$. A *model extraction* attack adaptively queries the neural network to obtain a set of input/output pairs $\{(x_i, y_i)\}$ that reveals information about the weights θ. Neural networks are not constructed by design to be resistant to such attacks.

Thus, viewed appropriately, performing a model extraction attack—learning the weights θ given oracle access to the function f_θ—is a similar problem to performing a *chosen-plaintext attack* on a nontraditional "encryption" algorithm.

Given that it took the field of cryptography decades to design encryption algorithms secure against chosen-plaintext attacks, it would be deeply surprising if neural networks, where such attacks are not even considered in their design, were *not* vulnerable. Worse, the *primary* objective of cipher design is robustness against such attacks. Machine learning models, on the other hand, are primarily designed to be *accurate* at some underlying task, making the design of chosen-plaintext secure neural networks an even more challenging problem.

There are three differences separating model extraction from standard cryptanalysis that make model extraction nontrivial and interesting to study.

First, the attack success criterion differs. While a cryptographic break can be successful even without learning key bits—for example by distinguishing the algorithm from a pseudo-random function, only "total breaks" that reveal (some of) the actual model parameters θ are interesting for model extraction.

Second, the earlier analogy to keyed ciphers is imperfect. Neural networks typically take high-dimensional inputs (e.g., images) and return low-dimensional outputs (e.g., a single probability). It is almost more appropriate to make an analogy to cryptanalysis of keyed many-to-one functions, such as MACs. However, the security properties of MACs are quite different from those of machine learning models, for example second preimages are expected rather than shunned in neural networks.

Finally, and the largest difference in practice, is that machine learning models deal in fixed- or floating-point reals rather than finite field arithmetic. As such, there are many components to our attack that would be significantly simplified given infinitely precise floating-point math, but given the realities of modern machine learning, require far more sophisticated attack techniques.

1.2   Our Results

We introduce a differential attack that is effective at performing *functionally-equivalent* neural network model extraction attacks. Our attack traces the neural network's evaluation on pairs of examples that differ in a few entries and uses this to recover the layers (analogous to the rounds of a block cipher) of a neural network one by one. To evaluate the efficacy of our attack, we formalize the definition of *fidelity* introduced in prior work [JCB+19] and quantify the degree to which a model extraction attack has succeeded:

Definition 1. *Two models f and g are (ϵ, δ)-functionally equivalent on S if*

$$\Pr_{x \in S} \left[|f(x) - g(x)| \leq \epsilon \right] \geq 1 - \delta.$$

Table 1 reports the results of our differential attack across a wide range of model sizes and architectures, reporting both (ϵ, δ)-functional equivalence on the set $S = [0, 1]^{d_o}$, the input space of the model, along with a direct measurement of $\max |\theta - \hat{\theta}|$, directly measuring the error between the actual model weights θ and the extracted weights $\hat{\theta}$ (as described in Sect. 6.2).

Table 1. Efficacy of our extraction attack which is orders of magnitude more precise than prior work and for deeper neural networks orders of magnitude more query efficient. Models denoted a-b-c are *fully connected* neural networks with input dimension a, one hidden layer with b *neurons*, and c outputs; for formal definitions see Sect. 2. Entries denoted with a † were unable to recover the network after ten attempts.

Architecture	Parameters	Approach	Queries	$(\epsilon, 10^{-9})$	$(\epsilon, 0)$	$\max |\theta - \hat{\theta}|$
784-32-1	25,120	[JCB+19]	$2^{18.2}$	$2^{3.2}$	$2^{4.5}$	$2^{-1.7}$
		Ours	$2^{19.2}$	$2^{-28.8}$	$2^{-27.4}$	$2^{-30.2}$
784-128-1	100,480	[JCB+19]	$2^{20.2}$	$2^{4.8}$	$2^{5.1}$	$2^{-1.8}$
		Ours	$2^{21.5}$	$2^{-26.4}$	$2^{-24.7}$	$2^{-29.4}$
10-10-10-1	210	[RK19]	2^{22}	$2^{-10.3}$	$2^{-3.4}$	2^{-12}
		Ours	$2^{16.0}$	$2^{-42.7}$	$2^{-37.98}$	2^{-36}
10-20-20-1	420	[RK19]	2^{25}	$\infty^{\dagger}$	$\infty^{\dagger}$	$\infty^{\dagger}$
		Ours	$2^{17.1}$	$2^{-44.6}$	$2^{-38.7}$	2^{-37}
40-20-10-10-1	1,110	Ours	$2^{17.8}$	$2^{-31.7}$	$2^{-23.4}$	$2^{-27.1}$
80-40-20-1	4,020	Ours	$2^{18.5}$	$2^{-45.5}$	$2^{-40.4}$	$2^{-39.7}$

The remainder of this paper is structured as follows. We introduce the notation, threat model, and attacker goals and assumptions used in Sect. 2. In Sect. 4 we introduce an idealized attack that extracts $(0, 0)$-functionally-equivalent neural networks assuming infinite precision arithmetic. Section 5 develops an instantiation of this attack that works in practice with finite-precision arithmetic to yield (ϵ, δ)-functionally equivalent attacks.

1.3   Related Work

Model extraction attacks are classified into two categories [JCB+19]: *task accuracy* extraction and *fidelity* extraction. The first paper to study task accuracy extraction [TZJ+16] introduced techniques to steal *similar* models that approximately solves the same underlying decision task on the natural data distribution, but do not necessarily match the predictions of the oracle precisely. While further work exists in this space [CCG+18,KTP+19], we instead focus on fidelity extraction where the adversary aims to faithfully reproduce the predictions of the oracle model, when it is incorrect with respect to the ground truth. Again, [TZJ+16] studied this problem and developed (what we would now call) functionally equivalent extraction for the case of completely linear models.

This attack was then extended by a theoretical result defining and giving a method for performing functionally-equivalent extraction for neural networks with one layer, assuming oracle access to the gradients [MSDH19]. A concrete implementation of this one layer attack that works in practice, handling floating point imprecision, was subsequently developed through applying finite differences to estimate the gradient [JCB+19]. Parallel work to this also extended on these results, focusing on deeper networks, but required tens to hundreds of millions of queries [RK19]; while the theoretical results extended to deep networks, the implementation in practice only extracts up to the first two layers. Our work builds on all of these four results to develop an approach that is 10^6 times more accurate, requiring 10^3 times fewer queries, and applies to larger models.

Even without query access, it is possible to steal models with just a cache side-channel [BBJP19], although with less fidelity than our attack that we introduce which are $2^{20}\times$ more precise. Other attacks target *hyperparameter* extraction— that is, extracting high-level details about the model: through what method it was trained, if it contains convolutions, or related questions [WG18]. It is further possible to steal hyperparameters with cache side channels [HDK+20].

Recent work has studied the learnability of deep neural networks with random weights in the statistical query (SQ) model [DGKP20], showing that learnability drops off exponentially with the depth of the network. This line of work does not address the *cryptographic* hardness of extraction in the non-SQ model—precisely the question addressed in this work in the empirical setting.

While not directly related to our problem, it is worth noting that we are not the first to treat neural networks as just another type of mathematical function that can be analyzed without any specific knowledge of machine learning. Shamir et al. [SSRD19] explain the existence of adversarial examples [SZS+14,BCM+13], which capture evasion attacks on machine learning classifiers, by considering an abstract model of neural networks.

In a number of places, our attack draws inspiration from the cryptanalysis of keyed block-ciphers, most prominently differential cryptanalysis [BS91]. We neither assume nor require familiarity with this field, but the informed reader may enjoy certain parallels.

2 Preliminaries

This paper studies an abstraction of neural networks as functions $f: \mathcal{X} \to \mathcal{Y}$. Our results are independent of any methods for selecting the function f (e.g., stochastic gradient descent), and are independent of any utility of the function f. As such, machine learning knowledge is neither expected nor necessary.

2.1 Notation and Definitions

Definition 2. *A k-deep neural network $f_\theta(x)$ is a function parameterized by θ that takes inputs from an input space $\mathcal{X}$ and returns values in an output space $\mathcal{Y}$. The function f is composed as a sequence of functions alternating between linear layers f_j and a nonlinear function (acting component-wise) σ:*

$$f = f_{k+1} \circ \sigma \circ \cdots \circ \sigma \circ f_2 \circ \sigma \circ f_1.$$

We exclusively study neural networks over $\mathcal{X} = \mathbb{R}^{d_0}$ and $\mathcal{Y} = \mathbb{R}^{d_k}$. (Until Sect. 5 we assume floating-point numbers can represent $\mathbb{R}$ exactly.)

Definition 3. *The jth* layer *of the neural network f_j is given by the affine transformation $f_j(x) = A^{(j)}x + b^{(j)}$. The weights $A^{(j)} \in \mathbb{R}^{d_j \times d_{j-1}}$ is a $d_j \times d_{j-1}$ matrix; the biases $b^{(j)} \in \mathbb{R}^{d_j}$ is a d_j-dimensional vector.*

While representing each layer f_j as a full matrix product is the most general definition of a layer, which is called *fully connected*, often layers have more structure. For example, it is common to use (discrete) *convolutions* in neural networks that operate on images. Convolutional layers take the input as a $n \times m$ matrix and convolve it with a kernel, such as a 3×3 matrix. Importantly, however, it is always possible to represent a convolution as a matrix product.

Definition 4. *The neurons $\{\eta_i\}_{i=1}^N$ are functions receiving an input and passing it through the* activation function σ. *There are a total of $N = \sum_{j=1}^{k-1} d_j$ neurons.*

In this paper we exclusively study the ReLU [NH10] activation function, given by $\sigma(x) = \max(x, 0)$. Our results are a fundamental consequence of the fact that ReLU neural networks are piecewise linear functions.

Definition 5. *The* architecture *of a neural network captures the structure of f: (a) the number of layers, (b) the dimensions of each layer $\{d_i\}_{i=0}^k$, and (c) any additional constraints imposed on the weights $A^{(i)}$ and biases $b^{(i)}$.*

We use the shorthand a-b-c neural network to denote the sizes of each dimension; for example a 10-20-5 neural network has input dimension 10, one layer with 20 neurons, and output dimension 5. This description completely characterizes the structure of f for fully connected networks. In practice, there are only a few architectures that represent most of the deployed deep learning models [ZL16], and developing new architectures is an extremely difficult and active area in research [HZRS16, SIVA17, TL19].

Definition 6. *The parameters θ of f_θ are the concrete assignments to the weights $A^{(j)}$ and biases $b^{(j)}$, obtained during the process of training the neural network.*

It is beyond the scope of this paper to describe the training process which produces the parameters θ: it suffices to know that the process of training is often computationally expensive and that training is a nondeterministic process, and so training the same model multiple times will give different sets of parameters.

2.2 Adversarial Goals and Resources

There are two parties in a model extraction attack: the oracle $\mathcal{O}$ who returns $f_\theta(x)$, and the adversary who generates queries x to the oracle.

Definition 7. *A model parameter extraction attack receives oracle access to a parameterized function f_θ (in our case a k-deep neural network) and the architecture of f, and returns a set of parameters $\hat{\theta}$ with the goal that $f_\theta(x)$ is as similar as possible to $f_{\hat{\theta}}(x)$.*

Throughout this paper we use the $\hat{}$ symbol to indicate an extracted parameter. For example, $\hat{\theta}$ refers to the extracted weights of a model θ.

There is a spectrum of similarity definitions between the extracted weights and the oracle model that prior work has studied [TZJ+16, JCB+19, KTP+19]; we focus on the setting where the adversarial advantage is defined by (ε, δ)-functionally equivalent extraction as in Definition 1.

Analogous to cryptanalysis of symmetric-key primitives, the degree to which a model extraction attack succeeds is determined by (a) the number of chosen inputs to the model, and (b) the amount of compute required.

Assumptions. We make several assumptions of the oracle $\mathcal{O}$ and the attacker's knowledge. (We believe many of these assumptions are not fundamental and can be relaxed. Removing these assumptions is left to future work.)

- **Architecture knowledge.** We require knowledge of the architecture of the neural network.
- **Full-domain inputs.** We feed arbitrary inputs from $\mathcal{X}$.
- **Complete outputs.** We receive outputs directly from the model f without further processing (e.g., by returning only the most likely class without a score).
- **Precise computations.** f is specified and evaluated using 64-bit floating-point arithmetic.
- **Scalar outputs.** Without loss of generality we require the output dimensionality is 1, i.e., $\mathcal{Y} = \mathbb{R}$.
- **ReLU Activations.** All activation functions (σ's) are ReLU's.[1]

---

[1] This is the only assumption *fundamental* to our work. Switching to any activation that is not piecewise linear would prevent our attack. However, as mentioned, all state-of-the-art models use exclusively (piecewise linear generalizations of) the ReLU activation function [SIVA17, TL19].

3   Overview of the Differential Attack

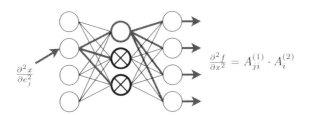

$$\frac{\partial^2 x}{\partial e_j^2} \qquad \frac{\partial^2 f}{\partial x^2} = A_{ji}^{(1)} \cdot A_i^{(2)}$$

Fig. 1. A schematic of our extraction attack on a 1-deep neural network. Let x be an input that causes exactly one neuron to have value zero. The second differential becomes zero at all other neurons—because they remain either fully-inactive or fully-active. Therefore the value of this differential is equal to the product of the weight going into the neuron at its critical point and the weight going out of this neuron.

Given oracle access to the function f_θ, we can estimate ∂f_θ through finite differences along arbitrary directions. For simple linear functions defined by $f(x) = a \cdot x + b$, its directional derivative satisfies $\frac{\partial f}{\partial e_i} = a_i$, where e_i is the basis vector and a_i is the ith entry of the vector a, allowing direct recovery of its weights through querying on these well-chosen inputs.

In the case of deep neural networks, we consider second partial directional derivatives. ReLU neural networks are piecewise linear functions with $\frac{\partial^2 f}{\partial x^2} \equiv 0$ almost everywhere, except when the function has some neuron η_j at the boundary between the negative and positive region (i.e., is at its *critical point*). We show that the value of the partial derivative $\frac{\partial^2 f}{\partial e_i^2}$ evaluated at a point x so that neuron η_j is at such a critical point actually directly reveals the weight $T(A_{i,j}^{(1)})$ for some transform T that is invertible—and therefore the adversary can learn $A_{i,j}^{(1)}$. By repeating this attack along all basis vectors e_i and for all neurons η_j we can recover the complete matrix $A^{(1)}$. Once we have extracted the first layer's weights, we are able to "peel off" that layer and re-mount our attack on the second layer of the neural network, repeating to the final layer. There are three core technical difficulties to our attack:

Recovering the neuron signs. For each neuron η, our attack does not exactly recover $A_i^{(l)}$, the ith row of $A^{(l)}$, but instead a scalar multiple $v = \alpha \cdot A_i^{(l)}$. While losing a constant $\alpha > 0$ keeps the neural network in the same equivalence class, the sign of α is important and we must distinguish between the weight vector $A_i^{(l)}$ and $-A_i^{(l)}$. We construct two approaches that solve this problem, but in the general case we require exponential work (but a linear number of queries).

Controlling inner-layer hidden state. On the first layer, we can directly compute the derivative entry-by-entry, measuring $\frac{\partial^2 f}{\partial e_i^2}$ for each standard basis vector e_i in order to recover $A_{ij}^{(1)}$. Deeper in the network, we can not move along standard basis vector vectors. Worse, for each input x on average half of the neurons are in the negative region and thus their output is identically 0; when this happens it is not possible to learn the weight along edges with value zero. Thus we are required to develop techniques to elicit behavior from every neuron, and techniques to cluster together partial recoveries of each row of $A_i^{(l)}$ to form a complete recovery.

Handling floating-point imprecision. Implementing our attack in practice with finite precision neural networks introduces additional complexity. In order to estimate the second partial derivative, we require querying on inputs that differ by only a small amount, reducing the precision of the extracted first weight matrix to twenty bits, or roughly 10^{-6}. This error of 10^{-6} is not large to begin with, but this error impacts our ability to recover the next layer, compounding multiplicatively the deeper we go in the network. Already in the second layer, the error is magnified to 10^{-4}, which can completely prevent reconstruction for the third layer: our predicted view of the hidden state is sufficiently different from the actual hidden state that our attack fails completely. We resolve this through two means. First, we introduce numerically stable methods assuming that all prior layers have been extracted to high precision. Second, we develop a precision-refinement technique that takes a prefix of the first $j \leq k$ layers of a neural network extracted to n bits of precision and returns the j-deep model extracted to $2n$ bits of precision (up to floating-point tolerance).

4   Idealized Differential Extraction Attack

We now introduce our $(0, 0)$-functionally-equivalent model extraction attack that assumes infinite precision arithmetic and recovers completely functionally equivalent models. Recall our attack assumptions (Sect. 2.2); using these, we present our attack beginning with two "reduced-round" attacks on 0-deep (Sect. 4.1) and 1-deep (Sect. 4.2) neural networks, and then proceeding to k-deep extraction for contractive (Sect. 4.3) and expansive (Sect. 4.4) neural networks. Section 5 refines this idealized attack to work with finite precision.

4.1   Zero-Deep Neural Network Extraction

Zero-deep neural networks are linear functions $f(x) \equiv A^{(1)} \cdot x + b^{(1)}$. Querying d_0 linearly independent suffices to extract f by solving the resulting linear system.

However let us view this problem differently, to illuminate our attack strategy for deeper networks. Consider the parallel evaluations $f(x)$ and $f(x + \delta)$, with

$$f(x + \delta) - f(x) = A^{(1)} \cdot (x + \delta) - A^{(1)} \cdot x = A^{(1)} \cdot \delta.$$

If $\delta = e_i$, the ith standard basis vector of $\mathbb{R}^{d_0}$ (e.g., $e_2 = \begin{bmatrix} 0 \ 1 \ 0 \ 0 \dots 0 \end{bmatrix}$), then

$$f(x + \delta) - f(x) = A^{(1)} \cdot \delta = A_i^{(1)}.$$

This allows us to directly read off the weights of $A^{(1)}$. Put differently, we perform finite differences to estimate the gradient of f, given by $\nabla_x f(x) \equiv A^{(1)}$.

4.2   One-Deep Neural Network Extraction

Many of the important problems that complicate deep neural network extraction begin to arise at 1-deep neural networks. Because the function is no longer completely linear, we require multiple phases to recover the network completely. To do so, we will proceed layer-by-layer, extracting the first layer, and then use the 0-deep neural network attack to recover the second layer.

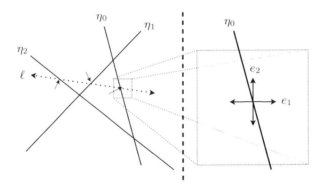

Fig. 2. (left) Geometry of a 1-deep neural network. The three solid line corresponds to "critical hyperplanes" of neurons. We identify one *witness* to each neuron with binary search on the dotted line ℓ. **(right)** For each discovered critical point, we compute the second partial derivative along axis e_1 and e_2 to compute the angle of the hyperplane.

For the remainder of this paper it will be useful to have two distinct mental models of the problem at hand. First is the *symbolic* view shown previously in Fig. 1. This view directly studies the flow of information through the neural networks, represented as an alternating sequence of linear layers and non-linear transformations. This view helps understanding the algebraic steps of our attack.

The second is the *geometric* view. Because neural networks operate over the real vector space, they can be visualized by plotting two dimensional slices of the landscape [MSDH19]. Figure 2 (left) contains an example of such a figure. Each solid black line corresponds to a change in gradient induced in the space by a neuron changing sign from positive to negative (or vice versa)— ignoring for now the remaining lines. The problem of neural network extraction corresponds to recovering the locations and angles of these neuron-induced *hyperplanes*: in general with input dimension d_0, the planes have dimension $d_0 - 1$.

Definition 8. *The function that computes the first j layers (up to and including f_j but not including σ) of f is denoted as $f_{1..j}$. In particular, $f = f_{1..k}$.*

Definition 9. *The* hidden state *at layer j is the output of the function $f_{1..j}$, before applying the nonlinear transformation σ.*

Layer f_j is a linear transformation of the $(j-1)$st hidden state after σ.

Definition 10. *$\mathcal{V}(\eta; x)$ denotes the input to neuron η (before applying σ) when evaluated at x. $\mathcal{L}(\eta)$ denotes the layer of neuron η. The first layer starts at 1.*

Definition 11. *A neuron η is at a* critical point *when $\mathcal{V}(\eta; x) = 0$. We refer to this input x as a* witness *to the fact that η is at a critical point, denoted by $x \in \mathcal{W}(\eta)$. If $\mathcal{V}(\eta; x) > 0$ then η is* active, *and otherwise* inactive.

In Fig. 2 the locations of these critical points correspond exactly to the solid black lines drawn through the plane. Observe that because we restrict ourselves to ReLU neural networks, the function f is piecewise linear and infinitely differentiable almost everywhere. The gradient $\nabla_x f(x)$ is well defined at all points x except when there exists a neuron that is at its critical point.

Extracting the rows of $A^{(1)}$ up to sign. Functionally, the attack as presented in this subsection has appeared previously in the literature [MSDH19,JCB+19]. By framing it differently, our attack will be extensible to deeper networks.

Assume we were given a witness $x^* \in \mathcal{W}(\eta_j)$ that caused neuron η_j to be at its critical point (i.e., its value is identically zero). Because we are using the ReLU activation function, this is the point at which that neuron is currently "inactive" (i.e., is not contributing to the output of the classifier) but would become "active" (i.e., contributing to the output) if it becomes slightly positive. Further assume that *only* this neuron η_j is at its critical point, and that for all others neurons $\eta \neq \eta_j$ we have $|\mathcal{V}(\eta, x_j)| > \delta$ for a constant $\delta > 0$.

Consider two parallel executions of the neural network on pairs of examples. Begin by defining e_i as the standard basis vectors of $\mathcal{X} = \mathbb{R}^N$. By querying on the two pairs of inputs $(x^*, x^* + \epsilon e_i)$ and $(x^*, x^* - \epsilon e_i)$ we can estimate

$$\alpha_+^i = \left.\frac{\partial f(x)}{\partial e_i}\right|_{x=x^*+\epsilon e_1} \quad \text{and} \quad \alpha_-^i = \left.\frac{\partial f(x)}{\partial e_i}\right|_{x=x^*-\epsilon e_1}$$

through finite differences.

Consider the quantity $|\alpha_+ - \alpha_-|$. Because x^* induces a critical point of η_j, exactly one of $\{\alpha_+, \alpha_-\}$ will have the neuron η_j in its active regime and the other will have η_j in its inactive regime. If no two columns of $A^{(1)}$ are collinear, then as long as $\epsilon < \frac{\delta}{\sum_{i,j}|A_{i,j}^{(1)}|}$, we are guaranteed that all other neurons in the neural network will remain in the same state as before—either active or inactive. Therefore, if we compute the difference $|\alpha_+^i - \alpha_-^i|$, the gradient information flowing into and out of all other neurons will cancel and we will be left with just the gradient information flowing along the edge from the input coordinate i to neuron η_j to the output. Concretely, we can write the 1-deep neural network as

$$f(x) = A^{(2)}\text{ReLU}(A^{(1)}x + b^{(1)}) + b^{(2)}.$$

and so either $\alpha_+^i - \alpha_-^i = A_{j,i}^{(1)} \cdot A^{(2)}$ or $\alpha_-^i - \alpha_+^i = A_{j,i}^{(1)} \cdot A^{(2)}$. However, if we repeat the above procedure on a new basis vector e_k then either $\alpha_+^k - \alpha_-^k = A_{j,k}^{(1)} \cdot A^{(2)}$ or $\alpha_-^k - \alpha_+^k = A_{j,k}^{(1)} \cdot A^{(2)}$ will hold. Crucially, whichever of the two relations that holds for along coordinate i will be the same relation that holds on coordinate k. Therefore we can divide out $A^{(2)}$ to obtain the ratio of pairs of weights

$$\frac{\alpha_+^k - \alpha_-^k}{\alpha_+^i - \alpha_-^i} = \frac{A_{j,k}^{(1)}}{A_{j,i}^{(1)}}.$$

This allows us to compute every row of $A^{(1)}$ up to a single scalar c_j. Further, we can compute $b_j^{(1)} = -\hat{A}_j^{(1)} \cdot x^*$ (again, up to a scaling factor) because we know that x^* induces a critical point on neuron η_j and so its value is zero.

Observe that the magnitude of c_j is unimportant. We can always push a constant $c > 0$ through to the weight matrix $A^{(2)}$ and have an a functionally equivalent result. However, the *sign* of c_j does matter.

Extracting row signs. Consider a single witness x_i for an arbitrary neuron η_i. Let $h = f_1(x)$, so that at least one element of h is identically zero. If we assume that $A^{(1)}$ is contractive (Sect. 4.4 studies non-contractive networks) then we can find a preimage x to any vector h. In particular, let e_i be the unit vector in the space $\mathbb{R}^{d_1}$. Then we can compute a preimage x_+ so that $\hat{f}_1(x_+) = h + e_i$, and a preimage x_- so that $\hat{f}_1(x_-) = h - e_i$.

Because x_i is a witness to neuron η_i being at its critical point, we will have that either $f(x_+) = f(x_i)$ or $f(x_-) = f(x_i)$. Exactly one of these equalities is true because $\sigma(h - e_i) = \sigma(h)$, but $\sigma(h + e_i) \neq \sigma(h)$ when $h_i = 0$. Therefore if the second equality holds true, then we know that our extracted guess of the ith row has the correct sign. However, if the first equality holds true, then our extracted guess of the ith row has the incorrect sign, and so we invert it (along with the bias $b_i^{(1)}$). We repeat this procedure with a critical point for every neuron η_i to completely recover the signs for the full first layer.

Finding witnesses to critical points. It only remains to show how to find witnesses $x^* \in \mathcal{W}(\eta)$ for each neuron η on the first layer. We choose a random line in input space (the dashed line in Fig. 2, left), and search along it for nonlinearities in the partial derivative. Any nonlinearity must have resulted from a ReLU changing signs, and locating the specific location where the ReLU changes signs will give us a critical point. We do this by binary search.

To begin, we take a random initial point $x_0, v \in \mathbb{R}^{d_0}$ together with a large range T. We perform a binary search for nonlinearities in $f(x_0 + tv)$ for $t \in [-T, T]$. That is, for a given interval $[t_0, t_1]$, we know a critical point exists in the interval if $\frac{\partial f(x + tv)}{\partial v}|_{t=t_0} \neq \frac{\partial f(x + tv)}{\partial v}|_{t=t_1}$. If these quantities are equal, we do not search the interval, otherwise we continue with the binary search.

Extracting the second layer. Once we have fully recovered the first layer weights, we can "peel off" the weight matrix $A^{(1)}$ and bias $b^{(1)}$ and we are left with extracting the final linear layer, which reduces to 0-deep extraction.

4.3 k-Deep Contractive Neural Networks

Extending the above attack to deep neural networks has several complications that prior work was unable to resolve efficiently; we address them one at a time.

Critical Points Can Occur Due to ReLUs on Different Layers. Because 1-deep networks have only one layer, all ReLUs occur on that layer. Therefore all critical points found during search will correspond to a neuron on that layer. For k-deep networks this is not true, and if we want to begin by extracting the first layer we will have to remove non-first layer critical points. (And, in general, to extract layer j, we will have to remove non-layer-j critical points.)

The Weight Recovery Procedure Requires Complete Control of the Input. In order to be able to directly read off the weights, we query the network on basis vectors e_i. Achieving this is not always possible for deep networks, and we must account for the fact that we may only be able to query on non-orthogonal directions.

Recovering Row Signs Requires Computing the Preimage of Arbitrary Hidden States. Our row-sign procedure requires that we be able to invert $A^{(1)}$, which in general implies we need to develop a method to compute a preimage of $f_{1..j}$.

4.3.1   Extracting Layer-1 Weights with Unknown Critical Point Layers

Suppose we had a function $\mathcal{C}_0(f) = \{x_i\}_{i=1}^M$ that returns at least one critical points for every neuron in the first layer (implying $M \geq d_1$), but never returns critical points for any deeper layer. We claim that the exact differential attack from above still correctly recovers the first layer of a deep neural network.

We make the following observation. Let $x^* \notin \bigcup_{\eta_i} \mathcal{W}(\eta_i)$ be an input that is a witness to no critical point, i.e., $|\mathcal{V}(\eta_i; x^*)| > \epsilon > 0$. Define f_{local} as the function so that for a sufficiently small region we have that $f_{\text{local}} \equiv f$, that is,

$$f_{\text{local}}(x) = \left(A^{(k+1)} \cdots \left(I^{(2)}(A^{(2)}(I^{(1)}(A^{(1)}x + b^{(1)})) + b^{(2)})\right) + \ldots\right) + b^{(k+1)}$$
$$= A^{(k+1)} I^{(k)} A^{(k)} \cdots I^{(2)} A^{(2)} I^{(1)} A^{(1)} x + \beta$$
$$= \Gamma x + \beta$$

Here, $I^{(j)}$ are 0–1 diagonal matrices with a 0 on the diagonal when the neuron is inactive and 1 on the diagonal when the neuron is active:

$$I_{n,n}^{(j)} = \begin{cases} 1 & \text{if } \mathcal{V}(\eta_n; x) > 0 \\ 0 & \text{otherwise} \end{cases}$$

where η_n is the nth neuron on the first layer. Importantly, observe that each $I^{(j)}$ is a constant as long as x is sufficiently close to x^*. While β is unknown, as long as we make only gradient queries $\partial f_{\text{local}}$ its value is unimportant. This observation so far follows from the definition of piecewise linearity.

Consider now some input that is a witness to exactly one critical point on neuron η^*. Formally, $x^* \in \mathcal{W}(\eta^*)$, but $x^* \notin \bigcup_{\eta_j \neq \eta^*} \mathcal{W}(\eta_j; x^*)$. Then

$$f_{\text{local}}(x) = A^{(k+1)} I^{(k)} A^{(k)} \cdots I^{(2)} A^{(2)} I^{(1)}(x) A^{(1)} x + \beta(x)$$

where again $I^{(j)}$ are 0–1 matrices, but except that now, $I^{(1)}$ (and only $I^{(1)}$) is a function of x returning a 0–1 diagonal matrix that has one of two values, depending on the value of $\mathcal{V}(\eta^*; x) > 0$. Therefore we can no longer collapse the matrix product into one matrix Γ but instead can only obtain

$$f_{\text{local}}(x) = \Gamma I^{(1)}(x) A^{(1)} x + \beta(x).$$

But this is exactly the case we have already solved for 1-deep neural network weight recovery: it is equivalent to the statement $f_{\text{local}}(x) = \Gamma \sigma(A^{(1)} x + b^{(1)}) + \beta_2$, and so by dividing out Γ exactly as before we can recover the ratios of $A^{(1)}_{i,j}$.

Finding first-layer critical points. Assume we are given a set of inputs $S = \{x_i\}$ so that each x_i is a witness to neuron η_{x_i}, with η_{x_i} unknown. By the coupon collector's argument (assuming uniformity), for $|S| \gg N \log N$, where N is the total number of neurons, we will have at least *two* witnesses to every neuron η.

Without loss of generality let $x_0, x_1 \in \mathcal{W}(\eta)$ be witnesses to the same neuron η on the first layer, i.e, that $\mathcal{V}(\eta; x_0) = \mathcal{V}(\eta; x_1) = 0$. Then, performing the weight recovery procedure beginning from each of these witnesses (through finite differences) will yield the correct weight vector $A^{(1)}_j$ up to a scalar.

Typically elements of S will *not* be witnesses to neurons on the first layer. Without loss of generality let x_2 and x_3 be witnesses to any neuron on a deeper layer. We claim that we will be able to detect these error cases: the outputs of the extraction algorithm will appear to be random and uncorrelated. Informally speaking, because we are running an attack designed to extract first-layer neurons on a neuron actually on a later layer, it is exceedingly unlikely that the attack would, by chance, give consistent results when run on x_2 and x_3 (or any arbitrary pair of neurons).

Formally, let $h_2 = f_1(x_2)$ and $h_3 = f_1(x_3)$. With high probability, $\text{sign}(h_2) \neq \text{sign}(h_3)$. Therefore, when executing the extraction procedure on x_2 we compute over the function $\Gamma_1 I^{(1)}(x_2) A^{(1)} x + \beta_1$, whereas extracting on x_3 computes over $\Gamma_2 I^{(1)}(x_3) A^{(1)} x + \beta_2$. Because $\Gamma_1 \neq \Gamma_2$, this will give inconsistent results.

Therefore our first layer weight recovery procedure is as follows. For all inputs $x_i \in S$ run the weight recovery procedure to recover the unit-length normal vector to each critical hyperplane. We should expect to see a large number of vectors only once (because they were the result of running the extraction of a layer 2 or greater neuron), and a small number of vectors that appear duplicated (because they were the result of successful extraction on the first layer). Given the first layer, we can reduce the neural network from a k-deep neural network to a $(k-1)$-deep neural network and repeat the attack. We must resolve two difficulties, however, discussed in the following two subsections.

4.3.2   Extracting Hidden Layer Weights with Unknown Critical Points

When extracting the first layer weight matrix, we were able to compute $\frac{\partial^2 f}{\partial e_i \partial e_j}$ for each input basis vectors e_i, allowing us to "read off" the ratios of the weights on the first layer directly from the partial derivatives. However, for deeper layers, it is nontrivial to exactly control the hidden layers and change just one coordinate in order to perform finite differences.[2] Let j denote the current layer we are extracting. Begin by sampling $d_j + 1$ directions $\delta_i \sim \mathcal{N}(0, \epsilon I_{d_0}) \in \mathcal{X}$ and let

$$\{y_i\} = \left\{ \frac{\partial^2 f(x)}{\partial \delta_1 \partial \delta_i} \bigg|_{x=x^*} \right\}_{i=1}^{d_j+1}.$$

From here we can construct a system of equations: let $h_i = \sigma(f_{1..j-1}(x + \delta_i))$ and solve for the vector w such that $h_i \cdot w = y_i$.

As before, we run the weight recovery procedure assuming that each witness corresponds to a critical point on the correct layer. Witnesses that correspond to neurons on incorrect layers will give uncorrelated errors that can be discarded.

Unifying partial solutions. The above algorithm overlooks one important problem. For a given critical point x^*, the hidden vector obtained from $f_{1..j}(x^*)$ is likely to have several (on average, half) neurons that are negative, and therefore $\sigma(f_{1..j}(x^*))$ and any $\sigma(f_{1..j}(x^* + \delta_i))$ will have neurons that are identically zero. This makes it impossible to recover the complete weight vector from just one application of least squares—it is only possible to compute the weights for those entries that are non-zero. One solution would be to search for a witness x^* such that component-wise $f_{1..j}(x^*) \geq 0$; however doing this is not possible in general, and so we do not consider this option further.

Instead, we combine together multiple attempts at extracting the weights through a *unification* procedure. If x_1 and x_2 are witnesses to critical points for the same neuron, and the partial vector $f_{1..j}(x_1)$ has entries $t_1 \subset \{1, \ldots, d_j\}$ and the partial vector $f_{1..j}(x_2)$ has entries $t_2 \subset \{1, \ldots, d_j\}$ defined, then it is possible to recover the ratios for all entries $t_1 \cup t_2$ by unifying together the two partial solutions as long as $t_1 \cap t_2$ is non-empty as follows.

Let r_i denote the extracted weight vector on witness x_1 with entries at locations $t_1 \subset \{1, \ldots, d_j\}$ (respectively, r_2 at x_2 with locations at t_2). Because the two vectors correspond to the solution for the same row of the weight matrix $A_i^{(j)}$, the vectors r_1 and r_2 must be consistent on $t_1 \cap t_2$. Therefore, we will have that $r_1[t_1 \cap t_2] = c \cdot r_2[t_1 \cap t_2]$ for a scalar $c \neq 0$. As long as $t_1 \cap t_2 \neq \emptyset$ we can compute the appropriate constant c and then recover the weight vector $r_{1,2}$ with entries at positions $t_1 \cup t_2$.

Observe that this procedure also allows us to *check* whether or not x_1 and x_2 are witnesses to the same neuron n reaching its critical point. If $|t_1 \cap t_2| \geq \gamma$, then as long as there do not exist two rows of $A^{(j)}$ that have $\gamma + 1$ entries that are scalar multiples of each other, there will be a unique solution that merges the

---

[2] For the expansive networks we will discuss in Sect. 4.4 it is actually impossible; therefore this section introduces the most general method.

two partial solutions together. If the unification procedure above fails—because there does not exist a single scalar c so that $c \cdot r_1[t_1 \cap t_2] = r_2[t_1 \cap t_2]$—then x_1 and x_2 are not witnesses to the same neuron being at a critical point.

4.3.3   Recovering Row Signs in Deep Networks

The 1-layer contractive sign recovery procedure can still apply to "sufficiently contractive" neural network where at layer j there exists an $\epsilon > 0$ so that for all $h \in \mathbb{R}^{d_j}$ with $\|h\| < \epsilon$ there exists a preimage x with $f_{1..j}(x) = h$. If a neural network is sufficiently contractive it is easy to see that the prior described attack will work (because we have assumed the necessary success criteria).

In the case of 1-deep networks, it suffices for $d_1 \leq d_0$ and $A^{(1)}$ to be onto as described. In general it is necessary that $d_k \leq d_{k-1} \leq \cdots \leq d_1 \leq d_0$ but it is not sufficient, even if every layer $A^{(i)}$ were an onto map. Because there is a ReLU activation after every hidden layer, it is not possible to send negative values *into* the second layer f_j when computing the preimage.

Therefore, in order to find a preimage of $h_i \in \mathbb{R}^{d_i}$ we must be more careful in how we mount our attack: instead of just searching for $h_{i-1} \in \mathbb{R}^{d_{i-1}}$ so that $f_{i-1}(h_{i-1}) = h_i$ we must additionally require that component-wise $h_{i-1} \geq 0$. This ensures that we will be able to recursively compute $h_{i-2} \rightarrow h_{i-1}$ and by induction compute $x \in \mathcal{X}$ such that $f_{1..j}(x) = h_j$.

It is simple to test if a network is sufficiently contractive without any queries: try the above method to find a preimage x; if this fails, abort and attempt the following (more expensive) attack procedure. Otherwise it is contractive.

4.4 k-Deep Expansive Neural Networks

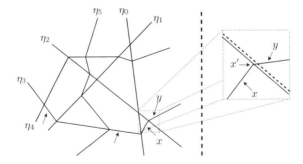

Fig. 3. (left) Geometry of a k-deep neural network, following [RK19]. Critical hyperplanes induced from neuron η_0, η_1, η_2 are on the first layer and are linear. Critical hyperplanes induced from neurons η_3, η_4 are on the second layer and are "bent" by neurons on the first layer. The critical hyperplane induced from neuron η_5 is a neuron on the third layer and is bent by neurons on the prior two layers. **(right)** Diagram of the hyperplane following procedure. Given an initial witness to a critical point x, follow the hyperplane to the double-critical point x'. To find where it goes next, perform binary search along the dashed line and find the witness y.

While most small neural networks are contractive, in practice almost all interesting neural networks are expansive: the number of neurons on some intermediate layer is larger than the number of inputs to that layer. Almost all of the prior methods still apply in this setting, with one exception: the column sign recovery procedure. Thus, we are required to develop a new strategy.

Recovering signs of the last layer. Observe that sign information is not lost for the final layer: because there is no ReLU activation and we can directly solve for the weights with least squares, we do not lose sign information.

Recovering signs on the second-to-last layer. Suppose we had extracted completely the function $\hat{f}_{1..k-1}$ (the third to last layer), and further had extracted the weights $\hat{A}^{(k)}$ and biases $\hat{b}^{(k)}$ up to sign of the rows. There are three unknown quantities remaining: a sign vector $s \in \{-1, 1\}^{d_k}$, $\hat{A}^{(k+1)}$ and $\hat{b}^{(k+1)}$. Suppose we were given $S \subset \mathcal{X}$ so that $|S| > d_k$. Then it would be possible to solve for all three unknown simultaneously through brute force.

Definition 12. *Let $v \odot M = M'$ denote multiplying rows of matrix $M \in \mathbb{R}^{a \times b}$ by the corresponding coordinate from $v \in \mathbb{R}^a$. Thus, $M'_{ij} = M_{ij} \cdot v_i$.*

Let $h_i = \sigma(f_{1..k-1}(x_i))$. Enumerate all 2^{d_k} assignments of s and compute $g_i = \sigma((s \odot \hat{A}^{(k)})h_i + (s \odot \hat{b}^{(k)}))$. We know that if we guessed the sign vector s correctly, then there would exist a solution to the system of equations $v \cdot g_i + b = f(x_i)$. This is the zero-deep extraction problem and solving it efficiently requires just a single call to least squares. This allows us to—through brute forcing the sign bits—completely recover both the signs of the second-to-last layer as well as the values (and signs) of the final layer.

Unfortunately, this procedure does not scale to recover the signs of layer $k-1$ and earlier. It relies on the existence of an efficient testing procedure (namely, least squares) to solve the final layer. If we attempted this brute-force strategy at layer $k - 3$ in order to test if our sign assignment was correct, we would need to run the complete layer $k - 2$ extraction procedure, thus incurring an exponential number of queries to the oracle.

However, we can use this idea in order to still recover signs even at earlier layers in the network with only a linear number of queries (but still exponential work in the width of the hidden layers).

Recovering signs of arbitrary hidden layers. Assume that we are given a collection of examples $\{x_i\} \subset \mathcal{W}(\eta)$ for some neuron η that is on the layer after we extracted so far: $\mathcal{L}(\eta) = j + 1$. Then we would know that there should exist a single unknown vector v and bias b such that $f_j(x_i) \cdot v + b = 0$ for all x_i.

This gives us an efficient procedure to test whether or not a given sign assignment on layer j is correct. As before, we enumerate all possible sign assignments and then check if we can recover such a vector v. If so, the assignment is correct; if not, it is wrong. It only remains left to show how to implement this procedure to obtain such a collection of inputs $\{x_i\}$.

4.4.1   The Polytope Boundary Projection Algorithm

Definition 13. *The* layer j polytope *containing x is the set of points $\{x + \delta\}$ so that $sign(\mathcal{V}(\eta; x)) = sign(\mathcal{V}(\eta; x + \delta))$ for all $\mathcal{L}(\eta) \leq j$.*

Observe that the layer j polytope around x is an open, convex set, as long as x is not a witness to a critical point. In Fig. 3, each enclosed region is a layer-k polytope and the triangle formed by η_0, η_1, and η_2 is a layer-$(k-1)$ polytope.

Given an input x and direction Δ, we can compute the distance α so that the value $x' = x + \alpha\Delta$ is at the boundary of the polytope defined by layers 1 to k. That is, starting from x traveling along direction Δ we stop the first time a neuron on layer j or earlier reaches a critical point. Formally, we define

$$\text{Proj}_{1..j}(x, \Delta) = \min_{\alpha \geq 0} \{\alpha : \exists\eta \text{ s.t. } \mathcal{L}(\eta) \leq j \land \mathcal{V}(\eta; x + \alpha\Delta) = 0\}$$

We only ever compute $\text{Proj}_{1..j}$ when we have extracted the neural network up to layer j. Thus we perform the computation with respect to the extracted function $\hat{f}$ and neuron-value function $\hat{\mathcal{V}}$, and so computing this function requires no queries to the oracle. In practice we solve for α via binary search.

4.4.2   Identifying a Single Next-Layer Witness

Given the correctly extracted network $\hat{f}_{1..j-1}$ and the weights (up to sign) of layer $j - 1$, our sign extraction procedure requires *some* witness to a critical point on layer j. We begin by performing our standard binary search sweep to find a collection $S \subset \mathcal{X}$, each of which is a witness to some neuron on an unknown layer. It is simple to filter out critical points on layers $j - 1$ or earlier by checking if any of $\hat{\mathcal{V}}(\eta; x) = 0$ for $\mathcal{L}(\eta) \leq j - 1$. Even though we have not solved for the sign of layer j, it is still possible to compute whether or not they are at a critical point because critical points of $\hat{A}^{(j)}$ are critical points of $-\hat{A}^{(j)}$. This removes any witnesses to critical points on layer j or lower.

Now we must filter out any critical points on layers strictly later than j. Let $x^* \in \mathcal{W}(\eta^*)$ denote a potential witness that is on layer j or later (having already filtered out critical points on layers $j - 1$ or earlier). Through finite differences, estimate $g = \pm\nabla_x f(x)$ evaluated at $x = x^*$. Choose any random vector r perpendicular to g, and therefore parallel to the critical hyperplane. Let $\alpha = \text{Proj}_{1..j}(x^*, r)$. If it turns out that x^* is a witness to a critical point on layer j then for all $\epsilon < \alpha$ we must have that $x^* + \epsilon r \in \mathcal{W}(\eta^*)$. Importantly, we also have the converse: with high probability for $\delta > \alpha$ we have that $x^* + \delta r \notin \mathcal{W}(\eta^*)$. However, observe that if x^* is *not* a witness to a neuron on layer j then one of these two conditions will be false. We have already ruled out witnesses on *earlier* neuron, so if x^* is a witness to a *later* neuron on layer $j' > j$ then it is unlikely that the layer-j' polytope is the same shape as the layer-j polytope, and therefore we will discover this fact. In the case that the two polytopes are actually identical, we can mount the following attack and if it fails we know that our initial input was on the wrong layer.

4.4.3   Recovering Multiple Witnesses for the Same Neuron

The above procedure yields a single witness $x^* \in \mathcal{W}(\eta^*)$ so that $\mathcal{L}(\eta^*) = j + 1$. We expand this to a collection of witnesses W where all $x \in W$ have $x \in \mathcal{W}(\eta^*)$, requiring the set to be *diverse*:

Definition 14. *A collection of inputs S is* fully diverse *at layer j if for all η with $\mathcal{L}(\eta) = j$ and for $s \in \{-1, 1\}$ there exists $x \in S$ such that $s \cdot \mathcal{V}(\eta; x) \geq 0$.*

Informally, being diverse at layer j means that if we consider the projection onto the space of layer j (by computing $f_{1..j}(x)$ for $x \in S$), for every neuron η there will be at least one input $x_+ \in S$ that the neuron is positive, and at least one input $x_- \in S$ so that the neuron is negative.

Our procedure is as follows. Let n be normal to the hyperplane x^* is on. Choose some r with $r \cdot n = 0$ and let $\alpha = \mathrm{Proj}_{1..j}(x^*, r)$ to define $x' = x^* + \alpha r$ as a point on the layer-j polytope boundary. In particular, this implies that we still have that $x' \in \mathcal{W}(\eta^*)$ (because r is perpendicular to n) but also $x' \in \mathcal{W}(\eta_u)$ for some neuron $\mathcal{L}(\eta_u) < j$ (by construction of α). Call this input x' the double-critical point (because it is a witness to two critical points simultaneously).

From this point x', we would like to obtain a new point y so that we still have $y \in \mathcal{W}(\eta^*)$, but that also y is on the other side of the neuron η_u, i.e., $\mathrm{sign}(\mathcal{V}(\eta_u; x^*)) \neq \mathrm{sign}(\mathcal{V}(\eta_u; y))$. Figure 3 (right) gives a diagram of this process. In order to follow x^* along its path, we first need to find it a critical point on the new hyperplane, having just been bent by the neuron η_u. We achieve this by performing a critical-point search starting ϵ-far away from, and parallel to, the hyperplane from neuron η_u (the dashed line in Fig. 3). This returns a point y from where we can continue the hyperplane following procedure.

The geometric view hurts us here: because the diagram is a two-dimensional projection, it appears that from the critical point y there are only two directions we can travel in: *away* from x' or *towards* x'. Traveling away is preferable—traveling towards x' will not help us construct a fully diverse set of inputs.

However, a d_0-dimensional input space has in general $(d_0 - 1)$ dimensions that remain on the neuron η^*. We defer to Sect. 5.5.1 an efficient method for selecting the continuation direction. For now, observe that choosing a random direction will eventually succeed at constructing a fully-diverse set, but is extremely inefficient: there exist better strategies than choosing the next direction.

4.4.4   Brute Force Recovery

Given this collection S, we can now—through brute force work—recover the correct sign assignment as follows. As described above, compute a fully diverse set of inputs $\{x_i\}$ and define $h_i = f_{1..j}(x_i)$. Then, for all possible 2^{d_j} assignments of signs $s \in \{-1, 1\}^{d_j}$, compute the guessed weight matrix $\hat{A}_s^{(j)} = s \odot \hat{A}^{(j)}$.

If we guess the correct vector s, then we will be able to compute $\hat{h}_i = \sigma(\hat{A}_v^{(j)} h_i + \hat{b}_v^{(j)}) = \sigma(\hat{A}_v^{(j)} f_{1..j-1}(x_i) + \hat{b}_v^{(j)})$ for each $x_i \in S$. Finally, we know that there will exist a vector $w \neq \mathbf{0}$ and bias $\hat{b}$ such that for all $\hat{h}_i$ we have $\hat{h}_i w + b = 0$. As before, if our guess of s is wrong, then with overwhelming probability there will not exist a valid linear transformation w, b. Thus we can recover sign with a linear number of queries and exponential work.

5   Instantiating the Differential Attack in Practice

The above idealized attack would efficiently extract neural network models but suffers from two problems. First, many of the algorithms are not numerically stable and introduce small errors in the extracted weights. Because errors in layer i compound and cause further errors at layers $j > i$, it is necessary to keep errors to a minimum. Second, the attack requires more chosen-inputs than is necessary; we develop new algorithms that require fewer queries or re-use previously-queried samples.

Reading this section. Each sub-section that follows is independent from the surrounding sub-sections and modifies algorithms introduced in Sect. 4. For brevity, we assume complete knowledge of the original algorithm and share the same notation. Readers may find it helpful to review the original algorithm before proceeding to each subsection.

5.1   Improving Precision of Extracted Layers

Given a precisely extracted neural network up to layer j so that $\hat{f}_{1..j-1}$ is functionally equivalent to $f_{1..j-1}$, but so that weights $\hat{A}^{(j)}$ and biases $\hat{b}^{(j)}$ are imprecisely extracted due to imprecision in the extraction attack, we will now show how to extend this to a *refined* model $\tilde{f}_{1..j}$ that is functionally equivalent to $f_{1..j}$. In an idealized environment with infinite precision floating point arithmetic this step is completely unnecessary; however empirically this step brings the relative error in the extracted layer's weights from 2^{-15} to 2^{-35} or better.

To begin, select a neuron η with $\mathcal{L}(\eta) = j$. By querying the already-extracted model $\hat{f}_{1..j}$, analytically compute witnesses $\{x_i\}_{i=1}^{d_j}$ so that each $x_i \in \hat{\mathcal{W}}(\eta)$. This requires no queries to the model as we have already extracted this partial model.

If the $\hat{A}^{(j)}$ and $\hat{b}^{(j)}$ were exactly correct then $\mathcal{W}(\eta; \cdot) \equiv \hat{\mathcal{W}}(\eta; \cdot)$ and so each computed critical point x_i would be exactly a critical point of the true model f and so $\mathcal{V}(\eta; x_i) \equiv 0$. However, if there is any imprecision in the computation, then in general we will have that $0 < |\mathcal{V}(\eta; x_i)| < \epsilon$ for some small $\epsilon > 0$.

Fortunately, given this x_i it is easy to compute x_i' so that $\mathcal{V}(\eta; x_i') = 0$. To do this, we sample a random $\Delta \in \mathcal{R}^{d_0}$ and apply our binary search procedure on the range $[x_i + \Delta, x_i - \Delta]$. Here we should select Δ so that $\|\Delta\|$ is sufficiently small that the only critical points it crosses is the one induced by neuron η, but sufficiently large that it does reliably find the true critical point of η.

Repeating this procedure for each witness x_i gives a set of witnesses $\{x_i'\}_{i=1}^{d_j}$ to the same neuron η. We compute $h_i = \hat{f}_{1..j-1}(x_i')$ as the hidden vector that layer j will receive as input. By assumption h_i is precise already and so $\hat{f}_{1..j-1} \approx f_{1..j-1}$. Because x_i' is a witness to neuron η having value zero, we know that that $A_n^{(j)} \cdot h_i = 0$ where n corresponds to the row of neuron η in $A^{(j)}$.

Ideally we would solve this resulting system with least squares. However, in practice, occasionally the conversion from $x \to x'$ fails because x' is no longer a witness to the same neuron η'. This happens when there is some other neuron (i.e., η') that is closer to x than the true neuron η. Because least squares is not robust to outliers this procedure can fail to improve the solution.

We take two steps to ensure this does not happen. First, observe that if Δ is smaller, the likelihood of capturing incorrect neurons η' decreases faster than the likelihood of capturing the correct neuron η. Thus, we set Δ to be small enough that roughly half of the attempts at finding a witness x' fails. Second, we apply a (more) robust method of determining the vector that satisfies the solution of equations [JOB+18]. However, even these two techniques taken together occasionally fail to find valid solutions to improve the quality. When this happens, we reject this proposed improvement and keep the original value.

Our attack could be improved with a solution to the following robust statistics problem: Given a (known) set $S \subset \mathbb{R}^N$ such that for some (unknown) weight vector w we have $\Pr_{x \in S}[|w \cdot x + 1| \le \epsilon] > \delta$ for sufficiently small ϵ, sufficiently large $\delta > 0.5$, and $\delta|S| > N$, efficiently recover the vector w to high precision.

5.2   Efficient Finite Differences

Most of the methods in this paper are built on computing second partial derivatives of the neural network f, and therefore developing a robust method for estimating the gradient is necessary. Throughout Sect. 4 we compute the partial derivative of f along direction α evaluated at x with step size ε as

$$\frac{\partial_\varepsilon}{\partial_\varepsilon \alpha} f(x) \stackrel{\text{def}}{=} \frac{f(x + \varepsilon \cdot \alpha) - f(x)}{\varepsilon}.$$

To compute the second partial derivative earlier, we computed α_+^i and α_-^i by first taking a step towards $x^* + \epsilon_0 e_1$ for a different step size ϵ_0 and then computed the first partial derivative at this location. However, with floating point imprecision it is not desirable to have two step sizes (ϵ_0 controlling the distance away from x^* to step, and ϵ controlling the step size when computing the partial derivative). Worse, we must have that $\epsilon \ll \epsilon_0$ because if $\frac{\partial f}{\partial e_1} \epsilon_0 > \frac{\partial f}{\partial e_i} \epsilon$ then when computing the partial derivative along e_i we may cross the hyperplane and estimate the first partial derivative incorrectly. Therefore, instead we compute

$$\alpha_+^i = \left.\frac{\partial f(x)}{\partial e_i}\right|_{x=x^*+\epsilon e_i} \quad \text{and} \quad \alpha_-^i = \left.\frac{\partial f(x)}{\partial -e_i}\right|_{x=x^*-\epsilon e_i}$$

where we both step along e_i and also take the partial derivative along the same e_i (and similarly for $-e_i$). This removes the requirement for an additional hyper-parameter and allows the step size ϵ to be orders of magnitude larger, but introduces a new error: we now lose the relative signs of the entries in the row when performing extraction and can only recover $\left|A_{i,j}^{(1)}/A_{i,k}^{(1)}\right|$.

Extracting column signs. We next recover the value $\text{sign}(A_{i,j}^{(1)}) \cdot \text{sign}(A_{i,k}^{(1)})$. Fortunately, the same differencing process allows us to learn this information, using the following observation: if $A_{i,j}^{(1)}$ and $A_{i,k}^{(1)}$ have the same sign, then moving in the $e_j + e_k$ direction will cause their contributions to add. If they have different signs, their contributions will cancel each other. That is, if

$$\left| \alpha_+^{j+k} - \alpha_-^{j+k} \right| = \left| \alpha_+^j - \alpha_-^j \right| + \left| \alpha_+^k - \alpha_-^k \right|,$$

we have that

$$\left| (A_{i,j}^{(1)} + A_{i,k}^{(1)}) \cdot A^{(2)} \right| = \left| A_{i,j}^{(1)} \cdot A^{(2)} \right| + \left| A_{i,k}^{(1)} \cdot A^{(2)} \right|,$$

and therefore that

$$\left| \frac{A_{i,j}^{(1)}}{A_{i,k}^{(1)}} \right| = \frac{A_{i,j}^{(1)}}{A_{i,k}^{(1)}}.$$

We can repeat this process to test whether each $A_{i,j}^{(1)}$ has the same sign as (for example) $A_{i,1}^{(1)}$. However, we still do not know whether any single $A_{i,j}^{(1)}$ is positive or negative—we still must recover the row signs as done previously.

5.3   Finding Witnesses to Critical Points

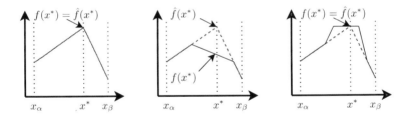

Fig. 4. Efficient and accurate witness discovery. **(left)** If x_α and x_β differ in only one ReLU (as shown left), we can precisely identify the location x^* at which the ReLU reaches its critical point. **(middle)** If instead more than one ReLU differs (as shown right), we can detect that this has happened: the predicted of $\hat{f}(\cdot)$ evaluated at x^* as inferred from intersecting the dotted lines does not actually equal the true value of $f(x^*)$. **(right)** This procedure is not *sound* and still may potentially incorrectly identify critical points; in practice we find these are rare.

Throughout the paper we require the ability to find witnesses to critical points. Section 4.2 uses simple binary search to achieve this which is (a) imprecise in practice, and (b) query inefficient. We improve on the witness-finding search procedure developed by [JCB+19]. Again we interpolate between two examples u, v and let $x_\alpha = (1-\alpha)u + \alpha v$. Previously, we repeatedly performed binary search as long as the partial derivatives were not equal $\partial f(x_\alpha) \neq \partial f(x_\beta)$, requiring p queries to obtain p bits of precision of the value x^*. However, observe that if x_α

and x_β differ in the sign of exactly one neuron i, then we can directly compute the location x^* at which $\mathcal{V}(\eta_i; x^*) = 0$ but so that for all other η_j we have

$$\text{sign}(\mathcal{V}(\eta_j; x_\alpha)) = \text{sign}(\mathcal{V}(\eta_j; x^*)) = \text{sign}(\mathcal{V}(\eta_j; x_\beta))$$

This approach is illustrated in Fig. 4 and relies on the fact that f is a piecewise linear function with two components. By measuring, $f(x_\alpha)$ and $\partial f(x_\alpha)$ (resp., $f(x_\beta)$ and $\partial f(x_\beta)$), we find the slope and intercept of both the left and right lines in Fig. 4 (left). This allows us to solve for their expected intersection $(x^*, \hat{f}(x^*))$. Typically, if there are more than two linear segments, as in the middle of the figure, we will find that the true function value $f(x^*)$ will not agree with the expected function value $\hat{f}(x^*)$ we obtained by computing the intersection; we can then perform binary search again and repeat the procedure.

However, we lose some soundness from this procedure. As we see in Fig. 4 (right), situations may arise where many ReLU units change sign between x_α and x_β, but $\hat{f}(x^*) = f(x^*)$. In this case, we would erroneously return x^* as a critical point, and miss all of the other critical points in the range. Fortunately, this error case is pathological and does not occur in practice.

5.3.1 Further Reducing Query Complexity of Witness Discovery

Suppose that we had already extracted the first j layers of the neural network and would like to perform the above critical-point finding algorithm to identify all critical points between x_α and x_β. Notice that we do not need to collect any more critical points from the first j layers, but running binary search will recover them nonetheless. To bypass this, we can analytically compute S as the set of all witnesses to critical points on the extracted neural network $\hat{f}_{1..j}$ between x_α and x_β. As long as the extracted network $\hat{f}$ is correct so far, we are guaranteed that all points in S are also witnesses to critical points of the true f.

Instead of querying on the range (x_α, x_β) we perform the $|S| + 1$ different searches. Order the elements of S as $\{s_i\}_{i=1}^{|S|}$ so that $s_i < s_j \implies |x_\alpha - s_i| < |x_\alpha - s_j|$. Abusing notation, let $s_1 = x_\alpha$ and $s_{|S|} = x_\beta$. Then, perform binary search on each disjoint range (S_i, S_{i+1}) for $i = 1$ to $|S| - 1$ and return the union.

5.4 Unification of Witnesses with Noisy Gradients

Recall that to extract $\hat{A}^{(l)}$ we extract candidates candidates $\{r_i\}$ and search for pairs r_i, r_j that agree on multiple coordinates. This allows us to merge r_i and r_j to recover (eventually) full rows of $\hat{A}^{(l)}$. With floating point error, the unification algorithm in Sect. 4.3 fails for several reasons.

Our core algorithm computes the normal to a hyperplane, returning pairwise ratios $\hat{A}_{i,j}^{(1)}/\hat{A}_{i,k}^{(1)}$; throughout Sect. 4 we set $\hat{A}_{i,1}^{(1)} = 1$ without loss of generality.

Unfortunately in practice there is loss of generality, due to the disparate impact of numerical instability. Consider the case where $A_{i,1}^{(l)} < 10^{-\alpha}$ for $\alpha \gg 0$, but $A_{i,k}^{(l)} \geq 1$ for all other k. Then there will be substantially more (relative) floating point imprecision in the weight $A_{i,1}^{(l)}$ than in the other weights. Before normalizing there is no cause for concern since the absolute error is no larger than for any other. However, the described algorithm now normalizes every *other* coordinate $A_{i,k}^{(l)}$ by dividing it by $A_{i,1}^{(l)}$—polluting the precision of these values.

Therefore we adjust our solution. At layer l, we are given a collection of vectors $R = \{r_i\}_{i=1}^n$ so that each r_i corresponds to the extraction of some (unknown) neuron η_i. First, we need an algorithm to cluster the items into sets $\{S_j\}_{j=1}^{d_l}$ so that $S_j \subset R$ and so that every vector in S_j corresponds to one neuron on layer l. We then need to unify each set S_j to obtain the final row of $\hat{A}_j^{(l)}$.

Creating the Subsets S with Graph Clustering. Let $r_m^{(a)} \in S_n$ denote the ath coordinate of the extracted row r_m from cluster n. Begin by constructing a graph $G = (V, E)$ where each vector r_i corresponds to a vertex. Let $\delta_{ij}^{(k)} = |r_i^{(k)} - r_j^{(k)}|$ denote the difference between row r_i and row r_j along axis k; then connect an edge from r_i to r_j when the approximate $\|\cdot\|_0$ norm is sufficiently large $\sum_k \mathbb{1}\left[\delta_{ij}^{(k)} < \epsilon\right] > \log d_0$. We compute the connected components of G and partition each set S_j as one connected component. Observe that if $\epsilon = 0$ then this procedure is exactly what was described earlier, pairing vectors whose entries agree perfectly; in practice we find a value of $\varepsilon = 10^{-5}$ suffices.

Unifying Each Cluster to Obtain the Row Weights. We construct the three dimensional $M_{i,a,b} = r_a^{(i)}/r_b^{(i)}$. Given M, the a good guess for the scalar c_{ab} so that $r_a^{(i)} = r_b^{(i)} \cdot C_{ab}$ along as many coordinates i as possible is the assignment $C_{ab} = \text{median}_i\, M_{i,a,b}$, where the estimated error is $e_{ab} = \text{stdev}_i\, M_{i,a,b}$.

If all r_a were complete and had no imprecision then C_{ab} would have no error and so $C_{ab} = C_{ax} \cdot C_{xb}$. However because it does have error, we can iteratively improve the guessed C matrix by observing that if the error $e_{ax} + e_{xb} < e_{ab}$ then the guessed assignment $C_{ax} \cdot C_{xb}$ is a better guess than C_{ab}. Thus we replace $C_{ab} \leftarrow C_{ax} \cdot C_{xb}$ and update $e_{ab} \leftarrow e_{ax} + e_{xb}$. We iterate this process until there is no further improvement. Then, finally, we choose the optimal dimension $a = \arg\min_a \sum_b e_{ab}$ and return the vector C_a. Observe that this procedure closely follows constructing the union of two partial entries r_i and r_j except that we perform it along the best axis possible for each coordinate.

5.5   Following Neuron Critical Points

Section 4.4.3 developed techniques to construct a set of witnesses to the same neuron being at its critical point. We now numerically-stabilize this procedure.

As before we begin with an input $x^* \in \mathcal{W}(\eta^*)$ and compute the normal vector n to the critical plane at x^*, and then choose r satisfying $r \cdot n = 0$. The computation of n will necessarily have some floating point error, so r will too.

This means when we compute $\alpha = \text{Proj}_{1..j}(x^*, r)$ and let $x' = x^* + r\alpha$ the resulting x' will be almost exactly a witness to some neuron η_u with $\mathcal{L}(\eta_u) < j$, (because this computation was performed analytically on a precisely extracted

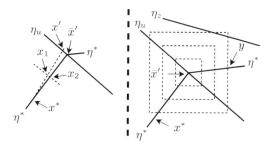

Fig. 5. Numerically stable critical-point following algorithm. **(left)** From a point x' compute a parallel direction along η^*, step part way to x_1 and refine it to x_2, and then finish stepping to x'. **(right)** From x' grow increasingly large squares until there are more than four intersection points; return y as the point on η^* on the largest square.

model), but x' has likely drifted off of the original critical plane induced by η^* (Fig. 5).

To address this, after computing α we initially take a smaller step and let $x_1 = x^* + r\sqrt{\alpha}$. We then refine the location of this point to a point x_2 by performing binary search on the region $x_1 - \epsilon n$ to $x_1 + \epsilon n$ for a small step ϵ. If there was no error in computing n then $x_1 = x_2$ because both are already witnesses to η^*. If not, any error has been corrected. Given x^* and x_2 we now can now compute $\alpha_2 = \mathrm{Proj}_{1..j}(x^*, x_2 - x^*)$ and let $\bar{x}' = x^* + (x_2 - x^*)\alpha_2$ which will actually be a witness to both neurons simultaneously.

Next we give a stable method to compute y that is a witness to η^* and on the other side of η_u. The previous procedure required a search parallel to η_u and infinitesimally displaced, but this is not numerically stable without accurately yet knowing the normal to the hyperplane given by η_u.

Instead we perform the following procedure. Choose two orthogonal vectors of equal length β, γ and and perform binary search on the line segments that trace out the perimeter of a square with coordinates $\bar{x}' \pm \beta \pm \gamma$.

When $\|\beta\|$ is small, the number of critical points crossed will be exactly four: two because of η_u and two because of η^*. As long as the number of critical points remains four, we double the length of β and γ.

Eventually we will discover more than four critical points, when the perimeter of the square intersects another neuron η_z. At this point we stop increasing the size of the box and can compute the continuation direction of η^* by discarding the points that fall on η_u. We can then choose y as the point on η^* that intersected with the largest square binary search.

5.5.1 Determining Optimal Continuation Directions

The hyperplane following procedure will *eventually* recover a fully diverse set of inputs W but it may take a large number of queries to do so. We can reduce the number of queries by several orders of magnitude by carefully choosing the continuation direction r instead of randomly choosing any value so that $r \cdot n = 0$.

Given the initial coordinate x and after computing the normal n to the hyperplane, we have $d_0 - 1$ dimensions that we can choose between to travel next. Instead of choosing a random $r \cdot n = 0$ we instead choose r such that we make progress towards obtaining a fully diverse set W.

Define W_i as the set of witnesses that have been found so far. We say that this set is diverse on neuron η if there exists an $x_+, x_- \in W_i$ such that $\mathcal{V}(\eta; x_+) \geq 0$ and $\mathcal{V}(\eta; x_-) < 0$. Choose an arbitrary neuron η_t such that W_i is not diverse on η_t. (If there are multiple such options, we should prefer the neuron that would be *easiest* to reach, but this is secondary.)

Our goal will be to choose a direction r such that (1) as before, $r \cdot n = 0$, however (2) $W_i \cup \{x + \alpha r\}$ is closer to being fully diverse. Here, "closer" means that $d(W) = \min_{x \in W} |\mathcal{V}(\eta_t; x)|$ is smaller. Because the set is not yet diverse on η_t, all values are either positive or negative, and it is our objective to switch the sign, and therefore become closer to zero. Therefore our procedure sets

$$r = \arg\min_{r:\ r \cdot n = 0} d(W_i \cup \{x + \alpha r\})$$

performing the minimization through random search over 1,000 directions.

6 Evaluation

We implement the described extraction algorithm in JAX [BFH+18], a Python library that mirrors the NumPy interface for performing efficient numerical computation through just in time compilation.

6.1 Computing $(\varepsilon, 10^{-9})$-Functional Equivalence

Computing $(\varepsilon, 10^{-9})$-functional equivalence is simple. Let $\bar{S} \subset S$ be a finite set consisting of $|\bar{S}| > 10^9$ different inputs drawn $x \in S$. Sort $\bar{S}$ by $|f(x) - \hat{f}(x)|$ and choose the lowest ε so that

$$\Pr_{x \in \bar{S}} \left[|f(x) - g(x)| \leq \epsilon \right] \geq 1 - \delta.$$

In practice we set $|\bar{S}| = 10^9$ and compute the max so that evaluating the function is possible under an hour per neural network.

6.2 Computing $(\varepsilon, 0)$-Functional Equivalence

Directly computing $(\varepsilon, 0)$-functional equivalence is infeasible, and is NP-hard (even to approximate) by reduction to Subset Sum [JCB+19]. We nevertheless propose two methods that efficiently give upper bounds that perform well.

Error bounds propagation. The most direct method to compute $(\varepsilon, 0)$-functional equivalence of the extracted neural network $\hat{f}$ is to compare the weights $A^{(i)}$ to the weights $\hat{A}^{(i)}$ and analytically derive an upper bound on the error when performing inference. Observe that (1) permuting the order of the neurons in the network does not change the output, and (2) any row can be multiplied by a positive scalar $c > 0$ if the corresponding column in the next layer is divided by c. Thus, before we can compare $\hat{A}^{(i)}$ to $A^{(i)}$ we must "align" them. We identify the permutation mapping the rows of $\hat{A}^{(l)}$ to the rows of $A^{(l)}$ through a greedy matching algorithm, and then compute a single scalar per row $s \in \mathbb{R}_+^{d_i}$. To ensure that multiplying by a scalar does not change the output of the network, we multiply the columns of the next layer $\hat{A}^{(l+1)}$ by $1/s$ (with the inverse taken pairwise). The process to align the bias vectors $b^{(l)}$ is identical, and the process is repeated for each further layer.

This gives an aligned $\tilde{A}^{(i)}$ and $\tilde{b}^{(i)}$ from which we can analytically derive upper bounds on the error. Let $\Delta_i = \tilde{A}^{(i)} - A^{(i)}$, and let δ_i be the largest singular value of Δ_i. If the ℓ_2-norm of the maximum error going into layer i is given by e_i then we can bound the maximum error going out of layer i as

$$e_{i+1} \leq \delta_i \cdot e_i + \|\tilde{b}^{(i)} - b^{(i)}\|_2.$$

By propagating bounds layer-by-layer we can obtain an upper bound on the maximum error of the output of the model.

This method is able to prove an upper bound on $(\epsilon, 0)$ functional equivalence for some networks, when the pairing algorithm succeeds. However, we find that there are some networks that are $(2^{-45}, 10^{-9})$ functionally equivalent but where the weight alignment procedure fails. Therefore, we suspect that there are more equivalence classes of functions than scalar multiples of permuted neurons, and so develop further methods for tightly computing $(\varepsilon, 0)$ functional equivalence.

Error overapproximation through MILP. The above analysis approach is loose. Our second approach gives exact bounds with an additive error at most 10^{-10}.

Neural networks are piecewise linear functions, and so can be cast as a mixed integer linear programming (MILP) problem [KBD+17]. We directly express Definition 1 as a MILP, following the process of [KBD+17] by encoding linear layers directly, and encoding ReLU layers by assigning a binary integer variable to each ReLU. Due to the exponential nature of the problem, this approach is limited to small networks.

State-of-the-art MILP solvers offer a maximum (relative, additive) error tolerance of 10^{-10}; for our networks the SVD upper bound is often 10^{-10} or better, so the MILP solver gives a *worse* bound, despite theoretically being tight.

7   Results

We extract a wide range of neural network architectures; key results are given in Table 1 (Sect. 1). We compute (ε, δ)-functional equivalence at $\delta = 10^{-9}$ and $\delta = 0$ on the domain $S = \{x \colon \|x\|_2 < d_0 \ \wedge \ x \in \mathcal{X}\}$, sufficient to explore both sides of every neuron.

8   Concluding Remarks

We introduce a cryptanalytic method for extracting the weights of a neural network by drawing analogies to cryptanalysis of keyed ciphers. Our differential attack requires multiple orders of magnitude fewer queries per parameter than prior work and extracts models that are multiple orders of magnitude more accurate than prior work. In this work, we do not consider defenses—promising approaches include detecting when an attack is occuring, adding noise at some stage of the model's computation, or only returning the label corresponding to the output, any of these easily break our presented attack.

The practicality of this attack has implications for many areas of machine learning and cryptographic research. The field of secure inference relies on the assumption that observing the output of a neural network does not reveal the weights. This assumption is false, and therefore the field of secure inference will need to develop new techniques to protect the secrecy of trained models.

We believe that by casting neural network extraction as a cryptanalytic problem, even more advanced cryptanalytic techniques will be able to greatly improve on our results, reducing the computational complexity, reducing the query complexity and reducing the number of assumptions necessary.

Acknowledgements. We are grateful to the anonymous reviewers, Florian Tramèr, Nicolas Papernot, Ananth Raghunathan, and Úlfar Erlingsson for helpful feedback.

References

[BBJP19] Batina, L., Bhasin, S., Jap, D., Picek, S.: CSI NN: reverse engineering of neural network architectures through electromagnetic side channel. In: 28th USENIX Security Symposium (2019)

[BCB15] Bahdanau, D., Cho, K., Bengio, Y.: Neural machine translation by jointly learning to align and translate. In: 3rd International Conference on Learning Representations (ICLR) (2015)

[BCM+13] Biggio, B., et al.: Evasion attacks against machine learning at test time. In: Blockeel, H., Kersting, K., Nijssen, S., Železný, F. (eds.) ECML PKDD 2013. LNCS (LNAI), vol. 8190, pp. 387–402. Springer, Heidelberg (2013). https://doi.org/10.1007/978-3-642-40994-3_25

[BFH+18] Bradbury, J., et al.: JAX: composable transformations of Python+NumPy programs (2018)

[BS91] Biham, E., Shamir, A.: Differential cryptanalysis of DES-like cryptosystems. J. Cryptol. **4**(1), 3–72 (1991). https://doi.org/10.1007/BF00630563

[CCG+18] Chandrasekaran, V., Chaudhuri, K., Giacomelli, I., Jha, S., Yan, S.: Exploring connections between active learning and model extraction. arXiv preprint arXiv:1811.02054 (2018)

[CLE+19] Carlini, N., Liu, C., Erlingsson, Ú., Kos, J., Song, D.: The secret sharer: evaluating and testing unintended memorization in neural networks. In: USENIX Security Symposium, pp. 267–284 (2019)

[DGKP20] Das, A., Gollapudi, S., Kumar, R., Panigrahy, R.: On the learnability of random deep networks. In: ACM-SIAM Symposium on Discrete Algorithms, SODA 2020, pp. 398–410 (2020)

[EKN+17] Esteva, A., et al.: Dermatologist-level classification of skin cancer with deep neural networks. Nature **542**(7639), 115–118 (2017)

[FJR15] Fredrikson, M., Jha, S., Ristenpart, T.: Model inversion attacks that exploit confidence information and basic countermeasures. In: ACM CCS, pp. 1322–1333 (2015)

[GBDL+16] Gilad-Bachrach, R., Dowlin, N., Laine, K., Lauter, K., Naehrig, M., Wernsing, J.: CryptoNets: applying neural networks to encrypted data with high throughput and accuracy. In: International Conference on Machine Learning, pp. 201–210 (2016)

[Gen09] Gentry, C.: A fully homomorphic encryption scheme. Ph.D. thesis, Stanford University (2009)

[HDK+20] Hong, S., Davinroy, M., Kaya, Y., Dachman-Soled, D., Dumitraş, T.: How to 0wn the NAS in your spare time. In: International Conference on Learning Representations (2020)

[HZRS16] He, K., Zhang, X., Ren, S., Sun, J.: Deep residual learning for image recognition. In: Proceedings of the IEEE Conference on Computer Vision and Pattern Recognition, pp. 770–778 (2016)

[JCB+19] Jagielski, M., Carlini, N., Berthelot, D., Kurakin, A., Papernot, N.: High-fidelity extraction of neural network models. arXiv:1909.01838 (2019)

[JOB+18] Jagielski, M., Oprea, A., Biggio, B., Liu, C., Nita-Rotaru, C., Li, B.: Manipulating machine learning: poisoning attacks and countermeasures for regression learning. In: 2018 IEEE Symposium on Security and Privacy (S&P), pp. 19–35. IEEE (2018)

[KBD+17] Katz, G., Barrett, C., Dill, D.L., Julian, K., Kochenderfer, M.J.: Reluplex: an efficient SMT solver for verifying deep neural networks. In: Majumdar, R., Kunčak, V. (eds.) CAV 2017. LNCS, vol. 10426, pp. 97–117. Springer, Cham (2017). https://doi.org/10.1007/978-3-319-63387-9_5

[KLA+19] Karras, T., Laine, S., Aittala, M., Hellsten, J., Lehtinen, J., Aila, T.: Analyzing and improving the image quality of StyleGAN. CoRR, abs/1912.04958 (2019)

[KTP+19] Krishna, K., Tomar, G.S., Parikh, A.P., Papernot, N., Iyyer, M.: Thieves on sesame street! Model extraction of BERT-based APIs. arXiv preprint arXiv:1910.12366 (2019)

[Lev14] Levinovitz, A.: The mystery of Go, the ancient game that computers still can't win. Wired, May 2014

[MLS+20] Mishra, P., Lehmkuhl, R., Srinivasan, A., Zheng, W., Popa, R.A.: DELPHI: a cryptographic inference service for neural networks. In: 29th USENIX Security Symposium (2020)

[MSDH19] Milli, S., Schmidt, L., Dragan, A.D., Hardt, M.: Model reconstruction from model explanations. In: Proceedings of the Conference on Fairness, Accountability, and Transparency, FAT* 2019, pp. 1–9 (2019)

[NH10] Nair, V., Hinton, G.E.: Rectified linear units improve restricted Boltzmann machines. In: Proceedings of the 27th International Conference on Machine Learning (ICML), pp. 807–814 (2010)

[RK19] Rolnick, D., Kording, K.P.: Identifying weights and architectures of unknown ReLU networks. arXiv preprint arXiv:1910.00744 (2019)

[RWT+18] Riazi, M.S., Weinert, C., Tkachenko, O., Songhori, E.M., Schneider, T., Koushanfar, F.: Chameleon: a hybrid secure computation framework for machine learning applications. In: ACM ASIACCS, pp. 707–721 (2018)

[SHM+16] Silver, D., et al.: Mastering the game of Go with deep neural networks and tree search. Nature **529**(7587), 484 (2016)

[SIVA17] Szegedy, C., Ioffe, S., Vanhoucke, V., Alemi, A.A.: Inception-v4, Inception-ResNet and the impact of residual connections on learning. In: Proceedings of the Thirty-First AAAI Conference on Artificial Intelligence, AAAI 2017, pp. 4278–4284. AAAI Press (2017)

[SSRD19] Shamir, A., Safran, I., Ronen, E., Dunkelman, O.: A simple explanation for the existence of adversarial examples with small Hamming distance. CoRR, abs/1901.10861 (2019)

[SZS+14] Szegedy, C., et al.: Intriguing properties of neural networks. In: 2nd International Conference on Learning Representations (ICLR 2014). arXiv:1312.6199 (2014)

[TL19] Tan, M., Le, Q.V.: EfficientNet: rethinking model scaling for convolutional neural networks. arXiv preprint arXiv:1905.11946 (2019)

[TZJ+16] Tramèr, F., Zhang, F., Juels, A., Reiter, M.K., Ristenpart, T.: Stealing machine learning models via prediction APIs. In: USENIX Security Symposium, pp. 601–618 (2016)

[Wen90] Wenskay, D.L.: Intellectual property protection for neural networks. Neural Netw. **3**(2), 229–236 (1990)

[WG18] Wang, B., Gong, N.Z.: Stealing hyperparameters in machine learning. In: 2018 IEEE Symposium on Security and Privacy (S&P), pp. 36–52. IEEE (2018)

[WSC+16] Wu, Y., et al.: Google's neural machine translation system: bridging the gap between human and machine translation. arXiv preprint arXiv:1609.08144 (2016)

[XHLL19] Xie, Q., Hovy, E., Luong, M.-T., Le, Q.V.: Self-training with noisy student improves ImageNet classification. arXiv preprint arXiv:1911.04252 (2019)

[Yao86] Yao, A.C.-C.: How to generate and exchange secrets. In: FOCS 1986, pp. 162–167. IEEE (1986)

[ZL16] Zoph, B., Le, Q.V.: Neural architecture search with reinforcement learning. arXiv preprint arXiv:1611.01578 (2016)

Automatic Verification of Differential Characteristics: Application to Reduced Gimli

Fukang Liu[1,3(✉)], Takanori Isobe[2,3], and Willi Meier[4]

[1] Shanghai Key Laboratory of Trustworthy Computing,
East China Normal University, Shanghai, China
liufukangs@163.com
[2] National Institute of Information and Communications Technology, Tokyo, Japan
[3] University of Hyogo, Hyogo, Japan
takanori.isobe@ai.u-hyogo.ac.jp
[4] FHNW, Windisch, Switzerland
willimeier48@gmail.com

Abstract. Since Keccak was selected as the SHA-3 standard, more and more permutation-based primitives have been proposed. Different from block ciphers, there is no round key in the underlying permutation for permutation-based primitives. Therefore, there is a higher risk for a differential characteristic of the underlying permutation to become incompatible when considering the dependency of difference transitions over different rounds. However, in most of the MILP or SAT based models to search for differential characteristics, only the difference transitions are involved and are treated as independent in different rounds, which may cause that an invalid one is found for the underlying permutation. To overcome this obstacle, we are motivated to design a model which automatically avoids the inconsistency in the search for differential characteristics. Our technique is to involve both the difference transitions and value transitions in the constructed model. Such an idea is inspired by the algorithm to find SHA-2 characteristics as proposed by Mendel et al. in ASIACRYPT 2011, where the differential characteristic and the conforming message pair are simultaneously searched. As a first attempt, our new technique will be applied to the Gimli permutation, which was proposed in CHES 2017. As a result, we reveal that some existing differential characteristics of reduced Gimli are indeed incompatible, one of which is found in the Gimli document. In addition, since only the permutation is analyzed in the Gimli document, we are lead to carry out a comprehensive study, covering the proposed hash scheme and the authenticated encryption (AE) scheme specified for Gimli, which has become a second round candidate of the NIST lightweight cryptography standardization process. For the hash scheme, a semi-free-start (SFS) collision attack can reach up to 8 rounds starting from an intermediate round. For the AE scheme, a state recovery attack is demonstrated to achieve up to 9 rounds. It should be emphasized that our analysis does not threaten the security of Gimli.

ⓒ International Association for Cryptologic Research 2020
D. Micciancio and T. Ristenpart (Eds.): CRYPTO 2020, LNCS 12172, pp. 219–248, 2020.
https://doi.org/10.1007/978-3-030-56877-1_8

Keywords: Gimli · Hash function · AE · MILP · Collision · State-recovery

1   Introduction

As the demand for lightweight cryptographic primitives in industry increases, NIST is currently holding a public Lightweight Cryptography Standardization process [1], aiming at lightweight cryptography standardization by combining the efforts from both academia and industry. Among the 32 second round candidates, Gimli was first proposed in CHES 2017 [4]. The main strategy to improve its performance is to process the 384-bit data in four 96-bit columns independently and make only a 32-bit word swapping among the four columns every two rounds. Such a design strategy soon received a doubt from Hamburg [13]. However, the attack in [13] works for an ad-hoc mode rather than the proposed hash scheme or AE scheme in the submitted Gimli document.

Along the development of differential attacks [7], several variants have been proposed. A very influential one was the modular differential attack on the MD-SHA hash family, which directly turned MD5 [23] and SHA-1 [20,22] into broken hash functions. To mount collision attacks on MD5 and SHA-1 as in [22,23], one challenging work is to find a proper differential characteristic, which was first finished by hand-craft [22,23]. Later, the guess-and-determine method to search for differential characteristics was proposed in ASIACRYPT 2006, together with its application to full SHA-1 [10]. However, when such a guess-and-determine technique is directly applied to reduced SHA-2, Mendel et al. pointed out in [18] that the discovered differential characteristics are always invalid since contradictions may easily occur in the set of conditions implied in the discovered differential characteristics. To overcome this obstacle, they finally developed an algorithm to search for the differential characteristic and the conforming message pair simultaneously to avoid the inconsistency.

Indeed, such a case does not only exist in the MD-SHA hash family. For the ARX construction, for instance, some differential characteristics of Blake-256 [8] and Skein-512 [3] are also proven to be invalid if taking some dependency into account, as revealed by Leurent [15]. To search for valid differential characteristics of reduced Skein, Leurent designed a dedicated algorithm in [16] using the improved generalized conditions [15] and the guess-and-determine technique [10].

In another direction, since the introduction of the MILP-based method to search for differential characteristics [21], the SAT-based method has also been developed [14]. However, in most of the MILP models or SAT models to search for differential characteristics [4,14,21,25], only the difference transitions are taken into account and are treated as independent in different rounds. Although such an assumption is commonly believed to be reasonable for block ciphers, it may not hold well for permutation-based primitives since there is no round key in the permutation. A similar problem has been investigated in [9]. Moreover, since Keccak [6] was selected as the SHA-3 standard, more and more permutation-based primitives have been proposed. However, whether similar cases once appearing in SHA-2 [18], Skein-512 [3] and Blake-256 [8] will occur in the commonly constructed MILP or SAT models to search for differential characteristics for the underlying permutation remains unknown. Therefore, it is vital to make an investigation for such a problem.

However, both the methods in [16,18] require a dedicated implementation of the heuristic search. In addition, how to achieve the simultaneousness is ambiguous in [18]. For [16], the inconsistency is avoided by using the improved generalized conditions [15]. As is known, the most convincing way is to provide a conforming message pair for the discovered differential characteristic.

Therefore, similar to the motivation to introduce the MILP-based method into cryptanalysis, it would be meaningful to utilize some off-the-shelf tools to reduce the workload. Consequently, we take Gimli as our first attempt and are motivated to tackle the problem of how to construct a model to **always** avoid the incompatibility in the search for differential characteristics. Moreover, since Gimli is one of the second round candidates in NIST Lightweight Cryptography Standardization process, we will provide some additional analysis of reduced Gimli. We noticed that there is a related work [19] for MD-SHA hash family published at SAT 2006 aiming at automatic message modification, though with ambiguous technical details.

Our Contributions. We made a comprehensive study of Gimli[1], as summarized below:

- We make the first step to investigate the properties of the SP-box. Such a work is meaningful since all the attacks in this paper heavily rely on them.
- A novel MILP model capturing the difference transitions and value transitions simultaneously is developed. To the best of our knowledge, this is the first model which takes both transitions into account. This model can be simply used to detect contradictions in the differential characteristic of Gimli. As a result, we prove that both the 12-round differential characteristic in the Gimli document [4] and the 6-round differential characteristic used for the collision attack on 6-round Gimli-Hash in [25] are invalid. The second usage of this model is to directly search for a valid differential characteristic and the conforming message pair simultaneously.
- For the hash scheme, we provide the first practical semi-free-start (SFS) colliding message pair for 6-round Gimli-Hash and develop several techniques to convert SFS collisions into collisions. Moreover, we also mount a SFS collision attack on the intermediate 8-round Gimli-Hash.
- For the AE scheme, we are curious why the designers only claim 128-bit security while a 256-bit key is used. Thus, we are motivated to devise an attack which can maximize the number of rounds with complexity below 2^{256}. Consequently, we mount a state-recovery attack on 9-round Gimli with a rather high time complexity 2^{192} and memory complexity 2^{190}.

The memory/data/time complexity of the above attacks are displayed in Table 1.

---

[1] The source code of our attacks can be referred to https://github.com/LFKOKAMI/ GimliAnalysis.git.

Organization. The Gimli permutation and some properties of the SP-box will be introduced in Sect. 2 and Sect. 3, respectively. Then, the MILP model capturing both difference transitions and value transitions will be described in Sect. 4. The (SFS) collision attack on 6-round and 8-round Gimli-Hash will be shown in Sect. 5 and Sect. 6, respectively. Then, we will investigate the security of the AE scheme and present the state-recovery attack on 9-round Gimli in Sect. 7. Finally, we conclude the paper in Sect. 8.

Table 1. The analytical results of reduced Gimli, where Z-S represents Zero-sum and Z-D represents Zero-internal-difference.

Target	Attack Type	Rounds	Memory	Data	Time	Ref.
Hash scheme	SFS collision	6	Practical			Sect. 5
Hash scheme	Collision	6	2^{64}	–	2^{64}	Sect. 5.3
Hash scheme	Collision	6	Negligible	–	$2^{91.4}$	[17][a]
Hash scheme	SFS collision	8	Negligible	–	2^{64}	Sect. 6
AE scheme	State-recovery	5	2^{126}	4	2^{128}	[17][a]
AE scheme	State-recovery	9	2^{190}	4	2^{192}	Sect. 7

[a]The full version of this paper.

2   Description of Gimli

The Gimli state can be viewed as a two-dimensional array $S = (S_{i,j})$ ($0 \leq i \leq 2, 0 \leq j \leq 3$), where $S_{i,j} \in F_2^{32}$, as illustrated in Fig. 1.

$S_{0,0}$	$S_{0,1}$	$S_{0,2}$	$S_{0,3}$
$S_{1,0}$	$S_{1,1}$	$S_{1,2}$	$S_{1,3}$
$S_{2,0}$	$S_{2,1}$	$S_{2,2}$	$S_{2,3}$

Fig. 1. The Gimli state

The 24-round permutation can be viewed as iterating the following sequence of operations for 6 times:

$$(SP \rightarrow S\_SW \rightarrow AC) \rightarrow (SP) \rightarrow (SP \rightarrow B\_SW) \rightarrow (SP),$$

where the SP-box operation, Small-Swap operation, Big-Swap operation and AddRoundConstant operation are denoted by SP, S_SW, B_SW and AC, respectively. For the SP-box operation, the SP-box will be applied to the four columns independently. For the AddRoundConstant operation, a 32-bit word is added to $S_{0,0}$. More details can be referred to [4]. For convenience, denote the internal state after r-round permutation by S^r and the input state by S^0. In other words, we have

$$S^{4i} \xrightarrow{SP} S^{4i+0.5} \xrightarrow{S\_SW} \xrightarrow{AC} S^{4i+1} \xrightarrow{SP} S^{4i+2} \xrightarrow{SP} \xrightarrow{S\_BW} S^{4i+3} \xrightarrow{SP} S^{4i+4},$$

where $0 \le i \le 5$. In addition, ΔS^r denotes the exclusive or difference in S^r ($0 \le r \le 24$). $Z[i]$ ($0 \le i \le 31$) denotes the $(i+1)$-th bit of the 32-bit word Z and $Z[0]$ is the least significant bit of Z. $Z[i \sim j](0 \le j < i \le 31)$ represents the $(j+1)$-th bit to the $(i+1)$-th bit of the 32-bit word Z. For example, $Z[1 \sim 0]$ represents the two bits $(Z[1],Z[0])$. Moreover, $\oplus$, $\ll$, $\lll$, $\vee$ and $\wedge$ represent the logic operations *exclusive or, shift left, rotate left, or, and*, respectively.

2.1 SP-box

The SP-box of Gimli takes a 96-bit value as input and outputs a 96-bit value. Denote the input and the output by $(IX, IY, IZ) \in F_2^{32 \times 3}$ and $(OX, OY, OZ) \in F_2^{32 \times 3}$, respectively. Then, the relation between (OX, OY, OZ) and (IX, IY, IZ) can be described as follows:

$$IX \leftarrow IX \lll 24$$
$$IY \leftarrow IY \lll 9$$
$$OZ \leftarrow IX \oplus IZ \ll 1 \oplus (IY \wedge IZ) \ll 2$$
$$OY \leftarrow IY \oplus IX \oplus (IX \vee IZ) \ll 1$$
$$OX \leftarrow IZ \oplus IY \oplus (IX \wedge IY) \ll 3$$

Based on the above relation, the following bit relations can be derived, where the indices are considered within modulo 32.

$$OX[i] = \begin{cases} IZ[i] \oplus IY[i-9] \ (0 \le i \le 2) \\ IZ[i] \oplus IY[i-9] \oplus (IX[i-27] \wedge IY[i-12]) \ (3 \le i \le 31) \end{cases} \quad (1)$$

$$OY[i] = \begin{cases} IY[i-9] \oplus IX[i-24] \ (i=0) \\ IY[i-9] \oplus IX[i-24] \oplus (IX[i-25] \vee IZ[i-1]) \ (1 \le i \le 31) \end{cases} \quad (2)$$

$$OZ[i] = \begin{cases} IX[i-24] \ (i=0) \\ IX[i-24] \oplus IZ[i-1] \ (i=1) \\ IX[i-24] \oplus IZ[i-1] \oplus (IY[i-11] \wedge IZ[i-2]) \ (2 \le i \le 31) \end{cases} \quad (3)$$

2.2 Linear Layer

The linear layer includes two different swap operations, namely Small-Swap and Big-Swap. Small-Swap occurs every 4 rounds starting from the 1st round. Big-Swap occurs every 4 rounds starting from the 3rd round. The illustration of Small-Swap and Big-Swap can be referred to Fig. 2.

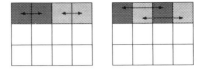

Fig. 2. The linear layer. The left/right one represent the Small-Swap/Big-Swap.

2.3 Gimli-Hash

How Gimli-Hash compresses a message is illustrated in Fig. 3. Specifically, Gimli-Hash initializes a 48-byte Gimli state to all-zero. It then reads sequentially through a variable-length input as a series of 16-byte input blocks, denoted by M_0, M_1, $\cdots$. After all message blocks are processed, the 256-bit hash value will be generated. More details can be referred to [1].

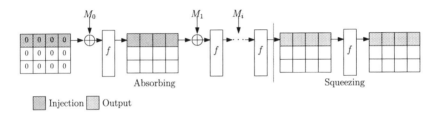

Fig. 3. The process to compress the message, where f is the Gimli permutation

3 Properties of the SP-box

Since several properties of the SP-box will be exploited in our collision attack and state-recovery attack, for convenience, we summarize them in this part. For simplicity, the input and output of the SP-box are denoted by (IX, IY, IZ) and (OX, OY, OZ), respectively.

Property 1. *If $IY[31 \sim 23] = 0$ and $IY[19 \sim 0] = 0$, OX will be independent of IX.*

Property 2. *A random triple (IY, IZ, OX) is potentially valid with probability $2^{-15.5}$ without knowing IX.*

Property 3. *Given a random triple (IX, OY, OZ), it is valid with probability 2^{-1}. Once it is valid, $(OX[30 \sim 0], IY, IZ[30 \sim 0])$ can be determined.*

Property 4. *Given a random triple (IY, IZ, OZ), (IX, OX, OY) can be uniquely determined. In addition, a random tuple (IY, IZ, OY, OZ) is valid with probability 2^{-32}.*

Property 5. *Suppose the pair (IY, IZ) and t bits of OY are known. Then t bits of information on IX can be recovered by solving a linear equation system of size t.*

The above properties will be frequently exploited in our attacks and therefore we list them ahead of time. The corresponding proofs can be referred to the full version of this paper [17]. Some other properties will be explained later.

4   The MILP Model Capturing Difference and Value Transitions

To search for a valid differential characteristic of reduced SHA-2, Mendel et al. developed a technique to search for the differential characteristic and conforming message pair simultaneously [18]. However, how to achieve the simultaneousness is not explained in [18]. Inspired by such an idea, different from many models where only the difference transitions are considered and are treated as independent in different rounds, we try to construct a model which can describe the difference transitions and value transitions simultaneously. The basic idea is simple. As shown in Fig. 4, the models to describe the difference transitions and value transitions will be independently constructed. Then, construct a model to describe the difference-value relations in the nonlinear operation and use it to connect the difference transitions and value transitions. The reason is that the difference transitions and value transitions are dependent only in the nonlinear operation. If such a model can be constructed, the contradictions can always be avoided in the search.

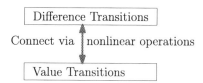

Fig. 4. Illustration of the model

4.1   Difference-Value Relations Through the SP-box

First of all, consider the relations between the difference and value. According to the bit relations between (IX, IY, IZ) and (OX, OY, OZ) as specified in Eq. 1, Eq. 2, and Eq. 3, one can easily observe that there are at most 4 types of Boolean expressions as follows, where $a[i] \in F_2$ and $0 \leq i \leq 4$.

Type-1: $a[1] = a[0]$.
Type-2: $a[2] = a[0] \oplus a[1]$.

Type-3: $a[4] = a[0] \oplus a[1] \oplus a[2] \wedge a[3]$.
Type-4: $a[4] = a[0] \oplus a[1] \oplus a[2] \vee a[3]$.

Specifically, Type-1 corresponds to the expression to calculate $OZ[0]$. Type-2 corresponds to the expressions to calculate $OX[0]$, $OX[1]$, $OX[2]$, $OY[0]$ and $OZ[1]$. Type-3 corresponds to the expression to compute $OX[i]$ $(3 \leq i \leq 31)$ and $OZ[j]$ $(2 \leq j \leq 31)$, while Type-4 corresponds to the expression to compute $OY[i]$ $(1 \leq i \leq 31)$.

For convenience, introduce another 5 bit variables $a' = \{a'[0], a'[1], a'[2], a'[3], a'[4]\}$ and let $\Delta a = a \oplus a'$, i.e. $\Delta a[i] = a[i] \oplus a'[i]$ for $0 \leq i \leq 4$. For better understanding, we explain the relations between the difference (Δa) and the value (a) for each of the 4 types.

Type-1. For this type, there is no relation between Δa and a. Only the following relation can be derived:

$$\Delta a[1] = \Delta a[0].$$

Type-2. Similar to Type-1, there is no relation between Δa and a. Only the following relation can be derived:

$$\Delta a[2] = \Delta a[0] \oplus \Delta a[1].$$

Type-3. Since a nonlinear operation exists in this expression, we can derive the relations between Δa and a, as specified below:

$$\Delta a[4] \oplus \Delta a[0] \oplus \Delta a[1] = 1, \Delta a[2] = 0, \Delta a[3] = 0 \Rightarrow Contradiction$$
$$\Delta a[4] \oplus \Delta a[0] \oplus \Delta a[1] = 1, \Delta a[2] = 0, \Delta a[3] = 1 \Rightarrow a[2] = 1$$
$$\Delta a[4] \oplus \Delta a[0] \oplus \Delta a[1] = 1, \Delta a[2] = 1, \Delta a[3] = 0 \Rightarrow a[3] = 1$$
$$\Delta a[4] \oplus \Delta a[0] \oplus \Delta a[1] = 1, \Delta a[2] = 1, \Delta a[3] = 1 \Rightarrow a[2] = a[3]$$
$$\Delta a[4] \oplus \Delta a[0] \oplus \Delta a[1] = 0, \Delta a[2] = 0, \Delta a[3] = 1 \Rightarrow a[2] = 0$$
$$\Delta a[4] \oplus \Delta a[0] \oplus \Delta a[1] = 0, \Delta a[2] = 1, \Delta a[3] = 0 \Rightarrow a[3] = 0$$
$$\Delta a[4] \oplus \Delta a[0] \oplus \Delta a[1] = 0, \Delta a[2] = 1, \Delta a[3] = 1 \Rightarrow a[2] \oplus a[3] = 1.$$

Type-4. Similar to Type-3, since a nonlinear operation exists in this expression, the following relations between Δa and a can be derived:

$$\Delta a[4] \oplus \Delta a[0] \oplus \Delta a[1] = 1, \Delta a[2] = 0, \Delta a[3] = 0 \Rightarrow Contradiction$$
$$\Delta a[4] \oplus \Delta a[0] \oplus \Delta a[1] = 1, \Delta a[2] = 0, \Delta a[3] = 1 \Rightarrow a[2] = 0$$
$$\Delta a[4] \oplus \Delta a[0] \oplus \Delta a[1] = 1, \Delta a[2] = 1, \Delta a[3] = 0 \Rightarrow a[3] = 0$$
$$\Delta a[4] \oplus \Delta a[0] \oplus \Delta a[1] = 1, \Delta a[2] = 1, \Delta a[3] = 1 \Rightarrow a[2] = a[3]$$
$$\Delta a[4] \oplus \Delta a[0] \oplus \Delta a[1] = 0, \Delta a[2] = 0, \Delta a[3] = 1 \Rightarrow a[2] = 1$$
$$\Delta a[4] \oplus \Delta a[0] \oplus \Delta a[1] = 0, \Delta a[2] = 1, \Delta a[3] = 0 \Rightarrow a[3] = 1$$
$$\Delta a[4] \oplus \Delta a[0] \oplus \Delta a[1] = 0, \Delta a[2] = 1, \Delta a[3] = 1 \Rightarrow a[2] \oplus a[3] = 1.$$

4.2 Constructing the MILP Model

It has been discussed above that there are only two cases when we need to consider the relations between the difference and value transitions through the SP-box. Thus, we first construct the MILP model to describe such relations. First of all, consider two minimal models called **AND-Model** and **OR-Model**.

Constructing AND-Model. Consider the following Boolean expression

$$a[2] = a[0] \wedge a[1].$$

Firstly, construct the truth table for $(a[0], a[1], \Delta a[0], \Delta a[1], \Delta a[2])$, which can be easily finished by enumerating all 16 possible values of $(a[0], a[1], \Delta a[0], \Delta a[1])$ and computing the corresponding $\Delta a[2]$. Details are given in the full version of this paper [17]. Using the greedy algorithm in [21], the corresponding truth table can be described with the following linear inequalities, where the remaining 16 invalid patterns can not satisfy at least one of them.

$$
\begin{cases}
-a[0] - a[1] - \Delta a[1] + \Delta a[2] + 2 \geq 0 \\
a[0] - a[1] - \Delta a[1] - \Delta a[2] + 2 \geq 0 \\
-a[0] + a[1] - \Delta a[0] - \Delta a[2] + 2 \geq 0 \\
a[0] + \Delta a[0] - \Delta a[2] \geq 0 \\
a[0] + a[1] - \Delta a[0] - \Delta a[1] + \Delta a[2] + 1 \geq 0 \\
\Delta a[0] + \Delta a[1] - \Delta a[2] \geq 0 \\
a[1] + \Delta a[1] - \Delta a[2] \geq 0 \\
-a[1] - \Delta a[0] + \Delta a[1] + \Delta a[2] + 1 \geq 0 \\
-a[0] + \Delta a[0] - \Delta a[1] + \Delta a[2] + 1 \geq 0
\end{cases}
\tag{4}
$$

Constructing OR-Model. Consider the following Boolean expression

$$a[2] = a[0] \vee a[1].$$

Similarly, construct the truth table for $(a[0], a[1], \Delta a[0], \Delta a[1], \Delta a[2])$ by enumerating all 16 possible values of $(a[0], a[1], \Delta a[0], \Delta a[1])$ and computing the corresponding $\Delta a[2]$. Details are given in the full version of this paper [17]. The corresponding truth table is equivalent to the following linear inequalities:

$$
\begin{cases}
-a[1] + \Delta a[1] - \Delta a[2] + 1 \geq 0 \\
-a[0] + \Delta a[0] - \Delta a[2] + 1 \geq 0 \\
a[1] - \Delta a[0] + \Delta a[1] + \Delta a[2] \geq 0 \\
a[0] + \Delta a[0] - \Delta a[1] + \Delta a[2] \geq 0 \\
a[0] + a[1] - \Delta a[1] + \Delta a[2] \geq 0 \\
\Delta a[0] + \Delta a[1] - \Delta a[2] \geq 0 \\
a[0] - a[1] - \Delta a[0] - \Delta a[2] + 2 \geq 0 \\
-a[0] - a[1] - \Delta a[0] - \Delta a[1] + \Delta a[2] + 3 \geq 0 \\
-a[0] + a[1] - \Delta a[1] - \Delta a[2] + 2 \geq 0
\end{cases}
\tag{5}
$$

Constructing MILP Model for Value Transitions. For the Gimli round function, the linear layer can be viewed as a simple permutation of bit positions. Thus, we only focus on the model to describe the value transitions through the SP-box in this part. As discussed above, there are at most 4 types of Boolean expressions when expressing the output bit in terms of the input bits for the SP-box. Now, we explain how to model such 4 types of expressions.

Modeling Type-1 Expression. The Type-1 Boolean expression is

$$a[1] = a[0].$$

Thus, it is rather simple to model the value relation by using the following linear equality:

$$a[1] = a[0]. \tag{6}$$

Modeling Type-2 Expression. The Type-2 Boolean expression is

$$a[2] = a[0] \oplus a[1].$$

Such a linear Boolean equation can be described with the following linear inequalities:

$$\begin{cases} a[0] + a[1] - a[2] \geq 0 \\ a[0] - a[1] + a[2] \geq 0 \\ -a[0] + a[1] + a[2] \geq 0 \\ -a[0] - a[1] - a[2] + 2 \geq 0 \end{cases} \tag{7}$$

Modeling Type-3 Expression. The Type-3 Boolean expression is

$$a[4] = a[0] \oplus a[1] \oplus a[2] \wedge a[3].$$

Such a linear Boolean equation can be described with the following linear inequalities:

$$\begin{cases} -a[0] + a[1] + a[3] + a[4] \geq 0 \\ a[0] - a[1] + a[3] + a[4] \geq 0 \\ a[0] + a[1] + a[2] - a[4] \geq 0 \\ a[0] + a[1] + a[3] - a[4] \geq 0 \\ a[0] - a[1] + a[2] + a[4] \geq 0 \\ -a[0] + a[1] + a[2] + a[4] \geq 0 \\ a[0] + a[1] - a[2] - a[3] + a[4] + 1 \geq 0 \\ -a[0] - a[1] + a[2] - a[4] + 2 \geq 0 \\ a[0] - a[1] - a[2] - a[3] - a[4] + 3 \geq 0 \\ -a[0] - a[1] - a[2] - a[3] + a[4] + 3 \geq 0 \\ -a[0] - a[1] + a[3] - a[4] + 2 \geq 0 \\ -a[0] + a[1] - a[2] - a[3] - a[4] + 3 \geq 0 \end{cases} \tag{8}$$

Modeling Type-4 Expression. The Type-4 Boolean expression is

$$a[4] = a[0] \oplus a[1] \oplus a[2] \vee a[3].$$

Such a linear Boolean equation can be described with the following linear inequalities:

$$\begin{cases} -a[0] + a[1] - a[3] - a[4] + 2 \geq 0 \\ a[0] - a[1] - a[3] - a[4] + 2 \geq 0 \\ -a[0] - a[1] - a[3] + a[4] + 2 \geq 0 \\ -a[0] + a[1] - a[2] - a[4] + 2 \geq 0 \\ a[0] - a[1] - a[2] - a[4] + 2 \geq 0 \\ -a[0] - a[1] - a[2] + a[4] + 2 \geq 0 \\ -a[0] + a[1] + a[2] + a[3] + a[4] \geq 0 \\ a[0] + a[1] - a[3] + a[4] \geq 0 \\ a[0] + a[1] - a[2] + a[4] \geq 0 \\ a[0] - a[1] + a[2] + a[3] + a[4] \geq 0 \\ a[0] + a[1] + a[2] + a[3] - a[4] \geq 0 \\ -a[0] - a[1] + a[2] + a[3] - a[4] + 2 \geq 0 \end{cases} \quad (9)$$

Constructing MILP Model for Difference Transitions. The value transitions through the SP-box have been discussed above. In the following, how to model the difference transitions will be detailed. Similarly, write the four possible types of expressions for differences as follows:

$$\Delta a[1] = \Delta a[0], \quad (10)$$
$$\Delta a[2] = \Delta a[0] \oplus \Delta a[1], \quad (11)$$
$$\Delta a[4] = \Delta a[0] \oplus \Delta a[1] \oplus \Delta na_0, \quad (12)$$
$$\Delta a[4] = \Delta a[0] \oplus \Delta a[1] \oplus \Delta na_1, \quad (13)$$

where na_0 and na_1 represent the output difference of the nonlinear operation $a[2] \wedge a[3]$ and $a[2] \vee a[3]$, respectively. It can be easily observed that the first two possible transitions (Eq. 10 and Eq. 11) share the same MILP model used to describe the value transitions for Type-1 expression and Type-2 expression. For the last two transitions, we need to construct a model to describe the following linear Boolean equation:

$$a[3] = a[0] \oplus a[1] \oplus a[2].$$

This task is also rather easy. The linear inequalities to describe the above linear Boolean equation in terms of four variables are specified as follows:

$$\begin{cases}
a[0] + a[1] - a[2] + a[3] \geq 0 \\
a[0] + a[1] + a[2] - a[3] \geq 0 \\
-a[0] + a[1] + a[2] + a[3] \geq 0 \\
a[0] - a[1] + a[2] + a[3] \geq 0 \\
-a[0] - a[1] + a[2] - a[3] + 2 \geq 0 \\
a[0] - a[1] - a[2] - a[3] + 2 \geq 0 \\
-a[0] + a[1] - a[2] - a[3] + 2 \geq 0 \\
-a[0] - a[1] - a[2] + a[3] + 2 \geq 0
\end{cases} \qquad (14)$$

One may observe that two **intermediate variables** na_0 and na_1 are introduced when constructing the model for difference transitions and they have not been connected with the actual variables, i.e. a and Δa in the constructed model. In fact, this is where our technique exists in order to model the difference and value transitions simultaneously. Specifically, the two intermediate variables na_0 and na_1 will be utilized to link the value transitions and difference transitions, together with the two minimal models AND-Model and OR-Model.

Connecting the Value Transitions and Difference Transitions. It can be observed that the current MILP models for value transitions and difference transitions are independently constructed. In this part, we will describe how to connect the value and difference transitions with the two intermediate variables (na_0, na_1) by using the AND-Model and OR-Model. Note that na_0 and na_1 denote the output difference of the nonlinear operations $a[2] \wedge a[3]$ and $a[2] \vee a[3]$, respectively.

Connecting the Two Transitions for Type-3 Expression. Consider the Type-3 expression:

$$a[4] = a[0] \oplus a[1] \oplus a[2] \wedge a[3].$$

Firstly, use Eq. 8 to model the relations of $(a[0], a[1], a[2], a[3], a[4])$. Then, use the AND-Model to describe the relations of $(a[2], a[3], \Delta a[2], \Delta a[3], na_0)$. Finally, use Eq. 14 to describe the relations of $(\Delta a[0], \Delta a[1], na_0, \Delta a[4])$. In this way, the value and difference transitions for Type-3 expression are connected.

Connecting the Two Transitions for Type-4 Expression. The Type-4 expression is specified as follows:

$$a[4] = a[0] \oplus a[1] \oplus a[2] \vee a[3].$$

Similarly, Eq. 9 is used to model the relations of $(a[0], a[1], a[2], a[3], a[4])$. Then, the OR-Model is used to model the relations of $(a[2], a[3], \Delta a[2], \Delta a[3], na_1)$. At last, Eq. 14 is used to describe the relations of $(\Delta a[0], \Delta a[1], na_1, \Delta a[4])$.

For the remaining two expressions (Type-1 and Type-2), the value and difference transitions are independent. Therefore, the corresponding two models are independent and there is no need to connect them. Obviously, the AND-Model and OR-Model are the core techniques to achieve the connection.

4.3 Detecting Contradictions

Since both the difference transitions and value transitions are taken into account in our MILP model, once given a specified differential characteristic of Gimli, the difference transitions are fixed. In addition, some constraints on the value of the internal states are fixed as well based on the AND-Model and OR-Model. Thus, the final inequality system in the whole model is only in terms of the variables representing the value of the internal states. If a solution can be returned by the solver, it simply means that there is a conforming message pair satisfying the differential characteristic. However, if the solver returns "infeasible", it implies that no conforming message pair can satisfy the differential characteristic, thus revealing that the differential characteristic is impossible.

We have used the above method to check the validity of two existing differential characteristics of Gimli. One is the 12-round differential characteristic proposed in the Gimli document [4], and the other is the 6-round differential characteristic used for a collision attack in [25]. Surprisingly, both of them are proven to be invalid, i.e. the Gurobi solver [2] returns "infeasible". To support the correctness of our model, detailed analysis of the contradictions are provided in the full version of this paper [17].

5   Collision Attack on 6-Round Gimli-Hash

Since the 6-round differential characteristic is invalid in [25], it is necessary to search for a valid one in order to mount a collision attack on 6-round Gimli-Hash. On the whole, our collision attack procedure can be divided into the following two phases:

Phase 1: Utilize our model to find a valid 6-round differential characteristic.
Phase 2: Use the linearization and start-from-the-middle techniques to find all the conforming message pairs satisfying the discovered differential characteristic and store them in a clever way. All these message pairs can be viewed as SFS colliding message pairs. Then, convert the SFS collisions into collisions with a divide-and-conquer method.

Obviously, both the way to search for a differential characteristic and the way to mount a collision attack are different from that in [25].

5.1   Searching a Valid 6-Round Differential Characteristic

It can be easily observed in [25] that, in order to eliminate the influence of linear layer (Big-Swap and Small-Swap) and to reduce the workload of the MILP model, the authors only considered the difference transitions in one column rather than the whole state. Specifically, as shown in Fig. 5, the target is to find the following valid difference transitions through the SP-box:

$$(D_0, 0, 0) \xrightarrow{SP} (0, D_1, D_2) \xrightarrow{SP} (D_3, D_4, D_5) \xrightarrow{SP}$$
$$(D_6, D_7, D_8) \xrightarrow{SP} (D_9, D_{10}, D_{11}) \xrightarrow{SP} (0, 0, D_{12}) \xrightarrow{SP} (D_{13}, 0, 0).$$

Once such a solution is found, it can be easily converted into a differential characteristic of the full state. However, as has been proved, the solution found in [25] is actually invalid if considering the dependency between the value transitions and difference transitions.

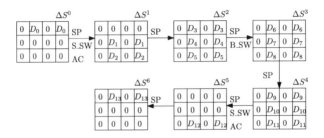

Fig. 5. The pattern of the difference transitions in [25]

Different from the optimal differential characteristic which may be sparse, the differential characteristic used for the collision attack is much denser, thus having a high probability that contradictions occur if only the difference transitions are considered. To avoid such a bad case, the differential characteristic and the conforming message pair will be simultaneously searched with our constructed MILP model. Similar to [4,25], a probability 1 two-round differential characteristic is first constructed in the last two rounds. Moreover, to reduce the workload, some additional constraints will be added when constructing the model, as specified below:

$$\Delta S_{i,0}^0 = \Delta S_{i,2}^0 = 0 \ (0 \le i \le 2). \tag{15}$$
$$\Delta S_{j,1}^0 = \Delta S_{j,3}^0 = 0 \ (1 \le j \le 2). \tag{16}$$
$$\Delta S_{i,0}^4 = \Delta S_{i,2}^4 = 0 \ (0 \le i \le 2). \tag{17}$$
$$\Delta S_{j,1}^4 = \Delta S_{j,3}^4 = 0 \ (1 \le j \le 2). \tag{18}$$
$$\Delta S_{i,j}^r = \Delta S_{i,j+2}^r \ (0 \le i \le 2, 0 \le j \le 1, 0 \le r \le 3). \tag{19}$$
$$\Delta S_{0,1}^4 = \Delta S_{0,3}^4 = \text{0x80}. \tag{20}$$
$$\Delta S_{1,1}^4 = \Delta S_{1,3}^4 = \text{0x400000}. \tag{21}$$
$$\Delta S_{2,1}^4 = \Delta S_{2,3}^4 = \text{0x80000000}. \tag{22}$$

Moreover, to reduce the search space, we further constrain the hamming weight of $(\Delta S^3_{0,1}, \Delta S^3_{1,1}, \Delta S^3_{2,1})$ as follows, i.e. the number of bits whose values are 1:

$$HW(\Delta S^3_{0,1}, \Delta S^3_{1,1}, \Delta S^3_{2,1}) \leq 8.$$

Specifically, the aim is to find a solution for the 32-bit words marked with "?" in Fig. 6.

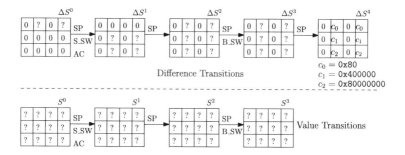

Fig. 6. Searching a valid 6-round differential characteristic

The 6-Round Differential Characteristic. Based on the above model, the Gurobi solver returns a solution in less than 4 h. In other words, a valid 6-round differential characteristic and a conforming message pair are obtained. For a better presentation, the differential characteristic is displayed in Table 2. The conforming message pair is displayed in Table 4. The conditions implied in the differential characteristic are shown in Table 3. Note that by using one more message block to eliminate the difference in the rate part, a full-state SFS collision is obtained. However, the SFS collision attack is still less meaningful than the collision attack. Therefore, we are further motivated to convert the SFS collisions into collisions.

5.2 Converting SFS Collision Attacks into Collision Attacks

First of all, as shown in Table 3, the conditions on $S^3_{0,1}$ and $S^3_{0,3}$ only involve the bits of $S^3_{0,1}$ and $S^3_{0,3}$, respectively. Due to the symmetry of the 6-round differential characteristic, the conditions on $S^3_{0,1}$ and $S^3_{0,3}$ are the same. Due to the influence of Big-Swap, $S^3_{0,3}$ is actually computed by using $(S^2_{0,1}, S^2_{1,1}, S^2_{2,1})$, while $S^3_{0,1}$ is computed by using $(S^2_{0,3}, S^2_{1,3}, S^2_{2,3})$. Thus, we define two sets of conditions which can be independently verified, as specified below:

Definition 1. *The internal state words* $(S^0_{0,1}, S^0_{1,1}, S^0_{2,1})$, $(S^1_{0,1}, S^1_{1,1}, S^1_{2,1})$, $(S^2_{0,1}, S^2_{1,1}, S^2_{2,1})$ *and* $(S^3_{0,3}, S^3_{1,1}, S^3_{2,1})$ *only depend on the input state words* $(S^0_{i,j})$ $(0 \leq i \leq 2, 0 \leq j \leq 1)$, *while the internal state words* $(S^0_{0,3}, S^0_{1,3}, S^0_{2,3})$,

Table 2. The 6-round differential characteristic

State	XOR Difference		
ΔS^0	0 0x7c2c642a	0 0x7c2c642a	
	0	0 0	0
	0	0 0	0
ΔS^1	0	0 0	0
	0 0x6e1c342c	0 0x6e1c342c	
	0 0x2a7c2c64	0 0x2a7c2c64	
ΔS^2	0 0x91143078	0 0x91143078	
	0 0x28785014	0 0x28785014	
	0 0x35288a58	0 0x35288a58	
ΔS^3	0 0x80010008	0 0x80010008	
	0 0x00002000	0 0x00002000	
	0 0x44400080	0 0x44400080	
ΔS^4	0 0x00000080	0 0x00000080	
	0 0x00400000	0 0x00400000	
	0 0x80000000	0 0x80000000	
ΔS^5	0	0 0	0
	0	0 0	0
	0 0x80000000	0 0x80000000	
ΔS^6	0 0x80000000	0 0x80000000	
	0	0 0	0
	0	0 0	0

$(S_{0,3}^1, S_{1,3}^1, S_{2,3}^1)$, $(S_{0,3}^2, S_{1,3}^2, S_{2,3}^2)$ and $(S_{0,1}^3, S_{1,3}^3, S_{2,3}^3)$ only depend on the input state words $(S_{i,j}^0)$ $(0 \leq i \leq 2, 2 \leq j \leq 3)$.

Therefore, by only knowing $(S_{i,j}^0)$ $(0 \leq i \leq 2, 0 \leq j \leq 1)$, we can fully compute $(S_{0,1}^0, S_{1,1}^0, S_{2,1}^0)$, $(S_{0,1}^1, S_{1,1}^1, S_{2,1}^1)$, $(S_{0,1}^2, S_{1,1}^2, S_{2,1}^2)$ and $(S_{0,3}^3, S_{1,1}^3, S_{2,1}^3)$. For simplicity, the conditions on these 12 internal state words in Table 3 are called **L-Conditions**.

Similarly, by only knowing $(S_{i,j}^0)$ $(0 \leq i \leq 2, 2 \leq j \leq 3)$, we can fully compute $(S_{0,3}^0, S_{1,3}^0, S_{2,3}^0)$, $(S_{0,3}^1, S_{1,3}^1, S_{2,3}^1)$, $(S_{0,3}^2, S_{1,3}^2, S_{2,3}^2)$ and $(S_{0,1}^3, S_{1,3}^3, S_{2,3}^3)$. For simplicity, the conditions on these 12 internal state words in Table 3 are called **R-Conditions**.

Therefore, the L-Conditions and R-Conditions can be verified independently. Now, we introduce a method to identify all the possible values for the capacity of the first two columns $(S_{i,j}^0)$ $(1 \leq i \leq 2, 0 \leq j \leq 1)$ which can fulfill the L-Conditions. Since the L-Conditions and R-Conditions are identical, the method works in the same way to find all the possible values for the capacity part of the last two columns $(S_{i,j}^0)$ $(1 \leq i \leq 2, 2 \leq j \leq 3)$ which can fulfill the R-Conditions.

Identifying All Possible Solutions. To obtain all valid values of $(S_{i,j}^0)$ $(1 \leq i \leq 2, 0 \leq j \leq 1)$, the following techniques will be exploited to accelerate the exhaustive search:

1. Merge the conditions in two consecutive rounds, which can significantly reduce the size of the search space.
2. Use a start-from-the-middle method and the properties of the SP-box to further accelerate the exhaustive search.

Table 3. The conditions implied in the 6-round differential characteristic

```
S^0_{0,1}  - - - - - - - - - - - - - - - - - - - - - - - - - - - - - - - -
S^0_{1,1}  - - 0 0 - - 0 - - - - - 0 - 0 - - 0 0 0 0 0 - - - - 0 - 0 0 -
S^0_{2,1}  - - 0 - 1 - 0 - - 1 0 0 1 1 - - - - 1 - 0 0 - - - 1 0 - - 0 - -
S^0_{0,3}  - - - - - - - - - - - - - - - - - - - - - - - - - - - - - - - -
S^0_{1,3}  - - 0 0 - - 0 - - - - - 0 - 0 - - 0 0 0 0 0 - - - - 0 - 0 0 -
S^0_{2,3}  - - 0 - 1 - 0 - - 1 0 0 1 1 - - - - 1 - 0 0 - - - 1 0 - - 0 - -
```

```
S^1_{0,1}  - 1 1 1 0 1 - - - 0 1 0 1 0 - - 1 0 0 1 1 0 - - - - 1 1 0 - 1 -
S^1_{1,1}  - - - 1 - - - - - - - - - - - 0 - - - - 1 - 1 - - - - 1 - - 1 -
S^1_{2,1}  - - - 1 - - - - - - - - - - - - 0 - 1 - - - - 1 - - 0 0 - - - -
S^1_{0,3}  - 1 1 1 0 1 - - - 0 1 0 1 0 - - 1 0 0 1 1 0 - - - - 1 1 0 - 1 -
S^1_{1,3}  - - - 1 - - - - - - - - - - - 0 - - - - 1 - 1 - - - - 1 - - 1 -
S^1_{2,3}  - - - 1 - - - - - - - - - - - - 0 - 1 - - - - 1 - - 0 0 - - - -
```

$S_{1,1}^1[2] \neq S_{2,1}^1[11]$, $S_{1,1}^1[10] \neq S_{2,1}^1[19]$, $S_{1,1}^1[12] = S_{2,1}^1[21]$
$S_{1,1}^1[13] = S_{2,1}^1[22]$, $S_{1,1}^1[18] = S_{2,1}^1[27]$, $S_{1,1}^1[20] \neq S_{2,1}^1[29]$
$S_{1,1}^1[25] = S_{2,1}^1[2]$, $S_{1,1}^1[29] \neq S_{2,1}^1[6]$, $S_{1,3}^1[2] \neq S_{2,3}^1[11]$
$S_{1,3}^1[10] \neq S_{2,3}^1[19]$, $S_{1,3}^1[12] = S_{2,3}^1[21]$, $S_{1,3}^1[13] = S_{2,3}^1[22]$
$S_{1,3}^1[18] = S_{2,3}^1[27]$, $S_{1,3}^1[20] \neq S_{2,3}^1[29]$, $S_{1,3}^1[25] = S_{2,3}^1[2]$
$S_{1,3}^1[29] \neq S_{2,3}^1[6]$

```
S^2_{0,1}  - - 1 - 0 - - - 0 - 1 - 0 - 0 - - 1 - - 1 - - - - - - - - 0 - 1
S^2_{1,1}  - - - 0 - 0 - - - - - - - - 1 1 - 1 - - - 1 0 - - 1 0 - - 1 - 1 0
S^2_{2,1}  - 0 - - 1 - - - 1 - - 0 - - - 1 - - 0 1 - 0 - - - - 0 - - - - -
S^2_{0,3}  - - 1 - 0 - - - 0 - 1 - 0 - 0 - - 1 - - 1 - - - - - - - - 0 - 1
S^2_{1,3}  - - - 0 - 0 - - - - - - - - 1 1 - 1 - - - 1 0 - - 1 0 - - 1 - 1 0
S^2_{2,3}  - 0 - - 1 - - - 1 - - 0 - - - 1 - - 0 1 - 0 - - - - 0 - - - - -
```

$S_{0,1}^2[4] \neq S_{2,1}^2[28]$, $S_{0,1}^2[5] \neq S_{2,1}^2[29]$, $S_{0,1}^2[12] = S_{2,1}^2[4]$
$S_{2,1}^2[31] = S_{1,1}^2[14]$, $S_{1,1}^2[2] \neq S_{2,1}^2[11]$, $S_{1,1}^2[12] = S_{2,1}^2[21]$
$S_{1,1}^2[19] = S_{2,1}^2[28]$, $S_{1,1}^2[20] \neq S_{2,1}^2[29]$, $S_{1,1}^2[27] \neq S_{2,1}^2[4]$
$S_{1,1}^2[29] \neq S_{2,1}^2[6]$, $S_{0,3}^2[4] \neq S_{2,3}^2[28]$, $S_{0,3}^2[5] \neq S_{2,3}^2[29]$
$S_{0,3}^2[12] = S_{2,3}^2[4]$, $S_{0,3}^2[31] = S_{1,3}^2[14]$, $S_{1,3}^2[2] \neq S_{2,3}^2[11]$
$S_{1,3}^2[12] = S_{2,3}^2[21]$, $S_{1,3}^2[19] = S_{2,3}^2[28]$, $S_{1,3}^2[20] \neq S_{2,3}^2[29]$
$S_{1,3}^2[27] \neq S_{2,3}^2[4]$, $S_{1,3}^2[29] \neq S_{2,3}^2[6]$

```
S^3_{0,1}  - 0 - - - - - - - - - - - - - - - - 0 - - - - - - - - 1 - - - 0 - -
S^3_{1,1}  0 0 - - - - - - - - - - - - - 1 0 - - 1 - - - - - - - - - - - -
S^3_{2,1}  - - - - 1 - - - 1 - - - - - - - - - - - - - - 1 - - - - - - - -
S^3_{0,3}  - 0 - - - - - - - - - - - - - - - - 0 - - - - - - - - 1 - - - 0 - -
S^3_{1,3}  0 0 - - - - - - - - - - - - - 1 0 - - 1 - - - - - - - - - - - -
S^3_{2,3}  - - - - 1 - - - 1 - - - - - - - - - - - - - - 1 - - - - - - - -
```

$S_{1,1}^3[13] \neq S_{2,1}^3[22]$, $S_{1,3}^3[13] \neq S_{2,3}^3[22]$

Instead of directly finding all valid values for $(S_{i,j}^0)$ $(1 \leq i \leq 2, 0 \leq j \leq 1)$, we will first search for all the valid solutions for $(S_{0,1}^1, S_{1,1}^1, S_{2,1}^1)$. It should be noted that once $(S_{0,1}^1, S_{1,1}^1, S_{2,1}^1)$ are known, $(S_{0,1}^1, S_{1,1}^1, S_{2,1}^1)$ and $(S_{0,3}^3, S_{1,1}^3, S_{2,1}^3)$ can be fully determined. In other words, we can first identify all the solutions for $(S_{0,1}^1, S_{1,1}^1, S_{2,1}^1)$ which can make the conditions on $(S_{0,1}^1, S_{1,1}^1, S_{2,1}^1)$, $(S_{0,1}^2, S_{1,1}^2, S_{2,1}^2)$ and $(S_{0,3}^3, S_{1,1}^3, S_{2,1}^3)$ hold.

Merging the Conditions. According to Table 3, there are 40 linearly independent conditions on $(S_{0,1}^1, S_{1,1}^1, S_{2,1}^1)$. Moreover, there are 41 linearly independent conditions on $(S_{0,1}^2, S_{1,1}^2, S_{2,1}^2)$. The basic idea to convert partial conditions on $(S_{0,1}^2, S_{1,1}^2, S_{2,1}^2)$ into those on $(S_{0,1}^1, S_{1,1}^1, S_{2,1}^1)$ is simple. Specifically, represent the conditions on $(S_{0,1}^1, S_{1,1}^1, S_{2,1}^1)$ using a matrix LM_1 at first. Then, represent

Table 4. The conforming message pair for the 6-round differential characteristic

The input state S^0			
0xff792f16	0x9a757bef	0xff792f16	0x9a757bef
0x37feedd1	0x0d8080e8	0x37feedd1	0x0d8080e8
0xaca93960	0x88cda05b	0xaca93960	0x88cda05b

The input state $S'^0 (S^0 \oplus \Delta S^0)$			
0xff792f16	0xe6591fc5	0xff792f16	0xe6591fc5
0x37feedd1	0x0d8080e8	0x37feedd1	0x0d8080e8
0xaca93960	0x88cda05b	0xaca93960	0x88cda05b

The output state S^6 after 6-round permutation for S^0			
0x0765a592	0xcda58e91	0xa5f12648	0xcf35aef1
0x2cecc20e	0xc11436eb	0xba243082	0xc0df1177
0xeda218de	0xeb3f7ab7	0xffb9fd21	0xebe4552b

The output state S'^6 after 6-round permutation for S'^0			
0x0765a592	0x4da58e91	0xa5f12648	0x4f35aef1
0x2cecc20e	0xc11436eb	0xba243082	0xc0df1177
0xeda218de	0xeb3f7ab7	0xffb9fd21	0xebe4552b

$\Delta S^6 = S'^6 \oplus S^6$			
0	0x80000000	0	0x80000000
0	0	0	0
0	0	0	0

the conditions on $(S_{0,1}^2, S_{1,1}^2, S_{2,1}^2)$ using another matrix LM_2. Consider the following relations between $(S_{0,1}^1, S_{1,1}^1, S_{2,1}^1)$ and $(S_{0,1}^2, S_{1,1}^2, S_{2,1}^2)$:

$$S_{0,1}^2[i] = \begin{cases} S_{2,1}^1[i] \oplus S_{1,1}^1[i-9] \ (0 \leq i \leq 2) \\ S_{2,1}^1[i] \oplus S_{1,1}^1[i-9] \oplus (S_{0,1}^1[i-27] \wedge S_{1,1}^1[i-12]) \ (3 \leq i \leq 31) \end{cases}$$

$$S_{1,1}^2[i] = \begin{cases} S_{1,1}^1[i-9] \oplus S_{0,1}^1[i-24] \ (i=0) \\ S_{1,1}^1[i-9] \oplus S_{0,1}^1[i-24] \oplus (S_{0,1}^1[i-25] \vee S_{2,1}^1[i-1]) \ (1 \leq i \leq 31) \end{cases}$$

$$S_{2,1}^2[i] = \begin{cases} S_{0,1}^1[i-24] \ (i=0) \\ S_{0,1}^1[i-24] \oplus S_{2,1}^1[i-1] \ (i=1) \\ S_{0,1}^1[i-24] \oplus S_{2,1}^1[i-1] \oplus (S_{1,1}^1[i-11] \wedge S_{2,1}^1[i-2]) \ (2 \leq i \leq 31) \end{cases}$$

Therefore, if there are conditions on $S_{0,1}^2[i]$ ($0 \leq i \leq 2$) or on $S_{1,1}^2[0]$ or on $S_{2,1}^2[i]$ ($0 \leq i \leq 1$), they can be directly converted into linear conditions on $(S_{0,1}^1, S_{1,1}^1, S_{2,1}^1)$. Thus, we can add these newly-generated conditions to LM_1 and apply the Gauss elimination. As for the remaining conditions on $(S_{0,1}^1, S_{1,1}^1, S_{2,1}^1)$, we first check whether the nonlinear part $S_{0,1}^1[i-27] \wedge S_{1,1}^1[i-12]$ or $S_{0,1}^1[i-25] \vee S_{2,1}^1[i-1]$ or $S_{1,1}^1[i-11] \wedge S_{2,1}^1[i-2]$ can be linearized based on the conditions on $(S_{0,1}^1, S_{1,1}^1, S_{2,1}^1)$. Specifically, if one bit of the nonlinear part is fixed in $(S_{0,1}^1, S_{1,1}^1, S_{2,1}^1)$, the corresponding conditions on $(S_{0,1}^2, S_{1,1}^2, S_{2,1}^2)$ can be directly converted into linear conditions on $(S_{0,1}^1, S_{1,1}^1, S_{2,1}^1)$. Then, we add these newly-generated linear conditions to LM_1 and again apply the Gauss elimination. Such a process is repeated until LM_1 becomes stable, i.e. no more conditions on $(S_{0,1}^2, S_{1,1}^2, S_{2,1}^2)$ can be converted into new linear conditions on

$(S_{0,1}^1, S_{1,1}^1, S_{2,1}^1)$. In this way, there will be finally 61 linearly independent conditions on $(S_{0,1}^1, S_{1,1}^1, S_{2,1}^1)$. In other words, the size of the solution space of $(S_{0,1}^1, S_{1,1}^1, S_{2,1}^1)$ is reduced to $2^{96-61} = 2^{35}$ from $2^{96-40} = 2^{56}$ after converting partial conditions on $(S_{0,1}^2, S_{1,1}^2, S_{2,1}^2)$ into those on $(S_{0,1}^1, S_{1,1}^1, S_{2,1}^1)$.

The Start-From-the-Middle Method. According to the above analysis, the solution space of $(S_{0,1}^1, S_{1,1}^1, S_{2,1}^1)$ can now be exhausted in practical time 2^{35}. For each of its possible values, the conditions on $(S_{0,1}^2, S_{1,1}^2, S_{2,1}^2)$ and $(S_{0,3}^3, S_{1,1}^3, S_{2,1}^3)$ can be fully verified. In this way, we find that there are in total 1632 solutions for $(S_{0,1}^1, S_{1,1}^1, S_{2,1}^1)$. By sorting the solutions according to $(S_{1,1}^1, S_{2,1}^1)$, we find that among all the 1632 solutions, there are 720 different values of $(S_{1,1}^1, S_{2,1}^1)$ and each different value of $(S_{1,1}^1, S_{2,1}^1)$ will correspond to 2 different values of $S_{0,1}^1$ on average. Record these 720 different values of $(S_{1,1}^1, S_{2,1}^1)$ in order to identify all the valid values of $(S_{1,1}^0, S_{2,1}^0)$.

It has been discussed in Property 4 that a random tuple $(S_{1,1}^0, S_{2,1}^0, S_{1,1}^1, S_{2,1}^1)$ is valid with probability 2^{-32}. Once it is valid, $(S_{0,1}^0, S_{0,1}^1)$ is determined. In other words, although the attacker can freely choose the values of $S_{0,1}^0$, whether the 720 different values of $(S_{1,1}^1, S_{2,1}^1)$ can be reached only depends on the value of $(S_{1,1}^0, S_{2,1}^0)$. According to Table 3, there are 27 linearly independent conditions on $(S_{1,1}^0, S_{2,1}^0)$. Thus, a naive way to find all the valid solutions of $(S_{1,1}^0, S_{2,1}^0)$ is to exhaust all the $2^{64-27} = 2^{37}$ possible values of $(S_{1,1}^0, S_{2,1}^0)$ since we can pre-assign values to $(S_{1,1}^0, S_{2,1}^0)$ to make the 27 linear conditions on them hold. For each guessed value, check whether there exists a tuple $(S_{1,1}^1, S_{2,1}^1)$ which can make the tuple $(S_{1,1}^0, S_{2,1}^0, S_{1,1}^1, S_{2,1}^1)$ valid. Obviously, the time complexity of this method is $720 \times 2^{37} = 2^{46.4}$ and therefore it still requires a significant amount of time. To accelerate this exhaustive search, we use the following property of the SP-box.

Property 6. *Given the triple (IZ, OY, OZ), IY can be recovered by solving a linear equation system of size 32.*

Proof. For simplicity, we omit the rotate shift of (IX, IY) and only focus on the following relations.

$$OZ \leftarrow IX \oplus IZ \lll 1 \oplus (IY \wedge IZ) \lll 2$$
$$OY \leftarrow IY \oplus IX \oplus (IX \vee IZ) \lll 1$$
$$OX \leftarrow IZ \oplus IY \oplus (IX \wedge IY) \lll 3$$

Therefore, we can obtain that

$$OY = IY \oplus (OZ \oplus IZ \lll 1 \oplus (IY \wedge IZ) \lll 2) \oplus ((OZ \oplus IZ \lll 1 \oplus (IY \wedge IZ) \lll 2) \vee IZ) \lll 1.$$

Since (IZ, OY, OZ) are known, 32 linearly independent equations in terms of the unknown 32 bits of IY can be derived. Consequently, IY can be recovered by solving a linear equation system of size 32.

Based on Property 6, the search space of $(S_{1,1}^0, S_{2,1}^0)$ can be significantly reduced, as specified below:

Step 1: Record the 13 conditions on $S_{1,1}^0$ displayed in Table 3 by a matrix LM_3. Keep the 14 conditions on $S_{2,1}^0$ displayed in Table 3 hold.

Step 2: Guess all possible values of the remaining unknown 18 bits of $S_{2,1}^0$. For each guess of $S_{2,1}^0$, exhaust the 720 different values of $(S_{1,1}^1, S_{2,1}^1)$. For each guessed value of $(S_{2,1}^0, S_{1,1}^1, S_{2,1}^1)$, according to Property 6, 32 linear equations in terms of $S_{1,1}^0$ can be derived. Add these 32 linear equations to LM_3 and check the consistency using Gauss elimination. If they are consistent, output the solution to $S_{1,1}^0$.

The time complexity of the above method is therefore $720 \times 2^{18} = 2^{27.4}$. With this method, we find that there are in total 0x34c8 valid values for $(S_{1,1}^0, S_{2,1}^0)$. Moreover, each solution of $(S_{1,1}^0, S_{2,1}^0)$ will correspond to 2 different values of $(S_{1,1}^1, S_{2,1}^1)$. Note that each $(S_{1,1}^1, S_{2,1}^1)$ can correspond to 2 different values of $S_{0,1}^1$ on average. Thus, each valid solution of $(S_{1,1}^0, S_{2,1}^0)$ can correspond to 4 different solutions of $S_{0,1}^1$ on average.

Calculating the Probability. It has been identified that there are in total 0x34c8 valid values for $(S_{1,1}^0, S_{2,1}^0)$, each of which will correspond to 4 different values of $S_{0,1}^1$. Note that $S_{0,1}^1$ is computed by using $(S_{0,0}^0, S_{1,0}^0, S_{2,0}^0)$ due to the effect of Small-Swap. It has been pointed out in Property 2 that a random tuple $(S_{1,0}^0, S_{2,0}^0, S_{0,1}^1)$ holds with probability $2^{-15.5}$. Thus, a random tuple $(S_{1,0}^0, S_{2,0}^0, S_{1,1}^1, S_{2,1}^1)$ is valid with probability $2^{-64} \times$ 0x34c8 $\times (4 \times 2^{-15.5}) \approx 2^{-63.8}$. It has been discussed above that L-Conditions and R-Conditions are identical. Consequently, the whole capacity part $(S_{i,j}^0)$ $(1 \le i \le 2, 0 \le j \le 3)$ is valid with probability $2^{-127.6}$. Once it is valid, a solution to $(S_{0,0}^0, S_{0,1}^0, S_{0,2}^0, S_{0,3}^0)$ can always be computed to make the L-Conditions and R-Conditions hold. In the following, how to find the solution to $(S_{0,0}^0, S_{0,1}^0, S_{0,2}^0, S_{0,3}^0)$ when $(S_{i,j}^0)$ $(1 \le i \le 2, 0 \le j \le 1)$ are valid will be described.

For better understanding, the corresponding illustrations for merging the conditions, the start-from-the-middle method and calculating the probability can be referred to the full version of this paper [17].

Storing the Solutions. Note that there is no need to enumerate all the valid solutions for $(S_{i,j}^0)$ $(1 \le i \le 2, 0 \le j \le 3)$, which will be very costly. Instead, we can construct 4 small tables to record all the valid solutions as follows.

1. Construct the table TA_0 to record the valid tuples $(S_{1,1}^0, S_{2,1}^0)$.
2. Construct the table TA_1 to record the valid tuples $(S_{0,1}^1, S_{1,1}^1, S_{2,1}^1)$.
3. Construct the table TA_2 to record the valid tuples $(S_{1,1}^0, S_{2,1}^0, S_{1,1}^1, S_{2,1}^1)$.
4. Construct the table TA_3 to record the valid tuples $(S_{1,1}^0, S_{2,1}^0, S_{0,1}^1)$.

In this way, once $(S_{i,j}^0)$ $(1 \le i \le 2, 0 \le j \le 3)$ are valid, we can retrieve the corresponding $(S_{1,1}^1, S_{2,1}^1, S_{1,3}^1, S_{2,3}^1)$ from TA_2. And once $(S_{1,1}^1, S_{2,1}^1, S_{1,3}^1, S_{2,3}^1)$ are known, we can retrieve valid $(S_{0,1}^1, S_{0,3}^1)$ from TA_1. Until this phase, $(S_{1,0}^0, S_{2,0}^0, S_{0,1}^1)$, $(S_{1,2}^0, S_{2,2}^0, S_{0,3}^1)$, $(S_{1,1}^0, S_{2,1}^0, S_{1,1}^1, S_{2,1}^1)$ and $(S_{1,3}^0, S_{2,3}^0, S_{1,3}^1, S_{2,3}^1)$ are known. Thus, we can compute the corresponding value of $(S_{0,0}^0, S_{0,1}^0, S_{0,2}^0, S_{0,3}^0)$ and they will always make the L-Conditions and R-Conditions hold.

Thus, the remaining work is how to find a valid value of the capacity part $(S^0_{i,j})$ $(1 \le i \le 2, 0 \le j \le 3)$.

5.3 Finding a Valid Capacity Part

According to the above analysis, converting a semi-free-start collision attack into a collision attack based on the 6-round differential characteristic in Table 2 is reduced to finding a valid capacity part of the output state after several message blocks are absorbed. Since the capacity part is valid with probability $2^{-127.6}$, a naive way is to try $2^{127.6}$ random messages, which is obviously too inefficient. In the following, a time-memory trade-off method will be introduced to efficiently find a message which can make the capacity part valid. Another method without time-memory trade-off can be referred to the full version of this paper [17].

The Exhaustive Search with Time-Memory Trade-Off. An illustration of the procedure can be referred to Fig. 7. Note that the valid values of $(S^6_{1,1}, S^6_{2,1})$ have been stored in TA_0 and $(S^6_{1,3}, S^6_{2,3})$ shares the same valid values with $(S^6_{1,1}, S^6_{2,1})$ due to the symmetry of the 6-round differential characteristic. Moreover, given a valid value of $(S^6_{1,1}, S^6_{2,1})$, by using TA_3 and the Property 2 of the SP-box, we can determine whether $(S^6_{1,0}, S^6_{2,0})$ is valid with only 4 times of check. Why 4 times are needed can be referred to the part to calculate the probability of a valid capacity part.

To efficiently find a valid value for S^6, some conditions on $(S^0_{i,j})$ $(1 \le i \le 2, 0 \le j \le 3)$ will be added, as specified below:

$$\begin{cases} (S^0_{1,0} \lll 9) \wedge \text{0x1fffffff} = 0, \\ (S^0_{1,1} \lll 9) \wedge \text{0x1fffffff} = 0, \\ (S^0_{1,2} \lll 9) \wedge \text{0x1fffffff} = 0, \\ (S^0_{1,3} \lll 9) \wedge \text{0x1fffffff} = 0. \end{cases} \tag{23}$$

In this way, $(S^1_{0,0}, S^1_{0,1}, S^1_{0,2}, S^1_{0,3})$ will be independent of $(S^0_{0,0}, S^0_{0,1}, S^0_{0,2}, S^0_{0,3})$ based on Property 1. For readability, how to find a message which can lead to an output whose capacity part satisfies Eq. 23 will be first skipped. In the following, we start from how to find a valid solution for the capacity part of S^6 when Eq. 23 has been fulfilled. We refer to Fig. 7 for better understanding. The corresponding procedure is as follows:

Step 1: Exhaust all 0x34c8 possible values of $(S^6_{1,1}, S^6_{2,1})$. For each value, guess $S^5_{2,1}$ and compute $S^5_{1,1}$. Store all $2^{32} \times \text{0x34c8} \approx 2^{45.7}$ possible values of $(S^5_{1,1}, S^5_{2,1}, S^6_{1,1}, S^6_{2,1})$ in the table TA_4. Due to the symmetry of the 6-round differential characteristic, $(S^5_{1,3}, S^5_{2,3}, S^6_{1,3}, S^6_{2,3})$ take the same possible values with that of $(S^5_{1,1}, S^5_{2,1}, S^6_{1,1}, S^6_{2,1})$.

Step 2: Exhaust all 2^{64} possible values of $(S^0_{0,0}, S^0_{0,2})$ and compute the corresponding $(S^5_{0,1}, S^5_{0,3})$. Record all the values of $(S^5_{0,1}, S^5_{0,3}, S^0_{0,0}, S^0_{0,2})$ in the table TA_5.

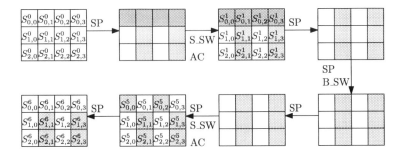

Fig. 7. Matching one valid capacity part

Step 3: Exhaust all 2^{64} possible values of $(S^0_{0,1}, S^0_{0,3})$. For each value, compute the corresponding $(S^5_{1,1}, S^5_{2,1}, S^5_{1,3}, S^5_{2,3})$. According to TA_4, retrieve the corresponding $(S^6_{1,1}, S^6_{2,1}, S^6_{1,3}, S^6_{2,3})$ if there is. Otherwise, try another guess of $(S^0_{0,1}, S^0_{0,3})$. It is expected that there will be $2^{64+(-64+45.7)\times 2} = 2^{27.4}$ valid values of $(S^0_{0,1}, S^0_{0,3}, S^6_{1,1}, S^6_{2,1}, S^6_{1,3}, S^6_{2,3})$. For each valid value, move to Step 4.

Step 4: Once $(S^6_{1,1}, S^6_{2,1}, S^6_{1,3}, S^6_{2,3})$ is known, compute the corresponding $(S^5_{0,1}, S^5_{0,3})$ according to Property 4. Then, retrieve the corresponding $(S^0_{0,0}, S^0_{0,2})$ from TA_5. Once $(S^0_{0,0}, S^0_{0,2})$ is determined, we can compute $(S^6_{1,0}, S^6_{2,0}, S^6_{1,2}, S^6_{2,2})$ and check its validity according to TA_3, which holds with probability $(4 \times 2^{-15.5})^2 = 2^{-27}$. Thus, it is expected to find one solution to $(S^0_{0,0}, S^0_{0,1}, S^0_{0,0}, S^0_{0,3})$ which can make the capacity part of S^6 valid.

It can be easily observed that the time and memory complexity of the above procedure are both 2^{64}.

Fulfilling Equation 24. It should be observed that the initial state of Gimli-Hash satisfies Eq. 23. Thus, we can start from an input state S^0 whose capacity part satisfies Eq. 23 and find a solution to $(S^0_{0,0}, S^0_{0,1}, S^0_{0,2}, S^0_{0,3})$ in order that the capacity part of S^6 satisfies Eq. 24. The procedure is almost the same with the above one.

$$\begin{cases} (S^6_{1,0} \lll 9) \wedge \texttt{0x1fffffff} = 0, \\ (S^6_{1,1} \lll 9) \wedge \texttt{0x1fffffff} = 0, \\ (S^6_{1,2} \lll 9) \wedge \texttt{0x1fffffff} = 0, \\ (S^6_{1,3} \lll 9) \wedge \texttt{0x1fffffff} = 0. \end{cases} \tag{24}$$

Step 1: Exhaust all 2^{64} possible values of $(S^0_{0,0}, S^0_{0,2})$ and compute the corresponding $(S^5_{0,1}, S^5_{0,3})$. Record all the values of $(S^5_{0,1}, S^5_{0,3}, S^0_{0,0}, S^0_{0,2})$ in the table TA_6.

Step 2: Exhaust all 2^{64} possible values of $(S^0_{0,1}, S^0_{0,3})$. For each possible value, $(S^5_{1,1}, S^5_{2,1}, S^5_{1,3}, S^5_{2,3})$ is computable. Then, based on the Property 5 of the SP-box, compute $(S^5_{0,1}, S^5_{0,3})$ which can make the conditions on

$(S_{1,1}^6, S_{1,3}^6)$ hold. Once $(S_{0,1}^5, S_{0,3}^5)$ is determined, we can retrieve from TA_6 the values of $(S_{0,0}^0, S_{0,2}^0)$. Then, we can compute the full value of S^6 and check whether the conditions on $(S_{1,0}^6, S_{1,2}^6)$ hold. Once it is valid, a solution to the rate part of S^0 which can make the $4 \times 29 = 116$ bit conditions on the capacity part of S^6 hold is found.

Obviously, the time complexity to find a conditional capacity part is upper bounded by 2^{64} and the memory complexity is 2^{64}. Consequently, the time and memory complexity to convert the SFS collisions into collisions are both 2^{64}.

5.4   Discussions on Our MILP Model

Similar to the MILP model for bit-based division property to find an integral distinguisher [24], our model is used to identify whether there exists a feasible solution instead of proving something optimal. If the model is infeasible, it simply implies that the corresponding differential characteristic is invalid. We also have to admit that the detection of contradictions can be performed manually, especially for the primitives with simple linear and nonlinear components. However, when the components become sophisticated, it is rather time-consuming to tackle this task. For example, the linear and nonlinear components of ASCON [11] are more complex than those of Gimli and we are not able to carry out a manual analysis of the 2-round differential characteristic for ASCON found in [25]. However, after constructing a similar model for ASCON, we immediately found that the 2-round differential characteristic [25] is invalid as well. The correctness of the model for ASCON is verified by setting a correct 4-round differential characteristic and its corresponding conforming message as inputs, which are found by the designers in [12]. However, we are not able to improve the results for ASCON.

We also notice that as the number of the attacked rounds increases, more variables and more related inequalities are involved, thus making the time to get a solution increase significantly. Consequently, it is difficult to estimate whether a differential characteristic can be verified in practical time. We believe that if there are simple contradictions in the differential characteristic, they can be found immediately. However, when the contradictions are complex, it may take more time to detect them. For example, we followed some truncated collision-producing differential characteristics for ASCON identified in [11]. For the dense parts, after we ensure that there is no contradiction for certain two consecutive rounds and get a solution for the differential characteristic, when three consecutive rounds are tested, contradictions start to appear and it takes some time for the solver to output "infeasible".

Therefore, we provide an insight on searching for differential characteristics for the permutation-based primitives. Suppose the target is to search for a characteristic for up to XR rounds. For such a task, one can involve the value transitions in a suitable place of the differential characteristics to avoid the inconsistency in this part. After a feasible solution is found, involve the value transitions in longer consecutive rounds and further check the consistency. However, it can not be guaranteed that we can always obtain a solution ("feasible") or no solution ("infeasible") in practical time.

6 SFS Collisions for Intermediate 8-Round Gimli-Hash

The collision attack on 6-round Gimli-Hash has been described above. To further understand the security of Gimli-Hash, a SFS collision attack on the intermediate 8 rounds of Gimli-Hash will be described in this section. Specifically, the following sequence of operations (8-round permutation) will be considered:

$$(\text{SP}) \to (\text{SP} \to \text{B\_SW}) \to (\text{SP})$$
$$\to (\text{SP} \to \text{S\_SW} \to \text{AC}) \to (\text{SP}) \to (\text{SP} \to \text{B\_SW}) \to (\text{SP})$$
$$\to (\text{SP} \to \text{S\_SW} \to \text{AC}).$$

In addition, our target is to find an inner collision, i.e. the collision in the capacity part, which can be trivially converted to a real SFS collision by using more message blocks to absorb the difference in the rate part.

Different from the collision attack on 6-round Gimli-Hash, this attack does not rely on a specific differential characteristic. Instead, the structure of the intermediate 8-round permutation will be exploited. As shown in Fig. 8, the message difference is only injected in $S_{0,3}^1$ and the difference of several internal state words are conditioned in order to generate an inner collision. In other words, finding a SFS collision is equivalent to finding a message pair which can make the conditions on these intermediate words hold.

6.1 Fulfilling $\Delta S_{0,1}^3 = 0$, $\Delta S_{1,3}^5 = 0$ and $\Delta S_{2,3}^5 = 0$

First of all, consider the conditions on ΔS^3 and ΔS^5, i.e. $\Delta S_{0,1}^3 = 0$, $\Delta S_{1,3}^5 = 0$ and $\Delta S_{2,3}^5 = 0$. The following facts should be noticed:

- $S_{0,1}^3$ only depends on $(S_{0,3}^1, S_{1,3}^1, S_{2,3}^1)$.
- $(S_{1,3}^5, S_{2,3}^5)$ only depend on $(S_{0,3}^3, S_{1,3}^3, S_{2,3}^3)$.
- $S_{0,3}^3$ only depends on $(S_{0,1}^1, S_{1,1}^1, S_{2,1}^1)$.
- $(S_{1,3}^3, S_{2,3}^3)$ only depend on $(S_{0,3}^1, S_{1,3}^1, S_{2,3}^1)$.

Therefore, the corresponding attack procedure to make the above three conditions hold can be described as below:

Step 1: Randomly choose a value for $(S_{1,3}^1, S_{2,3}^1)$, exhaust all 2^{32} possible values of $S_{0,3}^1$ and compute the corresponding $(S_{0,1}^3, S_{1,3}^3, S_{2,3}^3)$. Store these values in a table and sort it according to $S_{0,1}^3$.

Step 2: For each pair of $(S_{0,1}^3, S_{1,3}^3, S_{2,3}^3)$ colliding in $S_{0,1}^3$, exhaust all 2^{32} possible values of $S_{0,3}^3$. Then, we can compute a pair of $(S_{1,3}^5, S_{2,3}^5)$ and check whether they collide. If all possible values of $S_{0,3}^3$ are used up and there is no collision in $(S_{1,3}^5, S_{2,3}^5)$, goto Step 1. If a collision in $(S_{1,3}^5, S_{2,3}^5)$ is found, move to Step 3.

Step 3: Randomly choose a value for $(S_{1,1}^3, S_{2,1}^3)$ and compute backward to obtain $(S_{0,1}^1, S_{1,1}^1, S_{2,1}^1)$.

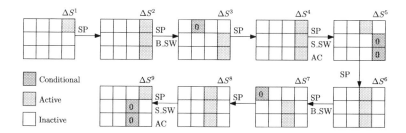

Fig. 8. SFS collision attack on the intermediate 8-round Gimli-Hash

Complexity Evaluation. Obviously, at Step 1, we can expect 2^{31} pairs of $(S_{0,1}^3, S_{1,3}^3, S_{2,3}^3)$ colliding in $S_{0,1}^3$. The time complexity and memory complexity to obtain these collisions are both 2^{32}. As for Step 2, we need to enumerate all possible values of $S_{0,3}^3$ for each colliding message pair. Therefore, the time complexity is 2^{64}. In addition, $\Delta S_{1,3}^5 = 0$ and $\Delta S_{2,3}^5 = 0$ hold with probability 2^{-64} while only 2^{32+31} pairs of $(S_{0,3}^3, S_{1,3}^3, S_{2,3}^3)$ will be checked at Step 2. Thus, Step 1 will be repeated twice. Since only half state is computed at this phase, the time complexity to make the conditions $\Delta S_{0,1}^3 = 0$, $\Delta S_{1,3}^5 = 0$ and $\Delta S_{2,3}^5 = 0$ hold is 2^{64}, while the memory complexity is 2^{32}.

6.2 Fulfilling $\Delta S_{0,0}^7 = 0$, $\Delta S_{1,2}^9 = 0$ and $\Delta S_{2,2}^9 = 0$

After the conditions on ΔS^3 and ΔS^5 are satisfied, some internal state words will be fixed, as can be noted in the above attack procedure to fulfill these conditions. In fact, the above method can be adjusted to fulfill $\Delta S_{0,0}^7 = 0$, $\Delta S_{1,2}^9 = 0$ and $\Delta S_{2,2}^9 = 0$. First of all, notice the following facts:

- $S_{0,0}^7$ only depends on $(S_{0,2}^5, S_{1,2}^5, S_{2,2}^5)$.
- $(S_{1,2}^9, S_{2,2}^9)$ only depend on $(S_{0,2}^7, S_{1,2}^7, S_{2,2}^7)$.
- $S_{0,2}^7$ only depends on $(S_{0,0}^5, S_{1,0}^5, S_{2,0}^5)$.
- $(S_{1,2}^7, S_{2,2}^7)$ only depend on $(S_{0,2}^5, S_{1,2}^5, S_{2,2}^5)$.
- $(S_{0,0}^5, S_{0,2}^5)$ have already been fixed.

Therefore, the procedure to fulfill the conditions $\Delta S_{0,0}^7 = 0$, $\Delta S_{1,2}^9 = 0$ and $\Delta S_{2,2}^9 = 0$ can be described as below:

Step 1: Exhaust all 2^{64} possible values of $(S_{1,2}^5, S_{2,2}^5)$. In this way, 2^{64} different pairs of $(S_{0,2}^5, S_{1,2}^5, S_{2,2}^5)$ can be obtained. For each pair, check whether they collide in $S_{0,0}^7$, which holds with probability 2^{-32}. Once they collide, move to Step 2.

Step 2: Exhaust all 2^{32} possible values of $S_{0,2}^7$. In this way, 2^{32} different pairs of $(S_{0,2}^7, S_{1,2}^7, S_{2,2}^7)$ can be generated. For each pair, check whether they collide in $(S_{1,2}^9, S_{2,2}^9)$, while occurs with probability 2^{-64}. Once they collide, move to Step 3. Otherwise, goto Step 1.

Step 3: Randomly choose values for $(S_{1,0}^5, S_{2,0}^5)$ and compute the corresponding $S_{0,2}^7$. Repeat until the computed $S_{0,2}^7$ is consistent with that obtained at Step 2. Finally, randomly choose a value for $S_{0,3}^5$ and the full state of S^5 is known. Compute backward to obtain the corresponding S^1.

Complexity Evaluation. At Step 1, it is expected that there will be 2^{32} pairs of $(S_{0,2}^5, S_{1,2}^5, S_{2,2}^5)$ colliding in $S_{0,0}^7$. The corresponding time complexity is 2^{64}. For each colliding pair, at Step 2, we will exhaust 2^{32} all possible values of $S_{0,2}^7$ and check whether the collision will occur in $(S_{1,2}^9, S_{2,2}^9)$. Thus, after traversing all possible solutions obtained at Step 1, we can expect a collision in $(S_{1,2}^9, S_{2,2}^9)$. Thus, the time complexity at Step 2 is 2^{32}. As for Step 3, it is obvious that the time complexity is 2^{32}. Therefore, the total time complexity to find a SFS collision for the intermediate 8-round Gimli-Hash is 2^{64}.

Remark. It can be noted that there is a minor difference between the methods to fulfill the conditions on (S^3, S^5) and on (S^7, S^9). Thus, when fulfilling the conditions on (S^3, S^5), there is actually no need to consume 2^{32} memory. Similar to the above method, one can simply first choose two different values for $S_{0,3}^1$ and then exhaust all possible values of $(S_{1,3}^1, S_{2,3}^1)$ to obtain 2^{32} pairs colliding in $S_{0,1}^3$. Thus, we do not take the memory complexity into account in the final complexity evaluation. On the other hand, 2^{32} memory is cheap as well.

6.3 Experimental Verification

One may doubt whether the above differential pattern for 8-round Gimli-Hash is valid. To confirm it, our MILP model is applied. Since the generic complexity we found is 2^{64}, it is reasonable that the solver cannot find a solution in practical time, except the case when there are some more clever algorithms to solve the corresponding inequalities in the solver. According to the output of the Gurobi solver, it keeps trying to solve the inequalities and does not output "infeasible" for such a differential pattern. Thus, we believe that the 8-round differential pattern is reasonable. As a counter-example, an impossible 7-round differential pattern is displayed in full version of this paper [17].

7 State Recovery Attack on 9-Round Gimli

For the AE scheme specified in the submitted Gimli document [1], which adopts the well-known duplex mode [5], the key length is 256 bits while the designers claim only 128-bit security. Such a security claim is strange since there is no generic attack matching this bound. Although there is a key-recovery attack on 22.5-round Gimli [13], it only works for an ad-hoc mode and cannot be directly applied to the official scheme. Thus, we are motivated to devise the following two attacks and we believe that they are meaningful to further understand the security of Gimli.

1. The attack on a round-reduced variant matching the 2^{128} security claim.
2. Maximize the number of rounds that can be attacked with complexity below 2^{256}.

For our state recovery attack, we aim at the encryption phase and only four 128-bit message blocks will be used, as shown in Fig. 9. The aim is to recover the secret state of P_1. To achieve it in less than 2^{256} time, a guess-and-determine method will be utilized.

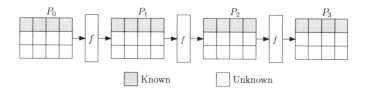

Fig. 9. Leaked information in the state recovery attack

Specifically, as shown in Fig. 10, our aim is to exhaust all possible values of $(S_{i,j}^9)$ ($1 \leq i \leq 2, 0 \leq j \leq 3$) and then compute backward to check whether the first row of S^0 can be matched. The complexity is required not to exceed 2^{256}. The corresponding attack procedure can be described as follows:

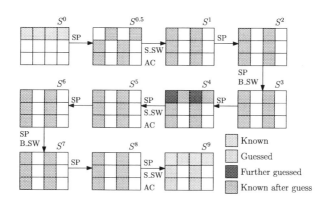

Fig. 10. State recovery attack on 9-round Gimli

Step 1: Guess $(S_{1,0}^9, S_{2,0}^9, S_{1,2}^9, S_{2,2}^9, S_{0,0}^4, S_{0,2}^4)$. For each guess, compute backward to obtain $(S_{1,0}^{0.5}, S_{2,0}^{0.5}, S_{1,2}^{0.5}, S_{2,2}^{0.5}, S_{0,1}^{0.5}, S_{0,3}^{0.5})$. Then, according to the Property 3 of the SP-box, the guess is correct with probability 2^{-2}. Once it is correct, compute $(S_{1,0}^0, S_{2,0}^0[30 \sim 0], S_{0,0}^{0.5}[30 \sim 0])$. For the correct guess, store the corresponding value of the tuple

$$(S_{0,0}^{0.5}[30 \sim 0], S_{0,1}^{0.5}, S_{0,2}^{0.5}[30 \sim 0], S_{0,3}^{0.5}, S_{0,0}^4, S_{0,1}^4, S_{0,2}^4, S_{0,3}^4, S_{1,0}^9, S_{2,0}^9, S_{1,2}^9, S_{2,2}^9)$$

in a table denoted by T_{49}. It is expected to have $2^{192-2} = 2^{190}$ valid values.

Step 2: Similarly, guess $(S_{1,1}^9, S_{2,1}^9, S_{1,3}^9, S_{2,3}^9, S_{0,1}^4, S_{0,3}^4)$ and compute the corresponding value of the tuple

$$(S_{0,0}^{0.5}, S_{0,1}^{0.5}[30 \sim 0], S_{0,2}^{0.5}, S_{0,3}^{0.5}[30 \sim 0], S_{0,0}^4, S_{0,1}^4, S_{0,2}^4, S_{0,3}^4).$$

Check whether there is a match between

$$(S_{0,0}^{0.5}[30 \sim 0], S_{0,1}^{0.5}[30 \sim 0], S_{0,2}^{0.5}[30 \sim 0], S_{0,3}^{0.5}[30 \sim 0], S_{0,0}^4, S_{0,1}^4, S_{0,2}^4, S_{0,3}^4)$$

in the table T_{49}. Once a match is found, a valid value of $(S_{i,j}^9)$ $(1 \leq i \leq 2, 0 \leq j \leq 3)$ is found. Since the matching probability is $2^{-31 \times 4 - 128} = 2^{-252}$ and there are in total $2^{190+190} = 2^{380}$ pairs, it is expected to find $2^{380-252} = 2^{128}$ valid values of $(S_{i,j}^9)$ $(1 \leq i \leq 2, 0 \leq j \leq 3)$.

Obviously, the time complexity and memory complexity to enumerate all valid values of $(S_{i,j}^9)$ $(1 \leq i \leq 2, 0 \leq j \leq 3)$ are 2^{192} and 2^{190}, respectively. The correctness of $(S_{i,j}^9)$ $(1 \leq i \leq 2, 0 \leq j \leq 3)$ can be simply further verified using the leaked information from (P_2, P_3).

8   Conclusion

A comprehensive study of Gimli has been made. Especially, a novel MILP model capturing both difference transitions and value transitions is developed. As far as we know, this is the first MILP model to search for a differential characteristic involving the value transitions. It would be interesting to apply this technique to other permutation-based cryptographic primitives. Based on this new model, we reveal that some existing differential characteristics of Gimli are incompatible. Moreover, a practical SFS colliding message pair for 6-round Gimli-Hash is found by utilizing this model and several techniques to convert the SFS collisions into collisions are developed. To test how far the SFS collision attack on Gimli-Hash can go, we also mount an attack on the intermediate 8-round Gimli-Hash with time complexity 2^{64}. For the authenticated encryption scheme, a state-recovery attack on 9-round Gimli can be mounted with time complexity 2^{192} and memory complexity 2^{190}. To the best of our knowledge, these are the best attacks on round-reduced Gimli, covering the proposed hash scheme and authenticated encryption scheme.

Acknowledgements. We thank the anonymous reviewers of CRYPTO 2020 for their many helpful comments. We thank Daniel J. Bernstein and Florian Mendel for some discussions on the cryptanalysis of Gimli. We also thank Xiaoyang Dong and Rui Zong for the discussions on the contradictions in the 6-round differential characteristic. Fukang Liu and Takanori Isobe are supported by Grant-in-Aid for Scientific Research (B) (KAKENHI 19H02141) for Japan Society for the Promotion of Science and SECOM science and technology foundation. In addition, Fukang Liu is partially supported by National Natural Science Foundation of China (Grant No. 61632012, 61672239) and the National Cryptography Development Fund [No. MMJJ20180201].

References

1. https://csrc.nist.gov/Projects/Lightweight-Cryptography/Round-2-Candidates
2. https://www.gurobi.com
3. Aumasson, J.-P., Çalık, Ç., Meier, W., Özen, O., Phan, R.C.-W., Varıcı, K.: Improved cryptanalysis of Skein. In: Matsui, M. (ed.) ASIACRYPT 2009. LNCS, vol. 5912, pp. 542–559. Springer, Heidelberg (2009). https://doi.org/10.1007/978-3-642-10366-7_32
4. Bernstein, D.J., et al.: GIMLI: a cross-platform permutation. In: Fischer, W., Homma, N. (eds.) CHES 2017. LNCS, vol. 10529, pp. 299–320. Springer, Cham (2017). https://doi.org/10.1007/978-3-319-66787-4_15
5. Bertoni, G., Daemen, J., Peeters, M., Van Assche, G.: Duplexing the sponge: single-pass authenticated encryption and other applications. In: Miri, A., Vaudenay, S. (eds.) SAC 2011. LNCS, vol. 7118, pp. 320–337. Springer, Heidelberg (2012). https://doi.org/10.1007/978-3-642-28496-0_19
6. Bertoni, G., Daemen, J., Peeters, M., Assche, G.V.: The Keccak reference (2011). http://keccak.noekeon.org
7. Biham, E., Shamir, A.: Differential cryptanalysis of DES-like cryptosystems. In: Menezes, A.J., Vanstone, S.A. (eds.) CRYPTO 1990. LNCS, vol. 537, pp. 2–21. Springer, Heidelberg (1991). https://doi.org/10.1007/3-540-38424-3_1
8. Biryukov, A., Nikolić, I., Roy, A.: Boomerang attacks on BLAKE-32. In: Joux, A. (ed.) FSE 2011. LNCS, vol. 6733, pp. 218–237. Springer, Heidelberg (2011). https://doi.org/10.1007/978-3-642-21702-9_13
9. Blondeau, C., Bogdanov, A., Leander, G.: Bounds in shallows and in miseries. In: Canetti, R., Garay, J.A. (eds.) CRYPTO 2013. LNCS, vol. 8042, pp. 204–221. Springer, Heidelberg (2013). https://doi.org/10.1007/978-3-642-40041-4_12
10. De Cannière, C., Rechberger, C.: Finding SHA-1 characteristics: general results and applications. In: Lai, X., Chen, K. (eds.) ASIACRYPT 2006. LNCS, vol. 4284, pp. 1–20. Springer, Heidelberg (2006). https://doi.org/10.1007/11935230_1
11. Dobraunig, C., Eichlseder, M., Mendel, F., Schläffer, M.: Ascon v1.2 (2018). https://ascon.iaik.tugraz.at/files/asconv12-nist.pdf
12. Dobraunig, C., Eichlseder, M., Mendel, F., Schläffer, M.: Preliminary analysis of Ascon-Xof and Ascon-Hash (version 0.1) (2019). https://ascon.iaik.tugraz.at/files/Preliminary_Analysis_of_Ascon-Xof_and_Ascon-Hash_v01.pdf
13. Hamburg, M.: Cryptanalysis of 22 1/2 rounds of Gimli. Cryptology ePrint Archive, Report 2017/743 (2017). https://eprint.iacr.org/2017/743
14. Kölbl, S., Leander, G., Tiessen, T.: Observations on the SIMON block cipher family. In: Gennaro, R., Robshaw, M. (eds.) CRYPTO 2015. LNCS, Part I, vol. 9215, pp. 161–185. Springer, Heidelberg (2015). https://doi.org/10.1007/978-3-662-47989-6_8
15. Leurent, G.: Analysis of differential attacks in ARX constructions. In: Wang, X., Sako, K. (eds.) ASIACRYPT 2012. LNCS, vol. 7658, pp. 226–243. Springer, Heidelberg (2012). https://doi.org/10.1007/978-3-642-34961-4_15
16. Leurent, G.: Construction of differential characteristics in ARX designs application to Skein. In: Canetti, R., Garay, J.A. (eds.) CRYPTO 2013. LNCS, Part I, vol. 8042, pp. 241–258. Springer, Heidelberg (2013). https://doi.org/10.1007/978-3-642-40041-4_14
17. Liu, F., Isobe, T., Meier, W.: Automatic verification of differential characteristics: application to reduced Gimli (full version). Cryptology ePrint Archive, Report 2020/591 (2020). https://eprint.iacr.org/2020/591

18. Mendel, F., Nad, T., Schläffer, M.: Finding SHA-2 characteristics: searching through a minefield of contradictions. In: Lee, D.H., Wang, X. (eds.) ASIACRYPT 2011. LNCS, vol. 7073, pp. 288–307. Springer, Heidelberg (2011). https://doi.org/10.1007/978-3-642-25385-0_16

19. Mironov, I., Zhang, L.: Applications of SAT solvers to cryptanalysis of hash functions. In: Biere, A., Gomes, C.P. (eds.) SAT 2006. LNCS, vol. 4121, pp. 102–115. Springer, Heidelberg (2006). https://doi.org/10.1007/11814948_13

20. Stevens, M., Bursztein, E., Karpman, P., Albertini, A., Markov, Y.: The first collision for full SHA-1. In: Katz, J., Shacham, H. (eds.) CRYPTO 2017. LNCS, Part I, vol. 10401, pp. 570–596. Springer, Cham (2017). https://doi.org/10.1007/978-3-319-63688-7_19

21. Sun, S., Hu, L., Wang, P., Qiao, K., Ma, X., Song, L.: Automatic security evaluation and (related-key) differential characteristic search: application to SIMON, PRESENT, LBlock, DES(L) and other bit-oriented block ciphers. In: Sarkar, P., Iwata, T. (eds.) ASIACRYPT 2014. LNCS, Part I, vol. 8873, pp. 158–178. Springer, Heidelberg (2014). https://doi.org/10.1007/978-3-662-45611-8_9

22. Wang, X., Yin, Y.L., Yu, H.: Finding collisions in the full SHA-1. In: Shoup, V. (ed.) CRYPTO 2005. LNCS, vol. 3621, pp. 17–36. Springer, Heidelberg (2005). https://doi.org/10.1007/11535218_2

23. Wang, X., Yu, H.: How to break MD5 and other hash functions. In: Cramer, R. (ed.) EUROCRYPT 2005. LNCS, vol. 3494, pp. 19–35. Springer, Heidelberg (2005). https://doi.org/10.1007/11426639_2

24. Xiang, Z., Zhang, W., Bao, Z., Lin, D.: Applying MILP method to searching integral distinguishers based on division property for 6 lightweight block ciphers. In: Cheon, J.H., Takagi, T. (eds.) ASIACRYPT 2016. LNCS, Part I, vol. 10031, pp. 648–678. Springer, Heidelberg (2016). https://doi.org/10.1007/978-3-662-53887-6_24

25. Zong, R., Dong, X., Wang, X.: Collision attacks on round-reduced Gimli-Hash/Ascon-Xof/Ascon-Hash. Cryptology ePrint Archive, Report 2019/1115 (2019). https://eprint.iacr.org/2019/1115

The MALICIOUS Framework: Embedding Backdoors into Tweakable Block Ciphers

Thomas Peyrin[✉] and Haoyang Wang[✉]

School of Physical and Mathematical Sciences, Nanyang Technological University,
Singapore, Singapore
thomas.peyrin@ntu.edu.sg, wang1153@e.ntu.edu.sg

Abstract. Inserting backdoors in encryption algorithms has long seemed like a very interesting, yet difficult problem. Most attempts have been unsuccessful for symmetric-key primitives so far and it remains an open problem how to build such ciphers.

In this work, we propose the MALICIOUS framework, a new method to build tweakable block ciphers that have backdoors hidden which allows to retrieve the secret key. Our backdoor is differential in nature: a specific related-tweak differential path with high probability is hidden during the design phase of the cipher. We explain how any entity knowing the backdoor can practically recover the secret key of a user and we also argue why even knowing the presence of the backdoor and the workings of the cipher will not permit to retrieve the backdoor for an external user. We analyze the security of our construction in the classical black-box model and we show that retrieving the backdoor (the hidden high-probability differential path) is very difficult.

We instantiate our framework by proposing the LowMC-M construction, a new family of tweakable block ciphers based on instances of the LowMC cipher, which allow such backdoor embedding. Generating LowMC-M instances is trivial and the LowMC-M family has basically the same efficiency as the LowMC instances it is based on.

Keywords: Tweakable block cipher · Backdoor · Differential cryptanalysis · LowMC-M

1 Introduction

A backdoor in an encryption algorithm enables an entity who knows it to circumvent the security guarantees so that he can obtain the secret information more efficiently than with a generic black-box attack. There are two categories of backdoors. The first one is the backdoor implemented in a security product at the protocol or key-management level, which is generally considered in practice.

In this article, we focus on the second type: a cryptographic backdoor. A cryptographic backdoor is embedded directly during the design phase of a

© International Association for Cryptologic Research 2020
D. Micciancio and T. Ristenpart (Eds.): CRYPTO 2020, LNCS 12172, pp. 249–278, 2020.
https://doi.org/10.1007/978-3-030-56877-1_9

cryptographic primitive and renders the cipher susceptible to some dedicated cryptanalysis. Cryptographic backdoors have been extensively studied by Young and Yung, introducing the term "Kleptography" [41,44]. However, despite some interest from the academic community about this topic, there are very few publicly known backdoored primitives. A concrete example is the pseudorandom number generator Dual_EC_DBRG [8] designed by NSA, whose backdoor was revealed by Edward Snowden in 2013 and also in some research works [10,37].

Embedding backdoors into block ciphers is a challenging problem since block ciphers are deterministic and thus it is complex to exploit randomness in computations. Young and Yung have designed several backdoors in secret block ciphers [42,43,45], where it is assumed that the cipher specifications are unknown to the adversary. In this work, we will not make such assumption and we will consider the specifications of the cipher to be fully public.

A backdoor should be computationally difficult to retrieve, even if its general form is known. More concretely, the backdoor security (the cost of retrieving the backdoor) should be the same as the security generically provided by the cipher (otherwise the backdoor would naturally reduce the security of the block cipher). Besides, the backdoor should ideally lead to a practical key recovery attack, or at least reduce the brute force search cost for the adversary. For example, if a backdoor could reduce the security of AES-256 to 2^{128}, it would be a great theoretical advance, but would be unusable in practice. Last but not least, the resulting block cipher also has to be secure in the classical sense, that is, it is able to resist state-of-the-art cryptanalysis techniques.

There have been only limited works focusing on this direction and to the best of the authors' knowledge there is no such design satisfying the above requirements simultaneously. In 1997, Rijmen and Preneel proposed a special Sbox design strategy which was used to hide a high-probability linear approximation in an Sbox [35]. The knowledge of this backdoor leads to an efficient key recovery attack based on linear cryptanalysis, but only a part of the key information can be obtained. They presented concrete instantiations by applying the Sbox design to CAST and LOKI91 ciphers and claimed that the embedded backdoors are undetectable even if the general form of the backdoor is known. However, this design was broken subsequently in 1998 [39] by Wu *et al.* who found a way to easily recover the backdoor and showed that the security and practicability of the backdoor can't be guaranteed at the same time. Later in 1999, Paterson suggested that if the group generated by round functions acts imprimitively on the message group, then it is possible to create a backdoor in the cipher [31]. Built upon this mechanism, he introduced a DES-like cipher which allows an entity knowing the backdoor to retrieve the key with 2^{41} computations. However, as mentioned by the author, the backdoor is detectable and the cipher is vulnerable to differential attacks. Following on this idea, a backdoor based on partitioning cryptanalysis was studied in [5] and a concrete instance of an AES-like cipher called BEA-1 was later proposed in [6], but no explicit backdoor security was provided. One can also mention the work from Patarin and Goubin [29,30] who proposed "2R–schemes", basically Sbox-based asymmetric schemes secretly consisting of a 2-round secret Substitution-Permutation Network (SPN) but publicly represented as its corresponding algebraic equations. However, this research direction also suffered from attacks [12,40]. Two more backdoor designs [4,13] have been introduced, but neither of them provide solid proof for the backdoor security and even the security of the cipher itself is questionable. Lastly, in a different setting, a backdoored version of the SHA-1 hash function was proposed in [1], where the attacker is allowed to pre-choose the constants used in the design, so he can prepare in advance some specific collision messages for that particular instance.

Apart from these public researches, one can naturally question if there are some public block ciphers that might contain backdoors not claimed by the designers. In particular, primitives whose detailed design rationale is not provided are naturally more suspicious, especially when the ciphers have been designed by governmental agencies (as can be seen by the difficulties encountered by the NSA lightweight block ciphers SIMON and SPECK [9] to become ISO standards). For example, Perrin found a very strong algebraic structure [32] that is hidden inside the Sbox employed in both the block cipher Kuznyechik [36] and the hash function Streebog [27], both primitives being selected as Russian standards (GOST). Even though there is currently no attack based on this result, it illustrates the issue of potential backdoor in foreign encryption algorithms and more research is required to better understand the possibilities and implications of cryptographic backdoor.

We emphasize that inserting backdoors in an encryption algorithm itself is very different from inserting backdoors in an implementations, being in software or in hardware (like hardware trojans).

Our Contributions. In this paper, we propose a new method to generate backdoor encryption algorithms. We bring together tweakable block ciphers (TBC) and Extendable-Output Function (XOF) in a common framework called MALICIOUS, which enables the designer to embed backdoors into the TBC. The general representation of our construction is similar to that of the TWEAKEY framework [22], but the tweak is handled separately by a XOF and the round function has to be partially non-linear.

Our backdoor is based on differential cryptanalysis: due to the partial non-linear layer, the designer can embed related-tweak differential characteristics with probability 1 over many rounds. In particular, the sub-tweak difference employed in an embedded differential characteristic is generated from a specific tweak pair that is chosen in advance by the designer. This malicious tweak pair is the backdoor, and the XOF applied in the tweak schedule is used to protect the malicious tweak pair: even knowing the high-probability related-tweak differential characteristic, it will remain computationally difficult to find a tweak pair that triggers it. More importantly, the backdoor security is ensured by the target-difference resistance ability of the chosen XOF. An attacker with the knowledge of the backdoor is able to retrieve the full key with negligible effort under the chosen-tweak scenario.

Based on the MALICIOUS framework, we also propose a concrete instantiation that we call LowMC-M. Our family of TBC LowMC-M is created based on some instances of the block cipher LowMC [2]. Compared to LowMC, our proposal LowMC-M has an additional sub-tweak addition in each round and the tweak schedule is a XOF, but the other parts of the round function and the number of rounds remain unchanged. Apart from its backdoor security that is naturally inherited from the MALICIOUS framework, we claim that its classical black-box security against state-of-the-art cryptanalysis is the same as the corresponding LowMC variants.

We believe this work is a first step in a new direction for the study of backdoors in encryption algorithms. We are confident that more exotic (based on other types of cryptanalysis techniques than plain differential cryptanalysis) and potentially more efficient instances following the MALICIOUS would be possible.

Paper Organization. In Sect. 2, we present the attacking scenario and some security notions for backdooring cryptographic primitives. In Sect. 3 the MALICIOUS framework is described and its backdoor security and design rationale are explained. We introduce a concrete instantiation of MALICIOUS (so-called LowMC-M) in Sect. 4. We then analyze LowMC-M with respect to the backdoor security and the classical black-box security in Sect. 5 and Sect. 6 respectively. Finally, we present our conclusions in Sect. 7.

2   Preliminaries

2.1   Attacking Scenario

For classical (tweakable) block ciphers, the attacking scenario considers only two entities: the *user* (or pair of users) who owns the secret key and the *attacker* who tries to break the cryptosystem, *i.e.*, to find out the secret key. For (tweakable) block ciphers with a backdoor, another entity has to be involved in the attacking scenario: the *designer*, who inserts the backdoor into the primitive. Thus, we have in total three entities: the designer (knows the backdoor, but not the secret key), the user (knows the secret key, but not the backdoor) and the attacker (neither backdoor nor key is known).

One can see that both the user and the attacker have some motivation to find out what is the backdoor. More importantly, in our model the backdoor is independent of the secret key, and therefore the user and the attacker possess the same capability in trying to uncover the backdoor (the cipher specifications are public known, so they can test the cipher with any chosen key they want). For the rest of this article, when considering the recovery of the backdoor, we will simply refer to both of them as the attacker.

2.2   Security Notions and More

We introduce below various notions regarding the security and the practicability of a backdoor:

- *Undetectability:* this security notion represents the inability for an external entity to realize the existence of the hidden backdoor.
- *Undiscoverability:* it represents the inability for an attacker to find the hidden backdoor, even if the general form of the backdoor is known.
- *Untraceability:* it states that an attack based on the backdoor should not reveal any information about the backdoor itself.
- *Practicability:* this usability notion stipulates that the backdoor is practical, in the sense that it is easy to recover the secret key once the backdoor is known.

If a cipher is publicly claimed as potentially backdoored, it will naturally increase the watchfulness of users, even if they do not know whether there is indeed backdoored or not embedded in the primitive. In this scenario, the undetectability notion models the incapacity of a user to find any hard evidence that a backdoor indeed exists.

For our proposal LowMC-M, the backdoor is claimed to be undetectable, undiscoverable and practicable, but not untraceable.

2.3   Notations

Given a bit string x, we will denote by $x[i]$ its i-th bit, counting from the least significant bit (LSB). Given two bit strings x and y, $x||y$ will represent the concatenation of x and y. Finally, we denote by k_j (respectively by t_j) the subkey (respectively sub-tweak) incorporated during the j-th round of the cipher, while k_0 and t_0 are added in as whitening material.

3   The MALICIOUS Framework

In this section, we introduce the MALICIOUS framework which allows to generate tweakable block ciphers that are embedded with hidden high-probability differential characteristics. This framework is based on partial non-linear layers for the internal state transformation and a tweak schedule based on an extendable-output function (XOF).

3.1   Block Ciphers with Partial Non-linear Layers

SPN-based block ciphers are usually designed to apply linear layers (L_i) and non-linear layers (S_i) to the entire state at every round i. In 2013, an irregular design was suggested by Gérard *et al.* [18], where the non-linear layer is only applied to a subpart of the state at each round. We consider such design with block size n bits and partial non-linear layers of size s ($< n$) bits. Assume, without loss of generality, that the non-linear layer is always applied before the linear layer at every round. Then, we can write $f_i(x) = L_i(S_i(x^{(0)})||x^{(1)})$ the round function f_i that transforms the state x at round i, the state being partitioned into two parts where the non-linear layer only operates on the part $x^{(0)}$ and not on the part $x^{(1)}$.

Such design allows efficient masking and thus can improve security against side-channel attacks. A concrete instantiation of this methodology named ZORRO was then proposed [18]. Even though ZORRO was rapidly broken [7,20,33,38], the general design strategy continued to attract interest from the research community: in 2015, another such design LowMC was proposed [2]. Its aim was to minimize the multiplicative complexity and depth of the cipher in order to have performance advantages in certain applications, including multi-party computation (MPC), fully homomorphic encryption (FHE) and zero-knowledge proofs (ZK). After a few tweaks due to security concerns, the current version v3 of LowMC remains solid after the several third party analysis [15,16,34].

Compared to a full non-linear layer, a partial non-linear layer inevitably weakens the security of a cipher. One notable property is that there will exist non-trivial differential characteristics that will not activate any Sboxes over one or more rounds of the cipher. In a single round, by setting the difference on $x^{(0)}$ to be 0, there are 2^{n-s} differences of x that do not differentially activate any Sboxes. Assuming a well designed linear layer with good mixing properties, one can still expect around 2^{n-2s} differences that will also not differentially activate any Sboxes in the second round. This reasoning can be continued until no difference survives and thus the maximal expected number of rounds that a deterministic differential characteristic can cover is $\lfloor \frac{n}{s} \rfloor$. Note that this number would of course vary depending on the specificities of the linear layers.

3.2   Tweakable Block Ciphers

The first formal treatment of tweakable block ciphers (TBC) was proposed by Liskov, Rivest and Wagner in [25,26]. The signature of a conventional block cipher can be described as $E : \{0,1\}^k \times \{0,1\}^n \to \{0,1\}^n$ where an n-bit plaintext is encrypted to an n-bit ciphertext using a k-bit secret key. A tweakable block cipher accepts an additional t-bit public input called tweak, its signature thus being $E : \{0,1\}^k \times \{0,1\}^t \times \{0,1\}^n \to \{0,1\}^n$. The introduction of a tweak input provides the ability for the user to select a permutation among a family of permutations even when the key is fixed.

Due to this extra degree of freedom that can potentially be leveraged by the attacker, designing a TBC is not straightforward. Block cipher-based TBC constructions have been studied, but comes with a non-negligible efficiency penalty. We can mention the TWEAKEY framework, a recent design strategy to build ad-hoc TBCs, that was proposed at ASIACRYPT 2014 by Jean *et al.* [22]. In this framework, the key and tweak inputs are treated equivalently in terms of design and this material is called tweakey: the tweakey input can be used as key or tweak value, which is up to the choice of the user.

Unlike the key input, the tweak does not need to be kept secret and therefore one should assume that an adversary has full control over it. Thus, besides the attack models of single-key (no difference in the key or tweak), related-key (difference in the key, but no difference in the tweak), related-tweak (no difference in the key, but difference in the tweak) and related-tweakey (difference in both the key and tweak), it is reasonable to consider the chosen-tweak model as a meaningful model in practice.

3.3 Extendable-Output Function

An extendable-output function (XOF) is a generalization of a hash function, where the output can be extended to any desired length. Similar to a hash function, it should be collision, preimage and second-preimage resistant. A XOF is a natural choice when an application requires a hash function to have non-standard digest length. Technically, it is also possible to use a XOF as a generic hash function by setting the output length fixed. Besides, it has some other applications, such as key derivation functions and stream ciphers.

Currently, there are many instances of XOF, such as SHAKE128 and SHAKE256 (defined in SHA-3 standard [17]) and the more efficient variant KangarooTwelve [11].

3.4 The MALICIOUS Construction

Motivation. Differential and linear cryptanalysis are among the most efficient and well-understood attacks against block ciphers, both in theory and in practice. Thus, it seems natural to try creating backdoors using these techniques. Yet, there have been only a few works focusing on this research direction. For example, [3] and [28] explored backdoors in hash functions based on differential cryptanalysis. As for block ciphers, to the best of our knowledge, there is only one work from 1997 [35] using linear cryptanalysis. In that paper, special Sboxes are designed to hide high-probability linear approximations, which then enable a practical linear cryptanalysis. However, this construction was easily broken by Wu *et al.* in the subsequent year [39]. The attack against this cipher shows that the higher the probability of the embedded linear approximation, the weaker the backdoor security. Consequently, the authors claimed that it is infeasible for such a cipher to build a practical backdoor while keeping acceptable backdoor security. They further noted that *"it seems that hiding differentials is more difficult than hiding linear relations"*.

Even though other block ciphers embedding backdoors have been proposed [4–6,13,31], their design methodologies are usually very dedicated. On the other hand, as the topic of backdoor ciphers has not drawn much attention from the cryptography community, the backdoor security of these ciphers has not been well analyzed yet.

Considering the above facts, we introduce the MALICIOUS framework which allows to build efficient backdoors based on differential cryptanalysis. Moreover, we will show that the backdoor security can be reduced to a variation of the collision resistance notion of the XOF used in the tweak schedule.

The Construction. MALICIOUS is a framework to build a tweakable block cipher with n-bit blocksize, k-bit key and tweak of arbitrary size. It consists of three components:

- a round function f_i with partial non-linear layer, which can be expressed as $f_i(x) = L_i(S_i(x^{(0)})||x^{(1)})$,
- a tweak schedule based on a XOF,
- a key schedule.

The sub-tweak and sub-key values are XORed only to the non-linear part of the state, but are XORed to full state at the whitening stage[1]. The cipher is composed of r consecutive rounds. The framework is depicted in Fig. 1.

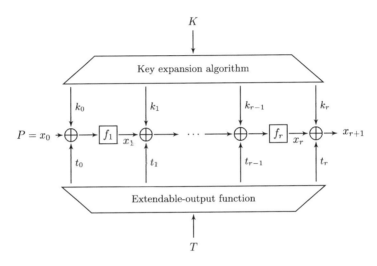

Fig. 1. The MALICIOUS framework

The backdoor introduced by MALICIOUS are related-tweak differential characteristics with probability 1 (deterministic). With the knowledge of this backdoor, a key recovery attack can be performed using various methods of differential cryptanalysis. It is to be noted that the attack is under the *chosen-tweak* model: both the designer and the attacker have complete freedom over the tweak values. This model is classical for TBC and realistic in practice.

We now describe how the backdoor can be embedded in the cipher. The core idea is that the sub-tweak difference of the backdoor chosen tweaks is used to cancel the difference of the non-linear part of the state in each round, so that the resulting differential characteristics will have no differentially active Sbox (as illustrated in Fig. 2). In Algorithm 1, we present the general steps to construct a MALICIOUS instance, in which a deterministic differential characteristic over r_0 ($\leq r$) rounds is embedded.

The key of the backdoor is the tweak pair generating these particular sub-tweak differences and the plaintext difference used in the embedded differential characteristic. We will use the prefix *malicious* to denote them. We also note that

---

[1] This is equivalent to a full state addition for all rounds, see Sect. 4.2 for details.

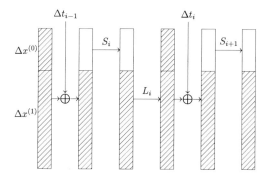

Fig. 2. Transitions of state difference in the embedded related-tweak differential characteristic. The differences of the hashed blocks can be zero or non-zero, while the differences of the white blocks are necessarily zero.

Algorithm 1: Constructing a MALICIOUS instance with an embedded deterministic differential characteristic over r_0 rounds

---

Select a XOF as the tweak schedule.

Choose uniformly at random a pair of tweak values (T_1, T_2) of arbitrary length.

Compute $t_0^1 || \ldots || t_r^1 \leftarrow \text{XOF}(T_1)$ and $t_0^2 || \ldots || t_r^2 \leftarrow \text{XOF}(T_2)$.

Evaluate the differences $\Delta t_i = t_i^1 \oplus t_i^2$ for all $i \in [0, \ldots, r]$.

Randomly select a plaintext difference $\Delta P = \Delta x_0$ for the linear part $x_0^{(1)}$ and set $\Delta x_0^{(0)} = \Delta t_0^{(0)}$.

for i *from 1 to r* **do**
    Determine a round function f_i with partial non-linear layers such that:
    if $i < r_0$ **then**
        Given the input difference $(\Delta x_{i-1} \oplus \Delta t_{i-1})$, the output difference after f_i has to satisfy $\Delta x_i^{(0)} = \Delta t_i$.
    end
end

Output the cipher description and the r_0-round related-tweak differential characteristic that is embedded into it (with related tweaks T_1 and T_2).

---

it is possible to embed multiple differential characteristics simultaneously. Then, the key recovery complexity will depend on the number of embedded differential characteristics and the cryptanalysis method.

We emphasize that the framework only focuses on the requirements of the cipher to embed a backdoor. However, a concrete instantiation would also have to take into account many other design principles so that the cipher could resist all state-of-the-art cryptanalysis as well as the attack against the backdoor described in the following section.

3.5   The Backdoor Security

In this section, we will evaluate two particular aspects of the backdoor security: (1) the complexity for the attacker to find the embedded differential characteristics, (2) whether additional backdoors exist in the resulting primitives, and if so, what is the complexity to find them.

Firstly, we will discuss the relation between the malicious tweak pair and its corresponding plaintext difference. We consider in this article that the number of rounds for the embedded differential characteristic is publicly known. On the one hand, if the malicious tweak pair is known to the attacker, then the corresponding sub-tweak differences can of course be computed. From these sub-tweak differences, he can obtain partial information about the state differences expected during the differential characteristic. Note that the embedded differential characteristic being deterministic indicates that the transformations of state differences are linear. Hence, by reversing the linear transformations, the malicious plaintext difference can eventually be recovered. That is, the leakage of the malicious tweak pair reveals the malicious plaintext difference.

On the other hand, if the malicious plaintext difference is known to the attacker, he can compute its transformation through the linear layer and obtain the required value for the sub-tweak difference such that it cancels the non-linear layer difference (since the sub-tweak is only XORed to the non-linear part, there is only one such candidate), and continue this process in the following rounds. Eventually, the embedded differential characteristic will be revealed. However, it remains difficult to recover the actual malicious tweak pair due to the XOF-based tweak schedule: given the embedded related-tweak differential characteristic, finding a tweak pair that leads to it through the XOF will be difficult. We define this new security notion as *target-difference resistance*:

Definition 1 (Target-difference resistance). *A hash function H is target-difference resistant if it is hard to find two inputs x and y such that $H(x) \oplus H(y) = \Delta$, where Δ is a given non-zero constant.*

To better understand target-difference resistance, we introduce the limited-birthday problem, which was first proposed in [19]:

Definition 2 (The limited-birthday problem [21]). *Let H be an n-bit output hash function that can be randomized by some input (IV or tweak or etc.) and that processes any input message of fixed size m bits, where $m > n$. Let IN be a set of admissible input differences and OUT be a set of admissible output differences, with the property that IN and OUT are closed sets with respect to $\oplus$ operation. Then, for the limited-birthday problem, the goal of the adversary is to generate a message pair (x, y) such that $x \oplus y \in IN$ and $H(x) \oplus H(y) \in OUT$ for a randomly chosen instance of H.*

Let 2^I and 2^O denote the sizes of IN and OUT respectively. The lower bound on the time complexity to find a solution for the limited-birthday problem is

$\max(2^{\frac{n-O+1}{2}}, 2^{n-I-O+1})^2$. If I is small, the complexity is $2^{n-I-O+1}$. However, even if I is very big, the complexity cannot be below $2^{\frac{n-O+1}{2}}$.

Target-difference resistance can be seen as a special case of the limited-birthday problem (as well as a generalisation of the classical collision resistance) where OUT is limited to a single value ($2^O = 1$) and IN is the full input space. Therefore, target-difference resistance has the same generic complexity as the classical collision resistance notion, that is the birthday bound $O(2^{n/2})$.

More generally, instead of the exact malicious tweak pair, the attacker could try to find another tweak pair whose sub-tweak differences are also the desired ones for the embedded differential characteristic. Yet, its complexity is still covered by the expected target-difference resistance of the XOF.

The above attack can possibly be applied to other plaintext differences. According to the construction of the MALICIOUS framework, the size of the input (tweak) to the XOF can be arbitrary long and thus any output of the XOF can potentially be obtained. For instance, if SHAKE128 is used as XOF, it can produce at most 2^b output streams (b being the state size between absorbing and squeezing phases in the sponge construction). Hence the number of possible sub-tweaks values is bounded by 2^b, no matter how many rounds it covers, and the number of sub-tweak differences is accordingly bounded by a greater value N ($\geq 2^b$). Thus, given a random plaintext difference and a certain number of rounds, if the size of the required sub-tweak differences for the deterministic related-tweak differential characteristic does not exceed $\log N$, then there will be a tweak pair matching the differential characteristic. We summarize this finding as follows:

Property 1. In addition to the embedded differential characteristics, there might exist other deterministic differential characteristics that would threaten the cipher security.

Consequently, we have to evaluate the security of the cipher with respect to all the potential deterministic differential characteristics, not only the planned ones. We consider a MALICIOUS instance that has a key size of 128 bits and employs SHAKE128 as tweak schedule. The security strength of SHAKE128 against collision attack is $\min(l/2, 128)$ bits, where l is the output length (or the length of the colliding part). In order to recover an r_0-round deterministic differential characteristic, the attacker has to find a tweak pair whose sub-tweak differences are the desired ones. The total size of these sub-tweak differences is $n + s \cdot (r_0 - 1)$ bits and thus the generic attack complexity is $2^{\min((n+s \cdot (r_0-1))/2, 128)}$, which becomes 2^{128} when $(n + s \cdot (r_0 - 1))/2 \geq 128$. The analysis is similar for the case where the key size is 256 bits and SHAKE256 is employed. We define r' to represent the value of r_0 that turns this inequality into an equality:

$$(n + s \cdot (r' - 1))/2 = k \tag{1}$$

All the deterministic related-tweak differential characteristics smaller than r' rounds can be recovered with a complexity smaller than the actual key size.

---

[2] The success probability here is about 0.63.

Therefore, in order to prevent these differential characteristics to weaken the cipher, r' must be taken into consideration when determining the number of rounds of the MALICIOUS instance. Actually, these related-tweak differential characteristics will decay exponentially in the remaining rounds as the corresponding sub-tweak differences are basically random.

3.6   Rationale Underlying the MALICIOUS Construction

When designing a backdoor for block ciphers, the first question that comes into mind is probably *what type of backdoor should be used?* While some existing backdoor designs directly insert a backdoor inside Sboxes or some other parts of the round function, we found out that the additional input tweak capability of a tweakable block cipher could be a perfect carrier of the backdoor. Suppose that a tweakable block cipher has a special property only when it is initiated with very specific tweak values, while it performs normally for all the other tweak values, then this property could be used as a backdoor. Moreover, if the tweak size is large enough, finding these special tweak values could be as hard as finding the secret key in the ideal case. One straightforward example of the special property is to build related-tweak differential characteristics using these tweaks. In the following, we provide more in-depth explanations on the design choices in MALICIOUS.

Components Rationale. When instantiating the MALICIOUS framework, some (security) notions have to be taken into account. The first and most important one is the undiscoverability: an entity who does not know the backdoor should not have increased chances to break the cipher. This requires that the backdoor security has to be as high as the cipher security. Thus, the MALICIOUS framework should provide a valid and solid security evaluation for the backdoor.

Another important notion is the practicability of the backdoor, and we will aim to make it as efficient as possible.

We detail in the following how the components of the MALICIOUS framework do follow these principles.

Tweak Schedule Based on XOF. As the malicious tweak values are the backdoor, the main task of the tweak schedule is to protect the malicious tweaks. According to the security analysis from Sect. 3.5, the backdoor security relies on the target-difference problem, where the attacker tries to find a tweak pair whose sub-tweak differences are the desired ones. This notion is simply a variation of the classical collision resistance for a hash function, so we expect a good cryptographic hash function to naturally provide this resistance.

Since MALICIOUS is a generalized framework, the total number of rounds will vary according to the different instantiations, so does the length of the sub-tweaks. Hence, the output length of the tweak schedule is expected to be flexible. Besides, if the tweak schedule was designed specifically for each MALICIOUS instantiation, it will render the backdoor evaluation much more difficult. Thus, for sake of simplicity of the analysis, it seems a better idea to make the tweak schedule uniform in the framework.

For all these reasons, a XOF seemed to be the best choice for our tweak schedule. The security of actual XOF functions such as SHAKE128 or SHAKE256 is rather well-analyzed and it can provide many choices in terms of security level.

Partial Non-linear Layers. The probability of a differential characteristic is determined by the number of differentially active Sboxes. Hence, in order to embed an efficient backdoor based on a differential characteristic, the best case is that the differential characteristic activates no Sbox at all. This is obviously very unlikely to happen in the MALICIOUS framework if the round functions are fully non-linear layers. Indeed, unless the related-key model is considered, a non-zero difference inserted in the plaintext would have to be cancelled by the first sub-tweak difference. However, when inserting differences in the tweak input, as the sub-tweak differences produced by the XOF will be random, they will force many active Sboxes in the subsequent rounds. Thus, it is unlikely for the MALICIOUS framework to be able to embed a deterministic related-tweak differential characteristic that covers more than a few rounds if full non-linear layers are utilized. Of course, it is possible to construct a differential characteristic with limited number of active Sboxes, but this is not the efficiency we are targeting.

We have also tried to modify the framework such that the sub-tweak addition is not performed every round. For example, an r rounds deterministic related-tweak differential characteristic can be realized by applying the tweak addition only once at the beginning, see Fig. 3. This way, the sub-tweak difference Δt_0 could neutralize the plaintext input difference Δx_0 and the resulting zero difference would get through the r rounds with probability 1. However, this candidate has an obvious fatal flaw: for any tweak pair the attacker can always set the plaintext input difference to be equal to Δt_0.

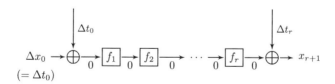

Fig. 3. A defective variant of the MALICIOUS framework. Key addition is omitted.

The above analysis shows that full non-linear layers seem not suitable for the MALICIOUS framework. On the contrary, partial non-linear layers satisfy our requirements. As in that case the Sbox only applies to a part of the internal state, the round function is able to map a non-zero input difference to a non-zero output difference while no active Sbox is activated. In term of building deterministic differential characteristics, we only have to set the difference of the non-linear part of the internal state to be zero rather than the full state. This allows to choose the linear transformation so that the output difference could satisfy the requirements from Algorithm 1.

4   Instantiating the **MALICIOUS** Framework with **LowMC**

In this section, we introduce a concrete instantiation of the MALICIOUS framework, called LowMC-M, which is based on the family of block ciphers LowMC.

4.1   LowMC

LowMC [2] is a family of block ciphers based on SPN structure with partial nonlinear layers. The parameters are flexible and we denote the block size by n, the key size by k, the number of Sboxes applied each round by m and the maximum allowed data complexity by d (d is the $\log_2$ of the allowable data complexity up to which the cipher is expected to give the claimed security). In order to reach the security claims, the number of rounds r is then derived from all these parameters using a round formula, the latest version being given in [34].

At the beginning of the encryption process, a key whitening is performed. The round function at round i consists of four operations in the following order:

- SboxLayer. A 3-bit Sbox is applied in parallel on the $s = 3m$ LSBs of the state, while the transformation for the remaining $n - s$ bits is the identity.
- LinearLayer(i). The state is multiplied in GF(2) with an invertible $n \times n$ binary matrix L_i which is chosen independently and uniformly at random.
- ConstantAddition(i). The state is XORed with an n-bit round constant C_i which is chosen independently and uniformly at random.
- KeyAddition(i). The state is XORed with an n-bit round key k_i. To generate k_i, the master key K is multiplied in GF(2) with an $n \times k$ binary matrix KL_i. This matrix is chosen independently and uniformly at random with rank $\min(n, k)$.

4.2   Equivalent Representation of **LowMC**

As discussed in [14,23,34], round keys and constants in LowMC can be compressed due to the fact that the non-linear layer is partial.

In the round function, it is possible to exchange the order of consecutive linear operations. We swap the order of LinearLayer and KeyAddition operations while keeping ConstantAddition as the last step in round i. Then, the equivalent round key can be written as $k_i' = L_i^{-1}(k_i)$. We observe that the Sbox only operates on the first s bits of the state and does not change the rest of the $n - s$ bits. Thus, we split k_i' into $k_i'^{(0)}$ and $k_i'^{(1)}$, and we can move the addition of $k_i'^{(1)}$ to the beginning of the round. Next, we observe that $k_i'^{(1)}$ can move further up to be combined with k_{i-1} in the previous round. The procedure is illustrated in Fig. 4. In general, if we start from the last round and iterate this procedure recursively until all the additions to the linear part have been moved to the beginning of the algorithm, we will end up with an equivalent representation where all the round keys are reduced to s bits apart from the whitening key. We remark that the same reasoning can be applied to the round constants.

This optimized representation can also reduce the implementation cost of the key schedule. Since all transformations performed during the optimization are linear and since the key schedule is itself linear, these transformations can be composed with the key schedule in order to compute the new $3m$-bit round keys directly. We refer to [14] for details.

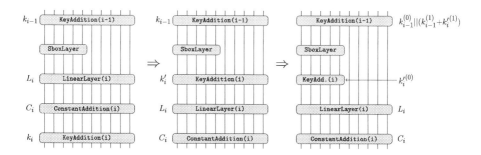

Fig. 4. Simplified representation of LowMC.

4.3 LowMC-M

We will directly use the simplified representation of LowMC as a starting point in our design, with a further modification: we move LinearLayer behind SboxLayer in every round[3].

LowMC-M is a family of tweakable block ciphers built upon LowMC with an additional transformation in each round:

– TweakAddition(i). The non-linear part of the state is XORed with an s-bit sub-tweak t_i just after KeyAddition. t_i is generated from a XOF whose input is the original tweak value T.

The XOF is based on SHAKE128 or SHAKE256, depending on the key size. All the other transformations of the round function are the same as for LowMC. The round function is finally composed of the following operations (Fig. 5):

TweakAddition(i) ∘ KeyAddition(i) ∘ ConstantAddition(i) ∘ LinearLayer(i) ∘ SboxLayer

The encryption starts with a key and tweak whitening and the sizes of k_0 and t_0 are both n. The derivation formula for the number of rounds r is the same as for LowMC.

---

[3] The resulting primitive is an equivalent representation of a LowMC instantiation with different linear layers, key schedule and round constants, because these components are chosen randomly.

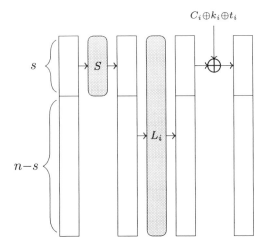

$C_i \oplus k_i \oplus t_i$

Fig. 5. A single round of LowMC-M.

Notations for LowMC-M. During a differential cryptanalysis, we denote by X_i the i-th round state difference before the LinearLayer transformation. Given a matrix L_i, we denote its j-th row by $L_i[j, *]$, and partition L_i into four submatrices:

$$L_i = \left[\begin{array}{c|c} L_i^{00} & L_i^{01} \\ \hline L_i^{10} & L_i^{11} \end{array} \right]$$

where $L_i^{00} \in \mathrm{GF}(2)^{s \times s}$, $L_i^{01} \in \mathrm{GF}(2)^{s \times (n-s)}$, $L_i^{10} \in \mathrm{GF}(2)^{(n-s) \times s}$, $L_i^{11} \in \mathrm{GF}(2)^{(n-s) \times (n-s)}$. With this notation, L_i^{00} and L_i^{01} will map $X_i^{(0)}$ and $X_i^{(1)}$ to the non-linear part of the state, respectively. And L_i^{10} and L_i^{11} will map $X_i^{(0)}$ and $X_i^{(1)}$ to the linear part of the state, respectively.

4.4 Embedding a Backdoor into LowMC-M

There are many forms of differential cryptanalysis that can perform a key recovery attack, such as the impossible differential attack, the boomerang attack, etc. For LowMC-M, we use the plain version where the attacker can deduce full or partial information about the r-th round key from a differential characteristic over $r-1$ rounds.

Since an $(r-1)$-round deterministic differential characteristic can only reveal the s-bit sub-key k_r of the r-th round, more deterministic differential characteristics should be added in order to eventually recover the full key. After k_r has been retrieved, the cipher can be reduced to $r-1$ rounds and thus another s-bit sub-key k_{r-1} can be recovered from an $(r-2)$-round deterministic differential characteristic. Finally, assume that there are a total of a such deterministic differential characteristics embedded in LowMC-M (one on $r-1$ rounds, one on $r-2$ rounds, etc., see Fig. 6), then $a \cdot s$ sub-key bits can be recovered. As the key schedule is fully linear and each matrix inside the key schedule is generated independently and uniformly at random, it implies that one will recover $a \cdot s$ bits of information about the key by solving a system of linear equations. Therefore, at most $a = \lceil k/s \rceil$ deterministic differential characteristics are needed to recover the full key.

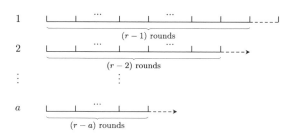

Fig. 6. The deterministic differential characteristics embedded into LowMC-M.

Now, we explain how to embed such differential characteristics into an instantiation of LowMC-M. The general procedure is given in Algorithm 1. The a malicious tweak pairs are chosen by the designer at the very beginning and the corresponding sub-tweak differences are computed. Then, the linear layer matrix L_i is generated along with the generation of the deterministic differential characteristics, **round by round**.

Firstly, we explain how to generate the linear layer matrices. Note that in order to have a deterministic differential characteristic over i rounds, only the linear layer matrices of the first $i - 1$ rounds have to be specifically designed as the matrix L_i has no impact on the differences of the i-th round Sboxes. Assuming we have already embedded a deterministic differential characteristics over i rounds, then all the linear layer matrices of the first $i - 1$ rounds of LowMC-M have been fixed accordingly. If we plan to extend b ($b \leq a$) of the a deterministic differential characteristics by one more round, the matrix L_i should be specified. Denote by SX_i the set of $X_i^{(1)}$ of those deterministic differential characteristics that will be extended in the next round. Here, SX_i refers to the b differential characteristics. Since the non-linear state difference $X_i^{(0)}$ equals to zero for all the b differential characteristics, the set SX_i will determine the differential in the following round. Given the difference set SX_i, the output differences after the multiplication by the matrix L_i^{01} should cancel the following sub-tweak differences so that the b differential characteristics will activate no Sbox in round $i + 1$. We detail the generation of L_i in Algorithm 2.

Denote the $b \times (n - s)$ matrix in Equation (2) by MX_i. We emphasize that the rank of MX_i should be $\min(b, n-s)$, otherwise Equation (2) is likely to have no solution. In practice, b is always smaller than $n - s$ for a normal parameters set of LowMC-M. Thus, this requirement also means that the binary vectors of $X_i^{(1)}$ in SX_i should be linearly independent.

Algorithm 2: Generate linear layer matrix L_i.

Input   : The set $SX_i = (X_{i,1}^{(1)}, X_{i,2}^{(1)}, \cdots, X_{i,b}^{(1)})$ and the sub-tweak differences $(\Delta t_i^1, \Delta t_i^2, \cdots, \Delta t_i^b)$ for the b differential characteristics.

Output: Matrix L_i

while *True* **do**

    for j *from* 1 *to* s **do**

        Solve the following system of linear equations and randomly pick one solution of $x = (x_1, x_2, ..., x_n)$ as $L_i^{01}[j, *]$.

$$\begin{pmatrix} X_{i,1}^{(1)}[1] \ X_{i,1}^{(1)}[2] \ ... \ X_{i,1}^{(1)}[n-s] \\ X_{i,2}^{(1)}[1] \ X_{i,2}^{(1)}[2] \ ... \ X_{i,2}^{(1)}[n-s] \\ \vdots \\ X_{i,b}^{(1)}[1] \ X_{i,b}^{(1)}[2] \ ... \ X_{i,b}^{(1)}[n-s] \end{pmatrix} \cdot \begin{pmatrix} x_1 \\ x_2 \\ \vdots \\ x_{n-s} \end{pmatrix} = \begin{pmatrix} \Delta t_i^1[j] \\ \Delta t_i^2[j] \\ \vdots \\ \Delta t_i^b[j] \end{pmatrix} \quad (2)$$

    end

    Randomly select the sub-matrices L_i^{00}, L_i^{10} and L_i^{11}.

    if L_i *is full rank* **then**

      | return L_i

    end

end

The whole process of generating an instance of LowMC-M is given here:

1. Select a different pairs of tweaks of any desired length and compute the corresponding sub-tweak differences in all rounds for each pair of tweaks.
2. For each tweak pair, choose an n-bit value of the plaintext difference ΔP as the input difference for the embedded differential characteristic, while setting the first s bits of ΔP to be equal to $\Delta t_0^{(0)}$.
3. For the a differential characteristics, compute $X_1^{(1)} = \Delta P^{(1)} \oplus \Delta t_0^{(1)}$ and if the binary vectors of SX_1 are not linearly independent, then go back to step 2.
4. For round i from 1 to $r-2$:
   - Generate the matrix L_i using Algorithm 2 with SX_i and the corresponding sub-tweak differences as inputs[4].
   - Except for the last loop, compute the set of SX_{i+1} through the matrix multiplication of L_i. If the binary vectors of SX_{i+1} are not linearly independent, repeat this loop.
5. Choose L_{r-1} and L_r independently and uniformly at random from all invertible $n \times n$ binary matrices.
6. For all rounds i, choose KL_i independently and uniformly at random from all $n \times k$ binary matrices of rank $\min(n, k)$ and the round constants C_i as well.

---

[4] Starting from round $r - a + 1$, the number of deterministic differential characteristics decrements by 1 at every loop.

Recovering the Secret Key With the Backdoor. The backdoor is the a malicious tweak pairs and the corresponding plaintext differences. With the knowledge of these related-tweak differential characteristics, the designer can recover the full key in a very short time. To create the a plaintext differences, the designer can firstly choose a random P, then compute $P_i = P \oplus \Delta P_i$ for $i \in \{1, \cdots, a\}$. We note the fact that for any non-zero probability differential (Δ_1, Δ_2) of LowMC-M Sbox, where $\Delta_1 \neq 0$ and $\Delta_2 \neq 0$, there is only one unordered pair of inputs/outputs of the Sbox satisfying the differential. If each plaintext difference is used only once in the attack, then two sub-key candidates will remain for each Sbox as we cannot determine which order of the input/output pair of the targeted Sbox should be in the attack. The wrong sub-key candidate can be filtered by repeating the attack with another pair of plaintexts of the same difference. By doing so, $a \cdot s$ bits of information of the key can be retrieved in the end. Later, the remaining $(k - a \cdot s)$ key bits, if they exist, can be brute forced. Finally, the key recovery requires $2(a + 1) + \max(k - a \cdot s, 0)$ encryptions and the data complexity is $2(a + 1)$.

Note that the bit length of $X_i^{(1)}$ is $n - s$. In order to ensure that Equation (2) is solvable, the number of differential characteristics that are embedded in LowMC-M should not be higher than $n - s$. Generally, this bound is much higher than the number of differential characteristics that is actually needed in a concrete instantiation. Last but not least, one may wonder why we chose different malicious tweak pairs for the a related-tweak differential characteristics (indeed using a single malicious tweak pair would work), but we recommend doing so for security reasons as we will explain in Sect. 5.1.

4.5   Parameters

The design goal of LowMC-M is to keep the backdoor and the cipher secure, but also to ensure the efficiency of the key recovery using the backdoor. Based on these principles, we selected some instantiation parameters[5] and we present them in Table 1. The security analysis is given in Sect. 5 and Sect. 6.

Regarding the performances, we evaluated the corresponding LowMC used in the LowMC-M instances. The LowMC implementations we benchmarked are optimized for AVX2 instructions. Measurements were performed on an AMD EPYC 7401 running Ubuntu 18.04. We tested several instances and we observed that a single encryption generally costs around 10000 to 30000 cycles depending on the parameters, the block size (= key size) ranging from 128 to 256 bits.

---

[5] The reference code of LowMC-M generation can be found at https://github.com/MaliciousLowmc/LowMC-M.

Table 1. A range of different parameters sets of LowMC-M instantiations. For each instantiation, the malicious tweak pair that triggers each embedded differential characteristic is unique. d is the log_2 of the allowed data complexity, a is the number of differential characteristics embedded.

block size n	non-linear s	key size k	data d	rounds r	#differentials a	XOF
128	3	128	64	208	43	SHAKE128
	6	128	64	104	21	SHAKE128
	9	128	64	70	14	SHAKE128
	30	128	64	23	5	SHAKE128
	90	128	64	14	2	SHAKE128
256	3	256	64	384	85	SHAKE256
	9	256	64	129	28	SHAKE256
	60	256	64	21	5	SHAKE256
	120	256	64	14	3	SHAKE256

5 Backdoor Security

In this section, we will discuss the backdoor security of LowMC-M with respect to the notions mentioned in Sect. 2.2: undetectability, undiscoverability, untraceability and practicability.

5.1 Undetectability

In this subsection, we discuss whether a LowMC-M instance containing a backdoor is distinguishable from a random LowMC-M with no backdoor embedded. Since the only difference between these two cases lies in the way the linear layer matrices are generated, we will investigate the properties of these matrices.

We now would like to show that all embedded differential characteristics must use distinct tweak pairs in order to maintain undetectability. Assuming there is a backdoored LowMC-M instance that is generated following the steps described in Sect. 4.4 and a total of a deterministic related-tweak differential characteristics are embedded, while only a' ($< a$) different tweak pairs are used during the generation phase. Let c_j denote the number of embedded differential characteristics triggered by the same tweak pair, with $j \in \{1, \ldots, a'\}$. We will show that some dependency will exist in the linear layer matrices for the first i ($\leq r - a$) rounds, consequently some additional deterministic related-tweak differential characteristics over the first i rounds can be recovered.

Definition 3. *For a* LowMC-M *instance,* A_i *is the matrix of dimension* $(i \cdot s) \times (n - s)$ *defined as:*

$$\begin{pmatrix} L_1^{01} \\ L_2^{01} \cdot L_1^{11} \\ L_3^{01} \cdot L_2^{11} \cdot L_1^{11} \\ \vdots \\ L_i^{01} \cdot L_{i-1}^{11} \cdot \ldots \cdot L_1^{11} \end{pmatrix}$$

We remark that a malicious plaintext difference ΔP can be retrieved if the corresponding malicious tweak pair is provided: in order to have a deterministic differential characteristic all Sboxes must be differentially inactive (*i.e.*, the input difference of each Sbox should be zero) and thus for a malicious tweak pair that takes any of the a' different values, recovering $\Delta P^{(0)}$ (the non-linear part of ΔP) is straightforward as it is equal to the sub-tweak difference $\Delta t_0^{(0)}$. After that, one just needs to retrieve the remaining part $\Delta P^{(1)}$. In order to have a deterministic differential characteristic over the first two rounds, $L_1^{01}(X_1^{(1)})$ should be equal to Δt_1, where $X_1^{(1)} = \Delta P^{(1)} \oplus \Delta t_0^{(1)}$. To extend the differential characteristic to the third round, $L_2^{01} \cdot L_1^{11}(X_1^{(1)})$ should be equal to Δt_2. Continuing this process until the i-th round, we can create a system of linear equations with $n - s$ binary variables:

$$\begin{pmatrix} L_1^{01} \\ L_2^{01} \cdot L_1^{11} \\ L_3^{01} \cdot L_2^{11} \cdot L_1^{11} \\ \vdots \\ L_{i-1}^{01} \cdot L_{i-2}^{11} \cdot \ldots \cdot L_1^{11} \end{pmatrix} \cdot (X_1^{(1)}) = A_{i-1} \cdot (X_1^{(1)}) = \begin{pmatrix} \Delta t_1 \\ \Delta t_2 \\ \Delta t_3 \\ \vdots \\ \Delta t_{i-1} \end{pmatrix} \qquad (3)$$

Solving Eq. (3) will output the solution of $X_1^{(1)}$, then the remaining part $\Delta P^{(1)}$ can be recovered naturally. However, there may be more solutions as the number of solutions is determined by the rank of A_{i-1}.

In cases where the number of rounds i is large enough such that $(i - 1) \cdot s \gg (n - s)$, if all the linear layer matrices are chosen independently and uniformly at random, the rank of A_{i-1} will be $n - s$ with very high probability. However, for a LowMC-M instance with backdoor embedded, since the linear layer matrices are specially designed, the rank of A_{i-1} can not be determined similarly.

Determining the Rank of A_{i-1}. We first introduce the following definition.

Definition 4. *If* M *is an* $n \times m$ *binary matrix and* v *is an* n-bit vector, the solution space $sol(M, v)$ is defined as: $sol(M, v) = \{x^T \in \{0, 1\}^m : Mx = v\}$.

Assume that a special LowMC-M instance is generated with c related-tweak deterministic differential characteristics over i rounds while only one malicious tweak pair is used. During the generation of L_j^{01}, $j \in \{1, \ldots, i-1\}$, Equation (2) could be simplified as:

$$MX_j \cdot x = \mathbf{1} \quad or \quad MX_j \cdot x = \mathbf{0} \tag{4}$$

where $\mathbf{0}$ and $\mathbf{1}$ are c-bit vectors full of zeros and ones, respectively.

Denote by V the union of $sol(MX_1, \mathbf{1})$ and $sol(MX_1, \mathbf{0})$, the rows of L_1^{01} are chosen from V. Since the dimensions of $sol(MX_1, \mathbf{1})$ and $sol(MX_1, \mathbf{0})$ are both $n - s - c$, then the dimension of V is $n - s - c + 1$. When $j = 2$, Eqs. (4) can be represented by:

$$MX_1 \cdot (L_1^{11})^T \cdot x = \mathbf{1} \quad or \quad MX_1 \cdot (L_1^{11})^T \cdot x = \mathbf{0}$$

because $X_2^{(1)} = L_1^{11} \cdot X_1^{(1)}$. The rows of L_2^{01} are chosen from $sol(MX_1 \cdot (L_1^{11})^T, \mathbf{1})$ or $sol(MX_1 \cdot (L_1^{11})^T, \mathbf{0})$. Before we continue, we will use the following lemma.

Lemma 1. *Let M_1 and M_2 be two binary matrices of dimension $(n \times m)$ and $(m \times m)$ respectively. If $x \in sol(M_1 \cdot M_2, v)$, then $x \cdot M_2^T \in sol(M_1, v)$ for any n-bit vector v.*

Proof. For any $x \in sol(M_1 \cdot M_2, v)$, we have $(M_1 \cdot M_2) \cdot x^T = v$. It can be represented by $M_1 \cdot (M_2 \cdot x^T) = v$, thus $(M_2 \cdot x^T)^T = x \cdot M_2^T \in sol(M_1, v)$. □

According to Lemma 1, if $x \in sol(MX_1 \cdot (L_1^{11})^T, \mathbf{1})$, then $x \cdot L_1^{11} \in sol(MX_1, \mathbf{1})$ and also if $x \in sol(MX_1 \cdot (L_1^{11})^T, \mathbf{0})$, then $x \cdot L_1^{11} \in sol(MX_1, \mathbf{0})$. Thus, all the rows of $L_2^{01} \cdot L_1^{11}$ are in the space V. Similarly, we can get the same results for $L_3^{01} \cdot L_2^{11} \cdot L_1^{11}, \cdots, L_{i-1}^{01} \cdot L_{i-2}^{11} \cdot \ldots \cdot L_1^{11}$. To summarize, all the rows of A_{i-1} for this special LowMC-M instance are chosen from the space V of dimension $n - s - c + 1$. Thus, the rank of A_{i-1} is $n - s - c + 1$.

Let us return back to the previous LowMC-M instance mentioned at the beginning of this subsection. We can divide the a differential characteristics into a' sub-groups where each sub-group includes c_j differential characteristics that are triggered with the same tweak pair, $j \in \{1, \ldots, a'\}$. Then, the space V will be the intersection of all the spaces that are determined by the a' sub-groups. We summarize the result as follows.

Proposition 1. *If there is a total of a' different malicious tweak pairs and each of them is used to build c_j deterministic differential characteristics over i rounds in an instance of LowMC-M, with $(i-1) \cdot s \gg (n-s)$, then the rank of A_{i-1} will be $n - s - \sum_{j=1}^{a'}(c_j - 1)$.*

As a result, the rank of A_{i-1} is $n - s - \sum_{j=1}^{a'}(c_j - 1)$ and a total of $2^{\sum_{j=1}^{a'}(c_j - 1)}$ deterministic differential characteristics for each of the a' tweak pairs can be recovered by the designer. Note that the rank of A_{i-1} can be easily computed by any entity. Compared to the full rank A_{i-1} for a random LowMC-M with no backdoor embedded, the unusual property of A_{i-1} for the backdoored LowMC-M will uncover the existence of the backdoor if $a' < a$. However, if $a' = a$, that is,

$c_j = 1$ for all $j \in \{1, \ldots, a'\}$, then A_{i-1} will be full rank. Therefore, in order to keep the backdoor of LowMC-M undetectable, we recommend to not use the same tweak pair for building more than one differential characteristics in the generation phase.

5.2 Undiscoverability

In this subsection, we discuss whether the backdoor from a LowMC-M instance can be efficiently recovered by an attacker. Recall that some unknown deterministic related-tweak differential characteristics potentially exist in LowMC-M, according to Property 1. Instead of considering the embedded backdoor exclusively, we evaluate the complexity of finding any useful deterministic related-tweak differential characteristics for an attacker. Basically, the complexity is based on the XOF security properties.

We simply adopt the security analysis for the general MALICIOUS framework in Sect. 3.5. For any LowMC-M instance, the bound r' derived from Formula 1 is much smaller compared to the total number of rounds, which poses no threat to the backdoor. We list the evaluation for some instances in Table 2.

We can examine the undiscoverability security from another perspective. Note that deterministic related-tweak differential characteristics can be derived as long as Eq. (3) is solvable. The requirement for the equation to be solvable is that the ranks of the coefficient matrix A_{i-1} and the augmented matrix of Eq. (3) are equal, which means that the vector on the right side of the equation, denoted as v, has to be a combination of the columns of A_{i-1}. Observe that the number of such combinations is 2^α, α being the rank of A_{i-1} and it can be computed according to Proposition 1. As for vector v, it is random due to the XOF and its size is $s \cdot (i-1)$. In conclusion, Eq. (3) is solvable with probability $2^{\alpha - s \cdot (i-1)}$, that is, the complexity of finding an i-round deterministic related-tweak differential characteristic is $2^{s \cdot (i-1) - \alpha}$. We define r'' to represent the value of i that turns the complexity to be equal to the key space size

$$r'' = \frac{k + \alpha}{s} + 1 \tag{5}$$

The maximal value is $r'' = \frac{k+n}{s}$ when A_{i-1} is full rank of $n - s$. Still, r'' is much smaller than the number of rounds of any LowMC-M instance, see examples in Table 2.

To summarize, the backdoor and the other potential deterministic related-tweak differential characteristics of the same length are fully protected by the XOF, and its recovery is as hard as brute forcing the key.

Table 2. Backdoor security evaluation for LowMC-M-n/s with block size n, key size n, non-linear layer size s and log_2 data complexity 64. r is the actual number of rounds of the instance, r' and r'' are defined in Formulas 1 and 5 respectively.

Parameters	r	r'	r''
LowMC-M-128/3	208	44	86
LowMC-M-128/6	104	23	43
LowMC-M-128/9	70	16	29
LowMC-M-128/30	23	6	9
LowMC-M-128/90	14	3	3
LowMC-M-256/3	384	87	170
LowMC-M-256/9	129	30	57
LowMC-M-256/60	21	6	9
LowMC-M-256/120	14	4	5

5.3   Untraceability and Practicability

As for practicability, only negligible data and computation are required to launch a full key recovery attack with the knowledge of the backdoor, as explained in Sect. 4.4. Thus, the full key can be recovered within seconds.

Since the usage of the backdoor requires chosen tweaks, the malicious tweaks can be detected by the user once the designer makes queries to attack him, which means the backdoor is traceable. Besides, as only a few queries are needed to launch an attack with the knowledge of the backdoor, the user is able to quickly brute force the queries to find out the malicious tweak pairs.

6   Cipher Security

In this section, we study the security of LowMC-M as a tweakable block cipher.

6.1   Attacks Based on Tweak

In comparison to LowMC, an additional tweak addition is introduced in LowMC-M. Theoretically, this feature will provide extra degrees of freedom for the attacker and might naturally weaken LowMC-M when compared to LowMC. However, since the tweak schedule is an XOF, the attacker cannot control its output. Even if the attacker could brute force some structures on the sub-tweaks for a few rounds, this will result in the remaining rounds containing completely random structure, which consequently prevent the attacker utilizing these remaining rounds for what should have been the best attack on LowMC. Hence, we believe that the extra degrees of freedom provided by the tweak is not easily usable and will not lead to any important improvement over classical attack, including the existing cryptanalysis [15, 16, 34] on LowMC.

6.2   Attacks Without Tweak

All the current attacks [15, 16, 34] on LowMC have been conducted under the assumption that the linear layer matrices of LowMC are chosen independently and uniformly at random. Except the tweak addition, LowMC-M has the equivalent specification to LowMC. The only difference lies in the way the linear layer matrices L_i are chosen during the generation phase. In order to prove that the security of LowMC-M is on par with that of LowMC, we need to show that the linear layer matrices of LowMC-M are indistinguishable from those of LowMC-M from the perspective of the attacker. We will evaluate this with respect to the randomness and independence.

Randomness of Linear Layer Matrices. The randomness of the linear layer matrix L_i is analyzed by scrutinizing its four sub-matrices one by one.

L_i^{00} **and** L_i^{10}. As described in Algorithm 2, the two sub-matrices L_i^{00} and L_i^{10} of L_i are chosen independently and uniformly at random for each round.

L_i^{11}. Even though L_i^{11} is chosen randomly in Algorithm 2, there is a supplementary requirement during the generation phase. That is, the binary vectors of SX_{i+1} have to be linearly independent, which adds an extra constraint to L_i^{11} since each binary vector of SX_{i+1} is obtained by:

$$X_{i+1}^{(1)} = L_i^{11} \cdot X_i^{(1)} \tag{6}$$

and thus the transformation of L_i^{11} should map a set of linearly independent vectors to another set of linearly independent vectors. Since L_i^{11} is chosen randomly and all the $X_i^{(1)}$ involved are linearly independent, every $X_{i+1}^{(1)}$ in SX_{i+1} produced by Formula 6 can be regarded as random binary vectors and are independent from each other. On the other hand, note that at most $a = \lceil k/s \rceil$ differential characteristics are embedded in LowMC-M, which means that the size of SX_{i+1} is $\lceil k/s \rceil$ at most. For any reasonable parameter set, we will have $\lceil k/s \rceil \ll (n-s)$. Based on Lemma 2 below, we can compute the probability that the set SX_{i+1} is linearly independent. As a result, the probability is almost 1, which is also verified from our experiments.

Hence, the constraint on L_i^{11} is very loose. The final selection of L_i^{11} will not introduce any special property.

Lemma 2. *[24, adapted] For m random n-bit vectors over $\mathbb{F}_2$ ($m \leqslant n$), the probability that they are linearly independent is $p(m) = \prod_{k=0}^{m-1}(1 - 2^{k-n})$. In particular, $p(n) > 0.2887$.*

L_i^{01}. L_i^{01} is the essential part for embedding backdoors, and thus it is the one specially designed. The row length of L_i^{01} is $n - s$ bits, while in the generation phase each row is chosen from a sub-space of dimension $n - s - b$ which is determined by the corresponding Equation (2), b being the size of SX_i. However, we will show that for the attacker this special chosen L_i^{01} is still indistinguishable from a randomly chosen one.

Observe that both MX_i and the sub-tweak difference vector in Equation (2) are unknown for the attacker, thus the solution space is unidentified. Moreover, the solution space for each row of L_i^{01} could be different due to the sub-tweak difference. Therefore, it is impossible for the attacker to trace some rows of L_i^{01} to the targeted hidden sub-space.

To summarize, the four sub-matrices are indistinguishable from random matrices for the attacker. The only connection between these four sub-matrices is that the combined matrix L_i should be invertible, which is also the same for LowMC, so it reveals no additional information. Hence, we conclude that for the attacker the matrix L_i is indistinguishable from a random matrix.

Independence Between Linear Layer Matrices. The definition of A_r captures partial information of the matrices that includes L_i^{10} and L_i^{11} over r consecutive rounds. If the linear layer matrices are chosen independently and uniformly at random, the resultant A_r should be random, thus the rank of A_r will be $n - s$ when $r \cdot s \gg (n - s)$. If the rank for a LowMC-M instance is smaller than $n - s$, it will imply a connection between these matrices. As suggested in Proposition 1, the rank of A_r can be computed by $n - s - \sum_{i=1}^{a'}(c_i - 1)$. In order to eliminate the connections, each c_i should equal to 1, that is, different malicious tweak pairs should be used to build different differential characteristics during the generation phase.

The two sub-matrices L_i^{00} and L_i^{10} are chosen randomly and independently, so it will not impose any connection between the matrices.

We remark that even if there is some dependence existing between the linear layer matrices, the cipher security is still unlikely to be threatened. Yet, we conservatively recommend to avoid such dependency in a LowMC-M instance.

7   Conclusion

In this article, we proposed the MALICIOUS framework for embedding backdoors into tweakable block ciphers. The backdoor is a set of related-tweak differential characteristics with probability 1, from which the secret key can be recovered fully and efficiently. Besides, the backdoor security of our proposal is reduced to the target-difference resistance (a variant of the classical collision resistance, with the same generic complexity) of the XOF employed in the cipher. We also proposed several concrete instances LowMC-M, which are directly inspired from the block cipher LowMC.

We have proved that it is possible to build a secure and efficient backdoor into tweakable block ciphers. Third party analysis is of course required to fully understand its security, but our proposal could be a new interesting direction towards building backdoors in symmetric-key primitives.

Not only this result will increase the community's awareness to potential backdoors in symmetric-key primitives, but it can also lead to new applications.

It has been shown in [35] that a backdoored block cipher is equivalent to a public key encryption where the backdoor is regarded as the secret key. Even though our proposal does not yet reach the usability of a public encryption scheme, building public-key primitives out of symmetric-key ones has been a long standing open problem.

We envision several future works after this first step. Other cryptanalysis techniques than just a plain differential attack (such as impossible differential attacks, boomerang attacks, integral attacks, etc.) might also be used to build backdoors and could allow us to build more efficient or more usable designs. It would also be interesting to build other types of backdoored primitives, such as Message Authentication Codes (MAC), Authenticated Encryption (AE), etc. which might require totally different design strategies. Finally, our proposal remains somewhat traceable (once the backdoor used against him, a user could try to check all of its tweak values queried and check which tweaks pair leads to a related-tweak differential with a very good probability) and it would be interesting to study new techniques or protocols to reduce this detection surface as much as possible.

Acknowledgements. The authors would like to thank the anonymous referees and Eik List for their helpful comments. We also thank Shiyao Chen for his help on automatic search tools. We furthermore thank the Picnic team for providing standalone optimized implementations of LowMC.

References

1. Albertini, A., Aumasson, J.-P., Eichlseder, M., Mendel, F., Schläffer, M.: Malicious hashing: Eve's variant of SHA-1. In: Joux, A., Youssef, A. (eds.) SAC 2014. LNCS, vol. 8781, pp. 1–19. Springer, Cham (2014). https://doi.org/10.1007/978-3-319-13051-4_1
2. Albrecht, M.R., Rechberger, C., Schneider, T., Tiessen, T., Zohner, M.: Ciphers for MPC and FHE. In: Oswald, E., Fischlin, M. (eds.) EUROCRYPT 2015. LNCS, vol. 9056, pp. 430–454. Springer, Heidelberg (2015). https://doi.org/10.1007/978-3-662-46800-5_17
3. AlTawy, R., Youssef, A.M.: Watch your constants: malicious Streebog. Cryptology ePrint Archive, Report 2014/879 (2014). https://eprint.iacr.org/2014/879
4. Angelova, V., Borissov, Y.: Plaintext recovery in DES-like cryptosystems based on S-boxes with embedded parity check. Serdica J. Comput. **7**(3), 257–270 (2013)
5. Bannier, A., Bodin, N., Filiol, E.: Partition-based trapdoor ciphers. Cryptology ePrint Archive, Report 2016/493 (2016). http://eprint.iacr.org/2016/493
6. Bannier, A., Filiol, E.: Mathematical backdoors in symmetric encryption systems-proposal for a backdoored AES-like block cipher. arXiv preprint arXiv:1702.06475 (2017)
7. Bar-On, A., Dinur, I., Dunkelman, O., Lallemand, V., Keller, N., Tsaban, B.: Cryptanalysis of SP networks with partial non-linear layers. In: Oswald, E., Fischlin, M. (eds.) EUROCRYPT 2015. LNCS, Part I, vol. 9056, pp. 315–342. Springer, Heidelberg (2015). https://doi.org/10.1007/978-3-662-46800-5_13

8. Barker, E.B., Kelsey, J.M.: Recommendation for random number generation using deterministic random bit generators (revised). US Department of Commerce, Technology Administration, National Institute of Standards and Technology, Computer Security Division, Information Technology Laboratory (2007)

9. Beaulieu, R., Shors, D., Smith, J., Treatman-Clark, S., Weeks, B., Wingers, L.: The SIMON and SPECK families of lightweight block ciphers. Cryptology ePrint Archive, Report 2013/404 (2013). http://eprint.iacr.org/2013/404

10. Bernstein, D.J., Lange, T., Niederhagen, R.: Dual EC: a standardized back door. In: Ryan, P.Y.A., Naccache, D., Quisquater, J.-J. (eds.) The New Codebreakers. LNCS, vol. 9100, pp. 256–281. Springer, Heidelberg (2016). https://doi.org/10.1007/978-3-662-49301-4_17

11. Bertoni, G., Daemen, J., Peeters, M., Van Assche, G., Van Keer, R., Viguier, B.: KangarooTwelve: fast hashing based on Keccak-p. In: Preneel, B., Vercauteren, F. (eds.) ACNS 2018. LNCS, vol. 10892, pp. 400–418. Springer, Cham (2018). https://doi.org/10.1007/978-3-319-93387-0_21

12. Biham, E.: Cryptanalysis of Patarin's 2-round public key system with S boxes (2R). In: Preneel, B. (ed.) EUROCRYPT 2000. LNCS, vol. 1807, pp. 408–416. Springer, Heidelberg (2000). https://doi.org/10.1007/3-540-45539-6_28

13. Calderini, M., Sala, M.: On differential uniformity of maps that may hide an algebraic trapdoor. In: Maletti, A. (ed.) CAI 2015. LNCS, vol. 9270, pp. 70–78. Springer, Cham (2015). https://doi.org/10.1007/978-3-319-23021-4_7

14. Dinur, I., Kales, D., Promitzer, A., Ramacher, S., Rechberger, C.: Linear equivalence of block ciphers with partial non-linear layers: application to LowMC. In: Ishai, Y., Rijmen, V. (eds.) EUROCRYPT 2019. LNCS, Part I, vol. 11476, pp. 343–372. Springer, Cham (2019). https://doi.org/10.1007/978-3-030-17653-2_12

15. Dinur, I., Liu, Y., Meier, W., Wang, Q.: Optimized interpolation attacks on LowMC. In: Iwata, T., Cheon, J.H. (eds.) ASIACRYPT 2015. LNCS, Part II, vol. 9453, pp. 535–560. Springer, Heidelberg (2015). https://doi.org/10.1007/978-3-662-48800-3_22

16. Dobraunig, C., Eichlseder, M., Mendel, F.: Higher-order cryptanalysis of LowMC. In: Kwon, S., Yun, A. (eds.) ICISC 2015. LNCS, vol. 9558, pp. 87–101. Springer, Cham (2016). https://doi.org/10.1007/978-3-319-30840-1_6

17. Dworkin, M.J.: SHA-3 standard: permutation-based hash and extendable-output functions. Technical report (2015)

18. Gérard, B., Grosso, V., Naya-Plasencia, M., Standaert, F.-X.: Block ciphers that are easier to mask: how far can we go? In: Bertoni, G., Coron, J.-S. (eds.) CHES 2013. LNCS, vol. 8086, pp. 383–399. Springer, Heidelberg (2013). https://doi.org/10.1007/978-3-642-40349-1_22

19. Gilbert, H., Peyrin, T.: Super-Sbox cryptanalysis: improved attacks for AES-like permutations. In: Hong, S., Iwata, T. (eds.) FSE 2010. LNCS, vol. 6147, pp. 365–383. Springer, Heidelberg (2010). https://doi.org/10.1007/978-3-642-13858-4_21

20. Guo, J., Nikolic, I., Peyrin, T., Wang, L.: Cryptanalysis of Zorro. Cryptology ePrint Archive, Report 2013/713 (2013). http://eprint.iacr.org/2013/713

21. Iwamoto, M., Peyrin, T., Sasaki, Y.: Limited-birthday distinguishers for hash functions. In: Sako, K., Sarkar, P. (eds.) ASIACRYPT 2013. LNCS, Part II, vol. 8270, pp. 504–523. Springer, Heidelberg (2013). https://doi.org/10.1007/978-3-642-42045-0_26

22. Jean, J., Nikolić, I., Peyrin, T.: Tweaks and keys for block ciphers: the TWEAKEY framework. In: Sarkar, P., Iwata, T. (eds.) ASIACRYPT 2014. LNCS, Part II, vol. 8874, pp. 274–288. Springer, Heidelberg (2014). https://doi.org/10.1007/978-3-662-45608-8_15

23. Kales, D., Perrin, L., Promitzer, A., Ramacher, S., Rechberger, C.: Improvements to the linear operations of LowMC: a faster picnic (2018)

24. Kolchin, V.: Random Graphs. Cambridge University Press, Cambridge (1999)

25. Liskov, M., Rivest, R.L., Wagner, D.: Tweakable block ciphers. In: Yung, M. (ed.) CRYPTO 2002. LNCS, vol. 2442, pp. 31–46. Springer, Heidelberg (2002). https://doi.org/10.1007/3-540-45708-9_3

26. Liskov, M., Rivest, R.L., Wagner, D.: Tweakable block ciphers. J. Cryptol. **24**(3), 588–613 (2011)

27. Matyukhin, D., Rudskoy, V., Shishkin, V.: A perspective hashing algorithm. In: Materials of XII Scientific Conference RusCrypto 2010 (2010)

28. Morawiecki, P.: Malicious Keccak. Cryptology ePrint Archive, Report 2015/1085 (2015). https://eprint.iacr.org/2015/1085

29. Patarin, J., Goubin, L.: Asymmetric cryptography with S-Boxes is it easier than expected to design efficient asymmetric cryptosystems? In: Han, Y., Okamoto, T., Qing, S. (eds.) ICICS 1997. LNCS, vol. 1334, pp. 369–380. Springer, Heidelberg (1997). https://doi.org/10.1007/BFb0028492

30. Patarin, J., Goubin, L.: Trapdoor one-way permutations and multivariate polynomials. In: Han, Y., Okamoto, T., Qing, S. (eds.) ICICS 1997. LNCS, vol. 1334, pp. 356–368. Springer, Heidelberg (1997). https://doi.org/10.1007/BFb0028491

31. Paterson, K.G.: Imprimitive permutation groups and trapdoors in iterated block ciphers. In: Knudsen, L. (ed.) FSE 1999. LNCS, vol. 1636, pp. 201–214. Springer, Heidelberg (1999). https://doi.org/10.1007/3-540-48519-8_15

32. Perrin, L.: Partitions in the S-Box of Streebog and Kuznyechik. IACR Trans. Symm. Cryptol. **2019**(1), 302–329 (2019)

33. Rasoolzadeh, S., Ahmadian, Z., Salmasizadeh, M., Aref, M.R.: Total break of Zorro using linear and differential attacks. Cryptology ePrint Archive, Report 2014/220 (2014). http://eprint.iacr.org/2014/220

34. Rechberger, C., Soleimany, H., Tiessen, T.: Cryptanalysis of low-data instances of full LowMCv2. IACR Trans. Symm. Cryptol. **2018**(3), 163–181 (2018)

35. Rijmen, V., Preneel, B.: A family of trapdoor ciphers. In: Biham, E. (ed.) FSE 1997. LNCS, vol. 1267, pp. 139–148. Springer, Heidelberg (1997). https://doi.org/10.1007/BFb0052342

36. Shishkin, V., Dygin, D., Lavrikov, I., Marshalko, G., Rudskoy, V., Trifonov, D.: Low-weight and hi-end: draft Russian encryption standard. CTCrypt **14**, 05–06 (2014)

37. Shumow, D., Ferguson, N.: On the possibility of a back door in the NIST SP800-90 Dual Ec Prng. In: Proceedings of Cryptology, vol. 7 (2007)

38. Wang, Y., Wu, W., Guo, Z., Yu, X.: Differential cryptanalysis and linear distinguisher of full-round Zorro. Cryptology ePrint Archive, Report 2013/775 (2013). http://eprint.iacr.org/2013/775

39. Wu, H., Bao, F., Deng, R.H., Ye, Q.-Z.: Cryptanalysis of Rijmen-Preneel trapdoor ciphers. In: Ohta, K., Pei, D. (eds.) ASIACRYPT 1998. LNCS, vol. 1514, pp. 126–132. Springer, Heidelberg (1998). https://doi.org/10.1007/3-540-49649-1_11

40. Ye, D.-F., Lam, K.-Y., Dai, Z.-D.: Cryptanalysis of "2 R" schemes. In: Wiener, M. (ed.) CRYPTO 1999. LNCS, vol. 1666, pp. 315–325. Springer, Heidelberg (1999). https://doi.org/10.1007/3-540-48405-1_20

41. Young, A., Yung, M.: The dark side of "Black-Box" cryptography or: should we trust capstone? In: Koblitz, N. (ed.) CRYPTO 1996. LNCS, vol. 1109, pp. 89–103. Springer, Heidelberg (1996). https://doi.org/10.1007/3-540-68697-5_8

42. Young, A., Yung, M.: Monkey: black-box symmetric ciphers designed for MONop-olizing KEYs. In: Vaudenay, S. (ed.) FSE 1998. LNCS, vol. 1372, pp. 122–133. Springer, Heidelberg (1998). https://doi.org/10.1007/3-540-69710-1_9

43. Young, A., Yung, M.: A subliminal channel in secret block ciphers. In: Handschuh, H., Hasan, M.A. (eds.) SAC 2004. LNCS, vol. 3357, pp. 198–211. Springer, Heidelberg (2004). https://doi.org/10.1007/978-3-540-30564-4_14

44. Young, A., Yung, M.: Malicious Cryptography: Exposing Cryptovirology. Wiley, New York (2004)

45. Young, A.L., Yung, M.: Backdoor attacks on black-box ciphers exploiting low-entropy plaintexts. In: Safavi-Naini, R., Seberry, J. (eds.) ACISP 2003. LNCS, vol. 2727, pp. 297–311. Springer, Heidelberg (2003). https://doi.org/10.1007/3-540-45067-X_26

Cryptanalysis of the Lifted Unbalanced Oil Vinegar Signature Scheme

Jintai Ding$^{(\boxtimes)}$, Joshua Deaton, Kurt Schmidt, Vishakha, and Zheng Zhang

University of Cincinnati, Cincinnati, OH, USA
jintai.ding@gmail.com,
{deatonju,schmidku,sharmav4,zhang2zh}@mail.uc.edu

Abstract. In 2017, Ward Beullens *et al.* submitted Lifted Unbalanced Oil and Vinegar (LUOV) [4], a signature scheme based on the famous multivariate public key cryptosystem (MPKC) called Unbalanced Oil and Vinegar (UOV), to NIST for the competition for post-quantum public key scheme standardization. The defining feature of LUOV is that, though the public key $\mathscr{P}$ works in the extension field of degree r of $\mathbb{F}_2$, the coefficients of $\mathscr{P}$ come from $\mathbb{F}_2$. This is done to significantly reduce the size of $\mathscr{P}$. The LUOV scheme is now in the second round of the NIST PQC standardization process.

In this paper we introduce a new attack on LUOV. It exploits the "lifted" structure of LUOV to reduce direct attacks on it to those over a subfield. We show that this reduces the complexity below the targeted security for the NIST post-quantum standardization competition.

1 Introduction

1.1 Background and Post-quantum Cryptography Standardization

A crucial building block for any free, secure, and *digital* society is the ability to authenticate digital messages. In their seminal 1976 paper [40], Whitfield Diffie and Martin Hellman described the mathematical framework to do such, which is now called a digital signature scheme. They proposed the existence of a function F so that for any given message D any party can easily check whether for any X that $F(X) = D$, *i.e.* verify a signature. However, only one party, who has a secret key, can find such an X, *i.e.* sign a document. Such a function F is called a trapdoor function. Following this idea, Rivest, Shamir, and Adleman proposed the first proof of concept of a signature scheme based on their now famous RSA public key encryption scheme, which relies on the difficulty of integer factorization [38].

Up to 2013, the National Institute of Standards and Technology (NIST)'s guidelines allowed for three different types of signature schemes: the Digital Signature Algorithm (DSA), RSA Digital Signature Algorithm, and The Elliptic Curve Digital Signature Algorithm [25]. However, a major drawback to these signature schemes is that in 1999 Peter Shor showed that they were weak to a sufficiently powerful quantum computer [39]. As research towards developing a

© International Association for Cryptologic Research 2020
D. Micciancio and T. Ristenpart (Eds.): CRYPTO 2020, LNCS 12172, pp. 279–298, 2020.
https://doi.org/10.1007/978-3-030-56877-1_10

fully fledged quantum computer continues, it has become increasingly clear that there is a significant need to prepare our current communication infrastructure for a post-quantum world. For it is not easy nor quick undergoing to transition our current infrastructure into a post quantum one. Thus, a significant effort will be required in order to develop, standardize, and deploy new post-quantum signature schemes.

As such in December 2016, NIST, under the direction of the NSA, put out a call for proposals of new post-quantum cryptosystems. NIST expects to perform multiple rounds of evaluations over a period of three to five years. The goal of this process is to select a number of acceptable candidate cryptosystems for standardization. These new standards will be used as quantum resistant counterparts to existing standards. The evaluation will be based on the following three criteria: Security, Cost, and Algorithm and Implementation Characteristics. We are currently in the second round of this process, and out of the original twenty-three signature schemes there are only nine left. LUOV is one of these remaining.

An additional complication to designing a post-quantum cryptosystem is quantifying security levels in a post quantum world for the exact capabilities of a quantum computer is not fully understood. In [34], NIST addresses this issue and quantifies the security strength of a given cryptosystem by comparing it to existing NIST standards in symmetric cryptography, which NIST expects to offer significant resistance to quantum cryptanalysis. Below are the relevant NIST security strength categories which we present the log base 2 of the complexity (Table 1).

Table 1. Description of different NIST security strength categories.

NIST Level	Security Description	Complexity
II	At least as hard to break as SHA256 (collision search)	146
IV	At least as hard to break as SHA384 (collision search)	210
V	At least as hard to break as AES256 (exhaustive key search)	272

1.2 Multivariate Public Key Cryptosystems

Since the work of Diffie and Hellman, mathematicians have found many other groups of cryptosystems that do not rely on Number Theory based problems. Some of these seem to be good candidates for a post-quantum system. One such group is Multivariate Public Key Cryptosystems (MPKC) [12,15]. The security of MPKC depends on the difficulty of solving a system of m multivariate polynomials in n variables over a finite field. Usually these polynomials are of degree two. Solving a set of random multivariate polynomial equations over a finite field is proven to be an NP-hard problem [27], thus lending a solid foundation for a post-quantum signature scheme. Furthermore, MPKCs in general can be computationally much more efficient than many other systems. However, as these systems need to be made into a trapdoor function they cannot be truly random.

They must be of a special form, which is generally hidden by composition with invertible linear maps. The difficulty lies in creating a hidden structure which does not impact the difficulty of solving the system.

A breakthrough in MPKC was proposed by Matsumoto and Imai in 1988 which is called either the MI cryptosystem or C^* [30]. They worked with a finite field k, but they did not work with the vector space k^n directly. Instead, they looked to a degree n extension of k where an inverse map can be constructed which is still a trapdoor function. As such this can be used to both encrypt and sign documents. This scheme was broken by Patarin using the Linearization Equation Attack which is the inspiration for all Oil and Vinegar Schemes [35]. To be brief, Patarin discovered that plain-text/cipher-text pairs $(\mathbf{x}, \mathbf{y})$ will satisfy equations (called the linearization equations) of the form

$$\sum \alpha_{ij} x_i y_j + \sum \beta_i x_i + \sum \gamma_i y_i + \delta = 0$$

Collecting enough such pairs and plugging them into above equations produces linear equations in the α_{ij}'s, β_i's, γ_i's, and δ which then can be solved for. Then for any cipher-text $\mathbf{y}$, its corresponding plain-text $\mathbf{x}$ will satisfy the linear equations found by plugging in $\mathbf{y}$ into the linearization equations. This will either solve for the $\mathbf{x}$ directly if enough linear equations were found or at least massively increase the efficiency of other direct attacks of solving for $\mathbf{x}$. Inspired by the attack, Patarin introduced the Oil and Vinegar scheme [36]. This has been one of the most studied schemes for multivariate cryptography.

1.3   A Brief Sketch and History of Oil and Vinegar Schemes

One of the most well known multivariate public key signature schemes is the Oil and Vinegar scheme. The key idea of the Oil and Vinegar signature scheme is to reduce signing a document into solving a linear system. This is done by separating the variables into two collections, the vinegar variables and the oil variables. Let $\mathbb{F}$ be a (generally small) finite field, o and v be two integers, and $n = o + v$. The central map $\mathscr{F} : \mathbb{F}^n \to \mathbb{F}^o$ is a quadratic map whose components $f_1, \ldots, f_o$ are in the form

$$f_k(\mathbf{x}) = \sum_{i=1}^{v} \sum_{j=i}^{n} \alpha_{i,j,k} x_i x_j + \sum_{i=1}^{n} \beta_{i,k} x_i + \gamma_k$$

where each coefficient is in $\mathbb{F}$. Here, $x_1, \ldots, x_v$ (which are called the vinegar variables) are potentially multiplied to all the other variables including themselves. However, the variables $x_{v+1}, \ldots, x_n$ (which are called the oil variables) are never multiplied to one another. Hence, if one guesses for all the vinegar variables, one is left with a system of o linear polynomials in o variables. This has a high probability of being invertible, and if it is not one can just take another guess for the vinegar variables. Hence to find pre-images for $\mathscr{F}$, one repeatedly guesses values for the vinegar variables until the resulting linear system is invertible. The public key $\mathscr{P}$ is the composition of $\mathscr{F}$ with an invertible affine map $\mathscr{T} : \mathbb{F}^n \to \mathbb{F}^n$.

$$\mathscr{P} = \mathscr{F} \circ \mathscr{T}.$$

The private key pair is $(\mathscr{F}, \mathscr{T})$. To find a signature for a message $\mathbf{y}$, one first finds an element z in $\mathscr{F}^{-1}(y)$, and then simply computes a signature by finding $\mathscr{T}^{-1}(z)$.

The security of Oil and Vinegar schemes relies on the fact that $\mathscr{P}$ is essentially as hard to find pre-images for as a random system (when one does not know the decomposition).

Patarin originally proposed that the number of oil variables would equal the number of vinegar variables. Hence the original scheme is now called Balanced Oil and Vinegar. However, Balanced Oil Vinegar was broken by Kipnis and Shamir using the method of invariant subspaces [28]. This attack, however, is thwarted by making the number of vinegar variables sufficiently greater then the number of oil variables. The other major attack using the structure of UOV is the Oil and Vinegar Reconciliation attack proposed by Ding *et al.* However, with appropriate parameters this attack can be avoided as well [18].

Proposed nearly twenty years ago, the Unbalanced Oil and Vinegar (UOV) scheme still remains unbroken. Further, this simple and elegant signature scheme boasts small signatures and fast signing times. Arguably, the only drawback to UOV is its rather large public key size. The work of Petzoldt mitigates this by generating the pair $((\mathscr{F}, \mathscr{T}), \mathscr{P})$ from a portion of the public key's Macaulay matrix and the map $\mathscr{T}$. By choosing this portion to be easy to store, *i.e.* if it is a cyclic matrix or generated from a pseudo-random number generator, the public key's bit size can be much reduced [37].

A large number of modern schemes are modifications to UOV that are designed to increase efficiency. This is in general hard to do as can be seen from the singularity attack by Ding *et al.* on HIMQ-3, which takes a large amount of its core design from UOV [19]. Out of the nine signature schemes that were accepted to round two of the NIST standardization program, two (LUOV and Rainbow) are based on UOV. Rainbow, originally proposed in 2005, reduces its keysize by forming multiple layers of UOV schemes, where oil variables in a higher layer become vinegar variables in the lower layers [16,18]. LUOV achieved a reduction in key size by forcing all the coefficients of the public key to either be 0 or 1. In this paper, we will show that such modifications used by LUOV allow for algebraic manipulations that result in an under-determined quadratic system over a much smaller finite field. We will further show that Rainbow and other UOV schemes are immune to such attacks.

1.4 Lifted Unbalanced Oil Vinegar Scheme (LUOV)

The LUOV scheme, as clear from its name, is a modification of the original UOV scheme. Its design was first proposed by Beullens *et al.* in [4]. The core design of LUOV is as follows:

Let $\mathbb{F}_{2^r}$ be a degree r extension of $\mathbb{F}_2$. Let o and v be two positive integers such that $o < v$ and $n = o + v$. The central map $\mathcal{F} : \mathbb{F}_{2^r}^n \to \mathbb{F}_{2^r}^o$ is a quadratic map whose components $f_1, \ldots, f_o$ are in the form:

$$f_k(\mathbf{x}) = \sum_{i=1}^{v} \sum_{j=i}^{n} \alpha_{i,j,k} x_i x_j + \sum_{i=1}^{n} \beta_{i,k} x_i + \gamma_k,$$

where the coefficients $\alpha_{i,j,k}'s$, $\beta_{i,k}'s$ and γ_k's are chosen randomly from the base field $\mathbb{F}_2$. As in standard UOV, To hide the Oil and Vinegar structure of these polynomials an invertible linear map $\mathcal{T} : \mathbb{F}_{2^r}^n \to \mathbb{F}_{2^r}^n$ is used to mix the variables. In particular, the authors of LUOV choose $\mathcal{T}$ in the form:

$$\begin{bmatrix} \mathbf{1}_v & \mathbf{T} \\ \mathbf{0} & \mathbf{1}_o \end{bmatrix}$$

where $\mathbf{T}$ is a $v \times o$ matrix whose entries are from the field $\mathbb{F}_2$. The public key is $\mathcal{P} = \mathcal{F} \circ \mathcal{T}$, where $\mathcal{T}$ and $\mathcal{F}$ are the private keys.

This choice of $\mathcal{T}$, first proposed by Czypek [10], speeds up the key generation and signing process as well as decreases storage requirements. This specific choice of $\mathcal{T}$ does not affect the security of the scheme in comparison to standard UOV due to the fact that for any UOV private key $(\mathcal{F}, \mathcal{T})$ key, there exists a with high probability an equivalent key $(\mathcal{F}', \mathcal{T}')$ such that $\mathcal{T}'$ is in the form chosen by above [42].

The third major modification is the use of the Petzoldt's aforementioned technique to use a pseudo-random number generator to generate both the private key and the public key. This modified key generation algorithm still produces the same distribution of key pairs, and thus the security of the scheme remains unaffected by this modification (assuming that the output of the PRNG is indistinguishable from true randomness). The keys, both public and private, are never directly stored. Each time are wishes to either generate or verify a signature, they are generated from the PRNG.

For the purpose of this paper, much of the details of LUOV are not important. In fact, we will ignore essentially most of the specified structure and focus purely on the "lifted" aspect of the design.

1.5   Our Contributions

We will present a new attack method called the Subfield Differential Attack (SDA). This attack does not rely on the Oil and Vinegar structure of LUOV but merely that the coefficients of the quadratic terms are contained in a small subfield. We will show that the attack will make it impossible for LUOV, as originally presented in the second round of the NIST competition, to fulfill NIST's security level requirements.

For public key $\mathcal{P} : \mathbb{F}_{2^r}^n \to \mathbb{F}_{2^r}^o$, we assert that with extremely high probability that for a randomly chosen $\mathbf{x}' \in \mathbb{F}_{2^r}^n$ and $\mathbf{y} \in \mathbb{F}_{2^r}^o$ there exists $\bar{\mathbf{x}} \in \mathbb{F}_{2^d}^n$ such that $\mathcal{P}(\mathbf{x}' + \bar{\mathbf{x}}) = \mathbf{y}$, where $\mathbb{F}_{2^d}$ is a subfield of $\mathbb{F}_{2^r}$. By the fact that the coefficients of

$\mathscr{P}$ are either 0 or 1 and by viewing $\overline{\mathscr{P}}(\bar{\mathbf{x}}) = \mathscr{P}(\mathbf{x}' + \bar{\mathbf{x}})$ as a system of equations over the smaller field $\mathbb{F}_{2^d}$, we will reduce the forging a signature to solving an under-determined quadratic system over $\mathbb{F}_{2^d}$. The complexity required for such is well under our target. For each proposed set of parameters, we will explicitly apply our attack. We will provide a small toy example. We will explain how UOV and Rainbow are unaffected by our attack. Finally, we will discuss the new parameter sets that LUOV uses in response to SDA.

2   The Subfield Differential Attack on LUOV

2.1   Transforming a LUOV Public by a Differential

The key idea of the attack is to transform the public key, $\mathscr{P}$, into a map over a subfield which is more efficient to work over but still contains a signature for a given message. Namely, maps of the form $\overline{\mathscr{P}} : \mathbb{F}_{2^d}^n \to \mathbb{F}_{2^r}^o$ defined by

$$\overline{\mathscr{P}}(\bar{\mathbf{x}}) = \mathscr{P}(\mathbf{x}' + \bar{\mathbf{x}})$$

where $\mathbf{x}'$ is a random point $\mathbb{F}_{2^r}^n$. We note that for any irreducible polynomial $g(t)$ of degree $r/d = s$,

$$\mathbb{F}_{2^d}[t]/(g(t)) \cong \mathbb{F}_{2^r}.$$

Henceforth, we will represent $\mathbb{F}_{2^r}$ by this quotient ring. Here, $\mathbb{F}_{2^d}$ is embedded as the set of constant polynomials. For more details see [29].

Consider a LUOV public key $\mathscr{P} = \mathscr{F} \circ \mathscr{T} : \mathbb{F}_{2^r}^n \to \mathbb{F}_{2^r}^o$. Then following the construction of all Oil Vinegar Schemes, $\mathscr{P}$ appears to be a random quadratic system except that all the coefficients are either 0 or 1.

$$\mathscr{P}(\mathbf{x}) = \begin{cases} \tilde{f}_1(\mathbf{x}) = \sum_{i=1}^{n}\sum_{j=i}^{n} \alpha_{i,j,1} x_i x_j + \sum_{i=1}^{n} \beta_{i,1} x_i + \gamma_1 \\ \tilde{f}_2(\mathbf{x}) = \sum_{i=1}^{n}\sum_{j=i}^{n} \alpha_{i,j,2} x_i x_j + \sum_{i=1}^{n} \beta_{i,2} x_i + \gamma_2 \\ \quad\quad\quad \vdots \\ \tilde{f}_o(\mathbf{x}) = \sum_{i=1}^{n}\sum_{j=i}^{n} \alpha_{i,j,o} x_i x_j + \sum_{i=1}^{n} \beta_{i,o} x_i + \gamma_o. \end{cases}$$

Randomly chose $\mathbf{x}' \in \mathbb{F}_{2^r}^n$ and define $\overline{\mathscr{P}}(\bar{\mathbf{x}}) = \mathscr{P}(\mathbf{x}' + \bar{\mathbf{x}})$. We see that the kth component of $\overline{\mathscr{P}}$ is of the form:

$$\tilde{f}_k(\mathbf{x}' + \bar{\mathbf{x}}) = \sum_{i=1}^{n}\sum_{j=i}^{n} \alpha_{i,j,k}(x_i' + \bar{x}_i)(x_j' + \bar{x}_j) + \sum_{i=1}^{n} \beta_{i,k}(x_i' + \bar{x}_i) + \gamma_k.$$

Expanding the above and separating the quadratic terms leads to

$$\tilde{f}_k(\mathbf{x}' + \bar{\mathbf{x}}) = \sum_{i=1}^{n} \sum_{j=i}^{n} \alpha_{i,j,k}(x_i'x_j' + x_i'\bar{x}_i + x_j'\bar{x}_j) + \sum_{i=1}^{n} \beta_{i,k}(x_i' + \bar{x}_i) + \gamma_k$$
$$+ \sum_{i=1}^{n} \sum_{j=i}^{n} \alpha_{i,j,k}\bar{x}_i\bar{x}_j.$$

On one hand, the coefficients of the quadratic terms in the variables $\bar{\mathbf{x}} = (\bar{x}_1, \ldots, \bar{x}_n)$ are still contained in $\mathbb{F}_2$. On the other hand, the x_i' are arbitrary elements of $\mathbb{F}_{2^r}$, and so the linear terms will have coefficients containing all the powers of t. We can thus regroup the above equation in terms of the powers of t, where the quadratic part is confined in the constant term. Meaning, for some linear polynomials $L_{i,k}(\bar{x}_1, \ldots, \bar{x}_n) \in \mathbb{F}_{2^d}[\bar{x}_1, \ldots, \bar{x}_n]$, and quadratic polynomials $Q_k(\bar{x}_1, \ldots, \bar{x}_n) \in \mathbb{F}_{2^d}[\bar{x}_1, \ldots, \bar{x}_n]$, we have that

$$\tilde{f}_k(\mathbf{x}' + \bar{\mathbf{x}}) = \sum_{i=1}^{s-1} L_{i,k}(\bar{x}_1, \ldots, \bar{x}_n)t^i + Q_k(\bar{x}_1, \ldots, \bar{x}_n).$$

2.2 Forging a Signature

Now suppose we want to forge a signature for a message $\mathbf{y} \in \mathbb{F}_{2^r}^o$ where $\mathbf{y} = (y_1, \ldots, y_m)$. Here $y_k = \sum_{i=0}^{s-1} w_{i,k}t^i$ where each $w_{i,k} \in \mathbb{F}_{2^d}$. We will achieve this by solving the system of equations

$$\overline{\mathscr{P}}(\bar{\mathbf{x}}) = \mathbf{y}.$$

This is solving the set of $(s-1)o$ linear equations

$$A = \left\{ L_{i,k}(\bar{x}_1, \ldots, \bar{x}_n) = w_{i,k} : 1 \leq i \leq s-1, 1 \leq k \leq o \right\}$$

and the set of o quadratic equations

$$B = \left\{ Q_k(\bar{x}_1, \ldots, \bar{x}_n) = w_{0,k} : 1 \leq k \leq o \right\}.$$

As A is a random system of linear equations, it has high probability to have rank $(s-1)o$ (or dimension n if $(s-1)o \geq n$). Let S be the solutions space to A. By the Rank Nullity Theorem, the dimension of S is $n - (s-1)o$. We see that our problem thus reduces to solving B over S. That is o quadratic equations in $n - (s-1)o$ variables over the subfield $\mathbb{F}_{2^d}$. Once we find a solution for $\bar{\mathbf{x}}$, the signature is then $\mathbf{x}' + \bar{\mathbf{x}}$ as

$$\mathscr{P}(\mathbf{x}' + \bar{\mathbf{x}}) = \overline{\mathscr{P}}(\bar{\mathbf{x}}) = \mathbf{y}.$$

2.3   The Choice of the Intermediate Field

Now that we know the method of the attack, we need to find the intermediate fields that ensures that $\overline{\mathscr{P}}(\bar{\mathbf{x}}) = \mathbf{y}$ has at least one solution. We wish to compute the probability that, when we define the map $\overline{\mathscr{P}} : \mathbb{F}_{2^d}^n \to \mathbb{F}_{2^r}^o$ as in the prior section, that $\overline{\mathscr{P}}^{-1}(\mathbf{y})$ is nonempty. We will achieve this by heuristically arguing that the quadratic map $\overline{\mathscr{P}}$ acts as a random map. So, we derive the following short lemma:

Lemma 1. *Let A and B be two finite sets and $\mathscr{Q} : A \to B$ be a random map. For each $b \in B$, the probability that $\mathscr{Q}^{-1}(b)$ is non-empty is approximately $1 - e^{-|A|/|B|}$.*

Proof. As the output of each element of A is independent, it is elementary that the probability for there to be at least one $a \in A$ such that $\mathscr{Q}(a) = b$ is

$$1 - \Pr(\mathscr{Q}(\alpha) \neq b, \forall \alpha \in A) = 1 - \prod_{\alpha \in A} \Pr(\mathscr{Q}(\alpha) \neq b) = 1 - \left(1 - \frac{1}{|B|}\right)^{|A|} = 1 - \left(1 - \frac{1}{|B|}\right)^{|B|\frac{|A|}{|B|}}.$$

Using $\lim_{n \to \infty} \left(1 - \frac{1}{n}\right)^n = e^{-1}$, we achieve the desired result.

As a result of this lemma, the probability that $\overline{\mathscr{P}}^{-1}(\mathbf{y})$ is non-empty is approximately $1 - e^{-2^{(dn)-(ro)}}$.

By far the largest cost in the attack is solving the final quadratic system over $\mathbb{F}_{2^d}$. The smaller the d is, the more efficient the cost is. So, we will minimize our choice of d such that the probability of finding a signature is high given our above estimate.

In Tables 6 and 3, we calculate the probability of success on the first guess for $\mathbf{x}'$ for the parameters as originally given for round 2 LUOV (the authors have since changed their parameters due to SDA) [3]. In the astronomically unlikely event that there is no signature, a different guess for $\mathbf{x}'$ can be used. Table 6 is given on parameters designed to reduce the size of signatures. These parameters are used in situations where many signatures are needed. Table 3 is given on parameters designed to reduce the cost of both signatures and public keys. These parameters are used when communicating both signatures and public keys is needed (Table 2).

Table 2. Estimated Probabilities of Success for Parameters Designed to Minimize the Size of the Signature

NIST Security Level	r	o	v	n	d	Probability of Success
II	8	58	237	295	2	$1 - \exp(-2^{126})$
IV	8	82	323	405	2	$1 - \exp(-2^{154})$
V	8	107	371	478	2	$1 - \exp(-2^{100})$

Table 3. Estimated Probabilities of Success for Parameters Designed to Minimize the Size of the Signature and Public Key

NIST Security Level	r	o	v	n	d	Probability of Success
II	48	43	222	265	8	$1 - \exp(-2^{56})$
IV	64	61	302	363	16	$1 - \exp(-2^{1904})$
V	80	76	363	439	16	$1 - \exp(-2^{944})$

3   Complexity of the Attack

While there is some slight overhead cost in computing $\overline{\mathscr{P}}(\overline{\mathbf{x}})$ and solving the linear system, the vast majority of the complexity is solving the quadratic system of $n - (s - 1)o$ variables and o equations over $\mathbb{F}_{2^d}$. Hence, to evaluate the effectiveness of our attack we will compute the complexity of finding a single solution to this quadratic system, which we will measure with the number of field multiplications. As this is a underdetermined system, the most effective strategy is first to use the method of Thomae and Wolf [41] to transform it by a linear change of variables to a determined system with fewer equations than before.

3.1   Statement and Results of Thomae and Wolf

Theorem 1 (Thomae and Wolf). *By a linear change of variables, the complexity of solving an underdetermined quadratic system of m equations and $n = \omega m$ variables can be reduced to solving a determined quadratic system of $m - \lfloor \omega \rfloor + 1$ equations. Further, if $\lfloor \omega \rfloor | m$ then the complexity can be further reduced to solving a determined quadratic system of $m - \lfloor \omega \rfloor$ equations.*

We calculate what these new determined systems will be in Table 4 for the various parameter sets representing each system as (number of variables) × (number of equations). The complexity will depend on direct methods of solving these systems of equations.

Table 4. Determined Systems to Solve after Thomae and Wolf

Table and Security	Finite Field	Original System	New System
(2, II)	$\mathbb{F}_{2^2}$	58×121	56×56
(2, IV)	$\mathbb{F}_{2^2}$	82×159	81×81
(2, V)	$\mathbb{F}_{2^2}$	107×157	106×106
(3, II)	$\mathbb{F}_{2^8}$	43×50	42×42
(3, IV)	$\mathbb{F}_{2^{16}}$	61×180	60×60
(3, V)	$\mathbb{F}_{2^{16}}$	76×135	75×75

3.2 Solving the Determined Systems

To find a solution to one of these determined systems, the best method is to use what is called the hybrid approach [1,2] which involves repeatedly fixing some of the values of the variables and then performing a direct attack on the new overdetermined system until a solution is found. The amount of variables guessed for depends on the algorithm and the finite field involved with a smaller finite field leading to more variables being guessed for.

The two main contenders for the best algorithm to use are one of the family of XL (eXtended Linearization) algorithms proposed by Courtois *et al.* [9] and either the F4/F5 algorithms proposed by Faugère [22,23] or algorithms developed from these two. In our case both will give comparable results though we will follow the work of Yet *et al.* [45] and favor the former using Wiedemann XL, the reason why we will explain shortly.

Let us give a brief description of the XL algorithm which, for simplicity, we will give for the case of quadratic systems. Let $\mathscr{P} : \mathbb{F}_q^n \to \mathbb{F}_q^m$ by a given quadratic system we want to solve where $\mathscr{P} = (p_1, \ldots, p_m)$. As in our case we will be working with overdetermined systems, we can assume that there will be at most one solution as can be justified by Lemma 1. We will denote a monomial $x_1^{b_1} x_2^{b_2} \cdots x_n^{b_n}$ by $\mathbf{x}^{\mathbf{b}}$ where $\mathbf{b} = (b_1, \ldots, b_n)$ and $|\mathbf{b}| = b_1 + b_2 + \cdots + b_n$. For a given natural number D, let us denote by $T^{(D)} = \{\mathbf{x}^{\mathbf{b}} : |\mathbf{b}| \leq D\}$ the set of all degree D or lower monomials. We note that $|T^{(D)}| = \binom{n+D}{D}$ as was shown in [9] but as we only seek a solution in the field $\mathbb{F}_q$ we can reduce this by equating $x_i^q = x_i$ leading to

$$|T^{(D)}| = [t^D] \frac{(1 - t^q)^n}{(1 - t)^{n+1}}$$

where $[t^D]g(t)$ is the coefficient of t^D in the series expansion $g(t)$ [44].

One begins by extending $\mathscr{P}$ to the set of relations $R^{(D)} = \{\mathbf{x}^{\mathbf{b}} p_i(\mathbf{x}) = 0 : 1 \leq i \leq m, \mathbf{x}^{\mathbf{b}} \in T^{(D-2)}\}$. Let us denote by $M^{(D)}$ the Macaulay matrix for $R^{(D)}$. One performs linear algebra techniques to attempt to solve $M^{(D)}$, and provided D is large enough one will either find a solution, a univariate polynomial for one of the variables which then can be solved for, or a contradiction. Obviously, the smallest such D will allow the lowest complexity in working with $M^{(D)}$ as the size of $M^{(D)}$ depends on D. We will denote this by D_0 which is called the operating degree of XL. Yeh *et al.* [45] stated that for random quadratic systems (which UOV systems behave like) over small fields (when the operating degree is larger than the size of the field) we will have

$$D_0 = \min \left\{ d : [t^d] \frac{(1 - t^q)^n (1 - t^2)^m}{(1 - t)^{n+1} (1 - t^{2q})^m} \leq 0 \right\}.$$

For larger fields we will instead have

$$D_0 = \min \left\{ d : [t^d](1 - t)^{m-n-1}(1 + t)^m < 0 \right\}.$$

The Macaulay matrix $M^{(D_0)}$ is a sparse matrix with total weight approximately equal to $|R^{(D_0)}|n^2/2$. This is one of the advantages of using XL as it allows one to solve the linear system by using the (block) Wiedemann matrix solver [8] in approximately $\frac{3}{2}|R^{(D_0)}||T^{(D_0)}|n^2$ field multiplications. By randomly discarding rows (most of of which are nonessential for solving the system) until there are $|T^{(D_0)}|$ left the number of field multiplications becomes $\frac{3}{2}|T^{(D_0)}|^2 n^2$ [43]. As $|T^{(D_0)}| \leq \binom{n+D_0}{D_0}$ and $\frac{n^2}{2} \approx \binom{n}{2}$ we can estimate this as $3 \times \binom{n+D_0}{D_0} \times \binom{n}{2}$.

Returning our focus to the determined systems we are dealing with in attacking LUOV, if we denote the number of variables we are guessing for as k and $D_0^{(k)}$ as the calculated operating degree after guessing for those variables, we have the following theorem with the additional factor of q^k accounting for the necessary repeated attempts due to the potential of incorrect guessing.

Theorem 2. *The complexity in terms of field multiplications of performing the XL algorithm on a determined quadratic system of m equations over a finite field of size q is*

$$Complexity_{XL} = min_k \left\{ q^k \times 3 \times \binom{m-k+D_0^{(k)}}{D_0^{(k)}}^2 \times \binom{m-k}{2} \right\}.$$

While there are other, more sophisticated, versions of XL like mutant XL and its sub-variants [11,31–33] that can also perform well in certain situations, the Wiedemann algorithm offers parallel compatibility and cheaper memory cost [7] that, along with its computation time, makes Wiedemann XL better than the other variants of XL for our case. It is for this same reason that we prefer Wiedemann XL over F4 and F5.

Now let us briefly describe our reasoning for preferring Wiedemann XL to either F4 or F5 in estimating the complexity of the attack. F4 [22] is an improvement of Buchberger's algorithm [6] for generating a Groebner for the ideal generated by the quadratic system $\mathscr{P}$. F4 also works with linear algebra techniques with a Macaulay matrix which allows it to do reduction steps in parallel to compute normal forms, eventually generating a Groebner basis. Thus its complexity will be determined the largest size of the matrix involved and the linear algebra cost in working with that matrix.

The size of the matrix will be determined by what is called the degree of regularity which is the degree at which the first non-trivial relation from the original polynomials $p_1, \cdots, p_m$ occurs. The trivial relations are $p_i^h p_j^h - p_j^h p_i^h = 0$ and $p_i^q - p_i = 0$. All others are nontrivial. We will denote this by D_{reg}. As F4 will have to deal with polynomial of degree D_{reg} [14], the size of the matrix will be roughly $|T^{(D_{reg})}| = \binom{n+D_{reg}}{D_{reg}}$ rows and columns.

The F5 algorithm [23] is an improvement on the F4 algorithm in that it too uses linear algebra techniques to construct a Groebner for the quadratic system. With the use of what Faugère calls signatures of the polynomials one can perform fewer reduction steps than F4. This is because some of the row reductions in F4 represent reductions to 0 meaning they are essentially useless in constructing the Groebner basis. The F5 algorithm uses the signatures to know beforehand not do these reductions. We note that we cannot find independent implementation of the F5 algorithm which meets the originally claimed levels of efficiency, and that the original "proof" of the termination of F5 was flawed. It was not until 2012 when Galkin [24] proved the termination (in fact in a more general case than originally proposed). There has been much research conducted on F5 inspired signature-based Groebner algorithms [21]. However, these improvements (some of which were not based on complexity at all but the issue of termination) are not large enough to overcome the largest determining factor in their complexity: the size of the Macaulay matrix involved. As the degree of regularity for F5 and F4 are the same D_{reg} [45], the matrix that F5 and F5 inspired algorithms will be working with is essentially the same size as F4 but having fewer rows due to the use of signatures.

The complexity for F4/F5 will then be approximately $\binom{n+D_{reg}}{D_{reg}}^{\omega}$ where $2 \leq \omega \leq 3$ is the complexity exponent of matrix multiplication. ω is likely to be about $\log_2(7) \approx 2.8$ though may be as low as 2.3727 [45]. We note that there has been work on improving the linear algebra cost involved in Groebner basis calculations due to the special shape of the matrices involved such as the GBLA library [5]. However, due to the fact that the matrix involved in XL is more sparse than that in F4 or F5 [45], the linear algebra for F4/F5 is more costly than that for Wiedemann XL and the memory size is greater for F4/F5 as well provided the size of the matrices are relatively close which happens when D_0 is very close to D_{reg} [45]. It is known that $D_{reg} \leq D_0$ so there will be fewer rows needed to work with when using F4 or F5. Further, for certain polynomial systems with specific (even if hidden) structure like HFE and its variants, D_{reg} may be much smaller for which there is much research [13,14,17,20,26]. In these cases, an F4/F5 type algorithm is the best to use. However, Yeh $et\ al.$ [45] has shown that for random overdetermined systems, like the ones we are attacking after we fix some variables, $D_0 - D_{reg}$ is most often ≤ 1 and in many cases 0. They give D_{reg} for quadratic systems over small fields as

$$D_{reg} = \min\left\{d : [t^d]\frac{(1-t^q)^n(1-t^2)^m}{(1-t)^n(1-t^{2q})^m} < 0\right\}$$

and for larger fields

$$D_{reg} = \min\left\{d : [t^d](1-t)^{m-n}(1+t)^m < 0\right\}.$$

As an example Fig. 1 shows both D_0 and D_{reg} after the different choices of variables to fix for the system of 56 variables and 56 equations over $\mathbb{F}_{2^2}$. We see that the difference is never more than 1 and often is 0. Thus we will use Theorem 2's estimate for the complexity of the attack using Wiedemann XL.

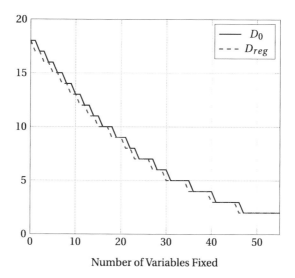

Fig. 1. D_0 and D_{reg} for the system with 56-k Variables and 56 Equations over $\mathbb{F}_{2^2}$

3.3   Calculating the Complexity

As an example, let's estimate the complexity of forging a signature for a LUOV public key with parameters $r = 8, o = 58, v = 237$ using Wiedemann XL. We need only to focus on solving the quadratic over the intermediate field as additional overhead is very small. As mentioned before, the optimal choice for the intermediate field is $\mathbb{F}_{2^2}$. The resulting quadratic system over this smaller field has $o = 58$ equations and $n - (s - 1)o = 121$ variables. As $\lfloor 121/58 \rfloor = 2$ which divides 58, we can use the stronger version of Theorem 1. So, the complexity is reduced to solving a determined system of $58 - 2 = 56$ equations.

We search through the complexities of the XL algorithm for the various choices of k, and we find the smallest is when $k = 31$. In this case,

$$\frac{(1 - t^q)^{m-k}(1 - t^2)^m}{(1 - t)^{m-k+1}(1 - t^{2q})^m} = 1 + 26t + 295t^2 + 1820t^3 + 5610t^4 - 1560t^5 + \cdots .$$

So the first power of t with a non-positive coefficient is t^5. Thus, $D_0^{(31)} = 5$.
Finally, we compute the complexity as

$$4^{31} \times 3 \times \binom{56 - 31 + 5}{5}^2 \times \binom{56 - 31}{2} = 842885418247230178100716240896000 \approx 2^{107}.$$

In Table 5 we compute the complexity for the various parameters found in the original round 2 submission. We round up the given log base 2 complexity. Recalling that NIST requires complexity $(2^{146}, 2^{210}, 2^{272})$ for security levels (II, IV, V) respectively, we see that LUOV fails to meet the security level requirements in all parameter sets given for their targeted security.

Table 5. Complexity in Terms of Number of Field Multiplications

Table and Security	Finite Field	Original System	New System	# of Guesses	$D_0^{(k)}$	Log_2 Complexity
(2, II)	$\mathbb{F}_{2^2}$	58×121	56×56	31	5	107
(2, IV)	$\mathbb{F}_{2^2}$	82×159	81×81	38	8	146
(2, V)	$\mathbb{F}_{2^2}$	107×157	106×106	51	9	184
(3, II)	$\mathbb{F}_{2^8}$	43×50	42×42	3	19	135
(3, IV)	$\mathbb{F}_{2^{16}}$	61×180	60×60	2	31	202
(3, V)	$\mathbb{F}_{2^{16}}$	76×135	75×75	2	38	244

The two schemes which claim to be of Level II security do not even satisfy the Level I security, which is supposed to be 2^{143}.

3.4   Toy Example

Let $o = 2$, $v = 8$, and $n = 10$. The size of the large extension field chosen by the public key generator will be $2^8 = 256$. In the attack, we will use our small field $\mathbb{F}_{2^2}$ denoting its elements by $\{0, 1, w_1, w_2\}$. We will then represent the field $\mathbb{F}_{2^8}$ by $\mathbb{F}_{2^2}[t]/f(t)$ where $f(t) = t^4 + t^2 + w_1 t + 1$.

Consider the LUOV public key $\mathscr{P} : \mathbb{F}_{2^8}^n \to \mathbb{F}_{2^8}^o$, where for simplicity sake, it will be homogeneous of degree two:

$$
\begin{aligned}
\tilde{f}_1(\mathbf{x}) =\;& x_1 x_4 + x_1 x_5 + x_1 x_6 + x_1 x_7 + x_1 x_8 + x_1 x_9 + x_2 x_4 + x_2 x_6 + x_2 x_9 + x_3^2 \\
& + x_3 x_6 + x_3 x_7 + x_3 x_{10} + x_4^2 + x_4 x_7 + x_4 x_8 + x_4 x_9 + x_4 x_{10} + x_5 x_6 + x_6 x_{10} \\
& + x_7^2 + x_7 x_8 + x_7 x_9 + x_8 x_9 + x_8 x_{10} + x_9^2 + x_9 x_{10} \\
\tilde{f}_2(\mathbf{x}) =\;& x_1 x_3 + x_1 x_4 + x_1 x_5 + x_1 x_9 + x_2 x_3 + x_2 x_6 + x_2 x_7 + x_2 x_9 + x_3^2 + x_3 x_4 \\
& + x_3 x_5 + x_3 x_6 + x_3 x_7 + x_3 x_9 + x_4^2 + x_4 x_5 + x_4 x_6 + x_4 x_7 + x_4 x_{10} + x_5^2 \\
& + x_5 x_6 + x_5 x_7 + x_5 x_8 + x_5 x_{10} + x_6 x_7 + x_7 x_9 + x_9 x_{10} + x_{10}^2
\end{aligned}
$$

We will attempt to find a signature for the message:

$$
\mathbf{y} = \begin{bmatrix} w_1 t^3 + w_2 t^2 + w_2 t \\ w_2 t^3 + w_2 t^2 + t \end{bmatrix}
$$

First, we randomly select our $\mathbf{x}'$ as

$$
\mathbf{x}' = \begin{bmatrix}
t^3 + w_2 t \\
w_1 t^3 + w_2 t^2 + w_2 t \\
t^3 + t + 1 \\
w_2 t^2 + w_1 \\
t^3 + t^2 + 1 \\
w_2 t^3 + t^2 + w_2 t + w_2 \\
w_1 t^3 + w_2 t + w \\
w_1 t^2 + w_2 t + 1 \\
t^3 + w_2 t + w_1 \\
w_2 t + w_2
\end{bmatrix}
$$

We then calculate $\mathscr{P}(\mathbf{x}' + \bar{\mathbf{x}})$ and represent it as a polynomial of t:

$$
\begin{aligned}
\tilde{f}_1(\mathbf{x}' + \bar{\mathbf{x}}) =& (\bar{x}_1 + w_1\bar{x}_2 + \bar{x}_3 + w_1\bar{x}_5 + w_2\bar{x}_6 + \bar{x}_7 + w_1\bar{x}_8 + \bar{x}_9 + w_2\bar{x}_{10})t^3 \\
&+ (\bar{x}_1 + w_1\bar{x}_2 + \bar{x}_3 + \bar{x}_4 + \bar{x}_5 + w_1\bar{x}_6 + \bar{x}_7 + w_2\bar{x}_8 + w_1\bar{x}_9)t^2 \\
&+ (w_2\bar{x}_3 + w_1\bar{x}_6 + w_1\bar{x}_7 + w_2\bar{x}_9 + w_1\bar{x}_{10})t \\
&+ Q_1(\bar{x}_1, \ldots, \bar{x}_n) \\
\tilde{f}_2(\mathbf{x}' + \bar{\mathbf{x}}) =& (\bar{x}_1 + \bar{x}_2 + w_1\bar{x}_3 + \bar{x}_5 + \bar{x}_8)t^3 \\
&+ (w_1\bar{x}_1 + \bar{x}_2 + \bar{x}_6 + \bar{x}_8 + w_2\bar{x}_9 + w_1\bar{x}_{10})t^2 \\
&+ (w_1\bar{x}_1 + w_1\bar{x}_2 + w_2\bar{x}_3 + \bar{x}_4 + w_1\bar{x}_5 + \bar{x}_6 + w_1\bar{x}_7 + \bar{x}_9 + w_2\bar{x}_{10})t \\
&+ Q_2(\bar{x}_1, \ldots, \bar{x}_n),
\end{aligned}
$$

where $Q_1(\bar{x}_1, \ldots, \bar{x}_n)$ and $Q_2(\bar{x}_1, \ldots, \bar{x}_n)$ are quadratic polynomials from $\mathbb{F}_{2^2}[\bar{x}_1, \ldots, \bar{x}_n]$. By comparing the coefficients of t^3, t^2, t^1 and assuming $\mathscr{P}(\mathbf{x}' + \bar{\mathbf{x}}) = \mathbf{y}$, we arrive at a system of linear equations over $\mathbb{F}_{2^2}$. This can be represented by a matrix equation $\mathbf{Ax} = \mathbf{y}$. In our case, this is the following:

$$
\begin{bmatrix}
1 & w_1 & 1 & 0 & w_1 & w_2 & 1 & w_1 & 1 & w_2 \\
1 & w_1 & 1 & 1 & 1 & w_1 & 1 & w_2 & w_1 & 0 \\
0 & 0 & w_2 & 0 & 0 & w_1 & w_1 & 0 & w_2 & w_1 \\
1 & 1 & w_1 & 0 & 1 & 0 & 0 & 1 & 0 & 0 \\
w_1 & 1 & 0 & 0 & 0 & 1 & 0 & 1 & w_2 & w_1 \\
w_1 & w_1 & w_2 & 1 & w_1 & 1 & w_1 & 0 & 1 & w_2
\end{bmatrix}
\begin{bmatrix}
\bar{x}_1 \\
\bar{x}_2 \\
\bar{x}_3 \\
\bar{x}_4 \\
\bar{x}_5 \\
\bar{x}_6 \\
\bar{x}_7 \\
\bar{x}_8 \\
\bar{x}_9 \\
\bar{x}_{10}
\end{bmatrix}
=
\begin{bmatrix}
w_1 \\
w_2 \\
w_2 \\
w_2 \\
w_2 \\
1
\end{bmatrix}
$$

The solution space for the equation above has dimension 4 over $\mathbb{F}_{2^2}$, as we would expect it to be $n - (s - 1)o = 4$. Thus, there are only $(2^2)^4 = 2^8$ possible choices for $\bar{\mathbf{x}}$. A quick search through these finds the signature

$$\sigma = \begin{bmatrix} t^3 + w_2 t + 1 \\ w_1 t^3 + w_2 t^2 + w_2 t + w_1 \\ t^3 + t + w_2 \\ w_2 t^2 \\ t^3 + t^2 + 1 \\ w_2 t^3 + t^2 + w_2 t + 1 \\ w_1 t^3 + w_2 t + w_1 \\ w_1 t^2 + w_2 t + 1 \\ t^3 + w_2 t + 1 \\ w_2 t \end{bmatrix}$$

4   The Inapplicability of the Subfield Differential Attack on Unbalanced Oil Vinegar

Now, let us discuss why the Subfield Differential Attack does not work on Unbalanced Oil Vinegar or Rainbow. Let $\mathscr{P} : \mathbb{F}_{q^r}^n \to \mathbb{F}_{q^r}^o$ be either a UOV public key or a Rainbow public key. Let us assume that $\mathbb{F}_{q^r}$ contains a non-trivial subfield $\mathbb{F}_{q^d}$. Again, construct the differential $\mathbf{x}' + \bar{\mathbf{x}}$ with $\mathbf{x}' \in \mathbb{F}_{q^r}$ and $\bar{\mathbf{x}} \in \mathbb{F}_{q^d}$, and evaluate the public key at the differential $\overline{\mathscr{P}}(\bar{\mathbf{x}}) = \mathscr{P}(\mathbf{x}' + \bar{\mathbf{x}})$. In the kth component of $\mathscr{P}$, we have that

$$\bar{f}_k(\mathbf{x}' + \bar{\mathbf{x}}) = \sum_{i=1}^{n}\sum_{j=i}^{n} \alpha_{i,j,k}(x_i' + \bar{x}_i)(x_j' + \bar{x}_j) + \sum_{i=1}^{n} \beta_{i,k}(x_i' + +\bar{x}_i) + \gamma_k.$$

Note that there are no restrictions on the coefficients, $\alpha_{i,j,k}, \beta_{i,k}$ and γ_k as they are randomly chosen from $\mathbb{F}_{q^r}$. If we multiply the polynomial out, then we get

$$\tilde{f}_k(\mathbf{x}' + \mathbf{x}) = \sum_{i=1}^{n}\sum_{j=i}^{n} \alpha_{i,j,k}(x_i' x_j' + x_i' \bar{x}_i + x_j' \bar{x}_j) + \sum_{i=1}^{n} \beta_{i,k}(x_i' + \bar{x}_i) + \gamma_k$$
$$+ \sum_{i=1}^{n}\sum_{j=i}^{n} \alpha_{i,j,k} \bar{x}_i \bar{x}_j.$$

The quadratic terms' coefficients will not be contained in the subfield $\mathbb{F}_{q^d}$. Thus, instead of having a clear separation of $(s-1)o$ linear polynomials and o quadratic polynomials over $\mathbb{F}_{2^d}$ as before for a LUOV public key, we instead have $s * o$ quadratic polynomials over $\mathbb{F}_{q^d}$. Thus it is not more efficient to direct attack than simply having o quadratic polynomials over $\mathbb{F}_{q^r}$, and so viewing the field as a quotient ring does not help for UOV or Rainbow. So the SDA attack does not apply to these schemes.

5   New Parameter Sets for LUOV in Response to SDA

We note that in response to the SDA attack, the authors of LUOV have submitted new parameters sets designed to avoid the existence of a sufficiently large intermediate field to perform SDA. In particular, they chose the extension $\mathbb{F}_{2^r}$ where r is a prime number. This means that only the trivial subfield $\mathbb{F}_2$ exists which is not large enough to find a signature over given their new parameters. Table 5 lists these new parameters.

Table 6. The New Parameter Sets for LUOV

Name	NIST Security Level	r	o	v	n
LUOV-7-57-197	I	7	57	197	254
LUOV-7-83-283	III	7	83	283	366
LUOV-7-110-374	V	7	110	374	484
LUOV-47-42-182	I	47	42	182	224
LUOV-61-60-261	III	61	60	261	321
LUOV-79-76-341	V	79	76	341	417

These new modifications are very new and untested. There is a good possibility that a more robust SDA variant utilizing special subsets of $\mathbb{F}_{2^r}$ instead of just subfields could handle a wider variety of parameters, including the current parameters of LUOV. Further research is needed in this area.

6   Conclusion

We proposed a new attack to a NIST round 2 candidate LUOV. All the parameters originally set for round 2 LUOV were broken according to the NIST standards. SDA only uses the basic structure of field extensions which is the core idea of LUOV. The idea of our attack is simple, however it has great potential. Its simple structure leaves room for improvement and modification to handle more cases more efficiently. Furthermore, one can see that the attack does not depend on the design of the central map. It can be applied to other schemes with a lifted structure and solving lifted quadratic systems in general. We believe that future study of SDA is warranted.

Acknowledgments. First we would like to thank Bo-Yin Yang for useful discussions, in particular, on the complexity analysis. Second, We would also like to thank partial support of NSF (Grant: #CNS-1814221) and NIST, and J. Ding would like to thank the TAFT Research Center for many years' support. Finally, we are grateful for the comments of the referees helping us improve the quality of this paper.

References

1. Bettale, L., Faugère, J.-C., Perret, L.: Hybrid approach for solving multivariate systems over finite fields. J. Math. Cryptol. **3**(3), 177–197 (2009)
2. Bettale, L., Faugère, J.-C., Perret, L.: Solving polynomial systems over finite fields: improved analysis of the hybrid approach. In: Proceedings of the 37th International Symposium on Symbolic and Algebraic Computation, pp. 67–74 (2012)

3. Beullens, W., Preneel, B., Szepieniec, A., Vercauteren, F.: LUOV: signature scheme proposal for NIST PQC project (round 2 version) (2018)
4. Beullens, W., Preneel, B.: Field lifting for smaller UOV public keys. In: Patra, A., Smart, N.P. (eds.) INDOCRYPT 2017. LNCS, vol. 10698, pp. 227–246. Springer, Cham (2017). https://doi.org/10.1007/978-3-319-71667-1_12
5. Boyer, B., Eder, C., Faugère, J.-C., Lachartre, S., Martani, F.: GBLA: Gröbner basis linear algebra package. In: Proceedings of the ACM on International Symposium on Symbolic and Algebraic Computation, pp. 135–142 (2016)
6. Buchberger, B.: A theoretical basis for the reduction of polynomials to canonical forms. ACM SIGSAM Bull. **10**(3), 19–29 (1976)
7. Cheng, C.-M., Chou, T., Niederhagen, R., Yang, B.-Y.: Solving quadratic equations with XL on parallel architectures - extended version. Cryptology ePrint Archive, Report 2016/412 (2016). https://eprint.iacr.org/2016/412
8. Coppersmith, D.: Solving homogeneous linear equations over GF(2) via block Wiedemann algorithm. Math. Comput. **62**(205), 333–350 (1994)
9. Courtois, N., Klimov, A., Patarin, J., Shamir, A.: Efficient algorithms for solving overdefined systems of multivariate polynomial equations. In: Preneel, B. (ed.) EUROCRYPT 2000. LNCS, vol. 1807, pp. 392–407. Springer, Heidelberg (2000). https://doi.org/10.1007/3-540-45539-6_27
10. Czypek, P.: Implementing multivariate quadratic public key signature schemes on embedded devices. Ph.D. thesis, Citeseer (2012)
11. Ding, J., Buchmann, J., Mohamed, M.S.E., Mohamed, W.S.A.E., Weinmann, R.-P.: MutantXL. In: Talk at the First International Conference on Symbolic Computation and Cryptography (SCC 2008) (2008)
12. Ding, J., Gower, J.E., Schmidt, D.: Multivariate Public Key Cryptosystems. Advances in Information Security, vol. 25. Springer, Boston (2006). https://doi.org/10.1007/978-0-387-36946-4
13. Ding, J., Hodges, T.J.: Inverting HFE systems is quasi-polynomial for all fields. In: Rogaway, P. (ed.) CRYPTO 2011. LNCS, vol. 6841, pp. 724–742. Springer, Heidelberg (2011). https://doi.org/10.1007/978-3-642-22792-9_41
14. Ding, J., Kleinjung, T.: Degree of regularity for HFE-. IACR Cryptology ePrint Archive, 2011:570 (2011)
15. Ding, J., Petzoldt, A.: Current state of multivariate cryptography. IEEE Secur. Priv. **15**(4), 28–36 (2017)
16. Ding, J., Schmidt, D.: Rainbow, a new multivariable polynomial signature scheme. In: Ioannidis, J., Keromytis, A., Yung, M. (eds.) ACNS 2005. LNCS, vol. 3531, pp. 164–175. Springer, Heidelberg (2005). https://doi.org/10.1007/11496137_12
17. Ding, J., Yang, B.-Y.: Degree of regularity for HFEv and HFEv-. In: Gaborit, P. (ed.) PQCrypto 2013. LNCS, vol. 7932, pp. 52–66. Springer, Heidelberg (2013). https://doi.org/10.1007/978-3-642-38616-9_4
18. Ding, J., Yang, B.-Y., Chen, C.-H.O., Chen, M.-S., Cheng, C.-M.: New differential-algebraic attacks and reparametrization of rainbow. In: Bellovin, S.M., Gennaro, R., Keromytis, A., Yung, M. (eds.) ACNS 2008. LNCS, vol. 5037, pp. 242–257. Springer, Heidelberg (2008). https://doi.org/10.1007/978-3-540-68914-0_15
19. Ding, J., Zhang, Z., Deaton, J., Vishakha: The singularity attack to the multivariate signature scheme HIMQ-3. Cryptology ePrint Archive, report 2019/895 (2019). https://eprint.iacr.org/2019/895
20. Dubois, V., Gama, N.: The degree of regularity of HFE systems. In: Abe, M. (ed.) ASIACRYPT 2010. LNCS, vol. 6477, pp. 557–576. Springer, Heidelberg (2010). https://doi.org/10.1007/978-3-642-17373-8_32

21. Eder, C., Faugère, J.-C.: A survey on signature-based algorithms for computing Gröbner bases. J. Symb. Comput. **80**, 719–784 (2017)
22. Faugère, J.-C.: A new efficient algorithm for computing Gröbner bases (F4). J. Pure Appl. Algebra **139**(1–3), 61–88 (1999)
23. Faugère, J.-C.: A new efficient algorithm for computing Gröbner bases without reduction to zero (F5). In: Proceedings of the 2002 International Symposium on Symbolic and Algebraic Computation, pp. 75–83 (2002)
24. Galkin, V.: Termination of original F5 (2012)
25. Gallagher, P.: Digital signature standard (DSS). Federal Information Processing Standards Publications, vol. FIPS, pp. 186–183 (2013)
26. Jiang, X., Ding, J., Hu, L.: Kipnis-Shamir attack on HFE revisited. In: Pei, D., Yung, M., Lin, D., Wu, C. (eds.) Inscrypt 2007. LNCS, vol. 4990, pp. 399–411. Springer, Heidelberg (2008). https://doi.org/10.1007/978-3-540-79499-8_31
27. Johnson, D.S., Garey, M.R.: Computers and Intractability: A Guide to the Theory of NP-Completeness. WH Freeman, New York (1979)
28. Kipnis, A., Shamir, A.: Cryptanalysis of the oil and vinegar signature scheme. In: Krawczyk, H. (ed.) CRYPTO 1998. LNCS, vol. 1462, pp. 257–266. Springer, Heidelberg (1998). https://doi.org/10.1007/BFb0055733
29. Lidl, R., Niederreiter, H.: Finite Fields, vol. 20. Cambridge University Press, Cambridge (1997)
30. Matsumoto, T., Imai, H.: Public quadratic polynomial-tuples for efficient signature-verification and message-encryption. In: Barstow, D., et al. (eds.) EUROCRYPT 1988. LNCS, vol. 330, pp. 419–453. Springer, Heidelberg (1988). https://doi.org/10.1007/3-540-45961-8_39
31. Mohamed, M.S.E., Cabarcas, D., Ding, J., Buchmann, J., Bulygin, S.: MXL$_3$: an efficient algorithm for computing Gröbner bases of zero-dimensional ideals. In: Lee, D., Hong, S. (eds.) ICISC 2009. LNCS, vol. 5984, pp. 87–100. Springer, Heidelberg (2010). https://doi.org/10.1007/978-3-642-14423-3_7
32. Mohamed, M.S.E., Ding, J., Buchmann, J., Werner, F.: Algebraic attack on the MQQ public key cryptosystem. In: Garay, J.A., Miyaji, A., Otsuka, A. (eds.) CANS 2009. LNCS, vol. 5888, pp. 392–401. Springer, Heidelberg (2009). https://doi.org/10.1007/978-3-642-10433-6_26
33. Mohamed, M.S.E., Mohamed, W.S.A.E., Ding, J., Buchmann, J.: *MXL2*: solving polynomial equations over GF(2) using an improved mutant strategy. In: Buchmann, J., Ding, J. (eds.) PQCrypto 2008. LNCS, vol. 5299, pp. 203–215. Springer, Heidelberg (2008). https://doi.org/10.1007/978-3-540-88403-3_14
34. National Institute of Standards and Technology: Submission requirements and evaluation criteria for the post-quantum cryptography standardization process. Technical report, National Institute of Standards and Technology (2017)
35. Patarin, J.: Cryptanalysis of the Matsumoto and Imai public key scheme of Eurocrypt88. In: Coppersmith, D. (ed.) CRYPTO 1995. LNCS, vol. 963, pp. 248–261. Springer, Heidelberg (1995). https://doi.org/10.1007/3-540-44750-4_20
36. Patarin, J.: The oil and vinegar algorithm for signatures. In: Dagstuhl Workshop on Cryptography 1997 (1997)
37. Petzoldt, A., Bulygin, S., Buchmann, J.: Linear recurring sequences for the UOV key generation. In: Catalano, D., Fazio, N., Gennaro, R., Nicolosi, A. (eds.) PKC 2011. LNCS, vol. 6571, pp. 335–350. Springer, Heidelberg (2011). https://doi.org/10.1007/978-3-642-19379-8_21
38. Rivest, R.L., Shamir, A., Adleman, L.: A method for obtaining digital signatures and public-key cryptosystems. Commun. ACM. **21**(2), 120–126 (1978)

39. Shor, P.W.: Polynomial-time algorithms for prime factorization and discrete logarithms on a quantum computer. SIAM Rev. **41**(2), 303–332 (1999)
40. Stallings, W.: Cryptography and Network Security, 4/E. Pearson Education India, London (2006)
41. Thomae, E., Wolf, C.: Solving underdetermined systems of multivariate quadratic equations revisited. In: Fischlin, M., Buchmann, J., Manulis, M. (eds.) PKC 2012. LNCS, vol. 7293, pp. 156–171. Springer, Heidelberg (2012). https://doi.org/10.1007/978-3-642-30057-8_10
42. Wolf, C., Preneel, B.: Equivalent keys in multivariate quadratic public key systems. J. Math. Cryptol. **4**(4), 375–415 (2011)
43. Yang, B.-Y., Chen, C.-H.O., Bernstein, D.J., Chen, J.-M.: Analysis of QUAD. In: Biryukov, A. (ed.) FSE 2007. LNCS, vol. 4593, pp. 290–308. Springer, Heidelberg (2007). https://doi.org/10.1007/978-3-540-74619-5_19
44. Yang, B.-Y., Chen, J.-M.: Theoretical analysis of XL over small fields. In: Wang, H., Pieprzyk, J., Varadharajan, V. (eds.) ACISP 2004. LNCS, vol. 3108, pp. 277–288. Springer, Heidelberg (2004). https://doi.org/10.1007/978-3-540-27800-9_24
45. Yeh, J.Y.-C., Cheng, C.-M., Yang, B.-Y.: Operating degrees for XL vs. F_4/F_5 for generic $\mathcal{MQ}$ with number of equations linear in that of variables. In: Fischlin, M., Katzenbeisser, S. (eds.) Number Theory and Cryptography. LNCS, vol. 8260, pp. 19–33. Springer, Heidelberg (2013). https://doi.org/10.1007/978-3-642-42001-6_3

Out of Oddity – New Cryptanalytic Techniques Against Symmetric Primitives Optimized for Integrity Proof Systems

Tim Beyne[1]([⊠]), Anne Canteaut[2]([⊠]), Itai Dinur[3]([⊠]), Maria Eichlseder[4,5]([⊠]), Gregor Leander[5]([⊠]), Gaëtan Leurent[2]([⊠]), María Naya-Plasencia[2]([⊠]), Léo Perrin[2]([⊠]), Yu Sasaki[7]([⊠]), Yosuke Todo[5,7]([⊠]), and Friedrich Wiemer[5,6]([⊠])

[1] imec-COSIC, KU Leuven, Leuven, Belgium
tim.beyne@student.kuleuven.be
[2] Inria, Paris, France
[3] Department of Computer Science, Ben-Gurion University, Beersheba, Israel
[4] Graz University of Technology, Graz, Austria
[5] Ruhr-Universität Bochum, Bochum, Germany
[6] cryptosolutions, Essen, Germany
[7] NTT Secure Platform Laboratories, Tokyo, Japan

Abstract. The security and performance of many integrity proof systems like SNARKs, STARKs and Bulletproofs highly depend on the underlying hash function. For this reason several new proposals have recently been developed. These primitives obviously require an in-depth security evaluation, especially since their implementation constraints have led to less standard design approaches. This work compares the security levels offered by two recent families of such primitives, namely GMiMC and HadesMiMC. We exhibit low-complexity distinguishers against the GMiMC and HadesMiMC permutations for most parameters proposed in recently launched public challenges for STARK-friendly hash functions. In the more concrete setting of the sponge construction corresponding to the practical use in the ZK-STARK protocol, we present a practical collision attack on a round-reduced version of GMiMC and a preimage attack on some instances of HadesMiMC. To achieve those results, we adapt and generalize several cryptographic techniques to fields of odd characteristic.

Keywords: Hash functions · Integrity proof systems · Integral attacks · GMiMC · HadesMiMC

1 Introduction

The emergence of cryptographic protocols with advanced functionalities, such as fully homomorphic encryption, multi-party computation and new types of proof systems, has led to a strong demand for new symmetric primitives offering good performance in the context of these specific applications. Indeed, as emphasized

© International Association for Cryptologic Research 2020
D. Micciancio and T. Ristenpart (Eds.): CRYPTO 2020, LNCS 12172, pp. 299–328, 2020.
https://doi.org/10.1007/978-3-030-56877-1_11

by Katz [26] in his invited lecture at CRYPTO 2019, symmetric-key cryptography has an important role to play in the further practical advancement of these applications. However, the standard criteria which govern the design of symmetric primitives are usually not appropriate in the context of these applications. For instance, the cost of the homomorphic evaluation of a symmetric primitive is mainly determined by its multiplicative size and depth [6]. Similarly, the area of integrity proof systems, like SNARKs, STARKs, Bulletproofs, is asking for symmetric primitives optimized for yet another cost metric. Moreover, the use of hash functions that are defined over finite fields of odd characteristic, in particular over prime fields is desirable in many such applications. One example of such a use case is the zero-knowledge proof system deployed in the Zcash cryptocurrency. Another very interesting example is the ZK-STARK protocol [13], which is expected to be deployed on top of the Ethereum blockchain within the next year: it uses as a building-block a collision-resistant hash function, and the performance of the proof system highly depends on the number of arithmetic operations required for describing the hash function (see [7] for details).

Therefore, several new ciphers and hash functions have been proposed in the last five years for these advanced protocols. They include several FHE-friendly symmetric encryption schemes such as LowMC [6], FLIP [31], Kreyvium [20] and Rasta [22], some MPC-friendly block ciphers such as MiMC [5] and its variants [3,24], and some primitives dedicated to proof systems such as the functions from the Marvellous family, including Jarvis, Friday [8], Vision and Rescue [7].

However, all these primitives are very innovative constructions and the implementation constraints which govern their designs may have introduced some unexpected weaknesses. This was the case for LowMC, which was broken a few weeks after its publication [21,23,32]. More recently, a practical attack against Jarvis has been mounted [2], showing that some of these designs are probably not mature enough for practical applications and require a more in-depth security evaluation. In particular, several of these primitives are defined over an odd prime field, a setting in which most of the classical cryptanalytic tools, and therefore also related security arguments, do not apply directly. This includes linear cryptanalysis and its variants, integral attacks and higher-order differential or cube attacks.

Our Contributions. This work analyses the security of two families of such primitives. To be concrete, we focus on the concrete proposals of STARK-friendly hash functions which have been specified in the context of a public competition launched by StarkWare Industries[1]. We aim to compare the security levels offered, for similar parameters, by two families of primitives: GMiMC [3,4] and HadesMiMC [24,25]. More precisely, we evaluate the resistance of these two primitives against several general types of attacks: attacks exploiting differential properties, integral attacks and advanced algebraic attacks. As a result, we present low-complexity distinguishers against the GMiMC and HadesMiMC

---

[1] https://starkware.co/hash-challenge/.

permutations for most parameters proposed in the challenges. In the more concrete setting of the sponge construction corresponding to the practical use in the ZK-STARK protocol, we describe a collision attack on a round-reduced version of GMiMC and a preimage attack on some instances of HADESMiMC. Our findings for the most efficient variants of the primitives are summarized in Table 1.

From a technical point, our results required to adapt and generalize several cryptanalytic techniques to fields of odd characteristic. In particular, for integral attacks, we demonstrate that instead of using sums over additive subgroups as usually done for ciphers over $\mathbb{F}_2^n$, it is possible to use any *multiplicative* subgroup of $\mathbb{F}_q^\times$ with similar impact. Interestingly, this seems to suggest that finite fields $\mathbb{F}_q$ with a limited number of multiplicative subgroups might be preferable, i.e. one might want to avoid $q-1$ being smooth. This implies that the fields which are suitable for implementing FFT may be more vulnerable to integral attacks. We expect that these general insights have applications beyond our concrete cryptanalytic results.

An additional technical contribution of this paper is the use of algebraic techniques for ensuring that transitions of a differential characteristic for a hash function hold for many rounds without paying the typical expensive probabilistic cost. In particular, we exploit the algebraic structure of the hash function to penetrate deep into its state and represent the conditions for the differential transitions as algebraic equations that can be efficiently solved. We refer to these attacks as *algebraically controlled differential attacks*. Algebraic techniques have been previously used in combination with differential attacks (for example, in the recent cryptanalysis of SHA-1 [36]). However, unlike prior work, in our setting each differential transition is very expensive to bypass probabilistically. Hence, our attacks are almost entirely algebraic and use dedicated techniques to ensure that the algebraic equations can be efficiently solved.

Organization of the Paper. The following section describes the two STARK-friendly primitives considered in the paper and their concrete instances. Section 3 details how integral attacks can be mounted over finite fields of any characteristic. Following this new framework, Sect. 4 exhibits low-complexity integral distinguishers on the full GMiMC permutation. Several differential attacks on round-reduced GMiMC are then detailed in Sect. 5, including a practical collision attack on the corresponding hash function. Section 6 presents two attacks on HADESMiMC: a general integral distinguisher covering all but two rounds of the permutation, and a preimage attack on the hash function which applies in the specific case where the MDS matrix defining the linear layer has a low multiplicative order.

2   STARK-Friendly Primitives

This paper focuses on two families of primitives, which are recent evolutions of the block cipher MiMC designed by Albrecht *et al.* in 2016 [5], and offer much more flexibility than the original construction:

Table 1. Distinguishers on the GMiMC and HadesMiMC permutations and attacks breaking the corresponding sponge hash functions. The variants aiming at 128-bit security operate on $t = 12$ elements in $\mathbb{F}_q$ with $q = 2^{61} + 20 \times 2^{32} + 1$. The variants aiming at 256-bit security operate on $t = 14$ elements in $\mathbb{F}_q$ with $q = 2^{125} + 266 \times 2^{64} + 1$. The last attack (*) only applies when the linear layer has a low multiplicative order. Attacks on full versions are typeset in bold.

Primitive (security)	Rounds		Attack			
			Type	Rounds	Cost	Sect.
GMiMC (128 bits)	101	permutation	integral distinguisher	70	2^{61}	4.1
			ZS distinguisher	**102**	$\mathbf{2^{48}}$	**4.3**
			ZS distinguisher	**128**	$\mathbf{2^{122}}$	**4.2**
			diff. distinguisher	64	2^{123}	5.2
			diff. distinguisher	66	practical	5.2
		hash function	collisions	40	practical	5.4
			collisions	42	2^{92}	5.4
			collisions	52	2^{83}	5.4
POSEIDON (128 bits)	8+40	permutation	ZS distinguisher	6+45	2^{61}	6.1
GMiMC (256 bits)	186	permutation	integral distinguisher	116	2^{125}	4.1
			ZS distinguisher	**206**	$\mathbf{2^{125}}$	**4.2**
			ZS distinguisher	**218**	$\mathbf{2^{250}}$	**4.2**
		hash function	collisions	50	2^{187}	5.3
POSEIDON (256 bits)	8+83	permutation	ZS distinguisher	6+87	2^{125}	6.1
		hash function*	**preimages**	**8+any**	$\mathbf{2^{160}}$	**6.2**

- **GMiMC**, designed by Albrecht *et al.* [3,4]
- **HadesMiMC**, proposed by Grassi *et al.* [24,25], for which two versions are distinguished depending on the characteristic of the underlying field: STARKAD over a field of characteristic 2, and POSEIDON over a prime field.

2.1   Expected Security Level

GMiMC and HadesMiMC are two block ciphers but both of them can be turned into permutations by replacing the round-keys by fixed independent and randomly chosen round-constants. Based on these primitives, hash functions are obtained by applying the sponge construction [14,15] depicted in Fig. 1 and using the primitive as an inner permutation.

In the following, we extensively use the following notation: the sponge operates on a state composed of t elements in a finite field $\mathbb{F}_q$. The main parameters which determine the security level of the sponge construction with respect to generic attacks are its *capacity* c and the size of the underlying alphabet $\mathbb{F}_q$. Namely, a random sponge whose capacity consists of c elements in $\mathbb{F}_q$ provides

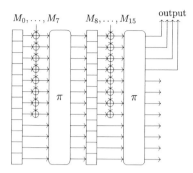

Fig. 1. Sponge construction with inner permutation π, internal state with $t = 12$ words and capacity $c = 4$.

a generic security level corresponding to $\frac{c}{2} \log_2 q$ queries both for collision and (second)-preimage resistance [14].

The primary cryptanalytic goal is to exhibit collision or preimage attacks on some weakened variants of the hash functions. However, the existence of a property which distinguishes a given cryptographic function from an ideal function of the same size is also commonly considered as a weakness (see e.g. [11, Page 19] for a discussion). In our context, since our attacks do not make any assumptions about the round-constants in the inner permutations, our *distinguishers* are related to the known-key model for block ciphers [28].

While a distinguisher on π cannot always be turned into a distinguisher for the hash function, it invalidates the security arguments provided by the indifferentiability proof of the sponge construction [15]. For this reason, the authors of KECCAK advocate following the so-called *hermetic sponge strategy* [16, Page 13], i.e. using the sponge construction with an inner permutation that should not have any structural distinguisher (other than the existence of a compact description).

2.2   Concrete Instances

The different members in each of these families are determined by the triple (c, t, q) representing respectively the number of words in the capacity, the number of words in the state and the field size. In the following, when referring to practical examples, we will focus on the values (c, t, q) considered in the Stark-Ware challenges given in Table 2. To each triple (c, t, q) correspond two variants: over a prime field and over a binary field, and the exact values of q are detailed in Table 2. Performance in terms of trace size, proving time, and verification cost, are essential criteria for choosing a STARK-friendly hash function. Implementation results show that, for each family of hash functions, the variant 128-d (for the target 128-bit security) is by far the most efficient [35]. For this reason, some attacks in the paper focus more specifically on this member in the three families, i.e., on sponges whose internal state consists of $t = 12$ words in a finite field $\mathbb{F}_q$ of order close to 2^{64} and with capacity $c = 4$. It is also worth noticing that, in

Table 2. Parameters proposed for the permutation and sponge construction.

Security level	$\log_2 q$	q (prime)	q (binary)	c	t	Variant
	64	$2^{61} + 20 \times 2^{32} + 1$	2^{63}	**4**	**12**	**128-d**
128 bits	128	$2^{125} + 266 \times 2^{64} + 1$	2^{125}	2	4	128-a
				2	12	128-c
	256	$2^{253} + 2^{199} + 1$	2^{255}	1	3	128-b
				1	11	128-e
256 bits	128	$2^{125} + 266 \times 2^{64} + 1$	2^{125}	4	8	256-a
				4	14	256-b

terms of performance and suitability, odd prime fields are more STARK-friendly than binary fields for a given size.

2.3 Specifications of GMiMC

GMiMC is a family of block ciphers designed by Albrecht *et al.* in 2019 [3] based on different types of Feistel networks using $x \mapsto x^3$ over the field corresponding to the branch alphabet as the round function. Among the variants proposed by the designers, we focus on the one chosen in the StarkWare challenges and depicted in Fig. 2, namely the variant using an unbalanced Feistel network with an expanding round function, named GMiMC$_{\text{erf}}$. In the whole paper, the rounds (and round constants) are numbered starting from 1, and the branches are numbered from 1 to t where Branch 1 is the leftmost branch. For the sake of simplicity, this particular variant will be called GMiMC. A specificity of GMiMC is that the designers' security claims concern the primitive instantiated over a prime field. They mention that "even if GMiMC can be instantiated over $\mathbb{F}_{2^n}$, [they] do not provide the number of rounds to guarantee security in this scenario".

In the block cipher setting with a key size equal to $n = \log_2 q$ bits, the key schedule is trivial, i.e. the master key is added to the input of the cube function at every round. This very simple key schedule is a major weakness [18]. However, it seems difficult to leverage the underlying property in the hash function setting we are focusing on.

2.4 Specifications of HADESMiMC

HadesMiMC is a family of permutations described by Grassi *et al.* in [25] which follows a new design strategy for block ciphers called HADES. The HADES construction aims to decrease the number of Sboxes relative to a traditional Substitution-Permutation Network, while guaranteeing that the cipher still resists all known attacks, including differential and linear cryptanalysis and algebraic attacks. Reducing the number of Sboxes is especially important in many applications and this was traditionally achieved by using a partial substitution-layer, i.e., an Sbox layer which does not operate on the whole internal state.

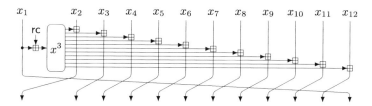

Fig. 2. One round of the GMiMC permutation with $t = 12$.

However, several attacks on this type of constructions, e.g. [12,21,23,32] show that it is much more difficult to estimate the security level of these constructions than that of classical SPNs. The basic principle of the HADES construction is then to combine both aspects: the inner rounds in the cipher have a partial Sbox layer to increase the resistance to algebraic attacks at a reduced implementation cost, whereas the outer rounds consist of traditional SPN rounds, with a full Sbox layer (Fig. 3). The resistance against statistical attacks is analyzed by removing the inner rounds, while the resistance to algebraic attacks, e.g. the evolution of the algebraic degree over the cipher, involves the inner rounds.

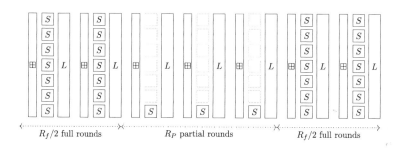

Fig. 3. The HADESMiMC construction with $t = 6$.

HADESMiMC [25, Section 3] is then a keyed permutation following the HADES construction dedicated to MPC applications or to STARK proof systems, where the Sbox is defined by the cube mapping over a finite field and the linear layer L corresponds to a $(t \times t)$-MDS matrix. Two concrete instantiations of HADESMiMC are then detailed by Grassi *et al.* in [24], namely:

- STARKAD operates on t elements in a binary field of odd absolute degree (which guarantees that the cube mapping is bijective);
- POSEIDON operates on t elements in a prime field $\mathbb{F}_p$ with $p \bmod 3 \neq 1$.

In both cases the partial rounds consist of a single Sbox operating on the last coordinate of the state. For all parameters we consider, the number of full rounds is equal to 8 and the number of partial rounds varies between 40 and 88.

3   Integral Attacks over Fields of Any Characteristic

The notion of *integral attacks* has been introduced by Knudsen and Wagner [29] and captures several variants including saturation attacks and higher-order differential attacks. These attacks have been used for cryptanalyzing many ciphers, but to our best knowledge, all of them operate on a binary field. Indeed, the main property behind these attacks is that, for any $F : \mathbb{F}_2^m \to \mathbb{F}_2^m$ and for any affine subspace $V \subset \mathbb{F}_2^m$,

$$\sum_{x \in V} F(x) = 0$$

when $\deg F < \dim V$. This comes from the fact that the sum of the images by F of all inputs in V corresponds to a value of a derivative of F of order $(\dim V)$ [30]. It follows that this derivative has degree at most $(\deg(F) - \dim V)$ and thus vanishes when $\deg F < \dim V$. It is then possible to *saturate* some input bits of F and to use as a distinguishing property the fact that the output bits are balanced, i.e. they sum to zero. The fact that the sum over all $x \in V$ of $F(x)$ corresponds to the value of a higher-order derivative does not hold anymore in odd characteristic, and the same technique cannot be applied directly.

Higher-order differentials over $\mathbb{F}_q$ then need to use a generalized notion of differentiation as analyzed in [34] (see also [1]). However, we can show that for the particular case of saturation attacks, the same technique can be used in the general case of a field $\mathbb{F}_q$ – even in odd characteristic. Indeed, we can exploit the following result.

Proposition 1. *For any $F : \mathbb{F}_q \to \mathbb{F}_q$ with $\deg(F) < q - 1$,*

$$\sum_{x \in \mathbb{F}_q} F(x) = 0 .$$

Proof. The result is due to following well-known property: for any exponent k with $1 \le k \le q - 2$, $\sum_{x \in \mathbb{F}_q} x^k = 0$. Moreover, when $k = 0$, we have $\sum_{x \in \mathbb{F}_q} x^0 = q = 0$. $\qquad\square$

Proposition 1 can be generalized to the multivariate case, i.e. to functions from $\mathbb{F}_q^k$ to $\mathbb{F}_q$.

Corollary 1. *For any $F : \mathbb{F}_q^t \to \mathbb{F}_q$ with $\deg(F) < k(q - 1)$ and any affine subspace $V \subseteq \mathbb{F}_q^t$ of dimension at least k, $\sum_{x \in V} F(x) = 0$.*

Proof. Let V be an affine space of dimension $\kappa \ge k$ and A an affine permutation over $\mathbb{F}_q^t$ such that $A(V) = \{(y, 0, \ldots, 0) \mid y \in \mathbb{F}_q^\kappa\}$. Then,

$$\sum_{x \in V} F(x) = \sum_{x \in V} (F \circ A^{-1})(A(x)) = \sum_{y_1, \ldots, y_\kappa \in \mathbb{F}_q} (F \circ A^{-1})(y_1, \ldots, y_\kappa, 0, \ldots, 0).$$

Since $\deg(F \circ A^{-1}) = \deg F < k(q - 1)$, $(F \circ A^{-1})$ consists of monomials of the form $y_1^{i_1} y_2^{i_2} \ldots y_\kappa^{i_\kappa}$ with at least one exponent $i_j < q - 1$. Then, $\sum_{y_j \in \mathbb{F}_q} y_j^{i_j} = 0$, implying that

$$\sum_{y_1, \ldots, y_\kappa \in \mathbb{F}_q} y_1^{i_1} y_2^{i_2} \ldots y_\kappa^{i_\kappa} = 0,$$

which leads to $\sum_{x \in V} F(x) = 0$.

Based on this observation, a saturation attack with data complexity q^k can be mounted whenever the degree of F as a polynomial over $\mathbb{F}_q$ is strictly less than $k(q-1)$, even if $\mathbb{F}_q$ is a field of odd characteristic.

Now, we generalize the notion of integral distinguishers to multiplicative subgroups using the following property.

Proposition 2. *Let $\mathbb{G}$ be a multiplicative subgroup of $\mathbb{F}_q^\times$. For any $F : \mathbb{F}_q \to \mathbb{F}_q$ such that $\deg(F) < |\mathbb{G}|$, $\sum_{x \in \mathbb{G}} F(x) - F(0) \cdot |\mathbb{G}| = 0$.*

This is a strict generalization of Proposition 1, for which $|\mathbb{G}| = q - 1$.

Proof. The result is a direct consequence of the following well-known property: for any exponent k with $1 \le k \le |\mathbb{G}| - 1$, $\sum_{x \in \mathbb{G}} x^k = 0$. Moreover, when $k = 0$, we have $\sum_{x \in \mathbb{G}} x^0 = |\mathbb{G}|$. □

We also note that Corollary 1 can be straightforwardly adapted to multiplicative subgroups. The power of summing over multiplicative subgroups (rather than over the entire field $\mathbb{F}_q$) comes from the fact that if $\mathbb{F}_q$ contains small multiplicative subgroups (as for the fields used for the concrete instances specified in Table 2), the complexity of the attacks may be fine-tuned and significantly reduced. In the next sections, such attacks will be applied to both GMiMC and HadesMiMC.

4 Integral Distinguishers on the Full GMiMC

4.1 Integral Distinguisher on GMiMC

Using Corollary 1, we can exhibit a distinguisher for $(3t - 4 + \lfloor \log_3(q-2) \rfloor)$ rounds of GMiMC. A remarkable property is that this distinguisher holds for any finite field. It is obtained by saturating a single branch of the Feistel network and consequently has data complexity q. Indeed, we choose a set of inputs where the $(t-2)$ leftmost branches are inactive, while the rightmost branch is determined by the value of Branch $(t-1)$. More precisely, we consider a set of inputs of the form

$$\mathcal{X} = \{(\alpha_1, \ldots, \alpha_{t-2}, x, f(x)) \mid x \in \mathbb{F}_q\} \tag{1}$$

where the α_i are arbitrary constants in $\mathbb{F}_q$ and f is defined by

$$f(x) = -\left(x + \sum_{i=1}^{t-2} \beta_i + \mathsf{RC}_{t-1}\right)^3 - x - 2\sum_{i=1}^{t-2} \beta_i - \mathsf{RC}_{t-1} - \mathsf{RC}_t$$

and $\beta_1, \ldots, \beta_{t-2}$ are constant values derived from $\alpha_1, \ldots, \alpha_{t-2}$ by

$$\beta_1 = (\alpha_1 + \mathsf{RC}_1)^3 \text{ and } \beta_{i+1} = \left(\alpha_{i+1} + \sum_{j=1}^{i} \beta_j + \mathsf{RC}_{i+1}\right)^3.$$

Let us first consider the first $(t - 2)$ rounds. We observe that, at Round i, $1 \leq i \leq t - 2$, the output of the Sbox corresponds to β_i and is added to all branches except the leftmost branch of the input. It follows that the output of Round $(t - 2)$ corresponds to

$$(x + \textstyle\sum_{i=1}^{t-2} \beta_i, f(x) + \sum_{i=1}^{t-2} \beta_i, \gamma_1, \ldots, \gamma_{t-2})$$

where $(\gamma_1, \ldots, \gamma_{t-2})$ are constants (see Figure 4 in [17]).

Therefore, if x' denotes the value of Branch 1, i.e., $x' = x + \sum_{i=1}^{t-2} \beta_i$, we have that Branch 2 corresponds to

$$f\left(x' - \sum_{i=1}^{t-2} \beta_i\right) + \sum_{i=1}^{t-2} \beta_i = -(x' + \mathsf{RC}_{t-1})^3 - x' - \mathsf{RC}_{t-1} - \mathsf{RC}_t .$$

The inputs of Round t are then

$$\{(-x' - \mathsf{RC}_t - \mathsf{RC}_{t-1}, \gamma_1 + (x' + \mathsf{RC}_{t-1})^3, \ldots, \gamma_{t-2} + (x' + \mathsf{RC}_{t-1})^3, x') \mid x' \in \mathbb{F}_q\}$$

and the inputs of Round $(t + 1)$ are

$$\{(\gamma_1, \ldots, \gamma_{t-2}, x' - (x' + \mathsf{RC}_{t-1})^3, -x' - \mathsf{RC}_t - \mathsf{RC}_{t-1}) \mid x' \in \mathbb{F}_q\} .$$

The following $(t - 2)$ rounds do not activate the Sbox, implying that the input set at Round $(2t - 1)$ has the form

$$\{(x' - (x' + \mathsf{RC}_{t-1})^3 + \delta_1, -x' + \delta_2, \delta_3, \ldots, \delta_t) \mid x' \in \mathbb{F}_q\} \tag{2}$$

for some fixed values $\delta_1, \ldots, \delta_t$ determined by the constants. Each coordinate of this input word can then be seen as a q-ary polynomial in x' of degree at most three. It follows that, after r additional rounds, the set (2) is transformed into a set of elements $(z_1, \ldots, z_t)$, whose coordinates have degree at most 3^{r+1}. Proposition 1 then implies that all z_i are balanced if $3^{r+1} \leq q - 2$, i.e., if $r \leq \lfloor \log_3(q - 2) \rfloor - 1$.

Adding $(t - 1)$ Rounds. We can add some more rounds by using the following relation over $(t - 1)$ rounds of GMiMC.

Proposition 3. *Let $(x_1, \ldots, x_t)$ and $(y_1, \ldots, y_t)$ denote the input and output of $(t - 1)$ rounds of GMiMC.*

$$\sum_{i=2}^{t} y_i - (t - 2)y_1 = \sum_{i=1}^{t-1} x_i - (t - 2)x_t . \tag{3}$$

Proof. Let $(x_1^\ell, \ldots, x_t^\ell)$ denote the input of Round ℓ. It can be observed that, for any $i, j \in \{1, \ldots, t - 1\}$,

$$x_i^\ell = x_{i+1}^{\ell-1} + (x_j^\ell - x_{j+1}^{\ell-1}) \text{ and } x_t^\ell = x_1^{\ell-1} .$$

It follows that, for any j, $1 \leq j \leq (t-1)$,

$$\sum_{i=1}^{t} x_i^{\ell} - (t-1)x_j^{\ell} = \sum_{i=1}^{t} x_i^{\ell-1} - (t-1)x_{j+1}^{\ell-1} .$$

By applying this equality $(t-1)$ times, we deduce (3).   □

From the previous proposition, we deduce that after a total of $R = 3t - 4 + \lfloor \log_3(q-2) \rfloor$ rounds the output $(v_1, \ldots, v_t)$ of GMiMC satisfies $\sum_{i=2}^{t} v_i - (t-2)v_1 = \sum_{i=1}^{t-1} z_i - (t-2)z_t$, which is a polynomial in x of degree at most $(q-2)$. This leads to a distinguisher with complexity q on R rounds, i.e., 70 rounds for the parameters we focus on.

4.2   Zero-Sum Distinguishers on the Full Permutation

Saturating a Single Branch. Since we are analyzing a permutation (or a family of permutations parameterized by the round-constants), there is no secret material involved in the computation, implying that a distinguisher can be built from some internal states in the middle of the primitive, not only from inputs and outputs, exactly as in the *known-key setting* for block ciphers [28]. This leads to *zero-sum distinguishers*, which were introduced by Aumasson and Meier [10] and exhibited for several hash functions, including SHA-3 [9,19].

The previously described distinguisher can be extended by $(t - 2 + \lfloor \log_3(q-2) \rfloor)$ rounds backwards. This is realized by choosing the internal states after $(t-2+\lfloor \log_3(q-2) \rfloor)$ rounds in $\mathcal{X}$, as defined by (1). The inverse of one round of GMiMC is still a round of a Feistel network of the same form and it has degree three over $\mathbb{F}_q$. Then, the coordinates $(y_1, \ldots, y_t)$ of the images of the elements in $\mathcal{X}$ by r backward rounds can be seen as univariate polynomials in x with degree at most 3^{r+1}. Exactly as in the forward direction, after $(\lfloor \log_3(q-2) \rfloor - 1)$ rounds, the degree of these polynomials cannot exceed $(q-2)$.

Based on Proposition 3, we can then add $(t-1)$ rounds backwards. Indeed, the input of the first round of the permutation $(u_1, \ldots, u_t)$ is related to the output of Round $(t-1)$, i.e. $(y_1, \ldots, y_t)$, by

$$\sum_{i=2}^{t} y_i - (t-2)y_1 = \sum_{i=1}^{t-1} u_i - (t-2)u_t ,$$

and the left-hand term of this equation is a polynomial in x of degree at most $(q-2)$, implying that $\left(\sum_{i=1}^{t-1} u_i - (t-2)u_t \right)$ sum to zero.

Similarly, we can apply the previously described distinguisher in the forward direction, and deduce that the outputs $(v_1, \ldots, v_t)$ of the permutation after $(3t - 4 + \lfloor \log_3(q-2) \rfloor)$ additional rounds are such that $\left(\sum_{i=2}^{t} v_i - (t-2)v_1 \right)$ sum to zero. This leads to a distinguisher with complexity q for a total of $(4t - 6 + 2\lfloor \log_3(q-2) \rfloor)$ rounds, which is higher than the number of rounds proposed in all StarkWare challenges, except in the case where q exceeds the claimed security level (see Table 3).

Saturating Two Branches. When $t \geq 4$, it is possible to exhibit a similar distinguisher on more rounds with complexity q^2 by saturating two branches. In this case, we start from Round m in the middle with a set of internal states

$$\mathcal{Y} = \{(\alpha_1, \ldots, \alpha_{t-4}, x, f(x), g(y), y) \mid x, y \in \mathbb{F}_q\}$$

where

$$f(x) = -\left(x + \sum_{i=1}^{t-4} \beta_i + \mathsf{RC}_{m+t-4}\right)^3 - x - 2\sum_{i=1}^{t-4} \beta_i - \mathsf{RC}_{m+t-4} - \mathsf{RC}_{m+t-3}$$

$$g(y) = (y + \mathsf{RC}_{m-1})^3 - y - \mathsf{RC}_{m-1} - \mathsf{RC}_{m-2}$$

and $\beta_1, \ldots, \beta_{t-4}$ are defined as before by replacing RC_i by RC_{m+i-1}.

Computing Forwards. As depicted on Figure 5 in [17], the corresponding set at the input of Round $(m + t - 4)$ is then of the form

$$\{(x', -(x' + \mathsf{RC}_{m+t-4})^3 - x' - \mathsf{RC}_{m+t-4} - \mathsf{RC}_{m+t-3}, \gamma_1(y), \ldots, \gamma_{t-2}(y)) \mid x', y \in \mathbb{F}_q\}$$

where $(\gamma_1, \ldots, \gamma_{t-2})$ are some values which depend on y only. After two more rounds, we then get some internal states whose $(t - 2)$ leftmost branches do not depend on x'. It follows that each coordinate of the input of Round $(m + 2t - 4)$ is a polynomial in x' and y of degree at most three in x'. After $(\lfloor \log_3(q-2) \rfloor - 1)$ rounds, we get that each coordinate is a polynomial of degree at most $(q - 2)$ in x'. Then, with the same technique as before, we can add $(t - 1)$ rounds and show that the output of the permutation $(v_1, \ldots, v_t)$ is such that the linear combination $\left(\sum_{i=1}^{t-1} v_i - (t - 2)v_t\right)$ sums to zero after $(3t - 6 + \lfloor \log_3(q - 2) \rfloor)$ rounds.

Computing Backwards. Starting from Round m and computing backwards, we get that the input of Round $(m - 1)$ is of the form

$$(y, \alpha_1 - (y + \mathsf{RC}_{m-1})^3, \ldots, x - (y + \mathsf{RC}_{m-1})^3, f(x) - (y + \mathsf{RC}_{m-1})^3, -y - \mathsf{RC}_{m-1} - \mathsf{RC}_{m-2})$$

and the input of Round $(m - 2)$ equals

$$(-y - \mathsf{RC}_{m-1} - \mathsf{RC}_{m-2}, y + (y + \mathsf{RC}_{m-1})^3, \alpha_1, \ldots, x, f(x)) .$$

Then, the following $(t-2)$ rounds do not activate the Sbox, implying that all the coordinates of the input of Round $(m - t)$ are polynomials in x and y of degree at most three in y. We deduce that the input $(u_1, \ldots, u_t)$ of Round $(m - 2t + 2 - \lfloor \log_3(q - 2) \rfloor)$ is such that the linear combination $\left(\sum_{i=1}^{t-1} u_i - (t - 2)u_t\right)$ sums to zero. This zero-sum distinguisher then covers a total of $(5t - 8 + 2\lfloor \log_3(q - 2) \rfloor)$ rounds which is detailed in Table 3 for the relevant parameters.

Table 3. Number of rounds of GMiMC covered by the zero-sum distinguishers of complexity q and q^2.

Security	Parameters		Full	ZS with complexity q	ZS with complexity q^2
	$\log_2 q$	t			Number of rounds
	61	12	101	118	128
	125	4	166	166	–
128 bits	125	12	182	198	–
	256	3	326	–	–
	256	11	342	–	–
256 bits	125	8	174	182	188
	125	14	186	206	218

4.3 Exploiting Integral Distinguishers over Multiplicative Subgroups

A noticeable shortcoming of the integral attacks over $\mathbb{F}_q$, as demonstrated by Table 3, is that they do not give any result for primitives over large fields $\mathbb{F}_q$ (for which $\log_2 q \approx 256$). However, by exploiting integral distinguishers over multiplicative subgroups of $\mathbb{F}_q$ (e.g., for the specific choice of $q = 2^{253} + 2^{199} + 1$), we obtain essentially the same results for GMiMC instances with large q as we obtain for instances with small q. For example, in Sect. 4.1 we derived an integral distinguisher on $R = 3t - 4 + \lfloor \log_3(q - 2) \rfloor$ rounds, with complexity q. By exploiting any multiplicative subgroup of size $|\mathbb{G}| = 2^s$ for $s \leq 199$ when $q = 2^{253} + 2^{199} + 1$, we obtain an integral distinguisher on $R = 3t - 4 + \lfloor \log_3(|\mathbb{G}| - 1) \rfloor$ with complexity $|\mathbb{G}| + 1$.

Moreover, even for smaller fields, we can fine-tune the size of $\mathbb{G}$ to reduce the complexity of the attack. This is relevant especially for cases where an attack with complexity q can reach more rounds than the ones used by the primitive (which is indeed the case, as shown in Table 3). For example, as derived in Sect. 4.2, we have a zero-sum property for $4t - 6 + 2\lfloor \log_3(q - 2) \rfloor$ rounds with complexity q. For the GMiMC variant with $q = 2^{61} + 20 \times 2^{32} + 1$ and $t = 12$, we use a subgroup of size $2^{33} \cdot 167 \cdot 211 \approx 2^{48}$ (which divides $q - 1$), and obtain a zero-sum property for $4t - 6 + 2\lfloor \log_3(2^{48} - 1) \rfloor = 102$ rounds, with complexity of about 2^{48} (which covers the full permutation).

5 Differential Attacks on Round-Reduced GMiMC

5.1 Impossible Differential Attacks

We present a new impossible differential for $(3t - 4)$ rounds, which improves the previous one for $(2t - 2)$ rounds presented by the designers [4, Page 46].

The previous impossible differential exploits the following probability one propagation for $(t - 1)$ rounds: $(0, \ldots, 0, \alpha) \rightarrow (\alpha, 0, \ldots, 0)$ where α is a non-zero difference. Hence, $(0, \ldots, 0, \alpha)$ never propagates to $(\beta, 0, \ldots, 0)$ after $2t - 2$

rounds for any β. The designers concluded that *conservatively $2t$ rounds are secure when the security level corresponds to the block size n.*

We show that $(0, \ldots, 0, \alpha_1) \xrightarrow{\mathcal{R}^{3t-4}} (\beta_1, 0, \ldots, 0)$ is an impossible propagation, where α_1, β_1 are non-zero differences satisfying $\alpha_1 \neq \beta_1$. That is, we include $t - 2$ more rounds in the middle compared to the property presented by the designers.

The intuition for why the above differential is impossible is as follows. When $(0, \ldots, 0, \alpha_1)$ is propagated, the output difference of the cube mapping is 0 for the first $t - 1$ rounds and is unpredictable for the next $t/2 - 1$ rounds. We denote them by $\alpha_2, \alpha_3, \ldots, \alpha_{t/2}$. Similarly, we extend $(0, \ldots, 0, \beta_1)$ by $t/2 - 1$ rounds backwards, using the notation $\beta_2, \beta_3, \ldots, \beta_{t/2}$. Here, to be a valid propagation, those differences must be equal in all the branches, which yields a system of t linear equations with $2(t/2 - 1) = t - 2$ variables. By solving the system, we obtain that $\alpha_1 = \beta_1$ is a necessary condition to obtain a valid differential propagation. In other words, for any α_1, β_1 with $\alpha_1 \neq \beta_1$, the propagation is impossible. A detailed analysis of this property is provided in [17].

5.2   A Differential Distinguisher

The original paper [4, Appendix D] analyzes the resistance of GMiMC against differential attacks. Most notably, the designers exhibit a differential characteristic over $(t+1)$ rounds with two active Sboxes, with probability $2^{-(2n+2)}$ where $n = \log_2 q$ and they conjecture that the corresponding differential is optimal. They deduce that

$$R = 2 + (t+1)\left\lceil \frac{tn}{2(n-1)} \right\rceil \text{ rounds}$$

are sufficient to resist differential cryptanalysis in the sense that the data complexity of the attack exceeds the size of the full codebook. For instance, when $t = 12$ and $n = 61$, this corresponds to 93 rounds out of 101.

A Better Differential. We exhibit another differential, over t rounds, which leads to a much more efficient attack. Let α and α' be two differences in $\mathbb{F}_q$. Then, the difference $(0, \ldots, 0, \alpha, \alpha')$ propagates through t rounds of the permutation as

$$(0, \ldots, 0, \alpha, \alpha') \xrightarrow{\mathcal{R}^{t-2}} (\alpha, \alpha', 0 \ldots, 0)$$
$$\xrightarrow{\mathcal{R}} (\alpha' + \beta, \beta, \ldots, \beta, \alpha)$$
$$\xrightarrow{\mathcal{R}} (\beta + \beta', \ldots, \beta + \beta', \alpha + \beta', \alpha' + \beta),$$

where $\alpha \xrightarrow{S} \beta$ denotes the Sbox transition occurring at Round $(t-1)$ and $\alpha' + \beta \xrightarrow{S} \beta'$ the Sbox transition occurring at Round t.

It follows that, for any possible value of β, we obtain the following t-round differential as soon as $\beta' = -\beta$, which occurs with probability 2^{-n} on average:

$$(0, \ldots, 0, \alpha, \alpha') \xrightarrow{\mathcal{R}^t} (0, \ldots, 0, \alpha - \beta, \alpha' + \beta) .$$

Since this probability does not depend on the choice of α and α', this differential can be iterated several times to cover more rounds.

For instance, when $t = 12$ and $n = 61$, the 101 rounds of GMIMC can be decomposed into 8 blocks of $t = 12$ rounds, followed by 5 rounds. We then get a differential of the form

$$(0, \ldots, 0, \alpha, \alpha') \longrightarrow (0, 0, 0, 0, 0, \gamma, \gamma', 0, 0, 0, 0, 0)$$

over the full cipher for some unknown γ, γ' with probability at least

$$P = (2^{-61})^8 = 2^{-488}$$

since the characteristic over the last 5 rounds has probability one. This leads to a differential distinguisher over the full permutation with complexity $P^{-1} = 2^{488}$ which is much lower than the size of the full codebook (2^{732}).

It is worth noticing that P is a lower bound on the probability of the 101-round differential since we considered pairs following some specific characteristics by fixing the forms of some differences at intermediate rounds. Some additional input pairs may lead to an output difference of the same form but not to these specific intermediate differences.

Improving the Complexity of the Distinguisher with Structures. The data complexity of the previous distinguisher can be improved by using structures of inputs. Here, a structure is a set of 2^{2n} inputs of the form $\mathcal{S}_c = \{(c_1, \ldots, c_{t-2}, x, y) \mid x, y \in \mathbb{F}_p\}$. The difference between any two elements in the same structure has the form $(0, \ldots, 0, \alpha, \alpha')$. It follows that, from any structure, we can construct 2^{4n-1} pairs of inputs whose difference conforms with the differential. Then, the number of structures required to obtain $P^{-1} = 2^{8n}$ pairs with an appropriate difference is

$$2^{8n-4n+1} = 2^{4n+1},$$

leading to an overall data complexity of $2^{6n+1} = 2^{367}$. The time complexity is equal to the data complexity here since the distinguisher consists in identifying the output pairs which coincide on all output words except the two in the middle. This does not require computing all pairs of elements in each structure, but only to store the values $\pi(x), x \in \mathcal{S}_c$ according to their first coordinates.

This differential distinguisher does not lead to an attack with complexity below the target security level. However, this must be considered as an unsuitable property since its complexity is much lower than what we expect for a randomly chosen permutation on a set of size 2^{732}.

It is worth noticing that, if we restrict ourselves to distinguishers with complexity below the target security level of 128 bits, then we can use at most $2^{128}/2^{2n} = 2^6$ structures. Therefore, we can derive from these structures 2^{6+4n-1} i.e. 2^{249} pairs of inputs conforming with the differential. These pairs be can used to distinguish 4 blocks of t rounds since the differential has probability at least 2^{-244}. Moreover, a valid pair propagates to a differential of the form

$(\gamma, \gamma', 0, 0, 0, 0, 0, 0, 0, 0, 0, 0)$ with probability one over $(t - 2)$ rounds, and we can extend it by a few more rounds by considering the number of state words that have the same difference. After another 6 rounds, the pair has a differential of the form

$$(\Delta, \Delta, \Delta, \Delta, \Delta, \Delta, *, *, *, *, *, *),$$

with probability one, where $*$ is an unknown difference that we do not care about. This differential form has a constraint of the size $5n$: the left-most six state words have an identical difference. The number of queries to satisfy the same property for a randomly chosen permutation is lower bounded by $2^{5n/2} \approx 2^{152.5}$. This implies that we can distinguish $4t + (t - 2) + (t - 6) = 64$ rounds of GMiMC from a randomly chosen permutation with complexity less than 2^{128}.

Improved Distinguisher Using Three Active Words. If we consider a differential with only two active words, the biggest structure we can build is of size 2^{2n}, which limits the advantage of using structures in reducing the cost of the distinguishers. Let us now consider the following differential:

$$
\begin{aligned}
&(0, \ldots, 0, \alpha, \alpha', \alpha'') \\
\xrightarrow{\mathcal{R}^{t-3}}\ &(\alpha, \alpha', \alpha'', 0 \ldots, 0) \\
\xrightarrow{\mathcal{R}}\ &(\alpha' + \beta, \alpha'' + \beta, \beta, \ldots, \beta, \alpha) \\
\xrightarrow{\mathcal{R}}\ &(\alpha'' + \beta + \beta', \beta + \beta', \beta + \beta', \ldots, \beta + \beta', \alpha + \beta', \alpha') \\
\xrightarrow{\mathcal{R}}\ &(\beta + \beta' + \beta'', \ldots, \beta + \beta' + \beta'', \alpha + \beta' + \beta'', \alpha' + \beta + \beta'', \alpha'' + \beta + \beta'),
\end{aligned}
$$

where $\alpha \xrightarrow{S} \beta$, $\alpha' + \beta \xrightarrow{S} \beta'$ and $\alpha'' + \beta + \beta' \xrightarrow{S} \beta''$ denote the Sbox transitions occurring at Round $(t - 2)$, at Round $(t - 1)$ and at Round t.

As with the previous differential, if $\beta + \beta' + \beta'' = 0$, which occurs with probability 2^{-n} on average, we have:

$$(0, \ldots, 0, \alpha, \alpha', \alpha'') \xrightarrow{\mathcal{R}^t} (0, \ldots, 0, \alpha - \beta, \alpha' + \beta + \beta'', \alpha'' - \beta'').$$

Again, the probability of this transition is independent of the values of α, α' and α'', so it can be iterated with probability 2^{-n}.

For this differential, we can build structures of size 2^{3n}. This will allow us to consider around 2^{6n} pairs with the required input differential, so we can expect to be able to iterate the characteristic for $6t$ rounds. The total distinguisher will cover $6t + (t - 3)$ rounds. As for the previous one, we can add 4 more rounds, generating an output state with 8 words having the same difference with a cost of 2^{3n}, compared to a cost of $2^{7n/2}$ for a random permutation. For GMiMC with $t = 12$, this allows to distinguish 85 rounds with a cost of 2^{3n}. By repeating this procedure 2^n times, we can expect t more round to be covered, and distinguish the whole permutation with 101 rounds with a complexity of $2^{5n} = 2^{320}$ and having 9 words with a zero difference (as we do not need to add the final four rounds).

Let us point out that using four instead of three words would not improve the number of rounds attacked on GMiMC-128-d, as the cost of one structure is already the same as the cost of obtaining the 8 non-zero differences in the output for a random permutation. Nevertheless, in the case of the GMiMC variant 256-b with $t = 14$, if we use a similar differential with four active words, we can distinguish up to $8t + (t - 4) = 122$ rounds while finding 10 words with no difference and with a complexity of about $2^{4n} = 2^{500}$.

To determine whether further improvements of these differentials are possible, we have searched for other differential characteristics with a Mixed-Integer Linear Programming (MILP) model. We conclude that the previously described characteristics are essentially optimal for the defined search space, and refer to [17] for details.

5.3   Algebraically Controlled Differential Attacks

In this section, we show how to use algebraic techniques to efficiently find inputs that satisfy a given differential characteristic. The basic idea is to represent the initial state of the permutation symbolically by assigning variables to some of its branches, while the remaining branches are assigned constant values. We then compute the permutation symbolically for several rounds. Namely, for each round, we derive a polynomial expression for each branch of the internal state in terms of the allocated variables.

We repeat this process starting from two initial states (representing two inputs to the permutation), perhaps assigning them different variables. We can now represent the difference between the internal states at each round in these two computations using polynomial expressions in the allocated variables. In particular, each differential transition of the given differential characteristic (whose probability is smaller than one) is expressed as a polynomial equation in the variables. Collecting the equations for all differential transitions, we obtain a system of polynomial equations, whose solution immediately gives two inputs to the permutation that satisfy the differential characteristic. For this approach to be useful, the equation system has to be efficiently solvable, which generally implies that we cannot allocate too many variables and need to minimize the algebraic degree of the polynomial equations.

Next, we discuss the complexity of solving equation systems of a specific form that we encounter in the remainder of this section. We then demonstrate the basic attack approach with an example and continue with more involved attacks.

Solving Polynomial Equation Systems with Few Variables. Some of our attacks in the remainder of this section reduce to solving equation systems over $\mathbb{F}_q$. When possible, we solved the systems in practice using the MAGMA software. However, it is also important to understand the complexity of our attacks on stronger variants of the cryptosystem, where they become impractical. In this section, we will only consider systems with one or two variables and estimate the complexity of solving such systems below. We note that in Sect. 6.2 we encounter equation systems with more variables. Solving such equations is more involved and we will have to use a different estimation, which is heuristic (but standard).

Solving a univariate polynomial equation over $\mathbb{F}_q$ of degree d is done by factoring the polynomial. Asymptotically, the best known algorithm for this problem was published in [27] and has complexity of about $d^{1.5+o(1)}$ bits operations. We note, however, that the $o(1)$ expression in the exponent hides a non-negligible term. Solving two bivariate polynomial equations $P_1(x, y) = 0$ and $P_2(x, y) = 0$ of total degrees d_1 and d_2 (respectively) can be done by computing the *resultant*[2] of the two polynomials, which is a univariate polynomial in x of degree $d_1 \cdot d_2$. We then compute the roots of the resultant (by factoring it) and for each such root $\bar{x}$, we compute the common roots of $P_1(\bar{x}, y)$ and $P_2(\bar{x}, y)$ (using a GCD algorithm). In general, the heaviest step in this process is factoring the resultant.

Satisfying $3t - 2$ Rounds. We show how to efficiently satisfy $3t - 2$ rounds of the iterative differential characteristic of Sect. 5,

$$(0, \ldots, 0, \mu_0, \mu_0') \xrightarrow{\mathcal{R}^{t-2}} (\mu_0, \mu_0', 0 \ldots, 0)$$
$$\xrightarrow{\mathcal{R}} (\mu_0' + \mu_1, \mu_1, \ldots, \mu_1, \mu_0)$$
$$\xrightarrow{\mathcal{R}} (\mu_1 + \mu_1', \ldots, \mu_1 + \mu_1', \mu_0 + \mu_1', \mu_0' + \mu_1),$$

where we require that $\mu_1 + \mu_1' = 0$.

Consider an initial state of the permutation of the form

$$X_0 = (\alpha_1, \ldots, \alpha_{t-2}, x, f(x)),$$

where the α_i are constants in $\mathbb{F}_q$, x is a variable and the function $f(x)$ is described in Sect. 4 (see (1)). Then, as described in Sect. 4, the internal state at Round $(t - 2)$ is described as

$$X_{t-2} = (x + \sum_{i=1}^{t-2} \beta_i, f(x) + \sum_{i=1}^{t-2} \beta_i, \gamma_1, \ldots, \gamma_{t-2}),$$

while the state at Round $(2t - 2)$ is described as

$$X_{2t-2} = (x' - (x' + \mathsf{RC}_{t-1})^3 + \delta_1, -x' + \delta_1, \delta_2, \ldots, \delta_t),$$

where $x' = x + \sum_{i=1}^{t-2} \beta_i$. Starting from Round $(2t - 2)$, the algebraic degree of the branches generally grows by a multiplicative factor of 3 per round, namely, the algebraic degree of Round $(2t - 2 + r)$ is at most 3^{r+1}.

Next, consider another initial state of the permutation of the form

$$Y_0 = (\alpha_1, \ldots, \alpha_{t-2}, y, f(y)),$$

where the initial constants α_i are identical to those of X_0. Note that the initial difference between the states is of the form

$$\Delta_0 = X_0 - Y_0 = (0, \ldots, 0, \mu_0(x, y), \mu_0'(x, y)).$$

---

[2] The resultant of two polynomials is itself a polynomial in their coefficients, whose zeroes coincide with the common roots of the two polynomials.

Then, the state Y_{2t-2} after Round $(2t-2)$ is described as

$$Y_{2t-2} = (y' - (y' + \mathsf{RC}_{t-1})^3 + \delta_1, -y' + \delta_2, \delta_3, \dots, \delta_t).$$

Therefore, the choice of the initial states of the two inputs, assures that $(2t-2)$ rounds of the differential characteristic are satisfied with probability one. At round $2t$, we have

$$\Delta_{2t} = X_{2t} - Y_{2t} =$$
$$(\mu_2(x,y) + \mu'_2(x,y), \dots, \mu_2(x,y) + \mu'_2(x,y), \mu_1(x,y) + \mu'_2(x,y), \mu'_1(x,y) + \mu_2(x,y)),$$

and we require $\mu_2(x,y) + \mu'_2(x,y) = 0$, which is a polynomial equation of degree $3^{2+1} = 27$ in the variables x, y. Since we have 2 variables and only one equation in $\mathbb{F}_q$, we can set one of the variables to an arbitrary constant and solve a univariate polynomial equation in the other variable. We expect one solution on average, which gives an input pair that satisfies the differential characteristic for $2t$ rounds. Since the next $(t-2)$ rounds are satisfied with probability one, we can satisfy $3t-2$ rounds at the cost of solving a univariate polynomial equation over $\mathbb{F}_q$ of degree 27 (which has very low complexity).

Satisfying $4t-2$ Rounds in an Inside-Out Setting. In an inside-out setting, the differential characteristic can be extended from $(3t-2)$ rounds to $(4t-2)$ rounds algebraically, by adding t rounds before the initial state. Indeed, since the initial state is described by polynomials of degree 3, the state at round (-2) can be described by polynomials of degree 27:

$$\Delta_{-2} = X_{-2} - Y_{-2} = (\mu_{-1}(x,y) + \mu'_{-1}(x,y), \dots,$$
$$\mu_{-1}(x,y) + \mu'_{-1}(x,y), \lambda_1(x,y) + \mu'_{-1}(x,y), \lambda'_1(x,y) + \mu_{-1}(x,y)).$$

Thus, we require $\mu_{-1}(x,y) + \mu'_{-1}(x,y) = 0$ in addition to $\mu_2(x,y) + \mu'_2(x,y) = 0$. This defines a system of two equations of degree 27 in two variables. Any solution with $x \neq y$ defines a pair of states that satisfies a differential characteristic from round $(-t)$ to round $(3t-2)$, because rounds $(-t)$ to (-2) are satisfied with probability 1.

To solve the system, we first divide each equation by $(y-x)$ to eliminate trivial solutions with $x = y$. Then we compute a Gröbner basis of the resulting system. Using the MAGMA software, this can be done in less than one minute on a standard PC (solving the system also has very low complexity by our theoretical estimate). Moreover, this can be extended to a distinguisher on 66 rounds by considering a truncated difference in the input and output. We give an example in Figure 6 of [17].

Satisfying $4t-4$ Rounds. If we want to use the differential in a collision attack, we must preserve the value of some initial state words, and we cannot use the inside-out technique. We describe an alternative technique, using a modified differential with four active state words:

$$(0, \ldots, 0, \mu_0, \mu_0', \mu_0'', \mu_0''')$$
$$\xrightarrow{\mathcal{R}^{t-4}} (\mu_0, \mu_0', \mu_0'', \mu_0''', 0 \ldots, 0)$$
$$\xrightarrow{\mathcal{R}} (\mu_0' + \mu_1, \mu_0'' + \mu_1, \mu_0''' + \mu_1, \mu_1, \ldots, \mu_1, \mu_0)$$
$$\xrightarrow{\mathcal{R}} (\mu_0'' + \mu_1 + \mu_1', \mu_0''' + \mu_1 + \mu_1', \mu_1 + \mu_1', \ldots, \mu_1 + \mu_1', \mu_0 + \mu_1', \mu_0' + \mu_1)$$
$$\xrightarrow{\mathcal{R}} (\mu_0''' + \mu_1 + \mu_1' + \mu_1'', \mu_1 + \mu_1' + \mu_1'', \ldots, \mu_1 + \mu_1' + \mu_1'', \mu_0 + \mu_1' + \mu_1'',$$
$$\mu_0' + \mu_1 + \mu_1'', \mu_0'' + \mu_1 + \mu_1')$$
$$\xrightarrow{\mathcal{R}} (\boldsymbol{\mu_1}, \ldots, \boldsymbol{\mu_1}, \mu_0 + \boldsymbol{\mu_1} - \mu_1, \mu_0' + \boldsymbol{\mu_1} - \mu_1', \mu_0'' + \boldsymbol{\mu_1} - \mu_1'', \mu_0''' + \boldsymbol{\mu_1} - \mu_1''')$$
with $\boldsymbol{\mu_1} = \mu_1 + \mu_1' + \mu_1'' + \mu_1'''$.

As in Sect. 5.2, we require that $\boldsymbol{\mu_1} = 0$. This happens with probability 2^{-n}, and results in an iterative truncated characteristic $(0, \ldots, 0, *, *, *, *) \xrightarrow{\mathcal{R}^t} (0, \ldots, 0, *, *, *, *)$.

As in the previous attack, we build an initial state with special relations to control the first t rounds with probability one:

$$X_0 = (\alpha_1, \ldots, \alpha_{t-4}, x, f(x), y, f(y)).$$

This ensures that the state at Round $(2t - 4)$ is of the form:

$$X_{2t-4} = (x' - (x' + \mathsf{RC}_{t-1})^3 + \delta_1, -x' + \delta_2, y' - (y' + \mathsf{RC}_{t-1})^3 + \delta_3, -y' + \delta_4, \delta_5, \ldots, \delta_t).$$

Instead of considering two different states with this shape (with four unknown in total), we will consider one variable state and one fixed state with $(x, y) = (0, 0)$. When we consider the state at Round $(2t)$, we have

$$\Delta_{2t} = X_{2t} - X_{2t}(0, 0) =$$
$$(\boldsymbol{\mu_2}, \ldots, \boldsymbol{\mu_2}, \mu_1 + \boldsymbol{\mu_2} - \mu_2, \mu_1' + \boldsymbol{\mu_2} - \mu_2', \mu_1'' + \boldsymbol{\mu_2} - \mu_2'', \mu_1''' + \boldsymbol{\mu_2} - \mu_2''')$$

Where $(\mu_1, \mu_1', \mu_1'', \mu_1''')$ are polynomials of degree 3, 1, 3, and 1 respectively (as seen in X_{2t-4}), and $(\mu_2, \mu_2', \mu_2'', \mu_2''')$ are polynomials of degree 9, 27, 81, and 243, with $\boldsymbol{\mu_2} = \mu_2 + \mu_2' + \mu_2'' + \mu_2'''$. All polynomials have variables x and x', and $X_{2t}(0, 0)$ is a vector of constants. We now require $\boldsymbol{\mu_2}(x, x') = 0$, and we can simplify the state using this assumption:

$$X_{2t} = X_{2t}(0, 0) + (0, \ldots, 0, \mu_1 - \mu_2, \mu_1' - \mu_2', \mu_1'' - \mu_2'', \mu_1''' + \mu_2 + \mu_2' + \mu_2'').$$

We obtain an expression of degree $(0, \ldots, 0, 9, 27, 81, 81)$.

When we focus on Round $(3t)$, we can now express the condition of the differential as a polynomial of degree 729. Therefore, we have a system of two equations of degree 243 and 729 in two variables. To estimate the complexity of solving the system, recall that we factor the resultant of these polynomials in time $d^{1.5+o(1)}$ bit operations. In our case, $d = 243 \cdot 729 = 177,147$.

Any solution with $(x, y) \neq (0, 0)$ defines a state such that $(X(x, y), X(0, 0))$ satisfies the differential characteristic up to round $(4t - 4)$, because rounds $(4t)$ to $(4t - 4)$ are satisfied with probability one.

Extending the Differentials. All these attacks can be extended probabilistically by finding about q different input pairs that satisfy the differential characteristic (each pair is found by choosing different constants α_i in the initial state). With high probability, one of these input pairs will also satisfy the next differential transitions, and follow the characteristic for t more rounds.

5.4   Reduced-Round Collision Attacks

We can build collisions on a reduced number of rounds by using the same ideas as for the previous structural or algebraic differential distinguishers. The additional constraint that we have now compared to distinguishers is that any values that need to be chosen must be assigned to the rate part, *i.e.* the 8 left-most words in GMiMC-128-d, and the capacity part, *i.e.* the 4 right-most words in GMiMC-128-d, will be fixed to a known value we cannot choose.

Building Collisions with Structures. We won't use the 3-word differential but the 2-word one, as using the full $2n$ structure from the 2-word one already implies a complexity equivalent to that of a generic collision attack. Instead of having $t = 12$ free rounds at the beginning, we will have only 8, due to the 4 words reserved for the capacity. With a cost of $2^{r \cdot n}$ we can then go through $r \cdot t$ rounds maintaining the same differential. Finally, we can freely add $(t-2)$ rounds that preserve the differences in the rate part and, consequently, can finally be cancelled:

$$(0,\ldots,0,\alpha,\alpha',0,0,0,0) \xrightarrow{\mathcal{R}^{t-6}} (\alpha,\alpha',0\ldots,0) \xrightarrow{\mathcal{R}^{r \cdot t}} (\beta,\beta',0\ldots,0),$$

This differential has a probability of $2^{-r \cdot t}$, and would allow to build collisions up to $3t - 6$ rounds, so for 30 rounds for GMiMC-128-d. If we use structures we can improve this: if we build a structure of size 2^x, with the cost of the structure we can verify a probability up to 2^{-2x}. If we choose structures of size $2^{3n/2}$, we can consider $r = 3$. This would provide collisions for $4t - 6$ rounds. For GMiMC-128-d this implies collisions on 42 rounds with a cost of 2^{92}, and for GMiMC-256 it implies collisions on 50 rounds with a complexity of 2^{187}.

Building Collisions with Algebraically Controlled Techniques. To use the algebraically controlled techniques in a collision attack, we must not use any difference in the inner part of the sponge. As noted, in the case of GMiMC-128-d, we have $c = 4$, therefore, we start from a state

$$X_0 = (\alpha_1, \ldots, \alpha_4, x, f(x), y, f(y), \alpha_9, \ldots, \alpha_{12})$$

and we have a characteristic over $4t - 4 - c = 40$ rounds. In MAGMA, this takes a few minutes using less than 3 GB of RAM. We give an example of a conforming pair in Figure AAA in [17], where all the α constants have been set to zero. This attack can be extended to t more rounds probabilistically, with (asymptotic) complexity of $q \cdot d^{1.5+o(1)}$ bit operations. In our case, $d = 177,147$ and we obtain an estimate of about 2^{90} if we ignore the $o(1)$ term.

6   Attacks on HADESMiMC

This section describes two types of attacks against HADESMiMC, which both exploit the propagation of affine subspaces over the partial rounds. The first one is an integral distinguisher covering all rounds except the first two rounds for most sets of parameters. The second one is a preimage attack on the full function which applies when the MDS matrix defining the linear layer has, up to multiplication by a scalar, a low multiplicative order. It is worth noticing that, while the designers of HADESMiMC do not mention any requirements on this MDS matrix, they provide several suggestions. For STARKAD and POSEIDON, Cauchy matrices are used [24]. In [17], we identify weak instances from this class of matrices. Alternatively, the HADESMiMC authors propose [25, Appendix B] the use of a matrix of the form $A \times B^{-1}$ where both A and B are Vandermonde matrices with generating elements a_i and b_i. In this case, if $a_i = b_i + r$ for some $r \in \mathbb{F}_q$, then the resulting MDS matrix will be an involution for $\mathbb{F}_q$ of characteristic two [33]. Similarly, in characteristic $p \neq 2$, one obtains an involution whenever $a_i = -b_i$.

6.1   Integral Distinguishers

In HADESMiMC, the number of rounds has been chosen by the designers in such a way that, when each coordinate of the output is expressed as a polynomial in t variables over $\mathbb{F}_q$, then the degree of this polynomial *in each input* is close to $(q - 1)$, which is the behaviour expected for a randomly chosen permutation. Assuming that the degree grows as 3^r for r rounds (which is an upper bound), $\lceil \log_3(t(q-1)) \rceil$ rounds are enough to get a polynomial of total degree $(q-1)t$. For the concrete parameters, i.e. $t = 12$ and $q = 2^{61} + 20 \times 2^{32} + 1$ for POSEIDON, we get that 41 rounds (out of 48 in total) are necessary to achieve maximal degree. For STARKAD with $t = 12$ and $q = 2^{63}$, 43 rounds (out of 51 in total) are necessary.

An Integral Property. Our idea to improve upon the trivial bound above by a few partial rounds is to choose a specific subspace of inputs. Indeed, we are going to construct a one-dimensional subspace V such that $t - 1$ partial rounds will map any coset $V + v_0$ onto a coset of another one-dimensional subspace W. Adding at most $\lfloor \log_3(q - 2) \rfloor$ rounds (either full or partial), ensures that the conditions of Corollary 1 are satisfied and thus the outputs sum to zero.

$$V + v_0 \xrightarrow{\mathcal{R}_p^{t-1}} W + w_0 \xrightarrow{\deg < q-1} \text{zero sum.}$$

Let us denote by V a linear subspace of internal states after the Sbox layer of the last of the first $R_f/2$ full rounds (see Fig. 4). Then, this subspace leads to an affine subspace at the input of the first partial round, which is a coset of $L(V)$. The following lemma guarantees the existence of a nontrivial vector space $L(V)$ such that any coset of $L(V)$ is mapped to a coset of $W = L^t(V)$ after $t - 1$ partial rounds.

Lemma 1. *Let $F : \mathbb{F}_q^t \to \mathbb{F}_q^t$ denote a permutation obtained from $r \geq 1$ partial* HADESMIMC *rounds instantiated with linear layer L. If L has multiplicative order h up to multiplication by a scalar, then there exists a vector space V with $\dim V \geq t - \min\{h, r\}$ such that $F(x + V) \subseteq F(x) + L^r(V)$ for all $x \in \mathbb{F}_q^t$.*

Proof. Let $V = \langle \delta_t, L^T(\delta_t), \ldots, (L^T)^{r-1}(\delta_t) \rangle^{\perp}$ where $\delta_t = (0, \ldots, 0, 1)$. Clearly, $\dim V$ satisfies the desired lower bound. It suffices to show that for all $x \in \mathbb{F}_q^t$ and $v \in V$, $F(x + v) = F(x) + L^r(v)$. Let $F = R_r \circ \cdots \circ R_1$. Since the last coordinate of any v in V is zero, i.e. $v \perp \delta_t$, the image of $x + V$ by the partial Sbox layer is a coset of V. It follows that $R_1(x + v) = R_1(x) + L(v)$. Similarly, for Round $i = 2, \ldots, r$, it holds that $R_i(x_i + L^{i-1}(v)) = R_i(x_i) + L^i(v)$ if $L^{i-1}(v) \perp \delta_t$ or equivalently $v \perp (L^T)^{i-1}(\delta_t)$. □

Let us consider any coordinate y of the output of the permutation after adding r additional (partial or full) rounds. When z_0 varies in V, these output words correspond to the images by the additional rounds of the elements z_1 in a coset of $W = L^t(V)$, which we denote by $\gamma + W$ (see Fig. 4). As the polynomial corresponding to the r additional rounds has degree at most 3^r, it then follows using Corollary 1 that

$$\sum_{z_0 \in V} y(z_0) = \sum_{z_1 \in \gamma + W} y(z_1) = \sum_{x \in \mathbb{F}_q} P(x) = 0 \,,$$

as long as r is at most $\lfloor \log_3(q - 2) \rfloor$.

Thus, in total this covers $(t - 1) + \lfloor \log_3(q - 2) \rfloor$ rounds, starting after the first full rounds. For most sets of concrete parameters, this actually exceeds the recommended number of rounds in the forward direction for both POSEIDON and STARKAD. Furthermore, Lemma 1 implies that if the linear layer L has multiplicative order less than $t - 1$, then the distinguisher covers an arbitrary number of partial rounds.

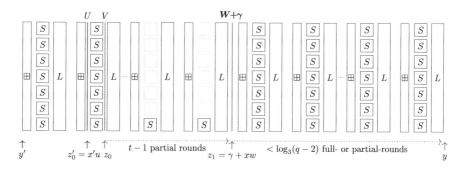

Fig. 4. Zero-sum distinguisher against POSEIDON and STARKAD covering $(2 + 4)$ full rounds and all partial rounds.

Zero-Sum Distinguishers over $\mathbb{F}_q$. By extending the above-mentioned approach in the backwards direction, we can construct a zero-sum distinguisher with a (slightly) extended number of rounds as depicted on Fig. 4. The problem is that contrary to the case of GMiMC, the inverse round function in HADESMiMC is very different from the round function itself, and it has a much higher degree. Indeed, the inverse of the cube mapping over $\mathbb{F}_q$ is the power function $x \mapsto x^{(2q-1)/3}$. By using classical bounds on the degree, we cannot guarantee a degree lower than $(q - 2)$ for more than a single round backwards.

However, V being one dimensional allows to overcome one additional layer of Sboxes, and thus one additional round. Namely, as V is a one-dimensional space there exists a vector $v = (v_1, \ldots, v_t) \in \mathbb{F}_q^t$ such that

$$V = \{(x\,v_1, x\,v_2, \ldots, x\,v_t) \mid x \in \mathbb{F}_q\}.$$

The image of V under the inverse of the full Sbox layer consists of all the vectors in $\mathbb{F}_q^t$ of the form

$$\left((x\,v_1)^{1/3}, \ldots, (x\,v_t)^{1/3}\right) = x^{1/3}\left(v_1^{1/3}, \ldots, v_t^{1/3}\right).$$

As a consequence, this image is again a one-dimensional vector space having the same form, namely $U = \{x'\,(u_1, \ldots, u_t) \mid x' \in \mathbb{F}_q\}$ where $u_i = v_i^{1/3}$ for all $0 \le i < t$. It is worth noticing that this particular structure does not propagate over more rounds because of the addition of a round constant. Then, any coordinate at the input of the previous round y' is the image of an element $z_0' = x'u$ in U by an affine layer, followed by the inverse of Sbox, i.e., by $x \mapsto x^{1/3}$ (see Fig. 4). We can then consider this mapping as a function of $x' \in \mathbb{F}_q$, and express it as a polynomial Q with coefficients in $\mathbb{F}_q$. Since the degree of this polynomial is the degree of the inverse Sbox, it does not exceed $(q - 2)$. Using the notion from Fig. 4, we then have

$$\sum_{z_0 \in V} y'(z_0) = \sum_{z_0' \in U} y'(z_0') = \sum_{x' \in \mathbb{F}_q} Q(x) = 0\,.$$

For most sets of proposed parameters, this provides a zero-sum distinguisher with data complexity q on HADESMiMC for all but the two initial rounds, i.e. for $2 + 4$ full rounds (2 at the beginning and 4 at the end), and all partial rounds, as detailed in Table 4. Again, for instantiations of HADESMiMC with a linear layer of multiplicative order less than $t - 1$, the distinguisher covers an arbitrary number of partial rounds.

6.2   Finding Preimages by Linearization of the Partial Rounds

This section shows that, when the linear layer in HADESMiMC has a low multiplicative order, the propagation of linear subspaces through all partial rounds leads to a much more powerful attack. Indeed, we now show that the existence of perfect linear approximations over the partial rounds of HADESMiMC, as detailed in Lemma 2, can be used to setup a simplified system of equations for finding preimages, leading to a full-round preimage attack.

Table 4. Number of rounds of HADESMIMC covered by the zero-sum distinguisher of complexity q.

security level	t		POSEIDON			STARKAD	
		$\log_2 q$	proposed R_f, R_P	nb of rounds of the ZS	$\log_2 q$	proposed R_f, R_P	nb of rounds of the ZS
128 bits	12	61	8, 40	2+4, 45	63	8, 43	2+4, 46
	4	125	8, 81	2+4, 77	125	8, 85	2+4, 77
	12	125	8, 83	2+4, 85	125	8, 86	2+4, 85
	3	253	8, 83	2+4, 157	255	8, 85	2+4, 158
	12	253	8, 85	2+4, 165	255	8, 88	2+4, 166
256 bits	8	125	8, 82	2+4, 81	125	8, 86	2+4, 81
	14	125	8, 83	2+4, 87	125	8, 83	2+4, 87

Lemma 2. *Let $F : \mathbb{F}_q^t \to \mathbb{F}_q^t$ denote a permutation obtained from $r \geq 1$ partial HADESMIMC rounds instantiated with linear layer L and round constants $c_1, \ldots, c_r$. Let $V \subset \mathbb{F}_q^t$ be the vector space $V = \langle L(\delta_t), L^2(\delta_t), \ldots, L^r(\delta_t) \rangle^\perp$, where $\delta_t = (0, \ldots, 0, 1)$. Then, for all $x \in \mathbb{F}_q^t$ and $v \in V$,*

$$v \cdot F(x) = v \cdot L^r(x) + \sum_{i=1}^{r} v \cdot L^{r+1-i}(c_i),$$

where $u \cdot v$ denotes the usual scalar product in $\mathbb{F}_q^t$. Furthermore, if L has multiplicative order h, then $\dim V \geq t - \min\{h, r\}$.

Proof. Let $F_r = R_r \circ R_{r-1} \circ \cdots \circ R_1$, where R_i denotes the ith partial round of HADESMIMC, namely $R_i(x) = L \circ S(x + c_i)$. We proceed by induction on r. For $r = 1$, we have, for any v and x,

$$v \cdot R_1(x) = L^T(v) \cdot S(x + c_1) = L^T(v) \cdot (x + c_1) = v \cdot L(x) + v \cdot L(c_1)$$

if the last coordinate of $L^T(v)$ is zero, or equivalently $L^T(v) \cdot \delta_t = v \cdot L(\delta_t) = 0$.

Let us now consider Round r and $v \in \langle L(\delta_t), L^2(\delta_t), \ldots, L^r(\delta_t) \rangle^\perp$. For any $y \in \mathbb{F}_q^t$, we have

$$v \cdot R_r(y) = L^T(v) \cdot S(y + c_r) = L^T(v) \cdot (y + c_r)$$

since $L^T(v) \cdot \delta_t = v \cdot L(\delta_t) = 0$. Letting $y = F_{r-1}(x)$, it follows that

$$v \cdot F_r(x) = L^T(v) \cdot F_{r-1}(x) + L^T(v) \cdot c_r = L^T(v) \cdot L^{r-1}(x) + \sum_{i=1}^{r-1} L^T(v) \cdot L^{r-i}(c_i) + L^T(v) \cdot c_r$$

where the last equality is deduced from the induction hypothesis using that $L^T(v)$ belongs to $\langle L(\delta_t), \ldots, L^{r-1}(\delta_t) \rangle^\perp$. Finally, it is easy to see that the dimension of $V^\perp$ can be upper bounded as $\dim V^\perp \leq \min\{h, r, t\}$. Hence, $\dim V \geq t - \min\{h, r\}$. □

Suppose that L is such that the vector space V from Lemma 2 is of dimension d. It will be shown that, if d is sufficiently large, such an instantiation of HADESMIMC is vulnerable to preimage attacks for some choices of the rate and capacity parameters of the sponge construction. In particular, when the MDS matrix L is an involution, we obtain $d = t - 2$.

By Lemma 2, there exists a matrix $U_1 \in \mathbb{F}_q^{d \times t}$ such that $U_1 F(x) = U_1(L^r(x) + a)$ for a known constant a. Indeed, let the rows of U_1 be a basis for V. Furthermore, let $U_2 \in \mathbb{F}_q^{(t-d) \times t}$ be a matrix with row space complementary to the row space of U_1. For each x, it holds that

$$
\begin{aligned}
U_1 y &= U_1(L^r(x) + \sum_{i=1}^{r} L^{r+1-i}(c_i)) \\
U_2 y &= U_2 F(x).
\end{aligned}
\tag{4}
$$

Consider a HADESMIMC permutation in a sponge construction with rate k and capacity $c = t - k$. Computing preimages of a one-block message $(y_1, \ldots, y_k) \in \mathbb{F}_q^k$ then corresponds to solving the system of equations $[F(x \| \mathsf{IV})]_i = y_i$, $i = 1, \ldots, k$ in the unknowns $x_1, \ldots, x_k$.

The idea of the attack is simple: for each guess of $U_2 F(x) \in \mathbb{F}_q^{t-d}$, replace the equations for the partial rounds by the affine relations (4) and solve the resulting system of equations. In order to ensure that the ideal generated by these equations is zero-dimensional, we should have $k \leq d$, which always holds when L is an involution unless $c = 1$. Note that we focus on the case where the number of output elements is equal to the rate. This is the most challenging setting. Indeed, if the output size is smaller than the rate – as in some of the StarkWare challenges – then the preimage problem will typically have many solutions. This allows the attacker to partially or completely avoid the guessing phase. If further degrees of freedom remain after fixing $U_2 F(x)$ completely, one or more input elements may be fixed to an arbitrary value.

In [17], we show that the total time cost of the attack can be estimated as

$$
2\gamma (2\pi)^{-\omega/2} k^{2-\omega/2} e^{\omega k} 3^{(\omega k+1)(R_F-1)} q^{t-d}
$$

where ω is the asymptotic exponent of the time complexity of matrix multiplication and γ is such that the cost of computing the row-reduced echelon form of an $m \times n$ matrix is $\gamma m n^\omega$.

For example, for an involutive L, $R_F = 8$ and an arbitrary number of partial rounds, Fig. 5a shows for which choices of q and t an improvement over the generic security of the sponge construction is obtained. The insecure instances are shaded in grey. Note that this domain corresponds to a conservative estimate for the cost of row-echelon reduction, i.e. $\omega = 3$ and $\gamma = 3/2$. The cost itself is shown in Fig. 5b. We stress that these figures correspond to the most challenging case, i.e. assuming that the hash output is of length k and no shorter.

For the concrete STARKAD and POSEIDON instances specified in Table 2, we obtain better-than-generic attacks on some variants assuming that the hash output has length $c \leq k$ (Table 5). Indeed, provided that $c \leq d/2 = t/2 - 1$, a sufficiently large number of preimages is likely to exist so that it is no

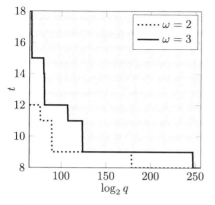

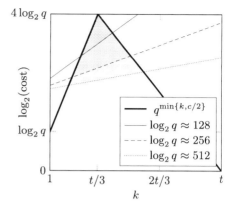

(a) Minimum t such that the cost is better than generic for some choice of k.

(b) Cost for different values of the rate k with $t = 12$ and $\omega = 3$.

Fig. 5. Cost analysis of the preimage attack on HADESMIMC with an involutive linear layer and $R_F = 8$. The shaded areas correspond to parameters for which the attack improves over the $q^{\min\{k,c/2\}}$ security level.

longer necessary to guess $U_2 F(x)$. In addition, input variables may be fixed until only c free variables remain. This leads to a computational cost of $2\gamma (2\pi)^{-\omega/2} c^{2-\omega/2} e^{\omega c} 3^{(\omega c+1)(R_F-1)}$. Note that, for these instances, we do not obtain relevant preimage attacks when the output size exceeds $t/2 - 1$.

Table 5. Overview of the computational cost (measured in $\mathbb{F}_q$ operations) of the preimage attack on different instances of POSEIDON and STARKAD, assuming an involutive linear layer. These estimates assume that the hash output has length c. For the variants 128-a, 128-b and 128-d, the attack does not improve over the generic security level of the sponge.

Variant	c	Computational cost	
		$\omega \approx 2.8$	$\omega = 3$
128-c	2	$2^{80.0}$	$2^{84.3}$
128-e	1	$2^{44.2}$	$2^{46.3}$
256-a	4	$2^{150.9}$	$2^{160.3}$
256-b	4	$2^{150.9}$	$2^{160.3}$

7   Conclusions

Our analysis of STARK-friendly primitives clearly shows that the concrete instances of GMIMC and HADESMIMC proposed in the StarkWare challenges present several major weaknesses, independently from the choice of the underlying finite field. At a first glance, the third contender involved in the challenges, namely VISION for the binary field and RESCUE for the prime fields [7], seems more resistant to the cryptanalytic techniques we have used against the other two primitives. This seems rather expected since VISION and RESCUE follow a more classical SPN construction with full Sbox layers; for similar parameters, they include a larger number of Sboxes which may prevent them from the unsuitable behaviours we have exhibited on the other primitives.

Another important aspect of our work is the extension of higher-order differential and integral attacks to primitives operating on any finite field, even with odd characteristic, while these attacks were previously defined over binary fields only. This points out that the notion of symmetric primitives over a prime field, which has been introduced very recently, needs to be further analyzed in order to get a rigorous assessment on its security. While decades of research have produced efficient cryptanalytic tools and security criteria for primitives defined over $\mathbb{F}_2$, establishing the right tools to analyze primitives over $\mathbb{F}_q$ for odd q raises many new and interesting open questions.

Acknowledgements. This research has received funding from StarkWare Industries and the Ethereum Foundation, as part of the process of selecting a STARK-friendly hash function. Tim Beyne is supported by a PhD Fellowship from the Research Foundation – Flanders (FWO). Itai Dinur is supported by the Israeli Science Foundation through grant no. 573/16. Part of this project has received funding from the European Research Council (ERC) under the European Union's Horizon 2020 research and innovation programme (grant agreements no. 714294 "QUASYModo", no. 757731 "LightCrypt", and no. 681402 "SOPHIA"). This work was partially supported by the German Federal Ministry of Education and Research (BMBF, project iBlockchain – 16KIS0901K) and by DFG under Germany's Excellence Strategy – EXC 2092 CASA – 390781972.

References

1. Agnesse, A., Pedicini, M.: Cube attack in finite fields of higher order. In: Boyd, C., Pieprzyk, J. (eds.) AISC 20111. CRPIT, vol. 116, pp. 9–14. Australian Computer Society (2011)
2. Albrecht, M.R., Cid, C., Grassi, L., Khovratovich, D., Lüftenegger, R., Rechberger, C., Schofnegger, M.: Algebraic cryptanalysis of STARK-friendly designs: application to MARVELlous and MiMC. In: Galbraith, S.D., Moriai, S. (eds.) ASIACRYPT 2019, Part III. LNCS, vol. 11923, pp. 371–397. Springer, Heidelberg (2019). https://doi.org/10.1007/978-3-030-34618-8_13
3. Albrecht, M.R., Grassi, L., Perrin, L., Ramacher, S., Rechberger, C., Rotaru, D., Roy, A., Schofnegger, M.: Feistel structures for MPC, and more. In: Sako, K., Schneider, S., Ryan, P.Y.A. (eds.) ESORICS 2019, Part II. LNCS, vol. 11736, pp. 151–171. Springer, Cham (2019). https://doi.org/10.1007/978-3-030-29962-0_8
4. Albrecht, M.R., Grassi, L., Perrin, L., Ramacher, S., Rechberger, C., Rotaru, D., Roy, A., Schofnegger, M.: Feistel structures for MPC, and more. Cryptology ePrint Archive, Report 2019/397 (2019). https://eprint.iacr.org/2019/397
5. Albrecht, M.R., Grassi, L., Rechberger, C., Roy, A., Tiessen, T.: MiMC: efficient encryption and cryptographic hashing with minimal multiplicative complexity. In: Cheon, J.H., Takagi, T. (eds.) ASIACRYPT 2016, Part I. LNCS, vol. 10031, pp. 191–219. Springer, Heidelberg (2016). https://doi.org/10.1007/978-3-662-53887-6_7

6. Albrecht, M.R., Rechberger, C., Schneider, T., Tiessen, T., Zohner, M.: Ciphers for MPC and FHE. In: Oswald, E., Fischlin, M. (eds.) EUROCRYPT 2015, Part I. LNCS, vol. 9056, pp. 430–454. Springer, Heidelberg (2015). https://doi.org/10.1007/978-3-662-46800-5_17

7. Aly, A., Ashur, T., Ben-Sasson, E., Dhooghe, S., Szepieniec, A.: Design of symmetric-key primitives for advanced cryptographic protocols. Cryptology ePrint Archive, Report 2019/426 (2019). https://eprint.iacr.org/2019/426

8. Ashur, T., Dhooghe, S.: MARVELlous: a STARK-friendly family of cryptographic primitives. Cryptology ePrint Archive, Report 2018/1098 (2018). https://eprint.iacr.org/2018/1098

9. Aumasson, J.-P., Käsper, E., Knudsen, L.R., Matusiewicz, K., Ødegård, R.S., Peyrin, T., Schläffer, M.: Distinguishers for the compression function and output transformation of Hamsi-256. In: Steinfeld, R., Hawkes, P. (eds.) ACISP 2010. LNCS, vol. 6168, pp. 87–103. Springer, Heidelberg (2010). https://doi.org/10.1007/978-3-642-14081-5_6

10. Aumasson, J.P., Meier, W.: Zero-sum distinguishers for reduced Keccak-f and for the core functions of Luffa and Hamsi. Presented at the Rump Session of Cryptographic Hardware and Embedded System – CHES 2009 (2009). https://131002.net/data/papers/AM09.pdf

11. Aumasson, J.-P., Phan, R.C.-W., Meier, W., Henzen, L.: The Hash Function BLAKE. ISC. Springer, Heidelberg (2014). https://doi.org/10.1007/978-3-662-44757-4

12. Bar-On, A., Dinur, I., Dunkelman, O., Lallemand, V., Keller, N., Tsaban, B.: Cryptanalysis of SP networks with partial non-linear layers. In: Oswald, E., Fischlin, M. (eds.) EUROCRYPT 2015, Part I. LNCS, vol. 9056, pp. 315–342. Springer, Heidelberg (2015). https://doi.org/10.1007/978-3-662-46800-5_13

13. Ben-Sasson, E., Bentov, I., Horesh, Y., Riabzev, M.: Scalable, transparent, and post-quantum secure computational integrity. Cryptology ePrint Archive, Report 2018/046 (2018). https://eprint.iacr.org/2018/046

14. Bertoni, G., Daemen, J., Peeters, M., Van Assche, G.: Sponge functions. In: ECRYPT Hash Workshop (2007). https://keccak.team/files/SpongeFunctions.pdf

15. Bertoni, G., Daemen, J., Peeters, M., Van Assche, G.: On the indifferentiability of the sponge construction. In: Smart, N. (ed.) EUROCRYPT 2008. LNCS, vol. 4965, pp. 181–197. Springer, Heidelberg (2008). https://doi.org/10.1007/978-3-540-78967-3_11

16. Bertoni, G., Daemen, J., Peeters, M., Van Assche, G.: Keccak sponge function family - main document. In: Submission to NIST (2009). https://keccak.team/obsolete/Keccak-main-2.0.pdf

17. Beyne, T., Canteaut, A., Dinur, I., Eichlseder, M., Leander, G., Leurent, G., Naya-Plasencia, M., Perrin, L., Sasaki, Y., Todo, Y., Wiemer, F.: Out of oddity - new cryptanalytic techniques against symmetric primitives optimized for integrity proof systems. Cryptology ePrint Archive, Report 2020/188 (2020). https://eprint.iacr.org/2020/188

18. Bonnetain, X.: Collisions on Feistel-MiMC and univariate GMiMC. Cryptology ePrint Archive, Report 2019/951 (2019). https://eprint.iacr.org/2019/951

19. Boura, C., Canteaut, A., De Cannière, C.: Higher-order differential properties of Keccak and Luffa. In: Joux, A. (ed.) FSE 2011. LNCS, vol. 6733, pp. 252–269. Springer, Heidelberg (2011). https://doi.org/10.1007/978-3-642-21702-9_15

20. Canteaut, A., Carpov, S., Fontaine, C., Lepoint, T., Naya-Plasencia, M., Paillier, P., Sirdey, R.: Stream ciphers: a practical solution for efficient homomorphic-ciphertext compression. J. Cryptol. 31(3), 885–916 (2018)

21. Dinur, I., Liu, Y., Meier, W., Wang, Q.: Optimized interpolation attacks on LowMC. In: Iwata, T., Cheon, J.H. (eds.) ASIACRYPT 2015, Part II. LNCS, vol. 9453, pp. 535–560. Springer, Heidelberg (2015). https://doi.org/10.1007/978-3-662-48800-3_22

22. Dobraunig, C., Eichlseder, M., Grassi, L., Lallemand, V., Leander, G., List, E., Mendel, F., Rechberger, C.: Rasta: a cipher with low ANDdepth and few ANDs per bit. In: Shacham, H., Boldyreva, A. (eds.) CRYPTO 2018, Part I. LNCS, vol. 10991, pp. 662–692. Springer, Cham (2018). https://doi.org/10.1007/978-3-319-96884-1_22

23. Dobraunig, C., Eichlseder, M., Mendel, F.: Higher-order cryptanalysis of LowMC. In: Kwon, S., Yun, A. (eds.) ICISC 2015. LNCS, vol. 9558, pp. 87–101. Springer, Cham (2016). https://doi.org/10.1007/978-3-319-30840-1_6

24. Grassi, L., Kales, D., Khovratovich, D., Roy, A., Rechberger, C., Schofnegger, M.: Starkad and Poseidon: new hash functions for zero knowledge proof systems. Cryptology ePrint Archive, Report 2019/458 (2019). https://eprint.iacr.org/2019/458

25. Grassi, L., Lüftenegger, R., Rechberger, C., Rotaru, D., Schofnegger, M.: On a generalization of substitution-permutation networks: the HADES design strategy. Cryptology ePrint Archive, Report 2019/1107 (2019). https://eprint.iacr.org/2019/1107

26. Katz, J.: Secure computation: When theory meets... Invited talk at CRYPTO 2019 (2019)

27. Kedlaya, K.S., Umans, C.: Fast modular composition in any characteristic. In: 49th FOCS, pp. 146–155. IEEE Computer Society Press (2008)

28. Knudsen, L.R., Rijmen, V.: Known-key distinguishers for some block ciphers. In: Kurosawa, K. (ed.) ASIACRYPT 2007. LNCS, vol. 4833, pp. 315–324. Springer, Heidelberg (2007). https://doi.org/10.1007/978-3-540-76900-2_19

29. Knudsen, L., Wagner, D.: Integral cryptanalysis. In: Daemen, J., Rijmen, V. (eds.) FSE 2002. LNCS, vol. 2365, pp. 112–127. Springer, Heidelberg (2002). https://doi.org/10.1007/3-540-45661-9_9

30. Lai, X.: Higher order derivatives and differential cryptanalysis. In: Proceedings of "Symposium on Communication, Coding and Cryptography", in Honor of J. L. Massey on the Occasion of his 60th Birthday. Kluwer Academic Publishers (1994)

31. Méaux, P., Journault, A., Standaert, F.-X., Carlet, C.: Towards stream ciphers for efficient fhe with low-noise ciphertexts. In: Fischlin, M., Coron, J.-S. (eds.) EUROCRYPT 2016, Part I. LNCS, vol. 9665, pp. 311–343. Springer, Heidelberg (2016). https://doi.org/10.1007/978-3-662-49890-3_13

32. Rechberger, C., Soleimany, H., Tiessen, T.: Cryptanalysis of low-data instances of full LowMCv2. IACR Trans. Symm. Cryptol. **2018**(3), 163–181 (2018)

33. Sajadieh, M., Dakhilalian, M., Mala, H., Omoomi, B.: On construction of involutory MDS matrices from Vandermonde matrices in $GF(2^q)$. Des. Codes Crypt. **64**(3), 287–308 (2012)

34. Sălăgean, A., Winter, R., Mandache-Sălăgean, M., Phan, R.C.-W.: Higher order differentiation over finite fields with applications to generalising the cube attack. Des. Codes Crypt. **84**(3), 425–449 (2016). https://doi.org/10.1007/s10623-016-0277-5

35. StarkWare Industries: Personal communication (2019)

36. Stevens, M., Bursztein, E., Karpman, P., Albertini, A., Markov, Y.: The first collision for full SHA-1. In: Katz, J., Shacham, H. (eds.) CRYPTO 2017, Part I. LNCS, vol. 10401, pp. 570–596. Springer, Cham (2017). https://doi.org/10.1007/978-3-319-63688-7_19

Improved Differential-Linear Attacks with Applications to ARX Ciphers

Christof Beierle[1], Gregor Leander[1], and Yosuke Todo[1,2(✉)]

[1] Ruhr University Bochum, Bochum, Germany
{christof.beierle,gregor.leander}@rub.de
[2] NTT Secure Platform Laboratories, Tokyo, Japan
yosuke.todo.xt@hco.ntt.co.jp

Abstract. We present several improvements to the framework of differential-linear attacks with a special focus on ARX ciphers. As a demonstration of their impact, we apply them to Chaskey and ChaCha and we are able to significantly improve upon the best attacks published so far.

Keywords: Symmetric cryptanalysis · ARX · Chaskey · ChaCha

1 Introduction

Symmetric cryptographic primitives play major roles in virtually any cryptographic scheme and any security-related application. The main reason for this massive deployment of symmetric primitives, i.e. (tweakable) block ciphers, stream ciphers, hash functions, or cryptographic permutations, is their significant performance advantage. Symmetric primitives usually outperform other cryptographic schemes by order(s) of magnitude.

One class of design of symmetric primitives that is inherently motivated by (software) efficiency is an *ARX-based* design. ARX is short for **a**ddition (modulo a power of two), word-wise **r**otation and **X**OR. Indeed, ciphers following this framework are composed of those operations and avoid the computation of smaller S-boxes through look-up tables. As most CPUs have hardware support for all those operations, in particular an addition unit and a barrel shifter implemented directly in hardware, executing them on such CPUs based on a suitable register size is inherently fast.

The block cipher FEAL [27] was probably the first ARX cipher presented in the literature and by now there are several state-of-the-art ciphers that follow this approach. One of the most important (family) of ARX ciphers is certainly the one formed by Salsa20, ChaCha and their variants (see [6,7]). Designed by Bernstein, those ciphers are now the default replacement for RC4 in TLS due to the high efficiency and simplicity of their implementations and are thus one of the most widely-used ciphers in practice. Besides being used in TLS, ChaCha is also deployed in several other products and in particular used as a building block in the popular hash functions Blake and Blake2 [2,3].

D. Micciancio and T. Ristenpart (Eds.): CRYPTO 2020, LNCS 12172, pp. 329–358, 2020.
https://doi.org/10.1007/978-3-030-56877-1_12

Clearly, the ARX-based design approach is not restricted to only stream-ciphers, but also allows the design of efficient block ciphers (e.g., Sparx [15]), cryptographic permutations (e.g., Sparkle [5]), and message authentication codes (MACs). For the latter, Chaskey [24] is among the most prominent examples.

Besides the advantage of having efficient implementations, there are also good reasons for ARX-based designs when it comes to security. The algebraic degree of ARX ciphers is usually high after only a very few rounds, as the carry bit within one modular addition already reaches almost maximal degree. Structural attacks like integral [18] or invariant attacks [28] are less of a concern and rotational cryptanalysis [17], originally invented for ARX ciphers, is in most cases very efficiently prevented by the XOR of constants.

When it comes to differential [9] and linear attacks [23], ARX-based designs often show a peculiar behaviour. For a small number of rounds, i.e., only very few modular additions, the differential probabilities (resp., absolute linear correlations) are very high. In particular for a single modular addition, those are equal to 1 due to the linear behaviour of the most and least significant bits. Moreover, for a single modular addition, the differential probabilities and linear correlations are well understood and we have at hand nice and efficient formulas for their computation [21,29]. In the case of (dependent) chains of modular additions and XORs, the situation is different and often checking the probabilities experimentally is the best way to evaluate the behaviour.

Thus, while a few rounds are very weak, for a well-crafted ARX scheme, the probabilities of differentials and the absolute correlations of linear approximations decrease very quickly with increasing the number of rounds. Indeed, this property led to the *long-trail strategy* for designing ARX-based ciphers [15].

Now, for symmetric primitives, the existence of strong differentials and linear approximations for a few rounds with a rapid decrease of probabilities (resp. absolute correlations) is exactly the situation in which considering differential-linear attacks [19] is promising. In a nutshell, differential-linear attacks combine a differential with probability p for the first r rounds of the cipher and a linear approximation with correlation q for the next t rounds into a linear approximation for $r+t$ rounds with correlation pq^2 that can be turned into an attack with data complexity of roughly $p^{-2}q^{-4}$.

Indeed, that said, it is not surprising that the best attacks against many ARX constructions, including ChaCha and Chaskey, are differential-linear attacks [11, 14,20]. Our work builds upon those ideas and improves differential-linear attacks on ARX ciphers along several dimensions.

1.1   Our Contribution

In this paper we present the best known attacks on ChaCha and Chaskey. Our improvements over prior work are based on improvements in the differential, as well as the linear part and the key-recovery part of differential-linear attacks.

Differential Part. For the differential part, our observation is both simple and effective. Recall that for a differential-linear attack, one needs many (roughly q^{-4}) pairs to fulfill the difference in the first part of the cipher, that is many

Table 1. (Partial) Key-Recovery Attacks on Chaskey and ChaCha.

	Key size	Rounds	Time	Data	Ref
Chaskey	128	6	$2^{28.6}$	2^{25}	[20]
		7	2^{67}	2^{48}	[20]
			$2^{51.21}$	$2^{40.21}$	Section 5.3
ChaCha	256	6	2^{139}	2^{30}	[1]
			2^{136}	2^{28}	[26]
			2^{116}	2^{116}	[11]
			$2^{77.4}$	2^{58}	Section 6.3
		7	2^{248}	2^{27}	[1]
			$2^{246.5}$	2^{27}	[26]
			$2^{238.9}$	2^{96}	[22]
			$2^{237.7}$	2^{96}	[11]
			$2^{235.22}$	–	[14]
			$2^{230.86}$	$2^{48.83}$	Section 6.4

right pairs for the differential. Now, imagine that an attacker could construct many right pairs with probability (close to) one, given only a single right pair. This would immediately reduce the data complexity of the attack by a factor of p^{-1}. As we will see, this situation is rather likely to occur for a few rounds of many ARX ciphers and in particular occurs for ChaCha and Chaskey. The details of those improvements are presented in Sect. 3.

Linear Part. For the linear part, our first observation is that often it is beneficial to not restrict to a single mask but rather consider *multiple* linear approximations. As we detail in Sect. 4, this nicely combines with an improved version of the partitioning technique for ARX ciphers [8,20], that splits the space of ciphertexts into subsets in order to increase the correlation of linear approximations. The starting point of our attacks is a new way of partitioning the ciphertexts, summarized in Lemma 3. Note that, although we use multiple linear masks in the attack, because of partitioning the ciphertexts, we use only a *single linear mask for each ciphertext*. In this way we avoid possible dependencies that would be hard to analyze otherwise.

Key Recovery. Related to the improvement in the linear part, we present a significant speed-up in the key recovery part. Here, the main observation is that after considering multiple masks and the partitioning technique, several key bits actually appear only *linearly* in the approximations. In particular, their value does not affect the absolute value of the correlation but rather the sign only. This observation allows us to, instead of guessing those keys as done in previous attacks, recover them by applying the Fast Walsh-Hadamard Transform (FWHT). Similar ideas have already been described in [12]. Details of this approach are given in Sect. 4.

Putting those improvements into one framework and applying the framework to round-reduced variants of ChaCha and Chaskey results in significantly reduced attack complexities. Our attacks with the corresponding complexities are summarized in Table 1, together with a comparison to the best attacks published so far.[1] In particular for ChaCha it is important to add that, as those attacks are on *round-reduced* variants of the ciphers only, they do not pose any threat on the full-round version of the ciphers. Rather, those attacks strengthen our trust in the design. We expect that our improvements have applications to other ciphers as well, especially ARX-based designs.

2   Preliminaries

By $\oplus$ we denote the XOR operation, i.e., addition in $\mathbb{F}_2^n$ and by $+$ we either denote the addition in $\mathbb{Z}$, or the modular addition $\mod 2^n$ for elements in $\mathbb{F}_2^n$, depending on the context. For $x \in \mathbb{F}_2^n$, we denote by $\bar{x}$ the bitwise complement of x. Given a set $\mathcal{S} \subseteq \mathbb{F}_2^n$ and a Boolean function $f \colon \mathbb{F}_2^n \to \mathbb{F}_2$, we define

$$\mathbf{Cor}_{x \in \mathcal{S}}\left[f(x)\right] := \frac{1}{|\mathcal{S}|} \sum_{x \in \mathcal{S}} (-1)^{f(x)}.$$

We denote the i-th unit vector of a binary vector space by $[i]$ and the sum of unit vectors $[i_1] \oplus [i_2] \oplus \cdots \oplus [i_t]$ by $[i_1, i_2, \ldots, i_t]$. Given a vector $x \in \mathbb{F}_2^n$, $x[i]$ denotes the i-th bit of x, and $x[i_1, i_2, \ldots, i_t]$ denotes $\bigoplus_{j=1}^{t} x[i_j]$. For $\gamma, x \in \mathbb{F}_2^n$, we define the inner product by $\langle \gamma, x \rangle = \bigoplus_{i=0}^{n-1} \gamma[i]x[i] \mod 2$. In particular, $x[i_1, i_2, \ldots, i_t] = \langle x, [i_1, i_2, \ldots, i_t] \rangle$.

In the remainder of this paper we assume that, when $\mathcal{S} \subseteq \mathbb{F}_2^n$ is a (sufficiently large) subset of $\mathbb{F}_2^n$ of random samples, $\mathbf{Cor}_{x \in \mathcal{S}}\left[f(x)\right]$ is a good approximation for $\mathbf{Cor}_{x \in \mathbb{F}_2^n}\left[f(x)\right]$. In other words, we assume that the empirical correlations obtained by sampling for a sufficiently large number of messages closely match the actual correlations.

We denote by $\mathcal{N}(\mu, \sigma^2)$ the normal distribution with mean μ and variance σ^2. By Φ we denote the cumulative distribution function of the standard normal distribution $\mathcal{N}(0, 1)$. Thus if $X \sim \mathcal{N}(\mu, \sigma^2)$, it holds that

$$\mathbf{Pr}(X \leq \Theta) = \Phi\left(\frac{\Theta - \mu}{\sigma}\right).$$

2.1   Differential-Linear Attacks

We first recall the basic variant of differential-linear cryptanalysis as introduced by Langford and Hellman [19]. Figure 1 shows the overview of the distinguisher. An entire cipher E is divided into two sub ciphers E_1 and E_2, such that

---

[1] After the submission of this paper, the authors of [13] independently found the same distinguisher without applying the technique for improving over the differential part, and the presented attack complexities are very close to ours.

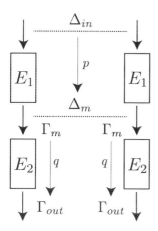
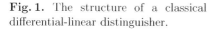

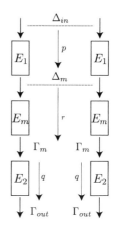

Fig. 1. The structure of a classical differential-linear distinguisher.

Fig. 2. A differential-linear distinguisher with experimental evaluation of the correlation r.

$E = E_2 \circ E_1$, and a differential distinguisher and a linear distinguisher are applied to the first and second parts, respectively.

In particular, assume that the differential $\Delta_{\mathrm{in}} \stackrel{E_1}{\to} \Delta_m$ holds with probability

$$\mathbf{Pr}_{x \in \mathbb{F}_2^n} \left[E_1(x) \oplus E_1(x \oplus \Delta_{\mathrm{in}}) = \Delta_m \right] = p.$$

Let us further assume that the linear approximation $\Gamma_m \stackrel{E_2}{\to} \Gamma_{\mathrm{out}}$ is satisfied with correlation $\mathbf{Cor}_{x \in \mathbb{F}_2^n} \left[\langle \Gamma_m, x \rangle \oplus \langle \Gamma_{\mathrm{out}}, E_2(x) \rangle \right] = q$. The differential-linear distinguisher exploits the fact that, under the assumption that $E_1(x)$ and $E(x)$ are independent random variables, we have

$$\mathbf{Cor}_{x \in \mathbb{F}_2^n} \left[\langle \Gamma_{\mathrm{out}}, E(x) \rangle \oplus \langle \Gamma_{\mathrm{out}}, E(x \oplus \Delta_{\mathrm{in}}) \rangle \right] = pq^2. \tag{1}$$

Therefore, by preparing $\epsilon p^{-2} q^{-4}$ pairs of chosen plaintexts $(x, \tilde{x})$, for $\tilde{x} = x \oplus \Delta_{\mathrm{in}}$, where $\epsilon \in \mathbb{N}$ is a small constant, one can distinguish the cipher from a PRP.

In practice, there might be a problem with the assumption that $E_1(x)$ and $E(x)$ are independent, resulting in wrong estimates for the correlation. To provide a better justification of this independence assumption (and in order to improve attack complexities) , adding a middle part is a simple solution and usually done in recent attacks (as well as in ours). Here, the cipher E is divided into three sub ciphers E_1, E_m and E_2 such that $E = E_2 \circ E_m \circ E_1$ and the middle part E_m is experimentally evaluated. In particular, let

$$r = \mathbf{Cor}_{x \in \mathcal{S}} \left[\langle \Gamma_m, E_m(x) \rangle \oplus \langle \Gamma_m, E_m(x \oplus \Delta_m) \rangle \right],$$

where $\mathcal{S}$ denotes the set of samples over which the correlation is computed. Then, the total correlation in Eq. 1 can be estimated as prq^2. Recently, as a theoretical support for this approach the Differential-Linear Connectivity Table (DLCT) [4] has been introduced. The overall attack framework is depicted in Fig. 2 and we will use this description in the remainder of the paper.

2.2 Partitioning Technique for ARX-Based Designs

Partitioning allows to increase the correlation of the differential-linear distinguisher by deriving linear equations that hold conditioned on ciphertext and key bits. We first recall the partitioning technique as used in [20]. Let $a, b \in \mathbb{F}_2^m$ and let $s = a + b$. When $i = 0$ (lsb), the modular addition for bit i becomes linear, i.e., $s[0] = a[0] \oplus b[0]$. Of course, for $i > 0$, computing the i-th output bit of modular addition is not linear. Still, by restricting (a, b) to be in a specific subset, we might obtain other linear relations. In previous work, the following formula on $s[i]$ was derived.

Lemma 1 ([20]). *Let* $a, b \in \mathbb{F}_2^m$ *and* $s = a + b$. *For* $i \geq 2$, *we have*

$$s[i] = \begin{cases} a[i] \oplus b[i] \oplus a[i-1] & \text{if } a[i-1] = b[i-1] \\ a[i] \oplus b[i] \oplus a[i-2] & \text{if } a[i-1] \neq b[i-1] \text{ and } a[i-2] = b[i-2]. \end{cases}$$

Let us now consider two m-bit words z_0 and z_1 and a modular addition operation

$$F \colon \mathbb{F}_2^{2m} \to \mathbb{F}_2^{2m}, \quad (z_1, z_0) \mapsto (y_1, y_0) = (z_1, z_0 + z_1),$$

as depicted in Fig. 5. F might correspond to a single branch of a wider ARX-based design. In the attacks we present later, we are interested in the value $z_0[i]$. For this, we cannot apply Lemma 1 directly since $z_0[i]$ is obtained by modular subtraction. However, for that case the following formula can be derived.

Lemma 2. *Let* $i \geq 2$ *and let* $\mathcal{S}_1 := \{(x_1, x_0) \in \mathbb{F}_2^{2m} \mid x_0[i-1] \neq x_1[i-1]\}$ *and* $\mathcal{S}_2 := \{(x_1, x_0) \in \mathbb{F}_2^{2m} \mid x_0[i-1] = x_1[i-1] \text{ and } x_0[i-2] \neq x_1[i-2]\}$. *Then,*

$$z_0[i] = \begin{cases} y_0[i] \oplus y_1[i] \oplus y_0[i-1] \oplus 1 & \text{if } (y_1, y_0) \in \mathcal{S}_1, \\ y_0[i] \oplus y_1[i] \oplus y_0[i-2] \oplus 1 & \text{if } (y_1, y_0) \in \mathcal{S}_2. \end{cases} \tag{2}$$

Clearly, $\mathcal{S}_1$ and $\mathcal{S}_2$ are disjoint sets. Note that Eq. 2 only holds for $\frac{3}{4}$ of the data, since $|\mathcal{S}_1| = 2^{-1} 2^{2m}$ and $|\mathcal{S}_2| = 2^{-2} 2^{2m}$.

Due to the propagation rules for linear trails over modular addition, we may end up with multiple linear trails that are closely related to each other. As an example, Fig. 3 shows two possible trails, where $[i]$ and $[i-1, i]$ denote the corresponding linear masks. The partitioning technique described above evaluates $z_0[i]$, but we can expect that there is a highly-biased linear trail in which $z_0[i-1] \oplus z_0[i]$ needs to be evaluated instead of $z_0[i]$. In the trivial method, we apply partitioning technique of Lemma 2 for $z_0[i]$ and $z_0[i-1]$ separately, which requires the knowledge of 3 bits of information from y in total. Our new

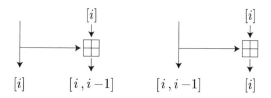

Fig. 3. Two linear trails with correlation 2^{-1}.

partitioning method allows us to determine the partition only by knowing the same 2 bits of information as needed for evaluating the case of $z_0[i]$, namely $(y_0[i-1] \oplus y_1[i-1])$ and $(y_0[i-2] \oplus y_1[i-2])$. This is especially helpful if y consists of the ciphertext XORed with the key, so we need to guess less key bits to evaluate the partition. In particular, the following relation holds, which is straightforward to proof. The intuition is that $z_0[i-1]$ corresponds to the carry bit $c[i-1]$ in the case of $(y_1, y_0) \in \mathcal{S}_3$ and $(y_1[i-2], y_1[i-1]) = (c[i-2], c[i-1])$ for $(y_1, y_0) \in \mathcal{S}_4$.

Lemma 3. *Let $i \geq 2$ and let $\mathcal{S}_3 = \{(x_1, x_0) \in \mathbb{F}_2^{2m} \mid x_0[i-1] = x_1[i-1]\}$ and $\mathcal{S}_4 = \{(x_1, x_0) \in \mathbb{F}_2^{2m} \mid x_0[i-1] \neq x_1[i-1]$ and $x_0[i-2] \neq x_1[i-2]\}$. Then,*

$$z_0[i] \oplus z_0[i-1] = \begin{cases} y_0[i] \oplus y_1[i] & \text{if } (y_1, y_0) \in \mathcal{S}_3, \\ y_0[i] \oplus y_1[i] \oplus y_0[i-1] \oplus y_0[i-2] \oplus 1 & \text{if } (y_1, y_0) \in \mathcal{S}_4. \end{cases}$$

Again, $\mathcal{S}_3$ and $\mathcal{S}_4$ are disjoint and the equation above holds for $\frac{3}{4}$ of the data.

3   The Differential Part – Finding Many Right Pairs

Let us be given a permutation $E_1 \colon \mathbb{F}_2^n \to \mathbb{F}_2^n$ and a differential $\Delta_{\text{in}} \overset{E_1}{\to} \Delta_m$ that holds with probability p. In other words,

$$|\{x \in \mathbb{F}_2^n \mid E_1(x) \oplus E_1(x \oplus \Delta_{\text{in}}) = \Delta_m\}| = p \cdot 2^n.$$

In a usual differential-linear attack on a permutation $E = E_2 \circ E_m \circ E_1$ as explained in Sect. 2.1, the internal structure of E_1 could be in general arbitrary and we would consider randomly chosen $x \in \mathbb{F}_2^n$ to observe the ciphertexts of the plaintext pairs $(x, x \oplus \Delta_{\text{in}})$. For each of those pairs, the differential over E_1 is fulfilled with probability p, which results in a data complexity of roughly $\epsilon p^{-2} r^{-2} q^{-4}$ for the differential-linear attack. In other words, we did not exploit the particular structure of E_1. In particular, it would be helpful to know something about the distribution of right pairs $(x, x \oplus \Delta_{\text{in}}) \in \mathbb{F}_2^n \times \mathbb{F}_2^n$ that fulfill the above differential.

Let us denote by $\mathcal{X}$ the set of all values that define right pairs for the differential, i.e.,

$$\mathcal{X} = \{x \in \mathbb{F}_2^n \mid E_1(x) \oplus E_1(x \oplus \Delta_{\text{in}}) = \Delta_m\}.$$

To amplify the correlation of a differential-linear distinguisher, instead of choosing random plaintexts from $\mathbb{F}_2^n$, we would consider only those that are in $\mathcal{X}$. In particular, we have[2]

$$\mathbf{Cor}_{x \in \mathcal{X}} [\langle \Gamma_{out}, E(x) \rangle \oplus \langle \Gamma_{out}, E(x \oplus \Delta_{in}) \rangle] = rq^2.$$

Since the set $\mathcal{X}$ might have a rather complicated structure, and is moreover key-dependent, we cannot use this directly for an arbitrary permutation E_1. However, if $\mathcal{X}$ employs a special structure such that, given one element $x \in \mathcal{X}$, we can generate many other elements in $\mathcal{X}$ for free,[3] independently of the secret key, we can use this to reduce the data complexity in a differential-linear attack. For example, if $\mathcal{X}$ contains a large affine subspace $\mathcal{A} = \mathcal{U} \oplus a$, given $x \in \mathcal{A}$, we can generate (roughly) $2^{|\dim \mathcal{U}|}$ elements in $\mathcal{X}$ for free, namely all elements $x \oplus u$, for $u \in \mathcal{U}$. In order to obtain an effective distinguisher, we must be able to generate enough plaintext pairs to observe the correlation of the differential-linear approximation. In particular, we need to require $|\mathcal{U}| > \epsilon r^{-2} q^{-4}$.

This will be exactly the situation we find in ChaCha. Here the number of rounds covered in the differential part is so small that it can be described by the independent application of two functions (see Sect. 3.1).

If $|\mathcal{U}|$ is smaller than the threshold of $\epsilon r^{-2} q^{-4}$, we can't generate enough right pairs for free to obtain a distinguisher by this method and we might use a probabilistic approach, see Sect. 3.2.

3.1   Fully Independent Parts

Let $E_1 \colon \mathbb{F}_2^n \to \mathbb{F}_2^n$ with $n = 2m$ be a parallel application of two block ciphers $E_1^{(i)} \colon \mathbb{F}_2^m \to \mathbb{F}_2^m$, $i \in \{0, 1\}$ (for a fixed key), i.e.,

$$E_1 \colon (x^{(1)}, x^{(0)}) \mapsto (E_1^{(1)}(x^{(1)}), E_1^{(0)}(x^{(0)})).$$

Suppose that, $E_1^{(0)}$ employs a differential $\alpha \xrightarrow{E_1^{(0)}} \beta$ with probability p. We consider the differential $\Delta_{in} \xrightarrow{E_1} \Delta_m$ with $\Delta_{in} = (0, \alpha)$ and $\Delta_m = (0, \beta)$, which also holds with probability p. Given one element $(x^{(1)}, x^{(0)}) \in \mathcal{X}$, any $(x^{(1)} \oplus u, x^{(0)})$ for $u \in \mathbb{F}_2^m$ is also contained in $\mathcal{X}$, thus we can generate 2^m right pairs for free.

If $2^m > \epsilon r^{-2} q^{-4}$, a differential-linear distinguisher on $E = E_2 \circ E_m \circ E_1$ would work as follows:

1. Choose $a = (a^{(1)}, a^{(0)}) \in \mathbb{F}_2^n$ uniformly at random.
2. Empirically compute

$$\mathbf{Cor}_{x \in a \oplus (\mathbb{F}_2^m \times \{0\})} [\langle \Gamma_{out}, E(x) \rangle \oplus \langle \Gamma_{out}, E(x \oplus \Delta_{in}) \rangle].$$

---

[2] Under the assumption that the sets $\{\langle \Gamma_{out}, E(x) \rangle \oplus \langle \Gamma_{out}, E(x \oplus \Delta_{in}) \rangle \mid x \in \mathcal{X}\}$ and $\{\langle \Gamma_{out}, E(x) \rangle \oplus \langle \Gamma_{out}, E(x \oplus \Delta_{in}) \rangle \mid x \in \mathcal{S}\}$ are indistinguishable, where $\mathcal{S}$ denotes a set of uniformly chosen samples of the same size as $\mathcal{X}$.

[3] Or at least with a cost much lower than p^{-1}, see Sect. 3.2.

3. If we observe a correlation of rq^2 using $\epsilon r^{-2}q^{-4}$ many x, the distinguisher succeeded. If not, start over with Step 1.

With probability p, we choose an element $a \in \mathcal{X}$ in Step 1. In that case, the distinguisher succeeds in Step 3. Therefore, the data complexity of the distinguisher is $\epsilon p^{-1}r^{-2}q^{-4}$, compared to $\epsilon p^{-2}r^{-2}q^{-4}$ as in the classical differential-linear attack.

3.2 Probabilistic Independent Parts

We are also interested in the situations in which the differential part cannot be simply written as the parallel application of two functions. Again, the goal is, given one element $x \in \mathcal{X}$, to be able to generate $\epsilon r^{-2}q^{-4}$ other elements in $\mathcal{X}$, each one with a much lower cost than p^{-1}. Suppose that $\mathcal{U} \subseteq \mathbb{F}_2^n$ is a subspace with $|\mathcal{U}| > \epsilon r^{-2}q^{-4}$ and suppose that $\mathbf{Pr}_{u \in \mathcal{U}}(x \oplus u \in \mathcal{X} \mid x \in \mathcal{X}) = p_1$, where p_1 is much larger than p. The data complexity of the improved differential-linear distinguisher would then be $\epsilon p^{-1}p_1^{-2}r^{-2}q^{-4}$. Note that the probability p_1 also depend on x. In particular, there might be $x \in \mathcal{X}' \subseteq \mathcal{X}$ for which p_1 is (almost) 1, but the probability to draw such an initial element x from $\mathbb{F}_2^n$ is p', which is smaller than p. Then, the data complexity would be $\epsilon p'^{-1}p_1^{-2}r^{-2}q^{-4}$. For instance, this will be the case for the attack on Chaskey (Sect. 5), where we have $p_1 \approx 1$ and $p' = p \times 222/256$.

In such situations, we propose an algorithmic way to experimentally detect suitable structures in the set of right pairs. This idea of the algorithm, see Algorithm 1 for the pseudo code, is to detect canonical basis vectors within the subspace $\mathcal{U}$. Running this algorithm for enough samples will return estimates of the probability γ_j that a right pair $x \in \mathcal{X}$ stays a right pair when the j-th bit is flipped, i.e.,

$$\gamma_i = \mathbf{Pr}\left(x \oplus [i] \in \mathcal{X} \mid x \in \mathcal{X}\right).$$

When applied to a few rounds of ARX ciphers it can be expected that there are some bits that will always turn a right pair into a right pair, i.e. $\gamma_i = 1$. Moreover, due to the property of the modular addition that the influence of bits on distant bits degrades quickly, high values of $\gamma_j \neq 1$ can also be expected. As we will detail in Sect. 5 this will be the case for the application to Chaskey.

4 The Linear Part – Advanced Partitioning and WHT-based Key-Recovery

In this section, we describe our improvements over the linear part of the attack which consists in exploiting multiple linear approximations and an advanced key-recovery technique using the partitioning technique and the fast Walsh-Hadamard transform. The overall structure of the advanced differential-linear attack is depicted in Fig. 4. Here F corresponds to the part of the cipher that we are going to cover using our improved key-guessing. Our aim is to recover parts of the last whitening key k by using a differential-linear distinguisher given

---

Algorithm 1. Computing probabilistic independent bits

Require: Number of samples T, input difference Δ_{in}, output difference Δ_m
Ensure: Probabilities $\gamma_0, \gamma_1, \ldots, \gamma_{n-1}$
 1: Let $s = 0$ and $c_j = 0$ for $j \in \{0, \ldots, n-1\}$.
 2: **for** $i = 1$ to T **do**
 3:     Pick a random X and compute $E_1(X)$ and $E_1(X \oplus \Delta_{in})$
 4:     **if** $E_1(X) \oplus E_1(X \oplus \Delta_{in}) = \Delta_m$ **then**
 5:         Increment s
 6:         **for** $j \in \{0, \ldots, n-1\}$ **do**
 7:             Prepare $\hat{X}$ where the j-th bit of X is flipped.
 8:             **if** $E_1(\hat{X}) \oplus E_1(\hat{X} \oplus \Delta_{in}) = \Delta_m$ **then**
 9:                 Increment c_j
10:             **end if**
11:         **end for**
12:     **end if**
13: **end for**
14: **for** $j \in \{0, \ldots, n-1\}$ **do**
15:     $\gamma_j = c_j / s$
16: **end for**

---

by s (multiple) linear approximations $\langle \Gamma_{\text{out}}^{(p_i)}, z \rangle \oplus \langle \Gamma_{\text{out}}^{(p_j)}, \tilde{z} \rangle$. In the following, we assume that the ciphertext space $\mathbb{F}_2^n$ is split into a direct sum $\mathcal{P} \oplus \mathcal{R}$ with $n_{\mathcal{P}} := \dim \mathcal{P}$ and $n_{\mathcal{R}} := \dim \mathcal{R} = n - n_{\mathcal{P}}$. Therefore, we can uniquely express intermediate states z as $z_{\mathcal{P}} \oplus z_{\mathcal{R}}$, where $z_{\mathcal{P}} \in \mathcal{P}$ and $z_{\mathcal{R}} \in \mathcal{R}$. The precise definition of $\mathcal{P}$ and $\mathcal{R}$ depends on the particular application of the attack.

4.1 Multiple Linear Approximations and Partitioning

The idea is to identify several tuples $(\mathcal{T}_{p_i}, \Gamma_{\text{out}}^{(p_i)}, \gamma^{(p_i)})$, $i \in \{1, \ldots, s\}$, where $\mathcal{T}_{p_i} = \mathcal{R} \oplus p_i$ is a coset of $\mathcal{R} \subseteq \mathbb{F}_2^n$, $\Gamma_{\text{out}}^{(p_i)} \in \mathbb{F}_2^n$ and $\gamma^{(p_i)} \in \mathcal{R}$, for which we can observe a high absolute correlation

$$\varepsilon_i := \mathbf{Cor}_{y \in \mathcal{T}_{p_i}} \left[\langle \Gamma_{\text{out}}^{(p_i)}, z \rangle \oplus \langle \gamma^{(p_i)}, y \rangle \right].$$

In the simplest case, we would have $\varepsilon_i = 1$, i.e.,

$$y \in \mathcal{T}_{p_i} \quad \Rightarrow \quad \left(\langle \Gamma_{\text{out}}^{(p_i)}, z \rangle = \langle \gamma^{(p_i)}, y \rangle = \langle \gamma^{(p_i)}, c \rangle \oplus \langle \gamma^{(p_i)}, k \rangle \right).$$

In other words, by considering only a specific subset of the ciphertexts (defined by $\mathcal{T}_{p_i}$) we obtain *linear relations* in the key with a high correlation.

Note that $y \in \mathcal{T}_{p_i} \Leftrightarrow c \in \mathcal{T}_{p_i} \oplus k_{\mathcal{P}}$, so we need to guess $n_{\mathcal{P}}$ bits of k to partition the ciphertexts into the corresponding $\mathcal{T}_{p_i}$. Note that there might be ciphertexts that are discarded,[4] i.e., there might be y which do not belong to

---

[4] Of course, the discarded data has to be considered in the data complexity of the attack.

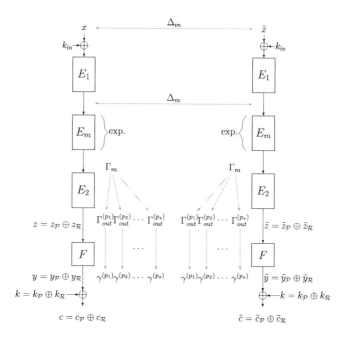

Fig. 4. The general structure of the attack.

any $\mathcal{T}_{p_i}$, for $i \in \{1, \ldots, s\}$. Note also that, since we require $\gamma^{(p_i)} \in \mathcal{R}$, we obtain linear relations only on $k_{\mathcal{R}}$.

By defining[5]

$$q_{i,j} := \underset{\substack{x \in \mathcal{X} \text{ such that} \\ (c,\tilde{c}) \in \mathcal{T}_{p_i} \times \mathcal{T}_{p_j} \oplus (k_{\mathcal{P}}, k_{\mathcal{P}})}}{\mathbf{Cor}} \left[\langle \Gamma_{\mathrm{out}}^{(p_i)}, z \rangle \oplus \langle \Gamma_{\mathrm{out}}^{(p_j)}, \tilde{z} \rangle \right],$$

we obtain

$$\underset{\substack{x \in \mathcal{X} \text{ such that} \\ (c,\tilde{c}) \in \mathcal{T}_{p_i} \times \mathcal{T}_{p_j} \oplus (k_{\mathcal{P}}, k_{\mathcal{P}})}}{\mathbf{Cor}} \left[\langle \gamma^{(p_i)}, c \rangle \oplus \langle \gamma^{(p_j)}, \tilde{c} \rangle \oplus \langle \gamma^{(p_i)} \oplus \gamma^{(p_j)}, k \rangle \right]$$

$$= \underset{\substack{x \in \mathcal{X} \text{ such that} \\ (c,\tilde{c}) \in \mathcal{T}_{p_i} \times \mathcal{T}_{p_j} \oplus (k_{\mathcal{P}}, k_{\mathcal{P}})}}{\mathbf{Cor}} \left[\langle \gamma^{(p_i)}, y \rangle \oplus \langle \gamma^{(p_j)}, \tilde{y} \rangle \right] = \varepsilon_i \varepsilon_j q_{i,j}.$$

For $r \in \mathbb{R}$, let us define $\mathrm{sgn}(r) = \begin{cases} 0 & \text{if } r \geq 0 \\ 1 & \text{if } r < 0 \end{cases}$. If we define

$$h_{i,j} := (-1)^{\mathrm{sgn}(\varepsilon_i \varepsilon_j q_{i,j})} \underset{\substack{x \in \mathcal{X} \text{ such that} \\ (c,\tilde{c}) \in \mathcal{T}_{p_i} \times \mathcal{T}_{p_j} \oplus (k_{\mathcal{P}}, k_{\mathcal{P}})}}{\mathbf{Cor}} \left[\langle \gamma^{(p_i)}, c \rangle \oplus \langle \gamma^{(p_j)}, \tilde{c} \rangle \right],$$

---

[5] If $|q_{i,j}|$ is not too small and if the number s of approximations is not too huge, we can empirically compute $q_{i,j}$ for all i, j. In other cases, we estimate $q_{i,j} = \mathbf{Cor}_{x \in \mathcal{X}} \left[\langle \Gamma_{\mathrm{out}}^{(p_i)}, z \rangle \oplus \langle \Gamma_{\mathrm{out}}^{(p_j)}, \tilde{z} \rangle \right]$ by assuming indistinguishability of the sets $\{ \langle \Gamma_{\mathrm{out}}^{(p_i)}, z \rangle \oplus \langle \Gamma_{\mathrm{out}}^{(p_j)}, \tilde{z} \rangle \mid x \in \mathcal{X} \text{ s.t. } (y, \tilde{y}) \in \mathcal{T}_{p_i} \times \mathcal{T}_{p_j} \}$ and $\{ \langle \Gamma_{\mathrm{out}}^{(p_i)}, z \rangle \oplus \langle \Gamma_{\mathrm{out}}^{(p_j)}, \tilde{z} \rangle \mid x \in \mathcal{S} \}$, where $\mathcal{S}$ is a set of uniformly random samples of $\mathcal{X}$ of suitable size.

we have $h_{i,j} = (-1)^{\langle \gamma^{(p_i)} \oplus \gamma^{(p_j)}, k \rangle} |\varepsilon_i \varepsilon_j q_{i,j}|$. Let us further assume that

$$\{x \in \mathcal{X} \mid (c, \tilde{c}) \in \mathcal{T}_{p_i} \times \mathcal{T}_{p_j} \oplus (k_{\mathcal{P}}, k_{\mathcal{P}})\}$$

is of equal size σ for all (i, j) and consider the scaled version of $h_{i,j}$, i.e.,

$$\alpha_{i,j} := \sigma \cdot h_{i,j} = (-1)^{\mathrm{sgn}(\varepsilon_i \varepsilon_j q_{i,j})} \sum_{\substack{x \in \mathcal{X} \text{ such that} \\ (c,\tilde{c}) \in \mathcal{T}_{p_i} \times \mathcal{T}_{p_j} \oplus (k_{\mathcal{P}}, k_{\mathcal{P}})}} (-1)^{\langle \gamma^{(p_i)}, c \rangle \oplus \langle \gamma^{(p_j)}, \tilde{c} \rangle}.$$

For each $\gamma \in W := \mathrm{Span}\{\gamma^{(p_i)} \oplus \gamma^{(p_j)} \mid i, j \in \{1, \ldots, s\}\}$, we define

$$\beta(\gamma) := \sum_{\substack{(i,j) \text{ such that} \\ \gamma^{(p_i)} \oplus \gamma^{(p_j)} = \gamma}} \alpha_{i,j}.$$

This function β now allows to efficiently recover $\dim W$ bits of information on $k_{\mathcal{R}}$. In other words, $k_{\mathcal{R}}$ can be uniquely expressed as $k_{\mathcal{L}} \oplus k_{\mathcal{R}'}$, where $k_{\mathcal{L}}$ is the part of the key that can be obtained from β. Finally, using the Fast Walsh-Hadamard transform on β, we compute for each tuple $(k_{\mathcal{P}}, k_{\mathcal{L}})$ a cumulative counter

$$\mathcal{C}(k_{\mathcal{P}}, k_{\mathcal{L}}) := \sum_{\gamma \in W} (-1)^{\langle \gamma, k_{\mathcal{L}} \rangle} \beta(\gamma).$$

Whenever this counter $\mathcal{C}$ is larger than some threshold Θ, we store the tuple $(k_{\mathcal{P}}, k_{\mathcal{L}})$ in the list of key candidates. Note that the idea of applying the Fast Walsh-Hadamard transform to gain a speed-up in the key-recovery phase of linear cryptanalysis has already been used before, see [12].

The attack is presented in Algorithm 2. Note that the actual correlations are approximated by sampling over N pairs of plaintexts, resp., ciphertexts.

A Note on the Walsh-Hadamard Transform. Given a real-valued function $f : \mathbb{F}_2^n \to \mathbb{R}$, the *Walsh-Hadamard transform* evaluates the function

$$\widehat{f} : \mathbb{F}_2^n \to \mathbb{R}, \quad \alpha \mapsto \sum_{y \in \mathbb{F}_2^n} (-1)^{\langle \alpha, y \rangle} f(y).$$

A naive computation needs $\mathcal{O}(2^{2n})$ steps (additions and evaluations of f), i.e., for each $\alpha \in \mathbb{F}_2^n$, we compute $(-1)^{\langle \alpha, y \rangle} f(y)$ for each $y \in \mathbb{F}_2^n$. The *Fast Walsh-Hadamard transform* is a well-known recursive divide-and-conquer algorithm that evaluates the Walsh-Hadamard transform in $\mathcal{O}(n2^n)$ steps. We refer to e.g., [10, Section 2.2] for the details.

Running Time and Data Complexity of Algorithm 2. Clearly, Algorithm 2 needs $2N$ queries to E as the data complexity. For the running time, the dominant part is the loop over the key guesses for $k_{\mathcal{P}}$, the collection of N data samples, and the Walsh-Hadamard transform. The overall running time can be estimated as $2^{n_{\mathcal{P}}}(2N + \dim W \cdot 2^{\dim W})$.

Algorithm 2. Key-recovery

Require: Cipher E, sample size N, threshold Θ.
Ensure: List of key candidates $(k'_{\mathcal{P}}, k_{\mathcal{L}})$ for $n_P + \dim W$ bit of information on k.
1: **for** $(i,j) \in \{1,\dots,s\} \times \{1,\dots,s\}$ **do**
2:     **for** $k'_{\mathcal{P}} \in \mathcal{P}$ **do**
3:         $\alpha_{i,j}^{(k'_{\mathcal{P}})} \leftarrow 0$
4:     **end for**
5: **end for**
6: Choose $a \xleftarrow{\$} \mathbb{F}_2^n$
7: **for** $\ell \in \{1,\dots,N\}$ **do**
8:     $x \xleftarrow{\$} U \oplus a$
9:     $(c,\tilde{c}) \leftarrow (E(x), E(x \oplus \Delta_{\mathrm{in}}))$
10:     **for** $k'_{\mathcal{P}} \in \mathcal{P}$ **do**
11:         Identify $\mathcal{T}_i \times \mathcal{T}_j$ for $(c \oplus k'_{\mathcal{P}}, \tilde{c} \oplus k'_{\mathcal{P}})$ and get corresponding $\gamma^{(p_i)}$ and $\gamma^{(p_j)}$
12:         $\alpha_{i,j}^{(k'_{\mathcal{P}})} \leftarrow \alpha_{i,j}^{(k'_{\mathcal{P}})} + (-1)^{\langle \gamma^{(p_i)}, c \rangle \oplus \langle \gamma^{(p_j)}, \tilde{c} \rangle}$ (where i,j are computed in line 11)
13:     **end for**
14: **end for**
15: **for** $k'_{\mathcal{P}} \in \mathcal{P}$ **do**
16:     Compute $\mathcal{C}(k'_{\mathcal{P}}, k_{\mathcal{L}})$ using the Fast Walsh-Hadamard Transform
17:     **if** $\mathcal{C}(k'_{\mathcal{P}}, k_{\mathcal{L}}) > \Theta$ **then**
18:         Save $(k'_{\mathcal{P}}, k_{\mathcal{L}})$ as a key candidate
19:     **end if**
20: **end for**

Success Probability of Algorithm 2. Two questions remain to be discussed here: (i) what is the probability that the right key is among the candidates and (ii) what is the expected size of the list of candidates? To answer those questions, we have to first establish a statistical model for the counter values $\mathcal{C}(k_{\mathcal{P}}, k_{\mathcal{L}})$.

For a key guess $k'_{\mathcal{L}}$, we first note that

$$\mathcal{C}(k_{\mathcal{P}}, k'_{\mathcal{L}}) = \sum_{\gamma \in W} (-1)^{\langle \gamma, k'_{\mathcal{L}} \rangle} \beta(\gamma)$$

$$= \sum_{\substack{\gamma \in W \\ \gamma^{(p_i)} \oplus \gamma^{(p_j)} = \gamma}} \sum_{\substack{(i,j) \text{ s. t.}}} (-1)^{\langle \gamma, k'_{\mathcal{L}} \rangle} (-1)^{\mathrm{sgn}(\varepsilon_i \varepsilon_j q_{i,j})} \sum_{\substack{x \in \mathcal{X} \text{ such that} \\ (c,\tilde{c}) \in \mathcal{T}_{p_i} \times \mathcal{T}_{p_j} \oplus (k_{\mathcal{P}}, k_{\mathcal{P}})}} (-1)^{\langle \gamma^{(p_i)}, c \rangle \oplus \langle \gamma^{(p_j)}, \tilde{c} \rangle}$$

$$= \sum_{\substack{\gamma \in W \\ \gamma^{(p_i)} \oplus \gamma^{(p_j)} = \gamma}} \sum_{\substack{(i,j) \text{ s. t.}}} (-1)^{\langle \gamma, k'_{\mathcal{L}} \rangle} (-1)^{\mathrm{sgn}(\varepsilon_i \varepsilon_j q_{i,j})} \sum_{\substack{x \in \mathcal{X} \text{ such that} \\ (c,\tilde{c}) \in \mathcal{T}_{p_i} \times \mathcal{T}_{p_j} \oplus (k_{\mathcal{P}}, k_{\mathcal{P}})}} (-1)^{\langle \gamma^{(p_i)}, y \oplus k_{\mathcal{R}} \rangle \oplus \langle \gamma^{(p_j)}, \tilde{y} \oplus k_{\mathcal{R}} \rangle}$$

$$= \sum_{\substack{\gamma \in W \\ \gamma^{(p_i)} \oplus \gamma^{(p_j)} = \gamma}} \sum_{\substack{(i,j) \text{ s. t.}}} (-1)^{\langle \gamma, k_{\mathcal{L}} \oplus k'_{\mathcal{L}} \rangle} (-1)^{\mathrm{sgn}(\varepsilon_i \varepsilon_j q_{i,j})} \sum_{\substack{x \in \mathcal{X} \text{ such that} \\ (c,\tilde{c}) \in \mathcal{T}_{p_i} \times \mathcal{T}_{p_j} \oplus (k_{\mathcal{P}}, k_{\mathcal{P}})}} (-1)^{\langle \gamma^{(p_i)}, y \rangle \oplus \langle \gamma^{(p_j)}, \tilde{y} \rangle}$$

$$= \sum_{\substack{\gamma \in W \\ \gamma^{(p_i)} \oplus \gamma^{(p_j)} = \gamma}} \sum_{\substack{(i,j) \text{ s. t.}}} (-1)^{\langle \gamma, k_{\mathcal{L}} \oplus k'_{\mathcal{L}} \rangle} |\varepsilon_i \varepsilon_j q_{i,j}| \cdot \sigma,$$

which implies that if $k'_\mathcal{L} = k_\mathcal{L}$ the partial counters add up, while if $k_\mathcal{L} \neq k'_\mathcal{L}$, the partial counters can be expected to cancel each other partially.

In the following, we assume that the distributions involved can be well estimated by normal approximations. This significantly simplifies the analysis. Note that we opted for a rather simple statistical model ignoring in particular the effect of the wrong key distribution and the way we sample our plain-texts (i.e. known vs. chosen vs. distinct plaintext). Those effects might have major impact on the performance of attacks when the data complexity is close to the full codebook and the success probability and the gain are limited. However, none of this is the case for our parameters. In our concrete applications, we have verified the behaviour experimentally wherever possible.

For the statistical model for the right key, this implies that the counter can be expected to approximately follow a normal distribution with parameters

$$\mathcal{C}(k_\mathcal{P}, k_\mathcal{L}) \sim \mathcal{N}(N^* h, N^*)$$

where

$$h = \frac{1}{s^2} \sum_{i,j} h_{i,j}$$

is the average correlation over all partitions and N^* is the effective data complexity, i.e. the data complexity N reduced by the invalid partitions. The wrong key counters (under the simple randomization hypothesis) is approximately normal distributed with parameters

$$\mathcal{C}(k'_\mathcal{P}, k'_\mathcal{L}) \sim \mathcal{N}(0, N^*).$$

With this we can deduce the following proposition.

Proposition 1. *After running Algorithm 2 for p^{-1}-times, the probability that the correct key is among the key candidates is*

$$p_{\text{success}} \geq \frac{1}{2} \Pr(\mathcal{C}(k_\mathcal{P}, k_\mathcal{L}) \geq \Theta) = \frac{1}{2}\left(1 - \Phi\left(\frac{\Theta - N^* h}{\sqrt{N^*}}\right)\right).$$

The expected number of wrong keys is $\frac{2^n}{p} \times \left(1 - \Phi\left(\frac{\Theta}{\sqrt{N^*}}\right)\right).$

4.2   A Simple Toy Example

We transfer the above terminology on the simple toy example given in Fig. 5 and already discussed earlier in Sect. 2.2. In this example, for a fixed $i \geq 2$, we want to evaluate $z_0[i]$ or $z_0[i] \oplus z_0[i-1]$ by using the partitioning rules as expressed in Lemma 2 and Lemma 3. For this, we say that $(z_0[i], z_0[i] \oplus z_0[i-1])$ defines a *partition point* ζ. This partition point gives rise to a 2-dimensional subspace $\mathcal{P}$ which can be defined by two parity check equations, i.e., $\mathcal{P}$ is a complement space of the space

$$\mathcal{R} = \{(x_1, x_0) \in \mathbb{F}_2^{2m} \mid x_0[i-1] \oplus x_1[i-1] = 0 \text{ and } x_0[i-2] \oplus x_1[i-2] = 0\}.$$

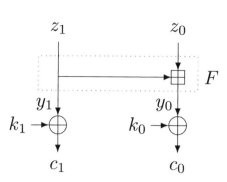

Fig. 5. A simple toy example.

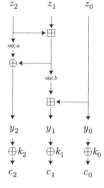

Fig. 6. A consecutive case.

For example, $\mathcal{P}$ can be chosen as $\{([],[]),([i-1],[]),([i-2],[]),([i-2,i-1],[])\}$.

To demonstrate the attack from the previous section, we split $\mathbb{F}_2^{2m}$ into the direct sum $\mathcal{P} \oplus \mathcal{R}$. By the isomorphism between $\mathcal{P}$ and $\mathbb{F}_2^2$, we can identify the elements $p \in \mathcal{P}$ by two-bit values $p \cong b_0 b_1$, where b_0 indicates the parity of $\bar{x}_0[i-1] \oplus x_1[i-1]$ and b_1 indicates the parity of $\bar{x}_0[i-2] \oplus x_1[i-2]$. We then consider the following four tuples $(\mathcal{T}_{b_0 b_1}, \Gamma_{\mathrm{out}}^{(b_0 b_1)}, \gamma^{(b_0 b_1)})$ and corresponding $\varepsilon_{b_0 b_1}$, whose definition come from the properties presented in Lemma 2 and Lemma 3:

$$
\begin{aligned}
&\mathcal{T}_{00} = \mathcal{R} \oplus 00 = \mathcal{S}_4 && \Gamma_{\mathrm{out}}^{(00)} = ([],[i,i-1]) && \gamma^{(00)} = ([i],[i,i-1,i-2]) && \varepsilon_{00} = -1 \\
&\mathcal{T}_{01} = \mathcal{R} \oplus 01 = \mathcal{S}_1 \setminus \mathcal{S}_4 && \Gamma_{\mathrm{out}}^{(01)} = ([],[i]) && \gamma^{(01)} = ([i],[i,i-1]) && \varepsilon_{01} = -1 \\
&\mathcal{T}_{10} = \mathcal{R} \oplus 10 = \mathcal{S}_2 && \Gamma_{\mathrm{out}}^{(10)} = ([],[i]) && \gamma^{(10)} = ([i],[i,i-2]) && \varepsilon_{10} = -1 \\
&\mathcal{T}_{11} = \mathcal{R} \oplus 11 = \mathcal{S}_3 \setminus \mathcal{S}_2 && \Gamma_{\mathrm{out}}^{(11)} = ([],[i,i-1]) && \gamma^{(11)} = ([i],[i]) && \varepsilon_{11} = 1.
\end{aligned}
$$

For example, to give an intuition for the choice of the first tuple,[6] when $(y_1, y_0) \in \mathcal{S}_4$, Lemma 3 tells us that $\langle \Gamma_{\mathrm{out}}^{(00)}, (z_1, z_0) \rangle = \langle \gamma^{(00)}, (y_1, y_0) \rangle \oplus 1$, i.e., $\varepsilon_{00} = \mathbf{Cor}_{y \in \mathcal{T}_{00}} \left[\langle \Gamma_{\mathrm{out}}^{(00)}, z \rangle \oplus \langle \gamma^{(00)}, y \rangle \right] = -1$.

We further have

$$
W = \mathrm{Span}\{\gamma^{(a)} \oplus \gamma^{(b)} \mid a, b \in \mathbb{F}_2^2\} = \{([],[]),([],[i-1]),([],[i-2]),([],[i-1,i-2])\}
$$

and we could recover the two bits $k_0[i-1]$ and $k_0[i-2]$ by the last step using the fast Walsh-Hadamard transform.

---

[6] Note that we might choose different $(\Gamma_{\mathrm{out}}^{(b_0 b_1)}, \gamma^{(b_0 b_1)})$ for $\mathcal{T}_{b_0 b_1}$. For example, for $\mathcal{T}_{00} = \mathcal{S}_4$, we might alternatively choose

$$
\Gamma_{\mathrm{out}}^{(00)} = ([],[i]) \quad \gamma^{(00)} = ([i],[i,i-1]) \quad \varepsilon_{00} = -1,
$$

which is obtained from Lemma 2. To verify, note that $\mathcal{S}_4 \subseteq \mathcal{S}_1$.

4.3 Another Toy Example Using Multiple Partition Points

Let us now look at another example which consists of two branches of the structure depiced in Fig. 5 in parallel, i.e., $(y_3, y_2, y_1, y_0) = (F(z_3, z_2), F(z_1, z_0))$ and $c_i = y_i \oplus k_i$. By using a single partition point as done in the above example, we can only evaluate the parity of at most two (consecutive) bits of $z = (z_3, z_2, z_1, z_0)$. Instead of just one single partition point, we can also consider multiple partition points. For example, if we want to evaluate the parity involving three non-consecutive bits of $z = (z_3, z_2, z_1, z_0)$, we can use three partition points, i.e.

$$\zeta_1 = (z_0[i], z_0[i] \oplus z_0[i-1]),$$
$$\zeta_2 = (z_0[j], z_0[j] \oplus z_0[j-1]),$$
$$\zeta_3 = (z_2[\ell], z_2[\ell] \oplus z_2[\ell-1]),$$

where $i, j, \ell \geq 2$. In a specific attack, the choice of the partition points depends on the definition of the linear trail. Those partition points give rise to three subspaces $\mathcal{P}_1$, $\mathcal{P}_2$, and $\mathcal{P}_3$, defined by two parity-check equations each, i.e., $\mathcal{P}_i$ is a complement space of $\mathcal{R}_i$, where

$$\mathcal{R}_1 = \{(x_3, x_2, x_1, x_0) \in \mathbb{F}_2^{4m} \mid x_0[i-1] \oplus x_1[i-1] = 0, x_0[i-2] \oplus x_1[i-2] = 0\}$$
$$\mathcal{R}_2 = \{(x_3, x_2, x_1, x_0) \in \mathbb{F}_2^{4m} \mid x_0[j-1] \oplus x_1[j-1] = 0, x_0[j-2] \oplus x_1[j-2] = 0\}$$
$$\mathcal{R}_3 = \{(x_3, x_2, x_1, x_0) \in \mathbb{F}_2^{4m} \mid x_2[\ell-1] \oplus x_3[\ell-1] = 0, x_2[\ell-2] \oplus x_3[\ell-2] = 0\}.$$

By defining[7] $\mathcal{P} = \mathcal{P}_1 \oplus \mathcal{P}_2 \oplus \mathcal{P}_3$ and $\mathcal{R}$ to be a complement space of $\mathcal{P}$, we split $\mathbb{F}_2^{4m}$ into the direct sum $\mathcal{P} \oplus \mathcal{R}$.

We can identify the elements $p \in \mathcal{P}$ by $n_{\mathcal{P}}$-bit values $p \cong b_0 b_1 \ldots b_{n_{\mathcal{P}}-1}$. We can then again define tuples

$$(\mathcal{T}_{b_0 b_1 \ldots b_{n_{\mathcal{P}}-1}}, \Gamma_{\text{out}}^{(b_0 b_1 \ldots b_{n_{\mathcal{P}}-1})}, \gamma^{(b_0 b_1 \ldots b_{n_{\mathcal{P}}-1})}) \tag{3}$$

by using the properties presented in Lemma 2 and Lemma 3. For example, if $n_{\mathcal{P}} = 6$, we can define

$$\mathcal{T}_{010101} = \{(x_3, x_2, x_1, x_0) \in \mathbb{F}_2^{4m} \mid x_0[i-1] \neq x_1[i-1], x_0[i-2] = x_1[i-2],$$
$$x_0[j-1] \neq x_1[j-1], x_0[j-2] = x_1[j-2],$$
$$x_2[\ell-1] \neq x_3[\ell-1], x_2[\ell-2] = x_3[\ell-2]\},$$

$\Gamma_{\text{out}}^{(010101)} = ([], [\ell], [], [i, j]),$ $\gamma^{(010101)} = ([\ell], [\ell-1, \ell], [i, j], [i-1, i, j-1, j]),$ and $\varepsilon_{010101} = -1$ by using the first case of Lemma 2.

We can also use the three partition points to compute the parity of more than three bits of z. For example, if $n_{\mathcal{P}} = 6$, by using Lemma 2 and 3, we can define

$$\mathcal{T}_{001011} = \{(x_3, x_2, x_1, x_0) \in \mathbb{F}_2^{4m} \mid x_0[i-1] \neq x_1[i-1], x_0[i-2] \neq x_1[i-2],$$
$$x_0[j-1] = x_1[j-1], x_0[j-2] \neq x_1[j-2],$$
$$x_2[\ell-1] = x_3[\ell-1], x_2[\ell-2] = x_3[\ell-2]\},$$

---

[7] Note that $\mathcal{P}$ is not necessarily a *direct* sum of $\mathcal{P}_1$, $\mathcal{P}_2$, and $\mathcal{P}_3$. In other words, the dimension of $\mathcal{P}$ might be smaller than 6, for instance if $i = j$, i.e., $\zeta_1 = \zeta_2$.

and

$$\Gamma_{\text{out}}^{(001011)} = ([], [\ell - 1, \ell], [], [i - 1, i, j])$$
$$\gamma^{(001011)} = ([\ell], [\ell], [i, j], [i - 2, i - 1, i, j - 2, j]), \quad \varepsilon_{001011} = 1,$$

which evaluates the parity of five bits of z. Again, several choices for the definition of the tuples in Eq. 3 are possible.

4.4   Analysis for Two Consecutive Modular Additions

To avoid the usage of long linear trails and to reduce the data complexity, we may use the partition technique for the more complicated structure of two consecutive modular additions. Inspired by the round function of Chaskey, we consider the case depicted in Fig. 6.

Suppose that we have the partition point $\zeta = (z_1[i], z_1[i] \oplus z_1[i - 1])$, i.e., we want to compute the parity $z_1[i]$ and $z_1[i, i - 1]$ from c_2, c_1, and c_0 (see Fig. 6). This partition point gives rise to a 5-dimensional subspace $\mathcal{P}$ which can be defined by five parity check equations, i.e., $\mathcal{P}$ is a complement space of the space

$$\mathcal{R} = \{(x_2, x_1, x_0) \in \mathbb{F}_2^{3m} \, | x_2[i_a - 1] \oplus x_1[i_b - 2] \oplus x_1[i_c - 2] = 0,$$
$$x_0[i_b - 1] \oplus x_1[i_b - 1] = 0, \; x_0[i_b - 2] \oplus x_1[i_b - 2] = 0,$$
$$x_0[i_c - 1] \oplus x_1[i_c - 1] = 0, \; x_0[i_c - 2] \oplus x_1[i_c - 2] = 0\},$$

where $i_a = i + a$, $i_b = i + b$, and $i_c = i + a + b$. Then, if $n_\mathcal{P} = 5$, we can identify the elements $p_i \in \mathcal{P}$ by five-bit values $p_i \cong b_0 b_1 b_2 b_3 b_4$, where $(b_0 b_1 b_2 b_3 b_4) = (y_2[i_a - 1] \oplus y_1[i_b - 2] \oplus y_1[i_c - 2], s[i_b - 1], s[i_b - 2], s[i_c - 1], s[i_c - 2])$ with $s = \bar{y}_0 \oplus y_1$. The whole $\mathbb{F}_2^{3m}$ is partitioned into 2^5 cosets $\mathcal{T}_{p_i} = \mathcal{R} \oplus p_i$ and these partitions can be constructed by guessing 5 bit of key information. The tuples as in Eq. 3 can be defined by $\Gamma_{\text{out}}^{(p_i)} \in \{([], [i], []), ([], [i, i - 1], [])\}$, and the corresponding linear mask $\gamma^{(p_i)}$ involves the bits

$$y_2[i_a], y_0[i_b], y_1[i_b], y_1[i_b - 1], y_1[i_b - 2], y_0[i_c], y_1[i_c], y_1[i_c - 1], y_1[i_c - 2].$$

When $i_a - 2$, $i_b - 2$, and $i_c - 2$ is not extremely close to 0, for each possible choice of $\Gamma \in \{([], [i], []), ([], [i, i - 1], [])\}$, we have 4 tuples corresponding to correlation $\varepsilon = \pm 1$, 8 tuples corresponding to correlation $\varepsilon = \pm 2^{-1}$, and 12 tuples corresponding to correlation $\varepsilon = \pm 2^{-0.263}$. In other words, a fraction of $24/32 = 3/4$ tuples with non-zero correlation is available, and the average absolute correlation is $(4 \times 1) + (8 \times 2^{-1}) + (12 \times 2^{-0.263}) \approx 2^{-0.415}$.

5   Application to Chaskey

Chaskey [24] is a lightweight MAC algorithm whose underlying primitive is an ARX-based permutation in an Even-Mansour construction, i.e., Chaskey-EM. The permutation operates on four 32-bit words and employs 12 rounds of the form as depicted in Fig. 7. The designers' claim security up to 2^{80} computations as long as the data is limited to 2^{48} blocks.

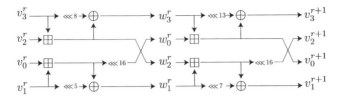

Fig. 7. The round function of Chaskey.

5.1   Overview of Our Attack

We first show the high-level overview of our attack. Similarly to the previous differential-linear attack from [20], we first divide the cipher into three sub ciphers, i.e, E_1 covering 1.5 rounds, E_m covering 4 rounds, and E_2 covering 0.5 rounds. The key-recovery is done over 1 round, thus the function F is covering 1 round to attack 7 rounds in total. The differential characteristic and the linear trail are applied to E_1 and E_2, respectively, while the experimental differential-linear distinguisher is applied to the middle part E_m. Note that, since the differential-linear distinguisher over E_m is constructed experimentally, its correlation must be high enough to be detectable by using a relatively small sampling space. Moreover, since it is practically infeasible to check *all* input difference and *all* output linear mask, we restricted ourselves to the case of an input difference of Hamming weight 1 and linear masks of the form $[i]$ or $[i, i+1]$, i.e., 1-bit or consecutive 2-bit linear masks. As a result, when there is a non-zero difference *only* in the 31st bit (msb) of w_0^1, i.e.,

$$\Delta_m = (([]), ([]), ([31]), ([])),$$

we observed the following two differential-linear distinguishers with correlations $2^{-5.1}$:

$$\mathbf{Cor}_{w^1 \in \mathcal{S}} \left[w_2^5[20] \oplus \tilde{w}_2^5[20] \right] \approx 2^{-5.1}, \tag{4}$$

$$\mathbf{Cor}_{w^1 \in \mathcal{S}} \left[w_2^5[20] \oplus w_2^5[19] \oplus \tilde{w}_2^5[20] \oplus \tilde{w}_2^5[19] \right] \approx 2^{-5.1}. \tag{5}$$

These correlations[8] are estimated using a set $\mathcal{S}$ consisting of 2^{26} random samples of w^1. This is significant enough since the standard deviation assuming a normal distribution is 2^{13}. For simplicity, only the first differential-linear distinguisher is exploited in our 7-round attack. That is

$$\Gamma_m = (([]), ([20]), ([]), ([])).$$

Note that we do not focus on the theoretical justification of this 4-round experimental differential-linear distinguisher in this paper and we start the analysis for E_1 and E_2 from the following subsection.

---

[8] The first case is the exactly same as the one shown in [20], but its correlation was reported as $2^{-6.1}$. We are not sure the reason of this gap, but we think that $2^{-6.1}$ refers to the bias instead of the correlation.

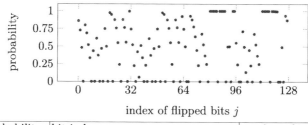

probability	bit index	number of indices
$\gamma_j = 1$	v_2 : 16,17,18,19,20,22,23,24,25,30,31 v_3 : 16,17,18,19,20,22,23	18
$0.95 \leq \gamma_j < 1$	v_0 : 19,20,31 v_3 : 24,25 v_1 : 19,20	7

Fig. 8. Probability that flipping $v_{j/32}^0[j \bmod 32]$ affects the output difference.

5.2 Differential Part

We need to construct a differential distinguisher $\Delta_{\text{in}} \to \Delta_m$ over E_1, where the output difference is equal to the 1-bit difference $\Delta_m = (([]), ([]), ([31]), ([]))$. We have 1.5-round differential characteristic of highest probability under this restriction and its probability is 2^{-17}, where

$$\Delta_{\text{in}} = (([8, 13, 21, 26, 30]), ([8, 18, 21, 30]), ([3, 21, 26]), ([21, 26, 27])).$$

If this differential characteristic is directly used in the differential-linear attack, the impact on the data complexity is $p^{-2} = 2^{34}$, which is quite huge given the restriction on the data complexity for Chaskey. In order to reduce the data complexity, we employ the new technique described in Sect. 3. Note that the previous analysis shown in [20] also employs the same differential characteristic, but the technique for reducing the data complexity is completely different. We will compare our technique to the previous technique at the end of this subsection.

Detecting an Appropriate Subspace $\mathcal{U}$. As described in Sect. 3, we want to detect a subspace $\mathcal{U}$ of the input space such that $E_1(v^0 \oplus u) \oplus E_1(v^0 \oplus u \oplus \Delta_{in}) = \Delta_m$ for all $u \in \mathcal{U}$ if $E_1(v^0) \oplus E_1(v^0 \oplus \Delta_{in}) = \Delta_m$. Then, for our attack to be effective, the condition is that $2^{|\dim \mathcal{U}|} > \epsilon r^{-2} q^{-4}$, where r and q denote the correlation of the differential-linear distinguisher over E_m and the linear distinguisher over E_2, respectively. If this condition is satisfied, we can reduce the total data complexity from $\epsilon p^{-2} r^{-2} q^{-4}$ to $\epsilon p^{-1} r^{-2} q^{-4}$.

Since the four branches are properly mixed with each other within 1.5 rounds, there is no trivial subspace as in the simple example in Sect. 3.1. However, the diffusion obtained by the modular addition, XOR and rotation is heavily biased. For example, let us focus on $v_2^0[31]$. This bit is independent of the 1.5-round differential trail. Thus, we will experimentally detect bits that do not, or only very rarely, effect the differential trail, as explained in Sect. 3 in Algorithm 1. We used this algorithm with a sampling parameter $T = 2^{32}$. Due to the differential probability of 2^{-17}, we find on average $2^{32} \times 2^{-17} = 2^{15}$ values of X such that $E_1(X) \oplus E_1(X \oplus \Delta_{in}) = \Delta_m$.

Figure 8 summarizes the result of the search. When the basis of the linear subspace $\mathcal{U}$ is chosen from the 18 indices i corresponding to a probability $\gamma_i = 1$, we are exactly in the setting as explained in Sect. 3 and the factor on the data complexity corresponding to the differential part would be p^{-1}. Unfortunately, 18 indices are not always sufficient to attack 7-round Chaskey. Therefore, we additionally add 7 indices, i.e., $v_0[19], v_0[20], v_0[31], v_1[19], v_1[20], v_3[24]$, and $v_3[25]$ to define the basis of $\mathcal{U}$. We then randomly picked 256 pairs $(X, X \oplus \Delta_{in})$ that result in the output difference Δ_m after E_1 and checked for how many of those pairs, the equation $E_1(X \oplus u) \oplus E_1(X \oplus u \oplus \Delta_{in}) = \Delta_m$ is satisfied *for all* $u \in \mathcal{U}$. As a result, this holds for 222 out of 256 pairs $(X, X \oplus \Delta_{in})$. In other words, we can estimate the factor on the data complexity corresponding to the differential part to be $(p \times 222/256)^{-1}$.

Comparison with the Technique of Leurent. In [20], Leurent applied the partitioning technique to the same 1.5-round differential characteristic. For applying the partitioning technique, 14 bit of key information need to be guessed and the impact on the data complexity from the differential part was estimated as $\left(\frac{17496}{2^{23}} \times 2^{10} \times 2^{-2 \times 11} \right)^{-1} \approx 2^{20.9}$ in [20]. In contrast, our technique does not need to guess any key bit and the impact on the data complexity from the differential part is estimated as $(p \times \frac{222}{256})^{-1} \approx 2^{17.2}$ when the size of $\mathcal{U}$ is 2^{25}.

5.3   Linear Part

In order to attack 7-round Chaskey, we consider as E_2 0.5-rounds of Chaskey and as F 1.5-rounds of Chaskey. For E_2 we consider two trails for the mask $\Gamma_m = ((\parallel), ([20]), (\parallel), (\parallel))$, namely

$$\psi^{(1)} = v_2^6[11, 10, 4] \oplus w_1^6[31, 0] \oplus w_0^6[16, 15],$$
$$\psi^{(0)} = v_2^6[11, 4, 3] \oplus w_1^6[0] \oplus w_0^6[16].$$

That is computing $\langle \Gamma_{out}^{p_i}, z \rangle$ corresponds to either $\psi^{(1)}$ or $\psi^{(0)}$

Similarly, we denote by $\tilde{\psi}^{(1)}$ and $\tilde{\psi}^{(0)}$ the corresponding parity bits for $\tilde{c}$. As discussed in Sect. 4, our attack uses only one of them (with highest absolute correlation) for each partition. For example, let us assume that $\psi^{(1)}$ is preferable for the partition belonging to c and $\psi^{(0)}$ is preferable for the partition belonging to $\tilde{c}$. Then, we compute $\psi^{(1)}$ and $\tilde{\psi}^{(0)}$ from c and $\tilde{c}$, respectively, and evaluate the probability satisfying $\psi^{(1)} = \tilde{\psi}^{(0)}$. We experimentally evaluated the correlations of any combination, i.e., the correlation of 2×2 differential-linear distinguishers. Similarly to the experiments in Sect. 5.1, we computed those correlations over a set $\mathcal{S}$ consisting of random samples of w^1, but the size of $\mathcal{S}$ had to be increased to 2^{28} because of the lower correlation. As a result, these empirical correlations are $\approx \pm 2^{-6.4}$.

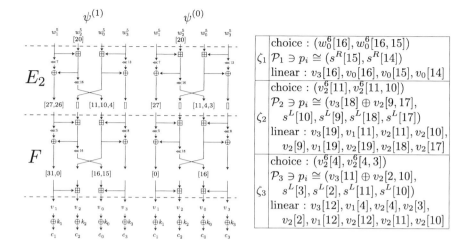

Fig. 9. Two 0.5-round linear trails and corresponding partition points.

For Chaskey, we use three partition points as shown in the right table of Fig. 9. The dimension of W for the FWHT is increased by 1 but it does not affect the size of partitions. As already presented in Sect. 4, the corresponding subspaces $\mathcal{P}_1$ can be defined by the bits summarized in Fig. 9, where $s^L := \bar{v}_1 \oplus v_2$ and $s^R := \bar{v}_3 \oplus v_0$. The same table also summarizes the linear bits that can be involved to a linear combination in the corresponding $\gamma^{(p_1)}$.

For ζ_2 and ζ_3, the situation is different since we have to evaluate two consecutive modular additions instead of just one. The major difference is that the corresponding subspace is now of dimension 5, i.e., the condition is defined by a 5-bit value. Further, the corresponding ε_i are not always ± 1.

Note that because there is a 1-bit interception in the defining bits for $\mathcal{P}_2$ and $\mathcal{P}_3$, we have $n_\mathcal{P} = \dim \mathcal{P} = \dim(\mathcal{P}_1 \oplus \mathcal{P}_2 \oplus \mathcal{P}_3) = 2 + 5 + 5 - 1 = 11$. Namely, the index p_i of the partition $\mathcal{T}_{p_i}$ is defined by the 11-bit value

$$(s^R[15], s^R[14], v_3[18] \oplus v_2[9, 17], s^L[10], s^L[9], s^L[18], s^L[17],$$
$$v_3[11] \oplus v_2[2, 10], s^L[3], s^L[2], s^L[11]).$$

It is difficult to evaluate the actual correlations of *all* $q_{i,j}, i, j \in \{1, \ldots, 2^{11}\}$ experimentally with a high significance. Therefore, we simply assume that these correlations are common for each partition, i.e., $q_{i,j} = 2^{-6.4}$ for all i and j.

Since we have two choices $\psi^{(0)}$ or $\psi^{(1)}$ for the linear mask $\Gamma_{\text{out}}^{(p_i)}$ that we use in each partition, we evaluated every correlation of possible $\Gamma_{\text{out}}^{(p_i)}$ and took the one with the highest absolute correlation. More precisely, we evaluated each subspace $\mathcal{P}_i$ step by step. We start our analysis from $\mathcal{P}_1$. For this, the condition is based on $s^R[15]$ and $s^R[14]$ and the available linear masks can be immediately determined as follows.

$$\begin{cases} \psi^{(1)}, \psi^{(0)} & \text{if } (s^R[15], s^R[14]) = (0,0), \\ \psi^{(0)} & \text{if } (s^R[15], s^R[14]) = (0,1), \\ \psi^{(1)}, \psi^{(0)} & \text{if } (s^R[15], s^R[14]) = (1,0), \\ \psi^{(1)}, & \text{if } (s^R[15], s^R[14]) = (1,1). \end{cases}$$

In other words, the number of available linear masks decreases from 2 to 1 for 2^{10} partitions, and the number is preserved for the other 2^{10} partitions. We next focus on $\mathcal{P}_2$, but it is more complicated because the index bit $s^L[10]$ also appears in the index for $\mathcal{P}_3$. Since $\dim(\mathcal{P}_2 \oplus \mathcal{P}_3) = 9$ is not large, we exhaustively evaluated the correlation of each partition. As a result, 1472 out of 2^{11} partitions show a significant correlation and the average of the absolute value of those correlations is $2^{-0.779}$. In the differential-linear attack, this partition analysis must be executed for both texts in each pair. Thus, when N pairs are used, the number of available pairs is $N^* = N \times (\frac{1472}{2048})^2 \approx N \times 2^{-0.953}$ and the correlation is $h = 2^{-6.4-0.779 \times 2} = 2^{-7.958}$.

We also need to evaluate the dimension of $W := \mathrm{Span}\{\gamma^{(p_i)} \oplus \gamma^{(p_j)} \mid i, j \in \{1, \ldots, s\}\}$ to evaluate the time complexity for the FWHT. Note that $\gamma \in W$ is always generated by XORing two linear masks. Therefore, bits that are always set to 1 in the linear masks $\gamma^{(p_i)}$ and $\gamma^{(p_j)}$ do not increase the dimension of W. For example, since both $\psi^{(1)}$ and $\psi^{(0)}$ involves $v_1[0]$, it does not increase the dimension of W. On the other hand, since $v_1[31]$ is involved only in $\psi^{(1)}$, it increases the dimension of W by 1. The same analysis can be applied to each partition point. For example, partition point ζ_1 involves four bits $v_3[16]$, $v_0[16]$, $v_0[15]$, and $v_0[14]$ in the key mask $\gamma^{(p_i)}$, but both $v_3[16]$ and $v_0[16]$ are always involved. As a result, the 10 bits

$$v_1[31], v_0[15], v_0[14], v_2[10], v_2[9], v_2[18], v_2[17], v_2[3], v_2[2], v_2[11]$$

are enough to construct any $\gamma \in W$, i.e., $\dim(W) \le 10$.

Experimental Reports. To verify our technique, we implemented the attack and estimated the experimental correlation if the linear masks are appropriately chosen for each partition. Then, for a right pair $(X, X \oplus \Delta_{in})$, we used 2^{28} pairs $(X \oplus u, X \oplus u \oplus \Delta_{in})$ for $u \in \mathcal{U}$. As a result, the number of available pairs is $2^{27.047}$, and the number well fits our theoretical estimation. On the other hand, there is a small (but important) gap between our theoretical analysis and experimental analysis. While this correlation was estimated as $2^{-7.958}$ in our theoretical analysis, the experimental correlation is $2^{-7.37}$, which is much higher than our theoretical estimation. We expect that this gap comes from *linear-hull effect* between $q_{i,j}$ and (ϵ_i, ϵ_j). The linear masks $\lambda^{(0)}$ and $\lambda^{(1)}$ are fixed in our theoretical estimation, but it allows to use multiple linear masks similarly to the conventional linear-hull effect. Moreover, as a consecutive modular addition causes much higher absolute correlation, we expect that our case also causes much higher absolute correlation. However, its detailed theoretical understanding is left as a open question in this paper.

Data and Time Complexities and Success Probability. We use the formula in Proposition 1 to estimate the data complexity and corresponding success probability. To find a right pair, we repeat Algorithm 2 for $(p \times 222/256)^{-1} = 2^{17.206}$ times, and we expect to find a right pair with probability $1/2$. For each iteration of Algorithm 2, we use $N = 2^{22}$ pairs, and $N^* = 2^{21.047}$. By using the threshold $\Theta = \sqrt{N^*} \times \Phi^{-1}(1 - \frac{p \times 222/256}{2^n})$, the expected number of wrong keys is 1, while[9] $p_{\text{success}} = 0.489$, where correlation $2^{-7.37}$ is used in this estimation. On this success probability, the data complexity is $2^{1+22+17.206} = 2^{40.206}$ and the time complexity is $2^{17.206} \times 2^{11} \times (2 \times 2^{22} + 10 \times 2^{10}) \approx 2^{51.208}$.

6   Application to ChaCha

The internal state of ChaCha is represented by a 4×4 matrix whose elements are 32-bit vectors. In this section, the input state for the r-th round function is represented as

$$\begin{pmatrix} v_0^r & v_1^r & v_2^r & v_3^r \\ v_4^r & v_5^r & v_6^r & v_7^r \\ v_8^r & v_9^r & v_{10}^r & v_{11}^r \\ v_{12}^r & v_{13}^r & v_{14}^r & v_{15}^r \end{pmatrix}.$$

In odd and even rounds, the QR function is applied on every column and diagonal, respectively. We also introduce the notion of a *half round*, in which the QR function is divided into two sub function depicted in Fig. 10. Let w^r be the internal state after the application of a half round on v^r. Moreover, we use the term *branches* for a, b, c and d, as shown in Fig. 10.

In the initial state of ChaCha, a 128-bit constant is loaded into the first row, a 128- or 256-bit secret key is loaded into the second and third rows, and a 64-bit counter and 64-bit nonce are loaded into the fourth row. In other words, the first three rows in v^0 are fixed. For r-round ChaCha, the odd and even round functions are iteratively applied, and the feed-forward values $v_i^0 \boxplus v_i^r$ is given as the key stream for all i. Note that we can compute v_i^r for $i \in \{0, 1, 2, 3, 12, 13, 14, 15\}$ because corresponding v_i^0 is known.

6.1   Overview of Our Attack

We use the same attack strategy as for Chaskey. The cipher is divided into the sub ciphers E_1 covering 1 round, E_m covering 2.5 rounds, and E_2 covering 1.5 rounds to attack 6 rounds, and F the key recovery is applied to the last one round. One difference to Chaskey is the domain space that can be controlled by the attacker. In particular, we cannot control branches a, b, and c because fixed constants and the fixed secret key is loaded into these states. Thus, only branch d can be varied. It implies that active bit positions for input differences

---

[9] It means that the success probability is $0.489 \times 2 = 0.978$ under the condition that the right pair is successfully obtained during $2^{17.206}$ iterations.

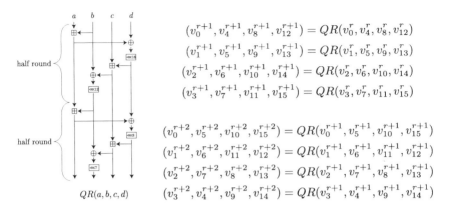

Fig. 10. The odd and even round functions of ChaCha.

are limited to branch d and a difference Δ_m after E_1 with Hamming weight is 1 will not be available due to the property of the round function. Therefore, we first need to generate consistent Δ_m whose Hamming weight is minimized. The following shows such differential characteristics over one QR function.

$$\Delta_{in} = (([\,]),([\,]),([\,]),([i])) \quad \rightarrow \quad \Delta_m = (([i+28]),([i+31,i+23,i+11,i+3]),$$
$$([i+24,i+16,i+4]),([i+24,i+4])).$$

The probability that pairs with input difference Δ_{in} satisfy this characteristic is 2^{-5} on average. We discuss the properties of this differential characteristic in Sect. 6.2 in more detail.

We next evaluate an experimental differential-linear distinguisher for the middle part E_m. When the Hamming weight of Γ_m is 1 and the active bit is in the lsb, it allows the correlation of linear trails for E_2 to be lower. For $i = 6$, i.e., $\Delta_m = (([2]),([5,29,17,9]),([30,22,10]),([30,10]))$, we find the following four differential-linear distinguishers.

$$\Delta(v_j^1, v_{j+4}^1, v_{j+8}^1, v_{j+12}^1) = \Delta_m \rightarrow \mathbf{Cor}[w_{(j+1) \bmod 4}^3[0] \oplus \tilde{w}_{(j+1) \bmod 4}^3[0]] = 2^{-8.3},$$

for $j \in \{0, 1, 2, 3\}$. When this experimental distinguisher is combined with the differential characteristic for E_1, it covers 3.5 rounds with a 1-bit output linear mask Γ_m. This differential-linear distinguisher is improved by 0.5 rounds from the previous distinguisher with 1-bit output linear mask (see [1,11]).

6.2   Differential Part

The QR function is independently applied to each column in the first round. Therefore, when the output difference of one QR function is restricted by Δ_m, the input of other three QR functions are trivially independent of the output difference. It implies that we have 96 independent bits, and we can easily amplify the probability of the differential-linear distinguisher. On the other hand, we face a different problem, namely that the probability of the differential characteristic (Δ_{in}, Δ_m) highly depends on the value of the secret key. For example, for $\Delta v_{12}^0[6] = 1$, we expect that there is a pair $(v_{12}^0, v_{12}^0 \oplus \texttt{0x00000020})$ satisfying $\Delta(v_0^1, v_4^1, v_8^1, v_{12}^1) = \Delta_m$, but it depends on the constant v_0^0 and the key values v_4^0 and v_8^0. In our experiments, we cannot find such a pair for 292 out of 1024 randomly generated keys. On the other hand, when we can find it, i.e., on 732 out of 1024 keys, the average probability satisfying $\Delta(v_0^1, v_4^1, v_8^1, v_{12}^1) = \Delta_m$ is $2^{-4.5}$. This experiment implies the existence of "strong keys" against our attack. However, note that we can vary the columns in which we put a difference, which involve different key values. Since the fraction of "strong keys" is not so high, i.e., 292/1024, we can assume that there is at least one column in which no "strong key" is chosen with very high probability.

To determine the factor p, for 1024 randomly generated keys, we evaluated p^{-1} randomly chosen iv and counter, where the branch that we induce the difference is also randomly chosen. As a result, we can find a right pair on 587 keys with $p^{-1} = 2^5$ iterations. Therefore, with $p = 2^{-5}$, we assume that we can find a right pair with probability 1/2 in this stage of the attack.

In the following, we explain our attack for the case that v_{12}^0 is active and $\Delta(v_0^1, v_4^1, v_8^1, v_{12}^1) = \Delta_m$. Note that the analysis for the other three cases follows the same argument.

6.3   Linear Part for 6-Round Attack

To attack 6-round ChaCha, we first construct a 5-round differential-linear distinguisher, where 1.5-round linear trails are appended (i.e. the E_2 part) to the 3.5-round experimental differential-linear distinguisher from the previous section. We have two 1.5-round linear trails given by

$$\mathbf{Cor}[w_1^3[0] \oplus \psi^{(1)}] = 2^{-1}, \qquad \mathbf{Cor}[w_1^3[0] \oplus \psi^{(0)}] = -2^{-1},$$

where $\psi^{(1)} = \psi \oplus v_{10}^5[6]$ and $\psi^{(0)} = \psi \oplus v_{14}^5[6]$, and

$$\psi = (v_5^5[19,7] \oplus v_{10}^5[19,7] \oplus v_{15}^5[8,0]) \oplus (v_1^5[0] \oplus v_6^5[26] \oplus v_{11}^5[0])$$
$$\oplus (v_{13}^5[0]) \oplus (v_3^5[0] \oplus v_9^5[12] \oplus v_{14}^5[7]).$$

Since their correlations are $\pm 2^{-1}$, we have 2×2 differential-linear distinguishers on 5 rounds whose correlations are $\pm 2^{-10.3}$. Note that the sign of each correlation is deterministic according to the output linear mask.

Our 6-round attack uses these 5-round differential-linear distinguishers, and the 1-round key recovery is shown in Fig. 11. Let $c = (c_0, \ldots, c_{15})$ be the corresponding output, and let $v = (v_0, \ldots, v_{15})$ be the sixteen 32-bit values before the secret key is added. Note that the secret key is only added with half of the state and public values are added with the other state. Therefore, we simply regard $v_i = c_i$ for $i \in \{0, 15, 1, 12, 2, 13, 3, 14\}$.

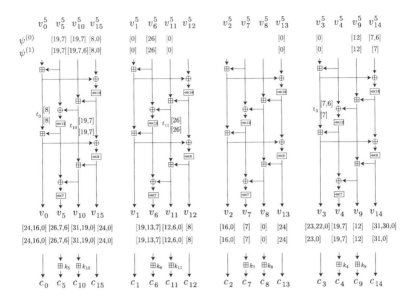

Fig. 11. Key recovery for 6-round ChaCha.

First, we partially extend two linear masks for the last round so that it can be linearly computed. Figure 11 summarizes the extended linear masks, where we need to compute the bits labeled by a red color. Moreover, for simplicity, we introduce t_0, t_{10}, t_{11}, and t_3 as depicted in Fig. 11.

Each bit in $\boldsymbol{v}$ in which the secret key is not added can be computed for free. For the other bits, we need to guess some key bits first. We first explain the simple case, i.e., we compute $v_i[j]$ from c_i. As an example, we focus on $v_7[7]$, which involves k_7 nonlinearly. We apply the partition technique to compute this bit, where $(3/4)$ data is available by guessing $k_7[6]$ and $k_7[5]$ (remember that $k_7[7]$ cancels out in the differential-linear approximation). Since $v_i[0]$ is linearly computed by $c_i[0]$, there are 13 simple partition points in which we need to guess key bits. In total, we need to guess a 26-bit key and $(3/4)^{13}$ data is available.

Computing bits in $\boldsymbol{v}^5$ and $\boldsymbol{t}$ is a bit more complicated than the simple case above. For example, let us consider $v_9^5[12]$, and this bit can be computed as

$$v_9^5[12] = (c_9 \boxminus k_9 \boxminus c_{14} \boxminus (c_3 \oplus (v_{14} \ggg 8)))[12]$$
$$= ((c_9 \boxminus c_{14} \boxminus (c_3 \oplus (v_{14} \ggg 8))) \boxminus k_9)[12].$$

Since we can compute $(c_9 \boxminus c_{14} \boxminus (c_3 \oplus (v_{14} \ggg 8)))$ for free, this case is equivalent to the simple case. We also use this equivalent transformation for t_{10}, t_{11}, and $v_{10}[19]$. In total, we have 6 such partition points, and some partition points can share the same key, e.g., 2-bit key $k_{10}[18]$ and $k_{10}[17]$ is already guessed to compute $v_{10}[19]$. Guessing 4 bits of additional key is enough to compute each bit.

Since we have two linear masks $\psi^{(0)}$ and $\psi^{(1)}$, the number of available partitions does not decrease for $v_{10}^5[7]/v_{10}^5[7,6]$. Therefore, $(3/4)^5$ data is available.

We cannot use the equivalent transformation to compute bits in t_0 and t_3. Then, we further extend this linear mask with correlation 2^{-1}. For example, we have the following approximations

$$t_0[8] \approx v_0[8,7] \oplus v_5[15] \oplus v_{10}[8] \oplus 1, \quad t_0[8] \approx v_0[8] \oplus v_5[15,14] \oplus v_{10}[8,7],$$

for $t_0[8]$ with correlation 2^{-1}, and we can use preferable approximations depending on the data. Namely, we first guess $k_{10}[7]$ and determine which linear approximations are available. Then, we guess $k_5[14]$ and $k_5[13]$ and compute $v_5[15]$ (resp. $v_5[15,14]$) with the fraction of available partitions $3/4$. In order words, we guess 3-bit key and $3/4$ data is available. We also use the same technique for $t_0[7]/t_0[7,6]$. Therefore, 6-bit additional key is required, $(3/4)^2$ data is available, but the correlation is $\pm 2^{-10.3-2\times 2} = \pm 2^{-14.3}$.

In summary, the fraction of available partitions is $(3/4)^{13+5+2} \approx 2^{-8.3}$. We need to guess 36-bit key in total.

We finally estimate the data and time complexities. When we use N pairs, the number of available pairs is $N^* = N \times 2^{2\times -8.3} \approx N2^{-16.6}$, and the average correlation is $\pm 2^{-14.3}$. Note that unlike Chaskey, once these key bits are correctly guessed, all linearly involved bits are either determined or cancelled out by XORing another text. It implies $\dim(W) = 0$ and we do not need to proceed with the FWHT.

Data and Time Complexities and Success Probability. We use the formula in Proposition 1 to estimate the data complexity and corresponding success probability. To find a right pair, we repeat Algorithm 2 for 2^5 times. For each pair, we use $N = 2^{52}$ pairs, and $N^* = 2^{35.4}$. For the threshold $\Theta = \sqrt{N^*} \times \Phi^{-1}(1 - \frac{2^{-5}}{2^{36}})$, the expected number of wrong keys is 1, but[10] $p_{\text{success}} = 0.499$. For this success probability, the data complexity is $2^{1+52+5} = 2^{58}$.

If we guess 2^{36} keys for each texts, the required time complexity is $2^{58+36} = 2^{94}$. However, note that once we get a pair, we can immediately compute those $k_{\mathcal{P}}$ values that correspond to valid partitions. Consequently, we only iterate through those $k_{\mathcal{P}}$ values for every pair. The time complexity is estimated as $1/p \times (2N + 2N^* \times 2^{n_P}) \approx 2^{77.4}$.

6.4   The 7-Round Attack

Unfortunately, 7-round ChaCha is too complicated to apply our technique for the linear part. On the other hand, thanks to our other contribution for the differential part, we find a new differential-linear distinguisher which is improved by 0.5 rounds. Therefore, to confirm the effect of our contribution for the differential part, we use the known technique, i.e., the probabilistic neutral bits (PNB)

---

[10] Note that it means that the success probability is $0.499 \times 2 = 0.999$ under the condition that the right pair is successfully obtained during 2^7 iterations.

approach, for the key-recovery attack against 7-round ChaCha. The PNB-based key recovery is a fully experimental approach. We refer to [1] for the details and simply summarize the technique as follows:

- Let the correlation in the forward direction (a.k.a, differential-linear distinguisher) after r rounds be ϵ_d.
- Let n be the number of PNBs given by a correlation γ. Namely, even if we flip one bit in PNBs, we still observe correlation γ.
- Let the correlation in the backward direction, where all PNB bits are fixed to 0 and non-PNB bits are fixed to the correct ones, is ϵ_a.

Then, the time complexity of the attack is estimated as $2^{256-n}N + 2^{256-\alpha}$, where the data complexity N is given as

$$N = \left(\frac{\sqrt{\alpha \log(4)} + 3\sqrt{1 - \epsilon_a^2 \epsilon_d^2}}{\epsilon_a \epsilon_d} \right)^2,$$

where α is a parameter that the attacker can choose.

In our case, we use a 4-round differential-linear distinguisher with correlation $\epsilon_d = 2^{-8.3}$. Under pairs generated by the technique shown in Sect. 6.2, we experimentally estimated the PNBs. With $\gamma = 0.35$, we found 74 PNBs, and its correlation $\epsilon_a = 2^{-10.6769}$. Then, with $\alpha = 36$, we have $N = 2^{43.83}$ and the time complexity is $2^{225.86}$. Again, since we need to repeat this procedure p^{-1} times, the data and time complexity is $2^{48.83}$ and $2^{230.86}$, respectively.

7   Conclusion and Future Work

We presented new ideas for differential-linear attacks and in particular the best attacks on ChaCha, one of the most important ciphers in practice. We hope that our framework finds more applications. In particular, we think that it is a promising future work to investigate other ARX designs with respect to our ideas.

Besides the plain application of our framework to more primitives, our work raises several more fundamental questions. As explained in the experimental verification, we sometimes observe absolute correlations that are higher than expected, which in turn make the attacks more efficient than estimated. Explaining those deviations from theory, likely to be caused by linear-hull effects, is an interesting question to tackle. Related to this, we feel that – despite interesting results initiated by [25] – the impact of dependent chains of modular additions on the correlations is not understood sufficiently well and requires further study.

Finally, we see some possible improvements to our framework. First, it might be beneficial to use multiple linear mask per partition, while we used only one in our applications. This of course rises the question of independence, but maybe a multidimensional approach along the lines of [16] might be possible. Second, one might improve the results further if the estimated values for $\beta(\gamma)$ are replaced by a weighted sum, where partitions and masks with higher correlations are given more weight than partitions and masks with a comparable low correlation.

Acknowledgments. We thank the anonymous reviewers for their detailed and helpful comments. We further thank Lukas Stennes for checking the application of our framework to ChaCha in a first version of this paper. This work was funded by *Deutsche Forschungsgemeinschaft (DFG)*, project number 411879806 and by DFG under Germany's Excellence Strategy - EXC 2092 CASA - 390781972.

References

1. Aumasson, J.-P., Fischer, S., Khazaei, S., Meier, W., Rechberger, C.: New features of latin dances: analysis of Salsa, ChaCha, and Rumba. In: Nyberg, K. (ed.) FSE 2008, Revised Selected Papers. LNCS, vol. 5086, pp. 470–488. Springer, Heidelberg (2008). https://doi.org/10.1007/978-3-540-71039-4_30

2. Aumasson, J.P., Henzen, L., Meier, W., Phan, R.C.W.: SHA-3 proposal Blake. In: Submission to NIST (2008)

3. Aumasson, J.-P., Neves, S., Wilcox-O'Hearn, Z., Winnerlein, C.: BLAKE2: simpler, smaller, fast as MD5. In: Jacobson, M., Locasto, M., Mohassel, P., Safavi-Naini, R. (eds.) ACNS 2013. LNCS, vol. 7954, pp. 119–135. Springer, Heidelberg (2013). https://doi.org/10.1007/978-3-642-38980-1_8

4. Bar-On, A., Dunkelman, O., Keller, N., Weizman, A.: DLCT: a new tool for differential-linear cryptanalysis. In: Ishai, Y., Rijmen, V. (eds.) EUROCRYPT 2019, Part I. LNCS, vol. 11476, pp. 313–342. Springer, Cham (2019). https://doi.org/10.1007/978-3-030-17653-2_11

5. Beierle, C., et al.: Lightweight AEAD and Hashing using the sparkle permutation family. IACR Trans. Symm. Cryptol. **2020**(S1), 208–261 (2020)

6. Bernstein, D.J.: ChaCha, a variant of Salsa20 (2008). http://cr.yp.to/chacha.html

7. Bernstein, D.J.: The Salsa20 family of stream ciphers. In: Robshaw, M., Billet, O. (eds.) New Stream Cipher Designs. LNCS, vol. 4986, pp. 84–97. Springer, Heidelberg (2008). https://doi.org/10.1007/978-3-540-68351-3_8

8. Biham, E., Carmeli, Y.: An improvement of linear cryptanalysis with addition operations with applications to FEAL-8X. In: Joux, A., Youssef, A. (eds.) SAC 2014, Revised Selected Papers. LNCS, vol. 8781, pp. 59–76. Springer, Cham (2014). https://doi.org/10.1007/978-3-319-13051-4_4

9. Biham, E., Shamir, A.: Differential cryptanalysis of DES-like cryptosystems. In: Menezes, A.J., Vanstone, S.A. (eds.) CRYPTO 1990. LNCS, vol. 537, pp. 2–21. Springer, Heidelberg (1991). https://doi.org/10.1007/3-540-38424-3_1

10. Carlet, C.: Boolean functions for cryptography and error correcting codes. In: Crama, Y., Hammer, P. (eds.) Boolean Methods and Models. Cambridge University Press (2007)

11. Choudhuri, A.R., Maitra, S.: Significantly improved multi-bit differentials for reduced round Salsa and ChaCha. IACR Trans. Symm. Cryptol. **2016**(2), 261–287 (2016)

12. Collard, B., Standaert, F.-X., Quisquater, J.-J.: Improving the time complexity of Matsui's linear cryptanalysis. In: Nam, K.-H., Rhee, G. (eds.) ICISC 2007. LNCS, vol. 4817, pp. 77–88. Springer, Heidelberg (2007). https://doi.org/10.1007/978-3-540-76788-6_7

13. Coutinho, M., Neto, T.C.S.: New multi-bit differentials to improve attacks against ChaCha. IACR Cryptology ePrint Archive 2020/350 (2020). https://eprint.iacr.org/2020/350

14. Dey, S., Sarkar, S.: Improved analysis for reduced round Salsa and ChaCha. Discrete Appl. Math. **227**, 58–69 (2017)

15. Dinu, D., Perrin, L., Udovenko, A., Velichkov, V., Großschädl, J., Biryukov, A.: Design strategies for ARX with provable bounds: SPARX and LAX. In: Cheon, J.H., Takagi, T. (eds.) ASIACRYPT 2016, Part I. LNCS, vol. 10031, pp. 484–513. Springer, Heidelberg (2016). https://doi.org/10.1007/978-3-662-53887-6_18

16. Hermelin, M., Cho, J.Y., Nyberg, K.: Multidimensional linear cryptanalysis. J. Cryptol. **32**(1), 1–34 (2019)

17. Khovratovich, D., Nikolić, I.: Rotational cryptanalysis of ARX. In: Hong, S., Iwata, T. (eds.) FSE 2010, Revised Selected Papers. LNCS, vol. 6147, pp. 333–346. Springer, Heidelberg (2010). https://doi.org/10.1007/978-3-642-13858-4_19

18. Knudsen, L., Wagner, D.: Integral cryptanalysis. In: Daemen, J., Rijmen, V. (eds.) FSE 2002, Revised Papers. LNCS, vol. 2365, pp. 112–127. Springer, Heidelberg (2002). https://doi.org/10.1007/3-540-45661-9_9

19. Langford, S.K., Hellman, M.E.: Differential-linear cryptanalysis. In: Desmedt, Y.G. (ed.) CRYPTO 1994. LNCS, vol. 839, pp. 17–25. Springer, Heidelberg (1994). https://doi.org/10.1007/3-540-48658-5_3

20. Leurent, G.: Improved differential-linear cryptanalysis of 7-round Chaskey with partitioning. In: Fischlin, M., Coron, J.-S. (eds.) EUROCRYPT 2016, Part I. LNCS, vol. 9665, pp. 344–371. Springer, Heidelberg (2016). https://doi.org/10.1007/978-3-662-49890-3_14

21. Lipmaa, H., Moriai, S.: Efficient algorithms for computing differential properties of addition. In: Matsui, M. (ed.) FSE 2001, Revised Papers. LNCS, vol. 2355, pp. 336–350. Springer, Heidelberg (2002). https://doi.org/10.1007/3-540-45473-X_28

22. Maitra, S.: Chosen IV cryptanalysis on reduced round ChaCha and Salsa. Discrete Appl. Math. **208**, 88–97 (2016)

23. Matsui, M.: Linear cryptanalysis method for DES cipher. In: Helleseth, T. (ed.) EUROCRYPT 1993. LNCS, vol. 765, pp. 386–397. Springer, Heidelberg (1994). https://doi.org/10.1007/3-540-48285-7_33

24. Mouha, N., Mennink, B., Van Herrewege, A., Watanabe, D., Preneel, B., Verbauwhede, I.: Chaskey: an efficient MAC algorithm for 32-bit microcontrollers. In: Joux, A., Youssef, A. (eds.) SAC 2014, Revised Selected Papers. LNCS, vol. 8781, pp. 306–323. Springer, Cham (2014). https://doi.org/10.1007/978-3-319-13051-4_19

25. Nyberg, K., Wallén, J.: Improved linear distinguishers for SNOW 2.0. In: Robshaw, M. (ed.) FSE 2006, Revised Selected Papers. LNCS, vol. 4047, pp. 144–162. Springer, Heidelberg (2006). https://doi.org/10.1007/11799313_10

26. Shi, Z., Zhang, B., Feng, D., Wu, W.: Improved key recovery attacks on reduced-round Salsa20 and ChaCha. In: Kwon, T., Lee, M.-K., Kwon, D. (eds.) ICISC 2012, Revised Selected Papers. LNCS, vol. 7839, pp. 337–351. Springer, Heidelberg (2013). https://doi.org/10.1007/978-3-642-37682-5_24

27. Shimizu, A., Miyaguchi, S.: Fast data encipherment algorithm FEAL. In: Chaum, D., Price, W.L. (eds.) EUROCRYPT 1987. LNCS, vol. 304, pp. 267–278. Springer, Heidelberg (1988). https://doi.org/10.1007/3-540-39118-5_24

28. Todo, Y., Leander, G., Sasaki, Yu.: Nonlinear invariant attack. In: Cheon, J.H., Takagi, T. (eds.) ASIACRYPT 2016, Part II. LNCS, vol. 10032, pp. 3–33. Springer, Heidelberg (2016). https://doi.org/10.1007/978-3-662-53890-6_1

29. Wallén, J.: Linear approximations of addition modulo 2^n. In: Johansson, T. (ed.) FSE 2003, Revised Papers. LNCS, vol. 2887, pp. 261–273. Springer, Heidelberg (2003). https://doi.org/10.1007/978-3-540-39887-5_20

Cryptanalysis Results on Spook
Bringing Full-Round Shadow-512 to the Light

Patrick Derbez[1(✉)], Paul Huynh[2], Virginie Lallemand[2],
María Naya-Plasencia[3], Léo Perrin[3], and André Schrottenloher[3]

[1] Univ Rennes, CNRS, IRISA, Rennes, France
`patrick.derbez@irisa.fr`
[2] Université de Lorraine, CNRS, Inria, LORIA, 54000 Nancy, France
`{paul.huynh,virginie.lallemand}@loria.fr`
[3] Inria, Paris, France
`{maria.naya_plasencia,leo.perrin,andre.schrottenloher}@inria.fr`

Abstract. Spook [BBB+19] is one of the 32 candidates that has made it
to the second round of the NIST Lightweight Cryptography Standardization
process, and is particularly interesting since it proposes differential
side channel resistance. In this paper, we present practical distinguishers of the full 6-step version of the underlying permutations of Spook,
namely Shadow-512 and Shadow-384, solving challenges proposed by the
designers on the permutation. We also propose practical forgeries with
4-step Shadow for the S1P mode of operation in the nonce misuse scenario, which is allowed by the CIML2 security game considered by the
authors. All the results presented in this paper have been implemented.

Keywords: Dedicated cryptanalysis · Differential attacks ·
Implemented attacks · Spook · Round constants · Lightweight
primitives · Distinguisher · Forgery

1 Introduction

The number of applications running on interconnected resource-constrained
devices increased exponentially during the last decade, bringing new challenges
to both the community and the industry. Sensor networks, Internet-of-Things,
smart cards and healthcare are a few examples which handle sensitive data that
should be protected.

These new platforms have their own specific sets of requirements, in particular in terms of implementation efficiency. As common cryptographic primitives
were not designed to satisfy these specific use cases, they can be ill-suited in
these contexts. A staggering number of algorithms has been proposed to fulfill
such requirements, such as PRESENT [BKL+07] (low gate count in hardware),

© IACR 2020. This article is the final version submitted by the authors to the IACR
and to Springer-Verlag on June 8th, 2020.

© International Association for Cryptologic Research 2020
D. Micciancio and T. Ristenpart (Eds.): CRYPTO 2020, LNCS 12172, pp. 359–388, 2020.
https://doi.org/10.1007/978-3-030-56877-1_13

PRINCE [BCG+12] (low latency in hardware), Midori [BBI+15] (low power consumption), or LEA [HLK+14] (low ROM and cycle count on micro-controllers). Such primitives have been nicknamed *lightweight*. Because the corresponding devices can often be expected to be physically interacted with by an attacker, an algorithm easing side channel resistance has a significant advantage. Hence many recent proposals were designed to be *naturally* resistant against side-channel attacks or, at least, protectable at low cost. For instance, the authenticated encryption (AE) scheme Pyjamask [GJK+19] was designed with a minimal number of non-linear gates to allow efficient masked implementations while the AE scheme ISAP [DEM+17] is resistant to differential power analysis, a powerful type of attack where the adversary try to deduce information about the secret key from power consumption.

This need for lightweight cryptographic primitives led the American National Institute of Standards and Technology (NIST) to initiate the Lightweight Cryptography Project, aiming at the standardization of hash functions and authenticated encryption algorithms suitable for constrained devices. It received 57 algorithm proposals in February 2019 and accepted 56 of them. In August 2019, 32 primitives were announced as the 2nd round candidates.

In this paper we study Spook, an Authenticated Encryption scheme with Associated Data (AEAD) which is among those 2nd round candidates. It was designed to achieve both resistance against side-channel analysis and low-energy implementations and is particularly interesting as it aims at providing strong integrity guarantees even in the presence of nonce misuse and leakage. AEAD is provided using three sub-components: the *Sponge One-Pass* mode of operation (S1P), the tweakable block cipher Clyde-128 and the permutation Shadow. Both Clyde and Shadow are based on simple extensions of the LS-design framework first introduced by the designers of the lightweight block ciphers Robin and Fantomas [GLSV15]. This strategy leads to efficient bitslicing and side-channel resistant implementations on a wide range of platforms. To further simplify the implementation, the permutation uses the round function of the tweakable block cipher as a sub-routine, effectively combining 3 or 4 parallel instances of a round-reduced cipher using a simple linear layer to construct a 384- or 512-bit permutation.

Motivation and Contributions. In Sect. 4.3 of the specification document of Spook [BBB+19], the designers explicitly point out that an important requirement for the permutation in the S1P mode of operation is that it provides collision resistance with respect to the 255 bits that generate the tag and they say:

> *"Hence, a more specific requirement is to prevent truncated differentials with probability larger than 2^{128} for those 255 bits. A conservative heuristic for this purpose is to require that no differential characteristic has probability better than 2^{-385}, which happens after twelve rounds (six steps)."*

In this paper we show that this heuristic is not conservative, providing practical truncated distinguishers on Shadow, the inner permutation of Spook. We exhibit non-random behavior for up to the full version of Shadow-512.

Moreover, the same technique would also distinguish Shadow-512 extended by 2 more rounds at the end. More precisely, we exhibit two particular subspaces E and F of co-dimension 128 and an efficient algorithm which returns pairs of messages (m, m') such that $m \oplus m' \in E$ and Shadow-512$(m) \oplus$Shadow-512$(m') \in F$. This implies in particular a practical collision on 128 bits of the output. This problem is a particular instance of the so-called *limited birthday* problem, which was first introduced by Gilbert and Peyrin when looking for known key distinguishers against the AES [GP10]. As a permutation can be seen as a block cipher with a known key, it is natural to borrow distinguishers from this field. While the complexity of a generic algorithm performing this task is around 2^{64} because of the birthday bound (see [IPS13] for more details), our un-optimized implementations of our distinguishers run in at most a few minutes on a regular desktop computer.

We also provide similar distinguishers targeting up to 10 (out of 12) rounds of Shadow-384, the small version of Shadow. Note that, as for Shadow-512, adding 2 more rounds at the end of the permutation would not increase its security as there would exist a similar distinguisher on the last 12 rounds (a 2-round shifted version of the proposed permutation).

As other several sponge-based lightweight algorithms[1], the authors purposefully relied on a permutation for which distinguishers could exist as this allows to use fewer permutation rounds (Spook designers pointed out for instance that 12 rounds were not enough to have 512 bits of security with respect to linear distinguishers) and thus an increase in the speed of data processing. Nevertheless, our distinguishers seem to prove that the behavior of Shadow is not compatible with the requirements given by the authors on the permutation for the S1P mode of operation.

The next important question is whether these distinguishers are a threat to Spook itself, as the impact is *a priori* not clear. For Spook, we are able to leverage the results we obtained to produce practical existential forgeries for the S1P mode of operation when Shadow-512 is reduced to 8 rounds out of 12 in the nonce misuse scenario, which is allowed by the CIML2 security game considered by the authors [BPPS17].

Distinguishers on both Shadow-512 and Shadow-384 along with the forgeries on 8-step Spook have been implemented and verified against the reference implementation provided by the designers.

Paper Organization. In Sect. 2 we describe Shadow and introduce some cryptanalysis techniques. Then in Sect. 3 we make some observations on the structure of the permutation that will play a crucial role in our cryptanalysis. Finally, in Sects. 4 and 5 we present the results of our analysis of both versions of Shadow, including a distinguisher on the full Shadow-512, as well as forgeries against Spook when Shadow-512 is reduced to 8 rounds.

---

[1] See for instance ASCON [DEMS16], Ketje [BDP+16], or SPARKLE [BBdS+19].

All the analyses presented in this paper are practical and have been implemented and tested. Their source code is available at: https://who.paris.inria.fr/Leo.Perrin/code/spook/index.html.

Our results have been acknowledged and discussed by the designers of Spook in [BBB+20].

2   Preliminaries

The specific mode of operation we target will be described in the relevant section. Here, we present the Shadow family of permutations and recall the definition of differential distinguishers.

2.1   Specification of Shadow-384 and Shadow-512

The Spook algorithm is based on a permutation named Shadow that exists in two flavors: Shadow-384 and Shadow-512, where Shadow-512 is the one used in the primary candidate to the NIST Lightweight competition. In both cases, the internal state is seen as a collection of m two-dimensional arrays (or bundles) each of dimensions 32×4: as depicted in Fig. 1, $m = 4$ for Shadow-512 and $m = 3$ for Shadow-384. The permutations have a Substitution Permutation Network (SPN) structure based on a 4-bit S-box layer and two distinct linear layers, each being used every second round.

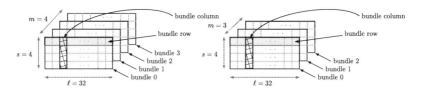

Fig. 1. State Organization of Shadow-512 (left) and of Shadow-384 (right).

The full versions of the permutations iterate 6 *steps*. As represented in Fig. 2, one step is made of two rounds, denoted round A and round B, interleaved with round constant additions. Shadow-384 and Shadow-512 only differ in the definition of the D layer.

Round A first applies a non-linear layer made by the application on each bundle column of the 4-bit S-box recalled in Table 1. It then applies the so-called L-box which calls the L' transformation to the first two and last two rows of each bundle. If we denote by (x, y) the input and by (a, b) the output the definition of L' is given by:

$$(a, b) = L'(x, y) = \begin{pmatrix} \mathrm{circ}(\texttt{0xec045008}) \cdot x^T \oplus \mathrm{circ}(\texttt{0x36000f60}) \cdot y^T \\ \mathrm{circ}(\texttt{0x1b0007b0}) \cdot x^T \oplus \mathrm{circ}(\texttt{0xec045008}) \cdot y^T \end{pmatrix}$$

where $\mathrm{circ}(A)$ stands for a circulant matrix whose first line is a row vector given by the binary decomposition of A.

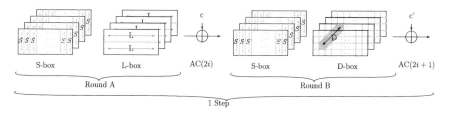

Fig. 2. Description of one step of Shadow-512.

Table 1. 4-bit S-box used in Shadow.

x	0 1 2 3 4 5 6 7 8 9 a b c d e f
S(x)	0 8 1 f 2 a 7 9 4 d 5 6 e 3 b c

Round B starts with the same S-layer as round A but uses a different linear layer, denoted D. The purpose of D is to provide diffusion between the m bundles of the state: as depicted in Fig. 2, it takes as input one bit of each bundle. It modifies them with the application of a near-MDS matrix (which previously appeared in the design of the ciphers Midori [BBI+15] and Mantis [BJK+16] for instance), respectively:

$$D(a, b, c, d) = \begin{pmatrix} 0 & 1 & 1 & 1 \\ 1 & 0 & 1 & 1 \\ 1 & 1 & 0 & 1 \\ 1 & 1 & 1 & 0 \end{pmatrix} \times \begin{pmatrix} a \\ b \\ c \\ d \end{pmatrix}$$

for Shadow-512 while for Shadow-384 we use:

$$D(a, b, c) = \begin{pmatrix} 1 & 1 & 1 \\ 1 & 0 & 1 \\ 1 & 1 & 0 \end{pmatrix} \times \begin{pmatrix} a \\ b \\ c \end{pmatrix}.$$

The **round constants** used in the permutation correspond to the internal state of a 4-bit LFSR. They are recalled in Table 2. At the end of every round (for rounds from 0 to 11), the 4-bit constant is XORed at 4 different positions, one time in each bundle: in bundle b (for $b = 0, 1, 2, 3$), the constant is XORed to the column number b. Without loss of generality, we hereafter position bit number 0 on the right of the state in our figures.

2.2 Differential Distinguishers

As indicated in the Spook specification, the black box security analysis of the mode of operation that is used in Spook (S1P) relies on the assumption that the permutations are random. In this paper we challenge this assumption by exhibiting distinguishers for the permutations – that is, algorithms that unveil a non-random behavior.

Table 2. Round constants used in Shadow. Note that the LSB is on the left.

Round	Constant	Round	Constant	Round	Constant	Round	Constant
0	(1,0,0,0)	1	(0,1,0,0)	2	(0,0,1,0)	3	(0,0,0,1)
4	(1,1,0,0)	5	(0,1,1,0)	6	(0,0,1,1)	7	(1,1,0,1)
8	(1,0,1,0)	9	(0,1,0,1)	10	(1,1,1,0)	11	(0,1,1,1)

Our distinguishers use the notion of differential, a technique that was introduced by Biham and Shamir in [BS91]. The idea is to find a couple of XOR differences (δ, Δ) such that if two messages differ from δ then with high probability their output difference after encryption is equal to Δ.

This idea was later extended by Knudsen in 1994 to define *truncated differentials* [Knu95], a variant in which only a portion of the difference is fixed (while the remaining part is undetermined). This technique is illustrated in Fig. 5 for instance, where we introduce a distinguisher that ends with a difference of the form $(*, *, *, 0)$ before the last D operation: the '$*$' symbol indicates that the difference between the messages is not determined over the first three bundles, while the '0' symbol indicates that the two messages are identical on the last bundle (128 bits).

3   Structural Observations

In this section we present the general properties we found that we will later exploit in our analysis. While our distinguisher is a truncated differential one, our method for finding right pairs does not rely on a high probability differential trail (whose very existence is disproved by the authors' wide trail argument). Instead, we exploit the similarity between the functions applied in parallel on each bundle. To better describe them, we introduce the notion of Super S-box (as it applies to Shadow) and we study the propagation of the following type of properties through the step function. Note that we next provide the details for Shadow-512 but that similar results apply to Shadow-384.

Definition 1 (*i*-identical state). *We call *i*-identical an internal state of Shadow in which i bundles are equal.*

3.1   Super S-Box

Given the fact that in every step only the D layer is mixing the bundles together, it is possible to rewrite Shadow as an SPN using four 128-bit *Super S-boxes* (each operating on one bundle) interleaved with a linear permutation D operating on the full state. If a, b, c and d are the 128-bit bundles, this linear permutation is represented as follows:

$$D(a,b,c,d) = \begin{pmatrix} 0 & I & I & I \\ I & 0 & I & I \\ I & I & 0 & I \\ I & I & I & 0 \end{pmatrix} \times \begin{pmatrix} a \\ b \\ c \\ d \end{pmatrix}.$$

D is an involution with branching number 4 (over 128-bit words) and it verifies that $\forall a \in \mathbb{F}_2^{128}, D(a,a,a,0) = (0,0,0,a)$.

We denote by σ_j for $j \in \{0,1,2,3\}$ the four parallel *Super S-boxes* of the cipher. They correspond to the first four operations of the step, namely: the S-layer and the linear operation L of round A, the constant addition (that is done on a different position for each Super S-box), and the S-layer of round B.

In the following, we show that even though the four bundles of a state go through different Super S-boxes it might be possible to have a Shadow state with four equal bundles that is transformed into a Shadow state of the same form at the output of a full step.

3.2   4-Identical States

In the discussion below we follow the evolution of the 4-identical property through a step and show the required conditions for it to remain in the end. This evolution is also summarized in Fig. 3.

Probability of Maintaining the 4-Identical Property Through a Step. We start from a 4-identical state X that we write $X = (x,x,x,x)$. Each bundle x is made of 32 columns: $x = (x^{31}, x^{30}, \cdots, x^1, x^0)$.

- **Application of the Super S-boxes.** The step starts with one non-linear layer followed by the L layer, applied in parallel (that is, independently) on each of the 4 bundles. Since these transformations are identical for each bundle the 4-identical property is followed with probability one up to this point and so we have $L \circ S(X) = (y,y,y,y)$ with $y = L \circ S(x)$. We next have the addition of the first round constant on column j of bundle j for $j \in \{0,1,2,3\}$, that we will call AC, and finally we apply another S-box layer. By denoting the round constant by[2] c, we obtain the following values for $S \circ AC(2i) \circ L \circ S(X)$:

$B_0:$	$S(y^{31})$	$\cdots$	$S(y^4)$	$S(y^3)$	$S(y^2)$	$S(y^1)$	$S(y^0 \oplus c)$
$B_1:$	$S(y^{31})$	$\cdots$	$S(y^4)$	$S(y^3)$	$S(y^2)$	$S(y^1 \oplus c)$	$S(y^0)$
$B_2:$	$S(y^{31})$	$\cdots$	$S(y^4)$	$S(y^3)$	$S(y^2 \oplus c)$	$S(y^1)$	$S(y^0)$
$B_3:$	$S(y^{31})$	$\cdots$	$S(y^4)$	$S(y^3 \oplus c)$	$S(y^2)$	$S(y^1)$	$S(y^0)$

where B_i is bundle i. At this stage, the 4 bundles stop being 4-identical but differ on the value of their 4 first columns.
- **D-box and second round constant addition.** The D layer mixes together the 4 bundles by XORing 3 of them together to form one output bundle, as

---

[2] Recall here that the value of the round constant depends on the round index.

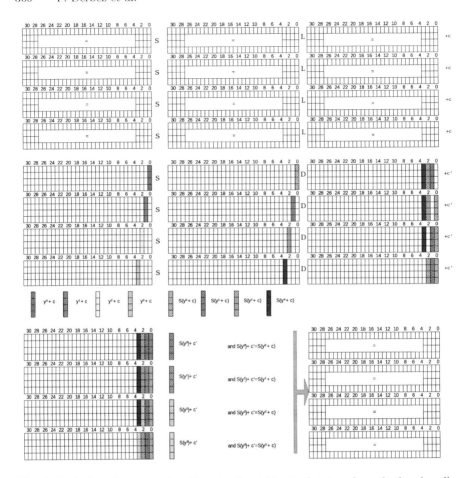

Fig. 3. Evolution of two rounds with a starting 4-identical state, where the four bundles are equal in the beginning.

described in Sect. 2.1. In the above representation of the state, it operates columnwise by replacing each column element with the XOR of the 3 others. The last operation is the addition of the second round constant, that we denote c', at the same positions as before (column j of bundle j for $j \in \{0,1,2,3\}$). Formally, the expression of the bundles of $AC(2i+1) \circ D \circ S \circ AC(2i) \circ L \circ S(X)$ is the following:

$$
\begin{array}{llllllll}
B_0: & S(y^{31}) & \cdots & S(y^4) & S(y^3 \oplus c) & S(y^2 \oplus c) & S(y^1 \oplus c) & S(y^0) \oplus c' \\
B_1: & S(y^{31}) & \cdots & S(y^4) & S(y^3 \oplus c) & S(y^2 \oplus c) & S(y^1) \oplus c' & S(y^0 \oplus c) \\
B_2: & S(y^{31}) & \cdots & S(y^4) & S(y^3 \oplus c) & S(y^2) \oplus c' & S(y^1 \oplus c) & S(y^0 \oplus c) \\
B_3: & S(y^{31}) & \cdots & S(y^4) & S(y^3) \oplus c' & S(y^2 \oplus c) & S(y^1 \oplus c) & S(y^0 \oplus c)
\end{array}
$$

To ensure a 4-identical state at this point, the following 4 equations need to be satisfied:

$$\begin{cases} S(y^3 \oplus c) = & S(y^3) \oplus c' \\ S(y^2 \oplus c) = & S(y^2) \oplus c' \\ S(y^1 \oplus c) = & S(y^1) \oplus c' \\ S(y^0 \oplus c) = & S(y^0) \oplus c'. \end{cases}$$

Depending on the values of c and c' – that vary with the index of the step – these 4 equations are either never verified or can be verified with a rather high probability. In fact, their number of solutions corresponds to the probability of the transition from a difference of c to a difference of c' through the S-box S. We computed the corresponding probabilities for all the steps and report the results in Table 3. Note that we experimentally verified these values.

Table 3. Probability that an output of step s of Shadow is 4-identical knowing that the input is.

s	0	1	2	3	4	5
Probability	0	0	0	2^{-12}	2^{-8}	0

3.3 3-Identical States

A similar reasoning applies to states for which only 3 (out of 4) bundles are equal. In this case, we have one fewer S-box transition to constrain, and then the probabilities of Table 3 increase to the ones provided in Table 4.

Table 4. Probability that an output of step s of Shadow is 3-identical knowing that the input is.

s	0	1	2	3	4	5
Probability	0	0	0	2^{-9}	2^{-6}	0

We detail the equations leading to the probabilities of Table 4 in Appendix A. These probabilities do not depend on the choice of the positions of the 3 input bundles that are identical. Instead, they are valid as soon as the 3 positions are the same in the input and in the output.

3.4 2-Identical States

We can follow a similar reasoning to obtain the probability of keeping a 2-identical state. We obtain two equations to solve, and the probabilities become the ones given in Table 3. Again, the position of the 2 identical bundles does not impact these probabilities but it has to be the same in the input and in the output.

Table 5. Probability that an output of step s of `Shadow` is 2-identical knowing that the input is.

s	0	1	2	3	4	5
Probability	0	0	0	2^{-6}	2^{-4}	0

4   A Distinguisher Against Full `Shadow-512` (and More)

In this section, we present a practical distinguisher which allows us to exhibit pairs (x, x') of 512-bit inputs of the `Shadow-512` permutation such that

$$x \oplus x' = (*, *, *, 0) \quad \text{and} \quad \pi(x) \oplus \pi(x') = D(0, 0, 0, *), \tag{1}$$

for the full version and such that

$$x \oplus x' = (*, *, *, 0) \quad \text{and} \quad \pi(x) \oplus \pi(x') = D(*, *, *, 0), \tag{2}$$

for a "round-extended" version of `Shadow-512` using 7 steps rather than 6. In other words, we efficiently solve a limited-birthday problem.

As proved by Iwamoto et al. [IPS13], generating such pairs for a random permutation would require roughly 2^{64} queries. However, we can produce pairs satisfying Property (1) for full `Shadow-512` using about 2^{15} calls to said permutation. The exact same technique finds pairs satisfying Property (2) for 7-step `Shadow-512`. The corresponding procedures are described in Sect. 4.2.

These distinguishers hinge on two properties: the propagation of 3-identical states which we described in Sect. 3.3, and a probability 1 truncated differential explained in Sect. 4.1. The latter can be used directly as a distinguisher for 10-round `Shadow-512`.

4.1   A 5-Step Truncated Differential Property

We start by devising a distinguisher of `Shadow-512` reduced to 5 steps out of 6. The truncated trail we use is summarized in Fig. 4. Starting from the middle, we can easily construct pairs of states such that their difference propagates with probability 1 over 2 forward and 2 backward steps.

All propagations are of probability 1, the only place where we would *a priori* have to pay for the cost of a transition is for the three Super S-box level transitions $\alpha \rightsquigarrow \beta$ in step 2. However, the high similarity between the Super S-boxes provides us with a simple way to obtain three such pairs of 128-bit blocks.

Building Pairs of Bundles That Follow the Same Differential for Different Super S-boxes. Recall that the only difference between two Super S-boxes lies in the constant addition operation that is done right after the L linear layer. The 4-bit constant c is added to the input of only one S-box of the second non-linear layer, and the index of this S-box depends on the Super S-box index.

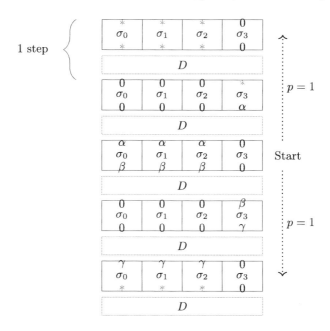

Fig. 4. A 5-step distinguisher against the 512-bit permutation Shadow.

Thanks to this limited difference between the Super S-boxes, we can easily build an input difference α so that the output difference of the S-box does not depend on its index. More precisely, this difference α should be chosen so that it does not diffuse to the last 4 columns of the bundle. This simple fact is formalized in the following lemma:

Lemma 1. *If $x \in \mathbb{F}_2^{128}$ and $\alpha \in \mathbb{F}_2^{128}$ are such that $(L \circ S)(x) \oplus (L \circ S)(x \oplus \alpha) = \beta$ and if β is set to 0 on the 4 S-boxes that can receive the round constant c, then the value of $\sigma_b(x) \oplus \sigma_b(x \oplus \alpha)$ does not depend on the bundle index b.*

Proof. We denote by y and $y \oplus \beta$ the respective values of $(L \circ S)(x)$ and $(L \circ S)(x \oplus \alpha)$. By expanding these into the column notation we get:

$$
\begin{array}{rccccccc}
y = & y^{31} & \cdots & y^4 & y^3 & y^2 & y^1 & y^0 \\
y \oplus \beta = & y^{31} \oplus \beta^{31} & \cdots & y^4 \oplus \beta^4 & y^3 & y^2 & y^1 & y^0
\end{array}
$$

Let us first look at σ_0. We have that

$$
\begin{array}{rccccccc}
\sigma_0(x) = & S(y^{31}) & \cdots & S(y^4) & S(y^3) & S(y^2) & S(y^1) & S(y^0 \oplus c) \\
\sigma_0(x \oplus \alpha) = & S(y^{31} \oplus \beta^{31}) & \cdots & S(y^4 \oplus \beta^4) & S(y^3) & S(y^2) & S(y^1) & S(y^0 \oplus c)
\end{array}
$$

so summing these equations yields

$$
\sigma_0(x) \oplus \sigma_0(x \oplus \alpha) = \quad \gamma^{31} \quad \cdots \quad \gamma^4 \quad 0 \quad 0 \quad 0 \quad 0
$$

Without loss of generality, let us now consider σ_1. We have

$$\begin{array}{ccccccccc} \sigma_1(x) = & S(y^{31}) & \cdots & S(y^4) & S(y^3) & S(y^2) & S(y^1 \oplus c) & S(y^0) \\ \sigma_1(x \oplus \alpha) = & S(y^{31} \oplus \beta^{31}) & \cdots & S(y^4 \oplus \beta^4) & S(y^3) & S(y^2) & S(y^1 \oplus c) & S(y^0) \end{array}$$

As we can see we have the exact same pairs of values, and thus the same output differences, unless we look at one of the first 4-bit nibbles. However, in this case, the values in $\sigma_1(x)$ and $\sigma_1(x \oplus \alpha)$ are identical to one another, meaning that their difference is equal to 0 as well.

This concludes the proof since the two differences are equal.   □

To put it differently, this lemma allows us to build pairs of messages that follow the same differential trail over one step whatever the index of the Super S-box.

Our distinguisher for 5 steps of Shadow-512 thus works by following the process described in Algorithm 1. As depicted in Fig. 4, the choice of the difference β ensures that the same transition is followed for the 3 first Super S-boxes of step 2. The differential pattern then propagates as expected with probability 1 through steps 1 then 0 (backward), and 3 then 4 (forward).

We have verified experimentally that this distinguisher works as predicted.

Algorithm 1. A distinguisher for 5-step Shadow.

---

1. Choose $\beta \in \mathbb{F}_2^{128}$ such that it is set to 0 on the 4 S-boxes of lowest weight
2. Choose a random $y \in \mathbb{F}_2^{128}$ and a random $z \in \mathbb{F}_2^{128}$
3. Compute $x = \sigma_0^{-1}(y)$ and $x + \alpha = \sigma_0^{-1}(y + \beta)$,
4. Set the two states at step 2 to be

$$X_2 = (x,\ x,\ x,\ z) \quad \text{and} \quad X_2' = (x + \alpha,\ x + \alpha,\ x + \alpha,\ z).$$

5. Invert step 1 and step 0 on X_2 and X_2' to obtain a pair of states (X_0, X_0') such that $\pi(X_0) \oplus \pi(X_0') = D(*, *, *, 0)$.

The differences in the output of the Super S-box layer of step 5 (denoted by $*$ in Fig. 4) are *a priori* different from one another, meaning that this approach cannot cover more rounds. Fortunately, we can use the property studied in Sect. 3.3 to our advantage, as explained below.

4.2 A Distinguisher for 6- and 7-Step Shadow

Using the truncated trail discussed in Sect. 4.1 with the observation in Sect. 3.3, we can build a distinguisher on 6 steps of Shadow, *i.e.* on the full permutation. It would naturally extend to a distinguisher on 7 steps if we defined such a "round-extended" variant of Shadow. This distinguisher is summarized in Fig. 5.

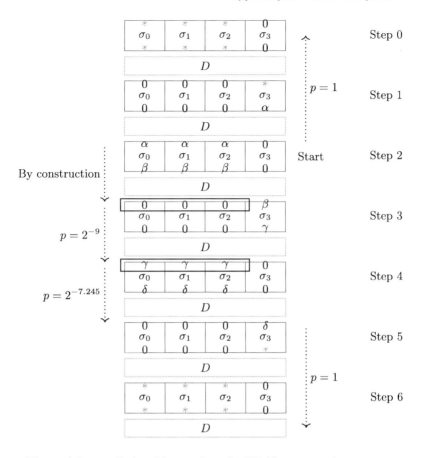

Fig. 5. A 7-step distinguisher against the 512-bit permutation Shadow.

Structure of the Distinguisher. Our distinguisher works as follows.

- We first focus on the input of step 2 and build a pair of messages that differ by $(\alpha, \alpha, \alpha, 0)$. This difference automatically sets the input difference of step 0 to be equal to 0 on the third bundle. Our choice of the two messages must also ensure that their difference at the end of step 2 is equal to $(0, 0, 0, \beta)$ and that the two output messages are 3-identical (the 3-identical property is depicted by the thick rectangle in Fig. 5).
- In step 3, we want to keep the 3-identical property in order to ease the following step. As we established before (see Table 4), this event has a probability equal to 2^{-9}. The input difference at the end of step 3 is then equal to $(\gamma, \gamma, \gamma, 0)$.
- We next aim for a difference equal to $(\delta, \delta, \delta, 0)$ at the output of the Super S-boxes of step 4, an event whose probability we later prove to be $2^{-7.245}$. When this condition is fulfilled we obtain a difference equal to $(0, 0, 0, \delta)$ at the output of step 4, which automatically leads to the required difference of the form $(*, *, *, 0)$ at the end of step 5.

Let us now show how we can efficiently find two states that verify the conditions at the input and the output of Step 3.

Suppose that there is an $x \in \mathbb{F}_2^{128}$ such that the following holds during step 2 for some 128-bit values α, β, ϵ and ϵ':

$$\begin{cases} \sigma_0(x) + \sigma_0(x + \alpha) & = \beta \\ \sigma_1(x + \epsilon) + \sigma_1(x + \epsilon + \alpha) & = \beta \\ \sigma_2(x + \epsilon') + \sigma_2(x + \epsilon' + \alpha) & = \beta, \end{cases} \quad (3)$$

these constraints corresponding to the differential trail at step 2 that is used in Fig. 5. Such an x would allow us to run the 5-round distinguisher described in Sect. 4.1. However, as we explained, the property would not extend beyond the fifth step. To achieve this, we add another set of constraints:

$$\begin{cases} (AC \circ D)\big(\sigma_0(x),\ \sigma_1(x + \epsilon),\ \sigma_2(x + \epsilon'),\ z\big) & = (y,\ y,\ y,\ z') \\ (AC \circ D)\big(\sigma_0(x + \alpha),\ \sigma_1(x + \alpha + \epsilon),\ \sigma_2(x + \alpha + \epsilon'),\ z\big) & = (y,\ y,\ y,\ z' + \beta). \end{cases} \quad (4)$$

In other words, we impose that each state we consider is 3-identical.

In this case, the difference between the states has to be equal to $(0, 0, 0, \beta)$ at the input of step 3. Furthermore, each state is 3-identical. This property is carried over to the next step with some probability. Should this happen, we would have at the input of step 4 that the difference between the states is equal to $(0, 0, 0, \gamma)$ for some $\gamma \in \mathbb{F}_2^{128}$, and that each state is 3-identical.

Finding Solutions for Properties (3) and (4). It turns out that a specific probability 1 truncated differential pattern allows us to trivially find solutions satisfying both Property (3) and Property (4).

Indeed, we remark that:

1. the impact of the constant additions both within the Super S-box layers and outside it (after the D layer) is limited to the S-boxes with indices in $\{0, 1, 2, 3\}$ (i.e. the 4 of lowest weight) within each Super S-box, and
2. the bits with indices 22 and 23 in each of the 4 input words of a Super S-box do not influence the output bits with indices in $\{0, 1, 2, 3\}$.

Using the reference implementation, we can indeed see that

$$\begin{aligned} L(0, e_{22}) &= (\texttt{1b880510},\ \texttt{6c06f000}) \\ L(e_{22}, 0) &= (\texttt{36037800},\ \texttt{1b880510}) \\ L(0, e_{23}) &= (\texttt{37100a20},\ \texttt{d80de000}) \\ L(e_{23}, 0) &= (\texttt{6c06f000},\ \texttt{37100a20}), \end{aligned}$$

where the 4 bits of lowest weight in each output are always equal to 0. We then define the vector space $\nabla \subset (\mathbb{F}_2^4)^{32}$ as

$$\nabla = \{a \times e_{22} + b \times e_{23}, a \in \mathbb{F}_2^4, b \in \mathbb{F}_2^4\},$$

where the multiplications are done in the finite field $\mathbb{F}_2^4$. As a consequence of our observations, we have the following lemma.

Lemma 2. *Let $x \in (\mathbb{F}_2^4)^{32}$ be a 128-bit vector and let $\alpha \in \nabla$ be a difference. Then for all steps and all bundle index i, we have that*

$$\sigma_i(x) + \sigma_i(x + \alpha) = (*, *, ..., *, 0, 0, 0, 0).$$

As evidenced by our experimental results (see below), this approach is efficient, and with the cost of computing 1 Super-Sbox we can obtain about 2^{16} internal states that verify the condition of step 2.

Description of the Full Distinguisher. Algorithm 2 details our distinguisher. Using the techniques described so far, we are able to find input differences that satisfy the truncated trail and are 3-identical where needed (see Fig. 5) from the beginning of step 0 to the end of step 2. Let us now see what happens in the remaining steps.

Algorithm 2. Our 7-step distinguisher against Shadow.

Output: A pair (x, y, z, t), (x', y', z', t) such that $\pi(x, y, z, t) \oplus \pi(x', y', z', t) = (*, *, *, 0)$ with probability at least $2^{-16.245}$ after 7-step Shadow-512.

1. Select a difference $\epsilon \in \nabla$.
2. Select a state (y_2, y_2, y_2, z_2) that will be a state after step 2.
3. Invert step 2 on (y_2, y_2, y_2, z_2), obtaining (x_1, y_1, z_1, t_1).
4. Invert step 1 on (x_1, y_1, z_1, t_1) and $(x_1 \oplus \epsilon, y_1 \oplus \epsilon, z_1 \oplus \epsilon, t_1)$, obtaining (x_0, y_0, z_0, t_0) and (x_0, y_0, z_0, t_0').
5. Invert step 0, obtaining a pair of Shadow-512 states with a zero-difference in the last bundle.
6. Return this pair of state. With high probability ($\geq 2^{-16.24}$), it satisfies the truncated trail in Figure 5.

Step 3. We start from two messages that are built such that at the end of step 2 they are 3-identical, and we want that the two messages are again 3-identical at the end of step 3. With a reasoning similar to the one given in Sect. 3.3, we obtain 6 equations to solve, while in fact only 3 are independent (the 3 equations obtained for the second message are the same as the 3 obtained for the first message since they only differ on the last bundle), and as detailed in Table 4 the probability is equal to 2^{-9} since this is step number 3.

Step 4. Our objective is to obtain a difference of the form $(0, 0, 0, \delta)$ for any non-zero δ in $\mathbb{F}_2^{128}$ at the beginning of step 5 (see Fig. 5). In order for this to happen, we need to have a difference equal to $(\delta, \delta, \delta, 0)$ at the end of step 4. To estimate the probability of this event, let us write the corresponding equations. We denote the two messages after the application of S and L of step 4 by (y, y, y, w) and (y', y', y', w) respectively. Since the input of step 4 is 3-identical, $y^i = y'^i$ for all $i > 3$. The expression of the last 4 column values at the end of step 4 (i.e. after applying D and AC) is then as follows for (y, y, y, w)

$$
\begin{array}{llll}
S(w^3 \oplus c) & S(y^2) \oplus S(y^2 \oplus c) \oplus S(w^2) & S(y^1) \oplus S(y^1 \oplus c) \oplus S(w^1) & S(w^0) \oplus c' \\
S(w^3 \oplus c) & S(y^2) \oplus S(y^2 \oplus c) \oplus S(w^2) & S(w^1) \oplus c' & S(y^0) \oplus S(y^0 \oplus c) \oplus S(w^0) \\
S(w^3 \oplus c) & S(w^2) \oplus c' & S(y^1) \oplus S(y^1 \oplus c) \oplus S(w^1) & S(y^0) \oplus S(y^0 \oplus c) \oplus S(w^0) \\
S(y^3) \oplus c' & S(y^2 \oplus c) & S(y^1 \oplus c) & S(y^0 \oplus c)
\end{array}
$$

and as follows for (y', y', y', w):

$S(w^3 \oplus c)$	$S(y'^2) \oplus S(y'^2 \oplus c) \oplus S(w^2)$	$S(y'^1) \oplus S(y'^1 \oplus c) \oplus S(w^1)$	$S(w^0) \oplus c'$
$S(w^3 \oplus c)$	$S(y'^2) \oplus S(y'^2 \oplus c) \oplus S(w^2)$	$S(w^1) \oplus c'$	$S(y'^0) \oplus S(y'^0 \oplus c) \oplus S(w^0)$
$S(w^3 \oplus c)$	$S(w^2) \oplus c'$	$S(y'^1) \oplus S(y'^1 \oplus c) \oplus S(w^1)$	$S(y'^0) \oplus S(y'^0 \oplus c) \oplus S(w^0)$
$S(y'^3) \oplus c'$	$S(y'^2 \oplus c)$	$S(y'^1 \oplus c)$	$S(y'^0 \oplus c)$

In order for the sum of these two states to be equal to $(0, 0, 0, \delta)$ (for any non-zero δ), the following relations have to be satisfied:

$$S(y'^2) \oplus S(y'^2 \oplus c) = S(y^2) \oplus S(y^2 \oplus c)$$
$$S(y'^1) \oplus S(y'^1 \oplus c) = S(y^1) \oplus S(y^1 \oplus c)$$
$$S(y'^0) \oplus S(y'^0 \oplus c) = S(y^0) \oplus S(y^0 \oplus c).$$

Since we are looking at step 4, the constant c is equal to $0x5$ and then each equality has a probability equal to $2^{-2.415}$ to be verified (assuming that the value of y and y' are independent).

Step 5. This last step is passed with probability one, so in the end we observe an output difference equal to $(*, *, *, 0)$ with a probability at least equal to $(2^{-2.415})^3 \times 2^{-9} = 2^{-16.245}$.

Step 6. One additional round can be added with probability one, since by inverting D we would find a difference equal to 0 in the last bundle with the same probability of $2^{-16.245}$.

Experimental Results. Experiments showed that the probability of the distinguisher is slightly higher than what we expected, since in fact the previously detailed trail is not the only one that leads to the required output difference (see Appendix B for a description of another valid trail). By running Algorithm 2 for 2^{22} times, we obtained 124 successful pairs, a probability close to 2^{-15}. Our unoptimized C++ implementation found all these pairs in less than 30 s on a desktop computer. Below is an example for 7 steps.

x_1				x_2			
9c7fbdf0	4a9a3523	90bd4f15	33e12e8f	b4764864	aaabc55e	2b65df83	33e12e8f
5554509d	5ea7c50d	db9fd14e	8cd31faf	30d8625c	6d513db3	9024c477	8cd31faf
5f0785c3	14ce1b1f	b9a7f521	336e44ba	89fb6758	5d19b594	e69ccd64	336e44ba
fcf630fb	82cafa8e	abf5b881	e5534b79	4f3d62a5	3e530b8b	f7ccf2b7	e5534b79
$x_1 \oplus x_2$				$\pi(x_1) \oplus \pi(x_2)$			
2809f594	e031f07d	bbd89096	00000000	39e368a5	03e51caf	f2d7ae55	00000000
658c32c1	33f6f8be	4bbb1539	00000000	2668956a	b1720999	00c93f81	00000000
d6fce29b	49d7ae8b	5f3b3845	00000000	4aed9270	2b317fb5	6f1a183b	00000000
b3cb525e	bc99f105	5c394a36	00000000	d902b8fd	5c7db7c2	2ef09921	00000000

4.3 A Distinguisher for 6-Step Shadow-384

In this section we show how to build a similar distinguisher on 6 steps of the 384-bit variant of Shadow shifted by one round (i.e. which works for steps from

1 to 6 but for no steps from 0 to 5 because of the round constants). As explained in the preliminaries, Shadow-384 is defined as a 3LS-design, and the D layer acts on three 128-bit bundles a, b, c as follows:

$$D(a, b, c) = \begin{pmatrix} I & I & I \\ I & 0 & I \\ I & I & 0 \end{pmatrix} \times \begin{pmatrix} a \\ b \\ c \end{pmatrix}$$

Interestingly, propagating identical states remains possible with this layer, more specifically for states in which the last 2 bundles are equal. Using this property, one can exhibit pairs (x, x') such that $x \oplus x' = (0, *, *)$ at step 1 and $\pi(x) \oplus \pi(x') = D(0, *, *)$ at the end of step 6. Note that in this case, we cannot cover step 0. Hence this is not a distinguisher on the full version of Shadow-384 for which we can cover only 5 steps. However, it shows that adding 1 more step at the end does not increase the security of Shadow-384. The distinguisher is summarized in Fig. 6.

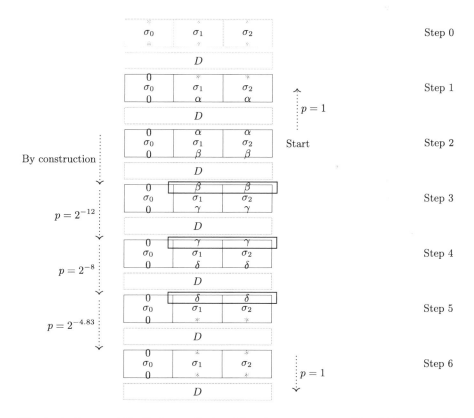

Fig. 6. A (1-step shifted) 6-step distinguisher for Shadow-384. The thick rectangles depict 2-identical states.

As previously described in Sect. 4.2, by picking an α in the vector space $\nabla = \{a \times e_{22} + b \times e_{23}, a \in \mathbb{F}_2^4, b \in \mathbb{F}_2^4\}$ we can easily find two states $(x_1, y_1, y_1 + \epsilon)$ and $(x_1, y_1 + \alpha, y_1 + \epsilon + \alpha)$ as inputs to step 2 that satisfy the following properties at input of step 3:

$$\begin{cases} \sigma_1(y_1) + \sigma_1(y_1 + \alpha) & = \beta \\ \sigma_2(y_1 + \epsilon) + \sigma_2(y_1 + \epsilon + \alpha) & = \beta, \end{cases} \tag{5}$$

and

$$\begin{cases} (AC \circ D)(x_1, \; \sigma_1(y_1), \; \sigma_2(y_1 + \epsilon)) & = (x_2, \; y_2, \; y_2) \\ (AC \circ D)(x_1, \; \sigma_1(y_1 + \alpha), \; \sigma_2(y_1 + \alpha + \epsilon)) & = (x_2, \; y_2 + \beta, \; y_2 + \beta). \end{cases} \tag{6}$$

By inverting step 1, we obtain a difference $(0, *, *)$ with probability 1.

Now at step 3, the input difference equals $(0, \beta, \beta)$ and the last two bundles of each state are identical. With probability 2^{-12} and 2^{-8} respectively, the 2-identical states are preserved through step 3 and 4. Using the same notations as in Sect. 3.2, these probabilities are explained below.

Starting from a 2-identical state $X = (x, y, y)$, let $(w, z, z) = L \circ S(X)$ with $w = L \circ S(x)$ and $z = L \circ S(y)$. The first round constant c is then added on column j of bundle j for $j \in \{0, 1, 2\}$, and another S-box layer is applied, and we obtain the following:

$$S \circ AC(2i) \circ L \circ S(X) = \begin{bmatrix} \cdots & S(w^i) & \cdots & S(w^2) & S(w^1) & S(w^0 \oplus c) \\ \cdots & S(z^i) & \cdots & S(z^2) & S(z^1 \oplus c) & S(z^0) \\ \cdots & S(z^i) & \cdots & S(z^2 \oplus c) & S(z^1) & S(z^0) \end{bmatrix}.$$

At this stage, the last 2 bundles of each state differ only on the value of their second and third columns. After the D layer and the addition of the second round constant c' at column j of bundle j for $j \in \{0, 1, 2\}$) as before, the expression of the bundles of $AC(2i+1) \circ D \circ S \circ AC(2i) \circ L \circ S(X)$ becomes:

$$\begin{matrix} \cdots S(w^i) & \cdots S(w^2) \oplus S(z^2) \oplus S(z^2 \oplus c) & S(w^1) \oplus S(z^1 \oplus c) \oplus S(z^1) & S(w^0 \oplus c) \oplus c' \\ \cdots S(w^i) \oplus S(z^i) & \cdots S(w^2) \oplus S(z^2 \oplus c) & S(w^1) \oplus S(z^1) \oplus c' & S(w^0 \oplus c) \oplus S(z^0) \\ \cdots S(w^i) \oplus S(z^i) & \cdots S(w^2) \oplus S(z^2) \oplus c' & S(w^1) \oplus S(z^1 \oplus c) & S(w^0 \oplus c) \oplus S(z^0). \end{matrix}$$

Thus, to ensure a 2-identical state, the following 2 equations need to be satisfied:

$$S(z^2 \oplus c) = S(z^2) \oplus c', \quad S(z^1 \oplus c) = S(z^1) \oplus c'.$$

We can then compute the probability of following each step of the truncated pattern in Fig. 6 starting from the end of step 2:

Step 3: each equation is satisfied with probability 2^{-3} for one state, thus 2^{-12} in total for the two states.

Step 4: the probability for one state becomes 2^{-2}, meaning 2^{-8} in total.

Step 5: the 2-identical property cannot be carried through because of the round constants. However, one can obtain a difference in the form $(0, *, *)$ between the two states with probability $2^{-4.83}$, as explained below.

By inverting the D layer of step 6, we should then observe a difference equal to 0 in the first bundle with a probability equal to $(2^{-2.415})^2 \times 2^{-8} \times 2^{-12} = 2^{-24.83}$.

Let us now compute the probability of going through step 5. If we denote (w, z, z) and (w, z', z') the two states after the application of S and L in step 5, then the expression of the column values at the end of that step for (w, z, z) becomes

$$
\begin{array}{lllll}
\cdots\, S(w^i) & \cdots\, S(w^2) \oplus S(z^2) \oplus S(z^2 \oplus c) & S(w^1) \oplus S(z^1 \oplus c) \oplus S(z^1) & S(w^0 \oplus c) \oplus c' \\
\cdots\, S(w^i) \oplus S(z^i) & \cdots\, S(w^2) \oplus S(z^2 \oplus c) & S(w^1) \oplus S(z^1) \oplus c' & S(w^0 \oplus c) \oplus S(z^0) \\
\cdots\, S(w^i) \oplus S(z^i) & \cdots\, S(w^2) \oplus S(z^2) \oplus c' & S(w^1) \oplus S(z^1 \oplus c) & S(w^0 \oplus c) \oplus S(z^0)
\end{array}
$$

and it takes the following value for (w, z', z')

$$
\begin{array}{lllll}
\cdots\, S(w^i) & \cdots\, S(w^2) \oplus S(z'^2) \oplus S(z'^2 \oplus c) & S(w^1) \oplus S(z'^1 \oplus c) \oplus S(z'^1) & S(w^0 \oplus c) \oplus c' \\
\cdots\, S(w^i) \oplus S(z'^i) & \cdots\, S(w^2) \oplus S(z'^2 \oplus c) & S(w^1) \oplus S(z'^1) \oplus c' & S(w^0 \oplus c) \oplus S(z'^0) \\
\cdots\, S(w^i) \oplus S(z'^i) & \cdots\, S(w^2) \oplus S(z'^2) \oplus c' & S(w^1) \oplus S(z'^1 \oplus c) & S(w^0 \oplus c) \oplus S(z'^0)
\end{array}
$$

For the first bundles to be equal for both states the following relations have to be satisfied:

$$
\begin{aligned}
S(z'^2) \oplus S(z'^2 \oplus c) &= S(z^2) \oplus S(z^2 \oplus c) \\
S(z'^1) \oplus S(z'^1 \oplus c) &= S(z^1) \oplus S(z^1 \oplus c),
\end{aligned}
$$

which occurs with probability $2^{-2.415}$ for each relation.

Experimental Results. Experiments showed that the probability of the distinguisher is very close to what we expected. By testing 2^{30} pairs, we obtained 31 successes, a probability close to 2^{-25}. Our unoptimized C++ implementation took less than 70 min on a desktop computer to find these pairs, i.e. about 2 min per pair on average. Below is an example.

x_1			x_2		
62544d56	60b9af6e	bd3ddabf	62544d56	48d12ffc	bb391a7d
019d0421	569ad0d3	e543b03f	019d0421	5efa911b	cb4ff1e5
5f8ba283	087f4892	f7b632d8	5f8ba283	265b098a	ffd272c0
116bb908	eef0b58d	97dc955a	116bb908	e0d8f55f	9790d5da
$x_1 \oplus x_2$			$\pi(x_1) \oplus \pi(x_2)$		
00000000	28688092	0604c0c2	00000000	d7ddf0cd	87ed7095
00000000	086041c8	2e0c41da	00000000	c4e25bec	df225a5c
00000000	2e244118	08644018	00000000	d3d67ba2	9416fab2
00000000	0e2840d2	004c4080	00000000	1cff6fdd	9cf7ed09

Difference with 7 Rounds. The main difference with our 7-round distinguisher on Shadow-512 is our inability to cover step 0, and it stems from D. The middle rounds of the attack cannot be moved, as they depend on our ability to cancel out the constants and maintain 2-identical states. In the 7-round attack, rounds alternate between 3 and 1 active Super S-box (bundle). The inverse step 1 takes in input a difference $\alpha, \alpha, \alpha, 0$ and the inverse application of D gives a difference $0, 0, 0, \alpha$. But since this difference is active in only one bundle, we can traverse one more round and have a difference active in only three bundles. Here, we used a different path, with two active bundles at each round. The inverse step 1 takes as input a difference $0, \alpha, \alpha$, the inverse of D maps to a difference $0, \alpha, \alpha$, but after the inverse Super S-box, we obtain two unknown differences, and we cannot traverse round 0.

5   Forgeries with 4-Step `Shadow` in the Nonce Misuse Setting

In this section, we show how to use the properties exploited in the distinguishers to create existential forgeries for the S1P mode of operation [BBB+19], in the single user setting, when used with 4-step `Shadow` (out of 6) shifted of two steps (starting at step 2 instead of 0). Hence, our attack targets the "aggressive parameters" specified in [BBB+19, Section 5].

One interesting feature of `Spook` is that it provides strong integrity guarantees in the presence of nonce misuse and leakage, which are formalized as CIML2 in the unbounded leakage model [BPPS17]. In our attack, we do not require leakage and instead exploit the nonce control. More specifically, we require the same nonce to be used three times. Our attack then creates two different messages with the same authentication tag. In particular, we are able to build collisions on the underlying hash function, which allows us to build the forgeries.

Attack Outline. S1P is a sponge-based mode of authenticated encryption with associated data represented in Fig. 7, that uses `Shadow` as its underlying permutation. It has a rate of size 256 bits and a capacity of size 256 bits. If we number the bundles of `Shadow` as in the reference implementation, bundles 0 and 1 are the rate part and bundles 2 and 3 are the capacity part.

For the sake of simplicity, we consider a version of the S1P mode of operation without associated data, and we only consider two-block messages M_0, M_1. This situation is depicted on Fig. 7, where π is the `Shadow` permutation, `Initialize` is a procedure combining π and the Clyde block cipher, that produces a 512-bit state from a nonce N and the secret key K, and `Finalize` is a procedure that, on input a 512-bit state, produces a 128-bit authentication tag.

Our goal is to output two plaintexts $(M_0, M_1), (M_0', M_1')$ and a nonce N that yield the same authentication tag. In order to do that, we obtain a collision on the internal state before `Finalize`. This means that any pair $(M_0, M_1, x_2, ..., x_\ell)$, $(M_0', M_1', x_2, ..., x_\ell)$ of messages built by appending the same blocks to our colliding pair would also yield the same tag provided that the nonce is reused. We can find (M_0, M_1) and (M_0', M_1') thanks to the following algorithm, that we will prove later.

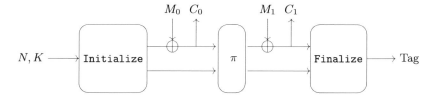

Fig. 7. S1P mode in our attack setting

Let π be the Shadow permutation restricted to rounds 2 to 5. Informally, the first queries allow us to find the difference between the states before π, the second ones to figure out the difference after π, and the third to cancel it out. The whole attack is presented in details in Algorithm 4. Before describing it, we present its main subroutine whose success probability is given by the following lemma.

Algorithm 3. Algorithm to generate candidate pairs for our 4-step property.

Output: two pairs of $(x_1, y_1), (x'_1, y'_1)$ such that $\pi(x_1, y_1, a, b) \oplus \pi(x'_1, y'_1, a, b) = (*, *, 0, 0)$ with probability p.

1. Select a random 128-bit bundle w_2.
2. Invert step 2 on $(w_2, w_2, 0, 0)$, obtaining $(x_1, y_1, *, *)$
3. Return $(x_1, y_1), (x_1 \oplus \epsilon, y_1 \oplus \epsilon)$ where $\epsilon \in \nabla$ (a difference that intervenes only in columns 22 and 23 of a bundle).

Lemma 3. *Let $(*, *, a, b)$ be a Shadow state. Then Algorithm 3 produces 4 bundles $(x_1, y_1), (x'_1, y'_1)$ such that $\pi(x_1, y_1, a, b) \oplus \pi(x'_1, y'_1, a, b) = (*, *, 0, 0)$ with a probability $p \simeq 2^{-24.83}$.*

In a nutshell, this property allows us to find a collision on the capacity part of the state after having applied π. Since we can control the differences in the rate before and after π, we then obtain a collision on the full 512-bit state. This is summarized in Algorithm 4. Notice that each plaintext and ciphertext "block" is comprised of two rate bundles.

4-Step Path. We will now prove Lemma 3. We are interested in pairs of 2-identical states for Shadow, where the first two bundles are equal. The following lemma stems immediately from the results in Table 5 (as both states in the pair must remain 2-identical, we take the squared probabilities).

Lemma 4. *Let t_1, t_2 be a pair of 2-identical states with difference $(\alpha, \alpha, 0, 0)$. Then after a step of Shadow, they remain 2-identical with probability 2^{-12} at step 3, 2^{-8} at step 4 and 0 otherwise.*

Algorithm 4. Collision attack on the S1P mode, with nonce reuse, and using 4-step Shadow.

---

1. Encrypt an arbitrary two-block (4-bundle) message, *e.g.* $(0,0),(0,0)$, and obtain ciphertexts $(d_0, d_1), (d_2, d_3)$. Let x_1, y_1, a, b be the 4-bundle state after Initialize (immediately before step 1). Then $d_0, d_1 = x_1, y_1$.
2. Use Algorithm 3 to obtain two pairs of rate bundles $(x'_1, y'_1), (x''_1, y''_1)$ such that $\pi(x'_1, y'_1, a, b) \oplus \pi(x''_1, y''_1, a, b) = (*, *, 0, 0)$ with probability p.
3. Encrypt (with the same nonce) $(x_1 \oplus x'_1, y_1 \oplus y'_1), (0, 0)$ and obtain $(c'_0, c'_1), (c'_2, c'_3)$. Then (c'_2, c'_3) is the value of the rate after the application of π on (x'_1, y'_1, a, b).
4. Encrypt (with the same nonce) $(x_1 \oplus x''_1, y_1 \oplus y''_1), (0, 0)$ and obtain $(c''_0, c''_1), (c''_2, c''_3)$. Then (c''_2, c''_3) is the value of the rate after the application of π on (x''_1, y''_1, a, b).
5. Output the two 4-bundle plaintexts: $(x_1 \oplus x'_1, y_1 \oplus y'_1), (c'_2, c'_3)$ and $(x_1 \oplus x''_1, y_1 \oplus y''_1), (c''_2, c''_3)$ and the nonce N that was used. Then these plaintexts, encrypted with this nonce, yield the same internal state before the Finalize procedure, and the same tag, with probability $p \simeq 2^{-24.83}$.

Using these probabilities, we can investigate Lemma 3.

Proof (of Lemma 3). We follow the convention of indexing bundles depending on the step that immediately precedes, *i.e.* w_2 is a bundle after step 2. The pattern used in this proof is summarized in Fig. 8.

We consider Shadow reduced to steps 2 to 5. We start with an input state $(*, *, a_1, b_1)$. We select a random bundle w_2 and invert step 2 on $(w_2, w_2, 0, 0)$. We denote by $(x_1, y_1, *, *)$ the state obtained after this inversion.

Now we consider the "mixed" state (x_1, y_1, a_1, b_1) passing through step 2. Applying the super-sboxes, D and adding the second round constant we obtain the state: $(\sigma_2(a_1) \oplus \sigma_3(b_1) \oplus w_2, \sigma_2(a_1) \oplus \sigma_3(b_1) \oplus w_2, *, *)$ which is 2-identical.

We also consider the state $(x_1 \oplus \epsilon, y_1 \oplus \epsilon, a_1, b_1)$, where ϵ belongs to the set ∇ of 2^{16} differences that modify only the columns 22 and 23 of a bundle. Then, as shown in our analysis from the previous section, the difference does not interact with the part of the state dealing with the round constant. Hence, the state after step 2 is also 2-identical and it has the same bundles in the capacity part.

We now have a pair of 2-identical states (x_2, x_2, a_2, b_2) and (y_2, y_2, a_2, b_2) in the output of step 2. It is mapped to a pair of 2-identical states (x_3, x_3, a_3, b_3) and (y_3, y_3, a_3, b_3) through step 3 with probability 2^{-12} and similarly through step 4 with probability 2^{-8}.

Before step 5, we have a 2-identical pair $(x_4, x_4, a_4, b_4), (y_4, y_4, a_4, b_4)$. Our goal is to obtain a zero-difference in the capacity part. By an analysis analogous to the one of Shadow-384, this happens with a probability approximately equal to $2^{-4.83}$. We then have a total probability of $\underbrace{1}_{\text{Step 2}} \times \underbrace{2^{-12}}_{\text{Step 3}} \times \underbrace{2^{-8}}_{\text{Step 4}} \times \underbrace{2^{-4.83}}_{\text{Step 5}}$. $\square$

Experimental Results. Lemmas 3 and 4 have been verified independently. Furthermore, we have fully implemented the attack against S1P itself. Using the

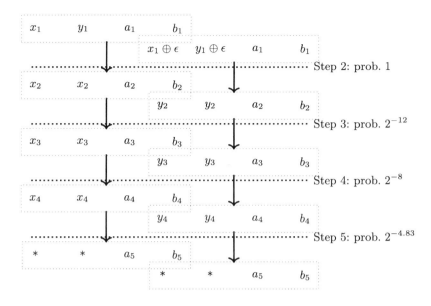

Fig. 8. 4-step path

reference implementation of S1P (but taking out the two first steps) we obtained the following example for a zero-key and a zero-nonce.

m_1 = aaf2fbf5334fdfc6c1ee182f593cc6e1 a5ebc70be994a1bc8b980410a3dae96a
        e93257859683265f20552e381b15c621 eb3257859783265f23552e381b15c621
m_2 = aaf2bbf5334fdfc6c1ee182f593cc6e1 a5eb870be994a1bc8b980410a3dae96a
        2f160415c118c8c174200434e93c2e83 2d160415c018c8c177200434e93c2e83
c_1 = 75235998b09dcbe55a97db04e29622e4 4e73577cdacccc3520d6d6b03b5f2f51
        00000000000000000000000000000000 00000000000000000000000000000000
        c6461d8861f434500882ac5dc3490ce1
c_2 = 75231998b09dcbe55a97db04e29622e4 4e73177cdacccc3520d6d6b03b5f2f51
        00000000000000000000000000000000 00000000000000000000000000000000
        c6461d8861f434500882ac5dc3490ce1

After 2^{30} trials, we obtained 41 successful collisions, with an experimental probability of success of $2^{-24.64}$ which backs the theoretical $2^{-24.83}$. In practice, our un-optimized C++ implementation needs about 15 min to find one collision.

Possible Extensions. Although using similar properties as the previous distinguishers (keeping 2-identical states with a cancellation of constants, using a difference in ∇), our attack suffers from the fact that we cannot control the input in the capacity part. This is the main reason why we cannot consider the steps before step 2, contrary to our distinguisher on full Shadow-512.

As a trivial extension, we remark that we can extend our reduced-step Shadow by one round (*i.e.* half a step) at the end of our 4-step path, since this round does not traverse D; but it falls outside the scope of the actual primitive. We could attack rounds 4 to 13 of `Shadow-512` instead of rounds 0 to 12.

Furthermore, the differences that we obtain at the input of step 2 are very sparse, since they belong to the space ∇. As the complexity of our attack is of the order of 2^{25}, and the generic complexity is of 2^{128} for a collision on the capacity, it might be possible to extend the attack 1 round at the beginning `Shadow`, but this seems far from trivial and would require advanced message modification techniques.

6 Conclusion

In this paper we have shown some new cryptanalysis results on the second round candidate of the lightweight NIST competition `Spook` based on the limited birthday problem. We can distinguish 5-step `Shadow-512` from a random permutation using only 2 queries. If we exploit the round constants, we are able to distinguish the full (6-step) `Shadow-512`, and we could even distinguish 7 steps if the number of rounds was increased (and regardless of the round constant values chosen for this step). Regarding `Shadow-384`, we are able to efficiently distinguish the 6-step permutation if its round constants are shifted, and a round-reduced 5-step version otherwise.

Using similar ideas we could build collisions on the underlying hash function for a 4-step version of the permutation, which means we can build forgeries for the S1P mode with nonce misuse, which is allowed by the CIML2 security game considered by the authors [BPPS17].

All the analyses presented are practical and have been implemented and verified. The corresponding source code is publicly available.

An interesting extension of this work would be to reach 5-step forgeries: as we presented, extending it one round is easy, but one more round for reaching 5-steps might be possible using some advanced message modification techniques. In any case, 6-steps do seem out of reach with our current techniques.

New Criterion. Our analysis provides a new simple criterion for choosing the round constants in LS-designs: besides trying to avoid invariant subspaces attacks, they should be introduced in such a way that their effect in the internal symmetries cannot be canceled out.

Possible Tweaks for `Shadow`. Though our findings do not represent a threat on the full-round authenticated encryption primitive, it is possible to tweak the permutation to counter the low complexity distinguisher and improve the security margin of `Spook`.

The first tweak we would suggest is to use denser constants. This change would not affect the 5-step distinguishers, but would counter the 6-step ones and the 4-step forgeries. Another option that might have the same effect as using less sparse constants is to only use one round constant per step instead of two as it is the case now. This would prevent us from canceling them out inside a step in order to build identical bundle states. This option could be more interesting than denser constants due to implementation reasons.

A second option is to change the D matrix in order to break the symmetry properties between the bundles. This approach was favored by the authors of Spook. After our results, they proposed a new version, Spook v2 [BBB+20], in which they replace the matrix D by an efficient MDS matrix (they also modify the round constants of Shadow for more efficiency). Thus, the attacks presented in this paper are a priori inapplicable to Spook v2.

Acknowledgments. The authors would like to thank the designers of Spook for many helpful discussions and useful comments. Part of this work was done during the symmetric cryptography seminars of FrisiaCrypt 2019 and Dagstuhl 2020 (Seminar 20041). This project has received funding from the European Research Council (ERC) under the European Union's Horizon 2020 research and innovation programme (grant agreement no. 714294 - acronym QUASYModo) and has been partly funded by the ANR under grant Decrypt ANR-18-CE39-0007.

A   Equations to Keep a 3-Identical State

Without loss of generality we consider that the 3 first bundles are identical so we start from a 3-identical state $X = (x, x, x, z)$. The step starts with the application of the same operations to each bundle, namely S and L, we denote the modified state as $L \circ S(X) = (y, y, y, w)$. Once the other operations are applied the output becomes:

$$S(w^{31}), \cdots, S(w^3 \oplus c), S(y^2) \oplus S(y^2 \oplus c) \oplus S(w^2), S(y^1) \oplus S(y^1 \oplus c) \oplus S(w^1), \qquad\qquad S(w^0) \oplus c',$$
$$S(w^{31}), \cdots, S(w^3 \oplus c), S(y^2) \oplus S(y^2 \oplus c) \oplus S(w^2), \qquad\qquad S(w^1) \oplus c', S(y^0) \oplus S(y^0 \oplus c) \oplus S(w^0),$$
$$S(w^{31}), \cdots, S(w^3 \oplus c), \qquad S(w^2) \oplus c', S(y^1) \oplus S(y^1 \oplus c) \oplus S(w^1), S(y^0) \oplus S(y^0 \oplus c) \oplus S(w^0),$$
$$S(y^{31}), \cdots, S(y^3) \oplus c', \qquad\qquad S(y^2 \oplus c), \qquad\qquad S(y^1 \oplus c), \qquad\qquad S(y^0 \oplus c)$$

To assure a 3-identical state the following equations have to be satisfied:

$$S(y^2 \oplus c) = \ \ S(y^2) \oplus c', \quad S(y^1 \oplus c) = \ \ S(y^1) \oplus c', \quad S(y^0 \oplus c) = \ \ S(y^0) \oplus c'.$$

B   Another High Probability Characteristic over 7 Steps

The trail we describe in Sect. 4.2 and that is represented in Fig. 5 is not the only one contributing to the probability of our 7-step distinguisher, as demonstrated by the fact that our experiments return a probability close to 2^{-15} while we expected $2^{-16.245}$. In this section we detail a second trail of high probability that benefits from the definition of L, namely from the fact that the bits in column 2 do not diffuse to column 0, 1 and 2.

Structure of the Trail. The trail is represented in Fig. 9 and works as follows:

- As previously, our construction at step 2 gives a pair of messages that leads with probability 1 to the desired difference $(*, *, *, 0)$ at the input of the permutation, while the states at the output of step 2 are 3-identical and differ by $(0, 0, 0, \beta)$.
- With probability 2^{-9} the two states keep their 3-identical property at the end of step 3, and their difference is $(\gamma, \gamma, \gamma, 0)$.
- We then require that at the end of step 4 the two states are 2-identical while they share the same third bundle value. As we detail next, this event is of probability $2^{-8.3}$.
- Step 5 ends with a null difference in the last bundle with probability 1 thanks to the definition of L. The distinguisher can be extended to a 7-step one for free.

The total probability of this trail is thus equal to $2^{-17.3}$. Adding it to the probability of the other trail discussed in Sect. 4.2 we obtain something closer to what is observed experimentally: $2^{-17.3} + 2^{-16.245} = 2^{-15.678}$. Note that other trails add up to this probability, for instance the ones with a difference of the form $(0, \tau, \tau, \kappa)$ or $(\tau, 0, \tau, \kappa)$ at the end of step 4.

Detail of the Probabilities.

Step 3. As for the trail described in Sect. 4.2, the probability that the states remain 3-identical is equal to 2^{-9}.

Step 4. At the end of step 4, we aim for a pair of messages that are 2-identical in their first 2 bundles and that have no difference in their third bundle. Formally, let us denote by (y, y, y, w) and (y', y', y', w) the two states after S and L. After applying the first constant addition, the second S-layer, the D operation and the second constant addition, we obtain:

$$
\begin{array}{llll}
S(w^{31}), \cdots, & S(w^3 \oplus c), & S(y^2) \oplus S(y^2 \oplus c) \oplus S(w^2), \ S(y^1) \oplus S(y^1 \oplus c) \oplus S(w^1), & S(w^0) \oplus c', \\
S(w^{31}), \cdots, & S(w^3 \oplus c), & S(y^2) \oplus S(y^2 \oplus c) \oplus S(w^2), & S(w^1) \oplus c', \ S(y^0) \oplus S(y^0 \oplus c) \oplus S(w^0), \\
S(w^{31}), \cdots, & S(w^3 \oplus c), & S(w^2) \oplus c', \ S(y^1) \oplus S(y^1 \oplus c) \oplus S(w^1), \ S(y^0) \oplus S(y^0 \oplus c) \oplus S(w^0), \\
S(y^{31}), \cdots, & S(y^3) \oplus c', & S(y^2 \oplus c), & S(y^1 \oplus c), & S(y^0 \oplus c)
\end{array}
$$

and

$$
\begin{array}{llll}
S(w^{31}), \cdots, & S(w^3 \oplus c), & S(y'^2) \oplus S(y'^2 \oplus c) \oplus S(w^2), \ S(y'^1) \oplus S(y'^1 \oplus c) \oplus S(w^1), & S(w^0) \oplus c', \\
S(w^{31}), \cdots, & S(w^3 \oplus c), & S(y'^2) \oplus S(y'^2 \oplus c) \oplus S(w^2), & S(w^1) \oplus c', \ S(y'^0) \oplus S(y'^0 \oplus c) \oplus S(w^0), \\
S(w^{31}), \cdots, & S(w^3 \oplus c), & S(w^2) \oplus c', \ S(y'^1) \oplus S(y'^1 \oplus c) \oplus S(w^1), \ S(y'^0) \oplus S(y'^0 \oplus c) \oplus S(w^0), \\
S(y'^{31}), \cdots, & S(y'^3) \oplus c', & S(y'^2 \oplus c), & S(y'^1 \oplus c), & S(y'^0 \oplus c)
\end{array}
$$

In order to obtain a 2-identical state the following relations have to hold:

$$
S(y^1) \oplus S(y^1 \oplus c) = c', \quad S(y^0) \oplus S(y^0 \oplus c) = c',
$$
$$
S(y'^1) \oplus S(y'^1 \oplus c) = c', \quad S(y'^0) \oplus S(y'^0 \oplus c) = c'.
$$

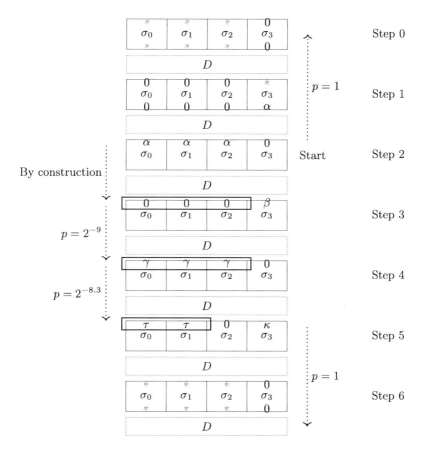

Fig. 9. Another trail contributing to the probability of the 7-step distinguisher of Shadow-512.

Given that we are looking at step number 4 we have $c = 0x5$ and $c' = 0xa$, so each equation is verified with probability 2^{-2}. Also, since we aim for a difference at the end of step 4 of the form $(\tau, \tau, 0, \kappa)$ with $\tau \neq 0$, we have to add the condition:

$$S(y^2) \oplus S(y^2 \oplus c) \oplus S(y'^2) \oplus S(y'^2 \oplus c) \neq 0.$$

That is verified with probability $2^{-0.3}$. Consequently, the probability of step 4 is equal to $2^{-8.3}$. Once these conditions are fulfilled, we automatically have an output difference of step 4 equal to $(\tau, \tau, 0, \kappa)$ and the actual value of τ is very sparse, only the second column is active:

$$\tau = (0, \cdots, \quad 0, \quad S(y'^2) \oplus S(y'^2 \oplus c) \oplus S(y^2) \oplus S(y^2 \oplus c), \quad 0, \quad 0)$$

This particular shape implies that step 5 is passed with probability 1.

Step 5. We denote the two input states by (u, u, v, x) and $(u \oplus \tau, u \oplus \tau, v, x')$. Our goal is to obtain a difference equal to zero in the last bundle at the end of the step. We first remark that after applying the first S-layer to the two states, we obtain two states (U, U, V, X) and (U', U', V, X') so that again the difference between U and U' is only positioned in the second column of the bundle (simply because the S-layer modifies each column independently). We denote the new difference by $T = U \oplus U'$.

Due to the linearity of the next step we can further trace the evolution of τ through the L layer: we have that $L(U) \oplus L(U') = L(T)$. Moreover, using the specification of L and the same notations as in Sect. 4.2 we observe that:

$$L(e_2, 0) = (\texttt{805101b8}, \texttt{6f0006c0})$$
$$L(0, e_2) = (\texttt{37800360}, \texttt{805101b8}).$$

These computations indicate that any difference positioned in column 2 does not propagate to any of the first 3 columns, and in particular that whatever the exact value of T the two first bundles of each state have the same value over their 3 first columns. To see how this leads to the required equality at the end of step 5, we can look at the formal expression of the two states. After applying L, the first round constant addition and the second non-linear layer we obtain:

$S(L(U)^{31}), \cdots,$	$S(L(U)^3),$	$S(L(U)^2),$	$S(L(U)^1),$	$S(L(U)^0 \oplus c),$
$S(L(U)^{31}), \cdots,$	$S(L(U)^3),$	$S(L(U)^2),$	$S(L(U)^1 \oplus c),$	$S(L(U)^0),$
$S(L(V)^{31}), \cdots,$	$S(L(V)^3),$	$S(L(V)^2 \oplus c),$	$S(L(V)^1),$	$S(L(V)^0),$
$S(L(X)^{31}), \cdots,$	$S(L(X)^3 \oplus c),$	$S(L(X)^2),$	$S(L(X)^1),$	$S(L(X)^0)$

for the first state, and the following for the second state:

$S(L(U')^{31}), \cdots,$	$S(L(U')^3),$	$S(L(U')^2),$	$S(L(U')^1),$	$S(L(U')^0 \oplus c),$
$S(L(U')^{31}), \cdots,$	$S(L(U')^3),$	$S(L(U')^2),$	$S(L(U')^1 \oplus c),$	$S(L(U')^0),$
$S(L(V)^{31}), \cdots,$	$S(L(V)^3),$	$S(L(V)^2 \oplus c),$	$S(L(V)^1),$	$S(L(V)^0),$
$S(L(X')^{31}), \cdots,$	$S(L(X')^3 \oplus c),$	$S(L(X')^2),$	$S(L(X')^1),$	$S(L(X')^0)$

The difference in the last bundle at the end of step 5 is thus given by the sum of the first 3 bundles of both states (since we are passing through D). It gives:

$$0, \cdots, 0, S(L(U)^1) \oplus S(L(U)^1 \oplus c) \oplus S(L(U')^1) \oplus S(L(U')^1 \oplus c), S(L(U)^0) \oplus S(L(U)^0 \oplus c) \oplus S(L(U')^0)$$
$$\oplus S(L(U')^0 \oplus c).$$

We then use the previous observation which implies that $L(U')^1 = L(U)^1$ together with $L(U')^0 = L(U)^0$ to conclude that the bundle difference is null with probability 1.

References

[BBB+19] Bellizia, D., et al.: Spook: sponge-based leakage-resilient authenticated encryption with a masked tweakable block cipher. In: Submission to the NIST Lightweight Cryptography project (2019). https://csrc.nist.gov/CSRC/media/Projects/lightweight-cryptography/documents/round-2/spec-doc-rnd2/Spook-spec-round2.pdf

[BBB+20] Bellizia, D., et al.: Spook: sponge-based leakage-resistant authenticated encryption with a masked tweakable block cipher. IACR Trans. Symm. Cryptol. Special Issue Des. NIST Lightweight Standardisation Process (2020). https://www.spook.dev/assets/TOSC_Spook.pdf

[BBdS+19] Beierle, C., et al.: SCHWAEMM and ESCH: lightweight authenticated encryption and hashing using the SPARKLE permutation family. In: Submission to the 2nd Round of the NIST Lightweight Process (2019)

[BBI+15] Banik, S., et al.: Midori: a block cipher for low energy. In: Iwata, T., Cheon, J.H. (eds.) ASIACRYPT 2015, Part II. LNCS, vol. 9453, pp. 411–436. Springer, Heidelberg (2015). https://doi.org/10.1007/978-3-662-48800-3_17

[BCG+12] Borghoff, J., et al.: PRINCE – a low-latency block cipher for pervasive computing applications extended abstract. In: Wang, X., Sako, K. (eds.) ASIACRYPT 2012. LNCS, vol. 7658, pp. 208–225. Springer, Heidelberg (2012). https://doi.org/10.1007/978-3-642-34961-4_14

[BDP+16] Bertoni, G., Daemen, J., Peeters, M., Van Assche, G., Van Keer, R.: CAESAR submission: Ketje v2. In: Submission to the CAESAR Competition (2016)

[BJK+16] Beierle, C., et al.: The SKINNY family of block ciphers and its low-latency variant MANTIS. In: Robshaw, M., Katz, J. (eds.) CRYPTO 2016, Part II. LNCS, vol. 9815, pp. 123–153. Springer, Heidelberg (2016). https://doi.org/10.1007/978-3-662-53008-5_5

[BKL+07] Bogdanov, A., et al.: PRESENT: an ultra-lightweight block cipher. In: Paillier, P., Verbauwhede, I. (eds.) CHES 2007. LNCS, vol. 4727, pp. 450–466. Springer, Heidelberg (2007). https://doi.org/10.1007/978-3-540-74735-2_31

[BPPS17] Berti, F., Pereira, O., Peters, T., Standaert, F.-X.: On leakage-resilient authenticated encryption with decryption leakages. IACR Trans. Symm. Cryptol. **2017**(3), 271–293 (2017)

[BS91] Biham, E., Shamir, A.: Differential cryptanalysis of DES-like cryptosystems. In: Menezes, A.J., Vanstone, S.A. (eds.) CRYPTO 1990. LNCS, vol. 537, pp. 2–21. Springer, Heidelberg (1991). https://doi.org/10.1007/3-540-38424-3_1

[DEM+17] Dobraunig, C., Eichlseder, M., Mangard, S., Mendel, F., Unterluggauer, T.: ISAP - towards side-channel secure authenticated encryption. IACR Trans. Symm. Cryptol. **2017**(1), 80–105 (2017)

[DEMS16] Dobraunig, C., Eichlseder, M., Mendel, F., Schläffer, M.: Ascon v1. 2. In: Submission to the CAESAR Competition (2016)

[GJK+19] Goudarzi, D., et al.: Submission to the NIST Lightweight Cryptography Project (2019). https://csrc.nist.gov/CSRC/media/Projects/lightweight-cryptography/documents/round-2/spec-doc-rnd2/pyjamask-spec-round2.pdf

[GLSV15] Grosso, V., Leurent, G., Standaert, F.-X., Varıcı, K.: LS-designs: bit-slice encryption for efficient masked software implementations. In: Cid, C., Rechberger, C. (eds.) FSE 2014. LNCS, vol. 8540, pp. 18–37. Springer, Heidelberg (2015). https://doi.org/10.1007/978-3-662-46706-0_2

[GP10] Gilbert, H., Peyrin, T.: Super-Sbox cryptanalysis: improved attacks for AES-like permutations. In: Hong, S., Iwata, T. (eds.) FSE 2010. LNCS, vol. 6147, pp. 365–383. Springer, Heidelberg (2010). https://doi.org/10.1007/978-3-642-13858-4_21

[HLK+14] Hong, D., Lee, J.-K., Kim, D.-C., Kwon, D., Ryu, K.H., Lee, D.-G.: LEA: a 128-bit block cipher for fast encryption on common processors. In: Kim, Y., Lee, H., Perrig, A. (eds.) WISA 2013. LNCS, vol. 8267, pp. 3–27. Springer, Cham (2014). https://doi.org/10.1007/978-3-319-05149-9_1

[IPS13] Iwamoto, M., Peyrin, T., Sasaki, Y.: Limited-birthday distinguishers for hash functions. In: Sako, K., Sarkar, P. (eds.) ASIACRYPT 2013, Part II. LNCS, vol. 8270, pp. 504–523. Springer, Heidelberg (2013). https://doi.org/10.1007/978-3-642-42045-0_26

[Knu95] Knudsen, L.R.: Truncated and higher order differentials. In: Preneel, B. (ed.) FSE 1994. LNCS, vol. 1008, pp. 196–211. Springer, Heidelberg (1995). https://doi.org/10.1007/3-540-60590-8_16

Cryptanalysis of LEDAcrypt

Daniel Apon[1(✉)], Ray Perlner[1], Angela Robinson[1], and Paolo Santini[2,3]

[1] National Institute of Standards and Technology, Gaithersburg, USA
{daniel.apon,ray.perlner,angela.robinson}@nist.gov
[2] Università Politecnica delle Marche, Ancona, Italy
p.santini@pm.univpm.it
[3] Florida Atlantic University, Boca Raton, USA

Abstract. We report on the concrete cryptanalysis of LEDAcrypt, a 2nd Round candidate in NIST's Post-Quantum Cryptography standardization process and one of 17 encryption schemes that remain as candidates for near-term standardization. LEDAcrypt consists of a public-key encryption scheme built from the McEliece paradigm and a key-encapsulation mechanism (KEM) built from the Niederreiter paradigm, both using a quasi-cyclic low-density parity-check (QC-LDPC) code.

In this work, we identify a large class of extremely weak keys and provide an algorithm to recover them. For example, we demonstrate how to recover 1 in $2^{47.72}$ of LEDAcrypt's keys using only $2^{18.72}$ guesses at the 256-bit security level. This is a major, practical break of LEDAcrypt. Further, we demonstrate a continuum of progressively less weak keys (from extremely weak keys up to all keys) that can be recovered in substantially less work than previously known. This demonstrates that the imperfection of LEDAcrypt is fundamental to the system's design.

Keywords: NIST PQC · LEDAcrypt · McEliece · QC-LDPC · Cryptanalysis

1 Introduction

Since Shor's discovery [27] of a polynomial-time quantum algorithm for factoring integers and solving discrete logarithms, there has been a substantial amount of research on quantum computers. If large-scale quantum computers are ever built, they will be able to break many of the public-key cryptosystems currently in use. This would gravely undermine the integrity and confidentiality of our current communications infrastructure on the Internet and elsewhere.

In response, the National Institute of Standards and Technology (NIST) initiated a process [1] to solicit, evaluate, and standardize one or more quantum-resistant, public-key cryptographic algorithms. This process began in late 2017 with 69 submissions from around the world of post-quantum key-establishment mechanisms or KEMs (resp. public-key encryption schemes or PKEs), and digital signature algorithms. In early 2019, the list of candidates was cut from 69

© International Association for Cryptologic Research 2020
D. Micciancio and T. Ristenpart (Eds.): CRYPTO 2020, LNCS 12172, pp. 389–418, 2020.
https://doi.org/10.1007/978-3-030-56877-1_14

to 26 (17 of which are PKEs or KEMs), and the 2nd Round of the competition began [2]. The conclusion of Round 2 is now rapidly approaching.

LEDAcrypt [16] is one of the 17 remaining candidates for standardization as a post-quantum PKE or KEM scheme. It is based on the seminal works of McEliece [20] in 1978 and Niederreiter [23] in 1986, which are based on the NP-complete problem of decoding an arbitrary linear binary code [5]. More precisely, LEDAcrypt is composed of a PKE scheme based on McEliece but instantiated with a particular type of codes (called QC-LDPC) and a KEM in the variant style of Niederreiter. The specific origins of LEDAcrypt – the idea of using QC-LDPC codes with the McEliece paradigm – dates back a dozen years to [15].

At a very high level, the private key of LEDAcrypt is a pair of binary matrices H and Q, where H is a sparse, quasi-cyclic, parity-check matrix of dimension $p \times p \cdot n_0$ for a given QC-LDPC code and where Q is a random, sparse, quasi-cyclic matrix of dimension $p \cdot n_0 \times p \cdot n_0$. Here p is a moderately large prime and n_0 is a small constant. The intermediate matrix $L = [L_0|...|L_{n_0-1}] = H \cdot Q$ is formed by matrix multiplication. The public key M is then constructed from L by multiplying each of the L_i by $L_{n_0-1}^{-1}$. Given this key pair, information can be encoded into codeword vectors, then perturbed by random error-vectors of a low Hamming weight.[1]

Security essentially relies on the assumption that it is difficult to recover the originally-encoded information from the perturbed codeword unless a party possesses the factorization of the public key as H and Q. To recover such matrices (or, equivalently, their product) one must find low-weight codewords in the public code (or in its dual) which, again, is a well-known NP-complete problem [5]. State-of-the-art algorithms to solve this problem are known as Information Set Decoding (ISD), and their expected computational complexity is indeed used as a design criteria for LEDAcrypt parameters.

The LEDAcrypt submission package in the 2nd Round of NIST's PQC process provides a careful description of the algorithm's history and specific design, a variety of concrete parameters sets tailored to NIST's security levels (claiming approximately 128-bit, 192-bit, and 256-bit security, under either IND-CPA or IND-CCA attacks), and a reference implementation in-code.

1.1   Our Results

In this work, we provide a novel, concrete cryptanalysis of LEDAcrypt. Note that, in LEDAcrypt design procedure, the time complexity of ISD algorithms is derived by assuming that the searched codewords are uniformly distributed over the set of all n-uples of fixed weight. However, as we show in Sect. 3, for LEDAcrypt schemes this assumption does not hold, since it is possible to identify many families of secret keys, i.e., matrices H and Q, for which the rows of $L = HQ$ (which represent low weight codewords in the dual code) are characterized by a strong bias in the distribution of set bits. We define such keys as *weak* since, intuitively, in such a case an ISD algorithm can be strongly improved by taking

---

[1] We refer the reader to [3], A.1 for further technical details of the construction.

into account the precise structure of the searched codeword. As a direct evidence, in Sect. 4 we consider a moderately-sized, very weak class of keys, which can be recovered with substantially less computational effort than expected. This is a major, practical break of the LEDAcrypt cryptosystem, which is encapsulated in the following theorem.

Theorem 1.1 (Section 4). *There is an algorithm that costs the same as* $2^{49.22}$ *AES-256 operations and recovers 1 in* $2^{47.72}$ *of LEDAcrypt's Category 5 (i.e. claimed 256-bit-secure) ephemeral/IND-CPA keys.*

Similarly, there is an algorithm that costs the same as $2^{57.50}$ *AES-256 operations and recovers 1 in* $2^{51.59}$ *of LEDAcrypt's Category 5 (i.e. claimed 256-bit-secure) long-term/IND-CCA keys.*

While most key-recovery algorithms can exchange computational time spent vs. fraction of the key space recovered, this trade-off will generally be 1-to-1 against a secure cryptosystem. (In particular this trade off is 1-to-1 for the AES cryptosystem which is used to define the NIST security strength categories for LEDAcrypt's parameter sets.) However, we note in the above that both $49.22 + 47.72 = 96.94 \ll 256$ and $57.49 + 51.59 = 109.08 \ll 256$, making this attack quite significant. Additionally, we note that this class of very weak keys is present in every parameter set of LEDAcrypt.

While the existence of classes of imperfect keys is a serious concern, one might ask:

Is it possible to identify such keys during KeyGen, reject them, and thereby save the scheme's design?

We are able to answer this in the negative.

Indeed, as we demonstrate in Sect. 3, the bias in the distribution of set bits in L, which is at the basis of our attack, is intrinsic in the scheme's design. Our results clearly show that the existence of weaker-than-expected keys in LEDAcrypt is *fundamental* in the system's formulation and cannot be avoided without a major re-design of the cryptosystem.

Finally, we apply our new attack ideas to attempting key recovery without considering a weak key notion. Here we analyze the asymptotic complexity of attacking *all* LEDAcrypt keys.

Theorem 1.2 (Section 5). *The asymptotic complexity of ISD using an appropriate choice of structured information sets, when attacking* all *LEDAcrypt keys in the worst case, is* $\exp(\tilde{O}(p^{\frac{1}{4}}))$.

This gives a significant asymptotic speed-up over running ISD with uniformly random information sets, which costs $\exp(\tilde{O}(p^{\frac{1}{2}}))$. We note that simply enumerating all possible values of H and Q actually leads to an attack running in time $\exp(\tilde{O}(p^{\frac{1}{4}}))$, and indeed similar attacks were considered in LEDAcrypt's submission documents for the NIST PQC process. However, this type of attack had worse concrete complexity than ordinary ISD with uniformly random information sets for all of the 2nd Round parameter sets.

1.2   Technical Overview of Our New Attacks

Basic Approach: Exploiting the Product Structure. The typical approach to recovering keys for LEDAcrypt-like schemes is to use ordinary ISD algorithms, a class of techniques which can be used to search for low weight codewords in an arbitrary code. Generally speaking, these algorithms symbolically consider a row of an unknown binary matrix corresponding to the secret key of the scheme. From this row, they randomly choose a set of bit positions uniformly at random in the hope that these bits will (mostly) be zero. If the guess is correct and, additionally, the chosen set is an *information set* (i.e., a set in which all codewords differ at least in one position), then the key will be recovered with linear algebra computation. If (at least) one of the two requirements on the set is not met, then the procedure resets and guesses again.

For our attacks, intuitively, we will choose the information set in a non-uniform manner in order to increase the probability that the support of HQ, i.e. the non-zero coefficients of HQ, is (mostly) contained in the complement of the information set. At a high level, we will guess two sets of polynomials $H'_0, ..., H'_{n_0-1}$ and $Q'_{0,0}, ..., Q'_{n_0-1,n_0-1}$, then (interpreting the polynomials as $p \times p$ circulant matrices) group them into quasi-cyclic matrices H' and Q'. These matrices will be structured analogously to H and Q, but with non-negative coefficients defined over $\mathbb{Z}[x]/\langle x^p - 1 \rangle$ rather than $\mathbb{F}_2[x]/\langle x^p + 1 \rangle$. The hope is that the support of $H'Q'$ will (mostly) contain the support of HQ. It should be noted that a sufficient condition for this to be the case is that the support of H' contains the support of H and the support of Q' contains the support of Q. Assuming the Hamming weight of $H'Q'$ (interpreted as a coefficient vector) is chosen to be approximately W, then the information set can be chosen as the complement of the support of $H'Q'$ and properly passed to an ISD subroutine in place of a uniform guess.

Observe that the probability that the supports of H' and Q' contain the supports of H and Q, respectively, is maximized by making the Hamming weight of H' and Q' as large as possible while still limiting the Hamming weight of $H'Q'$ to W. An initial intuition is that this can be done by choosing the 1-coefficients of the polynomials $H'_0, ..., H'_{n_0-1}$ and $Q'_{0,0}, ..., Q'_{n_0-1,n_0-1}$ to be in a single, consecutive chunk. For example, by choosing the Hamming weight of the polynomials (before multiplication) as some value $B \ll W$, we can take $H'_0 = x^a + x^{a+1} + ... + x^{a+B-1}$ and $Q'_{0,0} = x^c + x^{c+1} + ... + x^{c+B-1}$.

Note that the polynomials H'_0 and $Q'_{0,0}$ (chosen with consecutive 1-coefficients as above) have Hamming weight B, while their product only has Hamming weight $2B - 1$. In the most general case, uniformly chosen polynomials with Hamming weight B would be expected to have a product with Hamming weight much closer to $\min(B^2, p)$. That is, for a fixed weight W required of $H'Q'$ by the ISD subroutine, we can guess around $W/2$ positions at once in H' and Q' respectively instead of something closer to $\sqrt{W}$ as would be given by a truly uniform choice of information set. As a result, each individual guess of H' and Q' that's "close" to this outline of our intuition will be more rewarding for searching the keyspace than the "typical" case of uniformly guessing information sets.

This constitutes the core intuition for our attacks against LEDAcrypt, but additional considerations are required in order to make the attacks practically effective (particularly when concrete parameters are considered). We enumerate a few of these observations next.

Different Ring Representations. The idea of choosing the polynomials within H' and Q' with consecutive nonzero coefficients makes each iteration of an information set decoding algorithm using such an H' and Q' much more effective than an iteration with a random information set. However there is only a limited number of successful information sets with this form. We can vastly increase our range of options by observing that the ring $\mathbb{F}_2[x]/\langle x^p + 1 \rangle$ has $p - 1$ isomorphic representations which can be mapped to one another by the isomoprhism $f(x) \rightarrow f(x^\alpha)$. This allows us many more equally efficient choices of the information set, since rather than restricting our choices to have polynomials H'_0 and $Q'_{0,0}$ with consecutive ones in the standard ring representation, we have the freedom to choose them with consecutive ones in any ring representation (provided the same representation is used for H'_0 and $Q'_{0,0}$.)

Equivalent Keys. For each public key of LEDAcrypt, there exist many choices of private keys that produce the same public key. In particular, the same public key $M = (L_{n_0-1})^{-1}L$ produced by the private key

$$H = [H_0, H_1, \cdots, H_{n_0-1}],$$

$$Q = \begin{bmatrix} Q_{0,0} & Q_{0,1} & \cdots & Q_{0,n_0-1} \\ Q_{1,0} & Q_{1,1} & \cdots & Q_{1,n_0-1} \\ \vdots & \vdots & \ddots & \vdots \\ Q_{n_0-1,0} & Q_{n_0-1,1} & \cdots & Q_{n_0-1,n_0-1} \end{bmatrix};$$

would also be produced by any private key of the form

$$H' = [x^{a_0}H_0, x^{a_1}H_1, \cdots, x^{a_{n_0-1}}H_{n_0-1}],$$

$$Q' = \begin{bmatrix} x^{b-a_0}Q_{0,0} & x^{b-a_0}Q_{0,1} & \cdots & x^{b-a_0}Q_{0,n_0-1} \\ x^{b-a_1}Q_{1,0} & x^{b-a_1}Q_{1,1} & \cdots & x^{b-a_1}Q_{1,n_0-1} \\ \vdots & \vdots & \ddots & \vdots \\ x^{b-a_{n_0}}Q_{n_0-1,0} & x^{b-a_{n_0}}Q_{n_0-1,1} & \cdots & x^{b-a_{n_0}}Q_{n_0-1,n_0-1} \end{bmatrix};$$

for any integers $0 < a_i, b < p, i \in \{0, \ldots, n_0 - 1\}$. These p^{n_0+1} equivalent keys improve the success probability of key recovery attacks as detailed in the following sections.

Different Degree Constraints for H' and Q'. While we have so far described H' and Q' as having the same Hamming weight B, this does not necessarily need to be the case. In fact, there are many, equivalent choices of H' and Q' which produce the same product $H'Q'$ based on this observation. For example, the product of

$$H'_0 = x^a + x^{a+1} + \ldots + x^{a+B-1}$$
$$Q'_{0,0} = x^c + x^{c+1} + \ldots + x^{c+B-1}$$

is identical to the product of

$$H'_0 = x^a + x^{a+1} + \ldots + x^{a+B-1-\delta}$$
$$Q'_{0,0} = x^c + x^{c+1} + \ldots + x^{c+B-1+\delta}$$

for any integer $-B < \delta < B$. More generally, this relationship (that if H' shrinks and Q' proportionally grows, or vice versa, then the product $H'Q'$ is the same) is independently true for any set of $\{H'_i, Q'_{i,0}, \ldots, Q'_{i,n_0-1}\}$ for $i \in \{0, \ldots, n_0 - 1\}$.

Attacks for $n_0 = 2$ Imply Similar-Cost Attacks for $n_0 > 2$. Our attacks are more easily described (and more effective) in the case $n_0 = 2$. In this case, we apply ISD to find low-weight codewords in the row space of the public key $[M_0 \mid M_1]$ to recover a viable secret key for the system. Naively extending this approach for the case $n_0 > 2$ to the entire public key $[M_0 \mid \ldots \mid M_{n_0}]$ requires constraints on the support of $n_0 + n_0^2$ polynomials (n_0 polynomials corresponding to H' and n_0^2 polynomials corresponding to Q'), so the overall work in the attack would increase quadratically as n_0 grows. However, even in the case that $n_0 > 2$, we observe that it is sufficient to find low weight codewords in the row space of only $[M_0 \mid M_1]$ in order to recover a working key, implying that the attack only needs to consider $3n_0$ polynomials $H_i, Q_{j,0}, Q_{k,1}$. So, increasing n_0 will make all of our attacks less effective, but not substantially so. More importantly, any attack against $n_0 = 2$ parameters immediately implies a similar-cost attack against parameters with $n_0 > 2$. Therefore, we focus on the case of $n_0 = 2$ in the remainder of this work.

A Continuum of Progressively Less Weak Keys. The attacker can recover keys with the highest probability per iteration of ISD by using a very structured pattern for L'. As we will see in Sect. 4, in this pattern both L'_0 and L'_1 will have a single contiguous stretch of nonzero coefficients in some ring representation. The result is a practical attack, but one which is only capable of recovering weak keys representing something like 1 in 2^{40} or 1 in 2^{50} private keys.

However, if the attacker is willing to use a more complicated pattern for the information set, using different ring representations for different blocks of H' and Q', and possibly having multiple separate stretches of consecutive nonzero coefficients in each block, then the attacker will not recover keys with as high a probability per iteration, but the attack will extend to a broader class of slightly less weak keys. This may for example lead to a somewhat less practical attack that recovers 1 in 2^{30} keys, but still much faster than would be expected given the claimed security strength of the parameter set in question.

We do not analyze the multitude of possible cases here, but we show they must necessarily exist in Sect. 3 by demonstrating that bias is intrinsically present throughout the LEDAcrypt key space.

Improvements to Average-Case Key Recovery. In Sect. 5 we will take the continuum of progressively weaker keys to its logical extreme. We show that the attacks in this paper are asymptotically stronger than the standard attacks not just for weak keys, but for all keys.

As we move away from the simpler information set patterns used on the weakest keys, the analysis becomes more difficult. To fully quantify the impact of our attack on average keys would require extensive case analysis of all scenarios that might lead to a successful key recovery given a particular distribution of information sets used by the attacker, which we leave for future work.

1.3 Related Work

The main attack strategies against cryptosystems based on QC-LDPC codes are known as information set decoding (ISD) algorithms. These algorithms are also applicable to a variety of other code-based cryptosystems including the NIST 2nd round candidates BIKE [22], HQC [8], Classic McEliece [9], and NTS-KEM [17]. Initiated by Prange [25] in 1962, these algorithms have since experienced substantial improvements during the years [4,7,12,13,18,19,28]. ISD algorithms can also be used to find low-weight codewords in a given, arbitrary code. ISD main approach is that of guessing a set of positions where such codewords contain a very low number of set symbols; when this set is actually an information set, then linear algebra computations yield the searched codeword (see [3], Appendix A.3). ISD time complexity is estimated as the product between the expected number of required information set guesses and the cost of testing each set. Advanced ISD algorithms improve Prange's basic idea by reducing the average number of required guesses, at the cost of increasing the time complexity of the testing phase. Quantum ISD algorithms take into account Grover's algorithm [10] to quadratically accelerate the guessing phase. A quantum version of Prange's algorithm [6] was presented in 2010, while quantum versions of more advanced ISD algorithms were presented in 2017 [11].

In the case of QC-MDPC and QC-LDPC codes, ISD key recovery attacks can get a speed-up which is polynomial in the size of the circulant blocks [26]. This gain is due to the fact that there are more than one sparse vector in the row space of the parity check matrix, and no modification to the standard ISD algorithms is required to obtain this speed-up. Another example of gains due to the QC structure is that of [14] which, however, works only in the case of the circulant size having a power of 2 among its factors (which is not the case we consider here).

ISD can generally be described as a technique for finding low Hamming-weight codewords in a linear code. Most ISD algorithms are designed to assume that the low-weight codewords are random aside from their sparsity. However, in some cryptosystems that can be cryptanalyzed using ISD, these short codewords are not random in this respect, and modified versions of ISD have been used to break these schemes [21,24]. Our paper can be seen as a continuation of this line of work, since unlike the other 2nd Round NIST candidates where ISD is cryptanalytically relevant, the sparse codewords which lead to a key recovery of

LEDAcrypt are not simply random sparse vectors, but have additional structure due to the product structure of LEDAcrypt's private key.

2 Preliminaries

2.1 Notation

Throughout this work, we denote the finite field with 2 elements by $\mathbb{F}_2$. We denote the Hamming weight of a vector a (or a polynomial a, viewed in terms of its coefficient vector) as $\mathrm{wt}(a)$. For a polynomial a we use the representation $a = \sum_{i=0}^{p-1} a_i x^i$, and call a_i its i-th coefficient. We denote the support – i.e. the non-zero coordinates – of a vector (or polynomial) a by $\mathrm{S}(a)$. In similar way, we define the *antisupport* of a, and denote it as $\bar{\mathrm{S}}(a)$, as the set of positions i such that $a_i = 0$. Given a polynomial a and a set J, we denote as $a|_J$ the set of coefficients of a that are indexed by J. Given π, a permutation of $\{0, \cdots, n-1\}$, we represent it as the ordered set of integers $\{\ell_0, \cdots, \ell_{n-1}\}$, such that π places ℓ_i in position i. For a length-n vector a, $\pi(a)$ denotes the action of π on a, i.e., the vector whose i-th entry is a_{ℓ_i}. For a probability distribution $\mathcal{D}$, we write $X \sim \mathcal{D}$ if X is distributed according to $\mathcal{D}$.

2.2 Parameters

The parameter sets of LEDAcrypt that we explicitly consider in this work are shown in Table 1 (although similar forms of our results hold for all parameter sets). We refer the reader to [3], Appendix A.1 for further technical details of the construction.

Table 1. LEDAcrypt parameter sets that we consider in this paper.

NIST Category	Security Type	p	d_v	m_0	m_1	n_0
1 (128-bit)	IND-CPA	14,939	11	4	3	2
5 (256-bit)	IND-CPA	36,877	11	7	6	2
5 (256-bit)	IND-CCA	152,267	13	7	6	2

3 Existence of Weak Keys in LEDAcrypt

As we have explained in Sect. 1.3, key recovery attacks against cryptosystems based on codes with sparse parity-check matrices can be performed by searching for low weight codewords, either in the code or in its dual. For instance, such codewords in the dual correspond, with overwhelming probability, to the rows of the secret parity-check matrix, of weight $\omega \ll n$, where n denotes the code length. The most efficient way to solve this problem is to use ISD algorithms. To analyze the efficiency of such attacks, weight-ω codewords are normally modeled as independent random variables, sampled according to the uniform distribution of n-uples with weight ω, which we denote as $\mathcal{U}_\omega$. At each ISD iteration, the algorithm succeeds if the intersection between the chosen set T and the support of (at least) one of such codewords satisfies some properties. Regardless of the considered ISD variant, this intersection has to be small.

Let ϵ be the probability that a single ISD iteration can actually recover a specific codeword of the desired weight. When the code contains M codewords of weight ω, then the probability that a single ISD iteration can recover any of these codewords is $1 - (1 - \epsilon)^M$ which, if $\epsilon M \ll 1$, can be approximated as ϵM. This speed-up in ISD algorithm normally applies to the case of QC codes, where M corresponds to the number of rows in the parity-check matrix (that is, $M = n - k$).

In this section we show that the product structure in LEDAcrypt yields to a strong bias in the distribution of set symbols in the rows of the secret parity-check matrix $L = HQ$. As a consequence, the assumption on the uniform distribution of the searched codewords does not hold anymore, and this opens up for dramatic improvements in ISD algorithms. To provide evidence of this claim we analyze, without loss of generality, a simplified situation. We focus on the case $n_0 = 2$, and consider the success probability of ISD algorithms when applied on LEDAcrypt schemes, searching for a row of the secret L (say, the first row), with weight $\omega = 2d_v(m_0 + m_1)$.

In this case we expect to have the usual speed-up deriving from the presence of multiple low-weight codewords. However, quantifying this speed-up is not straightforward and requires cumbersome computations, since it also depends on the particular choice of the chosen set in ISD. Thus, to keep the description as general as possible and easy to follow, in this section we only focus on a single row of L. Exact computations for these quantities are performed in Sects. 4 and 5. Furthermore, we only consider the probability that a chosen set T does not overlap with the support of the searched codeword. With this choice, we essentially capture the essence of all ISD algorithms. An analysis on a specific variant, with optimized parameters and requirements on the chosen set, might significantly improve the results of this section which, however, are already significant for the security of LEDAcrypt schemes.

Let $T \subseteq \{0, \cdots, n-1\}$ be a set of dimension k: for $a \sim \mathcal{U}_\omega$, we have

$$\Pr\left[T \cap \mathrm{S}(a) = \varnothing \,\middle|\, a \sim \mathcal{U}_\omega\right] = \frac{\binom{n-\omega}{k}}{\binom{n}{k}}.$$

Note that this probability does not depend on the particular choice of T, but just on its size. When a purely random QC-MDPC code is used, as in BIKE [22], the first row of the secret parity-check matrix is well modeled as a random sample from $\mathcal{U}_\omega$. The previous probability can also be described as the ratio between the number of n-uples of weight ω whose support is disjoint with T, and that of all possible samples from $\mathcal{U}_\omega$; in schemes such as BIKE, this also corresponds to the probability that a secret key satisfies the requirement on an arbitrary set T.

As we show in the remainder of this section, in LEDAcrypt such a fraction can actually be made significantly larger, when T is properly chosen. To each choice, we can then associate a family of *weak keys*, that is, secret keys for which the corresponding first row of L does not overlap with T. We formally define the notion of weak keys in the following.

Definition 3.1. *Let $\mathcal{K}$ be the public key space of LEDAcrypt with parameters n_0, p, d_v, m_0, m_1. Let $T \subseteq \{0, \cdots, n_0 p - 1\}$ of cardinality $n - k = p$ and $\mathcal{W} \subseteq \mathcal{K}$ be the set of all public keys corresponding to secret keys $sk = (H, Q)$ such that the first row in the corresponding $L = HQ$ has support that is disjoint with T. Finally, we define $\omega = n_0(m_0 + m_1)d_v$ and $\mathcal{U}_\omega$ as the uniform distribution of $(n_0 p)$-tuples with weight ω. Then, we say that $\mathcal{W}$ is a set of weak-keys if*

$$\Pr\left[pk \in \mathcal{W}|(sk, pk) \leftarrow \mathsf{KeyGen}()\right] \gg \Pr\left[T \cap \mathrm{S}(a) = \varnothing | a \sim \mathcal{U}_\omega\right] = \frac{\binom{n_0 p - \omega}{p}}{\binom{n_0 p}{p}}.$$

Roughly speaking, we have a family of weak keys when, for a specific set choice, the number of keys meeting the requirement on the support is significantly larger than the one that we would have for the uniform case. Indeed, for all such keys, we will have a strongly bias in the matrix L, since null positions can be guessed with high probability; as we describe in Sects. 4 and 5, this fact opens up strong attacks against very large portions of keys.

3.1   Preliminary Considerations on Sparse Polynomials Multiplications

We now recall some basic fact about polynomial multiplication in the rings $\mathbb{F}_2[x]/\langle x^p + 1\rangle$ and $\mathbb{Z}[x]/\langle x^p - 1\rangle$, which will be useful for our treatment. Let $a, b \in \mathbb{F}_2[x]/\langle x^p + 1\rangle$ and $c = ab$; we then have

$$c_i = \bigoplus_{z=0}^{p-1} a_z b_{z'}, \quad z' = i - z \mod p,$$

where the operator $\bigoplus$ highlights the fact that the sum is performed over $\mathbb{F}_2$. Taking into account antisupports, we can rewrite the previous equation as

$$c_i = \bigoplus_{\substack{z \notin \bar{\mathrm{S}}(a) \\ z' = i - z \mod p, \ z' \notin \bar{\mathrm{S}}(b)}}^{p-1} a_z b_{z'}. \tag{1}$$

Let $N(a, b, i)$ denote the set of terms that contribute to the sum in Eq. (1), i.e.

$$N(a, b, i) = \left\{z \text{ s.t. } z \notin \bar{\mathrm{S}}(a) \text{ and } i - z \mod p \notin \bar{\mathrm{S}}(b)\right\}.$$

We now denote with $\tilde{a}$ and $\tilde{b}$ the polynomials obtained by lifting a and b over $\mathbb{Z}[x]/\langle x^p - 1\rangle$ i.e., by mapping the coefficients of a and b into $\{0, 1\} \subset \mathbb{Z}$. Let $\tilde{c} =$

$\tilde{a}\tilde{b}$: we straightforwardly have that $c \equiv \tilde{c} \mod 2$, $|N(a,b,i)| = \tilde{c}_i$ and $\sum_{i=0}^{p-1} \tilde{c}_i = \mathrm{wt}(a) \cdot \mathrm{wt}(b)$. Let $a' \in \mathbb{Z}[x]/\langle x^p + 1\rangle$ with coefficients in $\{0,1\}$, such that $S(a') \supseteq S(a)$, i.e., such that its support contains that of a (or, in another words, such that its antisupport is contained in that of a); an analogous definition holds for b'. Indeed, we can write $a' = \tilde{a} + s_a$, where $s_a \in \mathbb{Z}[x]/\langle x^p + 1\rangle$ and whose i-th coefficient is equal to 0 if $a'_i = a_i$, and equal to 1 otherwise; with analogous notation, we can write $b' = \tilde{b} + s_b$. Then

$$c' = a'b' = (\tilde{a} + s_a)(\tilde{b} + s_b) = \tilde{a}\tilde{b} + s_a\tilde{b} + s_b\tilde{a} + s_a s_b = \tilde{c} + s_a\tilde{b} + s_b\tilde{a} + s_a s_b.$$

Since $s_a\tilde{b}$, $s_b\tilde{a}$ and $s_a s_b$ have all non-negative coefficients, we have

$$c'_i \geq \tilde{c}_i = |N(a,b,i)| \geq 0, \forall i \in \{0, \cdots, p-1\}. \tag{2}$$

We now derive some properties that link the coefficients of c' to those of c; as we show, knowing portions of the antisupports of a and b is enough to gather information about the coefficients in their product.

Lemma 3.2. *Let $a, b \in \mathbb{F}_2[x]/\langle x^p + 1\rangle$, and $J_a, J_b \subseteq \{0, \cdots, p-1\}$ such that $J_a \supseteq S(a)$ and $J_b \supseteq S(b)$. Let $a', b' \in \mathbb{Z}[x]/\langle x^p - 1\rangle$ be the polynomials whose coefficients are null, except for those indexed by J_a and J_b, respectively, which are set as 1. Let $c = ab \in \mathbb{F}_2[x]/\langle x^p + 1\rangle$ and $c' = a'b' \in \mathbb{Z}[x]/\langle x^p - 1\rangle$; then*

$$c'_i = 0 \implies c_i = 0.$$

Proof. The result immediately follows from (2) by considering that if $c'_i = 0$ then necessarily $|N(a,b,i)| = 0$ and, subsequently, $c_i = 0$.   □

When the weight of $c = ab$ is maximum, i.e., equal to $\mathrm{wt}(a) \cdot \mathrm{wt}(b)$, the probability to have null coefficients in c_i can be related to the coefficients in c'_i; in analogous way, we can also derive the probability that several bits are simultaneously null. These relations are formalized in the following Lemma.

Lemma 3.3. *Let $a, b \in \mathbb{F}_2[x]/\langle x^p + 1\rangle$, with respective weights ω_a and ω_b, such that $\omega = \omega_a \omega_b \leq p$, and $c = ab$ has weight ω. Let $J_a, J_b \subseteq \{0, \cdots, p-1\}$ such that $J_a \supseteq S(a)$ and $J_b \supseteq S(b)$. Let $a', b' \in \mathbb{Z}[x]/\langle x^p - 1\rangle$ be the polynomials whose coefficients are null, except for those indexed by J_a and J_b, respectively, which are set as 1; finally, let $M = |J_a| \cdot |J_b|$.*

i) Let c'_i be the i-th coefficient of $c' = a'b'$; then

$$\Pr[c_i = 0 | c'_i] = \gamma(M, \omega, c'_i) = \left(1 + \omega \cdot \frac{c'_i}{M + 1 - \omega - c'_i}\right)^{-1}.$$

ii) For $V = \{v_0, \cdots, v_{t-1}\} \subseteq \{0, \cdots, p-1\}$, we have

$$\Pr[\mathrm{wt}(c|_V) = 0 \mid c'] = \zeta(V, c', \omega) = \prod_{\ell=0}^{t-1} \gamma\left(M - \sum_{j=0}^{\ell-1} c'_{v_j}, \omega, c'_{v_\ell}\right).$$

Proof. The results follow from a combinatorial argument. See [3], Appendix B.3 for details.   □

3.2   Identifying Families of Weak Keys

We are now ready to use the results presented in the previous section to describe how, in LEDAcrypt, families of weak keys as in Definition 3.1 can be identified. We base our strategy on the results of Lemmas 3.2 and 3.3. Briefly, we guess "containers" for each polynomial in the secret key, i.e., polynomials over $\mathbb{Z}[x]/\langle x^p - 1 \rangle$ whose support contains that of the corresponding polynomials in $\mathbb{F}_2[x]/\langle x^p + 1 \rangle$. We then combine such containers, to find positions that, with high probability, do not point at set coefficient in the polynomials in $L = HQ$. Assuming that the initial choice for the containers is right, we can then use the results of Lemmas 3.2 and 3.3 to determine such positions. For the sake of simplicity, and without loss of generality, we describe our ideas for the practical case of $n_0 = 2$.

Operatively, to build a set T defining an eventual set of weak keys, we rely on the following procedure.

1. Consider sets J_{H_i} such that $J_{H_i} \supseteq \mathrm{S}(H_i)$, for $i = 0, 1$; the cardinality of J_{H_i} is denoted as B_{H_i}. In analogous way, define sets $J_{Q_{i,j}}$, for $i = 0, 1$ and $j = 0, 1$, with cardinalities $B_{Q_{i,j}}$.
2. To each set J_{H_i}, associate a polynomial $H_i' \in \mathbb{Z}[x]/\langle x^p - 1 \rangle$, taking values in $\{0, 1\}$ and whose support corresponds to J_{H_i}; in analogous way, construct polynomials $J_{Q_{i,j}}$ from the sets $J_{Q_{i,j}}$. Compute

$$L_{i,j}' = H_j' Q_{j,i}' \in \mathbb{Z}[x]/\langle x^p - 1 \rangle, \quad (i,j) \in \{0,1\}^2.$$

3. Compute

$$L_i' = L_{i,0}' + L_{i,1}' = H_0' Q_{0,i}' + H_1' Q_{1,i}' \in \mathbb{Z}[x]/\langle x^p - 1 \rangle.$$

Let π_i, with $i = 0, 1$, be a permutation such that the coefficients of $\pi_i(L_i')$ are in non decreasing order. Group the first $\lfloor \frac{p}{2} \rfloor$ entries of π_0 in a set T_0, and the first $\lceil \frac{p}{2} \rceil$ ones of π_1 in a set T_1. Define T as $T = T_0 \cup \{p + \ell | \ell \in T_1\}$.

A visual representation of the above constructive method to search for weak keys is described in [3], Appendix C.

Essentially, our proposed procedure to find families of weak keys starts from the sets J_{H_i} and $J_{Q_{i,j}}$, which we think of as "containers" for the secret key, i.e., sets containing the support of the corresponding polynomial in the secret key. Their products yield polynomials $L_{i,j}'$, which are containers for the products $H_i Q_{j,i}$. Because of the maximum weight requirement in LEDAcrypt key generation, each $L_{i,j}'$ matches the hypothesis required by the Lemma 3.3: the lowest entries in $L_{i,j}'$ correspond to the coefficients that, with the highest probability, are null in $H_i' Q_{j,i}'$. We remark that, because of Lemma 3.2, a null coefficient in $L_{i,j}'$ means that the corresponding coefficients in $H_j Q_{j,i}$ must be null. Finally, we need to combine the coefficients of the polynomials $L_{i,j}'$, to identify positions that are very likely to be null in each L_i. The approach we consider consists in choosing the positions that correspond to coefficients with minimum values in the sums $L_{i,0}' + L_{i,1}'$. This simple criterion is likely to be not optimal, but allows to avoid cumbersome notation and computations; furthermore, as we show next, it already detects significantly large families of weak keys.

The number of secret keys that meet the requirements on T, i.e., keys leading to polynomials L_0 and L_1 that do not overlap with the chosen sets T_0 and T_1, respectively, clearly depends on the particular choice for the containers. In the remainder of this section, we describe how such a quantity can be estimated. For the sake of simplicity, we analyze the case in which the starting sets for the containers have constant size, i.e., $B_{H_i} = B_H$ and $B_{Q_{i,j}} = B_Q$, for all i and j; furthermore, we choose $J_{H_0} = J_{H_1}$, $J_{Q_{0,0}} = J_{Q_{1,1}}$ and $J_{Q_{1,0}} = J_{Q_{0,1}}$.

First of all, let $\mathcal{J}$ be the set of secret keys whose polynomials are contained in the sets J_{H_i} and $J_{Q_{i,j}}$; the cardinality of this set can be estimated as

$$|\mathcal{J}| = \eta\left(\binom{B_H}{d_v}\binom{B_Q}{m_0}\binom{B_Q}{m_1}\right)^2,$$

where η is the acceptance ratio in key generation, i.e., the probability that a random choice of matrices H and Q leads to a matrix L with full weight.

We now estimate the number of keys in $\mathcal{J}$ that produce polynomials L_0 and L_1 corresponding to a correct choice for T_0 and T_1, i.e., such that their supports are disjoint with T_0 and T_1, respectively. For each product $H_i Q_{i,j}$, we know i) that it has full weight, not larger than p, and ii) that sets J_{H_i}, $J_{Q_{i,j}}$ are containers for H_i and $Q_{i,j}$, respectively. Then, Lemma 3.3 can be used to estimate the portion of valid keys. For instance, we consider the polynomial $L_0 = H_0 Q_{0,0} + H_1 Q_{1,0}$: the coefficients that are indexed by T_0 will be null when both the supports of $H_0 Q_{0,0}$ and $H_1 Q_{1,0}$ are disjoint with T_0. If we neglect the fact that these two products are actually correlated (because of the full weight requirement on L_0), then the probability that L_0 does not overlap with T_0, which we denote as $\Pr[\mathtt{null}(T_0)]$, is obtained as

$$\Pr[\mathtt{null}(T_0)] = \zeta(T_0, L'_{0,0}, m_0 d_v) \cdot \zeta(T_0, L'_{0,1}, m_1 d_v),$$

where ζ is defined in Lemma 3.3. The above quantity can then be used to estimate the fraction of keys in $\mathcal{J}$ for which the support of L_0 does not overlap with T_0; we remark that, as highlighted by the above formula, this quantity strongly depends on the choices on J_{H_0}, J_{H_1}, $J_{Q_{0,0}}$, $J_{Q_{1,0}}$.

With the same reasoning, and with analogous notation, we compute $\Pr[\mathtt{null}(T_1)]$; because of the simplifying restrictions on $J_{Q_{i,j}}$, this probability is equal to $\Pr[\mathtt{null}(T_0)]$.

Then, if we neglect the correlation between L_0 and L_1 (since H_0 and H_1 are involved in the computation of both polynomials), the probability that a random key from $\mathcal{J}$ is associated to a valid L, i.e., that it leads to polynomials L_0 and L_1 that respectively do not overlap with T_0 and T_1, can be estimated as

$$\Pr[\mathtt{null}(T)] = \Pr[\mathtt{null}(T_0)] \cdot \Pr[\mathtt{null}(T_1)]$$
$$= \left(\Pr[\mathtt{null}(T_0)]\right)^2$$
$$= \left(\zeta(T_0, L'_{0,0}, m_0 d_v) \cdot \zeta(T_0, L'_{0,1}, m_1 d_v)\right)^2.$$

Thus we conclude that the number of keys whose polynomials are contained by the chosen sets, and such that the corresponding L does not overlap with T, can be estimated as $|\mathcal{J}| \cdot \Pr[\texttt{null}(T)]$.

Then, for the set of secret keys where T does not intercept the first row of L, which we denote with $\mathcal{W}$, we have

$$|\mathcal{W}| \geq |\mathcal{J}| \cdot \Pr[\texttt{null}(T)]. \tag{3}$$

The inequality comes from the fact the right term in the above formula only counts keys with polynomials contained by the initially chosen sets; even if such property is not satisfied, it may still happen that the resulting L does not overlap with T (thus, we are underestimating the cardinality of $\mathcal{W}$).

3.3   Results

In this section we provide practical examples on choices for containing sets, leading to actual families of weak keys. To this end, we need to define clear criteria on how the sets J_{H_i} and $J_{Q_{i,j}}$ can be selected. For the sake of simplicity, we restrict our attention to the cases $J_{H_0} = J_{H_1} = J_H$ and $J_{Q_{0.0}} = J_{Q_{0.1}} = J_{Q_{1.0}} = J_{Q_{1.1}} = J_Q$. We here consider two different strategies to pick these sets.

– *Type I*: for $i = 0, 1$, $\delta \in \{0, \cdots, p-1\}$ and $t \in \{1, \cdots, p-1\}$, we choose

$$J_H = \{\ell t \mod p \,|\, 0 \leq \ell \leq B_H - 1\},$$
$$J_Q = \{\delta + \ell t \mod p \,|\, 0 \leq \ell \leq B_Q - 1\}.$$

– *Type II*: for $i = 0, 1$, we choose $J_{H_0} = J_{H_1}$ as the union of disjoint sets, formed by contiguous positions. Analogous choice is adopted for J_Q.

To provide numerical evidences for our analysis, in Fig. 1 we compare the simulated values of $\Pr[\texttt{null}(T)]$ with the ones obtained with theoretical expression, for parameters of practical interest and for some Types I and II choices. The simulated probabilities have been obtained by generating random secret keys from $\mathcal{J}$ and, as our results show, are well approximated by the theoretical expression. This shows that Eq. 3 provides a good estimate for the fraction of keys in $\mathcal{J}$ that meet the requirement on the corresponding set T.

Tables 2, 3 display results testing various weak key families of Type I and II, for two different LEDAcrypt parameters sets. According to the reasoning in the previous section, the values reported in the last column can be considered as a rough (and likely conservative) estimate for the probability that a random key belongs to the corresponding set $\mathcal{W}$. Our results show that the identified families of keys meet Definition 3.1, so can actually be considered weak.

Remark 1. The results we have shown in this section only represent a qualitative evidence of the existence of families of weak keys in LEDAcrypt. There may exist many more families of weak keys, having a complete different structure from the ones we have studied. Additionally, the parameters we have considered for types

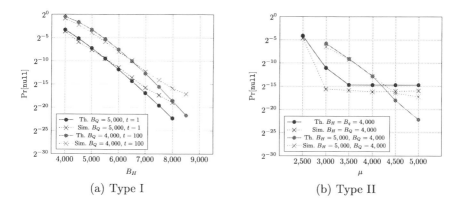

(a) Type I   (b) Type II

Fig. 1. Comparison between simulated and theoretical values for Pr[null], for $p = 14939$, $d_v = 11$, $m_0 = 4$, $m_1 = 3$. The values reported in Figure (a) are all referred to the case $\delta = 0$. In Figure (b), the blue curves correspond to the choice $J_H = J_Q = \{0, \cdots, 1999\} \cup \{\mu, \cdots, \mu + 1999\}$, while the red curves correspond to $J_H = \{0, \cdots, 2499\} \cup \{\mu, \cdots, \mu + 2499\}$ and $J_Q = \{0, \cdots, 3999\}$.

Table 2. Fraction of weak keys, for LEDAcrypt instances designed for 128-bit security, with parameters $n_0 = 2$, $p = 14939$, $d_v = 11$, $m_0 = 4$, $m_1 = 3$, for which $\eta \approx 0.7090$. For this parameter set, probability of randomly guessing a null set of dimension p, in a vector of length $2p$ and weight $2(m_0 + m_1)d_v$, is $2^{-154.57}$.

Type	Family Parameters	$\frac{|\mathcal{J}| \cdot \Pr[\mathtt{null}(T)]}{|\mathcal{K}|}$
I	$B_H = B_Q = 7470$ $\delta = 0, t = 1$	$2^{-99.88}$
I	$B_H = 8000, B_Q = 4000$ $\delta = 2000, t = 1$	$2^{-85.25}$
I	$B_H = 8500, B_Q = 4000$ $\delta = 0, t = 127$	$2^{-90.23}$
II	$J_H = \{0, \cdots, 4499\} \cup \{7000, \cdots, 11499\}$ $J_Q = \{0, \cdots, 2499\} \cup \{8000, \cdots, 10499\}$	$2^{-101.53}$

I and II may not be the optimal ones, but already identify families of weak keys. In the next sections we provide a detailed analysis for families of keys of type I and II, and furthermore specify the actual complexity of a full cryptanalysis exploiting such a key structure.

Table 3. Fraction of weak keys, for LEDAcrypt instances designed for 256-bit security, with parameters $n_0 = 2$, $p = 36877$, $d_v = 11$, $m_0 = 7$, $m_1 = 6$, for which $\eta \approx 0.614$. For this parameter set, probability of randomly guessing a null set of dimension p, in a vector of length $2p$ and weight $2(m_0 + m_1)d_v$, is $2^{-286.80}$.

Type	Family Parameters	$\frac{|\mathcal{J}| \cdot \Pr[\text{null}(T)]}{|\mathcal{K}|}$
I	$B_H = 18000, B_Q = 9000$ $\delta = 9000, t = 1$	$2^{-125.18}$
I	$B_H = 24000, B_Q = 12000$ $\delta = 0, t = 1$	$2^{-184.21}$
I	$B_H = 18000, B_Q = 9000$ $\delta = 0, t = 5$	$2^{-125.18}$
II	$J_H = \{0, \cdots, 20999\}$ $J_Q = \{0, \cdots, 3999\} \cup \{10000, \cdots, 13999\} \cup \{20000, \cdots, 23999\}$	$2^{-270.30}$

4 Explicit Attack on the Weakest Class of Keys

In the previous section we described how the product structure in LEDAcrypt leads to an highly biased distribution in set positions in L. As we have hinted, this property may be exploited to improve cryptanalysis techniques based on ISD algorithms. In this section, we present an attack against a class of weak keys in LEDAcrypt's design. We begin by identifying what appear to be the weakest class of keys (though large enough in number to constitute a serious, practical problem for LEDAcrypt). It is easily seen that the class of keys we consider in this section corresponds to a particular case of type I, introduced in Sect. 3.3. We proceed to provide a simple, single-iteration ISD algorithm to recover these keys, then analyze the fraction of all of LEDAcrypt's keys that would be recovered by this attack. Afterward, we show how to extend the ISD algorithm to more than one iteration, so as to enlarge the set of keys recovered by a similar enough of effort per key. We conclude by considering the effect of advanced ISD algorithms on the attack as well as the relationship between the rejection sampling step in LEDAcrypt's KeyGen and our restriction to attacking a subspace of the total key space.

4.1 Attacking an Example (sub)class of Ultra-Weak Keys

The simplest and, where it works, most powerful version of the attack dramatically speeds up ISD for a class of ultra-weak keys chosen under parameter sets where $n_0 = 2$. One example (sub)class of ultra-weak keys are those keys where the polynomials L_0 and L_1 are of degree at most $\frac{p}{2}$. Such keys can be found by a single iteration of a very simple ISD algorithm. We describe this simple attack as follows.

The attacker chooses the information set to consist of the last $\frac{p-1}{2}$ columns of the first block of M and the last $\frac{p+1}{2}$ columns of the second block. If the key being attacked is one of these weak keys, the attacker can correctly guess the top row of L as being identically zero within the information set and linearly solve for the nonzero linear combination of the rows of M meeting this condition. The cost of the attack is one iteration of an ISD algorithm.

A sufficient condition for this class of weak key to occur is for the polynomials H_0, H_1, $Q_{0,0}$, $Q_{0,1}$, $Q_{1,0}$, and $Q_{1,1}$ to have degree no more than $\frac{p}{4}$. Since each of the $2m_0 + 2m_1 + 2d_v$ nonzero coefficients of these polynomials has a $\frac{1}{4}$ probability of being chosen with degree less than $\frac{p}{4}$, these weak keys represent at least 1 part in $4^{2m_0+2m_1+2d_v}$ of the key space.

4.2   Enumerating Ultra-Weak Keys for a Single Information Set

In fact, there are significantly more weak keys than this that can be recovered by the basic, one-iteration ISD algorithm using the information set described above. Intuitively, this is for two reasons:

1. **Equivalent keys:** There are p^2 private keys, not of this same, basic form, which nonetheless produce the same public key.
2. **Different degree constraints:** The support of the top row of L will also fall entirely outside the information set if the degree of H_0 is less than $\frac{p}{4} - \delta$ and the degrees of $Q_{0,0}$ and $Q_{0,1}$ are both less than $\frac{p}{4} + \delta$ for any $\delta \in \mathbb{Z}$ such that $-\frac{p}{4} < \delta < \frac{p}{4}$. Likewise for H_1 and $Q_{1,0}$ and $Q_{1,1}$, for a total of p keys.

Concretely, we derive the number of distinct private keys that are recovered by the one-iteration ISD algorithm in the following theorem.

Remark 2. There are p columns of each block of M. For the sake of simplicity, instead of referring to pairs of $\frac{p-1}{2}$ and $\frac{p+1}{2}$ columns, we instead use $\frac{p}{2}$ for both cases. This has a negligible effect on our results.

Theorem 4.1. *The number of distinct private keys that can be found in a single iteration of the decoding algorithm described above (where the information set is chosen to consist of the last $\frac{p}{2}$ columns of each block of M) is*

$$
\begin{aligned}
p^3 \cdot & \sum_{A_0=d_v-1}^{\frac{p}{2}} \sum_{A_1=d_v-1}^{\frac{p}{2}} \left(\binom{A_0-1}{d_v-2}\binom{A_1-1}{d_v-2} \right. \\
& \cdot \left(\binom{\frac{p}{2}-A_0-2}{m_0-1}\binom{\frac{p}{2}-A_0-1}{m_1}\binom{\frac{p}{2}-A_1-1}{m_1}\binom{\frac{p}{2}-A_1-1}{m_0} \right. \\
& + \binom{\frac{p}{2}-A_0-1}{m_0}\binom{\frac{p}{2}-A_0-2}{m_1-1}\binom{\frac{p}{2}-A_1-1}{m_1}\binom{\frac{p}{2}-A_1-1}{m_0} \\
& + \binom{\frac{p}{2}-A_0-1}{m_0}\binom{\frac{p}{2}-A_0-1}{m_1}\binom{\frac{p}{2}-A_1-2}{m_1-1}\binom{\frac{p}{2}-A_1-1}{m_0} \\
& + \left. \left. \binom{\frac{p}{2}-A_0-1}{m_0}\binom{\frac{p}{2}-A_0-1}{m_1}\binom{\frac{p}{2}-A_1-1}{m_1}\binom{\frac{p}{2}-A_1-2}{m_0-1} \right) \right) \\
& \cdot \left(1 - O\left(\frac{m}{p}\right) \right).
\end{aligned}
\tag{4}
$$

Proof. We count the number of ultra-weak keys as follows. By assumption, all nonzero bits in each block of an ultra-weak key are contained in some consecutive stretch of size $\leq \frac{p}{2}$. Thus these ultra-weak keys contain a stretch of at least $\frac{p}{2}$ zero bits. This property applies directly to the polynomials $H_0 Q_{0,0} + H_1 Q_{1,0}$ and $H_0 Q_{0,1} + H_1 Q_{1,1}$, and must also hold for H_0 and H_1. We index the number of ultra-weak keys according to the first nonzero coefficient of these polynomials after the stretch of zero bits in cyclic ordering.

We begin by considering H, Q though not requiring HQ to have full weight. We are using an information set consisting of the same columns for both $H_0 Q_{0,0} + H_1 Q_{1,0}$ and $H_0 Q_{0,1} + H_1 Q_{1,1}$. Therefore we count according the first nonzero bit of the sum $H_0 Q_{0,0} + H_1 Q_{1,0} + H_0 Q_{0,1} + H_1 Q_{1,1}$. Let l be the location of the first nonzero bit of this sum.

Let j_0, j_1 be the locations of the first nonzero bit of H_0, H_1, respectively. Suppose that the nonzero bits of H_0, H_1 are located within a block of length A_0, A_1, respectively.

By LEDAcrypt's design, $d_v \leq A_i, i \in \{0, 1\}$ and by assumption on the chosen information set, $A_i \leq \frac{p}{2}, i \in \{0, 1\}$. Once j_0 is fixed, there are $\sum_{A_0 = d_v - 1}^{\frac{p}{2}} \binom{A_0 - 1}{d_v - 2}$ ways to arrange the remaining bits of H_0. Thus there are

$$\sum_{j_0 = 1}^{p-1} \sum_{A_0 = d_v - 1}^{\frac{p}{2}} \binom{A_0 - 1}{d_v - 2} \sum_{j_1 = 1}^{p-1} \sum_{A_1 = d_v - 1}^{\frac{p}{2}} \binom{A_1 - 1}{d_v - 2} \tag{5}$$

many bit arrangements of H_0, H_1.

Once j_0, j_1 are fixed, there are four blocks of Q which may influence the location l. We compute the probability that only one block of Q may influence l at a time.

If l is influenced by $Q_{0,0}$, there are $\binom{\frac{p}{2} - A_0 - 2}{m_0 - 1}$ ways the remaining bits of $Q_{0,0}$ can fall, $\binom{\frac{p}{2} - A_0 - 1}{m_1}$ arrangements of the bits of $Q_{0,1}$, $\binom{\frac{p}{2} - A_1 - 1}{m_1}$ arrangements of the bits of $Q_{1,0}$, and $\binom{\frac{p}{2} - A_1 - 1}{m_0}$ arrangements of the bits of $Q_{1,1}$. If l is influenced by $Q_{0,1}$, there are $\binom{\frac{p}{2} - A_0 - 2}{m_0}$ arrangements of the bits of $Q_{0,0}$, $\binom{\frac{p}{2} - A_0 - 1}{m_1 - 1}$ ways the remaining bits of $Q_{0,1}$ can fall, $\binom{\frac{p}{2} - A_1 - 1}{m_1}$ arrangements of the bits of $Q_{1,0}$, and $\binom{\frac{p}{2} - A_1 - 1}{m_0}$ arrangements of the bits of $Q_{1,1}$. Similar estimates hold for $Q_{1,0}$, or $Q_{1,1}$.

We sum over the l locations considering each of the blocks of Q and their respective weights. Then the overall sum is

$$\sum_{j_0=0}^{p-1} \sum_{A_0=d_v-1}^{\frac{p}{2}} \binom{A_0-1}{d_v-2} \sum_{j_1=0}^{p-1} \sum_{A_1=d_v-1}^{\frac{p}{2}} \binom{A_1-1}{d_v-2}$$

$$\cdot \sum_{l=0}^{p-1} \left(\left(\binom{\frac{p}{2}-A_0-2}{m_0-1} \binom{\frac{p}{2}-A_0-1}{m_1} \binom{\frac{p}{2}-A_1-1}{m_1} \binom{\frac{p}{2}-A_1-1}{m_0} \right) \right.$$

$$+ \binom{\frac{p}{2}-A_0-1}{m_0} \binom{\frac{p}{2}-A_0-2}{m_1-1} \binom{\frac{p}{2}-A_1-1}{m_1} \binom{\frac{p}{2}-A_1-1}{m_0} \tag{6}$$

$$+ \binom{\frac{p}{2}-A_0-1}{m_0} \binom{\frac{p}{2}-A_0-1}{m_1} \binom{\frac{p}{2}-A_1-2}{m_1-1} \binom{\frac{p}{2}-A_1-1}{m_0}$$

$$+ \left. \binom{\frac{p}{2}-A_0-1}{m_0} \binom{\frac{p}{2}-A_0-1}{m_1} \binom{\frac{p}{2}-A_1-1}{m_1} \binom{\frac{p}{2}-A_1-2}{m_0-1} \right) \right)$$

$$\cdot \left(1 - O\left(\frac{m}{p}\right) \right).$$

Failure to impose full weight requirements on HQ introduces double-counting. This occurs when more than one block of Q influences l, though the probability of this event will not exceed $O(\frac{m}{p})$. The constant sums yield the factor of p^3. □

We can now estimate the percentage of these recovered, ultra-weak keys out of all possible keys.

Theorem 4.2. *Let* $m = m_0 + m_1, x = \frac{A_0}{p}, y = \frac{A_1}{p}$. *Out of* $\binom{p}{d_v}^2 \binom{p}{m_0}^2 \binom{p}{m_1}^2$ *possible keys, we estimate the percentage of ultra-weak keys found in a single iteration of the decoding algorithm above as*

$$d_v^{\,2}(d_v-1)^2 m \int_{x=0}^{\frac{1}{2}} \int_{y=0}^{\frac{1}{2}} (xy)^{d_v-2} \left(\left(\frac{1}{2}-x\right)\left(\frac{1}{2}-y\right) \right)^m \left(\frac{1}{\frac{1}{2}-x} + \frac{1}{\frac{1}{2}-y} \right) dy dx.$$

Proof. Note that the lines 2–5 of (4) are approximately

$$\binom{\frac{p}{2}-A_0}{m_0} \binom{\frac{p}{2}-A_0}{m_1} \binom{\frac{p}{2}-A_1}{m_1} \binom{\frac{p}{2}-A_1}{m_0} \left(\frac{m_0+m_1}{\frac{p}{2}-A_1} + \frac{m_0+m_1}{\frac{p}{2}-A_0} \right). \tag{7}$$

For $b, c \in \{0,1\}$,

$$\binom{\frac{p}{2}-A_b}{m_c} \approx \binom{p}{m_c} \left(\frac{1}{2} - \frac{A_b}{p}\right)^{m_c} \tag{8}$$

and

$$\binom{A_b-1}{d_v-2} \approx \binom{p}{d_v-2} \left(\frac{A_b}{p}\right)^{d_v-2} \tag{9}$$

since p is much larger than m_0, m_1, d_v. We rewrite (4) using the approximations of expressions (7, 8) as

$$p^3 \sum_{A_0=d_v-1}^{\frac{p}{2}} \binom{A_0-1}{d_v-2} \sum_{A_1=d_v-1}^{\frac{p}{2}} \binom{A_1-1}{d_v-2} \binom{p}{m_0}^2 \left(\frac{1}{2}-\frac{A_0}{p}\right)^{m_0+m_1} \tag{10}$$

$$\binom{p}{m_1}^2 \left(\frac{1}{2}-\frac{A_1}{p}\right)^{m_0+m_1} \left(\frac{m_0+m_1}{\frac{p}{2}-A_1}+\frac{m_0+m_1}{\frac{p}{2}-A_0}\right). \tag{11}$$

Applying approximation (9) further reduces expression (10) to

$$p^3 \binom{p}{m_0}^2 \binom{p}{m_1}^2 \binom{p}{d_v-2}^2 \sum_{A_0=d_v-1}^{\frac{p}{2}} \left(\frac{A_0}{p}\right)^{d_v-2} \sum_{A_1=d_v-1}^{\frac{p}{2}} \left(\frac{A_1}{p}\right)^{d_v-2}$$

$$\left(\frac{1}{2}-\frac{A_0}{p}\right)^{m_0+m_1} \left(\frac{1}{2}-\frac{A_1}{p}\right)^{m_0+m_1} \left(\frac{m_0+m_1}{\frac{p}{2}-A_1}+\frac{m_0+m_1}{\frac{p}{2}-A_0}\right)$$

$$=p^2 \binom{p}{d_v-2}^2 \binom{p}{m_0}^2 \binom{p}{m_1}^2 m \sum_{A_0=d_v-1}^{\frac{p}{2}} \sum_{A_1=d_v-1}^{\frac{p}{2}} \left(\frac{A_0}{p}\frac{A_1}{p}\right)^{d_v-2} \left(\frac{1}{2}-\frac{A_0}{p}\right)^m$$

$$\left(\frac{1}{2}-\frac{A_1}{p}\right)^m \left(\frac{1}{\frac{1}{2}-\frac{A_0}{p}}+\frac{1}{\frac{1}{2}-\frac{A_1}{p}}\right).$$

Letting $x=\frac{A_0}{p}, y=\frac{A_1}{p}$, this is approximated by

$$p^2 \binom{p}{d_v}^2 \binom{p}{m_0}^2 \binom{p}{m_1}^2 m \frac{d_v^2(d_v-1)^2}{(p-d_v+2)^2(p-d_v+1)^2}$$

$$\cdot p^2 \int_{x=0}^{\frac{1}{2}} \int_{y=0}^{\frac{1}{2}} (xy)^{d_v-2} \left(\frac{1}{2}-x\right)^m \left(\frac{1}{2}-y\right)^m \left(\frac{1}{\frac{1}{2}-x}+\frac{1}{\frac{1}{2}-y}\right) dy dx.$$

Dividing by $\binom{p}{d_v}^2 \binom{p}{m_0}^2 \binom{p}{m_1}^2$, the result follows.   □

Evaluating this percentage with the claimed-256-bit ephemeral (CPA-secure) key parameters of LEDAcrypt—$d_v = 11, m = 13$—we determine that 1 in $2^{72.8}$ ephemeral keys are broken by one iteration of ISD. Similarly for the long-term (CCA-secure) key setting, we evaluate with the claimed 256-bit parameters—$d_v = 13, m = 13$—and conclude the number of long-term keys broken is 1 in $2^{80.6}$.

This result merely determines the number of keys that can be recovered given that the information set of both blocks of M is chosen to be the last $\frac{p}{2}$ columns.[2] In the following, we turn to demonstrating a class of additional information sets that are as effective as this one.

---

[2] For the reader, we point out that if, hypothetically, we had a sufficiently large number of *totally independent* information sets that were equally "rewarding" in recovering keys, this would straightforwardly imply $\approx 2^{72.8}$-time and $\approx 2^{80.6}$-time "full" attacks against LEDAcrypt's claimed-256-bit parameters rather than weak-key attacks.

Remark 3. We remind the reader that instead of referring to the pairs of $\frac{p-1}{2}, \frac{p+1}{2}$ columns of blocks of M, we use $\frac{p}{2}$ in both cases. This has a negligible effect on our results.

4.3   Enumerating Ultra-Weak Keys for All Information Sets

Now we will demonstrate a multi-iteration ISD attack that is effective against the class of all ultra-weak keys. To set up the discussion, we begin by highlighting two, further "degrees of freedom," which will allow us to find additional, relevant information sets to guess:

1. **Changing the ring representation:** Contiguity of indices depends on the choice of ring representation. The large family of ring isomorphisms on $\mathbb{Z}[x]/\langle x^p - 1 \rangle$ given by $f(x) \to f(x^t)$ for $t \in [0, p]$ preserves Hamming weight. For example, we can use the family of polynomials

$$H_i' = Q_{i,j}' = 1 + x^t + x^{2t} + \ldots + x^{\lfloor \frac{p}{4} \rfloor t}$$

   in this attack, since there exists one t such that H_i' has consecutive nonzero coefficients. Choices of $t \in \{1, \ldots, \frac{p-1}{2}\}$ yield independent information sets (noting that choices of t and $-t$ mod p yield equivalent information sets).

2. **Changing the relative offset of the two consecutive blocks:** We can also change the beginning index of the consecutive blocks produced within L_0' or L_1' (by modifying the beginning indices of H_i' and $Q_{i,j}'$ to suit). Note that shifting both L_0' and L_1' by the same offset will recover equivalent keys. However, if we fix the beginning index of L_0' and allow the beginning index of L_1' to vary, we can find more, mostly independent information sets in order to recover more, distinct keys. The exact calculation of how far one should shift L_1''s indices for a practically effective attack is somewhat complex; we perform this analysis below in the remainder of this subsection.

Recall that in the prior 1-iteration attack, we considered *one* example class of ultra-weak keys – namely, those keys where the polynomials L_0 and L_1 are of degree at most $\frac{p}{2}$. Here, we will now take a broader view on the weakest-possible keys.

Definition 4.3. *We define the* **class of ultra-weak keys** *to be those where, in some ring representation, both* $H_0 Q_{0,0} + H_1 Q_{1,0}$ *and* $H_0 Q_{0,1} + H_1 Q_{1,1}$ *have nonzero coefficients that lie within a block of* $\frac{p-1}{2}$*-many consecutive (modulo p) degrees.*

Our goal will be now to find a multi-iteration ISD algorithm—by estimating how far to shift the offset of L_1' per iteration—that recovers as much of the class of ultra-weak keys as possible without "overly wasting" the attacker's computational budget. Toward this end, recall that we have a good estimate in Theorem 4.2 of the fraction of keys $(2^{-72.8}, \text{resp. } 2^{-80.6})$ recovered by the best-case, single iteration of our ISD algorithm. In what follows, we will first calculate the fraction of ultra-weak keys as a part of the total key space.

Let 2^{-X} be the fraction of all keys recovered by the best-case, single itera-tion of our previous ISD algorithm. Let 2^{-Y} be the fraction of ultra-weak keys among all keys. On the assumption that every ring representation leads to inde-pendent information sets (chosen uniformly for each invocation of ISD) and on the assumption that independence of ISD key-recovery is maximized by shifting "as far as possible," we will compute an estimate of the number of index-shifts that should be performed by the optimal ultra-weak-key attacker as $2^Z = 2^{X-Y}$. Beyond 2^Z shifts per guess (but not until), the attacker should begin to experi-ence diminishing returns in how many keys are recovered per shifted guess.

Therefore, given an index beginning at 1 out of p positions, the attacker will shift by $\frac{p(\frac{p-1}{2})}{2^Z}$ indices at each invocation (where the factor $\frac{p-1}{2}$ accounts for the effect of the different possible ring representations). By assumption, each such guess will be sufficiently independent to recover as many keys in expectation as the initial, best-guess case described by the 1-iteration algorithm. We note that additional, ultra-weak keys will certainly be obtained by performing more work—specifically by shifting less than $\frac{p(\frac{p-1}{2})}{2^Z}$ per guess—but necessarily at a reduced rate of reward per guess.

Toward this end, we now calculate the number of ultra-weak keys then the fraction of ultra-weak keys among all keys following the format of the previous calculation.

Theorem 4.4. *The total number of ultra-weak keys is*

$$\frac{p-1}{2}p^2 \sum_{A_0=d_v-1}^{\frac{p}{2}} \sum_{A_1=d_v-1}^{\frac{p}{2}} \binom{A_0-1}{d_v-2}\binom{A_1-1}{d_v-2} \tag{12}$$

$$\cdot \sum_{l_0=0}^{p-1} \left(\binom{\frac{p}{2}-A_0-1}{m_0-1}\binom{\frac{p}{2}-A_1-1}{m_1} + \binom{\frac{p}{2}-A_0-1}{m_0}\binom{\frac{p}{2}-A_1-1}{m_1-1} \right) \tag{13}$$

$$\cdot \sum_{l_1=0}^{p-1} \left(\binom{\frac{p}{2}-A_0-1}{m_0}\binom{\frac{p}{2}-A_1-1}{m_1-1} + \binom{\frac{p}{2}-A_0-1}{m_0-1}\binom{\frac{p}{2}-A_1-1}{m_0} \right). \tag{14}$$

Proof. The proof technique follows as in Theorem 4.1. Details are found in [3], B.1. □

Theorem 4.5. *Let* $m = m_0 + m_1, x = \frac{A_0}{p}, y = \frac{A_1}{p}$. *The fraction of ultra-weak keys out of all possible keys is*

$$\frac{p-1}{2}d_v^2(d_v-1)^2 \int_{x=0}^{\frac{1}{2}} \int_{y=0}^{\frac{1}{2}} x^{d_v-2}y^{d_v-2} \left(\frac{1}{2}-x\right)^m \left(\frac{1}{2}-y\right)^m$$
$$\left(\frac{m_0^2+m_1^2}{(\frac{1}{2}-x)(\frac{1}{2}-y)} + \frac{m_0m_1}{(\frac{1}{2}-x)^2} + \frac{m_0m_1}{(\frac{1}{2}-y)^2} \right) dydx.$$

Proof. Similar techniques apply. See [3], B.2 for details. □

We evaluate the fraction of weak keys using the claimed CPA-secure parameters $p = 36877, m = 13, d_v = 11$ and determine that 1 in $2^{54.1}$ ephemeral keys are broken. Evaluating with one of the CCA-secure parameter sets $p = 152267, m = 13, d_v = 13$, approximately 1 in $2^{59.7}$ long-term keys are broken.

Given the above, we can make an estimate as to the optimal shift-distance per ISD invocation as $\frac{36,877\binom{\frac{36,876}{2}}{2}}{2^{72.8-54.1}} \approx 1597 \approx 2^{10.6}$ for the ephemeral key parameters and $\frac{152,267\binom{\frac{152,266}{2}}{2}}{2^{80.6-59.7}} \approx 5925 \approx 2^{12.5}$ for the long-term key parameters.

The multi-iteration ISD algorithm against the class of ultra-weak keys, then, makes its first guess (except, one in each ring representation) as in the case of the 1-iteration ISD algorithm. It then shifts the relative offset of the two consecutive blocks by the values calculated above and repeats (again, in each ring representation).

This will not recover all ultra-weak keys, but it will recover a significant fraction of them. In particular, if the support of each block of L, rather than fitting in $\frac{p}{2}$ consecutive bits fits in blocks that are smaller by at least $\frac{1}{4}$ of the shift distance. We can therefore lower bound the fraction of recovered keys by replacing factors of $\frac{1}{2}$ with factors of $\frac{p}{2}$ minus half or a quarter of the offset, all divided by p, to find the sizes of sets of private keys of which we are guaranteed to recover all, or at least half of respectively.

The multi-iteration ISD algorithm attacking the ephemeral key parameters will make $2^{72.8-54.1} \approx 2^{18.7}$ independent guesses and recover at least 1 in $2^{56.0}$ of the total keys. The multi-iteration ISD algorithm attacking the long-term key parameters will make $2^{80.6-59.7} \approx 2^{20.9}$ independent guesses and recover at least 1 in $2^{61.6}$ of the total keys.

4.4 Estimating the Effect of More Advanced Information-Set Decoding

Our attempts to enumerate all weak keys were based on the assumption that the adversary was using an ISD variant that required a row of L to be uniformly 0 on all columns of the information set. The state of the art in information set decoding still allows the adversary to decode provided that a row of L has weight no more than about 6 on the information set. For example, Stern's algorithm [28] with parameter 3 would attempt to find a low weight row of L as follows.

The information set is divided into two disjoint sets of $\frac{p}{2}$ columns. The first row of L to be recovered should have weight at most 3 within each of the two sets. Further, the same row of L should have have $\Omega(\log(p))$ many consecutive 0's in column-indices that are disjoint from those of the information set. If both of these conditions occur, then a matrix inversion is performed (even though 6 non-zero bits were contained in the information set).

Note that for reasonably large p, nearly a third of the sparse vectors having weight 6 in the information set will meet both conditions. The most expensive steps in the Stern's algorithm iteration are a matrix inversion of size p and a claw finding on functions with logarithmic cost in p and domain sizes of $\binom{\frac{p}{2}}{3}$. The claw finding step is similar in cost to the matrix inversion, both having computational cost $\approx p^3$. The matrix inversion step is present in all ISD algorithms. Therefore with Stern's algorithm we can recover in a single iteration with similar cost to a single iteration of a simpler ISD algorithm, $O(1)$ of the private keys where a row of L has weight no more than 6 on the information set columns.

Recall that we choose the information set to be of size $\approx \frac{p}{2}$ in L'. The distribution of the non-zero coordinates within a successful guess of information set will be more heavily weighted toward the middle of the set and approximately triangular shaped (since these coordinates are produced by convolutions of polynomials). In particular, we will *heuristically* model both of the tails of the distribution as small triangles containing 3 bits on the left side and three bits on the right that are missed by the choice of information set.

Let $W = 2d_v(m_0 + m_1)$ denote the number of non-zero bits in L'. Then the actual fraction ϵ that the information set (in the context of advanced information set decoding) should target within L, rather than $1/2$, can be estimated by geometric area as

$$\epsilon \cdot \left(1 - \sqrt{\frac{3}{W/2}} \right) = \frac{1}{2}$$

or, re-writing:

$$\epsilon = \frac{1}{2 \left(1 - \sqrt{\frac{3}{W/2}} \right)}.$$

For the claimed-256-bit ephemeral key parameters, we have $W_{\mathsf{CPA}} = 286$. For the claimed-256-bit long-term key parameters, we have $W_{\mathsf{CCA}} = 338$. Therefore,

$$\epsilon_{\mathsf{CPA}} = \frac{1}{2 \left(1 - \sqrt{\frac{3}{286/2}} \right)} \approx 0.585.$$

$$\epsilon_{\mathsf{CCA}} = \frac{1}{2 \left(1 - \sqrt{\frac{3}{338/2}} \right)} \approx 0.577.$$

So – heuristically – we can model the effect of using advanced information set decoding algorithms by replacing the $\frac{1}{2}$'s in the calculations of the theorems earlier in this section by ϵ_{CPA} or ϵ_{CCA} respectively.

4.5   Rejection Sampling Considerations

We recall that LEDACrypt's KeyGen algorithm explicitly requires that the parity check matrix L be *full weight*. Intuitively full weight means that no cancellations occur in the additions or the multiplications that are used to generate L from H and Q. Formally, the full weight condition on L can be stated as:

$$\forall i \in \{0, \ldots, n_0 - 1\}, \quad \mathsf{weight}(L_i) = d_v \sum_{j=0}^{n_0-1} m_j.$$

When a weak key notion causes rejections to occur significantly more often for weak keys than non-weak keys, we will effectively reduce the probability of weak key generation compared to our previous analysis. As an extreme example, if, for a given weak key notion, rejection sampling rejects all weak keys, then no weak keys will ever be sampled. We therefore seek to measure the probability of key rejection for both weak keys and keys in general in order to determine whether the effectiveness of this attack is reduced via rejection sampling.

Let $\mathcal{K}$, $\mathcal{W} \subset \mathcal{K}$, and KeyGen be the public key space, the weak key space, and the key generation algorithm of LEDACrypt, respectively. Let $\mathcal{K}'$, $\mathcal{W}' \subset \mathcal{K}'$, and KeyGen' be the associated objects if rejection sampling were omitted from LEDACrypt. We observe that since KeyGen samples uniformly from $\mathcal{K}$,

$$\Pr\left[pk \in \mathcal{W} | (pk, sk) \leftarrow \mathsf{KeyGen}()\right] = \frac{|\mathcal{W}|}{|\mathcal{K}|}.$$

This equality additionally holds when rejection sampling does not occur. Since, until now, all of our analysis has ignored rejection sampling we have effectively been measuring $|\mathcal{W}'|/|\mathcal{K}'|$. We therefore seek to find a relation that allows us determine $|\mathcal{W}|/|\mathcal{K}|$ from $|\mathcal{K}'|$ and $\mathcal{W}'|$. We observe that

$$\frac{|\mathcal{W}|}{|\mathcal{K}|} = \frac{|\mathcal{W}|}{|\mathcal{K}|}\frac{|\mathcal{W}'|}{|\mathcal{W}'|}\frac{|\mathcal{K}'|}{|\mathcal{K}'|} = \frac{|\mathcal{W}'|}{|\mathcal{K}'|}\frac{|\mathcal{W}|}{|\mathcal{W}'|}\frac{|\mathcal{K}'|}{|\mathcal{K}|}.$$

Therefore it holds that the probability of generating a weak key when we consider rejection sampling for the first time in our analysis changes by exactly a factor of $(|\mathcal{W}|/|\mathcal{W}'|) \cdot (|\mathcal{K}'|/|\mathcal{K}|)$. This is precisely the probability that a weak key will not be rejected due to weight concerns divided by the probability that key will not be rejected due to weight concerns.

We note that as long as the rejection probabilities for both keys and weak keys is not especially close to 0 or 1, then it is sufficient to sample many keys according to their distributions and observe the portion of these keys that would be rejected.

In order to practically measure the security gained by rejection sampling for the 1-iteration ISD attack against the ephemeral key parameters, we sample 10,000 keys according to KeyGen' and we sample 10,000 weak keys according to KeyGen' and we observe how many of them are rejected. We observe that approximately 39.2% of regular keys are rejected while approximately 67.4% of weak keys are rejected. We therefore conclude for this attack and this parameter set, $\frac{|\mathcal{W}|}{|\mathcal{K}|} = 0.582 \frac{|\mathcal{W}'|}{|\mathcal{K}'|}$. Therefore, rejection sampling grants less than 1 additional bit of security back to LEDACrypt.

This attack analysis can be efficiently reproduced for additional parameter sets and alternative notions of weak key with the same result.

4.6   Putting It All Together

Finally, we re-calculate the results of Sect. 4.2 using Theorems 4.2 and 4.5, but accounting for the attack improvement of using advanced information set decoding from Sect. 4.4 and accounting for the security improvement due to rejection sampling issues in Sect. 4.5. We re-write the formulas with the substitutions of ϵ_{CPA} (resp. ϵ_{CPA}) for the constant $\frac{1}{2}$ for the reader, and note that the definition of ultra-weak keys has been implicitly modified to have more liberal degree constraints to suit the advanced ISD subroutine being used now.

Let x, y, m be defined as in Theorem 4.5. For the case of claimed-256-bit security for ephemeral key parameters, the fraction of ultra-weak keys recovered by a single iteration of the advanced ISD algorithm is

$$d_v{}^2 (d_v - 1)^2 m \int_{x=0}^{\epsilon} \int_{y=0}^{\epsilon} (xy)^{d_v - 2} \left((\epsilon - x)(\epsilon - y) \right)^m \left(\frac{1}{\epsilon - x} + \frac{1}{\epsilon - y} \right) \mathrm{d}y\mathrm{d}x,$$

and the fraction of these ultra-weak keys out of all possible keys is

$$(\epsilon p) d_v{}^2 (d_v - 1)^2 \int_{x=0}^{\epsilon} \int_{y=0}^{\epsilon} x^{d_v - 2} y^{d_v - 2} (\epsilon - x)^m (\epsilon - y)^m$$
$$\left(\frac{m_0{}^2 + m_1{}^2}{(\epsilon - x)(\epsilon - y)} + \frac{m_0 m_1}{(\epsilon - x)^2} + \frac{m_0 m_1}{(\epsilon - y)^2} \right) \mathrm{d}y\mathrm{d}x.$$

Evaluating these formulae with ephemeral key parameters $d_v = 11, m_0 = 7, m_1 = 6, p = 36,877$ and substituting $\epsilon_{\mathsf{CPA}} = .585$ yields 1 key recovered in $2^{62.62}$ per single iteration, and 1 ultra-weak key in $2^{43.90}$ of all possible keys. This yields an algorithm making $2^{62.62-43.90} = 2^{18.72}$ guesses and recovering 1 in $2^{47.72}$ of the ephemeral keys (accounting for the loss due to rejection sampling and the limited number of iterations).

Substituting $\epsilon_{\mathsf{CCA}} = .577$ similarly and evaluating with long-term key parameters $d_v = 13, m_0 = 7, m_1 = 6, p = 152,267$ yields 1 key recovered in $2^{70.45}$ per single iteration and 1 ultra-weak key in $2^{49.55}$ of all possible keys. This yields an algorithm making $2^{70.45-49.55} = 2^{20.90}$ guesses and recovering 1 in $2^{52.54}$ of the long-term keys (accounting for the loss due to rejection sampling and the limited number of iterations).

To conclude, we would like to compare this result against the claimed security level of NIST Category 5. Formally, these schemes should be as hard to break as breaking 256-bit AES. Each guess in the ISD algorithms leads to a cost of approximately p^3 bit operations (due to linear algebra and claw finding operations combined). This is $2^{45.5}$ bit operations for the ephemeral key parameters and $2^{51.6}$ bit operations for the long-term key parameters. A single AES-256 operation costs approximately 2^{15} bit operations. This yields the main result of this section.

Theorem 4.6 (Main). *There is an advanced information set decoding algorithm that costs the same as $2^{49.22}$ AES-256 operations and recovers 1 in $2^{47.72}$ of LEDAcrypt's Category 5 ephemeral keys.*

Similarly, there is an advanced information set decoding algorithm that costs the same as $2^{57.50}$ AES-256 operations and recovers 1 in $2^{52.54}$ of LEDAcrypt's Category 5 long-term keys.

Remark 4. Note that $49.22 + 47.72 = 96.94 \ll 256$, $57.50 + 52.54 = 110.03 \ll 256$.

Remark 5. Finally, we recall that we used various heuristics to approximate the above numbers, concretely. However, these simplifying choices can only affect at most one or two bits of security compared to a fully formalized calculation (which would come at the expense of making the analysis significantly more burdensome to parse for the reader).

5   Attack on All Keys

To conclude, we briefly analyze the asymptotic complexity of our new attack strategy in the context of recovering keys in the average case. We first note that, assuming the LEDAcrypt approach is parameterized in a balanced way – that is, H and Q are similarly sparse, and further assuming that n_0 is a constant – the ordinary ISD attack (with a randomly chosen information set) has a complexity of $\exp(\tilde{O}(p^{\frac{1}{2}}))$. To see this, observe that all known ISD variants using a random information set to find an asymptotically sparse secret parity check matrix constructed like the LEDAcrypt private key, have complexity $O\left(\frac{n_0}{n_0-1}\right)^w$, where $w = n_0 d_v m$ is the row weight of the secret parity check matrix. Efficient decoding requires $w = O(p^{\frac{1}{2}})$. By inspection this complexity is $\exp(\tilde{O}(p^{\frac{1}{2}}))$

However, we obtain an improved asymptotic complexity when using structured information sets as follows.

Theorem 5.1. *The asymptotic complexity of ISD using an appropriate choice of structured information sets, when attacking all LEDAcrypt keys in the worst case, is* $\exp(\tilde{O}(p^{\frac{1}{4}}))$.

Proof. We analyze the situation with structured information sets. Imagine we are selecting the nonzero coefficients of H' and Q' completely at random, aside from a sparsity constraint. The sparsity constraint needs to be set in such a way that the row weight of the product $H'Q'$ (restricted to two cyclic blocks) has row weight no more than p. This further constrains the row weight of each cyclic block of H' and Q' to be approximately $\left(\frac{p\ln(2)}{n_0}\right)^{\frac{1}{2}} = O(p^{\frac{1}{2}})$. The probability of success per iteration is then at least $O\left(\left(\frac{\ln(2)}{pn_0}\right)^{\frac{1}{2}\cdot\left(\sum_{i=0}^{n_0-1} m_i + n_0 d_v\right)}\right)$. With balanced parameters, d_v and the m_i are $O(p^{\frac{1}{4}})$, thus the total complexity is indeed $\exp(\tilde{O}(p^{\frac{1}{4}}))$. Note that when H' and Q' are random aside from the sparsity constraint, the probability that the supports of H' and Q' contain the supports of H and Q respectively does not depend on H and Q, so the structured ISD algorithm is asymptotically better than the unstructured ISD algorithm, even when we ignore weak keys.

$\square$

Remark 6. The fact that there exists an asymptotically better attack than standard information set decoding against keys structured like those of LEDAcrypt is not itself particularly surprising. Indeed, the very simple attack that proceeds by enumerating all the possible values of H and Q is also asymptotically $\exp(\tilde{O}(p^{\frac{1}{4}}))$. However, this simple attack does not affect the concrete parameters presented in the Round 2 submission of LEDAcrypt.

In contrast, we strongly suspect, but have not rigorously proven, that our attack significantly improves on the complexity of standard information set decoding against typical keys randomly chosen for some of the submitted parameter sets of LEDAcrypt. In particular, our estimates suggest that the NIST category 5 parameters with $n_0 = 2$ can be attacked with an appropriately chosen distribution for H' and Q' (e.g. with each polynomial block of H' and Q' chosen to have 5 or 6 consecutive chunks of nonzero coefficients in some ring representation) and that typical keys will be broken at least a few hundred times faster than with ordinary information set decoding.

If it were the case that we were attacking an "analogously-chosen" parameter set for LEDAcrypt targeting higher security levels (512-bit security, 1024-bit security, and so on), we believe a much larger computational advantage would be obtained and (importantly) be very easy to rigorously demonstrate.

6   Conclusion

In this work, we demonstrated a novel, real-world attack against LEDAcrypt – one of 17 remaining 2nd Round candidates for standardization in NIST's Post-Quantum Cryptography competition. The attack involved a customized form of Information Set Decoding, which carefully guesses the information set in a non-uniform manner so as to exploit the unique product structure of the keys in LEDAcrypt's design. The attack was most effective against classes of weak keys in the proposed parameter sets asserted to have 256-bit security (demonstrating a trade-off between computational time and fraction of the key space recovered that was better than expected even of a 128-bit secure cryptosystem), but the attack also substantially reduced security of all parameter sets similarly.

Moreover, we demonstrated that these type of weak keys are present throughout the key space of LEDAcrypt, so that simple "patches" such as rejection sampling cannot repair the problem. This was done by demonstrating a continuum of progressively larger classes of less weak keys and by showing that the same style of attack reduces the average-case complexity of certain parameter sets.

Acknowledgements. We thank Corbin McNeill for his contributions to our analysis of rejection sampling on the weak key attack. We also thank the anonymous reviewers for very thorough editorial feedback. This work is funded in part by NSF grant award number 1906360.

References

1. National Institute of Standards and Technology: Post-quantum cryptography project (2016). https://csrc.nist.gov/projects/post-quantum-cryptography
2. Alagic, G., et al.: Status Report on the First Round of the NIST Post-Quantum Cryptography Standardization Process (2019)
3. Apon, D., Perlner, R.A., Robinson, A., Santini, P.: Cryptanalysis of LEDAcrypt. Cryptology ePrint Archive, Report 2020/455 (2020). https://eprint.iacr.org/2020/455
4. Becker, A., Joux, A., May, A., Meurer, A.: Decoding random binary linear codes in $2^{n/20}$: how $1 + 1 = 0$ improves information set decoding. In: Pointcheval, D., Johansson, T. (eds.) EUROCRYPT 2012. LNCS, vol. 7237, pp. 520–536. Springer, Heidelberg (2012). https://doi.org/10.1007/978-3-642-29011-4_31
5. Berlekamp, E., McEliece, R., Van Tilborg, H.: On the inherent intractability of certain coding problems (corresp.). IEEE Trans. Inf. Theory $\mathbf{24}$(3), 384–386 (1978)
6. Bernstein, D.J.: Grover vs. McEliece. In: Sendrier, N. (ed.) PQCrypto 2010. LNCS, vol. 6061, pp. 73–80. Springer, Heidelberg (2010). https://doi.org/10.1007/978-3-642-12929-2_6
7. Bernstein, D.J., Lange, T., Peters, C.: Smaller decoding exponents: ball-collision decoding. In: Rogaway, P. (ed.) CRYPTO 2011. LNCS, vol. 6841, pp. 743–760. Springer, Heidelberg (2011). https://doi.org/10.1007/978-3-642-22792-9_42
8. Melchor, C.A.: et al.: HQC. Technical report, National Institute of Standards and Technology (2019). https://csrc.nist.gove/projects/post-quantum-cryptography/round-2-submission
9. Bernstein, D.J.: Classic McEliece. Technical report, National Institute of Standards and Technology (2019). https://csrc.nist.gove/projects/post-quantum-cryptography/round-2-submission
10. Grover, L.K.: A fast quantum mechanical algorithm for database search. In: Proceedings of 28th Annual ACM Symposium on the Theory of Computing, pp. 212–219, Philadephia, PA, May 1996
11. Kachigar, G., Tillich, J.-P.: Quantum Information Set Decoding Algorithms, pp. 69–89, March 2017
12. Lee, P.J., Brickell, E.F.: An observation on the security of McEliece's public-key cryptosystem. In: Barstow, D., et al. (eds.) EUROCRYPT 1988. LNCS, vol. 330, pp. 275–280. Springer, Heidelberg (1988). https://doi.org/10.1007/3-540-45961-8_25
13. Leon, J.S.: A probabilistic algorithm for computing minimum weights of large error-correcting codes. IEEE Trans. Inf. Theory $\mathbf{34}$(5), 1354–1359 (1988)
14. Löndahl, C., et al.: Squaring attacks on McEliece public-key cryptosystems using quasi-cyclic codes of even dimension. Des. Codes Cryptogr. $\mathbf{80}$(2), 359–377 (2016)
15. Baldi, M., Bodrato, M., Chiaraluce, F.: A new analysis of the McEliece cryptosystem based on QC-LDPC codes. In: Ostrovsky, R., De Prisco, R., Visconti, I. (eds.) SCN 2008. LNCS, vol. 5229, pp. 246–262. Springer, Heidelberg (2008). https://doi.org/10.1007/978-3-540-85855-3_17
16. Baldi, M., Barenghi, A., Chiaraluce, F., Pelosi, G., Santini, P.: LEDAcrypt. Technical report, National Institute of Standards and Technology (2019). https://csrc.nist.gov/projects/post-quantum-cryptography/round-2-submissions
17. Albrecht, M., Cid, C., Paterson, K.G., Tjhai, C.J., Tomlinson, M.: NTS-KEM. Technical report, National Institute of Standards and Technology (2019). https://csrc.nist.gove/projects/post-quantum-cryptography/round-2-submission

18. May, A., Meurer, A., Thomae, E.: Decoding random linear codes in $\tilde{\mathcal{O}}(2^{0.054n})$. In: Lee, D.H., Wang, X. (eds.) ASIACRYPT 2011. LNCS, vol. 7073, pp. 107–124. Springer, Heidelberg (2011). https://doi.org/10.1007/978-3-642-25385-0_6

19. May, A., Ozerov, I.: On computing nearest neighbors with applications to decoding of binary linear codes. In: Oswald, E., Fischlin, M. (eds.) EUROCRYPT 2015. LNCS, vol. 9056, pp. 203–228. Springer, Heidelberg (2015). https://doi.org/10.1007/978-3-662-46800-5_9

20. McEliece, R.: A public-key cryptosystem based on algebraic coding theory. Deep Space Netw. (DSN) Prog. Rep. **44**, 114–116 (1978)

21. Moody, D., Perlner, R.: Vulnerabilities of "McEliece in the World of Escher". In: Takagi, T. (ed.) PQCrypto 2016. LNCS, vol. 9606, pp. 104–117. Springer, Cham (2016). https://doi.org/10.1007/978-3-319-29360-8_8

22. Aragon, N., et al.: BIKE. Technical report, National Institute of Standards and Technology (2019). https://csrc.nist.gove/projects/post-quantum-cryptography/round-2-submission

23. Niederreiter, H.: Knapsack-type cryptosystems and algebraic coding theory. Prob. Control Inf. Theory **15**(2), 159–166 (1986)

24. Perlner, R.: Optimizing information set decoding algorithms to attack cyclosymmetric MDPC codes. In: Mosca, M. (ed.) PQCrypto 2014. LNCS, vol. 8772, pp. 220–228. Springer, Cham (2014). https://doi.org/10.1007/978-3-319-11659-4_13

25. Prange, E.: The use of information sets in decoding cyclic codes. IRE Trans. Inf. Theory **8**(5), 5–9 (1962)

26. Sendrier, N.: Decoding one out of many. In: Yang, B.-Y. (ed.) PQCrypto 2011. LNCS, vol. 7071, pp. 51–67. Springer, Heidelberg (2011). https://doi.org/10.1007/978-3-642-25405-5_4

27. Shor, P.W.: Algorithms for quantum computation: discrete logarithms and factoring. In: Proceedings 35th Annual Symposium on Foundations of Computer Science (FOCS), pp. 124–134 (1994)

28. Jacques Stern. A method for finding codewords of small weight. In Coding Theory and Applications, 3rd International Colloquium, Toulon, France, November 2–4, 1988, Proceedings, pages 106–113, 1988

Alzette: A 64-Bit ARX-box
(Feat. CRAX and TRAX)

Christof Beierle[1], Alex Biryukov[2], Luan Cardoso dos Santos[2],
Johann Großschädl[2], Léo Perrin[3], Aleksei Udovenko[4], Vesselin Velichkov[5],
and Qingju Wang[2(✉)]

[1] Ruhr University Bochum, Bochum, Germany
christof.beierle@rub.de
[2] University of Luxembourg, Esch-sur-Alzette, Luxembourg
{alex.biryukov,luan.cardoso,johann.groszschaedl,qingju.wang}@uni.lu,
sparklegrupp@googlegroups.com
[3] Inria, Paris, France
leo.perrin@inria.fr
[4] CryptoExperts, Paris, France
aleksei@affine.group
[5] University of Edinburgh, Edinburgh, UK
vvelichk@ed.ac.uk

Abstract. S-boxes are the only source of non-linearity in many symmetric primitives. While they are often defined as being functions operating on a small space, some recent designs propose the use of much larger ones (e.g., 32 bits). In this context, an S-box is then defined as a subfunction whose cryptographic properties can be estimated precisely.

We present a 64-bit ARX-based S-box called Alzette, which can be evaluated in constant time using only 12 instructions on modern CPUs. Its parallel application can also leverage vector (SIMD) instructions. One iteration of Alzette has differential and linear properties comparable to those of the AES S-box, and two are at least as secure as the AES super S-box. As the state size is much larger than the typical 4 or 8 bits, the study of the relevant cryptographic properties of Alzette is not trivial.

We further discuss how such wide S-boxes could be used to construct round functions of 64-, 128- and 256-bit (tweakable) block ciphers with good cryptographic properties that are guaranteed even in the related-tweak setting. We use these structures to design a very lightweight 64-bit block cipher (CRAX) which outperforms SPECK-64/128 for short messages on micro-controllers, and a 256-bit tweakable block cipher (TRAX) which can be used to obtain strong security guarantees against powerful adversaries (nonce misuse, quantum attacks).

Keywords: (Tweakable) block cipher · Related-tweak setting · Long trail strategy · Alzette · MEDCP · MELCC

1 Introduction

It is well known that symmetric cryptographic primitives need to be non-linear. It is common to rely on so-called *S-boxes* to obtain this property. Typically

© International Association for Cryptologic Research 2020
D. Micciancio and T. Ristenpart (Eds.): CRYPTO 2020, LNCS 12172, pp. 419–448, 2020.
https://doi.org/10.1007/978-3-030-56877-1_15

these are functions S mapping $\mathbb{F}_2^n$ to $\mathbb{F}_2^m$ for a value of n small enough that it is possible to specify S using its lookup table. They are applied in parallel to the whole state as part of the *round function* of the primitive.

This common definition of S-boxes is being challenged by the recent use of larger S-boxes in some designs. First, the designers of the hash function WHIRL-WIND [5] used a 16-bit S-box based on the multiplicative inverse in the finite field $\mathbb{F}_{2^{16}}$. In this case, the intention of the implementers was not to use the 2^{17}-byte lookup table of the permutation but instead to rewrite the permutation using tower fields. More recently, large S-boxes have been proposed in SPARX [19] and in the NIST lightweight candidate SATURNIN [15]. In the latter case, a 16-bit S-box is constructed using a classical Substitution-Permutation Network (SPN): four 4-bit S-boxes are applied to a 16-bit word in parallel, followed by an MDS matrix, and another application of the 4-bit S-box layer. While there is no closed formula for the differential and linear properties of such a structure (unlike for the multiplicative inverse used in WHIRLWIND), 16-bit remains small enough that a direct computation is possible.

This is not the case for the 32-bit S-box of SPARX. In this cipher, the S-box consists of an Addition, Rotation, XOR (ARX) network operating on two 16-bit branches, and it is key-dependent. Furthermore, while the properties of the S-box are usually sufficient[1] to prove that the cipher meets some security criteria, it is not the case for the *ARX-box* of SPARX. Indeed, in order to achieve the security goals by its designers (following the *long trail* security argument), it was necessary to study several "S-boxes", namely A, $A \circ A$, $A \circ A \circ A$, etc.

Another significant difference between the 32-bit ARX-box of SPARX and 16-bit S-boxes is the fact that it is *not* possible to evaluate its cryptographic properties directly because the complexity of the algorithms involved is usually proportional to 2^{2n}, where n is the block size. Thus, the authors of SPARX instead considered their ARX-box like a small block cipher and used techniques borrowed from block cipher analysis [14] to investigate their ARX-box.

Our Contribution. In this paper, we present a new 64-bit S-box called Alzette (pronounced [alzɛt])) that satisfies a similar scope statement to that of the SPARX ARX-box: it is also an ARX-based S-box, and we analyze both A and $A \circ A$. Alzette is parameterized by a constant $c \in \mathbb{F}_2^{32}$ and is defined for each such c as a permutation of $\mathbb{F}_2^{32} \times \mathbb{F}_2^{32}$. The algorithm evaluating this permutation is given in Algorithm 1 and depicted in Fig. 1. Alzette has the following advantages:

- it relies on 32-bit rather than 16-bit operations, meaning that (according to [18, Sect. 5]) it is suitable for a larger number of architectures;
- it makes better use of barrel shift registers (when available) and has more efficient rotation constants (for platforms on which they have different costs);
- its differential and linear properties are superior to those of a scaled-up SPARX ARX-box;
- our analysis takes more attacks into account, and is confirmed experimentally whenever possible;

---

[1] Along with some conditions on the linear layer, in particular its branching number.

After providing a detailed design rationale of Alzette, we investigate its security against cryptanalytic attacks in more detail. Besides using state-of-the-art methods to conduct the analysis, we also developed new methods. In particular, to analyze the security against generalized integral attacks, we describe a new encoding of the bit-based division property [39] for modular addition.

Note that in some attack scenarios, the security of Alzette needs to be analyzed for the precise choice of round constants c used in the actual primitive. In this work, we provide experimental analysis for the round constants employed in the permutation SPARKLE, submitted to the NIST lightweight cryptography standardization process [8]. However, our methods can easily be applied for an arbitrary choice of round constants.

Large parts of the experimental analysis have been carried out on the UL HPC cluster [40]. The source code for our experimental analysis can be found at https://github.com/cryptolu/sparkle.

We provide software implementations of Alzette on 8-bit AVR and 32-bit ARM processors. To summarize, Alzette can be executed in only 12 cycles on a 32-bit ARM Cortex-M3 and 122 cycles on an 8-bit AVR ATmega128 processor. Besides, the code size is low: respectively 24 and 176 bytes on those platforms.

Finally, we discuss the suitability of Alzette as a building block in cryptographic primitives. Since we already know how to use Alzette to design a cryptographic permutation, i.e., SPARKLE, we show in this paper how it can be applied to design (tweakable) block ciphers operating on a variety of block lengths. In a nutshell, those ciphers use Alzette in a Feistel construction and interleave it with XORing the round keys. In a tweakable block cipher, the tweak will be XORed only to half the state and only every second round. Similar to how the long-trail strategy was applied to take into account cancellations of differences within the absorption phase in a cryptographic sponge construction [8], we use the same technique to provide security arguments against related-tweak attacks, by taking cancellations of differences through tweak injection into account.

Besides describing this more general design idea, we provide two concrete cipher instances CRAX and TRAX.

CRAX is a 64-bit block cipher that uses a 128-bit secret key. Since its key schedule is very simple and does not have to be precomputed, it is one of the fastest 64-bit lightweight block ciphers in software, beaten only for messages longer than 72 bytes by the NSA cipher SPECK [6]. Due to this simple key schedule, it consumes lower RAM than SPECK. While the family of tweakable block ciphers SKINNY [9] can be considered as an academic alternative to the NSA cipher SIMON [6] in terms of hardware efficiency, CRAX can be seen as an academic alternative to SPECK in terms of software efficiency.

TRAX is a tweakable block cipher operating on a larger state of 256-bit blocks. It applies a 256-bit key and 128-bit tweak. To the best of our knowledge, the only other large tweakable block cipher is Threefish which was used as a building for the SHA-3 candidate Skein [31]. Unlike this cipher, TRAX uses 32-bit words that are better suited for vectorized implementation as well as on microcontrollers. Another improvement of TRAX over Threefish is the fact that we provide strong bounds for the probability of all linear trails and all (related-tweak) differential trails. Because of its Substitution-Permutation Network structure, TRAX is indeed inherently easier to analyze. Such a large tweakable block cipher can provide robust authenticated encryption, meaning that it can retain a high security level even in case of nonce misuse or in the presence of quantum adversaries, as argued in [15]. The performance penalty of such guarantees can be minimized using vectorization and/or parallelism.

Algorithm 1. A_c

Input/Output: $(x, y) \in \mathbb{F}_2^{32} \times \mathbb{F}_2^{32}$

$x \leftarrow x + (y \ggg 31)$
$y \leftarrow y \oplus (x \ggg 24)$
$x \leftarrow x \oplus c$
$x \leftarrow x + (y \ggg 17)$
$y \leftarrow y \oplus (x \ggg 17)$
$x \leftarrow x \oplus c$
$x \leftarrow x + (y \ggg 0)$
$y \leftarrow y \oplus (x \ggg 31)$
$x \leftarrow x \oplus c$
$x \leftarrow x + (y \ggg 24)$
$y \leftarrow y \oplus (x \ggg 16)$
$x \leftarrow x \oplus c$
return (x, y)

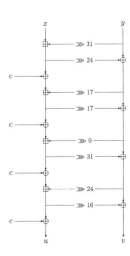

Fig. 1. The Alzette instance A_c.

Outline. The design process that we used to construct Alzette is explained in Sect. 2. In particular, we show that it offers resilience against a large variety of attacks. This analysis is confirmed experimentally in Sect. 3. We also discuss the efficiency of Alzette in Sect. 4. The discussion on the usage of Alzette as a building block, together with the specification of our (tweakable) block ciphers is given in Sect. 5.

Notation. By $\mathbb{F}_2$, we denote the finite field with two elements and by $\mathbb{F}_2^n$ the set of bitstrings of length n. We denote the set $\{0, 1, \ldots, n-1\}$ by $\mathbb{Z}_n$. We use $+$ to denote the addition modulo 2^{32} and $\oplus$ to denote the XOR of two bitstrings of the same size. The symbol $\&$ denotes the bit-wise AND. Further, by $x \ggg r$, we denote the cyclic rotation of the 32-bit word x to the right by the offset r.

Let E be a key alternating block cipher with r rounds, and round function R. In a differential attack [12] against E_k, an attacker exploits differences δ and Δ such that the probability that $E_k(x \oplus \delta) \oplus E_k(x) = \Delta$ is significantly higher than 2^{-n} (for an n-bit block cipher). For typical values of n (64, 128 or 256) the exact computation of this probability is infeasible. Instead, the common practise is to approximate this quantity by the maximum probability of a *differential trail/characteristic* averaged over all round keys. A differential trail is a sequence of differences $\{\delta_0, \delta_1, \ldots, \delta_r\}$ that specifies not only the input and output differences to the block cipher, but also the intermediate differences between the rounds such that $R(\delta_i \oplus x) \oplus R(x) = \delta_{i+1}$. The approximated probability (averaged over all round keys) is derived as the product of the probabilities of the transitions occurring in each round[2]. The maximum probability (across all trails) computed in this way is denoted *Maximum Expected Differential Characteristic Probability (MEDCP)*. An upper bound on the MEDCP is an approximation of the maximum differential probability and is called a *differential bound*.

By analogy to the differential case, for linear attacks [29] the aim is to find masks α and β such that $\beta \cdot E_k(x) = \alpha \cdot x + f(k)$, where "·" denotes the usual scalar product over $\mathbb{F}_2^n$ and where f is a function of the key bits. In practice, we look for a sequence of input, output and intermediate masks $\{\alpha_0, ..., \alpha_r\}$ called a *linear trail/characteristic* that has high absolute correlation, where $\alpha_{i+1} \cdot R(x) = \alpha_i \cdot x + f_i(k)$. Analogously to MEDCP and the differential bound, in the linear case we define a *Maximum Expected Linear Characteristic Correlation (MELCC)* and a *linear bound*.

2 The Design of **Alzette**

We now present both the design process and the main properties of Alzette. These are verified experimentally later in Sect. 3, and summarized in Sect. 3.6.

2.1 Block and Word Sizes

Our S-box should be efficient on a wide variety of platforms, while allowing a practical analysis of its relevant cryptographic properties. What would be the best word and block sizes in this context?

Word Size. In SPARX, the S-box operates on 32 bits, which are split into two 16-bit words. This word size allows a computationally cheap analysis of its cryptographic properties while facilitating efficient implementations on 8 and 16-bit micro-controllers. However, 16-bit words hamper performance on 32-bit platforms, simply because only half of their 32-bit registers and datapath can be used. The same holds when 16-bit operations are executed on a 64-bit processor. Furthermore, 16-bit operations can also incur a performance penalty on 8-bit micro-controllers; for example, rotating two 16-bit operands by n bits on an 8-bit AVR device is usually slower than rotating a single 32-bit operand by n bits (see e.g. [17, Appendix A, B, C] for details).

While 16-bit words are suboptimal because they are too small, it can also be argued that 64-bit word are too large. To establish why, we have to separately discuss the performance of 64-bit operations on 8/16/32-bit micro-controllers and on 64-bit processors. We start with three arguments for why 64-bit operations may not be a good choice on small micro-controllers.

1. 32-bit ARM micro-controllers allow one to perform a rotation "for free" since it can be executed together with another arithmetic/logical instruction.[3] Still,

---

[2] Under the *Markov assumption* which allows to treat the rounds as independent from each other.

[3] We exploit this property to design Alzette, as explained in Sect. 2.2.

a 32-bit ARM processor can only perform rotations of 32-bit operands for free, but not rotations of 64-bit words.

2. As discussed later, we will use word-wise modular additions. Some 32-bit architectures, most notably RISC-V and MIPS32, do not have an add-with-carry instruction. Adding two 64-bit operands on these platforms requires to first add the lower 32-bit parts of the operands and then compare the 32-bit sum with any of the operands to find out whether an overflow happened (i.e. to obtain a carry bit). Then, the two upper 32-bit words are added up together with the carry bit. A 64-bit addition requires at least four instructions (i.e. four cycles) on these platforms, whereas two 32-bit additions take only two instructions (i.e. two cycles).

3. Compilers for 8 and 16-bit micro-controllers are notoriously bad at handling 64-bit words, especially rotations of 64-bit words. The reason is simple: outside of cryptography, 64-bit words are of little to no use on an 8- or 16-bit platform, and therefore compiler designers have no incentive to optimize 64-bit operations.

A word size of 64 bits is naturally a good choice for 64-bit processors. For example, the authors of [21] established that SHA512 (which operates in 64-bit words) reaches much higher throughput on 64-bit Intel processors than SHA256 (operating on 32-bit words). However, this does not necessarily imply that ARX designs using 32-bit words are inferior to 64-bit variants on 64-bit processors. This can be justified with the fact that the best way to implement an ARX cipher on a 64-bit Intel or a 64-bit ARM processor is to use the vector (SIMD) extensions they provide, e.g. Intel SSE, AVX or ARM NEON. Most high-end 64-bit processors have such vector instruction sets, and all of them can execute additions, rotations and XORs on 32-bit words. The fact that a 32-bit word size allows peak performance on 64-bit processors was already used for instance by the designers of Gimli [11].

As a consequence, we chose to design an S-box that operates on 32-bit words as those offer the best performances across the board.

Block Size. Our S-box could a priori operate on any block size that is a multiple of 32. However, two criteria significantly narrow down the design space.

First, we need to be able to investigate the cryptographic properties of our S-box. We are not aware of any efficient combination of simple operations (AND, addition, rotation, XOR, etc.) on a single word that would allow us to give strong bounds on the differential and linear probabilities. On the other hand, computational technique that find such bounds tend to be less efficient if the state size is large as it implies a greater number of potential branches to explore in a tree. Our ability to find bounds thus imposes a number of words which is at least equal to 2 and as small as possible.

Second, in order to use vector instruction sets to their fullest extent, it is better to have a larger number of S-boxes that can be applied in parallel in each call to the round function. On smaller micro-controllers, limiting the block size makes it easier for implementers to keep one full S-box state (or maybe even several full S-box states) in the register file, thereby reducing the number of memory accesses. Finally, in order to build primitives with a small state size, it is necessary that the S-box size is at most equal to said state size. However, as mentioned before, it makes sense to aim for the smallest possible number of branches (and, consequently, a large number of S-boxes) to leverage SIMD-style parallelism.

Because of these requirements, we settled for the use of two words. Given that our discussion above set a 32-bit word size, our S-box operates on 64 bits.

2.2 Round Structure and Number of Rounds

We decided to build an ARX-box out of the operations *XOR of rotation* and *ADD of rotation*, i.e., $x \oplus (y \ggg s)$ and $x + (y \ggg r)$, because they can be executed in a single clock cycle on ARM processors and thus provide extremely good diffusion per cycle. As the ARX-boxes could be implemented with their rounds unrolled, we allowed the use of different rotations in every round. We observed that one can obtain much better resistance against differential and linear attacks in this case compared to having identical rounds.

In particular, we aimed for designing an ARX-box consisting of the composition of t rounds of the form

$$T_i : \begin{cases} \mathbb{F}_2^{32} \times \mathbb{F}_2^{32} & \rightarrow \mathbb{F}_2^{32} \times \mathbb{F}_2^{32} \\ (x,y) & \mapsto \left(x + (y \lll r_i), \; y \oplus \big((x + (y \lll r_i)) \lll s_i \big) \right) \oplus (\gamma_i^L, \gamma_j^R) \,, \end{cases}$$

where i-th round is defined by the rotation amounts $(r_i, s_i) \in \mathbb{Z}_{32} \times \mathbb{Z}_{32}$ and the round constant $(\gamma_i^L, \gamma_i^R) \in \mathbb{F}_2^{32} \times \mathbb{F}_2^{32}$. It is computed in three steps: $x \leftarrow x + (y \lll r_i)$, $y \leftarrow y \oplus (x \lll s_i)$, and finally $(x,y) \leftarrow (x \oplus \gamma_i^L, y \oplus \gamma_i^R)$.

In our final design, we decided to use $t = 4$ rounds. The reason is that, when it comes to designing primitives, for r-round ARX-boxes, usable bounds from the long-trail strategy can be obtained from the $2r$-round bounds of the ARX structure by concatenating two ARX-boxes. The complexity of deriving upper bounds on the differential trail probability or absolute linear trail correlation depends on the number of rounds considered. For 8 rounds, i.e., 2 times a 4-round ARX-box, it is feasible to compute strong bounds in reasonable time (i.e., several days up to few weeks on a single CPU). For 3-round ARX-boxes, the 6-round bounds of the best ARX-boxes we found seem not strong enough to build a secure cipher with a small number of iterations. Since we cannot arbitrarily reduce the number of round (step) iterations in a cryptographic function because of structural attacks, using ARX-boxes with more than four rounds would lead to worse efficiency overall. In other words, we think that four-round ARX-boxes provide the best balance between the number of ARX-box layers needed and rounds per ARX-box in order to build a secure primitive.

2.3 Criteria for Choosing the Rotation Amounts

We aimed for choosing the rotations (r_i, s_i) in Alzette in a way that maximizes security and efficiency. For efficiency reasons, we want to minimize the *cost* of the rotations, where we use the cost metric as given in Table 1. While each rotation has the same cost in 32-bit ARM processors (i.e., 0 because rotation is for free on top of XOR, resp., AND), we further aimed for minimizing the cost with regard to 8-bit and 16-bit architectures. Therefore, we restricted ourselves to rotations from the set $\{0, 1, 7, 8, 9, 15, 16, 17, 23, 24, 25, 31\}$, as those are the most efficient when implemented on 8 and 16-bit micro-controllers. We define the *cost* of a collection of rotation amounts (that is needed to define all the rounds of an ARX-box) as the sum of the costs of its contained rotations.

Table 1. For each rotation in $\{0, 1, 7, 8, 9, 15, 16, 17, 23, 24, 25, 31\}$, the table shows an estimation of the number of clock cycles needed to implement the rotation on top of XOR, resp. ADD. We associate the mean of those values for the three platforms to be the *cost* of a rotation.

rot (mod 32)	8-bit AVR	16-bit MSP	32-bit ARM	cost
0	0	0	0	0.00
±1	5	3	0	2.66
±7	5	9	0	4.66
8	0	6	0	2.00
±9	5	9	0	4.66
±15	5	3	0	2.66
16	0	0	0	0.00

For security reasons, we aim to minimize the provable upper bound on the expected differential trail probability (resp. expected absolute linear trail correlation) of a differential (resp. linear) trail. More precisely, our target was to obtain strong bounds, preferably at least as good as those of the round structure of the 64-bit block cipher SPECK, i.e., an 8-round differential bound of 2^{-29} and an 8-round linear bound of 2^{-17}. If possible, we aimed for improving upon those bounds. Note that for $r > 4$, the term *r-round bound* refers to the differential (resp. linear) bound for r rounds of an iterated ARX-box. As explained above, at the same time we aimed for choosing an ARX-box with a low cost. In order to reduce the search space, we relied on the following criteria as a heuristic for selecting the final choice for Alzette:

- The candidate ARX-box must fulfill the differential bounds $(-\log_2)$ of 0, 1, 2, 6, and 10 for 1, 2, 3, 4 and 5 rounds respectively, for *all four possible offsets*. We conjecture that those bounds are optimal for up to 5 rounds.
- The candidate must fulfill a differential bound of at least 16 for 6 rounds, also for all offsets.
- The 8-round linear bound $(-\log_2)$ of the candidate ARX-box should be at least 17.

By the term *offset* we refer to the round index of the starting round of a differential trail. Note that we are considering all offsets for the differential criteria because the bounds are computed using Matsui's branch and bound algorithm, which needs to use the $(r-1)$-round bound of the differential trail with starting round index 1 (second round) in order to compute the r-round bound of the trail.

We tested *all* rotation sets with a cost below 12 for the above conditions. None of those fulfilled the above criteria. For a cost below 15, we found the ARX-box with the following rotations:

$$(r_0, r_1, r_2, r_3, s_0, s_1, s_2, s_3) = (31, 17, 0, 24, 24, 17, 31, 16) .$$

This rotation set fulfills all the criteria. The differential and linear bounds for the respective ARX-box are summarized in Table 2.

Table 2. Differential and linear bounds for several rotation parameters. For each offset, the first line shows the differential bound and the second shows the linear one. The value set in parenthesis is the maximum absolute correlation of the linear hull taking clustering into account (see Sect. 3.2). The bounds [14, 20, 27, 28] for SPECK are given for comparison.

$(r_0, r_1, r_2, r_3, s_0, s_1, s_2, s_3)$	1	2	3	4	5	6	7	8	9	10	11	12
$(31, 17, 0, 24, 24, 17, 31, 16)$	0	1	2	6	10	18	≥ 24	≥ 32	≥ 36	≥ 42	≥ 46	≥ 52
	0	0	1	2	5	8	13 (11.64)	17 (15.79)	–	–	–	–
$(17, 0, 24, 31, 17, 31, 16, 24)$	0	1	2	6	10	17	≥ 25	≥ 31	≥ 37	≥ 41	≥ 47	–
	0	0	1	2	5	9	13	16	–	–	–	–
$(0, 24, 31, 17, 31, 16, 24, 17)$	0	1	2	6	10	18	≥ 24	≥ 32	≥ 36	≥ 42	–	–
	0	0	1	2	6	8	13	15	–	–	–	–
$(24, 31, 17, 0, 16, 24, 17, 31)$	0	1	2	6	10	17	≥ 25	≥ 31	≥ 37	–	–	–
	0	0	1	2	5	9	12	16	–	–	–	–
SPECK64	0	1	3	6	10	15	21	29	34	38	42	46
	0	0	1	3	6	9	13	17	19	21	24	27

2.4   On the Round Constants

The purpose of round constant additions, i.e., the XORs with γ_i^L, γ_i^R in the general ARX-box structure, is to ensure some independence between the rounds. They also break additive patterns that could arise on the left branch due to the chain of modular addition it would have without said constant additions. Perhaps even more importantly, they should also ensure that the Alzette instances called in parallel are different from one another to avoid symmetries.

For efficiency reasons, we decided to use the same round constant in every round of the ARX-box, i.e., $\forall i : \gamma_i^L = c$. As the rounds themselves are different from one another, we do not rely on γ_i^L or γ_i^R to prevent slide-style patterns. Thus, using the same constant in each round is not a problem. Moreover, we chose $\gamma_i^R = 0$ for all i. It is important to note that the experimental verification of the differential probabilities and absolute linear correlations we conducted (see Sects. 3.1 and 3.2 respectively) did not lead to significant differences when changing to a more complex round constant schedule. In other words, even for random choices of all γ_i^L and γ_i^R, we did not observe significantly different results that would justify the use of a more complex constant schedule (which would of course lead to worse efficiency in the implementation).

The analysis provided in the next section is dependent on the actual choice of round constants c. We conducted this analysis for the constants of SPARKLE:

$$
\begin{aligned}
c_0 &= \texttt{b7e15162}, \; c_1 = \texttt{bf715880}, \; c_2 = \texttt{38b4da56}, \; c_3 = \texttt{324e7738}, \\
c_4 &= \texttt{bb1185eb}, \; c_5 = \texttt{4f7c7b57}, \; c_6 = \texttt{cfbfa1c8}, \; c_7 = \texttt{c2b3293d} \; .
\end{aligned}
\tag{1}
$$

3 Analysis of Alzette

In this section, we study cryptographic properties of the ARX-box Alzette. The analysis is done for the round constants used in SPARKLE, except for analysis of differential/linear characteristic bounds and division property propagation, which are independent of the choice of the constants. All described methods can easily be applied to arbitrary choices of constants.

3.1 On the Differential Properties

Bounding the Maximum Expected Differential Trail Probability. We used the Algorithm 1 in [14] and adapted it to our round structure to compute the bounds on the maximum expected differential trail probabilities of the ARX-boxes which use the constants given in Eq. (1). The algorithm is basically a refined variant of Matsui's well-known branch and bound algorithm [30]. While the latter has been originally proposed for ciphers that have S-boxes (in particular the DES), the former is targeted at ARX-based designs that use modular addition, rather than an S-box, as a source of non-linearity.

Algorithm 1 [14] exploits the differential properties of modular addition to efficiently search for characteristics in a bitwise manner. Upon termination, it outputs a trail (characteristic) with the maximum expected differential trail probability (MEDCP). For Alzette, we obtain such trails for up to six rounds, where the 6-round bound is 2^{-18}. We further collected all trails corresponding to the maximum expected differential probability for 4 and 5 rounds and experimentally checked the actual probabilities of the differentials (for the constants used in SPARKLE), see below.

Note that for 7 and 8 rounds, we could not get a tight bound due to the high complexity of the search. In other words, the algorithm did not terminate in reasonable time. However, the algorithm exhaustively searched the range up to $-\log_2(p) = 24$ and $-\log_2(p) = 32$ for 7 and 8 rounds respectively, which proves that there are no valid differential trails with an expected differential trail probability larger than 2^{-24} and 2^{-32}, respectively. We evaluated similar bounds for up to 12 rounds.

Experiments on the Fixed-Key Differential Probabilities. As in virtually all block cipher designs, the security arguments against differential attacks are only average results when *averaging over all keys of the primitive*. When leveraging such arguments for a cryptographic permutation, i.e., a block cipher with a fixed key, it might be possible in theory that the actual fixed-key maximum differential probability is higher than the expected maximum differential probability. In particular, the variance of the distribution of the maximum fixed-key differential probabilities might be high.

For all of the 8 Alzette instances corresponding to the constants in Eq. (1), we conducted experiments in order to see if the expected maximum differential trail probabilities derived by Matsui's search are close to the actual differential probabilities of the fixed ARX-boxes. Our results are as follows.

By Matsui's search we found 7 differential trails for Alzette[4] that correspond to the maximum expected differential trail probability of 2^{-6} for 4 rounds, see Table 3. For any Alzette instance A_{c_i} and any such trails with input difference α and output difference β, we experimentally computed the actual differential probability of the differential $\alpha \to \beta$ by

$$\frac{|\{x \in S | A_{c_i}(x) \oplus A_{c_i}(x \oplus \alpha) = \beta\}|}{|S|} \, ,$$

where S is a set of 2^{24} inputs sampled uniformly at random. Our results show that the expected differential trail probabilities approximate the actual differential probabilities very well, i.e., all of the probabilities computed experimentally are in the range $[2^{-6} - 10^{-4}, 2^{-6} + 10^{-4}]$ for a sample size of 2^{24}.

For 5 rounds, i.e., one full Alzette instance and one additional first round of Alzette, there is only one trail with maximum expected differential trail probability $p = 2^{-10}$. In the case of SPARKLE, for all *combinations* of round constants that can occur in 5 rounds (one Alzette instance plus one round) that do not go into the addition of a step counter, i.e., corresponding to the twelve compositions

$$A_{c_2} \circ A_{c_0} \;\; A_{c_3} \circ A_{c_1} \;\; A_{c_3} \circ A_{c_0} \;\; A_{c_4} \circ A_{c_1} \;\; A_{c_5} \circ A_{c_2} \;\; A_{c_4} \circ A_{c_0}$$
$$A_{c_5} \circ A_{c_1} \;\; A_{c_6} \circ A_{c_2} \;\; A_{c_7} \circ A_{c_3} \;\; A_{c_2} \circ A_{c_3} \;\; A_{c_3} \circ A_{c_4} \;\; A_{c_2} \circ A_{c_7},$$

we checked whether the actual differential probabilities are close to the maximum expected differential trail probability. We found that all of the so computed probabilities are in the range $[2^{-10} - 10^{-5}, 2^{-10} + 10^{-5}]$ for a sample size of 2^{28}.

3.2 On the Linear Properties

Bounding Maximum Expected Absolute Linear Trail Correlation. We used the Mixed-Integer Linear Programming approach described in [20] and the Boolean satisfiability problem (SAT) approach in [27] in order to get bounds on the

---

[4] Note that those are independent of the actual round constants as the probability corresponds to the average probability over all keys when analyzing Alzette as a block cipher where independent subkeys are used instead of round constants.

Table 3. The input and output differences α, β (in hex) of all differential trails over Alzette corresponding to maximum expected differential trail probability $p = 2^{-6}$ and $p = 2^{-10}$ for four and five rounds, respectively.

rounds	α	β	$-\log_2(p)$
4	8000010000000080	8040410041004041	6
	8000010000000080	80c04100410040c1	6
	0080400180400000	8000018081808001	6
	0080400180400000	8000008080808001	6
	a0008140000040a0	8000010001008001	6
	8002010000010080	0101000000030101	6
	8002010000010080	0301000000030301	6
5	a0008140000040a0	8201010200018283	10

maximum expected absolute linear trail correlation. It was feasible to get tight bounds even for 8 rounds, where the 8-round bound of our final choice for Alzette is 2^{-17}. We were able to collect all linear trails that correspond to the maximum expected absolute linear trail correlation for 4 up to 8 rounds and experimentally checked the actual correlations of the corresponding linear approximations for the Alzette instances using the constants in Eq. (1), see below.

Experiments on the Fixed-Key Linear Correlations. Similarly as for the case of differentials, for all of the 8 Alzette instances used in SPARKLE, we conducted experiments in order to see whether the maximum expected absolute linear trail correlations derived by MILP and presented in Table 2 are close to the actual absolute correlations of the linear approximations over the fixed Alzette instances. Details of our results are presented in the full version, but they can be summarized as follows.

For a full Alzette instance, there are 4 trails with a maximum expected absolute trail correlation of 2^{-2}. For all of the eight Alzette instances, the actual absolute correlations are very close to the theoretical values and we did not observe any clustering. For more than four rounds (i.e., one full instance plus additional rounds), we again checked all combinations of ARX-boxes that do not get a step counter in SPARKLE. For five rounds, there are 16 trails with a maximum expected absolute trail correlation of 2^{-5}. In our experiments, we can observe a slight clustering. In fact, we chose the round constants c_i of SPARKLE such that, for all combinations of Alzette that occur over the linear layer, the linear hull effect is to our favor, i.e., the actual correlation tends to be *lower* than the theoretical value.[5]

This tendency also holds for the correlations over six rounds. There are 48 trails with a maximum expected absolute linear trail correlation of 2^{-8}.

---

[5] The constants in SPARKLE were derived from the fractional digits of e, excluding some blocks. For the excluded blocks, the actual absolute correlations are slightly higher than the theoretical bound, but all smaller than 2^{-8}.

For seven rounds, there are 2992 trails with a maximum expected absolute linear trail correlation of 2^{-13}. Over all the twelve combinations that do not add a step counter in SPARKLE and all of the 2992 approximations, the maximum absolute correlation we observed was $2^{-11.64}$ using a sample size of 2^{32} plaintexts chosen uniformly at random.

For eight rounds, there are 3892 trails with a maximum expected absolute linear trail correlation of 2^{-17}. Over all the twelve combinations that do not add a step counter and all of the 3892 approximations, the maximum absolute correlation we observed was $2^{-15.79}$ using a sample size of 2^{40} plaintexts chosen uniformly at random.

Overall, our correlation estimates based on linear trails seem to closely approximate the actual absolute correlations since our estimate is only $2^{1.21}$ times lower than the actual absolute correlation.

3.3 On the Algebraic Properties

Integral cryptanalysis exploits low algebraic degree or a more fine-grained algebraic degeneracy of the cryptographic primitive under attack. An *integral distinguisher* defines an input set X such that the analyzed function sums to zero over this set (at least in some bits) for any value of the secret key involved. In the case of a keyless permutation, such as an ARX-box, such distinguishers are trivial to find and are meaningless. However, an analysis of the growth of the algebraic degree (and the evolution of the algebraic structure in general) provides a useful information about the permutation. When the permutation is plugged into, for example, a block cipher, this information directly translates into information about integral distinguishers.

Division property is a technique introduced by Todo [37] to find *integral characteristics*. Later, Xiang *et al.* [41] discovered that the bit-based division property propagation can be efficiently encoded as *an mixed-integer linear programming* instance (MILP), and, surprisingly, can be solved on practice using modern optimization software (Gurobi Optimizer [22]) for practically all known block ciphers. Sun *et al.* [36] described a way to encode the modular addition operation using MILP inequalities, extending the framework to ARX-based primitives.

We briefly recall the MILP-aided bit-based division property framework.

Definition 1 (Block-Based Division Property). *Let n be an integer and let X be a set of n-bit vectors. Let k be an integer, $0 \leq k \leq n$. The set S satisfies division property $\mathcal{D}_k^n$ if and only if for all $u \in \mathbb{F}_2^n$ with $wt(u) < k$, we have $\bigoplus_{x \in X} x^u = 0$, where x^u is a shorthand for $x_0^{u_0} \ldots x_{n-1}^{u_{n-1}}$.*

Definition 2 (Bit-Based Division Property). *Let n be an integer and let X, K be two sets of n-bit vectors, $0 \notin K$. The set X satisfies division property $\mathcal{D}_K$ if and only if for all $u \in \mathbb{F}_2^n$ such that $u \prec k$ for all $k \in K$*

$$\bigoplus_{x \in X} x^u = 0 \,,$$

where $u \prec k$ if and only if $u \neq k$ and $u_i \leq k_i$ for all $i, 0 \leq i < n$.

For further information on division property propagation and its encoding using MILP inequalities, we refer to [41]. However, we describe briefly a new technique for encoding division property propagation through the modular addition. Our technique is simpler and more compact than the one proposed by Sun *et al.* [36].

Addition Modulo 2^{32}. The method by Sun *et al.* is based on expressing the modular addition as a Boolean circuit and applying the standard known encoding for XOR and AND operations. As a result, for each bit of a word at least 12 bit operations are produced. We propose a new simple method which requires only 2 *inequalities* per bit.

Our key idea is to compute the carry bits and the output bits in pairs using a 3×2 bit look-up table. The division property propagation through this look-up table can be encoded using only 2 inequalities.

Consider an addition of two n-bit words $a, b \in \mathbb{F}_2^n$ and let $y = a \boxplus b \mod 2^n$ (recall that a_0 denotes the most significant bit of a, a_{n-1} denotes the least significant bit of a, etc.). Define *carry* bits $c_i, 0 \leq i < n$ as follows: $c_{n-1} = 0$ and $c_i = \mathrm{Maj}(a_{i+1}, b_{i+1}, c_{i+1})$ for $-1 \leq i < n - 1$, where Maj is the 3-bit *majority* function. Then it is easy to verify that $y_i = a_i \oplus b_i \oplus c_i$ for all $0 \leq i < n$. Full modular addition can be computed sequentially from $i = n - 1$ to $i = 0$. Let $f : \mathbb{F}_2^3 \rightarrow \mathbb{F}_2^2$ be such that $f(a, b, c) = (\mathrm{Maj}(a, b, c), a \oplus b \oplus c)$, then we can write

$$(c_{i-1}, y_i) = f(a_i, b_i, c_i),$$

for all $0 \leq i < n$. The lookup table of f is given in Table 4. Note that no bits are copied in the sequential computation process. It follows that the division property propagation can be encoded directly by encoding n sequential applications of f (using the S-Box encoding methods by Xiang *et al.* [41]). Finally, an additional constraint is needed to ensure that the resulting division property is not active in the bit c_{-1}.

The division property propagation table is given in Table 5. This table can be characterized by the two following integer inequalities:

$$\begin{cases} -a - b - c + 2c' + y & \geq 0, \\ a + b + c - 2c' - 2y & \geq -1, \end{cases}$$

where $a, b, c \in \mathbb{Z}_2$ correspond to the values of the input division property and $c', y \in \mathbb{Z}_2$ correspond to the values of the output division property. In our experiments, these two inequalities applied for each bit position generate precisely the correct division property propagation table of the addition modulo 2^n for n up to 7. There are a few redundant transitions, but they do not affect the result.

An alternative to MILP-solvers that is used for division property analysis are SMT-solvers. To facilitate this alternative method, we characterize the division property propagation table of f by four Boolean propositions (obtained by

Table 4. Look-up table of f.   **Table 5.** Division property propagation table of f.

input	output	input	output
000	00	100	01
001	01	101	10
010	01	110	10
011	10	111	11

input	outputs	input	outputs
000	$\{00\}$	100	$\{01, 10\}$
001	$\{01, 10\}$	101	$\{10\}$
010	$\{01, 10\}$	110	$\{10\}$
011	$\{10\}$	111	$\{11\}$

enumerating all possible outputs and constraining respective inputs):

$$\begin{cases} c' \wedge y & \Rightarrow & a \wedge b \wedge c, \\ \neg c' \wedge \neg y & \Rightarrow & \neg a \wedge \neg b \wedge \neg c, \\ \neg c' \wedge y & \Rightarrow & (a \oplus b \oplus c) \wedge (\neg a \vee \neg b), \\ c' \wedge \neg y & \Rightarrow & (a \vee b \vee c) \wedge (\neg a \vee \neg b \vee \neg c). \end{cases} \quad \begin{array}{l} \triangleright\ a = b = c = 1 \\ \triangleright\ a = b = c = 0 \\ \triangleright\ a + b + c = 1 \\ \triangleright\ 1 \le a + b + c \le 2 \end{array}$$

We used this representation together with the Boolector SMT-solver [32] (version 3.1.0) to verify our results.

Finally, we note that subtraction modulo 2^n, used in the inverse of Alzette, is equivalent to the addition with respect to the division property propagation in our method. Indeed, let $f' : \mathbb{F}_2^3 \to \mathbb{F}_2^2$,

$$f'(a, b, c) = (c', y) = ([a - b - c < 0], a \oplus b \oplus c),$$

where the first coordinate of f' computes the subtraction carry bit. It is in fact equivalent to the first coordinate of f (the majority function) up to XOR with constants:

$$[a - b - c < 0] = [a + (1 - b) + (1 - c) < 2]$$
$$= 1 - [a + (1 - b) + (1 - c) \ge 2] = 1 \oplus f_0(a, 1 \oplus b, 1 \oplus c).$$

We conclude that f' has the same division property propagation table as f and thus division property propagation using our method is the same for modular addition and subtraction.

Division Property Propagation in Alzette. First, we evaluated the general algebraic degree of the ARX-box structure based on the division property. The 5th and 6th rounds rotation constants were chosen as the 1st and 2nd rounds rotation constants respectively, as this will happen when two Alzette instances will be chained. The inverse ARX-box structure starts with 4th round rotation constants, then 3rd, 2nd, 1st, 4th, etc. The minimum and maximum degree among coordinates of the ARX-box structure and its inverse are given in Table 6 Even though these are just upper bounds, we expect that they are close to the actual values, as the division property was shown to be rather precise [39]. Thus, the Alzette structure may have full degree in all its coordinates, but the inverse of an Alzette instance has a coordinate of degree 46.

The block-based division property of Alzette is such that, for any $1 \le k \le 62$, $\mathcal{D}_k^{64}$ maps to $\mathcal{D}_1^{64}$ after two rounds, and $\mathcal{D}_{63}^{64}$ maps to $\mathcal{D}_2^{64}$ after two rounds and to $\mathcal{D}_1^{64}$ after three rounds. The same holds for the inverse of an Alzette instance.

Table 6. The upper bounds on the minimum and maximum degree of the coordinates of Alzette and its inverse.

Rounds	1	2	3	4	Inverse rounds	1	2	3	4
min	1	10	42	63	min	1	2	32	46
max	32	62	63	63	max	32	62	63	63

The longest integral characteristic found with bit-based division property is for the 6-round ARX-box, where the input has 63 active bits and the inactive bit is at the index 44 (i.e., there are 44 active bits from the left and 19 active bits from the right), and in the output 16 bits are balanced:

input active bits:

11111111111111111111111111111111,111111111111011111111111111111111,

balanced bits after 6-round ARX-box (denoted by B) :

?????????????????????????BBBBBBBB,?????????BBBBBBBB??????????????????.

The inactive bit can be moved to indexes $45, 46, 47, 48$ as well, the balanced property after 6 round stays the same. For the 7-round ARX-box we did not find any integral distinguishers.

For the inverse ARX-box, the longest integral characteristic is for 5 rounds:

input active bits:

11111111111111111111111111101111,111111111111111111111111111111111,

balanced bits after 5-round ARX-box inverse:

??????????????????????????????B,???????BBBBBBBBB???????????????????.

For the ARX-box inverse with 6-rounds we did not find any integral characteristic.

As a conclusion, even though a single Alzette instance has integral characteristics, for two chained Alzette instances there are no integral characteristics that can be found using the state-of-the-art division property method.

Experimental Algebraic Degree Lower Bound. The modular addition is the only non-linear operation in Alzette. Its algebraic degree is 31 and thus, in each 4-round Alzette instance, there must exist some output bits of algebraic degree at least 32.

We experimentally checked that, for each instance A_{c_i} with c_i as in Eq. (1), the algebraic degree of *each* output bit is at least 32. In particular, for each output bit we found a monomial of degree 32 that occurs in its ANF. Note that for checking whether the monomial $\prod_{i=0}^{m-1} x_{i_m}$ occurs in the ANF of a Boolean function f one has to evaluate f on 2^m inputs.

3.4   Invariant Subspaces

Invariant subspace attacks were considered in [26]. For the round constants used in SPARKLE, using a similar "to and fro" method from [13,33], we searched for an affine subspace that is mapped by an Alzette instance A_{c_i} to a (possibly different) affine subspace of the same dimension. We could not find any such subspace of nontrivial dimension.

Note that the search is randomized so it does not result in a proof. As an evidence of the correctness of the algorithm, we found many such subspace trails for all 2-round reduced ARX-boxes, with dimensions from 56 up to 63. For example, let A denotes the first two rounds of A_{c_0}. Then for all $l, r, l', r' \in \mathbb{F}_2^{32}$ such that $A(l, r) = (l', r')$, it holds that

$$
(l_{29} + r_{21} + r_{30})(l_{30} + r_{31})(l_{31} + r_0)(r_{22})(r_{23}) = \\
(l'_4 + r'_{21})(l'_5 + r'_{22})(l'_6 + r'_{23})(l'_{28} + l'_{30} + l'_{31} + r'_{13} + 1)(l'_{29} + l'_{31} + r'_{14}).
$$

This equation defines a subspace trail of constant dimension 59.

3.5 Nonlinear Invariants

Nonlinear invariant attacks were considered recently in [38] to attack lightweight primitives. For the round constants used in SPARKLE, using linear algebra, we experimentally verified that for any ARX-box A_{c_i} and any non-constant Boolean function f of degree at most 2, the compositions $f \circ A_{c_i}$ and $f \circ A_{c_i}^{-1}$ have degree at least 10:

$$
\forall f : \mathbb{F}_2^{64} \to \mathbb{F}_2, 1 \le \deg(f) \le 2, \quad \deg(f \circ A_{c_i}) \ge 10, \deg(f \circ A_{c_i}^{-1}) \ge 10,
$$

and for functions f of degree at most 3, the compositions have degree at least 4:

$$
\forall f : \mathbb{F}_2^{64} \to \mathbb{F}_2, 1 \le \deg(f) \le 3, \quad \deg(f \circ A_{c_i}) \ge 4, \deg(f \circ A_{c_i}^{-1}) \ge 4.
$$

In particular, any A_{c_i} has no cubic invariants. Indeed, a cubic invariant f would imply that $f \circ A_{c_i} + \varepsilon = f$ is cubic (for a constant $\varepsilon \in \mathbb{F}_2$). The same holds for the inverse of any ARX-box A_{c_i}.

By using the same method, we also verified that there are no quadratic equations relating inputs and outputs of any A_{c_i}. However, there are quadratic equations relating inputs and outputs of 3-round reduced versions of each A_{c_i}.

3.6 Summary of the Properties of Alzette

Our experimental results validate our theoretical analysis of the properties of Alzette: in practice, the differential and linear trail probabilities (resp., absolute correlations) are as predicted. In the case of differential probabilities, the clustering is minimal. While it is not quite negligible in the linear case, our estimates remain very close to the quantities we measured experimentally.

The diffusion is fast: all output bits depend on all input bits after a single call of Alzette – though the dependency may be sometimes weak. After a double call of Alzette, diffusion is of course complete. More formally, as evidenced by our analysis of the division property, no integral distinguisher exist in this case.

While the two components have utterly different structures, Alzette has similar properties to one round of AES and the double iteration of Alzette to the AES super-S-box (see Table 7). The bounds for the (double) ARX-box come from Table 2. For the AES, the bounds for a single rounds are derived from the properties of its S-box, so its maximum differential probability is $4/256 = 2^{-6}$ and its maximum absolute linear correlation is 2^{-3}. For two rounds, we raise the quantities of the S-box to the power 5 because the branching number of the MixColumn operation is 5,

Table 7. A comparison of the properties of Alzette with those of the AES with a fixed key. MEDCP denotes the maximum expected differential trail probability and MELCC denotes the maximum expected absolute linear trail correlation.

	MEDCP	MELCC
Alzette	2^{-6}	2^{-2}
AES S-box layer	2^{-6}	2^{-3}
Double Alzette	$\leq 2^{-32}$	2^{-17}
AES super S-box layer	2^{-30}	2^{-15}

These experimental verifications were enabled by our use of a key-less structure. For a block cipher, we would need to look at all possible keys to reach the same level of confidence.

4   Implementation Aspects

4.1   Software Implementations

Alzette was designed to provide good security bounds, but also efficient implementation. The rotation amounts have been carefully chosen to be a multiple of eight bits or one bit from it. On 8 or 16 bit architectures these rotations can be efficiently implemented using move, swap, and 1-bit rotate instructions. On ARM processors, operations of the form $z \leftarrow x <op> (y \lll \ell)$ can be executed with a single instruction in a single clock cycle, irrespective of ℓ.

Alzette itself operates over two 32-bit words of data, with an extra 32-bit constant value. This allows the full computation to happen in-register in AVR, MSP and ARM architectures, whereby the latter is able to hold at least 4 Alzette instances entirely in registers. This in turn reduces load-store overheads and contributes to the performance of a primitive calling Alzette.

The consistency of operations allows one to either focus on small code size (by implementing the parallel Alzette instances in a substitution layer in a loop), or on architectures with more registers, execute two or more instances to exploit instruction pipelining. This consistency of operations also allows some degree of parallelism, namely by using Single Instruction Multiple Data (SIMD) instructions. SIMD is a type of computational model that executes the same operation on multiple operands. Due to the layout of Alzette, an SIMD implementation can be created by packing $x_0 \ldots x_{n_b}$, $y_0 \ldots y_{n_b}$, and $c_0 \ldots c_{n_b}$ each in a vector register. That allows 128-bit SIMD architectures such as NEON to execute four Alzette instances in parallel, or even eight instances when using x86 AVX2 instructions.

Table 8. Execution time (in clock cycles) and codes size (in bytes) of Alzette.

Platform	Execution time	Code size
8-bit AVR ATmega128	78	156
32-bit ARM Cortex-M3	12	48

Table 8 summarizes the execution time and code size of Alzette on an 8-bit AVR and a 32-bit ARM Cortex-M3 micro-controller. The assembler implementation of Alzette for the latter architecture consists of 12 instructions, which take 12 clock cycles to execute. The actual code size of Alzette may be less than 48 bytes since the Cortex-M3 supports Thumb2, which means some simple instructions can be only 16 bits long. However, whether an instruction is 16 or 32 bits long depends, among other things, on the register allocation. Our ARM implementation assumes that the two 32-bit branches of Alzette and the round constant are already in registers and not in memory, which is a reasonable assumption since the register file of a Cortex-M3 is big enough to accommodate a few instances of Alzette together with a few round constants.

The situation is a bit different for 8-bit AVR. The arithmetic/logical operations of Alzette amount to 78 instructions altogether, each of which executes in a single cycle, i.e. 78 clock cycles in total. Each of the used instructions has a length of 2 bytes, yielding a code size of 156 bytes. However, in contrast to ARM, we can not take it for granted that the whole state of a cipher fits into the register file of an AVR micro-controller, which means the load and store operations should be considered when evaluating the execution time. Loading a byte from RAM takes 2 cycles, while loading a byte from flash (e.g. for the round constants) requires 3 cycles. Storing a byte in RAM takes also 2 cycles. Consequently, when taking all loads/stores into account (including the loading of a round constant from flash), the execution time increases from 78 to 122 cycles and the code size from 156 to 196 bytes.

4.2 Hardware Implementations

A hardware implementation can, for example, use a 32-bit ALU that is able to execute the following set of basic arithmetic/logical operations: 32-bit XOR, addition of 32-bit words, and rotations of a 32-bit word by four different amounts, namely 16, 17, 24, and 31 bits. Since there are only four different rotation amounts, the rotations can be simply implemented by a collection of 32 4-to-1 multiplexers. There exist a number of different design approaches for a 32-bit adder; the simplest variant is a conventional Ripple-Carry Adder (RCA) composed of 32 Full Adder (FA) cells. RCAs are very efficient in terms of area requirements, but their delay increases linearly with the bit-length of the adder.

Alternatively, if an implementation requires a short critical path, the adder can also take the form of a Carry-Lookahead Adder (CLA) or Carry-Skip Adder (CSA), both of which have a delay that grows logarithmically with the word size. On the other hand, when reaching small silicon area is the main goal, one can "re-use" the adder for performing XOR operations. Namely, an RCA can output the XOR of its two inputs by simply suppressing the propagation of carries, which requires an ensemble of 32 AND gates. In summary, a minimalist ALU consists of 32 FA cells, 32 AND gates (to suppress the carries if needed), and 32 4-to-1 multiplexers (for the rotations). To minimize execution time, it makes sense to combine the addition (resp. XOR) with a rotation into a single operation that can be executed in a single clock cycle.

5   Alzette as a Building Block

Alzette is at the core of two families of lightweight algorithms that are among the second round candidates of the NIST lightweight cryptography standardization process, namely the hash functions ESCH and the authenticated ciphers with associated data SCHWAEMM (submission SPARKLE [8]). In this section, we show that it can also be used to easily construct block ciphers. This approach is flexible: combining Alzette with simple linear layers, we can simply build step functions operating on 64-, 128- and 256-bit blocks. We explain this approach and analyze the security of its result in Sect. 5.1. Specific instances are then given in Sect. 5.2, namely the 64-bit lightweight block cipher CRAX, and the 256-bit tweakable block cipher TRAX.

5.1   Skeletons for a Family of (Tweakable) Block Ciphers

Our approach relies on the long trail strategy pioneered by the designers of SPARX [19], and which was then used to build sLiSCP [3], sLiSCP-light [4] as well as the NIST lightweight candidates using them (SPIX [2], SPOC [1], SPARKLE [8]). Provided that the round function allows its use, this method provides a simple algorithm for bounding the probability of differential and linear trails. To achieve this, we loop over all possible truncated trails, and bound the probability of all differential (resp. linear) trails that conform to the truncated trail using the differential (resp. linear) bounds of the employed S-box, including those for multiple iterations when relevant. In all the algorithms listed above, variants of the Feistel structure have been applied because such round functions lend themselves well to such an analysis.

It is simple to adapt this framework to the design of Alzette-based block ciphers. Furthermore, the structure of a long trail argument allows for an efficient algorithm bounding the probability of *related-tweak* differentials.[6] Indeed, in our

---

[6] Note that, in a related-tweak differential, we allow non-zero input differences not only in the plaintext, but also in the tweak value. This is because the attacker can choose the tweak, i.e., he has access to an encryption oracle for the cipher instantiated with a tweak T and a (random) key K and to an encryption oracle for a cipher instantiated with tweak $T \oplus \Delta$ and key K, where Δ can be freely chosen.

case, the S-box used is 64 bit wide. Thus, the number of bits needed to describe a truncated differential in a given internal state is very small, only 4 suffice for a block size of 256 bits. Besides, the use of a Feistel structure implies that half of these bits are mere copies of the ones in the previous round. As a consequence, the total number of truncated trails that must be considered is low.

It also implies that the impact of a tweak difference is manageable: if the tweak difference activates a previously inactive S-box then its presence does not increase the number of truncated trails. On the other hand, a possible cancellation merely multiplies the number of possible trails by 2. An algorithm enumerating all related-tweak truncated trails such that the probability of all differential trails that conform to them is below a given threshold, is therefore easy to write and is efficient. In fact, our straight-forward Python implementation returned all the results needed for this paper in a matter of seconds at worst. Large S-boxes such as Alzette are therefore very convenient building blocks to construct tweakable block ciphers with strong security arguments.

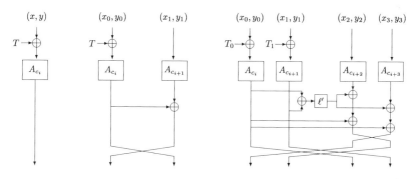

Fig. 2. The round functions of TRAX-S, TRAX-M, and TRAX-L, respectively. $\ell'(z_1, z_2, z_3, z_4) = (z_4, z_3 \oplus z_4, z_2, z_1 \oplus z_2)$, where z_i are 16-bit words. The tweak is added only in odd steps.

Below, we present three Alzette-based (tweakable) block cipher structures for which we provide upper bounds on the probability of the best differential trail in both the single-key and the related-tweak setting. Of course, we also investigate other attacks. The "S", "M" and "L" versions operate on 64, 128 and 256 bits respectively and their round functions are depicted in Fig. 2 (pseudo-code is provided in the full version). Their properties are summarized in Table 9:

- $r_e(c)$ rounds are needed to prevent the existence of known single-key distinguishers with a data complexity upper bounded by 2^c in total,
- $r_e^T(c)$ rounds are needed to prevent the existence of known related-tweak distinguishers with a data complexity upper bounded by 2^c in total (possibly spread across multiple tweak values), and

– r_d rounds are needed in order for all the bits of the state to depend on all the bits of the key.

For example, if the best single-key differential trail with a probability above 2^{-n} covers r rounds, then $r_e \geq r + 1$. It is assumed that n-bit subkeys are used.

It is assumed that there is no tweak schedule, i.e. that the tweak is simply XORed in the same part of the state each time it is added. As discussed below, we found that the security level was higher when this addition occurred every second step. The motivation for this simple tweak-schedule is simple: the tweak is expected to change far more often than the key, so using a trivial tweak-schedule will improve the performances of our algorithms.

Of course, we can set the tweak to a constant (e.g. 0) and obtain a tweak-less "regular" block cipher.[7] For the skeleton structures, we do not specify key schedules and leave it to cipher designers to come up with appropriate ones for their use cases. Related-key and related-tweak security will of course depend on the specifics of the key schedule chosen. We present concrete ciphers using these structures in Sect. 5.2 (along with their key schedules). Our best distinguishers against the various versions of our step function are summarized in Table 10. Related-tweak integral cryptanalysis is given in the full version of this paper.

Table 9. The properties of the different (tweakable) round functions.

Version	n	$|T|$	r_d	r_e	$r_e^T(n)$	$r_e^T(n/2)$
S	64	64	2	5	8	4
M	128	64	2	7	11	6
L	256	128	3	10	16	9

The S Version. It operates on 64 bits, meaning that it simply consists in iterating Alzette, interleaving it with key additions. The tweak is XORed every second step as it allows to ensure that at least one double Alzette is active during 4 steps. Thus, 8 steps are sufficient to prevent related-tweak differential distinguishers with a data complexity of 2^{64}. If we remove the tweak then we need 4 steps to argue the absence of differential distinguishers.

We start adding the tweak at the beginning of step 1 and not step 0 as it could otherwise trivially be cancelled out with chosen plaintexts.

As we saw in Sect. 3.2, linear distinguishers are in practice less predictable than differential ones. In particular, they exhibit some key-sensitivity that we did not observe in the differential case. As our bound for 4 steps is at the edge of being exploitable (2^{-34}), a small key-dependent deviation may allow 4-step distinguishers. As a consequence, we consider that 5 steps are needed to prevent linear distinguishers. Note that, allowing related tweaks does not give an advantage when looking for linear distinguisher, as established by Kranz et al. [24].

---

[7] We do *not* consider related-cipher attacks between the obtained block cipher and the corresponding tweakable block cipher.

Table 10. The number of steps $r_e(i)$ needed for the S, M and L step functions to prevent various distinguishers with a data complexity of at most 2^i. "RT" stands for "related-tweak" where the tweak is added in every odd step. As $r_e(n/2) \leq r_e(n)$, we use the latter if the former is not known and use "$\dagger$". For comparison, we give $r_e(i)$ for the AES using that it achieves 25 active S-boxes in any non-trivial 4-round (differential or linear) trail and plugging in the bounds for its S-box provided in Table 7.

	Distinguisher	Differential	Linear	Imp. diff.	RT differential
S	$r_e(n)$	4	5	2	8
	$r_e(n/2)$	2	3	$2^\dagger$	4
M	$r_e(n)$	7	7	4	11
	$r_e(n/2)$	4	4	$4^\dagger$	6
AES-128	$r_e(n)$	4	4	5	–
	$r_e(n/2)$	4	4	$5^\dagger$	–
L	$r_e(n)$	10	10	4	16
	$r_e(n/2)$	5	6	$4^\dagger$	9

The security against integral attacks and other attacks that would exploit a slow diffusion (like impossible differential attacks) also follows directly from our analysis of Alzette: our best integral distinguisher relies on the bit-based division property and covers only 6 rounds of Alzette, i.e. 1.5 steps. Extending it backwards, we can obtain at most an 11-round zero-sum distinguisher, i.e. one that covers 2.75 steps. Thus, 3 steps are sufficient to prevent them. Since we have full diffusion in one step, there cannot be an impossible differential found via a miss-in-the-middle that covers 2 steps.

Assuming that the key schedule uses statistically independent key bits in even and odd steps, we need only $r_d = 2$ steps to ensure that all bits depend (although possibly weakly) on all key bits. This result, along with all the distinguishers we investigated for this step function, are summarized in Table 10.

The M Version. In order to operate on 128 bits, we use a simple Feistel round as the linear layer that maps (x, y) to $(y \oplus x, x)$. This structure ensures long trails. To further foster the existence of long trails, we only XOR the tweak on half of the state, namely at the input of the Alzette instance which is always doubled due to the structure of the linear layer.

We have found using our long trail argument implementation that the best frequency for adding a tweak corresponds to an addition every second round (as for the S version). A smaller or larger number of steps between tweak additions would lead to worse differential bounds. As in the S version, we start adding the tweak at the beginning of step 1.

A long trail argument shows that differential and linear distinguishers become infeasible when the number of steps is at least equal to 7. Unlike in the S version, trail clustering is less of a concern here. Indeed, we observed the clustering within one Alzette to be minimal, and unlike in the S version, the linear masks are constrained in each step by the presence of the linear layer. It is not sufficient for the input and output masks of a double Alzette to be identical: in order to leverage clustering, we now need that the mask at the end of the first Alzette call is the same in all trails as well.

In the related-tweak setting, there could exist differential trail covering more than 7 steps with usable probabilities but none covering 11 steps (or more). If we restrict ourselves to attack with a data complexity at most equal to 2^{64} then no useful related-tweak trail can cover more than 6 steps.

This step function employs a Feistel structure with a bijective Feistel function but the well known 5-round impossible differential identified by Knudsen [23] cannot be used here. Indeed, our non-linear permutation (Alzette) is applied on both branches in each round, thus breaking the pattern used by this distinguisher. In fact, the best impossible differential we can find only covers 4 steps: the probability of the transition $(0, \delta) \rightsquigarrow (\Delta, \Delta)$ is equal to 0 for any non-zero 64-bit differences δ and Δ. It needs about 2^{32} chosen plaintexts to be exploited.

Since the key is of the same size as the block, the number of rounds needed for diffusion of the key material is the number of rounds needed all state bits to impact the whole state. In this case, it is $r_d = 2$.

The L Version. This round function operates on 256-bit using 4 Alzette instances in parallel. The round key is added in the full state. The best frequency for adding the tweak is every second step, for the same reason as for the M version: changing this frequency leads to worse differential bounds in the related-tweak setting.

This round function is similar to the one of SPARKLE: a lot of the cryptanalysis performed for this algorithm directly carries over (see [8]). In particular, the type of attacks for which we need the largest number of steps to prevent the existence of distinguishers is indeed the linear one in the single-tweak setting.

As for the M version, the number of rounds needed for diffusion of the key is the number needed for all state bits to impact the whole state. Here, it is $r_d = 3$.

5.2   Recommended Instances

Choosing the Number of Steps. In order to evaluate the number of steps needed to build a secure cipher, we observed that attacks against block ciphers are usually constructed using a specific distinguisher against a round-reduced version of the algorithm. Then, rounds are added at the top and at the bottom using key guesses. As a consequence, we used the following heuristic.

Heuristic (Number of rounds). *Suppose that a block cipher round function is such that:*

- *r_e rounds are needed to prevent the existence of known (and relevant) distinguishers, and*
- *r_d rounds are needed in order for all the bits of the state to depend on all the bits of the key.*

Then, we suggest using a number of rounds equal to $H_\eta = \lceil 2r_d + (1 + \eta)r_e \rceil$, where η is a security factor intended to take into account possible improvements of the relevant distinguishers.

This method is heuristic as it is impossible to foresee how the best distinguishers will be improved, if at all. At the same time, we think it makes more sense than an approach based e.g. on simply doubling the number of rounds needed to prevent known distinguisher since it takes into account the actual structure of the attacks known. Our restriction to "relevant" distinguisher allows for example designers to discard related-key distinguisher if those are not relevant for their design. On the other hand, in our case, we consider related-tweak distinguishers to be relevant. In our definition of r_d, we assume that the diffusion is equally fast in the forward and in the backward direction.

A Lightweight Block Cipher. We can use our round function to build CRAX-S-10, a lightweight block cipher operating on 64-bit using a 128-bit key intended for the most constrained micro-controllers. We claim that it provides 128 bits of security in the single-key setting. A reference implementation is provided in the full version. We used a security factor $\eta = 0.2$, so that the total number steps corresponds to $10 = \lceil 2 + 2 + r_e \times 1.2 \rceil$.

Our cipher uses a tweakless instance of the S step function described above. Since the step function has good diffusion and since we do not aim for related-key security, we use a very simple key schedule: the 64-bit round key k_i used at the beginning of step i is simply $k_i = K_{i \mod 2} \oplus i$, where the master key is (K_0, K_1). As there is no tweak, we do not need to worry about a bad interaction between tweak and key.

In order to prevent slide properties, we use the step counter in combination with a reduction of the number of round constants: instead of using all 8 of them, we only use 5. That way, in the first half of the cipher the steps involve c_i and $K_{i \mod 2}$ while in the second half they use c_i and $K_{(i+1) \mod 2}$. For other attacks, the security of CRAX-S-10 follows directly from our analysis of Alzette.

CRAX-S-10 is a very lightweight block cipher, arguably one of the the lightest ever reported in the literature when it comes to micro-controller implementations. The code size, RAM consumption, and execution time of CRAX-S-10 on an 8-bit AVR and a 32-bit ARM Cortex-M3 micro-controller are summarized in Table 11, along with those of SPECK-64/128 [7]. We obtained the results for SPECK from the best implementations contained in the FELICS project [18], namely the implementation "03" for ARM Cortex-M3 and the implementation "06" for the AVR architecture.[8] As SPECK has the best performances across micro-controllers, it serves as a good benchmark for comparison.

The ARM implementation of CRAX we benchmarked is the optimized C code included in the full version of this paper. Encrypting a single 64-bit block on a Cortex-M3 takes 239 cycles (including function-call overhead), and the decryption has exactly the same execution time. For comparison, SPECK-64/128 encrypts and decrypts at a rate of 184 and 254 cycles per block, respectively. However, since SPECK needs first to run its key schedule, CRAX-S-10 encryption

---

[8] The source code of these SPECK implementations and the complete benchmarking results are available on the CryptoLux wiki at http://www.cryptolux.org/index.php/FELICS_Block_Ciphers_Detailed_Results ("Scenario 0").

Table 11. A comparison of our implementation of CRAX-S-10 with SPECK-64/128. RAM and ROM consumption are measured in bytes and the time for processing a 64-bit block is given in clock cycles.

		Enc. 64-bit			Dec. 64-bit			Key schedule		
		ROM	RAM	Time	ROM	RAM	Time	ROM	RAM	Time
32-bit ARM	SPECK	340	132	184	448	132	254	48	132	514
(Cortex-M3)	CRAX-S	196	36	239	202	36	239	0	0	0
8-bit AVR	SPECK	542	132	997	706	132	1139	178	132	1401
(ATmega128)	CRAX-S	584	20	1257	582	20	1249	0	0	0

is faster than SPECK for short messages of up to 9 blocks (i.e. 72 bytes). The SPECK implementation occupies significantly more RAM than that of CRAX (mostly because of the round keys) and has a much smaller binary code size.

The results for the 8-bit AVR platform in Table 11 were both obtained with hand-written assembler implementations. When executed on an ATmega128 micro-controller, CRAX-S-10 is slower than SPECK-64/128 when we leave the key schedule aside, but is actually faster on short messages (up to 5 blocks). Similar to ARM, the round keys make SPECK significantly more RAM-demanding than CRAX. In terms of code size, the decryption CRAX is smaller than that of SPECK, while the encryption is slightly larger. However, when both functionalities are needed, CRAX consumes less code space than SPECK (including key schedule).

In summary, we can say that CRAX is at least as light as SPECK (lighter on ARM, comparable on AVR). Further, CRAX shines for short messages, which are common in real-world applications like simple challenge-response protocols for the authentication of RFID tags and other IoT devices.

A Wide Tweakable Block Cipher. We can build an efficient software-oriented 256-bit tweakable block cipher with a 256-bit key and a 128-bit tweak using TRAX-L-17 (pronounced "T-rax"). We claim related-tweak security as long as the total number of (x, T) queries to the encryption (or decryption) oracle for a given key k is at most equal to 2^{128}. We do not make any claim in the related-key setting. A reference implementation is provided in the full version.

The motivation for this bound on the data complexity is simple: while an attacker may have tremendous computing power, it is impossible that they obtain this many plaintext/ciphertext pairs. Furthermore, the security of many modes of operations drops when the amount of queries reaches the birthday bound—2^{128} in our case. Combining the fact that the best distinguisher in the related-tweak setting cannot cover 9 steps with the same security factor as CRAX-S-10 (namely $\eta = 0.2$), we use $\lceil 3 + 3 + 1.2 \times 9 \rceil = 17$ steps.

For the key schedule, we use a simple generalized Feistel structure to update the key state and thus derive $k_{i+1} = F_i(k_i)$, where k_0 is the 256-bit master key and where P_i is $\sigma \circ F_i$, with $\sigma(x_0, ..., x_7) = (x_1, x_2, x_3, x_4, x_5, x_6, x_7, x_0)$ and

$$F_i(x_0, x_1, x_2, x_3, x_4, x_5, x_6, x_7) = \big(x_0 + x_1 + c_{2i+1}, \ x_1, \ x_2 \oplus x_3 \oplus i, \ x_3,$$
$$x_4 + x_5 + c_{2i}, \ x_5, \ x_6 \oplus x_7 \oplus (i \ll 16), \ x_7\big),$$

where the constant indices are taken modulo 8. This key schedule ensures that the key material undergoes some transformation so as to break potential patterns linking subkeys and tweak.

A tweakable block cipher lends itself well to a parallelizable mode of operation such as ΘCB [25], a variant of OCB which saves its complex overhead needed to turn a regular block cipher into a tweakable one. Since our block size is equal to 256 bits, attacks relying on collisions obtained via the birthday paradox are non-issue with TRAX-L-17. Some modes such as the Synthetic Counter-in-Tweak [35] can retain a security level up to the birthday bound in case of nonce misuse. As suggested in [15], using a 256-bit block cipher can also help providing post-quantum security in cases where the attacker is given a lot of power (e.g. if the primitive runs on a quantum computer).[9]

In summary, TRAX-L-17 can be used in SCT mode to provide 128 bits of security in case of nonce-misuse, and its large block size can frustrate some quantum attacks when used in the same mode as SATURNIN: it can be used to offer a very robust authenticated encryption. On a Cortex-M3 micro-controller, the generation of sub-keys takes 980 cycles and the encryption has an execution time of 2506 cycles (both results are based on a standard C implementation). For comparison, SATURNIN is more than two times slower on ARM (a detailed comparison can be found in the full version).

The use of 32-bit operations implies that it is possible to vectorize the computation of several parallel TRAX-L-17 instances on many platforms, meaning that its speed can be multiplied whenever e.g. AVX instructions are available.

6   Conclusion

Alzette is a component of a new kind, a wide S-box operating on 64 bits that can nevertheless be argued to provide strong security against many attacks. Because of its reliance on ARX operations with carefully chosen rotations, a constant-time implementation is both easy to write and very efficient on a wide class of processors and micro-controllers.

The NIST LWC submission SPARKLE [8] provides the first application of the Alzette S-box, but we showed that Alzette can also be used to design software-efficient (tweakable) block ciphers on a variety of block lengths. A modified long-trail argument allows us to estimate the number of rounds needed to provide security with regard to (related-tweak) differential and linear attacks. We provided two concrete instances of this approach: the 64-bit block cipher CRAX and the 256-bit tweakable block cipher TRAX. Due to its very simple key schedule, CRAX is competitive compared to the block cipher SPECK: it consumes less

---

[9] We remark that in several modes of operations, like ΘCB, it is necessary to take care of domain separation. For instance, a few bits of the tweak can be reserved for this purpose. For example, the NIST lightweight AEAD candidate SKINNY-AEAD [10] simply dedicates one byte of the tweak for domain separation. Therefore, if a full 256-bit tweak needs to be exploited, a tweakable block cipher with a (slightly) larger tweak length of $256 + x$ would be beneficial.

RAM and is faster for short messages consisting of up to nine 64-bit blocks. On the other hand, the large block size of TRAX can be used to obtain strong security guarantees in settings where the attacker is quite powerful (nonce-misuse, quantum computing) while its use of a tweak eases the use of parallelizable modes of operation that can better leverage vector instructions.

Acknowledgements. Part of the work of Christof Beierle was funded by *Deutsche Forschungsgemeinschaft (DFG)*, project number 411879806, and part of the work of Christof Beierle was performed while he was at the University of Luxembourg and funded by the SnT CryptoLux RG budget. Luan Cardoso dos Santos is supported by the Luxembourg National Research Fund through grant PRIDE15/10621687/SPsquared. Part of the work of Aleksei Udovenko was performed while he was at the University of Luxembourg and funded by the Fonds National de la Recherche Luxembourg (project reference 9037104). Part of the work by Vesselin Velichkov was performed while he was at the University of Luxembourg. The work of Qingju Wang is funded by the University of Luxembourg Internal Research Project (IRP) FDISC. The experiments presented in this paper were carried out using the HPC facilities of the University of Luxembourg [40] – see https://hpc.uni.lu.

References

1. AlTawy, R., et al.: SpoC: an authenticated cipher. NIST round 2 lightweight candidate (2019). https://csrc.nist.gov/CSRC/media/Projects/lightweight-cryptography/documents/round-2/spec-doc-rnd2/spoc-spec-round2.pdf

2. AlTawy, R., Gong, G., He, M., Mandal, K., Rohit, R.: SPIX: an authenticated cipher. NIST round 2 lightweight candidate (2019). https://csrc.nist.gov/CSRC/media/Projects/lightweight-cryptography/documents/round-2/spec-doc-rnd2/spix-spec-round2.pdf

3. AlTawy, R., Rohit, R., He, M., Mandal, K., Yang, G., Gong, G.: sLiSCP: Simeck-based permutations for lightweight sponge cryptographic primitives. In: Adams, C., Camenisch, J. (eds.) SAC 2017. LNCS, vol. 10719, pp. 129–150. Springer, Cham (2018). https://doi.org/10.1007/978-3-319-72565-9_7

4. Altawy, R., Rohit, R., He, M., Mandal, K., Yang, G., Gong, G.: SLISCP-light: towards hardware optimized sponge-specific cryptographic permutations. ACM Trans. Embed. Comput. Syst. **17**(4), 81:1–81:26 (2018)

5. Barreto, P., Nikov, V., Nikova, S., Rijmen, V., Tischhauser, E.: Whirlwind: a new cryptographic hash function. Des. Codes Cryptogr. **56**(2), 141–162 (2010). https://doi.org/10.1007/s10623-010-9391-y

6. Beaulieu, R., Shors, D., Smith, J., Treatman-Clark, S., Weeks, B., Wingers, L.: The SIMON and SPECK families of lightweight block ciphers. IACR Cryptology ePrint Archive 2013, 404 (2013). http://eprint.iacr.org/2013/404

7. Beaulieu, R., Shors, D., Smith, J., Treatman-Clark, S., Weeks, B., Wingers, L.: The SIMON and SPECK block ciphers on AVR 8-bit microcontrollers. Cryptology ePrint Archive, Report 2014/947 (2014). http://eprint.iacr.org/2014/947

8. Beierle, C., et al.: SCHWAEMM and ESCH: lightweight authenticated encryption and hashing using the Sparkle permutation family. NIST round 2 lightweight candidate (2019). https://csrc.nist.gov/CSRC/media/Projects/lightweight-cryptography/documents/round-2/spec-doc-rnd2/sparkle-spec-round2.pdf

9. Beierle, C., et al.: The SKINNY family of block ciphers and its low-latency variant MANTIS. In: Robshaw, M., Katz, J. (eds.) CRYPTO 2016. Part II. LNCS, vol. 9815, pp. 123–153. Springer, Heidelberg (2016). https://doi.org/10.1007/978-3-662-53008-5_5

10. Beierle, C., et al.: SKINNY-AEAD and SKINNY-Hash. NIST round 2 lightweight candidate (2019). https://csrc.nist.gov/CSRC/media/Projects/lightweight-cryptography/documents/round-2/spec-doc-rnd2/SKINNY-spec-round2.pdf

11. Bernstein, D.J., et al.: GIMLI: a cross-platform permutation. In: Fischer, W., Homma, N. (eds.) CHES 2017. LNCS, vol. 10529, pp. 299–320. Springer, Cham (2017). https://doi.org/10.1007/978-3-319-66787-4_15

12. Biham, E., Shamir, A.: Differential cryptanalysis of DES-like cryptosystems. In: Menezes, A.J., Vanstone, S.A. (eds.) CRYPTO 1990. LNCS, vol. 537, pp. 2–21. Springer, Heidelberg (1991). https://doi.org/10.1007/3-540-38424-3_1

13. Biryukov, A., De Cannière, C., Braeken, A., Preneel, B.: A toolbox for cryptanalysis: linear and affine equivalence algorithms. In: Biham, E. (ed.) EUROCRYPT 2003. LNCS, vol. 2656, pp. 33–50. Springer, Heidelberg (2003). https://doi.org/10.1007/3-540-39200-9_3

14. Biryukov, A., Velichkov, V., Corre, Y.L.: Automatic search for the best trails in ARX: application to block cipher speck. In: Peyrin [34], pp. 289–310

15. Canteaut, A., et al.: Saturnin: a suite of lightweight symmetric algorithms for post-quantum security. NIST round 2 lightweight candidate (2019). https://csrc.nist.gov/CSRC/media/Projects/lightweight-cryptography/documents/round-2/spec-doc-rnd2/saturnin-spec-round2.pdf

16. Cheon, J.H., Takagi, T. (eds.): ASIACRYPT 2016. Part I. LNCS, vol. 10031. Springer, Heidelberg (2016). https://doi.org/10.1007/978-3-662-53887-6

17. Dinu, D.: Efficient and secure implementations of lightweight symmetric cryptographic primitives. Ph.D. thesis, University of Luxembourg (2017). https://orbilu.uni.lu/handle/10993/33803

18. Dinu, D., Corre, Y.L., Khovratovich, D., Perrin, L., Großschädl, J., Biryukov, A.: Triathlon of lightweight block ciphers for the Internet of things. J. Cryptogr. Eng. 9(3), 283–302 (2018). https://doi.org/10.1007/s13389-018-0193-x

19. Dinu, D., Perrin, L., Udovenko, A., Velichkov, V., Großschädl, J., Biryukov, A.: Design strategies for ARX with provable bounds: Sparx and LAX. In: Cheon and Takagi [16], pp. 484–513

20. Fu, K., Wang, M., Guo, Y., Sun, S., Hu, L.: MILP-based automatic search algorithms for differential and linear trails for speck. In: Peyrin [34], pp. 268–288

21. Gueron, S., Johnson, S., Walker, J.: SHA-512/256. Cryptology ePrint Archive, Report 2010/548 (2010). http://eprint.iacr.org/2010/548

22. Gurobi Optimization, LLC: Gurobi optimizer reference manual (2018). http://www.gurobi.com

23. Knudsen, L.: Deal - a 128-bit block cipher. NIST AES Proposal (1998)

24. Kranz, T., Leander, G., Wiemer, F.: Linear cryptanalysis: key schedules and tweakable block ciphers. IACR Trans. Symmetric Cryptol. 2017(1), 474–505 (2017)

25. Krovetz, T., Rogaway, P.: The software performance of authenticated-encryption modes. In: Joux, A. (ed.) FSE 2011. LNCS, vol. 6733, pp. 306–327. Springer, Heidelberg (2011). https://doi.org/10.1007/978-3-642-21702-9_18

26. Leander, G., Abdelraheem, M.A., AlKhzaimi, H., Zenner, E.: A cryptanalysis of PRINTCIPHER: the invariant subspace attack. In: Rogaway, P. (ed.) CRYPTO 2011. LNCS, vol. 6841, pp. 206–221. Springer, Heidelberg (2011). https://doi.org/10.1007/978-3-642-22792-9_12

27. Liu, Y., Wang, Q., Rijmen, V.: Automatic search of linear trails in ARX with applications to SPECK and Chaskey. In: Manulis, M., Sadeghi, A.-R., Schneider, S. (eds.) ACNS 2016. LNCS, vol. 9696, pp. 485–499. Springer, Cham (2016). https://doi.org/10.1007/978-3-319-39555-5_26

28. Liu, Z.: Automatic tools for differential and linear cryptanalysis of ARX ciphers. Ph.D. thesis, University of Chinese Academy of Science (2017). (in Chinese)

29. Matsui, M.: Linear cryptanalysis method for DES cipher. In: Helleseth, T. (ed.) EUROCRYPT 1993. LNCS, vol. 765, pp. 386–397. Springer, Heidelberg (1994). https://doi.org/10.1007/3-540-48285-7_33

30. Matsui, M.: On correlation between the order of S-boxes and the strength of DES. In: Santis, A.D. (ed.) EUROCRYPT 1994. LNCS, vol. 950, pp. 366–375. Springer, Heidelberg (1995). https://doi.org/10.1007/BFb0053451

31. Niels, F., et al.: The Skein hash function family. Submission to the NIST SHA-3 competition (round 3) (2010)

32. Niemetz, A., Preiner, M., Biere, A.: Boolector 2.0 system description. J. Satisf. Boolean Model. Comput. 9, 53–58 (2014 (published 2015)). https://github.com/boolector/boolector

33. Patarin, J., Goubin, L., Courtois, N.: Improved algorithms for isomorphisms of polynomials. In: Nyberg, K. (ed.) EUROCRYPT 1998. LNCS, vol. 1403, pp. 184–200. Springer, Heidelberg (1998). https://doi.org/10.1007/BFb0054126

34. Peyrin, T. (ed.): FSE 2016. LNCS, vol. 9783. Springer, Heidelberg (2016). https://doi.org/10.1007/978-3-662-52993-5

35. Peyrin, T., Seurin, Y.: Counter-in-tweak: authenticated encryption modes for tweakable block ciphers. In: Robshaw, M., Katz, J. (eds.) CRYPTO 2016. Part I. LNCS, vol. 9814, pp. 33–63. Springer, Heidelberg (2016). https://doi.org/10.1007/978-3-662-53018-4_2

36. Sun, L., Wang, W., Wang, M.: Automatic search of bit-based division property for ARX ciphers and word-based division property. In: Takagi, T., Peyrin, T. (eds.) ASIACRYPT 2017. Part I. LNCS, vol. 10624, pp. 128–157. Springer, Cham (2017). https://doi.org/10.1007/978-3-319-70694-8_5

37. Todo, Y.: Structural evaluation by generalized integral property. In: Oswald, E., Fischlin, M. (eds.) EUROCRYPT 2015. Part I. LNCS, vol. 9056, pp. 287–314. Springer, Heidelberg (2015). https://doi.org/10.1007/978-3-662-46800-5_12

38. Todo, Y., Leander, G., Sasaki, Y.: Nonlinear invariant attack - practical attack on full SCREAM, iSCREAM, and Midori64. In: Cheon, J.H., Takagi, T. (eds.) ASIACRYPT 2016. Part II. LNCS, vol. 10032, pp. 3–33. Springer, Heidelberg (2016). https://doi.org/10.1007/978-3-662-53890-6_1

39. Todo, Y., Morii, M.: Bit-based division property and application to Simon family. In: Peyrin [34], pp. 357–377

40. Varrette, S., Bouvry, P., Cartiaux, H., Georgatos, F.: Management of an academic HPC cluster: the UL experience. In: Proceedings of the 2014 International Conference on High Performance Computing & Simulation (HPCS 2014), pp. 959–967. IEEE, Bologna, July 2014

41. Xiang, Z., Zhang, W., Bao, Z., Lin, D.: Applying MILP method to searching integral distinguishers based on division property for 6 lightweight block ciphers. In: Cheon and Takagi [16], pp. 648–678

Delay Functions

Order-Fairness for Byzantine Consensus

Mahimna Kelkar[1,2,3]($\boxtimes$), Fan Zhang[1,2,3], Steven Goldfeder[1,2,3],
and Ari Juels[1,2,3]

[1] Cornell Tech, New York, USA
{mahimna,fanz}@cs.cornell.edu,
{goldfeder,juels}@cornell.edu
[2] Cornell University, Ithaca, USA
[3] The Initiative for CryptoCurrencies & Contracts (IC3), New York, USA

Abstract. Decades of research in both cryptography and distributed systems has extensively studied the problem of state machine replication, also known as Byzantine consensus. A consensus protocol must satisfy two properties: *consistency* and *liveness*. These properties ensure that honest participating nodes agree on the same log and dictate when fresh transactions get added. They fail, however, to ensure against adversarial manipulation of the actual *ordering* of transactions in the log. Indeed, in leader-based protocols (almost all protocols used today), malicious leaders can directly choose the final transaction ordering.

To rectify this problem, we propose a third consensus property: *transaction order-fairness*. We initiate the first formal investigation of order-fairness and explain its fundamental importance. We provide several natural definitions for order-fairness and analyze the assumptions necessary to realize them.

We also propose a new class of consensus protocols called Aequitas. Aequitas protocols are the first to achieve order-fairness in addition to consistency and liveness. They can be realized in a black-box way using existing broadcast and agreement primitives (or indeed using any consensus protocol), and work in both synchronous and asynchronous network models.

1 Introduction

The abstraction of state machine replication has been investigated in cryptography and distributed systems literature for the past three decades. At a high level, the goal of a state machine replication protocol is for a set of nodes to agree on an ever-growing, linearly ordered log of messages (transactions). Two properties need to be satisfied by such a protocol: (1) *Consistency* - all honest nodes must have the same view of the agreed upon log—that is, they must output messages

---

The full version of this paper is available at https://eprint.iacr.org/2020/269 [27].

D. Micciancio and T. Ristenpart (Eds.): CRYPTO 2020, LNCS 12172, pp. 451–480, 2020.
https://doi.org/10.1007/978-3-030-56877-1_16

in the same order; and (2) *Liveness* - messages submitted by clients are added to the log within a reasonable amount of time. In this paper, we will use the terms *state machine replication* and *consensus*[1] interchangeably.

Unfortunately, neither consistency nor liveness says anything about the actual ordering of transactions in the final log. A protocol that ensures that all nodes agree on the same ordering is deemed consistent regardless of how the ordering is generated. This leaves room for the definition to be satisfied even if an adversary directly chooses the actual transaction ordering, which is discomforting considering that the ordering is often easy to manipulate [7]. Moreover, in all existing protocols that rely on a designated "leader" node (e.g., [15,34,44]), which includes most used in practice, an adversarial leader may choose to propose transactions in any order.

In this paper, we formulate a new property for byzantine consensus which we call *order-fairness*. Intuitively, order-fairness denotes the notion that if a large number of nodes receive a transaction tx_1 before another one tx_2, then this should somehow be reflected in the final ordering.

Importance of Fair Transaction Ordering. The need for a notion of fair transaction ordering is immediately clear when looking at financial systems. Here, the execution order can determine the validity and/or profitability of a given transaction. Suppose Bob has $0, and two transactions are initiated: tx_0, which sends $5 from Alice to Bob, and tx_1, which sends $5 from Bob to Carol. If tx_0 is sequenced before tx_1, then both transactions are valid; the opposite ordering invalidates tx_1. Manipulation of transaction ordering is a well known phenomenon on Wall Street [32], but recent work has shown it to also be commonplace in consensus-based systems such as permissionless blockchains. A recent paper by Daian et al. [20], for example, reports rampant adversarial manipulation of transactions in the Ethereum network [23] by bots extracting upwards of USD 6M in revenue from unsophisticated users.

Comparison to Validity in Byzantine Agreement. Beyond its critical practical importance, we believe that order-fairness is a key missing theoretical concept in existing consensus literature. To underscore this point, consider Byzantine agreement [30], or *single-shot* agreement, another well-studied problem in consensus literature. For Byzantine agreement, each node starts with a single value within a set $\mathcal{V}$. The goal is for all nodes to agree on the same value. *Validity* requires that if all honest nodes start with the same value v, then the agreed upon value should also be v.

The property of *order-fairness* is a natural analog of validity formulated for the consensus problem, i.e., extension of Byzantine agreement to multiple rounds. If all honest nodes start with the belief that a transaction tx_1 precedes another transaction tx_2, by natural analogy with validity, the final output log

---

[1] The term "consensus" has been used in systems literature for a number of related primitives, including "single-shot" consensus. However, in this paper, we use "consensus" to refer to the problem of "state machine replication."

should sequence tx_1 before tx_2. Consequently, we maintain that *order-fairness* is a natural property of independent theoretical interest in the consensus literature.

1.1 Our Contributions

The main contributions of our paper are three-fold: (1) First, we investigate a natural notion of fair transaction ordering and show why it is impossible to realize. (2) Second, we investigate slightly weaker notions of fair ordering that are intuitive yet achievable. Still, we find that no existing consensus protocol achieves them. (3) Third, we introduce a new class of consensus protocols that we refer to as Aequitas[2]. Aequitas protocols achieve fair transaction ordering while also providing the usual consistency and liveness. We discuss Aequitas protocols in both synchronous and asynchronous settings.

Defining Order-Fairness and Impossibility Results. To model our consensus protocols, we use an approach similar to prior work by Pass et al. [39,40], wherein protocol nodes *receive* transactions from clients and need to *output* or *deliver* them in a way that satisfies consistency and liveness. We detail our model in Sect. 2. Within this model, we provide the first formalization of the property of order-fairness (Sect. 4). We start with a natural definition based on when transactions are received by nodes.

Definition 1 (Receive-Order-Fairness, informal; formalized in Definition 9). *If sufficiently many (at least γ-fraction) nodes receive a transaction tx before another transaction tx', then all honest nodes must output tx before tx'.*

While Definition 1 is intuitive, it turns out that it is impossible to achieve unless we assume very strong synchrony properties and/or a non-corrupting adversary. This result draws from a surprising connection with voter preferences in social choice theory. To highlight this using a simple example, consider three nodes, A, B, and C, that each receive 3 transactions, x, y, and z. A receives them in the order $[x, y, z]$, B in the order $[y, z, x]$ and C in the order $[z, x, y]$. Notice that a majority of nodes have received $(x$ before $y)$, $(y$ before $z)$ and $(z$ before $x)$! This scenario, often called the Condorcet paradox [18], can cause a non-transitive global ordering *even when* all local orderings are transitive. This is problematic for the notion of receive-order-fairness. Theorem 1 gives an informal description of our impossibility result.

Theorem 1 (Impossibility of receive-order-fairness, informal; formalized in Theorem 2). *Consider a system with n nodes where the external network (between users and protocol nodes) is either asynchronous or the maximum delay δ is at least n rounds. Then, no protocol can achieve all of consistency, liveness, and receive-order-fairness.*

Given this impossibility result, we consider a natural relaxation of receive-order-fairness that we call *block-receive-order-fairness*, or simply *block-order-fairness*. To see the primary difference between the two definitions, we look

---

[2] Aequitas (IPA pronunciation: /ˈae̯.kʷi.taːs/) is the Roman personification of fairness.

at two transactions, tx and tx′, where sufficiently many nodes have received tx before tx′. While receive-order-fairness requires that tx be output "*before*" tx′, block-order-fairness relaxes this to "*before or at the same time as.*" We refer to transactions delivered at the same time as being in the same "block."

Definition 2 (Block-Order-Fairness, informal; formalized in Definition 11). *If sufficiently many nodes (at least γ-fraction) receive a transaction tx before another transaction tx′, then no honest node can deliver tx in a block after tx′.*

This small relaxation allows us to evade the Condorcet paradox by a simple trick: placing paradoxical orderings into the same "block." We emphasize that block order-fairness does not mean that transactions are partially ordered. Consistency still requires that all nodes output transactions in the same order (within the same block or not). The only difference is that unfair ordering of a set of transactions in our definition without blocks is now, with the use of blocks, considered fair, provided that these transactions appear in the same block.

Further, we note that while receive-order-fairness is impossible to achieve (as pointed out informally in Theorem 1 and formalized later in the paper in Theorem 2), block-order-fairness is not and we provide protocols that guarantee it. We would also like to highlight that our proposed Aequitas protocols actually make minimal use of this relaxation. In particular, they achieve the stronger notion of receive-order-fairness except when non-transitive preferences are observed.

Aequitas: Achieving order-fairness. We present a new class of consensus protocols, Aequitas, that achieve block-order-fairness, in addition to providing consistency and liveness. Aequitas protocols make use of two basic primitives in a black-box way: (1) FIFO Broadcast (FIFO-BC) [26], which is a basic extension of standard reliable broadcast; and (2) Set Byzantine Agreement (Set-BA; defined in Sect. 3), which can be achieved from Byzantine agreement.

We note that these are weak primitives and any standard consensus protocol (that achieves consistency and liveness) can also be used to build the FIFO-BC and Set-BA primitives. This results in an interesting observation: The Aequitas technique provides a generic compiler that takes any standard consensus protocol and converts it into one that also provides order-fairness. At a high level, Aequitas protocols proceed in three major stages. Each transaction tx goes through these stages before being delivered.

1. **Gossip Stage.** Nodes gossip transactions in the order that they are received. That is, each node gossips its *local* transaction ordering.

   For this purpose, we use the FIFO broadcast primitive (FIFO-BC), which guarantees that broadcasts by an honest node are delivered by other honest nodes in the same order that they were broadcast. Even if the sender is dishonest, FIFO-BC guarantees that all honest nodes deliver messages in the same order. As a result, nodes have a consistent view of the transaction orderings of other nodes.

   We use Log_i^j to denote node i's view of the order in which node j received transactions, according to how j gossiped them. Note that if node j is malicious, Log_i^j may arbitrarily differ from the actual order in which j *received* transactions, but FIFO-BC prevents j from equivocating, i.e., any two honest nodes i and k will have consistent Log_i^j and Log_k^j. When i records enough logs Log_i^k that contain tx, we say that the "gossip phase" for tx is complete.

2. **Agreement Stage.** Nodes agree on the set of nodes whose local orderings should be considered for deciding on the global ordering of a particular transaction.

   To elaborate, at the end of the gossip stage for a transaction tx, a node i ends up with a set U_i^{tx} of other nodes whose local orderings i has obtained. That is, $k \in U_i^{\mathsf{tx}}$ if tx $\in \mathsf{Log}_i^k$. Note that different nodes may end up with a slightly different set U, but agreement proceeds when enough honest nodes are present in each set. Nodes perform Byzantine agreement to agree on a set L^{tx} of nodes whose ordering will be used to finalize the ordering for tx. For this, we define a new primitive Set-BA whose validity condition guarantees that if $k \in U_i^{\mathsf{tx}}$ for all i, then $k \in L^{\mathsf{tx}}$. It is easy to see how Set-BA can be realized by using standard Byzantine agreement to determine the inclusion of each possible value k individually.

3. **Finalization Stage.** Nodes finalize the global ordering of a transaction tx using the set of local orderings decided on in the agreement stage.

   Suppose that the agreement stage for a transaction tx resulted in the set L^{tx}. Now, if there is any other transaction tx$'$ such that tx$'$ is ordered before tx in a large number of these local logs, it signifies that tx should be delivered after tx$'$. In other words, the finalization of tx depends on waiting until tx$'$ has been delivered.

   To characterize such ordering dependencies between transactions, a node i maintains a directed graph G_i, where vertices represent transactions and an edge from a to b denotes that b is waiting for a. Since nodes are building this graph on the same "data" (the set of local logs agreed upon in the agreement phase), nodes will have consistent graphs. That is, if an edge (a, b) exists in G_i, then it will also (eventually) exist in G_j, if i and j are both honest.

   We present two finalization techniques, a leader-based one and a leaderless one. For the leader-based technique, resolving any partial ordering within the graph is delegated to a leader node. We emphasize that order-fairness is not lost. The leader is only able to choose the ordering for transactions that are not required to be ordered a certain way. We present another, leaderless technique that requires no further communication between nodes. We find that both realize a slightly weaker notion of liveness than the standard one, even in the synchronous setting. Specifically, future transactions are required to be input to the system in order to "flush out" earlier transactions. We formally define "weak-liveness" in Sect. 2.

It is worth pointing out that the first two stages (gossip and agreement) are fairly straightforward to understand and easy to achieve. The third stage is somewhat complex, as it needs to avoid the Condorcet paradox while continuing to maintain both consistency and order-fairness.

Aequitas **Protocols.** In summary, we present the first consensus protocols that provide order-fairness. We provide a leader-based and a leaderless protocol each for the synchronous and asynchronous settings, for a total of four protocols that follow the same general outline. These protocols all provide consistency, block order-fairness, and some form of liveness. Figure 1 shows a comparison.

Protocol	Style	Network	Corruption Bound[†]	Consistency	Liveness	Order-Fairness
$\Pi_{\text{Aequitas}}^{\text{sync,lead}}$	Leader	Synchronous*	$n > \frac{2f}{2\gamma-1}$	✓	✓ (Weak)	✓
$\Pi_{\text{Aequitas}}^{\text{sync,nolead}}$	Leaderless	Synchronous*	$n > \frac{2f}{2\gamma-1}$	✓	✓ (Weak)	✓
$\Pi_{\text{Aequitas}}^{\text{async,lead}}$	Leader	Any	$n > \frac{4f}{2\gamma-1}$	✓	✓ (Eventual, Weak)	✓
$\Pi_{\text{Aequitas}}^{\text{async,nolead}}$	Leaderless	Any	$n > \frac{4f}{2\gamma-1}$	✓	✓ (Eventual, Weak)	✓

* Completely Synchronous Setting (See Section 2)

† $\frac{1}{2} < \gamma \leq 1$ is the order-fairness parameter (See Section 4)

Fig. 1. The Aequitas protocols

Paper Organization. The rest of the paper is organized as follows. We discuss our results in the context of related work in Sect. 1.2. We describe our formal framework, along with other preliminaries, in Sect. 2. In Sect. 3, we provide the building blocks for our protocol constructions. Section 4 formally introduces our notion of order-fairness. Section 5 provides a general overview of our constructions; we detail our leaderless construction for the synchronous setting in Sect. 6. Due to space constraints, we defer other constructions and results, as well as several proofs to the full version [27] of our paper.

1.2   Related Work

While there is an extensive literature on consensus protocols, to the best of our knowledge, no previous work formally captures a notion of order-fairness like the one we introduce. The term "fairness" has been used widely in blockchain and cryptography literature, but for properties unrelated to ours.

Broadcast Primitives. Byzantine broadcast, or the Byzantine Generals Problem [30], is the elementary broadcast primitive where a designated sender broadcasts a single value to a set of receiving nodes. In a Byzantine broadcast protocol with the key property of *consistency*, all honest receivers output the same value. Reliable broadcast is a continuous version of Byzantine broadcast where the sender broadcasts multiple values which must be eventually delivered by nodes if the sender is honest. Three orthogonal properties can be added onto reliable broadcast to give stronger notions. FIFO-ordering provides first-in first-out ordering on the messages broadcast by an honest sender. We refer to such a protocol as FIFO Broadcast or OARcast [26]. Local-ordering (also called causal-ordering) ensures that if a node broadcasts a message m' after receiving some other message m, then m will be ordered before m'. The total-ordering property ensures that all honest nodes deliver messages broadcast potentially by different senders in the same order. This notion is usually called *atomic broadcast* [19], which is well-known to be equivalent to the consensus problem. Adding all three properties to reliable broadcast results in the notion of Causal FIFO Atomic Broadcast which still does not provide the *order-fairness* property that we are looking for. The main problem is none of the requirements consider a global notion of FIFO ordering based on multiple senders.

Our order-fairness property does enforce such a notion according to the following idea: If enough nodes broadcast a message m before another message m', then honest nodes will respect this ordering. Adding this property to atomic broadcast results in a *new broadcast* notion, which we call "Global FIFO Atomic Broadcast." Consequently, requiring order-fairness along with standard consensus properties of consistency and liveness will be equivalent to this new notion of Global FIFO Atomic Broadcast.

We note that our setup is also slightly different than earlier notions. We assume that any message broadcast by an honest node is also eventually broadcast by all honest nodes. This allows us to redefine liveness in terms of being broadcast by enough nodes. This also means that identical messages broadcast by different nodes can now be delivered together as a single message. Global FIFO ordering is defined on the ordering of these messages. Note that it no longer makes sense to talk about (single source) FIFO order or causal order as identical messages, potentially broadcast at different positions by different nodes, are now delivered as a single message.

Consensus Protocols. Hundreds of Byzantine fault tolerant consensus protocols have been proposed over the years, with PBFT [15] being perhaps the most well known. Multiple survey papers [7,10] have aimed to systematize this vast literature. Many papers provide efficiency improvements while maintaining the basic leader-based structure of PBFT. That is, a *leader* or *primary* node is responsible for proposing the transactions in the current round. In such leader-based protocols ([2,3,5,8,17,34,42–44], just to name a few), the leader node can propose transactions in the order of its choosing. The leader is also capable of suppressing transactions, at least temporarily, until an honest node becomes the new leader. We highlight that in previously explored leader-based protocols, nodes do not know the ordering in which transactions were received by everyone. This means that a leader's proposal can only be rejected based on validity of transactions rather than the fairness of their ordering. Order-fairness is thus not achieved in existing leader-based protocols.

Some protocols provide *transaction censorship resistance*, such that malicious nodes cannot censor specific transactions based on their content. For this, in protocols like [4,11,36], transactions are encrypted, and the contents are revealed only once their ordering is fixed. Separately, protocols like [4,29,31] rely on a reputation based system to detect unfair censorship. Censorship resistance is strictly weaker than the order-fairness we consider for three reasons. First, in practice, even if transaction data is temporarily encrypted, metadata such as a user identifier or a client IP address can be used to censor a particular transaction. Second, a malicious leader can still *blindly* reorder or censor transactions based on just their ciphertext. But perhaps more importantly, a malicious leader colluding with a user will know the ciphertext corresponding to the user's transaction and can thus unfairly order this transaction before others.

Other Uses of the Word *Fairness*. The term *fairness* has been used before in consensus literature for notions unrelated to ours. One popular use case relates to *fairness in block mining* in Proof-of-Work (PoW) blockchains, which intuitively requires that a node's mining rewards be proportional to its relative computational power. That is, no node should be able to mine *selfishly* [24] to obtain more rewards than its fair share. This fairness notion is met by protocols in [1,31,33,35,37], among others.

Another related definition considers fairness in terms of the opportunities each node gets to append transactions to the ledger. This includes both fair leader election (in leader based protocols) and fair committee election (in hybrid consensus protocols). This definition is considered in [1,25,28,31,38]. We note that even if the leader election process is fair, the current leader still has the power to manipulate transaction ordering.

Fairness has also been used in the context of "fair exchange," which provides a way for mutually distrusting parties to exchange digital goods in a secure way. This notion is unrelated to ours but we mention it for completeness.

Works That Mention Fair Transaction Ordering. Helix [4] alludes to fair transaction ordering, but only considers censorship resistance and fair committee election. It uses threshold encryption to choose a random set of pending transactions for inclusion in the current block. Hashgraph [6] considers our notion of receive-order fairness, but provides no formal definitions. Moreover, it *fails to realize the impossibility* of this notion of fairness resulting from the Condorcet paradox [18]. As a result, we identify an elementary attack on the Hashgraph protocol that allows an adversarial node to control transaction ordering. The main problem in Hashgraph is the use of timestamp based ordering. In Sect. 5, we provide a brief explanation for why this does not work and defer the description of our attack to the full version [27].

2   Definitions, Framework, and Preliminaries

In this section, we describe the general execution framework that we will use for expressing and analyzing consensus protocols. We adopt an approach like that of Pass and Shi [39,40] and Chan et al. [16]. We focus on the "permissioned" setting, where the number of consensus nodes n, as well as their identities, are known a priori to all participants. While arbitrary clients can send messages to these nodes, only a fixed set of nodes will take part in the consensus protocol. We are interested in protocols for several network settings (e.g. synchronous, partially synchronous, and asynchronous) and define constrained environments for these settings by imposing restrictions that an adversary must respect. Due to space constraints, we only include the relevant formalism for the constructions in this paper. For the complete details of the model, we refer the reader to the full version [27].

2.1 Protocol Execution Model

Interactive Turing Machines (ITMs). We adopt the widely used Interactive Turing Machine (ITM) approach rooted in the Universal Composability framework [12]. Informally, a protocol details how nodes interact with each other, where each node is represented by an ITM. As standard practice in cryptography literature [12–14], we use an environment $\mathcal{Z}(1^\kappa)$ (where κ is the security parameter) to direct the protocol execution. $\mathcal{Z}$ is responsible for activating nodes as either *honest* or *corrupt*, providing messages as inputs to nodes, and delivering messages between nodes. Honest nodes follow the protocol description while corrupt nodes are assumed to be controlled by an adversary, denoted by $\mathcal{A}$. $\mathcal{A}$ is able to read all inputs/messages sent to corrupt nodes and can set all outputs/messages to be sent. The adversary also decides when messages sent over the network get delivered, subject to any network assumptions.

Rounds. We assume that $\mathcal{Z}$ maintains a global clock. The clock is a global functionality [14] that contains a simple monotonic counter which can be updated adversarially by the environment. In the synchronous setting, we can model protocol execution in discrete time steps or rounds. At the start of each round, each node receives a set txs of transactions from the environment $\mathcal{Z}$. Transactions are assumed to be submitted by clients, but using the environment abstraction avoids having to model clients explicitly. At the end of each round, each node outputs an ordered log LOG to $\mathcal{Z}$ which intuitively represents the list of transactions ordered by the node so far. We assume that $\mathcal{Z}$ always signals the start of a new round to each node. Rounds in the partially synchronous setting work similarly to the synchronous setting. In the asynchronous setting, the clock is not accessible to the protocol nodes. $\mathcal{Z}$ can provide user transactions and communication messages to nodes at any time. Any protocol that works in the asynchronous setting should not rely on the current time. Throughout the paper, we may use the terms "time" and "round" interchangeably.

Notational Conventions. We use κ to denote the security parameter. $\mathcal{N}$ denotes the set of protocol nodes. For a protocol Π, $\mathsf{EXEC}^\Pi(\mathcal{A}, \mathcal{Z}, \kappa)$ represents the random variable for all possible execution traces of Π w.r.t. adversary $\mathcal{A}$ and environment $\mathcal{Z}$. We use view $\leftarrow_{\$} \mathsf{EXEC}^\Pi(\mathcal{A}, \mathcal{Z}, \kappa)$ to denote randomly sampling an execution. |view| denotes the number of rounds in view.

Corruption Model. Since we are concerned only with the permissioned setting, we consider environments $\mathcal{Z}$ that spawn a set of nodes, numbered from 1 to n at the start, and never spawn additional nodes. At any point, $\mathcal{A}$ can ask $\mathcal{Z}$ to corrupt a particular node for which $\mathcal{Z}$ sends a `corrupt` signal to that node. When this happens, the internal state of the node gets exposed to $\mathcal{A}$ and $\mathcal{A}$ henceforth fully controls the node. A node is said to be *honest* in a given view if it is never under adversarial control. Otherwise, it is said to be *corrupt* or *Byzantine*. $\mathcal{A}$ can corrupt nodes at any point during the protocol's execution; but once a node is corrupted, it cannot become honest at a later point. The corruption parameter f denotes the maximum number of nodes that $\mathcal{A}$ can corrupt.

Communication and Network Model. As mentioned before, $\mathcal{Z}$ provides transactions sent by users as inputs to nodes and also handles communication between nodes. We assume that a node can broadcast messages to others through authenticated channels. Furthermore, we assume that the adversary $\mathcal{A}$ cannot modify messages sent by honest nodes but can reorder or delay messages, possibly constrained by the specific setting.

We differentiate between two networks in our model—an *internal* network for communication between nodes and an *external* network for how external users send transactions to nodes. We emphasize that $\mathcal{A}$ is only in charge of scheduling message delivery for the internal network. The external network may reside in other parts of the application (not relevant to the consensus protocol) and is managed by $\mathcal{Z}$ (and possibly by some other network adversary). For both networks, we consider the synchronous setting [22] (where the network delay bound is known), the partially synchronous setting [21] (where the network delay bound is finite but unknown), and the asynchronous setting [9] (where the network delay is unbounded).

2.2   Execution Environments

Clients submit transactions by sending them to all nodes. As mentioned before, we do not explicitly model clients, but rather have transactions input by $\mathcal{Z}$.

External Network. The external network models the channel between the system clients and the protocol nodes. By a synchronous external network, we mean that any transaction that is received from $\mathcal{Z}$ by a node reaches all other nodes within a known time. This is formally defined in Definition 3.

Definition 3 (External Synchronous Setting). *We say that $(\mathcal{A}, \mathcal{Z})$ respects $\Delta_{\mathsf{ext}} = (\mathsf{full}, \delta)$ ext-synchrony w.r.t. protocol Π if for every $\kappa \in \mathbb{N}$ and view in the support of $\mathsf{EXEC}^{\Pi}(\mathcal{A}, \mathcal{Z}, \kappa)$, the following conditions hold: (1) $\mathcal{Z}$ provides δ to all nodes upon spawning; (2) If $\mathcal{Z}$ provides an input message m to a node in the txs set at time t, then at any time $t' \geq t + \delta$, all other nodes will also have received message m as input.*

For the partially synchronous setting, we assume that δ exists but is unknown to the nodes, and not provided by $\mathcal{Z}$. For the asynchronous setting, we only assume that transactions are not dropped by the network—they eventually get delivered to all the nodes.

Internal Network. The internal network represents the network between nodes and is usually the standard network considered for consensus problems. We formalize the internal synchrony assumption in Definition 4. The partially synchronous and asynchronous settings are defined similarly to the corresponding notions for the external network.

Definition 4 (Internal Synchronous Setting). *We say that* $(\mathcal{A}, \mathcal{Z})$ *respects* $\Delta_{\text{int}} = (\text{full}, \delta)$ int-*synchrony w.r.t. protocol* Π *if for every* $\kappa \in \mathbb{N}$ *and* view *in the support of* $\text{EXEC}^{\Pi}(\mathcal{A}, \mathcal{Z}, \kappa)$, *the following conditions hold: (1)* $\mathcal{Z}$ *provides* δ *to all nodes upon spawning; (2) If an honest node sends a message at time* t, *then at any time* $t' \geq t + \delta$, *all recipient(s) will have received the message.*

Network Nomenclature. We say that the network is *completely synchronous* (resp. *completely asynchronous*) if both the external and the internal network are synchronous (resp. asynchronous). We use not-async to denote both the synchronous setting and the partially synchronous setting.

Permissioned Setting. For the "permissioned" or "classical" environment, we require that $\mathcal{Z}$ spawn all nodes up front and not spawn any new nodes during the protocol execution. Furthermore, all nodes know the identity of all other nodes in the protocol. We define the permissioned environment in Definition 5.

Definition 5 (Classical Permissioned Environment). *We say that* $(\mathcal{A}, \mathcal{Z})$ *respects* $(n, f, \Delta_{\text{int}}, \Delta_{\text{ext}})$-*classical execution w.r.t. a protocol* Π *if it respects* Δ_{int} int-*synchrony,* Δ_{ext} ext-*synchrony and for every* $\kappa \in \mathbb{N}$ *and* view *in the support of* $\text{EXEC}^{\Pi}(\mathcal{A}, \mathcal{Z}, \kappa)$, *the following conditions hold: (1)* $\mathcal{Z}$ *spawns a set of nodes numbered from* 1 *to* n *at the start of the protocol and never spawns any nodes later; (2)* $\mathcal{Z}$ *does not corrupt more than* f *nodes; (3)* $\mathcal{Z}$ *provides all nodes* n, f *as well as any other public parameters upon spawning.*

For all constraints on $(\mathcal{A}, \mathcal{Z})$, when the context is clear, we may choose to exclude the protocol we are referring to.

2.3 The State Machine Replication Abstraction

In the state machine replication or consensus problem, a set of nodes try to agree on a growing, linearly ordered log. At the start of each round, $\mathcal{Z}$ provides a set txs (possibly empty) of transactions to protocol nodes. We assume that the transactions input by $\mathcal{Z}$ are unique. At any time, nodes may also choose to deliver transactions by outputting a LOG to $\mathcal{Z}$. The LOG can be thought of as a totally ordered sequence where each element is an ordered set of transactions. We refer to the set of transactions at an index of the LOG as a "block." The LOG represents the set of transactions committed by a node so far.

Transaction Nomenclature. When discussing the trajectory of a transaction, we say that a transaction tx is *received* by a node when it is given as input to the node by $\mathcal{Z}$. A transaction tx is *delivered* or *output* by a node when it is included in a LOG output by the node to $\mathcal{Z}$.

Notation for the Ordered Log. $\mathcal{T}$ denotes the space of all possible transactions. Let LOG_i represent the most recent log output by node i to the environment, i.e., the ordered list of transactions that node i has delivered so far. For two logs LOG and LOG', we define a relation $\preceq$ which intuitively signifies a "prefix" notion. $\mathsf{LOG} \preceq \mathsf{LOG}'$ stands for "LOG is a prefix of LOG'." We assume that for any x, we have $x \preceq x$ and $\emptyset \preceq x$. $\mathsf{LOG}[p]$ denotes the pth element in LOG. $\mathsf{LOG}(m)$ denotes the number p such that $\mathsf{LOG}[p]$ contains m.

The security of a state machine replication protocol is now defined as follows:

Definition 6 (Security of state machine replication [40]). *We say that a protocol Π satisfies consistency (resp. $(T_{\text{warmup}}, T_{\text{confirm}})$-liveness) w.r.t. $(\mathcal{A}, \mathcal{Z})$ if there exists a negligible function $\mathsf{negl}(\cdot)$ such that for any $\kappa \in \mathbb{N}$, consistency (resp. $(T_{\text{warmup}}, T_{\text{confirm}})$-liveness) is satisfied except with $\mathsf{negl}(\kappa)$ probability over the choice of $\mathsf{view} \leftarrow_\$ \mathsf{EXEC}^\Pi(\mathcal{A}, \mathcal{Z}, \kappa)$ where negl is negligible in κ. For a particular view, we define the properties as below:*

- *(**Consistency**) A view satisfies consistency if the following holds:*
  - *Common Prefix. If an honest node i outputs LOG to $\mathcal{Z}$ at time t and an honest node j outputs LOG' to $\mathcal{Z}$ at time t', then it holds that either $\mathsf{LOG} \preceq \mathsf{LOG}'$ or $\mathsf{LOG}' \preceq \mathsf{LOG}$.*
  - *Future Self Consistency. If a node that is honest between times t and t', outputs LOG at time t and LOG' at time $t' \geq t$ to the environment $\mathcal{Z}$, then it holds that $\mathsf{LOG} \preceq \mathsf{LOG}'$.*

- *(**Liveness**) A view satisfies $(T_{\text{warmup}}, T_{\text{confirm}})$-liveness if the following holds: At a time t such that $T_{\text{warmup}} < t \leq |\mathsf{view}|$, if an honest node either received a transaction m from $\mathcal{Z}$ or output m in its log to $\mathcal{Z}$, then for any honest node i and any time $t' \geq t + T_{\text{confirm}}; t' \leq |\mathsf{view}|$, it holds that m is in the log output by node i at time t'.*

Here, T_{confirm} and T_{warmup} are polynomial functions in κ, n, f, any maximum network delay bounds as defined in Δ_{ext} and Δ_{int}, as well as the actual network delay. T_{warmup} is the protocol's warmup time, until which point liveness need not be satisfied. T_{confirm} is the maximum time it takes for a transaction (input after the warmup time) to be delivered by all honest nodes.

Weak Liveness. The standard definition of liveness of a transaction tx (from Definition 6) is independent of what happens in the rest of the protocol's execution. Sometimes however, it may be enough for a protocol to be live only if transactions continue to be received by the system. For example, a transaction tx will only be delivered if there is some transaction that is received by all nodes sufficiently after tx. Intuitively, later transactions will cause earlier ones to be "flushed out" of the system. We note that this subtle distinction between the two liveness definitions is rarely considered in the literature. We found that some leaderless protocols (i.e. those that are not based on a leader node) like [6,41] implicitly ignore this distinction. Along similar lines, we define a weaker version of conventional liveness, which we call "weak-liveness." Despite the technical difference, we think that it should be acceptable in most real world systems. For a particular view, we define weak-liveness below.

– **(Weak Liveness)** A view satisfies $(T_{\mathrm{warmup}}, T_{\mathrm{confirm}})$-weak-liveness if the following holds: Suppose that at a time t such that $t > T_{\mathrm{warmup}}$, an honest node either received a transaction m from $\mathcal{Z}$ or output m in its log to $\mathcal{Z}$. Let T be a set built recursively as follows: (1) Add m to T; (2) For $m_0 \in \mathsf{T}$, add to T, all transactions m_0' that were received by at least one honest node before m_0. Now if another transaction m' was received at time t' and is such that it was first received by a node after all nodes received all transactions in T, then for any honest node i and any time $t'' \geq t' + T_{\mathrm{confirm}}; t'' \leq |\mathsf{view}|$, it holds that m is in the log output by node i at time t''.

3   Building Blocks

We start by describing some useful primitives that will form the foundation for designing our fair ordering consensus protocols. More specifically, we will utilize two primitives: (1) Set Byzantine Agreement (Set-BA); and (2) FIFO Broadcast (FIFO-BC). We show how to build Set-BA from Byzantine agreement and FIFO-BC from reliable broadcast in the full version [27].

Subroutines and Composition. We follow standard conventions to enable secure composition. Each instance of a protocol is spawned with a session identifier sid. We use $\Pi[\mathsf{sid}]$ to denote the instance of protocol Π with session id sid. Each protocol may take inputs from and return outputs to an environment. Note that this "environment" may be different for any subroutines called.

3.1   Set Byzantine Agreement

Definitions. In a (poly) Set Byzantine Agreement protocol (Set-BA), participating nodes will try to agree on a set of values. At the start of the protocol, each node receives any public parameters from $\mathcal{Z}$. Each node i in the set $\mathcal{P}$ of participating nodes also receives a set $U_i \subseteq S$ as input from $\mathcal{Z}$. The set S is also known to all nodes and its description is polynomial in κ. At the end of the protocol, each honest node $j \in \mathcal{P}$ outputs a set of the agreed upon values O_j.

Definition 7 (Security of Set-BA). *A Set-BA protocol Π_{sba} satisfies agreement, inclusion validity, and exclusion validity w.r.t. $(\mathcal{A}, \mathcal{Z})$ if for all $\kappa \in \mathbb{N}$, the following properties hold except with negligible probability over $\mathsf{view} \leftarrow_{\$} EXEC^{\Pi_{\mathrm{sba}}}(\mathcal{A}, \mathcal{Z}, \kappa)$.*

– *(**Agreement**) If honest nodes i and j output the sets O_i and O_j respectively, then $O_i = O_j$.*
– *(**Inclusion Validity**) If an element is in the input sets of all nodes, then it will also be in the output sets of all honest nodes.*

- **(Exclusion Validity)** *If an element is not in any input set, then it is not in any honest output set.*

For a given view, we also say that Π_{sba} satisfies $T^{\text{sba}}_{\text{confirm}}$-liveness, if all honest nodes output in at most $T^{\text{sba}}_{\text{confirm}}$ rounds after all honest nodes have input their starting value. Lemma 1 shows a helpful result that any outputs are "honestly proposed."

Lemma 1. *Consider any set Byzantine agreement protocol Π_{sba} that satisfies agreement, inclusion validity, and exclusion validity (w.r.t $(\mathcal{A}, \mathcal{Z})$). Except for a negligible number of views, Π_{sba} also satisfies the following:*

- **(Honest Proposal)** *If an honest node outputs the set O, then for every $c \in O$, there exists $i \in \mathcal{P}$ such that i is honest and $c \in U_i$.*

3.2 FIFO Broadcast

Single source FIFO (first in, first out) broadcast (also called Ordered Authenticated Reliable broadcast or OARcast in [26]) is a broadcast primitive in which all honest nodes in the protocol need to deliver messages in the same order as they were broadcast by the sender. In one instantiation of a FIFO broadcast protocol, we consider a single designated sender who broadcasts a sequence of messages to all other nodes. If the sender is honest, each honest node must deliver the messages in the same order as they were broadcast. If the sender is dishonest, all honest nodes must deliver messages in the same order as each other; except now, this order may be different than the one broadcast by the sender. When composing several FIFO broadcast primitives together with different senders, FIFO order is maintained for each individual sender but different honest nodes may deliver messages from different senders in different orders.

Definitions. At the start of the FIFO Broadcast (FIFO-BC) protocol, each node receives the appropriate public parameters from the environment. At any time, the designated sender may also receive as input a message m from the environment. At any time, nodes can choose to deliver messages.

Definition 8 (Security of (FIFO-BC)). *A FIFO-BC protocol Π_{fifocast} satisfies liveness, agreement, and FIFO-order w.r.t. $(\mathcal{A}, \mathcal{Z})$ if for all $\kappa \in \mathbb{N}$, the following properties hold except with negligible probability over* view $\leftarrow_{\$}$ $EXEC^{\Pi_{\text{fifocast}}}$ $(\mathcal{A}, \mathcal{Z}, \kappa)$.

- $((T^{\text{fifocast}}_{\text{warmup}}, T^{\text{fifocast}}_{\text{confirm}})$-**Liveness**) *If the sender is honest and receives a message m as input in round $r > T^{\text{fifocast}}_{\text{warmup}}$, or if an honest node delivers m in round $r > T^{\text{fifocast}}_{\text{warmup}}$, then all honest nodes will have delivered m by round $r + T^{\text{fifocast}}_{\text{confirm}}$.*
- **(Agreement)** *If an honest node delivers a message m before m', then no honest node delivers m' unless it has already delivered m.*
- **(FIFO-Order)** *If the sender is honest and is input a message m before m', then no honest node delivers m' unless it has already delivered m.*

$T_{\text{confirm}}^{\text{fifocast}}$ *is a polynomial in* κ, n, f *and the internal network delay.*

Notation. Let $\Pi_{\text{fifocast}}[(\text{sid}, j)]$ denote the instance of the protocol Π_{fifocast} where node j is the designated sender. In a consensus protocol that invokes $\Pi_{\text{fifocast}}[(\text{sid}, j)]$, we assume that each node i keeps track of the messages delivered (i.e. messages broadcast by node j) in a local log $\text{Log}_i^{(\text{sid}, j)}$. This represents node i's view of broadcasts from node j in the session sid. When the session id is clear from context, we may simply write Log_i^j. Two local logs Log and Log' are called "equal until tx", denoted by $\approx_{\text{tx}}$, if they are equivalent until the occurrence of tx. $\text{Log}[p]$ denotes the pth element in Log. $\text{Log}(m)$ denotes the number p such that $\text{Log}[p]$ contains m. Consequently, $\text{Log}(m) < \text{Log}(m')$ signifies that m appears before m' in Log.

4 Defining Fair Ordering

We formally define fair ordering in this section. As it turns out, providing a definition that is achievable by protocols, yet intuitive, is not trivial. Some natural definitions are not achievable except under strong assumptions. We use this section to also go through these definitions that led to our final definition.

(Attempt 1) – Send-order-fairness. A strawman approach is to require ordering to be in terms of when transactions were *sent* by clients. For instance, if a transaction tx_1 was sent by a client before another transaction tx_2 (possibly by another client), then tx_1 should appear before tx_2 in the agreed upon log. Not surprisingly, this can lead to several problems: most importantly, there needs to be a trusted way to timestamp a transaction at the client side. We discuss the possibility of achieving it in practice using trusted hardware in the full version [27].

(Attempt 2) – Receive-order-fairness. The challenges of send-order-fairness suggest it would be more prudent to define fair ordering in terms of when the consensus nodes actually *receive* transactions. Intuitively, "receive order" means that the fair ordering is defined by looking at when *enough* nodes receive a particular transaction. For instance, if sufficiently many nodes receive a transaction tx_1 before another transaction tx_2, then tx_1 must appear before tx_2 in the final log. "Sufficiently many" is parameterized using γ.

Definition 9 (Receive-order-fairness, restatement of Definition 1). *For a view in the support of* $\mathsf{EXEC}^{\Pi}(\mathcal{A}, \mathcal{Z}, \kappa)$, *define receive-order-fairness as follows:*

– *A view satisfies* $(\gamma, T_{\text{warmup}})$ *receive-order-fairness if the following holds: For any two transactions* m *and* m', *let* η *be the number of nodes that received both transactions between times* T_{warmup} *and* $|\text{view}|$. *If at least* $\gamma\eta$ *of those nodes received* m *before* m' *from* $\mathcal{Z}$, *then for all honest nodes* i, i *does not deliver* m' *unless it has previously delivered* m.

A protocol Π *satisfies* $(\gamma, T_{\text{warmup}})$ *receive-order-fairness w.r.t* $(\mathcal{A}, \mathcal{Z})$ *if there is a negligible function* $\mathsf{negl}(\cdot)$ *such that for any* $\kappa \in \mathbb{N}$, *the order-fairness property is satisfied except with probability* $\mathsf{negl}(\kappa)$ *over* $\text{view} \leftarrow_{\$} \mathsf{EXEC}^{\Pi}(\mathcal{A}, \mathcal{Z}, \kappa)$.

4.1 Condorcet Paradox and the Impossibility of Fair Ordering

The Condorcet paradox [18], or the "voting paradox", is a result in social choice theory that shows how some situations can lead to non-transitive collective voting preferences even if the preferences of individual voters are transitive. To illustrate how this applies to fair ordering, let us look at a simple example:

Example 1. Suppose that there are 3 nodes: A, B, and C. In the protocol execution, 3 transactions, tx_1, tx_2, and tx_3 are sent by clients to all the nodes.

 – Node A receives transactions in the order tx_1, tx_2, tx_3.
 – Node B receives transactions in the order tx_2, tx_3, tx_1.
 – Node C receives transactions in the order tx_3, tx_1, tx_2.

Now, 2 nodes (A and C) received tx_1 before tx_2, 2 nodes (A and B) received tx_2 before tx_3, and 2 nodes (B and C) received tx_3 before tx_1. It is easy to see that no protocol can satisfy fair ordering for $\gamma \leq \frac{2}{3}$, since such a protocol would have to include tx_1 before tx_2; tx_2 before tx_3; and tx_3 before tx_1 in its final log.

Theorem 2 generalizes this observation to show an impossibility for $\gamma \leq \frac{n-1}{n}$. Furthermore, it also shows that when $f \geq 1$, even $\gamma = 1$ receive-order-fairness is impossible to achieve.

Theorem 2 (Restatement of Theorem 1). *Consider any $n, f \geq 1, \Delta_{\mathsf{int}}, \Delta_{\mathsf{ext}}$ where Δ_{ext} is either asynchronous or (**not-async**, $\delta_{\mathsf{ext}} \geq n$). Let $\gamma \leq 1$. If a consensus protocol Π satisfies consistency and $(T_{\mathrm{warmup}}, T_{\mathrm{confirm}})$ liveness w.r.t. all $(\mathcal{A}, \mathcal{Z})$ that respect $(n, f, \Delta_{\mathsf{int}}, \Delta_{\mathsf{ext}})$-classical execution, then it cannot also satisfy $(\gamma, T_{\mathrm{warmup}})$ receive-order-fairness.*

Proof (Sketch). Taking inspiration from the counterexample in Example 1, we first show the result for $\gamma \leq \frac{n-1}{n}$. Denote the nodes in the system by the numbers 1 to n. Suppose that clients submit n transactions tx_1 to tx_n. Further, suppose that node 1 receives the transactions in the order $tx_1, tx_2, \cdots, tx_n$ and any node $i \neq 1$ receives the transactions in the order $tx_i, \cdots, tx_n, tx_1, \cdots, tx_{i-1}$.

Now, it is straightforward to see that all nodes except node 2 received tx_1 before tx_2, all nodes except node 3 received tx_2 before tx_3 and so on. Finally, all nodes except node 1 received tx_n before tx_1. This means that any consensus protocol that provides order-fairness for $\gamma \leq \frac{n-1}{n}$ must order tx_1 before tx_2, $\cdots$, tx_{n-1} before tx_n, and tx_n before tx_1 which is a contradiction.

To see the result for $\gamma = 1$, since $f \geq 1$, we observe that the adversary $\mathcal{A}$ can simply crash a single node N. Suppose that all other nodes receive tx_1 before tx_2. Now, since the node N sends no messages, other nodes do not know the order in which it received tx_1 and tx_2. Therefore, any protocol that satisfies receive-order-fairness for $\gamma = 1$ would order tx_1 before tx_2 even when N actually received tx_2 first. In other words it would also need to satisfy receive-order-fairness for $\gamma = \frac{n-1}{n}$, which we showed to be impossible.

4.2   Environments that Support Receive-Order-Fairness

We find that the Condorcet paradox can be circumvented in a few ways by assuming specific network properties.

External Synchrony Assumption. The primary reason for the impossibility of fair-ordering is that different nodes may receive the same client transaction several rounds apart, resulting in non-transitive collective ordering. Suppose that $\Delta_{\text{ext}} = (\text{full}, \delta)$ where $\delta \leq 1$ (e.g., an instant synchronous external network). Then, any client transaction that a node receives will reach all other nodes within 1 round. This implies that if some node receives transactions tx_1, tx_2 and tx_3 in that order, then no node can receive tx_3 before tx_1. It is now straightforward to see how this circumvents the Condorcet paradox.

Non-corrupting Adversary and $\gamma = 1$. If the adversary does not corrupt any nodes, and its power is restricted to influencing network delays, we find that it is possible to achieve receive-order-fairness for $\gamma = 1$. In this setting, a single leader can receive the transaction orderings from individual nodes, and decide on a final ordering that preserves receive order-fairness.

4.3   Towards Weaker Definitions for Order-Fairness

We give two natural relaxations of the original definition. The first is *approximate receive order-fairness* (or simply *approximate-order-fairness*) while the second is *block receive order-fairness* (or simply *block-order-fairness*). For approximate-order-fairness, we only look at unfairness in the ordering of two transactions if they were received sufficiently apart in time. We emphasize that approximate-order-fairness only makes sense in synchronous and partially synchronous settings. On the other hand, for block-order-fairness, we choose to ignore the ordering within a block while considering fair ordering. Notably, this allows us to circumvent the Condorcet paradox by aggregating any transactions with non-transitive orderings into the same block. This is reasonable to consider even in asynchronous environments. First, we look at approximate-order-fairness. For a given view in the support of $\text{EXEC}^{\Pi}(\mathcal{A}, \mathcal{Z}, \kappa)$, we define the property below.

Definition 10 (Approximate-Order-Fairness). *A view satisfies $(\gamma, T_{\text{warmup}}, \xi)$ approximate-order-fairness if the following holds: For any two transactions m and m', let η be the number of nodes that received both transactions between times T_{warmup} and $|\text{view}|$. If at least $\gamma\eta$ of those nodes received m more than ξ rounds before m' from $\mathcal{Z}$, then for all honest nodes i, i does not deliver m', unless it has previously delivered m.*

A protocol Π satisfies $(\gamma, T_{\text{warmup}}, \xi)$ approximate-order-fairness w.r.t $(\mathcal{A}, \mathcal{Z})$ if there is a negligible function $\text{negl}(\cdot)$ such that for any $\kappa \in \mathbb{N}$, the above property is satisfied except with probability $\text{negl}(\kappa)$ over $\text{view} \xleftarrow{\$} \text{EXEC}^{\Pi}(\mathcal{A}, \mathcal{Z}, \kappa)$.

Quickly, we notice a protocol that satisfies $(T_{\text{warmup}}, T_{\text{confirm}})$-liveness, also satisfies $(1, T_{\text{warmup}}, \xi)$ approximate order-fairness for any $\xi \geq T_{\text{confirm}}$. Clearly, if a transaction tx_2 was received after tx_1 was delivered by all nodes, then tx_2

will be delivered after tx_1. Moreover, we also find that if $\xi < T_{\text{confirm}}$, then any protocol that satisfies $(\gamma, T_{\text{warmup}}, \xi)$ approximate-order-fairness must also satisfy $(\gamma, T_{\text{warmup}})$ receive-order-fairness (for environments with a different network synchrony bound).

Theorem 3. *Consider any* $n, f \geq 1, \Delta_{\text{int}}, \Delta_{\text{ext}}$. *Let* $\Delta_{\text{int}} = (\textsf{not-async}, \delta_{\text{int}})$ *and* $\Delta_{\text{ext}} = (\textsf{not-async}, \delta_{\text{ext}} \geq 1)$. *Also consider* $\gamma \leq 1$ *and* $\xi < T_{\text{confirm}}$. *If a protocol* Π *achieves consistency,* $(T_{\text{warmup}}, T_{\text{confirm}})$-*liveness, and* $(\gamma, T_{\text{warmup}}, \xi)$ *approximate-order-fairness. w.r.t. all* $(\mathcal{A}, \mathcal{Z})$ *that respect* $(n, f, \Delta_{\text{int}}, \Delta_{\text{ext}})$-*classical execution, then it also satisfies* $(\gamma, T_{\text{warmup}})$ *receive-order-fairness w.r.t all* $(\mathcal{A}', \mathcal{Z}')$ *that respect* $(n, f, \Delta'_{\text{int}}, \Delta'_{\text{ext}})$-*classical execution where* $\Delta'_{\text{int}} = (\textsf{not-async}, \delta'_{\text{int}} = \frac{\delta_{\text{int}}}{\xi+1})$ *and* $\Delta'_{\text{ext}} = (\textsf{not-async}, \delta'_{\text{ext}} = \frac{\delta_{\text{ext}}}{\xi+1})$.

Consequently, approximate-order-fairness doesn't turn out to be very useful since it suffers from the same problems as the previously defined receive-order-fairness. Note that from Sect. 4.2, we can infer that approximate-order-fairness can be achieved when $\delta_{\text{ext}} \leq \xi$. Still, since it only applies to non-asynchronous networks, we propose a second definition, block-order-fairness, that performs much better since it provides a way to handle any cycles in transaction ordering and also applies to asynchronous networks. We note that our synchronous protocol (Sect. 6) also satisfies approximate-order-fairness for $\xi \geq \delta_{\text{ext}}$.

For a given view in the support of $\textsf{EXEC}^{\Pi}(\mathcal{A}, \mathcal{Z}, \kappa)$, we state the block-order-fairness property below.

Definition 11 (Block Order-Fairness). *A* view *satisfies* $(\gamma > \frac{1}{2}, T_{\text{warmup}})$-*block-order-fairness if the following holds: For any two transactions* m *and* m', *let* η *be the number of nodes that received both transactions between times* T_{warmup} *and* $|\textsf{view}|$. *If at least* $\gamma\eta$ *of those nodes received* m *before* m' *from* $\mathcal{Z}$, *then for all honest nodes* i, i *does not deliver* m *at a later index than it delivers* m'.

A protocol Π *satisfies* $(\gamma, T_{\text{warmup}})$-*block-order-fairness w.r.t* $(\mathcal{A}, \mathcal{Z})$ *if there is a negligible function* $\textsf{negl}(\cdot)$ *such that for any* $\kappa \in \mathbb{N}$, *the above property is satisfied except with probability* $\textsf{negl}(\kappa)$ *over* $\textsf{view} \leftarrow_{\$} \textsf{EXEC}^{\Pi}(\mathcal{A}, \mathcal{Z}, \kappa)$.

5   Overview of the **Aequitas** Protocols

We provide a general overview of our Aequitas protocols in this section. Specifically, we give four constructions:

- $\Pi_{\text{Aequitas}}^{\text{sync,nolead}}$ is a leaderless protocol that provides consistency, (weak) liveness, and block-order-fairness in the completely synchronous setting.
- $\Pi_{\text{Aequitas}}^{\text{sync,lead}}$ is a leader-based protocol that provides consistency, (weak) liveness, and block-order-fairness in the completely synchronous setting.
- $\Pi_{\text{Aequitas}}^{\text{async,nolead}}$ is a leaderless protocol that provides consistency, eventual (weak) liveness, and block-order-fairness in any setting.
- $\Pi_{\text{Aequitas}}^{\text{async,lead}}$ is a leader-based protocol that provides consistency, eventual (weak) liveness, and block-order-fairness in any setting.

We present a detailed account only for the synchronous leaderless protocol $\Pi_{\text{Aequitas}}^{\text{sync,nolead}}$ in this paper (Sect. 6) and defer the other constructions to the full version [27].

Construction Overview. Our Aequitas protocols utilize the FIFO-broadcast (FIFO-BC) and the set Byzantine agreement (Set-BA) primitives described in Sect. 3 in a black-box way to provide order-fairness. We elaborate on the three major stages of our Aequitas protocols below:

- **Stage I: Gossip/Broadcast**. Each node FIFO-broadcasts transactions as they are received as input from the environment. When a node i receives a set of transactions txs from $\mathcal{Z}$, it sends txs as input to the protocol $\Pi_{\text{fifocast}}[(\text{sid}, i)]$ with i as the designated sender. Note that all broadcasts can be sent in the same session sid. Different session ids need to be used only when considering composition of several protocols in the system.

  In parallel to broadcasting transactions, a node also receives and processes broadcasts from other nodes. For a node i, broadcasts sent by node j are appended to a local log Log_i^j when they get delivered to i by $\Pi_{\text{fifocast}}[(\text{sid}, j)]$. Intuitively, Log_i^j denotes node i's view of how transactions were received by node j.

- **Stage II: Agreement on local logs**. To determine the ordering for a particular transaction tx, a node i waits until it has received tx from sufficiently many other nodes. In other words, node i waits until there are sufficiently many k such that its local log Log_i^k contains tx. When both the external and internal networks are synchronous, this can alternatively be achieved by waiting for enough *time*. The properties of FIFO-BC guarantee that if two honest nodes i and j have local logs Log_i^k and Log_j^k respectively that both contain tx, then $\text{Log}_i^k \approx_{\text{tx}} \text{Log}_j^k$. We state this fact as Lemma 2. Recall that $\text{Log}_i^k \approx_{\text{tx}} \text{Log}_j^k$ holds when Log_i^k and Log_j^k are identical until tx occurs.

  Now, the next step is for all nodes to agree on which local logs to use to determine the ordering for tx. For a node i, let U_i^{tx} denote the set of nodes k such that Log_i^k contains tx. Node i starts an instance of the protocol $\Pi_{\text{sba}}[(\text{sid}, \text{tx})]$ and provides it the input U_i^{tx}. Upon the completion of the Set-BA protocol, all honest nodes receive the same set L^{tx}. Intuitively, Set-BA is used to agree which nodes' orderings should be used to determine the final ordering for transaction tx. Recall that Lemma 1 guarantees that if $k \in L^{\text{tx}}$, then there is some honest node j such that $\text{tx} \in \text{Log}_j^k$. This, along with the liveness property for FIFO-BC ensures that all honest nodes will eventually receive tx broadcast by node $k \in L^{\text{tx}}$ (even if k is malicious).

  Finally, we note that at the end of the agreement phase, every honest node has agreed on a set of nodes L^{tx} whose transaction orderings should be used to determine the final ordering for the transaction tx in consideration. We say that a node i has received the agreed logs for tx if for all $k \in L^{\text{tx}}$, it holds that $\text{tx} \in \text{Log}_i^k$.

- **Stage III: Finalization.** To decide on the final ordering for a transaction tx, we provide two options for the finalization step: a leader based one and a

leaderless one. For both the leader-based and leaderless finalizations, nodes
first build a graph that represents any ordering dependencies between transactions. Specifically, a node i maintains a directed graph G_i, where vertices
represent transactions and edges represent ordering dependencies. We refer
to G_i as the "dependency graph" or the "waiting graph" maintained by i.
After the agreement stage for tx is completed, the protocol now uses the
local logs to see if some other transaction might have come before. If there
is another transaction tx′ that appears before tx in sufficiently many local
logs (e.g., $n - f$ times), then i adds an edge from tx′ to tx in G_i. Intuitively,
an edge $(a, b) \in G_i$ denotes that the finalization stage for b is "waiting" for
a to be delivered. Since the same L^{tx} is used by all honest nodes, if an edge
(a, b) exists in G_i, then it will at some point exist in G_j, when nodes i and j
are both honest. However, we note that G_i is neither guaranteed to be complete nor acyclic. Two vertices in G_i might never have an edge between them.
Moreover, the Condorcet paradox can still create cycles in G_i. To break ties
between transactions without an edge, we use the following two techniques.

- **Finalization via leader-based proposal.** $\Pi_{\text{Aequitas}}^{\text{sync,lead}}$ and $\Pi_{\text{Aequitas}}^{\text{async,lead}}$ both use
  a leader-based approach to finalize transactions in the graph. For this, any
  leader-based consensus protocol can be run along with the gossip and agreement stages above. When a designated leader proposes and broadcasts a new
  block, instead of just checking the syntactical validity of transactions, each
  node i checks that the proposal does not conflict with any required order-
  fairness in the graph G_i. That is, node i checks that for any transaction tx
  in the proposed block, if (tx′, tx) is in G_i, then either tx′ has already been
  delivered or tx′ is also in the current proposed block.
  Abstractly, we allow the leader node to choose the transaction ordering but
  only as long as order-fairness is still satisfied. For transactions among which
  there is no clear winner, the leader may choose any ordering.
- **Finalization via local computation.** $\Pi_{\text{Aequitas}}^{\text{sync,nolead}}$ and $\Pi_{\text{Aequitas}}^{\text{async,nolead}}$ both use
  a leaderless approach to finalize transactions in the graph and require no
  further communication. At a high level, to order transactions tx_1 and tx_2
  between whom there in no edge in G_i, the protocol will wait until tx_1 and
  tx_2 have a common descendant, with the final ordering being based on which
  transaction vertex has the most descendants. We prove that any other graph
  vertex that is a descendant of only one of tx_1 and tx_2 is present in G_i when
  node i makes the decision for ordering tx_1 and tx_2. This will ensure that all
  honest nodes will order tx_1 and tx_2 the same way.

We highlight that the above description of the finalization stage is a simplified
one. As described, it is not sufficient to avoid the Condorcet paradox. Furthermore, adversarial transactions could result in a node waiting for unbounded
periods of time. The actual technique to get around these obstacles is quite
nuanced and we dedicate Sect. 5.1 to its details.

Lemma 2. *If two honest nodes i and j have local logs Log_i^k and Log_j^k respectively where k is any other node such that both logs contain a transaction tx, then $\mathsf{Log}_i^k \approx_{tx} \mathsf{Log}_j^k$.*

Proof. This result follows directly from the agreement property of FIFO-BC.

Before diving into the details of the finalization step, we take a step back to understand why it turns out to be quite non-trivial. We look at a simple straw-man protocol based on transaction timestamping that looks intuitive and analyze why it does not work.

The Problem with Timestamp-Based Ordering. Consider a simple synchronous protocol $\Pi_{\text{timestamp}}$ that works as follows:

1. When an honest node i receives a transaction tx from $\mathcal{Z}$ in round t, it assigns tx the timestamp t and broadcasts (tx, t) to all other nodes.
2. Upon waiting for $\delta_{\text{ext}} + T_{\text{confirm}}$ rounds where δ_{ext} is the network delay bound for the external network and T_{confirm} is the liveness polynomial for the broadcast primitive, nodes reach agreement on the set of timestamps T to use to calculate the final timestamp for tx.
3. Each node calculates the final timestamp for tx as the median of all the timestamps in T. We represent this final timestamp by $\mathsf{final}(tx)$.

Notice how the first two steps almost perfectly resemble the gossip and agreement stages. The finalization (third) step is also surprisingly simple, but unfortunately can lead to easy manipulation of final timestamps by a single adversary. To see why, consider 5 nodes, A, B, C, D and E, where E is malicious and two transactions, tx_1 and tx_2. tx_1 is received by nodes $A, \ldots, E$ at rounds $1, 1, 4, 4, 2$ while tx_2 is received by the nodes at rounds $2, 2, 5, 5, 3$. Now, all nodes have received tx_1 before tx_2 and consequently, $\mathsf{final}(tx_1) < \mathsf{final}(tx_2)$ should hold. However, notice how E can invert the ordering of the final timestamps simply by switching around its own timestamps for tx_1 and tx_2. E can make $\mathsf{final}(tx_1) = 3$ and $\mathsf{final}(tx_2) = 2$ which results in a timestamp of 3 for tx_1 (median of $(1, 1, 3, 4, 4)$) and 2 for tx_2 (median of $(2, 2, 2, 5, 5)$), and thus an unfair ordering.

5.1 The Finalization Stage

We describe the general theme of the finalization stage here.

Ordering Two Transactions. For a pair of transactions tx and tx', how does a node i choose which one to deliver first? Suppose that the agreement phases for tx and tx' result in the outputs L^{tx} and $L^{tx'}$. Define $l_{(tx,tx')}$ as below.

$$l_{(tx,tx')} = \left| \left\{ k \in L^{tx} \cup L^{tx'} \mid \mathsf{Log}_i^k(tx) \leq \mathsf{Log}_i^k(tx') \right\} \right|$$

$l_{(tx,tx')}$ denotes the number of logs Log_i^k where tx was ordered at or before tx'. Now, if $l_{(tx,tx')}$ is "small," it means that a large number of nodes have received tx' before tx. This means that the finalization stage for tx should wait until tx' has been delivered. This provides a partial ordering between any two transactions.

Additional Notation. Let tx $\lhd_i$ tx$'$ represent that i is waiting to deliver tx$'$ before proceeding with the finalization phase for tx. Lemma 3 shows that $l_{(\text{tx},\text{tx}')}$ and $l_{(\text{tx}',\text{tx})}$ cannot both be "small". Consequently, both tx and tx$'$ will not wait for each other or equivalently, at most one of tx $\lhd_i$ tx$'$ and tx$'$ $\lhd_i$ tx will be true.

Lemma 3. $l_{(\text{tx},\text{tx}')} + l_{(\text{tx}',\text{tx})} \geq \left| L^{\text{tx}} \cup L^{\text{tx}'} \right|$

Proof. Let $X = L^{\text{tx}} \cup L^{\text{tx}'}$. For any $k \in X$, at least one of $\mathsf{Log}_i^k(\text{tx}) \leq \mathsf{Log}_i^k(\text{tx}')$ and $\mathsf{Log}_i^k(\text{tx}') \leq \mathsf{Log}_i^k(\text{tx})$ is true. k is therefore counted in either $l_{(\text{tx},\text{tx}')}$ or $l_{(\text{tx}',\text{tx})}$ which proves the required result.

Adversarial Transactions. The calculation of $l_{(\text{tx},\text{tx}')}$ needs to wait for the agreement phases of both tx and tx$'$ to finish. Now, if an adversarial node FIFO-broadcasts a transaction tx_{fake} claiming it to be a real user transaction, then the ordering between tx_{fake} and a real transaction tx cannot be calculated since the agreement phase for tx_{fake} will never finish. So that this does not happen, the protocol needs to ensure that at least one honest node has received tx_{fake} before tx (from $\mathcal{Z}$). For the synchronous protocol, this is done by checking that a transaction tx$'$ is added to the graph only when there is another transaction tx that has finished its agreement stage and tx$'$ is present in at least $|L^{\text{tx}}| - (n - f) + 1$ among the local logs in L^{tx}. Note that the agreement stage will only finish for honest transactions.

Non-transitive Waiting. The Condorcet paradox can still cause non-transitive waiting. It is still possible to have transactions $\text{tx}_1, \text{tx}_2,$ and tx_3 such that $\text{tx}_1 \lhd \text{tx}_2$; $\text{tx}_2 \lhd \text{tx}_3$; and $\text{tx}_3 \lhd \text{tx}_1$. The way we get around this is by delivering such transactions at the same time—by placing them in the same block.

Graph Based Approach. Instead of a separate thread waiting for the resolution of each transaction, representing the "waiting" between transactions as a graph provides a nice way to modularize the protocol. Suppose that each node i maintains a directed graph $G_i = (G_i.V, G_i.E)$ where $G_i.V$ denotes the set of vertices and $G_i.E$ denotes the set of edges in G_i. Each vertex represents a transaction and an edge from y to x (equiv. $(y, x) \in G_i.E$) represents that x is waiting on y i.e. $x \lhd_i y$. When the agreement phase for a transaction tx completes, i does the following:

- Add tx to the graph G_i if it does not already exist.
- For all transactions tx$'$ such tx $\lhd_i$ tx$'$, first, if tx$'$ does not exist in the graph, add a new vertex. Then, add the edge (tx$'$, tx) to G_i.

As mentioned before, G_i may not be acyclic. In order to deal with the Condorcet paradox, we consider the *strongly connected components* of G_i. Recall that a subgraph G' of a directed graph G is called strongly connected if every vertex in G' can reach every other vertex in G'. A strongly connected component is a maximal strongly connected subgraph.

Intuitively, all transactions in a strongly connected component will be delivered in the same block. A cycle that exists in G_i (due to non-transitivity of transactions) will be entirely contained in the same strongly connected component. On the other hand, if a transaction does not need to wait on any other one, then it will be in a strongly connected component by itself. We can collapse G_i into a new graph G_i^* where each strongly connected component is represented as a single vertex. G_i^* is also called the *condensation* of G_i. Each vertex in G_i^* will now denote a set of transactions. We note that G_i^* will now be acyclic.

Graph Notation. Since a vertex in G_i contains a single transaction, we may use a transaction and its corresponding vertex interchangeably when referring to the vertex in G_i. Let $\mathsf{TXS}_i(v)$ be the set of transactions for a vertex $v \in G_i^*.V$. Let $\mathsf{SCC}_i(v)$ denote the strongly connected component of G_i that contains the vertex v. $\mathsf{SCC}_i(v)$ also denotes the corresponding vertex in the condensation graph G_i^*.

Ordering Incomparable Vertices in G_i^* and Breaking Ties. As mentioned before, not all pairs of vertices in G_i^* are connected by an edge. This only gives a partial ordering for delivering transactions. We still need a way to totally order vertices in G_i^*. In the leader-based version of the finalization step, we delegate this responsibility to the leader node. We elaborate on the technique used in the synchronous leaderless protocol in Sect. 6.

Delivering a Transaction. Recall that a transaction enters the *finalization* stage when it has completed the agreement stage, while it is *delivered* when it gets output to $\mathcal{Z}$ as part of the LOG. For the leaderless protocols, the set of transactions $\mathsf{TXS}_i(v)$ corresponding to the vertex $v \in G_i^*.V$ can be delivered in the LOG output to $\mathcal{Z}$ when it is not waiting for any other transaction and is preferred over any other transaction that it is incomparable with in the graph. For this, care must be taken to ensure that the set of transactions that tx is incomparable with is the same when all honest nodes are deciding to deliver tx, which we defer to the actual protocol description in Sect. 6.

6 The Synchronous **Aequitas** Protocol

We describe $\Pi_{\mathsf{Aequitas}}^{\mathsf{sync},\mathsf{nolead}}$, the leaderless Aequitas protocol for the completely synchronous setting. By "complete synchrony," we mean that both the external and internal networks are synchronous. For this section, we assume that $(\mathcal{A}, \mathcal{Z})$ respects $\Delta_{\mathsf{ext}} = (\mathsf{full}, \delta_{\mathsf{ext}})$ ext-synchrony and $\Delta_{\mathsf{int}} = (\mathsf{full}, \delta_{\mathsf{int}})$ int-synchrony.

To build the $\Pi_{\mathsf{Aequitas}}^{\mathsf{sync},\mathsf{nolead}}$ protocol, we assume a secure FIFO-BC protocol Π_{fifocast} (from Definition 8) and a secure Set-BA protocol Π_{sba} (from Definition 7) that both work for any $(\mathcal{A}, \mathcal{Z})$ that respects $(n, f, \Delta_{\mathsf{int}}, \Delta_{\mathsf{ext}})$-classical execution. Let $(T_{\mathsf{warmup}}^{\mathsf{fifocast}}, T_{\mathsf{confirm}}^{\mathsf{fifocast}})$ and $T^{\mathsf{Set}}\text{-}\mathsf{BA}_{\mathsf{confirm}}$ denote the liveness parameters for Π_{fifocast} and Π_{sba} respectively. We note that any bound for the number of corruptions f will be at least as restrictive as bounds required by Π_{fifocast} and Π_{sba}.

6.1   Protocol Description

The $\Pi_{\text{Aequitas}}^{\text{sync,nolead}}$ protocol follows much of the same general techniques from Sect. 5. The gossip and agreement stage take place exactly as described there. In the gossip stage, a node i forks an instance of $\Pi_{\text{fifocast}}[(\text{sid}, i)]$ and uses it to broadcast transactions as they are received from $\mathcal{Z}$. After broadcasting a transaction tx, it waits until the broadcasts from all honest nodes would have arrived. Let U_i^{tx} denote the set of nodes k such that $\text{tx} \in \text{Log}_i^k$. Note that all honest nodes are present in U_i^{tx}. In the agreement stage, i forks an instance of $\Pi_{\text{sba}}[(\text{sid}, \text{tx})]$ to agree on a set L^{tx} indicating the nodes whose logs to use to order tx.

For the finalization stage, we now present the remaining details that were deferred from Sect. 5.1. Please refer to Sect. 5 for any notation.

Building the "Waiting" Graph G_i. Recall that each node i builds a graph G_i where vertices are transactions and edges denote ordering dependencies between transactions. For two transactions tx and tx′, an edge (tx', tx) is added to G_i if $l_{(\text{tx,tx}')} \leq \left| L^{\text{tx}} \cup L^{\text{tx}'} \right| - \gamma n + f$. Each node i also maintains the condensation graph G_i^* where each strongly connected component in G_i is condensed to a single vertex.

Ordering Incomparable Vertices in G_i^*. Suppose that v and v' are two vertices in G_i^* that are currently not comparable i.e. they do not have an edge between them. To determine which vertex to deliver first, we wait until they have a common descendant, after which we order based on number of descendants. We note that once a common descendant arrives, any other transaction that arrives will also be a descendant of both v and v'. In other words, the vertex with the higher number of descendants will become fixed allowing for a consistent ordering across protocol nodes. Lemma 4 shows a helpful result on when vertices can be "incomparable."

A subtle point to note here is that the common descendant itself can cause v and v' to be combined into the same strongly connected component if it creates a cycle containing them. This is precisely why our protocol achieves weak-liveness, where we achieve liveness, if a transaction arrives late enough that it cannot create a cycle with transactions in v and v'. Effectively, we need to wait for a transaction to arrive sufficiently late in order to "flush out" earlier transactions.

Lemma 4. *Let v_1 and v_2 be two vertices in G_i^* that do not have an edge between them. Let r_{first} denote the time when any transaction in $\text{TXS}_i(v_1)$ was first received by a node. Let r_{last} denote the time when any transaction in $\text{TXS}_i(v_2)$ was last received by a node. Then $r_{\text{last}} - r_{\text{first}} \leq 2\delta_{\text{ext}}$.*

Breaking Ties. We use an a priori known ordering relation to break any ties that arise (e.g., two vertices with equal number of descendants). In particular, suppose that Ord is a binary relation on $2^{\mathcal{T}} \times 2^{\mathcal{T}}$ that is known a priori to all nodes. $2^{\mathcal{T}}$ represents the power set of $\mathcal{T}$. The relation is defined on sets of transactions (rather than individual transactions only) since we may deliver several transactions at once. We assume that Ord is supplied to all nodes on initialization by $\mathcal{Z}$. We will use this function to deterministically break ties between two sets of transactions when neither should clearly come before the other. For two sets S_1 and S_2, $(S_1, S_2) \in$ Ord implies that all nodes agree S_1 should come before S_2 if there is no clear winner. Ord can also be used to order transactions in the same block. We note that Ord can be defined using a simple alphabetical or ascending order. In general, Ord needs to satisfy two properties:

- $\forall (a, b) \in 2^T \times 2^T; a \neq b$, exactly one of (a, b) and (b, a) is in Ord.
- $\forall a, b, c \in 2^T$, if $(a, b) \in$ Ord and $(b, c) \in$ Ord then $(a, c) \in$ Ord.

Delivering Transactions. The transactions $\mathsf{TXS}_i(v)$ of a vertex v in G_i^* can be delivered when:

- v is a source vertex i.e., it has no incoming edge. This ensures that v is not waiting on any other transaction to be delivered first.
- $2\delta_{\mathsf{ext}}$ rounds have passed since v was added to the graph. This ensures that any other vertex v' that v is incomparable to, is also present in the graph.
- For any other source vertex v', v has a common descendant with v' and either has more descendants or has an equal number of descendants and $(\mathsf{TXS}_i(v), \mathsf{TXS}_i(v')) \in$ Ord holds. This ensures that every node will order v before v'.

Bound on f. Suppose that $(\gamma, \cdot)$ order-fairness needs to be realized. This implies that if γn nodes receive transactions in a particular order, it must be reflected in the final ordering. Since f nodes can be adversarial, the output must be the same even if $\gamma n - f$ of those orderings are seen. Now, as we don't want a bi-directed edge to be added to G_i, $\gamma n - f > \frac{n}{2}$ must hold. Equivalently, $n > \frac{2f}{2\gamma - 1}$. For block-order-fairness with $\gamma = 1$, we require an honest majority.

6.2   Protocol Pseudocode

Initialization. At the start of the protocol, we assume that i receives the identities of other protocol nodes, n, f, the maximum network delays $\delta_{\mathsf{int}}, \delta_{\mathsf{ext}}$, and the binary relation Ord. A FIFO-BC protocol Π_{fifocast} and a Set-BA protocol Π_{sba} have also been agreed upon a priori. Let $T_{\mathsf{confirm}}^{\mathsf{fifocast}}$ and $T_{\mathsf{confirm}}^{\mathsf{sba}}$ represent the liveness bounds for Π_{fifocast} and Π_{sba} respectively. Now, for each $j \in \mathcal{N}$, i initializes $\mathsf{Log}_i^j \leftarrow []$. It also initializes an empty graph G_i and a final output log LOG_i.

- At the start of round r, when a node i receives a set of transactions txs from $\mathcal{Z}$, it does the following:

1. **(Gossip)**
   (a) Fork an instance of $\Pi_{\mathsf{fifocast}}[(\mathsf{sid}, i)]$, if it does not already exist.
   (b) Send txs as input to $\Pi_{\mathsf{fifocast}}[(\mathsf{sid}, i)]$.
   (c) Record $(\mathsf{sid}, \mathsf{gossip\text{-}end}, \mathsf{txs}, r + \delta_{\mathsf{ext}} + T_{\mathsf{confirm}}^{\mathsf{fifocast}})$

2. **(Agreement)**
    (a) Check if there is any recorded tuple $(\mathsf{sid}, \mathsf{gossip\text{-}end}, \mathsf{txs'}, r')$ such that $r = r'$.
    (b) For such a tuple for $\mathsf{txs'}$, for each $\mathsf{tx} \in \mathsf{txs'}$, fork an instance of $\Pi_{\mathsf{sba}}[(\mathsf{sid}, \mathsf{tx})]$ and provide it the input U_i^{tx}.
    (c) Record $(\mathsf{sid}, \mathsf{agreement\text{-}end}, \mathsf{tx}, \mathsf{r} + \mathsf{T}_{\mathrm{confirm}}^{\mathrm{sba}})$ for each $\mathsf{tx} \in \mathsf{txs'}$.

3. **(Build Graph)**
    (a) Check if there is any recorded tuple $(\mathsf{sid}, \mathsf{agreement\text{-}end}, \mathsf{tx}, r')$ such that $r = r'$.
    (b) For such a tuple for tx, first add a vertex denoted by tx to G_i if it does not already exist. Now, for any other transaction $\mathsf{tx'}$ seen so far that has not yet been delivered,
        i. Let $u = \left| \left\{ k \in L^{\mathsf{tx}} \mid \mathsf{tx'} \in \mathsf{Log}_i^k \right\} \right|$.
        ii. If $u \geq |L^{\mathsf{tx}}| - (n - f) + 1$, compute $l_{(\mathsf{tx},\mathsf{tx'})}$ as per Sect. 5.1.
        iii. If $l_{(\mathsf{tx},\mathsf{tx'})} \leq \left| L^{\mathsf{tx}} \cup L^{\mathsf{tx'}} \right| - \gamma n + f$, then record $\mathsf{tx} \lhd \mathsf{tx'}$. Add an edge $(\mathsf{tx'}, \mathsf{tx})$ to G_i if it does not already exist.
    (c) Record $(\mathsf{sid}, \mathsf{graph\text{-}end}, \mathsf{tx}, r + 2\delta_{\mathsf{ext}})$ for tx.

4. **(Finalization)**
    (a) Compute the *condensation* graph G_i^* of G_i by collapsing each strongly connected component into a single vertex.
    (b) Let V_{source} be the set of vertices in G_i^* where $v \in V_{\mathsf{source}}$ if it satisfies:
        • All transactions in $\mathsf{TXS}(v)$ have been received.
        • v is a source vertex in G_i^*. That is, v has no incoming edges.
    (c) Let $V_{\mathsf{finalize}} \subseteq V_{\mathsf{source}}$ be the set of vertices v that also satisfy:
        • For all $\mathsf{tx}^* \in \mathsf{TXS}(v)$, there is any previously recorded tuple $(\mathsf{sid}, \mathsf{graph\text{-}end}, \mathsf{tx}^*, r')$ with $r \geq r'$
    (d) For $v \in V_{\mathsf{source}}$, let $\mathsf{Desc}(v)$ denote the descendants of v in G_i^*. Let $\mathsf{nDesc}(v) = |\mathsf{Desc}(v)|$ i.e. the number of descendants.
    (e) For $v \in V_{\mathsf{finalize}}$ and $v' \in V_{\mathsf{source}}$, let $\mathsf{common\text{-}desc}_{(v,v')}$ be a boolean that denotes whether v and v' have a common descendant. That is, we define $\mathsf{common\text{-}desc}_{(v,v')} := (\mathsf{Desc}(v) \cap \mathsf{Desc}(v') \neq \emptyset)$
    (f) If there is a $v \in V_{\mathsf{finalize}}$ such that for all other $v' \in V_{\mathsf{source}}$,
        • $\mathsf{common\text{-}desc}_{(v,v')} = \mathsf{true}$
        • Either $\mathsf{nDesc}(v) > \mathsf{nDesc}(v')$ holds or $(\mathsf{nDesc}(v) = \mathsf{nDesc}(v')) \wedge (\mathsf{TXS}(v), \mathsf{TXS}(v')) \in \mathsf{Ord}$.
        then, deliver transactions in v by appending $\mathsf{TXS}(v)$ to LOG_i. Remove v from G_i^* and the corresponding vertices form G_i.
    (g) Repeat steps 4b to 4f until there is no such v in step 4f.
    (h) Output the current LOG_i to $\mathcal{Z}$.

• When i receives txs from $\Pi_{\mathsf{fifocast}}[(\mathsf{sid}, j)]$, it appends txs to Log_i^j and adds j to the set U_i^{tx}.
• When i receives the output from $\Pi_{\mathsf{sba}}[(\mathsf{sid}, \mathsf{tx})]$, it stores it as L^{tx}.

Transaction Lifecycle. Suppose that a transaction tx is input to node i in round r_0. Since the external network is synchronous, by round $r_0 + \delta_{\text{ext}}$, all nodes will have been input tx by $\mathcal{Z}$. Consequently, by round $r_1 = r_0 + \delta_{\text{ext}} + T^{\text{fifocast}}_{\text{confirm}}$, node i will have received the gossip broadcasts from all other honest nodes. By round $r_2 = r_1 + T^{\text{sba}}_{\text{confirm}}$, node i will receive the output of the agreement stage for tx, and tx can be added to the graph G_i. Now by round $r_3 = r_2 + 2\delta_{\text{ext}}$, any other transaction that tx could be incomparable with will also get added to G_i. Waiting for this time ensures that tx does not get delivered before ensuring that all relevant transactions have been placed in the graph.

6.3   Consistency, Liveness, and Order-Fairness Results

We present the consistency, liveness, and order-fairness results for $\Pi^{\text{sync,nolead}}_{\text{Aequitas}}$ in Theorem 4. We provide brief proof sketches, and defer the formal proofs to the full version [27]. As a corollary, we also note that $\Pi^{\text{sync,nolead}}_{\text{Aequitas}}$ also satisfies receive-order-fairness, and (conventional) liveness when the external network has $\delta_{\text{ext}} = 1$, since non-transitive Condorcet cycles can no longer arise.

Theorem 4 (Consistency, Liveness, and Order-Fairness of $\Pi^{\text{sync,nolead}}_{\text{Aequitas}}$). *Consider any $n, f, \gamma > \frac{1}{2}, \Delta_{\text{ext}} = (\text{full}, \delta_{\text{ext}}), \Delta_{\text{int}} = (\text{full}, \delta_{\text{int}})$ with $n > \frac{2f}{2\gamma - 1}$. Let Π_{fifocast} be a secure FIFO-BC protocol and Π_{sba} be a secure Set-BA protocol. Further, suppose that Π_{fifocast} satisfies $(T^{\text{fifocast}}_{\text{warmup}}, T^{\text{fifocast}}_{\text{confirm}})$ liveness, and Π_{sba} satisfies $T^{\text{sba}}_{\text{confirm}}$ liveness. Then $\Pi^{\text{sync,nolead}}_{\text{Aequitas}}$ satisfies consistency, $(T^{\text{fifocast}}_{\text{warmup}}, T^*_{\text{confirm}})$ weak-liveness where $T^*_{\text{confirm}} = 2\delta_{\text{ext}} + T^{\text{fifocast}}_{\text{confirm}} + T^{\text{sba}}_{\text{confirm}}$, and $(\gamma, T^{\text{fifocast}}_{\text{warmup}})$ block-order-fairness w.r.t. any $(\mathcal{A}, \mathcal{Z})$ that respects $(n, f, \Delta_{\text{int}}, \Delta_{\text{ext}})$-classical execution.*

Consistency Proof Sketch. To show consistency, we need to prove that two honest nodes i and j remove transactions from their graphs G^*_i and G^*_j in the same order. For this, we first present a helpful lemma (Lemma 5).

Lemma 5. *Suppose that when an honest node i delivers tx, $v = \text{SCC}_i(\text{tx})$ is the vertex that contains tx in G^*_i. Now, if another honest node j delivers tx and $v' = \text{SCC}_j(\text{tx})$ at that point, then $\text{TXS}_i(v) = \text{TXS}_j(v')$, or equivalently $\text{SCC}_i(\text{tx}) = \text{SCC}_j(\text{tx})$ when tx is output by each of the nodes. This means that we can drop the node subscripts.*

Now, suppose that node i delivers a transaction tx_1 before another one tx_2. Let $v_1 = \text{SCC}_i(\text{tx}_1)$ and $v_2 = \text{SCC}_i(\text{tx}_2)$ be vertices in G^*_i when tx_1 and tx_2 were delivered. Note that by Lemma 5, we can also use v_1 and v_2 to denote the vertices when j delivers tx_1 and tx_2. Now, either tx_1 was delivered even before tx_2 was added to G_i, or there is an edge from v_1 to v_2 in G^*_i (which caused tx_1 to be output before) or v_1 and v_2 are incomparable.

- If tx_1 was delivered before tx_2 was added to G_i, then at least $\gamma n - f$ nodes received tx_1 before tx_2. Therefore, even if tx_2 gets added to G_j before tx_1, there will be an edge from tx_1 to tx_2 in G_j. By Lemma 5, tx_1 cannot be in the same SCC as tx_2 either, which implies that j cannot deliver tx_2 first.

- If (v_1, v_2) is an edge in G_i^*, then it will also be in G_j^* when j delivers $\mathsf{TXS}(v_2)$. This means that j cannot deliver $\mathsf{TXS}(v_2)$ before it delivers $\mathsf{TXS}(v_1)$.
- If there is no edge between v_1 and v_2 in G_i^*, then node i delivers $\mathsf{TXS}(v_1)$ before because v_1 had more descendants (or because of the deterministic tie-breaker). Since j waits for $2\delta_{\mathsf{ext}}$ time, both v_1 and v_2 are present in its graph G_j^* when j outputs $\mathsf{TXS}(v_2)$, causing j to wait for a common descendant of v_1 and v_2 to be added. By this time, any other vertex that is not a common descendant will also be in G_j^*, and the difference in the number of descendants of v_1 and v_2 will remain constant henceforth. This means that j will take the same decision as i to deliver $\mathsf{TXS}(v_1)$ before $\mathsf{TXS}(v_2)$.

Weak-Liveness Proof Sketch. To show weak-liveness for a transaction tx, first, in Lemma 6, we prove that if a transaction is input sufficiently after tx, it cannot be coalesced into the same strongly connected component as tx.

Lemma 6. *Consider a transaction* tx *and build the set* T *as per the weak-liveness definition. Now, let* tx' *be a transaction that is input to all nodes after all transactions in* T. *Then* $\mathsf{SCC}_i(\mathrm{tx}) \neq \mathsf{SCC}_i(\mathrm{tx}')$ *for any honest i.*

Now, suppose that tx was first input by $\mathcal{Z}$ in round $r > T_{\mathsf{warmup}}^{\mathsf{fifocast}}$. Consider the set T built form tx as in the weak-liveness definition. Suppose now that a transaction $\mathrm{tx}_{\mathsf{flush}}$ is input to all nodes after all transactions in T. Let r_{flush} be the round that $\mathrm{tx}_{\mathsf{flush}}$ is first input to some node. Then, $\mathrm{tx}_{\mathsf{flush}}$ is received by all nodes by round $r_{\mathsf{flush}} + \delta_{\mathsf{ext}}$ and therefore added to all honest graphs G_i by round $r_{\mathsf{flush}} + 2\delta_{\mathsf{ext}} + T_{\mathsf{confirm}}^{\mathsf{fifocast}} + T_{\mathsf{confirm}}^{\mathsf{sba}}$. From Lemma 6, $v = \mathsf{SCC}_i(\mathrm{tx}) \neq \mathsf{SCC}_i(\mathrm{tx}_{\mathsf{flush}})$ for any honest i. Now, any transaction tx' that tx is incomparable was input to at least one honest node no later than tx, i.e. $\mathrm{tx}_{\mathsf{flush}}$ was received after tx' by all honest nodes. Consequently, $\mathrm{tx}_{\mathsf{flush}}$ will be a descendant of both tx and tx'. This means that node i can deliver $\mathsf{TXS}_i(\mathrm{tx})$ when $\mathrm{tx}_{\mathsf{flush}}$ gets added to its graph, which happens by round $r_{\mathsf{flush}} + T_{\mathsf{confirm}}^*$.

Order-Fairness Proof Sketch. First, we note that if γn nodes receive tx_1 before tx_2, then at least $\gamma n - f$ honest ones do. This means that there will be an edge from tx_1 to tx_2 in all honest G_i. Consequently, either tx_1 will be delivered before tx_2 by all nodes, or it will end up in the same strongly connected component as tx_2 and be delivered at the same time.

Acknowledgements. This work was funded by NSF grants CNS-1564102, CNS-1704615, and CNS-1933655 as well as support from IC3 industry partners. We would also like to thank Mic Bowman at Intel for drawing attention to potential applications.

References

1. Abraham, I., et al.: Solida: a blockchain protocol based on reconfigurable byzantine consensus. In: OPODIS, pp. 25:1–25:19 (2017)
2. Abraham, I., et al.: Sync HotStuff: simple and practical synchronous state machine replication. Cryptology ePrint Archive, Report 2019/270 (2019)

3. Amir, Y., et al.: Prime: byzantine replication under attack. IEEE TDSC **8**(4), 564–577 (2011)

4. Asayag, A., et al.: A fair consensus protocol for transaction ordering. In: ICNP, pp. 55–65 (2018)

5. Aublin, P.-L., Mokhtar, S.B., Quéma, V.: RBFT: redundant byzantine fault tolerance. In: ICDCS, pp. 297–306 (2013)

6. Baird, L.: The Swirlds Hashgraph Consensus Algorithm: Fair, Fast, Byzantine Fault Tolerance (2016). https://www.swirlds.com/downloads/SWIRLDS-TR-2016-01.pdf

7. Bano, S., et al.: Consensus in the age of blockchains. arXiv:1711.03936 (2017)

8. Bessani, A., Sousa, J., Alchieri, E.E.P.: State machine replication for the masses with BFT-SMART. In: DSN, pp. 355–362 (2014)

9. Bracha, G., Toueg, S.: Asynchronous consensus and broadcast protocols. J. ACM **32**(4), 824–840 (1985)

10. Cachin, C., Vukolić, M.: Blockchain consensus protocols in the wild. arXiv:1707.01873 (2017)

11. Cachin, C., Kursawe, K., Petzold, F., Shoup, V.: Secure and efficient asynchronous broadcast protocols. In: Kilian, J. (ed.) CRYPTO 2001. LNCS, vol. 2139, pp. 524–541. Springer, Heidelberg (2001). https://doi.org/10.1007/3-540-44647-8_31

12. Canetti, R.: Universally composable security: a new paradigm for cryptographic protocols. In: FOCS, pp. 136–147 (2001)

13. Canetti, R., Rabin, T.: Universal composition with joint state. In: Boneh, D. (ed.) CRYPTO 2003. LNCS, vol. 2729, pp. 265–281. Springer, Heidelberg (2003). https://doi.org/10.1007/978-3-540-45146-4_16

14. Canetti, R., Dodis, Y., Pass, R., Walfish, S.: Universally composable security with global setup. In: Vadhan, S.P. (ed.) TCC 2007. LNCS, vol. 4392, pp. 61–85. Springer, Heidelberg (2007). https://doi.org/10.1007/978-3-540-70936-7_4

15. Castro, M., Liskov, B.: Practical byzantine fault tolerance. In: OSDI, pp. 173–186 (1999)

16. Hubert Chan, T.-H., Pass, R., Shi, E.: Consensus through herding. In: Ishai, Y., Rijmen, V. (eds.) EUROCRYPT 2019. LNCS, vol. 11476, pp. 720–749. Springer, Cham (2019). https://doi.org/10.1007/978-3-030-17653-2_24

17. Clement, A., et al.: Making byzantine fault tolerant systems tolerate byzantine faults. In: NDSI, pp. 153–168 (2009)

18. Condorcet Paradox. https://wikipedia.org/wiki/Condorcet_paradox

19. Cristian, F., et al.: Atomic broadcast: from simple message diffusion to byzantine agreement. Inf. Comput. **118**(1), 158–179 (1995)

20. Daian, P., et al.: Flash boys 2.0: frontrunning in decentralized exchanges, miner extractable value, and consensus instability. In: IEEE S&P, pp. 585–602 (2020)

21. Dolev, D., Raymond Strong, H.: Authenticated algorithms for byzantine agreement. SIAM J. Comput. **12**, 656–666 (1983)

22. Dwork, C., Lynch, N., Stockmeyer, L.: Consensus in the presence of partial synchrony. J. ACM **35**(2), 288–323 (1988)

23. Ethereum. https://ethereum.org/

24. Eyal, I., Sirer, E.G.: Majority is not enough: bitcoin mining is vulnerable. In: Christin, N., Safavi-Naini, R. (eds.) FC 2014. LNCS, vol. 8437, pp. 436–454. Springer, Heidelberg (2014). https://doi.org/10.1007/978-3-662-45472-5_28

25. Gilad, Y., et al.: Algorand: scaling byzantine agreements for cryptocurrencies. In: SOSP, pp. 51–68 (2017)

26. Ho, C., Dolev, D., van Renesse, R.: Making distributed applications robust. In: Tovar, E., Tsigas, P., Fouchal, H. (eds.) OPODIS 2007. LNCS, vol. 4878, pp. 232–246. Springer, Heidelberg (2007). https://doi.org/10.1007/978-3-540-77096-1_17

27. Kelkar, M., et al.: Order-fairness for byzantine consensus. Cryptology ePrint Archive, Report 2020/269 (2020)

28. Kiayias, A., Russell, A., David, B., Oliynykov, R.: Ouroboros: a provably secure proof-of-stake blockchain protocol. In: Katz, J., Shacham, H. (eds.) CRYPTO 2017. LNCS, vol. 10401, pp. 357–388. Springer, Cham (2017). https://doi.org/10.1007/978-3-319-63688-7_12

29. Kokoris-Kogias, E., et al.: OmniLedger: a secure, scale-out, decentralized ledger via sharding. In: IEEE S&P, pp. 583–598 (2018)

30. Lamport, L., Shostak, R., Pease, M.: The byzantine generals problem. TOPLAS **4**(3), 382–401 (1982)

31. Lev-Ari, K., et al.: FairLedger: a fair blockchain protocol for financial institutions. In: OPODIS, pp. 1:1–1:16 (2019)

32. Lewis, M.: Flash Boys: A Wall Street Revolt. WW Norton & Company, New York (2014)

33. Luu, L., et al.: SmartPool: practical decentralized pooled mining. In: USENIX Security, pp. 1409–1426 (2017)

34. Martin, J.-P., Alvisi, L.: Fast byzantine consensus. IEEE TDSC **3**(3), 202–215 (2006)

35. Miller, A., et al.: Non-outsourceable scratch-off puzzles to discourage bitcoin mining coalitions. In: ACM CCS, pp. 680–691 (2015)

36. Miller, A., et al.: The honey badger of BFT protocols. In: ACM CCS, pp. 31–42 (2016)

37. Pass, R., Shi, E.: FruitChains: a fair blockchain. In: PODC, pp. 315–324 (2017)

38. Pass, R., Shi, E.: Hybrid consensus: efficient consensus in the permissionless model. In: DISC, pp. 1–16 (2017)

39. Pass, R., Shi, E.: Rethinking large-scale consensus. In: CSF, pp. 15–129 (2017)

40. Pass, R., Shi, E.: Thunderella: blockchains with optimistic instant confirmation. In: Nielsen, J.B., Rijmen, V. (eds.) EUROCRYPT 2018. LNCS, vol. 10821, pp. 3–33. Springer, Cham (2018). https://doi.org/10.1007/978-3-319-78375-8_1

41. Rocket, T., et al.: Scalable and probabilistic leaderless BFT consensus through metastability. arXiv:1906.08936 (2019)

42. Veronese, G.S., et al.: Efficient byzantine fault-tolerance. IEEE Trans. Comput. **62**(1), 16–30 (2013)

43. Veronese, G.S., et al.: Spin one's wheels? Byzantine fault tolerance with a spinning primary. In: SRDS, pp. 135–144 (2009)

44. Yin, M., et al.: HotStuff: BFT consensus with linearity and responsiveness. In: PODC, pp. 347–356 (2019)

Generically Speeding-Up Repeated Squaring Is Equivalent to Factoring: Sharp Thresholds for All Generic-Ring Delay Functions

Lior Rotem[(✉)] and Gil Segev

School of Computer Science and Engineering, Hebrew University of Jerusalem,
Jerusalem 91904, Israel
{lior.rotem,segev}@cs.huji.ac.il

Abstract. Despite the fundamental importance of delay functions, repeated squaring in RSA groups (Rivest, Shamir and Wagner '96) is the only candidate offering both a useful structure and a realistic level of practicality. Somewhat unsatisfyingly, its sequentiality is provided directly by assumption (i.e., the function is assumed to be a delay function).

We prove sharp thresholds on the sequentiality of all generic-ring delay functions relative to an RSA modulus based on the hardness of factoring in the standard model. In particular, we show that generically speeding-up repeated squaring (even with a preprocessing stage and any polynomial number parallel processors) is equivalent to factoring.

More generally, based on the (essential) hardness of factoring, we prove that any generic-ring function is in fact a delay function, admitting a sharp sequentiality threshold that is determined by our notion of *sequentiality depth*. Moreover, we show that generic-ring functions admit not only sharp sequentiality thresholds, but also sharp pseudorandomness thresholds.

1 Introduction

The recent and exciting notion of a verifiable delay function, introduced by Boneh et al. [BBB+18], and the classic notion of time-lock puzzles, introduced by Rivest, Shamir and Wagner [RSW96], are gaining significant interest due to a host of thrilling applications. These include, for example, randomness beacons, resource-efficient blockchains, proofs of replication and computational times-tamping. A fundamental notion underlying both of these notions is that of a cryptographic delay function: For a delay parameter T, evaluating a delay function on a randomly-chosen input should require at least T sequential steps (even

L. Rotem and G. Segev—Supported by the European Union's Horizon 2020 Framework Program (H2020) via an ERC Grant (Grant No. 714253).
L. Rotem—Supported by the Adams Fellowship Program of the Israel Academy of Sciences and Humanities.

D. Micciancio and T. Ristenpart (Eds.): CRYPTO 2020, LNCS 12172, pp. 481–509, 2020.
https://doi.org/10.1007/978-3-030-56877-1_17

with a polynomial number of parallel processors and with a preprocessing stage), yet the function can be evaluated on any input in time polynomial in T.

A delay function can be easily constructed by iterating a cryptographic hash function. A major benefit of this construction is that its sequentiality is supported by an idealized-model proof of security: When the hash function is modeled as a random oracle, its sequentiality is guaranteed in an information-theoretic sense. Alas, the lack of structure exhibited by this construction seems to disable its practical use for realizing time-lock puzzles or verifiable delay functions. Specifically, for time-lock puzzles, iterated hashing does not seem to admit sufficiently fast generation of input-output pairs [MMV11]; and for verifiable delay functions it does not seem to enable sufficiently fast verification.[1]

The only known construction of a delay function that offers both a useful structure for realizing time-lock puzzles or verifiable delay functions and a realistic level of practicality is the "repeated squaring" function in RSA groups, defined via $x \mapsto x^{2^T} \bmod N$, underlying the time-lock puzzle of Rivest et al. [RSW96].[2] This delay function was recently elegantly extended by Pietrzak [Pie19] and Wesolowski [Wes19] to additionally yield a verifiable delay function.

The sequentiality of this function, however, is provided directly by assumption. That is, the function is assumed to be a delay function, and there is currently no substantial evidence relating its sequentiality to any other, more standard, assumptions such as the RSA or factoring assumptions. This highly unsatisfying state of affairs raises the important challenge of obtaining a better understanding of the sequentiality of repeated squaring in RSA groups. Clearly, given the factorization of the RSA modulus N, it is possible to speed up the computation of the repeated squaring function by reducing 2^T modulo the order of the multiplicative group $\mathbb{Z}_N^*$. Thus, the hardness of factoring is essential for the sequentiality of repeated squaring in RSA groups, leading to the following ambitious question:

Is speeding-up repeated squaring equivalent to factoring?

More generally, and given that delay functions have become a basic primitive underlying a variety of evolving applications, this urges at exploring other candidate delay functions, and obtaining a rigorous understanding of the cryptographic assumptions underlying their sequentiality.

---

[1] Although, asymptotically, for any concrete instantiation of the hash function, such verification can be based on succinct non-interactive arguments for NP languages [Kil92, Mic94, GW11], as suggested by Döttling et al. [DGM+19] and Boneh et al. [BBB+18].

[2] There are additional constructions of delay functions which enable extensions to time-lock puzzles and to verifiable delay functions, but these rely on computational hardness within algebraic structures that are less-explored from a cryptographic standpoint. These include the class groups of imaginary quadratic fields [BW88, BBB+18, Pie19, Wes19] and isogenies of supersingular elliptic curves [FMP+19, Sha19].

1.1   Our Contributions

We resolve the above-mentioned challenges within the generic-ring model relative to an RSA modulus, capturing all computations that ignore any specific property of the representation of ring elements. Our main result is a sharp threshold on the sequentiality of all generic-ring delay functions based on the hardness of factoring in the standard model.

Trade-offs between sequentiality and parallelism are still not sufficiently understood from the complexity-theoretic perspective for computations in the standard model, and the generic-ring model provides a framework in which the nature of computation is somewhat better understood on the one hand, and which captures a wide variety of practical constructions and attacks on the other hand. In particular, our results apply to the repeated squaring function, for which we obtain the following theorem:

Theorem 1.1 (informal). *Generically speeding-up repeated squaring is equivalent to standard-model factoring.*

That is, we prove that any generic-ring algorithm that has a non-negligible probability in computing the function $x \mapsto x^{2^T} \bmod N$ for a uniformly chosen input $x \leftarrow \mathbb{Z}_N^*$ using a preprocessing stage and any polynomial number of parallel processors, each of which performs less than T sequential ring operations, yields a polynomial-time standard-model factoring algorithm with polynomially-related success probability and running time.

Sharp Sequentiality Thresholds. More generally, as mentioned above, we prove sharp thresholds on the sequentiality of all generic-ring delay functions based on the hardness of factoring in the standard model. These include, in particular, all rational (partial) multivariate functions over the ring, as well as more expressive functions which may depend on the equality pattern among all intermediate values in the computation.

We prove that every generic-ring function is in fact a delay function, whose sequentiality depends on the notion *sequentiality depth*, which we put forward. For rather simple polynomials, this notion essentially coincides with the logarithm of their degree (thus leading to Theorem 1.1 for the case of repeated squaring). For general generic-ring functions, our notion of sequentiality depth can be viewed as approximating the minimal degree of a rational function that is equivalent modulo N to the given function. Even for rational functions, however, defining a notion of equivalence is quite subtle given that the ring we consider is not an integral domain.

Equipped with our notion of sequentiality depth for any generic-ring function, we show that it serves as a sharp threshold for the number of sequential ring operations required in order to evaluate the function on a uniformly-chosen input.

Theorem 1.2 (informal). *Let F be a generic-ring function of sequentiality depth d. Assuming the hardness of factoring in the standard model, it holds that:*

– *F can be generically evaluated on any input with d sequential rounds of ring operations issued by a polynomial number of parallel processors.*
– *F cannot be generically evaluated on a uniformly-chosen input with less than d sequential rounds of ring operations, even with a preprocessing stage and any polynomial number of parallel processors.*

Sharp Pseudorandomness Thresholds. Moreover, we prove that for generic attackers who preform two few sequential rounds of ring operations, generic-ring functions provide not only unpredictability but in fact pseudorandomness. We explore the pseudorandomness of delay functions not merely as a natural strengthening of sequentiality, but also given that various applications of delay functions may directly benefit from it (e.g., randomness beacons [BCG15, BGZ16, PW18, BBB+18]).

Complementing our notion of sequentiality depth, we put forward the notion of *pseudorandomness depth* of a generic-ring function, which can be viewed as an indistinguishability-based variant of sequentiality depth. As above, for rather simple polynomials the notion of pseudorandomness depth essentially coincides with the logarithm of their degree (thus leading to a variant of Theorem 1.1 that considers the pseudorandomness of repeated squaring instead of its sequentiality). For general generic-ring functions, the pseudorandomness depth is always upper bounded by the sequentiality depth, and exploring the exact relation between these two notions is an interesting direction for future research.

We prove that the pseudorandomness depth of any generic-ring function serves as a sharp threshold for the number of sequential rounds of ring operations required in order to distinguish between a uniformly chosen ring element and the output of the function when evaluated on a uniformly-chosen input.

Theorem 1.3 (informal). *Let F be a k-variate generic-ring function of pseudorandomness depth d. Assuming the hardness of factoring in the standard model, it holds that:*

– *$F(x_1, \ldots, x_k)$ can be generically distinguished from a uniform ring element y, where $x_1, \ldots, x_k$ are uniformly chosen in the ring, with d sequential rounds of ring operations issued by a polynomial number of parallel processors,*
– *$F(x_1, \ldots, x_k)$ cannot be generically distinguished from a uniform ring element y, where $x_1, \ldots, x_k$ are uniformly chosen in the ring, with less than d sequential rounds of ring operations, even with a preprocessing stage and any polynomial number of parallel processors.*

1.2   Related Work

We prove our results within the generic-ring model introduced by Aggarwal and Maurer [AM09] and further studied by Jager and Schwenk [JS13], as part of the line of research on idealized models for capturing algebraic constructions and hardness assumptions (see [Nec94, Sho97, BL96, MW98, Mau05, JS08, JR10, FKL18] and the references therein). Within their model, which is more suitable for capturing RSA-based constructions compared to the generic-group model, Aggarwal and Maurer proved that any generic algorithm that is able to compute roots of random ring elements relative to an RSA modulus can be used to produce a standard-model factoring algorithm. That is, they showed that the hardness of the RSA problem in the generic-ring model is equivalent to the hardness of factoring in the standard model. Following-up on previous work on the relationship between the RSA and factoring assumptions (e.g., [BV98, DK02, Bro05, LR06, JNT07]), this provided substantial evidence towards the security of RSA-based constructions, showing that under the factoring assumption they are not vulnerable to a wide variety of practical cryptanalytic attacks.

Our work is directly inspired by the work of Aggarwal and Maurer in relating the capabilities of generic attackers to the hardness of factoring. The key difference, however, both conceptually and technically is that, based on the hardness of factoring, Aggarwal and Maurer proved that certain functions are completely infeasible to compute in polynomial time, whereas we show a more fine-grained result: It is infeasible to *speed-up* functions that can be computed in polynomial time (even with a preprocessing stage and with any polynomial number of parallel processors).

Following-up on the work of Aggarwal and Maurer, Jager and Schwenk [JS13] proved that generically computing the Jacobi symbol of a random $\mathbb{Z}_N$ element is equivalent to factoring, although Jacobi symbols are easy to compute non-generically given the standard integer representation of $\mathbb{Z}_N$ elements. As pointed out by Jager and Schwenk, and as discussed above, lower bounds in the generic-ring model nevertheless capture a wide variety of practical constructions and cryptanalytic attacks.[3]

In an independent work, Katz, Loss and Xu [KLX20] proved that within a quantitative variant of the algebraic group model [FKL18], speeding-up repeated squaring in the group $\mathbb{QR}_N$ of quadratic residues modulo N is equivalent to factoring N, where N is a bi-prime integer. Our results differ from theirs in a few aspects. Firstly, our result holds for any function which may be defined in the generic-ring model, whereas they consider only the repeated squaring function; and we consider both unpredictability and pseudorandomness, whereas they consider only unpredictability. Secondly, the model in which Katz et al. prove their result is incomparable to the model in which we prove our results: On the one hand, in the algebraic group model the adversary may use the concrete representation of group elements (which is unavailable to the adversary in the generic-ring model); but on the other hand, the adversary's output must be explained by a sequence of *group operations* (in $\mathbb{QR}_N$ this translates to a sequence of multiplications modulo N), whereas the generic-ring model permits the two

---

[3] Aggarwal and Maurer also point out that lower bounds in the generic-ring model remain interesting specifically for problems in which the adversary is required to output elements in the ring, which is the case for evaluation of delay functions and for computing roots in the ring, bit is not the case for computing the Jacobi symbol of ring elements.

ring operations and their inverses (i.e., in addition to multiplication, it also allows for addition, subtraction and division modulo N). Finally, they consider the group $\mathbb{QR}_N$, whereas we consider its super-group $\mathbb{Z}_N^*$. From a technical standpoint, their proof inherently relies on the fact that $\mathbb{QR}_N$ is cyclic, which is not the case for $\mathbb{Z}_N^*$.

Various cryptographic notions that share a somewhat similar motivation with delay functions have been proposed over the years, such as the above-discussed notions of time-lock puzzles and verifiable delay functions (e.g., [RSW96, BGJ+16, BBB+18, BBF18, Pie19, Wes19, EFK+20, FMP+19]), as well as other candidate functions [DN92, LW15] and other notions such as sequential functions and proofs of sequential work (e.g., [MMV11, MMV13, CP18]). It is far beyond the scope of this work to provide an overview of these notions and constructions, and we refer the reader to the work of Boneh et al. [BBB+18] for an in-depth discussion of these notions and of the relations among them.

In the generic-*group* model, Rotem, Segev and Shahaf [RSS20] have recently ruled out the possibility of constructing delay functions in cyclic groups, where the group's order is known to the attacker. In the random-oracle model, Döttling, Garg, Malavolta and Vasudevan [DGM+19], and Mahmoody, Smith and Wu [MSW19] recently proved impossibility results for certain classes of *verifiable* delay functions. Our work is of a different flavor, as these works provide negative evidence for the existence of delay functions and verifiable delay functions, whereas our work provides positive evidence for the existence of generic-ring delay functions. Our work is also different from the work of Rotem et al. [RSS20] in that it considers the generic-ring model in order to capture the RSA group which is believed to be of an *unknown order* from a computational perspective; and from the works of Döttling et al. [DGM+19] and Mahmoody et al. [MSW19] both in terms of focusing on the seemingly weaker notion of delay functions (i.e., we do not require verifiability), and in terms of characterizing the sequentiality and pseudorandomness of all functions in the more structured and expressive generic-ring model, based on the hardness of factoring in the standard model.

1.3   Paper Organization

The remainder of the paper is organized as follows. First, in Sect. 2 we present the generic-ring model, and in Sect. 3 we describe our framework for generic-ring delay functions. In Sect. 4 we prove our sharp threshold on the sequentiality of straight-line delay functions. Due to space limitations, our extension of this threshold to arbitrary generic-ring delay functions, as well as our sharp threshold on the pseudorandomness of delay functions, are formally presented and proven in the full version of this paper.

2   The Generic-Ring Model

In this section we present the idealized model of computation that we consider in this work, slightly refining the generic-ring model introduced by Aggarwal and

Maurer [AM09] as we discuss below (mainly for the purpose of a more detailed accounting of parallelism vs. sequentiality). Informally, a generic-ring algorithm which receives one or more ring elements as input is restricted to handling these elements only via the two ring binary operations and their inverses, and by checking equality between two ring elements.

More formally, we consider generic computations in a ring R. Concretely, following Aggarwal and Maurer, the ring R we consider is that of integers modulo N, denoted $\mathbb{Z}_N$, for N which is the product of two primes and is generated by a modulus-generation algorithm $\mathsf{ModGen}(1^\lambda)$, where $\lambda \in \mathbb{N}$ is the security parameter. All generic-ring algorithms in this paper receive the modulus N as an explicit bit-string input. Any computation in this model is associated with a table $\mathbf{B}$, where each entry of this table stores an element of R, and we denote by V_i the ring element that is stored in the ith entry.

Generic-ring algorithms access this table via an oracle $\mathcal{O}$, providing black-box access to $\mathbf{B}$ as follows. A generic-ring algorithm A that takes d ring elements as input does not receive an explicit representation of these elements, but instead, has oracle access to the table $\mathbf{B}$, whose first d entries store the elements of R corresponding to the d ring elements that are included in $\mathcal{A}$'s input. That is, if the input of an algorithm A consists of d ring elements $x_1, \ldots, x_d$, then from A's point of view the input consists of "pointers" $\widehat{x_1}, \ldots, \widehat{x_d}$ to the ring elements $x_1, \ldots, x_d$ (these elements are stored in the table $\mathbf{B}$). Accordingly, when a generic-ring algorithm outputs a ring element $y \in R$, it actually outputs a pointer which we denote by $\widehat{y}$, pointing to an entry in $\mathbf{B}$ containing y.[4] The oracle $\mathcal{O}$ allows for two types of queries:

- **Ring-operation queries:** These queries enable computation of the binary ring operations and their inverses. On input $(i, j, \circ)$ for $i, j \in \mathbb{N}$ and $\circ \in \{+, -, \cdot, /\}$, the oracle checks that the ith and jth entries of the table $\mathbf{B}$ are not empty and are not $\perp$, and in case that $\circ$ is $/$ (i.e., the inverse of the multiplication operation), the oracle also checks that the result of V_j is invertible in the ring. If all checks pass, then the oracle computes $V_i \circ V_j$ and stores the result in the next available entry. Otherwise, it stores $\perp$ in the next available entry.
- **Equality queries:** On input $(i, j, =)$ for $i, j \in \mathbb{N}$, the oracle checks that the ith and jth entries in $\mathbf{B}$ are not empty and are not $\perp$, and then returns 1 if $V_i = V_j$ and 0 otherwise. If either the ith or the jth entries are empty or are $\perp$, the oracle ignores the query.

Straight-Line Functions. Looking ahead, we will first prove our results for the case in which the delay function is a straight-line program, which is a deterministic generic-ring algorithm that does not issue any equality queries. We refer to such delay functions as straight-line delay functions. Then, we will extend our

---

[4] We assume that all generic-ring algorithms receive a pointer to the multiplicative identity 1 and a pointer to the additive identity 0 as their first two inputs (we capture this fact by always assuming that the first two entries of $\mathbf{B}$ are occupied by $1 \in R$ and $0 \in R$), and we will forgo noting this explicitly from this point on.

result to arbitrary generic-ring functions that may issue both ring-operations queries and equality queries.

Parallel Computation. In order to reason about delay functions in this model, we need to extend it in a way which accommodates parallel computation. A generic-ring algorithm with w parallel processors invokes the oracle $\mathcal{O}$ with ring-operation queries in "rounds", where in each round, at most w parallel ring-operation queries may be issued. We assume some order on the processors so that the results of the queries are also placed in the table $\mathbf{B}$ according to this order. We emphasize, however, that the action that the oracle takes in response to each of the queries in a certain round is with respect to the contents of the table $\mathbf{B}$ *before* this round; meaning, the elements passed as input in the query issued by a processor in some round cannot depend on the result of a query made by any other processor in the same round. We emphasize that parallelism will not play a role when it comes to equality queries, as we allow algorithm to issue all possible such queries and do not account for their sequentiality (i.e., we prove our thresholds for the number of ring-operation queries considering only the total number of equality queries in our lower bound, and without issuing any equality queries in our upper bound).

We are interested in three main efficiency measures when considering generic-ring algorithms: (1) The number of parallel processors; (2) the number of sequential rounds in which ring-operation queries are issued; and (3) the algorithm's internal computation, measured via its running time.

Interactive Computations. We consider interactive computations in which multiple algorithms pass ring elements (as well as non-ring elements) as inputs to one another. This is naturally supported by the model as follows: When a generic-ring algorithm A outputs k ring elements (along with a potential bit-string σ), it outputs the indices of k (non-empty) entries in the table $\mathbf{B}$ (together with σ). When these outputs (or some of them) are passed on as inputs to a generic-ring algorithm C, the table $\mathbf{B}$ is re-initialized, and these values (and possibly additional group elements that C receives as input) are placed in the first entries of the table.

Polynomial Interpretation. Every ring element computed by the oracle $\mathcal{O}$ in response to a ring-operation query made by a generic-ring algorithm, can be naturally identified with a pair of polynomials in the ring elements given as input to the algorithm. Formally, for a generic-ring algorithm which receives d ring elements as input (in addition to the multiplicative identity 1 and the additive identity 0), we identify the ith input element with the pair $(X_i, 1)$ where X_i is an indeterminate of the polynomials we will consider (the 1 and 0 elements are identified with the pairs $(1, 1)$ and $(0, 1)$, respectively). The rest of the polynomials are defined recursively: For a ring-operation query $(i, j, \circ)$, let $(P_i(\mathbf{X}), Q_i(\mathbf{X}))$ and $(P_j(\mathbf{X}), Q_j(\mathbf{X}))$ be the pairs of polynomials identified with V_i and with V_j, where $\mathbf{X} = (X_1, \ldots, X_d)$. We define the pair of polynomials identified with the result of the query as:

$$(P(\mathbf{X}), Q(\mathbf{X})) = \begin{cases} (P_i(\mathbf{X}) \cdot Q_j(\mathbf{X}) + P_j(\mathbf{X}) \cdot Q_i(\mathbf{X}), Q_i(\mathbf{X}) \cdot Q_j(\mathbf{X})), \text{ if } \circ \text{ is } + \\ (P_i(\mathbf{X}) \cdot Q_j(\mathbf{X}) - P_j(\mathbf{X}) \cdot Q_i(\mathbf{X}), Q_i(\mathbf{X}) \cdot Q_j(\mathbf{X})), \text{ if } \circ \text{ is } - \\ (P_i(\mathbf{X}) \cdot P_j(\mathbf{X}), Q_i(\mathbf{X}) \cdot Q_j(\mathbf{X})) \qquad\qquad\quad, \text{ if } \circ \text{ is } \cdot \\ (P_i(\mathbf{X}) \cdot Q_j(\mathbf{X}), Q_i(\mathbf{X}) \cdot P_j(\mathbf{X})) \qquad\qquad\quad, \text{ if } \circ \text{ is } / \end{cases}$$

Note that this definition extends to the interactive case, in which one generic-ring algorithm A receives d ring elements $x_1, \ldots, x_d$ as input, computes some ring element from them which is associated with the pair of polynomials $(P(\mathbf{X}), Q(\mathbf{X}))$, and then passes this ring element as input to another generic-ring algorithm C. Then, this definition allows us to reason about the values computed by C as pairs of polynomials in the elements $x_1, \ldots, x_d$.

Each pair of polynomials is naturally interpreted as a rational function (by setting the first polynomial to be the numerator and the second to be the denominator). For the time being, however, we simply think of these polynomials as polynomials in $\mathbb{Z}[\mathbf{X}]$, and so the problem of division by 0 does not arise yet, since the second polynomial is always non-zero as a polynomial in $\mathbb{Z}[\mathbf{X}]$. For a straight-line program S, we will denote by $(P_\sigma^S[i, j], Q_\sigma^S[i, j])$ the pair of polynomials computed by the jth query of the ith processor of S, when invoked on explicit input $\sigma \in \{0, 1\}^*$. For the special case of a straight-line program S that outputs a single ring element, the pair of polynomials corresponding to this element is fixed for every explicit input σ, and we denote it by (P_σ^S, Q_σ^S). When we are working in the ring $\mathbb{Z}_N$, we will sometimes consider all of the aforementioned polynomials as polynomials in $\mathbb{Z}_N[\mathbf{X}]$ (instead of allowing arbitrary integer coefficients). This is naturally done by reducing all coefficients of the polynomial modulo N, and will be clear from context.

Passing Ring Elements Explicitly. Throughout the paper we refer to values as either "explicit" ones or "inexplicit"/"implicit" ones. Explicit values are all values whose representation (e.g., binary strings of a certain length) is explicitly provided to the generic algorithms under consideration. Inexplicit values are all values that correspond to ring elements and that are stored in the table $\mathbf{B}$ – thus generic algorithms can access them only via oracle queries. We will sometimes interchange between providing ring elements as input to generic-ring algorithms inexplicitly, and providing them explicitly. Note that moving from the former to the latter is well defined, since a generic-ring algorithm A that receives some of its input ring elements explicitly can always simulate the computation as if they were received as part of the table $\mathbf{B}$. For a ring element x, we will differentiate between the case where x is provided explicitly and the case where it is provided implicitly via the table $\mathbf{B}$, using the notation x in the former case, and the notation $\hat{x}$ in the latter.

In cases where all inputs to a generic-ring element A are provided explicitly, we may be interested in obtaining its outputs explicitly as well (note that this is indeed possible, since in this case the algorithm may preform all ring operations internally in an explicit manner). When this is the case, we will use the oracle notation A^R instead of $A^\mathcal{O}$, where R is the ring being considered. For example, consider a generic-ring algorithm A which receives two ring elements x_1 and

x_2 as input, and outputs $x_1 + x_2$, and the is ring $\mathbb{Z}_{15}$ of integers modulo 15. The notation $A^{\mathbb{Z}_{15}}(7, 10)$ indicates that the output of A (i.e., the integer 2) is obtained explicitly as an integer.

Finally, note that if we replace a proper subset of the input ring-elements to a generic algorithm A with explicit integers, than the intermediate ring elements which A computes via the oracle $\mathcal{O}$ can be interpreted as pairs of polynomials in the remaining inexplicit ring elements, as described above.

Comparison with the Model of Aggarwal and Maurer. Our model slightly refines that of Aggarwal and Maurer [AM09] in the following natural respects:

- As mentioned above, we consider algorithms with possibly many parallel processors, whereas Aggarwal and Maurer consider algorithms which may invoke the oracle on a single query at a time. Considering multiple processors is essential when reasoning about delay function, as their security guarantees should hold even against parallel adversaries.
- Algorithms in our model may receive multiple ring elements as input, as opposed to a single ring element in the model of Aggarwal and Maurer. This allows us to reason about the sequentiality of computing arbitrary generic functions in the ring (e.g., multivariate rational functions).
- We consider interactive computations, which allows us to reason about security properties which are defined via an interactive security experiment. In particular, it allows us to account for a preprocessing stage when reasoning about delay functions.
- Algorithms in our model may receive an explicit bit-string input (in addition to the modulus N), which allows us to consider families of functions (via the delay parameter T passed to the function evaluation algorithm), and explicit states passed from one adversarial algorithm to another in interactive security experiments.

In addition to the above extensions, it should be noted that Aggarwal and Maurer present graph-based definitions for straight-line programs and generic-ring algorithms, which we forgo here. However, both our definitions and the ones in the work of Aggarwal and Maurer can be rendered as special cases of Maurer's generic model of computation [Mau05]; and when restricting our definitions to single-processor algorithms with one ring element input, they are equivalent to the ones found in the work of Aggarwal and Maurer.

The reason we choose to base our definitions on oracle-aided algorithms is that we find it more convenient to explicitly consider the running time of such algorithms in terms of their internal computational efforts. This comes up when analyzing the running time of our factorization algorithms (in the plain model) outputted by the reduction. Even when considering the simple case where the input to the reduction is a straight-line program; once this program receives an explicit input (e.g., the modulus N) in addition to ring elements, its queries may be (and are indeed expected to be) a function of this input. Since this function is not necessarily efficiently computable, reasoning about the running time of the underlying straight-line program is necessary.

3   Generic-Ring Delay Functions

A generic-ring delay function in the ring $\mathbb{Z}_N$ is given by a generic-ring algorithm DF. This is a deterministic generic-ring algorithm, which receives as input the modulus N, the delay parameter T and implicit access, as defined in Sect. 2, to k_{in} ring elements $x_1, \ldots, x_{k_{\mathsf{in}}}$, and outputs (implicitly) a single ring element.[5] In this section, we define the security of generic-ring delay functions (see Sect. 3.1) and our notions of sequentially depth and pseudorandomness depth (see Sect. 3.2).

3.1   The Security of Generic-Ring Delay Functions

We consider two definitions that capture the fact that a generic-ring delay function needs to be "inherently sequential". The first requires that for a delay parameter T, no algorithm which makes less than T sequential rounds of ring-operation queries should be successful with non-negligible probability in evaluating a delay function on a randomly-chosen input – even with any polynomial number of parallel processors and with a preprocessing stage. This definition is an adaptation of the sequentiality definition for verifiable delay functions of Boneh et al. [BBB+18] to the generic-ring model.

Definition 3.1 (Sequentiality). *Let* $k_{\mathsf{in}} = k_{\mathsf{in}}(\lambda), T = T(\lambda)$ *and* $w = w(\lambda)$ *be functions of the security parameter* $\lambda \in \mathbb{N}$. *A generic-ring delay function* DF *is* (T, w)-*sequential if for every polynomial* $q = q(\cdot, \cdot)$ *and for every pair* $A = (A_0, A_1)$ *of generic-ring algorithms, where* A_0 *issues at most* $q(\lambda, T)$ *ring-operation queries and* A_1 *consists of at most* $w(\lambda)$ *parallel processors each of which issues at most* T *sequential rounds of ring-operation queries, there exists a negligible function* $\nu(\cdot)$ *such that*

$$\Pr\left[\mathsf{Exp}^{\mathsf{Seq}}_{\mathsf{DF}, A}(\lambda) = 1\right] \leq \nu(\lambda)$$

for all sufficiently large $\lambda \in \mathbb{N}$, *where the experiment* $\mathsf{Exp}^{\mathsf{Seq}}_{\mathsf{DF}, A}(\lambda)$ *is defined as follows:*

1. $N \leftarrow \mathsf{ModGen}(1^\lambda)$.
2. $\mathsf{st} \leftarrow A_0^{\mathcal{O}}(N, T)$.
3. $\widehat{y} := \mathsf{DF}^{\mathcal{O}}(N, T, \widehat{x_1}, \ldots, \widehat{x_{k_{\mathsf{in}}}})$, *where* $x_1, \ldots, x_{k_{\mathsf{in}}} \leftarrow \mathbb{Z}_N$.
4. $\widehat{y'} \leftarrow A_1^{\mathcal{O}}(N, \mathsf{st}, \widehat{x_1}, \ldots, \widehat{x_{k_{\mathsf{in}}}})$.
5. *Output* 1 *if* $y' = y$, *and otherwise output* 0.

Note that the state st passed from A_0 to A_1 in the definition of $\mathsf{Exp}^{\mathsf{Seq}}_{\mathsf{DF}, A}(\lambda)$ may include both explicit bit-strings and implicit ring elements.

Our second definition is a seemingly stronger one, and it requires that the for a delay parameter T, no algorithm which makes less than T sequential rounds

---

[5] For concreteness, we consider the case where the output consists of a single ring element, and note that all of our bounds easily extend to the case where the output consists of several ring elements and an explicit bit-string.

of ring-operation queries should be successful with non-negligible probability in distinguishing between the true output of the function and a uniformly chosen ring element – even with any polynomial number of parallel processors and with a preprocessing stage. Satisfying this definition is desirable not merely because it is stronger in principal, but also because applications of delay functions often do rely on the assumption that the output of the function is pseudorandom for any algorithm which runs in sequential time which is less than the delay parameter T. Such application include for example the use of verifiable delay-functions for constructing randomness beacons (see, for example [BCG15, BGZ16, PW18, BBB+18] and the references within).

Definition 3.2 (Pseudorandomness). *Let $k_{in} = k_{in}(\lambda), T = T(\lambda)$ and $w = w(\lambda)$ be functions of the security parameter $\lambda \in \mathbb{N}$. A generic-ring delay function DF whose input includes k_{in} ring elements is (T, w)-pseudorandom if for every polynomial $q = q(\cdot, \cdot)$ and for every pair $A = (A_0, A_1)$ of generic-ring algorithms, where A_0 issues at most $q(\lambda, T)$ ring-operation queries and A_1 consists of at most $w(\lambda)$ parallel processors each of which issues at most T sequential rounds of ring-operation queries, there exists a negligible function $\nu(\cdot)$ such that*

$$\mathsf{Adv}_{\mathsf{DF},A}(\lambda) \overset{\text{def}}{=} \left| \Pr\left[\mathsf{Exp}^{\mathsf{SP}}_{\mathsf{DF},A,0}(\lambda) = 1 \right] - \left[\mathsf{Exp}^{\mathsf{SP}}_{\mathsf{DF},A,1}(\lambda) = 1 \right] \right| \leq \nu(\lambda)$$

for all sufficiently large $\lambda \in \mathbb{N}$, where for $b \in \{0, 1\}$, the experiment $\mathsf{Exp}^{\mathsf{SP}}_{\mathsf{DF},A,0}(\lambda)$ is defined as:

1. $N \leftarrow \mathsf{ModGen}(1^\lambda)$.
2. $\mathsf{st} \leftarrow A_0^{\mathcal{O}}(N, T)$.
3. $y_0 \leftarrow \mathbb{Z}_N$.
4. $\widehat{y_1} := \mathsf{DF}^{\mathcal{O}}(N, T, \widehat{x_1}, \ldots, \widehat{x_{k_{in}}})$, *where* $x_1, \ldots, x_{k_{in}} \leftarrow \mathbb{Z}_N$.
5. $b' \leftarrow A_1^{\mathcal{O}}(N, \mathsf{st}, \widehat{x_1}, \ldots, \widehat{x_{k_{in}}}, \widehat{y_b})$.
6. *Output b'.*

3.2   The Depth of Generic-Ring Delay Functions

Our bounds on the sequentiality and pseudorandomness of generic-ring delay functions depend on the notions of sequentiality depth and pseudorandomness depth that we now introduce. We will begin by defining these notions for straight-line functions, and then we will extend them to arbitrary generic-ring functions.

Straight-Line Delay Functions. We begin, in Definition 3.3, by defining the sequentiality depth of a straight-line delay function. Informally, if a straight-line delay function DF has sequentiality depth at most d, it means that it is possible (with high probability and with a preprocessing stage) to compute a rational function which is equivalent modulo N to the rational function computed by DF using d or less sequential rounds of ring operations. By equivalence of rational functions, we mean that the numerator of the difference between the two functions is the zero polynomial modulo N.

We remind the reader that for a straight-line program S and explicit input σ, the pair (P_σ^S, Q_σ^S) describes the output of S on the explicit input σ, as a pair of polynomials (which we may think of as a rational function) in the ring elements given as input to S (see Sect. 2).

Definition 3.3. *Let $T = T(\lambda)$ and $d = d(\lambda)$ be functions of the security parameter $\lambda \in \mathbb{N}$, and let DF be a straight-line delay function. We say that DF has sequentiality depth at least d if for every pair $G = (G_0, G_1)$ of polynomial-time generic-ring algorithms, where G_1 is a straight-line program with polynomially-many parallel processors each of which issues at most $d - 1$ sequential rounds of ring-operation queries, there exists a negligible function $\nu(\cdot)$ such that*

$$\Pr\left[\mathsf{Exp}_{\mathsf{DF},G}^{\mathsf{SeqDepth}}(\lambda) = 1\right] \leq \nu(\lambda),$$

for all sufficiently large $\lambda \in \mathbb{N}$, where the experiment $\mathsf{Exp}_{\mathsf{DF},G}^{\mathsf{SeqDepth}}(\lambda)$ is defined as follows:

1. *$N \leftarrow \mathsf{ModGen}(1^\lambda)$.*
2. *$\mathsf{st} \leftarrow G_0^{\mathcal{O}}(N, T)$, where $\mathsf{st} = (\mathsf{st}_0, \widehat{\mathsf{st}_1}, \dots, \widehat{\mathsf{st}_\ell})$.*
3. *Output 1 if*

$$g_{\mathsf{num}}, g_{\mathsf{den}} \not\equiv 0 \ (mod \ N)$$

and

$$P_{N,T}^{\mathsf{DF}} \cdot g_{\mathsf{den}} - Q_{N,T}^{\mathsf{DF}} \cdot g_{\mathsf{num}} \equiv 0 \ (mod \ N),$$

where $(g_{\mathsf{num}}(\mathbf{X}), g_{\mathsf{den}}(\mathbf{X})) = (P_{N,T,\mathsf{st}_0}^{G_1}(\mathsf{st}_1, \dots, \mathsf{st}_\ell, \mathbf{X}), Q_{N,T,\mathsf{st}_0}^{G_1}(\mathsf{st}_1, \dots, \mathsf{st}_\ell, \mathbf{X}))$. Otherwise, output 0.

If the sequentiality depth of DF is not at least $d + 1$, we say that it is at most d. If the sequentiality depth of DF is at least d and at most d, we say that DF has sequentiality depth d.

We clarify that g_{num} and g_{den} are polynomials only in the formal variables replacing the input elements to the function DF, and are obtained from G_1 by fixing its explicit input to be (N, T, st_0) and assigning the integer values $\mathsf{st}_1, \dots, \mathsf{st}_\ell$ to the variables replacing the ring elements passed from G_0 to G_1 as part of the state. By the notation $P \equiv 0 \ (mod \ N)$ for a polynomial P, we mean that all of the coefficients of P are 0 modulo N. Note that a k-variate polynomial might have a value of 0 for all inputs in $(\mathbb{Z}_N)^k$, but still have non-zero coefficients modulo N.

Intuitively, Definition 3.3 captures the fact that if we multiply both the numerator and the denominator of the function computed by DF by the same polynomial p, then this does not change the number of sequential ring operations required to evaluate the function. For example, the function $f_{N,T}(X_1, X_2, X_3) = \left(X_1^{2^T} \cdot X_2\right) \Big/ \left(X_1^{2^T} \cdot X_3\right) \ (mod \ N)$ can be evaluated using a single ring operation, since it is equivalent to the function $g_{N,T}(X_1, X_2, X_3) = X_2/X_3 \ (mod \ N)$. On the other hand, the function $f_{N,T}(X) = X^{\varphi(N)} \ (mod \ N)$ (where φ is

Euler's totient function) is not equivalent under our definition to the function $g_{N,T}(X) = 1$, even though the two functions agree almost everywhere in the ring.

Note that since we wish to relate Definition 3.3 to Definition 3.1, allowing for a preprocessing stage is paramount. Consider for example the function $f_{N,T}(X) = 2^T \cdot X \pmod{N}$. Without preprocessing, trivially evaluating this function requires $T + 1$ ring operations. However, T of them are independent of the input, and may be moved to the preprocessing stage, leaving just a single ring operation to be computed in the online stage.

We now define, in Definition 3.3, the pseudorandomness depth of a straight-line delay function. The definition will use the notation $P_{N,T,\text{st}_0}^{G_1}(\text{st}_1, \ldots, \text{st}_\ell, \mathbf{X},$ $P_{N,T}^{\text{DF}}(\mathbf{X})/Q_{N,T}^{\text{DF}}(\mathbf{X}))$ for a straight-line program G_1. This can be seen as the polynomial obtained by invoking G_1 on explicit input (N, T, st_0), ℓ explicit state ring elements, k_{in} input ring elements $\widehat{x_1}, \ldots, \widehat{x_{k_{\text{in}}}}$, and an ring element $\widehat{y}$ which is the output of DF on $\widehat{x_1}, \ldots, \widehat{x_{k_{\text{in}}}}$, and looking at the numerator of the output of G_1 as a polynomial in the variables $X_1, \ldots, X_{k_{\text{in}}}$ replacing $\widehat{x_1}, \ldots, \widehat{x_{k_{\text{in}}}}$ (as discussed in Sect. 2).

Definition 3.4. *Let $T = T(\lambda)$ and $d = d(\lambda)$ be functions of the security parameter $\lambda \in \mathbb{N}$, and let DF be a straight-line delay function. We say that DF has pseudorandomness depth at least d if for every pair $G = (G_0, G_1)$ of polynomial-time generic-ring algorithms, where G_1 is a straight-line program with polynomially-many parallel processors each of which issues at most $d - 1$ rounds of ring-operation queries, there exists a negligible function $\nu(\cdot)$ such that*

$$\Pr\left[\text{Exp}_{\text{DF},G}^{\text{PRDepth}}(\lambda) = 1\right] \le \nu(\lambda),$$

for all sufficiently large $\lambda \in \mathbb{N}$, where the experiment $\text{Exp}_{\text{DF},G}^{\text{PRDepth}}(\lambda)$ is defined as follows:

1. $N \leftarrow \text{ModGen}(1^\lambda)$.
2. $\text{st} \leftarrow G_0^\mathcal{O}(N, T)$, where $\text{st} = (\text{st}_0, \widehat{\text{st}_1}, \ldots, \widehat{\text{st}_\ell})$.
3. *Output 1 if*
$$P_{N,T,\text{st}_0}^{G_1}(\text{st}_1, \ldots, \text{st}_\ell, \mathbf{X}, Y) \not\equiv 0 \pmod{N}$$

   and

$$P_{N,T,\text{st}_0}^{G_1}\left(\text{st}_1, \ldots, \text{st}_\ell, \mathbf{X}, \frac{P_{N,T}^{\text{DF}}(\mathbf{X})}{Q_{N,T}^{\text{DF}}(\mathbf{X})}\right) \equiv 0 \pmod{N}$$

   Otherwise, output 0.

If the pseudorandomness depth of DF is not at least $d + 1$, we say that it is at most d. If the pseudorandomness depth of DF is at least d and at most d, we say that DF has pseudorandomness depth d.

Informally, if the pseudorandomness depth of a straight-line delay function DF which takes in k_{in} ring elements is at most d, it means that it is possible (with high probability and with a preprocessing stage) to compute a $(k_{\mathsf{in}} + 1)$-variate polynomial p which is not the zero polynomial, but becomes the zero $(k_{\mathsf{in}}$-variate) polynomial when the last variable is replaced with the output of the rational function computed by DF (in the previous k_{in} input variables). Intuitively, this notion captures the following trivial attack: Given access to $\widehat{x_1}, \ldots, \widehat{x_{k_{\mathsf{in}}}}$ and $\widehat{y}$, evaluate p at these inputs and zero test the result. Note that if the sequentiality depth of DF is at most d, then so is its pseudorandomness depth.

Sequentiality and Pseudorandomness Depths vs. Degree. The sequentiality and pseudorandomness depths of a straight-line delay function are inherently related to the degree the rational function it computes. For a rational function $f = f_{\mathsf{num}}/f_{\mathsf{den}}$, we let its degree be the difference (in absolute value) between the degrees of its numerator and denominator polynomials, where by degree of a multi-variate polynomial, we mean its *total* degree;[6] i.e.,

$$\deg(f) = |\deg(f_{\mathsf{num}}) - \deg(f_{\mathsf{den}})|.$$

Informally, the following claim establishes that the sequentiality and pseudorandomness depths of a straight-line delay function DF are lower bounded by the logarithm of the degree of the rational function it computes.

Before stating the claim (which is proved in the full version of the paper), we introduce the following notation. For a concrete modulus $N \in \mathbb{N}$ outputted by $\mathsf{ModGen}(1^\lambda)$, denote by $\mathsf{Exp}_{\mathsf{DF},G}^{\mathsf{SeqDepth}}(\lambda, N)$ and $\mathsf{Exp}_{\mathsf{DF},G}^{\mathsf{PRDepth}}(\lambda, N)$ the experiments obtained from $\mathsf{Exp}_{\mathsf{DF},G}^{\mathsf{SeqDepth}}(\lambda)$ and $\mathsf{Exp}_{\mathsf{DF},G}^{\mathsf{PRDepth}}(\lambda)$ by fixing the modulus to be N (instead of sampling it at the onset), respectively.

Claim 3.5. *Let $T = T(\lambda), d = d(\lambda)$ and $k_{\mathsf{in}} = k_{\mathsf{in}}(\lambda)$ be functions of the security parameter $\lambda \in \mathbb{N}$, let N be an integer outputted by $\mathsf{ModGen}(1^\lambda)$ and let DF be a straight-line delay function. Let $f_{\mathsf{num}}, f_{\mathsf{den}} \in \mathbb{Z}_N[X_1, \ldots, X_k]$ such that $f = f_{\mathsf{num}}/f_{\mathsf{den}}$ is the rational function computed by DF on explicit input (N, T). If all coefficients of f_{num} and of f_{den} are coprime to N, then for every pair $G = (G_0, G_1)$ of polynomial-time generic-ring algorithms, where G_1 is a straight-line program with polynomially-many parallel processors each of which issues at most d sequential rounds of ring-operation queries, it holds that*

1. If $\Pr\left[\mathsf{Exp}_{\mathsf{DF},G}^{\mathsf{SeqDepth}}(\lambda, N) = 1\right] > 0$ then $d(\lambda) \geq \log(\deg(f))$.

2. If $\Pr\left[\mathsf{Exp}_{\mathsf{DF},G}^{\mathsf{PRDepth}}(\lambda, N) = 1\right] > 0$ then $d(\lambda) \geq \log(\deg(f))$.

The Depth of Repeated Squaring. As discussed in Sect. 1.1, for rather simple polynomials our notions of sequentiality depth and pseudorandomness depth essentially coincides with the logarithm of their degree. This is the case with the repeated squaring function of Rivest, Shamir and Wagner [RSW96], where both notions exactly coincide with the logarithm of its degree. Specifically, consider the repeated squaring function: For a modulus N and a delay parameter $T = T(\lambda)$, the function

---

[6] E.g., the degree of the polynomial $X_1 X_2$ is 2.

is defined by $f_{N,T}^{\mathsf{RSW}}(X) = X^{2^T} \pmod{N}$. Of course, $f_{N,T}^{\mathsf{RSW}}$ may be evaluated using T ring operations, so its sequentiality depth is at most T. Claim 3.5 shows that it is exactly T, since any function computed with less than T ring operations will not be equivalent (as specified by Definition 3.3) to $f_{N,T}^{\mathsf{RSW}}$. Moreover, Claim 3.5 shows that the pseudorandomness depth of repeated squaring is also exactly T.

Arbitrary Generic-Ring Delay Functions. We now extend the above notions to arbitrary generic-ring delay functions. Informally, in case that a delay function DF issues equality queries, we consider the straight-line program obtained from DF by setting the responses to all equality queries to be negative, except those which are trivially satisfied. As formally defined below, by a trivially satisfied equality query we mean that the polynomial it induces is the all-zero polynomial modulo N.

More formally, for a generic-ring delay function DF, we denote by SLP(DF) the straight-line program obtained from DF by setting the responses to all nontrivial equality queries to be negative (and to all trivial queries to be positive). This may be done one query at a time: At each step, consider the first of the equality queries remaining (recall that DF is deterministic), and let (P, Q) and (P', Q') be the pairs of polynomials associated with it. If $P \cdot Q' - P' \cdot Q \equiv 0 \pmod{N}$, then assume (without querying) that the answer is answered affirmatively, and otherwise assume that it is answered negatively (if any of P, Q, P' and Q' is $\bot$, then treat the query as ignored). Note that this transformation is not necessarily efficient, but it need not be, since it is only used to *define* the notions of sequentiality depth and pseudorandomness depth for arbitrary generic-ring delay functions. Equipped with this notation, Definition 3.6 captures the above informal description.

Definition 3.6. *Let $T = T(\lambda)$, $d_{\mathsf{Seq}} = d_{\mathsf{Seq}}(\lambda)$ and $d_{\mathsf{PR}} = d_{\mathsf{PR}}(\lambda)$ be functions of the security parameter $\lambda \in \mathbb{N}$, and let DF be a generic-ring delay function. We say that DF has sequentiality depth at least (resp. at most) d_{Seq} if SLP(DF) has sequentiality depth at least (resp. at most) d_{Seq}. We say that DF has pseudorandomness depth at least (resp. at most) d_{PR} if SLP(DF) has sequentiality depth at least (resp. at most) d_{PR}.*

4   A Sharp Sequentiality Threshold for Straight-Line Delay Functions

In this section we present our sharp threshold for the number of sequential rounds of ring-operation queries that are required for evaluating straight-line delay functions (i.e., rational functions in their input elements). Our lower bound is proven in Sect. 4.1, and its matching upper bound is proven in Sect. 4.2.

4.1   From Speeding up Straight-Line Delay Functions to Factoring

Let DF be a straight-line delay function that has sequentiality depth at least d, for some function $d = d(\lambda)$ of the security parameter (recall Definition 3.3).

We prove the following theorem, showing that any generic-ring algorithm that computes DF on a uniform input with a non-negligible probability in less than d sequential rounds of ring-operation queries, can be transformed into a factoring algorithm in the standard model.

Theorem 4.1. *Let $T = T(\lambda)$ and $k_{in} = k_{in}(\lambda)$ be functions of the security parameter $\lambda \in \mathbb{N}$, and let DF be a straight-line program delay function receiving k_{in} ring elements as input. Then, for every function $\epsilon = \epsilon(\lambda)$, for every polynomial $p(\cdot)$, and for every pair $G = (G_0, G_1)$ of probabilistic polynomial-time generic-ring algorithms such that G_1 has polynomially many parallel processors each of which issues at most $q_{op} = q_{op}(\lambda)$ sequential rounds of ring-operation queries and the sequentiality depth of DF is at least $q_{op} + 1$, there exists an algorithm A running in time $\mathsf{poly}(\lambda, \log(1/\epsilon))$ for which the following holds: For all sufficiently large $\lambda \in \mathbb{N}$, if*

$$\Pr\left[\mathsf{Exp}^{\mathsf{Seq}}_{\mathsf{DF},G}(\lambda) = 1\right] \geq \frac{1}{p(\lambda)}$$

then

$$\Pr_{\substack{N \leftarrow \mathsf{ModGen}(1^\lambda) \\ (a,b) \leftarrow A(N,T)}} [(N = a \cdot b) \wedge (a, b \in [N-1])] > 1 - \epsilon(\lambda).$$

The proof of Theorem 4.1 makes use of Lemma 4.2 stated below. We first introduce some notation: For an integer $N \in \mathbb{N}$ and for a k-variate polynomial P, we denote by $\alpha_N(P)$ the density of roots of P in $\mathbb{Z}_N$; i.e.,

$$\alpha_N(P) = \Pr_{x_1,\ldots,x_k \leftarrow \mathbb{Z}_N} [P(x_1,\ldots,x_k) = 0 \ (\mathrm{mod}\ N)].$$

Roughly speaking, Lemma 4.2 states that given any straight-line program whose output is a polynomial P in its input elements, we can construct a standard-model algorithm which succeeds in factoring N with probability which is proportional to $\alpha_N(P)$. Recall that for a straight-line program S, the pair $(P^S_{N,\sigma}, Q^S_{N,\sigma})$ denotes the output of S on explicit input (N, σ), as a pair of polynomials in the input ring elements to S (see Sect. 2).

Lemma 4.2. *Let $k = k(\lambda), t = t(\lambda), w = w(\lambda), \ell = \ell(\lambda)$ and $q = q(\lambda)$ be functions of the security parameter $\lambda \in \mathbb{N}$. For any generic-ring straight-line program S which takes as input k ring elements, a modulus N and an additional explicit ℓ-bit string, and runs in time t with w parallel processors, while making at most q sequential rounds of ring-operation queries, there exists an algorithm A_S which runs in time $O\left(t + \lambda^5 \cdot k^3 + w^3 \cdot q^3\right)$, such that the following holds: For every $\lambda \in \mathbb{N}$, for every N which is outputted with positive probability by $\mathsf{ModGen}(1^\lambda)$ and for every bit-string $\sigma \in \{0,1\}^\ell$ which S may receive as an additional explicit input, if $P^S_{N,\sigma} \not\equiv 0 \ (\mathrm{mod}\ N)$ then*

$$\Pr_{(a,b) \leftarrow A_S(N,\sigma)}\left[\begin{matrix} N = a \cdot b \\ a, b \in [N-1] \end{matrix}\right] \geq \frac{\alpha_N(P^S_{N,\sigma}) - (k-1) \cdot 2^{-\lambda+1}}{(1 - 2^{-\lambda})^{k-1} \cdot 8k \cdot (2\lambda \cdot k + w \cdot q)}.$$

We first prove Theorem 4.1 assuming Lemma 4.2 and then turn to prove Lemma 4.2. We start by giving a high-level overview of the proof, which ignores many of the technical difficulties arising in the formal analysis. Given $G = (G_0, G_1)$, our factoring algorithm A operates in three stages. In the first stage, it invokes G_0 in order to sample a state st,[7] samples random coins ρ for G_1, and initializes a data structure η which will be used in order to keep track of the likely response pattern to G_1's equality queries. The second stage proceeds in iterations – one per each equality query made by G_1. Each such equality query naturally induces a polynomial when fixing st, ρ and the responses to all previous equality queries according to the information in η. In the ith iteration, A tries to factor N using the factoring algorithm guaranteed by Lemma 4.2 for the polynomial induced by the ith equality query. If unsuccessful, A updates η with the likely response to the ith query, by checking it on a uniformly sampled input. In the third stage, A considers the polynomial induced by an equality between the output of DF and the output of G_1 when it is ran on the state st and with random coins ρ, and when the responses to its equality queries are in accordance with the learned η. Our algorithm then tries to factor N using the factoring algorithm guaranteed by Lemma 4.2 for the straight-line program computing this induced polynomial.

The analysis considers two cases. In the first case, there exists an equality query which is "balanced" in the sense that it is affirmatively answered with probability which is sufficiently bounded away from both 0 and 1, conditioned on all previous queries being answered with the more likely response. When this is the case, we show that in the iteration which corresponds to the first such query in the second stage of A, it succeeds in factoring N with high probability since: (1) with high probability the information in η indeed reflects the likely responses to previous queries; and (2) the polynomial induced by the this query is non-trivial and has a high rate of roots. In the second case, all equality queries of G_1 are sufficiently non-balanced so that the success probability of G is not reduced by too much when conditioning on all of these queries being answered in the more likely manner. If this is the case, then whenever the information in η is consistent with the likely responses (which happens with high enough probability), the rate of roots of the polynomial considered in the third stage of A is proportional to the success probability of G. We use the fact that G_1 makes less ring-operation queries than the sequentiality depth of DF to argue that this polynomial is non-trivial. We proceed to the formal proof.

Proof of Theorem 4.1. Let $G = (G_0, G_1)$ be a pair of generic-ring algorithms as in the statement of Theorem 4.1. Let $q_{eq} = q_{eq}(\lambda)$ and $w = w(\lambda)$ denote the bound on the number of equality queries made by G_1, and the number of parallel processors of G_1, respectively, and let $r = r(\lambda)$ be a bound on the number of random coins used by G_1. For a modulus N, a state st outputted by $G_0^{\mathbb{Z}_N}(N, T)$, an index $i \in [q_{eq}]$, random coins $\rho \in \{0, 1\}^r$ and a binary string η of

---

[7] For the sake of this high-level overview, assume that st does not include any implicit ring elements. In the full proof, this assumption is lifted by noting that since A is the one that runs G_0 it has explicit knowledge of the integer values of these elements.

length at most q_{eq} bits, we define a related polynomial $f[G_1, N, \mathsf{st}, i, \rho, \eta]$. This is the polynomial obtained from G_1 by running it on explicit input (N, T, st) and randomness ρ up to (and not including) the ith equality query, while setting the reply to each of the first $i - 1$ equality queries of G_1 according to η: The reply to the jth equality query is positive if and only if the jth bit of η is 1. Let (P, Q) and (P', Q') be the pairs of polynomials corresponding to the two ring elements compared in the jth equality query in this computation. Then, we define $f[G_1, N, \mathsf{st}, i, \rho, \eta] = P \cdot Q' - P' \cdot Q$. Finally, for $\rho \in \{0,1\}^r$ and $\eta \in \{0,1\}^{q_{eq}}$, denote by $\mathsf{SLP}(G_1)$ the straight-line program obtained from G_1 in the following manner: On explicit input $(N, T, \mathsf{st}, \rho, \eta)$, the program $\mathsf{SLP}(G_1)$ runs G_1 on explicit input (N, T, st) and randomness ρ, while setting the responses to all equality queries according to the bits of η. Consider the following standard-model factoring algorithm A_G:

Algorithm A_G

Input: An integer N sampled by $\mathsf{ModGen}(1^\lambda)$, and a delay parameter $T \in \mathbb{N}$.

1. Sample $\mathsf{st} \leftarrow G_0^{\mathbb{Z}_N}(N, T)$, and $\rho \leftarrow \{0,1\}^r$.
2. Initialize η_0 to be the empty string.
3. For $i = 1, \ldots, q_{eq}$:
   (a) Let $f_i^{(N,\mathsf{st},\rho,\eta_{i-1})}(\mathbf{X}) = f[G_1, N, \mathsf{st}, i, \rho, \eta_{i-1}](\mathbf{X})$, let S_i be the straight-line program that on explicit input $(N, T, \mathsf{st}, \rho, \eta_{i-1})$ computes the pair $\left(f_i^{(N,\mathsf{st},\rho,\eta_{i-1})}(\mathbf{X}), 1 \right)$, and let A_{S_i} be the corresponding factorization algorithm guaranteed by Lemma 4.2. Run $A_{S_i}(N, T, \mathsf{st}, \rho, \eta_{i-1})$ to obtain (a_i, b_i). If $a_i, b_i \in [N-1]$ and $a_i \cdot b_i = N$, output (a_i, b_i) and terminate.
   (b) Sample $x_1, \ldots, x_{k_{in}} \leftarrow \mathbb{Z}_N$.
   (c) If $f_i^{(N,\mathsf{st},\rho,\eta_{i-1})}(x_1, \ldots, x_{k_{in}}) = 0$, set $\eta_i := \eta_{i-1}\|1$ and otherwise, set $\eta_i := \eta_{i-1}\|0$.
4. Let $\eta = \eta_{q_{eq}}$, let $S = \mathsf{SLP}(G_1)$ and let $f_{out}^{(N,\mathsf{st},\rho,\eta)} = P_{N,T,\mathsf{st},\rho,\eta}^S \cdot Q_{N,T}^{DF} - Q_{N,T,\mathsf{st},\rho,\eta}^S \cdot P_{N,T}^{DF}$. Let S_{out} be the straight-line program that on explicit input $(N, T, \mathsf{st}, \rho, \eta)$ computes $\left(f_{out}^{(N,\mathsf{st},\rho,\eta)}(\mathbf{X}), 1 \right)$ and let $A_{S_{out}}$ be the corresponding factorization algorithm guaranteed by Lemma 4.2. Run $A_{S_{out}}(N, T, \mathsf{st}, \rho, \eta)$ to obtain (a, b). If $a, b \in [N-1]$ and $a \cdot b = N$, output (a, b). Otherwise, output $\bot$.

Denote $\Pr\left[\mathsf{Exp}_{\mathsf{DF},G}^{\mathsf{Seq}}(\lambda) = 1 \right]$ by β. We show that the probability that A_G outputs a valid factorization of N is at least $\Omega\left(\beta^2/\mathrm{poly}(\lambda)\right)$. Then, repeating the attack described by A_G for $\Omega\left(\ln(1/\epsilon) \cdot \beta^{-2} \cdot \mathrm{poly}(\lambda)\right)$ iterations yields Theorem 4.1.

For a modulus N, an index $i \in [q_{eq}]$, a state st passed by G_0, randomness $\rho \in \{0,1\}^r$ and a string $\eta \in \{0,1\}^{i-1}$, we say that the polynomial $f_i^{(N,\mathsf{st},\rho,\eta)}$ is *heavy* if $\Pr_{\mathbf{x}}\left[f_i^{(N,\mathsf{st},\rho,\eta)}(\mathbf{x}) = 0 \right] \geq 1 - \beta/(4 \cdot q_{eq})$, and we say that it is *light* if $\Pr_{\mathbf{x}}\left[f_i^{(N,\mathsf{st},\rho,\eta)}(\mathbf{x}) = 0 \right] \leq \beta/(4 \cdot q_{eq})$. Otherwise, we say that it is *balanced*. For the same parameters, we also define an i-character string $\eta_{N,\mathsf{st},\rho,i}^* \in \{0, 1, \bot\}^i$ recursively; we let $\eta_{N,\mathsf{st},\rho,0}^*$ be the empty string, and for $i \in [q_{eq}]$ we define:

$$\eta^*_{N,\text{st},\rho,i} = \begin{cases} \eta^*_{N,\text{st},\rho,i-1} \| \perp, & \text{if } \perp \in \eta^*_{N,\text{st},\rho,i-1} \text{ or } f_i^{(N,\text{st},\rho,\eta^*_{N,\text{st},\rho,i-1})} \text{ is balanced} \\ \eta^*_{N,\text{st},\rho,i-1} \| 0, & \text{if } \perp \notin \eta^*_{N,\text{st},\rho,i-1} \text{ and } f_i^{(N,\text{st},\rho,\eta^*_{N,\text{st},\rho,i-1})} \text{ is light} \\ \eta^*_{N,\text{st},\rho,i-1} \| 1, & \text{if } \perp \notin \eta^*_{N,\text{st},\rho,i-1} \text{ and } f_i^{(N,\text{st},\rho,\eta^*_{N,\text{st},\rho,i-1})} \text{ is heavy} \end{cases}$$

Denote $\eta^*_{N,\text{st},\rho} = \eta^*_{N,\text{st},\rho,i_{\text{eq}}}$, and denote by Bal the event in which $\eta^*_{N,\text{st},\rho}$ contains a $\perp$ symbol. We will prove the bound on A_G's success probability separately for the following two cases.

Case 1: $\Pr[\text{Bal}] \geq \beta/2$. Let Factor be the event in which $A_G(N,T)$ successfully outputs a factorization of N. By total probability, it holds that

$$\Pr[\text{Factor}] \geq \Pr[\text{Factor}|\text{Bal}] \cdot \Pr[\text{Bal}] \geq \frac{\beta}{2} \cdot \Pr[\text{Factor}|\text{Bal}], \qquad (1)$$

and so we wish to bound $\Pr[\text{Factor}|\text{Bal}]$. For $i \in [q_{\text{eq}}]$, let E_i and E_i^* be the random variables corresponding to η_i in the execution of A_G and to $\eta^*_{N,\text{st},\rho,i}$ described above. Let i^* be the minimal index in which $\eta^*_{N,\text{st},\rho}$ has a $\perp$ symbol (if there are no $\perp$ symbols, then $i^* = 0$; note that i^* is also a random variable), and let Typ be the event in which $E_{i^*-1} = E^*_{i^*-1}$. Then,

$$\Pr[\text{Factor}|\text{Bal}] \geq \Pr[\text{Factor}|\text{Bal} \wedge \text{Typ}] \cdot \Pr[\text{Typ}|\text{Bal}]$$

$$\geq \Pr[\text{Factor}|\text{Bal} \wedge \text{Typ}] \cdot \left(1 - \frac{\beta}{4}\right) \qquad (2)$$

$$\geq \frac{3}{4} \cdot \Pr[\text{Factor}|\text{Bal} \wedge \text{Typ}] \qquad (3)$$

where (2) follow by union bound on all indices up to i^* and the fact that it is always the case that $i^* \leq q_{\text{eq}}$.

Let Factor(i^*) denote the event in which $A_{S_{i^*}}(N,T,\text{st},\rho,\eta_{i^*-1})$ successfully outputs a factorization of N. It holds that

$$\Pr[\text{Factor}|\text{Bal} \wedge \text{Typ}] \geq \Pr[\text{Factor}(i^*)|\text{Bal} \wedge \text{Typ}]. \qquad (4)$$

To complete the analysis of Case 1, we wish to bound $\Pr[\text{Factor}(i^*)|\text{Bal} \wedge \text{Typ}]$, and to this end, we would like to invoke Lemma 4.2. In order to so, we need to argue two things: (1) That the (first) polynomial outputted by S_{i^*} – meaning, the polynomial $f_{i^*}^{(N,\text{st},\rho,\eta_{i^*-1})}$ – is non-trivial modulo N; and (2) That this polynomial has many roots modulo N in $\mathbb{Z}_N$. This is indeed the case, since assuming both Bal and Typ occur, it holds that $E_{i^*-1} = E^*_{i^*-1}$ and hence the polynomial $f_{i^*}^{(N,\text{st},\rho,\eta_{i^*-1})}$ is equal to the polynomial $f_{i^*}^{(N,\text{st},\rho,\eta^*_{N,\text{st},\rho,i^*-1})}$. But since the i^*th bit of $\eta^*_{\text{st},\rho}$ is $\perp$, it means that $\alpha_N\left(f_{i^*}^{(N,\text{st},\rho,\eta^*_{N,\text{st},\rho,i^*-1})}\right) > \beta/(4 \cdot q_{\text{eq}})$. Hence, by Lemma 4.2,

$$\Pr[\text{Factor}(i^*)|\text{Bal} \wedge \text{Typ}] \geq \frac{\alpha_N\left(f_{i^*}^{(N,\text{st},\rho,\eta^*_{N,\text{st},\rho,i^*-1})}\right) - (k_{\text{in}} - 1) \cdot 2^{-\lambda+1}}{8 \cdot (1 - 2^{-\lambda})^{k_{\text{in}}-1} \cdot k_{\text{in}} \cdot (2\lambda \cdot k_{\text{in}} + w \cdot q_{\text{op}})}$$

$$\geq \frac{\beta - (k_{\text{in}} - 1) \cdot 2^{-\lambda+3} \cdot q_{\text{eq}}}{32 \cdot q_{\text{eq}} \cdot (1 - 2^{-\lambda})^{k_{\text{in}}-1} \cdot k_{\text{in}} \cdot (2\lambda \cdot k_{\text{in}} + w \cdot q_{\text{op}})}. \qquad (5)$$

Combining inequalities (1), (3) and (5) concludes the analysis of Case 1.

Case 2: $\Pr[\mathsf{Bal}] < \beta/2$. In this case, it holds that

$$\Pr\left[\mathsf{Exp}^{\mathsf{Seq}}_{\mathsf{DF},G}(\lambda) = 1|\overline{\mathsf{Bal}}\right] \geq \Pr\left[\left(\mathsf{Exp}^{\mathsf{Seq}}_{\mathsf{DF},G}(\lambda) = 1\right) \wedge \overline{\mathsf{Bal}}\right]$$

$$= \beta - \Pr\left[\left(\mathsf{Exp}^{\mathsf{Seq}}_{\mathsf{DF},G}(\lambda) = 1\right) \wedge \mathsf{Bal}\right]$$

$$\geq \beta - \Pr[\mathsf{Bal}]$$

$$> \frac{\beta}{2}. \tag{6}$$

Let AllTyp be the event in which $\eta = \eta^*_{N,\mathsf{st},\rho}$, and let $\mathsf{FactorOut}$ denote the event in which $A_{S_{\mathrm{out}}}(N, T, \mathsf{st}, \rho, \eta)$ successfully outputs a factorization of N. Then,

$$\Pr[\mathsf{Factor}] \geq \Pr[\mathsf{FactorOut}]$$

$$\geq \Pr\left[\mathsf{FactorOut}|\overline{\mathsf{Bal}} \wedge \mathsf{AllTyp}\right] \cdot \Pr\left[\overline{\mathsf{Bal}}\right] \cdot \Pr\left[\mathsf{AllTyp}|\overline{\mathsf{Bal}}\right]$$

$$> \Pr\left[\mathsf{FactorOut}|\overline{\mathsf{Bal}} \wedge \mathsf{AllTyp}\right] \cdot \left(1 - \frac{\beta}{2}\right) \cdot \left(1 - \frac{\beta}{4}\right) \tag{7}$$

$$\geq \frac{3}{8} \cdot \Pr\left[\mathsf{FactorOut}|\overline{\mathsf{Bal}} \wedge \mathsf{AllTyp}\right], \tag{8}$$

where (7) follows from union bound over $i \in [q_{\mathsf{eq}}]$.

We again wish to invoke Lemma 4.2, so we wish to argue that conditioned on $\overline{\mathsf{Bal}} \wedge \mathsf{AllTyp}$, the polynomial $f^{(N,\mathsf{st},\rho,\eta)}_{\mathrm{out}} = P^S_{N,T,\mathsf{st},\rho,\eta} \cdot Q^{\mathsf{DF}}_{N,T} - Q^S_{N,T,\mathsf{st},\rho,\eta} \cdot P^{\mathsf{DF}}_{N,T}$ which the straight-line program S (from Step 4 of the algorithm A_G) computes is non-trivial modulo N with overwhelming probability. Assume that the contrary is true; i.e., that $f^{(N,\mathsf{st},\rho,\eta)}_{\mathrm{out}} \equiv 0 \pmod{N}$ with non-negligible probability conditioned on $\overline{\mathsf{Bal}} \wedge \mathsf{AllTyp}$. But, conditioned on $\overline{\mathsf{Bal}} \wedge \mathsf{AllTyp}$, it holds that $\eta = \eta^*_{N,\mathsf{st},\rho}$, and the responses pattern induced by $\eta^*_{N,\mathsf{st},\rho}$ to G_1's equality queries occurs with probability at least $3/4$ in $\mathsf{Exp}^{\mathsf{Seq}}_{\mathsf{DF},G}(\lambda)$. This means that the straight-line program S corresponds to a valid execution of G_1, and thus makes at most q_{op} operation queries, when given as input the ring elements in st implicitly (as elements in the oracle table $\mathbf{B}$). Consider the pair of algorithms (B_0, S), where B_0 computes st, ρ and η as in the definition of A_G and passes them to S, where the ring elements in st are passed implicitly. By Definition 3.3, this is a contradiction to the fact that DF has sequentiality depth at least $q_{\mathsf{op}} + 1$. Hence, for all sufficiently large $\lambda \in \mathbb{N}$, the polynomial $f^{(N,\mathsf{st},\rho,\eta)}_{\mathrm{out}}$ is non-trivial modulo N with all but negligible probability, and there exists an negligible function $\nu(\cdot)$ such that by Lemma 4.2,

$$\Pr\left[\mathsf{factor}(N, \mathsf{out})|\overline{\mathsf{Bal}} \wedge \mathsf{AllTyp}\right]$$

$$\geq \frac{\alpha_N\left(f^{(N,\mathsf{st},\rho,\eta)}_{\mathrm{out}}\right) - (k_{\mathsf{in}} - 1) \cdot 2^{-\lambda+1} - \nu(\lambda)}{8 \cdot (1 - 2^{-\lambda})^{k_{\mathsf{in}}-1} \cdot k_{\mathsf{in}} \cdot (2\lambda \cdot k_{\mathsf{in}} + w \cdot q_{\mathsf{op}})}$$

$$= \frac{\alpha_N\left(f^{(N,\mathsf{st},\rho,\eta^*_{N,\mathsf{st},\rho})}_{\mathrm{out}}\right) - (k_{\mathsf{in}} - 1) \cdot 2^{-\lambda+1} - \nu(\lambda)}{8 \cdot (1 - 2^{-\lambda})^{k_{\mathsf{in}}-1} \cdot k_{\mathsf{in}} \cdot (2\lambda \cdot k_{\mathsf{in}} + w \cdot q_{\mathsf{op}})} \tag{9}$$

We are left with bounding $\alpha_N\left(f_{\text{out}}^{(N,\text{st},\rho,\eta^*_{N,\text{st},\rho})}\right)$ for N, st and ρ for which $\overline{\text{Bal}}$ holds. Consider the experiment $\text{Exp}_{\text{DF},G}^{\text{Seq}}(\lambda)$, and let Con be the event in which the all equality queries made by G_1 in this experiment are answered consistently with $\eta^*_{N,\text{st},\rho}$. Conditioned on $\overline{\text{Bal}}$ and on Con, the output of G_1 is exactly $\left(P_{N,\text{st},\rho,\eta^*_{N,\text{st},\rho}}^S, Q_{N,\text{st},\rho,\eta^*_{N,\text{st},\rho}}^S\right)$, and hence for every $\mathbf{x} \in (\mathbb{Z}_N)^{k_{\text{in}}}$ for which G_1 successfully evaluates the function, it is also the case that $f_{\text{out}}^{N,\text{st},\rho,\eta^*_{N,\text{st},\rho}}(\mathbf{x}) = 0 \pmod{N}$. Since the input N given to A_G is sampled as in $\text{Exp}_{\text{DF},G}^{\text{Seq}}(\lambda)$, and the st and ρ are sampled by A_G as in $\text{Exp}_{\text{DF},G}^{\text{Seq}}(\lambda)$, this means that for N, st and ρ for which $\overline{\text{Bal}}$ holds, it holds that

$$
\alpha_N\left(f_{\text{out}}^{N,\text{st},\rho,\eta^*_{N,\text{st},\rho}}\right)
$$

$$
\geq \Pr\left[\text{Exp}_{\text{DF},G}^{\text{Seq}}(\lambda) = 1 \middle| \overline{\text{Bal}} \wedge \text{Con}\right]
$$

$$
\geq \Pr\left[\left(\text{Exp}_{\text{DF},G}^{\text{Seq}}(\lambda) = 1\right) \wedge \text{Con}\middle|\overline{\text{Bal}}\right]
$$

$$
= \Pr\left[\text{Exp}_{\text{DF},G}^{\text{Seq}}(\lambda) = 1\middle|\overline{\text{Bal}}\right] - \Pr\left[\left(\text{Exp}_{\text{DF},G}^{\text{Seq}}(\lambda) = 1\right) \wedge \overline{\text{Con}}\middle|\overline{\text{Bal}}\right]
$$

$$
\geq \frac{\beta}{2} - \Pr\left[\overline{\text{Con}}\middle|\overline{\text{Bal}}\right] \tag{10}
$$

$$
\geq \frac{\beta}{4}. \tag{11}
$$

Inequality (10) follows from (6) and inequality (11) follows by union bound over all $i \in [q_{\text{eq}}]$. Combining inequalities (8), (9) and (11) concludes the analysis of case 2.

We complete the proof by analyzing the running time of A_G. To that end, we use the following proposition, which states that any single-output straight-line program S can be converted into a related straight-line program S' which computes the pairs $(P_{N,\sigma}^S, 1)$ and $(Q_{N,\sigma}^S, 1)$ in two different oracle queries, using roughly the same running time, parallelism and query complexity as S. In other words, one can "decouple" the numerator from the denominator which a straight-line program computes, with very little overhead. An almost identical proposition (in the univariate, single processor setting) was proven in [Jag07] and was also used in [AM09].

Proposition 4.3. *Let $w = w(\lambda), q = q(\lambda), t = t(\lambda)$ and $\ell = \ell(\lambda)$ be functions of the security parameter $\lambda \in \mathbb{N}$, let $N \leftarrow \text{ModGen}(1^\lambda)$ and let $\sigma \in \{0,1\}^\ell$. For any single-output straight-line program S which runs in time t with w parallel processors, each of which making at most q sequential oracle queries, there exits a straight-line program S' which runs in time $O(t)$ with $3w$ parallel processors, each of which making at most $2q$ sequential oracle queries, and there exist indices*

$i_1, i_2 \in [3w]$ and $j_1, j_2 \in [2q]$, such that $(P_{N,\sigma}^{S'}[i_1, j_1], Q_{N,\sigma}^{S'}[i_1, j_1]) = (P_{N,\sigma}^S, 1)$ and $(P_{N,\sigma}^{S'}[i_2, j_2], Q_{N,\sigma}^{S'}[i_2, j_2]) = (Q_{N,\sigma}^S, 1)$.

We turn to the runtime analysis. Steps 1 and 2 of A_G take $\mathsf{poly}(\lambda)$ time. The dominant part in each iteration of Step 3 is Step (a): The straight-line program S_i runs in time $\mathsf{poly}(\lambda)$ and makes at most $O(\mathsf{poly}(\lambda) + q_{\mathsf{op}})$ ring-operation queries per processor. This is by: (1) first, converting the explicit elements in st (of which there are at most $\mathsf{poly}(\lambda)$) to elements in the table (each conversion takes at most 2λ queries), and then (2) running the straight-line program guaranteed by Proposition 4.3 for the straight-line program which runs G_1 until the ith equality query (answering all equality queries up to that point according to η) and then outputting $z_1 - z_2$ where z_1 and z_2 are the ring elements being compared. Hence, the factorization algorithm A_{S_i} runs in time polynomial in λ by Lemma 4.2. Similarly, the factorization algorithm $A_{S_{\mathsf{out}}}$ from Step 5 runs in time polynomial in λ as well. This concludes the proof of Theorem 4.1. ∎

We now conclude this section by presenting the proof of Lemma 4.2. In order to prove Lemma 4.2, we reduce the case of straight-line programs with multiple input elements and multiple parallel processors, to single-processor straight-line programs receiving just one ring element as input. In the latter setting, Aggarwal and Maurer [AM09] proved the following special case of Lemma 4.2.[8]

Lemma 4.4. ([AM09]). *Let $t = t(\lambda), q = q(\lambda)$ and $\ell = \ell(\lambda)$ be functions of the security parameter $\lambda \in \mathbb{N}$. For any straight-line program S which takes as input a single ring element and an explicit bit-string in $\{0, 1\}^\ell$, and runs in time t with a single processor making at most q ring-operation queries, there exists an algorithm A_S which runs in time $O(t + q^3 \cdot \lambda^2)$, such that the following holds: For every $\lambda \in \mathbb{N}$, for every N which is outputted with positive probability by $\mathsf{ModGen}(1^\lambda)$ and for every $\sigma \in \{0, 1\}^\ell$ which S may receive as an explicit input, if $P_{N,\sigma}^S \not\equiv 0 \pmod{N}$ then*

$$\Pr_{(a,b) \leftarrow A_S(N,\sigma)} \left[\begin{array}{c} N = a \cdot b \\ a, b \in [N-1] \end{array} \right] \geq \frac{\alpha_N \left(P_{N,\sigma}^S(x) \right)}{8q}.$$

Equipped with this lemma, we turn to prove the general case of Lemma 4.2.

Proof of. Lemma 4.2. Let $k = k(\lambda), t = t(\lambda), w = w(\lambda), \ell = \ell(\lambda)$ and $q = q(\lambda)$ be functions of the security parameter $\lambda \in \mathbb{N}$, and let S be a straight-line program which receives as input k ring elements, a modulus N and an additional ℓ-bit string, and runs in time t with w parallel processors, each making at most q oracle queries. Consider the following algorithm A_S:

---

[8] The lemma of Aggarwal and Maurer is stated in [AM09] in the terminology of their graph-based language for generic-ring algorithms, and without explicitly considering additional bit-string inputs (alongside the implicit access to ring elements). However, Lemma 4.4 as stated here follows directly from their proof.

Algorithm A_S

Input: An integer N sampled by $\mathsf{ModGen}(1^\lambda)$, and an ℓ-bit string σ.

1. Sample $i \leftarrow [k]$, and sample $\mathbf{x} = (x_1, \ldots, x_{i-1}, x_{i+1}, \ldots, x_k) \leftarrow (\mathbb{Z}_N \setminus \{0\})^{k-1}$.
2. For every $j \in [k] \setminus \{i\}$, compute $g_i = \gcd(x_j, N)$, and if $g_j \notin \{1, N\}$, then output $(g_j, N/g_j)$ and terminate.
3. Let $f_{\mathbf{x}} := P^S_{N,\sigma}(x_1, \ldots, x_{i-1}, X, x_{i+1}, \ldots, x_k)$ be the uni-variate polynomial in the indeterminate X obtained from $P^S_{N,\sigma}$ by fixing X_j to be x_j for each $j \in [k] \setminus \{i\}$, let $S_{f_{\mathbf{x}}}$ be the single-processor straight-line which on explicit input (N, σ) outputs $(f_{\mathbf{x}}(X), 1)$, and let $A_{S_{f_{\mathbf{x}}}(N)}$ be the factoring algorithm guaranteed by Lemma 4.4. Invoke $(a, b) \leftarrow A_{S_{f_{\mathbf{x}}}}(N, \sigma)$ and output (a, b).

Let N be the input modulus to A_S, and let $a^*, b^* \in \{0, 1\}^\lambda$ be its prime factors and assume that $P^S_{N,\sigma} \not\equiv 0 \pmod{N}$ (as otherwise the lemma trivially holds). Let success be the event in which A_S outputs the correct factors of N, and denote the event in which X_i (where i is the index chosen by A_S in Step 1) has non-zero degree in $P^S_{N,\sigma}$ by nonzero. Observe that since $P^S_{N,\sigma} \not\equiv 0 \pmod{N}$, then the probability of nonzero is at least $1/k$. By total probability it holds that

$$\Pr[\text{sucess}] \geq \Pr[\text{sucess}|\text{nonzero}] \cdot \frac{1}{k}.$$

Denote by hit the event in which A_S terminates in Step 2 (hence, $\overline{\text{hit}}$ is the event in which it terminates in Step 3). Since hit and nonzero are independent events, it holds that

$$\begin{aligned}
\Pr[\text{success}|\text{nonzero}] &= \Pr[\text{success}|\text{hit} \wedge \text{nonzero}]\Pr[\text{hit}] \\
&\quad + \Pr\left[\text{success}|\overline{\text{hit}} \wedge \text{nonzero}\right] \cdot \Pr\left[\overline{\text{hit}}\right] \\
&= 1 \cdot \Pr[\text{hit}] + \Pr\left[\text{success}|\overline{\text{hit}} \wedge \text{nonzero}\right] \cdot (1 - \Pr[\text{hit}]) \\
&\geq \Pr\left[\text{success}|\overline{\text{hit}} \wedge \text{nonzero}\right].
\end{aligned}$$

We now wish to lower bound $\Pr\left[\text{success}|\overline{\text{hit}} \wedge \text{nonzero}\right]$. We observe that since $P^S_{N,\sigma} \not\equiv 0 \pmod{N}$, then conditioned on $\overline{\text{hit}}$ and nonzero it is also the case that $f_{\mathbf{x}} \not\equiv 0 \pmod{N}$. To see why that is, assume that $\overline{\text{hit}}$ and nonzero hold, and assume towards contradiction that $f_{\mathbf{x}} \equiv 0 \pmod{N}$. In this case, since X_i has non-zero degree in $P^S_{N,\sigma}$, there exists in $P^S_{N,\sigma}$ a monomial of the form $c \cdot X_{i_1} \cdots X_{i_m} \cdot X_i^\delta$ (where $c \in \mathbb{Z}$, $m \in \mathbb{N}$, $\delta > 0$ and $i_j \in [k]$ for every $j \in [m]$) such that c is not divisible by N. Assume without loss of generality that c is not divisible by a^* (if c is divisible by a^*, then it is not divisible by b^* and the proof is symmetric). But since $f \equiv 0 \pmod{N}$ it holds that $c \cdot x_{i_1} \cdots x_{i_m}$ is divisible by N. Finally, since $0 < x_{i_1}, \ldots, x_{i_m} < N$, there exists at least one $h \in [m]$ such that x_{i_h} is divisible by a^*. Therefore, $\gcd(x_{i_h}, N) = a^*$ and A_S outputs (a^*, b^*) in Step 2 with probability 1, in contradiction to the fact that we are conditioning on $\overline{\text{hit}}$. Moreover, the single-processor straight-line program $S_{f_{\mathbf{x}}}$ makes at most $2\lambda \cdot k + w \cdot q$ oracle queries: 2λ queries to obtain each element in $\mathbf{x}$, and then

$w \cdot q$ operations to compute the polynomial $f_\mathbf{x}$ (by a serialization of the multi-processor program S). Hence, if $P_{N,\sigma}^S \not\equiv 0 \pmod{N}$ then by Lemma 4.4 it holds that

$$
\begin{aligned}
\Pr[\mathsf{success}] &\geq \frac{1}{k} \cdot \Pr[\mathsf{success}|\overline{\mathsf{hit}} \wedge \mathsf{nonzero}] \\
&\geq \frac{\Pr_{\substack{\mathbf{x} \leftarrow (\mathbb{Z}_N \setminus \{0\})^{k-1} \\ x \leftarrow \mathbb{Z}_N}}\left[P_N^{A_{S_{f_\mathbf{x}}}(N)}(x) = 0 \pmod{N}\right]}{8k \cdot (2\lambda \cdot k + w \cdot q)} \qquad (12) \\
&= \frac{\Pr_{\substack{\mathbf{x} \leftarrow (\mathbb{Z}_N \setminus \{0\})^{k-1} \\ x \leftarrow \mathbb{Z}_N}}\left[f_\mathbf{x}(x) = 0 \pmod{N}\right]}{8k \cdot (2\lambda \cdot k + w \cdot q)} \\
&= \frac{\Pr_{\substack{\mathbf{x} \leftarrow (\mathbb{Z}_N)^{k-1} \\ x \leftarrow \mathbb{Z}_N}}\left[f_\mathbf{x}(x) = 0 \pmod{N} \mid \forall x_j \in \mathbf{x}, x_j \neq 0\right]}{8k \cdot (2\lambda \cdot k + w \cdot q)} \\
&\geq \frac{\Pr_{\substack{\mathbf{x} \leftarrow (\mathbb{Z}_N)^{k-1} \\ x \leftarrow \mathbb{Z}_N}}\left[f_\mathbf{x}(x) = 0 \pmod{N}\right] - \Pr_{\mathbf{x} \leftarrow (\mathbb{Z}_N)^{k-1}}\left[\exists x_j \in \mathbf{x}, x_j = 0\right]}{\left(\Pr_{\mathbf{x} \leftarrow (\mathbb{Z}_N)^{k-1}}\left[\forall x_j \in \mathbf{x}, x_j \neq 0\right]\right) \cdot 8k \cdot (2\lambda \cdot k + w \cdot q)} \\
&\geq \frac{\Pr_{\substack{\mathbf{x} \leftarrow (\mathbb{Z}_N)^{k-1} \\ x \leftarrow \mathbb{Z}_N}}\left[f_\mathbf{x}(x) = 0 \pmod{N}\right] - (k-1) \cdot 2^{-\lambda+1}}{(1 - 2^{-\lambda})^{k-1} \cdot 8k \cdot (2\lambda \cdot k + w \cdot q)} \qquad (13) \\
&\geq \frac{\alpha_N(P_{N,\sigma}^S) - (k-1) \cdot 2^{-\lambda+1}}{(1 - 2^{-\lambda})^{k-1} \cdot 8k \cdot (2\lambda \cdot k + w \cdot q)}, \qquad (14)
\end{aligned}
$$

where (12) follows from Lemma 4.4, (13) holds since $2^{\lambda-1} \leq N < 2^\lambda$ and (14) follows from the definition of $f_\mathbf{x}$.

We conclude by analyzing the running time of A_S. Steps 1 and 2 can be executed in time $O(k \cdot \lambda)$. The significant step is Step 3: $S_{f_\mathbf{x}}$ runs in time t and makes at most $2\lambda \cdot k + w \cdot q$ oracle queries. Hence, by Lemma 4.4, invoking $A_{S_{f_\mathbf{x}}}$ in Step 3 can be done in time $O\left(t + (2\lambda \cdot k + w \cdot q)^3 \cdot \lambda^2\right) = O\left(t + \lambda^5 \cdot k^3 + w^3 \cdot q^3\right)$. This concludes the proof of Lemma 4.2. ∎

4.2   A Matching Upper Bound

In this section we prove a matching upper bound to the lower bound from Sect. 4.1. Roughly speaking, Theorem 4.5 states that for $q_{\mathsf{op}} = q_{\mathsf{op}}(\lambda)$, if DF has sequentiality depth at most q_{op}, then there is a generic attack which evaluates DF (according to Definition 3.1) while issuing at most q_{op} rounds of ring-operation queries (after a preprocessing stage), or else factoring is easy.

Theorem 4.5. Let $T = T(\lambda)$ and $q_{\mathsf{op}} = q_{\mathsf{op}}(\lambda)$ be functions of the security parameter $\lambda \in \mathbb{N}$, and let DF be a straight-line delay function whose sequentiality depth is at most q_{op}. Then, there exist a pair $G = (G_0, G_1)$ of generic-ring algorithms where G_1 has polynomially-many parallel processors each of which issues at most q_{op} rounds of ring-operation queries, a standard-model probabilistic *polynomial-time algorithm A, and a polynomial $p(\cdot)$, such that at least one of the following holds for infinitely many values of $\lambda \in \mathbb{N}$:*

1. $\Pr\left[\mathsf{Exp}_{\mathsf{DF},G}^{\mathsf{Seq}}(\lambda) = 1\right] \geq 1/(2 \cdot p(\lambda))$.
2. $\Pr_{\substack{N \leftarrow \mathsf{ModGen}(1^\lambda) \\ (a,b) \leftarrow A(N,T)}}\left[(N = a \cdot b) \wedge (a, b \in [N-1])\right] > 1/(2 \cdot p(\lambda))$.

Proof. Since DF has sequentiality depth at most q_{op}, it means that there exists a pair $G = (G_0, G_1)$ of polynomial-time generic-ring algorithms, where G_1 is a straight-line program with polynomially-many parallel processors making at most q_{op} rounds of operation queries, and there exists a polynomial $p(\cdot)$ such that

$$\Pr\left[\mathsf{Exp}_{\mathsf{DF},G}^{\mathsf{SeqDepth}}(\lambda) = 1\right] > \frac{1}{p(\lambda)},$$

for infinitely many values of $\lambda \in \mathbb{N}$. Let $k_{\mathsf{in}} = k_{\mathsf{in}}(\lambda)$ be the number of ring elements which DF receives as input, and consider the following standard-model factoring algorithm A.

Algorithm A

Input: An integer N sampled by $\mathsf{ModGen}(1^\lambda)$, and the delay parameter $T \in \mathbb{N}$.

1. Sample $\mathbf{x} = (x_1, \ldots, x_{k_{\mathsf{in}}}) \leftarrow (\mathbb{Z}_N)^{k_{\mathsf{in}}}$.
2. Compute $y = Q_{N,T}^{\mathsf{DF}}(x_1, \ldots, x_{k_{\mathsf{in}}})$, and compute $a = \gcd(y, N)$. If $a \notin \{1, N\}$, then output $(a, N/a)$ and terminate.
3. Run $G_0^{\mathbb{Z}_N}(N, T)$ to obtain a state $\mathsf{st} = (\mathsf{st}_0, \mathsf{st}_1, \ldots, \mathsf{st}_\ell)$, where $\mathsf{st}_1, \ldots, \mathsf{st}_\ell$ are ring elements.
4. Compute $z = Q_{N,T,\mathsf{st}_0}^{G_1}(\mathsf{st}_1, \ldots, \mathsf{st}_\ell, x_1, \ldots, x_{k_{\mathsf{in}}})$, and compute $b = \gcd(z, N)$. If $b \notin \{1, N\}$, then output $(b, N/b)$ and terminate.
5. Output $\perp$.

Denote by Factor the event in which A outputs a valid factorization of N, and denote by Inv the event in which both $y = Q_{N,T}^{\mathsf{DF}}(x_1, \ldots, x_{k_{\mathsf{in}}})$ and $z = Q_{N,T,\mathsf{st}_0}^{G_1}(\mathsf{st}_1, \ldots, \mathsf{st}_\ell, x_1, \ldots, x_{k_{\mathsf{in}}})$ are invertible modulo N. Observe that conditioned on $\mathsf{Exp}_{\mathsf{DF},G}^{\mathsf{SeqDepth}}(\lambda) = 1$ and on Inv, it holds that

$$\frac{Q_{N,T}^{\mathsf{DF}}(x_1, \ldots, x_{k_{\mathsf{in}}})}{P_{N,T}^{\mathsf{DF}}(x_1, \ldots, x_{k_{\mathsf{in}}})} = \frac{P_{N,T,\mathsf{st}_0}^{G_1}(\mathsf{st}_1, \ldots, \mathsf{st}_\ell, x_1, \ldots, x_{k_{\mathsf{in}}})}{Q_{N,T,\mathsf{st}_0}^{G_1}(\mathsf{st}_1, \ldots, \mathsf{st}_\ell, x_1, \ldots, x_{k_{\mathsf{in}}})}.$$

In other words, G_1 successfully outputs the output of DF.

On the other hand, conditioned on $\mathsf{Exp}_{\mathsf{DF},G}^{\mathsf{SeqDepth}}(\lambda) = 1$ and on $\overline{\mathsf{Inv}}$, at least one of y and z are not invertible modulo N. In this case, $a = \gcd(y, N)$ or $b = \gcd(z, N)$ are a prime factor of N and A outputs a valid factorization of N. Hence, by total probability, for infinitely many values of $\lambda \in \mathbb{N}$ it holds that

$$\Pr\left[\mathsf{Exp}_{\mathsf{DF},G}^{\mathsf{SeqDepth}}(\lambda) = 1\right] = \Pr\left[\mathsf{Exp}_{\mathsf{DF},G}^{\mathsf{SeqDepth}}(\lambda) = 1 \wedge \mathsf{Inv}\right]$$
$$+ \Pr\left[\mathsf{Exp}_{\mathsf{DF},G}^{\mathsf{SeqDepth}}(\lambda) = 1 \wedge \overline{\mathsf{Inv}}\right]$$
$$\leq \Pr\left[\mathsf{Exp}_{\mathsf{DF},G}^{\mathsf{Seq}}(\lambda) = 1\right] + \Pr\left[\mathsf{Factor}\right]. \qquad (15)$$

Therefore, at least one of the addends in (15) is greater than $1/(2p(\lambda))$ for infinitely many values of $\lambda \in \mathbb{N}$, concluding the proof.   ∎

References

[AM09] Aggarwal, D., Maurer, U.: Breaking RSA generically is equivalent to factoring. In: Joux, A. (ed.) EUROCRYPT 2009. LNCS, vol. 5479, pp. 36–53. Springer, Heidelberg (2009). https://doi.org/10.1007/978-3-642-01001-9_2

[BBB+18] Boneh, D., Bonneau, J., Bünz, B., Fisch, B.: Verifiable delay functions. In: Shacham, H., Boldyreva, A. (eds.) CRYPTO 2018. LNCS, vol. 10991, pp. 757–788. Springer, Cham (2018). https://doi.org/10.1007/978-3-319-96884-1_25

[BBF18] Boneh, D., Bünz, B., Fisch, B.: A survey of two verifiable delay functions. Cryptology ePrint Archive, Report 2018/712 (2018)

[BCG15] Bonneau, J., Clark, J., Goldfeder, S.: On bitcoin as a public randomness source. Cryptology ePrint Archive, Report 2015/1015 (2015)

[BGJ+16] Bitansky, N., Goldwasser, S., Jain, A., Paneth, O., Vaikuntanathan, V., Waters, B.: Time-lock puzzles from randomized encodings. In: Proceedings of the 7th Conference on Innovations in Theoretical Computer Science, pp. 345–356 (2016)

[BGZ16] Bentov, I., Gabizon, A., Zuckerman, D.: Bitcoin beacon. arXiv:605.04559 (2016)

[BL96] Boneh, D., Lipton, R.J.: Algorithms for black-box fields and their application to cryptography. In: Koblitz, N. (ed.) CRYPTO 1996. LNCS, vol. 1109, pp. 283–297. Springer, Heidelberg (1996). https://doi.org/10.1007/3-540-68697-5_22

[Bro05] Brown, D.R.L.: Breaking RSA may be as difficult as factoring. Cryptology ePrint Archive, Report 2005/380 (2005)

[BV98] Boneh, D., Venkatesan, R.: Breaking RSA may not be equivalent to factoring. In: Nyberg, K. (ed.) EUROCRYPT 1998. LNCS, vol. 1403, pp. 59–71. Springer, Heidelberg (1998). https://doi.org/10.1007/BFb0054117

[BW88] Buchmann, J., Williams, H.C.: A key-exchange system based on imaginary quadratic fields. J. Cryptol. **1**(2), 107–118 (1988). https://doi.org/10.1007/BF02351719

[CP18] Cohen, B., Pietrzak, K.: Simple proofs of sequential work. In: Nielsen, J.B., Rijmen, V. (eds.) EUROCRYPT 2018. LNCS, vol. 10821, pp. 451–467. Springer, Cham (2018). https://doi.org/10.1007/978-3-319-78375-8_15

[DGM+19] Döttling, N., Garg, S., Malavolta, G., Vasudevan, P.N.: Tight verifiable delay functions. Cryptology ePrint Archive, Report 2019/659 (2019)

[DK02] Damgård, I., Koprowski, M.: Generic lower bounds for root extraction and signature schemes in general groups. In: Knudsen, L.R. (ed.) EUROCRYPT 2002. LNCS, vol. 2332, pp. 256–271. Springer, Heidelberg (2002). https://doi.org/10.1007/3-540-46035-7_17

[DN92] Dwork, C., Naor, M.: Pricing via processing or combatting junk mail. In: Brickell, E.F. (ed.) CRYPTO 1992. LNCS, vol. 740, pp. 139–147. Springer, Heidelberg (1993). https://doi.org/10.1007/3-540-48071-4_10

[EFK+20] Ephraim, N., Freitag, C., Komargodski, I., Pass, R.: Continuous verifiable delay functions. In: Canteaut, A., Ishai, Y. (eds.) EUROCRYPT 2020. LNCS, vol. 12107, pp. 125–154. Springer, Cham (2020). https://doi.org/10.1007/978-3-030-45727-3_5

[FKL18]   Fuchsbauer, G., Kiltz, E., Loss, J.: The algebraic group model and its applications. In: Shacham, H., Boldyreva, A. (eds.) CRYPTO 2018. LNCS, vol. 10992, pp. 33–62. Springer, Cham (2018). https://doi.org/10.1007/978-3-319-96881-0_2

[FMP+19] De Feo, L., Masson, S., Petit, C., Sanso, A.: Verifiable delay functions from supersingular isogenies and pairings. In: Galbraith, S.D., Moriai, S. (eds.) ASIACRYPT 2019. LNCS, vol. 11921, pp. 248–277. Springer, Cham (2019). https://doi.org/10.1007/978-3-030-34578-5_10

[GW11]   Gentry, C., Wichs, D.: Separating succinct non-interactive arguments from all falsifiable assumptions. In: Proceedings of the 43rd Annual ACM Symposium on Theory of Computing, pp. 99–108 (2011)

[Jag07]   Jager, T.: Generic group algorithms. Master's thesis, Ruhr Universität Bochum (2007)

[JNT07]   Joux, A., Naccache, D., Thomé, E.: When e-th roots become easier than factoring. In: Kurosawa, K. (ed.) ASIACRYPT 2007. LNCS, vol. 4833, pp. 13–28. Springer, Heidelberg (2007). https://doi.org/10.1007/978-3-540-76900-2_2

[JR10]   Jager, T., Rupp, A.: The semi-generic group model and applications to pairing-based cryptography. In: Abe, M. (ed.) ASIACRYPT 2010. LNCS, vol. 6477, pp. 539–556. Springer, Heidelberg (2010). https://doi.org/10.1007/978-3-642-17373-8_31

[JS08]   Jager, T., Schwenk, J.: On the equivalence of generic group models. In: Baek, J., Bao, F., Chen, K., Lai, X. (eds.) ProvSec 2008. LNCS, vol. 5324, pp. 200–209. Springer, Heidelberg (2008). https://doi.org/10.1007/978-3-540-88733-1_14

[JS13]   Jager, T., Schwenk, J.: On the analysis of cryptographic assumptions in the generic ring model. J. Cryptol. **26**(2), 225–245 (2012). https://doi.org/10.1007/s00145-012-9120-y

[Kil92]   Kilian, J.: A note on efficient zero-knowledge proofs and arguments. In: Proceedings of the 24th Annual ACM Symposium on Theory of Computing, pp. 723–732 (1992)

[KLX20]   Katz, J., Loss, J., Xu, J.: On the security of time-locked puzzles and timed commitments. Cryptology ePrint Archive, Report 2020/730 (2020)

[LR06]   Leander, G., Rupp, A.: On the equivalence of RSA and factoring regarding generic ring algorithms. In: Lai, X., Chen, K. (eds.) ASIACRYPT 2006. LNCS, vol. 4284, pp. 241–251. Springer, Heidelberg (2006). https://doi.org/10.1007/11935230_16

[LW15]   Lenstra, A.K., Wesolowski, B.: A random zoo: sloth, unicorn, and trx. Cryptology ePrint Archive, Report 2015/366 (2015)

[Mau05]   Maurer, U.: Abstract models of computation in cryptography. In: Smart, N.P. (ed.) Cryptography and Coding 2005. LNCS, vol. 3796, pp. 1–12. Springer, Heidelberg (2005). https://doi.org/10.1007/11586821_1

[Mic94]   Micali, S.: CS proofs. In: Proceedings of the 35th Annual IEEE Symposium on the Foundations of Computer Science, pp. 436–453 (1994)

[MMV11]   Mahmoody, M., Moran, T., Vadhan, S.: Time-lock puzzles in the random oracle model. In: Rogaway, P. (ed.) CRYPTO 2011. LNCS, vol. 6841, pp. 39–50. Springer, Heidelberg (2011). https://doi.org/10.1007/978-3-642-22792-9_3

[MMV13]   Mahmoody, M., Moran, T., Vadhan, S.P.: Publicly verifiable proofs of sequential work. In: Proceedings of the 4th Conference on Innovations in Theoretical Computer Science, pp. 373–388 (2013)

[MSW19] Mahmoody, M., Smith, C., Wu, D.J.: A note on the (im)possibility of verifiable delay functions in the random oracle model. Cryptology ePrint Archive, Report 2019/663 (2019)

[MW98] Maurer, U., Wolf, S.: Lower bounds on generic algorithms in groups. In: Nyberg, K. (ed.) EUROCRYPT 1998. LNCS, vol. 1403, pp. 72–84. Springer, Heidelberg (1998). https://doi.org/10.1007/BFb0054118

[Nec94] Nechaev, V.I.: Complexity of a determinate algorithm for the discrete logarithm. Math. Notes **55**(2), 91–101 (1994)

[Pie19] Pietrzak, K.: Simple verifiable delay functions. In: Proceedings of the 10th Conference on Innovations in Theoretical Computer Science, pp. 60:1–60:15 (2019)

[PW18] Pierrot, C., Wesolowski, B.: Malleability of the blockchain's entropy. Cryptogr. Commun. **10**(1), 211–233 (2018). https://doi.org/10.1007/s12095-017-0264-3

[RSS20] Rotem, L., Segev, G., Shahaf, I.: Generic-group delay functions require hidden-order groups. In: Canteaut, A., Ishai, Y. (eds.) EUROCRYPT 2020. LNCS, vol. 12107, pp. 155–180. Springer, Cham (2020). https://doi.org/10.1007/978-3-030-45727-3_6

[RSW96] Rivest, R.L., Shamir, A., Wagner, D.A.: Time-lock puzzles and timed-release crypto (1996)

[Sha19] Shani, B.: A note on isogeny-based hybrid verifiable delay functions. Cryptology ePrint Archive, Report 2019/205 (2019)

[Sho97] Shoup, V.: Lower bounds for discrete logarithms and related problems. In: Fumy, W. (ed.) EUROCRYPT 1997. LNCS, vol. 1233, pp. 256–266. Springer, Heidelberg (1997). https://doi.org/10.1007/3-540-69053-0_18

[Wes19] Wesolowski, B.: Efficient verifiable delay functions. In: Ishai, Y., Rijmen, V. (eds.) EUROCRYPT 2019. LNCS, vol. 11478, pp. 379–407. Springer, Cham (2019). https://doi.org/10.1007/978-3-030-17659-4_13

Zero Knowledge

Compressed Σ-Protocol Theory and Practical Application to Plug & Play Secure Algorithmics

Thomas Attema[1,2,3]([✉]) and Ronald Cramer[1,2]([✉])

[1] CWI, Cryptology Group, Amsterdam, The Netherlands
thomas.attema@tno.nl, cramer@cwi.nl, cramer@math.leidenuniv.nl
[2] Mathematical Institute, Leiden University, Leiden, The Netherlands
[3] Cyber Security and Robustness, TNO, The Hague, The Netherlands

Abstract. Σ-Protocols provide a well-understood basis for secure algorithmics. Recently, Bulletproofs (Bootle et al., EUROCRYPT 2016, and Bünz et al., S&P 2018) have been proposed as a *drop-in* replacement in case of zero-knowledge (ZK) for arithmetic circuits, achieving logarithmic communication instead of linear. Its *pivot* is an ingenious, logarithmic-size proof of knowledge BP for certain *quadratic* relations. However, reducing ZK for *general* relations to it forces a somewhat cumbersome "reinvention" of cryptographic protocol theory.

We take a rather different viewpoint and *reconcile* Bulletproofs with Σ-Protocol Theory such that (a) simpler circuit ZK is developed *within* established theory, while (b) achieving exactly the same logarithmic communication.

The natural key here is *linearization*. First, we repurpose BPs as a blackbox *compression* mechanism for standard Σ-Protocols handling ZK proofs of general *linear relations* (on compactly committed secret vectors); *our pivot*. Second, we reduce the case of general *nonlinear* relations to *blackbox* applications of our pivot via a novel variation on *arithmetic secret sharing based techniques for Σ-Protocols* (Cramer et al., ICITS 2012). Orthogonally, we enhance versatility by enabling scenarios not previously addressed, e.g., when a secret input is dispersed across several commitments. Standard implementation platforms leading to logarithmic communication follow from a Discrete-Log assumption or a generalized Strong-RSA assumption. Also, under a Knowledge-of-Exponent Assumption (KEA) communication drops to *constant*, as in ZK-SNARKS.

All in all, our theory should more generally be useful for modular ("plug & play") design of practical cryptographic protocols; this is further evidenced by our separate work (2020) on proofs of partial knowledge.

Keywords: Σ-protocols · Bulletproofs · Zero-knowledge · Plug-and-play · Secure algorithmics · ZK-SNARKS · Verifiable computation

© International Association for Cryptologic Research 2020
D. Micciancio and T. Ristenpart (Eds.): CRYPTO 2020, LNCS 12172, pp. 513–543, 2020.
https://doi.org/10.1007/978-3-030-56877-1_18

1   Introduction

The theory of Σ-Protocols provides a well-understood basis for *plug-and-play* secure algorithmics.[1] Recently, Bulletproofs [5,7] have been introduced as a "drop-in replacement" for Σ-Protocols in several important applications. Notably, this includes ZK for arithmetic circuits with communication $O(\log |C| \cdot \kappa)$ bits where $|C|$ is the circuit size[2] and κ is the security parameter, down from $O(|C| \cdot \kappa)$ bits. A similar result holds for range proofs.

At the heart of Bulletproofs is an interactive proof of knowledge between a Prover and Verifier showing that a Pedersen commitment to a vector of large length n satisfies a multi-variate polynomial equation of degree 2, defined with an inner product. We refer to this PoK by BP. Concretely, suppose $\mathbb{G}$ is a cyclic group of prime order q (denoted multiplicatively) supporting discrete-log-based cryptography. Suppose, furthermore, that $\mathbf{g} = (g_1, \ldots, g_n) \in \mathbb{G}^n$ and $h \in \mathbb{G}$ (each g_i as well as h generators of $\mathbb{G}$) have been set up once-and-for-all such that, for parties that may subsequently act as provers, finding nontrivial linear relations between them is computationally as hard as computing discrete logarithms in $\mathbb{G}$. For each $\mathbf{x} \in \mathbb{Z}_q^n$, define $\mathbf{g}^{\mathbf{x}} = \prod_{i=1}^n g_i^{x_i}$. A Pedersen-commitment P to a vector $\mathbf{x} \in \mathbb{Z}_q^n$ is then computed as $P = \mathbf{g}^{\mathbf{x}} \cdot h^{\rho}$ where $\rho \in \mathbb{Z}_q$ is selected uniformly at random. This commitment is information-theoretically hiding and, on account of the set-up, computationally binding. Note that it is compact in the sense that, independently of n, a commitment is a single $\mathbb{G}$-element. Suppose that n is even and write $n = 2m$. Setting $\mathbf{x} = (\mathbf{x}_0, \mathbf{x}_1) \in \mathbb{Z}_q^m \times \mathbb{Z}_q^m$, a Bulletproof allows the prover to prove that it can open P such that the inner-product $\langle \mathbf{x}_0, \mathbf{x}_1 \rangle$ equals some value claimed by the prover.[3]

BPs stand out in that they ingeniously reduce communication to $O(\log n)$ elements from $O(n)$ via traditional methods. Although this is at the expense of introducing logarithmic number of moves (instead of constant), its public-coin nature ensures that it can be rendered non-interactive using the Fiat-Shamir heuristic [16]. However, design of BP *applications* meet with a number of *technical difficulties*. First, BPs are not zero-knowledge, and second, cryptographic protocol theory has to be "reinvented" with the quadratic constraint proved as its "pivot". This leads to practical yet rather opaque, complex protocols where applying natural plug-and-play intuition appears hard.

1.1   Summary of Our Contributions

In this work we take a different approach. We reconcile Bulletproofs with theory of Σ-Protocols such that (a) applications can follow (established) cryptographic protocol theory, thereby dispensing with the need for "reinventing" it, while

---

[1] Loosely speaking, we refer to modular design of "cryptographic realizations" of standard "algorithmic tasks". In other words, this entails porting algorithms for standard tasks to cryptographic scenarios, e.g., MPC and zero-knowledge.

[2] Actually, the result only depends on the number of inputs and multiplication gates.

[3] Alternatively, this inner-product value may be taken as part of the committed vector.

(b) enjoying exactly the same communication reduction. We do this by giving a precise perspective on BPs as a *significant strengthening* of the power of Σ-protocols. We believe this novel perspective is rather useful for intuitive, plug-and-play or modular design of practical secure algorithmics. Perhaps surprisingly our approach yields the same communication complexity; up to and including the constants.

We combine two essential components. First, we isolate a natural, *alternative pivot*: compact commitment with "arbitrary linear form openings". Given a Pedersen commitment to a long vector $\mathbf{x}$, consider a ZKPoK that the prover knows $\mathbf{x}$, while also revealing, for an *arbitrary, public, linear form L*, the scalar $L(\mathbf{x})$ correctly and nothing else. This has a simple Σ-Protocol. We then *compress* it by replacing the final (long) prover-message with an appropriate BP that the prover *knows it*. Indeed, the relation that this message is required to satisfy turns out amenable to deployment of a suitable BP. As a result, PoK and honest-verifier ZK are preserved, but *overall communication* drops from linear to logarithmic. In the process, we simplify, for a portion of the full parameter space relevant to our applications, known run-time analyses of knowledge extractors involved and give concrete estimates. For the remainder, we continue to rely on known analyses. On top of this, we introduce further necessary utility enhancements. First, without increasing overall complexity, we show, using the pivot as black-box, how to open several linear form evaluations instead of just one. Second, using this and by plug & play with our basic theory, we show how to handle the application scenario where the secret, long vector is initially "dispersed" across several commitments, by compactifying these into a single compact commitment first. This is useful in important applications. *From this point on, the only fact about the pivot that we will need is that we have access to a compact commitment scheme that allows a ZKPoK with low overall communication, showing that the prover knows the long secret committed vector and showing the correct openings of several linear evaluations on that committed vector;* the technical details do not matter anymore.

Second, the pivot's *significance* now surfaces when integrated with a novel variation on – hitherto largely overlooked – *arithmetic secret sharing based techniques for Σ-Protocols* [12], inspired by MPC. These techniques allow for *linearization* of "nonlinear relations". Mathematically, solving the linear instances first and then "linearizing" the non-linear ones is perhaps among the most natural problem solving strategies; here, this fits seamlessly with Sigma-protocol theory and our adaptation of [12]. It is in these adaptations that free choice of linear forms in the pivot is fully exploited; the maps arising from our adaptation of [12] do not form a well-structured subclass of maps. All in all, this yields *simple* logarithmic communication solutions for circuit ZK. Similarly for range proofs, which are now trivial to design. We also offer trade-offs, i.e., "square-root" complexity in constant rounds. Our results are based on either of three assumptions, the Discrete Logarithm assumption, an assumption derived from the Strong-RSA assumption, or a Knowledge-of-Exponent derived assumption.

We proceed as follows. We start by outlining our program, in nearly exclusively conceptual fashion. We believe that the fact that it is possible to do so further underscores our main points. Later on we detail how this program deviates exactly from the paths taken in the recent literature.

1.2 A More Detailed View of Our Program

A. Our Pivotal Σ-Protocol

We isolate a basic Σ-protocol Π_0 that, given a compact commitment to a secret vector $\mathbf{x}$ of large length n, allows to *partially* open it. Concretely, given an *arbitrary, public, linear form* L, only the value $L(\mathbf{x})$ is released and nothing else. Briefly, the prover has a compact commitment P to a long secret vector $\mathbf{x}$. By a simple twist on basic Σ-protocol theory, the prover then selects a compact commitment A to a secret random vector $\mathbf{r}$. The prover sends, as first move, this commitment A *and* the values $y = L(\mathbf{x})$ and $y' = L(\mathbf{r})$. In the second move, the verifier sends a random challenge $c \in \mathbb{Z}_q$. In the third, final move, the prover then opens the commitment AP^c to a vector $\mathbf{z}$ (i.e., $\mathbf{z}$ is its committed vector; we leave the randomness underlying the commitment implicit here). Finally, the verifier checks the opening of the commitment and checks that $L(\mathbf{z}) = cy + y'$. The communication in this Σ-protocol is dominated by the *opening of AP^c*. The latter amounts to $O(n\kappa)$ bits (where κ is the security parameter), whereas the remainder of the protocol has $O(\kappa)$ bits *in total*. That said, it is an honest-verifier zero-knowledge proof of knowledge (with unconditional soundness). In addition, we describe an amortized version of this basic Σ-protocol, i.e., a Σ-protocol Π_0^{Am} that, given s compact commitments to secret vectors $\mathbf{x}_1, \ldots, \mathbf{x}_s$ and a linear form L, allows to open $L(\mathbf{x}_1), \ldots, L(\mathbf{x}_s)$ and nothing else. The communication costs of this amortized Σ-protocol are exactly $s - 1$ elements more than that of the basic Σ-protocol (i.e., the evaluations at the $s - 1$ additional input vectors).

Using the pivotal Σ-protocol as a black-box, its utility can be *enhanced*, which will be important later on. More concretely, *many linear forms* can be opened for essentially the price of a *single one*. First, by deploying a "polynomial amortization trick" (known, e.g., from MPC) we can do any number of *nullity* checks without any substantial increase in complexity. Second, building on this trick, we can extend the utility to the opening of *several* arbitrary linear forms $L_1, \ldots, L_s$ instead of a single one, at the cost of increasing the communication by exactly $s - 1$ values in $\mathbb{Z}_q$ (i.e., the evaluations of $s - 1$ additional forms). Finally, we note the entire discussion on these enhancements holds *verbatim* when we replace linear forms by *affine forms*.[4]

Note that we have identified two distinct *intractability assumptions*, each of which supports this pivot: the Discrete Logarithm assumption (as used in prior work involving Bulletproofs [5,7]) but also one derived from the Strong-RSA assumption (as nailed down in a recent work [8] on Bulletproofs and their improved applications). The introduction focuses on the DL assumption, but

---

[4] I.e., a linear form plus a constant.

the Σ-protocol for the solution derived from the Strong-RSA assumption follows similarly. Our program can be based on either platform. In addition, we show how to base the program on a specific knowledge of exponent assumption. However, such assumptions are known to be unfalsifiable and, therefore, not without controversy. The details of our pivotal Σ-protocol can be found in Sect. 3, and the utility enhancements are described in Sect. 5.

B. Compressing the Pivot

We argue that protocol Π_0 can be *compressed* using the ideas underlying Bulletproofs, yielding a protocol Π_c that has the same functionality and is still an honest-verifier zero-knowledge proof of knowledge for the relation in question, but that has communication $O(\kappa \log n)$ bits *instead*, and $O(\log n)$ moves. Technically the compression degrades the soundness from unconditional to computational, and protocols with computational soundness are called arguments of knowledge. However, we will use the terms proof and argument of knowledge interchangeably. The compression techniques directly carry over to amortized Σ-protocol Π_0^{Am}. See below for variations achieving unconditional soundness.

Main Compression Idea. The idea is simply as follows, starting from Π_0. Suppose that P is the commitment in question. The linear forms are constants as they are part of the relation proved, so they will not be made explicit for now. Furthermore suppose that the prover has sent the message a as first move of Π_0, and that the verifier has subsequently sent challenge c as the second move. Thus, in the third –and final– move, the prover would be required to send the reply z. The verifier would, finally, apply the verification function ϕ attached to Π_0 to check that $\phi(P; a, c, z) = 1$, and accept only if this is the case. To define the compressed protocol Π_c, instead of requiring the prover to send the long vector z, a suitable adaptation of Bulletproof's PoK (BP) will be deployed to let the prover convince the verifier that it *knows* some z such that $\phi(P; a, c, z) = 1$, which is much more efficient. Note that it is immaterial that the Bulletproof part is not zero knowledge as, in Π_0, the prover would have *revealed* z anyway.

This will ensure the claimed communication reduction, i.e., $O(\kappa \log n)$ bits in $O(\log n)$ moves. We show that, as a *trade-off*, we may opt for *constant* number of rounds (instead of logarithmic) and $O(\kappa \sqrt{n})$ communication (instead of logarithmic). But of course, in non-interactive Fiat-Shamir mode (which clearly applies here), the logarithmic variant may be preferable.

Note that this compression idea equally applies to the enhancements of the basic utility as discussed above. It gives essentially the same complexities. Of course, this assumes that the number of openings of linear forms is not too large; it is not sensitive to the number of nullity checks though. The details of the compression idea can be found in Sect. 4.

Refined Analysis of Knowledge Extractors. In the theory of Σ-protocols [9], it is well known that *special soundness* implies knowledge soundness with knowledge error $1/q$, where q is the size of the challenge set. Depending on a choice for the definition of knowledge soundness, this result can either be shown by an application [9] of Jensen's inequality, or by a more intricate variation of the classical heavy-row type approach [14].

Recently, and particularly for the above mentioned compression techniques, natural generalizations of special soundness have become relevant. However, the mentioned proof techniques are no longer directly applicable. The nature of the compression techniques namely significantly reduces the efficiency of the corresponding knowledge extractors. For this reason prior works [5,7] resort to alternative arguments without computing the exact knowledge error. See also [29] and [23] for a discussion on extractor efficiency and knowledge errors.

Here, we show that an adaptation of the proof using Jensen's inequality does apply for a portion of the full parameter space relevant to our applications. This results in a simple proof and an exact knowledge error for this portion of the parameter space. For parameters that do not fall in this range we resort to prior results [5,7]. The details of the extractor analysis can be found in the full-version of this paper [1].

Compressed Pivot with Unconditional Soundness. In addition, we show two approaches for realizing our compressed pivot with *unconditional* soundness, rather than computational. In our first approach we simply omit the step of the BP compression in which the linear-form evaluation is incorporated into the commitment, and execute that part "in the open". This works for us here since we only consider linear constraints in the compressed pivot and no quadratic ones. As a result, unconditional soundness is achieved. This approach increases the communication costs by a factor 2.

Our second approach is based on the observation that an unconditionally sound ZKPoK for opening linear forms can be based on *black-box access* to an unconditionally sound ZKPoK for just proving knowledge of an opening of a Pedersen vector commitment. The reduction uses structural information of a given linear form (i.e., it depends on the null-space and selection of a basis for it). By removing the provisions for linear forms from the compressed pivot Π_c the required black-box is realized. The details can be found in the full-version of this paper [1].

C. Compactifying a Vector of Commitments

Our compressed pivot may be summarized as compact commitments to long secret vectors that allow for very efficient partial openings, i.e., arbitrary linear forms applied to the secret committed vector. As we show later on, this is sufficient for proving any (nonlinear) relation. To make this work, all relevant prover data (secret data vector plus secret auxiliary data, such a random coins) is required to be committed to in a *single compact commitment*.

However, in many relevant practical scenarios, we must assume that the commitment to the prover's secret data vector, about which something is to be proved in zero knowledge, has already been produced *before* the zero knowledge protocol is run. In order to handle this, we require the prover to *compactify* these commitments together with the secret auxiliary data in a single commitment.

We consider two extreme scenarios: (1) the prover has a single compact commitment to the secret data vector about which some zero knowledge proof is to be conducted and (2) same, except that the prover has *individual* commitments to the coordinates of that secret data vector. For each scenario we give a conceptually clean realization by plug & play with our basic theory. We note that scenario 1 has not been addressed by previous work.

For the first scenario the prover uses new generators to commit to the auxiliary information. Using the compressed Σ-protocol, the prover shows that this is indeed a commitment that *exclusively* involves the new generators. Prover and verifier multiply the two compact commitments to obtain a single compact commitment to all relevant data.

For the second scenario, a basic (amortized) Σ-protocol shows that the prover knows openings to all individual commitments. From this basic protocol, we define a new Σ-protocol as follows. The prover appends the first message a of the basic protocol with a compact commitment containing all relevant data *and* the randomness sampled in the first move of the basic Σ-protocol. After receiving the challenge the prover's response can now be computed as a public linear form (parameterized by the challenge c) evaluated at the vector to which the prover committed. Instead of sending this message directly, the prover and verifier run the interactive protocol to open the associated linear form on the compact vector commitment. The verifier checks that the opening of the vector commitment is also an opening of the commitment in the Σ-protocol. As a result the prover has shown that it knows openings to all the individual commitments and that these openings are contained in the compact commitment together with the auxiliary data. The details on the compactification of vector commitments can be found in Sect. 5.3.

D. Plug-and-Play Secure Algorithmics from Compressed Pivot

We will now explain the power of our compressed pivot. It will turn out that we only need *black-box access*. Our key point is to show how to combine this with a hitherto largely overlooked part of Σ-protocol theory, namely the work of [12] that shows how to prove *arbitrary constraints* on committed vectors by exploiting techniques from secure multi-party computation based on arithmetic secret sharing, more concretely, the ideas underlying the Commitment Multiplication Protocol from [10]. For more information, see Section 12.5.3 in [11] for a general description of efficient zero-knowledge verification of secret multiplications in terms of arbitrary (strongly-multiplicative) arithmetic secret sharing. It is this *combination* of "compact commitments with linear openings" and arithmetic secret sharing that allows for "linearizing nonlinear relations". So this explains also why our compressed pivot does not need any "direct" provision to handle nonlinearity.

We need to make some appropriate adaptations to make this work for us here. We first outline the technique from [12] and then we discuss adaptations. The work of [12] considers homomorphic commitment schemes where the secret committed to is not a vector of large length, but a *single element* of $\mathbb{Z}_q$ instead. The primary result is a Σ-protocol showing the correctness of commitments to m multiplication triples $(\alpha_i, \beta_i, \gamma_i := \alpha_i \beta_i)$, with *low amortized complexity* for large m. In other words, the protocol verifies the multiplicative relations, and the costs per triple are relatively small.

Each of the α_i's (resp., the β_i's and γ_i's) is individually committed to. Their solution employs strongly-multiplicative packed-secret sharing. For instance, consider Shamir's scheme over $\mathbb{Z}_q$, with privacy parameter $t = 1$, but with secret-space dimension m. This uses random polynomials of degree $\leq m$, subject to the evaluations on the points $1, \ldots, m$ comprising the desired secret vector. Note that, for each sharing, a single random $\mathbb{Z}_q$-element is required (which can be taken as the evaluation at 0).

It is important to note that, given secret vector and random element, it holds by Lagrange Interpolation that, for each $c \in \mathbb{Z}_q$, the evaluation $f(c)$ of such polynomial $f(X)$ is some public $\mathbb{Z}_q$-linear combination over the coordinates of the secret vector and the random element. Namely, consider the map that takes $m + 1$ arbitrary evaluations on the points $0, \ldots, m$ and that outputs the unique polynomial $f(X)$ of degree $\leq m$ interpolating them to the evaluations of $f(X)$ in all other points. A transformation matrix describing this map does not correspond to a Vandermonde-matrix, but it can be determined from it.

Now, assume that $2m < q$ (for strong-multiplicativity). The protocol goes as follows.

- The vectors of commitments to the multiplication triples are assumed to be part of the common input.
- The prover selects a random polynomial $f(X)$ that defines a packed secret sharing of the vector $(\alpha_1, \ldots, \alpha_m)$. The prover also selects a random polynomial $g(X)$ that defines a packed secret sharing of the vector $(\beta_1, \ldots, \beta_m)$. Finally, the prover computes the product polynomial $h(X) := f(X)g(X)$ of degree $\leq 2m < q$.
- The prover commits to the random $\mathbb{Z}_q$-element for the sharing based on $f(X)$, i.e., $f(0)$, and commits to the random $\mathbb{Z}_q$-element for the sharing based on $g(X)$, i.e., $g(0)$. The prover also commits the evaluations of $h(X)$ on the points $0, m+1, \ldots, 2m$.[5] Note that the "absent" evaluations at $1, \ldots, m$ comprise the γ_i's and their commitments are already assumed to be part of the common input.
- The prover sends these commitments to the verifier.
- The verifier selects a random challenge $c \in \mathbb{Z}_q$ distinct from $1, \ldots, m$ and sends it to the prover.
- By public linear combinations, both prover and verifier can compute three commitments: one to $u := f(c)$, one to $v := g(c)$ and one to $w := h(c)$. The prover opens each of these (assuming, of course, that c is in the right range). The verifier checks each of these three openings and checks whether $w = uv$. If the committed polynomials do not satisfy $f(X)g(X) = h(X)$, and under the assumption that the commitment scheme is binding, there are at most $2m$ values of c out of the $q-m$ possibilities such that the final check goes through. So a lying prover is caught with probability greater than $1 - 2m/(q - m)$. With q exponential in the security parameter and m, say, polynomial in it, this is exponentially close to 1. Honest-verifier zero-knowledge essentially follows from 1-privacy of the secret sharing scheme.

---

[5] By Lagrange interpolation these points, together with the γ_i's, determine $h(X)$.

Our *first observation here* is as follows. *In the above protocol, the prover may as well use our compressed pivot as a black-box.* Indeed, the entire vector

$$\mathbf{y} = (\alpha_1, \ldots, \alpha_m, \beta_1, \ldots, \beta_m, f(0), g(0), h(0), h(1), \ldots, h(2m)) \in \mathbb{Z}_q^{4m+3}$$

of data that the prover commits to in the protocol above can be committed to in a *single* compact commitment. Note that, by definition, $\gamma_i = h(i)$ for all $1 \le i \le m$. Furthermore, all of the data *opened* to the verifier is some fixed linear form on the (long) secret committed vector $\mathbf{y}$. Indeed:

1. Each of the values u, v correspond to an opening of a public linear form applied to $\mathbf{y}$. The linear form is determined by some row in a transformation matrix as addressed above, under the convention that the form takes zeros on the portion of the coordinates of $\mathbf{y}$ not relevant to the computation.
2. Similarly for the value w, except that this simply corresponds to an "evaluation of a polynomial whose coefficients are defined by a part of $\mathbf{y}$". So evaluation is a public linear form as well.

Overall, we get an honest-verifier proof of knowledge for showing correctness of m secret multiplication-triples with $O(k \log m)$ bits communication in $O(\log m)$ moves (or in constant rounds but with $O(k\sqrt{m})$ bits communication).

Our *second observation here* is as follows. Suppose we have an arithmetic circuit[6] C over $\mathbb{Z}_q$ with n inputs, s outputs and m multiplication gates.[7] We can easily turn the observation above into a solution for "circuit zero-knowledge", i.e., the prover convinces the verifier that the committed vector $\mathbf{x} \in \mathbb{Z}_q^n$ satisfies some constraint captured by a given circuit C which (w.l.o.g.) returns 0. We note that [12] also gives a solution for circuit zero-knowledge. But that one does not work for us here as it gives too large complexity. So we make some changes.

By the aforementioned compactification techniques it is *sufficient* to consider the ZK scenario where the prover wants to demonstrate that C is satisfiable; this means that we may assume that the prover commits to all relevant data (inputs *and* all auxiliary data) in a *single* compact commitment. Other ZK scenarios, in which the prover has already committed to input data, are dealt with by first *compactifying* existing commitments and auxiliary information into a single compact commitment.

The protocol goes as follows. The prover first determines the computation graph implied by instantiating the circuit C with its input vector $\mathbf{x} \in \mathbb{Z}_q^n$. The m multiplication gates in C will be handled as above, i.e., via polynomials $f(X)$, $g(X)$ and $h(X)$ defining packed-secret sharings of the left inputs, the right inputs and outputs of the multiplication gates. The prover commits to each of the coordinates of $\mathbf{x}$ and to the auxiliary data $\mathsf{aux} = (f(0), g(0), h(0), h(1), \ldots, h(2m)) \in \mathbb{Z}_q^{2m+3}$ in one single compact commitment. *The length γ of the committed vector $\mathbf{y}$ thus equals $n + 2m + 3$.*

---

[6] Each gate of the circuit has fan-in two, but unbounded fan-out.
[7] We only count multiplication gates with *variable* inputs. Additions and multiplications by constants are implicitly handled and immaterial to the communication.

A simple fact about arithmetic circuits shows that all wire values are accessible as affine combinations of the coefficients committed to. These affine combinations are uniquely defined by the addition and scalar multiplication gates of the circuit. This explains why, *in contrast to the discussion above*, it is no longer necessary to commit explicitly to the α_i's and the β_i's as these are now implicitly committed to via said affine functions of $\mathbf{y}$. Therefore, since the values $f(0), g(0)$ are still included in $\mathbf{y}$, the polynomials $f(X), g(X)$ and $h(X)$ are well-defined by $\mathbf{y}$, and their evaluations are, by composition of the appropriate maps, also affine evaluations on $\mathbf{y}$.

With the above observations in hand, the protocol is reduced to opening the affine map Φ that, on input $\mathbf{y}$, outputs $(C(\mathbf{x}), f(c), g(c), h(c))$ for a challenge $c \in \mathbb{Z}_q \setminus \{1, \ldots, m\}$ sampled uniformly at random by the verifier. First, the verifier checks that $h(c) = f(c)g(c)$ which, as above, shows that the required multiplicative relations hold with high probability. Second, the verifier checks that $C(\mathbf{x}) = 0$, which shows that the circuit is satisfiable and that the prover knows a witness $\mathbf{x}$. By the amortized nullity checks (A) the costs of these openings can be amortized. As a result, circuit zero knowledge can be done $O(\kappa \log \gamma)$ bits in $O(\log \gamma)$ moves. In particular, the communication costs are independent of the number of output vertices s. Trade-off between communication and moves applies as above. More details on circuit ZK can be found in Sect. 6.

E. Range Proofs

In a basic range proof a prover wishes to commit to a secret integer v and show that this integer is in a public range, say $[0, 2^{n-1}]$. From the above circuit ZK protocols, range proofs immediately follow. A prover simply considers the bit decomposition $\mathbf{b} \in \mathbb{Z}^n$ of the integer v, the length of this decomposition determines the range. Note that v can be accessed as a linear form evaluated at $\mathbf{b}$ and thereby a commitment to $\mathbf{b}$ is an implicit commitment to v. Prover and verifier run the above circuit satisfiability protocol to commit to $\mathbf{b}$ and prove that $C(\mathbf{b}) = 0$ for $C : \mathbb{Z}_q^n \to \mathbb{Z}_q^n, \quad x \mapsto x * (1-x)$, where $*$ represents the component-wise product. The nullity check for C shows that the committed coefficients are indeed bits. The communication complexity of this range proof is $O(\kappa \log n)$ bits. Using the techniques described in Sect. 5.3, this functionality can be extended to scenario where a prover has to prove that a Pedersen commitment to $v \in \mathbb{Z}_q$ is in a certain range. The details can be found in Sect. 7 and the full-version of this paper.

F. Our Program from the Strong-RSA Assumption

Thus far, we have implemented our program in the discrete log setting, starting from Pedersen commitments and their basic Σ-protocols. Besides some minor details in the compressed pivot, we show that the above discussion holds *verbatim* for a commitment scheme based on an assumption derived from the Strong-RSA assumption. More precisely, we show how the polynomial commitment scheme from a recent work [8] can be adapted to open arbitrary linear forms. Our adaptations of the linearization techniques from [12] are directly applicable to the Strong-RSA derived pivot. The details can be found in Sect. 7 and the full-version of this paper.

G. Our Program from the Knowledge-of-Exponent Assumption

In addition to the discrete log and strong-RSA derived assumptions, our program can also be based on an assumption derived from the Knowledge-of-Exponent Assumption (KEA). Note that KEA is unfalsifiable and its application is not completely without controversy [4,26]. Moreover, this approach introduces a trusted set-up phase, which might be undesirable. The main benefit of the KEA based approach is that it reduces the communication complexity from logarithmic to constant, i.e., independent of the dimension of the committed vector. In Sect. 9 we describe the main techniques and for more details we refer to [22].

H. Proofs of Partial Knowledge from Compressed Σ-Protocol Theory

In a ZK proof of (k, n)-partial knowledge, a prover knowing witnesses for some k-subset of n given public statements can convince the verifier of this fact without revealing which k-subset. In separate work [2], we construct logarithmic size proofs of partial knowledge *for all k, n*, by adapting our compressed Σ-protocols and repurposing ideas from [13].

I. Our program from Lattice Assumptions

From the work of [6] we can extract an instantiation of our compressed pivot based on lattice assumptions. Based on this, our framework can therefore be instantiated from lattice assumptions. However, lattice based proofs of knowledge in general are typically subject to a so called soundness slack that is further increased by the compression in [6]. Therefore, whether or not one follows our framework, selection of *larger* implementation parameters is warranted. Further research is required to determine if and how the implementation parameters can be improved.

1.3 Comparison with Earlier Work

Traditional solutions for circuit ZK in the discrete logarithm setting have a communication complexity that is linear in the circuit size. Building on the work of Groth [20], an ingenious recursive approach achieved logarithmic communication complexity [5]. At its heart lies an earlier version of the BP protocol discussed earlier. Further improvements were introduced in [7] and later revisited in [23]. Recently, Bünz, Fisch and Szepieniec [8] show that similar results can be derived from the Strong-RSA assumption. The main merit of the Strong-RSA derived solutions is a reduction in the number of public parameters. In addition, [8] deploys proofs of exponentiation [28] to reduce the computational complexity.

A common denominator in the aforementioned works is the use of a quadratic constraint as a main pivot. In [20], a specific inner-product relation is introduced, and it is shown how basic Σ-protocols for this relation can be enhanced to achieve sub-linear communication complexity. A similar inner-product relation lies at the foundation of the logarithmic size protocols of [5], except that it also uses an earlier version of the BP idea. In [7], it is subsequently shown that a modification of the quadratic relation leads to better constants. In [23], more general quadratic constraints were considered with a view towards reducing *computational* complexity in specific ZK scenarios. Also they strive for a more modular approach. However, this induces (minor) communication overhead in comparison to Bulletproofs [7].

Furthermore, it is worth mentioning that in [5], as an intermediate stepping stone, a polynomial commitment scheme is constructed. A polynomial commitment is a commitment to the coefficient vector of a polynomial together with the functionality of opening the evaluation at any given point. The solution derived from the Strong-RSA assumption [8] bases itself entirely on this polynomial functionality. For general relations it uses recent, but complicated, reductions [18,25,30]. Constructing protocols from quadratic constraints, either directly or via a polynomial commitment scheme, leads to a complex theory in which plug-and-play secure algorithmics appears hard. Significant effort is required to realize higher level applications such as circuit ZK or range proofs.

As for zero-knowledge, the work of [7] and [23] establishes this property at a higher level, and not, as do the other works, at the level of their main pivot, which leads to additional difficulties in designing ZK protocols. In fact, in [23], zero-knowledge, reduced communication and reduced computation is achieved in an integrated manner.

The most significant difference between our approach and that of the aforementioned works is our simple and direct construction of a compressed pivot to open *arbitrary* linear forms and to combine this with the simple (MPC inspired) linearization techniques from [12]. The compression is achieved by a suitable adaptation of the BP ideas [7], and the linearization techniques discard the need for a direct provision to handle nonlinearity. Moreover, plug and play design of applications according to this compressed Σ-protocol theory is just as easy as with the standard Σ-protocol theory. Despite the conceptual simplicity, the communication complexities of our approach are, even including the constants, equal to that of Bulletproofs [7].

Note that polynomial evaluation, as used in some of the other works, of course also comes down to the evaluation of a linear form, albeit a specific one. Therefore these approaches are not amenable to the linearization techniques we use. Opening *arbitrary* linear forms therefore seems to be a sweet spot in that it achieves conceptual simplicity, both in designing ZK protocols and in implementing the pivot.

2   Preliminaries

In this section we introduce the basic notation, definitions and conventions used in the remainder of the paper.

Interactive Protocols. Let $R = \{(x, w)\}$ be some NP-relation. Here, x is called a *statement* and w is called a *witness* for x. An interactive protocol Π for relation R is a protocol that allows a prover to convince a verifier that it knows a witness w for given statement x. Protocol Π takes x as public input and w as prover's private input, which we write as either $\Pi(x; w)$ or, in the graphical protocol description, as INPUT$(x; w)$. The verifier always implicitly outputs reject or accept. Optionally, the protocol can output a public string y to both verifier and prover, and a private string w' only to the prover. In this case we write $\mathrm{OUTPUT}(y; w')$. In addition to the input and output of the protocol, the prover's claim (i.e, $(x; w) \in R$) is made explicit in the graphical protocol description. An interactive protocol in which the verifier chooses all its messages uniformly at random and independent from the prover's messages is called a *public coin* protocol. All protocols in this work are public coin and can therefore be made non-interactive by applying the Fiat-Shamir transformation [16].

Special Soundness and Zero-Knowledge. A public coin protocol is said to be (unconditionally) $(k_1, \ldots, k_\mu)$-*special sound* if there exists a polynomial time algorithm that on input a statement x and a $(k_1, k_2, \ldots, k_\mu)$-*tree of accepting transcripts*, outputs a witness w for x. See [5] for a detailed definition. In brief, a $(k_1, k_2, \ldots, k_\mu)$-tree of accepting transcripts is a set of $\prod_{i=1}^{\mu} k_i$ accepting transcripts that are arranged in a tree structure. The edges in this three correspond to the verifier's challenges and vertices to the prover's messages, which can be empty. Every node at depth i has precisely k_i children corresponding to k_i pairwise distinct challenges. Every transcript corresponds to exactly one path from the root node to a leaf node. Note that this notion is, in two ways, a natural generalization of the standard notion *special soundness*: (1) from a colliding pair of transcripts to a k-collision and (2) from 1 challenge protocols to protocols with $\mu \geq 1$ challenges. In [5] it is shown that $(k_1, \ldots, k_\mu)$-special soundness implies *witness extended emulation* [24]. A protocol is said to have this property if for any prover $\mathcal{P}^*$ there exists an efficient algorithm, with rewindable oracle access to $\mathcal{P}^*$, that outputs a transcript and, if this transcript is accepting then it outputs, with overwhelming probability, a witness as well. The transcripts generated by this algorithm are required to be indistinguishable from conversations between $\mathcal{P}^*$ and an honest verifier. We show that all protocols in this work are $(k_1, k_2, \ldots, k_\mu)$-special sound for some μ and some set of k_i's. From the result of [5] it then follows that the protocols in this work are *proofs of knowledge*.

The protocol's public parameters are typically a set of generators $g_1, \ldots, g_n, h$ of a group $\mathbb{G}$ of prime order q. We assume that, in the setup phase, these generators are sampled uniformly at random such that the prover does not know a non-trivial DL relation between them. We say that the protocol is *computationally* $(k_1, k_2, \ldots, k_\mu)$-special sound, under the DL assumption, if there exists an efficient algorithm that *either* extracts a witness *or* finds a non-trivial DL relation between the public parameters $g_1, \ldots, g_n, h$. Protocols that satisfy this computational variant of soundness are also called *arguments of knowledge*. Later we will also consider different set up assumptions, based on Strong-RSA of Knowledge of Exponent derived assumptions. Finally, we will consider standard notions of zero-knowledge such *special honest verifier zero-knowledge* (SHVZK).

3   The Basic Pivot

This section formally describes the Pedersen vector commitment scheme and our pivotal Σ-protocol, as discussed in Sect. 1.2 (A). In addition, we describe a standard amortized Σ-protocol for opening a linear form on many commitments.

3.1   The Basic Σ-protocol

The primary commitment scheme under consideration in this paper is the Pedersen vector commitment scheme.

Definition 1. (Pedersen Vector Commitment [27]). *Let $\mathbb{G}$ be an Abelian group of prime order q. Pedersen vector commitments are defined by the following setup and commitment phase:*

- *Setup:* $\mathbf{g} = (g_1, \ldots, g_n) \leftarrow_R \mathbb{G}^n, \ h \leftarrow_R \mathbb{G}$.
- *Commit:* $\mathrm{COM} : \mathbb{Z}_q^n \times \mathbb{Z}_q \to \mathbb{G}, \quad (\mathbf{x}, \gamma) \mapsto h^\gamma \mathbf{g}^{\mathbf{x}} := h^\gamma \prod_{i=1}^n g_i^{x_i}$.

We define $\mathbf{g}^{\mathbf{x}} := \prod_{i=1}^n g_i^{x_i}$ and $\mathbf{g}^c := (g_1^c, g_2^c, \ldots, g_n^c)$ for any $\mathbf{g} \in \mathbb{G}^n$, $\mathbf{x} \in \mathbb{Z}_q^n$ and $c \in \mathbb{Z}_q$. Moreover, the component-wise product between two vectors $\mathbf{g}, \mathbf{h} \in \mathbb{G}^n$ is written as $\mathbf{g} * \mathbf{h} = (g_1 h_1, g_2 h_2, \ldots, g_n h_n)$.

Pedersen vector commitments are perfectly hiding and computationally binding under the assumption that the prover does not know a non-trivial discrete log relation between the generators $g_1, \ldots, g_n, h$.

To open a commitment to a linear form $L : \mathbb{Z}_q^n \to \mathbb{Z}_q$ means that the prover wishes to reveal $L(\mathbf{x})$ together with a proof of validity without revealing any additional information on $\mathbf{x}$. Achieving this functionality amounts for the prover to send the value $L(\mathbf{x})$ along with a ZKPoK for the relation

$$R = \big\{ \big(P \in \mathbb{G}, L \in \mathcal{L}\left(\mathbb{Z}_q^n\right), y \in \mathbb{Z}_q; \mathbf{x} \in \mathbb{Z}_q^n, \gamma \in \mathbb{Z}_q \big): \\ P = \mathbf{g}^{\mathbf{x}} h^\gamma, y = L(\mathbf{x}) \big\}, \tag{1}$$

where we use the following definition for the set of linear forms on $\mathbb{Z}_q^n$.

Definition 2. $\mathcal{L}\left(\mathbb{Z}_q^n\right) := \{(L : Z_q^n \to \mathbb{Z}_q) : L \text{ is a } \mathbb{Z}_q\text{-linear map}\}$. Protocol 1, denoted by Π_0, shows a basic Σ-protocol for relation R. Π_0 was informally described in Sect. 1.2 (A). Theorem 1 shows that Π_0 is indeed a special honest-verifier zero-knowledge (SHVZK) Proof of Knowledge (PoK). Both the communication costs from the prover $\mathcal{P}$ to the verifier $\mathcal{V}$ and vice versa are given. Note that in the non-interactive Fiat-Shamir [16] mode the communication costs from verifier to prover might be irrelevant.

Theorem 1 (Basic Pivot). *Π_0 is a 3-move protocol for relation R. It is perfectly complete, special honest-verifier zero-knowledge and unconditionally special sound. Moreover, the communication costs are:*

- *$\mathcal{P} \to \mathcal{V}$: 1 element of $\mathbb{G}$ and $n + 2$ elements of $\mathbb{Z}_q$.*
- *$\mathcal{V} \to \mathcal{P}$: 1 element of $\mathbb{Z}_q$.*

3.2   Amortization over Many Commitments

A standard amortization technique for Σ-protocols allows a prover to show correctness of s evaluations of the linear form L on s committed vectors for essentially the costs of one evaluation. For details we refer to the full-version of this paper [1].

Protocol 1 Σ-protocol Π_0 for relation R

Σ-protocol to prove correctness of a linear form evaluation.

PUBLIC PARAMETERS : $\mathbf{g} \in \mathbb{G}^n, h \in \mathbb{G}$

INPUT$(P, L, y; \mathbf{x}, \gamma)$

$$P = \mathbf{g}^{\mathbf{x}} h^{\gamma} \in \mathbb{G}$$
$$y = L(\mathbf{x}) \in \mathbb{Z}_q$$

Prover		Verifier

$\mathbf{r} \leftarrow_R \mathbb{Z}_q^n, \rho \leftarrow_R \mathbb{Z}_q$

$t = L(\mathbf{r})$

$A = \mathbf{g}^{\mathbf{r}} h^{\rho}$ $\qquad \xrightarrow{\quad t, A \quad}$

$\qquad\qquad\qquad\qquad\qquad\qquad\qquad c \leftarrow_R \mathbb{Z}_q$

$\qquad\qquad\qquad\qquad \xleftarrow{\quad c \quad}$

$\mathbf{z} = c\mathbf{x} + \mathbf{r}$

$\phi = c\gamma + \rho$

$\qquad\qquad\qquad \xrightarrow{\quad \mathbf{z}, \phi \quad}$

$\qquad\qquad\qquad\qquad\qquad\qquad\qquad \mathbf{g}^{\mathbf{z}} h^{\phi} \overset{?}{=} AP^c$

$\qquad\qquad\qquad\qquad\qquad\qquad\qquad L(\mathbf{z}) \overset{?}{=} cy + t$

---

4   Compressing the Pivot

This section shows how Bulletproof techniques can be applied to compress our pivotal Σ-protocol Π_0, as mentioned in Sect. 1.2 (B). The key observation is that sending the final message $\widehat{\mathbf{z}} := (\mathbf{z}, \phi) \in \mathbb{Z}_q^{n+1}$ is actually a (trivial) proof of knowledge for the relation

$$R_1 = \left\{ \left(\widehat{P}, \widehat{L}, \widehat{y}; \widehat{\mathbf{z}} \right) : \widehat{\mathbf{g}}^{\widehat{\mathbf{z}}} = \widehat{P} \wedge \widehat{y} = \widehat{L}(\widehat{\mathbf{z}}) \right\}, \tag{2}$$

where, with respect to relation R, $\widehat{\mathbf{g}} := (g_1, \ldots, g_n, h) \in \mathbb{G}^{n+1}, \widehat{P} := AP^c, \widehat{y} := cy + t$ and $\widehat{L}(\mathbf{z}, \phi) := L(\mathbf{z})$ for all $(\mathbf{z}, \phi)$. Another PoK would also suffice, in particular a PoK with a smaller communication complexity. Moreover, it is immaterial that the PoK is zero-knowledge as the original PoK clearly is not. In [5] this observation was applied to Groth's Σ-protocol [20]. The main difference is that we start with linear form relation R, whereas Groth's Σ-protocol is for a specific quadratic relation.

Let Π be a PoK for relation R_1. We call the new protocol obtained by replacing the final move of protocol Π_0 by protocol Π the *composition* and write $\Pi \diamond \Pi_0$. Since Π_0 is SHVZK it immediately follows that the composition is also SHVZK.

The essence of Bulletproofs is a PoK, denoted by BP, with logarithmic communication complexity for the following inner product relation,

$$R_{\text{bullet}} = \left\{ \left(P \in \mathbb{G}, u \in \mathbb{Z}_q; \mathbf{a}, \mathbf{b} \in \mathbb{Z}_q^n \right) : P = \mathbf{g}^{\mathbf{a}} \mathbf{h}^{\mathbf{b}} \wedge u = \langle \mathbf{a}, \mathbf{b} \rangle \right\}, \tag{3}$$

where $\mathbf{g}, \mathbf{h} \in \mathbb{G}^n$ are the public parameters. The quadratic relation R_{bullet} is quite similar to the relation R_1 and it turns out that minor adaptations of BP give a logarithmic size PoK for relation R_1. We will now describe the components of the BP protocol, while simultaneously adapting these to our relation R_1.

4.1   Reduction from Relation R_1 to Relation R_2

The first step of the BP PoK is to incorporate the linear form into the Pedersen vector commitment. For this step an additional generator $k \in \mathbb{G}$ is required such that the prover does not know a discrete log relation between the generators $g_1, \ldots, g_n, h, k$. More precisely, the problem of finding a proof for relation R_1 is reduced to the problem of finding a proof for relation

$$R_2 = \left\{ \left(Q \in \mathbb{G}, \widetilde{L} \in \mathcal{L}\left(\mathbb{Z}_q^{n+1}\right) ; \widehat{\mathbf{z}} \in \mathbb{Z}_q^{n+1} \right) : Q = \widehat{\mathbf{g}}^{\widehat{\mathbf{z}}} k^{\widetilde{L}(\widehat{\mathbf{z}})} \right\}. \tag{4}$$

where, $Q := \widehat{P} k^{\widehat{y}}$ and $\widetilde{L} := c\widehat{L}$ for a random challenge $c \in \mathbb{Z}_q$ sampled by the verifier. The reduction is described in Protocol 2 and denoted by Π_1. Lemma 1 shows that Π_1 is an argument of knowledge for relation R_1.

Lemma 1. Π_1 *is a 2-move protocol for relation* R_1. *It is perfectly complete and computationally special sound, under the discrete logarithm assumption. Moreover, the communication costs are:*

- $\mathcal{P} \to \mathcal{V}$: $n + 1$ *elements of* $\mathbb{Z}_q$.
- $\mathcal{V} \to \mathcal{P}$: 1 *element of* $\mathbb{Z}_q$.

Proof. **Completeness** follows directly.

Special Soundness: We show that there exists an efficient algorithm χ that, on input two accepting transcripts, either extracts a witness for R_1, or finds a non-trivial discrete log relation. So let $(c_1, \widehat{\mathbf{z}}_1)$ and $(c_2, \widehat{\mathbf{z}}_2)$ be two accepting transcripts with $c_1 \neq c_2$, then $\widehat{\mathbf{g}}^{\widehat{\mathbf{z}}_1 - \widehat{\mathbf{z}}_2} k^{c_1 \widehat{L}(\widehat{\mathbf{z}}_1) - c_2 \widehat{L}(\widehat{\mathbf{z}}_2)} = k^{(c_1 - c_2)\widehat{y}}$. Hence, either we have found a non-trivial discrete log relation, or $\widehat{\mathbf{z}}_1 = \widehat{\mathbf{z}}_2$ and $c_1 \widehat{L}(\widehat{\mathbf{z}}_1) - c_2 \widehat{L}(\widehat{\mathbf{z}}_2) = (c_1 - c_2)\widehat{y}$. In the latter case, it follows that $\widehat{L}(\widehat{\mathbf{z}}_1) = \widehat{L}(\widehat{\mathbf{z}}_2) = \widehat{y}$. Moreover, from this it follows that $\widehat{\mathbf{g}}^{\widehat{\mathbf{z}}_1} k^{c_1 \widehat{L}(\widehat{\mathbf{z}}_1)} = \widehat{P} k^{c_1 \widehat{y}}$ which implies $\widehat{\mathbf{g}}^{\widehat{\mathbf{z}}_1} = \widehat{P}$. Hence, $\widehat{\mathbf{z}}_1$ is a witness for relation R_1, which completes the proof.

4.2   Logarithmic Size PoK for Linear Relation R_2

Next we deploy the main technique of the Bulletproof protocol to construct an efficient PoK for relation R_2. For simplicity let us assume that $n + 1$ is a power of 2. If this is not the case the vector can be appended with zeros. The protocol is recursive and in each iteration the dimension of the witness is halved until its dimension equals 2. We could add one additional step to the recursion and only send the response when the dimension equals 1. This would reduce the

---

Protocol 2 Argument of Knowledge Π_1 for R_1
Reduction from relation R_1 to relation R_2.

PUBLIC PARAMETERS $: \widehat{\mathbf{g}} \in \mathbb{G}^{n+1}, k \in \mathbb{G}$
INPUT$(\widehat{P}, \widehat{L}, \widehat{y}; \widehat{\mathbf{z}})$

$$\widehat{P} = \widehat{\mathbf{g}}^{\widehat{\mathbf{z}}} \in \mathbb{G}$$
$$\widehat{y} = \widehat{L}(\widehat{\mathbf{z}}) \in \mathbb{Z}_q$$

Prover		Verifier
	$\xleftarrow{\quad c \quad}$	$c \leftarrow_R \mathbb{Z}_q$
	$\xrightarrow{\quad \widehat{\mathbf{z}} \quad}$	
		$\widehat{\mathbf{g}}^{\widehat{\mathbf{z}}} k^{c\widehat{L}(\widehat{\mathbf{z}})} \overset{?}{=} \widehat{P} k^{c\widehat{y}}$

---

communication costs by one field element, but it would increase the number of group elements sent by the prover by 2.

For any even dimension m and vector $\mathbf{g} \in \mathbb{G}^m$, we define $\mathbf{g}_L = (g_1, \ldots, g_{m/2})$ as its left half and $\mathbf{g}_R = (g_{m/2+1}, \ldots, g_m)$ as its right half. The same notation is used for vectors in $\mathbb{Z}_q^m$. For a linear form $L : \mathbb{Z}_q^m \to \mathbb{Z}_q$, we define

$$L_L : \mathbb{Z}_q^{m/2} \to \mathbb{Z}_q, \quad \mathbf{x} \mapsto L(\mathbf{x}, 0), \qquad L_R : \mathbb{Z}_q^{m/2} \to \mathbb{Z}_q, \quad \mathbf{x} \mapsto L(0, \mathbf{x}), \qquad (5)$$

where $(\mathbf{x}, 0), (0, \mathbf{x}) \in \mathbb{Z}_q^m$ are the vectors $\mathbf{x}$ appended with $m/2$ zeros on the right and left, respectively. Recall that the component-wise product between two vectors is denoted by $*$.

The compression is described in Protocol 3 and denoted by Π_2. Theorem 2 shows that protocol Π_2 is a proof of knowledge for relation R_2. Note that, in contrast to the compression mechanism of [7], protocol Π_2 is unconditionally $(3, \ldots, 3)$-special sound.

Theorem 2 (Compression Mechanism). Π_2 *is a* $(2\mu + 1)$*-move protocol for relation* R_2*, where* $\mu = \lceil \log_2(n+1) \rceil - 1$*. It is perfectly complete and unconditionally* $(k_1, \ldots, k_\mu)$*-special sound, where* $k_i = 3$ *for all* $1 \le i \le \mu$*. Moreover, the communication costs are:*

- $\mathcal{P} \to \mathcal{V}$: $2\lceil \log_2(n+1) \rceil - 2$ *elements of* $\mathbb{G}$ *and* 2 *elements of* $\mathbb{Z}_q$.
- $\mathcal{V} \to \mathcal{P}$: $\lceil \log_2(n+1) \rceil - 1$ *elements of* $\mathbb{Z}_q$.

Proof. **Completeness** follows directly.

Special Soundness follows in a similar manner as it does for the amortized Σ-protocol mentioned in Sect. 3.2. Namely, by the same "polynomial amortization trick" the commitments A, Q, B are combined in a single commitment $Q' := AQ^c B^{c^2}$ where c is a random challenge. Informally, if a prover can open commitment Q', it follows, with high probability, that a prover can open all three commitments A, Q and B. For completeness we include the detailed proof.

For simplicity we assume that we only run one of the recursive steps, i.e., we consider the 3-move variant of protocol Π_2, where the prover sends the response $\mathbf{z}'$ regardless of its dimension, and we show that this protocol is 3-special sound. From there $(3, \ldots, 3)$-special soundness follows by an inductive argument of which we omit the details.

So let us show that there exists an efficient algorithm χ that, on input 3 accepting transcripts $(A, B, c_1, \mathbf{z}_1)$, $(A, B, c_2, \mathbf{z}_2)$, $(A, B, c_3, \mathbf{z}_3)$, with $c_i \neq c_j$ for all i, j, outputs a witness for relation R_2. Given these transcripts let us define Vandermonde matrix

$$V = \begin{pmatrix} 1 & 1 & 1 \\ c_1 & c_2 & c_3 \\ c_1^2 & c_2^2 & c_3^2 \end{pmatrix}, \tag{6}$$

with $\det(V) = (c_3 - c_1)(c_3 - c_1)(c_3 - c_2)$. Since $c_i \neq c_j$ for all i, j, it follows that V is invertible and that we can define

$$\begin{pmatrix} a_1 & a_2 & a_3 \end{pmatrix}^T := V^{-1} \begin{pmatrix} 0 & 1 & 0 \end{pmatrix}^T. \tag{7}$$

Now it is easily seen that, for $\bar{\mathbf{z}} := \left(\sum_{i=1}^3 a_i \mathbf{z}_i, \sum_{i=1}^3 a_i c_i \mathbf{z}_i \right)$, it holds that $\mathbf{g}^{\bar{\mathbf{z}}} k^{\tilde{L}(\bar{\mathbf{z}})} = Q$. Hence, $\mathbf{z}$ is a witness for relation R_2, which proves the claim.

Protocol 3 Compressed Proof of Knowledge Π_2 for R_2

PUBLIC PARAMETERS : $\widehat{\mathbf{g}}, k$
INPUT$(Q, \widetilde{L}; \widehat{\mathbf{z}})$
$Q = \widehat{\mathbf{g}}^{\widehat{\mathbf{z}}} k^{\tilde{L}(\widehat{\mathbf{z}})}$

Prover   Verifier

$A = \widehat{\mathbf{g}}_R^{\widehat{\mathbf{z}}_L} k^{\tilde{L}_R(\widehat{\mathbf{z}}_L)}$
$B = \widehat{\mathbf{g}}_L^{\widehat{\mathbf{z}}_R} k^{\tilde{L}_L(\widehat{\mathbf{z}}_R)}$ $\xrightarrow{\quad A,B \quad}$

                                                                        $c \leftarrow_R \mathbb{Z}_q$

                                                                $\xleftarrow{\quad c \quad}$

                        $\mathbf{g}' := \widehat{\mathbf{g}}_L^c * \widehat{\mathbf{g}}_R \in \mathbb{G}^{(n+1)/2}$
                        $Q' := A Q^c B^{c^2}$
                        $L' := c\tilde{L}_L + \tilde{L}_R$

$\mathbf{z}' = \widehat{\mathbf{z}}_L + c\widehat{\mathbf{z}}_R$
if $\left(\mathbf{z}' \in \mathbb{Z}_q^2 \right)$: $\xrightarrow{\quad \mathbf{z}' \quad}$ $(\mathbf{g}')^{\mathbf{z}'} k^{L'(\mathbf{z}')} \stackrel{?}{=} Q'$

else :   Run $\Pi_2(Q', L'; \mathbf{z}')$ with
                                PUBLIC PARAMETERS : $\mathbf{g}', k$

4.3   Composing the Building Blocks

The compressed Σ-protocol Π_c for relation R is the composition of the previously mentioned protocols, i.e., $\Pi_c := \Pi_2 \diamond \Pi_1 \diamond \Pi_0$. For a graphical protocol description of Π_c we refer to the full-version of this paper [1]. Theorem 3 shows that Π_c is indeed a SHVZK argument of knowledge for relation R with a logarithmic communication complexity.

Theorem 3 (Compressed Pivot). *Π_c is a $(2\mu+3)$-move protocol for relation R, where $\mu = \lceil \log_2(n+1) \rceil - 1$. It is perfectly complete, special honest-verifier zero-knowledge and computationally $(2, 2, k_1, \ldots, k_\mu)$-special sound, under the discrete logarithm assumption, where $k_i = 3$ for all $1 \le i \le \mu$. Moreover, the communication costs are:*

 – *$\mathcal{P} \to \mathcal{V}$: $2 \lceil \log_2(n+1) \rceil - 1$ elements of $\mathbb{G}$ and 3 elements of $\mathbb{Z}_q$.*
 – *$\mathcal{V} \to \mathcal{P}$: $\lceil \log_2(n+1) \rceil + 1$ elements of $\mathbb{Z}_q$.*

Proof. **Completeness** follows directly from the completeness of Π_0, Π_1 and Π_2.

SHVZK follows since Π_0 is SHVZK. The simulator for Π_c namely runs the simulator for Π_0 and continues with honest executions of Π_1 and Π_2.

Special soundness follows from a straightforward combination of the extraction algorithms of protocols Π_0, Π_1 and Π_2.

In a completely analogous manner, the amortized Σ-protocol Π_0^{Am} of Sect. 3.2 can be compressed. For the properties of the amortized and compressed Σ-protocol we refer to the full-version of this paper [1].

4.4 Compressed Pivot with Unconditional Soundness

Note that since protocol Π_1 has computational soundness so does the compressed pivot Π_c. In the full-version of this paper [1] we show two approaches for deriving an unconditionally sound compressed pivot.

4.5 A Remark on Sublinear Communication Complexity

A straightforward adaptation of the compression techniques from Sect. 4 allows the round complexity of the compressed pivot to be reduced from logarithmic to constant. However, this reduction comes at the cost of increasing the communication complexity from $O(\log(n))$ to $O(\sqrt{n})$ elements. For more details on this trade-off we refer to the full-version of this paper [1].

5 The Compressed Pivot as a Black-Box

From this point on, the only facts about the pivot that we need is that we have access to a compact vector commitment scheme that allows a prover to open *arbitrary* linear forms on *multiple* commitments. Hence, we assume black-box access to such a pivot. First, we treat the utility enhancements mentioned in Sect. 1.2 (A). Second, we describe the compactification techniques as discussed in Sect. 1.2 (C).

We use the following notation. We write $[\mathbf{x}]$ for a compact commitment to a vector $\mathbf{x} \in \mathbb{Z}_q^n$, and for a (public) linear form L we write $\Pi_{\mathrm{OPEN}}([\mathbf{x}], L; \mathbf{x})$ for the interactive protocol that reveals $L(\mathbf{x})$ and nothing else to the verifier. Recall that our notation $\Pi_{\text{OPEN}}([\mathbf{x}], L; \mathbf{x})$ means that interactive protocol Π_{OPEN} takes as public input $[\mathbf{x}]$ and L and as prover's private input $\mathbf{x}$. The communication costs of Π_{OPEN} are equal to the cost of the underlying interactive protocol (Π_c) plus 1 field element from $\mathcal{P}$ to $\mathcal{V}$ (the output of L), unless of course the output is known in advance. Similarly, we write $\Pi_{\text{OPEN}}([\mathbf{x}_1], \ldots, [\mathbf{x}_s], L; \mathbf{x}_1, \ldots, \mathbf{x}_s)$ for the (amortized) interactive protocol that exclusively reveals $L(\mathbf{x}_i)$ for $1 \leq i \leq s$ to the verifier.

At this point, the implementation details of the compact commitment scheme do not matter anymore. However, when we give soundness properties and communication costs it is implicitly assumed that $[\cdot]$ is instantiated with Pedersen vector commitments and compressed Σ-protocol Π_c.

5.1   Many Nullity Checks for the Price of One

A "polynomial amortization trick" (known, e.g., from MPC) allows us to do many nullity checks on the committed vector $\mathbf{x}$ without a substantial increase in complexity. Consider linear forms $L_1, \ldots, L_s$ and *suppose the prover claims that $L_i(\mathbf{x}) = 0$ for $i = 1 \ldots, s$*. The verifier then samples $\rho \in \mathbb{Z}_q$ uniformly at random and asks the prover to open the linear form $L(\mathbf{x}) := \sum_{i=1}^{s} L_i(\mathbf{x})\rho^{i-1}$, i.e., prover and verifier run $\Pi_{\text{OPEN}}([\mathbf{x}], L; \mathbf{x})$. The opening of $L(\mathbf{x})$ equals the evaluation of some polynomial of degree at most $s - 1$. If this polynomial is non-zero, it has at most $s - 1$ zero's. Hence, $L(\mathbf{x}) = 0$ implies that $L_i(\mathbf{x}) = 0$ for all i with probability at least $1 - (s - 1)/q$. When q is exponential and s is polynomial in the security parameter this probability is exponentially close to 1. We write $\Pi_{\text{NULLITY}}([\mathbf{x}], L_1, \ldots, L_s; , \mathbf{x})$ for this protocol. The communication costs are equal to the costs of a single nullity-check ($s = 1$) plus one additional $\mathbb{Z}_q$ element from $\mathcal{V}$ to $\mathcal{P}$ (the challenge ρ).

The above discussion holds *verbatim* when we replace the linear forms by affine forms $\Phi_1, \ldots, \Phi_s$, for which we also write $\Pi_{\text{NULLITY}}([\mathbf{x}], \Phi_1, \ldots, \Phi_s; \mathbf{x})$. Moreover, by the amortized and compressed Σ-protocol Π_c^{Am} these techniques directly carry over to the scenario where the prover makes the *same* nullity claims over many *different* commitments.

5.2   Opening Affine Maps

Many ZK scenarios can be reduced to nullity-checks and, as such, the above utility enhancement is extremely powerful. As an often encountered example, we specifically mention the functionality of opening arbitrary affine maps $\Phi : \mathbb{Z}_q^n \to \mathbb{Z}_q^s$, $\mathbf{x} \mapsto A\mathbf{x} + b$, at the cost of increasing the communication by exactly $s - 1$ values in $\mathbb{Z}_q$ in comparison to opening one linear form (i.e., the evaluations of $s-1$ additional outputs). Note that Φ is the combination of s affine forms. The protocol goes as follows. The prover reveals the evaluation $\mathbf{y} = \Phi(\mathbf{x})$ followed by an amortized nullity-check on the affine forms $\Phi_1(\mathbf{x}) - y_1, \ldots, \Phi_s(\mathbf{x}) - y_s$. For the interactive protocol that opens an affine map Φ we write $\Pi_{\text{OPEN}}([\mathbf{x}], \Phi; \mathbf{x})$.

As before, this protocol directly caries over the scenario where a prover opens the evaluations of Φ on many committed vectors. The communications costs are only increased by the additional evaluations, i.e., the communication costs of the underlying compressed Σ-protocol remain the same. Note that in this case amortization is applied twice. First, at the Σ-protocol level, allowing many commitments to be considered. Second, only requiring black-box access to the pivotal Σ-protocols, allowing many affine forms to be considered.

5.3   Compactifying a Vector of Commitments

So far, we have shown how to open many linear forms L applied to a compactly committed secret vector $\mathbf{x}$ with low complexity. Dealing with nonlinear functions of a secret-vector-of-interest $\mathbf{x}$ will, as shown in Sect. 6, require that the prover, at the starting point, is *also* committed to a vector aux consisting of *correlated secret randomness*. As the method will consist of opening appropriate linear forms on the *entire vector* given by the pair $(\mathbf{x}, \text{aux})$, it will be assumed that the prover is committed to this pair via a *single* compact commitment.

Now, from a practical application perspective, it is likely that the prover is *already* committed to $\mathbf{x}$ before the start of a ZK proof. Consider, for example, the following two extreme cases:

- **Case 1:** The prover is committed to $\mathbf{x}$ in a *single* compact commitment. This scenario may be said to correspond to a "textbook" ZK setting.
- **Case 2:** The prover is committed to the coordinates of $\mathbf{x}$ *individually*. This scenario is relevant in practical situations with a natural dynamic where provers deliver committed data in subsequent transactions and only periodically prove in ZK some property on the compound information.

In order to deal with each of these scenarios, we need some further utility enhancements of the compressed pivot in order to bring about the desired starting point for the methods from Sect. 6, *without too much loss in communication*. It turns out that this is just a matter of "technology", i.e., plug and play with our compressed pivot and its basic theory suffices.

Besides these extreme cases one can consider hybrid scenarios in which the secret-vector-of-interest $\mathbf{x}$ is dispersed over various compact commitments. The methods described below *both* carry over to hybrid scenarios. The optimal approach depends on specific properties of the scenario. Namely, the communication complexity of the "Case 1 enhancement" is linear in the number of commitments, whereas the communication complexity of the "Case 2 enhancement" is linear in the (maximum) dimension of the committed vectors.

Case 1. We describe a straightforward approach. *We use the homomorphic property of Pedersen commitments*. The prover has a compact commitment P to $\mathbf{x}$. Taking from the public set-up information a new set of generators *disjoint* from the initial set that, supposedly, underlies P, the prover creates a compact commitment Q to aux. Eventually, the prover will set $P' := P \cdot Q$ as the compact commitment to the secret pair $(\mathbf{x}, \text{aux})$, a *join*. But, first, the prover must show that **x** and aux "live on disjoint sets of generators". This is just a nullity check, basically. The prover shows that, in P, there is a window of zeros w.r.t. the new generators, i.e., each occurs to the power 0. Similarly for Q but with a window of zeros w.r.t. the initial set of generators. By the methods for amortized nullity checks described earlier, this is handled with logarithmic communication. In fact, for the methods of Sect. 6 to work, it is easy to see that it suffices to perform the check on Q only. However, since the methods of Sect. 6 would be applied *serially*, i.e., *after* the join above, this would incur a constant multiplicative factor 2 loss in communication efficiency. We show how it can be done *in parallel*, thereby avoiding any such loss.

The amortized pivot allows a prover to open *one* linear form on *many* compact commitments efficiently. By the amortized nullity checks a prover can open *many* linear forms on *one* compact commitments efficiently. Together these amortization techniques almost suffice, except that they force a prover to open linear forms "intended" for one particular commitment on *other* commitments as well; they reveal the *cross-terms*. Thus, to prevent a privacy breach, we need to mask these cross-terms appropriately and we do this by constructing a small *shell* around commitments containing sufficient randomness. Masking the appropriate cross-terms returns us to the "standard" amortization scenario where the prover wishes to open one affine map on multiple compact commitments. The shells cause unintended evaluations to return random values, whereas intended evaluations are left unaltered. For the details we refer to the full-version of this paper [1].

Case 2. In this case we describe a simple, single protocol that integrates the compactification of a vector of commitments to individual coordinates of **x** together with a compact commitment to aux. See the full-version of this paper [1] for the details. Performing this integration in parallel with the methods of Sect. 6 is a straightforward application of the amortized nullity checks.

6   Proving Nonlinear Relations via Arithmetic Circuits

Using our compressed pivot as a black-box, this section describes how to obtain efficient zero-knowledge arguments for arbitrary arithmetic circuits. We consider arithmetic circuits C over $\mathbb{Z}_q$ with n inputs, s outputs and m multiplication gates. Addition and multiplication gates have fan-in 2 and unbounded fan-out. The number of addition gates is immaterial, as is the number of gates for scalar multiplication. For this reason m only refers to the multiplication gates that take two variable inputs. We fix an ordering $1, \ldots, n$ of the inputs and an ordering $1, \ldots, m$ of the multiplication gates.

The approach is to combine the compressed pivot with an adaptation of the work of [12] that shows how to prove arbitrary constraints on vectors of committed elements by exploiting techniques from secure multi-party computation. Concretely, we use the ideas underlying the Commitment Multiplication

Protocol from [10].[8] A detailed overview of the approach has been given in Sect. 1.2 (D). Here, we summarize the key points and formalize the main properties of the resulting protocols.

6.1 Basic Circuit Satisfiability

First, we consider the basic circuit satisfiability scenario in which a prover shows that it knows an input $\mathbf{x} \in \mathbb{Z}_q^n$ for which the arithmetic circuit C evaluates to 0. More precisely, we construct a ZK protocol for the following circuit satisfiability relation: $R_{cs} = \{(C; \mathbf{x}) : C(\mathbf{x}) = 0\}$.

Our approach follows the *commit and prove* paradigm, i.e., the prover commits to the witness $\mathbf{x}$ and subsequently proves that it satisfies the required relation. The terminology *circuit satisfiability* seems to suggest that we are only considering circuits for which it is hard to compute a satisfying witness $\mathbf{x}$. However, many practical scenarios consider circuits C for which it is easy to compute an $\mathbf{x}$ such that $C(\mathbf{x}) = 0$. In these scenarios the arithmetic circuit allows the prover to show that a committed vector satisfies certain properties.

If C is an affine map, i.e., without multiplication gates, the protocol follows directly from the (enhanced) functionality of our pivot. Namely, the prover commits to $\mathbf{x}$ and runs $\Pi_{\text{NULLITY}}([\mathbf{x}], C; \mathbf{x})$. Hence, addition gates and scalar multiplications, are implicitly handled since our pivot allows the opening of *arbitrary* linear forms.

Multiplication gates are handled by an appropriate adaptation of the techniques from [12]. Their primary result is a Σ-protocol showing correctness of m multiplication triples $(\alpha_i, \beta_i, \gamma_i)$. First, we recall the adaptation of their approach that uses our compressed pivot as a black-box. See also the first observation made in Sect. 1.2 (D). The protocol goes as follows.

- The prover selects a random polynomial $f(X) \in \mathbb{Z}_q[X]_{\leq m}$ that defines a packed secret sharing of the vector $(\alpha_1, \ldots, \alpha_m)$. The prover also selects a random polynomial $g(X) \in \mathbb{Z}_q[X]_{\leq m}$ that defines a packed secret sharing of the vector $(\beta_1, \ldots, \beta_m)$. Finally, the prover computes the product polynomial $h(X) := f(X)g(X)$ of degree $\leq 2m < q$.
- The prover commits to the vector

$$\mathbf{y} = (\alpha_1, \ldots, \alpha_m, \beta_1, \ldots, \beta_m, f(0), g(0), h(0), h(1), \ldots, h(2m)) \in \mathbb{Z}_q^{4m+3}$$

in a single compact commitment and sends the commitment to the verifier. Note that, by Lagrange interpolation, the polynomials $f(X)$, $g(X)$ and $h(X)$ are uniquely defined by the vector $\mathbf{y}$.
- The verifier selects a random challenge $c \in \mathbb{Z}_q$ distinct from $1, \ldots, m$ and sends it to the prover.

---

[8] For a general description of efficient ZK verification of secret multiplications, in terms of (strongly-multiplicative) arithmetic secret sharing, see Section 12.5.3 [11].

– Public linear combinations of the coefficients of $\mathbf{y}$ define three values: $u :=$ $f(c)$, $v := g(c)$ and $w := h(c)$. These values are opened and the verifier checks whether $w = uv$. A cheating prover is caught with probability greater than $1 - 2m/(q - m)$ and honest-verifier zero-knowledge essentially follows from 1-privacy of the secret sharing scheme.

Now we adapt this approach to the circuit satisfiability scenario, where we let $C : \mathbb{Z}_q^n \rightarrow \mathbb{Z}_q^s$ be an arbitrary arithmetic circuits with m multiplication gates. We use a simple fact about a circuit C. Consider the computation graph induced by evaluation at *input-vector* $\mathbf{x} \in \mathbb{Z}_q^n$. Write $\gamma_1, \ldots, \gamma_m \in \mathbb{Z}_q$ for the resulting *outputs of the multiplication gates*. For each i, write $(\alpha_i, \beta_i) \in \mathbb{Z}_q^2$ for the resulting *inputs to the i-th multiplication gate*. Finally, write $\omega \in \mathbb{Z}_q^s$ for the resulting *output of the circuit*. Then, for each i, there are *affine forms*[9] $u_i, v_i : \mathbb{Z}_q^{n+m} \rightarrow \mathbb{Z}_q$, depending only on C, such that, for all $\mathbf{x} \in \mathbb{Z}_q^n$, it holds that $\alpha_i = u_i(\mathbf{x}, \gamma_1, \ldots, \gamma_m)$ and $\beta_i = v_i(\mathbf{x}, \gamma_1, \ldots, \gamma_m)$. These forms are uniquely determined by the addition and scalar multiplication gates. Similarly, there is an affine function $w : \mathbb{Z}_q^{n+m} \rightarrow \mathbb{Z}_q^s$ such that, for all $\mathbf{x} \in \mathbb{Z}_q^n$, it holds that $\omega = w(\mathbf{x}, \gamma_1, \ldots, \gamma_m)$. In other words, a given pair $(\mathbf{x}, \gamma_1, \ldots, \gamma_m) \in \mathbb{Z}_q^n \times \mathbb{Z}_q^m$ can be completed to an accepting computation graph if and only if $u_i(\mathbf{x}, \gamma_1, \ldots, \gamma_m) \cdot v_i(\mathbf{x}, \gamma_1, \ldots, \gamma_m) = \gamma_i$ (for $i = 1, \ldots, m$) and $w(\mathbf{x}, \gamma_1, \ldots, \gamma_m) = 0$.

The vector $\mathbf{y}$, from the above multiplication-triples approach, is now adapted as follows. The prover includes the input vector $\mathbf{x}$. *However*, the α_i's and the β_i's are *omitted* from $\mathbf{y}$. Otherwise, the vector $\mathbf{y}$ is unchanged. In particular,

$$\mathbf{y} = (\mathbf{x}, f(0), g(0), h(0), h(1), \ldots, h(2m)) \in \mathbb{Z}_q^{n+2m+3}$$

and $(\mathbf{x}, \gamma_1, \ldots, \gamma_m) := (\mathbf{x}, h(1), \ldots, h(m))$ is a subvector of $\mathbf{y}$. Subsequently, the prover compactly commits to this adapted vector $\mathbf{y}$. By the handle discussed above, the prover needs to convince the verifier that (1) $w(\mathbf{x}, \gamma_1, \ldots, \gamma_m) = 0$, and that (2) $\alpha_i \cdot \beta_i = \gamma_i$ for all $1 \leq i \leq m$. *The α_i's and β_i's are now taken as the evaluation at* $(\mathbf{x}, \gamma_1, \ldots, \gamma_m)$ *of the affine functions* u_i, v_i *introduced above.* Note that we may capture all these as affine functions *evaluated at* $\mathbf{y}$.

As for (1), checking that $w(\mathbf{x}, \gamma_1, \ldots, \gamma_m) = 0$ is just a nullity check as provided by the pivot. As for (2), the polynomials $f(X)$, $g(X)$ are *still* well-defined by the prover's compact commitment to $\mathbf{y}$. Namely, $\rho := f(0)$, i.e., the randomness underlying its selection, is *still* included in $\mathbf{y}$. As the α_i's thus defined are affine functions of $\mathbf{y}$, the prover is still (implicitly) committed to a polynomial $f(X)$ of degree $\leq m$ such that $f(0) = \rho$ and $f(i) = \alpha_i$ ($i = 1, \ldots, m$) and evaluation of $f(X)$ in a point c is *still*, by composition of appropriate maps, an affine evaluation at $\mathbf{y}$, as enabled by the pivot. Since $\rho' := g(0)$ is also still included in $\mathbf{y}$, a similar conclusion is drawn about the β_i's, $g(X)$, and evaluation of the latter. As no changes with respect to $h(X)$ were made in $\mathbf{y}$, we conclude that the required check can be performed in the same way as before.

The costs of the different openings are reduced by applying the amortized nullity checks of Sect. 5.1. In fact, the communication costs are independent of the number of outputs s.

---

[9] $\mathbb{Z}_q$-linear forms plus a constant.

The protocol is formally described in Protocol 4 and denoted by Π_{cs}. Protocol Π_{cs} only requires black-box access to the commitment scheme $[\cdot]$. For notational convenience, we write

$$\Pi_{\text{NULLITY}}\left([\mathbf{y}], C(\mathbf{x}), f(c) - y_1, g(c) - y_2, h(c) - y_3; \mathbf{y}\right) \qquad (8)$$

for the amortized nullity check on the affine forms associated to the $s + 3$ coefficients of $(C(\mathbf{x}), f(c) - z_1, g(c) - z_2, h(c) - z_3)$.

Theorem 4 shows that, when $[\cdot]$ is instantiated with Pedersen vector commitments and compressed Σ-protocol Π_c, Π_{cs} is a SHVZK argument of knowledge for relation R_{cs}. The theorem also shows that the special soundness property depends on the number of multiplication gates in the circuit. If the circuit size is polynomial in the security parameter and q is exponential, then witness extended emulation follows from the special soundness property of Π_{cs}.

Theorem 4 (Basic Circuit ZK). *Π_{cs} is a $(2\mu + 7)$-move protocol for the circuit relation R_{cs}, where $\mu = \lceil \log_2(n + 2m + 4) \rceil - 1$. It is perfectly complete, special honest-verifier zero-knowledge and computationally $(2m + 1, s + 3, 2, 2, k_1, \ldots, k_\mu)$-special sound, under the discrete logarithm assumption, where $k_i = 3$ for all $1 \le i \le \mu$. Moreover, the communication costs are:*

- *$\mathcal{P} \to \mathcal{V}$: $2\lceil \log_2(n + 2m + 4) \rceil$ elements of $\mathbb{G}$ and 6 elements of $\mathbb{Z}_q$.*
- *$\mathcal{V} \to \mathcal{P}$: $\lceil \log_2(n + 2m + 4) \rceil + 3$ elements of $\mathbb{Z}_q$.*

Proof (Sketch). **Completeness** follows directly.

Special soundness: By Lagrange interpolation there exists an efficient algorithm to reconstruct a polynomial of degree t given $t + 1$ evaluations. Hence, the packed secret sharing and the amortized nullity-checks are $(2m + 1)$-special sound and $(s + 3)$-special sound, respectively. The soundness in these steps is computational, i.e., it is essential that the prover does not know a non-trivial discrete log relation. The special soundness claim now from the properties of protocol Π_c.

SHVZK follows from 1-privacy of the secret sharing scheme and the fact that Π_c is SHVZK.

6.2 Circuit ZK from Compactification

Thus far, we have restricted ourselves to the basic circuit satisfiability scenario where the prover commits to all input and auxiliary data at once. However, there is a great variety of other scenarios, where the circuit takes as input committed values. As in Sect. 5.3 we consider two extreme cases for circuit ZK:

- **Case 1.** Prove that $C(\mathbf{x}) = 0$ for a vector commitment $[\mathbf{x}]$ with $\mathbf{x} \in \mathbb{Z}_q^n$.
- **Case 2.** Prove that $C(x_1, \ldots, x_n) = 0$ for commitments $[x_i]$ with $x_i \in \mathbb{Z}_q$ for all i.

Protocol 4 Circuit Satisfiability Argument Π_{cs} for Relation R_{cs}

The polynomials f and g are sampled uniformly at random such that their evaluations in $1, \ldots, m$ coincide with the left and, respectively, right inputs of the m multiplication gates of C evaluated at $\mathbf{x}$.

$$\text{INPUT}(C; \mathbf{x})$$

$$C : \mathbb{Z}_q^n \to \mathbb{Z}_q^s$$
$$C(\mathbf{x}) = 0$$

Prover   Verifier

$f, g \leftarrow_R \mathbb{Z}_q[X]_{\leq m}$
$h(X) := f(X)g(X)$
$\mathbf{y} = (\mathbf{x}, f(0), g(0), h(0),$
$\quad h(1), \ldots, h(2m))$ $\xrightarrow{\quad [\mathbf{y}] \quad}$

                                                                $c \leftarrow_R \mathbb{Z}_q \setminus \{1, \ldots, m\}$

$z_1 = f(c)$ $\xleftarrow{\quad c \quad}$
$z_2 = g(c)$
$z_3 = h(c)$ $\xrightarrow{\quad z_1, z_2, z_3 \quad}$

                                                                $z_3 \stackrel{?}{=} z_1 z_2$

$$\Pi_{\text{NULLITY}} \left([\mathbf{y}], \begin{pmatrix} C(\mathbf{x}) \\ f(c) - z_1 \\ g(c) - z_2 \\ h(c) - z_3 \end{pmatrix}; \mathbf{z} \right)$$

These cases are dealt with by compactifying the commitments into a single compact commitment to all relevant data. The resulting protocol for Case 1 is denoted by $\Pi_{cs}^{(1)}$ with corresponding relation $R_{cs}^{(1)}$ and its properties are given by Theorem 5. Recall that we consider arithmetic circuits C over $\mathbb{Z}_q$ with n input, s output and m multiplication gates.

Theorem 5 (Circuit ZK Case 1). $\Pi_{cs}^{(1)}$ *is a* $(2\mu + 9)$*-move protocol for circuit relation* $R_{cs}^{(1)}$*, where* $\mu = \lceil \log_2(n + 2m + 6) \rceil - 1$*. It is perfectly complete, special honest-verifier zero-knowledge and computationally* $(2m + 1, \max(n, s + 3) + 1, 2, 2, 3, 2, k_1, \ldots, k_\mu)$*-special sound, under the discrete logarithm assumption, where* $k_i = 3$ *for all* $1 \leq i \leq \mu$*. Moreover, the communication costs are:*

- $\mathcal{P} \to \mathcal{V}$: $2 \lceil \log_2(n + 2m + 6) \rceil + 4$ *elements of* $\mathbb{G}$ *and* 12 *elements of* $\mathbb{Z}_q$.
- $\mathcal{V} \to \mathcal{P}$: $\lceil \log_2(n + 2m + 6) \rceil + 5$ *elements of* $\mathbb{Z}_q$.

The protocol for Case 2 is denoted by $\Pi_{cs}^{(2)}$ with corresponding relation $R_{cs}^{(2)}$ and its properties are given by Theorem 6. Note that in this case we can restrict ourselves to $n \leq 2m$. For if n is larger than the number of inputs to multiplication gates there must exist linear reductions that can be applied directly to the Pedersen commitments $[x_i]$ using its homomorphic properties. Therefore, the communication costs from prover to verifier are upper-bounded by

$2 \lceil \log_2(4m + 5) \rceil + 9 \leq 2 \lceil \log_2(m + 2) \rceil + 13$ elements. Bulletproofs achieve a communication cost of $2 \lceil \log(m) \rceil + 13$ elements. Hence, perhaps surprisingly, our plug-and-play approach almost never increases the communication costs.

Theorem 6 (Circuit ZK Case 2). $\Pi_{cs}^{(2)}$ *is a $(2\mu + 7)$-move protocol for circuit relation $R_{cs}^{(2)}$, where $\mu = \lceil \log_2(n + 2m + 5) \rceil - 1$. It is perfectly complete, special honest-verifier zero-knowledge and computationally $(2m + 1, n + 1, s + 4, 2, 2, k_1, \ldots, k_\mu)$-special sound, under the discrete logarithm assumption, where $k_i = 3$ for all $1 \leq i \leq \mu$. Moreover, the communication costs are:*

- $\mathcal{P} \to \mathcal{V}$: $2 \lceil \log_2(n + 2m + 5) \rceil + 1$ *elements of $\mathbb{G}$ and 8 elements of $\mathbb{Z}_q$.*
- $\mathcal{V} \to \mathcal{P}$: $\lceil \log_2(n + 2m + 5) \rceil + 4$ *elements of $\mathbb{Z}_q$.*

7   Range Proofs

In a range proof a prover wishes to show that a secret committed integer v is in a public range, say $[0, 2^{n-1}]$. For our range proofs, we invoke the circuit ZK protocols of Sect. 6 in a black-box manner and thereby achieve a conceptual simplification of earlier solutions such as those in [5,7]. Note that this black-box approach for range proofs can also be instantiated from the circuit ZK protocols of (e.g.) [5] and [7]. For details we refer to the full-version of this paper [1].

8   Our Program from the Strong-RSA Assumption

In this section we describe how our program can be based on Strong-RSA derived assumptions, as mentioned in Sect. 1.2 (F). We treat the main differences and refer to the full-version of this paper [1] and [8] for more details.

A disadvantage of the Pedersen vector commitment scheme is the number of generators required. In fact, to commit to an n-dimensional vector, $n + 1$ generators of the group $\mathbb{G}$ are required. Moreover, the compressed Σ-protocol Π_c has a verification time that is linear in the dimension n.

Alternatively, vector commitment schemes can be constructed via integer commitment schemes [15,17]. A commitment to the vector $\mathbf{x} \in \mathbb{Z}_q^n$ is then a commitment to an integer representation $\widehat{\mathbf{x}} \in \mathbb{Z}$ of $\mathbf{x}$. The integer commitment schemes of [15,17] are constructed by using groups $\mathbb{G}$ of unknown order.

This is precisely the approach followed in a recent work of Bünz, Fisch and Szepieniec [8]. They construct a polynomial commitment scheme allowing a prover to commit to a polynomial $f \in \mathbb{Z}_q[X]$ of arbitrary degree, via a unique integer representation of its coefficient vector. A commitment to such a representation only requires two group elements $g, h \in \mathbb{G}$.

The work of [8] shows how to open arbitrary evaluations $f(a) \in \mathbb{Z}_q$ of a committed polynomial without revealing any additional information about f. Their polynomial evaluation protocol uses recursive techniques similar to those used in Bulletproofs. This approach results in a logarithmic communication complexity. In addition, [8] deploys Proofs of Exponentiation (PoE) [28] to achieve logarithmic verification time.

Their work refers to generic constructions that can be used to obtain more general ZK protocols from polynomial commitment schemes. However, we argue that these constructions are overly complicated and that a stronger functionality (vector commitment scheme with linear form openings) avoids many difficulties in the design of ZK protocols. Moreover, it turns out that the protocols of [8] only require minor adaptations to accommodate this stronger functionality. From this, an instantiation of the black-box functionality of Sect. 5 is derived, now based on the hardness assumptions related to the Strong-RSA assumption [3]. The techniques of Sect. 6 and Sect. 7 directly apply, and the higher level applications inherit the logarithmic communication and computation complexity of the vector commitment scheme. The compactification methods of Sect. 5.3 are tailored to Pedersen (vector) commitments. Minor modifications are required to adapt these techniques to the Strong-RSA setting.

9   Our Program from the KEA

If one desires our program can also be instantiated from the Knowledge-of-Exponent Assumption (KEA), i.e., we construct a KEA based vector commitment scheme with compact linear form openings. The techniques from Sect. 6 apply as before, resulting in ZK protocols for arbitrary arithmetic circuits. Basing our program on KEA reduces communication complexity from logarithmic to *constant*. The protocols do require a trusted setup that depends on the arithmetic circuit under consideration.

We stress that KEA is of a different nature than the DL or strong-RSA assumption. KEA is not an intractability assumption and it is unfalsifiable [4,26]. For these reasons, its application is not completely without controversy.

We now, informally, describe the main components of the KEA based vector commitment scheme together with its ZK protocol for opening linear forms. Our approach uses the techniques of [22] and only minor adaptations are required.

A compact commitment to a vector $\mathbf{x} \in \mathbb{Z}_q^n$ is, as before, a Pedersen vector commitment $P = h^\gamma \mathbf{g}^\mathbf{x}$. A ZKPoK for knowing an opening to P is another Pedersen commitment P' to $\mathbf{x}$, under the same randomness γ, using a different set of generators $h' := h^\alpha, g_1' := g_1^\alpha, \ldots, g_n' := g_n^\alpha$. The value $\alpha \in \mathbb{Z}_q$ is sampled uniformly at random in the trusted setup phase and is only shared with a *designated* verifier. Both sets of generators are public and part of the common reference string. The proof P' is verified by checking that $P' = P^\alpha$.

The Knowledge-of-Exponent Assumption states that an adversary capable of computing pairs (P, P') with $P' = P^\alpha$, either knows α or an opening to P. From this assumption knowledge soundness follows. Correctness and zero-knowledge are immediate. Note that the resulting ZKPoK is non-interactive and its size is independent of the dimension n.

Given a bilinear pairing $e : \mathbb{G} \times \mathbb{G} \to \mathbb{G}_T$ the verification can be done without knowledge of α, eliminating the restriction to a designated verifier. In this case verification amounts to checking that $e(P, h') = e(h, P')$.

To prove that the committed vector $\mathbf{x}$ satisfies a linear form relation $L(\mathbf{x}) = u$, the generators are taken of a specific form. More precisely, the generators are sampled under the condition that $g_i = h^{\beta^i}$, for some secret $\beta \in \mathbb{Z}_q$, for all $1 \le i \le n$. The associated KEA derived assumption is the n-power Knowledge-of-Exponent Assumption (n-PKEA).

Groth showed that, using this additional structure, together with the bilinear pairing, efficient circuit ZK protocols exist [22]. His protocols are easily adapted to our situation, where we simply wish to prove correctness of a linear form evaluation. The adaptation relies on the following observation. Suppose that $\mathbf{a} = (a_1, \ldots, a_n) \in \mathbb{Z}_q^n$ is such that $L(\mathbf{z}) = \langle \mathbf{a}, \mathbf{z} \rangle$ for all $\mathbf{z} \in \mathbb{Z}_q^n$, and let us define the following polynomials: $f(Y) := \gamma + \sum_{i=1}^{n} x_i Y^i$, $g(Y) := \sum_{i=0}^{n-1} a_{n-i} Y^i$ and $h(Y) := f(Y)g(Y) = \sum_{i=0}^{2n-1} c_i Y^i$. The n-th coefficient of $h(Y)$ equals $c_n = \langle \mathbf{x}, \mathbf{a} \rangle = L(\mathbf{x})$. This observation allows for a straightforward adaptation of the product argument in [22, Section 6], resulting in a constant size ZKPoK for the correctness of a linear form evaluation. We omit further details and refer the reader to [22].

For circuit ZK protocols we apply the techniques from Sect. 6 to linearize the non-linearities in a black-box manner. In contrast, other KEA based approaches use a protocol for proving quadratic relations as their main pivot and translate arithmetic circuit relations to so called quadratic span programs or QSPs [19,21]. This translation, also called arithmetization, is not required when applying our linearization techniques. However, in contrast to other KEA based protocols, the linearization techniques render our solution interactive (although in a setting where Fiat-Shamir applies). Additionally, we note that this approach achieves constant verification complexity, in contrast to the linear complexity of the DL based approach, i.e., our KEA based protocol is a ZK-SNARK.

Acknowledgements. We thank Serge Fehr, Toon Segers and Thijs Veugen for extensive commenting at an early stage. We also thank Jens Groth for useful editorial comments and pointers. We are grateful for a comment by Michael Klooß that our exact analysis of knowledge error is only meaningful for a portion of the full parameter space relevant to our application. Thomas Attema has been supported by EU H2020 project No 780701 (PROMETHEUS). Ronald Cramer has been supported by ERC ADG project No 74079 (ALGSTRONGCRYPTO) and by the NWO Gravitation project QSC.

References

1. Full-version of this paper. IACR ePrint 2020/152
2. Attema, T., Cramer, R., Fehr, S.: Compressing proofs of k-out-of-n partial knowledge. IACR ePrint 2020/753
3. Barić, N., Pfitzmann, B.: Collision-free accumulators and fail-stop signature schemes without trees. In: Fumy, W. (ed.) EUROCRYPT 1997. LNCS, vol. 1233, pp. 480–494. Springer, Heidelberg (1997). https://doi.org/10.1007/3-540-69053-0_33
4. Bitansky, N., Canetti, R., Paneth, O., Rosen, A.: On the existence of extractable one-way functions. In: STOC, pp. 505–514. ACM (2014)

5. Bootle, J., Cerulli, A., Chaidos, P., Groth, J., Petit, C.: Efficient zero-knowledge arguments for arithmetic circuits in the discrete log setting. In: Fischlin, M., Coron, J.-S. (eds.) EUROCRYPT 2016. Part II. LNCS, vol. 9666, pp. 327–357. Springer, Heidelberg (2016). https://doi.org/10.1007/978-3-662-49896-5_12

6. Bootle, J., Lyubashevsky, V., Nguyen, N.K., Seiler, G.: A non-PCP approach to succinct quantum-safe zero-knowledge. IACR ePrint 2020/737

7. Bünz, B., Bootle, J., Boneh, D., Poelstra, A., Wuille, P., Maxwell, G.: Bulletproofs: short proofs for confidential transactions and more. In: IEEE S&P 2018, pp. 315–334 (2018)

8. Bünz, B., Fisch, B., Szepieniec, A.: Transparent SNARKs from DARK compilers. In: Canteaut, A., Ishai, Y. (eds.) EUROCRYPT 2020. Part I. LNCS, vol. 12105, pp. 677–706. Springer, Cham (2020). https://doi.org/10.1007/978-3-030-45721-1_24

9. Cramer, R.: Modular design of secure yet practical cryptographic protocols. Ph.D. thesis, CWI and University of Amsterdam (1996)

10. Cramer, R., Damgård, I., Maurer, U.M.: General secure multi-party computation from any linear secret-sharing scheme. In: Preneel, B. (ed.) EUROCRYPT 2000. LNCS, vol. 1807, pp. 316–334. Springer, Heidelberg (2000). https://doi.org/10.1007/3-540-45539-6_22

11. Cramer, R., Damgård, I., Nielsen, J.B.: Secure Multiparty Computation and Secret Sharing. Cambridge University Press, Cambridge (2015)

12. Cramer, R., Damgård, I., Pastro, V.: On the amortized complexity of zero knowledge protocols for multiplicative relations. In: Smith, A. (ed.) ICITS 2012. LNCS, vol. 7412, pp. 62–79. Springer, Heidelberg (2012). https://doi.org/10.1007/978-3-642-32284-6_4

13. Cramer, R., Damgård, I., Schoenmakers, B.: Proofs of partial knowledge and simplified design of witness hiding protocols. In: Desmedt, Y.G. (ed.) CRYPTO 1994. LNCS, vol. 839, pp. 174–187. Springer, Heidelberg (1994). https://doi.org/10.1007/3-540-48658-5_19

14. Damgård, I.: On sigma-protocols. Lecture Notes, Aarhus University, Department of Computer Science (2010)

15. Damgård, I., Fujisaki, E.: A statistically-hiding integer commitment scheme based on groups with hidden order. In: Zheng, Y. (ed.) ASIACRYPT 2002. LNCS, vol. 2501, pp. 125–142. Springer, Heidelberg (2002). https://doi.org/10.1007/3-540-36178-2_8

16. Fiat, A., Shamir, A.: How to prove yourself: practical solutions to identification and signature problems. In: Odlyzko, A.M. (ed.) CRYPTO 1986. LNCS, vol. 263, pp. 186–194. Springer, Heidelberg (1987). https://doi.org/10.1007/3-540-47721-7_12

17. Fujisaki, E., Okamoto, T.: Statistical zero knowledge protocols to prove modular polynomial relations. In: Kaliski, B.S. (ed.) CRYPTO 1997. LNCS, vol. 1294, pp. 16–30. Springer, Heidelberg (1997). https://doi.org/10.1007/BFb0052225

18. Gabizon, A., Williamson, Z.J., Ciobotaru, O.: PLONK: permutations over Lagrange-bases for oecumenical noninteractive arguments of knowledge. IACR ePrint 2019/953

19. Gennaro, R., Gentry, C., Parno, B., Raykova, M.: Quadratic span programs and succinct NIZKs without PCPs. In: Johansson, T., Nguyen, P.Q. (eds.) EUROCRYPT 2013. LNCS, vol. 7881, pp. 626–645. Springer, Heidelberg (2013). https://doi.org/10.1007/978-3-642-38348-9_37

20. Groth, J.: Linear algebra with sub-linear zero-knowledge arguments. In: Halevi, S. (ed.) CRYPTO 2009. LNCS, vol. 5677, pp. 192–208. Springer, Heidelberg (2009). https://doi.org/10.1007/978-3-642-03356-8_12

21. Groth, J.: On the size of pairing-based non-interactive arguments. In: Fischlin, M., Coron, J.-S. (eds.) EUROCRYPT 2016. Part II. LNCS, vol. 9666, pp. 305–326. Springer, Heidelberg (2016). https://doi.org/10.1007/978-3-662-49896-5_11

22. Groth, J.: Short pairing-based non-interactive zero-knowledge arguments. In: Abe, M. (ed.) ASIACRYPT 2010. LNCS, vol. 6477, pp. 321–340. Springer, Heidelberg (2010). https://doi.org/10.1007/978-3-642-17373-8_19

23. Hoffmann, M., Klooß, M., Rupp, A.: Efficient zero-knowledge arguments in the discrete log setting, revisited. In: ACM CCS (2019)

24. Lindell, Y.: Parallel coin-tossing and constant-round secure two-party computation. J. Cryptol. **16**(3), 143–184 (2003). https://doi.org/10.1007/s00145-002-0143-7

25. Maller, M., Bowe, S., Kohlweiss, M., Meiklejohn, S.: Sonic: zero-knowledge snarks from linear-size universal and updatable structured reference strings. In: ACM CCS, pp. 2111–2128 (2019)

26. Naor, M.: On cryptographic assumptions and challenges. In: Boneh, D. (ed.) CRYPTO 2003. LNCS, vol. 2729, pp. 96–109. Springer, Heidelberg (2003). https://doi.org/10.1007/978-3-540-45146-4_6

27. Pedersen, T.P.: Non-interactive and information-theoretic secure verifiable secret sharing. In: Feigenbaum, J. (ed.) CRYPTO 1991. LNCS, vol. 576, pp. 129–140. Springer, Heidelberg (1992). https://doi.org/10.1007/3-540-46766-1_9

28. Wesolowski, B.: Efficient Verifiable Delay Functions. In: Ishai, Y., Rijmen, V. (eds.) EUROCRYPT 2019. Part III. LNCS, vol. 11478, pp. 379–407. Springer, Cham (2019). https://doi.org/10.1007/978-3-030-17659-4_13

29. Wikström, D.: Special soundness revisited. IACR ePrint 2018/1157

30. Xie, T., Zhang, J., Zhang, Y., Papamanthou, C., Song, D.: Libra: succinct zero-knowledge proofs with optimal prover computation. In: Boldyreva, A., Micciancio, D. (eds.) CRYPTO 2019. Part III. LNCS, vol. 11694, pp. 733–764. Springer, Cham (2019). https://doi.org/10.1007/978-3-030-26954-8_24

A Tight Parallel Repetition Theorem for Partially Simulatable Interactive Arguments via Smooth KL-Divergence

Itay Berman[1], Iftach Haitner[2], and Eliad Tsfadia[2]($\boxtimes$)

[1] MIT, Cambridge, USA
itayberm@mit.edu
[2] School of Computer Science, Tel Aviv University, Tel Aviv, Israel
iftachh@cs.tau.ac.il, eliadtsf@tau.ac.il

Abstract. Hardness amplification is a central problem in the study of interactive protocols. While "natural" parallel repetition transformation is known to reduce the soundness error of some special cases of interactive arguments: three-message protocols (Bellare, Impagliazzo, and Naor [FOCS '97]) and public-coin protocols (Håstad, Pass, Wikström, and Pietrzak [TCC '10], Chung and Liu [TCC '10] and Chung and Pass [TCC '15]), it fails to do so in the general case (the above Bellare et al.; also Pietrzak and Wikström [TCC '07]).

The only known round-preserving approach that applies to all interactive arguments is Haitner's *random-terminating* transformation [SICOMP '13], who showed that the parallel repetition of the transformed protocol reduces the soundness error at a *weak* exponential rate: if the original m-round protocol has soundness error $1 - \varepsilon$, then the n-parallel repetition of its random-terminating variant has soundness error $(1 - \varepsilon)^{\varepsilon n/m^4}$ (omitting constant factors). Håstad et al. have generalized this result to *partially simulatable interactive arguments*, showing that the n-fold repetition of an m-round δ-simulatable argument of soundness error $1 - \varepsilon$ has soundness error $(1 - \varepsilon)^{\varepsilon\delta^2 n/m^2}$. When applied to random-terminating arguments, the Håstad et al. bound matches that of Haitner.

In this work we prove that parallel repetition of random-terminating arguments reduces the soundness error at a much stronger exponential rate: the soundness error of the n parallel repetition is $(1 - \varepsilon)^{n/m}$, only an m factor from the optimal rate of $(1 - \varepsilon)^n$ achievable in public-coin and three-message arguments. The result generalizes to δ-simulatable

Due to space limitations, the reader is referred to the full version [2].

I. Berman—Research supported in part by NSF Grants CNS-1413920 and CNS-1350619, and by the Defense Advanced Research Projects Agency (DARPA) and the U.S. Army Research Office under contracts W911NF-15-C-0226 and W911NF-15-C-0236.

I. Haitner—Member of the Check Point Institute for Information Security.

I. Haitner and E. Tsfadia—Research supported by ERC starting grant 638121 and Israel Science Foundation grant 666/19.

© International Association for Cryptologic Research 2020
D. Micciancio and T. Ristenpart (Eds.): CRYPTO 2020, LNCS 12172, pp. 544–573, 2020.
https://doi.org/10.1007/978-3-030-56877-1_19

arguments, for which we prove a bound of $(1 - \varepsilon)^{\delta n/m}$. This is achieved by presenting a tight bound on a relaxed variant of the KL-divergence between the distribution induced by our reduction and its ideal variant, a result whose scope extends beyond parallel repetition proofs. We prove the tightness of the above bound for random-terminating arguments, by presenting a matching protocol.

Keywords: Parallel repetition · Interactive argument · Partially simulatable · Smooth KL-divergence

1 Introduction

Hardness amplification is a central question in the study of computation: can a somewhat secure primitive be made fully secure, and, if so, can this be accomplished without loss (i.e., while preserving certain desirable properties the original primitive may have). In this paper we focus on better understanding the above question with respect to interactive arguments (also known as, computationally sound proofs). In an interactive argument, a prover tries to convince a verifier in the validity of a statement. The basic properties of such proofs are *completeness* and *soundness*. Completeness means that the prover, typically using some extra information, convinces the verifier to accept valid statements with high probability. Soundness means that a cheating *polynomial-time* prover cannot convince the verifier to accept invalid statements, except with small probability. Interactive arguments should be compared with the related notion of *interactive proofs*, whose soundness should hold against *unbounded* provers. Interactive argument are important for being "sufficiently secure" proof system that sometimes achieve properties (e.g., compactness) that are beyond the reach of interactive proofs. Furthermore, the security of many cryptographic protocols (e.g., binding of a computationally binding commitment) can be cast as the soundness of a related interactive argument, but (being computational) cannot be cast as the soundness of a related interactive proof.

The question of hardness amplification with respect to interactive arguments is whether an argument with *non-negligible* soundness error, i.e., a cheating prover can convince the verifier to accept false statements with some non-negligible probability, can be transformed into a new argument, with similar properties, of negligible soundness error (i.e., the verifier almost never accepts false statements). The most common paradigm to obtain such an amplification is via *repetition*: repeat the protocol multiple times with independent randomness, and the verifier accepts only if the verifiers of the original protocol accept in *all* executions. Such repetitions can be done in two different ways, sequentially (known as *sequential repetition*), where the $(i+1)$ execution of the protocol starts only after the ith execution has finished, or in parallel (known as *parallel repetition*), where the executions are all simultaneous. Sequential repetition is known to reduce the soundness error in most computational models (cf., Damgård and Pfitzmann [9]), but has the undesired effect of increasing the round complexity of the protocol. Parallel repetition, on the other hand, does preserve the round complexity, and reduces the soundness error for (single-prover) interactive proofs (Goldreich [16]) and two-prover interactive proofs (Raz [25], Holenstein [19] Rao [24]). Parallel repetition was also shown to reduce the soundness error in three-message arguments ([1]) and public-coin arguments (Håstad, Pass, Wikström, and Pietrzak [18], Chung and Lu [5], Chung and Pass [8]). Unfortunately, as shown by Bellare et al. [1], and by Pietrzak and Wikström [23], parallel repetition *might not* reduce the soundness error of any interactive argument: assuming common cryptographic assumptions, [23] presented an 8-message interactive proof with constant soundness error, whose parallel repetition, for *any* polynomial number of repetitions, still has a constant soundness error.

Faced with the above barrier, Haitner [17] presented a simple method for transforming any interactive argument π into a slightly modified protocol $\widetilde{\pi}$, such that the parallel repetition of $\widetilde{\pi}$ does reduce the soundness error. Given any m-round interactive protocol $\pi = (P, V)$, let $\widetilde{V}$ be the following *random-terminating variant* of V: in each round, $\widetilde{V}$ flips a coin that takes one with probability $1/m$ and zero otherwise. If the coin outcome is one, $\widetilde{V}$ accepts and aborts the execution. Otherwise, $\widetilde{V}$ acts as V would, and continues to the next round. At the end of the prescribed execution, if reached, $\widetilde{V}$ accepts if and only if V would. Observe that if the original protocol π has soundness error $1 - \varepsilon$, then the new protocol $\widetilde{\pi} = (P, \widetilde{V})$ has soundness error $1 - \varepsilon/4$ (i.e., only slightly closer to one). Haitner [17] proved that the parallel repetition of $\widetilde{\pi}$ does reduce the soundness error (for any protocol π). Håstad, Pass, Wikström, and Pietrzak [18] have generalized the above to *partially-simulatable interactive arguments*, a family of interactive arguments that contains the random-terminating variant protocols as a special case. An interactive argument $\pi = (P, V)$ is δ-simulatable if given any partial view v of an efficient prover P* interacting with V, the verifier's future messages in (P*, V) can be simulated with probability δ. This means that one can efficiently sample a random continuation of the execution conditioned on an event of density δ over V's coins consistent with v. It is easy to see that the random-terminating variant of any protocol is $1/m$ simulatable. Unfortunately, the soundness bound proved by Haitner [17], Håstad et al. [18] lags way behind what one might have hoped for, making parallel repetition impractical in many typical settings. Assuming a δ-simulatable argument π has soundness error is $1 - \varepsilon$, then π^n, the n-parallel repetition of π, was shown to have soundness error $(1 - \varepsilon)^{\varepsilon \delta^2 n / m^2}$ (equals $(1 - \varepsilon)^{\varepsilon n / m^4}$ if π is a random-terminating variant), to be compared with the $(1 - \varepsilon)^n$ bound achieved by parallel repetition of interactive proofs, and by three-message and public-coin interactive arguments.[1] Apart from the intellectual challenge, improving the above bound is important since repeating the random-termination variant in parallel is the

---

[1] As in all known amplifications of computational hardness, and proven to be an inherent limitation (at least to some extent) in Dodis et al. [11], the improvement in the soundness error does not go below negligible. We ignore this subtly in the introduction. We also ignore constant factors in the exponent.

only known unconditional round-preserving amplification method for arbitrary interactive arguments.

1.1 Proving Parallel Repetition

Let $\pi = (P, V)$ be an interactive argument with assumed soundness error $1 - \varepsilon$, i.e., a polynomial time prover cannot make the verifier accept a false statement with probability larger than $1 - \varepsilon$. Proving amplification theorems for such proof systems is done via reduction: assuming the existence of a cheating prover P^{n*} making all the n verifiers in n-fold protocol $\pi^n = (P^n, V^n)$ accept a false statement "too well" (e.g., more than $(1 - \varepsilon)^n$), this prover is used to construct a cheating prover P^* making V accept this false statement with probability larger than $1 - \varepsilon$, yielding a contradiction. Typically, the cheating prover P^* emulates an execution of (P^{n*}, V^n) while *embedding* the (real) verifier V as one of the n verifiers (i.e., by embedding its messages). Analyzing the success probability of this P^* is directly reduced to bounding the "distance" (typically statistical distance or KL-divergence) between the following Winning and Attacking distributions: the Winning distribution is the n verifiers' messages distribution in a winning (all verifiers accept) execution of (P^{n*}, V^n). The Attacking distribution is the n verifiers' messages distribution in the emulated execution done by P^* (when interacting with V).

If the verifier is public-coin, or if the prover is unrestricted (as in single-prover interactive proofs), an optimal strategy for P^* is sampling the emulated verifiers messages uniformly at random conditioned on all verifiers accept, and the messages so far. Håstad et al. [18] have bounded the statistical distance between the induced Winning and Attacking distributions in such a case, while Chung and Pass [8] gave a tight bound for the KL-divergence between these distributions, yielding an optimal result for public-coin arguments.

For non public-coin protocols, however, a computationally bounded prover cannot always perform the above sampling task (indeed, this inability underneath the counter examples for parallel repetition of such arguments). However, if the argument is random terminating, the cheating prover can sample the following "skewed" variant of the desired distribution: it samples as described above, but conditioned that the real verifier *aborts at the end of the current round*, making the simulation of its future messages trivial. More generally, for partially-simulatable arguments, the cheating prover samples the future messages of the real verifier using the built-in mechanism for sampling a skewed sample of its coins. Analyzing the prover success probability for such an attack, and thus upper-bounding the soundness error of the parallel repetition of such arguments, reduces to understanding the (many-round) skewed distributions induced by the above attack. This will be discussed in the next section.

1.2 Skewed Distributions

The Attacking distribution induced by the security proof of parallel repetition of partially-simulatable arguments discussed in Sect. 1.1, gives rise to the following notion of (many-round) skewed distributions. Let $P = P_X$ be a distribution over an $m \times n$ size matrices, letting P_{X_i} and P_{X^j} denoting the induced distribution over the ith row and j^{th} column of X, respectively. For an event W, let $\widetilde{P} = P|W$. The following distribution $Q_{X,J}$ is a skewed variant of $\widetilde{P}$ induced by an event family $\mathcal{E} = \{E_{i,j}\}_{i\in[m],j\in[n]}$ over P: let $Q_J = U_{[n]}$, and let

$$Q_{X|J} = \prod_{i=1}^{m} P_{X_{i,J}|X_{<i,J}} \widetilde{P}_{X_{i,-J}|X_{<i},X_{i,J},E_{i,J}} \tag{1}$$

for $X_{<i} = (X_1, \ldots, X_{i-1})$, $X_{<i,j} = (X_{<i})^j = (X_{1,j}, \ldots, X_{i-1,j})$ and $X_{i,-j} = X_{i,[n]\setminus\{j\}}$. That is, Q induced by first sampling $J \in [n]$ uniformly at random, and then sampling the following skewed variant of $\widetilde{P}$: At round i

1. Sample $X_{i,J}$ according to $P_{X_{i,J}|X_{<i,J}}$ (rather than $P_{X_{i,J}|X_{<i},W}$ as in $\widetilde{P}$),
2. Sample $X_{i,-J}$ according $\widetilde{P}_{X_{i,-J}|X_{<i},X_{i,J},E_{i,J}}$ (rather than $\widetilde{P}_{X_{i,J}|X_{<i},X_{i,J}}$).

At a first glance, the distribution Q looks somewhat arbitrary. Nevertheless, as we explain below, it naturally arises in the analysis of parallel repetition theorem of partially-simulatable interactive arguments, and thus of random-terminating variants. Somewhat similar skewed distributions also come up when proving parallel repetition of two-prover proofs, though there we only care for single round distributions, i.e., $m = 1$.

The distributions $\widetilde{P}$ and Q relate to the Winning and Attacking distributions described in Sect. 1.1 in the following way: let $\pi = (\text{P}, \text{V})$ be an m-round δ-simulatable argument, and let P^{n*} be an efficient (for simplicity) deterministic cheating prover for π^n. Let P to be the distribution of the n verifiers messages in a random execution of π^n, and let W be the event that P^{n*} wins in $(\text{P}^{n*}, \text{V}^n)$. By definition, $\widetilde{P} = P|W$ is just the Winning distribution. Assume for sake of simplicity that V is a random-termination variant (halts at the end of each round with probability $1/m$), let $E_{i,j}$ be the set of coins in which the jth verifier halts at the end of the ith round of (P^n, V^n), and let $Q = Q(P, W, \{E_{i,j}\})$ be according to Eq. (1). Then, ignoring some efficiency concerns, Q is just the Attacking distribution. Consequently, a bound on the soundness error of π^n can be proved via the following result:

Lemma 1 (informal). *Let π be a partially simulatable argument of soundness error $(1 - \varepsilon)$. Assume that for every efficient cheating prover for π^n and every event T, it holds that*

$$\Pr_{Q_X}[T] \leq \Pr_{\widetilde{P}_X}[T] + \gamma$$

where W, $\widetilde{P}$ and Q are as defined above with respect to this adversary, and that Q is efficiently samplable. Then π^n has soundness error $(1 - \varepsilon)^{\log(1/P[W])/\gamma}$.

It follows that proving a parallel repetition theorem for partially simulatable arguments, reduces to proving that low probability events in $\widetilde{P}_X$ have low probability in Q_X (for the sake of the introduction, we ignore the less fundamental samplability condition assumed for Q). One can try to prove the latter, as implicitly done in [17,18], by bounding the *statistical distance* between $\widetilde{P}$ and Q (recall that $\mathrm{SD}(P,Q) = \max_E(\Pr_P[E] - \Pr_Q[E])$). This approach, however, seems doomed to give non-tight bounds for several reasons: first, statistical distance is not geared to bound non-product distributions (i.e., iterative processes) as the one defined by Q, and one is forced to use a wasteful hybrid argument in order to bound the statistical distance of such distributions. A second reason is that statistical distance bounds the difference in probability between the two distributions for *any* event, where we only care that this difference is small for low (alternatively, high) probability events. In many settings, achieving this (unneeded) stronger guarantee inherently yields a weaker bound.

What seems to be a more promising approach is bounding the *KL-divergence* between $\widetilde{P}$ and Q (recall that $D(P\|Q) = \mathrm{E}_{x\sim P}\log\frac{P(x)}{Q(x)}$). Having a chain rule, KL-divergence is typically an excellent choice for non-product distributions. In particular, bounding it only requires understanding the non-product nature (i.e., the dependency between the different entries) of the left-hand-side distribution. This makes KL-divergence a very useful measure in settings where the iterative nature of the right-hand-side distribution is much more complicated. Furthermore, a small KL-divergence guarantees that low probability events in $\widetilde{P}$ happen with almost the same probability in Q, but it only guarantees a weaker guarantee for other events (so it has the potential to yield a tighter result). Chung and Pass [8] took advantage of this observation for proving their tight bound on parallel repetition of public-coin argument by bounding the KL-divergence between their variants of $\widetilde{P}$ and Q. Unfortunately, for partially simulatable (and for random terminating) arguments, the KL-divergence between these distributions might be infinite.

Faced with the above difficulty, we propose a relaxed variant of KL-divergence that we name *smooth KL-divergence*. On the one hand, this measure has the properties of KL-divergence that make it suitable for our settings. However, on the other hand, it is less fragile (i.e., oblivious to events of small probability), allowing us to tightly bound its value for the distributions under consideration.

1.3   Smooth KL-divergence

The KL-divergence between distributions P and Q is a very sensitive distance measure: an event x with $P(x) \gg Q(x)$ might make $D(P\|Q)$ huge even if $P(x)$ is tiny (e.g., $P(x) > 0 = Q(x)$ implies $D(P\|Q) = \infty$). While events of tiny probability are important in some settings, they have no impact in ours. So we seek a less sensitive measure that enjoys the major properties of KL-divergence, most notably having chain-rule and mapping low probability events to low probability events. A natural attempt would be to define it as $\inf_{P',Q'}\{D(P'\|Q')\}$, where the infimum is over all pairs of distributions such that both $\mathrm{SD}(P,P')$ and $\mathrm{SD}(Q,Q')$ are small. This relaxation, however, requires an upper bound on the probability of events with respect to Q, which in our case is the complicated skewed distribution Q. Unfortunately, bounding the probability of events with respect to the distribution Q is exactly the issue in hand.

Instead, we take advantage of the asymmetric nature of the KL-divergence to propose a relaxation that only requires upper-bounding events with respect to P, which in our case is the much simpler $\widetilde{P}$ distribution. Assume P and Q are over a domain $\mathcal{U}$. The α-smooth KL-divergence of P and Q is defined by

$$D^\alpha(P||Q) = \inf_{(F_P, F_Q) \in \mathcal{F}} \{D(F_P(P)||F_Q(Q))\}$$

for $\mathcal{F}$ being the set of randomized function pairs, such that for any $(F_P, F_Q) \in \mathcal{F}$: (1) $\Pr_{x \sim P}[F_P(x) \neq x] \leq \alpha$, and (2) $\forall x \in \mathcal{U}$ and $C \in \{P, Q\}$: $F_C(x) \in \{x\} \cup \overline{\mathcal{U}}$. Note that for any pair $(F_P, F_Q) \in \mathcal{F}$ and any event B over $\mathcal{U}$, it holds that $\Pr_Q[B] \geq \Pr_{F_Q(Q)}[B]$, and $\Pr_{F_P(P)}[B] \geq \Pr_P[B] - \alpha$. Thus, if $\Pr_P[B]$ is low, a bound on $D(F_P(P)||F_Q(Q))$ implies that $\Pr_Q[B]$ is also low. Namely, low probability events in P happen with low probability also in Q.

Bounding Smooth KL-Divergence. Like the (standard) notion of KL-divergence, the power of smooth KL-divergence is best manifested when applied to non-product distributions. Let P and Q be two distributions for which we would like to prove that small events in $P_{X=(X_1,\ldots,X_m)}$ are small in $Q_{X=(X_1,\ldots,X_m)}$ (as a running example, let P and Q be the distributions $\widetilde{P}_X$ and $Q_{X,J}$ from the previous section, respectively). By chain rule of KL-divergence, it suffices to show that for some events $B_1, \ldots, B_m$ over Q (e.g., B_i is the event that $J|X_{<i}$ has high min entropy) it holds that

$$\sum_{i=1}^m D(P_{X_i}||Q_{X_i|B_{\leq i}} \mid P_{X_{<i}}) \quad \left(\text{i.e.,} \sum_{i=1}^m \mathrm{E}_{x \leftarrow P_{X_{<i}}} \left[D\left(P_{X_i|X_{<i}=x}||Q_{X_i|X_{<i}=x, B_{\leq i}}\right)\right]\right) \tag{2}$$

is small, and $Q[B_{\leq m}]$ is large. Bounding Eq. (2) only requires understanding P and simplified variants of Q (in which all but the ith entry is sampled according to P). Unfortunately, bounding $Q[B_{\leq m}]$ might be hard since it requires a good understanding of the distribution Q itself. We would have liked to relate the desired bound to $P[B_{\leq m}]$, but the events $\{B_i\}$ might not even be defined over P (in the above example, P has no J part). However, smooth KL-divergence gives us the means to do almost that.

Lemma 2 (Bounding smooth KL-divergence, informal). *Let P, Q and $\{B_i\}$ be as above. Associate the events $\{\widetilde{B}_i\}$ with P, each $\widetilde{B}_i$ (independently) occur with probability $Q[B_i \mid B_{<i}, X_{<i}]$. Then*

$$D^{1-P[\widetilde{B}_{\leq m}]}(P_X||Q_X) \leq \sum_{i=1}^m D\left(P_{X_i}||Q_{X_i|B_{\leq i}} \mid P_{X_{<i}|\widetilde{B}_{\leq i}}\right).$$

Namely, $\{\widetilde{B}_i\}$ mimics the events $\{B_i\}$, defined over Q, in (an extension of) P. It follows that bounding the smooth KL-divergence of P_X and Q_X (and thus guarantee that small events in P_X are small in Q_X), is reduced to understanding P and *simplified* variants of Q.

1.4   Main Results

We prove the following results (in addition to Lemmas 1 and 2). The first result, which is the main technical contribution of this paper, is the following bound on the smooth KL-divergence between a distribution and its many-round skewed variant.

Theorem 1 (Smooth KL-divergence for skewed distributions, informal). *Let $P = P_X$ be a distribution over an $m \times n$ matrices with independent columns, and let W and $\mathcal{E} = \{E_{i,j}\}$ be events over P. Let $\widetilde{P} = P|W$ and let $Q = Q(P, W, \mathcal{E})$ be the skewed variant of $\widetilde{P}$ defined in Eq. (1). Assume $\forall (i,j) \in [m] \times [n]$: (1) $E_{i,j}$ is determined by X^j and (2) There exists $\delta_{i,j} \in (0,1]$ such that $P[E_{i,j}|X_{\leq i,j}] = \delta_{i,j}$ for any fixing of $X_{\leq i,j}$. Then (ignoring constant factors, and under some restrictions on n and $P[W]$)*

$$D^{\varepsilon m + 1/\delta n}(\widetilde{P}_X \| Q_X) \leq \varepsilon m + m/\delta n$$

for $\delta = \min_{i,j}\{\delta_{i,j}\}$ and $\varepsilon = \log(\frac{1}{P[W]})/\delta n$. In a special case where $E_{i,j}$ is determined by $X_{\leq i+1,j}$, it holds that

$$D^{\varepsilon + 1/\delta n}(\widetilde{P}_X \| Q_X) \leq \varepsilon + m/\delta n.$$

Combining Lemma 1 and Theorem 1 yields the following bound on parallel repetition of partially simulatable arguments. We give separate bounds for partially simulatable argument and for *partially prefix-simulatable arguments*: a δ-simulatable argument is δ-prefix-simulatable if for any i-round view, the event E guaranteed by the simulatable property for this view is determined by the coins used in the first $i + 1$ rounds. It is clear that the random-termination variant of an m-round argument is $1/m$-prefix-simulatable.

Theorem 2 (Parallel repetition for partially simulatable arguments, informal). *Let π be an m-round δ-simulatable interactive argument with soundness error $1 - \varepsilon$, and let $n \in \mathbb{N}$. Then π^n has soundness error $(1 - \varepsilon)^{\delta n/m}$. Furthermore, if π is δ-prefix-simulatable, then π^n has soundness error $(1 - \varepsilon)^{\delta n}$.*[2]

A subtlety that arises when proving Theorem 2 is that a direct composition of Lemma 1 and Theorem 1 only yields the desired result when the number of repetitions n is "sufficiently" large compared to the number of rounds m (roughly, this is because we need the additive term $m/\delta n$ in Theorem 1 to be smaller than ε). We bridge this gap by presenting a sort of upward-self reduction from a few

---

[2] Throughout, we assume that the protocol transcript contains the verifier's Accept/Reject decision (which is without loss of generality for random-terminating variants). We deffer the more general case for the next version.

repetitions to many repetitions. The idea underlying this reduction is rather general and applies to other proofs of this type, and in particular to those of [6,17,18].[3]

We complete the picture by showing that an δ factor in the exponent in Theorem 2 is unavoidable.

Theorem 3 (lower bound, informal). *Under suitable cryptographic assumptions, for any $n, m \in \mathbb{N}$ and $\varepsilon \in [0,1]$, there exists an m-round δ-prefix-simulatable interactive argument π with soundness error $1 - \varepsilon$, such that π^n has soundness error at least $(1 - \varepsilon)^{\delta n}$. Furthermore, protocol π is a random-terminating variant of an interactive argument.*

It follows that our bound for partially prefix-simulatable arguments and random-termination variants, given in Theorem 2, is tight.

1.4.1 Proving Theorem 1

We highlight some details about the proof of Theorem 1. Using Lemma 2, we prove the theorem by showing that the following holds for a carefully chosen events $\{B_i\}$ over $Q_{X,J}$:

- $\sum_{i=1}^{m} D\left(\widetilde{P}_{X_i} \| Q_{X_i | B_{\leq i}} \mid \widetilde{P}_{X_{<i} | \widetilde{B}_{\leq i}}\right)$ is small, and
- $\widetilde{P}[\widetilde{B}_{\leq m}]$ is large,

where $\{\widetilde{B}_i\}$ are events over (extension of) $\widetilde{P}$, with $\widetilde{B}_i$ taking the value 1 with probability $Q[B_i \mid B_{<i}, X_{<i}]$. We chose the events $\{B_i\}$ so that we have the following guarantees on $Q_{X_i, J | B_{\leq i}, X_{<i}}$:

1. $J | X_{<i}$ has high entropy (like it has without any conditioning), and
2. $P[W \mid X_{<i}, X_{i,J}, E_{i,J}] \geq P[W | X_{<i}]/2$.

Very roughly, these guarantees make the task of bounding the required KL-divergence much simpler since they guarantee that the skewing induced by Q does not divert it too much (compared to $\widetilde{P}$). The remaining challenge is therefore lower-bounding $\widetilde{P}[\widetilde{B}_{\leq m}]$. We bound the latter distribution by associating a martingale sequence with the distribution Winning. In order to bound this sequence, we prove a new concentration bound for "slowly evolving" martingale sequences, Lemma 3, that we believe to be of independent interest.

---

[3] Upward-self reductions trivially exist for interactive proof: assume the existence of a cheating prover P^{n*} breaking the α soundness error of π^n, then $(P^{n*})^{\ell}$, i.e., the prover using P^{n*} in parallel for ℓ times, violates the assumed α^{ℓ} soundness error of $\pi^{n\ell}$. However, when considering interactive arguments, for which we cannot guarantee a soundness error below negligible (see Footnote 1), this approach breaks down when α^{ℓ} is negligible.

1.5   Related Work

1.5.1   Interactive Arguments

Positive Results. Bellare et al. [1] proved that the parallel repetition of three-message interactive arguments reduces the soundness error at an exponential, but not optimal, rate. Canetti et al. [4] later showed that parallel repetition does achieve an optimal exponential decay in the soundness error for such arguments. Pass and Venkitasubramaniam [22] have proved the same for constant-round public-coin arguments. For public-coin arguments of any (polynomial) round complexity, Håstad et al. [18] were the first to show that parallel repetition reduces the soundness error exponentially, but not at an optimal rate. The first optimal analysis of parallel repetition in public-coin arguments was that of Chung and Liu [6], who showed that the soundness error of the k repetitions improves to $(1 - \varepsilon)^k$. Chung and Pass [8] proved the same bound using KL-divergence. For non-public coin argument (of any round complexity), Haitner [17] introduced the random-terminating variant of a protocol, and proved that the parallel repetition of these variants improves the soundness error at a weak exponential rate. Håstad et al. [18] proved the same, with essentially the same parameters, for partially-simulatable arguments, that contain random-terminating protocols as a special case. All the above results extend to "threshold verifiers" where the parallel repetition is considered accepting if the number of accepting verifiers is above a certain threshold. Our result rather easily extends to such verifiers, but we defer the tedious details to the next version. Chung and Pass [7] proved that full independence of the parallel executions is not necessary to improve the soundness of public-coin arguments, and that the verifier can save randomness by carefully correlating the different executions. It is unknown whether similar savings in randomness can be achieved for random-terminating arguments. Finally, the only known round-preserving alternative to the random-terminating transformation is the elegant approach of Chung and Liu [6], who showed that a fully-homomorphic encryption (FHE) can be used to compile any interactive argument to a one (with the same soundness error) for which parallel repetition improves the soundness error at ideal rate, i.e., $(1 - \varepsilon)^n$. However, in addition to being conditional (and currently it is only known how to construct FHE assuming hardness of learning with errors [3]), the compiled protocol might lack some of the guarantees of the original protocol (e.g., fairness). Furthermore, the reduction is *non* black box (the parties homomorphically evaluate *each* of the protocol's gates), making the resulting protocol highly impractical, and preventing the use of this approach when only black-box access is available (e.g., the weak protocol is given as a DLL or implemented in hardware).

Negative Results. Bellare et al. [1] presented for any $n \in \mathbb{N}$, a four-message interactive argument of soundness error $1/2$, whose n-parallel repetition soundness remains $1/2$. Pietrzak and Wikström [23] ruled out the possibility that enough repetitions will eventually improve the soundness of an interactive argument. They presented a *single* 8-message argument for which the above phenomenon holds for all polynomial n simultaneously. Both results hold under common cryptographic assumptions.

1.5.2 Two-Prover Interactive Proofs

The techniques used in analyzing parallel-repetition of interactive arguments are closely related to those for analyzing parallel repetition of two-prover one-round games. Briefly, in such a game, two unbounded *isolated* provers try to convince a verifier in the validity of a statement. Given a game of soundness error $(1-\varepsilon)$, one might expect the soundness error of its n parallel repetition to be $(1-\varepsilon)^n$, but as in the case of interactive arguments, this turned out to be false [13–15]. Nonetheless, Raz [25] showed that parallel repetition does achieve an exponential decay for any two-prover one-round game, and in particular reduces the soundness error to $(1-\varepsilon)^{\varepsilon^{O(1)}n/s}$, where s is the provers' answer length. These parameters were later improved by Holenstein [19], and improved further for certain types of games by Rao [24], Dinur and Steurer [10], Moshkovitz [20]. The core challenge in the analysis of parallel repetition of interactive arguments and of multi-prover one-round games is very similar: how to simulate a random accepting execution of the proof/game given the verifier messages. In interactive arguments, this is difficult since the prover lacks computational power. In multi-prover one-round games, the issue is that the different provers cannot communicate.

Open Questions

While our bound for the parallel repetition of partially prefix-simulatable arguments is tight, this question for (non prefix) partially simulatable arguments is still open (there is a $1/m$ gap in the exponent). A more important challenge is to develop a better (unconditional) round-preserving amplification technique for arbitrary interactive arguments (which cannot be via random termination), or alternatively to prove that such an amplification does not exist.

Paper Organization

Basic notations, definitions and tools used throughout the paper are stated in Sect. 2. The definition of smooth KL-divergence and some properties of this measure are given in Sect. 3. The definition of many-round skewed distributions and our main bound for such distributions are given in Sect. 4. A proof sketch of the aforementioned bound is given in Sect. 6, and is used in Sect. 5 for proving our bound on the parallel repetition of partially simulatable arguments. Due to space limitations, the full proof of our main bound, the matching lower bound (Theorem 3) and other missing proofs are only given in the full version of this paper [2].

2 Preliminaries

2.1 Notation

We use calligraphic letters to denote sets, uppercase for random variables, and lowercase for values and functions. All logarithms considered here are natural logarithms (i.e., in base e). For $n \in \mathbb{N}$, let $[n] := \{1, \ldots, n\}$. Given a vector

$v \in \Sigma^m$, we let v_i be its ith entry, and let $v_{<i} = v_{1,\ldots,i-1}$ and $v_{\leq i} = v_{1,\ldots,i}$. For $v \in \{0,1\}^n$, let $1_v = \{i \in [n]: v_i = 1\}$. For $m \times n$ matrix x, let x_i and x^j denote their i^{th} row and j^{th} column respectively, and defined $x_{<i}$, $x_{\leq i}$, $x^{<j}$ and $x^{\leq j}$ respectively. Given a Boolean statement S (e.g., $X \geq 5$), let 1_S be the indicator function that outputs 1 if S is a true statement and 0 otherwise.

Let poly denote the set of all polynomials, PPT denote for probabilistic polynomial time, and PPTM denote a PPT algorithm (Turing machine). A function $\nu \colon \mathbb{N} \to [0,1]$ is *negligible*, denoted $\nu(n) = \text{neg}(n)$, if $\nu(n) < 1/p(n)$ for every $p \in \text{poly}$ and large enough n. Function ν is *noticeable*, denoted $\nu(n) \geq 1/\text{poly}(n)$, if exists $p \in \text{poly}$ such that $\nu(n) \geq 1/p(n)$ for all n.

2.2 Distributions and Random Variables

A discrete random variable X over $\mathcal{X}$ is sometimes defined by its probability mass function (pmf) P_X (P is an arbitrary symbol). A conditional probability distribution is a function $P_{Y|X}(\cdot|\cdot)$ such that for any $x \in \mathcal{X}$, $P_{Y|X}(\cdot|x)$ is a pmf over $\mathcal{Y}$. The joint pmf P_{XY} can be written the product $P_X P_{Y|X}$, where $(P_X P_{Y|X})(x,y) = P_X(x) P_{Y|X}(y|x) = P_{XY}(xy)$. The marginal pmf P_Y can be written as the composition $P_{Y|X} \circ P_X$, where $(P_{Y|X} \circ P_X)(y) = \sum_{x \in \mathcal{X}} P_{Y|X}(y|x) P_X(x) = P_Y(y)$. We sometimes write $P_{\cdot,Y}$ to denote a pmf $P_{X,Y}$ for which we do not care about the random variable X. We denote by $P_X[W]$ the probability that an event W over P_X occurs, and given a set $\mathcal{S} \subseteq \mathcal{X}$ we define $P_X(\mathcal{S}) = P_X[X \in \mathcal{S}]$. Distribution P'_{XY} is an extension of P_X if $P'_X \equiv P_X$. Random variables and events defined over P_X are defined over the extension P'_{XY} by ignoring the value of Y. We sometimes abuse notation and say that P_{XY} is an extension of P_X.

The support of a distribution P over a finite set $\mathcal{X}$, denoted $\text{Supp}(P)$, is defined as $\{x \in \mathcal{X} : P(x) > 0\}$. The *statistical distance* of two distributions P and Q over a finite set $\mathcal{X}$, denoted as $\text{SD}(P,Q)$, is defined as $\max_{\mathcal{S} \subseteq \mathcal{X}} |P(\mathcal{S}) - Q(\mathcal{S})| = \frac{1}{2} \sum_{x \in \mathcal{S}} |P(x) - Q(x)|$. Given a set $\mathcal{S}$, let $U_{\mathcal{S}}$ denote the uniform distribution over the elements of $\mathcal{S}$. We sometimes write $x \sim \mathcal{S}$ or $x \leftarrow \mathcal{S}$, meaning that x is uniformly drawn from $\mathcal{S}$. For $p \in [0,1]$, let $\text{Bern}(p)$ be the Bernoulli distribution over $\{0,1\}$, taking the value 1 with probability p.

2.3 KL-Divergence

Definition 1. *The* KL-divergence *(also known as, Kullback-Leibler divergence and relative entropy) between two distributions P, Q on a discrete alphabet $\mathcal{X}$ is*

$$D(P\|Q) = \sum_{x \in \mathcal{X}} P(x) \log \frac{P(x)}{Q(x)} = \mathbb{E}_{x \sim P} \log \frac{P(x)}{Q(x)},$$

where $0 \cdot \log \frac{0}{0} = 0$ and if $\exists x \in \mathcal{X}$ such that $P(x) > 0 = Q(x)$ then $D(P\|Q) = \infty$.

Definition 2. *Let P_{XY} and Q_{XY} be two probability distributions over $\mathcal{X} \times \mathcal{Y}$. The* conditional divergence *between $P_{Y|X}$ and $Q_{Y|X}$ is*

$$D(P_{Y|X}||Q_{Y|X}|P_X) = \mathrm{E}_{x \sim P_X}[D(P_{Y|X=x}||Q_{Y|X=x})] = \sum_{x \in \mathcal{X}} P_X(x) D(P_{Y|X=x}||Q_{Y|X=x}).$$

Fact 4 (Properties of divergence). P_{XY} and Q_{XY} be two probability distributions over $\mathcal{X} \times \mathcal{Y}$. It holds that:

1. (Information inequality) $D(P_X||Q_X) \geq 0$, with equality holds iff $P_X = Q_X$.
2. (Monotonicity) $D(P_{XY}||Q_{XY}) \geq D(P_Y||Q_Y)$.
3. (Chain rule) $D(P_{X_1 \cdots X_n}||Q_{X_1 \cdots X_n}) = \sum_{i=1}^{n} D(P_{X_i|X_{<i}}||Q_{X_i|X_{<i}}|P_{X_{<i}})$ If $Q_{X_1 \cdots X_n} = \prod_{i=1}^{n} Q_{X_i}$ then

$$D(P_{X_1 \cdots X_n}||Q_{X_1 \cdots X_n}) = D(P_{X_1 \cdots X_n}||P_{X_1} P_{X_2} \cdots P_{X_n}) + \sum_{i=1}^{n} D(P_{X_i}||Q_{X_i}).$$

4. (Conditioning increases divergence) If $Q_Y = Q_{Y|X} \circ P_X$ (and $P_Y = P_{Y|X} \circ P_X$), then $D(P_Y||Q_Y) \leq D(P_{Y|X}||Q_{Y|X}|P_X)$.
5. (Data-processing) If $Q_Y = P_{Y|X} \circ Q_X$ (and $P_Y = P_{Y|X} \circ P_X$), it holds that $D(P_Y||Q_Y) \leq D(P_X||Q_X)$.

Fact 5. Let X be random variable drawn from P and let W be an event defined over P. Then $D\left(P_{X|W}||P_X\right) \leq \log \frac{1}{P[W]}$.

Definition 3. For $p, q \in [0,1]$ let $D(p||q) := D(\mathrm{Bern}(p)||\mathrm{Bern}(q))$.

Fact 6 ([21, Implicit in Corollary 3.2 to 3.4]). For any $p \in [0,1]$:

1. $D((1-\delta)p||p) \geq \delta^2 p/2$ for any $\delta \in [0,1]$.
2. $D((1+\delta)p||p) \geq \min\{\delta, \delta^2\}p/4$ for any $\delta \in [0, \frac{1}{p}-1]$.

The proof of the following proposition, which relies on Donsker and Varadhan [12]'s inequality, is given in the full version.

Proposition 1. Let X be a random variable drawn form either P or Q. Assume that $\Pr_P[|X| \leq 1] = 1$ (i.e., if X is drawn from P then $|X| \leq 1$ almost surely) and that there exist $\varepsilon, \sigma^2, K_1, K_2 > 0$ such that $\Pr_Q[|X| \leq 1] \geq 1 - \varepsilon$ and

$$\Pr_Q[|X| \geq t] \leq K_2 \cdot \exp\left(-\frac{t^2}{K_1 \sigma^2}\right) \quad \text{for all } 0 \leq t \leq 1.$$

Then, $\exists K_3 = K_3(K_1, K_2, \varepsilon) > 0$ such that $\mathrm{E}_P[X^2] \leq K_3 \cdot \sigma^2 \cdot (D(P||Q) + 1)$.

2.4   Concentration Bounds

The following concentration bound is proven in the full version.

Fact 7. Let $L_1, \ldots, L_n$ be independent random variables over $\mathbb{R}$ with $|L_i| \leq \ell$ for all $i \in [n]$ and let $Z_i = (L_i/p_i) \cdot \mathrm{Bern}(p_i)$ with $p_i > 0$ for all $i \in [n]$. Let $L = \sum_{i=1}^{n} L_i$, let $Z = \sum_{i=1}^{n} Z_i$, let $\mu = \mathrm{E}[L]$ and let $p = \min_{i \in [n]}\{p_i\}$. Finally, let $\Gamma = Z/\mu - 1$. Then for any $\gamma \in [0,1]$ it holds that

$$\Pr[|\Gamma| \geq \gamma] \leq 4 \exp\left(-\frac{p\mu^2\gamma^2}{5\ell^2 n}\right)$$

2.4.1   Martingales

Definition 4. *A sequence of random variables* $Y_0, Y_1, \ldots, Y_n$ *is called a **martingale sequence with respect to** a sequence* $X_0, X_1, \ldots, X_n$, *if* $\forall i \in [n]$: *(1)* Y_i *is a deterministic function of* $X_0, \ldots, X_i$, *and (2)* $\mathrm{E}[Y_i \mid X_0, \ldots, X_{i-1}] = Y_{i-1}$.

The following lemma (proven in the full version) is a new concentration bound on "slowly evolving" martingales.

Lemma 3 (A bound on slowly evolving martingales). *Let* $Y_0 = 1, Y_1, \ldots, Y_n$ *be a martingale w.r.t* $X_0, X_1, \ldots, X_n$ *and assume that* $Y_i \geq 0$ *for all* $i \in [n]$. *Then for every* $\lambda \in (0, \frac{1}{4}]$ *it holds that*

$$\Pr[\exists i \in [n] \text{ s.t. } |Y_i - 1| \geq \lambda] \leq \frac{23 \cdot \mathrm{E}\left[\sum_{i=1}^n \min\{|R_i|, R_i^2\}\right]}{\lambda^2}$$

for $R_i = \frac{Y_i}{Y_{i-1}} - 1$, *letting* $R_i = 0$ *in case* $Y_{i-1} = Y_i = 0$.

That is, if Y_i is unlikely to be far from Y_{i-1} in a multiplicative manner, then the sequence is unlikely to get far from 1.

2.5   Interactive Arguments

Definition 5 (Interactive arguments). *A* PPT *protocol* (P, V) *is an* interactive argument *for a language* $\mathrm{L} \in \mathrm{NP}$ *with* completeness α *and* soundness error β, *if the following holds:*

- $\Pr[(\mathrm{P}(w), \mathrm{V})(x) = 1] \geq \alpha(|x|)$ *for any* $(x, w) \in R_\mathrm{L}$.
- $\Pr[(\mathrm{P}^*, \mathrm{V})(x) = 1] \leq \max\{\beta(|x|), \mathrm{neg}(|x|)\}$ *for any* PPT P^* *and large enough* $x \notin \mathrm{L}$.

We refer to party P *as the* prover, *and to* V *as the* verifier.

Soundness against *non-uniform* provers is analogously defined, and all the results in this paper readily extend to this model.

Since in our analysis we only care about soundness amplification, in the following we fix L to be the empty language, and assume the input to the protocol is just a string of ones, which we refer to as the *security parameter*, a parameter we omit when cleared from the context.

2.5.1   Random-Terminating Variant

Definition 6 (Random-terminating variant, [17]). *Let* V *be a* m-*round randomized interactive algorithm. The* random-terminating variant *of* V, *denoted* $\widetilde{\mathrm{V}}$, *is defined as follows: algorithm* V *acts exactly as* V *does, but adds the following step at the end of each communication round: it tosses an* $(1 - 1/m, 1/m)$ *biased coin (i.e., 1 is tossed with probability* $1/m$), *if the outcome is one then it outputs* 1 *(i.e., accept) and halts. Otherwise, it continues as* V *would.*

For a protocol $\pi = (\mathrm{P}, \mathrm{V})$, *the protocol* $\widetilde{\pi} = (\mathrm{P}, \widetilde{\mathrm{V}})$ *is referred to as the* random-terminating variant *of* π.

2.5.2 Partially Simulatable Interactive Arguments

Definition 7 (Partially simulatable protocols, [18]). *A randomized inter-active algorithm* V *is* δ-simulatable, *if there exists an oracle-aided* S *(simulator) such that the following holds: for every strategy* P* *and a partial view* v *of* P* *in an interaction of* (P*, V)(1^κ)*, the output of* $\mathsf{S}^{\mathrm{P}^*}(1^\kappa, v)$ *is* P* *'s view in a random continuation of* (P*, V)(1^κ) *conditioned on* v *and* Δ, *for* Δ *being a* δ-dense sub-set of the coins of* V *that are consistent with* v. *The running time of* $\mathsf{S}^{\mathrm{P}^*}(1^\kappa, v)$ *is polynomial in* κ *and the running time of* P*(1^κ).

Algorithm V *is* δ-prefix-simulatable *if membership in the guaranteed event* Δ *is determined by the coins* V *uses in the first* $\mathrm{round}(v) + 1$ *rounds.*[4]

An interactive argument (P, V) *is* δ-simulatable/ δ-prefix-simulatable, *if* V *is.*

It is clear that random termination variant of an m-round interactive argument is $1/m$-prefix-simulatable.

Remark 1. One can relax the above definition and allow a different (non-black) simulator per P*, and then only require it to exists for poly-time P*. While our proof readily extends to this relaxation, we prefer to use the above definition for presentation clarity.

2.5.3 Parallel Repetition

Definition 8 (Parallel repetition). *Let* (P, V) *be an interactive protocol, and let* $n \in \mathbb{N}$. *We define the* n-parallel-repetition *of* (P, V) *to be the protocol* (P^n, V^n) *in which* P^n *and* V^n *execute* n *copies of* (P, V) *in parallel, and at the end of the execution,* V^n *accepts if all copies accept.*

Black-box soundness reduction. As in most such proofs, our proof for the parallel repetition of partially-simulatable arguments has the following black-box form.

Definition 9 (Black-box reduction for parallel repetition). *Let* $\pi = $ (P, V) *be an interactive argument. An oracle-aided algorithm* R *is a* black-box reduction *for the* g-soundness of the parallel repetition of* π, *if the following holds for any poly-bounded* n: *let* $\kappa \in \mathbb{N}$ *and* P^{n*} *be deterministic cheating prover breaking the soundness of* $\pi^{n=n(\kappa)}(1^\kappa)$ *with probability* $\varepsilon' \geq g(n, \varepsilon = \varepsilon(\kappa))$. *Then*

Sucesss probability. R = $\mathsf{R}^{\mathrm{P}^{n*}}(1^\kappa, 1^n)$ *breaks the soundness of* π *with proba-bility at least* $1 - \varepsilon/3$.

Running time. *Except with probability* $\varepsilon/3$, *the running time of* R *is polynomial in* κ, *the running time of* P^{n*}(1^κ) *and* $1/\varepsilon'$.

We use the following fact (proven in the full version).

---

[4] $\Delta = \Delta_1 \times \Delta_2$, for Δ_1 being a (δ-dense) subset of the possible values for first $\mathrm{round}(v) + 1$ round coins, and Δ_2 is the set of all possible values for the coins used in rounds $\mathrm{round}(v) + 2, \ldots, m$, for m being the round complexity of V.

Proposition 2. *Assume there exists a black-box reduction for the g-soundness of the parallel repetition of any δ-simulatable [resp., δ-prefix-simulatable] interactive argument, then for any poly-bounded n, the soundness error of the n-fold repetition of any such argument is bounded by $g(n, \varepsilon)$.*

3   Smooth KL-Divergence

In this section we formally define the notion of smooth KL-divergence, state some basic properties of this measure in Sect. 3.1, and develop a tool to help bounding it in Sect. 3.2.

Definition 10. (α-*smooth* divergence). *Let P and Q be two distributions over a universe $\mathcal{U}$ and let $\alpha \in [0, 1]$. The α-smooth divergence of P and Q, denoted $D^{\alpha}(P\|Q)$, is defined as $\inf_{(F_P, F_Q) \in \mathcal{F}}\{D(F_P(P)\|F_Q(Q))\}$, for $\mathcal{F}$ being the set of randomized functions pairs such that for every $(F_P, F_Q) \in \mathcal{F}$:*

1. $\Pr_{x \sim P}[F_P(x) \neq x] \leq \alpha$, where the probability is also over the coins of F_P.
2. $\forall x \in \mathcal{U}$: $\mathrm{Supp}(F_P(x)) \cap \mathcal{U} \subseteq \{x\}$ and $\mathrm{Supp}(F_Q(x)) \cap \mathcal{U} \subseteq \{x\}$.

See the full version for comparison to the H-technique.

3.1   Basic Properties

The following proposition (proven in the full version) states that small smooth KL-divergence guarantees that small events with respect to the left-hand-side distribution are also small with respect to the right-hand-side distribution.

Proposition 3. *Let P and Q be two distributions over $\mathcal{U}$ with $D^{\alpha}(P\|Q) < \beta$. Then for every event E over $\mathcal{U}$, it holds that $Q[E] < 2 \cdot \max\{\alpha + P[E], 4\beta\}$.*

Like any useful distribution measure, smooth KL-divergence posses a data-processing property. The following proposition is proven in the full version.

Proposition 4 (Data processing of smooth KL-divergence). *Let P and Q be two distributions over a universe $\mathcal{U}$, let $\alpha \in [0, 1]$ and let H be a randomized function over $\mathcal{U}$. Then $D^{\alpha}(H(P)\|H(Q)) \leq D^{\alpha}(P\|Q)$.*

3.2   Bounding Smooth KL-Divergence

The following lemma allow us to bound the smooth KL-divergence between P and Q, while only analyzing simpler variants of Q.

Lemma 4 (Bounding smooth KL-Divergence, restatement of Lemma 2).
Let P and Q be distributions with P_X and Q_X being over universe $\mathcal{U}^m$, and let $A_1, \ldots, A_m$ and $B_1, \ldots, B_m$ be two sets of events over P and Q respectively. Let $P_{\cdot,XY}$ be an extension of $P = P_{\cdot,X}$ defined by $P_{Y|\cdot,X} = \prod_i P_{Y_i|X}$ for $P_{Y_i|X} =$

$\text{Bern}\,(P[A_i \mid X, A_{<i}] \cdot Q[B_i \mid X_{<i}, B_{<i}])$, *letting* $P_{Y_i|X} = 0$ *if* $P[A_{<i} \mid X] = 0$ *or* $Q[B_{<i} \mid X_{<i}] = 0$, *and let* $C_i = \{Y_i = 1\}$. *Then*[5]

$$D^{1-P[C_{\leq m}]}(P_X \| Q_X) \leq \sum_{i=1}^{m} D(P_{X_i|A_{\leq i}} \| Q_{X_i|B_{\leq i}} \mid P_{X_{<i}|C_{\leq i}}).$$

Proof. Let $Q_{\cdot, XY}$ be an extension of $Q = Q_{\cdot, X}$ defined by $Q_{Y|\cdot, X} = \prod_i Q_{Y_i|X}$ for $Q_{Y_i|X} = \text{Bern}\,(P[A_i \mid X_{<i}, A_{<i}] \cdot Q[B_i \mid X, B_{<i}])$, letting $Q_{Y_i|X} = 0$ if $P[A_{<i} \mid X_{<i}] = 0$ or $Q[B_{<i} \mid X] = 0$. Our goal is to show that

$$D^{1-P[C_{\leq m}]}(P_{Y_1, X_1, \ldots, Y_m, X_m} \| Q_{Y_1, X_1, \ldots, Y_m, X_m}) \leq \sum_{i=1}^{m} D(P_{X_i|A_{\leq i}} \| Q_{X_i|B_{\leq i}} \mid P_{X_{<i}|C_{\leq i}}) \tag{3}$$

The proof then follows by data processing of smooth KL-divergence (Proposition 4). By definition, for any $i \in [m]$:

$$P_{X_{<i}|Y_{\leq i}=1^i} \equiv P_{X_{<i}|C_{\leq i}} \tag{4}$$

and for any fixing of $x_{<i} \in \text{Supp}(P_{X_{<i}|Y_{\leq i}=1^i})$:

$$P_{X_i|Y_{\leq i}=1^i, X_{<i}=x_{<i}} \equiv P_{X_i|X_{<i}, A_{\leq i}} \tag{5}$$

$$Q_{X_i|Y_{\leq i}=1^i, X_{<i}=x_{<i}} \equiv Q_{X_i|X_{<i}, B_{\leq i}} \tag{6}$$

and for any fixing of $x_{<i} \in \text{Supp}(P_{X_{<i}|Y_{<i}=1^{i-1}})$:

$$P_{Y_i|Y_{<i}=1^{i-1}, X_{<i}=x_{<i}}(1) \tag{7}$$
$$\equiv \mathbf{E}_{x \leftarrow P_{X|Y_{<i}=1^{i-1}, X_{<i}=x_{<i}}} [P[A_i \mid X = x, A_{<i}] \cdot Q[B_i \mid X_{<i} = x_{<i}, B_{<i}]]$$
$$\equiv P[A_i \mid X_{<i} = x_{<i}, A_{<i}] \cdot Q[B_i \mid X_{<i} = x_{<i}, B_{<i}]$$
$$\equiv \mathbf{E}_{x \leftarrow Q_{X|Y_{<i}=1^{i-1}, X_{<i}=x_{<i}}} [P[A_i \mid X_{<i} = x_{<i}, A_{<i}] \cdot Q[B_i \mid X = x, B_{<i}]]$$
$$\equiv Q_{Y_i|Y_{<i}=1^{i-1}, X_{<i}=x_{<i}}(1).$$

By Eqs. (4) to (6):

$$\mathbf{E}_{P_{X_{<i}|Y_{\leq i}=1^i}} \left[D\left(P_{X_i|X_{<i}, Y_{\leq i}=1^i} \| Q_{X_i|X_{<i}, Y_{\leq i}=1^i} \right) \right] = \mathbf{E}_{P_{X_{<i}|C_{\leq i}}} \left[D\left(P_{X_i|X_{<i}, A_{\leq i}} \| Q_{X_i|X_{<i}, B_{\leq i}} \right) \right] \tag{8}$$

and by Eq. (7), for any fixing of $x \in \text{Supp}(P_{X_{<i}|Y_{<i}=1^{i-1}})$:

$$D\left(P_{Y_i|X_{<i}=x, Y_{<i}=1^{i-1}} \| Q_{Y_i|X_{<i}=x, Y_{<i}=1^{i-1}} \right) = 0 \tag{9}$$

---

[5] Note that Lemma 2 is a special case of Lemma 4 that holds when choosing $A_1, \ldots, A_m$ with $P[A_{\leq m}] = 1$.

We use Eqs. (8) and (9) for proving Eq. (3), by applying on both distributions a function that "cuts" all values after the first appearance of $Y_i = 0$. Let $f_{\mathsf{cut}}(y_1, x_1, \ldots y_m, x_m) = (y_1, x_1, \ldots y_m, x_m)$ if $y = (y_1, \ldots, y_m) = 1^m$, and $f_{\mathsf{cut}}(y_1, x_1, \ldots y_m, x_m) = (y_1, x_1, \ldots y_{i-1}, x_{i-1}, y_i, \perp^{2n-2i+1})$ otherwise, where i is the minimal index with $y_i = 0$, and $\perp$ is an arbitrary symbol $\notin \mathcal{U}$. By definition,

$$\Pr_{s \sim P_{Y_1, X_1, \ldots, Y_m, X_m}} [f_{\mathsf{cut}}(s) \neq s] = P[Y \neq 1^m] = 1 - P[C_{\leq m}],$$

and by Eqs. (8) and (9) along with data-processing of standard KL-divergence (Fact 4(3)),

$$D\left(f_{\mathsf{cut}}\left(P_{Y_1, X_1, \ldots, Y_m, X_m}\right) \| f_{\mathsf{cut}}\left(Q_{Y_1, X_1, \ldots, Y_m, X_m}\right)\right) \leq \sum_{i=1}^{m} D(P_{X_i | A_{\leq i}} \| Q_{X_i | B_{\leq i}} \mid P_{X_{<i} | C_{\leq i}}).$$

That is, f_{cut} is the function realizing the stated bound on the smooth KL-divergence of P_X and Q_X.

4   Skewed Distributions

In this section we formally define the notion of many-round skewed distributions and state our main result for such distributions.

Definition 11 (The skewed distribution Q). *Let P be a distribution with P_X being a distribution over $m \times n$ matrices, and let W and $\mathcal{E} = \{E_{i,j}\}_{i \in [m], j \in [n]}$ be events over P. We define the skewed distribution $Q_{X,J} = Q(P, W, \mathcal{E})$ of $\tilde{P}_X = P|W$, by $Q_J = U_{[n]}$ and*

$$Q_{X|J} = \prod_{i=1}^{m} P_{X_{i,J} | X_{<i,J}} \tilde{P}_{X_{i,-J} | X_{<i}, X_{i,J}, E_{i,J}}$$

Definition 12 (dense and prefix events). *Let P_X be a distribution over $m \times n$ matrices, and let $\mathcal{E} = \{E_{i,j}\}_{i \in [m], j \in [n]}$ be an event family over P_X such that $E_{i,j}$, for each i, j, is determined by X^j. The family $\mathcal{E}$ has* density δ *if $\forall (i, j) \in [m] \times [n]$ and for any fixing of $X_{\leq i,j}$, it holds that $P[E_{i,j} | X_{\leq i,j}] = \delta_{i,j} \geq \delta$. The family $\mathcal{E}$ is a* prefix family *if $\forall (i, j) \in [m] \times [n]$ the event $E_{i,j}$ is determined by $X_{\leq i+1, j}$.*

Bounding Smooth KL-Divergence of Smooth Distributions. The following theorem states our main result for skewed distributions. In Sect. 6 we give a proof sketch of Theorem 8, and in the full version we give the full details.

Theorem 8. *Let P be a distribution with P_X being a distribution over $m \times n$ matrices with independent columns, let W be an event over P and let $\mathcal{E} = \{E_{i,j}\}$ be a δ-dense event family over P_X. Let $\tilde{P} = P|W$ and let $Q_{X,J} = Q(P, W, \mathcal{E})$ be the skewed variant of $\tilde{P}$ defined in Definition 11. Let $Y_i = (Y_{i,1}, \ldots, Y_{i,n})$ for $Y_{i,j}$ being the indicator for $E_{i,j}$, and let $d = \sum_{i=1}^{m} D(\tilde{P}_{X_i Y_i} \| P_{X_i Y_i} | \tilde{P}_{X_{<i}})$. Assuming $n \geq c \cdot m/\delta$ and $d \leq \delta n/c$, for a universal constant $c > 0$, then*

$$D^{\frac{c}{\delta n}(d+1)}(\tilde{P} \| Q) \leq \frac{c}{\delta n}(d + m).$$

We now prove that Theorem 1 is an immediate corollary of Theorem 8.

Corollary 1 (Restatement of Theorem 1). *Let $P, \widetilde{P}, Q, W, \mathcal{E}, \delta$ and c be as in Theorem 8, and let $\varepsilon = \log(\frac{1}{P[W]})/\delta n$. Then the following hold assuming $n \geq c \cdot m/\delta$:*

- *if $P[W] \geq \exp(-\delta n/cm)$, then $D^{c \cdot (\varepsilon m + 1/\delta n)}(\widetilde{P}||Q) \leq c \cdot (\varepsilon m + m/\delta n)$, and*
- *if $P[W] \geq \exp(-\delta n/2c)$ and $\mathcal{E}$ is a prefix family, then $D^{2c \cdot (\varepsilon + 1/\delta n)}(\widetilde{P}||Q) \leq 2c \cdot (\varepsilon + m/\delta n)$.*

Proof. Let $\{Y_{i,j}\}$ be as in Theorem 8. Note that for each $i \in [m]$:

$$D(\widetilde{P}_{X_i Y_i}||P_{X_i Y_i} \mid \widetilde{P}_{X_{<i}}) \leq D(\widetilde{P}_{X_{\geq i}}||P_{X_{\geq i}} \mid \widetilde{P}_{X_{<j}}) \leq D(\widetilde{P}_X||P_X) \leq \log \frac{1}{P[W]}.$$

The first inequality holds by data-processing of KL-divergence (Fact 4(5)). The second inequality holds by chain-rule of KL-divergence (Fact 4(3)). The last inequality holds by Fact 5. Assuming $P[W] \geq \exp(-\delta n/cm)$, it holds that

$$d \leq m \cdot \log \frac{1}{P[W]} \leq \delta n/c,$$

concluding the proof of the first part.

Assuming $P[W] \geq \exp(-\delta n/c)$ and $\mathcal{E}$ is a prefix family (i.e., $E_{i,j}$ is a function of $X_{\leq i+1}$), then

$$
\begin{aligned}
d &\leq \sum_{i=1}^{m-1} D(\widetilde{P}_{X_i X_{i+1}}||P_{X_i X_{i+1}} \mid \widetilde{P}_{X_{<i}}) + D(\widetilde{P}_{X_m}||P_{X_m} \mid \widetilde{P}_{X_{<m}}) \\
&= \sum_{i \in [m-1] \cap \mathbb{N}_{even}} D(\widetilde{P}_{X_i X_{i+1}}||P_{X_i X_{i+1}} \mid \widetilde{P}_{X_{<i}}) + \sum_{i \in [m-1] \cap \mathbb{N}_{odd}} D(\widetilde{P}_{X_i X_{i+1}}||P_{X_i X_{i+1}} \mid \widetilde{P}_{X_{<i}}) \\
&\quad + D(\widetilde{P}_{X_m}||P_{X_m} \mid \widetilde{P}_{X_{<m}}) \leq 2 \cdot D(\widetilde{P}_X||P_X) \\
&\leq 2 \cdot \log \frac{1}{P[W]} \leq \delta n/c,
\end{aligned}
$$

concluding the proof of the second part. The first inequality holds by data-processing of KL-divergence, and the second one holds by chain-rule and data-processing of KL-divergence.

In order to show that the attacking distribution Q can be carried out efficiently, it suffice to show that with high probability over $(x, j) \sim Q_{X,J}$, we have for all $i \in [m]$ that $P[W \mid (X_{<i}, X_{i,j}) = (x_{<i}, x_{i,j}), E_{i,j}]$ is not much smaller than $P[W]$. The following lemma (proven in the full version) states that the above holds under $\widetilde{P}_X$. Namely, when sampling $x \sim \widetilde{P}_X$ (instead of $x \sim Q_X$) and then $j \sim Q_{J|X=x}$, then $P[W \mid (X_{<i}, X_{i,j}) = (x_{<i}, x_{i,j}), E_{i,j}]$ is indeed not too low.

Lemma 5. *Let* $P, \widetilde{P}, Q, W, \mathcal{E}, \delta, d$ *be as in Theorem 8, let* $t > 0$ *and let*

$$p_t := \Pr_{x \sim \widetilde{P}_X \; ; \; j \sim Q_{J|X=x}} \left[\exists i \in [m] : P[W \mid (X_{<i}, X_{i,j}) = (x_{<i}, x_{i,j}), E_{i,j}] < P[W]/t \right]$$

Assuming $n \geq c \cdot m/\delta$ *and* $d \leq \delta n/c$, *for a universal constant* $c > 0$, *then*

$$p_t \leq 2m/t + c(d+1)/(\delta n).$$

As an immediate corollary, we get the following result.

Corollary 2. *Let* $P, \widetilde{P}, Q, W, \mathcal{E}, \delta$ *be as in Theorem 8, let* $\varepsilon = \log(\frac{1}{P[W]})/\delta n$, *let* $t > 0$ *and let* c *and* p_t *as in Lemma 5. Assuming* $n \geq c \cdot m/\delta$, *it holds that*

- *if* $P[W] \geq \exp(-\delta n/cm)$, *then* $p_t \leq 2m/t + c \cdot (\varepsilon m + 1/\delta n)$.
- *if* $P[W] \geq \exp(-\delta n/2c)$ *and* $\mathcal{E}$ *is a prefix family, then* $p_t \leq 2m/t + 2c \cdot (\varepsilon + 1/\delta n)$.

5   The Parallel Repetition Theorem

In this section, we use Theorem 8 to prove Theorem 2, restated below.

Theorem 9 (Parallel repetition for partially simulatable arguments, restatement of Theorem 2). *Let* π *be an* m-*round* δ-*simulatable [resp., prefix* δ-*simulatable] interactive argument of soundness error* $1 - \varepsilon$. *Then* π^n *has soundness error* $(1 - \varepsilon)^{cn\delta/m}$ *[resp.,* $(1 - \varepsilon)^{cn\delta}$*], for a universal constant* $c > 0$.

Since the random terminating variant of an m-round interactive argument is $1/m$-prefix-simulatable, the (tight) result for such protocols immediately follows. The proof of Theorem 9 follows from our bound on the smooth KL-divergence of skewed distributions, Theorem 8, and Lemma 6, stated and proven below.

Definition 13 (bounding function for many-round skewing). *A function* f *is a* bounding function for many-round skewing *if there exists a polynomial* $p(\cdot, \cdot)$ *such that the following holds for every* $\delta \in (0,1]$ *and every* $m, n \in \mathbb{N}$ *with* $n > p(m, 1/\delta)$: *let* P *be a distribution with* P_X *being a column independent distribution over* $m \times n$ *matrices. Let* W *be an event and let* $\mathcal{E}$ *be a* δ-*dense [resp., prefix* δ-*dense] event family over* P *(see Definition 12). Let* $\widetilde{P} = P|W$ *and let* $Q = Q(P, W, \mathcal{E})$ *be according to Definition 11. Then the following holds for* $\gamma = \log(1/P[W])/f(n, m, \delta)$:

1. $Q_X[T] \leq 2 \cdot \widetilde{P}_X[T] + \gamma$ *for every event* T,[6] *and*
2. $\forall t > 0 : \Pr_{x \sim \widetilde{P}_X \; ; \; j \sim Q_{J|X=x}} [(x,j) \in \mathsf{Bad}_t] \leq p(m, 1/\delta)/t + \gamma$, *letting*

   $\mathsf{Bad}_t := \{(x,j) : \exists i \in [m] : P[W \mid (X_{<i}, X_{i,j}) = (x_{<i}, x_{i,j}), E_{i,j}] < P[W]/t\}$.

---

[6] The constant 2 can be replaced with any other constant without changing (up to a constant factor) the decreasing rate which is promised by Lemma 6.

Lemma 6 (Restatement of Lemma 1). *Let π be an m-round δ-simulatable [resp., prefix δ-simulatable] interactive argument of soundness error $1 - \varepsilon$, let f be a bounding function for many-round skewing (according to Definition 13). Then π^n has soundness error $(1 - \varepsilon)^{f(n,m,\delta)/80}$.*

That is, Lemma 6 tells us that the task of maximizing the decreasing rate of π^n directly reduces to the task of maximizing a bounding function for many-round skewing. A larger bounding function yields a smaller γ in Definition 13. This γ both defines an additive bound on the difference between a small event in $\widetilde{P}$ to a small event in Q, and bounds a specific event in $\widetilde{P}$ that captures the cases in which an attack can be performed efficiently.

We first prove Theorem 9 using Lemma 6.

Proof of Theorem 9.

Proof. We prove for δ-simulatable arguments, the proof for δ-prefix-simulatable arguments follows accordingly. Let $m, n, P, \delta, \mathcal{E}, W, \widetilde{P}$ and Q be as in Lemma 6, where $\mathcal{E}$ is δ-dense, and let $c = \max\{c', c''\}$ where c' is the constant from Corollary 1 and c'' is the constant from Corollary 2. By Corollary 1, if $n \geq c \cdot m/\delta$ and $P[W] \geq \exp(-\delta n/cm)$, then

$$D^{3cm\mu}(\widetilde{P} \| Q) \leq 3cm\mu \tag{10}$$

for $\mu = \log(1/P[W])/\delta n$, where we assumed without loss of generality that $P[W] \leq 1/2$. Hence, assuming that $n \geq c \cdot m/\delta$ and $P[W] \geq \exp(-\delta n/cm)$, Proposition 3 Eq. (10) yields that for every event T:

$$Q[T] \leq 2 \cdot \widetilde{P}[T] + \gamma, \tag{11}$$

where $\gamma = \log(1/P[W])/f(n, m, \delta)$ for $f(n, m, \delta) = \delta n/(24cm)$. For an event W of smaller probability, it holds that $\gamma \geq 24$, and therefore Eq. (11) trivially holds for such events. In addition, by Corollary 2, if $n \geq c \cdot m/\delta$ then

$$\Pr_{x \sim \widetilde{P}_X \; ; \; j \sim Q_{J|X=x}} [\exists i \in [m] : P[W \mid (X_{<i}, X_{i,j}) = (x_{<i}, x_{i,j}), E_{i,j}] < P[W]/t] \leq 2m/t + \gamma \tag{12}$$

(We assume $P[W] \geq \exp(-\delta n/cm)$, as otherwise Eq. (12) trivially holds.) By Eqs. (11) and (12), f is a bounding function for many-round skewing with the polynomial $p(m, 1/\delta) = c \cdot m/\delta$. Therefore, Lemma 6 yields that the soundness error of π^n is bounded by $(1 - \varepsilon)^{f(n,m,\delta)/80} = (1 - \varepsilon)^{\delta n/(c'm)}$, for $c' = 1920c$.

5.1 Proving Lemma 6

Let f be a bounding function for many-round skewing with the polynomial $p(\cdot, \cdot) \in \text{poly}$. We first prove the case when the number of repetition n is at least $p(m, 1/\delta)$, and then show how to extend the proof for the general case.

Many Repetitions Case.

Proof (Proof of Lemma 6, many repetitions). Fix an m-round δ-simulatable interactive argument $\pi = (P, V)$ of soundness error $1-\varepsilon$ (the proof of the δ-prefix-simulatable case follows the same lines), and let $n = n(\kappa) > p(m(\kappa), 1/\delta(\kappa))$. Note that without loss of generality $\varepsilon(\kappa) \geq 1/\text{poly}(\kappa)$.

Our proof is a black-box reduction according to Definition 9: we present an oracle-aided algorithm that given access to a deterministic cheating prover for π^n violating the claimed soundness of π^n, uses it to break the assumed soundness of π while not running for too long. The lemma then follows by Proposition 2.

Let S be the oracle-aided simulator guaranteed by the δ-simulatablily of V. For a cheating prover P^{n*} for π^n, let P^* be the cheating prover that when interacting with V, emulates a random execution of (P^{n*}, V^n), letting V plays one of the n verifiers at a random location. (Clearly, P^* only requires oracle access to P^{n*}.) Assume without loss of generality that in each round V flips $t = t(\kappa)$ coins. The oracle-aided algorithm P^* is defined as follows.

Algorithm 10 (P^*)
Input: 1^κ, $m = m(\kappa)$ and $n = n(\kappa)$.
Oracles: cheating prover P^{n*} for π^n.
Operation:

1. *Let $j \leftarrow [n]$.*
2. *For $i = 1$ to m do:*
    (a) Let a_i be the ith message sent by V.
    (b) Do the following ("rejection continuation"):
        i. Let $x_{i,-j} \leftarrow (\{0,1\}^t)^{n-1}$
        ii. Let $v = S^{P^{n*}}(1^\kappa, (j, x_{\leq i,-j}, a_{\leq i}))$.
        iii. If all n verifiers accept in v, break the inner loop.
    (c) Send to V the ith message P^{n*} sends in v.

Fix a cheating prover P^{n*}. We also fix $\kappa \in \mathbb{N}$, and omit it from the notation. Let $P = P_X$ denotes the coins V^n uses in a uniform execution of (P^{n*}, V^n). (Hence P_X is uniformly distributed over $m \times n$ matrices.) Let W be the event over P that P^{n*} wins in (P^{n*}, V^n) (i.e., all verifiers accept), and let $\tilde{P}_X = P_X|W$. For an i rounds view $v = (j, \cdot)$ of P^{n*} in (P^{n*}, V), let Δ_v be the δ-dense subset of V's coins describing the output distribution of $S^{P^{n*}}(v)$. Let $\mathcal{T}_{i,j}$ be all possible i round views of P^{n*} in (P^{n*}, V) that are starting with j. Finally, let $\mathcal{E} = \{E_{i,j}\}_{i\in[m], j\in[n]}$ be the event family over P defined by $E_{i,j} = \bigcup_{v\in\mathcal{T}_{i,j}} \Delta_v$, and let $Q_{X,J}$ be the e (skewed) distribution described in Definition 11 with respect to $P, W, \mathcal{E}$. By inspection, Q describes the distribution of $(j, x_{\leq m})$ in a random execution of (P^*, V^n), where $x_{\leq m,j}$ denotes the coins of V, and $x_{\leq m,-j}$ denote the final value of this term in the execution. Assume

$$\Pr[(P^{n*}, V^n) = 1] = P[W] > (1 - \varepsilon)^{f(n,m,\delta)/80}, \tag{13}$$

and let $\gamma = \log\left(1/P[W]\right)/f(n, m, \delta)$. By Eq. (13) it holds that

$$\gamma < -\log(1-\varepsilon)/80 \leq \varepsilon/80 \tag{14}$$

Since $\widetilde{P}[W] = 1$, we deduce by Property 13(1) of f on the event $\neg W$ that

$$\Pr\left[(\mathrm{P}^*, \mathrm{V}) = 1\right] \geq Q_X[W] > 1 - \gamma > 1 - \varepsilon/80 \tag{15}$$

So it is left to argue about the running time of P^*. By Property 13(2) of f on $t = 80 \cdot p(m, 1/\delta)/\varepsilon$ it holds that

$$\Pr_{x \sim \widetilde{P}_X \;;\; j \sim Q_{J|X=x}} \left[(x, j) \in \mathsf{Bad}_t\right] \quad \leq \quad p(m, 1/\delta)/t + \gamma < \varepsilon/40 \tag{16}$$

Consider the extension $\widetilde{P}_{XJ}$ of $\widetilde{P}_X$, where $\widetilde{P}_{J|X} = Q_{J|X}$. Note that by Property 13(1), for any event T over (X, J) it holds that $Q_{XJ}[T] \leq 2 \cdot \widetilde{P}_{XJ}[T] + \gamma$. In particular, this holds for the event $(X, J) \in \mathsf{Bad}_t$. Therefore, we deduce from Eqs. (14) and (16) that

$$\Pr_{x \sim Q_X \;;\; j \sim Q_{J|X=x}} \left[(x, j) \in \mathsf{Bad}_t\right] \quad \leq \quad 2\varepsilon/40 + \gamma < \varepsilon/10 \tag{17}$$

By Eqs. (15) and (17) we obtain that

$$\Pr_{(x,j) \sim Q_{X,J}} \left[W \wedge ((x, j) \notin \mathsf{Bad}_t)\right] > 1 - \varepsilon/5 \tag{18}$$

Namely, with probability larger than $1 - \varepsilon/5$, the attacker P^* wins and its expected running time in each round is bounded by $O(t/P[W]) \leq \mathrm{poly}(\kappa)$. This contradicts the soundness guaranty of π.

Any Number of Repetitions. See the full version.

6   Bounding Smooth KL-Divergence of Skewed Distributions - Proof Sketch

In this section we give a rather detailed proof sketch (more accurately, an attempt proof sketch) for proving Theorem 8 in which we explain the difficulties that arise. The actual proof appears in the full version due to page limitation.

Fix a distribution P with P_X being a distribution over $\mathcal{U}^{m \times n}$ matrices with independent columns, event W over P and δ-dense event family $\mathcal{E} = \{E_{i,j}\}$ over P_X. Let $\widetilde{P} = P|W$ and let $Q_{X,J} = Q(P, W, \mathcal{E})$ be the skewed variant of $\widetilde{P}$ defined in Definition 11. Let $Y_i = (Y_{i,1}, \ldots, Y_{i,n})$ for $Y_{i,j}$ be the indicator for $E_{i,j}$, and let $d = \sum_{i=1}^m D(\widetilde{P}_{X_i Y_i} \| P_{X_i Y_i} | \widetilde{P}_{X_{<i}})$.

In the following we present an attempt to bound the divergence between $\widetilde{P}$ and Q. That is, to show that

$$D(\widetilde{P} \| Q) \leq O\left(\frac{1}{\delta n}\right) \cdot (d + m) \tag{19}$$

We try to do so by showing that for every $i \in [m]$ it holds that

$$D(\widetilde{P}_{X_i}||Q_{X_i}|\widetilde{P}_{X_{<i}}) \leq O\left(\frac{1}{\delta n}\right) \cdot (d_i + 1) \tag{20}$$

for $d_i = D(\widetilde{P}_{X_i Y_i}||P_{X_i Y_i}|\widetilde{P}_{X_{<i}})$, and applying chain-rule of KL-divergence for deducing Eq. (19). By data-processing of KL-divergence (Fact 4(5)), it holds that

$$D(\widetilde{P}_{X_i}||Q_{X_i}|\widetilde{P}_{X_{<i}}) \leq D(\widetilde{P}_{X_i Y_i}||Q'_{X_i Y_i}|\widetilde{P}_{X_{<i}}), \tag{21}$$

where

$$Q'_{X_i Y_i|X_{<i}} = \widetilde{P}_{X_i Y_i|X_{<i}, X_{i,J}, Y_{i,J}=1} \circ Q_{J, X_{i,J}|X_{<i}} \equiv P_{X_{i,J}|X_{<i}} \widetilde{P}_{X_i Y_i|X_{<i}, X_{i,J}, Y_{i,J}=1} \circ Q_{J|X_{<i}}$$

(note that $Q'_{X_i} \equiv Q_{X_i}$ and that $P_{X_{i,J}|X_{<i}} \equiv P_{X_{i,J}|X_{<i,J}}$ because the columns under P are independent). By definition of Q', for any fixing of $x_{\leq i} y_i \in \text{Supp}(\widetilde{P}_{X_{\leq i} Y_i})$ it holds that

$$Q'_{X_i Y_i|X_{<i}=x_{<i}}(x_i y_i) \tag{22}$$

$$= E_{j \sim Q_{J|X_{<i}=x_{<i}}}\left[P_{X_{i,j}|X_{<i}=x_{<i}}(x_{i,j}) \cdot \widetilde{P}_{X_i Y_i|X_{<i}=x_{<i}, X_{i,j}=x_{i,j}, Y_{i,j}=1}(x_i y_i)\right]$$

$$= \sum_{j=1}^{n} Q_{J|X_{<i}=x_{<i}}(j) \cdot P_{X_{i,j}|X_{<i}=x_{<i}}(x_{i,j}) \cdot \frac{\widetilde{P}_{X_i Y_i X_{i,j} Y_{i,j}|X_{<i}=x_{<i}}(x_i y_i x_{i,j} 1)}{\widetilde{P}_{X_{i,j}, Y_{i,j}|X_{<i}=x_{<i}}(x_{i,j}, 1)}$$

$$= \sum_{j \in 1_{y_i}} Q_{J|X_{<i}=x_{<i}}(j) \cdot P_{X_{i,j}|X_{<i}=x_{<i}}(x_{i,j}) \cdot \frac{\widetilde{P}_{X_i Y_i|X_{<i}=x_{<i}}(x_i y_i)}{\widetilde{P}_{X_{i,j}, Y_{i,j}|X_{<i}=x_{<i}}(x_{i,j}, 1)}$$

$$= \sum_{j \in 1_{y_i}} Q_{J|X_{<i}=x_{<i}}(j) \cdot \frac{\beta_{i,j}(x_{i,j}) \cdot \widetilde{P}_{X_i Y_i|X_{<i}=x_{<i}}(x_i y_i)}{\tilde{\delta}_{i,j}},$$

for $\beta_{i,j}(x_{i,j}) = \beta_{i,j}(x_{i,j}; x_{<i}) = \frac{P_{X_{i,j}|X_{<i}=x_{<i}}(x_{i,j})}{\widetilde{P}_{X_{i,j}|X_{<i}=x_{<i}, Y_{i,j}=1}(x_{i,j})}$ and $\tilde{\delta}_{i,j} = \tilde{\delta}_{i,j}(x_{<i}) = \widetilde{P}_{Y_{i,j}|X_{<i}=x_{<i}}(1) \, (= \widetilde{P}[E_{i,j} \mid X_{<i} = x_{<i}])$, where recall that we denote $1_{y_i} = \{j \in [n]: y_{i,j} = 1\}$. We now use the following claim (proven in the full version) that calculates the probability to get j in the conditional distribution $Q_{J|X_{<i}=x_{<i}}$.

Claim. Let $\omega'_{i,j} = \omega'_{i,j}(x_{<i}) := \prod_{s=1}^{i-1} \frac{P[X_{s,j}=x_{s,j}|X_{<s}=x_{<s}]}{\widetilde{P}[X_{s,j}=x_{s,j}|X_{<s}=x_{<s}]}$ and let

$$\omega_{i,j} = \omega_{i,j}(x_{<i}) := \frac{n \cdot \omega'_{i,j}}{\sum_{t=1}^{n} \omega'_{i,t}} \cdot \prod_{s=1}^{i-1} \frac{\widetilde{P}[E_{s,j} \mid X_{<s} = x_{<s}]}{\widetilde{P}[E_{s,j} \mid X_{<s} = x_{<s}, X_{s,j} = x_{s,j}]} \cdot \frac{\widetilde{P}[E_{s,j} \mid X_{<s} = x_{<s}]}{P[E_{s,j} \mid X_{<s} = x_{<s}]}.$$

Then it holds that

$$Q_{J|X_{<i}=x_{<i}}(j) = \frac{\omega_{i,j}}{\sum_{t=1}^{n} \omega_{i,t}}.$$

Note that $\omega_{i,j}$ is basically a relative "weight" for the column j, where a large $\omega_{i,j}$ with respect to the other $\omega_{i,t}$'s means that $Q_{J|X_{<i}=x_{<i}}(j)$ is higher. In an extreme case it is possible that $\omega_{i,j} = \infty$, meaning that $Q_{J|X_{<i}=x_{<i}}(j) = 1$. However, we assume for now that all $\omega_{i,j} < \infty$. Later in this proof attempt we even assume that all the terms are close to 1, meaning that $Q_{J|X_{<i}=x_{<i}}$ has high min entropy (assumptions that are eliminated in the full version). As a side note, observe that $\omega_{1,j} = 1$ for all $j \in [n]$ (meaning that Q_J, without any conditioning, is the uniform distribution over $[n]$). At this point, we just mention that we added (the same) multiplicative factor of $\frac{n}{\sum_{t=1}^{n} \omega'_{i,t}}$ to all $\{\omega_{i,j}\}_{j=1}^{n}$. On the one hand this does not change the relative weight, but on the other hand it will help us to claim in the full version that these $\omega_{i,j}$'s are indeed close to 1. By Eqs. (21) and (22) and Claim 6, it holds that

$$D(\widetilde{P}_{X_i} \| Q_{X_i} | \widetilde{P}_{X_{<i}}) \leq D(\widetilde{P}_{X_i Y_i} \| Q'_{X_i Y_i} | \widetilde{P}_{X_{<i}}) \tag{23}$$

$$= E_{x_{<i} \sim X_{<i}} E_{x_i y_i \sim \widetilde{P}_{X_i Y_i | X_{<i} = x_{<i}}} \left[\log \frac{\widetilde{P}_{X_i Y_i | X_{<i} = x_{<i}}(x_i y_i)}{Q_{X_i Y_i | X_{<i} = x_{<i}}(x_i y_i)} \right]$$

$$= E_{x_{<i} \sim X_{<i}} E_{x_i y_i \sim \widetilde{P}_{X_i Y_i | X_{<i} = x_{<i}}} \left[\log \frac{\sum_{j=1}^{n} \omega_{i,j}}{\sum_{j \in 1_{y_i}} \frac{\omega_{i,j} \cdot \beta_{i,j}(x_{i,j})}{\delta_{i,j}}} \right]$$

$$= E_{x_{<i} \sim X_{<i}} E_{x_i y_i \sim \widetilde{P}_{X_i Y_i | X_{<i} = x_{<i}}} \left[-\log\left(1 + \gamma_i(x_i y_i)\right) \right],$$

for

$$\gamma_i(x_i y_i) = \gamma_i(x_i y_i; x_{<i}) = \left(\sum_{j \in 1_{y_i}} \frac{\omega_{i,j} \cdot \beta_{i,j}(x_{i,j})}{\delta_{i,j}} \right) \Big/ \left(\sum_{j=1}^{n} \omega_{i,j} \right) - 1 \tag{24}$$

Naturally, we would like to approximate the logarithm in the above equation with a low-degree polynomial. However, we can only do if γ_i is far away from -1. In particular, if $\widetilde{P}[\gamma_i(X_i Y_i; X_{<i}) = -1] > 0$ (which happens if the event W allows for none of the events $\{E_{i,j}\}_{i=1}^{n}$ to occur), the above expectation is unbounded. At that point, we only show how to bound Eq. (23) under simplifying assumptions, while in the full version we present how to eliminate the assumptions via smooth KL-divergence. We now assume that for any $x_{<i} \in \mathrm{Supp}(\widetilde{P}_{X_{<i}})$ and any $j \in [n]$, the following holds:

Assumption 11

1. $|\gamma_i(x_i y_i)| \leq 1/2$ for any $x_i y_i \in \mathrm{Supp}(\widetilde{P}_{X_i Y_i | X_{<i} = x_{<i}})$.
2. $\tilde{\delta}_{i,j} \geq 0.9 \delta_{i,j}$ (recall that $\delta_{i,j} = P[E_{i,j}] = P[E_{i,j} \mid X_{\leq i}]$ for any fixing of $X_{\leq i}$).
3. $\omega_{i,j} \in 1 \pm 0.1$.
4. $\mathrm{Supp}(P_{X_{i,j}|X_{<i}=x_{<i}}) \subseteq \mathrm{Supp}(\widetilde{P}_{X_{i,j}|X_{<i}=x_{<i}, Y_{i,j}=1})$.
5. $\beta_{i,j}(x_{i,j}) \leq 1.1$ for any $x_{i,j} \in \mathrm{Supp}(\widetilde{P}_{X_{i,j}|X_{<i}=x_{<i}})$.

Note that Assumption 3 implies that $Q_{J|X_{<i}}$ has high min-entropy, and Assumptions 2 along with 5 imply that for all j:

$$P[W \mid (X_{<i}, X_{i,j}) = (x_{<i}, x_{i,j}), E_{i,j}]$$

$$= \frac{\widetilde{P}_{X_{i,j}|X_{<i}=x_{<i}, E_{i,j}}(x_{i,j})}{P_{X_{i,j}|X_{<i}=x_{<i}, E_{i,j}}(x_{i,j})} \cdot \frac{\widetilde{P}[E_{i,j} \mid X_{<i} = x_{<i}]}{P[E_{i,j} \mid X_{<i} = x_{<i}]} \cdot P[W \mid X_{<i} = x_{<i}]$$

$$= \beta_{i,j}(x_{i,j}) \cdot \left(\tilde{\delta}_{i,j}/\delta_{i,j}\right) \cdot P[W \mid X_{<i} = x_{<i}] \geq P[W \mid X_{<i} = x_{<i}]/2,$$

which fits the explanation in Sect. 1.4.1 (note that in the second equality we used the fact that $P_{X_{i,j}|X_{<i}=x_{<i}, E_{i,j}}(x_{i,j}) = P_{X_{i,j}|X_{<i}=x_{<i}}(x_{i,j})$ by assumption).
By Eq. (23), note that in order to prove Eq. (20), it is enough to show that for any $x_{<i} \in \mathrm{Supp}(\widetilde{P}_{x_{<i}})$ it holds that

$$\tag{25}$$

$$\mathrm{E}_{x_i y_i \sim \widetilde{P}_{X_i Y_i | X_{<i} = x_{<i}}} [-\log(1 + \gamma_i(x_i y_i))] \leq O\left(\frac{1}{\delta n}\right) \cdot \left(D(\widetilde{P}_{X_i Y_i | X_{<i}=x_{<i}} \| P_{X_i Y_i | X_{<i}=x_{<i}}) + 1\right)$$

In the following, fix $x_{<i} \in \mathrm{Supp}(\widetilde{P}_{x_{<i}})$. We now focus on proving Eq. (25). Using the inequality $-\log(1+x) \leq -x + x^2$ for $|x| \leq \frac{1}{2}$, we deduce from Assumption 1 that

$$\mathrm{E}_{x_i y_i \sim \widetilde{P}_{X_i Y_i | X_{<i} = x_{<i}}} [-\log(1 + \gamma_i(x_i y_i))] \leq \mathrm{E}_{x_i y_i \sim \widetilde{P}_{X_i Y_i | X_{<i} = x_{<i}}} \left[-\gamma_i(x_i y_i) + \gamma_i(x_i y_i)^2\right] \tag{26}$$

Note that

$$\mathrm{E}_{x_i y_i \sim \widetilde{P}_{X_i Y_i | X_{<i} = x_{<i}}} \left[\sum_{j \in 1_{y_i}} \frac{\omega_{i,j} \cdot \beta_{i,j}(x_{i,j})}{\tilde{\delta}_{i,j}}\right] \tag{27}$$

$$= \sum_{j=1}^{n} \mathrm{E}_{x_{i,j} y_{i,j} \sim \widetilde{P}_{X_{i,j} Y_{i,j} | X_{<i} = x_{<i}}} \left[y_{i,j} \cdot \frac{\omega_{i,j} \cdot \beta_{i,j}(x_{i,j})}{\tilde{\delta}_{i,j}}\right]$$

$$= \sum_{j=1}^{n} \omega_{i,j} \cdot \mathrm{E}_{x_{i,j} \sim \widetilde{P}_{X_{i,j} | X_{<i} = x_{<i}, Y_{i,j}=1}} [\beta_{i,j}(x_{i,j})]$$

$$= \sum_{j=1}^{n} \omega_{i,j} \cdot \mathrm{E}_{x_{i,j} \sim \widetilde{P}_{X_{i,j} | X_{<i} = x_{<i}, Y_{i,j}=1}} \left[\frac{P_{X_{i,j}|X_{<i}=x_{<i}}(x_{i,j})}{\widetilde{P}_{X_{i,j}|X_{<i}=x_{<i}, Y_{i,j}=1}(x_{i,j})}\right]$$

$$= \sum_{j=1}^{n} \omega_{i,j} \cdot P_{X_{i,j}|X_{<i}=x_{<i}}(\mathrm{Supp}(\widetilde{P}_{X_{i,j}|X_{<i}=x_{<i}, Y_{i,j}=1})) = \sum_{j=1}^{n} \omega_{i,j}.$$

The second equality holds since $y_{i,j} \in \{0,1\}$ and since Assumption 2 implies that $\widetilde{P}_{Y_{i,j}|X_{<i}=x_{<i}}(1) = \tilde{\delta}_{i,j} > 0$ for all $j \in [n]$, and the last equality holds by Assumption 4. Therefore, we deduce from Eq. (27) that

$$\mathrm{E}_{x_i y_i \sim \widetilde{P}_{X_i Y_i | X_{<i} = x_{<i}}} \left[\gamma_i(x_i y_i) \right] \tag{28}$$

$$= \left(\mathrm{E}_{x_i y_i \sim \widetilde{P}_{X_i Y_i | X_{<i} = x_{<i}}} \left[\sum_{j \in 1_{y_i}} \frac{\omega_{i,j} \cdot \beta_{i,j}(x_{i,j})}{\tilde{\delta}_{i,j}} \right] \right) \bigg/ \left(\sum_{j=1}^{n} \omega_{i,j} \right) - 1 = 0.$$

Hence, in order to prove Eq. (25), we deduce from Eqs. (26) and (28) that it is left to prove that

$$\mathrm{E}_{x_i y_i \sim \widetilde{P}_{X_i Y_i | X_{<i} = x_{<i}}} \left[\gamma_i(x_i y_i)^2 \right] \leq O\left(\frac{1}{\delta n} \right) \cdot \left(D(\widetilde{P}_{X_i Y_i | X_{<i} = x_{<i}} \| P_{X_i Y_i | X_{<i} = x_{<i}}) + 1 \right) \tag{29}$$

In the following, rather than directly bounding the expected value of $\gamma_i(x_i y_i)^2$ under $\widetilde{P}_{X_i Y_i | X_{<i} = x_{<i}}$, we show that under the product of the marginals of $\widetilde{P}_{X_i Y_i | X_{<i} = x_{<i}}$ (namely, under the distribution $\prod_{j=1}^{n} \widetilde{P}_{X_{i,j} Y_{i,j} | X_{<i} = x_{<i}}$), the value of $\gamma_i(x_i y_i)$ is well concentrated around its mean (i.e., zero), and the proof will follow by Proposition 1. More formally, let Γ be the value of $\gamma_i(x_i y_i)$ when $x_i y_i$ is drawn from either $\widetilde{P} = \widetilde{P}_{X_i Y_i | X_{<i} = x_{<i}}$ or $\widetilde{P}^{II} = \prod_{j=1}^{n} \widetilde{P}_{X_{i,j} Y_{i,j} | X_{<i} = x_{<i}}$. We prove that there exist two constants $K_1, K_2 > 0$ such that for any $\gamma \in [0, 1]$:

$$\widetilde{P}^{II}[|\Gamma| \geq \gamma] \leq K_2 \cdot \exp\left(-\frac{\gamma^2}{K_1 \cdot \sigma^2} \right) \tag{30}$$

for $\sigma^2 = 1/\delta n$. Using Eq. (30) and the fact that $|\Gamma| \leq 1$ (Assumption 1), Proposition 1 yields that

$$\mathrm{E}_{x_i y_i \sim \widetilde{P}_{X_i Y_i | X_{<i} = x_{<i}}} \left[\gamma_i(x_i y_i)^2 \right] = \mathrm{E}_{\widetilde{P}} \left[\Gamma^2 \right] \leq \frac{K_3}{\delta n} \cdot \left(D(\widetilde{P} \| \widetilde{P}^{II}) + 1 \right) \tag{31}$$

$$= \frac{K_3}{\delta n} \cdot \left(D(\widetilde{P}_{X_i Y_i | X_{<i} = x_{<i}} \| \prod_{j=1}^{n} \widetilde{P}_{X_{i,j} Y_{i,j} | X_{<i} = x_{<i}}) + 1 \right)$$

$$\leq \frac{K_3}{\delta n} \cdot \left(D(\widetilde{P}_{X_i Y_i | X_{<i} = x_{<i}} \| P_{X_i Y_i | X_{<i} = x_{<i}}) + 1 \right).$$

The last inequality holds by chain rule of KL-divergence when the right-hand side distribution is product (Fact 4(3), where recall that $P_{X_i Y_i | X_{<i} = x_{<i}} = \prod_{j=1}^{n} P_{X_{i,j} Y_{i,j} | X_{<i} = x_{<i}}$). This concludes the proof of Eq. (29). It is left to prove Eq. (30). In the following, given $x_i y_i$ which are drawn from either $\widetilde{P}^{II} = \prod_{j=1}^{n} \widetilde{P}_{X_{i,j} Y_{i,j} | X_{<i} = x_{<i}}$ or $\widetilde{P}^{II'} = \prod_{j=1}^{n} \widetilde{P}_{Y_{i,j} | X_{<i} = x_{<i}} \cdot \widetilde{P}_{X_{i,j} | X_{<i} = x_{<i}, Y_{i,j} = 1}$, we define the random variables L_j, Z_j, L and Z (in addition to Γ), where L_j is the value of $\omega_j \cdot \beta_j(x_{i,j})$, $L = \sum_{j=1}^{n} L_j$, $Z_j = \begin{cases} L_j / \tilde{\delta}_j & y_{i,j} = 1 \\ 0 & y_{i,j} = 0 \end{cases}$ and $Z = \sum_{j=1}^{n} Z_j$, letting $\omega_j = \omega_{i,j}$, $\beta_j(\cdot) = \beta_{i,j}(\cdot)$ and $\tilde{\delta}_j = \tilde{\delta}_{i,j}$. Note that by definition, $Z = (1 + \Gamma)\mu$ for $\mu = \sum_{j=1}^{n} \omega_j$. Namely, Γ measures how far Z is from its expected value μ (follows by Eq. (27) that calculates $\mathrm{E}_{\widetilde{P}}[Z]$, which also equals to $\mathrm{E}_{\widetilde{P}^{II}}[Z]$ and $\mathrm{E}_{\widetilde{P}^{II'}}[Z]$). Note that the distribution of Z and Γ when $x_i y_i$ is

drawn from $\widetilde{P}^{II}$ is identical to the distribution of Z and Γ (respectively) when $x_i y_i$ is drawn from $\widetilde{P}^{II'}$. Therefore, in particular it holds that

$$\widetilde{P}^{II}[|\Gamma| \geq \gamma] = \widetilde{P}^{II'}[|\Gamma| \geq \gamma] \tag{32}$$

Under $\widetilde{P}^{II'}$, the L_j's are independent random variables with $\mathrm{E}_{\widetilde{P}^{II'}}[L_j] = \omega_j$ and $\mathrm{E}_{\widetilde{P}^{II'}}[L] = \mu$ where $\mu = \sum_{j=1}^n \omega_j \geq n/2$ and $|L_j| \leq 2$ (by Assumptions 3 and 5). Moreover, for all $j \in [n]$, $Z_j = (L_j/\tilde{\delta}_j) \cdot \mathrm{Bern}(\tilde{\delta}_j)$ where $\tilde{\delta}_j \geq 0.9\delta_{i,j} \geq 0.9\delta$ (by Assumption 2). Hence, Fact 7 yields that

$$\widetilde{P}^{II'}[|\Gamma| \geq \gamma] \leq 4 \exp\left(-\frac{\delta n \gamma^2}{100}\right) \tag{33}$$

The proof of Eq. (30) now follows by Eqs. (32) and (33), which ends the proof of Theorem 8 under the assumptions in 11.

6.1 Eliminating the Assumptions

The assumptions we made in 11 may seem unjustified at first glance. For instance, even for $j = 1$, there could be "bad" columns $j \in [n]$ with $\tilde{\delta}_{1,j} < 0.9\delta_{1,j}$. We claim, however, that the probability that a uniform J (chosen by Q) will hit such a "bad" column j is low. For showing that, let $\mathcal{B}_1 = \{j \in [n]: \tilde{\delta}_{1,j} < 0.9\delta_{1,j}\}$ be the set of "bad" columns $j \in [n]$ for $i = 1$. A simple calculation yields that

$$d_1 = D(\widetilde{P}_{X_1 Y_1} || P_{X_1 Y_1}) \geq D(\widetilde{P}_{Y_1} || P_{Y_1}) \geq \sum_{j=1}^n D(\widetilde{P}_{Y_{1,j}} || P_{Y_{1,j}})$$

$$= \sum_{j=1}^n D(\tilde{\delta}_{1,j} || \delta_{1,j}) \geq \sum_{j \in \mathcal{B}_1} D(\tilde{\delta}_{1,j} || \delta_{1,j}) \geq \sum_{j \in \mathcal{B}_1} \delta_{1,j}/200 \geq |\mathcal{B}_1| \cdot \delta/200.$$

The second inequality holds by chain-rule of KL-divergence when the right-hand side distribution is product (Fact 4(3))) and the penultimate inequality holds by Fact 6(1). This implies that $|\mathcal{B}_1| \leq 200 d_1/\delta$, and hence, $Q_J[J \in \mathcal{B}_1] < 200 d_1/(\delta n)$. Extending the above argument for a row $i > 1$ is a much harder task. As we saw in Claim 6, the conditional distribution $Q_{J|X_{<i}}$ is much more complicated, and it also seems not clear how to bound $|\mathcal{B}_i|$ (now a function of $X_{<i}$) as we did for $i = 1$, when $X_{<i}$ is drawn from Q. Yet, we show in the full version that when $X_{<i}$ is drawn from $\widetilde{P}$ (and not from Q), then we are able to understand $Q_{J|X_{<i}}$ and $\mathcal{B}_i(X_{<i})$ better and bound by $O(d/(\delta n))$ the probability of hitting a "bad" column for all $i \in [m]$. This is done by relating martingale sequences for each sequence $\{\omega_{i,j}\}_{i=1}^m$ under $\widetilde{P}$, and by showing (using Lemma 3) that with high probability, the sequences of most $j \in [n]$ remains around 1.

Following the above discussion, the high level plan of our proof is to define the "good" events $A_1, \ldots, A_n$ for $\widetilde{P}$ and $B_1, \ldots, B_n$ for Q such that for all $i \in [m]$, the conditional distributions $\widetilde{P}_{X_i|A_{\leq i}}$ and $Q_{X_i|B_{\leq i}}$ satisfy the assumptions in 11. Then, by only bounding the probability of "bad" events under $\widetilde{P}$, the proof of Theorem 8 will follow by Lemma 4. For details, see the full version.

References

1. Bellare, M., Impagliazzo, R., Naor, M.: Does parallel repetition lower the error in computationally sound protocols? In: 38th Annual Symposium on Foundations of Computer Science, FOCS 1997, Miami Beach, Florida, USA, 19–22 October 1997, pp. 374–383 (1997)
2. Berman, I., Haitner, I., Tsfadia, E.: A tight parallel repetition theorem for partially simulatable interactive arguments via smooth KL-divergence. Cryptology ePrint Archive, Report 2019/393 (2019). https://eprint.iacr.org/2019/393
3. Brakerski, Z., Vaikuntanathan, V.: Efficient fully homomorphic encryption from (standard) LWE. J. ACM 43(2), 831–871 (2014)
4. Canetti, R., Halevi, S., Steiner, M.: Hardness amplification of weakly verifiable puzzles. In: Kilian, J. (ed.) TCC 2005. LNCS, vol. 3378, pp. 17–33. Springer, Heidelberg (2005). https://doi.org/10.1007/978-3-540-30576-7_2
5. Chung, F., Lu, L.: Connected components in random graphs with given expected degree sequences. Ann. Comb. 6, 125–145 (2002). https://doi.org/10.1007/PL00012580
6. Chung, K.-M., Liu, F.-H.: Parallel repetition theorems for interactive arguments. In: Micciancio, D. (ed.) TCC 2010. LNCS, vol. 5978, pp. 19–36. Springer, Heidelberg (2010). https://doi.org/10.1007/978-3-642-11799-2_2
7. Chung, K.M., Pass, R.: The randomness complexity of parallel repetition. In: Proceedings of the 52nd Annual Symposium on Foundations of Computer Science (FOCS), pp. 658–667 (2011)
8. Chung, K.-M., Pass, R.: Tight parallel repetition theorems for public-coin arguments Using KL-divergence. In: Dodis, Y., Nielsen, J.B. (eds.) TCC 2015, Part II. LNCS, vol. 9015, pp. 229–246. Springer, Heidelberg (2015). https://doi.org/10.1007/978-3-662-46497-7_9
9. Damgård, I.B., Pfitzmann, B.: Sequential iteration arguments and an efficient zero-knowledge argument for NP. In: Annual International Colloquium on Automata, Languages and Programming (ICALP), pp. 772–783 (1998)
10. Dinur, I., Steurer, D.: Analytical approach to parallel repetition. In: Symposium on Theory of Computing, STOC 2014, New York, NY, USA, 31 May–03 June 2014, pp. 624–633 (2014)
11. Dodis, Y., Jain, A., Moran, T., Wichs, D.: Counterexamples to hardness amplification beyond negligible. In: Cramer, R. (ed.) TCC 2012. LNCS, vol. 7194, pp. 476–493. Springer, Heidelberg (2012). https://doi.org/10.1007/978-3-642-28914-9_27
12. Donsker, M.D., Varadhan, S.R.S.: Asymptotic evaluation of certain markov process expectations for large time. IV. Commun. Pure Appl. Math. 36(2), 183–212 (1983)
13. Feige, U.: On the success probability of the two provers in one-round proof systems. In: Proceedings of the Sixth Annual Structure in Complexity Theory Conference, Chicago, Illinois, USA, 30 June–3 July 1991, pp. 116–123 (1991)
14. Feige, U., Verbitsky, O.: Error reduction by parallel repetition - a negative result. Combinatorica 22(4), 461–478 (2002)
15. Fortnow, L., Rompel, J., Sipser, M.: Errata for on the power of multi-prover interactive protocols. In: Proceedings: Fifth Annual Structure in Complexity Theory Conference, Universitat Politècnica de Catalunya, Barcelona, Spain, 8–11 July 1990, pp. 318–319 (1990)
16. Goldreich, O.: Modern Cryptography Probabilistic Proofs and Pseudorandomness. Springer, Heidelberg (1999). https://doi.org/10.1007/978-3-662-12521-2

17. Haitner, I.: A parallel repetition theorem for any interactive argument. SIAM J. Comput. **42**(6), 2487–2501 (2013). https://doi.org/10.1137/100810630
18. Håstad, J., Pass, R., Wikström, D., Pietrzak, K.: An efficient parallel repetition theorem. In: Micciancio, D. (ed.) TCC 2010. LNCS, vol. 5978, pp. 1–18. Springer, Heidelberg (2010). https://doi.org/10.1007/978-3-642-11799-2_1
19. Holenstein, T.: Parallel repetition: simplification and the no-signaling case. Theory Comput. **5**(1), 141–172 (2009)
20. Moshkovitz, D.: Parallel repetition from fortification. In: 55th IEEE Annual Symposium on Foundations of Computer Science, FOCS 2014, Philadelphia, PA, USA, 18–21 October 2014, pp. 414–423 (2014)
21. Mulzer, W.: Chernoff bounds (2018). https://page.mi.fu-berlin.de/mulzer/notes/misc/chernoff.pdf
22. Pass, R., Venkitasubramaniam, M.: A parallel repetition theorem for constant-round Arthur-Merlin proofs. TOCT **4**(4), 10:1–10:22 (2012)
23. Pietrzak, K., Wikström, D.: Parallel repetition of computationally sound protocols revisited. J. Cryptol. **25**(1), 116–135 (2012). https://doi.org/10.1007/s00145-010-9090-x
24. Rao, A.: Parallel repetition in projection games and a concentration bound. SIAM J. Comput. **40**(6), 1871–1891 (2011)
25. Raz, R.: A parallel repetition theorem. SIAM J. Comput. **27**(3), 763–803 (1998)

Interactive Proofs for Social Graphs

Liran Katzir[1(✉)], Clara Shikhelman[2], and Eylon Yogev[3]

[1] Google Research, Tel Aviv, Israel
lirank@google.com
[2] Chaincode Labs, New York City, USA
clara.shikhelman@gmail.com
[3] BU and TAU, Boston, USA
eylony@gmail.com

Abstract. We consider interactive proofs for social graphs, where the verifier has only oracle access to the graph and can query for the ith neighbor of a vertex v, given i and v. In this model, we construct a doubly-efficient public-coin two-message interactive protocol for estimating the size of the graph to within a multiplicative factor $\varepsilon > 0$. The verifier performs $\widetilde{O}(1/\varepsilon^2 \cdot \tau_{mix} \cdot \Delta)$ queries to the graph, where τ_{mix} is the mixing time of the graph and Δ is the average degree of the graph. The prover runs in quasi-linear time in the number of nodes in the graph.

Furthermore, we develop a framework for computing the quantiles of essentially any (reasonable) function f of vertices/edges of the graph. Using this framework, we can estimate many health measures of social graphs such as the clustering coefficients and the average degree, where the verifier performs only a small number of queries to the graph.

Using the Fiat-Shamir paradigm, we are able to transform the above protocols to a non-interactive argument in the random oracle model. The result is that social media companies (e.g., Facebook, Twitter, etc.) can publish, once and for all, a short proof for the size or health of their social network. This proof can be publicly verified by any single user using a small number of queries to the graph.

Keywords: Interactive proofs · Social graphs · Succinct arguments

1 Introduction

Social networks have become a large and influential part of the everyday lives of billions of people. The study and analysis of social networks is a modern approach to understand human relationships and, as such, it has gained a vast amount of attention from researchers in areas spanning from psychology and public policy to game theory and computer science. As many of these networks contain immense amounts of data [CEKLM15], new tools ought to be developed to facilitate new demands.

From a computational point of view, a social network is modeled as a graph. Very abstractly, a node represents an individual (or an entity), and an edge

© International Association for Cryptologic Research 2020
D. Micciancio and T. Ristenpart (Eds.): CRYPTO 2020, LNCS 12172, pp. 574–601, 2020.
https://doi.org/10.1007/978-3-030-56877-1_20

represents a relationship between two individuals (we note that a social graph can represent other entities as well, such as companies, objects of interest, or virtual asserts such as a webpage and more). This abstraction is limited yet has been shown very fruitful for studying social relationships with applications ranging from economics to health. Social networks usually share common structural properties such as homophily, the existence of clusters, the small-world phenomena, heterogeneous distributions of friends, and community structure [Bre12, EK10, Kle00]. Some of these properties can be explained using known measures of graphs such as small mixing time (e.g., a random walk converges rapidly to its stationary distribution), small average distance between a pair of nodes (the "small world" phenomenon), and small average degree.

The company or the network's provide (the entity in hold of the data of the network) in most cases regularly publishes data (either to the public or to a group of interest) regarding the number of (active) users and other "health" measures for various commercial and sociological purposes. However, as a community, it is crucial to have an *independent* estimate of these measures, and in particular, one that does not have a blind trust in the provider's reports, which are amenable by financial or political incentives. For example, Facebook has acquired WhatsApp at a steep price of 16 billion dollars which was computed by a 40 dollar evaluation per user of the platform [Wha], giving WhatsApp incentive to increase their network size in the reports[1].

Two main challenges stand in the path to performing independent estimates of social graphs health measures. First, the graphs are huge, which makes it infeasible to simply obtained the data on a standard machine and perform arbitrary computations. Second, and perhaps more importantly, the data is usually not freely available to obtain, but instead, is accessible via the *public interface of the network*. Typically, and as considered in this work, the interface includes queries to check membership of a specific node's ID, querying for the node's neighbors, fetching meta-data as its degree, and so on. Furthermore, for security and data proprietary reasons, access to this interface is throttled where it is forbidden to perform a large number of queries in a short time.

As a result, to face these challenges, there has been a line of work focused on estimating the size of social graphs, and other measures, via its public interface while performing few queries as possible. The main ingredient in these works is that the public interface allows performing a "random walk" in the graph and since such graphs have good mixing-time one can reach the stationary distribution with only a few queries. For example, the public interfaces have been used in [GKBM10, HRH09, RT10] to estimate the assortativity coefficient, degree distribution, and clustering coefficients of online social networks, as well as in [YW11, HRH09, KLSC14, KBM12, KH15] to estimate the number of registered users.

Similar techniques are used for search engines as well, as they provide a public interface as part of their service. Web results (documents) which fit a

---

[1] We are not suggesting that WhatsApp behave untruthfully, but merely that they had the incentive to do so.

search engine queries induces a bipartite query-document graph structure. Search engine public interfaces have been used in [BYG08,Bro+06,BYG11] to estimate corpus size, index freshness, and density of duplicates using search engine queries. In [BYG09] the authors provide a way to estimate the impression rank of a webpage. In [ZLAZ11] the number of YouTube videos is estimated by sampling link prefixes.

One of the most basic property of a social graph that one would study is the *size* of the graph (the number of nodes in the network). If the graph has n nodes, then using birthday paradox techniques, the number of queries required to estimate n is roughly $\sqrt{n}$, assuming queries return a uniform node at random [YW11]. In a more recent work, [KLSC14] have shown that the random walks provide a biased sampling of the nodes in the graph which, under certain assumptions on the graph, allow to get a biased version of the birthday paradox that uses only (roughly) $O(n^{1/4})$ queries. In [KMV17] it is shown that this bound is tight, if one insists on solely using the public interface. This is a huge improvement over a naïve $O(n)$ solution but still leaves much to be desired. This leads us to ask:

Can we estimate social graph measures using **few** *queries to the network while having* **no** *trust in the graph's provider?*

We propose a way to, on the one hand, use the power of the network provider (e.g., Facebook, Twitter, YouTube, Linkedin, etc.) for computation, and on the other hand, put no trust in them. That is, we propose *interactive proof for social graphs*, as a solution to this problem and as a generalization of the known interactive protocols [GMR89]. In this model, we request the network's provider to not only provide measures such as the size of the graph but, in addition, provide a "proof" of their claims. The proof will come in the form of an interactive protocol between a verifier (a weak computation device that can perform a small number of queries to the public interface) and a prover (the network's provider that has full access to the graph).

As the verifier cannot query the entire graph, we cannot hope to compute the precise graph size. Instead, we relax this requirement and settle for an approximation of the size of any measure in mind. As is often the case in interactive proofs, we require two properties from the interactive protocol. Completeness: if the prover is honest and provides the right measures with the prescribed proof, then the verifier will accept the claims (with high probability). Soundness: if a cheating prover submits claims that are *far* from the correct ones, then no matter what proof it provides, the verifier will reject its claims (with high probability). This way, we can efficiently estimate the graph's size without putting any trust in the network itself.

Our model assumes that the graph itself is fixed, and we only interact with a prover that has access to this graph but cannot make changes to it. One could imagine that a social network could create an alternative fake view of the network with a large number of fake users and connections which would fool the verifier. However, there are several reasons why this would not happen and we stress two points.

First, it is impossible to distinguish between queries issued by a verifier and by legitimate users. Thus, in order for the prover to cheat the cheating prover must consistently change the graph for all users, and not only for a specific verifier. Second, without our protocol, the social network can cheat simply by publishing wrong reports about their network (which happens in many cases). Using our protocol, any cheating report has to be materialized and maintained in the network in a way that affects all users. While this is still possible, it puts a huge burden on the cheating party.

1.1 Our Results

We develop a framework for interactive proofs for social graphs. The first main result is a public-coin interactive protocol for estimating the size of a social graph, up to a small multiplicative error ε for any $\varepsilon > 0$. Let G be a graph of size n and let $\widetilde{n}$ be the claimed size. The protocol verifies that $\widetilde{n} \in (1 \pm \varepsilon)n$. The verifier performs a small number of queries (depending on the mixing-time and average degree of the graph), and the prover is quasi-linear in the size of the graph. This improves upon all previous works in terms of the number of queries (however, with the help of a prover).

We stress that we have no precise definition of a "social graph" and instead our results apply to any graph where the complexity of the protocol depends on different measures of the graph (e.g., mixing time) which are relatively small for social graphs. We show the following theorem.

Theorem 1 (informal). *Let G be a graph with n nodes, mixing time τ_{mix} and average degree Δ, and let $\varepsilon > 0$. There is a two message public-coin interactive proof for estimating the size of a graph in the social graph model, within an error of ε where the verifier's query complexity, running-time and the communication complexity are all bounded by $\widetilde{O}(1/\varepsilon^2 \cdot \tau_{mix} \cdot \Delta)$, and the prover runs in time $\widetilde{O}(n \cdot 1/\varepsilon^2)$.*

The theorem above is shown via a more general technique of estimating the size of any set S where the verifier has limited access to the set, in our case, the set will be the set of vertices in the graph. The verifier has membership queries to the set and an efficient procedure that can sample a uniform element from the set (which in our case corresponds to a random walk in the graph). The precise theorem is given in Theorem 5.

Estimating the size of a social graph (or in general a set) is perhaps the first and most basic property one would like to know about the graph. However, many other more involved complexity measures are desired as well, including the average degree, the local clustering coefficients, and others. Towards this end, we develop a general framework for estimating a large class of measures that include the most popular and studied ones, such as the examples given above.

For essentially any computable function f which is applied on a single vertex of the graph, let $A_f(q)$ a value that is the q-th quantile of the vertices of the graph when applying the function f. As the first theorem, this theorem, too, is shown via a more general approach to estimate the average value $f(x)$ for any set S.

Theorem 2 (informal). *Let G be a graph with n nodes and mixing time τ_{mix}, and let f be a computable function. There is a two-message protocol that (given n) computes $\widetilde{A}_f(q)$ such that*

$$\widetilde{A}_f(q) \in [A_f((1 - \varepsilon)q), A_f((1 + \varepsilon)q)],$$

with soundness error $1/3$, completeness error $1/3$, communication complexity $\widetilde{O}(1/\varepsilon^2)$, verifier query complexity $\widetilde{O}(1/\varepsilon^2 \cdot \tau_{mix})$, and prover running-time $\widetilde{O}(1/\varepsilon^2 \cdot n)$.

The precise theorem (for general sets) is given in Theorem 8.

Applications of Our Framework. The structure of social networks is studied via a set of common structural measures which reflect the health and authenticity of the network (see [CRTB06] for a survey of major structural measurement). In [MMGDB07] a large-scale measurement study and analysis of the structure of multiple online social networks. Our framework is useful for estimating various different structural measures of social graphs. The core measures are average degree; degree distribution; and local clustering coefficient distribution. [CRTB06]. In Sect. 5 we elaborate on these applications.

Social Graphs and Society. Social media companies are subject to severe public critique in the past years. As the understanding of the effects of social media grows, the companies are expected to fight bots pretending to be users, echo chambers, and other unfavorable phenomena (see, e.g., [GDFMGM18, ACELP13] and references therein). The protocol proposed in this paper can be used by the companies to prove that the issues are under control, and by society to hold the companies accountable. In Sect. 5.5 we elaborate on this further.

Non-interactive Arguments for Social Graphs. One important property of our protocols is that they are public-coin protocols, meaning that the verifier has no secret random coins and the messages it sends are merely the random coins he flips. This has two main benefits. First, it ensures that the protocol is secure even if the social graph observes the verifier's queries. The verifier might perform queries that are later not sent to the prover and leak information about its private randomness. Since the social graph is the entity that implements these oracles to the graph, these private queries are indeed leaked to it. Our public-coin protocol removes any concern of this type.

Second, and even more importantly, public-coin protocols can be transformed, via the Fiat-Shamir transformation, to non-interactive arguments systems, in the random oracle model. This is achieved by having the prover use the random oracle for getting the random challenge for a specific prover message. The result is a short (e.g., polylog-sized) "proof" that can be published once and for all by a social graph company (Facebook, Twitter, etc.) and can be later *publicly* verified by any single user using only few (i.e., polylog) queries to the network (in the random oracle model, the scheme is even more practical and does not hide any large constants). These proofs can be used for publishing the company's annual report and even possibly used in court.

1.2   Related Work

Goldwasser and Sipsers [GS89] presented a general technique that transforms any interactive protocol to a public coin protocol. At the heart of their transformation is a public-coin interactive proof for lower bounding the size of a specific set that is given implicitly to the verifier (he has only membership access to the set). Our work strengthens this result in several ways. First, we provide an upper bound together with the lower bound, which gives a complete estimation of the size of the set (in [GS89] a lower bound was sufficient for their proof). Second, we provide an arbitrary approximation with ratio ε where in [GS89] the ratio was assumed to be 2. We note that the protocol given in [GS89] does not work for better approximations ratios (it is not merely a matter of better analysis, but a protocol change is required).

There is a generic way to reduce a general approximation ratio of ε to 2, by taking the Cartesian product of the set with itself. That is, if S is the set, we estimate the size of S^k which contains all k tuples from S. The main problem with this is that the set S^k has size $|S|^k$, and thus, the running time of the prover is at least $|S|^k$, which is not realistic for most sets S and appropriate values k.

Fortnow [For87] also gave a protocol for estimating the size of a general set (he gives a lower bound and an upper bound), however, in his work the approximation ratio assumed is super-constant (in fact, his protocol allows distinguishing between a set of size n and a set of size n^2). Moreover, the upper bound he gives is a *private-coin* protocol where our protocol is public-coin. As discussed, a public-coin protocol is desirable, in part for applying the Fiat-Shamir transformation to get a corresponding non-interactive argument. Note that one cannot simply apply the [GS89] transformation to make the protocol of [For87] public-coin as this transformation is proven in the standard model (where the verifier has full access to the input) and, moreover, this transformation does not preserve the running-time of the prover (where we aim to have an efficient and practical prover).

Interactive Proofs of Proximity. In our protocol, the verifier is sublinear in its input and soundness condition only asserts that what we compute is close to the real value. This can be modeled as an *interactive proof of proximity* (IPP) [EKR04, RVW13]. One can view IPPs as the property testing analogue of interactive proofs. More concretely, consider the representation of the graph as a long indicator vector of size $|U|$ where U is the universe of all possible vertex IDs. Then, what we develop here is an IPP for the hamming weight of this vector, which corresponds to the size of the graph. However, there are critical differences in our goal compared to what is known for IPPs. Our protocols achieve a multiplicative error ε with respect to the *size of the graph*. On the other hand, in an IPP, the distance and error are with respect to $|U|$, the size of this long vector. Thus, any hamming weight IPP would not be useful in our setting.

1.3   Paper Organization

In Sect. 2 we give a formal definition of the graph query model in which our interactive protocols take place, and provide additional required preliminaries.

In Sect. 3 we show our first main result which is a general protocol for estimating the size of any set, where the verifier is given only oracle access to the set. The proof is split into two parts, one for the lower bound and one for the upper bound (each in its own subsection).

Then, in Sect. 4 we build upon this protocol and construct a general framework for estimating a large class of functions. The section begin with an overview of our techniques and then the formal statement and proof.

In Sect. 5 we combine the previous sections (that apply to any set) and show how to instantiate them on a social graph using random walks and get our final theorem statements. Additionally, we demonstrate the usefulness of our framework and show how to estimate various different social graph measures.

Finally, in Sect. 6 we show how to apply the Fiat-Shamir transformation to get a corresponding non-interactive version of our protocols, in the random oracle model.

2   Model Definition and Preliminaries

Graph Notations. Throughout the paper, we will consider a social graph. The graph is denoted by G, its set or vertices is denoted by V and the set of edges is denoted by E. Usually, n represents the size of the graph, i.e., the number of vertices in the graph, where m usually represents the number of edges. Using this notation, $|V| = n$ and $|E| = m$. Additionally, we denote by d_i the degree of vertex i and the sum of degrees by $D = \sum_{i=1}^{n} d_i = 2|E|$. The maximum degree of a graph is noted by $d_{\max} = \max_{i=1}^{n} d_i$.

2.1   Interactive Proofs

An interactive protocol (P, V) for a language L is a pair of interactive Turing machines; for a instance x we denote by $\langle P(x), V(x) \rangle$ the output of V in an interaction between P and V on common input x.

Definition 1. *An interactive protocol (P, V) is an interactive argument system for a language $L \subset \{0, 1\}^*$, if V is PPT and the following conditions hold:*

- **Completeness:** *For every $x \in L$: $\Pr[\langle P(x), V(x) \rangle = 1] \geq 2/3$.*
- **Soundness:** *For every P^*, for every $x \notin L$: $\Pr[\langle P^*(x), V(x) \rangle = 1] \leq 1/3$.*

We refer to (P, V) as a public-coin proof system if V simply sends the outcomes of its coin tosses to the prover (and only performs computation to determine its final verdict). Note that the soundness error and completeness error can be arbitrary amplified to 2^{-k} by repeating the protocol in parallel $O(k)$ times.

2.2   The Graph Query Model

In this paper, we construct interactive protocols for languages where the verifier is sublinear and has specific oracle access to the input. In particular, we consider languages of graphs. Let U be a universe of elements (e.g., U is the set of all possible IDs of a vertex in the graph). Let $G = (V, E)$ be a graph where $V \subseteq U$ and let $n = |V|$. Every element in $x \in V$ is described using $\log |U|$ bits and this will be our "word" size $w = \log |U|$. In our model of computation, we assume that algorithms can perform operations on words of size w in constant time. The verifier has oracle access to such a graph G where the oracle ρ_G is given as follows:

$$\rho_G : U \times \{0, 1, \dots, |U|\} \longrightarrow U \cup \{0, 1, \dots, |U|\} \cup \{\bot\}.$$

The oracle ρ_G gets an element x and an index i and returns the ith neighbor of x in the graph G. If x is not in the graph then it returns $\bot$. If x has less than i neighbors then it returns $\bot$. If $i = 0$ then it returns the number of neighbors that x has in the graph (this is why the range of ρ_G is $U \cup 0, 1, ..., |U|$). Formally, we define

$$\rho_G(x, i) = \begin{cases} \bot & \text{if } x \notin V \text{ or } \deg(x) < i \\ \deg(v) & \text{if } x \in V \text{ and } i = 0 \\ u & \text{if } x \in V \text{ and } u \text{ is the } i^{th} \text{ neighbor of } v. \end{cases}$$

We consider algorithms that have oracle access to ρ_G. An oracle algorithm A with oracle ρ_G can perform queries to ρ_G and get a response in a single time unit cost. Thus, the running time of A is a bound on the actual computation time and the number of oracle queries it performs. Using this, we can define an interactive protocol between a verifier and a prover where the prover has complete access to the graph and the verifier has only ρ_G query access, and performs a small number of queries.

Definition 2 (Interactive proofs in the graph query model). *Let G be a graph and let $\langle P(G), V(G) \rangle$ be an interactive protocol where the instance is the graph G. We say that the protocol is in the **graph query model** if the verifier V has only oracle access to ρ_G (the prover has explicit access to G). Additionally, we give the verifier V an arbitrary node x_0 in the graph.*

Formally, we write the completeness and soundness conditions as follows.

- **Completeness:** *For every $G \in L$:*

$$\Pr[\langle P(G), V^{\rho_G}(x_0) \rangle = 1] \geq 2/3.$$

- **Soundness:** *For every unbounded P^*, and every $G \notin L$,*

$$\Pr[\langle P^*(G), V^{\rho_G}(x_0) \rangle = 1] \leq 1/3.$$

2.3　Additional Preliminaries

Theorem 3 (Chernoff-Hoeffding). *Let* $X = \sum_{i=1}^{m} X_i$ *be the mean of* m *independent Bernoulli (indicator) random variables where* $\mathbb{E}[X_i] = p_i$. *Let* $\mu = \mathbb{E}[X] = \sum_{i=1}^{m} p_i$. *Then,*

1. $\Pr[X \geq (1+\delta)\mu] \leq e^{-\frac{\delta^2}{2+\delta} \cdot \mu}$ *for all* $\delta > 0$.
2. $\Pr[X \leq (1-\delta)\mu] \leq e^{-\frac{\delta^2}{2} \cdot \mu}$ *for all* $0 < \delta < 1$.

Limited Independence. A family of functions $\mathcal{H}$ mapping domain $\{0,1\}^n$ to range $\{0,1\}^m$ is k-wise independent if for every distinct elements $x_1, \ldots, x_k \in \{0,1\}^n$, $y_1, \ldots, y_k \in \{0,1\}^m$, we have $\Pr_{h \in \mathcal{H}}[h(x_1) = y_1 \wedge \ldots \wedge h(x_k) = y_k] \leq \frac{1}{2^{km}}$.

Theorem 4. *There exists a family* $\mathcal{H}$ *of* k-*wise independent functions from* $\{0,1\}^n$ *to* $\{0,1\}^m$ *such that choosing a random function from* $\mathcal{H}$ *requires* $O(k \cdot n)$ *bits.*

Definition 3. *We say that* $G : \{0,1\}^d \to \{0,1\}^n$ ε-*fools a circuit class* $\mathcal{C}$ *if for every* $C \in \mathcal{C}$ *it holds that*

$$\left| \Pr_{s \leftarrow \{0,1\}^d}[C(G(s)) = 1] - \Pr_{x \leftarrow \{0,1\}^n}[C(X) = 1] \right| \leq \varepsilon. \tag{1}$$

3　Set Cardinality Interactive Proof

In this section, we provide a general interactive protocol for estimating the size of a (large) given set, with a sublinear verifier that has only oracle access to the set. Looking ahead, we will apply this protocol on the nodes (and edges) of the social graph. The task is formulated as follows. There is a universe U and a subset $S \subset U$ of interest. Our goal is to (approximately) compute the size of the set to within a multiplicative error ε. The prover has complete access to the set S while the verifier has only limited access to S given by two methods. The first method is a *membership* oracle where the verifier can specify an element $x \in U$ and gets as response whether $x \in S$ or not. The second method is an efficient random algorithm $\mathcal{D}$ that samples a *uniformly* random element in the set. We say that $\mathcal{D}$ is a sampler for the set S that uses ℓ bits if $\mathcal{D}$ can sample a uniform element in S using at most ℓ random bits.

One can easily observe that it is impossible to verify that indeed the size of the set S is *exactly* n while using a sublinear (in n) number of queries. However, here our goal is to verify that the size of the set is *approximately* n. That is, for every $\varepsilon > 0$ we want a protocol that assures that a given alleged size $\tilde{n}$ satisfies $\tilde{n} \in (1 \pm \varepsilon)|S|$ with probability at least $2/3$.

To formally define this as an interactive proof for a specific language, we define the language $L_{S,\varepsilon}$

$$L_{S,\varepsilon} = \{(S, \tilde{n}) : (1 - \varepsilon)|S| \leq \tilde{n} \leq (1 + \varepsilon)|S|\}.$$

The main focus is to minimize the number of queries the verifier performs (both membership queries and sampling queries). For practical use cases, we additionally want the running-time of the prover to actually be quasi-linear in the size of the set S (which is achieved in our protocol). In the following theorem the notation $\widetilde{O}$ hides polylog(n) factors.

Theorem 5. *Let S be a set of size n with a sampler $\mathcal{D}$ that uses ℓ random bits. Let $\varepsilon > 0$ be a parameter and let $L_{S,\varepsilon}$ be the language defined as above. Then, there is an public-coin protocol for $L_{S,\varepsilon}$ with the following properties: (1) The protocol has two messages (first the verifier then the prover); (2) The verifier performs at most $\widetilde{O}(1/\varepsilon^2)$ queries (to both $\mathcal{D}$ and the membership oracle); (3) The verifier's running time and the communication complexity are bounded by $\widetilde{O}(1/\varepsilon^2 \cdot \ell)$; and (4) The prover runs in time $\widetilde{O}(n \cdot 1/\varepsilon^2)$.*

We split the proof into two parts, one for the lower bound and one for the upper bound. The protocols are described separately for ease of presentation and since each might be used independently in different contexts. The final protocol is obtained by simply running the two subprotocols in parallel (without a cost in the round complexity).

Let n be the *real* number of nodes in the graph and let $\widetilde{n}$ be the number of nodes in the graph *claimed* by the prover. Throughout, assume for simplicity that $0 < \varepsilon \le 1/2$. Recall, our goal is to verify that $\widetilde{n} \in n \pm \varepsilon n$. We begin with the lower bound.

3.1   Lower Bound

Overview. The general idea of the protocol is inspired by the Goldwasser-Sipser protocol [GS89]. Goldwasser and Sipser provide a method to compile any private coin protocol to a corresponding public-coin protocol. At the heart of their transformation was a protocol proving that a certain exponentially large set, given implicitly to the verifier, is indeed large enough. The verifier has only membership access to this set.

In the protocol, the verifier sends a (pairwise independent) hash function $h \in \mathcal{H}$ that hashes the elements of the set to a range of size $\widetilde{n}$. The prover is asked to find an element that is mapped to a specific bin (i.e., an element in the range of the hash). Their main observation is that is the set is indeed large enough, then such an element exists with higher probability than if the set is smaller. This suffices for catching a cheating prover (with some probability) and at the end the soundness and completeness of the protocol are amplified.

A Better Statistical Measure. Put in more general terms, the verifier picks a random hash function, and is concerned with how the elements of the set are distributed among the different bins. The Goldwasser-Sipser protocol asks the prover to send a simple "statistical measure" of proving that a random bin is not empty. This measure was sufficient for their protocol as they had a factor of 2 separating from a large set and a small set, however, their protocol cannot separate smaller differences in the sizes, and in our case, we only have a factor of $(1 + \varepsilon)$.

There is a generic way to amplify this factor by taking the Cartesian product of the set with itself. That is, if S is the set, we estimate the size of S^k which contains all k tuples from S. The main problem with this approach is that it does maintain the running of the prover which is now at least $O(|S|^k)$ (k is not even a constant in general, and we aim for linear time prover).

Instead, we look at a more involved statistic, namely, *the size of the preimage*. The verifier samples a single hash function $h \in \mathcal{H}$ which is sent to the prover. The prover responds with all the preimages z of fixed output y with respect to h. The verifier asserts that z is indeed a set of preimages, and then counts the number of elements in z and accepts if and only if it is higher than its expectation (minus a small fraction).

The hash family we use is a t-wise independence hash family. Let $\mathcal{H} = \{h : U \to [c \cdot \tilde{n}/k]\}$ be a family of t-wise independent hash functions, where t and c are a parameters that will be defined later. The c parameter is used to ensure the h's co-domain(range) is a power of 2 and also to control the error probability. It would be easier for the reader to think of the hash functions as being completely random, and moreover, the analysis will be first shown under this assumption. Then, in Sect. 3.3 we show how the same analysis (with negligible changes in the soundness and completeness) holds for our family of t-wise independent hash functions.

The formal description of the protocol is given in Fig. 1.

Set cardinality lower bound

Parameters: c and $k = \frac{4^3}{\varepsilon^2}$.

1. V $\Rightarrow$ P: Verifier samples $h \in \mathcal{H}$ where $h : U \to [c \cdot \tilde{n}/k]$, and $y \in [c \cdot \tilde{n}/k]$ and sends them to the prover.
2. P $\Rightarrow$ V: Prover sends the set of preimages $Z = h^{-1}(y)$.
3. Verifier checks that:
   (a) $Z \subseteq S$ (by a membership query to each element $z \in Z$); and
   (b) $\forall z \in Z$, $h(z) = y$ (and rejects otherwise).
4. The verifier accepts iff $|Z| > (1 - \varepsilon/4) \cdot c \cdot k$.

Fig. 1. Our lower bound protocol for the approximate size of a set.

Formally, this protocol is an interactive protocol for a similar language of $L_{S,\varepsilon}$ only where we consider only the lower bound. Thus, we define

$$L'_{S,\varepsilon} = \{(S, \tilde{n}) : (1 - \varepsilon)|S| \leq \tilde{n}\}.$$

We show the following lemma which specifies the properties of the protocol with respect to parameter c.

Lemma 1. *Given a parameter c, and ε the protocol in Fig. 1 is an interactive protocol for $L'_{S,\varepsilon}$ with the following properties: soundness error e^{-2c}; completeness error e^{-4c}; total communication $O(c/\varepsilon^2 \cdot \mathrm{polylog}(n))$; verifier running time $O(c/\varepsilon^2 \cdot \mathrm{polylog}(n))$; prover running time $O(1/\varepsilon^2 \cdot n \cdot \mathrm{polylog}(n))$.*

We turn to analyze the protocol (i.e., Fig. 1). As mentioned, the completeness and soundness are first analyzed under the assumption that each h is a truly random function. After the proof, in Sect. 3.3 we show that the limited independence hash function suffices and compute its complexity (both in terms of the key size and the evaluation time), as this affects the communication complexity of the protocol and the verifier's running time.

Completeness. Assume that $\tilde{n} = n$ and that the prover behaves honestly according to the protocol. Denote the elements of the set by $S = (x_1, \dots, x_n)$. Let Z_i be the indicator $h(x_i) = y$. Namely, $Z_i = 1$ iff $h(x_i) = y$. Then, since the hash function is random we get that $\mathbb{E}[Z_i] = c \cdot k/n$. Clearly $|Z| = \sum_i Z_i$, and thus we get

$$\mathbb{E}[|Z|] = \sum_{i=1}^{n} \mathbb{E}[Z_i] = n \cdot \frac{c \cdot k}{n} = c \cdot k.$$

Since we assumed that h is a completely random function, we get that we the random variables $Z_1, \dots, Z_n$ are independent. Using a Chernoff-Hoeffding bound (see Theorem 3) we entail

$$\Pr[\text{reject}] = \Pr[Z \leq (1 - \varepsilon/4) \cdot c \cdot k] \leq e^{-\frac{\varepsilon^2}{2 \cdot 4^2} \cdot c \cdot k} = e^{-2c}.$$

Soundness. Assume that the instance is not in the language, that is, $\tilde{n} > (1+\varepsilon)n$. Let $\tilde{Z}$ be the set sent by the prover (i.e., the alleged Z). If the verifier did not reject at step (3) then it must be that $\tilde{Z} \subseteq S$ and $\tilde{Z} \subseteq Z$, and therefore $|\tilde{Z}| \leq |Z|$. Again, let Z_i be the indicator $h(x_i) = y$. In this case, we have that

$$\mathbb{E}[|Z|] = \sum_{i=1}^{n} \mathbb{E}[Z_i] = n \cdot \frac{c \cdot k}{\tilde{n}} = c \cdot k < c \cdot k \frac{n}{(1+\varepsilon)n} = \frac{c \cdot k}{1+\varepsilon}.$$

We bound from above the probability that the verifier accepts in this case.

$$\begin{aligned}
\Pr[\text{accept}] &\leq \Pr\left[|\tilde{Z}| > (1 - \varepsilon/4) \cdot c \cdot k\right] \\
&\leq \Pr[|Z| > (1 - \varepsilon/4) \cdot c \cdot k] \\
&= \Pr[|Z| - \mathbb{E}[|Z|] > (1 - \varepsilon/4) \cdot c \cdot k - \mathbb{E}[|Z|]] \\
&\leq \Pr[|Z| - \mathbb{E}[|Z|] > (1 - \varepsilon/4)(1 + \varepsilon)\mathbb{E}[|Z|] - \mathbb{E}[|Z|]] \\
&= \Pr[|Z| - \mathbb{E}[|Z|] > (\varepsilon - \varepsilon/4 - \varepsilon^2/4)\mathbb{E}[|Z|]] \\
&\leq \Pr[|Z| - \mathbb{E}[|Z|] > \varepsilon/2 \cdot \mathbb{E}[|Z|]] < e^{-4c}.
\end{aligned}$$

This shows the soundness error and completeness error of the protocol. Notice that one can set c to be a small constant (e.g., $c = 2$) to get the standard $1/3$

and 2/3 soundness error and completeness requirements. We now turn to show the other complexity measures of the protocol.

Complexity Measures

- *Queries.* The verifier performs $c \cdot k = O(c/\varepsilon^2)$ membership queries, one to each $z \in Z$. Note that there is no need for the prover to send Z whose size is bigger than $c \cdot k$. That is, if Z is larger than $c \cdot k$ then the prover simply sends an arbitrary subset $Z' \subset Z$ of size $c \cdot k$. This way, the verifier performs at most $O(c \cdot k)$, and it also bounds the communication complexity.
- *Communication.* We bound the total amount of communication in the protocol (both from prover to verifier and from verifier to prover). The verifier sends a hash function with $O(t)$ bits, where $t = \text{polylog}(n)$ is the independence of the hash function. The prover replies with a set that have total size of $O(c \cdot k)$ (see argument above) and thus can be specified using $O(c \cdot k \cdot \log n)$ bits. The total communication is thus $O(c \cdot k \cdot \text{polylog}(n)) = O(c/\varepsilon^2 \cdot \text{polylog}(n))$.
- *Verifier running-time.* The verifier is rather simple and its only computation besides choosing randomness and reading the communication is to compute the hash function h on all $z \in Z$. The hash function can be computed in time $\text{polylog}(n)$ for a single element, there are $O(c \cdot k)$ elements and thus the total running time of the verifier is $O(c/\varepsilon^2 \cdot \text{polylog}(n))$.
- *Prover running-time.* The prover runs over all n nodes in the graph and checks if it a preimage of y. This takes time $O(1/\varepsilon^2 \cdot n \cdot \text{polylog}(n))$.

3.2   Upper Bound

Overview. In the previous subsection, we have devised a protocol for a lower bound on the set size. In this subsection, we provide a protocol for an *upper bound* on the size of the set. An upper bound for a set is somewhat counterintuitive, as the prover can always act honestly on a small subset. Since the verifier has limited access to the set, it would be hard to notice this.

Here, we exploit the fact that the verifier has uniform random access to the set. If the prover ignores an ε fraction of the set, and the verifier samples $1/\varepsilon$ random elements then the verifier has a good chance of sampling an element that was ignored by the prover. However, even if this happens, how can the verifier check if the prover included this element in this proof? After all, the proof is very short compared to the large set (the set is of size n and the proof is roughly logarithmic in the size of the set).

A Simple but Expensive Solution. Our protocol is based on the "birthday paradox" and works as follows. We begin with a simple and not query efficient protocol. We have the verifier sample roughly $O(\sqrt{\tilde{n}})$ random elements from the set. If indeed $n = \tilde{n}$, then we expect to see a collision (i.e., two samples that ended with the same element). However, if the set is much larger, then such a collision is less likely. This is a good protocol, however, the verifier has a very high query complexity.

The Actual Protocol. Instead, we let the prover simulate this process for us. We ask the prover to perform $O(\sqrt{\widetilde{n}})$ samples and tell us if he saw a collision. This is very naive, as it is hard to force that prover to behave this way. Thus, we again use a random hash function. Here the goal of the hash is fixed some common randomness that is used in order to perform the $O(\sqrt{\widetilde{n}})$ samples.

Let $\mathcal{H} = \{h\colon U \to [\ell]\}$ be a family of hash functions (recall that ℓ is the number of bits used by the algorithm $\mathcal{D}$). Then, the prover uses the values of the hash function $h(i)$ as random bits to use to run the $\mathcal{D}$, and finds $1 \leq i \neq j \leq \widetilde{n}$ such that running the sampler with random coins $h(i)$ results in the same elements as with the coins $h(j)$, namely, $\mathcal{D}(h(i)) = \mathcal{D}(h(j))$. The prover sends i and j to the verifier which can easily verifier that $\mathcal{D}(h(i)) = \mathcal{D}(h(j))$ (and that $i \neq j$) with merely 2 queries!

The description above heavily uses the fact that the hash function h is truly random. Again, in Sect. 3.3 we show that a limited independent hash function suffices for this analysis as well. Formally, the protocol is given in Fig. 2.

An upper bound for estimating the size of a general set

1. V $\Rightarrow$ P: Verifier samples $h \in \mathcal{H}$ and sends it to the prover.
2. P $\Rightarrow$ V: Prover does the following:
   (a) compute randomness $r_i = h(i)$ for all $i \in \sqrt{\widetilde{n}}$.
   (b) let $v_i \leftarrow \mathcal{D}(r_i)$.
   (c) sends the minimal $i \neq j \in \sqrt{\widetilde{n}}$ such that $v_i = v_j$.
3. V: Verifier computes $r_i = \mathcal{D}(h(i))$ and $r_j = \mathcal{D}(h(j))$ and asserts that: (1) $\mathcal{D}(r_i) = \mathcal{D}(r_j)$; (2) $i \neq j$; and (3) $i, j \in [\sqrt{\widetilde{n}}]$ and accepts.

Fig. 2. An interactive protocol for ensuring an upper bound of the set size.

Completeness and Soundness. We turn to analyze the protocol. Here, we do not argue completeness and soundness separately but rather in a single joint argument. We denote the completeness by α and the soundness error by β and show that $\alpha - \beta = \gamma$, where γ is not too small. Then, using parallel repetition, we can expand the gap between the completeness and soundness error by an arbitrary constant of our choice. In particular, if γ is the gap, then, to get the desired completeness $2/3$ and soundness error $1/3$, the number of repetitions required is $O(1/\gamma)$ (see e.g., [HPWP10]). In our case, we show that $\gamma \geq \Omega(\epsilon)$ which means that we need $O(1/\varepsilon)$ repetitions of the protocol we describe above.

Define α and β as follows:

$$\alpha = \Pr\left[\exists i, j \in [\sqrt{\widetilde{n}}] : D(r_i) = D(r_j) \mid \widetilde{n} = n\right],$$

$$\beta = \Pr\left[\exists i, j \in [\sqrt{\widetilde{n}}] : D(r_i) = D(r_j) \mid \widetilde{n} \leq (1 - \varepsilon)n\right].$$

Note that α and β are indeed the completeness and soundness parameters of the protocol. We consider what is known to be "the birthday paradox". Given m uniformly chosen items $r_1, \ldots, r_m$ from a set of size n we have that

$$\Pr[r_1, \ldots, r_m \text{ are distinct}] = \prod_{i=0}^{m-1} \left(1 - \frac{i}{n}\right).$$

We are interested in analyzing this formula. Thus, before we continue the proof of the completeness and soundness we provide the following technical lemma.

Lemma 2. *For any integer* $1 \le k \le \frac{n}{2}$,

$$e^{-\frac{k(k+1)}{2n} - \frac{(k+1)^3}{3n^2}} < \prod_{i=0}^{k} \left(1 - \frac{i}{n}\right) < e^{-\frac{k(k+1)}{2n}}.$$

Proof. First, we observe that

$$\prod_{i=0}^{k} \left(1 - \frac{i}{n}\right) = \exp\left(\sum_{i=0}^{k} \ln\left(1 - \frac{i}{n}\right)\right).$$

Next, we note that $-x - x^2 < \ln(1 - x) < -x$ holds for $0 < x \le 1/2$ (the second inequality even holds for $0 < x < 1$). In addition, for every positive k we have $k(k+1)(2k+1) < 2(k+1)^3$. Finally,

$$-\frac{k(k+1)}{2n} - \frac{k(k+1)(2k+1)}{6n^2} < \sum_{i=0}^{k} \ln\left(1 - \frac{i}{n}\right) < -\frac{k(k+1)}{2n}.$$

$\square$

Claim 3.2. For any $x \ge 1$, $c > 0$ and $\varepsilon > 0$,

$$ce^{-x} - e^{-\frac{x}{1-\varepsilon}} > e^{-x}[c - (1 - \varepsilon)].$$

Proof.

$$ce^{-x} - e^{-\frac{x}{1-\varepsilon}} = e^{-x}\left[c - e^{-\frac{x}{1-\varepsilon} + x}\right] = e^{-x}\left[c - e^{-x\frac{\varepsilon}{1-\varepsilon}}\right]$$
$$> e^{-x}\left[c - (1 - \varepsilon)^x\right] \ge e^{-x}\left[c - (1 - \varepsilon)\right].$$

The for first inequality we used $e^{-\frac{z}{1-z}} < 1 - z$ for $z > 0$. The for second inequality we used $x \ge 1$.

$\square$

We choose k as the smallest integer such that $k(k+1) \ge 2n$. Using the Lemma 2 and Claim 3.2, we get

$$\alpha - \beta > e^{-\frac{k(k+1)}{2n} - \frac{(k+1)^3}{3n^2}} - e^{-\frac{k(k+1)}{2n(1-\varepsilon)}}$$
$$> e^{-\frac{k(k+1)}{2n}} \left(e^{-\frac{(k+1)^3}{3n^2}} - (1 - \varepsilon)\right)$$
$$> e^{-\frac{k(k+1)}{2n}} \left(1 - \frac{(k+1)^3}{3n^2} - (1 - \varepsilon)\right)$$
$$= e^{-\frac{k(k+1)}{2n}} \left(\varepsilon - \frac{(k+1)^3}{3n^2}\right),$$

where the three inequalities follow since: (1) the first inequality is due to Lemma 2 and the definition of α and β; (2) the second inequality is due to Claim 3.2 for $x = \frac{k(k+1)}{2n}$, $c = e^{-\frac{(k+1)^3}{3n^2}}$ and ε (and the choice of k); and (3) the third inequality is due to $e^{-x} > 1 - x$. Since $(k-1)^2 < (k-1)k < 2n \leq k(k+1)$, we get that $k < 1 + \sqrt{2n}$ which yields

1. $\frac{k(k+1)}{2n} < 1 + \frac{2+3\sqrt{2n}}{2n}$;
2. $\frac{(k+1)^3}{3n^2} < \frac{(2+\sqrt{2n})^3}{3n^2} < \frac{2}{\sqrt{n}}$.

For any $n \geq 1000$, we get $e^{-\frac{k(k+1)}{2n}}\left(\varepsilon - \frac{(k+1)^3}{3n^2}\right) > \frac{1}{4}\left(\varepsilon - \frac{2}{\sqrt{n}}\right)$. Assuming $\varepsilon \geq \frac{2}{\sqrt{n}}$, we have $\alpha - \beta \geq \frac{\varepsilon}{12}$, as desired.

Complexity Measures. We compute the complexity measures of the underlying protocol and then its cost for the amplified protocol. Recall that we perform parallel repetitions for $O(1/\varepsilon)$ repetitions. All the complexity measures below are actually subsumed by the upper bound.

- *Queries.* The verifier performs only two queries, for the given i and j. After amplification, the number of queries is $O(1/\varepsilon)$.
- *Communication.* The verifier sends h which takes polylog(n) bits. The prover simply sends i and j which are $O(\log n)$ bits. After amplification, the communication complexity is $O(1/\varepsilon \cdot \text{polylog}(n))$.
- *Verifier running-time.* The verifier's running time is mainly the running time of $\mathcal{D}$, which is $O(\ell \cdot \text{polylog}(n))$, and computing the hash function h which takes time polylog(n). After amplification, the running time is $O(1/\varepsilon \cdot \ell \cdot \text{polylog}(n))$.
- *Prover running-time.* The prover runs over all $i \in [\sqrt{n}]$ and runs $\mathcal{D}$ on $h(i)$ and searches for collisions. The running time is $O(\sqrt{n} \cdot \text{polylog}(n))$, and after amplification it is $O(1/\varepsilon \cdot \sqrt{n} \cdot \text{polylog}(n))$.

3.3   Using Explicit Hash Functions

The analysis of the above upper bound and lower bound were performed in a model where the sampled hash functions $h \in \mathcal{H}$ were assumed to be truly random functions. This approach is useful for making the analysis easy to read and is a complete proof in the random oracle model. Practically speaking, one could implement the protocol above using a heuristic hash function such as SHA256 and similar implementations as the random oracle. This would heuristically be secure and save a lot in terms of communication since the random oracle serves a large common source of randomness and thus eliminating the need of the verifier to send random coins.

Nevertheless, we show how to use *explicit* limited independent hashes functions to make the analysis *provably* secure where the description of the hash is small (it will be polylog(n)). Thus, our protocol is secure in the standard model with no heuristics or any further assumptions.

We give different arguments for the lower bound and upper bound, but in both cases we rely on pseudorandom generators. The main idea in both the lower bound and upper bound is similar. The analysis of the protocols relies on the probability of a certain event. For example, in the lower bound, we relied on the probability of Z to be large enough for completeness and to be small enough for soundness. Instead of using a completely random hash function, we use pseudo-random hash function. The main question is which definition of "pseudo" suffices for our protocol, which we now argue separately.

What we show here is that the event we rely on can be identified by a low depth circuit. Thus, it will suffice to use $\text{polylog}(n)$ wise independent hash function as these fool AC^0 circuits.

Lower Bound. Consider the event $\mathcal{E}$ that the set $Z = h^{-1}(y)$ has size at least $(1 - \varepsilon/4) \cdot c \cdot k$. The completeness of the protocol shows that if the instance is in the language then the probability of $\mathcal{E}$ is high, and the soundness of the protocol shows that when the instance is not in the language then the probability of this event is low. The probability is taken over a truly random hash function h, where takes at most $|U| \cdot \log n$ bits to describe.

The key point is that this event can be identified by a low space algorithm, and thus we can use a pseudorandom generator to fool it. Define an algorithm C that has gets $x_1, \ldots, x_n$ and y and outputs 1 if and only if

$$|h^{-1}(y)| > (1 - \varepsilon/4) \cdot c \cdot k,$$

where h is a truly random function defined by the random coins of the algorithm. What the analysis of the completeness of the protocol shows is that for any $x_1, \ldots, x_n$ and y it holds that $\Pr[C(x_1, \ldots, x_n, y) = 1] \geq 1 - e^{-4c}$. The soundness shows that in the "no" case it holds that $\Pr[C(x_1, \ldots, x_n, y) = 1] \leq e^{-2c}$.

It is easy to see that this algorithm C can be implemented in $O(\log n)$ space. Indeed, the algorithm enumerates over all $x_1, \ldots, x_n$ and for each computes $h(x_i)$ by tossing coins (no need to remember the coins) and counting how many of them equal $h(x_i) = y$ (where or course counting can be done in small space).

Thus, it suffices to use Nisan's pseudorandom generator to fool algorithm C.

Theorem 6. *Let C be the family of algorithms computable in $\log m$ space. There is a PRG $G: \{0,1\}^{\log^2 m} \to \{0,1\}^m$ that $1/m$-fools C.*

That is, we do not need the verifier to send $|U| \log n = \text{poly}(n) = m$ random bits. Instead, it suffices for the verifier to send a seed of length $O(\log^2 n)$ to the prover which will then act the same on the m pseudorandom bits which the generator G provides. This has a negligible effects in the completeness and soundness error of the protocol and reduces the description of the hash function to $O(\log^2 n)$ bits.

Upper Bound. We now move to the upper bound. In this protocol, we used the truly random property of the hash function where we claimed that for $r_i = \mathcal{D}(h(i))$ it holds that

$$\Pr[r_1, \ldots, r_m \text{ are distinct}] = \prod_{i=0}^{m-1} \left(1 - \frac{i}{n}\right).$$

To argue this with an explicit hash function, we will the following theorem due to Braverman [Bra10] and its improvement by Tal [Tal17] and Harsha and Srinivasan [HS19].

Theorem 7 (Follows from [Bra10, Tal17, HS19]**).** *Let C be an AC^0 circuit of size m and depth d over n bits. Let μ be a distribution that is $r = r(m, d)$-independent over n bits and let U be the uniform distribution over n bits. Then, $|\mathbb{E}_{x \leftarrow \mu}[C(x)] - \mathbb{E}_{x \leftarrow U}[C(x)]| \leq \frac{1}{m}$ where $r = (\log m)^{O(d)}$.*

Let C be a circuit that gets an input a random string $R = r_1, \ldots, r_{\sqrt{n}}$, and works as follows:

$$C(r_1, \ldots, r_{\sqrt{n}}) = 1 \text{ if and only if } \mathcal{D}(r_i) \neq \mathcal{D}(r_j) \text{ for all } i \neq j.$$

Recall that $\mathcal{D}$ uses at most ℓ bits of randomness assume, without loss of generality, that $\log m \leq \ell$. Then, the circuit C can be implemented as an AC^0 circuit (constant depth) of size $|C| = 2^{O(\ell)}$ by precomputing $\mathcal{D}(r)$ for all $r \in \{0, 1\}^\ell$ and then searching for collisions. Thus, there exists a constant c such that ℓ^c-wise independence $1/n$-fools C. Therefore, we set $\mathcal{H}$ to be a family of ℓ^c-wise independent hash functions from Theorem 4. Each function $h \in \mathcal{H}$ maps $[n]$ to $\{0, 1\}^\ell$ and can be described using $O(\ell^c \cdot \log n)$ bits. In particular, if $\ell = \text{polylog}(n)$ then each hash function can be described using $\text{polylog}(n)$ bits and the difference in the soundness and completeness is at most $1/n$.

4   The General Framework

We have seen an interactive protocol for estimating the size of a set while given only oracle access to the set. In this section, building on this protocol, we extend it to get a more general framework for computing arbitrary function quantiles of the set (the precise definition is below). Then, the framework is used to estimate other interesting measures of the graph, such as degree distribution, the local clustering coefficients distribution and more (see Sect. 5), given that the size of the set has already been established.

Fix a set S of interest. Let $S_{\leq u}$ be the set of all elements in S whose f value is less or equal u. Formally, $S_{\leq u} = \{x \in S \mid f(x) \leq u\}$. Moreover, we given a similar definition for other operations such as greater than, equal and so on. Formally, for any $\circ \in \{\geq, >, =, <, \leq\}$ we define $S_{\circ u}$ to be $S_{\circ u} = \{x \in S \mid f(x) \circ u\}$.

Given a function f, a set S of known size n, and a parameter q we seek to compute the q-th quantile of f which is a value $A_f(q)$ such that:

$$\left| S_{\leq A_f(q)} \right| \geq n \cdot q; \text{ and}$$

$$\left| S_{\geq A_f(q)} \right| \geq n \cdot (1 - q)$$

In particular, if $q = 1/2$ then $A_f(q)$ is the median of the set S with respect to the function f. As before, we will not compute $A_f(q)$ exactly (which is impossible with a sublinear-time verifier), but rather give an approximation $\widetilde{A}_f$ which with high probability satisfies

$$\widetilde{A}_f(q) \in [A_f((1-\varepsilon)q), A_f((1+\varepsilon)q)].$$

Note that the approximation above is with respect to the quantile and not the value $A_f(q)$.

Overview. We begin with a high-level overview of the protocol. We divide the elements into three "buckets" (or bins) according to their $f(x)$ values. Each bucket includes all nodes with values in a specific range, where the ranges are $(-\infty, \widetilde{A}_f(q))$, $[\widetilde{A}_f(q), \widetilde{A}_f(q)]$, and $(\widetilde{A}_f(q), \infty)$. The size of each bucket can be communicated using the lower bound protocol (Sect. 3.1).

Therefore, our goal now is to learn the size of each bucket. Actually, approximate values suffice as well. Here we reduce the problem to our lower bound protocol. To run the cardinality protocol, we need to implement the two oracle queries for the verifier. The membership queries are easy to implement, as we simply check that the element x is in the set, then compute $f(x)$ and see that its value is in the buckets range (given $\widetilde{A}_f(q)$ the ranges are fixed and known to the verifier).

Multiple q Values. The framework can be extended to multiple q values. We can reduce the number of queries if we perform the protocol for buckets induced by the ranges intersection together instead of one-by-one.

An interactive protocol for estimating A_f for a set S and a function f

Parameters: ε, q.

1. P $\Rightarrow$ V: The prover sends the values $\widetilde{A}_f(q)$; $\widetilde{n}_{<q}$; $\widetilde{n}_{=q}$; and $\widetilde{n}_{>q}$, where (allegedly) $\widetilde{A}_f(q) = A_f(q)$; $\widetilde{n}_{<q} = \left|S_{<A_f(q)}\right|$; $\widetilde{n}_{=q} = \left|S_{=A_f(q)}\right|$; and $\widetilde{n}_{>q} = \left|S_{>A_f(q)}\right|$.
2. V: Verifier assets that: (a) $\widetilde{n}_{<q}, \widetilde{n}_{=q}, \widetilde{n}_{>q} \in \mathbb{N}$; (b) $n = \widetilde{n}_{<q} + \widetilde{n}_{=q} + \widetilde{n}_{>q}$; (c) $\widetilde{n}_{<q} + \widetilde{n}_{=q} \geq n \cdot q$; and (d) $\widetilde{n}_{=q} + \widetilde{n}_{>q} > n \cdot (1-q)$.
3. P $\Longleftrightarrow$ V: The prover and verifier run the lower bound protocol (Figure 1) on the sets $S_{<A_f(q)}$, $S_{=A_f(q)}$, $S_{>A_f(q)}$ with approximation parameter ε.
4. V returns $\widetilde{A}_f(q)$.

Fig. 3. A detailed description of our interactive protocol for estimating the quantile q of a function f on the elements of a given set S of known size n.

Theorem 8. *The protocol described above (See Fig. 3) asserts that*

$$\widetilde{A}_f(q) \in [A_f((1-\varepsilon)q), A_f((1+\varepsilon)q)],$$

with soundness error $1/3$, completeness error $1/3$, communication complexity $\widetilde{O}(1/\varepsilon^2)$, verifier running-time $\widetilde{O}(1/\varepsilon^2)$, and prover running-time $\widetilde{O}(1/\varepsilon^2 \cdot n)$.

Proof of Theorem 8. The lower bound protocol (see Fig. 1) is invoked three time. To correct for potentially increased error we use a large enough constant c (as specified in Lemma 1) such we can union bound over all invocations of the protocol (e.g., $c \approx 3$). Thereby, soundness is guaranteed with probability $3e^{-2c} < 1/3$ (by union bound) and completeness guaranteed with probability $e^{-4c} < 1/3$.

Given the guarantees of the lower bound protocol we can conclude that:

$$\left| S_{\leq \tilde{A}_f(q)} \right| = \left| S_{< \tilde{A}_f(q)} \right| + \left| S_{= \tilde{A}_f(q)} \right| \geq (1 - \varepsilon)\,(\tilde{n}_{<q} + \tilde{n}_{=q}) \geq (1 - \varepsilon)n \cdot q.$$

This implies that $\tilde{A}_f(q) \geq A_f((1 - \varepsilon)q)$. On the other hand, we have that

$$\left| S_{\geq \tilde{A}_f(q)} \right| = \left| S_{> \tilde{A}_f(q)} \right| + \left| S_{= \tilde{A}_f(q)} \right| \geq (1 - \varepsilon)\,(\tilde{n}_{=q} + \tilde{n}_{>q}) \geq (1 - \varepsilon)n \cdot (1 - q).$$

This implies that $\tilde{A}_f(q) \leq A_f((1 + \varepsilon)q)$. Together, this concludes the proof.

□

Approximating n. This section assumes that the size n of the set has already been established, and is known to the verifier. If this is not the case, then one can run our protocol for estimating the size of the set first, getting an approximation of n and then running the protocols in this section. Note that if one wants to compute many different functions f, then it suffices to estimate n once, and then run these protocols for any f. For this reason, we did not explicitly include running the cardinality estimation protocol in this section but assumed that it was already established. Finally, note that if one has only an approximation of the size n, then the error of the approximation will be added to the error of the protocol in this section. Thus, in order to get a desired error of ε then one should use $\varepsilon/2$ in each protocol.

5   Applications to Social Graphs

The framework we developed can be used to estimate the size of any set S. Moreover, the suggested framework can be used to approximate the values distribution of any arbitrary function on elements of S. In order to implement these protocols, the verifier needs to have access to the set via the two methods of membership and random sampling. In this section, we show how to implement this access with a *social graph* and hence get a protocol to estimate the size of a social graph and other complexity measures.

Suppose we have a social graph G with vertex set V and edge set E. We are interested in estimating the size of the graph, that is, we let the set S be the set V of vertices. First, notice that implementing membership access is easy, as such a query is included in the interface of a social graph. Given an element x, we can check if $x \in S$ by checking if x is a valid vertex in V using a single query to the graph. The more involved part is sampling a uniformly random vertex in the graph, as this is not part of the interface given by a social graph. However, using random walks on the graph, we can implement sampling a random vertex using a small number of queries to the graph. This strongly relates to the mixing time of the graph, and we elaborate below on how to do this and its cost.

5.1   Generating Random Samples

Let $G = (V, E)$ be an undirected graph with n vertices, and let d_x be the degree of a node $v_x \in V$. A random walk with r steps on G, denoted by $R = (x_1, x_2, \ldots, x_r)$, is defined as follows: start from an arbitrary node v_{x_1}, then choose a uniformly random neighbor (i.e., x_{i+1} is chosen with probability $\frac{1}{d_{x_i}}$) and repeat this process $r - 1$ times. As r grows to infinity, the probability that the last step of this random walk lands on a specific node v_i, i.e., $\Pr[x_r = i]$, converges to $p_i \triangleq d_i/D$. The vector $\pi = (p_1, p_2, \ldots, p_n)$ is called the stationary distribution of G. We recommend the book [LPW08] and additionally the survey [LLE96] for an excellent overview on random walks and their properties.

The actual number of steps needed to converge to the stationary distribution depends on what is called as *the mixing time* of G. There are several different definitions of mixing time, many of which are known to be equivalent up to constant factors [LPW08]. All definitions take an ε parameter to measure the distance between the stationary and the induced distribution by the random walk. We denote the mixing time of graph G by $\tau_{mix}(\varepsilon)$. We use the following definition:

Definition 4. *Let p be a distribution over the vertices of the graph G. Let $\pi_r(p)$ be the distribution of the end point of an r step random walk starting from a vertex chosen in accordance with p. Then we say that ϵ-mixing time of the graph is $\tau_{mix}(\epsilon)$ if for any p we have that the total variation is less than ϵ. Namely,*

$$\left\| \pi_{\tau_{mix}(\epsilon)}(p) - \pi \right\|_1 \leq \epsilon.$$

It is customary to define the mixing time to be $\tau_{mix} := \tau_{mix}(1/4)$. Choosing this (or any other constant) is not very significant as the value of ε affects the value by at most a logarithmic amount [LPW08]:

$$\tau_{mix}(\varepsilon) \leq \lceil \log_2 1/\varepsilon \rceil \tau_{mix}.$$

Social network graphs are known to have low mixing times. Recently, Addario-Berry et al. [ABL12] proved rigorously that the mixing time of Newman-Watts [NW99a, NW99b] small world networks is $\Theta(\log^2 n)$. Mohaisen et al. [MYK10] provide numerical evaluation of the mixing time of several networks. The empirical evidence provided by [MYK10] support the claim that the theoretical argument by Addario-Berry et al. [ABL12] extends to real world social networks. Specifically, in [MYK10, Table 1 and Figure 2] it is shown that to get total variation close to 0, the number of steps should be $r = \log^2 n$ for the Facebook network, $r = 3\log^2 n$ for the DBLP and youtube networks, and $r = 10\log^2 n$ for the Live Journal network.

Sampling a Random Vertex. There are three popular ways to sample a *node uniformly at random* [CDKLS16] (and matching lower bounds [CH18]). As in this model we do not have any prior knowledge of the graph, we use *rejection sampling.*

In this processes we start by performing a random walk for $r = \tau_{mix}(\epsilon)$ steps. The stationary distribution is proportional to the degree of the vertex, that is $\Pr[x_r = v_i] = d_i/D$. To fix the dependency on the degree, after preforming the random walk, we accept the vertex with probability $1/d_i$ and reject it otherwise. Thus, the expected probability for rejection is $\sum_{i=1}^{n} 1/d_i \cdot d_i/D = n/D = 1/\Delta$, and the expected number of trials until acceptance is Δ. Using this approach to sample random vertices, we get the following theorem.

Theorem 9. *Let G be a graph of size n with mixing time τ_{mix} and average degree Δ. For every $\varepsilon > 0$, there is a two-message public-coin interactive protocol to estimate the size of the graph within an error ε, in the graph query model where the verifier's query complexity and communication are bounded by $O(\frac{1}{\varepsilon^2} \cdot \log 1/\varepsilon \cdot \tau_{mix} \cdot \Delta)$ queries, and the prover runs in $\tilde{O}(n \cdot 1/\varepsilon^2)$ time.*

Sampling a Random Edge. Sampling an *edge uniformly at random* from the graph can be achieved as follows: (1) generate a random node v_i from the stationary distribution; (2) pick one of v_i's neighbors uniformly at random. The probability for sampling an edge $e = (v_i, v_j)$ is $\frac{d_i}{D} \cdot \frac{1}{d_i} + \frac{d_j}{D} \cdot \frac{1}{d_j} = \frac{1}{|E|}$.

The mixing time of the edges is bounded by the mixing time of the nodes[2]. Note that no rejection is needed here. Thus, an edge is sampled using $O(\tau_{mix})$ queries, without a dependency on the average degree of the graph. We apply the framework on the set of *edges* of the graph and get the following theorem.

Theorem 10. *Let G be a graph with m edges and mixing time τ_{mix}. For every $\varepsilon > 0$, there is a two-message public-coin interactive protocol to estimate m within an error ε, in the graph query model where the verifier' query complexity and communication are bounded by $O(\frac{1}{\varepsilon^2} \cdot \log 1/\varepsilon \cdot \tau_{mix})$ queries, and the prover runs in $\tilde{O}(m \cdot 1/\varepsilon^2)$ time.*

5.2   The Average Degree

For a graph with n nodes and m edges, the average degree is m/n. The average degree is a crucial property of a social graph ([DKS14]). Estimating the average degree can be done using Theorems 9 and 10 when using $\varepsilon' = \varepsilon/4$, where one can obtain the following bounds:

$$\frac{m}{n}(1 - 2\varepsilon') < \frac{m(1-\varepsilon')}{n(1+\varepsilon')} < \frac{\tilde{m}}{\tilde{n}} < \frac{m(1+\varepsilon')}{n(1-\varepsilon')} < \frac{m}{n}(1 + 4\varepsilon').$$

The number of queries required by the prover for this is then $O(\frac{1}{\varepsilon^2} \cdot \log 1/\varepsilon \cdot \tau_{mix} \cdot \Delta)$.

---

[2] Since any ε deviation is further divided by the v_i's degree.

5.3   Degree Distribution

In this subsection, we show how to use our framework to estimate the degree distribution of the graph, given that we have already established the size of the graph. We set the function $f(v) = d(v)$ and the use of the framework (Theorem 8) immediately yields the nodes degree distribution. For a parameter b, the framework returns all quantiles $\boldsymbol{q} = (1/b, 2/b, \ldots, (b-1)/b)$. This is a very robust surrogate for the full nodes' degree distribution.

Theorem 11. *Let G be a graph of size n. Let b be an integer and let $\varepsilon > 0$. Let $A_f(\boldsymbol{q}) = (A_f(1/b), A_f(2/b), \ldots, A_f((b-1)/b))$ be the quantiles of the nodes' degree. There is a three-message protocol for estimating $A_f(\boldsymbol{q})$ (given n) to within a factor of ε in the graph query model where the verifier performs $\widetilde{O}(\varepsilon^{-2})$ queries to the graph (this also bounds the communication complexity and the verifier's run-time).*

5.4   Local Clustering Coefficients

Besides the degree distribution, one of the interesting measures for social graph is the distribution of the *local clustering coefficients* [CRTB06, UKBM11]. The local clustering coefficient of a node quantifies how close the sub-graph of the node and its neighbors to being a clique. The notion of social graph composed by small overlapping mini-communities is captured by this node-centric view. In turn, the local clustering coefficients can be used to quantify how close is a graph to a small-world network.

Let N_i be the set of neighbor nodes of the node v_i. The number of edges between any two nodes in N_i is at least 0 and at most $d_i(d_i - 1)/2$. The local clustering coefficient C_i measures the fraction between the actual number of edges between nodes in N_i and the maximum number of such edges. Thus, $0 \le C_i \le 1$. Formally,

$$C_i = \frac{|\{(j, k) : (v_j, v_k) \in E, v_k, v_j \in N_i, j \ne k\}|}{d_i(d_i - 1)}.$$

We set the function $f(v_i) = C_i$ and the use of the framework (Theorem 8) immediately yields the local clustering coefficient distribution. The computation of $f(v_i)$ in our model requires $O(d_i^2)$ queries. For simplicity, we assume that we additionally have oracle access to the mutual neighbors of two vertices, or alternatively, can get the full list of neighbors in a single query which reduces the cost to $O(d_i)$ queries. We denote by $d_{\max}$ the maximum degree of any node in the graph.

Theorem 12. *Let G be a graph of size n. Let b be an integer and let $\varepsilon > 0$. Let $A_f(\boldsymbol{q}) = (A_f(1/b), A_f(2/b), \ldots, A_f((b-1)/b))$ be the quantiles of $\{C_1, C_2, \ldots, C_n\}$. There is a three-message protocol for estimating $A_f(\boldsymbol{q})$ (given n) to within a factor of ε in the graph query model where the verifier performs $\widetilde{O}(\varepsilon^{-2} \cdot d_{max})$ queries to the graph (this also bounds the communication complexity and the verifier's run-time).*

5.5   Social Graphs and Society

As a result of the growing influence of social networks, the question of the companies obligations and responsibilities is a subject of a heightened discussion. Various companies were required to prove that they are following various laws and guidelines, and to back their claims with data. Our protocol can be applied to some of these claims and we elaborate on two examples that are of particular interest.

Bots and Fake Accounts. Companies, political organizations and other entities are known to use bots to fabricate support, notion of validity or image of popularity. Malicious actors use fake accounts for various attacks on private people or groups of users. In light of public outrage on various events in the recent years, social networks are making efforts to fight this issue.

The detection of fake accounts is the subject of many studies in recent years (see, e.g. [XFH15, EAKA17]). These studies, together with our protocol, can be used to publicly prove that the proportion of fake users is low, or at least decreasing after certain policies were brought into effect.

For example, in many cases, fake accounts appear in *clusters* that share similar emails, dates of joining the network and other features. One can apply our framework with a function $f(v)$ that returns a "similarity" measure of a vertex v to its neighbors, for some appropriate definition of similarity. In a healthy network we would expect the average similarity to be somewhat high but beneath a certain trivial threshold. We also expect the number of individual vertices with a suspiciously high neighbor-similarity to be low. It is crucial to require social networks both to keep track of these and other "red flags" and *prove* that they are indeed fighting the phenomenon.

Echo Chambers. Social networks are one of the main stages for political debate, compared by many to a virtual "town square" where different people have a chance to debate their opinions. In contrast to this, others claim that instead of introducing various opinions, social networks close people in echo chambers where the only opinions that they are exposed to are similar to theirs.

Extensive research has been done on this subject for various social network (see, e.g., Facebook [QSS16] or Twitter [BJNTB15]). In many cases, it is possible to determine the standing of users on controversial subjects, and explore the connection between various parties. One might make use of use protocol to estimate the number of edges in the graph where each endpoint of the edge has a user with a different stand. This might be useful to track how much diversity are users exposed to in the network.

The above are only two of the many phenomena that social media exhibits. Our protocol allows researchers from various fields to demand reliable data and use it to improve our interaction with social media in the upcoming future.

6   Non-interactive Succinct Arguments for Social Graphs

We have described an interactive protocol for estimating the size of a social graph and other complexity measures. Our protocols are AM protocols – they are public-coin and consist of a constant number of rounds. One might ask if this already limited interaction can be further reduced to a completely non-interactive setting where the prover sends a proof and the verifier (probabilistically) decides whether to accepts or reject (an MA protocol). Such a non-interactive protocol is very mush desirable: a social graph provider can publish a proof, once and for all, and any user can later verify the proof on its own, using a small number of queries to the graph. This eliminates the need of the prover to interact with each verifier and to be online on time of verification.

Towards this end, we observe that our protocols can be compiled to non-interactive argument systems in the random oracle model. In such an argument system, proofs of false statements *exist*, but it is *computationally hard* to find them. Here, computation is measured by the number of queries performed to the random oracle. We apply the common approach to eliminate interaction, which is called the Fiat-Shamir transformation or heuristic (first used in [FS86]), that is applicable to any public-coin protocol (this is another reason why we insisted on having a protocols public-coin). In the Fiat-Shamir setting, the parties have access to a random oracle, and the prover is computationally limited: it can only perform a (polynomially) bounded number of queries to the random oracle.

The security of the compiled protocol, in general, is not clear and requires careful analysis [Can+19, CCRR18, CCHLRR18, KRR17]. However, in our case, since our protocols have only a constant number of rounds (it is either a single round for estimating the size of the graph, or two rounds for the general case), it is easy to argue about its soundness. In general, the compiler uses the random oracle to define the randomness sent by the verifier. Very roughly, on prover message Π, the prover uses the randomness in $\rho(\Pi)$ as the verifier's next message, where ρ is the random oracle (see [Mic00, BCS16] and [NPY18, Section 8.1] for a more precise description). As long as the protocol had negligible soundness, then the compiled protocol will be sound (against cheating prover that can perform at most polynomially many queries to the random oracle). Recall that to achieve soundness $2^{-\lambda}$ it suffices to perform parallel repetition of the protocol $O(\lambda)$, which yields a multiplicative overhead of λ in the communication complexity and query complexity of all protocols. The resulting argument size is simply the communication complexity of the amplified protocol.

The result of this compilation is quite remarkable. A company or social network provider (e.g., facebook, twitter, linkedin, youtube) can provide, in their public report, a proof of the health of its network, in terms of the number of users from different communities and other health measures such as local clustering coefficient, distribution of degrees and so on. The proof is written once in the report without a specific verifier in mind. Then, any individual (a private citizen, shareholders, potential buyer) can look at the report and verify its validity. This might have an effect on the way such provides manage their network, with the aim to more transparent and truthful reports. These reports are also critical for business development issues, choosing between networks for advertisement campaigns or for launching social applications.

Acknowledgments. This work was done (in part) while the second and third authors were visiting the Simons Institute for the Theory of Computing. Eylon Yogev is funded by the ISF grants 484/18, 1789/19, Len Blavatnik and the Blavatnik Foundation, and The Blavatnik Interdisciplinary Cyber Research Center at Tel Aviv University.

References

[ABL12] Addario-Berry, L., T, Lei.: "The mixing time of the Newman-Watts small world". In

[ACELP13] Alvisi, L., Clement, A., Epasto, A., Lattanzi, S., Panconesi, A.: Sok: the evolution of sybil defense via social networks. IEEE (2013)

[BCS16] Ben-Sasson, E., Chiesa, A., Spooner, N.: Interactive Oracle proofs. In: Hirt, M., Smith, A. (eds.) TCC 2016. LNCS, vol. 9986, pp. 31–60. Springer, Heidelberg (2016). https://doi.org/10.1007/978-3-662-53644-5_2

[BJNTB15] Barberá, P., Jost, J.T., Nagler, J., Tucker, J.A., Bonneau, R.: Tweeting from left to right: is online political communication more than an echo chamber? Psychol. Sci. **26**, 1531–1542 (2015)

[BYG08] Bar-Yossef, Z., Gurevich, M.: Random sampling from a search engine's index. J. ACM **55**, 1–74 (2008)

[BYG09] Bar-Yossef, Z., Gurevich, M.: Estimating the ImpressionRank of web pages (2009)

[BYG11] Bar-Yossef, Z., Gurevich, M.: Efficient search engine measurements. TWEB **5**, 1–48 (2011)

[Bra10] Braverman, M.: Polylogarithmic independence fools AC^0 circuits. J. ACM **57**, 1–10 (2010)

[Bre12] Brede, M.: Networks-an introduction. In: Newman, M.E.J. (ed.) 2010 Artificial Life. Oxford University Press (2012)

[Bro+06] Broder, A., et al.: Estimating corpus size via queries. In: Association for Computing Machinery (2006)

[CCHLRR18] Canetti, R., Chen, Y., Holmgren, J., Lombardi, A., Rothblum, G.N., Rothblum, R.D.: Fiat-Shamir from simpler assumptions. IACR Cryptology ePrint Archive (2018)

[CCRR18] Canetti, R., Chen, Y., Reyzin, L., Rothblum, R.D.: Fiat-Shamir and correlation intractability from strong KDM-secure encryption. In: Nielsen, J.B., Rijmen, V. (eds.) EUROCRYPT 2018. LNCS, vol. 10820, pp. 91–122. Springer, Cham (2018). https://doi.org/10.1007/978-3-319-78381-9_4

[CDKLS16] Chiericetti, F., Dasgupta, A., Kumar, R., Lattanzi, S., Sarlós, T.: On sampling nodes in a network (2016)

[CEKLM15] Ching, A., Edunov, S., Kabiljo, M., Logothetis, D., Muthukrishnan, S.: One trillion edges: graph processing at Facebook-scale. PVLDB **8**, 1804–1815 (2015)

[CH18] Chierichetti, F., Haddadan, S.: On the complexity of sampling vertices uniformly from a graph (2018)

[CRTB06] da F Costa, L., Rodrigues, F.A., Travieso, G., Boas, P.R.V.: Characterization of complex networks: a survey of measurements. Adv. Phys. **56**, 167–242 (2006)

[Can+19] Canetti, R., et al.: Fiat-Shamir: from practice to theory (2019)

[DKS14]   Dasgupta, A., Kumar, R., Sarlós, T.: On estimating the average degree. ACM (2014)

[EAKA17]   Ersahin, B., Aktas, Ö., Kilinç, D., Akyol, C.: Twitter fake account detection. IEEE (2017)

[EK10]   Easley, D.A., Kleinberg, J.M.: Networks, Crowds, and Markets - Reasoning About a Highly Connected World. Cambridge University Press, Cambridge (2010)

[EKR04]   Ergün, F., Kumar, R., Rubinfeld, R.: Fast approximate probabilistically checkable proofs. Inf. Comput. **189**, 135–159 (2004)

[FS86]   Fiat, A., Shamir, A.: How to prove yourself: practical solutions to identification and signature problems. In: Odlyzko, A.M. (ed.) CRYPTO 1986. LNCS, vol. 263, pp. 186–194. Springer, Heidelberg (1987). https://doi.org/10.1007/3-540-47721-7_12

[For87]   Fortnow, L.: The complexity of perfect zero-knowledge. In: STOC 1987 (1987)

[GDFMGM18] Garimella, K., De Francisci Morales, G., Gionis, A., Mathioudakis, M.: Political discourse on social media: echo chambers, gatekeepers, and the price of bipartisanship (2018)

[GKBM10]   Gjoka, M., Kurant, M., Butts, C.T., Markopoulou, A.: Walking in Facebook: a case study of unbiased sampling of OSNs. In: Proceedings of IEEE INFOCOM 2010 (2010)

[GMR89]   Goldwasser, S., Micali, S., Rackoff, C.: The knowledge complexity of interactive proof systems. SIAM J. Comput. **18**, 186–208 (1989)

[GS89]   Goldwasser, S., Sipser, M.: Private coins versus public coins in interactive proof systems. In: Advances in Computing Research (1989)

[HPWP10]   Håstad, J., Pass, R., Wikström, D., Pietrzak, K.: An efficient parallel repetition theorem. In: Micciancio, D. (ed.) TCC 2010. LNCS, vol. 5978, pp. 1–18. Springer, Heidelberg (2010). https://doi.org/10.1007/978-3-642-11799-2_1

[HRH09]   Hardiman, S.J., Richmond, P., Hutzler, S.: Calculating statistics of complex networks through random walks with an application to the on-line social network Bebo. Eur. Phys. J. B **71**, 611 (2009)

[HS19]   Harsha, P., Srinivasan, S.: On polynomial approximations to AC. Random Struct. Algorithms **54**, 289–303 (2019)

[KBM12]   Kurant, M., Butts, C.T., Markopoulou, A.: Graph size estimation. CoRR (2012)

[KH15]   Katzir, L., Hardiman, S.J.: Estimating clustering coefficients and size of social networks via random walk. ACM Trans. Web **9**, 1–20 (2015)

[KLSC14]   Katzir, L., Liberty, E., Somekh, O., Cosma, I.A.: Estimating sizes of social networks via biased sampling. Internet Math. **10**, 335–359 (2014)

[KMV17]   Kanade, V., Mallmann-Trenn, F., Verdugo, V. How large is your graph? (2017)

[KRR17]   Kalai, Y.T., Rothblum, G.N., Rothblum, R.D.: From obfuscation to the security of Fiat-Shamir for proofs. In: Katz, J., Shacham, H. (eds.) CRYPTO 2017. LNCS, vol. 10402, pp. 224–251. Springer, Cham (2017). https://doi.org/10.1007/978-3-319-63715-0_8

[Kle00]   Kleinberg, J.M.: The small-world phenomenon: an algorithmic perspective (2000)

[LLE96]   Lovász, L., Lov, L., Erdos, O.: Random walks on graphs: a survey (1996)

[LPW08] Levin, D.A., Peres, Y., Wilmer, E.L.: Markov Chains and Mixing Times. American Mathematical Society (2008)

[MMGDB07] Mislove, A., Marcon, M., Gummadi, K.P., Druschel, P., Bhattacharjee, B.: Measurement and analysis of online social networks (2007)

[MYK10] Mohaisen, A., Yun, A., Kim, Y.: Measuring the mixing time of social graphs (2010)

[Mic00] Micali, S.: Computationally sound proofs. SIAM J. Comput. **30**, 1253–1298 (2000)

[NPY18] Naor, M., Parter, M., Yogev, E.: The power of distributed verifiers in interactive proofs. In: Electronic Colloquium on Computational Complexity (ECCC) (2018)

[NW99a] Newman, M., Watts, D.: Renormalization group analysis of the small-world network model. Phys. Lett. A **263**, 341–346 (1999)

[NW99b] Newman, M., Watts, D.: Scaling and percolation in the small-world network model. Phys. Rev. E **60**, 7332 (1999)

[QSS16] Quattrociocchi, W., Scala, A., Sunstein, C.R.: Echo chambers on Facebook. Available at SSRN 2795110 (2016)

[RT10] Ribeiro, B.F., Towsley, D.F.: Estimating and sampling graphs with multidimensional random walks (2010)

[RVW13] Rothblum, G.N., Vadhan, S.P., Wigderson, A.: Interactive proofs of proximity: delegating computation in sublinear time. In: Boneh, D., Roughgarden, T., Feigenbaum, J. (eds.) ACM (2013)

[Tal17] Tal, A.: Tight bounds on the fourier spectrum of AC0 (2017)

[UKBM11] Ugander, J., Karrer, B., Backstrom, L., Marlow, C.: The anatomy of the Facebook social graph. CoRR (2011)

[Wha] List of mergers and acquisitions by Facebook. https://en.wikipedia.org/wiki/List_of_mergers_and_acquisitions_by_Facebook

[XFH15] Xiao, C., Freeman, D.M., Hwa, T.: Detecting clusters of fake accounts in online social networks (2015)

[YW11] Ye, S., Wu, S.F.: Estimating the size of online social networks. IJSCCPS **1**, 160–179 (2011)

[ZLAZ11] Zhou, J., Li, Y., Adhikari, V.K., Zhang, Z.-L.: Counting YouTube videos via random prefix sampling. In: Association for Computing Machinery, New York (2011). ISBN 9781450310130

The Measure-and-Reprogram Technique 2.0: Multi-round Fiat-Shamir and More

Jelle Don[1(✉)], Serge Fehr[1,2], and Christian Majenz[1,3]

[1] Centrum Wiskunde & Informatica (CWI), Amsterdam, The Netherlands
{jelle.don,serge.fehr}@cwi.nl, c.majenz@uva.nl
[2] Mathematical Institute, Leiden University, Leiden, The Netherlands
[3] QuSoft, Amsterdam, The Netherlands

Abstract. We revisit recent works by Don, Fehr, Majenz and Schaffner and by Liu and Zhandry on the security of the Fiat-Shamir (FS) transformation of Σ-protocols in the quantum random oracle model (QROM). Two natural questions that arise in this context are: (1) whether the results extend to the FS transformation of *multi-round* interactive proofs, and (2) whether Don et al.'s $O(q^2)$ loss in security is optimal.

Firstly, we answer question (1) in the affirmative. As a byproduct of solving a technical difficulty in proving this result, we slightly improve the result of Don et al., equipping it with a cleaner bound and an even simpler proof. We apply our result to digital signature schemes showing that it can be used to prove strong security for schemes like MQDSS in the QROM. As another application we prove QROM-security of a non-interactive OR proof by Liu, Wei and Wong.

As for question (2), we show via a Grover-search based attack that Don et al.'s quadratic security loss for the FS transformation of Σ-protocols is optimal up to a small constant factor. This extends to our new multi-round result, proving it tight up to a factor depending on the number of rounds only, i.e. is constant for constant-round interactive proofs.

1   Introduction

Reprogramming the Quantum Random Oracle. We reconsider the recent work of Don, Fehr, Majenz and Schaffner [9] on the quantum random oracle model (QROM). On a technical level, they showed how to reprogram the QROM adaptively at *one* input. More precisely, for any oracle quantum algorithm $\mathcal{A}^H$, making q calls to a random oracle H and outputting a pair (x, z) so that some predicate $V(x, H(x), z)$ is satisfied, they showed existence of a "simulator" $\mathcal{S}$ that mimics the random oracle, extracts x from $\mathcal{A}^H$ by measuring one of the oracle queries to H, and then reprograms $H(x)$ to a given value Θ so that z output by $\mathcal{A}^H$ now satisfies $V(x, \Theta, z)$, except with a multiplicative $O(q^2)$ loss in probability (plus a negligible additive loss). We emphasize that the challenging aspect of this problem is that $\mathcal{A}^H$'s queries to H may be in quantum superposition, and thus measuring such a query disturbs the state and thus the behavior of $\mathcal{A}^H$. Still, Don et al. managed to control this disturbance sufficiently. In independent work

D. Micciancio and T. Ristenpart (Eds.): CRYPTO 2020, LNCS 12172, pp. 602–631, 2020.
https://doi.org/10.1007/978-3-030-56877-1_21

and using very different techniques, Liu and Zhandry [13] showed a similar kind of result, but with a $O(q^9)$ loss.

As an immediate application of this technique, it is then concluded that the Fiat-Shamir (FS) transformation of a Σ-protocol is as secure (in the QROM) as the original Σ-protocol (in the standard model), up to a $O(q^2)$ loss, i.e., any of the typically considered security notions is preserved under the FS transformation, even in the quantum setting. In combination with prior work on simulating signature queries [11,18], security (in the QROM) of FS signatures that arise from ordinary Σ-protocols then follows as a corollary.

Given important examples of *multi-round* public-coin interactive proofs, used in, e.g., MQDSS [5] and for Bulletproofs [4][1], a natural question that arises is whether these techniques and results extend to the reprogrammability of the QROM at *multiple* inputs and the security of the FS transformation (in the QROM) of *multi-round* public-coin interactive proofs. Another question is whether the $O(q^2)$ loss (for the original Σ-protocols) is optimal, or whether one might hope for a linear loss as in the classical case.

In this work, we provide answers to both these natural questions—and more.

A technical hurdle for generalizing[9] to multi-round Fiat-Shamir. To start with, we observe that the naive approach of applying the original result of [9] inductively to reprogram multiple inputs one by one does not work . This is due to a subtle technical issue that has to do with the precise statement of the original result. In more detail, the statement involves an additive error term $\varepsilon_x \geq 0$ that depends on the choice of the point x, which is (adaptively) chosen to be the input on which the random oracle (RO) is reprogrammed. The guarantee provided by [9] is that this error term stays negligible even *when summed over all x's*, i.e., $\sum_x \varepsilon_x = negl$. The formulation of the result for individual x's with control over $\sum_x \varepsilon_x$ is important for the later applications to the FS transformation. However, when applying the result twice in a row, with the goal being to reprogram the RO at two inputs x_1, x_2, then we end up with two error terms ε_{x_1} and $\varepsilon_{x_2}^{x_1}$ (with the second one depending on x_1), where the first one stays negligible when summed over x_1 and the second one stays negligible when summed over x_2 (for any x_1); but it is unclear that the sum $\varepsilon_{x_1,x_2} := \varepsilon_{x_1} + \varepsilon_{x_2}^{x_1}$ stays negligible when summed over x_1 *and* x_2, which is what we would need to get the corresponding generalized statement.

Our Results. As a first contribution, we revise the *original* result from [9] of reprogramming the QROM at one input by showing an *improved* version that has *no* additive error term, but only the original multiplicative $O(q^2)$ loss. For typical direct cryptographic applications, this improvement makes no big quantitative difference due to the error term being negligible, but: (1) it makes the statement cleaner and easier to formulate, (2) somewhat surprisingly, the proof is simpler than that of the original result in [9], and (3) most importantly, it removes the

---

[1] The security of the original Bulletproofs protocol relies on the hardness of discrete-log; however, work in progress considers post-quantum secure versions [2].

technical hurdle to extend to multiple inputs. Indeed, we then get the desired multi-input reprogrammability result by means of a not too difficult, though somewhat tedious, induction argument.

Building on our multi-input reprogrammability result above, our next goal then is to show the security of the FS transformation (in the QROM) of multi-round public-coin interactive proofs. In contrast to the original result in [DFMS19] for the FS transformation of Σ-protocols some additional work is needed here, to deal with the order of the messages extracted from the FS adversary. Thus, as a stepping stone, we consider and analyze a variant of the above multi-input reprogrammability result, which enforces the right order of the extracted messages. As a simple corollary of this, we then obtain the desired security of multi-round FS. Here, the multiplicative loss becomes $O(q^{2n})$ for a $(2n+1)$-round public-coin interactive proof with constant n.

In the context of digital signatures, the original motivation for the FS transformation, we extend previous results by Unruh [18] and Don et al. [9] to show that FS signature schemes based on a multi-round, honest-verifier zero knowledge public-coin interactive quantum proof of knowledge have standard signature security (existential unforgeability under chosen message attacks, UF-CMA) in the QROM. Assuming the additional collision-resistance-like property of computationally unique responses, they are even strongly unforgeable. We go on to apply this result to the signature scheme MQDSS [5], a candidate in the ongoing NIST standardization process for post-quantum cryptographic schemes [1], providing its first QROM proof. Another application of our multi-round FS result would for instance be to Bulletproofs [4].

As a second application of our multi-input reprogrammability result, we show QROM-security of the non-interactive OR-proof introduced by Liu, Wei and Wong [12], further analyzed by Fischlin, Harasser and Janson [10]. While the well-known (interactive) OR-proof by Cramer, Damgård and Schoenmakers [7] is a Σ-protocol and thus the results from [9] apply, the inherently non-interactive OR-proof by Liu et al. does *not* is not obtained as the FS transformation of a Σ-protocol (though in some sense it is "close" to being of this form). We show here how the 2-input version of our multi-input reprogrammability result implies security of this OR-proof in the QROM.

Our last contribution is a lower bound that shows that the multiplicative $O(q^2)$ loss in the security argument of the FS transformation of Σ-protocols is tight (up to a factor 4). Thus, the $O(q^2)$ loss is unavoidable in general. Furthermore, we extend this lower bound to the FS transformation of multi-round interactive proofs as considered in this work, and we show that the obtained loss $O(q^{2n})$ is in general optimal as well here, up to a constant depending on n only.

Related Work. Before the recently obtained reduction [9,13] was available, the FS tranform in the QROM was studied in a number of works [8,11,18], where weaker security properties were shown. In addition, Unruh developed an alternative transform [16] that provided QROM security at the expense of an increased proof size. The Unruh transform was later generalized to apply to 5-round public coin interactive proof systems [6].

2   Notation

Up to some modifications, we follow closely the notation used in [9]. We consider a (purified) oracle quantum algorithm $\mathcal{A}$ that makes q queries to an *oracle*, i.e., an unspecified function $H : \mathcal{X} \to \mathcal{Y}$ with finite non-empty sets $\mathcal{X}, \mathcal{Y}$. Formally, $\mathcal{A}$ is described by a sequence of unitaries $A_1, \ldots, A_q$ and an initial state $|\phi_0\rangle$.[2] For technical reasons that will become clear later, we actually allow (some of) the A_i's to be a *projection* followed by a unitary (or vice versa). One can think of such a projection as a measurement performed by the algorithm, with the algorithm aborting except in case of a particular measurement outcome.

For any concrete choice of $H : \mathcal{X} \to \mathcal{Y}$, the algorithm $\mathcal{A}$ computes the state

$$|\phi_q^H\rangle := \mathcal{A}^H|\phi_0\rangle := A_q \mathcal{O}^H \cdots A_1 \mathcal{O}^H |\phi_0\rangle,$$

where $\mathcal{O}^H$ is the unitary defined by $\mathcal{O}^H : |c\rangle|x\rangle|y\rangle \mapsto |c\rangle|x\rangle|y \oplus c \cdot H(x)\rangle$ for any triple $c \in \{0, 1\}$, $x \in \mathcal{X}$ and $y \in \mathcal{Y}$, with $\mathcal{O}^H$ acting on appropriate registers. We emphasize that we allow *controlled* queries to H. Per se, this gives the algorithm more power, and thus will make our result only stronger. It is, however, easy to see that controlled queries to the standard quantum oracle for a function can be simulated using ordinary queries, at the price of one additional query.[3] The final state $\mathcal{A}^H|\phi_0\rangle$ is considered to be a state over registers $X = X_1 \ldots X_n$, Z and E.

We introduce some notation following [9]. For $0 \leq i, j \leq q$ we set

$$\mathcal{A}_{i \to j}^H := A_j \mathcal{O}^H \cdots A_{i+1} \mathcal{O}^H ,$$

where, by convention, $\mathcal{A}_{i \to j}^H$ is set to $\mathbb{1}$ if $j \leq i$. Furthermore, we let

$$|\phi_i^H\rangle := \left(\mathcal{A}_{0 \to i}^H\right)|\phi_0\rangle$$

be the state of $\mathcal{A}$ after the i-th step but right before the $(i+1)$-st query, which is consistent with $|\phi_q^H\rangle$ above.

For a given function $H : \mathcal{X} \to \mathcal{Y}$ and for fixed $x \in \mathcal{X}$ and $\Theta \in \mathcal{Y}$, we define the *reprogrammed* function $H * \Theta x : \mathcal{X} \to \mathcal{Y}$ that coincides with H on $\mathcal{X} \setminus \{x\}$ but maps x to Θ. With this notation at hand, we can then write

$$\left(\mathcal{A}_{i \to q}^{H * \Theta x}\right)\left(\mathcal{A}_{0 \to i}^H\right)|\phi_0\rangle = \left(\mathcal{A}_{i \to q}^{H * \Theta x}\right)|\phi_i^H\rangle$$

for an execution of $\mathcal{A}$ where the oracle is reprogrammed at a given point x after the i-th query. We stress that $\left(\mathcal{A}_{i \to q}^{H * \Theta x}\right)\left(\mathcal{A}_{0 \to i}^H\right)$ can again be considered

---

[2] Alternatively, we may regard $|\phi_0\rangle$, as an additional input given to $\mathcal{A}$.

[3] Allowing controlled queries to the random oracle is also the more natural model compared to restricting to plain access to the unitary After all, the motivation for the QROM is that in the real world, an attacker can implement hash functions on a quantum computer, allowing them to implement the controlled version as well.

to be an oracle quantum algorithm $\mathcal{B}$, which depends on $\Theta \in \mathcal{Y}$, that makes q queries to (the unprogrammed) function H. Indeed, the (controlled) queries to the reprogrammed oracle $H * \Theta x$ can be simulated by means of controlled queries to H (using one additional "work qubit").[4] Exploiting that, in addition to unitaries, we allow projections as elementary operations, we can also understand $(\mathcal{A}_{i \to q}^{H * \Theta x}) X (\mathcal{A}_{0 \to i}^{H})$ to be an oracle quantum algorithm that makes oracle queries to H, where X is the projection $X = |x\rangle\langle x|$, acting on the oracle query register.

More generally, for any $\mathbf{x} = (x_1, \ldots, x_n) \in \mathcal{X}^n$ *without duplicate entries*, i.e., $x_i \neq x_j$ for $i \neq j$, and for any $\Theta \in \mathcal{Y}^n$, we define

$$H * \boldsymbol{\Theta}\mathbf{x} = H * \Theta_1 x_1 * \cdots * \Theta_n x_n : \mathcal{X} \to \mathcal{Y}$$

$$x \mapsto \begin{cases} \Theta_i & \text{if } x = x_i \text{ for some } i \in \{1, \ldots, n\} \\ H(x) & \text{otherwise.} \end{cases}$$

This will then allow us to consider $(\mathcal{A}_{i_2 \to q}^{H * \Theta_1 x_1 * \Theta_2 x_2}) X_2 (\mathcal{A}_{i_1 \to i_2}^{H * \Theta_1 x_1}) X_1 (\mathcal{A}_{0 \to i_1}^{H})$ as an oracle quantum algorithm with oracle queries to H, etc.

Eventually, we are interested in the probability that after the execution of the original algorithm $\mathcal{A}^H$, and upon measuring register X in the computational basis to obtain $\mathbf{x} = (x_1, \ldots, x_n) \in \mathcal{X}^n$, the state of register Z is of a certain form dependent on $\mathbf{x}$ and $H(\mathbf{x}) = (H(x_1), \ldots, H(x_n))$. Such a requirement (for a fixed $\mathbf{x}$) is captured by a projection

$$G_{\mathbf{x}}^H = |\mathbf{x}\rangle\langle\mathbf{x}| \otimes \Pi_{\mathbf{x}, H(\mathbf{x})},$$

where $\{\Pi_{\mathbf{x}, \Theta}\}_{\mathbf{x}, \Theta}$ is a family of projections with $\mathbf{x} \in \mathcal{X}^n$ and $\Theta \in \mathcal{Y}^n$, and with the understanding that $|\mathbf{x}\rangle\langle\mathbf{x}|$ acts on X and $\Pi_{\mathbf{x}, H(\mathbf{x})}$ on register Z. We refer to such a family of projections as a *quantum predicate*. We use $G_{\mathbf{x}}^{\boldsymbol{\Theta}}$ as a short hand for $G_{\mathbf{x}}^{H * \boldsymbol{\Theta}\mathbf{x}}$, and we write G_x^H and G_x^{Θ} with $x \in \mathcal{X}$ and $\Theta \in \mathcal{Y}$ for the case $n = 1$.

For an arbitrary but fixed $\mathbf{x}_\circ \in \mathcal{X}^n$, we are then interested in the probability

$$\Pr\left[\mathbf{x} = \mathbf{x}_\circ \wedge V(\mathbf{x}, H(\mathbf{x}), z) : (\mathbf{x}, z) \leftarrow \mathcal{A}^H\right] = \left\|G_{\mathbf{x}_\circ}^H |\phi_q^H\rangle\right\|_2^2.$$

where the left hand side is our notation for this probability, where we understand $\mathcal{A}^H$ to be an algorithm that outputs the measured $\mathbf{x}$ together with the quantum state z in register Z, and V to be the quantum predicate specified by the projections $\Pi_{\mathbf{x}, \Theta}$. Correspondingly, $\Pr\left[x = x_\circ \wedge V(x, H(x), z) : (x, z) \leftarrow \mathcal{A}^H\right] = \|G_{x_\circ}^H |\phi_q^H\rangle\|_2^2$ for the $n = 1$ case.

3   An Improved Single-Input Reprogramming Result

For the case $n = 1$, Don et al. [9] show the existence of a black-box *simulator* $\mathcal{S}$ such that for any oracle quantum algorithm $\mathcal{A}$ as considered above with oracle access to a *uniformly random* H, it holds that

---

[4] Here it is crucial that we allow *controlled* queries to H.

$$\Pr_{\Theta}\left[x=x_\circ \wedge V(x,\Theta,z) : (x,z) \leftarrow \langle \mathcal{S}^{\mathcal{A}},\Theta\rangle\right]$$

$$\geq \frac{1}{2(q+1)(2q+3)} \Pr_{H}\left[x=x_\circ \wedge V(x,H(x),z) : (x,z) \leftarrow \mathcal{A}^{H}\right] - \varepsilon_{x_\circ}, \tag{1}$$

for any $x_\circ \in \mathcal{X}$, where the $\varepsilon_{x_\circ}$'s are non-negative and their sum over $x_\circ \in \mathcal{X}$ is bounded by $1/(2q|\mathcal{Y}|)$, i.e., negligible whenever $|\mathcal{Y}|$ is superpolynomial. The notation $(x,z) \leftarrow \langle \mathcal{S}^{\mathcal{A}},\Theta\rangle$ is to be understood in that in a first stage $\mathcal{S}^{\mathcal{A}}$ outputs x, and then on input Θ it outputs z. At the core, Eq. (1) follows from Lemma 1 of [9] which shows that

$$\mathop{\mathbb{E}}_{\Theta,i,b}\left[\left\|(|x\rangle\langle x| \otimes \Pi_{x,\Theta})\left(\mathcal{A}^{H*\Theta x}_{i+b\to q}\right)\left(\mathcal{A}^{H}_{i\to i+b}\right)X|\phi^{H}_i\rangle\right\|^2_2\right]$$

$$\geq \frac{\mathbb{E}_{\Theta}\left[\left\|(|x\rangle\langle x| \otimes \Pi_{x,\Theta})|\phi^{H*\Theta x}_q\rangle\right\|^2_2\right]}{2(q+1)(2q+3)} - \frac{\left\|X|\phi^{H}_q\rangle\right\|^2_2}{2(q+1)|\mathcal{Y}|}, \tag{2}$$

and from which the construction of $\mathcal{S}$ can be extracted. The bound (1) on the "success probability" of $\mathcal{S}$ then follows from the observation that $\mathcal{S}$ can simulate the calls to H and to $H*\Theta x$ by means of a $2(q+1)$-wise independent hash function, and that H and $H*\Theta x$ are indistinguishable for random H and Θ.

In this section we show an improved variant of Eq. (1), which avoids the additive error term $\varepsilon_{x_\circ}$. While having negligible quantitative effect in typcial situations, it makes the statement simpler. In addition it circumvents a technical issue one encounters when trying to extend to the multi-input case. Furthermore, our improved version comes with a simpler proof.[5]

The approach is to avoid the additive error term in Eq. (2). We achieve this by slightly tweaking the simulator $\mathcal{S}$. From the technical perspective, while on the left hand side of Eq. (2) the expectation is over a random $i \in \{0,\dots,q\}$, selecting one of the $q+1$ queries of $\mathcal{A}$ at random (where the X register of the output state is considered to be a final query), and a random $b \in \{0,1\}$, our new version has syntactically the same left hand side, but with the expectation over a random pair $(i,b) \in (\{0,\dots,q\text{-}1\} \times \{0,1\}) \cup \{(q,0)\}$ instead. This absorbs the additive error term into the simulator's success probability. Furthermore, it holds for any *fixed* choice of Θ (and not only on average for a random choice).

Lemma 1. *Let $\mathcal{A}$ be a q-query oracle quantum algorithm. Then, for any function $H : \mathcal{X} \to \mathcal{Y}$, any $x \in \mathcal{X}$ and $\Theta \in \mathcal{Y}$, and any projection $\Pi_{x,\Theta}$, it holds that*

$$\mathop{\mathbb{E}}_{i,b}\left[\left\|(|x\rangle\langle x| \otimes \Pi_{x,\Theta})\left(\mathcal{A}^{H*\Theta x}_{i+b\to q}\right)\left(\mathcal{A}^{H}_{i\to i+b}\right)X|\phi^{H}_i\rangle\right\|^2_2\right] \geq \frac{\left\|(|x\rangle\langle x| \otimes \Pi_{x,\Theta})|\phi^{H*\Theta x}_q\rangle\right\|^2_2}{(2q+1)^2},$$

where the expectation is over uniform $(i,b) \in (\{0,\dots,q\text{-}1\} \times \{0,1\}) \cup \{(q,0)\}$.

---

[5] We thank Dominique Unruh for the idea that it might be possible to avoid the additive error term, and for proposing an argument for achieving that, which inspired us to find the simpler argument we eventually used.

This new version of Eq. (2) translates to a simulator $\mathcal{S}$ that works by running $\mathcal{A}$, but with the following modifications. First, one of the $q + 1$ queries of $\mathcal{A}$ (also counting the final output in register X) is measured, and the measurement outcome x is output by (the first stage of) $\mathcal{S}$. We emphasize that the crucial difference to [9] is that each of the q actual queries is picked with probability $\frac{2}{2q+1}$, while the final output is picked with probability $\frac{1}{2q+1}$. Then, very much as in [9], this very query of $\mathcal{A}$ is answered either using the original H *or* using the reprogrammed oracle $H * \Theta x$, with the choice being made at random[6], while all the remaining queries of $\mathcal{A}$ are answered using oracle $H * \Theta x$. Finally, (the second stage of) $\mathcal{S}$ outputs whatever $\mathcal{A}$ outputs.

In line with Theorem 1 in [9], i.e. Equation (1) above, we obtain the following result from Lemma 1.

Theorem 2 (Measure-and-reprogram, single input). *Let $\mathcal{X}$ and $\mathcal{Y}$ be finite non-empty sets. There exists a black-box two-stage quantum algorithm $\mathcal{S}$ with the following property. Let $\mathcal{A}$ be an arbitrary oracle quantum algorithm that makes q queries to a uniformly random $H : \mathcal{X} \to \mathcal{Y}$ and that outputs some $x \in \mathcal{X}$ and a (possibly quantum) output z. Then, the two-stage algorithm $\mathcal{S}^{\mathcal{A}}$ outputs some $x \in \mathcal{X}$ in the first stage and, upon a random $\Theta \in \mathcal{Y}$ as input to the second stage, a (possibly quantum) output z, so that for any $x_\circ \in \mathcal{X}$ and any (possibly quantum) predicate V:*

$$\Pr_{\Theta}\left[x = x_\circ \wedge V(x, \Theta, z) : (x, z) \leftarrow \langle \mathcal{S}^{\mathcal{A}}, \Theta \rangle\right]$$

$$\geq \frac{1}{(2q + 1)^2} \Pr_{H}\left[x = x_\circ \wedge V(x, H(x), z) : (x, z) \leftarrow \mathcal{A}^{H}\right].$$

Furthermore, $\mathcal{S}$ runs in time polynomial in q, $\log |\mathcal{X}|$ and $\log |\mathcal{Y}|$.

The proof of Lemma 1 follows closely the proof of Eq. (1) in [9], but the streamlined statement and simulator allow to cut some corners.

Proof (of Lemma 1). For any $0 \leq i \leq q$, inserting a resolution of the identity and exploiting that

$$\left(\mathcal{A}_{i+1 \to q}^{H*\Theta x}\right)\left(\mathcal{A}_{i \to i+1}^{H}\right)\left(\mathbb{1} - X\right)|\phi_i^H\rangle = \left(\mathcal{A}_{i \to q}^{H*\Theta x}\right)\left(\mathbb{1} - X\right)|\phi_i^H\rangle,$$

we can write

$$\left(\mathcal{A}_{i+1 \to q+1}^{H*\Theta x}\right)|\phi_{i+1}^H\rangle$$
$$= \left(\mathcal{A}_{i+1 \to q+1}^{H*\Theta x}\right)\left(\mathcal{A}_{i \to i+1}^{H}\right)\left(\mathbb{1} - X\right)|\phi_i^H\rangle + \left(\mathcal{A}_{i+1 \to q+1}^{H*\Theta x}\right)\left(\mathcal{A}_{i \to i+1}^{H}\right)X|\phi_i^H\rangle$$
$$= \left(\mathcal{A}_{i \to q+1}^{H*\Theta x}\right)\left(\mathbb{1} - X\right)|\phi_i^H\rangle \qquad\qquad + \left(\mathcal{A}_{i+1 \to q+1}^{H*\Theta x}\right)\left(\mathcal{A}_{i \to i+1}^{H}\right)X|\phi_i^H\rangle$$
$$= \left(\mathcal{A}_{i \to q+1}^{H*\Theta x}\right)|\phi_i^H\rangle - \left(\mathcal{A}_{i \to q+1}^{H*\Theta x}\right)X|\phi_i^H\rangle + \left(\mathcal{A}_{i+1 \to q+1}^{H*\Theta x}\right)\left(\mathcal{A}_{i \to i+1}^{H}\right)X|\phi_i^H\rangle$$

---

[6] If it is the final output that is measured then there is nothing left to reprogram, so no choice has to be made.

Rearranging terms, applying $G_x^\Theta = (|x\rangle\langle x| \otimes \Pi_{x,\Theta})$ and using the triangle equality, we can thus bound

$$\left\| G_x^\Theta \left(\mathcal{A}_{i \to q}^{H*\Theta x} \right) |\phi_i^H\rangle \right\|_2 \leq \left\| G_x^\Theta \left(\mathcal{A}_{i+1 \to q}^{H*\Theta x} \right) |\phi_{i+1}^H\rangle \right\|_2$$
$$+ \left\| G_x^\Theta \left(\mathcal{A}_{i \to q}^{H*\Theta x} \right) X |\phi_i^H\rangle \right\|_2$$
$$+ \left\| G_x^\Theta \left(\mathcal{A}_{i+1 \to q}^{H*\Theta x} \right) \left(\mathcal{A}_{i \to i+1}^H \right) X |\phi_i^H\rangle \right\|_2.$$

Summing up the respective sides of the inequality over $i = 0, \ldots, q-1$, we get

$$\left\| G_x^\Theta |\phi_q^{H*\Theta x}\rangle \right\|_2 \leq \left\| G_x^\Theta |\phi_q^H\rangle \right\|_2 + \sum_{\substack{0 \leq i < q \\ b \in \{0,1\}}} \left\| G_x^\Theta \left(\mathcal{A}_{i+b \to q}^{H*\Theta x} \right) \left(\mathcal{A}_{i \to i+b}^H \right) X |\phi_i^H\rangle \right\|_2.$$

By squaring both sides, dividing by $2q+1$ (i.e., the number of terms on the right hand side), and using Jensen's inequality on the right hand side, we obtain

$$\frac{\left\| G_x^\Theta |\phi_q^{H*\Theta x}\rangle \right\|_2^2}{2q+1} \leq \left\| G_x^\Theta |\phi_q^H\rangle \right\|_2^2 + \sum_{\substack{0 \leq i < q \\ b \in \{0,1\}}} \left\| G_x^\Theta \left(\mathcal{A}_{i+b \to q}^{H*\Theta x} \right) \left(\mathcal{A}_{i \to i+b}^H \right) X |\phi_i^H\rangle \right\|_2^2$$

and thus, noting that we can write $\left\| G_x^\Theta |\phi_q^H\rangle \right\|_2^2$ as

$$\left\| G_x^\Theta \left(\mathcal{A}_{i+b \to q+1}^{H*\Theta x} \right) \left(\mathcal{A}_{i \to i+b}^H \right) X |\phi_i^H\rangle \right\|_2^2$$

with $i = q$ and $b = 0$,

$$\frac{\left\| G_x^\Theta |\phi_q^{H*\Theta x}\rangle \right\|_2^2}{(2q+1)^2} \leq \mathop{\mathbb{E}}_{i,b} \left[\left\| G_x^\Theta \left(\mathcal{A}_{i+b \to q}^{H*\Theta x} \right) \left(\mathcal{A}_{i \to i+b}^H \right) X |\phi_i^H\rangle \right\|_2^2 \right].$$

$\square$

For completeness, let us spell out how Theorem 8 of [9] on the generic security of the FS transformation (in the QROM) can now be re-phrased, avoiding the negligible error term present in [9]. We refer to [9] or to our later Sect. 5 for the details on the FS transformation.

Theorem 3. *There exists a black-box quantum polynomial-time two-stage quantum algorithm $\mathcal{S}$ such that for any adaptive FS adversary $\mathcal{A}$, making q queries to a uniformly random function H with appropriate domain and range, and for any $x_\circ \in \mathcal{X}$:*

$$\Pr\left[x = x_\circ \wedge v = accept : (x, v) \leftarrow \langle \mathcal{S}^\mathcal{A}, \mathcal{V} \rangle \right]$$
$$\geq \frac{1}{(2q+1)^2} \Pr_H\left[x = x_\circ \wedge V_{FS}^H(x, \pi) : (x, \pi) \leftarrow \mathcal{A}^H \right].$$

4   Multi-input Reprogrammability

In this section, we extend our (improved) results on adaptively reprogramming the quantum random oracle at *one* point $x \in \mathcal{X}$ to *multiple* points $x_1, \ldots, x_n \in \mathcal{X}$. This in turn will allow us to extend the results on the security of the FS transformation to *multi-round* protocols. We point out again that the improvement of Lemma 1 over Lemma 1 in [9] plays a crucial role here, in that it circumvents the trouble with the negligible error term that occurs when trying to extend the result from [9] to the setting considered here.

The starting point is the following generalized version of the problem considered in Sect. 3. We assume an oracle quantum algorithm $\mathcal{A}^H$ that makes q queries to a random oracle $H : \mathcal{X} \to \mathcal{Y}$ and then produces an output of the form $(x_1, \ldots, x_n, z)$, where z may be quantum, such that a certain (quantum) predicate $V(x_1, H(x_1), \ldots, x_n, H(x_n), z)$ is satisfied with some probability. The goal then is to turn such an $\mathcal{A}^H$ into a multi-stage quantum algorithm $\mathcal{S}$ (the *simulator*) that, stage by stage, outputs the x_i's and takes corresponding Θ_i's as input, and eventually outputs a (possibly quantum) z with the property that $V(x_1, \Theta_1, \ldots, x_n, \Theta_n, z)$ is satisfied with similar probability.

4.1   The General Case

Naively, one might hope for an $\mathcal{S}$ that outputs x_1 in the first stage (obtained by measuring one of the queries of $\mathcal{A}^H$), and then on input Θ_1 proceeds by outputting x_2 in the second stage (obtained by measuring one of the subsequent queries of $\mathcal{A}^H$), etc. However, since $\mathcal{A}^H$ may query the hashes of $x_1, \ldots, x_n$ in an arbitrary order, we cannot hope for this to work. Therefore, we have to allow $\mathcal{S}$ to produce $x_1, \ldots, x_n$ in an arbitrary order as well.[7] Formally, we consider $\mathcal{S}$ with the following syntactic behavior: in the first stage it outputs a permutation π together with $x_{\pi(1)}$ and takes as input $\Theta_{\pi(1)}$, and then for every subsequent stage $1 < i \leq n$ it outputs $x_{\pi(i)}$ and takes as input $\Theta_{\pi(i)}$; eventually, in the final stage (labeled by $n + 1$) it outputs z. In line with earlier notation, but taking this additional complication into account, we denote such an execution of $\mathcal{S}$ as $(\pi, \pi(\mathbf{x}), z) \leftarrow \langle \mathcal{S}^{\mathcal{A}}, \pi(\boldsymbol{\Theta}) \rangle$.

A final issue is that if $x_i = x_j$ then $H(x_i) = H(x_j)$ as well, whereas Θ_i and Θ_j may well be different. Thus, we can only expect $\mathcal{S}$ to work well when $x_1, \ldots x_n$ has no duplicates.

For us to be able to mathematically reason about the simulator described above, we introduce some additional notation. For the basic simulator from Lemma 1 we write, using $r_1 = (b_1, i_1)$, as

$$\mathcal{S}^{H,\mathcal{A}}_{\Theta_1, x_1, r_1} := \mathcal{S}^{H,\mathcal{A},\Theta_1, x_1, r_1} := \left(\mathcal{A}^{H * \Theta_1 x_1}_{i_1 + b_1 \to q} \right) \left(\mathcal{A}^H_{i_1 \to i_1 + b_1} \right) X_1 \left(\mathcal{A}^H_{0 \to i_1} \right).$$

---

[7] Looking ahead, in Sect. 4.2 we will force $\mathcal{A}^H$ to query, and thus $\mathcal{S}$ to extract, $x_1, \ldots, x_n$ in the *right* order by requiring x_2 to contain $H(x_1)$ as a substring, x_3 to contain $H(x_2)$ as a substring, etc. This will be important for the multi-round FS application.

This can be recursively extended by applying it to $\mathcal{A}^H$ now being $\mathcal{S}^{H,\mathcal{A}}_{\Theta_1,x_1,r_1}$ so as to obtain

$$\mathcal{S}^{H,\mathcal{A}}_{\Theta_{1,2},x_{1,2},r_{1,2}} := \left(\mathcal{S}^{H*\Theta_2 x_2,\mathcal{A},\Theta_1,x_1,r_1}_{i_2+b_2\to q}\right)\left(\mathcal{S}^{H,\mathcal{A},\Theta_1,x_1,r_1}_{i_2\to i_2+b_2}\right)X_2\left(\mathcal{S}^{H,\mathcal{A},\Theta_1,x_1,r_1}_{0\to i_2}\right).$$

In general, we can consider the following operator, which simulates $\mathcal{A}$ and performs n measurements:

$$\mathcal{S}^{H,\mathcal{A}}_{\Theta,\mathbf{x},\mathbf{r}} := \left(\mathcal{S}^{H*\Theta_n x_n,\mathcal{A},\overline{\Theta},\overline{\mathbf{x}},\overline{\mathbf{r}}}_{i_n+b_n\to q}\right)\left(\mathcal{S}^{H,\mathcal{A},\overline{\Theta},\overline{\mathbf{x}},\overline{\mathbf{r}}}_{i_n\to i_n+b_n}\right)X_n\left(\mathcal{S}^{H,\mathcal{A},\overline{\Theta},\overline{\mathbf{x}},\overline{\mathbf{r}}}_{0\to i_n}\right).$$

where, for arbitrary but fixed n and $\Theta = (\Theta_1,\ldots,\Theta_n) \in \mathcal{Y}^n$, the notation $\overline{\Theta}$ is understood as $\overline{\Theta} = (\Theta_1,\ldots,\Theta_{n-1}) \in \mathcal{Y}^{n-1}$, and correspondingly for $\mathbf{x}$ etc. Finally, when considering *fixed* $\Theta \in \mathcal{Y}^n$ and $\mathbf{x} \in \mathcal{X}^n$, we write

$$S^H_{\mathbf{r}}(\mathcal{A}) := \mathcal{S}^{H,\mathcal{A}}_{\Theta,\mathbf{x},\mathbf{r}}.$$

At the core of our multi-round result will be the following technical lemma, which generalizes Lemma 1.

Lemma 4. *Let $\mathcal{A}$ be a q-query oracle quantum algorithm. Then, for any function $H : \mathcal{X} \to \mathcal{Y}$, any $\mathbf{x} \in \mathcal{X}^n$ and $\Theta^n \in \mathcal{Y}^n$, and any projection $\Pi_{\mathbf{x},\Theta}$, it holds that*

$$\frac{\left\|(|\mathbf{x}\rangle\langle\mathbf{x}| \otimes \Pi_{\mathbf{x},\Theta})\mathcal{A}^{H*\Theta\mathbf{x}}|\phi_0\rangle\right\|^2_2}{(2q+1)^{2n}} \leq \mathbb{E}_{\mathbf{r}}\left[\left\|(|\mathbf{x}\rangle\langle\mathbf{x}|_A \otimes \Pi_{\mathbf{x},\Theta})S^H_{\mathbf{r}}(\mathcal{A})|\phi_0\rangle\right\|^2_2\right].$$

Proof. The proof is by induction on n, where the base case is given by Lemma 1. For the induction step we first apply the base case, substituting x_n for x_1, Θ_n for Θ_1, r_n for r_1, $H*\overline{\Theta}\overline{\mathbf{x}}$ for H, and $\hat{\Pi}_{x_n,\Theta_n}$ for Π_{x_1,Θ_1}, where

$$\hat{\Pi}_{x_n,\Theta_n} = |x_1\rangle\langle x_1| \otimes \ldots \otimes |x_{n-1}\rangle\langle x_{n-1}| \otimes \Pi_{\mathbf{x},\Theta}$$

to obtain

$$\frac{\left\|(|x_n\rangle\langle x_n| \otimes \hat{\Pi}_{x_n,\Theta_n})\mathcal{A}^{(H*\overline{\Theta}\overline{\mathbf{x}})*\Theta_n x_n}|\phi_0\rangle\right\|^2_2}{(2q+1)^2}$$
$$\leq \mathbb{E}_{r_n}\left[\left\|(|x_n\rangle\langle x_n|_A \otimes \hat{\Pi}_{x_n,\Theta_n})S^{H*\overline{\Theta}\overline{\mathbf{x}}}_{r_n}(\mathcal{A})|\phi_0\rangle\right\|^2_2\right]$$

which we can write as

$$\frac{\left\|(|\mathbf{x}\rangle\langle\mathbf{x}| \otimes \Pi_{\mathbf{x},\Theta})\mathcal{A}^{H*\Theta\mathbf{x}}|\phi_0\rangle\right\|^2_2}{(2q+1)^{2n}} \leq \frac{\mathbb{E}_{r_n}\left[\left\|(|\mathbf{x}\rangle\langle\mathbf{x}| \otimes \Pi_{\mathbf{x},\Theta})S^{H*\overline{\Theta}\overline{\mathbf{x}}}_{r_n}(\mathcal{A})|\phi_0\rangle\right\|^2_2\right]}{(2q+1)^{2(n-1)}} \quad (3)$$

dividing both sides by $(2q+1)^{2(n-1)}$ and swapping registers appropriately (to make sure that the register which contains x_n comes after the others).

Now fix r_n. We define

$$\hat{\Pi}_{\overline{\mathbf{x}},\overline{\Theta}} := |x_n\rangle\langle x_n| \otimes \Pi_{\mathbf{x},\Theta}.$$

and apply the induction hypothesis for $n-1$, substituting $\mathcal{S}_{r_n}^{H*\overline{\Theta x}}(\mathcal{A})$ for $\mathcal{A}^{H*\overline{\Theta x}}$, and $\hat{\Pi}_{\overline{x},\overline{\Theta}}$ for $\Pi_{\overline{x},\overline{\Theta}}$, in order to derive

$$\frac{\left\|(|\mathbf{x}\rangle\langle\mathbf{x}| \otimes \Pi_{\mathbf{x},\Theta})\mathcal{S}_{r_n}^{H*\overline{\Theta x}}(\mathcal{A})|\phi_0\rangle\right\|_2^2}{(2q+1)^{2(n-1)}} = \frac{\left\|(|\overline{\mathbf{x}}\rangle\langle\overline{\mathbf{x}}| \otimes \hat{\Pi}_{\overline{\mathbf{x}},\overline{\Theta}})\mathcal{S}_{r_n}^{H*\overline{\Theta x}}(\mathcal{A})|\phi_0\rangle\right\|_2^2}{(2q+1)^{2(n-1)}}$$

$$\leq \mathop{\mathbb{E}}_{\overline{\mathbf{r}}}\left[\left\|(|\overline{\mathbf{x}}\rangle\langle\overline{\mathbf{x}}| \otimes \hat{\Pi}_{\overline{\mathbf{x}},\overline{\Theta}})\mathcal{S}_{\overline{\mathbf{r}}}^{H}(\mathcal{S}_{r_n}(\mathcal{A}))|\phi_0\rangle\right\|_2^2\right]$$

$$= \mathop{\mathbb{E}}_{\overline{\mathbf{r}}}\left[\left\|(|\mathbf{x}\rangle\langle\mathbf{x}| \otimes \Pi_{\mathbf{x},\Theta})\mathcal{S}_{\mathbf{r}}^{H}(\mathcal{A})|\phi_0\rangle\right\|_2^2\right].$$

Since this inequality holds for any fixed r_n, it also holds in expectation over r_n. Substituting it in Eq. 3, we retrieve the statement of the lemma. □

Remark 5. In case of $\mathbf{x} = (x_1,\ldots,x_n) \in \mathcal{X}^n$ *without duplicate entries*, it follows from the resulting mutual orthogonality of the projections X_j and the definition of $\mathcal{S}_{\mathbf{r}}^{H}(\mathcal{A})$ that the following holds. The term in the expectation $\mathbb{E}_{\mathbf{r}}$ in the inequality of Lemma 4 vanishes for any $\mathbf{r} = (\mathbf{i},\mathbf{b})$ for which there exist two distinct coordinates $j \neq k$ with $i_j = i_k$. As such, we may well understand this expectation to be over $\mathbf{r} = (\mathbf{i},\mathbf{b})$ for which $i_j \neq i_k$ whenever $j \neq k$; this only increases the expectation.[8] In other words, we may assume that random *distinct* queries are measured in order to extract $x_1,\ldots,x_n$.

Theorem 6 (Measure-and-reprogram, multiple inputs). *Let n be a positive integer, and let $\mathcal{X},\mathcal{Y}$ be finite non-empty sets. There exists a black-box polynomial-time $(n+1)$-stage quantum algorithm $\mathcal{S}$ with the syntax as outlined at the start of this section, satisfying the following property. Let $\mathcal{A}$ be an arbitrary oracle quantum algorithm that makes q queries to a uniformly random $H : \mathcal{X} \to \mathcal{Y}$ and that outputs a tuple $\mathbf{x} \in \mathcal{X}^n$ and a (possibly quantum) output z. Then, for any $\mathbf{x}° \in \mathcal{X}^n$ without duplicate entries and for any predicate V:*

$$\mathop{\Pr}_{\Theta}\left[\mathbf{x}=\mathbf{x}° \wedge V(\mathbf{x},\Theta,z) : (\pi,\pi(\mathbf{x}),z) \leftarrow \langle\mathcal{S}^{\mathcal{A}},\pi(\Theta)\rangle\right]$$

$$\geq \frac{1}{(q+1)^{2n}}\mathop{\Pr}_{H}\left[\mathbf{x}=\mathbf{x}° \wedge V(\mathbf{x},H(\mathbf{x}),z) : (\mathbf{x},z) \leftarrow \mathcal{A}^H\right].$$

Proof. We consider the inequality of Lemma 4 with the expectation over $\mathbf{r}$ understood as in Remark 5. Additionally taking the expectation over H and Θ on both sides, we obtain

$$\mathop{\mathbb{E}}_{H,\Theta}\left[\frac{\left\|(|\mathbf{x}\rangle\langle\mathbf{x}| \otimes \Pi_{\mathbf{x},\Theta})\mathcal{A}^{H*\Theta x}|\phi_0\rangle\right\|_2^2}{(2q+1)^{2n}}\right] \leq \mathop{\mathbb{E}}_{H,\Theta,\mathbf{r}}\left[\left\|(|\mathbf{x}\rangle\langle\mathbf{x}| \otimes \Pi_{\mathbf{x},\Theta})\mathcal{S}_{\mathbf{r}}^{H}(\mathcal{A})|\phi_0\rangle\right\|_2^2\right]$$

and note that this is equivalent to

$$\mathop{\mathbb{E}}_{H}\left[\frac{\left\|(|\mathbf{x}\rangle\langle\mathbf{x}| \otimes \Pi_{\mathbf{x},H(\mathbf{x})})\mathcal{A}^{H}|\phi_0\rangle\right\|_2^2}{(2q+1)^{2n}}\right] \leq \mathop{\mathbb{E}}_{H,\Theta,\mathbf{r}}\left[\left\|(|\mathbf{x}\rangle\langle\mathbf{x}| \otimes \Pi_{\mathbf{x},\Theta})\mathcal{S}_{\mathbf{r}}^{H}(\mathcal{A})|\phi_0\rangle\right\|_2^2\right].$$

---

[8] One might try to exploit this actual improvement in the bound; however, for typical choices of parameters, with n a small constant and q large, this is insignificant.

since all values Θ_j and $H(x_j)$ have the same distribution. The term $\mathcal{S}_{\mathbf{r}}^H(\mathcal{A})|\phi_0\rangle = \mathcal{S}_{\Theta,\mathbf{x},\mathbf{r}}^{H,\mathcal{A}}|\phi_0\rangle$ corresponds to the output of the simulator that uses oracle access to H to run $\mathcal{A}$ on an initial state $|\phi_0\rangle$, while measuring queries i_j (finding x_j as the outcome) and reprogramming the oracle at x_j to Θ_j from the $(i_j + b_j)$-th query onwards, with $(i_j, b_j) = r_j$.

Next, we note that the value of the right hand side does not change [19] when instead of giving $\mathcal{S}$ oracle access to H, we let it choose a random instance from a family of $2q$-wise[9] independent hash functions to simulate $\mathcal{A}$ on. The choice of $\mathbf{r}$ uniquely determines the permutation π with the property $i_{\pi(1)} < \cdots < i_{\pi(n)}$; by definition of $\mathcal{S}_{\Theta,\mathbf{x},\mathbf{r}}^{H,\mathcal{A}}$, the values $\mathbf{x} = (x_1, \ldots, x_n)$ are then extracted from the adversary's queries in the order $\pi(\mathbf{x}) = (x_{\pi(1)}, \ldots, x_{\pi(n)})$. Since $\mathcal{S}$ chooses this $\mathbf{r}$ itself, we can assume that it includes π in its output. Likewise, the simulator takes as input to every stage—from the second to the $(n+1)$-st—a fresh random value, in the order given by $\pi(\Theta)$. However, by definition of $\Pi_{\mathbf{x},\Theta}$ the final output of the simulator satisfies the predicate V with respect to the given order (without π), i.e. such that $V(\mathbf{x}, \Theta, z) = 1$, as is the claim of the theorem. $\square$

4.2   The Time-Ordered Case

In some applications, like the multi-round version of the FS transformation, we need that the simulator extracts the messages in the right order. This can be achieved by replacing the hash *list* $H(\mathbf{x}) = \big(H(x_1), \ldots, H(x_n)\big)$, consisting of individual hashes, by a hash *chain*, where subsequent hashes depend on previous hashes. Intuitively, this enforces $\mathcal{A}$ to query the oracle in the given order.

Formally, considering a function $H : (\mathcal{X}_0 \cup \mathcal{Y}) \times \mathcal{X} \to \mathcal{Y}$ and given a tuple $\mathbf{x} = (x_0, x_1, \ldots, x_n)$ in $\mathcal{X}_0 \times \mathcal{X}^n$, we define the *hash chain* $\mathbf{h}^{H,\mathbf{x}} = \big(h_1^{H,\mathbf{x}}, \ldots, h_n^{H,\mathbf{x}}\big)$ given by

$$h_1^{H,\mathbf{x}} = H(x_0, x_1) \qquad \text{and} \qquad h_i^{H,\mathbf{x}} := H\big(h_{i-1}^{H,\mathbf{x}}, x_i\big)$$

for $2 \leq i \leq n$.

Theorem 7 (Measure-and-reprogram, enforced extraction order). *Let n be a positive integer, and let $\mathcal{X}_0, \mathcal{X}$ and $\mathcal{Y}$ be finite non-empty sets. There exists a black-box polynomial-time $(n+1)$-stage quantum algorithm $\mathcal{S}$, satisfying the following property. Let $\mathcal{A}$ be an arbitrary oracle quantum algorithm that makes q queries to a uniformly random $H : (\mathcal{X}_0 \cup \mathcal{Y}) \times \mathcal{X} \to \mathcal{Y}$ and that outputs a tuple $\mathbf{x} = (x_0, x_1, \ldots, x_n) \in (\mathcal{X}_0 \times \mathcal{X}^n)$ and a (possibly quantum) output z. Then, for any $\mathbf{x}^\circ \in (\mathcal{X}_0 \times \mathcal{X}^n)$ without duplicate entries and for any predicate V:*

$$\Pr_{\Theta}\big[\mathbf{x} = \mathbf{x}^\circ \wedge V(\mathbf{x}, \Theta, z) : (\mathbf{x}, z) \leftarrow \langle \mathcal{S}^A, \Theta \rangle\big]$$

$$\geq \frac{n!}{(q + n + 1)^{2n}} \Pr_H\big[\mathbf{x} = \mathbf{x}^\circ \wedge V(\mathbf{x}, \mathbf{h}^{H,\mathbf{x}}, z) : (\mathbf{x}, z) \leftarrow \mathcal{A}^H\big] - \epsilon_{\mathbf{x}^\circ}.$$

where $\epsilon_{\mathbf{x}^\circ}$ is equal to $\frac{n!}{|\mathcal{Y}|}$ when summed over all $\mathbf{x}^\circ$.

---

[9] It is easy to see that the result of [19] also holds for controlled-query algorithms. Alternatively, the q controlled queries can be simulated using $q + 1$ plain queries, and a $2(q + 1)$-wise independent function can be used.

Remark 8. The additive error term $n!/|\mathcal{Y}|$ stems from the fact that the extraction in the right order fails if $\mathcal{A}$ succeeds in guessing one (or more) of the hashes in the hash chain. The claimed term can be improved to $(n-1)^2/|\mathcal{Y}|+n!/|\mathcal{Y}|^2$ by doing a more fine-grained analysis, distinguishing between permutations $\pi \neq \text{id}$ that bring 2 elements "out of order" or more. In any case, it can be made arbitrary small by extending the range $\mathcal{Y}$ of H for computing the hash chain.

Proof. First, we note that $V(\mathbf{x}, \mathbf{h}^{H,\mathbf{x}}, z) = V'(\mathbf{v}, H(\mathbf{v}), z)$ for $\mathbf{v} = (v_1, \ldots, v_n)$ given by $v_1 = (x_0, x_1)$ and $v_i = \left(h_{i-1}^{H,\mathbf{x}}, x_i\right) = \left(H(v_{i-1}), x_i\right)$ for $i \geq 2$, and $V'(\mathbf{v}, \mathbf{h}, z) := \left[V(\mathbf{x}, \mathbf{h}, z) \wedge h_i' = h_{i-1} \forall i \geq 2\right]$ for any $\mathbf{v}$ of the form $v_1 = (x_0, x_1)$ and $v_i = \left(h_i', x_i\right)$ for $i \geq 2$. Next, at the cost of n additional queries, we can extend $\mathcal{A}$ to an algorithm $\mathcal{A}_+$ that actually outputs $(\mathbf{v}, z)$, since $\mathcal{A}_+$ can easily obtain the $H(v_i)$'s by making n queries to H. These observations together give

$$\Pr_H\left[\mathbf{x} = \mathbf{x}^\circ \wedge V(\mathbf{x}, \mathbf{h}^{H,\mathbf{x}}, z) : (\mathbf{x}, z) \leftarrow \mathcal{A}^H\right] =$$
$$\Pr_H\left[\mathbf{x} = \mathbf{x}^\circ \wedge V'(\mathbf{v}, H(\mathbf{v}), z) : (\mathbf{v}, z) \leftarrow \mathcal{A}_+^H\right].$$

Let $\mathbf{v}^\circ = (v_1^\circ, \ldots, v_n^\circ)$ with $v_i^\circ := (h_i^\circ, x_i^\circ)$, where $h_1^\circ = x_0^\circ$ and $h_i^\circ \in \mathcal{Y}$ is arbitrary but fixed for $i \geq 2$. Let $\boldsymbol{\Theta}$ be uniformly random in $\mathcal{Y}^n$. An application of Theorem 6 yields a simulator $\hat{\mathcal{S}}$ with

$$\Pr_{\boldsymbol{\Theta}}\left[\mathbf{v} = \mathbf{v}^\circ \wedge V'(\mathbf{v}, \boldsymbol{\Theta}, z) : (\pi, \pi(\mathbf{v}), z) \leftarrow \langle \hat{\mathcal{S}}^{\mathcal{A}_+}, \pi(\boldsymbol{\Theta}) \rangle\right]$$
$$\geq \frac{1}{(q+n+1)^{2n}} \Pr_H\left[\mathbf{v} = \mathbf{v}^\circ \wedge V'(\mathbf{v}, H(\mathbf{v}), z) : (\mathbf{v}, z) \leftarrow \mathcal{A}_+^H\right].$$

Summing both sides of the inequality over h_i° for $i \geq 2$ yields

$$\Pr_{\boldsymbol{\Theta}}\left[\mathbf{x} = \mathbf{x}^\circ \wedge V'(\mathbf{v}, \boldsymbol{\Theta}, z) : (\pi, \pi(\mathbf{v}), z) \leftarrow \langle \hat{\mathcal{S}}^{\mathcal{A}_+}, \pi(\boldsymbol{\Theta}) \rangle\right]$$
$$\geq \frac{1}{(q+n+1)^{2n}} \Pr_H\left[\mathbf{x} = \mathbf{x}^\circ \wedge V'(\mathbf{v}, H(\mathbf{v}), z) : (\mathbf{v}, z) \leftarrow \mathcal{A}_+^H\right] \quad (4)$$
$$= \frac{1}{(q+n+1)^{2n}} \Pr_H\left[\mathbf{x} = \mathbf{x}^\circ \wedge V(\mathbf{x}, \mathbf{h}^{H,\mathbf{x}}, z) : (\mathbf{x}, z) \leftarrow \mathcal{A}^H\right].$$

Recalling its construction, the simulator $\hat{\mathcal{S}}^{\mathcal{A}_+}$ begins by sampling a uniformly random permutation π, so we can write

$$\Pr_{\boldsymbol{\Theta}}\left[\mathbf{x} = \mathbf{x}^\circ \wedge V'(\mathbf{v}, \boldsymbol{\Theta}, z) : (\pi, \pi(\mathbf{v}), z) \leftarrow \langle \hat{\mathcal{S}}^{\mathcal{A}_+}, \pi(\boldsymbol{\Theta}) \rangle\right]$$
$$= \frac{1}{n!} \sum_{\sigma \in S_n} \Pr_{\boldsymbol{\Theta}}\left[\mathbf{x} = \mathbf{x}^\circ \wedge V'(\mathbf{v}, \boldsymbol{\Theta}, z) : (\pi, \pi(\mathbf{v}), z) \leftarrow \langle \hat{\mathcal{S}}^{\mathcal{A}_+}, \pi(\boldsymbol{\Theta}) \rangle | \pi = \sigma\right].$$
$$(5)$$

By definition, the predicate $V'(\mathbf{v}, \boldsymbol{\Theta}, z)$ (with $\mathbf{v}$ of the form as explained above) is false whenever there exists an $i \geq 2$ such that $h_i \neq \Theta_{i-1}$. Now suppose that $\pi \neq \text{id}$, then there must be some j such that $\pi(j) < \pi(j-1)$. This implies that the first $\pi(j)$ stages of $\hat{\mathcal{S}}^{\mathcal{A}+}$ which together (in the $\pi(j)$-th stage) produce $v_j = (h_j, x_j)$ are independent of Θ_{j-1}, since Θ_{j-1} is given as input only at the *later* stage $\pi(j-1)$. We thus have the following, taking it as understood, here and in the sequel, that the random variables $\pi, \mathbf{v}, \Theta$ and z are as in (5).

$$\Pr\big[\mathbf{x}=\mathbf{x}^\circ \wedge V'(\mathbf{v},\Theta,z)\big|\pi \neq \mathrm{id}\big]$$

$$\leq \Pr\big[\mathbf{x}=\mathbf{x}^\circ \wedge h_j = \Theta_{j-1}\big|\pi \neq \mathrm{id}\big] = \frac{\Pr\big[\mathbf{x}=\mathbf{x}^\circ\big|\pi \neq \mathrm{id}\big]}{|\mathcal{Y}|}.$$

Using Eq. (5), we can bound

$$\frac{1}{n!}\sum_{\sigma \in S_n} \Pr\big[\mathbf{x}=\mathbf{x}^\circ \wedge V'(\mathbf{v},\Theta,z)\big|\pi=\sigma\big]$$

$$\leq \frac{1}{n!}\Pr\big[\mathbf{x}=\mathbf{x}^\circ \wedge V'(\mathbf{v},\Theta,z)\big|\pi=\mathrm{id}\big] + \frac{\Pr\big[\mathbf{x}=\mathbf{x}^\circ\big|\pi\neq\mathrm{id}\big]}{|\mathcal{Y}|}.$$

We note that by definition of V',

$$\Pr\big[\mathbf{x}=\mathbf{x}^\circ \wedge V(\mathbf{x},\Theta,z)\big|\pi=\mathrm{id}\big] \geq \Pr\big[\mathbf{x}=\mathbf{x}^\circ \wedge V'(\mathbf{v},\Theta,z)\big|\pi=\mathrm{id}\big].$$

Furthermore, we may define a new simulator $\mathcal{S}$ which takes oracle access to $\mathcal{A}$ and turns it into $\mathcal{A}_+$, and always chooses $\pi = \mathrm{id}$ instead of a random permutation. Where $\hat{\mathcal{S}}$ would output $(\mathbf{v}, z)$, $\mathcal{S}$ ignores the $\mathbf{h}$-part of $\mathbf{v}$ and simply outputs $(\mathbf{x}, z)$. We then have

$$\Pr_{\Theta}\big[\mathbf{x}=\mathbf{x}^\circ \wedge V(\mathbf{x},\Theta,z) : (\mathbf{x},z) \leftarrow \langle \mathcal{S}^{\mathcal{A}},\Theta\rangle\big]$$

$$\geq \frac{n!}{(q+n+1)^{2n}} \Pr_H\big[\mathbf{x}=\mathbf{x}^\circ \wedge V(\mathbf{x},\mathbf{h}^{H,\mathbf{x}},z) : (\mathbf{x},z) \leftarrow \mathcal{A}^H\big] - \epsilon_{\mathbf{x}^\circ}.$$

with $\epsilon_{\mathbf{x}^\circ}$ given by $\epsilon_{\mathbf{x}^\circ} := n! \cdot \Pr_\Theta\big[\mathbf{x} = \mathbf{x}^\circ\big|\pi \neq \mathrm{id}\big]/|\mathcal{Y}|$. $\qquad \square$

5   The Multi-round Fiat-Shamir Transformation

A straightforward generalization of the FS transformation can be applied to arbitrary (i.e., multi-round) public-coin interactive proof systems (PCIP). We show here security of this multi-round FS transformation in the QROM.

5.1   Public Coin Interactive Proofs and Multi-round Fiat-Shamir

We begin by defining PCIPs, mainly to fix notation, and the corresponding multi-round FS transformation.

Definition 9 (Public coin interactive proof system (PCIP)). *Let $\mathcal{C}$ be a finite non-empty set, and V a predicate. A $(2n+1)$-round public coin interactive proof system (PCIP) $\Pi = (\mathcal{P}, \mathcal{V})$ for a language $\mathcal{L}$ is a $(2n+1)$-round two-party interactive protocol that proceeds as follows. In round $2r-1$, $\mathcal{P}$ sends a_r to $\mathcal{C}$, who answers with $c_r \overset{\$}{\leftarrow} \mathcal{C}$ (round $2r$), for $r = 1, ..., n$. Finally, $\mathcal{P}$ sends z (round $2n+1$) which is accepted iff $V(x, a_1, c_1, ..., a_n, c_n, z) = 1$.*

Remark 10. If the language $\mathcal{L}$ is definied by means of an (efficiently verifiable) witness relation $R \subseteq \mathcal{X} \times \mathcal{W}$, then the prover typcially gets a witness w for x as an additional input. We then also say that Π is a PCIP *for the relation R*. In case of a $(2n+1)$-round PCIP Π for a witness relation R that is *hard on average*, meaning that there exists an instance generator Gen with the property that for $(w, x) \leftarrow$ Gen it holds that $(w, x) \in R$, but given x alone it is computationally hard to find w with $(w, x) \in R$, Π is also called an *identification scheme*.

Just as in the ordinary FS transformation, the interaction used to enforce the time order between the prover committing to the message a_i and receiving the challenge c_i can be replaced by a hash function. In addition, we can include the previous challenge (i.e. the previous hash value) in the hash determining the next challenge to enforce the ordering of the n pairs (a_i, c_i) according to increasing i. We thus obtain the following non-interactive proof system.

Definition 11 (Fiat-Shamir transformation for general PCIP (mFS)). *Given an $(2n+1)$-round PCIP $\Pi = (\mathcal{P}, \mathcal{V})$ for a language $\mathcal{L}$ and a hash function H with appropriate domain, and range equal to $\mathcal{C}$, we define the non-interactive proof system* $\mathsf{FS}[\Pi] = (\mathcal{P}_{FS}^H, \mathcal{V}_{FS}^H)$ *as follows. The prover $\mathcal{P}$ outputs*

$$(x, a_1, ..., a_n, z) \leftarrow \mathcal{P}_{FS}^H$$

where z and a_i for $i = 1, ..., n$ are computed using $\mathcal{P}$, and the challenges are computed as

$$c_1 = H(0, x, a_1) \qquad and \qquad c_i = H(i - 1, c_{i-1}, a_i) \text{ for } i = 2, ..., n,$$

The verifier outputs 'accept' iff $V(x, a_1, c_1, ..., a_n, c_n, z) = 1$ for $c_1 = H(0, x, a_1)$ and $c_i = H(i - 1, c_{i-1}, a_i)$, $i = 2, ..., n$, denoted by $V_{FS}(x, a_1, c_1, ..., a_n, c_n, z) = 1$.

Remark 12. The challenge number i (minus 1) is included in the hash input to ensure that the challenges are generated using distinct inputs to H with probability 1. This is to enable us to apply Theorem 7, which only holds for duplicate-free lists of hash inputs. In fact, any additional strings can be included in the argument when computing c_i using H, without influencing the security properties of the non-interactive proof system in a detrimental way. In the literature one sometimes sees that the entire previous transcript is hashed (in which case the counter number i may then be omitted).

5.2   General Security of Multi-round Fiat-Shamir in the QROM

When constructing a reduction for mFS, this reduction is participating as a prover in the underlying PCIP, and is hence only provided with random challenges one at a time. We thus need the special simulator from Theorem 7, which always outputs the corresponding messages in the right order. The success of this simulator is based on the very essence of the FS transformation, namely the fact that the intractability of the hash function takes the role of the interaction in enforcing a time order in the transcript of the PCIP.

The security of the multi-round FS transformation follows as a simple Corollary of Theorem 7.

Corollary 13. *There exists a black-box quantum polynomial-time $(n+1)$-stage quantum algorithm $\mathcal{S}$ such that for any adaptive adversary $\mathcal{A}$ against the multi-round FS transformed version $\mathsf{FS}[\Pi]$ of a $(2n+1)$-round PCIP Π, making q queries to a uniformly random function H with appropriate domain and range equal $\mathcal{C}$, and for any $x^\circ \in \mathcal{X}$:*

$$\Pr\big[x = x^\circ \wedge v = accept : (x, v) \leftarrow \langle \mathcal{S}^\mathcal{A}, \mathcal{V} \rangle \big]$$
$$\geq \frac{n!}{(2q + n + 1)^{2n}} \Pr_H\big[x = x^\circ \wedge V_{FS}^H(x, \pi) : (x, \pi) \leftarrow \mathcal{A}^H \big] - \epsilon_{x^\circ}.$$

where the additive error term ϵ_{x° is equal to $\frac{n!}{|\mathcal{C}|}$ when summed over all x°.

Proof. We may simply set $\mathbf{x}^\circ = (x^\circ, (0, a_1), \ldots, (n - 1, a_n))$ for arbitrary $a_1, \ldots, a_n$, apply Theorem 7 and then sum over all choices of $a_1, \ldots, a_n$ to obtain the claimed inequality. Note that the round indices ensure that every such $\mathbf{x}^\circ$ is duplicate free, satisfying the corresponding requirement of Theorem 7.

Note that the additive error terms reflect the fact that the random oracle only *approximately* succeeds in enforcing the original time order in the transcript of the PCIP. However, it can be made arbitrarily small, as discussed below.

Remark 14. There exist PCIPs with soundness error much smaller than $1/|\mathcal{C}|$. As an example, consider the sequential repetition of a Σ-protocol with special soundness. Here, the soundness error is $1/|\mathcal{C}|^n$. In this case, the term proportional to $1/|\mathcal{C}|$ renders the bound from the above theorem trivial. Note however, that (i) this situation is extremely artificial, as there is absolutely no reason to repeat sequentially instead of in parallel, and (ii) the additive error term can be made arbitrarily small by considering a variant Π' of Π where the random challenges are enlarged with a certain number of bits that are ignored otherwise, see Remark 8.

In fact, we suspect that the observation from (i) is true in a much broader sense: if a PCIP still has negligible soundness error when allowing the adversary to learn one of the challenges c_i in advance of sending the corresponding commitment-type message a_i, it seems like the number of rounds can be reduced and the loss in soundness error can be won back by parallel repetition.

As for the case of the FS transformation for Σ-protocols, the general reduction implies that security properties that protect against dishonest provers carry over from the interactive to the non-interactive proof system. For a definition of the properties considered in the following theorem, see, e.g. [9]. The quantum proof-of-knowledge-property was intoduced in [15].

Corollary 15 (Preservation of Soundness/PoK). *Let Π be a constant-round PCIP that has (statistical/computational) soundness, and/or the (statistical/computational) quantum proof-of-knowledge-property, respectively. Then, in* the QROM, FS[Π] *has (statistical/computational) soundness, and/or the (statistical/computational) quantum proof-of-knowledge-property, too.*

Proof. Corollary 13 turns any dishonest prover $\mathcal{A}_{\mathsf{FS}[\Pi]}$ for FS[Π] with success probability ϵ into a dishonest prover $\mathcal{A}_\Pi$ for Π, with success probability $\epsilon \cdot (2q + 1)^{-2n}$, where $2n + 1$ is the number of rounds in Π. Since n is constant and q is polynomial in the security parameter, the success probabilities of the respective provers are polynomially related. The claimed implications follow now using the same arguments as in Corollaries 13 and 16 in [9].   □

6   Tightness of the Reductions

Here, we show tightness of our results. We start with proving tightness of Theorems 2 and 3 (up to essentially a factor 4). This implies that a $O(q^2)$-loss is unavoidable in general. Indeed, the following result shows that for a large and natural class of Σ-protocols Σ, there exists an attack against FS[Σ] that succeeds with a probability q^2 times larger than the best attack against Σ. The attack is based on an application of Grover's quantum algorithm for unstructured search.

To our surprise, we could not find an analysis of Grover's algorithm in the regime we require in the literature. Grover search has been analyzed in the case of an unknown number of solutions [3], but the focus of that work is on analyzing the expected number of queries required to find a solution, while we analyze the probability with which the Grover search algorithm succeeds for a *fixed but arbitrary* number of queries.

Theorem 16. *Let $\mathcal{L}$ be a language, and let Σ be a Σ-protocol for $\mathcal{L}$ with challenge set $\mathcal{C}$, special soundness and perfect honest-verifier zero-knowledge. Furthermore, we assume that the triples (a, c, z) produced by the simulator $\mathcal{S}_{\mathrm{ZK}}(x)$ are always accepted by the verifier even for instances $x \notin \mathcal{L}$, and that a has min-entropy γ.[10] Then for any q such that $(q^2 + 1) \cdot e^2 \cdot (5q)^6 < |\mathcal{C}|$ and $2^\gamma/(5q)^3 > 2$, there exists a q-query dishonest prover that succeeds with probability $q^2/|\mathcal{C}|$ in producing a valid FS[Σ]-proof for an instance $x \notin \mathcal{L}$.*

The idea of the attack against FS[Σ] is quite simple. For a Σ-protocol that is *special* honest-verifier zero-knowledge, meaning that the simulation works by first sampling the challenge c and the repsonse z and then computing a fitting answer a as a function $a(c, z)$, one simply does a Grover search to find a pair (c, z) for which $H(x, a(c, z)) = c$. For a typical H, this will give a quadratic improvement over the classical search, which, for a random H, succeeds with probability $q/|\mathcal{C}|$ (due to the special soundness). A subtle issue is that, for some (unlikely) choices of H, there are actually *many* (c, z) for which $H(x, a(c, z)) = c$, in which case

---

[10] These additional assumptions on the simulator could be avoided, but they simplify the proof. Furthermore, for typical Σ-protocols they are satisfied. In particular, the simulated transcripts for hard instances are accepted by the verifier with high probability. Otherwise, the two polynomial-time algorithms could otherwise be used to solve the hard instances, a contradiction.

the Grover search "overshoots". In the formal proof below, this is dealt with by controlling the probability of H having this (unlikely) property. Also, it removes the *special* honest-verifier zero-knowledge property by doing the Grover search over the randomness of the simulator, which requires some additional caution.

Remark 17. It is not hard to see that Theorem 16 still holds in the following two variations of the statement. (1) $H(x, a)$ is random and independent for different choices of a, but is *not* necessarily independent for different choices of x. (2) The Σ-protocol Σ is replaced by Σ', which has its challenge enlarged with a certain number of bits that are ignored otherwise, in line with Remark 14, and $\mathsf{FS}[\Sigma']$ then uses an H with a correspondingly enlarged range.[11]

Proof. Let $\mathcal{S}_{\mathrm{ZK}}$ be the zero-knowledge simulator given by the perfect honest-verifier zero-knowledge property of Σ. Consider an adversary $\mathcal{A}_{FS}$ against $\mathsf{FS}[\Sigma]$, that works as follows for an arbitrary instance $x \notin \mathcal{L}$:

- Define the function $f^H : R \to \{0, 1\}$ (where R is the set of random coins for $\mathcal{S}_{\mathrm{ZK}}$) as

$$f^H(\rho) = \begin{cases} 1 & \text{for } \mathcal{S}_{\mathrm{ZK}}(x; \rho) \to (a, c, z) \land H(x||a) = c \\ 0 & \text{otherwise.} \end{cases}$$

- Use Grover's algorithm for q steps, to try and find ρ s.t. $f(\rho) = 1$
- Run $\mathcal{S}_{\mathrm{ZK}}(x; \rho) \to (a, c, z)$ and output $(x, a||z)$.

Let p_1^H be the fraction of random coins from R that map to 1 under f^H. Note that by the special soundness of Σ, in any accepting triple a determines c and we thus have $\mathbb{E}_H[p_1^H] = \frac{1}{|\mathcal{C}|}$. By the way Grover works, after q iterations (requiring q queries to H) the probability p_2^H of finding such an input is $\sin^2((2q+1)\Theta^H)$, where $0 \le \Theta^H \le \pi/2$ is such that $\sin^2(\Theta^H) = p_1^H$. Now as long as Θ is not too large to begin with (i.e. as long as the Grover search will not 'overshoot'), p_2^H is approximately a factor q^2 larger than p_1^H. Our goal will be to show that also on average over H, the improvement is at least q^2. To this end we define $H_{\mathrm{bad}} := \{H : p_1^H > \sin^2(\frac{\pi}{6q+3})\}$ and H_{good} its complement. Then,

$$\mathbb{E}_H[p_2^H] = (1 - \alpha) \cdot \mathbb{E}_H\left[p_2^H | H \in H_{\mathrm{good}}\right] + \alpha \cdot \mathbb{E}_H\left[p_2^H | H \in H_{\mathrm{bad}}\right]$$

$$\ge (1 - \alpha) \cdot \mathbb{E}_H\left[p_2^H | H \in H_{\mathrm{good}}\right]$$

where $\alpha = \Pr_H[H \in H_{\mathrm{bad}}]$ and $1 - \alpha = \Pr_H[H \in H_{\mathrm{good}}]$.

---

[11] While (1) follows by inspecting the proof, (2) holds more generically: the dishonest prover attacking $\mathsf{FS}[\Sigma']$ simply runs the prover attacking $\mathsf{FS}[\Sigma]$ but enlarges the output register of the hash queries, with the corresponding state being set to be the fully mixed state in each query, and then dismisses these additional qubits again.

We first compute $\mathbb{E}_{H_{\text{good}}}\left[p_2^H\right]$. Let $H \in H_{\text{good}}$. We have $(2q+1)\Theta^H \leq \frac{\pi}{3}$. Since $\frac{d}{d\Theta}\sin(\Theta) = \cos(\Theta) \geq 1/2$ for $\Theta \in [0, \frac{\pi}{3}]$, and $\Theta \geq \sin(\Theta)$, it follows that

$$\sin((2q+1)\cdot\Theta^H) \quad \geq \quad \sin(\Theta^H) + \frac{2q\cdot\Theta^H}{2} \quad \geq \quad (q+1)\cdot\sin(\Theta^H).$$

Using $\sin(\Theta) \geq 0$ for $\Theta \in [0, \frac{\pi}{3}]$, we obtain

$$p_2^H = \sin^2((2q+1)\cdot\Theta^H) \geq (q+1)^2 \cdot \sin^2(\Theta^H) = (q+1)^2 \cdot p_1^H.$$

Therefore,

$$
\begin{aligned}
\mathbb{E}_H[p_2^H] \quad &\geq \quad \mathbb{E}_H\left[p_2^H \mid H \in H_{\text{good}}\right] \cdot \Pr_H[H \in H_{\text{good}}] \\
&\geq \quad (q+1)^2 \cdot \mathbb{E}_H\left[p_1^H \mid H \in H_{\text{good}}\right] \cdot \Pr_H[H \in H_{\text{good}}] \\
&\geq \quad (q+1)^2 \cdot \left(\mathbb{E}_H[p_1^H] - \Pr_H[H \in H_{\text{bad}}]\right)
\end{aligned}
\tag{6}
$$

Next we bound $\alpha = \Pr_H[H \in H_{\text{bad}}] = \Pr_H[p_1^H > \sin^2(\frac{\pi}{6q+3})]$. Note that for p_1^H to be large, we need that for many first messages a, $H(a)$ must be the unique challenge c for which there exist an accepting response. For a random H this is unlikely to happen. Formally, we argue as follows, using the Chernoff bound eventually.

We first define the following equivalence relation:

$$\rho \sim \rho' \text{ iff } \mathcal{S}_{\text{ZK}}(\rho) = (a, c, z) \wedge \mathcal{S}_{\text{ZK}}(\rho') = (a, c', z') \text{ for } \rho, \rho' \in R.$$

$R/_\sim$ then denotes the set of equivalence classes $[\rho] = \{\rho' \in R \mid \rho \sim \rho'\}$. By the perfect special soundness property and the assumptions on $\mathcal{S}_{\text{ZK}}$, we have that a determines c (remember that $x \notin \mathcal{L}$), and therefore f^H is constant on elements within a given equivalence class. Thus, $f^H : R/_\sim \to \{0,1\}$. For two distinct equivalence classes $[\rho] \neq [\rho']$, we have

$$\Pr_H[f^H([\rho]) = 1 \wedge f^H([\rho']) = 1] = \Pr_H[f^H([\rho]) = 1] \cdot \Pr_H[f^H([\rho']) = 1],$$

since $H(x\|a)$ is chosen independently for different a. Taking $X^H := \sum_{[\rho]} f^H([\rho])$ we then have

$$
\begin{aligned}
p_1^H = \Pr_\rho[f^H(\rho) = 1] &= \frac{\sum_\rho f(\rho)}{|R|} \\
&= \frac{\sum_{[\rho]} \left(f^H([\rho]) \cdot |[\rho]|\right)}{|R|} \leq \frac{|[\rho_{\max}]| \cdot \sum_{[\rho]} f^H([\rho])}{|R|} = X^H \cdot 2^{-\gamma}
\end{aligned}
$$

where $[\rho_{\max}]$ is the $[\rho]$ that maximizes $|[\rho]|$. It follows that

$$
\begin{aligned}
\alpha = \Pr_H[p_1^H > \sin^2\left(\frac{\pi}{6q+3}\right)] \\
\leq \Pr_H\left[X^H > \sin^2\left(\frac{\pi}{6q+3}\right) \cdot 2^\gamma\right] \leq \Pr_H\left[X^H > \frac{2^\gamma}{|C|} + \frac{2^\gamma}{(5q)^3}\right]
\end{aligned}
$$

where we used $\sin^2(x) > x^3$ for $0 \leq x \leq 0.80$ and $\frac{\pi}{6q+3} > \frac{1}{5q} + \sqrt[3]{\frac{1}{|\mathcal{C}|}}$ for $|\mathcal{C}| > (5q)^3$ in the last inequality. By definition of f, for any $[\rho]$ we have $\Pr_H[f(\rho) = 1] = \frac{1}{|\mathcal{C}|}$, hence

$$\mathbb{E}_H[X] = \sum_{[\rho]} \mathbb{E}_H[f^H([\rho])] = \sum_{[\rho]} \Pr_H[f^H([\rho]) = 1] = \frac{|R/\sim|}{|\mathcal{C}|} \geq \frac{2^\gamma}{|\mathcal{C}|}.$$

We use the following Chernoff bound:

$$\Pr_H\left[X^H > (1+\delta) \cdot \mathbb{E}_H[X^H]\right] < \left(\frac{e^\delta}{(1+\delta)^{1+\delta}}\right)^{\mathbb{E}_H[X^H]} < \left(\frac{e^{1+\delta}}{\delta^{1+\delta}}\right)^{\mathbb{E}_H[X^H]}$$
$$= \left(\frac{e}{\delta}\right)^{\mathbb{E}_H[X^H]\cdot(1+\delta)}.$$

Setting $\delta := \frac{|\mathcal{C}|}{(5q)^3}$, together with the inequalities derived above this leads to

$$\alpha \leq \left(\frac{e \cdot (5q)^3}{|\mathcal{C}|}\right)^{\frac{2^\gamma}{|\mathcal{C}|} + \frac{2^\gamma}{(5q)^3}} < \frac{e^2 \cdot (5q)^6}{|\mathcal{C}|^2} < \frac{1}{|\mathcal{C}| \cdot (q^2 + 1)}$$

where we used $\frac{2^\gamma}{(5q)^3} > 2$ in the second to last, and $|\mathcal{C}| > (q^2 + 1) \cdot e^2 \cdot (5q)^6$ in the last inequality. Plugging this bound into Eq. 6, we get

$$\mathbb{E}_H[p_2^H] \geq (q^2 + 1) \cdot \left(p_1 - \frac{1}{|\mathcal{C}| \cdot (q^2 + 1)}\right) = \frac{q^2}{|\mathcal{C}|} + \frac{1}{|\mathcal{C}|} - \frac{1}{|\mathcal{C}|} = \frac{q^2}{|\mathcal{C}|}.$$

Thus, the success probability of our adversary $\mathcal{A}_{FS}$ after making q queries to H is at least $\frac{q^2}{|\mathcal{C}|}$. □

The tightness of Corollary 13 follows from the above tightness result for the case of Σ-protocols in a fairly straightforward manner.

Theorem 18. *For every positive integer n, there exists a $(2n+1)$-round PCIP Π with soundness error ϵ and challenge space $\mathcal{C}$ such that $|\mathcal{C}| \geq 1/\epsilon$ and such that there exists a q-query dishonest prover $\mathcal{A}$ on $\mathsf{FS}(\Pi)$ with success probability $n^{-2n}q^{2n}\epsilon$.*

Before proving the theorem, we show how it implies the tightness of Theorem 13.

Corollary 19. *The security loss in the bound in Corollary 13 is optimal, up to a multiplicative factor that depends on n only.*

Proof. Let Π be a PCIP as shown to exist in Theorem 18. Let ϵ_Π, and $\epsilon_{\mathsf{FS}(\Pi)}(q)$, be the soundness error of Π, and the one of its Fiat Shamir transformation against q-query adversaries, respectively. By Theorem 18,

$$\epsilon_{\mathsf{FS}(\Pi)}(q) \geq n^{-2n}q^{2n}\epsilon_\Pi. \tag{7}$$

Theorem 13, on the other hand, yields

$$\epsilon_\Pi \geq \frac{n!}{(2q+n+1)^{2n}}\epsilon_{\mathsf{FS}(\Pi)}(q) - \frac{n!}{|\mathcal{C}|} \geq \frac{n!}{(2q+n+1)^{2n}}\epsilon_{\mathsf{FS}(\Pi)}(q) - n!\epsilon_\Pi, \quad (8)$$

where we used the condition on the challenge space size from Theorem 18 in the last line. Rearranging terms we obtain

$$\epsilon_{\mathsf{FS}(\Pi)}(q) \leq (2q+n+1)^{2n}\left(1+\frac{1}{n!}\right)\epsilon_\Pi(q) \leq 2(n+3)^2 q^{2n}\epsilon_\Pi(q), \quad (9)$$

where we have used $1 \leq q$ in the last line. In summary, we have constants $c_1 = n^{-2n}$ and $c_2 = 2(n+3)^{2n}$ such that

$$c_1 q^{2n}\epsilon_\Pi \leq \epsilon_{\mathsf{FS}(\Pi)}(q) \leq c_2 q^{2n}\epsilon_\Pi. \quad (10)$$

$\square$

Proof. (of Theorem 18). Let $\hat{\Sigma}$ be a Σ-protocol for a language $\mathcal{L}$ fulfilling the requirements of Theorem 16. Let the challenge space be denoted by $\hat{\mathcal{C}}$. Given an arbitrary positive integer, we define an $(2n+1)$-round PCIP Π for the same language $\mathcal{L}$ by means of n sequential independent executions of $\hat{\Sigma}$. Concretely, the $2n+1$ messages of Π are given in terms of the messages $\hat{a}_i, \hat{c}_i$ and $\hat{z}_i$ of the i-th repetition of $\hat{\Sigma}$ as

$$a_1 = \hat{a}_1, \qquad c_i = (\hat{c}_i, r_i) \text{ for } i = 1, ..., n,$$
$$a_i = (\hat{a}_i, \hat{z}_{i-1}) \text{ for } i = 2, ..., n, \qquad \text{and} \qquad z = \hat{z}_n,$$

where r_i is an independent random string of arbitrary (but fixed) length, which is ignored otherwise (in line with Remark 14). The purpose of r_i is to make the challenge space $\mathcal{C}$ of Π arbitrary large, as required. The verification procedure of Π simply checks if all the triples $(\hat{a}_i, \hat{c}_i, \hat{z}_i)$ are accepted by $\hat{\Sigma}$. By the special soundness property of $\hat{\Sigma}$, the soundness error of this PCIP is $\epsilon = |\hat{\mathcal{C}}|^{-n}$.

Using Theorem 16, we can attack the FS transformation of $\hat{\Sigma}$ repeatedly to devise an attack agains $\mathsf{FS}(\Pi)$: first use Theorem 16 to find $\hat{a}_1$ and $\hat{z}_1$, then use it again to find $\hat{a}_2$ and $\hat{z}_2$, etc., having the property that with the correctly computed challenges these form valid triples for an instance $x \notin \mathcal{L}$. In each invocation of Theorem 16 we use a q'-query attack, which then succeeds with probability $q'^2/|\hat{\mathcal{C}}|$. Thus, using in total $q = nq'$ queries, we succeed in breaking $\mathsf{FS}[\Pi]$ with probability $q'^{2n}/|\hat{\mathcal{C}}|^n = n^{-2n}q^{2n}\epsilon$, as claimed.

There are two issues we neglected in the above argument. First, we actually employ Theorem 16 for attacking a *variant* of $\hat{\Sigma}$ that has its challenge enlarged (and thus is not special sound); and, second, the challenge c_i is computed as

$$c_i = H(i-1, ..., H(1, H(0, x, \hat{a}_1), \hat{a}_2), ..., \hat{a}_i),$$

which is *not* a uniformly random function of x and $\hat{a}_i$ (but only of $\hat{a}_i$). However, by Remark 17, the attack from Theorem 16 still applies. $\square$

7   Applications

7.1   Digital Signature Schemes from Multi-round Fiat-Shamir

One of the prime applications of the FS transformation is the construction of digital signature schemes from interactive identification schemes. In this context, multi-round variants have also been used. An example where a QROM reduction is especially desirable is MQDSS [5], a candidate digital signature scheme in the ongoing NIST standardization process for post-quantum cryptographic schemes [1]. This digital signature scheme is constructed by applying the multi-round FS transformation to the 5-round identification scheme by Sakumoto, Shirai, and Hiwatari [14] based on the hardness of solving systems of multivariate quadratic equations.

In this section, we present a generic construction of a digital signature scheme based on multi-round FS, and give a proof sketch of its strong unforgeability under chosen message attacks. We refrain from giving a full, self-contained proof here so as to not distract from our main technical result and its implications. Many, though not all, parts of the argument are very similar to the ones made elsewhere for the 3-round case.

The following construction is a straightforward generalization of the original construction of Fiat and Shamir.

Definition 20 (Fiat-Shamir signatures from a general PCIP). *Given an $(2n+1)$-round public coin identification scheme $\Pi = (\mathsf{Gen}, \mathcal{P}, \mathcal{V})$ for a witness relation R and a hash function H with appropriate domain and range equal to $\mathcal{C}$, we define the digital signature scheme $\mathsf{Sig}[\Pi] = (\mathsf{Gen}, \mathsf{Sign}, \mathsf{Verify})$ as follows. The key generation algorithm Gen is just the one from Π. The signing algorithm Sign, on input a secret key sk and a message m, outputs*

$$\sigma = (a_1, ..., a_n, z) \leftarrow \mathsf{Sign}_{sk}(m)$$

where z and a_i for $i = 1, ..., n$ are computed using $\mathcal{P}(pk)$, and the challenges are computed as

$$c_1 = H(0, pk, m, a_1) \qquad and \qquad c_i = H(i-1, c_{i-1}, a_i) \text{ for } i = 2, ..., n.$$

The verification algorithm Verify, on input a public key pk, a message m and a signature $\sigma = (a_1, ..., a_n, z)$, computes c_i as specified above, outputs 'accept' iff $\mathcal{V}_{pk}(a_1, c_1, ..., a_n, c_n, z) = 1$, denoted by $\mathsf{Verify}_{pk}(m, \sigma) = 1$.

We note that the above definition is equivalent to the following, alternative formulation: Let $\mathsf{Sign}_{sk}(m)$ produce σ by running $P_{FS}^H(x||m)$, and let $\mathsf{Verify}(m, \sigma)$ be equal to the outcome of $V_{FS}^H(x||m)$, where $(P_{FS}^H, V_{FS}^H) = \mathsf{FS}[\Pi^*]$ and $\Pi^* = (\mathcal{P}^*, \mathcal{V}^*)$ is the identification scheme obtained from Π by setting $\mathcal{P}^*(x||m) = \mathcal{P}(x)$ and $\mathcal{V}^*(x||m) = \mathcal{V}(x)$ for any m. This alternative formulation will be convenient in the proof of Theorem 23.

Remark 21. As in the case of the plain multi-round FS transformation, one can include arbitrary additional strings in the argument when computing the challenges c_i. Examples where this is done include the MQDSS signature scheme [5], where the message m and the first commitment a_1 are also included in the argument for computing the second challenge, and Bulletproofs, where the challenges are computed by hashing the entire transcript up to that point [4].

As an identification scheme is an interactive honest-verifier zero knowledge proof of knowledge of a secret key, the above signature scheme is a non-interactive zero knowledge proof of knowledge of a secret key according to Corollary 13. For a digital signature scheme, however, the stronger security notion of (strong) unforgeability against chosen message ((s)UF-CMA) attacks is required.

In the following, we give a proof sketch for the fact that the above signature scheme is (s)UF-CMA. This fact follows immediately once we have convinced ourselves that a certain result by Unruh about the FS transformation holds for the multi-round case as well: For the FS transformation of Σ-protocols, extractability implies a stronger notion of extractability enabling a proof of (s)UF-CMA [18]. Here, we just patch the parts of the proof from [18] that make use of the fact that the underlying PCIP has only three rounds.

For the following we need the notion of a PCIP having computationally unique responses.

Definition 22. (Computationally unique responses - PCIP). *A $(2n+1)$-round PCIP $\Pi = (\mathcal{P}, \mathcal{V})$ is said to have* computationally unique responses *if given a partial transcript $(x, a_1, c_1, \ldots a_i, c_i)$ it is computationally hard to find two accepting conversations that both extend the partial transcript but differ in (at least) a_{i+1} (here we consider z to be equal to a_{n+1}), i.e. for $con_i = x, a_1, c_1, \ldots a_i, c_i, a_{i+1}^{(j)}, c_{i+1}^{(j)} \ldots, a_n^{(j)}, c_n^{(j)}, z^{(j)}$, $j = 1, 2$ we have that*

$$\Pr\left[\mathcal{V}(con_1) = 1 \wedge \mathcal{V}(con_2) = 1 : (con_1, con_2) \leftarrow \mathcal{A}\right]$$

is negligible for computationally bounded (quantum) $\mathcal{A}$, where $a_{i+1}^{(1)} \neq a_{i+1}^{(2)}$.

Equipped with this definition, we can state the main result of this section.

Theorem 23. ((s)UF-CMA of multi-round FS signatures). *Let Π be a PCIP for some hard relation R, which is a quantum proof of knowledge and satisfies completeness, HVZK, and has unpredictable commitments[12] as well as a superpolynomially large challenge space. Then $\mathsf{Sig}[\Pi]$ is existentially unforgeable under chosen message attack (UF-CMA). If Π in addition has computationally unique responses, $\mathsf{Sig}[\Pi]$ is strongly existentially unforgeable under chosen message attack (sUF-CMA).*

In [18] (Theorem 24, and 25, respectively), it is proven that an extractable FS proof system (of an HVZK Σ-protocol, and of an HVZK Σ-protocol with computationally unique responses, respectively) satisfies the stronger notion of *(strong) simulation-sound extractability*. In addition, it is shown that such a

---

[12] We take unpredictable commitments for PCIP's to be exactly the same as for Σ-protocols, with the first message playing the role of the commitment.

FS proof system gives rise to a (s)UF-CMA signature scheme if the underlying relation is hard. Corollary 15 implies that $\mathsf{FS}[\Pi^*]$ is indeed extractable if Π is extractable. Below we rely on the proof in [18] to argue simulation-sound extractability, only pointing out a particular difference for the multi-round case.

Proof (sketch). Since Π is a quantum proof of knowledge, so is Π^*. By Corollary 15, $\mathsf{FS}[\Pi^*]$ is a quantum proof of knowledge (extractable), and by Theorem 20 in [18] (which easily generalizes to the multi-round setting), completeness, unpredictable commitments[13] and HVZK of Π^* together imply ZK for $\mathsf{FS}[\Pi^*]$. For the proof that $\mathsf{FS}[\Pi^*]$ is also simulation-sound extractable, we refer to the proof of Theorem 24 in [18], noting only that in the hop from Game 1 to Game 2 we have to adjust the argument as follows: Let $\mathcal{S}_{ZK}$ be the zero-knowledge simulator that runs the HVZK simulator from Π^* and reprograms the oracle as necessary. We write H_f for the oracle H after it has been reprogrammed by $\mathcal{S}_{ZK}$, at the end of the run of $\mathcal{A}$. We have to show that $V_{FS}^{H_f}(x, a_1, \ldots, a_n, z) = 1$ implies $V_{FS}^{H}(x, a_1, \ldots, a_n, z) = 1$, where $(x, a_1, \ldots, a_n, z)$ is the final output of $\mathcal{A}$. Suppose the implication does not hold. Then either (i) $H_f(0, x, a_1) \neq H(0, x, a_1)$ or (ii) $H_f(i-1, c_{i-1}, a_i) \neq H(i-1, c'_{i-1}, a_i)$ for some i, where c_{i-1} is the $(i-1)$-st challenge as recomputed by $V_{FS}^{H_f}$ and c'_{i-1} is the one computed by V_{FS}^{H}. In case (i) holds, $\mathcal{A}$ has queried x and the corresponding forged proof that was output by $\mathcal{S}_{ZK}$ starts with a_1. In case (ii), assume that $H_f(j-1, c_{j-1}, a_j) = H(j-1, c_{j-1}, a_j)$ for all $j < i$, so that $c_{i-1} = c'_{i-1}$. Then,

$$H_f(i-1, \ldots, H(1, H(0, x, a_1), a_2), \ldots, a_i) \neq H(i-1, \ldots, H(1, H(0, x, a_1), a_2), \ldots, a_i)$$

which means that $\mathcal{A}$ either queried x and the corresponding forged proof that was output by $\mathcal{S}_{ZK}$ starts with a_1, or else $\mathcal{A}$ has queried some x' such that

$$H(i-2, \ldots, H(1, H(0, x', a'_1), a'_2), \ldots a'_{i-1})$$
$$= H(i-2, \ldots, H(1, H(0, x, a_1), a_2), \ldots, a_{i-1})$$

and $a_i = a'_i$, where $(a'_1, \ldots, a'_i)$ is part of the $\mathcal{S}_{ZK}$ proof resulting from query x'. By the fact that H is a random oracle, it is infeasible for $\mathcal{A}$ to find such an x'.

In the context of weak simulation-sound extractability, the fact that $\mathcal{A}$ has queried x is enough to derive a contradiction. For the strong variant, we now have that $\mathcal{S}_{ZK}$ has output $(x, a_1, a'_2, \ldots, a'_n, z')$ such that

$$\mathcal{V}(x, a_1, H_f(0, x, a_1), a'_2, c'_2 \ldots, a'_n, c'_n, z') = 1$$

and $\mathcal{A}$ has output $(x, a_1, a_2, \ldots, a_n, z)$ such that

$$\mathcal{V}(x, a_1, H_f(0, x, a_1), a_2, c_2, \ldots, a_n, c_n, z) = 1$$

---

[13] This property is required to have sufficient entropy on the inputs to the oracle that are reprogrammed by the zero-knowledge simulator $\mathcal{S}_{ZK}$. While $\mathcal{S}_{ZK}$ may reprogram the oracle on inputs $(i-1, c_{i-1}, a_i)$ for $i > 1$, it is enough to require the first message a_1 to have sufficient entropy, since with c_{i-1}, these later inputs all include a uniformly random element from the superpolynomially large challenge space.

(and $\mathcal{A}$ knows both since it interacted with $\mathcal{S}_{ZK}$). By the computationally unique responses property of Π, it must be that $a_2 = a_2'$. But then it follows that

$$c_2 = H_f(1, H_f(0, x, a_1), a_2) = H_f(1, H_f(0, x, a_1), a_2') = c_2'$$

(remember that both proofs are accepting with respect to H_f) which in turn implies that $a_3 = a_3'$, etc. Thus, we obtain that $\mathcal{A}$ has output a proof that was produced by $\mathcal{S}_{ZK}$, yielding a contradiction. We conclude that

$$V_{FS}^{H_f}(x, a_1, \ldots, a_n, z) = 1 \text{ implies } V_{FS}^{H}(x, a_1, \ldots, a_n, z) = 1$$

except with negligible probability.

In the rest of the proof of Theorems 24 and 25 in [18], no properties specific to a three-round scheme are used, and so the results extend to the PCIP context, that is, $FS[\Pi^*]$ is (strongly) simulation-sound extractable. Now applying Theorem 31 from [18], we obtain that $Sig[\Pi]$ is (s)UF-CMA. $\square$

Together with the fact that commit-and-open PCIPs can easily be made quantum extractable in the right sense by using standard hash-based commitments based on a collapsing hash function, we obtain the security of the MQDSS signature scheme. Recall that the standard hash-based commitment scheme works as follows. On input s, the commitment algorithm samples a random opening string u and outputs it together with the commitment $c = H(s, u)$. Opening just works by recomputing the hash and comparing it with c. Note that, while this commitment scheme is collapse-binding [17], we need the stronger property of collapsingness of the function defined by the commitment algorithm that, on input a string and some randomness, outputs a commitment (collapse-binding only requires the collapsingness with respect to the committed string, not the opening information).

Corollary 24 (sUF-CMA of MQDSS). *Let Π_{SSH} be the 5-round identification scheme from [14] repeated in parallel a suitable number of times and instantiated with the standard hash-based commitment scheme using a collapsing hash function. Then the FS signature scheme constructed from Π_{SSH} is sUF-CMA.*

Proof (sketch). In Π_{SSH}, the honest prover's first message consists of two commitments, and the second and final messages contain functions of the strings committed to in the first message. This structure, together with the computational binding property (implied by the collapse binding property) of the commitments, immediately implies that Π_{SSH} has computationally unique responses. According to Corollary 30 in the appendix, Π_{SSH} is a quantum proof of knowledge. It also has HVZK according to [14]. Finally, the first message of Π_{SSH} is clearly unpredictable. An application of Theorem 23 finishes the proof. $\square$

7.2 Sequential OR Proofs

A second application of our multi-input version of the measure-and-reprogram result is to the OR-proof as introduced by Liu, Wei and Wong [12] and further analyzed by Fischlin, Harasser and Janson [10]. This is an alternative (non-interactive) proof for proving existence/knowledge of (at least) one of two witnesses without revealing which one, compared to the well known technique by Cramer, Damgård and Schoenmakers [7].

Formally, given two Σ-protocols Σ_0, and Σ_1, for languages $\mathcal{L}_0$, and $\mathcal{L}_1$, respectively, [12] proposes as a non-interactive proof for the OR-language $\mathcal{L}_\vee = \{(x_0, x_1) : x_0 \in \mathcal{L}_0 \vee x_1 \in \mathcal{L}_1\}$ a quadruple $\pi_\vee = (a_0, a_1, z_0, z_1)$ such that

$$V_\vee^H(x_0, x_1, \pi_\vee) := \left[V_0\big(x_0, a_0, H(1, x_0, x_1, a_1), z_0\big) \wedge V_1\big(x_1, a_1, H(0, x_0, x_1, a_0), z_1\big)\right]$$

is satisfied. Fischlin et al. call this construction *sequential OR proof*. We emphasize that the two challenges c_0 and c_1 are computed "over cross", i.e., the challenge c_0 for the execution of Σ_0 is computed by hashing a_1, and vice versa. It is straightforward to verify that if Σ_0 and Σ_1 are special honest-verifier zero-knowledge, meaning that for any challenge c and response z one can efficiently compute a first message a such that (a, c, z) is accepted, then it is sufficient to be able to succeed in *one* of the two *interactive* protocols Σ_0 and Σ_1 in order to honestly produce such an OR-proof $\pi_\vee$. Thus, depending on the context, it is sufficient that one instance is in the corresponding language, or that the prover knows one of the two witnesses, to produce $\pi_\vee$. Indeed, if, say, $x_0 \in \mathcal{L}_0$ (and a witness w_0 is available), then $\pi_\vee$ can be produced as follows. Prepare a_0 according to Σ_0, compute $c_1 := H(0, x_0, x_1, a_0)$ and simulate z_1 and a_1 using the special honest-verifier zero-knowledge property of Σ_1 so that $V_1(x_1, a_1, c_1, z_1)$ is satisfied, and then compute the response z_0 for the challenge $c_0 := H(1, x_0, x_1, a_1)$ according to Σ_0.

On the other hand, intuitively one expects that one of the two instances must be true in order to be able to successfully produce a proof. Indeed, [12] shows security of the sequential OR in the (classical) ROM. [10] go a step further and show security in the (classical) *non-programmable* ROM. Here we show that our multi-input version of the measure-and-reprogram result (as a matter of fact the 2-input version) implies security in the QROM.

Theorem 25. *There exists a black-box quantum polynomial-time interactive algorithm $\hat{\mathcal{P}}$, which first outputs a bit b and two instances x_0, x_1, and in a second stage acts as an interactive prover that runs Σ_b on instance x_b, such that for any adversary $\mathcal{A}$ making q queries to a uniformly random function H and for any x_0°, x_1°:*

$$\Pr\left[x_0 = x_0^\circ \wedge x_1 = x_1^\circ \wedge v_b = accept : (b, x_0, x_1, v_b) \leftarrow \langle \hat{\mathcal{P}}^{\mathcal{A}}, \mathcal{V}_b \rangle\right]$$
$$\geq \frac{1}{(2q+1)^4} \Pr_H\left[x_0 = x_0^\circ \wedge x_1 = x_1^\circ \wedge V_\vee^H(x_0, x_1, \pi_\vee) : (x_0, x_1, \pi_\vee) \leftarrow \mathcal{A}^H\right].$$

As explained above, the execution $(b, x_0, x_1, v_b) \leftarrow \langle \hat{\mathcal{P}}^{\mathcal{A}}, \mathcal{V}_b \rangle$ should be understood in that $\hat{\mathcal{P}}^{\mathcal{A}}$ first outputs x_0, x_1 and b, and then it engages with $\mathcal{V}_b$ to execute Σ_b on instance x_b. Thus, the statement ensures that if $\mathcal{A}^H$ succeeds to produce a convincing proof $\pi_\vee$ then $\hat{\mathcal{P}}^{\mathcal{A}}$ succeeds to convincingly run Σ_0 *or* Σ_1 (with similar success probability), where it is up to $\hat{\mathcal{P}}^{\mathcal{A}}$ to choose which one it wants to do.

Of course, the statement translates to the *static* setting where the two instances x_0 and x_1 are *fixed* and not produced by the dishonest prover.

Proof. The algorithm $\mathcal{A}$ fits into the statement of Theorem 6 with the two extractable inputs $\tilde{x}_0 = (0, x_0, x_1, a_0)$ and $\tilde{x}_1 = (1, x_0, x_1, a_1)$. Thus, we can consider the 3-stage algorithm $\mathcal{S}$ ensured by Theorem 6, which behaves as follows with at least the probability given by the right hand side of the claimed inequality. In the first stage, it outputs a permutation on the set $\{0, 1\}$, represented by a bit $b \in \{0, 1\}$ with $b = 0$ corresponding to the identity permutation, as well as $\tilde{x}_b = (b, x_0, x_1, a_b)$. On input a random $\Theta_b = c_{1-b}$ ("locally" chosen by $\hat{\mathcal{P}}$), $\mathcal{S}$ then outputs $\tilde{x}_{1-b} = (1 - b, x_0, x_1, a_{1-b})$. Finally, on input a random $\Theta_{1-b} = c_b$ (provided by $\mathcal{V}_b$ as challenge upon the first message a_b), $\mathcal{S}$ outputs z_0, z_1 so that $V_\vee$ is satisfied with the challenges c_b and c_{1-b}, and thus in particular $V_b(x_b, a_b, c_b, z_b)$ is satisfied. This shows the existence of $\hat{\mathcal{P}}$ as claimed. □

Acknowledgement. We thank Dominque Unruh for hinting towards the possibility of the improved Theorem 2 (compared to [DFMS19]), see also Footnote 8, and Andreas Hülsing for helpful discussions. CM was funded by a NWO VENI grant (Project No. VI.Veni.192.159). SF was partly supported by the EU Horizon 2020 Research and Innovation Program Grant 780701 (PROMETHEUS). JD was funded by ERC-ADG project 740972 (ALGSTRONGCRYPTO).

A   Quantum extractability of q2 identification schemes

A class of identification schemes that is of particular interest are so-called q2-identification schemes. The NIST candidate signature scheme MQDSS, for example, is obtained from such an identification scheme via the multi-round FS transformation from Definition 20 (with some additional strings included in the hash arguments). In this section, we will prove that a PCIP with a so-called "q2 extractor" [5, Definition 4.6] is a quantum proof of knowledge if it has an additional collapsingness property. This is necessary for its FS transformation to fulfill (s)UF-CMA in the QROM (for (s)UF-CMA in the ROM, the q2-extractor alone is sufficient [5]).

We begin by defining q2 identification schemes and their extractors.

Definition 26. *A 5-round identification scheme is a q2 identification scheme, if the second challenge is a single bit. A q2 identification scheme is called q2-extractable if there exists a polynomial-time algorithm that, on input four transcripts* $t^{(i)} = (a_1^{(i)}, c_1^{(i)}, a_2^{(i)}, c_2^{(i)}, z^{(i)})$, $i = 1, 2, 3, 4$, *such that*

$$c_1^{(1)} = c_1^{(2)} \neq c_1^{(3)} = c_1^{(4)} \qquad \text{and} \qquad c_2^{(1)} = c_2^{(3)} \neq c_2^{(2)} = c_2^{(4)}, \qquad (11)$$

outputs the secret key with non-negligible probability.

For ease of exposition we have assumed that the different challenges of a single PCIP come all from the same challenge space. A q2 identification scheme can be brought into this form by having the prover compute the second challenge by selecting the first bit of an augmented second challenge that is as large as the first one. For classical provers, four transcripts as required by the above definition can be obtained by straightforward rewinding. In the following, we show that, if the q2 identification scheme has an additional property similar to the quantum-computationally unique responses property introduced in [9,13], then the existence of a q2 extractor implies that there exists a quantum extractor. This makes the scheme a quantum proof of knowledge. The argument follows the same lines as the one given in [9] to prove that t-soundness and quantum-computationally unique responses imply the quantum proof-of-knowledge-property, which in turn is an extension of the result by Unruh for Σ-protocols with perfect unique responses [15].

Recall the definition of a collapsing relation, [9, Definition 23], a generalization of the notion of a collapsing hash function [17]. We define the notion of collapsingness for interactive proof systems as follows:

Definition 27. *A $(2n+1)$-round interactive proof system Π is called collapsing, if the relation $R_\Pi : \mathcal{X} \times \mathcal{Y} \to \{0,1\}$ with $\mathcal{X} = \mathcal{C}^n \times \mathcal{A}_1$ and $\mathcal{Y} = \mathcal{A}_2 \times ... \times \mathcal{A}_n \times \mathcal{Z}$ given by the verification predicate V_Π of Π is collapsing from $\mathcal{X}$ to $\mathcal{Y}$.*

Note that for $n = 1$, this notion of collapsingness coincides with the notion of quantum-computationally unique responses from [9].

Given a q2-identification scheme Π, consider the following straightforward (first stage of a) quantum extractor $\mathcal{E}_\Pi^\mathcal{A}$. The extractor runs the prover $\mathcal{A}$ using honestly sampled challenges to obtain a first transcript $t^{(1)}$. Now it rewinds three times and reruns $\mathcal{A}$, each time with a fresh pair of challenges, chosen such as to obtain $t^{(i)}$, $i = 2, 3, 4$ such that the four transcripts fulfill the conditions (11). For this extractor, we obtain the following

Theorem 28. *Let Π a q2-extractable q2-identification scheme that is also collapsing. Then the success probability of the extractor $\mathcal{E}_\Pi^\mathcal{A}$ is lower-bounded in terms of the success probability of the prover $\mathcal{A}$ as*

$$\Pr[\mathcal{E}_\Pi^\mathcal{A} \text{ extracts}] \geq \left(\Pr\left[v = accept : (x, v) \leftarrow \langle \mathcal{A}, V_\Pi \rangle \right] \right)^7 \qquad (12)$$

The proof of this theorem is essentially the same as for Theorem 25 in [9], which is a slight modification of an argument from [15].

As a corollary, we obtain the fact that for q2 identification schemes, q2-extractability and collapsingness imply the quantum proof of knowledge property as defined in [15].

Corollary 29. *Let Π a q2-extractable q2-identification scheme that is also collapsing. Then it is a quantum proof of knowledge.*

In particular, the 5-round identification scheme Π_{SSH} from [14] which is used to construct the post-quantum digital signature scheme MQDSS has these properties under plausible assumptions, namely that it is instantiated with the standard hash-based commitment scheme using a collapsing hash function [17] (see discussion towards the end of Sect. 7.1). For MQDSS, this is no additional assumption, as the FS transformation uses the QROM anyway, and a quantum accessible random oracle is collapsing by [17].

Corollary 30. *If the 5-round identification scheme from [14] is instantiated with the standard hash-based commitment scheme using a collapsing hash function, it is a quantum proof of knowledge.*

Proof (sketch). According to [5], Π_{SSH} is a q2-extractable q2 identification scheme. In Π_{SSH}, the honest prover's first message consists of two commitments, and the second and final messages contain functions of the strings commited to in the first message, and some opening information, respectively. Measuring a function of a register is equivalent to a partial computational basis measurement of that register. According to the collapsing property of the hash function, no efficient algorithm can distinguish whether the committed string and the opening information are measured or not. This clearly implies the same indistinguishability for partial measurements of the string register, which implies that Π_{SSH} is collapsing. □

Note that the above proof works for any multi-round PCIP that has a similar commit-and-open structure.

References

1. Nist post-quantum cryptography standardization. https://csrc.nist.gov/projects/post-quantum-cryptography/round-1-submissions
2. Bootle, J.: Recursive techniques for lattice-based zero-knowledge. https://www.youtube.com/watch?v=NEayIq_k4ks. Accessed 06 Feb 2020
3. Boyer, M., Brassard, G., Høyer, P., Tapp, A.: Tight bounds on quantum searching. Fortschritte der Physik **46**(4–5), 493–505 (1998)
4. Bünz, B., Bootle, J., Boneh, D., Poelstra, A., Wuille, P., Maxwell, G.: Bulletproofs: short proofs for confidential transactions and more. In: 2018 IEEE Symposium on Security and Privacy (SP), pp. 315–334, May 2018
5. Chen, M.-S., Hülsing, A., Rijneveld, J., Samardjiska, S., Schwabe, P.: From 5-pass $\mathcal{MQ}$-based identification to $\mathcal{MQ}$-based signatures. In: Cheon, J.H., Takagi, T. (eds.) ASIACRYPT 2016. LNCS, vol. 10032, pp. 135–165. Springer, Heidelberg (2016). https://doi.org/10.1007/978-3-662-53890-6_5
6. Chen, M.-S., Hülsing, A., Rijneveld, J., Samardjiska, S., Schwabe, P.: SOFIA: $\mathcal{MQ}$-based signatures in the QROM. In: Abdalla, M., Dahab, R. (eds.) PKC 2018. LNCS, vol. 10770, pp. 3–33. Springer, Cham (2018). https://doi.org/10.1007/978-3-319-76581-5_1
7. Cramer, R., Damgård, I., Schoenmakers, B.: Proofs of partial knowledge and simplified design of witness hiding protocols. In: Desmedt, Y.G. (ed.) CRYPTO 1994. LNCS, vol. 839, pp. 174–187. Springer, Heidelberg (1994). https://doi.org/10.1007/3-540-48658-5_19

8. Dagdelen, Ö., Fischlin, M., Gagliardoni, T.: The Fiat–Shamir transformation in a quantum world. In: Sako, K., Sarkar, P. (eds.) ASIACRYPT 2013. LNCS, vol. 8270, pp. 62–81. Springer, Heidelberg (2013). https://doi.org/10.1007/978-3-642-42045-0_4

9. Don, J., Fehr, S., Majenz, C., Schaffner, C.: Security of the Fiat-Shamir transformation in the quantum random-oracle model. In: Boldyreva, A., Micciancio, D. (eds.) CRYPTO 2019. LNCS, vol. 11693, pp. 356–383. Springer, Cham (2019). https://doi.org/10.1007/978-3-030-26951-7_13

10. Fischlin, M., Harasser, P., Janson, C.: Signatures from sequential-OR proofs. In: Canteaut, A., Ishai, Y. (eds.) EUROCRYPT 2020. LNCS, vol. 12107, pp. 212–244. Springer, Cham (2020). https://doi.org/10.1007/978-3-030-45727-3_8

11. Kiltz, E., Lyubashevsky, V., Schaffner, C.: A concrete treatment of Fiat-Shamir signatures in the quantum random-oracle model. In: Nielsen, J.B., Rijmen, V. (eds.) EUROCRYPT 2018. LNCS, vol. 10822, pp. 552–586. Springer, Cham (2018). https://doi.org/10.1007/978-3-319-78372-7_18

12. Liu, J.K., Wei, V.K., Wong, D.S.: Linkable spontaneous anonymous group signature for Ad Hoc groups. In: Wang, H., Pieprzyk, J., Varadharajan, V. (eds.) ACISP 2004. LNCS, vol. 3108, pp. 325–335. Springer, Heidelberg (2004). https://doi.org/10.1007/978-3-540-27800-9_28

13. Liu, Q., Zhandry, M.: Revisiting post-quantum Fiat-Shamir. In: Boldyreva, A., Micciancio, D. (eds.) CRYPTO 2019. LNCS, vol. 11693, pp. 326–355. Springer, Cham (2019). https://doi.org/10.1007/978-3-030-26951-7_12

14. Sakumoto, K., Shirai, T., Hiwatari, H.: Public-key identification schemes based on multivariate quadratic polynomials. In: Rogaway, P. (ed.) CRYPTO 2011. LNCS, vol. 6841, pp. 706–723. Springer, Heidelberg (2011). https://doi.org/10.1007/978-3-642-22792-9_40

15. Unruh, D.: Quantum proofs of knowledge. In: Pointcheval, D., Johansson, T. (eds.) EUROCRYPT 2012. LNCS, vol. 7237, pp. 135–152. Springer, Heidelberg (2012). https://doi.org/10.1007/978-3-642-29011-4_10

16. Unruh, D.: Non-interactive zero-knowledge proofs in the quantum random oracle model. In: Oswald, E., Fischlin, M. (eds.) EUROCRYPT 2015. LNCS, vol. 9057, pp. 755–784. Springer, Heidelberg (2015). https://doi.org/10.1007/978-3-662-46803-6_25

17. Unruh, D.: Computationally binding quantum commitments. In: Fischlin, M., Coron, J.-S. (eds.) EUROCRYPT 2016. LNCS, vol. 9666, pp. 497–527. Springer, Heidelberg (2016). https://doi.org/10.1007/978-3-662-49896-5_18

18. Unruh, D.: Post-quantum security of Fiat-Shamir. In: Takagi, T., Peyrin, T. (eds.) ASIACRYPT 2017. LNCS, vol. 10624, pp. 65–95. Springer, Cham (2017). https://doi.org/10.1007/978-3-319-70694-8_3

19. Zhandry, M.: How to construct quantum random functions. In: 2012 IEEE 53rd Annual Symposium on Foundations of Computer Science, pp. 679–687. IEEE, October 2012

Fiat-Shamir for Repeated Squaring with Applications to PPAD-Hardness and VDFs

Alex Lombardi[(⊠)] and Vinod Vaikuntanathan

MIT, Cambridge, MA, USA
{alexjl,vinodv}@mit.edu

Abstract. The Fiat-Shamir transform is a methodology for compiling a (public-coin) interactive proof system for a language L into a *non-interactive* argument system for L. Proving security of the Fiat-Shamir transform in the standard model, especially in the context of *succinct* arguments, is largely an unsolved problem. The work of Canetti et al. (STOC 2019) proved the security of the Fiat-Shamir transform applied to the Goldwasser-Kalai-Rothblum (STOC 2008) succinct interactive proof system under a very strong "optimal learning with errors" assumption. Achieving a similar result under standard assumptions remains an important open question.

In this work, we consider the problem of compiling a different succinct interactive proof system: Pietrzak's proof system (ITCS 2019) for the iterated squaring problem. We construct a hash function family (with evaluation time roughly 2^{λ^c}) that guarantees the soundness of Fiat-Shamir for this protocol assuming the sub-exponential ($2^{-n^{1-\epsilon}}$)-hardness of the n-dimensional learning with errors problem. (The latter follows from the worst-case $2^{n^{1-\epsilon}}$ hardness of lattice problems.) More generally, we extend the "bad-challenge function" methodology of Canetti et al. for proving the soundness of Fiat-Shamir to a class of protocols whose bad-challenge functions are *not* efficiently computable.

As a corollary (following Choudhuri et al., ePrint 2019 and Ephraim et al., EUROCRYPT 2020), we construct hard-on-average problems in the complexity class **CLS** $\subset$ **PPAD** under the 2^{λ^c}-hardness of the repeated squaring problem and the $2^{-n^{1-\epsilon}}$-hardness of the learning with errors problem. Under the additional assumption that the repeated squaring problem is "inherently sequential", we also obtain a Verifiable Delay Function (Boneh et al., EUROCRYPT 2018) in the standard model. Finally, we give additional PPAD-hardness and VDF

A. Lombardi—Research supported in part by an NDSEG fellowship and by the second author's grants listed below.

V. Vaikuntanathan—Research was supported in part by NSF Grants CNS- 1350619 and CNS-1414119, an NSF-BSF grant CNS-1718161, the Defense Advanced Research Projects Agency (DARPA) and the U.S. Army Research Office under contracts W911NF-15-C-0226 and W911NF-15-C-0236, an IBM-MIT grant and a Microsoft Trustworthy and Robust AI grant.

D. Micciancio and T. Ristenpart (Eds.): CRYPTO 2020, LNCS 12172, pp. 632–651, 2020.
https://doi.org/10.1007/978-3-030-56877-1_22

instantiations demonstrating a broader tradeoff between the strength of the repeated squaring assumption and the strength of the lattice assumption.

1   Reference to Full Version

The full version of this paper [LV20] is freely available on the Cryptology ePrint Archive. We refer the reader to this version for a complete description of our results and proofs.

2   Introduction

The Fiat-Shamir transform [FS86] is a methodology for compiling a public-coin interactive proof (or argument) system for a language L into a non-interactive argument system for L. While originally developed in order to convert 3-message identification schemes into signature schemes, the methodology readily generalized [BR93] to apply to a broad, expressive class of interactive protocols, with applications including non-interactive zero knowledge for **NP** [BR93], succinct non-interactive arguments for **NP** [Mic00, BCS16], and widely used/practically efficient signature schemes [Sch89].

However, these constructions and results come with a big caveat: the security of the Fiat-Shamir transformation is typically *heuristic*. While the transformation has been proved secure (in high generality) in the random oracle model [BR93, PS96, Mic00, BCS16], it is known that some properties that hold in the random oracle model – including the soundness of Fiat-Shamir for certain contrived interactive arguments – cannot be instantiated at all in the standard model [CGH04, DNRS99, Bar01, GK03, BBH+19].

Given these negative results, security in the random oracle model is by no means the end of the story. Indeed, the question of whether Fiat-Shamir can be instantiated for any given interactive argument system (and under what computational assumptions this can be done) has been a major research direction over the last twenty years [DNRS99, Bar01, GK03, BLV06, CCR16, KRR17, CCRR18, HL18, CCH+19, PS19, BBH+19, BFJ+19, JJ19, LVW19]. After much recent work, some positive results are known, falling into three categories (in the decreasing order of strength of assumptions required):

1. We can compile *arbitrary* (constant-round, public-coin) interactive proofs under extremely strong assumptions [KRR17, CCRR18] that are *non-falsifiable* in the sense of [Nao03].
2. We can compile certain succinct interactive proofs [LFKN92, GKR08] – and variants of other interactive proofs not captured in item (3) below, such as [GMW91] – under extremely strong but *falsifiable* assumptions [CCH+19].
3. We can compile variants of some classical 3-message zero knowledge proof systems [GMR85, Blu86, FLS99] under *standard* cryptographic assumptions [CCH+19, PS19].

Elaborating on item (2) above, what is currently known is that the sum-check protocol [LFKN92] and the related Goldwasser-Kalai-Rothblum (GKR) [GKR08] interactive proof system can be compiled under an "optimal security assumption" related to (secret-key) Regev encryption. Roughly speaking, an optimal hardness assumption is the assumption that some search problem cannot be solved with probability significantly better than repeatedly guessing a solution at random. This is an extremely strong assumption that (in the context of Regev encryption) requires careful parameter settings to avoid being trivially false.

In this work, we focus on improving item (2); in particular, we ask:

Under what computational assumptions can we instantiate Fiat-Shamir for an interesting succinct *interactive proof?*

Instead of considering the [LFKN92, GKR08] protocols, we work on compiling a protocol of Pietrzak [Pie18] for the "repeated-squaring language" [RSW96]. At a high level, Pietrzak constructs a "sumcheck-like" succinct interactive proof system for the computation $f_{N,g}(T) = g^{2^T} \pmod{N}$ over an RSA modulus $N = pq$. Compiling this protocol turns out to have applications related to verifiable delay functions (VDFs) [BBBF18] and hardness in the complexity class **PPAD** [CHK+19a, CHK+19b, EFKP19], which we elaborate on below.

Applications. We consider two apparently different questions: the first is that of establishing the hardness of the complexity class **PPAD** ("polynomial parity arguments on directed graphs") [Pap94] that captures the hardness of finding Nash equilibria in bimatrix games [DGP09, CDT09]; the second is that of constructing verifiable delay functions (VDFs), a recently introduced cryptographic primitive [BBBF18] which gives us a way to introduce delays in decentralized applications such as blockchains.

The Hardness of **PPAD**. Establishing the hardness of **PPAD** [Pap94], possibly under cryptographic assumptions, is a long-standing question in the foundations of cryptography and computational game theory. After two decades of little progress on the question, a recent sequence of works [BPR15, HY17, CHK+19a, CHK+19b, EFKP19] has managed to prove that there are problems in **PPAD** (and indeed a smaller complexity class, **CLS** [DP11]) that are hard (even *on average*) under *strong* cryptographic assumptions. The results so far fall roughly into two categories, depending on the techniques used.

1. **Program Obfuscation.** Bitansky, Paneth and Rosen [BPR15], inspired by an approach outlined in [AKV04], showed that **PPAD** is hard assuming the existence of subexponentially secure indistinguishability obfuscation (IO) [BGI+01, GGH+13] and one-way functions. This was later improved [GPS16, HY17] to rely on polynomially-secure functional encryption and to give hardness in **CLS** $\subset$ **PPAD**.

2. **Unambiguously Sound Incrementally Verifiable Computation.** The recent beautiful work [CHK+19a] constructs a hard-on-average **CLS** instance assuming the existence of a special kind of incrementally verifiable computation (IVC) [Val08]. Instantiating this approach, they show that **CLS** ⊂ **PPAD** is hard-on-average if there exists a hash function family that soundly instantiates the Fiat-Shamir heuristic [FS86] for the sumcheck interactive proof system for #P [LFKN92]. Two follow-up works [CHK+19b, EFKP19] show the same conclusion if Fiat-Shamir for Pietrzak's interactive proof system [Pie18] can be soundly instantiated (and if the underlying "repeated squaring language" is hard).

Regarding the first approach [BPR15, GPS16, HY17], secure indistinguishability obfuscators have recently been constructed based on the veracity of a number of non-standard assumptions (see, e.g., [AJL+19, BDGM20]). Regarding the second approach [CHK+19a, CHK+19b, EFKP19], the hash function can be instantiated in the random oracle model, or under "optimal KDM-security" assumptions [CCRR18, CCH+19].

In summary, despite substantial effort, there are no known constructions of hard **PPAD** instances from standard cryptographic assumptions (although see Section 2.3 for a recent independent work [KPY20] that shows such a result under a new assumption on bilinear groups).

Verifiable Delay Functions. A Verifiable Delay Function (VDF) [BBBF18] is a function f with the following properties:

- f can be evaluated in some (moderately large) time T.
- Computing f (on average) requires time close to T, *even given a large amount of parallelism*.
- There is a time $T + o(T)$ procedure that computes $y = f(x)$ on an input x along with a proof π that $y = f(x)$ is computed correctly. This proof (argument) system should be verifiable in time $\ll T$ (ideally poly$(\lambda, \log T)$)) and satisfy standard (computational) soundness.

Since their introduction [BBBF18], there have been a few proposed candidate VDF constructions [BBBF18, Pie18, Wes19, dFMPS19, EFKP19]. There are currently no constructions based on standard cryptographic assumptions, but this is somewhat inherent to the primitive: a secure VDF implies the existence of a problem which can be solved in time T and also requires (sequential) time close to T. Nonetheless, one can ask[1] whether VDFs can be constructed from "more standard-looking" assumptions, a question partially answered by [Pie18, Wes19]. In particular, each of their constructions relies on two assumptions:

(1) The T-repeated squaring problem [RSW96] requires sequential time close to T.

---

[1] [BBBF18] explicitly suggested this.

(2) The Fiat-Shamir heuristic for some specific public-coin interactive proof/argument[2] can be soundly instantiated.

The techniques used in both the construction of hard **PPAD** instances and the construction of VDFs are similar, and so are the underlying assumptions (this is due to the connection between **PPAD** and incrementally verifiable computation [Val08, CHK+19a]). In particular, the works of [CHK+19b, EFKP19] construct hard **PPAD** (and even **CLS**) instances under two assumptions:

(1′) The T-repeated squaring problem [RSW96] requires super-polynomial (standard) time for some $T = \lambda^{\omega(1)}$.
(2′) The Fiat-Shamir heuristic for a variant of the [Pie18] interactive proof system can be soundly instantiated.

The assumption (1) (and its weakening, assumption (1′)) is the foundation of the Rivest-Shamir-Wagner time-lock puzzle [RSW96] and has been around for over 20 years. In particular, breaking the RSW assumption has received renewed cryptanalytic interest recently [Riv99, Fab19].

On the other hand, as previously discussed, the assumptions $(2, 2')$ are not well understood. Indeed, our main question about Fiat-Shamir for succinct arguments (if specialized to the [Pie18] protocol) is intimately related to the following question.

*Can we construct hard **PPAD** instances and VDFs under more well-studied assumptions?*

2.1 Our Results

We show how to instantiate the Fiat-Shamir heuristic for the [Pie18] protocol under a quantitatively strong (but relatively standard) variant of the Learning with Errors (LWE) assumption [Reg09]. We give a family of constructions of hash functions that run in subexponential (or even quasi-polynomial or polynomial) time, and prove that they soundly instantiate Fiat-Shamir for this protocol under a sufficiently strong LWE assumption.

More generally, we extend the "bad-challenge function" methodology of [CCH+19] for proving the soundness of Fiat-Shamir to a class of protocols whose bad-challenge functions are not efficiently computable. We elaborate on this below in the technical overview (Sect. 2.4).

As a consequence, we obtain **CLS**-hardness and VDFs from a pair of quantitatively related assumptions on the [RSW96] repeated squaring problem and on the learning with errors (LWE) problem [Reg09]; the latter can in turn be based on the worst-case hardness of the (approximate) shortest vector problem

---

[2] The two works [Pie18, Wes19] consider qualitatively different interactive argument systems. In this work, we focus on the [Pie18] protocol since (1) it has unconditional soundness and therefore is more conducive to provable Fiat-Shamir compilation, and (2) it is more closely related to **PPAD**-hardness.

(GapSVP) on lattices. In particular, we can base the hardness of **CLS** $\subset$ **PPAD**, as well as the security of a VDF, on the hardness of two relatively well-studied problems.

Fiat-Shamir for Pietrzak's Protocol. For our main result, we show that for any $\epsilon > 0$, an LWE assumption of quantitative strength $2^{n^{1-\epsilon}}$ allows for a Fiat-Shamir instantiation with verification runtime $2^{\tilde{O}(n^{\epsilon})}$ on a repeated squaring instance with security parameter $\lambda = O(n \log n)$. Such a result is meaningful as long as the verification runtime is smaller than the time it takes to solve the repeated squaring problem; the current best known algorithms for repeated squaring run in heuristic time $2^{\tilde{O}(\lambda^{1/3})} = 2^{\tilde{O}(n^{1/3})}$ [LLMP90].

Here and throughout the paper, we will use (t, δ)-hardness to denote that a cryptographic problem is hard for t-time algorithms to solve with δ probability (or distinguishing advantage).

Theorem 2.1. *Let $\epsilon > 0$ be arbitrary. Assume that (decision) LWE is $\left(2^{\tilde{O}(n^{1/2})}, 2^{-n^{1-\epsilon}}\right)$-hard (or alternatively, $\left(2^{\tilde{O}(n^{\epsilon})}, 2^{-n^{1-\epsilon}}\right)$-hard for non-uniform algorithms). Then, there exists a hash family $\mathcal{H}$ that soundly instantiates the Fiat-Shamir heuristic for Pietrzak's interactive proof system [Pie18]. When the proof system is instantiated for repeated squaring over groups of size $2^{O(\lambda)}$ with $\lambda = O(n \log n)$, the hash function h from the family $\mathcal{H}$ can be evaluated in time $2^{\tilde{O}(\lambda^{\epsilon})}$.*

Under the assumption that (decision) LWE is $\left(2^{\tilde{O}(n^{1/2})}, 2^{-\frac{n}{\log^c n}}\right)$-hard for some constant $c > 0$ (or alternatively, $\left(\text{quasipoly}(n), 2^{-\frac{n}{\log^c n}}\right)$-hard for non-uniform algorithms), there exists such a hash family $\mathcal{H}$ with quasi-polynomial evaluation time.

Moreover, the LWE assumption that we make falls into the parameter regime where we know worst-case to average-case reductions [Reg09, BLP+13, PRS17], so we obtain the following corollary.

Corollary 2.1. *The conclusions of Theorem 2.1 (with parameter $\epsilon < \frac{1}{2}$) follow from the assumption that the worst case problem $\text{poly}(n)$-GapSVP for rank n lattices requires time $2^{\omega(n^{1-\epsilon})}$. Similarly, the protocol with quasi-polynomial verification time is sound under the assumption that $\text{poly}(n)$-GapSVP requires time $2^{\frac{n}{\log(n)^c}}$ for some $c > 0$.*

The Shortest Vector Problem (SVP) on integer lattices is a well-studied problem (see discussion in [Pei16, ADRS15]); despite a substantial effort, all known $\text{poly}(n)$-approximation algorithms for the problem have exponential run-time $2^{\Omega(n)}$. As a result, our current understanding of the approximate-SVP landscape is consistent with the following conjecture.

Conjecture 2.1. (Exponential Time Hypothesis for GapSVP). For any fixed $\gamma(n) = \text{poly}(n)$, the $\gamma(n)$-*GapSVP* problem cannot be solved in time $2^{o(n)}$.

Assuming Conjecture 2.1, the conclusion of Theorem 2.1 holds for every $\epsilon > 0$; moreover, the variant of the Theorem 2.1 protocol with quasi-polynomial time evaluation is sound as well.

What about polynomial-time verification? Given a non-interactive protocol for repeated squaring with $2^{\tilde{O}(\lambda^\epsilon)}$ verification time (or quasi-polynomial evaluation time), one can always define a new security parameter $\kappa = 2^{\tilde{O}(\lambda^\epsilon)}$ (or $\kappa = 2^{\log(\lambda)^c}$) to obtain a protocol with *polynomial-time* verification. However, this makes use of *complexity leveraging* [CGGM00], so (i) this requires making the assumption that repeated squaring (on instances with security parameter λ) is hard for poly($\kappa(\lambda)$)-time adversaries, and (ii) the resulting protocol cannot have security subexponential in κ.

If one does not wish to use complexity leveraging, we give an alternative construction that has (natively) polynomial-time verification, at the cost of a stronger LWE assumption.

Theorem 2.2. *Let $\delta > 0$ be arbitrary and $q(n) = \text{poly}(n)$ be a fixed (sufficiently large) polynomial in n. Assume that (decision) LWE is $\left(\text{poly}(n), q^{-\delta n}\right)$-hard for non-uniform distinguishers (or $\left(2^{\tilde{O}(n^{1/2})}, q^{-\delta n}\right)$-hard for uniform distinguishers). Then, there exists a hash family $\mathcal{H}$ that soundly instantiates the Fiat-Shamir heuristic for Pietrzak's interactive proof system [Pie18] with $\text{poly}(\lambda) = \text{poly}(n \log n)$-time verification. More specifically, the verification time is $\lambda^{O(1/\delta)}$.*

Moreover, this strong LWE assumption *still* falls into the parameter regime with a meaningful worst-case to average-case reduction:

Corollary 2.2. *The conclusion of Theorem 2.2 follows from the assumption that worst-case $\gamma(n)$-GapSVP (for a fixed $\gamma(n) = \text{poly}(n)$) cannot be solved in time $n^{o(n)}$ with $\text{poly}(n)$ space and $\text{poly}(n)$ bits of nonuniform advice (independent of the lattice).*

Polynomial-space algorithms for GapSVP have themselves been an object of study for over 25 years [Kan83, KF16, BLS16, ABF+20], but the current best (poly-space) algorithms for this problem run in time $n^{\Omega(\epsilon n)}$ for approximation factor $n^{1/\epsilon}$. Therefore, under a sufficiently strong (and plausible) worst-case assumption about GapSVP, we have a polynomial-time Fiat-Shamir compiler without complexity leveraging.

By combining Theorems 2.1 and 2.2 with the results of [CHK+19b, EFKP19], we obtain the following construction of hard-on-average **CLS** instances.

Theorem 2.3. *For a constant $\epsilon > 0$, suppose that*

– *n-dimensional LWE (with polynomial modulus) is $\left(2^{\tilde{O}(n^{1/2})}, 2^{-n^{1-\epsilon}}\right)$-hard, and*

- *The repeated squaring problem on an instance of size 2^λ requires $2^{\lambda^\epsilon \log(\lambda)^{\omega(1)}}$ time.*

Then, there is a hard-on-average problem in **CLS** $\subset$ **PPAD**. *The same conclusion holds if for some $c > 0$,*

- LWE *is* $\left(2^{\tilde{O}(n^{1/2})}, 2^{-\frac{n}{\log(n)^c}}\right)$-*hard, and*
- *The repeated squaring problem is hard for quasi-polynomial time algorithms.*

The same conclusion also holds if for some $\delta > 0$,

- LWE *is* $\left(\text{poly}(n), q^{-\delta n}\right)$-*hard for non-uniform distinguishers, and*
- *The repeated squaring problem is hard for polynomial time algorithms.*

We obtain Theorem 2.3 by plugging our standard model Fiat-Shamir instantiation into the complexity-theoretic reduction of [CHK+19b].[3] For use in this reduction, our non-interactive protocol must satisfy a stronger security notion called *(adaptive) unambiguous soundness* [RRR16,CHK+19a], which we show is indeed the case.

Note that the two hardness assumptions in the theorem statement are in opposition to each other. As ϵ becomes smaller, the repeated squaring assumption becomes weaker, but the LWE assumption becomes stronger. In particular, we cannot set $\epsilon \geq 1/3$ as there are known algorithms [LLMP90] solving repeated squaring in (heuristic) time $2^{\widetilde{O}(\lambda^{1/3})}$.

Additionally, as a direct consequence of Theorem 2.1, we obtain VDFs in the standard model as long as the underlying repeated squaring problem is sufficiently (sequentially) hard. Recall that the repeated squaring problem [RSW96] is the computation of the function $f_{N,g}(T) = g^{2^T} \pmod{N}$, for the appropriate distribution on $N = pq$ and g.

Theorem 2.4. *For a constant $\epsilon > 0$, suppose that*

- LWE *is* $\left(2^{\tilde{O}(n^{1/2})}, 2^{-n^{1-\epsilon}}\right)$-*hard, and*
- *The repeated squaring problem [RSW96] over groups of size $2^{O(\lambda)}$ requires $T(1 - o(1))$ sequential time for $T \gg 2^{\tilde{O}(\lambda^\epsilon)}$.*

Then, the repeated squaring function $f_{N,g}$ can be made into a VDF with verification time $2^{\tilde{O}(\lambda^\epsilon)}$ on groups of size $2^{O(\lambda)}$ (with $\lambda = O(n \log n)$). Similarly, if for some $c > 0$,

- LWE *is* $\left(2^{\tilde{O}(n^{1/2})}, 2^{-\frac{n}{\log(n)^c}}\right)$-*hard, and*
- *The repeated squaring problem requires $T(1 - o(1))$ sequential time for $T \gg 2^{\tilde{O}(\log(\lambda)^{c+1})}$,*

---

[3] Our protocol differs very slightly from the formulation in [CHK+19b], but the difference is irrelevant to the reduction.

Then, $f_{N,g}$ can be made into a VDF with verification time $2^{\tilde{O}(\log(\lambda)^{c+1})}$. Finally, if for some $\delta > 0$,

- LWE *(with modulus q) is $\left(\text{poly}(n), q^{-\delta n}\right)$-hard for non-uniform distinguishers, and*
- *The repeated squaring problem requires $T(1 - o(1))$ sequential time for all $T = \text{poly}(\lambda)$.*

Then, $f_{N,g}$ can be made into a VDF with $\lambda^{O(1/\delta)}$-time verification.

Theorem 2.4 follows immediately from Theorem 2.1 along with the construction of Pietrzak [Pie18]. While many of the VDFs in Theorem 2.4 have super-polynomial verification time (and therefore do not fit the standard definition), they can be converted into (standard) VDFs with polynomial verification time via complexity leveraging; however, the leveraged VDFs will only support quasi-polynomial (respectively, $2^{2^{\text{poly} \log \log \kappa}}$) time computation (and soundness of the VDF will only hold against adversaries running in time quasi-polynomial in the new security parameter κ). Because of this, we consider the formulation in terms of super-polynomial time verification to be more informative.

2.2 Comparison with Prior Work

Cryptographic Hardness of **PPAD**. As described in the introduction, prior works on the cryptographic hardness of **PPAD** fall into two categories – those based on obfuscation and ones based on incrementally verifiable computation (IVC). The obfuscation-based constructions all make cryptographic assumptions related to the existence of indistinguishability obfuscation or closely related primitives that we currently do not know how to instantiate based on well-studied assumptions. (For the latest in obfuscation technology, we refer the reader to [JLMS19, JLS19].) We therefore focus on comparing to the previous IVC-based constructions.

- [CHK+19a] constructs hard problems in **CLS** under the polynomial hardness of #SAT with poly-logarithmically many variables along with the assumption that Fiat-Shamir can be soundly instantiated for the sumcheck protocol [LFKN92]. The latter follows either in the random oracle model or under the assumption that a LWE-based fully homomorphic encryption scheme is "optimally circular-secure" [CCH+18, CCH+19] for quasi-polynomial time adversaries.

  While the hardness of #SAT (with this parameter regime) is a weaker assumption than the subexponential hardness of repeated squaring, the [CHK+19a] (standard model) result has the drawback of relying on an optimal hardness assumption. Roughly speaking, an optimal hardness assumption is the assumption that some search problem cannot be solved with probability significantly better than repeatedly guessing a solution at random. This is an extremely strong assumption that requires careful parameter settings to avoid being trivially false.

In contrast, our main LWE assumption is *subexponential* (concerning distinguishing advantage $2^{-n^{1-\epsilon}}$) and follows from the worst-case hardness of $poly(n)$-GapSVP for time $2^{n^{1-\epsilon}}$ algorithms. Even our most optimistic LWE assumption (as in Theorem 2.2) follows from a form of worst-case hardness quantitatively far from the corresponding best known algorithms.

- [CHK+19b, EFKP19] construct hard problems in **CLS** assuming the polynomial hardness of repeated squaring along with a generic assumption that the Fiat-Shamir heuristic can be instantiated for round-by-round sound (see [CCH+18, CCH+19]) public-coin interactive proofs. The latter can be instantiated either in the random oracle model, or under the assumption that Regev encryption (or ElGamal encryption) is "optimally KDM-secure" for unbounded KDM functions [CCRR18].

  The [CCRR18] assumption is (up to minor technical details) stronger than the optimal security assumption used in [CHK+19a] (because the security game additionally involves an unbounded function), so the [CHK+19b, EFKP19] are mostly framed in the random oracle model. In this work, we give a new Fiat-Shamir instantiation to plug into the [CHK+19b, EFKP19] framework.

VDFs. We compare our construction of VDFs to previous constructions [BBBF18, Pie18, Wes19, dFMPS19, EFKP19].

- [BBBF18] and [dFMPS19] give constructions of VDFs from new cryptographic assumptions related to permutation polynomials and isogenies over supersingular elliptic curves, respectively. These assumptions are certainly incomparable to ours, but we rely on the hardness of older, more well-studied problems.
- [Pie18, EFKP19] have the same basic VDF construction as ours; the main difference is that they use a random oracle to instantiate their hash function, while we use a hash function in the standard model and prove its security under a quantitatively strong variant of LWE.
- [Wes19] also builds a VDF based on the hardness of repeated squaring, but by building a different interactive argument for computing the function and assuming that Fiat-Shamir can be instantiated for this argument. Again, this assumption holds in the random oracle model, but we know of no instantiation of this VDF in the standard model.

On the negative side, our main VDF (for the natural choice of security parameter) has verification time $2^{\tilde{O}(\lambda^\epsilon)}$; this can be thought of as polynomial-time via complexity leveraging, but this results in a VDF that is only quasi-polynomially secure. Alternatively, based on our optimistic LWE assumption, we only obtain a VDF with large polynomial (i.e. $\lambda^{1/\delta}$ for small δ) verification time. As a result, we consider our VDF construction to be a proof-of-concept regarding whether VDFs can be built based on "more standard-looking assumptions", in particular, without invoking the random oracle model.

2.3   Additional Related Work

[BG20] constructs hard instances in the complexity class **PLS** – which contains **CLS** and is incomparable to **PPAD** – under a falsifiable assumption on bilinear maps introduced in [KPY19] (along with the randomized exponential time hypothesis (ETH)).

    In recent independent work, [KPY20] constructs hard-on-average **CLS** instances under the (quasi-polynomial) [KPY19] assumption. In fact, they give a protocol for unambiguous and incrementally verifiable computation for all languages decidable in space-bounded and slightly super-polynomial time.

2.4   Technical Overview

We now discuss the ideas behind our main result, Theorem 2.1, which is an instantiation of the Fiat-Shamir heuristic for the [Pie18] repeated squaring protocol. In obtaining this result, we also broaden the class of interactive proofs for which we have Fiat-Shamir instantiations under standard assumptions.

    The main tool used by our construction is a hash function family $\mathcal{H}$ that is correlation intractable [CGH04] for *efficiently computable functions* [CLW18, CCH+19]. Recall that a hash family $\mathcal{H}$ is correlation intractable for t-time computable functions if for every function f computable time t, the following computational problem is hard: given a description of a hash function h, find an input x such that $h(x) = f(x)$. We now know [PS19] that such hash families can be constructed under the LWE assumption.

Correlation Intractability and Fiat-Shamir. In order to describe our result, we first sketch the [CCH+19] paradigm for using such a hash family $\mathcal{H}$ to instantiate the Fiat-Shamir heuristic.

    For simplicity, consider a three-message (public-coin) interactive proof system (Σ-protocol)

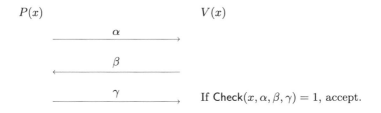

Fig. 1. A Σ-protocol Π.

as well as its corresponding Fiat-Shamir round-reduced protocol $\Pi_{\mathrm{FS},\mathcal{H}}$ for a hash family $\mathcal{H}$.

    Moreover, suppose that this protocol Π satisfies the following soundness property (sometimes referred to as "special soundness"): for every $x \notin L$ and

$P_{\mathsf{FS}}(x, h)$ $\qquad\qquad\qquad\qquad\qquad\qquad$ $V_{\mathsf{FS}}(x, h)$

$$\xrightarrow{\quad\alpha, \beta := h(\alpha), \gamma\quad}$$

If $\beta = h(\alpha)$

and $\mathsf{Check}(x, \alpha, \beta, \gamma) = 1$, accept.

Fig. 2. The Protocol $\Pi_{\mathsf{FS},\mathcal{H}}$.

every prover message α, there exists at most one verifier message $\beta^*(x, \alpha)$ allowing the prover to cheat.[4]

It then follows that if a hash family $\mathcal{H}$ is correlation intractable for the function family $f_x(\alpha) = \beta^*(x, \alpha)$, then $\mathcal{H}$ instantiates the Fiat-Shamir heuristic for Π.[5] This is because a cheating prover P^*_{FS} breaking the soundness of $\Pi_{\mathsf{FS},\mathcal{H}}$ must find a first message α such that its corresponding challenge $h(x, \alpha)$ is equal to the bad challenge $f_x(\alpha)$ (or else it has no hope of successfully cheating).

Therefore, using the hash family of [PS19], we can (under the LWE assumption) do Fiat-Shamir for any protocol Π whose "bad-challenge function" $f_x(\alpha)$ is computable in polynomial time; this has the important caveat that the complexity of computing the hash function h is at least the complexity of computing $f_x(\alpha)$.

This paradigm seems to run into the following roadblock: intuitively, for protocols Π of interest, computing $f_x(\alpha)$ appears to be *hard* rather than easy. For example,

1. For a standard construction of zero-knowledge proofs for **NP** such as [Blu86], computing $f_x(\alpha)$ involves breaking a cryptographically secure commitment scheme.
2. For (unconditional) statistical zero knowledge protocols such as the [GMR85] Quadratic Residuosity protocol, computing $f_x(\alpha)$ involves deciding the underlying hard language L.
3. For doubly efficient interactive proofs such as the [GKR08] interactive proof for logspace-uniform NC, computing $f_x(\alpha)$ again involves deciding the underlying language L; in this case, L is in P, but this Fiat-Shamir compiler would result in a non-interactive argument whose verifier runs in time longer than it takes to decide L.

The work [CCH+19] resolves issues (1) and (2) in the following way: in both cases, we can arrange for $f_x(\alpha)$ to be efficiently computable *given an appropriate trapdoor*: in the case of [Blu86], the commitment scheme can have a trapdoor allowing for efficient extraction, while in the case of [GMR85], $f_x(\alpha)$ is efficient

---

[4] The prover can cheat on a pair (α, β) if and only if there *exists* a third message γ such that $(x, \alpha, \beta, \gamma)$ is accepted by the verifier.

[5] To obtain *adaptive soundness*, we modify the protocol to set $\beta = h(x, \alpha)$ and instead consider the function $f(x, \alpha) = \beta^*(x, \alpha)$.

given an appropriate **NP**-witness for the complement language $\overline{L}$. However, we have no analogous resolution to (3), which is the setting of interest to us.[6]

The bad-challenge function of the [Pie18] *protocol.* With this context in mind, we now consider the [Pie18] protocol.[7] This protocol (like the [GKR08] protocol and the related sumcheck protocol [LFKN92]) is not a constant-round protocol, but is instead composed of up to polynomially many "reduction steps" of the following form.

– The prover, given (N, g, T), computes and sends $u = g^{2^{T/2}}$, the (supposed) "halfway point" of the computation.
– The message u indicates (to the verifier) two derivative claims: $u = g^{2^{T/2}}$ and $h = u^{2^{T/2}}$.
– The verifier then challenges the prover to prove a random linear combination of the two statements: $h \cdot u^r = (u \cdot g^r)^{2^{T/2}}$.

Soundness can then be analyzed in a "round-by-round" fashion [CCH+19]: if you start with a false statement (or if you start with a true statement but send an incorrect value $\tilde{u} \neq u$), there is at most one[8] bad challenge r^* resulting in a recursive call on a true statement.

To invoke the [CCH+19] paradigm, we ask: how efficiently can we compute the function $f(N, T, g, h, u) = r^*$? To answer this question, let $\tilde{g}$ denote a fixed group element of order $\phi(N)/2$ such that $g, h, u \in \langle \tilde{g} \rangle$. Letting γ, η, ω denote the discrete logs of g, h, and u in base $\tilde{g}$, we see that (for corresponding challenge r) the statement $(N, T/2, g', h')$ is true if and only if

$$\eta + r \cdot \omega \equiv 2^{T/2}(\omega + r \cdot \gamma) \pmod{\phi(N)/2}.$$

As a result, we see that r can be efficiently computed from the following information:

– The discrete logarithms η, ω, γ, and
– The factorization of N.

While the factorization of N can be known a priori in the security reduction (similar to prior work), the discrete logarithms depend on the prover message u and (adaptively chosen) statement (g, h). We conclude that the "bottleneck" for computing f is the problem computing a constant number of discrete logarithms in $\mathbb{Z}_p^\times$.

---

[6] The only current known Fiat-Shamir instantiation for the [GKR08] protocol utilizes a *compact* correlation intractable hash family (in the sense that the hash evaluation time is independent of the time to compute the correlation function/relation) which we only know how to build from an optimal security assumption [CCH+19].

[7] For this overview, we ignore the details of working over the group $\mathbb{QR}_N \subset \mathbb{Z}_N^\times$ and the corresponding technical challenges.

[8] To guarantee this property, r is selected from a range smaller than either of the prime factors of N.

Since computing discrete logarithms over $\mathbb{Z}_p^\times$ is believed to be hard, and is not known to have a trapdoor, it appears unlikely that this approach would allow us to rely on the polynomial hardness of the [PS19] hash family. However, it *is* plausible that we could use a variant of the [PS19] hash family supporting *super-polynomial* time computation (proven secure under a super-polynomial variant of LWE) to capture the complexity of computing discrete logarithms.

Unfortunately, the naive version of this approach fails: the best known run-time bounds[9] for computing discrete logarithms over $\mathbb{Z}_p^\times$ for $p = 2^{O(\lambda)}$ are of the form $2^{\tilde{O}(\lambda^{1/2})}$ [Adl79,Pom87], and the best known heuristic algorithms (plausibly) run in time $2^{\tilde{O}(\lambda^{1/3})}$ [LLMP90]. If we were to instantiate the [PS19] hash family to support functions of this complexity, we could prove the soundness of Fiat-Shamir for the [Pie18] protocol, but the resulting non-interactive protocol would run in time $2^{\tilde{O}(\lambda^{1/2})}$ (or in time $2^{\tilde{O}(\lambda^{1/3})}$ with a heuristic security proof); these are the same runtime bounds for the best known algorithms for solving the repeated squaring problem [Dix81,Pom87,LLMP90] (via factoring the modulus N). In other words, the verifier would run in enough time to be able to solve the repeated squaring problem itself. This is a very similar problem to issue (3) regarding the [LFKN92,GKR08] protocols, so we appear to be stuck.

Computing bad-challenge functions with low probability. We overcome the above problem with the following idea:

> What if we give up on computing the bad-challenge function *exactly*, and instead use a *faster* randomized algorithm with *low success probability*?

In other words, we consider a new variant of the [CCH+19] framework for instantiating Fiat-Shamir in the standard model, where:

- An interactive protocol Π is characterized by some bad-challenge function f,
- f can be computed by a time t algorithm (or size s circuit) with some small but non-trivial probability δ.
- The hash function $\mathcal{H}$ is assumed to be correlation intractable – with sufficiently strong quantitative security – against adversaries running in time t (or with size s).

Then, it turns out that the resulting non-interactive protocol is sound! Informally, this is because if f "approximated" by a time t-computable randomized function g_r (in the sense that $g_r(x)$ and $f(x)$ agree with probability δ on a worst-case input), then an adversary breaking the protocol $\Pi_{\mathrm{FS},\mathcal{H}}$ will break the correlation intractability of $\mathcal{H}$ with respect to g (rather than f) with probability δ. More formally, a cheating prover P_{FS}^* yields an algorithm that breaks the correlation intractability of $\mathcal{H}$ with respect to f, which in turn breaks the correlation intractability of $\mathcal{H}$ with respect to g_r (for hard-coded randomness

---

[9] See [JOP14] for a detailed discussion of the state-of-the-art on discrete logarithm algorithms.

r) with probability $\delta \cdot \frac{1}{\text{poly}(\lambda)}$ (since g_r and f agree on an arbitrary input with probability at least δ). Therefore, if $\mathcal{H}$ is $(t, \delta \cdot \lambda^{-\omega(1)})$-secure, we conclude that $\Pi_{\text{FS},\mathcal{H}}$ is sound.

This modification allows us to instantiate Fiat-Shamir for the [Pie18] protocol. In particular, we make use of folklore[10] [CCRR18] *preprocessing algorithms* for the discrete logarithm problem over $\mathbb{Z}_p^\times$ that run in time 2^{λ^ϵ} and have success probability $2^{-\lambda^{1-\epsilon}}$. More specifically, we consider a computation of the bad challenge function $f(N, T, g, h, u)$ in the following model:

- Hard-code (1) the factorization $N = pq$, (2) an appropriately chosen group element $\tilde{g}$ of high order, and (3) $2^{\tilde{O}(\lambda^\epsilon)}$ discrete logarithms (of fixed numbers modulo p and modulo q, respectively) in base $\tilde{g}$.
- Compute a (constant-size) collection of worst-case discrete logarithms by the standard index calculus algorithm [Adl79] in time $2^{\tilde{O}(\lambda^\epsilon)}$ with success probability $2^{-\lambda^{1-\epsilon}}$.

This can be thought of as either a non-uniform $2^{\tilde{O}(\lambda^\epsilon)}$-time algorithm, or a $2^{\tilde{O}(\lambda^\epsilon)}$-time algorithm with $2^{\tilde{O}(\lambda^{1/2})}$-time preprocessing.[11] By using this algorithm for the computation of the bad-challenge function $f(N, T, g, h, u)$, we obtain a Fiat-Shamir instantiation with verification time $2^{\tilde{O}(\lambda^\epsilon)}$ – a meaningful result as long as this runtime does not allow for solving the repeated squaring problem. Finally, the required assumption is that the [PS19] hash function is correlation intractable for adversaries that succeed with probability $2^{-\lambda^{1-\epsilon}}$, which holds under the claimed LWE assumption with parameters (n, q) for $\lambda = n \log q$.

Generalizations. In this overview, we focused specifically on the [Pie18] protocol, but our techniques give general blueprints for obtaining Fiat-Shamir instantiations. We believe these blueprints may be useful in future work, so we state them (as "meta-theorems") explicitly here:

- **Fiat-Shamir for protocols with low success probability bad-challenge functions**. Our approach shows that if an interactive protocol Π is governed by a bad-challenge function f that is computable by an efficient randomized algorithm that is only correct with (potentially very) low probability, it is still possible to instantiate Fiat-Shamir for Π under a sufficiently strong LWE assumption.
- **Fiat-Shamir for discrete-log based bad-challenge functions**. Our approach also shows that if a protocol Π is governed by a bad-challenge function

---

[10] We are not aware of prior work considering this particular time-probability trade-off, but the necessary smooth number bounds appear in [CEP83,Gra08]. Quite curiously, [CCRR18] considers the poly(λ)-time variant of this algorithm to give evidence against the optimal hardness of computing discrete logarithms over $\mathbb{Z}_p^\times$. That was bad for them, but for us, the non-optimal hardness is a feature!.

[11] This second variant allows for an invocation of correlation intractability against uniform adversaries in the security proof.

f that is efficiently computable given *oracle access*[12] to a *discrete log solver* (over $\mathbb{Z}_p^\times$ for $p \leq 2^{O(\lambda)}$), then it is possible to instantiate Fiat-Shamir for Π under a sufficiently strong LWE assumption.

We formalize both of these "meta-theorems" in the language of correlation intractability (rather than Fiat-Shamir) in the full version of this paper.

References

[ABF+20] Albrecht, M., Bai, S., Fouque, P.-A., Kirchner, P., Stehlé, D., Wen, W.: Faster enumeration-based lattice reduction: root Hermite factor $k^{1/(2k)}$ in time $k^{k/8+o(k)}$. In: CRYPTO (2020)

[Adl79] Adleman, L.: A subexponential algorithm for the discrete logarithm problem with applications to cryptography. In: 20th Annual Symposium on Foundations of Computer Science (SFCS 1979), pp. 55–60. IEEE (1979)

[ADRS15] Aggarwal, D., Dadush, D., Regev, O., Stephens-Davidowitz, N.: Solving the shortest vector problem in 2n time using discrete gaussian sampling. In: STOC 2015, pp. 733–742 (2015)

[AJL+19] Ananth, P., Jain, A., Lin, H., Matt, C., Sahai, A.: Indistinguishability obfuscation without multilinear maps: new paradigms via low degree weak pseudorandomness and security amplification. In: CRYPTO (2019)

[AKV04] Abbot, T., Kane, D., Valiant, P.: On algorithms for nash equilibria. Unpublished Manuscript 1 (2004). http://web.mit.edu/tabbott/Public/final.pdf

[Bar01] Barak, B.: How to go beyond the black-box simulation barrier. In: Proceedings 42nd IEEE Symposium on Foundations of Computer Science, pp. 106–115. IEEE (2001)

[BBBF18] Boneh, D., Bonneau, J., Bünz, B., Fisch, B.: Verifiable delay functions. In: Shacham, H., Boldyreva, A. (eds.) CRYPTO 2018. LNCS, vol. 10991, pp. 757–788. Springer, Cham (2018). https://doi.org/10.1007/978-3-319-96884-1_25. (EUROCRYPT 2018)

[BBH+19] Bartusek, J., Bronfman, L., Holmgren, J., Ma, F., Rothblum, R.D.: On the (in)security of Kilian-based SNARGs. In: Hofheinz, D., Rosen, A. (eds.) TCC 2019. LNCS, vol. 11892, pp. 522–551. Springer, Cham (2019). https://doi.org/10.1007/978-3-030-36033-7_20

[BCS16] Ben-Sasson, E., Chiesa, A., Spooner, N.: Interactive oracle proofs. In: Hirt, M., Smith, A. (eds.) TCC 2016. LNCS, vol. 9986, pp. 31–60. Springer, Heidelberg (2016). https://doi.org/10.1007/978-3-662-53644-5_2

[BDGM20] Brakerski, Z., Döttling, N., Garg, S., Malavolta, G.: Candidate iO from homomorphic encryption schemes. In: Canteaut, A., Ishai, Y. (eds.) EUROCRYPT 2020. LNCS, vol. 12105, pp. 79–109. Springer, Cham (2020). https://doi.org/10.1007/978-3-030-45721-1_4

[BFJ+19] Badrinarayanan, S., Fernando, R., Jain, A., Khurana, D., Sahai, A.: Statistical ZAP arguments. In: Canteaut, A., Ishai, Y. (eds.) EUROCRYPT 2020. LNCS, vol. 12107, pp. 642–667. Springer, Cham (2020). https://doi.org/10.1007/978-3-030-45727-3_22

---

[12] Crucially, we must also bound the number of calls that can be made to the oracle to be at most poly $\log(\lambda)$ to get a meaningful result.

[BG20]   Bitansky, N., Gerichter, I.: On the cryptographic hardness of local search. In: 11th Innovations in Theoretical Computer Science Conference (ITCS 2020). Schloss Dagstuhl-Leibniz-Zentrum für Informatik (2020)

[BGI+01] Barak, B., Goldreich, O., Impagliazzo, R., Rudich, S., Sahai, A., Vadhan, S., Yang, K.: On the (im)possibility of obfuscating programs. In: Kilian, J. (ed.) CRYPTO 2001. LNCS, vol. 2139, pp. 1–18. Springer, Heidelberg (2001). https://doi.org/10.1007/3-540-44647-8_1. Journal version appears in JACM 2012

[BLP+13] Brakerski, Z., Langlois, A., Peikert, C., Regev, O., Stehlé, D.: Classical hardness of learning with errors. In: STOC 2013, pp. 575–584. ACM (2013)

[BLS16]   Bai, S., Laarhoven, T., Stehlé, D.: Tuple lattice sieving. LMS J. Comput. Math. **19**(A), 146–162 (2016)

[Blu86]   Blum, M.: How to prove a theorem so no one else can claim it. In: Proceedings of the International Congress of Mathematicians, vol. 1, pp. 2. Citeseer (1986)

[BLV06]   Barak, B., Lindell, Y., Vadhan, S.: Lower bounds for non-black-box zero knowledge. J. Comput. Syst. Sci. **72**(2), 321–391 (2006)

[BPR15]   Bitansky, N., Paneth, O., Rosen, A.: On the cryptographic hardness of finding a nash equilibrium. In: FOCS 2015. IEEE (2015)

[BR93]   Bellare, M., Rogaway, P.: Random oracles are practical: a paradigm for designing efficient protocols. In: Proceedings of the 1st ACM Conference on Computer and communications security, pp. 62–73. ACM (1993)

[CCH+18] Canetti, R., Chen, Y., Holmgren, J., Lombardi, A., Rothblum, G.N., Rothblum, R.D.: Fiat-Shamir from simpler assumptions. IACR Cryptol. ePrint Arch. **2018**, 1004 (2018)

[CCH+19] Canetti, R., et al.: Fiat-Shamir: from practice to theory. In: STOC 2019. ACM (2019). Merge of [CCH+18] and [CLW18]

[CCR16]   Canetti, R., Chen, Y., Reyzin, L.: On the correlation intractability of obfuscated pseudorandom functions. In: Kushilevitz, E., Malkin, T. (eds.) TCC 2016. LNCS, vol. 9562, pp. 389–415. Springer, Heidelberg (2016). https://doi.org/10.1007/978-3-662-49096-9_17

[CCRR18] Canetti, R., Chen, Y., Reyzin, L., Rothblum, R.D.: Fiat-Shamir and correlation intractability from strong KDM-secure encryption. In: Nielsen, J.B., Rijmen, V. (eds.) EUROCRYPT 2018. LNCS, vol. 10820, pp. 91–122. Springer, Cham (2018). https://doi.org/10.1007/978-3-319-78381-9_4

[CDT09]   Chen, X., Deng, X., Teng, S.-H.: Settling the complexity of computing two-player nash equilibria. J. ACM (JACM) **56**(3), 1–57 (2009)

[CEP83]   Canfield, E.R., Erdös, P., Pomerance, C.: On a problem of oppenheim concerning "factorisatio numerorum". J. Number Theory **17**(1), 1–28 (1983)

[CGGM00] Canetti, R., Goldreich, O., Goldwasser, S., Micali, S.: Resettable zero-knowledge. In: STOC 2000, pp. 235–244 (2000)

[CGH04]   Canetti, R., Goldreich, O., Halevi, S.: The random oracle methodology, revisited. J. ACM (JACM) **51**(4), 557–594 (2004)

[CHK+19a] Choudhuri, A.R., Hubáček, P., Kamath, C., Pietrzak, K., Rosen, A., Rothblum, G.N.: Finding a nash equilibrium is no easier than breaking Fiat-Shamir. In: STOC 2019 (2019)

[CHK+19b] Choudhuri, A.R., Hubáček, P., Kamath, C., Pietrzak, K., Rosen, A., Rothblum, G.N.: PPAD-hardness via iterated squaring modulo a composite. Cryptology ePrint Archive, Report 2019/667, 2019 (2019)

[CLW18] Canetti, R., Lombardi, A., Wichs, D.: Fiat-shamir: from practice to theory, part II (non-interactive zero knowledge and correlation intractability from circular-secure FHE). IACR Cryptol. ePrint Arch. **2018**, 1248 (2018)

[dFMPS19] De Feo, L., Masson, S., Petit, C., Sanso, A.: Verifiable delay functions from supersingular isogenies and pairings. In: Galbraith, S.D., Moriai, S. (eds.) ASIACRYPT 2019. LNCS, vol. 11921, pp. 248–277. Springer, Cham (2019). https://doi.org/10.1007/978-3-030-34578-5_10

[DGP09] Daskalakis, C., Goldberg, P.W., Papadimitriou, C.H.: The complexity of computing a nash equilibrium. SIAM J. Comput. **39**(1), 195–259 (2009)

[Dix81] Dixon, J.D.: Asymptotically fast factorization of integers. Math. Comput. **36**(153), 255–260 (1981)

[DNRS99] Dwork, C., Naor, M., Reingold, O., Stockmeyer, L.: Magic functions. In: FOCS (1999)

[DP11] Daskalakis, C., Papadimitriou, C.: Continuous local search. In: SODA 2011, pp. 790–804. SIAM (2011)

[EFKP19] Ephraim, N., Freitag, C., Komargodski, I., Pass, R.: Continuous verifiable delay functions. In: EUROCRYPT 2020 (2019)

[Fab19] After 20 years, someone finally solved this MIT puzzle (2019)

[FLS99] Feige, U., Lapidot, D., Shamir, A.: Multiple noninteractive zero knowledge proofs under general assumptions. SIAM J. Comput. **29**(1), 1–28 (1999)

[FS86] Fiat, A., Shamir, A.: How to prove yourself: practical solutions to identification and signature problems. In: Odlyzko, A.M. (ed.) CRYPTO 1986. LNCS, vol. 263, pp. 186–194. Springer, Heidelberg (1987). https://doi.org/10.1007/3-540-47721-7_12

[GGH+13] Garg, S., Gentry, C., Halevi, S., Raykova, M., Sahai, A., Waters, B.: Candidate indistinguishability obfuscation and functional encryption for all circuits. In: FOCS 2013 (2013)

[GK03] Goldwasser, S., Kalai, Y.T.: On the (in)security of the Fiat-Shamir paradigm. In: FOCS 2003, pp. 102–113. IEEE (2003)

[GKR08] Goldwasser, S., Kalai, Y.T., Rothblum, G.N.: Delegating computation: interactive proofs for muggles. In: STOC 2008, pp. 113–122. ACM (2008)

[GMR85] Goldwasser, S., Micali, S., Rackoff, C.: The knowledge complexity of interactive proof-systems. In: STOC 1985, pp. 291–304. ACM (1985)

[GMW91] Goldreich, O., Micali, S., Wigderson, A.: Proofs that yield nothing but their validity or all languages in NP have zero-knowledge proof systems. J. ACM (JACM) **38**(3), 690–728 (1991)

[GPS16] Garg, S., Pandey, O., Srinivasan, A.: Revisiting the cryptographic hardness of finding a nash equilibrium. In: Robshaw, M., Katz, J. (eds.) CRYPTO 2016. LNCS, vol. 9815, pp. 579–604. Springer, Heidelberg (2016). https://doi.org/10.1007/978-3-662-53008-5_20

[Gra08] Granville, A.: Smooth numbers: computational number theory and beyond. Algorithm. Number Theory Lattices Number Fields Curves Cryptograph. **44**, 267–323 (2008)

[HL18] Holmgren, J., Lombardi, A.: Cryptographic hashing from strong one-way functions. In: FOCS 2018 (2018)

[HY17] Hubáček, P., Yogev, E.: Hardness of continuous local search: query complexity and cryptographic lower bounds. In: SODA 2017, pp. 1352–1371. SIAM (2017)

[JJ19] Jain, A., Jin, Z.: Statistical zap arguments from quasi-polynomial LWE. In: EUROCRYPT 2020 (2019)

[JLMS19] Jain, A., Lin, H., Matt, C., Sahai, A.: How to leverage hardness of constant-degree expanding polynomials over $\mathbb{R}$ to build $i\mathcal{O}$. In: Ishai, Y., Rijmen, V. (eds.) EUROCRYPT 2019. LNCS, vol. 11476, pp. 251–281. Springer, Cham (2019). https://doi.org/10.1007/978-3-030-17653-2_9

[JLS19] Jain, A., Lin, H., Sahai, A.: Simplifying constructions and assumptions for $i\mathcal{O}$. Cryptology ePrint Archive, Report 2019/1252 (2019)

[JOP14] Joux, A., Odlyzko, A., Pierrot, C.: The past, evolving present, and future of the discrete logarithm. In: Koç, Ç.K. (ed.) Open Problems in Mathematics and Computational Science, pp. 5–36. Springer, Cham (2014). https://doi.org/10.1007/978-3-319-10683-0_2

[Kan83] Kannan, R.: Improved algorithms for integer programming and related lattice problems. In: STOC 1983, pp. 193–206 (1983)

[KF16] Kirchner, P., Fouque, P.-A.: Time-memory trade-off for lattice enumeration in a ball. IACR Cryptol. ePrint Arch. **2016**, 222 (2016)

[KPY19] Kalai, Y.T., Paneth, O., Yang, L.: How to delegate computations publicly. In: STOC 2019, pp. 1115–1124 (2019)

[KPY20] Kalai, Y., Paneth, O., Yang, L.: PPAD-hardness and delegation with unambiguous and updatable proofs. In: CRYPTO 2020 (2020)

[KRR17] Kalai, Y.T., Rothblum, G.N., Rothblum, R.D.: From obfuscation to the security of Fiat-Shamir for proofs. In: Katz, J., Shacham, H. (eds.) CRYPTO 2017. LNCS, vol. 10402, pp. 224–251. Springer, Cham (2017). https://doi.org/10.1007/978-3-319-63715-0_8

[LFKN92] Lund, C., Fortnow, L., Karloff, H.J., Nisan, N.: Algebraic methods for interactive proof systems. J. ACM **39**(4), 859–868 (1992)

[LLMP90] Lenstra, A.K., Lenstra Jr., H.W., Manasse, M.S., Pollard, J.M.: The number field sieve. In: STOC 1990, pp. 564–572 (1990)

[LV20] Lombardi, A., Vaikuntanathan, V.: Fiat-Shamir for repeated squaring with applications to PPAD-hardness and VDFs. IACR Cryptology ePrint Archive, Report 2020/772 (2020). https://eprint.iacr.org/2020/772

[LVW19] Lombardi, A., Vaikuntanathan, V., Wichs, D.: 2-message publicly verifiable WI from (subexponential) LWE. Cryptology ePrint Archive, Report 2019/808 (2019)

[Mic00] Micali, S.: Computationally sound proofs. SIAM J. Comput. **30**(4), 1253–1298 (2000)

[Nao03] Naor, M.: On cryptographic assumptions and challenges. In: Boneh, D. (ed.) CRYPTO 2003. LNCS, vol. 2729, pp. 96–109. Springer, Heidelberg (2003). https://doi.org/10.1007/978-3-540-45146-4_6

[Pap94] Papadimitriou, C.H.: On the complexity of the parity argument and other inefficient proofs of existence. J. Comput. Syst. Sci. **48**(3), 498–532 (1994)

[Pei16] Peikert, C.: A decade of lattice cryptography. Found. Trends Theor. Comput. Sci. **10**(4), 283–424 (2016)

[Pie18] Pietrzak, K.: Simple verifiable delay functions. In: ITCS 2019 (2018)

[Pom87] Pomerance, C.: Fast, rigorous factorization and discrete logarithm algorithms. In: Discrete Algorithms and Complexity, pp. 119–143. Elsevier (1987)

[PRS17] Peikert, C., Regev, O., Stephens-Davidowitz, N.: Pseudorandomness of ring-LWE for any ring and modulus. In: STOC 2017, pp. 461–473. ACM (2017)

[PS96] Pointcheval, D., Stern, J.: Security proofs for signature schemes. In: Maurer, U. (ed.) EUROCRYPT 1996. LNCS, vol. 1070, pp. 387–398. Springer, Heidelberg (1996). https://doi.org/10.1007/3-540-68339-9_33

[PS19]   Peikert, C., Shiehian, S.: Noninteractive zero knowledge for NP from (Plain) learning with errors. In: Boldyreva, A., Micciancio, D. (eds.) CRYPTO 2019. LNCS, vol. 11692, pp. 89–114. Springer, Cham (2019). https://doi.org/10.1007/978-3-030-26948-7_4

[Reg09] Regev, O.: On lattices, learning with errors, random linear codes, and cryptography. J. ACM (JACM) **56**(6), 34 (2009)

[Riv99] Description of the LCS35 time capsule crypto-puzzle (1999)

[RRR16] Reingold, O., Rothblum, G.N., Rothblum, R.D.: Constant-round interactive proofs for delegating computation. SIAM J. Comput. STOC16-255 (2016)

[RSW96] Rivest, R.L., Shamir, A., Wagner, D.A.: Time-lock puzzles and timed-release crypto (1996)

[Sch89] Schnorr, C.P.: Efficient identification and signatures for smart cards. In: Brassard, G. (ed.) CRYPTO 1989. LNCS, vol. 435, pp. 239–252. Springer, New York (1990). https://doi.org/10.1007/0-387-34805-0_22

[Val08] Valiant, P.: Incrementally verifiable computation or proofs of knowledge imply time/space efficiency. In: Canetti, R. (ed.) TCC 2008. LNCS, vol. 4948, pp. 1–18. Springer, Heidelberg (2008). https://doi.org/10.1007/978-3-540-78524-8_1

[Wes19] Wesolowski, B.: Efficient verifiable delay functions. In: Ishai, Y., Rijmen, V. (eds.) EUROCRYPT 2019. LNCS, vol. 11478, pp. 379–407. Springer, Cham (2019). https://doi.org/10.1007/978-3-030-17659-4_13

Delegation with Updatable Unambiguous Proofs and PPAD-Hardness

Yael Tauman Kalai[1,3], Omer Paneth[2], and Lisa Yang[3(✉)]

[1] Microsoft Research, Cambridge, USA
[2] Tel Aviv University, Tel Aviv, Israel
[3] MIT, Cambridge, USA
lisayang1297@gmail.com

Abstract. In this work, we construct an *updatable* and *unambiguous* delegation scheme based on the decisional assumption on bilinear groups introduced by Kalai, Paneth and Yang [STOC 2019]. Using this delegation scheme, we show **PPAD**-hardness (and hence the hardness of computing Nash equilibria) based on the quasi-polynomial hardness of this bilinear group assumption and any hard language that is decidable in quasi-polynomial time and polynomial space.

The delegation scheme is for super-polynomial time deterministic computations and is publicly verifiable and non-interactive in the common reference string (CRS) model. It is *updatable* meaning that given a proof for the statement that a Turing machine reaches some configuration C in T steps, it is *efficient* to update it into a proof for the statement that the machine reaches the next configuration C' in $T + 1$ steps. It is *unambiguous* meaning that it is hard to find two different proofs for the same statement.

Keywords: PPAD-hardness · Delegation · Unambiguous proofs · Zero-testable encryption.

O. Paneth—Member of the Check Point Institute of Information Security. Suported by an Azrieli Faculty Fellowship, by Len Blavatnik and the Blavatnik Foundation, by the Blavatnik Interdisciplinary Cyber Research Center at Tel Aviv University, and ISF grant 1789/19. Part of this research was done while at MIT and Northeastern University and supported by NSF Grants CNS-1413964, CNS-1350619 and CNS-1414119, and the Defense Advanced Research Projects Agency (DARPA) and the U.S. Army Research Office (ARO) under contracts W911NF-15-C-0226 and W911NF-15-C-0236. Any opinions, findings and conclusions or recommendations expressed in this material are those of the author(s) and do not necessarily reflect the views of the DARPA and ARO.

L. Yang—Part of this research was done at Microsoft Research. This material is based upon work supported by the National Science Foundation Graduate Research Fellowship grant 174530, NSF/BSF grant 1350619, an MIT-IBM grant, and a DARPA Young Faculty Award.

D. Micciancio and T. Ristenpart (Eds.): CRYPTO 2020, LNCS 12172, pp. 652–673, 2020.
https://doi.org/10.1007/978-3-030-56877-1_23

1   Introduction

The computational complexity of finding a Nash equilibrium in bimatrix games has been the subject of extensive research in recent years. In his seminal work, Papadimitriou [27] defined the complexity class **PPAD** and showed that it contains the problem NASH. Daskalakis, Goldberg and Papadimitriou [14], and Chen, Deng and Teng [11] proved that NASH is **PPAD**-complete.

   Currently polynomial (or even subexponential) time algorithms for **PPAD** are not known and NASH is conjectured to be intractable. A promising approach to proving the hardness of **PPAD**, proposed by Papadimitriou, is to base its hardness on assumptions from cryptography. Despite tremendous progress in this direction over the past five years, **PPAD**-hardness is only known under very strong and "non-standard" cryptographic assumptions. Building on [1], Bitanski, Paneth and Rosen [6] show that **PPAD** is hard on average assuming sub-exponentially secure indistinguishability obfuscation. Hubáček and Yogev [19] extended this result to **CLS**, a subclass of **PPAD**. The assumption was relaxed in [18,23] from indistinguishability obfuscation to strong assumptions related to functional encryption. Very recently, Choudhuri et al. [12,13] and Ephraim et al. [17] showed average-case hardness of **PPAD** under an assumption closely related to the soundness of the Fiat-Shamir heuristic when applied to specific protocols. See Sect. 2.3 for more details on related work.

   Basing **PPAD**-hardness on weaker, well-studied cryptographic assumptions remains an important goal.

This work. We prove hardness of **CLS** and **PPAD**, under the following assumptions:

1. A decisional assumption on groups with bilinear maps (Assumption 1.3). This is a quasi-polynomial version of an assumption recently introduced by [20]. It is falsifiable (in quasi-polynomial time) and it holds in the generic group model.
2. The existence of a hard language L that can be decided in time $n^{(\log n)^\epsilon}$ for some $\epsilon < 1$ and polynomial space. For example, the assumption that SAT over $m = (\log n)^{1+\epsilon}$ variables is hard for 2^{m^c}-size circuits for some $c < 1$ suffices. If L is hard on average we show average-case hardness of **PPAD**.

   Our result follows a similar approach to that of Choudhuri et al. [13] exploiting a folklore connection between **PPAD** and the notion of incrementally verifiable computation [32]. Specifically, we consider delegation schemes that are both *updatable* and *unambiguous*. Loosely speaking, a delegation scheme for T-time computations is a computationally sound proof system that can be verified in time $<< T$. For the purpose of proving **PPAD**-hardness, in this work we focus on publicly verifiable non-interactive schemes in the CRS model for delegating super-polynomial time computations with polynomial-time verification.[1] A dele-

---

[1] More generally, in the literature delegation may also refer to privately verifiable schemes and interactive schemes. The focus is often on delegating polynomial-time computations with near linear-time verification.

gation scheme is said to be *updatable* if given a proof of correctness for the first t steps of a computation, we can extend it to a proof of correctness of the first $t+1$ steps without recomputing the proof from scratch (that is, in time independent of t). A delegation scheme is said to be *unambiguous* if it is computationally hard to construct two different accepting proofs for the same statement.

We show that the existence of such a delegation scheme for a hard language L as above, implies the hardness of a problem known as RELAXED-SINK-OF-VERIFIABLE-LINE (rSVL) that was defined and reduced to a problem in **CLS** in [13].

Theorem 1.1 (Informal). *Let L be a hard (resp. hard on average) language decidable by a deterministic Turing machine running in time $T(n) = n^{\omega(1)}$ and space $S(n) = \mathrm{poly}(n)$. If there exists an updatable and unambiguous delegation scheme for L then rSVL is hard (resp. hard on average).*

We refer the reader to Theorem 4.1 for the formal statement, to Definitions 3.1–3.3 for updatable and unambiguous delegation schemes, and to Definition 4.1 for the rSVL problem.

Our main technical and conceptual contribution is the construction of such a delegation scheme. Specifically, we show that for any $\epsilon < 1$ and $T = T(n) \leq n^{(\log n)^{\epsilon}}$ there exists an updatable and unambiguous delegation scheme for any T-time polynomial-space computation under Assumption 1.3 below.

Theorem 1.2 (Informal). *For any deterministic Turing machine $\mathcal{M}$ that runs in time $T(n) \leq n^{(\log n)^{\epsilon}}$ for some $0 \leq \epsilon < 1$ and space $S(n) = \mathrm{poly}(n)$ the following holds: Under Λ-hardness of Assumption 1.3 for $\Lambda(\kappa) = 2^{(\log \kappa)^{\frac{1+\epsilon}{1-\epsilon}}}$, there exists an updatable and unambiguous delegation scheme for $\mathcal{M}$ with setup time and proof length $\mathrm{poly}(S(n))$. The prover runs in time $T(n) \cdot \mathrm{poly}(S(n))$ and the verifier runs in time $\mathrm{poly}(S(n))$.*

We refer the reader to Sect. 5 for the formal statement (and a more general setting of parameters). We note that in Theorem 1.2 the efficiency of the delegation scheme grows with the space of the computation. We believe that this dependence can be removed using standard techniques [20, 22]. However, we did not pursue this in the current work since it would complicate the proof and it is not needed for showing **PPAD**-hardness.

Assumption 1.3 is a version of the bilinear group assumption from [20] with a hardness parameter $\Lambda = \Lambda(\kappa)$. We mention that [20] rely on this assumption for $\Lambda(\kappa) = \mathrm{poly}(\kappa)$ to construct a delegation scheme for polynomial-time computations. To construct a delegation scheme for super-polynomial time computations, towards showing **PPAD**-hardness, we rely on this assumption for super-polynomial $\Lambda(\kappa)$.

Assumption 1.3. *Let G be a group of prime order $p = 2^{\Theta(\kappa)}$ equipped with a bilinear map. For every $\alpha(\kappa) = O(\log \Lambda(\kappa))$ given the following 3-by-α matrix of group elements:*

$$\left(g^{s^j t^i}\right)_{\substack{i\in[0,2]\\j\in[0,\alpha]}} = \begin{pmatrix} g^{s^0} & g^{s^1} & \cdots & g^{s^\alpha} \\ g^{s^0 t} & g^{s^1 t} & \cdots & g^{s^\alpha t} \\ g^{s^0 t^2} & g^{s^1 t^2} & \cdots & g^{s^\alpha t^2} \end{pmatrix},$$

for random $g \in G$ and $s \in \mathbb{Z}_p$, it is $\Lambda(\kappa)$-hard to distinguish between the case where $t = s^{2\alpha+1}$ and the case where t is a random independent element in $\mathbb{Z}_p$.

2 Technical Overview

In this section we give an overview of our delegation scheme with unambiguous and updatable proofs. We build on the non-interactive delegation scheme of [20] (KPY) and we start by recalling the high-level structure of their scheme.

2.1 The KPY Delegation Scheme

The KPY construction consists of two steps: first, they construct *quasi-arguments* for **NP** which, following [22], are known to imply delegation for **P**. The KPY quasi-arguments have a long CRS which results in a delegation scheme for **P** with a long CRS (of length proportional to the running time of the computation). Then they use quasi-arguments again to "bootstrap" a delegation scheme with a long CRS to get a delegation scheme with a short CRS.

Quasi-arguments. A quasi-argument is a relaxation of an argument-of-knowledge: in a quasi-argument, the standard knowledge extraction requirement is replaced by a weaker requirement called *non-signaling (local) extraction*. To argue about locality, the definition specifically considers the **NP** complete language 3SAT. Roughly speaking, in an argument-of-knowledge for 3SAT, for any prover that convinces the verifier to accept a formula φ there exists an extractor that produces a satisfying assignment for φ. In a quasi-argument, however, the extractor is not required to produce a full assignment. Rather it is given a *small* set of variables $\mathbf{S}$ and it produces an assignment only for the variables in $\mathbf{S}$. This partial assignment is required to be *locally consistent*, satisfying every clause of φ over variables in $\mathbf{S}$. Furthermore, the partial assignments produced by the extractor should satisfy the *non-signaling* property. Loosely speaking, this property requires that for any subsets $\mathbf{S} \subset \mathbf{S}'$ the distribution of the assignments produced by the extractor for the variables in $\mathbf{S}'$, when restricted to the variables in $\mathbf{S}$, is independent of the variables in $\mathbf{S}' \setminus \mathbf{S}$. The notion of a quasi-argument was introduced in [26] under the name "core protocol with a local assignment generator". Prior works including [8,21,22] (implicitly) construct *privately verifiable two-message* quasi-arguments for **NP**.

The BMW heuristic. The KPY quasi-argument is inspired by the BMW heuristic [2] for converting a multi-prover interactive proof (MIP) into a two-message privately verifiable delegation scheme. In this delegation scheme, the verifier generates the MIP queries, encrypts each query using a homomorphic encryption scheme (with a fresh key), and sends the encrypted queries to the prover. The prover then homomorphically computes the encrypted answers, and the verifier decrypts and checks the answers. While this heuristic is known to be insecure in general [15,16], the work of [21] shows that it is sound for MIPs satisfying a strong soundness condition called non-signaling soundness.

From private to public verification. To obtain a publicly verifiable non-interactive delegation scheme, KPY follow the blueprint of Paneth and Rothblum (PR) [26] and place the encrypted queries in the CRS. Now, since the verifier does not encrypt the queries itself, it can no longer decrypt the answers. Instead, the queries are encrypted using a special homomorphic encryption equipped with a *weak zero-test* that allows the verifier to check the validity of the prover's answers without decrypting them. Modularizing the analysis of [21,22], PR show that the resulting protocol is a quasi-argument for **NP**.

The CRS length. Unlike the PR solution that was based on mulilinear maps, KPY construct a zero-testable homomorphic encryption scheme based only on bilinear maps. In the KPY scheme, however, the ciphertext length grows exponentially with the length of the encrypted query. This results in a quasi-argument with a long CRS. To shorten the CRS, KPY use an idea known as "bootstrapping" that was previously used to obtain succinct arguments of knowledge for **NP** (SNARKs) with a sort CRS [3,32]. In this setting, a SNARK with a long CRS is recursively composed with itself yielding a SNARK with a short CRS. In contrast, KPY compose a delegation scheme for **P** and a quasi-argument for **NP**, both with a long CRS to obtain a delegation scheme for **P** with a short CRS.

2.2   Our Delegation Scheme

We modify the KPY delegation scheme to make its proofs updatable and unambiguous. Obtaining updatability is fairly straightforward. Previous work [3,32] used recursive proof composition to merge proofs and applied this technique both for bootstrapping proofs (with the goal of shortening the CRS), and for creating updatable proofs. In the setting of delegation for **P**, the work of KPY shows how to use quasi-arguments to merge proofs for bootstrapping. Following KPY, our work shows how to use quasi-arguments to merge proofs for updatability.

The main technical challenge and the focus of the following overview is achieving unambiguity. We first construct quasi-arguments for **NP** with a long CRS that satisfy a notion of unambiguity. Then we argue that unambiguity is preserved in the bootstrapping step. We mention that in addition to satisfying the unambiguity property, our quasi-arguments are also more efficient than the quasi-arguments in KPY. As a result, we can delegate $n^{\log n^\epsilon}$-time polynomial-space computations with a $\mathrm{poly}(n)$-size CRS, as opposed to KPY that could only delegate $n^{O(\log \log n)}$-time computations.

Unambiguous delegation. The KPY delegation scheme is obtained by recursively composing a quasi-argument. Abstracting away the details of this bootstrapping step, the final delegation scheme has the following structure: the description of the deterministic computation is translated into a sequence of formulas, and the proof consists of one quasi-argument proof for each formula. Therefore, to get an unambiguous delegation scheme we focus on constructing unambiguous quasi-arguments.

Unambiguous quasi-arguments. In contrast to delegation for deterministic computations, quasi-arguments argue about non-deterministic formulas. We therefore need to take care in defining the required notion of unambiguity. The strongest requirement would be that the prover cannot find two accepting proofs for the same formula, even if the formula has multiple satisfying assignments. This notion, however, is only known under very strong assumptions [10, 31]. A natural relaxation is to ask for unambiguous proofs only for formulas where the satisfying assignment is unique, or where finding multiple satisfying assignments is intractable. However, even this relaxation seems outside the reach of our techniques. The issue is that there exist formulas where the full satisfying assignment is unique, however, there exists an efficient non-signaling local extractor that can produce multiple locally consistent assignments for every small set of variables (without violating the non-signaling property). We therefore further relax the unambiguity requirement for quasi-arguments to only require that it is hard to find multiple accepting proofs for formulas where any efficient non-signaling local extractor can only produce a unique assignment to each small set of variables. We refer to such formulas as *locally unambiguous*. We observe that instantiating the KPY delegation scheme with a quasi-argument satisfying this notion results in an unambiguous delegation scheme. Indeed, inspecting their soundness proof reveals that each quasi-argument argues about a locally unambiguous formula.

Unambiguous answers and ciphertexts. Next we describe our high-level strategy for making the KPY quasi-argument unambiguous. Recall that in KPY the quasi-argument CRS consists of encrypted MIP queries and the proof contains encrypted answers. Our construction has two steps: first we modify the quasi-argument so the answers encrypted in the proof are unambiguous. That is, for an honestly generated CRS, it is hard to find two accepting proofs for the same locally unambiguous formula that, when decrypted, result in different answers. Then we proceed to argue the unambiguity of the ciphertexts themselves. We show that in the KPY encryption scheme it is hard to find two different ciphertexts that decrypt to the same value without knowing the secret key. Moreover, this task is hard even given the ciphertexts in the CRS. Together, these two steps imply the unambiguity of the quasi-argument proof. We first explain how to achieve unambiguous answers which is the main challenge.

Unambiguity of answers. The MIP queries in the KPY quasi-argument come from $\mathbb{F}^\ell$ where $\mathbb{F}$ is a large field and ℓ is logarithmic in the number of variables in the formula. The prover's answers are given by low-degree polynomials in the queries. The first polynomial evaluated is denoted by X and it encodes the prover's assignment. Specifically, $X : \mathbb{F}^\ell \to \mathbb{F}$ is the multilinear extension of the assignment. That is, X is multilinear, and for every variable Z of the formula there exists a Boolean input $y \in \{0, 1\}^\ell$ such that the assignment to Z is $X(y)$. For each encrypted query in the CRS, the proof contains the evaluation of X on that query as well as evaluations of additional "proof polynomials" that help convince the verifier that the X evaluations are locally consistent. We first show how to make the evaluations of X unambiguous and then extend these techniques to the evaluations of the proof polynomials as well.

Unambiguity of X. Our first goal is to ensure unambiguity of the X evaluations. That is, for a locally unambiguous formula and an honestly generated CRS it should be hard to find two accepting proofs that encrypt different evaluations of X. In fact, we show that for any fixed query $q \in \mathbb{F}^\ell$, the evaluation $X(q)$ is unambiguous regardless of the other queries encrypted in the CRS. We first observe that the KPY quasi-argument already guarantees the unambiguity of $X(q)$ for each Boolean query $q \in \{0, 1\}^\ell$. This follows from the fact that the formula is locally unambiguous and from the construction of their local extractor. To see this, recall that for a Boolean q, the evaluation $X(q)$ gives the assignment to some variable Z of the formula. The KPY extractor, given a small set of variables that contains Z, samples a CRS that contains an encryption of q, evaluates the prover on the CRS and obtains an accepting proof. (If the proof is rejecting, the extractor tries again with fresh randomness.) It then decrypts the value $X(q)$ and returns it as the assignment to Z. Since the formula is locally unambiguous, the value the extractor assigns to Z is unambiguous. Since the CRS sampled by the extractor has the same distribution as an honestly generated CRS that contains an encryption of q, it follows that the evaluation $X(q)$ in the proof is also unambiguous for Boolean q.

Unambiguity of X on general queries. For general non-Boolean queries the KPY quasi-argument does not guarantee unambiguity. To produce a second accepting proof, an adversarial prover can compute a different polynomial $\widetilde{X} \neq X$ that agrees with X on all inputs in $\{0, 1\}^\ell$ such that following the honest prover's strategy using $\widetilde{X}$ instead of X still results in an accepting proof. Note that, unlike X, the individual degree of $\widetilde{X}$ must be > 1 since a multilinear polynomial is completely determined by its evaluations on $\{0, 1\}^\ell$.

Intuitively, our approach is to force the prover to evaluate a polynomial X that is multilinear. Following this intuition, however, is tricky. Recall that the prover does not explicitly specify the polynomial X (this would result in a long proof) and it only evaluates X on a small set of queries. In fact, given a set of queries and answers, there typically exists a multilinear polynomial X that is consistent with them. may not know X in the clear, since he only gets encryptions of these queries. However, this polynomial depends on the queries and answers, in particular, the prover does not know X in the clear. A possible fix is to have the prover provide a short proof of knowledge of the multilinear polynomial X.

In the non-interactive setting, however, such a proof of knowledge is only known based on non-falsifiable knowledge assumptions [4].

A proof of multilinearity. In order to avoid knowledge assumptions, we introduce a new notion of a multilinearity proof that allows us to argue the unambiguity of X on general queries. We then construct such proofs based on our bilinear assumption. In a multilinearity proof the CRS contains an encrypted input $q \leftarrow \mathbb{F}^\ell$. The prover can homomorphically evaluate any multilinear polynomial X on q and provide the encrypted evaluation together with a proof of multilinearity for the question-answer pair. The soundness requirement of our multilinearity proof is defined based on the notion of unambiguity. Roughly speaking, consider an efficient adversarial prover that, with non-negligible probability, produces two different encrypted evaluations and an accepting multilinearity proof for each of the evaluations with respect to the same encrypted input. We require that there exists a Boolean input $q \in \{0,1\}^\ell$ such that the prover continues to produce two distinct evaluations even when given an encryption of q. (Note that this requirement does not follow from the security of the encryption since checking that the answers are distinct requires the secret key.) By adding such a multilinearity proof to each evaluation of X in the KPY quasi-argument, we can directly extend the unambiguity of X on Boolean queries to unambiguity on general queries.

To see why this soundness requirement intuitively captures multilinearity, consider an adversarial prover that evaluates some polynomial $\widetilde{X}$ of individual degree > 1. If the prover was able to provide an accepting multilinearity proof for its evaluation, we would have been able to use this prover to break the soundness requirement as follows: choose a multilinear polynomial X that agrees with $\widetilde{X}$ on all inputs in $\{0,1\}^\ell$, homomorphically evaluate X on the input and compute a multilinearity proof honestly. Output both evaluations and their proofs. This contradicts the soundness of the multi-linearity test since for every Boolean q the two evaluations would always agree, whereas there exists $q \in \mathbb{F}^\ell$ where X and $\widetilde{X}$ disagrees resulting in different evaluations. By the security of the encryption, the prover must output an accepting multilinearity proof with the same probability, regardless of the encrypted input.

Zero-testable encryption. Our multilinearity proof relies on the weak zero-test of the homomorphic encryption used in KPY.[2] Before describing the construction, we describe the properties of this test. The weak zero-test is a public procedure (not using the secret key) that given a ciphertext, tests if it encrypts zero or not. A perfectly accurate zero-test clearly contradicts semantic security. We therefore consider a weak zero-test that has false negatives: it never passes on encryptions of non-zero values, however, it may fail on some encryptions of zero. The test is only guaranteed to pass on "trivial" encryptions of zero which are ciphertexts

---

[2] As a homomorphic encryption scheme, the KPY construction has several drawbacks: it can only encrypt short messages, and it is limited to arity-one one-hop homomorphic computations. For simplicity, in this overview we ignore these limitations.

that result from homomorphically evaluating a polynomial that is identically zero over $\mathbb{F}$ on some fresh ciphertext.

We demonstrate how to use the weak zero-test with the following dummy protocol: the CRS contains an encryption of some input $q \in \mathbb{F}^\ell$. The honest prover homomorphically evaluates three polynomials $A, B, C : \mathbb{F}^\ell \to \mathbb{F}$ on q and sends the verifier the encrypted evaluations a, b, c respectively. The prover claims that its polynomials satisfy the identity $A \cdot B \equiv C$ and therefore also $a \cdot b = c$. The verifier can test this (without the secret key) by homomorphically computing the value $a \cdot b - c$ and zero-testing the resulting ciphertext. If $A \cdot B - C$ is indeed the zero polynomial over $\mathbb{F}$, the verifier evaluates a trivial encryption of zero and the weak zero-test is guaranteed to pass. If, however, $a \cdot b \neq c$ then the verifier's ciphertext encrypts a non-zero value and therefore the weak zero-test fails.

Multilinearity proof from zero-testable encryption. We proceed to construct a multilinearity proof using the zero-testable encryption. To explain the high-level idea, we first describe a simple flawed construction. The CRS contains an input $q \in \mathbb{F}^\ell$ encrypted under a key sk. Given a multilinear polynomial $X : \mathbb{F}^\ell \to \mathbb{F}$, the prover homomorphically computes the evaluation $y = X(q)$. Additionally, for every $i \in [\ell]$ the prover computes the two multilinear polynomials $A_i, B_i : \mathbb{F}^{\ell-1} \to \mathbb{F}$ such that for every $z \in \mathbb{F}^\ell$, $X(z) = A_i(z_{-i}) \cdot z_i + B_i(z_{-i})$ where z_i is the i-th coordinate of z and $z_{-i} \in \mathbb{F}^{\ell-1}$ is z with the i-th coordinate removed. The prover homomorphically evaluates $a_i = A_i(q_{-i})$ and $b_i = B_i(q_{-i})$ and sends these 2ℓ evaluations to the verifier as the proof of multilinearity. Given the encrypted query q, the encrypted evaluation y and the proof, the verifier homomorphically computes the value $a_i \cdot q_i + b_i - y$ for every $i \in [\ell]$, and checks that all the resulting ciphertexts pass the weak zero-test.

The completeness of the proof follows from the properties of the weak zero-test. However, the proposed multilinearity proof is not sound: a cheating prover can evaluate a polynomial $\widetilde{X}$ of individual degree > 1 together with an accepting multilinearity proof by homomorphically computing the values a_i, b_i as a function of the entire query q rather than just q_{-i}. To prevent this, we need to somehow force the prover to compute the evaluations a_i, b_i without using the encryption of q_i. Our solution is to add to the CRS another input q' encrypted under a different key sk'. In addition to the encrypted evaluations y and $\{a_i, b_i\}$, the prover provides the evaluations $\{a_i' = A_i(q_{-i}'), b_i' = B_i(q_{-i}')\}$ which are encrypted under sk'. Now imagine that we set q' to be the same as q except that $q_i' = 0$. Since $q_{-i} = q_{-i}'$, we have that the honest $(a_i, b_i) = (a_i', b_i')$. We would like the prover to somehow convince the verifier that indeed $(a_i, b_i) = (a_i', b_i')$. Intuitively, since q' contains no information about q_i, such a proof would mean that the evaluations a_i, b_i were computed without using q_i. However, proving this equality is clearly impossible: the prover and verifier have neither of the secret keys, and therefore they cannot even test that indeed $q_{-i} = q_{-i}'$. Instead we ask the prover to argue a conditional claim: if $q_{-i} = q_{-i}'$ then $(a_i, b_i) = (a_i', b_i')$. To prove this claim we design a sub-protocol that we call an equality proof.

Soundness of the multilinearity proof. Before delving into the equality proof, we first argue the soundness of the multilinearity proof. The adversarial prover is given the inputs q and q' encrypted under keys sk and sk' respectively, and it outputs the evaluations y, $\{a_i, b_i\}$ and $\{a'_i, b'_i\}$ together with equality proofs that for every $i \in [\ell]$, if $q_{-i} = q'_{-i}$ then $(a_i, b_i) = (a'_i, b'_i)$. We assume that for any Boolean input $q \in \{0,1\}^\ell$ the evaluation y is unambiguous. That is, the prover cannot produce two distinct evaluations together with accepting proofs. We need to show that the same holds for general inputs $q \in \mathbb{F}^\ell$. Focusing on $i = 1$, for every $z_1 \in \{0,1\}$, consider an experiment where the CRS encrypts $q = (z_1, 0^{\ell-1})$ and $q' = 0^\ell$. We first argue that the line given by a'_1, b'_1 is also unambiguous. Since $q_{-1} = q'_{-1}$, when the proof is accepted we have that $(a_1, b_1) = (a'_1, b'_1)$ and therefore $y = a'_1 \cdot z_1 + b'_1$. If the prover could produce two different lines a'_1, b'_1, since y is unambiguous, the two lines must agree on z_1. Therefore, given only sk' we can decrypt the two lines and recover their unique intersection point z_1, thereby contradicting semantic security under sk. Now consider the same experiment except that z_1 is in $\mathbb{F}$ instead of $\{0,1\}$. Again by semantic security, the proof must continue to be accepting and the line a'_1, b'_1 must remain unambiguous (since this can be tested without sk). The equality $q_{-1} = q'_{-1}$ still holds and hence also $y = a'_1 \cdot z_1 + b'_1$. Therefore, this argument shows y must remain unambiguous even for $q \in \mathbb{F} \times \{0,1\}^{\ell-1}$. More generally, for each $i \in [0, \ell - 1]$ we use this argument to show that the unambiguity of y for $q \in \mathbb{F}^i \times \{0,1\}^{\ell-i}$ implies its unambiguity for $q \in \mathbb{F}^{i+1} \times \{0,1\}^{\ell-i-1}$ until we get unambiguity for general inputs $q \in \mathbb{F}^\ell$.

Equality proof. In an equality proof the CRS contains a pair of inputs $q, q' \leftarrow \mathbb{F}^\ell$ each encrypted independently under a different key. The prover can homomorphically evaluate a multilinear[3] polynomial X on both q and q' and provide the encrypted evaluations $y = X(q)$ and $y' = X(q')$ together with a proof of equality. The soundness requirement of our equality proof is that if $q = q'$ and the verifier accepts then $y = y'$ with overwhelming probability. Intuitively, the equality proof does not guarantee that the encrypted evaluations are equal, but that the prover computed both evaluations using the same polynomial.

We construct such an equality proof using the zero-testable encryption. The first challenge is that the inputs q and q' are encrypted under different keys. Fortunately, the zero-testable homomorphic encryption from KPY is multi-key homomorphic[4] and therefore we can compute jointly over q and q' under both keys.

A natural approach to implementing the equality proof is to simply have the verifier homomorphically compute the value $y - y'$ and zero-test the resulting ciphertext. This approach, however, does not achieve completeness. Even if the prover is honestly evaluating the same polynomial X on both inputs, since q

---

[3] Our equality proof supports any polynomial of low individual degree. For simplicity, in this overview we focus on the multilinear case.

[4] In KPY, as well as in this work, multi-key homomorphism is also used to evaluate the proof polynomials over multiple queries that are encrypted under different keys.

are q' are encrypted independently the verifier's ciphertext would be a non-trivial encryption of zero and would fail the zero-test. In more detail, the tested ciphertext is obtained by evaluating the polynomial $D(z, z') = X(z) - X(z')$ on a ciphertext encrypting (q, q'). Unless X is constant, we have that $D(z, z') \neq 0$ for some $z \neq z'$ and hence, starting from a CRS encrypting z and z' would lead the zero-test to fail. Therefore, by semantic security the test must also fail when the CRS encrypts $q = q'$.

Equality proof from zero-testable encryption. Instead we take a different approach. Suppose that the prover's polynomial X is sparse. In this case, the prover can simply send X's coefficients and the verifier can evaluate X on both inputs by itself. For a general polynomial X our idea is inspired by the interactive sum-check proof [25]. In a nutshell, we restrict X to a sequence of axis-parallel lines transitioning from q to q'. Each restriction is sparse and its consistency can be checked by the verifier using the weak zero-test.

In more detail, for every $i \in [\ell]$ the prover computes the polynomials $A_i, B_i :$ $\mathbb{F}^{\ell-1} \to \mathbb{F}$ where $X(z) = A_i(z_{-i}) \cdot z_i + B_i(z_{-i})$. We denote by $\tilde{q}^{(i)}$ the vector whose first i coordinates are from q and whose last $\ell - i$ coordinates are from q' (so $\tilde{q}^{(0)} = q'$ and $\tilde{q}^{(\ell)} = q$). The prover homomorphically computes the evaluations $y = X(q)$ and $y' = X(q')$ and the equality proofs that contain for every $i \in [\ell]$ the encrypted evaluations:

$$y_i = X\left(\tilde{q}^{(i)}\right), \quad a_i = A_i\left(\tilde{q}^{(i)}_{-i}\right), \quad b_i = B_i\left(\tilde{q}^{(i)}_{-i}\right),$$
$$y'_i = X\left(\tilde{q}^{(i-1)}\right), \quad a'_i = A_i\left(\tilde{q}^{(i-1)}_{-i}\right) \quad b'_i = B_i\left(\tilde{q}^{(i-1)}_{-i}\right).$$

The verifier uses the weak zero-test to check that $y' = y'_1$, $y = y_\ell$, and $y_i = y'_{i+1}$ for every $i \in [\ell - 1]$. Additionally, for every $i \in [\ell]$ the verifier checks that $y_i = a_i \cdot q_i + b_i$, $y'_i = a'_i \cdot q'_i + b'_i$, and $(a_i, b_i) = (a'_i, b'_i)$. The completeness of the proof follows from the properties of the weak zero-test together with the fact that, by construction, $\tilde{q}^{(i)}_{-i}$ and $\tilde{q}^{(i-1)}_{-i}$ are encrypted by the same ciphertext. To show soundness, we assume that $q = q'$ and use the equalities tested by the verifier to deduce that $y = y'$.

Unambiguity of the multilinearity proof. To achieve the unambiguity of the evaluations of X we added multilinearity proofs. Thus, to show the unambiguity of the quasi-argument proof, we must also guarantee that the multilinearity proofs themselves are unambiguous.

Unambiguity of the proof polynomials. In addition to the evaluations of X the KPY quasi-argument contains the evaluations of the proof polynomials which must also be made unambiguous. To argue the unambiguity of these evaluations we rely on the tests performed by the KPY verifier designed to check the consistency between the proof polynomials and X. We show that if the evaluations of X are unambiguous and the evaluations of the proof polynomials pass the verifier's zero-tests, then the evaluations of the proof polynomials must also be unambiguous.

Towards both ends, we use some of the techniques discussed above as well as additional tools, some of which use modifications of the KPY encryption scheme. We refer the reader to the full version for more details.

Unambiguity of ciphertexts. So far we focused on the unambiguity of the encrypted answers. Next, we argue the unambiguity of the ciphertexts themselves. That is, we show that given the CRS that contains an encryption of a random query $q \in \mathbb{F}^\ell$, an adversarial prover cannot find two different ciphertexts that decrypt to the same value under the same key. Together with the unambiguity of the answers (in the multilinearity proof and proof polynomials), this implies the unambiguity of the entire quasi-argument proof. We show that the KPY encryption scheme already satisfies the unambiguity of ciphertexts property. In the KPY encryption scheme, the secret key is a random element $\mathsf{sk} \in \mathbb{F}$ and a ciphertext encrypting an element $q \in \mathbb{F}$ is given by an injective encoding of a random low-degree polynomial P such that $P(\mathsf{sk}) = q$. Therefore, the encryption of the random query $q \in \mathbb{F}^\ell$ in the CRS is just an encoding of random polynomials and therefore, it does not reveal any information about sk. Finding two ciphertexts that encrypt the same value requires finding two encoded low-degree polynomials that agree on sk which is information theoretically impossible. Note that this unambiguity of ciphertexts only holds when the CRS contains encryptions of random queries in $\mathbb{F}^\ell$ and therefore it is crucial that we prove the unambiguity of the encrypted answers for general queries and not just for Boolean queries.

Bootstrapping preserves unambiguity. Finally, to go from the unambiguity of the quasi-argument to that of the delegation scheme, we need to show that the bootstrapping step preserves unambiguity. In more detail, the bootstrapping step uses the quasi-argument recursively: at the base of the recursion each quasi-argument is for a formula that encodes a small block of the delegated computation. We can directly show that each of these base formulas is locally unambiguous and therefore their quasi-argument proofs are also unambiguous. Then, to reduce the number of quasi-argument proofs, KPY use the quasi-argument again to argue about a formula that verifies multiple lower-level quasi-argument proofs. The fact that this formula is also locally unambiguous follows from the unambiguity of these lower-level proofs. Therefore, its quasi-argument proof is also unambiguous and the unambiguity of the entire delegation scheme proof follows by induction.

2.3   Related Work

Comparison with Choudhuri et al. and followup work. The **PPAD**-hardness proof of Choudhuri et al. [13] and followup work [12,17,24] can all be seen as as constructing an updatable and unambiguous delegation scheme for some particular contrived language. In [13] the language is related to the computation of a round-collapsed sum-check proof and [12,17] start from the protocol of Pietrzak [28] instead of sum-check. In contrast, this work constructs updatable and unambiguous delegation scheme for general (bounded space) deterministic computations.

The delegation schemes in [12,13,17,24] are based on an interactive protocol that is made non-interactive via the Fiat-Shamir transform. The unambiguity property is inherited from that of the original protocol. Updatability relies on the recursive structure of the interactive protocol and requires augmenting the language to depend on the protocol itself. In comparison, the delegation scheme in our work is based on the scheme from [20] for general computation and relies on a quasi-polynomial version of their assumption on bilinear groups. Updatability follows from the bootstrapping technique developed in [20] and the focus of this work is on achieving ambiguity.

Following the work of Canetti et al. [9] on instantiating the Fiat-Shamir huristic from simpler assumptions, Choudhuri et al. [13] show that that the security of their sum-check based scheme follows from a strong assumption on the "optimal security" of Learning with Errors against quasi polynomial attacks. In a recent work (concurrent to ours) Lombardi and Vaikuntanathan [24] start from Pietrzak's protocol and replace the Fiat-Shamir assumption by sub-exponential hardness of Learning with Errors.

In addition to the assumption behind the delegation scheme, previous work as well as ours rely on the hardness of the underlying language. Choudhuri et al. [13] assume hardness of #SAT with poly-logarithmic number of variables, while [12,17,24] rely on super-polynomial or sub-exponential hardness of the repeated squaring problem that is behind Pietrzak's protocol and the time-lock puzzle of [30]. Since our delegation scheme supports general languages we can rely on any hard language that can be decided in quasi-polynomial time and polynomial space.

Hardness of local search. Recently, Bitansky and Gerichter [5] showed the hardness of the class Polynomial Local Search (**PLS**), which is a different subclass of **TFNP** that contains **CLS**, based on the delegation scheme of KPY [20]. They observe that the KPY delegation scheme can be made incremental and use this to show **PLS** hardness. For hardness in **PPAD** and **CLS**, however, we need the unambiguity property achieved in this work.

3   Delegation

In this section we define the notion of a non-interactive delegation scheme for deterministic Turing machines.

Fix any Turing machine $\mathcal{M}$. Let $T(n)$ be an upper bound on the running time of $\mathcal{M}$ on inputs of length n and let $S(n)$ be an upper bound on the size of $\mathcal{M}$'s configuration which includes the machine's state, input tape and all of the work tapes. We always assume, without loss of generality, that $T(n) \geq S(n) \geq n$. Let $\mathcal{U}^{\mathcal{M}}$ denote the language such that $(\mathsf{cf}, \mathsf{cf}', t) \in \mathcal{U}^{\mathcal{M}}$ if and only if $\mathcal{M}$ transitions from configuration cf to configuration cf' in exactly t steps. Let $\mathcal{U}_n^{\mathcal{M}} \subseteq \mathcal{U}^{\mathcal{M}}$ be the set of instances $(\mathsf{cf}, \mathsf{cf}', t) \in \mathcal{U}^{\mathcal{M}}$ such that the input tapes in $\mathsf{cf}, \mathsf{cf}'$ are of length n.

A non-interactive delegation scheme for $\mathcal{U}^{\mathcal{M}}$ consists of algorithms $(\mathsf{Del.S}, \mathsf{Del.P}, \mathsf{Del.V})$ with the following syntax:

Setup: The probabilistic setup algorithm $\mathsf{Del.S}$ takes as input a security parameter $\kappa \in \mathbb{N}$ and an input length $n \in \mathbb{N}$, and outputs a pair of public keys: a prover key pk and a verifier key vk.

Prover: The deterministic prover algorithm $\mathsf{Del.P}$ takes as input a prover key pk and an instance $x \in \mathcal{U}^{\mathcal{M}}$. It outputs a proof Π.

Verifier: The deterministic verifier algorithm $\mathsf{Del.V}$ takes as input a verifier key vk, an instance $x \in \mathcal{U}^{\mathcal{M}}$ and a proof Π. It outputs a bit indicating if it accepts or rejects.

Definition 3.1. *A non-interactive delegation scheme* $(\mathsf{Del.S}, \mathsf{Del.P}, \mathsf{Del.V})$ *for* $\mathcal{U}^{\mathcal{M}}$ *with setup time* $T_S = T_S(\kappa, n)$ *and proof length* $L_\Pi = L_\Pi(\kappa, n)$ *satisfies the following requirements:*

Completeness. *For every* $\kappa, n \in \mathbb{N}$ *such that* $T(n) \leq 2^\kappa$ *and* $x = (\mathsf{cf}, \mathsf{cf}', t) \in \mathcal{U}_n^{\mathcal{M}}$:

$$\Pr\left[\mathsf{Del.V}(\mathsf{vk}, x, \Pi) = 1 \;\middle|\; \begin{array}{l} (\mathsf{pk}, \mathsf{vk}) \leftarrow \mathsf{Del.S}(\kappa, n) \\ \Pi \leftarrow \mathsf{Del.P}(\mathsf{pk}, x) \end{array}\right] = 1.$$

Efficiency. *In the completeness experiment above:*
- *The setup algorithm runs in time* $T_S(\kappa, n)$.
- *The prover runs in time* $t \cdot O(L_\Pi(\kappa, n))$ *and outputs a proof of length* $L_\Pi(\kappa, n)$.
- *The verifier runs in time* $O(|x| + L_\Pi(\kappa, n))$.

(Λ, n)**-Soundness.** *For every* $\mathrm{poly}(\Lambda(\kappa))$*-size adversary* Adv *there exists a negligible function* μ *such that for every* $\kappa \in \mathbb{N}$:

$$\Pr\left[\begin{array}{l} \mathsf{Del.V}(\mathsf{vk}, x, \Pi) = 1 \\ x \notin \mathcal{U}_{n(\kappa)}^{\mathcal{M}} \end{array} \;\middle|\; \begin{array}{l} (\mathsf{pk}, \mathsf{vk}) \leftarrow \mathsf{Del.S}(\kappa, n(\kappa)) \\ (x, \Pi) \leftarrow \mathsf{Adv}(\mathsf{pk}, \mathsf{vk}) \end{array}\right] \leq \mu(\Lambda(\kappa)).$$

Next we define the notion of an unambiguous delegation scheme [29]. We adapt the definition to our setting.

Definition 3.2 $((\Lambda, n)$**-Unambiguity).** *A non-interactive delegation scheme* $(\mathsf{Del.S}, \mathsf{Del.P}, \mathsf{Del.V})$ *for* $\mathcal{U}^{\mathcal{M}}$ *is* (Λ, n)*-unambiguous if for every* $\mathrm{poly}(\Lambda(\kappa))$*-size adversary* Adv *there exists a negligible function* μ *such that for every* $\kappa \in \mathbb{N}$:

$$\Pr\left[\begin{array}{l} \mathsf{Del.V}(\mathsf{vk}, x, \Pi) = 1 \\ \mathsf{Del.V}(\mathsf{vk}, x, \Pi') = 1 \\ \Pi \neq \Pi' \end{array} \;\middle|\; \begin{array}{l} (\mathsf{pk}, \mathsf{vk}) \leftarrow \mathsf{Del.S}(\kappa, n(\kappa)) \\ (x, \Pi, \Pi') \leftarrow \mathsf{Adv}(\mathsf{pk}, \mathsf{vk}) \end{array}\right] \leq \mu(\Lambda(\kappa)).$$

Lastly we define the notion of an updatable delegation scheme.

Definition 3.3 (Updatability). *A non-interactive delegation scheme* (Del.S, Del.P, Del.V) *for* $\mathcal{U}^{\mathcal{M}}$ is updatable *if there exists a deterministic polynomial-time algorithm* Del.U *such that for every* $\kappa, n \in \mathbb{N}$ *such that* $T(n) \le 2^{\kappa}$, *and* $x_1, x_2 \in \mathcal{U}_n^{\mathcal{M}}$ *of the form* $x_1 = (\mathsf{cf}, \mathsf{cf}_1, t)$ *and* $x_2 = (\mathsf{cf}, \mathsf{cf}_2, t+1)$:

$$\Pr \left[\begin{array}{c} \mathsf{cf}'_2 = \mathsf{cf}_2 \\ \Pi'_2 = \Pi_2 \end{array} \middle| \begin{array}{l} (\mathsf{pk}, \mathsf{vk}) \leftarrow \mathsf{Del.S}(\kappa, n) \\ \Pi_1 \leftarrow \mathsf{Del.P}(\mathsf{pk}, x_1) \\ \Pi_2 \leftarrow \mathsf{Del.P}(\mathsf{pk}, x_2) \\ (\mathsf{cf}'_2, \Pi'_2) \leftarrow \mathsf{Del.U}(\mathsf{pk}, x_1, \Pi_1) \end{array} \right] = 1.$$

4   PPAD-Hardness

The complexity class **PPAD** is a subclass of **TFNP** that consists of all problems that are polynomial-time reducible to the End-of-the-Line problem. We show **PPAD**-hardness by following the blueprint of Choudhuri *et al.* [13] and refer the reader to their work for background material. Specifically, we show the hardness of the subclass **CLS** that lies in the intersection of **PPAD** and **PLS**. Towards this end, we consider the Relaxed-Sink-of-Verifiable-Line problem that was defined and proven to be reducible to a problem in **CLS** in [13].

Definition 4.1 ([13]). *A* Relaxed-Sink-of-Verifiable-Line *(rSVL) instance* (Succ, Ver, T, v_0) *consists of* $T \in [2^m]$, $v_0 \in \{0,1\}^m$, *and circuits* Succ : $\{0,1\}^m \to \{0,1\}^m$ *and* Ver : $\{0,1\}^m \times [T] \to \{0,1\}$ *with the guarantee that for every* $(v, i) \in \{0,1\}^m \times [T]$ *such that* $v = \mathsf{Succ}^i(v_0)$, *it holds that* $\mathsf{Ver}(v, i) = 1$. *A solution consists of one of the following:*

1. **The sink:** *A vertex* $v \in \{0,1\}^m$ *such that* $\mathsf{Ver}(v, T) = 1$.
2. **A false positive:** *A pair* $(v, i) \in \{0,1\}^m \times [2^m]$ *such that* $v \ne \mathsf{Succ}^i(v_0)$ *and* $\mathsf{Ver}(v, i) = 1$.

Lemma 4.1 ([13]). Relaxed-Sink-of-Verifiable-Line *is polynomial-time reducible to a problem in* **CLS**.

Hard search problems. We say that a search problem given by a relation $\mathcal{R}$ is T-hard in the worst-case if for every $\mathrm{poly}(T(n))$-size circuit $\mathsf{Adv} = \{\mathsf{Adv}_n\}$ there exists an $x \in \{0,1\}^n$ such that $(x, \mathsf{Adv}_n(x)) \notin \mathcal{R}$.

We say the problem is T-hard in the average-case if there exists an efficiently (polynomial-time) sampleable distribution $\mathsf{D} = \{\mathsf{D}_n\}$ such that for every $\mathrm{poly}(T(n))$-size circuit $\mathsf{Adv} = \{\mathsf{Adv}_n\}$ there exists a negligible function μ such that for every $n \in \mathbb{N}$:

$$\Pr_{x \leftarrow \mathsf{D}_n} [(x, \mathsf{Adv}_n(x)) \in \mathcal{R}] \le \mu(T(n)).$$

Next we show the existence of a hard search problem and the existence of a non-interactive delegation scheme that is unambiguous and updatable implies rSVL is hard.

We say a function $\widehat{T}$ is well-behaved if for every polynomial p, it holds that $\widehat{T}(p(n)) = \mathrm{poly}(\widehat{T}(n))$.

Theorem 4.1. *Let $\mathcal{R}$ be a search problem that is solvable by a deterministic Turing machine $\mathcal{M}$ that runs in time $T = T(n) = n^{\omega(1)}$ and space $S = S(n) = \mathrm{poly}(n)$, and let $\widehat{T} = \widehat{T}(n)$ be a well-behaved function such that $\mathcal{R}$ is $\widehat{T}$-hard in the average-case (respectively in the worst-case).*

If there exists a non-interactive delegation scheme for $\mathcal{U}^{\mathcal{M}}$ with setup time $T_{\mathsf{S}}(\kappa, n) = \mathrm{poly}(n)$ and proof length $L_{\Pi}(\kappa, n) = \mathrm{poly}(n)$, and functions $\Lambda = \Lambda(\kappa)$ and $n = n(\kappa)$ such that $T(n(\kappa)) \leq \Lambda(\kappa)$ and the delegation scheme is (Λ, n)-sound, (Λ, n)-unambiguous, and updatable, then rSVL is $\widehat{T}$-hard in the average-case (respectively in the worst-case).

Proof. We focus on the setting of average-case hardness. The proof for worst-case hardness is similar.

Let $\mathcal{R}$ be $\widehat{T}$-hard with respect to a distribution $\mathsf{D} = \{\mathsf{D}_n\}$. Let $(\mathsf{Del.S}, \mathsf{Del.P}, \mathsf{Del.V}, \mathsf{Del.U})$ be a delegation scheme as in the theorem statement. Let A' denote a circuit for solving rSVL. We construct a circuit A that uses A' to solve $\mathcal{R}$.

Given as input an instance $x \in \{0, 1\}^n$, the algorithm A proceeds as follows:

1. Set the security parameter κ such that $|x| = n(\kappa)$. Sample $(\mathsf{pk}, \mathsf{vk}) \leftarrow \mathsf{Del.S}(\kappa, n)$. Let $m = S(n) + L_{\Pi}(\kappa, n)$.
2. Let cf_0 be the initial configuration of the Turing machine $\mathcal{M}$ on input x. We assume without loss of generality that at every time step, the configuration of $\mathcal{M}$ contains an index $i \in [T]$ corresponding to the current time step. Let $v_0 = (\mathsf{cf}_0, \Pi_0)$ where $\Pi_0 \leftarrow \mathsf{Del.P}(\mathsf{pk}, (\mathsf{cf}_0, \mathsf{cf}_0, 0))$.
3. Let $\mathsf{Succ} = \mathsf{Succ}_{x, \mathsf{pk}} : \{0, 1\}^m \to \{0, 1\}^m$ be the circuit that on input (cf_i, Π_i), parses the index $i \in [0, T]$ from cf_i and outputs $(\mathsf{cf}_{i+1}, \Pi_{i+1}) \leftarrow \mathsf{Del.U}(\mathsf{pk}, (\mathsf{cf}_0, \mathsf{cf}_i, i), \Pi_i)$.
4. Let $\mathsf{Ver} = \mathsf{Ver}_{x, \mathsf{vk}} : \{0, 1\}^m \times [T] \to \{0, 1\}$ be the circuit that on input $(v, i) \in \{0, 1\}^m \times [T]$, parses $v = (\mathsf{cf}, \Pi)$ and returns the output of $\mathsf{Del.V}(\mathsf{vk}, (\mathsf{cf}_0, \mathsf{cf}, i), \Pi)$.
5. Run A' on $(\mathsf{Succ}, \mathsf{Ver}, T, v_0)$.
   (a) If A' outputs $v \in \{0, 1\}^m$ such that $\mathsf{Ver}(v, T) = 1$ (the sink), then parse $v = (\mathsf{cf}, \Pi)$ and output the solution for x contained in cf.
   (b) Otherwise output $\perp$.

We construct the following $\widehat{T}$-hard distribution D' of rSVL instances: sample $x \leftarrow \mathsf{D}_n$ and run Steps 1 to 4 of A to generate $(\mathsf{Succ}, \mathsf{Ver}, T, v_0)$ of length $\ell = \ell(n) \geq n$.

First we show $\mathsf{D}' = \{\mathsf{D}'_\ell\}$ is efficiently sampleable. By the efficiency guarantees of the delegation scheme $(\mathsf{Del.S}, \mathsf{Del.P}, \mathsf{Del.V}, \mathsf{Del.U})$ (given by the theorem statement, Definition 3.1, Definition 3.3), Steps 1 to 4 take $\mathrm{poly}(n) = \mathrm{poly}(\ell)$ steps. Since D is efficiently sampleable, this shows D' is efficiently sampleable.

Next we argue that D' is supported on valid rSVL instances. We show that for any $x \in \{0, 1\}^n$, A generates $(\mathsf{Succ}, \mathsf{Ver}, T, v_0)$ such that for every $i \in [T]$ it holds that $\mathsf{Ver}(\mathsf{Succ}^i(v_0), i) = 1$. Consider any $i \in [T]$ and let $v = (\mathsf{cf}, \Pi) = \mathsf{Succ}^i(v_0)$. Let cf_i be the unique configuration such that $(\mathsf{cf}_0, \mathsf{cf}_i, i) \in \mathcal{U}_n^{\mathcal{M}}$ and let $\Pi_i = \mathsf{Del.P}(\mathsf{pk}, (\mathsf{cf}_0, \mathsf{cf}_i, i))$. By the updatability of the delegation scheme (Definition 3.3), $(\mathsf{cf}, \Pi) = (\mathsf{cf}_i, \Pi_i)$ so by the completeness of the delegation scheme (Definition 3.1), $\mathsf{Ver}(v, i) = 1$, as desired.

To show that $\mathcal{R}$ is $\widehat{T}$-hard with respect to D, assume towards contradiction there exists a $\mathrm{poly}(\widehat{T}(\ell))$-size circuit $\mathsf{A}' = \{\mathsf{A}'_\ell\}$ and polynomial function p' such that for infinitely many $\ell \in \mathbb{N}$, given an rSVL instance sampled from D'_ℓ, A'_ℓ outputs a solution (the sink or a false positive) with probability at least $1/p'(\widehat{T}(\ell))$. Since Steps 1 to 4 take $\mathrm{poly}(n)$ steps, $\ell = \mathrm{poly}(n)$ so $\widehat{T}(\ell) = \mathrm{poly}(\widehat{T}(n))$. Let p be a polynomial such that $p'(\widehat{T}(\ell)) \leq p(\widehat{T}(n))$. Since D' is efficiently sampleable and A' is a circuit of size $\mathrm{poly}(\widehat{T}(n))$, A is a circuit of size $\mathrm{poly}(\widehat{T}(n))$. It follows from our assumption that for $x \leftarrow \mathsf{D}$, A' outputs a rSVL solution (the sink or a false positive) in Step 5 with probability at least $1/p(\widehat{T}(n))$. Below we show A' outputs a false positive with probability at most $1/2p(\widehat{T}(n))$ and therefore it outputs the sink with probability at least $1/2p(\widehat{T}(n))$. In this case, we use the sink to recover a solution for x.

Assume towards contradiction that for infinitely many $n \in \mathbb{N}$, A' outputs a false positive (v, i) with probability at least $1/2p(\widehat{T}(n)) \geq 1/2p(\Lambda(\kappa))$ (since $\widehat{T}(n) < T(n) \leq \Lambda(\kappa)$). If $(v = (\mathsf{cf}, \Pi), i)$ is a false positive, then $\mathsf{Del.V}(\mathsf{vk}, (\mathsf{cf}_0, \mathsf{cf}, i), \Pi) = \mathsf{Ver}(v, i) = 1$ and $(\mathsf{cf}, \Pi) \neq (\mathsf{cf}_i, \Pi_i) = \mathsf{Succ}^i(v_0)$, so either $\mathsf{cf} \neq \mathsf{cf}_i$, or $\mathsf{cf} = \mathsf{cf}_i$ and $\Pi \neq \Pi_i$. One of the two cases must occur for infinitely many $\kappa \in \mathbb{N}$ with probability at least $1/4p(\Lambda(\kappa))$. In the first case, $\mathsf{cf} \neq \mathsf{cf}_i$, and A' can be used to break the (Λ, n)-soundness of the delegation (Definition 3.1): $(\mathsf{cf}_0, \mathsf{cf}, i) \notin \mathcal{U}_n^{\mathcal{M}}$ but $\mathsf{Del.V}(\mathsf{vk}, (\mathsf{cf}_0, \mathsf{cf}, i), \Pi)$ accepts. In the second case, $\mathsf{cf} = \mathsf{cf}_i$ and $\Pi \neq \Pi_i$, and A' can be used to break the (Λ, n)-unambiguity of the delegation (Definition 3.2): by the efficiency of the delegation (cf_i, Π_i) can be computed in time $T(n) \cdot \mathrm{poly}(n) \leq \mathrm{poly}(\Lambda(\kappa))$, and $\mathsf{Del.V}(\mathsf{vk}, (\mathsf{cf}_0, \mathsf{cf}_i, i), \Pi)$ and $\mathsf{Del.V}(\mathsf{vk}, (\mathsf{cf}_0, \mathsf{cf}_i, i), \Pi_i)$ both accept.

This shows A' outputs a false positive with probability at most $1/2p(\widehat{T}(n))$. Thus for infinitely many $n \in \mathbb{N}$, with probability at least $1/2p(\widehat{T}(n))$, A' outputs the sink $v = (\mathsf{cf}, \Pi)$ and $(\mathsf{cf}, \Pi) = \mathsf{Succ}^T(v_0)$. By the updatability of the delegation (Definition 3.3), $(\mathsf{cf}_0, \mathsf{cf}, T) \in \mathcal{U}_n^{\mathcal{M}}$, i.e. cf is the configuration of $\mathcal{M}$ on input x after T steps so it contains a solution for x. In this case, A outputs this solution, contradicting the $\widehat{T}$-hardness of $\mathcal{R}$.

5   Our Results

In the full version of this work we construct a non-interactive delegation scheme that is unambiguous and updatable, proving the theorem below. This theorem is a generalization of Theorem 1.2. The delegation scheme relies on the following decisional assumption on groups with bilinear maps (also stated in Assumption 1.3). The assumption is parameterized by a function $\Lambda = \Lambda(\kappa)$.

Assumption 5.1. *There exists an ensemble of groups $G = \{G_\kappa\}$ of prime order $p = p(\kappa) = 2^{\Theta(\kappa)}$ with a non-degenerate bilinear map such that for every $d(\kappa) =$*

$O(\log \Lambda(\kappa))$ and $\mathrm{poly}(\Lambda(\kappa))$-size adversary Adv, there exists a negligible function μ such that for every $\kappa \in \mathbb{N}$:

$$
\Pr\left[b' = b \ \middle| \ \begin{array}{l} b \leftarrow \{0,1\} \\ g \leftarrow G \\ s \leftarrow \mathbb{Z}_p \\ t_0 \leftarrow \mathbb{Z}_p \\ t_1 \leftarrow s^{2d+1} \\ \\ b' \leftarrow \mathsf{Adv}\left(\left(g^{s^i \cdot t_b^j} \right)_{\substack{i \in [0,d] \\ j \in [0,2]}} \right) \end{array} \right] \leq \frac{1}{2} + \mu(\Lambda(\kappa)).
$$

Theorem 5.2. *For any deterministic Turing machine $\mathcal{M}$ that runs in time $T = T(n)$ and space $S = S(n) \geq n$, and for every $\Lambda = \Lambda(\kappa)$ and $n = n(\kappa)$ such that $T(n(\kappa)) \leq \Lambda(\kappa)$, let $d = d(\kappa) = \log_n T(n)$ and let $\Lambda^*(\kappa) = \max\{\Lambda(\kappa), S(n(\kappa))^d, \kappa^{d^2}\}$. Under the Λ^*-hardness of Assumption 5.1, there exists a non-interactive delegation scheme for $\mathcal{U}^{\mathcal{M}}$ with setup time $T_\mathsf{S}(\kappa, n) = \mathrm{poly}(S(n), \kappa^d)$ and proof length $L_\Pi(\kappa, n) = \mathrm{poly}(S(n), \kappa^d)$ that is (Λ, n)-sound, (Λ, n)-unambiguous, and updatable.*

Next we state corollaries of Theorem 5.2 for different settings of parameters.

Corollary 5.1. *For any deterministic Turing machine $\mathcal{M}$ that runs in time $T = T(n)$ and space $S = S(n) = \mathrm{poly}(n)$, and for every $\Lambda = \Lambda(\kappa)$ and $n = n(\kappa) \geq 2^{\sqrt{\log \Lambda \cdot \log \kappa}}$ such that $T(n(\kappa)) \leq \Lambda(\kappa)$, under the Λ-hardness of Assumption 5.1, there exists a non-interactive delegation scheme for $\mathcal{U}^{\mathcal{M}}$ with setup time $T_\mathsf{S}(\kappa, n) = \mathrm{poly}(n)$ and proof length $L_\Pi(\kappa, n) = \mathrm{poly}(n)$ that is (Λ, n)-sound, (Λ, n)-unambiguous, and updatable.*

Proof. It suffices to prove that $\max\{\Lambda(\kappa), S(n(\kappa))^d, \kappa^{d^2}\} \leq \mathrm{poly}(\Lambda(\kappa))$ where $d = d(\kappa) = \log_n T(n)$, as follows:

$$
S(n(\kappa))^d = n(\kappa)^{O(d)} = n(\kappa)^{O(\log_n T(n))} = \mathrm{poly}(T(n)) \leq \mathrm{poly}(\Lambda(\kappa))
$$

$$
\kappa^d = \kappa^{\log_n T(n)} \leq \kappa^{\log_n \Lambda(\kappa)} = 2^{\frac{\log \Lambda \cdot \log \kappa}{\log n}} \leq n^{\frac{\sqrt{\log \Lambda \cdot \log \kappa}}{\log n}} \leq n
$$

$$
\kappa^{d^2} \leq n^d = n^{\log_n T(n)} = T(n) \leq \Lambda(\kappa).
$$

Corollary 5.2 (Quasi-polynomial security). *For any constant $c \geq 1$ and any deterministic Turing machine $\mathcal{M}$ that runs in time $T = T(n) \leq n^{(\log n)^a}$ where $a = (c-1)/(c+1)$ and space $S = S(n) = \mathrm{poly}(n)$, let $\Lambda = \Lambda(\kappa) = 2^{(\log \kappa)^c}$ and $n = n(\kappa) = 2^{\sqrt{\log \Lambda \cdot \log \kappa}}$. Under the Λ-hardness of Assumption 5.1, there exists a non-interactive delegation scheme for $\mathcal{U}^{\mathcal{M}}$ with setup time $T_\mathsf{S}(\kappa, n) = \mathrm{poly}(n)$ and proof length $L_\Pi(\kappa, n) = \mathrm{poly}(n)$ that is (Λ, n)-sound, (Λ, n)-unambiguous, and updatable.*

Proof. By Corollary 5.1, it suffices to prove that $T(n) \leq \Lambda(\kappa)$ by showing:

$$
n^{(\log n)^a} = 2^{(\log n)^{a+1}} \leq 2^{(\log \kappa)^c} \quad \text{for} \quad a = (c-1)/(c+1).
$$

It suffices to prove that:

$$(\log n)^{a+1} \leq (\log \kappa)^c \quad \text{for} \quad a = (c-1)/(c+1).$$

This follows from the calculation:

$$(\log n)^{a+1} = (\log \Lambda \cdot \log \kappa)^{\frac{a+1}{2}} = ((\log \kappa)^c \cdot \log \kappa)^{\frac{a+1}{2}} = (\log \kappa)^{\frac{(c+1)(a+1)}{2}} = (\log \kappa)^c.$$

By Corollary 5.2, Theorem 4.1 implies the following corollary.

Corollary 5.3. *Assume Assumption 5.1 is Λ-hard for $\Lambda = \Lambda(\kappa) = 2^{(\log \kappa)^c}$ for some $c \geq 1$. If there exists a search problem $\mathcal{R}$ that is solvable by a deterministic Turing machine $\mathcal{M}$ that runs in time $T = T(n) \leq n^{(\log n)^a}$ where $a = (c-1)/(c+1)$ and space $S = S(n) = \text{poly}(n)$, and a well-behaved function $\widehat{T} = \widehat{T}(n)$ such that $\mathcal{R}$ is $\widehat{T}$-hard in the average-case (respectively in the worst-case), then $rSVL$ is $\widehat{T}$-hard in the average-case (respectively in the worst-case).*

Corollary 5.4 (Sub-exponential security). *For any constant $\epsilon < 1$ and any deterministic Turing machine $\mathcal{M}$ that runs in time $T = T(n) \leq n^{\frac{\log n}{\log \log n}}$ and space $S = S(n) = \text{poly}(n)$, let $\Lambda = \Lambda(\kappa) = 2^{\kappa^\epsilon}$ and $n = n(\kappa) = 2^{\sqrt{\log \Lambda \cdot \log \kappa}}$. Under the Λ-hardness of Assumption 5.1, there exists a non-interactive delegation scheme for $\mathcal{U}^{\mathcal{M}}$ with setup time $T_S(\kappa, n) = \text{poly}(n)$ and proof length $L_\Pi(\kappa, n) = \text{poly}(n)$ that is (Λ, n)-sound, (Λ, n)-unambiguous, and updatable.*

Proof. By Corollary 5.1, it suffices to prove that $T(n) \leq \Lambda(\kappa)$ by showing:

$$n^{\frac{\epsilon}{2} \cdot \frac{\log n}{\log \log n}} = 2^{\frac{\epsilon \cdot (\log n)^2}{2 \log \log n}} \leq 2^{\kappa^\epsilon}.$$

It suffices to prove that:

$$\frac{\epsilon \cdot (\log n)^2}{2 \log \log n} \leq \kappa^\epsilon.$$

This follows from the calculation:

$$\log n = (\log \Lambda \cdot \log \kappa)^{1/2} = (\kappa^\epsilon \cdot \log \kappa)^{1/2} \geq \kappa^{\epsilon/2}$$

$$\frac{\epsilon \cdot (\log n)^2}{2 \log \log n} = \frac{\epsilon \cdot \kappa^\epsilon \cdot \log \kappa}{2 \log \log n} \leq \frac{\epsilon \cdot \kappa^\epsilon \cdot \log \kappa}{2 \cdot (\epsilon/2) \cdot \log \kappa} = \kappa^\epsilon.$$

By Corollary 5.4, Theorem 4.1 implies the following corollary.

Corollary 5.5. *Assume Assumption 5.1 is Λ-hard for $\Lambda = \Lambda(\kappa) = 2^{\kappa^\epsilon}$ for some $\epsilon < 1$. If there exists a search problem $\mathcal{R}$ that is solvable by a deterministic Turing machine $\mathcal{M}$ that runs in time $T = T(n) \leq n^{\frac{\epsilon}{2} \cdot \frac{\log n}{\log \log n}}$ and space $S = S(n) = \text{poly}(n)$, and a well-behaved function $\widehat{T} = \widehat{T}(n)$ such that $\mathcal{R}$ is $\widehat{T}$-hard in the average-case (respectively in the worst-case), then $rSVL$ is $\widehat{T}$-hard in the average-case (respectively in the worst-case).*

References

1. Abbot, T., Kane, D., Valiant, P.: On algorithms for Nash equilibria (2004). http://web.mit.edu/tabbott/Public/final.pdf. Unpublished manuscript
2. Biehl, I., Meyer, B., Wetzel, S.: Ensuring the integrity of agent-based computations by short proofs. In: Rothermel, K., Hohl, F. (eds.) MA 1998. LNCS, vol. 1477, pp. 183–194. Springer, Heidelberg (1998). https://doi.org/10.1007/BFb0057658
3. Bitansky, N., Canetti, R., Chiesa, A., Tromer, E.: Recursive composition and bootstrapping for SNARKS and proof-carrying data. In: Boneh et al. [7], pp. 111–120 (2013). https://doi.org/10.1145/2488608.2488623, https://doi.acm.org/10.1145/2488608.2488623
4. Bitansky, N., Chiesa, A., Ishai, Y., Paneth, O., Ostrovsky, R.: Succinct non-interactive arguments via linear interactive proofs. In: Sahai, A. (ed.) TCC 2013. LNCS, vol. 7785, pp. 315–333. Springer, Heidelberg (2013). https://doi.org/10.1007/978-3-642-36594-2_18
5. Bitansky, N., Gerichter, I.: On the cryptographic hardness of local search. In: Vidick, T. (ed.) 11th Innovations in Theoretical Computer Science Conference, ITCS 2020. LIPIcs, Seattle, Washington, USA, 12–14 January 2020, vol. 151, pp. 6:1–6:29. Schloss Dagstuhl - Leibniz-Zentrum für Informatik (2020). https://doi.org/10.4230/LIPIcs.ITCS.2020.6
6. Bitansky, N., Paneth, O., Rosen, A.: On the cryptographic hardness of finding a Nash equilibrium. In: IEEE 56th Annual Symposium on Foundations of Computer Science, FOCS 2015, Berkeley, CA, USA, 17–20 October 2015, pp. 1480–1498 (2015). https://doi.org/10.1109/FOCS.2015.94
7. Boneh, D., Roughgarden, T., Feigenbaum, J. (eds.): Symposium on Theory of Computing Conference, STOC 2013, Palo Alto, CA, USA, 1–4 June 2013. ACM (2013). http://dl.acm.org/citation.cfm?id=2488608
8. Brakerski, Z., Holmgren, J., Kalai, Y.T.: Non-interactive delegation and batch NP verification from standard computational assumptions. In: Proceedings of the 49th Annual ACM SIGACT Symposium on Theory of Computing, STOC 2017, Montreal, QC, Canada, 19–23 June 2017, pp. 474–482 (2017). https://doi.org/10.1145/3055399.3055497, https://doi.acm.org/10.1145/3055399.3055497
9. Canetti, R., et al.: Fiat-Shamir: from practice to theory. In: Proceedings of the 51st Annual ACM SIGACT Symposium on Theory of Computing, STOC 2019, Phoenix, AZ, USA, 23–26 June 2019, pp. 1082–1090 (2019). https://doi.org/10.1145/3313276.3316380
10. Chakraborty, S., Prabhakaran, M., Wichs, D.: Witness maps and applications. In: Kiayias, A., Kohlweiss, M., Wallden, P., Zikas, V. (eds.) PKC 2020, Part I. LNCS, vol. 12110, pp. 220–246. Springer, Cham (2020). https://doi.org/10.1007/978-3-030-45374-9_8
11. Chen, X., Deng, X., Teng, S.: Settling the complexity of computing two-player Nash equilibria. J. ACM. **56**(3), 14:1–14:57 (2009). https://doi.org/10.1145/1516512.1516516
12. Choudhuri, A.R., Hubáček, P., Kamath, C., Pietrzak, K., Rosen, A., Rothblum, G.N.: PPAD-hardness via iterated squaring modulo a composite. IACR Cryptology ePrint Archive 2019/667 (2019). https://eprint.iacr.org/2019/667
13. Choudhuri, A.R., Hub'avcek, P., Kamath, C., Pietrzak, K., Rosen, A., Rothblum, G.N.: Finding a Nash equilibrium is no easier than breaking Fiat-Shamir. In: Proceedings of the 51st Annual ACM SIGACT Symposium on Theory of Computing, STOC 2019, Phoenix, AZ, USA, 23–26 June 2019, pp. 1103–1114 (2019). https://doi.org/10.1145/3313276.3316400

14. Daskalakis, C., Goldberg, P.W., Papadimitriou, C.H.: The complexity of computing a Nash equilibrium. SIAM J. Comput. **39**(1), 195–259 (2009). https://doi.org/10.1137/070699652

15. Dodis, Y., Halevi, S., Rothblum, R.D., Wichs, D.: Spooky encryption and its applications. In: Robshaw, M., Katz, J. (eds.) CRYPTO 2016, Part III. LNCS, vol. 9816, pp. 93–122. Springer, Heidelberg (2016). https://doi.org/10.1007/978-3-662-53015-3_4

16. Dwork, C., Naor, M., Reingold, O., Stockmeyer, L.J.: Magic functions. J. ACM **50**(6), 852–921 (2003)

17. Ephraim, N., Freitag, C., Komargodski, I., Pass, R.: Continuous verifiable delay functions. IACR Cryptology ePrint Archive 2019/619 (2019). https://eprint.iacr.org/2019/619

18. Garg, S., Pandey, O., Srinivasan, A.: Revisiting the cryptographic hardness of finding a Nash equilibrium. In: Robshaw, M., Katz, J. (eds.) CRYPTO 2016, Part II. LNCS, vol. 9815, pp. 579–604. Springer, Heidelberg (2016). https://doi.org/10.1007/978-3-662-53008-5_20

19. Hubáček, P., Yogev, E.: Hardness of continuous local search: query complexity and cryptographic lower bounds. In: Proceedings of the Twenty-Eighth Annual ACM-SIAM Symposium on Discrete Algorithms, SODA 2017, Barcelona, Spain, Hotel Porta Fira, 16–19 January, pp. 1352–1371 (2017). https://doi.org/10.1137/1.9781611974782.88

20. Kalai, Y.T., Paneth, O., Yang, L.: How to delegate computations publicly. In: Proceedings of the 51st Annual ACM SIGACT Symposium on Theory of Computing, STOC 2019, Phoenix, AZ, USA, 23–26 June 2019, pp. 1115–1124 (2019). https://doi.org/10.1145/3313276.3316411

21. Kalai, Y.T., Raz, R., Rothblum, R.D.: Delegation for bounded space. In: Boneh et al. [7], pp. 565–574 (2013). https://doi.org/10.1145/2488608.2488679, https://doi.acm.org/10.1145/2488608.2488679

22. Kalai, Y.T., Raz, R., Rothblum, R.D.: How to delegate computations: the power of no-signaling proofs. In: STOC, pp. 485–494. ACM (2014)

23. Komargodski, I., Segev, G.: From minicrypt to obfustopia via private-key functional encryption. In: Coron, J.-S., Nielsen, J.B. (eds.) EUROCRYPT 2017, Part I. LNCS, vol. 10210, pp. 122–151. Springer, Cham (2017). https://doi.org/10.1007/978-3-319-56620-7_5

24. Lombardi, A., Vaikuntanathan, V.: Personal communication (2020)

25. Lund, C., Fortnow, L., Karloff, H.J., Nisan, N.: Algebraic methods for interactive proof systems. In: 31st Annual Symposium on Foundations of Computer Science, St. Louis, Missouri, USA, 22–24 October 1990, vol. I, pp. 2–10. IEEE Computer Society (1990). https://doi.org/10.1109/FSCS.1990.89518

26. Paneth, O., Rothblum, G.N.: On zero-testable homomorphic encryption and publicly verifiable non-interactive arguments. In: Kalai, Y., Reyzin, L. (eds.) TCC 2017, Part II. LNCS, vol. 10678, pp. 283–315. Springer, Cham (2017). https://doi.org/10.1007/978-3-319-70503-3_9

27. Papadimitriou, C.H.: On the complexity of the parity argument and other inefficient proofs of existence. J. Comput. Syst. Sci. **48**(3), 498–532 (1994). https://doi.org/10.1016/S0022-0000(05)80063-7

28. Pietrzak, K.: Simple verifiable delay functions. In: 10th Innovations in Theoretical Computer Science Conference, ITCS 2019, San Diego, California, USA, 10–12 January 2019, pp. 60:1–60:15 (2019). https://doi.org/10.4230/LIPIcs.ITCS.2019.60

29. Reingold, O., Rothblum, G.N., Rothblum, R.D.: Constant-round interactive proofs for delegating computation. In: Proceedings of the 48th Annual ACM SIGACT Symposium on Theory of Computing, STOC 2016, Cambridge, MA, USA, 18–21 June 2016, pp. 49–62 (2016). https://doi.org/10.1145/2897518.2897652
30. Rivest, R.L., Shamir, A., Wagner, D.A.: Time-lock puzzles and timed-release crypto. Technical report, USA (1996)
31. Sahai, A., Waters, B.: How to use indistinguishability obfuscation: deniable encryption, and more. In: Shmoys, D.B. (ed.) Symposium on Theory of Computing, STOC 2014, 31 May –03 June 2014, pp. 475–484. ACM, New York (2014). https://doi.org/10.1145/2591796.2591825
32. Valiant, P.: Incrementally verifiable computation or proofs of knowledge imply time/space efficiency. In: Canetti, R. (ed.) TCC 2008. LNCS, vol. 4948, pp. 1–18. Springer, Heidelberg (2008). https://doi.org/10.1007/978-3-540-78524-8_1

New Techniques for Zero-Knowledge: Leveraging Inefficient Provers to Reduce Assumptions, Interaction, and Trust

Marshall Ball[1]($\boxtimes$), Dana Dachman-Soled[2], and Mukul Kulkarni[3]

[1] Columbia University, New York City, USA
marshall@cs.columbia.edu
[2] University of Maryland, College Park, USA
danadach@umd.edu
[3] University of Massachusetts, Amherst, USA
mukul@cs.umass.edu

Abstract. We present a transformation from NIZK with *inefficient provers* in the uniform random string (URS) model to ZAPs (two message witness indistinguishable proofs) with *inefficient provers*. While such a transformation was known for the case where the prover is efficient, the security proof breaks down if the prover is inefficient. Our transformation is obtained via new applications of Nisan-Wigderson *designs*, a combinatorial object originally introduced in the derandomization literature.

We observe that our transformation is applicable both in the setting of super-polynomial provers/poly-time adversaries, as well as a new fine-grained setting, where the prover is polynomial time and the verifier/simulator/zero knowledge distinguisher are in a lower complexity class, such as NC^1. We also present NC^1-fine-grained NIZK in the URS model for all of NP from the worst-case assumption $\oplus L/\mathrm{poly} \not\subseteq \mathsf{NC}^1$.

Our techniques yield the following applications:

1. ZAPs for AM from Minicrypt assumptions (with super-polynomial time provers),
2. NC^1-fine-grained ZAPs for NP from worst-case assumptions,
3. Protocols achieving an "offline" notion of NIZK (oNIZK) in the standard (no-CRS) model with uniform soundness in both the super-polynomial setting (from Minicrypt assumptions) and the NC^1-fine-grained setting (from worst-case assumptions). The oNIZK notion is sufficient for use in indistinguishability-based proofs.

1 Introduction

A long and important line of research has been dedicated to understanding the necessary and sufficient assumptions for the existence of computational zero

M. Kulkarni—Part of this work was done while the author was a student at the University of Maryland.

© International Association for Cryptologic Research 2020
D. Micciancio and T. Ristenpart (Eds.): CRYPTO 2020, LNCS 12172, pp. 674–703, 2020.
https://doi.org/10.1007/978-3-030-56877-1_24

knowledge (CZK) proofs (with potentially unbounded provers) for a language $\mathcal{L}$ [13,49,60]. This line of research culminated with the work of Ong and Vadhan [59] which fully resolved the question by proving that a language in NP has a CZK protocol if and only if the language has an "instance-dependent" commitment scheme. The minimal assumptions required in the *non-interactive* zero knowledge (NIZK) setting—assuming unbounded provers and a common *reference* string (CRS)[1] (sometimes called the "public parameters" setting)—are also well-understood. Pass and Shelat [61], showed that (non-uniform) one-way functions are sufficient for NIZK with unbounded provers in the CRS model for all of AM, whereas NIZK with unbounded provers in the CRS model for a hard-on-average language implies the existence of (non-uniform) one-way functions.

While the NIZK of Pass and Shelat [61] indeed minimizes interaction and assumptions, it critically utilizes trusted setup to generate a structured CRS sampled from a particular distribution. In contrast, motivated by concerns of subversion of public parameters [12] and considerations from the blockchain community [16–18], a recent line of research has focused on "transparent" setup that does not require a trusted party, but simply access to a shared source of public randomness such the NIST randomness beacon, or a uniform random string (URS).[2] In the URS model, it is well known that NIZK with unbounded provers follows from one-way permutations (OWP) [34]. However, even agreeing upon a genuinely random string to implement the URS model may be infeasible in some cases.

We investigate what can be proven with "zero-knowledge" in a truly trust-free setting, with *minimal interaction and assumptions*. In particular, we extend the above line of work on minimizing assumptions to other types of "zero knowledge" primitives, such as *ZAPs* (two message witness indistinguishable (WI) proofs), non-interactive witness indistinguishable proofs (NIWI), and, ultimately, a type of NIZK with uniform soundness (and no URS/CRS).

Our primary goal is to understand the relationship between ZAPs and zero-knowledge primitives that can be constructed from minimal assumptions in the *inefficient prover* setting. Once we construct ZAPs, we will show that NIWI and a type of NIZK with uniform soundness can also be constructed (note that while these implications are already known in the efficient-prover setting [8,10], hurdles are introduced by removing this constraint). Ultimately, we are interested in obtaining constructions of ZAPs from *Minicrypt* [45] assumptions only[3]. To

---

[1] Throughout this work we make a distinction between common *reference* string denoted as CRS and uniform random string denoted as URS. URS is sometimes referred to common *random* string in literature. We write URS to avoid the confusion and overloading.

[2] Note that recent work on transparent or trustless (succinct) proofs, typically assumes existence of a public random oracle. We will only consider (at most) *short* public random strings in this work.

[3] We understand Minicrypt to be chiefly characterized by the lack of key agreement (KA), and note that one-way permutations (OWP) are separated from KA via the original Impagliazzo and Rudich separation [46] For the same reason, we consider Collision-Resistant Hashing to be in Minicrypt.

further motivate our focus on the *inefficient prover* setting, note that barriers are known for constructions of ZAPs from Minicrypt assumptions when the prover is required to be efficient. Indeed, efficient-prover ZAPs are known to be equivalent to efficient-prover NIZK in the URS model [32] (assuming one-way functions exist), and efficient-prover NIZKs, in turn, are only known to be achievable from Cryptomania [45] primitives such as (enhanced) trapdoor permutations. (See Sect. 1.2 for details.).

Because of this dichotomy, we consider the setting where the prover is computationally *more powerful* than the simulator/zero knowledge distinguisher. We refer to this setting as the *inefficient prover* setting. This covers both the setting of super-polynomial provers/polynomial adversary, as well as a new fine-grained setting that we consider for the first time (to the best of our knowledge), where the prover is polynomial time and the verifier/simulator/zero knowledge distinguisher are in a lower complexity class, such as NC^1 (logarithmic depth, polynomial-size circuits with constant fan-in). Our main technical contribution is a new transformation from inefficient prover NIZK in the URS model to inefficient prover ZAPs. A single transformation works both for the unbounded prover and fine-grained settings. Our transformation is obtained via new applications of Nisan-Wigderson *designs*, a combinatorial object originally introduced in the derandomization literature [58]. We also show that fine-grained NIZK in the URS model is achievable from worst-case assumptions ($\oplus L/\mathrm{poly} \not\subseteq \mathsf{NC}^1$). Given the well-known construction of unbounded prover NIZK in the URS model from one-way permutations (via the hidden bits model), we obtain (1) super-poly prover ZAPs for AM from Minicrypt assumptions and (2) fine-grained ZAPs for NP from worst-case assumptions.

Technical Hurdles Introduced by Inefficient Provers. When dealing with inefficient provers, one must proceed with care, as many "folklore" results no longer hold. We make the following surprising observation (discussed in more detail in Sect. 1.1): While it is known that NIZKs in the uniform random string (URS) model imply ZAPs for the case of *efficient provers* [32], the transformation of [32] fails when the NIZK prover is inefficient. Briefly, this occurs because the *reduction* from the zero knowledge of the underlying NIZK to the witness indistinguishability of the ZAP does not have the computational power to run the *honest* prover's algorithm. Furthermore, as we will explain in Sect. 1.1, the honest proofs cannot simply be pre-computed and hardwired into the reduction. Instead, we must develop new techniques for the inefficient prover case.

Our Notions of Zero Knowledge: The "Fine-Grained" Setting. We introduce fine-grained analogues of zero knowledge and witness indistinguishability. In fine-grained zero knowledge, we are concerned with (very) low complexity verifiers. We wish the honest verifier to have low complexity (we will use NC^1 as a running example), but we also want to scale down the claim "no additional knowledge" leaked (beyond validity of the statement) to what can be computed in this low complexity class (NC^1). The standard definition of zero knowledge simply requires that real transcripts can be simulated in probabilistic polynomial time. But if the verifier is in NC^1 the simulation complexity could in fact be substantially larger than that of the verifier, which does not capture the idea that "no additional knowledge" was leaked. While such a notion of simulation is stronger, we only require interactions with malicious verifiers in NC^1 to be simulatable. Moreover, simulation is only required to be indistinguishable from real to NC^1 distinguishers. In this sense, our notion of fine-grained zero knowledge is orthogonal to the standard, poly-time zero knowledge.[4] We also define a notion of fine-grained witness indistinguishability, where indistinguishability of interactions is only required to hold for low complexity distinguishers/verifiers.

We note that interactive fine-grained zero knowledge is straightforward to achieve using fine-grained commitments (which follow from the work of [29]) and a commitment-based ZK protocol (e.g. Blum-Hamiltonicity). We therefore focus on fine-grained ZAPs and NIZK.

NIZK Imply ZAPs for Inefficient Provers. Our main contribution is to prove that NIZK in the URS model implies ZAPs, even in the case of *inefficient provers*. Specifically, we show the following:

Theorem 1 (Informal). *Assuming the existence of an NIZK proof system for a language $\mathcal{L} \in \mathsf{AM}$ with provers running in time T in the URS model, there exists a ZAP for $\mathcal{L}$ with provers running in time $\mathrm{poly}(T, n)$, where n is security parameter.*

Our proof surprisingly leverages a type of *design*—a combinatorial object that was used in the derandomization of BPP by Nisan and Wigderson [58]. To the best of our knowledge, this is a novel application of designs to the cryptographic setting.

We also briefly discuss here the notion of a "witness" for an AM language and the meaning of witness indistinguishability. Recall that a language is in AM iff it has an AM protocol (Prover, Verifier) and so AM languages are inherently tied to protocols. Therefore, similarly to tying witnesses for NP languages to a specific verification algorithm, the notion of a "witness" for an AM language will be tied to the protocol. Specifically, we assume that there is an AM-protocol for a language $\mathcal{L}$. Given the first message r from the verifier, we can consider the Circuit-SAT problem w.r.t. the first message r and the verifier's circuit. Specifically, a witness w is a Prover's message that causes the verifier to output 1, when the first message r is fixed. Thus, witness-indistinguishability means that

---

[4] Note that this is very different from other fine-grained flavors of zero knowledge such as "knowledge tightness" or "precise zero knowledge" [30,31,36,37,57] which look for a simulation complexity that is tight to *each* simulator. Under these notions, if a malicious verifier, V, runs for n^{c_V} steps, then the interaction with the prover should simulatable with order $O(n^{c_V})$ steps. These verifier-by-verifier notions, in some sense, recover fine-grained zero knowledge with respect to $\mathsf{TIME}(n^c)$ for all c simultaneously. In this work, we aren't concerned with such verifier-by-verifier simulation of malicious poly-time verifiers, but instead what can be achieved if one is *only* concerned with (very) simple malicious verifiers (in order to minimize assumptions).

if there are two possible Prover messages w_1, w_2 that can be sent in response to r and such that the verifier accepts both, then the transcript of the ZAP should be indistinguishable when the Prover uses witness w_1 or w_2.

As a concrete example, consider the Goldwasser-Sipser (GS) protocol [40] for proving lower bounds on the size of NP sets. The verifier sends a random hash value and the prover responds with an element in the set that hashes to that value. WI is meaningful if there are multiple elements in the set that hash to the target value, since it guarantees that the verifier cannot distinguish which pre-image was used.[5]

Since it is well-known that NIZK with inefficient provers in the URS model can be constructed from one-way permutations (OWP) (see e.g. [61]), our result immediately yields ZAPs with subexponential provers from the Minicrypt assumption of OWP.

Theorem 2 (Informal). *Assuming the existence of one-way permutations, if* $\mathcal{L} \in$ AM *with prover run-time* T, *then there exists a ZAP for* $\mathcal{L}$ *with prover run-time* $\mathrm{poly}(T, \mathsf{subexp}(n))$.

Extending to the Fine-Grained Setting. Next, we observe that our same transformation can be applied to obtain *fine-grained* ZAPs from fine-grained NIZK in the URS model. Here, we assume that the prover is polynomial-time, but that the verifier and distinguisher are in a lower complexity class, $\mathcal{F}$. We then require that zero knowledge/witness indistinguishability hold against distinguishers from complexity class $\mathcal{F}$. For the proof technique from above to work, we require the class $\mathcal{F}$ to satisfy some mild compositional requirements, which are, in particular, satisfied by the class NC^1. We thus obtain the following:

Theorem 3 (Informal). *Assuming the existence of non-adaptive* NC^1*-fine-grained NIZK proof systems for* NP *in the URS model, there exist* NC^1*-fine-grained ZAPs for* NP.

We next show how to construct NC^1-fine-grained NIZK in the URS model for all of NP, assuming the *worst-case assumption* that $\oplus L/\mathrm{poly} \not\subseteq \mathsf{NC}^1$. Our result begins by converting the NIZK construction of [3] that works for languages $\mathcal{L}$ with randomized encodings from the CRS model to the URS model.[6] Since randomized encodings are known for the class $\oplus L/\mathrm{poly}$, this yields an NIZK proof system in the URS model (which actually achieves *statistical zero*

---

[5] We note that the GS protocol is used to prove that MA is contained in AM (by proving that the set of accepting coins of the verifier is sufficiently large). Recall that MA is like NP except the verifier can be randomized. It is not difficult to observe that our notion under the above transformation yields proofs for MA where witnesses that make the randomized verifier accept w.h.p. are indistinguishable.

[6] Recently, [33] constructed one-way permutations in the fine-grained setting. However, their results cannot be extended in straight-forward manner to construct fine-grained NIZKs and therefore are unlikely to lead to simpler constructions without using other techniques. For more discussion on this, we refer the interested readers to Sect. 1.2.

knowledge). We then introduce a new primitive, which we call a $\mathcal{G}$-*extractable*, $\mathcal{F}$-*Fine-Grained Commitment*. This is a commitment that is perfectly binding, hiding against $\mathcal{F}$, but extractable by $\mathcal{G}$. We show how to construct $\oplus L/$poly-extractable, NC^1-Fine-Grained Commitment under the *worst-case* assumption that $\oplus L/$poly $\not\subseteq \mathsf{NC}^1$ using techniques of [29]. Then, using $\oplus L/$poly-extractable, NC^1-Fine-Grained Commitment we show how to bootstrap the NIZK proof system in the URS model for the class $\oplus L/$poly to an $\mathcal{F}$-fine-grained NIZK proof system for NP in the URS model. We obtain the following theorem:

Theorem 4 (Informal). *Assuming that* $\oplus L/$poly $\not\subseteq \mathsf{NC}^1$, *there exist non-adaptive* NC^1-*fine-grained NIZK proof systems for* NP *in the URS model.*

Beyond ZAPs. One reason that ZAPs are a crucial tool in cryptography, is that they can be used as a building block to construct NIWI in the standard (no trusted setup) model under certain types of assumptions that are common in the derandomization literature. Indeed, the seminal work of Barak et al. [8] was the first to establish this connection between derandomization assumptions and NIWI. Furthermore, NIWI in the standard model can be used to construct NIZK with soundness against uniform adversaries in the standard model.

The constructions of NIWI from ZAPs and derandomization techniques go through in the inefficient-prover setting, since parallel repetition of 2-message protocols retains WI even in the inefficient prover setting (though this is not necessarily true for protocols with more than 2-messages).

We are not able to convert NIWI into fully standard NIZK with uniform soundness. The reason is that the transformation from NIWI to NIZK with uniform soundness in the no-CRS model employs the well-known FLS paradigm [34]. In this paradigm, the ZK simulator runs the honest prover with a trapdoor witness. However, in our case, the simulator cannot run the honest prover as it does not have enough computational power. Fortunately, we are able to show that if the simulator is given non-uniform advice that *does not depend on the statement being proved* then the simulator can perfectly simulate the honest prover's output on the trapdoor witness. Thus, we introduce offline NIZK (oNIZK), which requires existence of a distribution $\mathcal{D}_{\mathsf{Sim}}$ over small circuit simulators Sim, such that for any statement $x \in \mathcal{L}$, the distribution over (URS', π') obtained by drawing Sim from $\mathcal{D}_{\mathsf{Sim}}$ and outputting $(\mathsf{URS}', \pi') \leftarrow \mathsf{Sim}(x)$ is computationally indistinguishable from honest CRS's and proofs (URS, π). We note that this notion is sufficient for indistinguishability-based applications. We next state our results for the oNIZK setting:

Theorem 5 (Informal). *Assuming the existence of one-way permutations, appropriate derandomization assumptions,*[7] *and sub-exponentially-hard uniform collision resistant hash functions, then for any constant $0 < \epsilon < 1$ and constant $c \geq 1$, there exist oNIZK in the standard model for* NP *with honest provers run-*

---

[7] Specifically, the existence of efficient $1/2$-hitting set generators (HSG) against co-nondeterministic uniform algorithms [8].

ning in uniform time $2^{n'}$ and soundness against uniform adversaries running in time 2^{n^c}, where n is security parameter.

Theorem 6 (Informal). *Assuming that $\oplus L/\text{poly} \not\subseteq \mathsf{NC}^1$, appropriate derandomization assumptions as above, and the existence of uniform collision resistant hash functions, there exist NC^1-fine-grained oNIZK in the standard model for NP.*

1.1   Technical Overview

ZAPs from NIZK with inefficient provers. Let us begin by recapping the construction of ZAPs from a non-adaptive NIZK proof system with an efficient prover in the URS model.

The public coin verifier sends a random string r, which is partitioned into n' sections $r_1 || \cdots || r_{n'}$. Each r_i is a bitstring of length n, where n is also the bit length of the URS for the underlying NIZK proof system. Upon receiving $r_1 || \cdots || r_{n'}$, the prover chooses a string $x \in \{0,1\}^n$. For $i \in [n']$, the prover then sets $\mathsf{URS}_i := r_i \oplus x$ and runs the prover of the underlying NIZK proof system on the input statement, witness and URS_i, to produce proof π_i. The prover then sends $x, \pi_1, \ldots, \pi_{n'}$ to the verifier. For $i \in [n']$, the verifier recomputes $\mathsf{URS}_i := r_i \oplus x$ and runs the verifier of the underlying NIZK proof system on URS_i, π_i. If all the proofs accept, then the verifier accepts; otherwise, it rejects.

To prove soundness of the above proof system, a counting argument is employed. Specifically, fix any statement st that is not in the language. Since the underlying NIZK is statistically sound, the number of "bad" URS's for which there exists a proof π that accepts for st is small; say the fraction of "bad" URS's is at most $1/2$. This means that for a fixed statement st not in the language and a fixed x, the probability over random choice of $r_1, \ldots, r_{n'}$ that there exists an accepting proof π_i relative to each $\mathsf{URS}_i, i \in [n']$ is at most $2^{-n'}$. Taking a union bound over all possible choices for x, we have that for a fixed st, the probability over choice of $r_1, \ldots, r_{n'}$ that there *exists* an x of length n for which there exists an accepting proof relative to each $\mathsf{URS}_i, i \in [n']$ is at most $2^{n-n'}$. Setting $n' = 2n$ provides us with negligible statistical soundness in n.

On the other hand, to prove witness indistinguishability, one proceeds via a hybrid argument. In the original hybrid, witness w_1 is used for each of the n' number of honestly generated proofs $\pi_1, \ldots, \pi_{n'}$. In the final hybrid, witness w_2 is used for each of the n' number of honestly generated proofs $\pi_1, \ldots, \pi_{n'}$. In each intermediate hybrid, we switch from honestly generating a proof using w_1 to using w_2. Indistinguishability of intermediate hybrids is proved by showing that an efficient distinguisher between the hybrids implies an efficient distinguisher between real and simulated proofs of the underlying NIZK system. Specifically, a *reduction* is constructed as follows: Given the verifier's string $r = r_1 || \cdots || r_{n'}$ and a real or simulated URS/proof pair (URS^*, π^*), the reduction sets x such that $\mathsf{URS}_i = x \oplus r_i = \mathsf{URS}^*$. The reduction then runs the honest prover with w_2 for the first $i - 1$ proofs, runs the honest prover with w_1 for the last $n' - i$ proofs, and embeds π^* in the i-th location. The reduction then applies the distinguisher between Hybrids $i-1$ and i to the resulting transcript, and outputs whatever it does. Since a distinguisher between Hybrids $i-1$ and i must either distinguish the above when (URS^*, π^*) were generated using the honest prover and w_1 versus using the simulator or when (URS^*, π^*) were generated using the honest prover and w_2 versus using the simulator, the above reduction succeeds in one of those cases. If one of the cases succeeds, we obtain a contradiction to the zero knowledge property.

Note that to prove soundness of the ZAP, soundness against unbounded provers in the underlying NIZK is crucial since we use a counting argument based on the number of "bad" URS's for which there exists an accepting proof of the false statement. Furthermore, the fact that the prover in the underlying NIZK is *efficient* is crucial for arguing witness indistinguishability. The reason can be seen from the sketch of the hybrid argument above, where we have a hybrid in which we reduce to the zero knowledge of the underlying NIZK (note that the zero knowledge must always be *computational*, since we require the soundness to be statistical). This means that existence of a distinguisher for consecutive hybrids must imply a ZK distinguisher, and the ZK distinguisher that is constructed, given an efficient distinguisher for consecutive hybrids, must be efficient. But in the approach outlined above, to generate the correct hybrid distributions for the efficient distinguisher, we must run the honest prover with witness w_2 for the first $i-1$ proofs and run the honest prover with witness w_1 for the last $n'-i$ proofs. This cannot be done efficiently if the honest prover is inefficient. An immediate thought would be to use non-uniform advice to hardcode all the proofs except the i-th proof into the ZK distinguisher. However, this does not work because $\mathsf{URS}_{i'}$ for $i' \neq i$ *depends* on URS^*, which is part of the input to the ZK distinguisher. Specifically, on input (URS^*, π^*), x is set to $\mathsf{URS}^* \oplus r_i$ and only once x is fixed do we learn $\mathsf{URS}_{i'} := r_{i'} \oplus x$ for $i' \neq i$. So we cannot know the URS's $\mathsf{URS}_{i'}, i' \neq i$ ahead of time and therefore cannot hope to hardcode the proofs $\pi_{i'}$ as non-uniform advice.

We will resolve this issue and show that non-uniform advice *can* help in our setting, by allow limited pairwise dependency across the URS's. Specifically, our construction leverages the notion of a *design*, introduced by Nisan and Wigderson in their seminal work [58]. A *design* with parameters (l, n, c, n') is a set of n' sets $\mathcal{S}_1, \ldots, \mathcal{S}_{n'}$, where each $\mathcal{S}_i, i \in [n']$ is a subset of $[l]$ and has size $|\mathcal{S}_i| = n$. Moreover for every pair $i, j \in [n']$, $i \neq j$, it holds that $|\mathcal{S}_i \cap \mathcal{S}_j| \leq c$. It is known how to construct designs with $l = n^2$, constant c and $n' := n^c$ (see e.g. [58]). Let us see how a design with parameters $(l = n^2, n, c = 3, n' = n^3)$ can be used to resolve our problems above. Upon receiving string $r = r_1 || \cdots || r_{n'}$ from the verifier, we now allow the prover to choose a bit string $x = [x_j]_{j \in [l]}$ of length l. URS_i is then defined as $r_i \oplus [x_j]_{j \in \mathcal{S}_i}$, where $[x_j]_{j \in \mathcal{S}}$ for a set $\mathcal{S} \subseteq [l]$ denotes the substring of x corresponding to the positions $j \in \mathcal{S}$ and $\mathcal{S}_i$ is the corresponding set in the design. Now, soundness is ensured by the same argument as above (i.e. via a union bound), since $2^{-n'} \cdot 2^l = 2^{-n^3} \cdot 2^{n^2} = 2^{-n^3 + n^2}$ is negligible in n. Furthermore, since for each pair $i, j \in [n']$, $i \neq j$, it holds that $|\mathcal{S}_i \cap \mathcal{S}_j| \leq 3$, we can use the following proof strategy to argue indistinguishability of consecutive hybrids: In the i-th hybrid, we fix the string $[x_j]_{j \notin S_i}$ at random. We then generate $n' - 1$ truth tables with constant input length. The input to the i'-th truth table ($i' \in [n'], i' \neq i$) is at most 3 bits, corresponding to $[x_j]_{j \in S_{i'} \cap S_i}$. For $i' < i$, the output of the truth table $T_{i'}$ is a proof $\pi_{i'}$ that is honestly computed using witness w_2 and $\mathsf{URS}_{i'} = [x_j]_{j \in S_{i'}}$. For $i' > i$, the output of the truth table $T_{i'}$ is a proof $\pi_{i'}$ that is honestly computed using witness w_1 and $\mathsf{URS}_{i'} = [x_j]_{j \in S_{i'}}$. Note that since everything is fixed (including all the bits of $[x_j]_{j \in S_{i'}}$ except for $[x_j]_{j \in S_{i'} \cap S_i}$), each truth table can be computed by an NC^0 circuit.

Now, given a real or simulated URS/proof pair (URS^*, π^*), the reduction will set $[x_j]_{j \in S_i}$ such that $\mathsf{URS}_i = [x_j]_{j \in S_i} \oplus r_i = \mathsf{URS}^*$. The reduction will then use the truth table $T_{i'}$ to generate proof $\pi_{i'}$ for $i' \neq i$, and will embed π^* in the i-th location. The reduction will then evaluate the distinguisher D (represented as a poly-sized circuit) on the resulting transcript and output whatever it outputs. Note that the reduction can now be represented as a poly-sized circuit and note that it outputs exactly the correct distribution to the distinguisher. Thus, an efficient distinguisher for intermediate hybrids yields a poly-sized circuit that breaks the zero knowledge property of the underlying NIZK, resulting in contradiction.

Fine-Grained ZAPs. As discussed previously, fine-grained ZAPs relative to a class $\mathcal{F}$ are ZAPs that have a poly-time prover and provide witness indistinguishability against class $\mathcal{F}$ that is conjectured to not contain P. The same difficulty of converting a single-theorem fine-grained NIZK in the common random string model into a ZAP arises as above. Luckily, if circuits $f \in \mathcal{F}$ composed with NC^0 circuits are also in $\mathcal{F}$, then the same proof as above can work (since the reduction sketched above can be implemented with a NC^0 circuit. Thus, given a non-adaptive, fine-grained NIZK in the URS model against NC^1, we obtain a fine-grained ZAP relative to NC^1.

Fine-Grained NIZK in Uniform Random String (URS) Model. We first modify a construction of [3] in the CRS model to yield a construction in the URS model. This is done by observing that a random string is a good CRS for the construction of [47] with probability $1/2$ (which follows from the fact that randomized encodings of [47] are "balanced"). We then construct a URS by sampling many reference strings at random, and having the prover either prove that the reference string is invalid or provide a proof of the statement relative to the reference string. Note that this yields a construction with a poly-time prover and provides *statistical*-zero knowledge as well as soundness against unbounded provers. However, this construction only allows proving statements for languages that have randomized encodings (such as languages in $\oplus L/\text{poly}$). We would like to obtain a proof system for all languages in NP, while sacrificing the statistical zero knowledge property and obtaining a fine-grained NIZK with poly-time prover against the class NC^1. It turns out that to obtain this, we can use the fact that, assuming $\oplus L/\text{poly} \neq NC^1$, there exist "commitments" with the following properties: (1) Commitments can be constructed in the class NC^1. (2) Given a commitment, extracting the committed value can be performed in the class $\oplus L/\text{poly}$

(i.e. the decision problem $\mathcal{L}_{det}$ which, given a commitment *com* outputs 1 if it is a commitment to 1 is in $\oplus L/\text{poly}$). (3) Commitments are hiding against a NC^1 adversary. Such commitments can be easily constructed by computing the randomized encoding of a "canonical" 0 (resp. 1) input to commit to 0 (resp. 1). Now, using the fact that $\oplus L/\text{poly}$ is closed under negation, disjunction and conjunction (see [11]), we can use the statistical-zero knowledge NIZK in the URS model for languages in $\oplus L/\text{poly}$ to obtain a fine-grained NIZK in the URS model against NC^1 for all of NP as follows: Given a circuit-SAT instance $\mathcal{C}$, where $\mathcal{C}$ is a circuit consisting of NAND gates and we assume that it has z wires. the prover will commit to the values of all the wires of $\mathcal{C}$ for some satisfying assignment. This commitment will be performed using the "commitment" scheme described above. The prover will then prove that the sequence of "commitments" $com_1, \ldots, com_z$ is in the language $\mathcal{L}_{\mathcal{C}}$, where $com_z \in \mathcal{L}_{det}$, and for each NAND gate, with input wires i, j and output wire k, com_i, com_j, com_k are commitments to valid inputs/outputs for a NAND gate (i.e. $(com_i, com_j, com_k) \in \mathcal{L}_{gate}$). Since $\mathcal{L}_{\mathcal{C}}$ will consist of negation/conjunction/disjunction of languages in $\oplus L/\text{poly}$ and since $\oplus L/\text{poly}$ is closed under negation/conjunction/disjunction, we have that $\mathcal{L}_{\mathcal{C}} \in \oplus L/\text{poly}$. Moreover, given $com_1, \ldots, com_z$, we can simulate a proof in NC^1 (using the simulator for the NIZK for languages in $\oplus L/\text{poly}$), indicating that the NIZK provides zero knowledge against NC^1.

1.2   Related Work

Zero Knowledge. Zero knowledge (ZK) proofs were introduced by Goldwasser, Micali, and Rackoff [39]. Since its introduction, ZK proof systems and its variants have been studied with great interest. Some of the notable results related to ZK proofs are – [37] which showed ZK proofs exist for all languages in NP, and [38] which showed that interaction is crucial for achieving zero knowledge property in case of non-trivial languages. Specifically, [38] showed that if for language $\mathcal{L}$, 2-message ZK proof system exists then $\mathcal{L} \in \mathsf{BPP}$. The research aimed at minimizing the interaction has since relied on either constructing Non-Interactive Zero Knowledge proof systems (NIZKs) with the help of trusted setup assumptions such as uniform random string (URS) [21] or constructing non-interactive protocols with weaker security guarantees such as *non-interactive witness indistinguishability* (NIWI). Intuitively, witness indistinguishability ensures that the verifier does not learn which witness (out of multiple valid witnesses) is used by the prover to generate the proof. Dwork and Naor [32] showed introduced two-message, witness indistinguishable proof systems (ZAPs) and showed that ZAPs (in a no-CRS model) are equivalent to NIZKs in uniform *random* string (URS) model.

Zero Knowledge Primitives and Underlying Assumptions. Blum et al. [21], gave the first construction of NIZK in CRS model from number-theoretic assumptions (e.g. quadratic residuosity). Since then, NIZKs have been constructed in URS model from one-way permutations and certified trapdoor permutations [34], whereas Lapidot and Shamir [55], constructed publicly verifiable NIZK from one-way permutations in URS model, Groth et al. [42] constructed NIZK from DLIN assumption in URS model. Recently, Peikert and Shiehian [62] constructed NIZK from LWE assumption in URS model.

NIZKs have also been studied in other models [15,26,27], and models which consider preprocessing along with other assumptions such as one-way encryption schemes exist [28], lattices (LWE) [54], and DDH/CDH [53]. Few of the other works on NIZKs include [1,14,19,25,41,44,61]. For more details on NIZK related research, we refer the interested readers to [65]

The notion of witness indistinguishable proofs was introduced by [35]. As discussed earlier, Dwork and Naor [32] introduced ZAP (two-message, witness indistinguishable proofs) and presented a construction in plain (no-CRS) model assuming the existence of certified trapdoor permutations. Barak et al. [8] gave a construction of NIWI based on derandomization assumptions and certified trapdoor permutations (by derandomizing the verifier of [32] construction). Groth et al. [43] constructed first non-interactive ZAP from DLIN assumption, whereas Bitansky and Paneth [20] showed a construction of ZAP based on indistinguishabliy obfuscation (iO) and one-way functions, and NIWI from iO and one-way permutations. Recently ZAP were constructed assuming quasi-polynomial hardness of DDH [51,52], and quasi-polynomial hardness of LWE [4,50].

Fine-Grained Cryptography. Fine-grained cryptography refers to construction of primitives which provide security guarantees against adversaries with sharper complexity bounds than simply "polynomial time." Both adversaries with *specific* polynomial runtime bounds (e.g. $\mathsf{TIME}[O(n^2)]$) and adversaries with *specific* parallel-time complexity (e.g. NC^1) have been considered under this moniker in the literature. In [29] Degwekar et al. constructed primitives like one-way functions, pseudo-random generators, collision-resistant hash functions and public key encryption schemes based on well-studied complexity theoretic assumptions. Ball et al. [6,7] worst-case to average-case reduction for different type of fine-grained hardness problems and then extended their work to construct Proofs of Work. Campanelli and Gennaro [23] initiated the study of fine-grained secure computation by constructing a verifiable computation protocol secure against NC^1 adversaries based on worst-case assumptions. LaVigne et al. [56] constructed a fine-grained key-exchange protocol.

Comparison with Egashira et al. [33]. Recently, Egashira et al. [33] constructed one-way permutations, hash-proof systems, and trapdoor one-way functions, all of which can be computed in NC^1 and are secure against adversaries in NC^1, from the same assumptions that we consider in this work ($\oplus L/\mathrm{poly} \nsubseteq \mathsf{NC}^1$). Their results do not directly extend to construct NC^1-fine-grained NIZK systems in the URS model, as (1) to the best of our knowledge it is not known how to construct NIZK in URS model from trapdoor one-way functions, and (2) their one-way permutation does not directly allow instantiation of the hidden bits model [34], which could then be used to construct NC^1-fine-grained NIZK in the URS model. Specifically, the domain/range of their OWP includes only full rank matrices and does not include *all* strings of a given length. Furthermore, whether a given string is contained in the domain/range cannot be determined by a NC^1 circuit (assuming $\oplus L/\mathrm{poly} \not\subseteq \mathsf{NC}^1$) and strings that are not in the range can have multiple pre-images. So to implement the hidden bits model, a prover would need to prove that a string is or is not contained in the domain/range, without compromising the one-wayness of unopened bits, which would itself require a NC^1-fine-grained NIZK proof system in the URS model. In contrast, our construction of NC^1-fine-grained NIZK in the URS model is direct and does not require fine-grained OWP nor implementing a fine-grained hidden bits model.

2   Definitions

Definition 1. *Let $\mathcal{F} = \{\mathcal{F}_n\}_{n\in\mathbb{N}}$ be a class of circuits parameterized by n with input length $\ell(n)$. We say that two distribution ensembles $\{\mathcal{D}_n^0\}_{n\in\mathbb{N}}, \{\mathcal{D}_n^0\}_{n\in\mathbb{N}}$, with support $\{0,1\}^{\ell(n)}$, are indistinguishable by $\mathcal{F}$ if*

$$\max_{f_n\in\mathcal{F}_n} \left| \Pr[f_n(x) = 1 \mid x \sim \mathcal{D}_n^0] - \Pr[f_n(x) = 1 \mid x \sim \mathcal{D}_n^1] \right| \le \mathsf{negl}(n).$$

We refer the interested reader to the full version of this paper [5], for additional definitions of fine-grained pseudorandom generator (PRG), as well as the standard definitions of witness indistinguishability (WI), and non-interactive witness indistinguishability (NIWI).

Definition 2 ($\mathcal{G}$-Extractable, $\mathcal{F}$-Fine-Grained Commitment Scheme). *A commitment scheme comprising of three algorithms (Commit, Open, Extract) is called $\mathcal{G}$-Extractable, $\mathcal{F}$-Fine-Grained Commitment Scheme if the following hold:*

– Commit $\in \mathcal{F}$ and Open $\in \mathcal{F}$ for class $\mathcal{F}$.
– **Correctness:** *For all $n \in \mathbb{N}$ and for $b \in \{0,1\}$:*

$$\Pr[(com, d) \leftarrow \mathsf{Commit}(1^n, b) : \mathsf{Open}(com, d) = b] = 1$$

– **Perfect Binding:** *There does not exist a tuple (com, d, d') such that*

$$\mathsf{Open}(com, d) = 0 \wedge \mathsf{Open}(com, d') = 1.$$

– $\mathcal{F}$**-Hiding:** *For any Open$^* \in \mathcal{F}$,*

$$\left| \Pr_{b\leftarrow\{0,1\}}[(com, d) \leftarrow \mathsf{Commit}(1^n, b) : \mathsf{Open}^*(c) = b] - \frac{1}{2} \right| \le \mathsf{negl}(n)$$

– $\mathcal{G}$**-Extractability:** *There exists Extract $\in \mathcal{G}$ such that for any string com,*

$$\mathsf{Extract}(com) = b \text{ iff } \exists d \text{ s.t. } \mathsf{Open}(com, d) = b.$$

An $\mathcal{F}$-Fine-Grained Commitment Scheme is the same as the above definition, but does not enjoy the $\mathcal{G}$-Extractability property.

2.1 NIZK and Fine-Grained NIZK in the URS Model

Definition 3 (Non-interactive Proofs in the URS Model). *A pair of algorithms* (Prover, Verifier) *is called a non-interactive proof system in the URS model for a language* $\mathcal{L}$ *if the algorithm* Verifier *is deterministic polynomial-time, there exists a polynomial* $p(\cdot)$ *and a negligible function* $\mu(\cdot)$ *such that the following two conditions hold:*

– **Completeness:** *For every* $x \in \mathcal{L}$

$$\Pr[\mathsf{URS} \leftarrow \{0,1\}^{p(|x|)}; \pi \leftarrow \mathsf{Prover}(x, \mathsf{URS}) : \mathsf{Verifier}(x, \mathsf{URS}, \pi) = 1] \geq 1 - \mu(|x|).$$

– **Soundness:** *For every* $x \notin \mathcal{L}$, *every algorithm* P^*

$$\Pr[\mathsf{URS} \leftarrow \{0,1\}^{p(|x|)}; \pi' \leftarrow P^*(x, \mathsf{URS}) : \mathsf{Verifier}(x, \mathsf{URS}, \pi') = 1] \leq \mu(|x|).$$

Definition 4 (Non-interactive Zero-Knowledge with Offline Simulation (oNIZK) in the URS Model). *Let* (Prover, Verifier) *be a non-interactive proof system in the URS model for the language* $\mathcal{L}$. *We say that* (Prover, Verifier) *is* non-adaptively zero-knowledge with offline simulation *in the URS model if there exists a distribution* $\mathcal{D}_{\mathsf{Sim}}$ *over polynomial-sized circuits* Sim *such that the following two distribution ensembles are computationally indistinguishable by polynomial-sized circuits (when the distinguishing gap is a function of* $|x|$)

$$\{(\mathsf{URS}, \pi) : \mathsf{URS} \leftarrow \{0,1\}^{p(|x|)}; \pi \leftarrow \mathsf{Prover}(\mathsf{URS}, x)\}_{x \in \mathcal{L}}$$
$$\{(\mathsf{URS}', \pi') \leftarrow \mathsf{Sim}(x) : \mathsf{Sim} \leftarrow \mathcal{D}_{\mathsf{Sim}}\}_{x \in \mathcal{L}}.$$

A useful property of oNIZK is the following: Let $\mathcal{D}_{\mathsf{yes}}$ be a distribution over statements $x \in \mathcal{L}$ and let $\mathcal{D}_{\mathsf{no}}$ be a distribution over statements $x \in \overline{\mathcal{L}}$. If $\mathcal{D}_{\mathsf{yes}}$ and $\mathcal{D}_{\mathsf{no}}$ are computationally indistinguishable by polynomial-sized circuits then the following two distribution ensembles are computationally indistinguishable by polynomial-sized circuits (when the distinguishing gap is a function of $|x|$)

$$\{(x, (\mathsf{URS}, \pi) \leftarrow \mathsf{Sim}(x)) : \mathsf{Sim} \leftarrow \mathcal{D}_{\mathsf{Sim}}, x \leftarrow \mathcal{D}_{\mathsf{yes}}\}$$
$$\{(x', (\mathsf{URS}', \pi') \leftarrow \mathsf{Sim}(x')) : \mathsf{Sim} \leftarrow \mathcal{D}_{\mathsf{Sim}}, x' \leftarrow \mathcal{D}_{\mathsf{no}}\}.$$

The above allows a typical usage of oNIZK in hybrid style proofs: In the first hybrid, one can leave the statement the same and switch from proofs generated by the honest prover to proofs generated by the simulator, in the second step, one can switch the statement from a true statement to a false statement.

For more details on the relationship between Definition 4 and the notions of *witness hiding* (WH) and *weak zero knowledge* (WZK), see [5].

Definition 5 (Fine-Grained Non-interactive Proofs in the URS Model). *A pair of algorithms* (Prover, Verifier) *is called a* $\mathcal{F}$-*fine-grained non-interactive proof system in the URS model for a language* $\mathcal{L}$ *if the algorithm* Prover *is polynomial-time, (uniformly generated)* Verifier $\in \mathcal{F}_{|x|}$ *(*Verifier *can be uniformly generated), there exists a polynomial* $p(\cdot)$ *and a negligible function* $\mu(\cdot)$ *such that the following two conditions hold:*

- **Completeness:** For every $x \in \mathcal{L}$

  $$\Pr[\mathsf{URS} \leftarrow \{0,1\}^{p(|x|)}; \pi \leftarrow \mathsf{Prover}(x, \mathsf{URS}) : \mathsf{Verifier}(x, \mathsf{URS}, \pi) = 1] \geq 1 - \mu(|x|).$$

- **Soundness:** For every $x \notin \mathcal{L}$, every algorithm P^*

  $$\Pr[\mathsf{URS} \leftarrow \{0,1\}^{p(|x|)}; \pi' \leftarrow P^*(x, \mathsf{URS}) : \mathsf{Verifier}(x, \mathsf{URS}, \pi') = 1] \leq \mu(|x|).$$

Definition 6 (Fine-Grained Non-interactive Zero-Knowledge in the URS Model). *Let* (Prover, Verifier) *be a $\mathcal{F}$-fine-grained non-interactive proof system in the URS model for the language $\mathcal{L}$. We say that* (Prover, Verifier) *is a $\mathcal{F}$-fine-grained non-adaptively zero-knowledge in the URS model if there exists a randomized circuit* Sim *in $\mathcal{F}$ such that the following two distribution ensembles are computationally indistinguishable by circuits in $\mathcal{F}$ (when the distinguishing gap is a function of $|x|$)*

$$\{(\mathsf{URS}, \pi) : \mathsf{URS} \leftarrow \{0,1\}^{p(|x|)}; \pi \leftarrow \mathsf{Prover}(\mathsf{URS}, x)\}_{x \in \mathcal{L}}$$
$$\{(\mathsf{URS}', \pi') \leftarrow \mathsf{Sim}(x)\}_{x \in \mathcal{L}}.$$

We say that a fine-grained non-interactive proof system in the URS model is a *statistical NIZK protocol* (or alternatively *achieves statistical zero knowledge*) if the above distribution ensembles are statistically close.

Definition 7 (Fine-Grained Non-interactive Zero-Knowledge with Offline Simulation (oNIZK) in the URS Model). *Let* (Prover, Verifier) *be a $\mathcal{F}$-fine-grained non-interactive proof system in the URS model for the language $\mathcal{L}$. We say that* (Prover, Verifier) *is a $\mathcal{F}$-fine-grained non-adaptively zero-knowledge with offline simulation in the URS model if there exists a distribution $\mathcal{D}_{\mathsf{Sim}}$ over circuits in $\mathcal{F}$ such that the following two distribution ensembles are computationally indistinguishable by circuits in $\mathcal{F}$ (when the distinguishing gap is a function of $|x|$)*

$$\{(\mathsf{URS}, \pi) : \mathsf{URS} \leftarrow \{0,1\}^{p(|x|)}; \pi \leftarrow \mathsf{Prover}(\mathsf{URS}, x)\}_{x \in \mathcal{L}}$$
$$\{(\mathsf{URS}', \pi') \leftarrow \mathsf{Sim}(x) : \mathsf{Sim} \leftarrow \mathcal{D}_{\mathsf{Sim}}\}_{x \in \mathcal{L}}.$$

Note that by the same argument as above, our fine-grained NIZK definition (for $\mathcal{F} = \mathsf{NC}^1$) implies witness hiding and weak zero knowledge with inverse-polynomial distinguishing advantage. Specifically, for the witness hiding case: Let $\mathcal{D}$ be a distribution over statements $x \in \mathcal{L}$. Assume that $\mathcal{L}$ has witness relation $\mathcal{R}$ such that $x \in \mathcal{L}$ if and only if there exists a witness w such that $(x, w) \in \mathcal{R}$. Note that WLOG we can assume that $\mathcal{R} \in \mathsf{NC}^1$. Assume that for all circuits $C \in \mathsf{NC}^1$,

$$\Pr_{x \sim \mathcal{D}}[R(x, C(x)) = 1] \leq \mathsf{negl}(|x|).$$

Then we have that for all circuits $C' \in \mathsf{NC}^1$

$$\Pr_{x \sim \mathcal{D}}[R(x, C'(x, \mathsf{URS}, \pi)) = 1] = 1 : \mathsf{URS} \leftarrow \{0,1\}^{p(|x|)}; \pi \leftarrow \mathsf{Prover}(\mathsf{URS}, x)] \leq \mathsf{negl}(|x|).$$

2.2 Fine-Grained Witness Indistinguishability

Definition 8 ($\mathcal{F}$-fine-grained Witness Indistinguishability). *A proof system* $\langle$Prover, Verifier$\rangle$ *for a language* $\mathcal{L}$ *is* $\mathcal{F}$-*fine-grained witness-indistinguishable if* Prover *is polynomial-time,* Verifier *is in the class* $\mathcal{F}$ *and for any* $V^* \in \mathcal{F}$, *for all* $x \in \mathcal{L}$, *for all* $w_1, w_2 \in w(x)$, *and for all auxiliary inputs* z *to* V^*, *the distribution on the views of* V^* *following an execution* $\langle$Prover, Verifier$\rangle(x, w_1, z)$ *is indistinguishable from the distribution on the views of* V^* *following an execution* $\langle$Prover, Verifier$\rangle(x, w_2, z)$ *to a non-uniform distinguisher in class* $\mathcal{F}$ *receiving one of the above transcripts as well as* (x, w_1, w_2, z).

2.3 ZAPs and Fine-Grained ZAPs

Definition 9 (ZAP). *A ZAP is a 2-round (2-message) protocol for proving membership of* $x \in \mathcal{L}$, *where* $\mathcal{L}$ *is a language in* NP. *Let the first-round (verifier to prover) message be denoted* ρ *and the second-round (prover to verifier) response be denoted* π *satisfying the following conditions:*

- **Public Coins:** *There is a polynomial* $p(\cdot)$ *such that the first round messages form a distribution on strings of length* $p(|x|)$. *The verifier's decision whether to accept or reject is a polynomial time function of* x, ρ, *and* π *only.*
- **Completeness:** *Given* x, *a witness* $w \in w(x)$, *and a first-round* ρ, *the prover generates a proof* π *that will be accepted by the verifier with overwhelming probability over the choices made by the prover and the verifier.*
- **Soundness:** *With overwhelming probability over the choice of* ρ, *there exists no* $x' \notin \mathcal{L}$ *and second round message* π *such that the verifier accepts* (x', ρ, π).
- **Witness-Indistinguishability:** *Let* $w, w' \in w(x)$ *for* $x \in L$. *Then* $\forall \rho$, *the distribution on* π *when the prover has input* (x, w) *and the distribution on* π *when the prover has input* (x, w') *are nonuniform probabilistic polynomial time (in* $|x|$) *indistinguishable, even given both witnesses* w, w'.

Definition 10 ($\mathcal{F}$-fine-grained ZAP). *A* $\mathcal{F}$-*fine-grained ZAP is a 2-round (2-message) protocol for proving membership of* $x \in \mathcal{L}$, *where* $\mathcal{L}$ *is a language in* NP. *Let the first-round (verifier to prover) message be denoted* ρ *and the second-round (prover to verifier) response be denoted* π *satisfying the following conditions:*

- **Public Coins and Fine-Grained Verifier:** *There is a polynomial* $p(\cdot)$ *such that the first round messages form a distribution on strings of length* $p(|x|)$. *The verifier's decision whether to accept or reject is a function of* x, ρ, *and* π *only, and is contained in* $\mathcal{F}_{|x|}$.
- **Completeness:** *Given* x, *a witness* $w \in w(x)$, *and a first-round* ρ, *the prover, running in time polynomial in* $|x|$, *can generates a proof* π *that will be accepted by the verifier with overwhelming probability over the choices made by the prover and the verifier.*
- **Soundness:** *With overwhelming probability over the choice of* ρ, *there exists no* $x' \notin \mathcal{L}$ *and second round message* π *such that the verifier accepts* (x', ρ, π).

– $\mathcal{F}$-**fine-grained Witness-Indistinguishability:** *Let* $w, w' \in w(x)$ *for* $x \in L$. *Then* $\forall \rho$, *the distribution on* π *when the prover has input* (x, w) *and the distribution on* π *when the prover has input* (x, w') *are indistinguishable to nonuniform algorithms in the class* $\mathcal{F}_{|x|}$, *even given both witnesses* w, w'.

2.4   Fine-Grained NIWI

Definition 11 ($\mathcal{F}$-**fine-grained NIWI**). *A* $\mathcal{F}$-*fine-grained NIWI is a non-interactive protocol for proving membership of* $x \in \mathcal{L}$, *where* $\mathcal{L}$ *is a language in* NP. *A single message* π *is sent from the prover to the verifier.*

– **Fine-Grained Verifier:** *The verifier's decision whether to accept or reject is a function of the statement* x *and proof* π *only, and the verifier's circuit is contained in* $\mathcal{F}_{|x|}$.
– **Completeness:** *Given* x, *and a witness* $w \in w(x)$ *the prover, running in time polynomial in* $|x|$, *can generate a proof* π *that will be accepted by the verifier with overwhelming probability over the choices made by the prover and the verifier.*
– **Soundness:** *There exists no* $x' \notin \mathcal{L}$ *and message* π *such that the verifier accepts* (x', π).
  $\mathcal{F}$-**fine-grained Witness-Indistinguishability:** *Let* $w, w' \in w(x)$ *for* $x \in L$. *Then the distribution on* π *when the prover has input* (x, w) *and the distribution on* π *when the prover has input* (x, w') *are indistinguishable by the class* $\mathcal{F} := \{\mathcal{F}_{|x|}\}_{|x| \in \mathbb{N}}$, *even given both witnesses* w, w'.

2.5   NIZK and Fine-Grained NIZK Without CRS and with Uniform Soundness

Definition 12 (**Non-interactive Proofs with uniform soundness**). *A pair of algorithms* (Prover, Verifier) *is called a non-interactive proof system with uniform soundness* $T := T(|x|)$, *for a language* $\mathcal{L}$ *if the algorithm* Verifier *is deterministic polynomial-time, there exists a polynomial* $p(\cdot)$ *and a negligible function* $\mu(\cdot)$ *such that the following two conditions hold:*

– **Completeness:** *For every* $x \in \mathcal{L}$

$$\Pr[\pi \leftarrow \mathsf{Prover}(x) : \mathsf{Verifier}(x, \pi) = 1] \geq 1 - \mu(|x|).$$

– **Soundness:** *For every* $x \notin \mathcal{L}$, *every algorithm* P^* *running in uniform time* T,

$$\Pr[\pi' \leftarrow P^*(x) : \mathsf{Verifier}(x, \pi') = 1] \leq \mu(|x|).$$

Definition 13 (**Non-interactive Zero-Knowledge with Offline Simulation (oNIZK) in the standard model with uniform soundness**). *Let* (Prover, Verifier) *be a non-interactive proof system with uniform soundness* $T := T(|x|)$ *for the language* $\mathcal{L}$. *We say that* (Prover, Verifier) *is* zero-knowledge *with* offline simulation *if there exists a distribution $\mathcal{D}_{\mathsf{Sim}}$ over polynomial-sized circuits* Sim *such that the following two distribution ensembles are computationally indistinguishable by polynomial-sized circuits (when the distinguishing gap is a function of $|x|$)*

$$\{\pi \leftarrow \mathsf{Prover}(x)\}_{x \in \mathcal{L}}$$
$$\{\pi' \leftarrow \mathsf{Sim}(x) : \mathsf{Sim} \leftarrow \mathcal{D}_{\mathsf{Sim}}\}_{x \in \mathcal{L}}.$$

As discussed previously, our NIZK definition above implies witness hiding, via the same argument.

Definition 14 (Fine-Grained Non-interactive Proofs with uniform soundness). *A pair of algorithms* (Prover, Verifier) *is called a $\mathcal{F}$-fine-grained non-interactive proof system with uniform soundness for a language $\mathcal{L}$ if the algorithm* Prover *is polynomial-time, (uniformly generated)* Verifier $\in \mathcal{F}_{|x|}$, *there exists a polynomial $p(\cdot)$ and a negligible function $\mu(\cdot)$ such that the following two conditions hold:*

– **Completeness:** *For every $x \in \mathcal{L}$*

$$\Pr[\pi \leftarrow \mathsf{Prover}(x, \mathsf{URS}) : \mathsf{Verifier}(x, \pi) = 1] \geq 1 - \mu(|x|).$$

– **Soundness:** *For every $x \notin \mathcal{L}$, every uniform, PPT algorithm P^**

$$\Pr[\pi' \leftarrow P^*(x) : \mathsf{Verifier}(x, \pi') = 1] \leq \mu(|x|).$$

Definition 15 (Fine-Grained Non-interactive Zero-Knowledge with Offline Simulation (oNIZK) in the standard model with uniform soundness). *Let* (Prover, Verifier) *be a $\mathcal{F}$-fine-grained non-interactive proof system with uniform soundness for the language $\mathcal{L}$. We say that* (Prover, Verifier) *is $\mathcal{F}$-fine-grained zero-knowledge with offline simulation if there exists a distribution $\mathcal{D}_{\mathsf{Sim}}$ over circuits in $\mathcal{F}$ such that the following two distribution ensembles are computationally indistinguishable by circuits in $\mathcal{F}$ (when the distinguishing gap is a function of $|x|$)*

$$\{\pi \leftarrow \mathsf{Prover}(x)\}_{x \in \mathcal{L}}$$
$$\{\pi' \leftarrow \mathsf{Sim}(x) : \mathsf{Sim} \leftarrow \mathcal{D}_{\mathsf{Sim}}\}_{x \in \mathcal{L}}.$$

As discussed previously, our fine-grained NIZK definition above implies witness hiding, via the same argument.

3   ZAPs from NIZK

For our construction of ZAPs from oNIZK in the URS model, we will require a certain type of *design*, defined next and first used by Nisan and Wigderson in their derandomization of BPP [58].

Definition 16 (Design). *A* (l, n', n, c)-*design consists of sets* $\mathcal{S}_1, \ldots, \mathcal{S}_{n'} \subseteq [l]$ *such that the following hold:*

- *For each* $i \in [n']$, $|\mathcal{S}_i| = n$,
- *For each* i, i' *s.t.* $i \neq i'$, $|\mathcal{S}_i \cap \mathcal{S}_{i'}| \leq c$.

(l, n', n, c) designs are known for $l := n^2$, constant $c \in \mathbb{N}$, and $n' := n^c$ [58].

Let $\Pi = (\mathsf{Prover}^{NIZK}, \mathsf{Verifier}^{NIZK})$ be a non-adaptive oNIZK in the URS model with inefficient prover for language $\mathcal{L}$ that has soundness $1/2$ or better. Let sets $\mathcal{S}_1, \ldots, \mathcal{S}_{n'} \subseteq [l]$ form a (l, n', n, c)-design, where $l := n^2$, $c := 3$, and $n' := n^3$.

Verifier's First Round Message: Recall that in the first round of a ZAP, the Verifier sends a random string r to the Prover.

Prover Algorithm: On input statement $\mathsf{st} \in \mathcal{L}$, witness w, and random string $r = r_1 || \cdots || r_{n'}$ from the Verifier:

1. Choose bits $[x_j]_{j \in [l]}$ at random. For a set $\mathcal{S} \subseteq [l]$, let $[x_j]_{j \in \mathcal{S}}$ denote the substring of $[x_1, \ldots, x_l]$ corresponding to indices in set $\mathcal{S}$.
2. For each $i \in [n']$, let $\mathsf{URS}_i = r_i \oplus [x_j]_{j \in \mathcal{S}_i}$, where each r_i has length n and each $|\mathcal{S}_i| = n$ (recall that the sets $\mathcal{S}_i$ are the sets of the design).
3. For $i \in [n']$, run Prover^{NIZK} on input URS_i and witness w, outputting proof π_i.
4. Output $[\pi_i]_{i \in [n']}$ along with $[x_1, \ldots, x_l]$.

Verifier's Algorithm after the Second Round: Recall that the Verifier's first message is denoted r and that the verifier gets input statement st. After observing the Prover's message consisting of $[\pi_i]_{i \in [n']}$, $[x_1, \ldots, x_l]$, the Verifier does the following:

1. For $i \in [n']$, set $\mathsf{URS}_i = r_i \oplus [x_j]_{j \in \mathcal{S}_i}$
2. For $i \in [n']$, verify proof π_i relative to URS_i by running the verifier $\mathsf{Verifier}^{NIZK}$.
3. If all checks accept, then accept. Otherwise reject.

Theorem 7. *Assume* $\Pi = (\mathsf{Prover}^{NIZK}, \mathsf{Verifier}^{NIZK})$ *is a non-adaptive oNIZK proof system for language* $\mathcal{L}$ *with an inefficient prover in the URS model. Then the above construction is a ZAP for language* $\mathcal{L}$ *with an inefficient prover.*

Soundness Proof: We say that a URS is "bad" relative to a statement $\mathsf{st} \notin \mathcal{L}$ that is not in the language, if there exists an accepting proof relative to that URS (recall that the verifier is deterministic). For statement $\mathsf{st} \notin \mathcal{L}$ and fixed $[x_j]_{j \in [l]}$, the probability over choice of r that *every* URS_i, $i \in [n']$ is bad is at most $2^{-n'}$. Since there are at most 2^l choices for $[x_j]_{j \in [l]}$ (where $l := n^2$), the probability over random choice of r that there exists a setting of $[x_j]_{j \in [l]}$ such that each URS_i is bad is at most $2^{n^2} \cdot 2^{-n'}$. Since we have set $n' := n^3$, we have that $2^{n^2} \cdot 2^{-n'} = 2^{-n^3 + n^2}$ is negligible.

Witness Indistinguishability Proof: We consider the following distributions:

Hybrid H^{w_1}: This is the real distribution with statement st and witness w_1.

Hybrid H^{w_2}: This is the real distribution with statement st and witness w_2.

To prove WI, we must show that for every malicious verifier V^*.

$$H^{w_1} \approx H^{w_2}.$$

Towards this goal, we define the following sequences of hybrid distributions:

Hybrid H^{i,w_1,w_2}, for $i \in [n']$: Proofs with $\mathsf{URS}_{i'}$ for $i' \leq i$ are honest proofs using w_2. Proofs with $\mathsf{URS}_{i'}$ for $i' > i$ are honest proofs using w_1.
Note that $H^{w_1} = H^{0,w_1,w_2}$ and $H^{w_2} = H^{n',w_1,w_2}$.

Claim. For $i \in [n']$,
$$H^{i-1,w_1,w_2} \approx H^{i,w_1,w_2}.$$

Proof. Consider the distribution $H^{*,i,w_1,w_2}(\mathsf{URS}^*, \pi^*)$, where a draw from the distribution is defined as follows:

- Run V^* to produce $r = r^1 || \cdots || r^{n'}$, sample $[x_j]_{j \in [l] \setminus \mathcal{S}_i}$
- Set $[x_j]_{j \in \mathcal{S}_i} := \mathsf{URS}^* \oplus r^i$.
- Set $\pi_i := \pi^*$.
- For each $i' \in [i-1]$, run the honest prover Prover^{NIZK} on witness w_2 and $\mathsf{URS}_{i'} = r^{i'} \oplus [x_j]_{j \in \mathcal{S}_{i'}}$ to obtain proof $\pi_{i'}$.
- For each $i' \in \{i+1, \ldots, n'\}$, run the honest prover Prover^{NIZK} on witness w_1 and $\mathsf{URS}_{i'} = r^{i'} \oplus [x_j]_{j \in \mathcal{S}_{i'}}$ to obtain proof $\pi_{i'}$.
- Output $[\pi_{i'}]_{i' \in [n']}$ and $x := [x_j]_{j \in [l]}$.

Note that when $(\mathsf{URS}^* = \mathsf{URS}_{\mathsf{honest}}, \pi^* = \pi_{w_1})$ (resp. $(\mathsf{URS}^* = \mathsf{URS}_{\mathsf{honest}}, \pi^* = \pi_{w_2})$) are generated as honest CRS/proofs with witness w_1 (resp. w_2), then $H^{*,i,w_1,w_2}(\mathsf{URS}_{\mathsf{honest}}, \pi_{w_1})$ (resp. $H^{*,i,w_1,w_2}(\mathsf{URS}_{\mathsf{honest}}, \pi_{w_2})$) is equivalent to H^{i-1,w_1,w_2} (resp. H^{i,w_1,w_2}). We must also have that $H^{*,i,w_1,w_2}(\mathsf{URS}_{\mathsf{honest}}, \pi_{w_1})$ (resp. $H^{*,i,w_1,w_2}(\mathsf{URS}_{\mathsf{honest}}, \pi_{w_2})$) is indistinguishable from $H^{*,i,w_1,w_2}(\mathsf{URS}_{\mathsf{Sim}}, \pi_{\mathsf{Sim}})$ (where $\mathsf{URS}_{\mathsf{Sim}}, \pi_{\mathsf{Sim}}$ are generated by drawing a simulator from the oNIZK distribution and obtaining its output), since otherwise we obtain a non-uniform PPT adversary that breaks the zero knowledge of the underlying NIZK proof system. We will elaborate on how this indistinguishability is proved below. Assuming that this is the case, we conclude that H^{i-1,w_1,w_2} and H^{i-1,w_1,w_2} are indistinguishable, which completes the proof.

We now show that $H^{*,i,w_1,w_2}(\mathsf{URS}_{\mathsf{honest}}, \pi_{w_1})$ (resp. $H^{*,i,w_1,w_2}(\mathsf{URS}_{\mathsf{honest}}, \pi_{w_2})$) is indistinguishable from $H^{*,i,w_1,w_2}(\mathsf{URS}_{\mathsf{Sim}}, \pi_{\mathsf{Sim}})$ (where $\mathsf{URS}_{\mathsf{Sim}}, \pi_{\mathsf{Sim}}$ are generated by drawing a simulator from the oNIZK distribution and obtaining its output). Towards contradiction, assume the existence of non-uniform PPT verifier V^* and non-uniform PPT distinguisher D distinguishing $H^{*,i,w_1,w_2}(\mathsf{URS}_{\mathsf{honest}}, \pi_{w_1})$ (resp. $H^{*,i,w_1,w_2}(\mathsf{URS}_{\mathsf{honest}}, \pi_{w_2})$) from

$H^{*,i,w_1,w_2}(\mathsf{URS}_\mathsf{Sim}, \pi_\mathsf{Sim})$. Using V^*, D as above, we construct the following distribution over poly-sized circuits that receive as input (URS^*, π^*):

- Run V^* to produce $r = r^1 || \cdots || r^{n'}$, sample $[x_j]_{j \in [l] \setminus \mathcal{S}_i}$ uniformly at random as well as any auxiliary state state_{V^*}, which will be used by the distinguishing circuit D.
- **Hardwired values:**
  1. Statement s and witnesses w_1, w_2.
  2. Auxiliary state state_{V^*}.
  3. $r = r^1 || \cdots || r^{n'}$, $[x_j]_{j \in [l] \setminus \mathcal{S}_i}$.
  4. For each $i' \in [i]$, hardwire truthtable $T_{i'}$ that takes as input $[x_j]_{j \in \mathcal{S}_i \cap \mathcal{S}_{i'}}$ (at most 3 input bits) and outputs $\mathsf{URS}_{i'} = r_{i'} \oplus [x_j]_{j \in \mathcal{S}_{i'}}$, and proof $\pi_{i'}$ honestly computed with statement st and witness w_2.
  5. For each $i' \in \{i + 1, \ldots, n'\}$, hardwire truthtable $T_{i'}$ that takes as input $[x_j]_{j \in \mathcal{S}_i \cap \mathcal{S}_{i'}}$ and outputs $\mathsf{URS}_{i'} = r_{i'} \oplus [x_j]_{j \in \mathcal{S}_{i'}}$, and proof $\pi_{i'}$ honestly computed with statement st and witness w_1.
- **Circuit Evaluation:** On input (URS^*, π^*), do the following:
  - **Embed** (URS^*, π^*): Set $[x_j]_{j \in \mathcal{S}_i} := r_i \oplus \mathsf{URS}^*$. Set $\pi_i := \pi^*$.
  - **Compute Honest Proofs:** Use the truthtables to compute $\mathsf{URS}_{i'}$ and $\pi_{i'}$ for all $i' \neq i$, where the i'-th truthtable $T_{i'}$ takes input $[x_j]_{j \in \mathcal{S}_i \cap \mathcal{S}_{i'}}$.
  - **Output of Prover:** Combine the above two steps to obtain the Prover's message: $([\pi_{i'}]_{i' \in [n'']}, x := [x_j]_{j \in [l]})$.
  - **Application of Distinguisher:** Apply D (which may require state_{V^*} as auxiliary input) to the transcript and output $D(r, [\pi_{i'}]_{i' \in [n'']}, x := [x_j]_{j \in [l]})$.

Note that since each of the truth tables $T_{i'}$ takes a constant number of input bits, and since all the truth tables can be evaluated in parallel, the above is a distribution over circuits corresponding to a (non-uniform) NC^0 circuit composed with the distinguisher D. When D is a poly-sized circuit, the resulting circuit drawn from the distribution is poly-sized. Moreover, the expected distinguishing probability of a circuit drawn from the above distribution is exactly equal to D's distinguishing probability (which is assumed to be non-negligible). But this contradicts the zero knowledge property of the underlying oNIZK.

Note the same proof as above holds for the case of $\mathcal{F}$-fine-grained oNIZK, as long as the distribution defined above is a distribution over circuits contained in $\mathcal{F}$, whenever D is contained in $\mathcal{F}$. This holds when instantiating $\mathcal{F}$ with the class non-uniform NC^1 since, as discussed above, the depth of "Embed" + "Compute Honest Proofs" + "Output of Prover" is constant. So if the depth of D in the "Application of Distinguisher" is logarithmic, then the depth of the entire "Circuit Evaluation" is logarithmic. We therefore obtain:

Theorem 8. *Assume $\Pi = (\mathsf{Prover}^{NIZK}, \mathsf{Verifier}^{NIZK})$ is a NC^1-fine-grained, non-adaptive oNIZK proof system in the URS model. Then the above construction is a NC^1-fine-grained ZAP.*

We present the results related to ZAPs, NIWI and oNIZK for AM or NP with polynomial security in the full version of this paper [5].

4   Fine-Grained NIZK and ZAPs for NP

This section is focuses on constructing NC^1-fine-grained zero-knowledge non-interactive proofs for NP. Our general approach is to bootstrap a *statistical* NIZK for languages in $\oplus\mathsf{L/poly}$ to a fine-grained NIZK for all of NP. The NISZK protocol we bootstrap is a variant of NISZK protocol from [3], in turn constructed from the randomized encodings of [47,48], adapted to work in the URS setting. Next we repurpose the randomized encodings to construct a perfectly binding commitment scheme which is (a) hiding for NC^1, yet (b) extractable in $\oplus\mathsf{L/poly}$. Finally, to prove a circuit is satisfiable, the prover simply commits to a witness and the ensuing circuit evaluation and appends a NISZK that the commitments indeed open to a satisfying evaluation (which, when using such a special commitment scheme, is a $\oplus\mathsf{L/poly}$ statement). The fine-grained ZAP follows from the fine-grained NIZK by Theorem 8.

4.1   Background on Randomized Encodings of [47,48]

We begin by reviewing some of the ingredients we require from the work of Ishai and Kushilevitz [47,48]. Our exposition in this subsection follows that of [2].

Let $BP = (G, \phi, s, t)$ be a mod-2 BP of size ℓ, computing a Boolean function $f : \{0,1\}^n \rightarrow \{0,1\}$; that is, $f(x) = 1$ if and only if the number of paths from s to t in G_x equals 1 modulo 2, where G_x is the subgraph of G specified momentarily. Fix some topological ordering of the vertices of G, where the source vertex s is labeled 1 and the terminal vertex t is labeled ℓ. Let $A(x)$ be the $\ell \times \ell$ adjacency matrix of G_x viewed as a formal matrix whose entries are degree-1 polynomials in the input variables, $x_1, \ldots, x_n = x$. Specifically, the (i,j) entry of $A(x)$ contains the value of $\phi_{i,j}(x)$, where $\phi_{i,j}(x)$ is equal to either a constant function 1 or some literal, such as x_k or $\bar{x}_k$. We constrain ϕ such that if (i,j) is not an edge, the entry is necessarily 0. Define $L(x)$ as the submatrix of $A(x) - I$ obtained by deleting column s and row t (i.e., the first column and the last row). As before, each entry of $L(x)$ is a degree-1 polynomial in a single input variable x_i; moreover, $L(x)$ contains the constant $-1 = 1 \mod 2$ in each entry of its second diagonal (the one below the main diagonal) and the constant 0 below this diagonal (see Fig. 1).

Let $r^{(1)}$ and $r^{(2)}$ be vectors of $\mathbb{F}_2$ of length $\sum_{i=1}^{\ell-2} i = \binom{\ell-1}{2}$ and $\ell - 2$, respectively. Let $R_1(r^{(1)})$ be an $(\ell-1) \times (\ell-1)$ matrix with 1's on the main diagonal, 0's below it, and $r^{(1)}$'s elements in the remaining $\binom{\ell-1}{2}$ entries above the diagonal (a unique element of $r^{(1)}$ is assigned to each matrix entry). Let $R_2(r^{(2)})$ be an $(\ell-1) \times (\ell-1)$ matrix with 1's on the main diagonal, $r^{(2)}$'s elements in the rightmost column, and 0's in each of the remaining entries (see Fig. 1). We will also need the following facts. Note that in all that follows, we consider all arithmetic over $\mathbb{F}_2$, including determinants.

$$\begin{pmatrix} 1 & r_1^{(1)} & r_2^{(1)} & \cdot & \cdot & r_{\ell-2}^{(1)} \\ 0 & 1 & \cdot & \cdot & \cdot & \cdot \\ 0 & 0 & 1 & \cdot & \cdot & \cdot \\ 0 & 0 & 0 & 1 & \cdot & \cdot \\ 0 & 0 & 0 & 0 & 1 & r_{\binom{\ell-1}{2}}^{(1)} \\ 0 & 0 & 0 & 0 & 0 & 1 \end{pmatrix} \begin{pmatrix} \phi_{1,2}(x) & \phi_{1,3}(x) & \cdot & \cdot & \cdot & \phi_{1,\ell}(x) \\ & 1 & \cdot & \cdot & \cdot & \cdot \\ & 0 & 1 & \cdot & \cdot & \cdot \\ & 0 & 0 & 1 & \cdot & \cdot \\ & 0 & 0 & 0 & 1 & \cdot \\ & 0 & 0 & 0 & 0 & 1 & \phi_{\ell-1,\ell}(x) \end{pmatrix} \begin{pmatrix} 1 & 0 & 0 & 0 & 0 & r_1^{(2)} \\ 0 & 1 & 0 & 0 & 0 & r_2^{(2)} \\ 0 & 0 & 1 & 0 & 0 & \cdot \\ 0 & 0 & 0 & 1 & 0 & \cdot \\ 0 & 0 & 0 & 0 & 1 & r_{\ell-2}^{(2)} \\ 0 & 0 & 0 & 0 & 0 & 1 \end{pmatrix}$$

Fig. 1. The matrices $R_1(r^{(1)})$, $A(x)$, and $R_2(r^{(2)})$.

Fact 1 ([2]). *Let M, M' be $(\ell - 1) \times (\ell - 1)$ matrices that contain the constant $-1 = 1 \mod 2$ in each entry of their second diagonal and the constant 0 below this diagonal. Then, $\det(M) = \det(M')$ if and only if there exist $r^{(1)}$ and $r^{(2)}$ such that $R_1(r^{(1)}) M R_2(r^{(2)}) = M'$.*

Lemma 1 ([2]). *Let BP be a mod-2 branching program computing the Boolean function f. Define a function $\hat{f}(x, (r^{(1)}, r^{(2)})) := R_1(r^{(1)}) L(x) R_2(r^{(2)})$. Then $\hat{f}$ is a perfect randomized encoding of f.*

Define M_0 and M_1 as matrices that are all 0 except for the lower diagonal which is 1, and the top right entry which is 1 (resp. 0) in M_1 (resp. M_0).

$$M_0 := \begin{pmatrix} 0 & 0 & 0 & 0 & 0 & 0 \\ 1 & 0 & 0 & 0 & 0 & 0 \\ 0 & 1 & 0 & 0 & 0 & 0 \\ 0 & 0 & 1 & 0 & 0 & 0 \\ 0 & 0 & 0 & 1 & 0 & 0 \\ 0 & 0 & 0 & 0 & 1 & 0 \end{pmatrix} \qquad M_1 := \begin{pmatrix} 0 & 0 & 0 & 0 & 0 & 1 \\ 1 & 0 & 0 & 0 & 0 & 0 \\ 0 & 1 & 0 & 0 & 0 & 0 \\ 0 & 0 & 1 & 0 & 0 & 0 \\ 0 & 0 & 0 & 1 & 0 & 0 \\ 0 & 0 & 0 & 0 & 1 & 0 \end{pmatrix}$$

Lemma 2. *Assuming $\oplus L/\text{poly} \not\subseteq \mathsf{NC}^1$, the distributions $R_1(r^{(1)}) M_0 R_2(r^{(2)})$ and $R_1(r^{(1)}) M_1 R_2(r^{(2)})$ cannot be distinguished by NC^1 circuits, where $r^{(1)}, r^{(2)}$ are chosen at random.*

4.2 Statistical NIZK Protocol in the URS Model for $\oplus L/\text{poly}$

Due to properties of the randomized encoding construction of [47], we can construct a statistical NIZK protocol in the uniform *random* string (URS) model for languages in $\oplus L/\text{poly}$. Our protocol is heavily based on the protocol of Applebaum and Raykov [3], which gave a NISZK construction in the common *reference* string (CRS) model for languages that have (statistical) randomized encodings. Our protocol is described next:

- **URS Generation:** The URS consists of λ random strings, each from $\{0,1\}^t = \{0,1\}^{\binom{\ell-1}{2}+\ell-1}$.
- **Prover:** On input statement matrix $M = L(x)$ (as defined in Sect. 4.1), the prover does the following:

1. For $i \in [\lambda]$, use the i-th block of t bits to populate the upper-triangular entries of a matrix M_i' that has -1's on its second diagonal and 0's below.

2. For $i \in [\lambda]$, if $\det(M_i') = 0$, reveal $r_i^{(1)}, r_i^{(2)}$ of the correct form such that $R_1(r_i^{(1)})M_0 R_2(r_i^{(2)}) = M_i'$, where M_0 is a determinant 0 matrix of "canonical form." Otherwise, reveal $r^{(1)}, r^{(2)}$ of the correct form, such that $R_1(r_i^{(1)})M R_2(r_i^{(2)}) = M_i'$.

3. Output $\pi = [(r_i^{(1)}, r_i^{(2)})]_{i \in [\lambda]}$.

– **Verifier:** On input $(\mathsf{URS}, M, \pi = [(r_i^{(1)}, r_i^{(2)})]_{i \in [\lambda]})$, the verifier checks that for all $i \in [\lambda]$, either $M_i' = R_1(r_i^{(1)})M_0 R_2(r_i^{(2)})$ or $M_i' = R_1(r_i^{(1)})M R_2(r_i^{(2)})$.

Lemma 3. *The protocol above is a NIZK proof system with statistical soundness and statistical zero knowledge in the URS for languages $\mathcal{L} \in \oplus L/\mathrm{poly}$. Moreover, the NIZK simulator can be instantiated by sampling a NC^1 circuit Sim from an efficiently samplable distribution $\mathcal{D}_{\mathsf{Sim}}$.*

We present the proof of Lemma 3 in the full version of this paper [5].

4.3 $\mathcal{G}$-extractable, $\mathcal{F}$-Fine-Grained Commitments for NC^1

$\mathcal{G}$-extractable, $\mathcal{F}$-Fine-Grained Commitments are are commitments that are perfectly binding and have the following properties (see also Definition 2):

– The commitments can be computed and opened in class $\mathcal{F}$.
– Given a commitment, the committed value can be extracted in class $\mathcal{G}$.
– The hiding property of the commitment holds against $\mathcal{F}$.

For our purposes, we will consider $\mathcal{G}$ to be the class $\oplus L/\mathrm{poly}$ and the class $\mathcal{F}$ to be the class NC^1.

Define the following languages $\mathcal{L}_{det}, \overline{\mathcal{L}_{det}}$. $\mathcal{L}_{det}$ is the set of $\ell - 1 \times \ell - 1$ matrices M with -1 on the second diagonal, 0's below the second diagonal, 0 or 1 elements on the diagonal and above such that M has determinant 1 over $\mathbb{F}_2$. $\overline{\mathcal{L}_{det}}$ is the set of $\ell - 1 \times \ell - 1$ matrices M with -1 on the second diagonal, 0's below the second diagonal, 0 or 1 elements on the diagonal and above such that M has determinant 0 over $\mathbb{F}_2$.

Lemma 4. *The languages $\mathcal{L}_{det}$ and $\overline{\mathcal{L}_{det}}$ are contained in $\oplus L/\mathrm{poly}$.*

Toda [64] showed that the determinant is complete for #L by demonstrating NC^1-computable projection from the determinant to counting paths in acyclic graphs. It follows that evaluating the determinant in $\mathbb{F}_2$ can be done in $\oplus L/\mathit{poly}$. *Construction of $\oplus L/\mathrm{poly}$-extractable, NC^1-Fine-Grained Commitment Scheme:* To commit to a 1, choose random $(r^{(1)}, r^{(2)})$ of appropriate length and output $R_1(r^{(1)})M_0 R_2(r^{(2)})$. To commit to a 0, choose random $(r^{(1)}, r^{(2)})$ of appropriate length and output $R_1(r^{(1)})M_1 R_2(r^{(2)})$.

The required properties of the $\oplus L/\mathrm{poly}$-extractable, NC^1-Fine-Grained Commitment Scheme follow from Lemma 4 and from the assumption that $\oplus L/\mathrm{poly} \not\subseteq \mathsf{NC}^1$, as shown by [29].

4.4 NC^1-Fine-Grained NIZK for Circuit SAT

Assume $\mathcal{C}$ is represented as a circuit consisting of NAND gates and assume it has z number of wires. The value of each wire is committed (using the $\oplus L/$poly-extractable, NC^1-fine-grained commitment scheme from the previous section) as $com_1, \ldots, com_z$. Recall that com_i commits to 1 iff $com_1 \in \mathcal{L}_{det}$ and com_1 commits to 0 iff $com_1 \in \overline{\mathcal{L}_{det}}$. Additionally, recall that $\mathcal{L}_{det}$ (and therefore also $\overline{\mathcal{L}_{det}}$) is contained in $\oplus L/$poly. The language $\mathcal{L}_{\mathcal{C}}$ consists of strings $com_1, \ldots, com_z$ which satisfy all of the following:

- $com_z \in \mathcal{L}_{det}$
- For each gate G_ℓ with input wires i, j and output wire k:

$$\left(com_i \in \overline{\mathcal{L}_{det}} \wedge com_k \in \mathcal{L}_{det}\right) \vee \left(com_j \in \overline{\mathcal{L}_{det}} \wedge com_k \in \mathcal{L}_{det}\right) \vee$$
$$\left(com_i \in \mathcal{L}_{det} \wedge com_j \in \mathcal{L}_{det} \wedge com_k \in \overline{\mathcal{L}_{det}}\right).$$

We denote this as $(com_i, com_j, com_k) \in \mathcal{L}_{gate}$.

Due to closure of $\oplus L/$poly w.r.t. negation, conjunction and disjunction [11], we have that $\mathcal{L}_{\mathcal{C}} \in \oplus L/$poly.

Construction of NC^1-Fine-Grained NIZK for Circuit SAT. Given a circuit-SAT instance with circuit C, commit to the witness w using the above type of commitment (i.e. the witness corresponds to the values of all wires in the circuit C and the commitment is a wire-by-wire commitment to those values as above). We have shown above that the following language $\mathcal{L}_{\mathcal{C}}$ is then in $\oplus L/$poly $\mathcal{L}_{\mathcal{C}} : \{(com_1, \ldots, com_z) : com_1, \ldots, com_z$ are commitments to $w = w_1, \ldots, w_z$ and w is a circuit-SAT witness for $C\}$.

Now, applying the argument system from before to proving statement $(com_1, \ldots, com_z)$ is contained in language $\mathcal{L}_{\mathcal{C}}$ yields a fine-grained NIZK in the URS model for circuit SAT.

In more detail, the construction proceeds as follows: The Prover commits to witness $w = w_1, \ldots, w_z$ using a $\oplus L/$poly-extractable, NC^1-Fine-Grained Commitment Scheme, yielding $(com_1, \ldots, com_z)$. The Prover then runs the statistical NIZK protocol given above in Section 4.2 to prove that $(com_1, \ldots, com_z) \in \mathcal{L}_{\mathcal{C}}$.

Theorem 9. *The construction above is a NC^1-fine-grained NIZK proof system for the circuit SAT language.*

Note that the above implies a NC^1-fine-grained NIZK proof system for all of NP. This is because given an NP language, L, with a canonical polynomial size verification circuit $V(x, w)$, the prover can simply prove that the circuit $V_x(\cdot) := V(x, \cdot)$ is satisfiable. Because each bit of V_x is computable in NC^0, the NIZK verifier can generate V_x independently of the prover.

To argue zero knowledge of the NIZK against a NC^1 distinguisher, we define the following randomized circuit $Sim' \in NC^1$. Sim' takes as input the instance, represented by NAND circuit $\mathcal{C}$ consisting of z number of wires, and a sufficiently long string of random coins and does as follows:

- Generate z commitments to garbage $(com_1, \ldots, com_z)$.
- Let Sim be the zero knowledge simulator defined in Sect. 4.2 for languages in $\oplus L/\text{poly}$.
- Sim$'$ runs the simulator Sim on input statement $(com_1, \ldots, com_z)$ and language $\mathcal{L}_\mathcal{C}$.
- Sim$'$ outputs whatever Sim outputs.

Note that Sim$' \in \mathsf{NC}^1$, since Sim $\in \mathsf{NC}^1$. If a NC^1 adversary can distinguish simulated and real proofs, then we can use the adversary to break the hiding property of the $\oplus L/\text{poly}$-extractable, NC^1-Fine-Grained Commitment Scheme, a contradiction.

We require an alternative construction of NC^1-fine-grained NIZK in the URS model (deferred to the full version [5]), to construct NC^1-fine-grained oNIZK with uniform soundness in the standard model. We use either construction above together with Theorem 8 to obtain the following:

Theorem 10. *Assuming that $\oplus L/\text{poly} \not\subseteq \mathsf{NC}^1$, there exist NC^1-fine-grained ZAPs for* NP.

4.5 NC^1-Fine-Grained NIWI for NP

We use the transformation of Barak et al. [8,9] from ZAPs to NIWI, that relies on the existence of hitting set generators (HSG) against co-nondeterministic uniform algorithms. Note that this transformation retains statistical soundness (due to the properties of the HSG) and retains its witness indistinguishability against NC^1 adversaries. However, the verifier may no longer be in NC^1, since the verifier must evaluate the HSG in order to check that the prover is using the correct URS for each of the sub-proofs. To remedy this situation, the prover evaluates the HSG and then sends a tableau of the computation (which can be verified in AC^0) to the verifier, who can then verify that the URS being used is indeed consistent with the output of the HSG.

Theorem 11. *Assuming that $\oplus L/\text{poly} \not\subseteq \mathsf{NC}^1$, the existence of efficient 1/2-HSG against co-nondeterministic uniform algorithms, there exist NC^1-fine-grained NIWI for* NP.

4.6 NC^1-Fine-Grained oNIZK with Uniform Soundness

We now assume existence of a uniform collision resistant hash function h. Let $\mathcal{C}_h$ be the circuit that takes two inputs x_1, x_2 and outputs 1 if $x_1 \neq x_2$ and $h(x_1) = h(x_2)$. On input circuit SAT circuit $\mathcal{C}$, the prover now proves circuit satisfiability of the circuit $\mathcal{C}'$, where $\mathcal{C}'$ is defined as follows: $\mathcal{C}'$ takes public input $\mathsf{desc}(\mathcal{C})$, which is a description of the circuit $\mathcal{C}$, and private input x. $\mathcal{C}'$ outputs 1 on input $(\mathsf{desc}(\mathcal{C}), x)$ if and only if x is a satisfying assignment for $\mathcal{C}$ or x is a satisfying assignment for $\mathcal{C}_h$. Note that $\mathcal{C}'$ is a NC^1 circuit.

On input statement $\mathcal{C}$, the Prover uses the NIWI based on the alternate construction of the NC^1-fine-grained NIZK proof system with statistical soundness for the Circuit SAT language to prove that (1) $(com_1, \ldots, ,_z)$ is a satisfying assignment for $\mathcal{C}'$ and (2) The commitments corresponding to the public input decommit to values that are consistent with $\mathsf{desc}(\mathcal{C})$. The verifier runs the verifier of the NIWI to verify the proof for the statements (1) and (2) above.

To prove zero knowledge with offline simulation (oNIZK), we must show a distribution $\mathcal{D}_{\mathsf{Sim}}$ over NC^1 circuits such that a circuit drawn from this distribution, evaluated on input statement $\mathcal{C}$ produces a distribution over proofs that is indistinguishable from real proofs for a NC^1 circuit.

A draw from $\mathcal{D}_{\mathsf{Sim}}$ is defined as follows:

- Sample colliding inputs x_1, x_2 for h.
- For each wire i of $\mathcal{C}'$, sample a commitment to 0 and a commitment to 1: (com_i^0, com_i^1).
- For each public wire i of $\mathcal{C}'$, compute honest proofs $\pi_{in,i}^0, \pi_{in,i}^1$ proving that $com_i^0 \in \overline{\mathcal{L}_{det}}$ and that $com_i^1 \in \mathcal{L}_{det}$, respectively.
- For the output wire z of $\mathcal{C}'$, compute an honest proof π_{out} that $com_z^1 \in \mathcal{L}_{det}$.
- For each gate with input wires i, j and output wire k of $\mathcal{C}'$, compute 4 honest proofs $[\pi_{gate,i,j,k}^{b_1,b_2}]_{b_1,b_2 \in \{0,1\}}$ proving that $com_i^{b_1}, com_j^{b_2}, com_k^{1-b_1 \wedge b_2} \in \mathcal{L}_{gate}$, for $b_1, b_2 \in \{0,1\}$.
- **Hardwired Values:** A satisfying assignment y (using colliding inputs x_1, x_2) for $\mathcal{C}_h$ and $[com_i^0, com_i^1]_{i \in [z]}$, $(\pi_{in,i}^0, \pi_{in,i}^1)$, π_{out}, $[\pi_{gate,i,j,k}^{b_1,b_2}]_{i,j,k,b_1,b_2}$.
- **Circuit Evaluation:** On input $\mathsf{desc}(\mathcal{C})$, choose the appropriate public inputs corresponding to that input. Additionally, chose the private inputs corresponding to the satisfying assignment y. Let $b_{in}(i)$ denote the value of the i-th public input wire. Assume there are a total of z' input wires. Using these, compute the values of all wires of $\mathcal{C}'$ (this can be done in NC^1, since $\mathcal{C}'$ is a NC^1 circuit). Let $b(i)$ denote the value of the i-th wire of $\mathcal{C}'$. Output commitments $[com_i^{b(j)}]_{i \in [z]}$ and proofs $[\pi_{in,i}^{b_{in}(i)}]_{i \in [z']}$, $[\pi_{gate,i,j,k}^{b(i),b(j)}]_{i,j,k}$.

Note that the outputted distribution is identical to an honest proof with witness corresponding to a satisfying assignment of $\mathcal{C}_h$. Thus, by the witness indistinguishability property of the proof system, the simulated proof is indistinguishable from the real proof. Moreover, note that by the collision resistance of h, soundness still holds against uniform, poly-time provers.

Acknowledgments. We thank Tal Malkin for helpful discussions and suggestions to improve this work. The first author is supported in part by an IBM Research PhD Fellowship. This work is based upon work supported in part by the Office of the Director of National Intelligence (ODNI), Intelligence Advanced Research Projects Activity (IARPA) via Contract No. 2019-1902070006 and by the Defense Advanced Research Projects Agency (DARPA) under Contract No. HR001120C0085. The views and conclusions contained herein are those of the authors and should not be interpreted as necessarily representing the official policies, either express or implied, of ODNI, IARPA, DAPRA, or the U.S. Government. The U.S. Government is authorized to reproduce and distribute reprints for governmental purposes notwithstanding any copyright annotation therein. The second and third authors are supported in part by NSF grants #CNS-1933033, #CNS-1840893, #CNS-1453045 (CAREER), by a research partnership award from Cisco and by financial assistance award 70NANB15H328 and 70NANB19H126 from the U.S. Department of Commerce, National Institute of Standards and Technology.

References

1. Ananth, P., Deshpande, A., Kalai, Y.T., Lysyanskaya, A.: Fully homomorphic NIZK and NIWI proofs. Cryptology ePrint Archive, Report 2019/732 (2019). https://eprint.iacr.org/2019/732
2. Applebaum, B.: Cryptography in Constant Parallel Time. ISC. Springer, Heidelberg (2014). https://doi.org/10.1007/978-3-642-17367-7
3. Applebaum, B., Raykov, P.: On the relationship between statistical zero-knowledge and statistical randomized encodings. In: Robshaw and Katz [63], pp. 449–477
4. Badrinarayan, S., Fernando, R., Jain, A., Khurana, D., Sahai, A.: Statistical ZAP arguments. Cryptology ePrint Archive, Report 2019/780 (2019). https://eprint.iacr.org/2019/780
5. Ball, M., Dachman-Soled, D., Kulkarni, M.: New techniques for zero-knowledge: leveraging inefficient provers to reduce assumptions and interaction. Cryptology ePrint Archive, Report 2019/1464 (2019). https://eprint.iacr.org/2019/1464
6. Ball, M., Rosen, A., Sabin, M., Vasudevan, P.N.: Average-case fine-grained hardness. In: Hatami, H., McKenzie, P., King, V. (eds.) 49th ACM STOC, pp. 483–496. ACM Press, June 2017
7. Ball, M., Rosen, A., Sabin, M., Vasudevan, P.N.: Proofs of work from worst-case assumptions. In: Shacham, H., Boldyreva, A. (eds.) CRYPTO 2018, Part I. LNCS, vol. 10991, pp. 789–819. Springer, Cham (2018). https://doi.org/10.1007/978-3-319-96884-1_26
8. Barak, B., Ong, S.J., Vadhan, S.: Derandomization in cryptography. SIAM J. Comput. **37**(2), 380–400 (2007)
9. Barak, B., Ong, S.J., Vadhan, S.P.: Derandomization in cryptography. In: Boneh, D. (ed.) CRYPTO 2003. LNCS, vol. 2729, pp. 299–315. Springer, Heidelberg (2003). https://doi.org/10.1007/978-3-540-45146-4_18
10. Barak, B., Pass, R.: On the possibility of one-message weak zero-knowledge. In: Naor, M. (ed.) TCC 2004. LNCS, vol. 2951, pp. 121–132. Springer, Heidelberg (2004). https://doi.org/10.1007/978-3-540-24638-1_7
11. Beimel, A., Gál, A.: On arithmetic branching programs. J. Comput. Syst. Sci. **59**(2), 195–220 (1999)
12. Bellare, M., Fuchsbauer, G., Scafuro, A.: NIZKs with an untrusted CRS: security in the face of parameter subversion. In: Cheon, J.H., Takagi, T. (eds.) ASIACRYPT 2016, Part II. LNCS, vol. 10032, pp. 777–804. Springer, Heidelberg (2016). https://doi.org/10.1007/978-3-662-53890-6_26
13. Bellare, M., Micali, S., Ostrovsky, R.: Perfect zero-knowledge in constant rounds. In: 22nd ACM STOC, pp. 482–493. ACM Press, May 1990
14. Bellare, M., Yung, M.: Certifying permutations: noninteractive zero-knowledge based on any trapdoor permutation. J. Cryptol. **9**(3), 149–166 (1996). https://doi.org/10.1007/BF00208000
15. Ben-Or, M., Gutfreund, D.: Trading help for interaction in statistical zero-knowledge proofs. J. Cryptol. **16**(2), 95–116 (2003). https://doi.org/10.1007/s00145-002-0113-0

16. Ben-Sasson, E., et al.: Computational integrity with a public random string from quasi-linear PCPs. In: Coron, J.-S., Nielsen, J.B. (eds.) EUROCRYPT 2017, Part III. LNCS, vol. 10212, pp. 551–579. Springer, Cham (2017). https://doi.org/10.1007/978-3-319-56617-7_19

17. Ben-Sasson, E., Bentov, I., Horesh, Y., Riabzev, M.: Scalable, transparent, and post-quantum secure computational integrity. Cryptology ePrint Archive, Report 2018/046 (2018). https://eprint.iacr.org/2018/046

18. Ben-Sasson, E., Bentov, I., Horesh, Y., Riabzev, M.: Scalable zero knowledge with no trusted setup. In: Boldyreva and Micciancio [22], pp. 701–732

19. Bitansky, N., Lin, H.: One-message zero knowledge and non-malleable commitments. In: Beimel, A., Dziembowski, S. (eds.) TCC 2018, Part I. LNCS, vol. 11239, pp. 209–234. Springer, Cham (2018). https://doi.org/10.1007/978-3-030-03807-6_8

20. Bitansky, N., Paneth, O.: ZAPs and non-interactive witness indistinguishability from indistinguishability obfuscation. In: Dodis, Y., Nielsen, J.B. (eds.) TCC 2015, Part II. LNCS, vol. 9015, pp. 401–427. Springer, Heidelberg (2015). https://doi.org/10.1007/978-3-662-46497-7_16

21. Blum, M., Feldman, P., Micali, S.: Non-interactive zero-knowledge and its applications (extended abstract). In: 20th ACM STOC, pp. 103–112. ACM Press, May 1988

22. Boldyreva, A., Micciancio, D. (eds.): CRYPTO 2019, Part III. LNCS, vol. 11694. Springer, Cham (2019). https://doi.org/10.1007/978-3-030-26954-8

23. Campanelli, M., Gennaro, R.: Fine-grained secure computation. In: Beimel, A., Dziembowski, S. (eds.) TCC 2018, Part II. LNCS, vol. 11240, pp. 66–97. Springer, Cham (2018). https://doi.org/10.1007/978-3-030-03810-6_3

24. Canetti, R. (ed.): TCC 2008. LNCS, vol. 4948. Springer, Heidelberg (2008)

25. Canetti, R., Chen, Y., Holmgren, J., Lombardi, A., Rothblum, G.N., Rothblum, R.D., Wichs, D.: Fiat-Shamir: from practice to theory. In: Charikar, M., Cohen, E. (eds.) 51st ACM STOC, pp. 1082–1090. ACM Press, June 2019

26. Chailloux, A., Ciocan, D.F., Kerenidis, I., Vadhan, S.P.: Interactive and noninteractive zero knowledge are equivalent in the help model. In: Canetti [24], pp. 501–534

27. Ciocan, D.F., Vadhan, S.: Interactive and noninteractive zero knowledge coincide in the help model. Cryptology ePrint Archive, Report 2007/389 (2007). http://eprint.iacr.org/2007/389

28. De Santis, A., Micali, S., Persiano, G.: Non-interactive zero-knowledge with preprocessing. In: Goldwasser, S. (ed.) CRYPTO 1988. LNCS, vol. 403, pp. 269–282. Springer, New York (1990). https://doi.org/10.1007/0-387-34799-2_21

29. Degwekar, A., Vaikuntanathan, V., Vasudevan, P.N.: Fine-grained cryptography. In: Robshaw and Katz [63], pp. 533–562

30. Ding, N., Gu, D.: Precise time and space simulatable zero-knowledge. In: Boyen, X., Chen, X. (eds.) ProvSec 2011. LNCS, vol. 6980, pp. 16–33. Springer, Heidelberg (2011). https://doi.org/10.1007/978-3-642-24316-5_4

31. Ding, N., Gu, D.: On constant-round precise zero-knowledge. In: Chim, T.W., Yuen, T.H. (eds.) ICICS 2012. LNCS, vol. 7618, pp. 178–190. Springer, Heidelberg (2012). https://doi.org/10.1007/978-3-642-34129-8_16

32. Dwork, C., Naor, M.: Zaps and their applications. SIAM J. Comput. **36**(6), 1513–1543 (2007)

33. Egashira, S., Wang, Y., Tanaka, K.: Fine-grained cryptography revisited. In: Galbraith, S.D., Moriai, S. (eds.) ASIACRYPT 2019, Part III. LNCS, vol. 11923, pp. 637–666. Springer, Cham (2019). https://doi.org/10.1007/978-3-030-34618-8_22

34. Feige, U., Lapidot, D., Shamir, A.: Multiple noninteractive zero knowledge proofs under general assumptions. SIAM J. Comput. **29**(1), 1–28 (1999)
35. Feige, U., Shamir, A.: Zero knowledge proofs of knowledge in two rounds. In: Brassard, G. (ed.) CRYPTO 1989. LNCS, vol. 435, pp. 526–544. Springer, New York (1990). https://doi.org/10.1007/0-387-34805-0_46
36. Goldreich, O.: The Foundations of Cryptography - Volume 1: Basic Techniques. Cambridge University Press, Cambridge (2001)
37. Goldreich, O., Micali, S., Wigderson, A.: Proofs that yield nothing but their validity or all languages in np have zero-knowledge proof systems. J. ACM (JACM) **38**(3), 690–728 (1991)
38. Goldreich, O., Oren, Y.: Definitions and properties of zero-knowledge proof systems. J. Cryptol. **7**(1), 1–32 (1994). https://doi.org/10.1007/BF00195207
39. Goldwasser, S., Micali, S., Rackoff, C.: The knowledge complexity of interactive proof systems. SIAM J. Comput. **18**(1), 186–208 (1989)
40. Goldwasser, S., Sipser, M.: Private coins versus public coins in interactive proof systems. In: 18th ACM STOC, pp. 59–68. ACM Press, May 1986
41. Goyal, V., Jain, A., Sahai, A.: Simultaneous amplification: the case of non-interactive zero-knowledge. In: Boldyreva, A., Micciancio, D. (eds.) CRYPTO 2019, Part II. LNCS, vol. 11693, pp. 608–637. Springer, Cham (2019). https://doi.org/10.1007/978-3-030-26951-7_21
42. Groth, J., Ostrovsky, R., Sahai, A.: Non-interactive zaps and new techniques for NIZK. In: Dwork, C. (ed.) CRYPTO 2006. LNCS, vol. 4117, pp. 97–111. Springer, Heidelberg (2006). https://doi.org/10.1007/11818175_6
43. Groth, J., Ostrovsky, R., Sahai, A.: New techniques for noninteractive zero-knowledge. J. ACM (JACM) **59**(3), 11 (2012)
44. Groth, J., Sahai, A.: Efficient non-interactive proof systems for bilinear groups. In: Smart, N.P. (ed.) EUROCRYPT 2008. LNCS, vol. 4965, pp. 415–432. Springer, Heidelberg (2008). https://doi.org/10.1007/978-3-540-78967-3_24
45. Impagliazzo, R.: A personal view of average-case complexity. In: Tenth Annual IEEE Conference on Proceedings of Structure in Complexity Theory, pp. 134–147. IEEE (1995)
46. Impagliazzo, R., Rudich, S.: Limits on the provable consequences of one-way permutations. In: 21st ACM STOC, pp. 44–61. ACM Press, May 1989
47. Ishai, Y., Kushilevitz, E.: Randomizing polynomials: a new representation with applications to round-efficient secure computation. In: 41st FOCS, pp. 294–304. IEEE Computer Society Press, November 2000
48. Ishai, Y., Kushilevitz, E.: Perfect constant-round secure computation via perfect randomizing polynomials. In: Widmayer, P., Eidenbenz, S., Triguero, F., Morales, R., Conejo, R., Hennessy, M. (eds.) ICALP 2002. LNCS, vol. 2380, pp. 244–256. Springer, Heidelberg (2002). https://doi.org/10.1007/3-540-45465-9_22
49. Itoh, T., Ohta, Y., Shizuya, H.: Language dependent secure bit commitment. In: Desmedt, Y.G. (ed.) CRYPTO 1994. LNCS, vol. 839, pp. 188–201. Springer, Heidelberg (1994). https://doi.org/10.1007/3-540-48658-5_20
50. Jain, A., Jin, Z.: Statistical zap arguments from quasi-polynomial LWE. Cryptology ePrint Archive, Report 2019/839 (2019). https://eprint.iacr.org/2019/839
51. Jain, A., Kalai, Y.T., Khurana, D., Rothblum, R.: Distinguisher-dependent simulation in two rounds and its applications. In: Katz, J., Shacham, H. (eds.) CRYPTO 2017, Part II. LNCS, vol. 10402, pp. 158–189. Springer, Cham (2017). https://doi.org/10.1007/978-3-319-63715-0_6

52. Kalai, Y.T., Khurana, D., Sahai, A.: Statistical witness indistinguishability (and more) in two messages. In: Nielsen, J.B., Rijmen, V. (eds.) EUROCRYPT 2018. LNCS, vol. 10822, pp. 34–65. Springer, Cham (2018). https://doi.org/10.1007/978-3-319-78372-7_2

53. Katsumata, S., Nishimaki, R., Yamada, S., Yamakawa, T.: Designated verifier/prover and preprocessing NIZKs from Diffie-Hellman assumptions. In: Ishai, Y., Rijmen, V. (eds.) EUROCRYPT 2019, Part II. LNCS, vol. 11477, pp. 622–651. Springer, Cham (2019). https://doi.org/10.1007/978-3-030-17656-3_22

54. Kim, S., Wu, D.J.: Multi-theorem preprocessing NIZKs from lattices. In: Shacham, H., Boldyreva, A. (eds.) CRYPTO 2018, Part II. LNCS, vol. 10992, pp. 733–765. Springer, Cham (2018). https://doi.org/10.1007/978-3-319-96881-0_25

55. Lapidot, D., Shamir, A.: Publicly verifiable non-interactive zero-knowledge proofs. In: Menezes, A.J., Vanstone, S.A. (eds.) CRYPTO 1990. LNCS, vol. 537, pp. 353–365. Springer, Heidelberg (1991). https://doi.org/10.1007/3-540-38424-3_26

56. LaVigne, R., Lincoln, A., Williams, V.V.: Public-key cryptography in the fine-grained setting. In: Boldyreva and Micciancio [22], pp. 605–635

57. Micali, S., Pass, R.: Local zero knowledge. In: STOC, pp. 306–315. ACM (2006)

58. Nisan, N., Wigderson, A.: Hardness vs. randomness (extended abstract). In: 29th FOCS, pp. 2–11. IEEE Computer Society Press, October 1988

59. Ong, S.J., Vadhan, S.P.: An equivalence between zero knowledge and commitments. In: Canetti, R. (ed.) TCC 2008. LNCS, vol. 4948, pp. 482–500. Springer, Heidelberg (2008). https://doi.org/10.1007/978-3-540-78524-8_27. [24]

60. Ostrovsky, R., Wigderson, A.: One-way fuctions are essential for non-trivial zero-knowledge. In: Proceedings of Second Israel Symposium on Theory of Computing Systems, ISTCS 1993, Natanya, Israel, 7–9 June 1993, pp. 3–17 (1993)

61. Pass, R., Shelat, A.: Unconditional characterizations of non-interactive zero-knowledge. In: Shoup, V. (ed.) CRYPTO 2005. LNCS, vol. 3621, pp. 118–134. Springer, Heidelberg (2005). https://doi.org/10.1007/11535218_8

62. Peikert, C., Shiehian, S.: Noninteractive zero knowledge for NP from (plain) learning with errors. In: Boldyreva, A., Micciancio, D. (eds.) CRYPTO 2019, Part I. LNCS, vol. 11692, pp. 89–114. Springer, Cham (2019). https://doi.org/10.1007/978-3-030-26948-7_4

63. Robshaw, M., Katz, J. (eds.): CRYPTO 2016, Part III. LNCS, vol. 9816. Springer, Heidelberg (2016). https://doi.org/10.1007/978-3-662-53015-3

64. Toda, S.: Counting problems computationally equivalent to. SIAM J. Comput. **13**, 423–439 (1984)

65. Wu, H., Wang, F.: A survey of noninteractive zero knowledge proof system and its applications (2014). https://doi.org/10.1155/2014/560484

Spartan: Efficient and General-Purpose zkSNARKs Without Trusted Setup

Srinath Setty[✉]

Microsoft Research, Redmond, USA
`srinath@microsoft.com`

Abstract. This paper introduces Spartan, a new family of zero-knowledge succinct non-interactive arguments of knowledge (zkSNARKs) for the rank-1 constraint satisfiability (R1CS), an NP-complete language that generalizes arithmetic circuit satisfiability. A distinctive feature of Spartan is that it offers the first zkSNARKs without trusted setup (i.e., transparent zkSNARKs) for NP where verifying a proof incurs sub-linear costs—without requiring uniformity in the NP statement's structure. Furthermore, Spartan offers zkSNARKs with a time-optimal prover, a property that has remained elusive for nearly all zkSNARKs in the literature.

To achieve these results, we introduce new techniques that we compose with the sum-check protocol, a seminal interactive proof protocol: (1) *computation commitments*, a primitive to create a succinct commitment to a description of a computation; this technique is crucial for a verifier to achieve sub-linear costs after investing a one-time, public computation to preprocess a given NP statement; (2) SPARK, a cryptographic compiler to transform any existing extractable polynomial commitment scheme for multilinear polynomials to one that efficiently handles *sparse* multilinear polynomials; this technique is critical for achieving a time-optimal prover; and (3) a compact encoding of an R1CS instance as a low-degree polynomial. The end result is a public-coin succinct interactive argument of knowledge for NP (which can be viewed as *a succinct variant of the sum-check protocol*); we transform it into a zkSNARK using prior techniques. By applying SPARK to different commitment schemes, we obtain several zkSNARKs where the verifier's costs and the proof size range from $O(\log^2 n)$ to $O(\sqrt{n})$ depending on the underlying commitment scheme (n denotes the size of the NP statement). These schemes do not require a trusted setup except for one that requires a universal trusted setup.

We implement Spartan as a library in about 8,000 lines of Rust. We use the library to build a transparent zkSNARK in the random oracle model where security holds under the discrete logarithm assumption. We experimentally evaluate it and compare with recent zkSNARKs for R1CS instance sizes up to 2^{20} constraints. Among schemes without trusted setup, Spartan offers the fastest prover with speedups of 36–$152\times$ depending on the baseline, produces proofs that are shorter by 1.2–$416\times$, and incurs the lowest verification times with speedups of 3.6–$1326\times$. When compared to the state-of-the-art zkSNARK with trusted setup, Spartan's prover is $2\times$ faster for arbitrary R1CS instances and $16\times$ faster for data-parallel workloads.

© International Association for Cryptologic Research 2020
D. Micciancio and T. Ristenpart (Eds.): CRYPTO 2020, LNCS 12172, pp. 704–737, 2020.
https://doi.org/10.1007/978-3-030-56877-1_25

1   Introduction

We revisit the problem of designing zero-knowledge succinct non-interactive arguments of knowledge (zkSNARKs) [22,48] for the complexity class NP: they enable a computationally-bounded prover to convince the membership of a problem instance in an NP language by producing a proof—*without* revealing anything besides the validity of the statement. Furthermore, the proof size and the verifier's costs are sub-linear in the size of the statement. We are motivated to design zkSNARKs because they enable many applications that involve various forms of delegation of computation for scalability or privacy [12,26,29,31,38,39,41,46,59,61,70,73–79,87].

Specifically, we are interested in zkSNARKs that prove the satisfiability of R1CS instances over a finite field $\mathbb{F}$ (an NP-complete language that generalizes arithmetic circuit satisfiability; see Sect. 2.1 for details): given a problem instance $\mathbb{x} = (\mathbb{F}, A, B, C, io, m, n)$, we desire a proof that demonstrates the knowledge of a witness w such that $\mathsf{Sat}_{\mathrm{R1CS}}(\mathbb{x}, w) = 1.$[1] We desire zkSNARKs for R1CS because there exist efficient toolchains to transform high-level applications of interest to R1CS [13,15,18,31,60,70,73,77,83].

There are many approaches to construct such arguments in the literature, starting with the work of Kilian [58] who provided the first construction of a succinct interactive argument protocol by employing probabilistically checkable proofs (PCPs) [5–7,42,44,54] in conjunction with Merkle trees [67]. Micali [68] made a similar protocol non-interactive in the random oracle model, thereby obtaining the first zkSNARK. Unfortunately, the underlying PCP machinery remains extremely expensive for the prover and the verifier—despite foundational advances [14,19–21].

Thus, the first works with an explicit motivation to make proof systems practical [38,74,76,77,79] refine and implement interactive protocols of Ishai et al. [55] and Goldwasser et al. [49], which do not require asymptotically-efficient PCPs. The principal downside is that they achieve practicality for only a restricted class of NP statements.

Gennaro, Gentry, Parno, and Raykova (GGPR) [47] address the above issue with a new characterization of NP called *quadratic arithmetic programs (QAPs)*. By building on the work of Ishai et al. [55], Groth [50], and Lipmaa [65], GGPR construct a zkSNARK for R1CS in which the prover's running time is $O(n \log n)$, the size of a proof is $O(1)$, and the verifier incurs $O(|io|)$ computation to verify a proof, where n is the size of the statement, and io denotes the public input and output. Unfortunately, GGPR's zkSNARK requires a per-statement *trusted setup* that produces an $O_\lambda(n)$-sized structured common reference string and the trapdoor used in the setup process must be kept secret to ensure soundness. Relying on such a trusted setup is often infeasible, especially for applications that do not have trusted authorities. There exist several advances atop GGPR, but they retain a trusted setup [15,18,23,51,52,70], or require interaction [75].

---

[1] Although we use the word "proof", we mean proofs that are computationally sound [30].

The above state of affairs has motivated another class of works, called *transparent* zkSNARKs, that aim to eliminate the requirement of a trusted setup. They prove security in the random oracle model, which is acceptable in practice. First, Hyrax [84] extends a line of work [38,78–82] that refines the doubly-efficient interactive proofs (IPs) of Goldwasser et al. [49]. Second, STARK [10] and Aurora [16] build on interactive oracle proofs (IOPs) [17,71]. Third, Ligero [3] builds on the "MPC in the head" paradigm [56]. Fourth, Bulletproofs [32] builds on the work of Bootle et al. [27].

Unfortunately, they face the following problems.

- The computational model of Hyrax [83] is layered arithmetic circuits, where the verifier's costs and the proof sizes scale linearly in the depth of the circuit. Converting an arbitrary circuit into a layered form can increase its size quadratically [49],[2] so Hyrax is restricted to low-depth circuits. Also, Hyrax [83] achieves sub-linear verification costs only for circuits with a uniform structure (e.g., data-parallel circuits).
- STARK [10] requires circuits with a sequence of identical sub-circuits, otherwise it does not achieve sub-linear verification costs. Any circuit can be converted to this form [13,15], but the transformation increases circuit sizes by 10–1000×, which translates to a similar factor increase in the prover's costs [83].
- Ligero [3], Bulletproofs [33], and Aurora [16] incur $O(n)$ verification costs.

Our work addresses these problems.

1.1   Summary of Contributions

This paper presents a new family of zkSNARKs, which we call *Spartan*, for proving the satisfiability of NP statements expressed in R1CS. Spartan offers the first transparent zkSNARK that achieves sub-linear verification costs for arbitrary NP statements.[3] Spartan also offers zkSNARKs with a time-optimal prover, a property that has remained difficult to achieve in nearly all prior zkSNARKs.

In a nutshell, Spartan introduces a new public-coin succinct interactive argument of knowledge where the verifier incurs sub-linear costs for arbitrary R1CS instances by employing *computation commitments* (which we describe below). Our argument makes a black box use of an extractable polynomial commitment scheme in conjunction with an information-theoretic protocol, so its soundness holds under the assumptions needed by the polynomial commitment scheme (there exist many polynomial commitment schemes that can be instantiated under standard cryptographic assumptions [32,84,86]). The interactive argument is public-coin, so we add zero-knowledge using existing compilers [84,85,88],

---

[2] For a depth-d circuit, converting to a layered form increases the circuit size by a factor of $O(d)$.

[3] To our knowledge, short PCP-based transparent zkSNARKs [58,68] do not achieve sub-linear verification costs unless one uses uniform circuits, which is undesirable as noted above.

which themselves build on prior theory [9,35,40]. We then make the result-ing zero-knowledge argument of knowledge non-interactive in the random ora-cle model using the Fiat-Shamir transform [45]. Since our interactive argument employs a polynomial commitment scheme as a black box, we obtain a family of zkSNARKs where each variant employs a different polynomial commitment scheme.

In more detail, Spartan makes the following contributions.

(1) A new family of public-coin succinct interactive arguments of knowledge. Our core insight is that the sum-check protocol [66], a sem-inal interactive proof protocol (where soundness holds unconditionally), when applied to a suitably-constructed low-degree polynomial yields a powerful—but *highly inefficient*—interactive proof protocol, but the inefficiency can be tamed with new techniques. Specifically, we introduce three techniques (Fig. 1 offers a visual depiction of how these techniques work together):

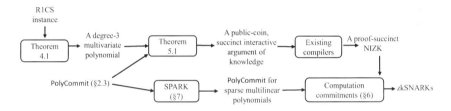

Fig. 1. Overview of our techniques for constructing zkSNARKs.

(i) *Computation commitments*, a primitive for creating succinct cryptographic commitments to a mathematical description of an NP statement, which is critical for achieving sub-linear verification costs.

Achieving sub-linear verification costs appears fundamentally unrealizable because the verifier must process an NP statement for which the proof is produced before it can verify a purported proof. Our observation is that this cost can be made sub-linear in the size of an NP statement by introducing a *public preprocessing step*.

Specifically, our observation is that when verifying a proof under our inter-active argument, the verifier must evaluate a low-degree polynomial that encodes the NP statement, which incurs $O(n)$ costs to the verifier. Our prim-itive, computation commitments, enables verifiably delegating the necessary polynomial evaluations to the prover. Specifically, in Spartan, the verifier reads an R1CS instance (without the *io* component) for which the proof is produced and retains a short cryptographic commitment to a set of sparse multilinear polynomials that encode the R1CS structure. Later, when pro-ducing a proof, the prover evaluates the necessary polynomials and proves that the sparse polynomial evaluations are consistent with the commitment retained by the verifier. While the verifier incurs $O(n)$ cost to compute a computation commitment, the cost is amortized over *all* future proofs produced for all R1CS instances with the same structure. This amortization is similar to that of GGPR [47]. However, unlike GGPR's trusted setup, creating a computation commitment does not involve any secret trapdoors. Section 6 provides details.

(ii) SPARK, a cryptographic compiler to transform any existing extractable polynomial commitment scheme for multilinear polynomials to one that efficiently handles sparse multilinear polynomials. Using the compiler, we obtain schemes with time-optimal costs for both creating commitments to sparse multilinear polynomials and to produce proofs of evaluations of the committed polynomials. This compiler is crucial for achieving a time-optimal prover in Spartan. In more detail, SPARK employs an existing extractable polynomial commitment scheme as a black box, and uses it in conjunction with a special-purpose zkSNARK and a carefully-constructed circuit (that employs offline memory checking techniques [4,24,37,43,73]) to efficiently prove evaluations of sparse multilinear polynomials. Section 7 provides details.

(iii) A compact encoding of an R1CS instance as a degree-3 multivariate polynomial that can be decomposed into four multilinear polynomials. The decomposition into multilinear polynomials is critical for achieving a time-optimal prover in the sum-check protocol by employing prior ideas [78,85]. Section 4 provides details.

(2) An optimized implementation and experimental evaluation. We implement Spartan as a library in about 8,000 lines of Rust. We use the library to build a transparent zkSNARK that employs an extractable polynomial commitment scheme due to Wahby et al. [84] where soundness holds under the hardness of computing discrete logarithms. Our experimental evaluation demonstrates that, among schemes without trusted setup, Spartan offers the fastest prover with speedups of 36–$152\times$ depending on the baseline, produces proofs that are shorter by 1.2–$416\times$, and incurs the lowest verification times with speedups of 3.6–$1326\times$. When compared to the state-of-the-art zkSNARK with trusted setup, Spartan's prover is $2\times$ faster for arbitrary R1CS instances and $16\times$ faster for data-parallel workloads.

(3) A unified understanding of different strands of theory. Spartan exposes inter-connections among different lines of work on probabilistic proofs—from the perspective of zkSNARKs—including doubly-efficient IPs, MIPs, and short PCPs [72, §3.2].

(4) Improvements in zkSNARKs with universal setup. While our focus is transparent zkSNARKs, Spartan improves on prior zkSNARKs with universal trusted setup.

By employing a different polynomial commitment scheme [69,87], which requires q-type, knowledge of exponent assumptions, in SPARK, Spartan offers an alternative to Libra [85]; we refer to this variant as $\text{Spartan}_{\text{KE}}$. Compared to Libra, $\text{Spartan}_{\text{KE}}$ supports arbitrary R1CS instances instead of layered arithmetic circuits. Furthermore, unlike Libra, the proof sizes and the verifier's running times in $Spartan_{KE}$ do not scale linearly with the circuit depth. Finally, Libra achieves sub-linear verification costs only for low-depth uniform circuits whereas $Spartan_{KE}$ achieves sub-linear verification costs for arbitrary R1CS instances via computation commitments.

	setup	prover	proof length	verifier	computational model
GGPR [47]	private	$O(n \log n)$	$O(1)$	$O(1)$	R1CS
Libra [85]	private*	$O(n)$	$O(d \log n)$	$O(d \log n)$	uniform circuits
Ligero [3]	public	$O(n \log n)$	$O(\sqrt{n})$	$O(n)$	arithmetic circuits
Hyrax [82]	public	$O(n + m \cdot g)$	$O(m + \sqrt{w})$	$O(m + \sqrt{w})$	data-parallel circuits
Bulletproofs [33]	public	$O(n)$	$O(\log n)$	$O(n)$	arithmetic circuits
STARK [10]	public	$O(n \log^2 n)$	$O(\log^2 n)$	$O(\log^2 n)$	uniform circuits
Aurora [16]	public	$O(n \log n)$	$O(\log^2 n)$	$O(n)$	R1CS
Fractal [36]	public	$O(n \log n)$	$O(\log^2 n)$	$O(\log^2 n)$	R1CS
Virgo [86]	public	$O(n \log n)$	$O(d \log n)$	$O(d \log n)$	uniform circuits
SuperSonic [32]	public	$O(n \log n)$	$O(\log n)$	$O(\log n)$	arithmetic circuits
Variants in Spartan's family of zkSNARKs:					
$Spartan_{DL}$	public	$O(n)$	$O(\sqrt{n})$	$O(\sqrt{n})$	R1CS
$Spartan_{KE}$	private*	$O(n)$	$O(\log^2 n)$	$O(\log^2 n)$	R1CS
$Spartan_{RO}$	public	$O(n \log n)$	$O(\log^2 n)$	$O(\log^2 n)$	R1CS
$Spartan_{CL}$	public	$O(n \log n)$	$O(\log^2 n)$	$O(\log^2 n)$	R1CS

Fig. 2. A comparison of prior and recent zkSNARKs, where n denotes the size of the NP statement. For Hyrax [84], we assume a layered arithmetic circuit $\mathcal{C}$ of depth d, width g, and β copies (i.e., $n = d \cdot g \cdot \beta$); w denotes the size of a witness to $\mathcal{C}$; and $m = d \cdot \log g$. Hyrax and $Spartan_{DL}$ can achieve sub-sqrt proofs at the cost of increasing $\mathcal{V}$'s time. For Libra and Virgo, we assume a depth-d layered uniform circuit. The verifier incurs $O(|io|)$ additional cost in all schemes where io denotes the public inputs and outputs of the NP relation being proved. Furthermore, all transparent zkSNARKs achieve non-interactivity in the random oracle model using the Fiat-Shamir heuristic [45]. Private* means that the trusted setup is universal. Ligero, Virgo, STARK, Aurora, Fractal, and $Spartan_{RO}$ are plausibly post-quantum secure. Finally, $Spartan_{CL}$ applies SPARK to the commitment scheme of Bünz et al. [32], but the commitment scheme requires an adaptation (Sect. 5.1).

1.2   Additional Related Work

Figure 2 compares the asymptotic costs of Spartan-based zkSNARKs with other schemes.

Recent schemes. Following our preprint, there are three transparent zkSNARKs: Fractal [36], SuperSonic [32], and Virgo [86]. Virgo's model of computation is same as Hyrax's, so it achieves sub-linear verification costs only for low-depth, uniform circuits.

Fractal and SuperSonic achieve sub-linear verification costs for arbitrary NP statements. In these schemes, the verifier preprocesses an NP statement—without secret trapdoors—to create a commitment to the structure of the statement. In other words, they instantiate the computation commitments primitive. Unfortunately, both schemes incur orders of magnitude higher expense than Spartan (Sect. 9).

2   Preliminaries

We use $\mathbb{F}$ to denote a finite field (e.g., the prime field $\mathbb{F}_p$ for a large prime p) and λ to denote the security parameter. We use $\mathsf{negl}(\lambda)$ to denote a negligible function in λ. Throughout the paper, the depicted asymptotics depend on λ, but we elide this for brevity. We use "PPT algorithms" to refer to probabilistic polynomial time algorithms.

2.1   Problem Instances in R1CS

Recall that for any problem instance $\mathbb{x}$, if $\mathbb{x}$ is in an NP language $\mathcal{L}$, there exists a witness w and a deterministic algorithm Sat such that:

$$\mathsf{Sat}_{\mathcal{L}}(\mathbb{x}, w) = \begin{cases} 1 & \text{if } \mathbb{x} \in \mathcal{L} \\ 0 & \text{otherwise} \end{cases}$$

Alternatively, the set of tuples of the form $\langle \mathbb{x}, w \rangle$ form a set of NP relations. The subset of those for which $\mathsf{Sat}_{\mathcal{L}}(\mathbb{x}, w) = 1$ are called *satisfiable instances*, which we denote as: $\mathcal{R}_{\mathcal{L}} = \{\langle \mathbb{x}, w \rangle : \mathsf{Sat}_{\mathcal{L}}(\mathbb{x}, w) = 1\}$.

As an NP-complete language, we focus on the rank-1 constraint satisfiability (R1CS). As noted earlier, R1CS is a popular target for compiler toolchains that accept applications expressed in high-level languages [70,75,77,83]. R1CS is implicit in the QAPs of GGPR [47], but it is used with (and without) QAPs in subsequent works [16,64,75].

Definition 2.1 (R1CS instance).   An R1CS instance is a tuple $(\mathbb{F}, A, B, C, io, m, n)$, where io denotes the public input and output of the instance, $A, B, C \in \mathbb{F}^{m \times m}$, where $m \geq |io|+1$ and there are at most n non-zero entries in each matrix.

Note that matrices A, B, C are defined to be square matrices for conceptual simplicity. Below, we use the notation $z = (x, y, z)$ (where each of x, y, z is a vector over $\mathbb{F}$) to mean that z is a vector that concatenates the three vectors in a natural way. WLOG, we assume that $n = O(m)$ throughout the paper.

Definition 2.2 (R1CS).   An R1CS instance $(\mathbb{F}, A, B, C, io, m, n)$ is said to be *satisfiable* if there exists a witness $w \in \mathbb{F}^{m-|io|-1}$ such that $(A \cdot z) \circ (B \cdot z) = (C \cdot z)$, where $z = (io, 1, w)$, $\cdot$ is the matrix-vector product, and $\circ$ is the Hadamard (entry-wise) product.

Note that R1CS generalizes arithmetic circuit satisfiability because the entries in matrices A, B, C can be used to encode addition and multiplication gates over $\mathbb{F}$. Furthermore, they can be used to encode a class of degree-2 constraints of the form $L(z) \cdot R(z) = O(z)$, where L, R, O are degree-1 polynomials over variables that take values specified by $z = (io, 1, w)$. In other words, R1CS supports arbitrary fan-in addition gates, and multiplication gates that verify arbitrary bilinear relations over the entire z.

Definition 2.3. For an R1CS instance $\mathbb{x} = (\mathbb{F}, A, B, C, io, m, n)$ and a purported witness $w \in \mathbb{F}^{m-|io|-1}$, we define:

$$
\mathsf{Sat}_{\mathrm{R1CS}}(\mathbb{x}, w) = \begin{cases} 1 & (A \cdot (io, 1, w)) \circ (B \cdot (io, 1, w)) = (C \cdot (io, 1, w)) \\ 0 & \text{otherwise} \end{cases}
$$

The set of satisfiable R1CS instances can be denoted as:

$$
\mathcal{R}_{\mathrm{R1CS}} = \{\langle (\mathbb{F}, A, B, C, io, m, n), w \rangle : \mathsf{Sat}_{\mathrm{R1CS}}((\mathbb{F}, A, B, C, io, m, n), w) = 1\}
$$

Definition 2.4. For a given R1CS instance $\mathbb{x} = (\mathbb{F}, A, B, C, io, m, n)$, the NP statement that $\mathbb{x}$ is satisfiable (i.e., $\mathbb{x} \in \mathcal{R}_{\mathrm{R1CS}}$) is of size $O(n)$.

2.2 Polynomials and Low-Degree Extensions

Definition 2.5 (Multilinear polynomial). A multivariate polynomial is called a multilinear polynomial if the degree of the polynomial in each variable is at most one.

Definition 2.6 (Low-degree polynomial). A multivariate polynomial $\mathcal{G}$ over a finite field $\mathbb{F}$ is called low-degree polynomial if the degree of $\mathcal{G}$ in each variable is exponentially smaller than $|\mathbb{F}|$.

Low-degree extensions (LDEs). Suppose $g : \{0,1\}^m \to \mathbb{F}$ is a function that maps m-bit elements into an element of $\mathbb{F}$. A *polynomial extension* of g is a low-degree m-variate polynomial $\widetilde{g}(\cdot)$ such that $\widetilde{g}(x) = g(x)$ for all $x \in \{0,1\}^m$.

A *multilinear* polynomial extension (or simply, a multilinear extension, or MLE) is a low-degree polynomial extension where the extension is a multilinear polynomial (i.e., the degree of each variable in $\widetilde{g}(\cdot)$ is at most one). Given a function $Z : \{0,1\}^m \to \mathbb{F}$, the multilinear extension of $Z(\cdot)$ is the unique multilinear polynomial $\widetilde{Z} : \mathbb{F}^m \to \mathbb{F}$. It can be computed as follows.

$$
\begin{aligned}
\widetilde{Z}(x_1, \ldots, x_m) &= \sum_{e \in \{0,1\}^m} Z(e) \cdot \prod_{i=1}^{m} (x_i \cdot e_i + (1 - x_i) \cdot (1 - e_i)) \\
&= \sum_{e \in \{0,1\}^m} Z(e) \cdot \widetilde{\mathrm{eq}}(x, e) \\
&= \langle (Z(0), \ldots, Z(2^m - 1)), (\widetilde{\mathrm{eq}}(x, 0), \ldots, \widetilde{\mathrm{eq}}(x, 2^m - 1)) \rangle
\end{aligned}
$$

Note that $\widetilde{\mathrm{eq}}(x, e) = \prod_{i=1}^{m}(e_i \cdot x_i + (1 - e_i) \cdot (1 - x_i))$, which is the MLE of the following function:

$$\mathrm{eq}(x, e) = \begin{cases} 1 & \text{if } x = e \\ 0 & \text{otherwise} \end{cases}$$

For any $r \in \mathbb{F}^m$, $\widetilde{Z}(r)$ can be computed in $O(2^m)$ operations in $\mathbb{F}$ [78,80].

Dense representation for multilinear polynomials. Since the MLE of a function is unique, it offers the following method to represent any multilinear polynomial. Given a multilinear polynomial $\mathcal{G}(\cdot) : \mathbb{F}^m \to \mathbb{F}$, it can be represented uniquely by the list of evaluations of $\mathcal{G}(\cdot)$ over the Boolean hypercube $\{0,1\}^m$ (i.e., a function that maps $\{0,1\}^m \to \mathbb{F}$). We denote such a representation of $\mathcal{G}$ as $\mathrm{DenseRepr}(\mathcal{G})$.

Definition 2.7. A multilinear polynomial $\mathcal{G} : \mathbb{F}^m \to \mathbb{F}$ is a sparse multilinear polynomial if $|\mathrm{DenseRepr}(\mathcal{G})|$ is sub-linear in $O(2^m)$. Otherwise, it is a dense multilinear polynomial.

2.3   A Polynomial Commitment Scheme for Multilinear Polynomials

We adopt our definitions from Bünz et al. [32] where they generalize the definition of Kate et al. [57] to allow interactive evaluation proofs. We also borrow their notation: in a list of arguments or returned tuples, variables before the semicolon are public and the ones after are secret; when there is no secret information, semicolon is omitted.

WLOG, below, when algorithms accept as input a multilinear polynomial, they use the dense representation of multilinear polynomials (Sect. 2.2).

A polynomial commitment scheme for multilinear polynomials is a tuple of four protocols $\mathsf{PC} = (\mathsf{Setup}, \mathsf{Commit}, \mathsf{Open}, \mathsf{Eval})$:

- $pp \leftarrow \mathsf{Setup}(1^\lambda, \mu)$: takes as input μ (the number of variables in a multilinear polynomial); produces public parameters pp.
- $(\mathcal{C}; \mathcal{S}) \leftarrow \mathsf{Commit}(pp; \mathcal{G})$: takes as input a μ-variate multilinear polynomial over a finite field $\mathcal{G} \in \mathbb{F}[\mu]$; produces a public commitment $\mathcal{C}$ and a secret opening hint $\mathcal{S}$.
- $b \leftarrow \mathsf{Open}(pp, \mathcal{C}, \mathcal{G}, \mathcal{S})$: verifies the opening of commitment $\mathcal{C}$ to the μ-variate multilinear polynomial $\mathcal{G} \in \mathbb{F}[\mu]$ with the opening hint $\mathcal{S}$; outputs a $b \in \{0,1\}$.
- $b \leftarrow \mathsf{Eval}(pp, \mathcal{C}, r, v, \mu; \mathcal{G}, \mathcal{S})$ is an interactive public-coin protocol between a PPT prover $\mathcal{P}$ and verifier $\mathcal{V}$. Both $\mathcal{V}$ and $\mathcal{P}$ hold a commitment $\mathcal{C}$, the number of variables μ, a scalar $v \in \mathbb{F}$, and $r \in \mathbb{F}^\mu$. $\mathcal{P}$ additionally knows a μ-variate multilinear polynomial $\mathcal{G} \in \mathbb{F}[\mu]$ and its secret opening hint $\mathcal{S}$. $\mathcal{P}$ attempts to convince $\mathcal{V}$ that $\mathcal{G}(r) = v$. At the end of the protocol, $\mathcal{V}$ outputs $b \in \{0,1\}$.

Definitions of properties of polynomial commitments as well as definitions of interactive arguments of knowledge are in an extended report [72].

3 The Sum-Check Protocol: Opportunities and Challenges

An interactive proof is an interactive argument, where the soundness holds unconditionally. We now describe a seminal interactive proof protocol that we employ in Spartan, called the sum-check protocol [66]. Suppose there is an μ-variate low-degree polynomial, $\mathcal{G} : \mathbb{F}^\mu \to \mathbb{F}$ where the degree of each variable in $\mathcal{G}$ is at most ℓ. Suppose that a verifier $\mathcal{V}_{SC}$ is interested in checking a claim of the following form by an untrusted prover $\mathcal{P}_{SC}$:

$$T = \sum_{x_1 \in \{0,1\}} \sum_{x_2 \in \{0,1\}} \cdots \sum_{x_\mu \in \{0,1\}} \mathcal{G}(x_1, x_2, \ldots, x_\mu)$$

Of course, given $\mathcal{G}(\cdot)$, $\mathcal{V}_{SC}$ can deterministically evaluate the above sum and verify whether the sum is T. But, this computation takes time exponential in μ.

Lund et al. [66] describe the sum-check protocol that requires far less computation on $\mathcal{V}_{SC}$'s behalf, but provides a probabilistic guarantee. In the protocol, $\mathcal{V}_{SC}$ interacts with $\mathcal{P}_{SC}$ over a sequence of μ rounds. At the end of this interaction, $\mathcal{V}_{SC}$ outputs $b \in \{0,1\}$. The principal cost to $\mathcal{V}_{SC}$ is to evaluate $\mathcal{G}$ at a random point in its domain $r \in \mathbb{F}^\mu$. We denote the sum-check protocol as $b \leftarrow \langle \mathcal{P}_{SC}, \mathcal{V}_{SC}(r) \rangle (\mathcal{G}, \mu, \ell, T)$. For any μ-variate polynomial $\mathcal{G}$ with degree at most ℓ in each variable, the following properties hold.

- **Completeness.** If $T = \sum_{x \in \{0,1\}^\mu} \mathcal{G}(x)$, then for a correct $\mathcal{P}_{SC}$ and for all $r \in \{0,1\}^*$, $\Pr\{\langle \mathcal{P}_{SC}(\mathcal{G}), \mathcal{V}_{SC}(r) \rangle (\mu, \ell, T) = 1\} = 1$.
- **Soundness.** If $T \neq \sum_{x \in \{0,1\}^\mu} \mathcal{G}(x)$, then for any $\mathcal{P}_{SC}^\star$ and for all $r \in \{0,1\}^*$, $\Pr_r\{\langle \mathcal{P}_{SC}^\star(\mathcal{G}), \mathcal{V}_{SC}(r) \rangle (\mu, \ell, T) = 1\} \leq \ell \cdot \mu / |\mathbb{F}|$.
- **Succinctness.** The communication between $\mathcal{P}_{SC}$ and $\mathcal{V}_{SC}$ is $O(\mu \cdot \ell)$ elements of $\mathbb{F}$.

An alternate formulation. In the rest of the paper, it is natural to view the sum-check protocol as a mechanism to reduce a claim of the form $\sum_{x \in \{0,1\}^m} \mathcal{G}(x) \overset{?}{=} T$ to the claim $\mathcal{G}(r) \overset{?}{=} e$. This is because in most cases, the verifier uses an auxiliary protocol to verify the latter claim, so this formulation makes it easy to describe our end-to-end protocols. We denote this reduction protocol with $e \leftarrow \langle \mathcal{P}_{SC}(\mathcal{G}), \mathcal{V}_{SC}(r) \rangle (\mu, \ell, T)$.

3.1 Challenges with Using the Sum-Check Protocol for Succinct Arguments

To build a succinct interactive argument of knowledge for R1CS, we need an interactive protocol for the verifier $\mathcal{V}$ to check if the prover $\mathcal{P}$ knows a witness w to a given R1CS instance $\mathbb{x} = (\mathbb{F}, A, B, C, io, m, n)$ such that $\mathtt{Sat}_{R1CS}(\mathbb{x}, w) = 1$.

At first glance, the sum-check protocol [66] seems to offer the necessary building block (it is public-coin, incurs succinct communication, etc.). However, to build a succinct interactive argument of knowledge (that can in turn be compiled into a zkSNARK), we must solve the following sub-problems:

1. **Encode R1CS instances as sum-check instances.** For any R1CS instance $\mathbb{x} = (\mathbb{F}, A, B, C, io, m, n)$, we must devise a degree-ℓ, μ-variate polynomial that sums to a specific value T over $\{0,1\}^\mu$ *if and only if* there exists a witness w such that $\mathrm{Sat}_{R1CS}(\mathbb{x}, w) = 1$, where $\mu = O(\log m)$ and ℓ is a small constant (e.g., 3).
2. **Achieve communication-succinctness.** Although the sum-check protocol offers succinctness (if the first sub-problem is solved with constraints on μ and ℓ noted above), building a succinct interactive argument is non-trivial. This is because after the sum-check reduction, $\mathcal{V}$ must verify $\mathcal{G}(r) \overset{?}{=} e$. Unfortunately, $\mathcal{G}(r)$ depends on the $\mathcal{P}$'s witness w to $\mathbb{x}$. Thus, a naive evaluation of $\mathcal{G}(r)$ requires $O(m)$ communication to transmit w. Transmitting w is also incompatible with zero-knowledge.
3. **Achieve verifier-succinctness.** To compile an interactive argument to a zkSNARK, $\mathcal{V}$'s costs must be sub-linear in the size of an NP statement, but evaluating $\mathcal{G}(r)$ requires $O(n)$ computation if the statement has no structure (e.g., data-parallelism). A potential way around this fundamental issue is for $\mathcal{V}$ to preprocess the structure of the R1CS instance to accelerate all future verification of proofs for different R1CS instances with the same structure. However, to avoid any form of trusted setup, the preprocessing must not involve secret trapdoors.

We describe prior solutions to the three sub-problems in an extended report [72].

4   An Encoding of R1CS Instances as Low-Degree Polynomials

This section describes a compact encoding of an R1CS instance as a degree-3 multivariate polynomial. The following theorem summarizes our result, which we prove below.

Theorem 4.1. *For any R1CS instance $\mathbb{x} = (\mathbb{F}, A, B, C, io, m, n)$, there exists a degree-3 $\log m$-variate polynomial $\mathcal{G}$ such that $\sum_{x \in \{0,1\}^{\log m}} \mathcal{G}(x) = 0$ if and only if there exists a witness w such that $\mathrm{Sat}_{R1CS}(\mathbb{x}, w) = 1$ (except for a soundness error that is negligible in λ) under the assumption that $|\mathbb{F}|$ is exponential in λ and $m = O(\lambda)$.*

For a given R1CS instance $\mathbb{x} = (\mathbb{F}, A, B, C, io, m, n)$, let $s = \lceil \log m \rceil$. Thus, we can view matrices $A, B, C \in \mathbb{F}^{m \times m}$ as functions with the following signature: $\{0,1\}^s \times \{0,1\}^s \to \mathbb{F}$. Specifically, any entry in them can be accessed with a $2s$-bit identifier (or two s-bit identifiers). Furthermore, given a purported witness w to $\mathbb{x}$, let $Z = (io, 1, w)$. It is natural to interpret Z as a function with the following signature: $\{0,1\}^s \to \mathbb{F}$, so any element of Z can be accessed with an s-bit identifier.

We now describe a function $F_{io}(\cdot)$ that can be used to encode w such that $F_{io}(\cdot)$ exhibits a desirable behavior *if and only if* $\text{Sat}_{\text{R1CS}}(\mathbb{x}, w) = 1$.

$$F_{io}(x) = \left(\sum_{y \in \{0,1\}^s} A(x,y) \cdot Z(y) \right) \cdot \left(\sum_{y \in \{0,1\}^s} B(x,y) \cdot Z(y) \right) - \sum_{y \in \{0,1\}^s} C(x,y) \cdot Z(y)$$

Lemma 4.1. $\forall x \in \{0,1\}^s$, $F_{io}(x) = 0$ *if and only if* $\text{Sat}_{R1CS}(\mathbb{x}, w) = 1$.

Proof. This follows from the definition of $\text{Sat}_{\text{R1CS}}(\mathbb{x}, w)$ (Sect. 2.1) and of $Z(\cdot)$. $\qquad\square$

Unfortunately $F_{io}(\cdot)$ is a function, *not* a polynomial, so it cannot be directly used in the sum-check protocol. But, consider its polynomial extension $\widetilde{F}_{io}$: $\mathbb{F}^s \to \mathbb{F}$.

$$\widetilde{F}_{io}(x) = \left(\sum_{y \in \{0,1\}^s} \widetilde{A}(x,y) \cdot \widetilde{Z}(y) \right) \cdot \left(\sum_{y \in \{0,1\}^s} \widetilde{B}(x,y) \cdot \widetilde{Z}(y) \right) - \sum_{y \in \{0,1\}^s} \widetilde{C}(x,y) \cdot \widetilde{Z}(y)$$

Lemma 4.2. $\forall x \in \{0,1\}^s$, $\widetilde{F}_{io}(x) = 0$ *if and only if* $\text{Sat}_{R1CS}(\mathbb{x}, w) = 1$.

Proof. For any $x \in \{0,1\}^s$, $\widetilde{F}_{io}(x) = F_{io}(x)$, so the result follows from Lemma 4.1. $\qquad\square$

Since $\widetilde{F}_{io}(\cdot)$ is a low-degree multivariate polynomial over $\mathbb{F}$ in s variables, a verifier $\mathcal{V}$ could check if $\sum_{x \in \{0,1\}^s} \widetilde{F}_{io}(x) = 0$ using the sum-check protocol with a prover $\mathcal{P}$. But, this is insufficient: $\sum_{x \in \{0,1\}^s} \widetilde{F}_{io}(x) = 0$ does not imply that $\widetilde{F}_{io}(x)$ is zero $\forall x \in \{0,1\}^s$. This is because the 2^s terms in the sum might cancel each other making the final sum zero—even when some of the individual terms are not zero.

We addresses the above issue using a prior idea [8,25,34]. Consider:

$$Q_{io}(t) = \sum_{x \in \{0,1\}^s} \widetilde{F}_{io}(x) \cdot \widetilde{\text{eq}}(t, x),$$

where $\widetilde{\text{eq}}(t, x) = \prod_{i=1}^{s} (t_i \cdot x_i + (1 - t_i) \cdot (1 - x_i))$.

Observe that $Q_{io}(\cdot)$ is a multivariate polynomial such that $Q_{io}(t) = \widetilde{F}_{io}(t)$ for all $t \in \{0,1\}^s$. Thus, $Q_{io}(\cdot)$ is a *zero-polynomial* (i.e., it evaluates to zero for all points in its domain) *if and only if* $\widetilde{F}_{io}(\cdot)$ evaluates to zero at all points in the s-dimensional Boolean hypercube (and hence *if and only if* $\widetilde{F}_{io}(\cdot)$ encodes a witness w such that $\text{Sat}_{\text{R1CS}}(\mathbb{x}, w) = 1$). To check if $Q_{io}(\cdot)$ is a zero-polynomial, it suffices to check if $Q_{io}(\tau) = 0$ where $\tau \in_R \mathbb{F}^s$. This introduces a soundness error, which we quantify below.

Lemma 4.3. $\Pr_\tau \{Q_{io}(\tau) = 0 | \exists x \in \{0,1\}^s \text{ s.t. } \widetilde{F}_{io}(x) \neq 0\} \leq \log m / |\mathbb{F}|$

Proof. If $\exists x \in \{0,1\}^s$ such that $\widetilde{F}_{io}(x) \neq 0$, then $Q_{io}(t)$ is not a zero-polynomial. By the Schwartz-Zippel lemma, $Q_{io}(t) = 0$ for at most $d/|\mathbb{F}|$ values of t in the domain of $Q_{io}(\cdot)$, where d is the degree of $Q_{io}(\cdot)$. Here, $d = s = \log m$. □

Proof of Theorem 4.1. For a given R1CS instance $\mathbb{x} = (\mathbb{F}, A, B, C, io, m, n)$, define, $\mathcal{G}_{io,\tau}(x) = \widetilde{F}_{io}(x) \cdot \widetilde{eq}(\tau, x)$, so $Q_{io}(\tau) = \sum_{x \in \{0,1\}^s} \mathcal{G}_{io,\tau}(x)$. Observe that $\mathcal{G}_{io,\tau}(\cdot)$ is a degree-3 s-variate polynomial if multilinear extensions of A, B, C, and Z are used in $\widetilde{F}_{io}(\cdot)$. In the terminology of the sum-check protocol, $T = 0, \mu = s = \log m$, and $\ell = 3$. Furthermore, if $\tau \in_R \mathbb{F}^s$, $\sum_{x \in \{0,1\}^s} \mathcal{G}_{io,\tau}(x) = 0$ if and only $\widetilde{F}_{io}(x) = 0 \ \forall x \in \{0,1\}^s$—except for soundness error that is negligible in λ under the assumptions noted above (Lemma 4.3). This combined with Lemma 4.2 implies the desired result.

5   A Family of NIZKs with Succinct Proofs for R1CS

We first design an interactive argument with succinct communication costs and then compile it into a family of NIZKs in the random oracle model using prior transformations.

5.1   A New Public-Coin Succinct Interactive Argument of Knowledge

The following theorem summarizes our result in this section.

Theorem 5.1. *Given an extractable polynomial commitment scheme for multilinear polynomials, there exists a public-coin succinct interactive argument of knowledge where security holds under the assumptions needed for the polynomial commitment scheme and assuming $|\mathbb{F}|$ is exponential in λ and the size parameter of R1CS instance $n = O(\lambda)$.*

To prove the above theorem, we first provide a construction of a public-coin succinct interactive argument of knowledge, and then analyze its costs and security. The proof of Theorem 4.1 established that for $\mathcal{V}$ to verify if an R1CS instance $\mathbb{x} = (\mathbb{F}, A, B, C, io, m, n)$ is satisfiable, it can check if $\sum_{x \in \{0,1\}^s} \mathcal{G}_{io,\tau}(x) = 0$. By using the sum-check protocol, we can reduce the claim about the sum to $e_x \stackrel{?}{=} \mathcal{G}_{io,\tau}(r_x)$ where $r_x \in \mathbb{F}^s$, so $\mathcal{V}$ needs a mechanism to evaluate $\mathcal{G}_{io,\tau}(r_x)$—without incurring $O(m)$ communication from $\mathcal{P}$ to $\mathcal{V}$.

Recall that $G_{io,\tau}(x) = \widetilde{F}_{io}(x) \cdot \widetilde{eq}(\tau, x)$. Thus, to evaluate $G_{io,\tau}(r_x)$, $\mathcal{V}$ must evaluate $\widetilde{F}_{io}(r_x)$ and $\widetilde{eq}(\tau, r_x)$. The latter can be evaluated in $O(\log m)$ time. Furthermore, recall:

$$\widetilde{F}_{io}(r_x) = \left(\sum_{y \in \{0,1\}^s} \widetilde{A}(r_x, y) \cdot \widetilde{Z}(y) \right) \cdot \left(\sum_{y \in \{0,1\}^s} \widetilde{B}(r_x, y) \cdot \widetilde{Z}(y) \right) - \sum_{y \in \{0,1\}^s} \widetilde{C}(r_x, y) \cdot \widetilde{Z}(y)$$

To evaluate $\widetilde{F}_{io}(r_x)$, $\mathcal{V}$ needs to evaluate the following $\forall y \in \{0,1\}^s$: $\widetilde{A}(r_x, y)$, $\widetilde{B}(r_x, y)$, $\widetilde{C}(r_x, y)$, and $\widetilde{Z}(y)$. However, the evaluations of $\widetilde{Z}(y)$ for all $y \in \{0,1\}^s$ is the same as $(io, 1, w)$, so the communication from $\mathcal{P}$ to $\mathcal{V}$ is $\geq O(|w|)$. We now address this issue.

Our solution is a combination of three protocols: the sum-check protocol, a randomized mini protocol, and a polynomial commitment scheme. Our first observation is that the structure of the individual terms in $F_{x,y}(\cdot)$ evaluated at r_x are in a form suitable for the application of a second instance of the sum-check protocol. Specifically, let $\widetilde{F}_{io}(r_x) = \overline{A}(r_x) \cdot \overline{B}(r_x) - \overline{C}(r_x)$, where

$$\overline{A}(r_x) = \sum_{y \in \{0,1\}^s} \widetilde{A}(r_x, y) \cdot \widetilde{Z}(y)$$

$$\overline{B}(r_x) = \sum_{y \in \{0,1\}^s} \widetilde{B}(r_x, y) \cdot \widetilde{Z}(y)$$

$$\overline{C}(r_x) = \sum_{y \in \{0,1\}^s} \widetilde{C}(r_x, y) \cdot \widetilde{Z}(y)$$

This observation opens up the following solution: the prover can make three separate claims to $\mathcal{V}$, say that $\overline{A}(r_x) = v_A$, $\overline{B}(r_x) = v_B$, and $\overline{C}(r_x) = v_C$. Then, $\mathcal{V}$ can evaluate:

$$\mathcal{G}_{io,\tau}(r_x) = (v_A \cdot v_B - v_C) \cdot \widetilde{\mathrm{eq}}(r_x, \tau),$$

which in turn enables $\mathcal{V}$ to verify $\mathcal{G}_{io,\tau}(r_x) \overset{?}{=} e_x$. Of course, $\mathcal{V}$ must still verify three new claims from $\mathcal{P}$: $\overline{A}(r_x) \overset{?}{=} v_A$, $\overline{B}(r_x) \overset{?}{=} v_B$, and $\overline{C}(r_x) \overset{?}{=} v_C$. To do so, $\mathcal{V}$ and $\mathcal{P}$ can run three independent instances of the sum-check protocol to verify these claims. Instead, we use a prior idea [35,84] to combine three claims into a single claim:

- $\mathcal{V}$ samples $r_A, r_B, r_C \in_R \mathbb{F}$ and computes $c = r_A \cdot v_A + r_B \cdot v_B + r_C \cdot v_C$.
- $\mathcal{V}$ uses the sum-check protocol with $\mathcal{P}$ to verify $r_A \cdot \overline{A}(r_x) + r_B \cdot \overline{B}(r_x) + r_C \cdot \overline{C}(r_x) \overset{?}{=} c$. In more detail, let $L(r_x) = r_A \cdot \overline{A}(r_x) + r_B \cdot \overline{B}(r_x) + r_C \cdot \overline{C}(r_x)$.

$$L(r_x) = \sum_{y \in \{0,1\}^s} r_A \cdot \widetilde{A}(r_x, y) \cdot \widetilde{Z}(y) + r_B \cdot \widetilde{B}(r_x, y) \cdot \widetilde{Z}(y) + r_C \cdot \widetilde{C}(r_x, y) \cdot \widetilde{Z}(y)$$

$$= \sum_{y \in \{0,1\}^s} M_{r_x}(y)$$

$M_{r_x}(y)$ is an s-variate polynomial with degree at most 2 in each variable. In the terminology of the sum-check protocol, $\mu = s, \ell = 2$, and $T = c$.

Lemma 5.1. $\mathrm{Pr}_{r_A, r_B, r_C}\{r_A \cdot \overline{A}(r_x) + r_B \cdot \overline{B}(r_x) + r_C \cdot \overline{C}(r_x) = c | \overline{A}(r_x) \neq v_A \vee \overline{B}(r_x) \neq v_B \vee \overline{C}(r_x) \neq v_C\} \leq 1/|\mathbb{F}|$, where $c = r_A \cdot v_A + r_y \cdot v_B + r_C \cdot v_C$.

Proof. The LHS is a polynomial in r_A, r_B, r_C of total degree 1; the same holds for the RHS. So, the desired result follows from the Schwartz-Zippel lemma. □

$\mathcal{V}$ is not out of the woods. At the end of the second instance of the sum-check protocol, $\mathcal{V}$ must evaluate $M_{r_x}(r_y)$ for $r_y \in \mathbb{F}^s$:

$$M_{r_x}(r_y) = r_A \cdot \widetilde{A}(r_x, r_y) \cdot \widetilde{Z}(r_y) + r_B \cdot \widetilde{B}(r_x, r_y) \cdot \widetilde{Z}(r_y) + r_C \cdot \widetilde{C}(r_x, r_y) \cdot \widetilde{Z}(r_y)$$

$$= (r_A \cdot \widetilde{A}(r_x, r_y) + r_B \cdot \widetilde{C}(r_x, r_y) + r_C \cdot \widetilde{C}(r_x, r_y)) \cdot \widetilde{Z}(r_y)$$

Observe that the only term in $M_{r_x}(r_y)$ that depends on the prover's witness is $\widetilde{Z}(r_y)$. This is because all other terms in the above expression can be computed locally by $\mathcal{V}$ using $\mathbb{x} = (\mathbb{F}, A, B, C, io, m, n)$ in $O(n)$ time (Sect. 6 discusses how to reduce the cost of those evaluations to be sub-linear in n). Our second observation is that to evaluate $\widetilde{Z}(r_y)$ without incurring $O(|w|)$ communication from $\mathcal{P}$ to $\mathcal{V}$, we can employ an extractable polynomial commitment scheme for multilinear polynomials (Sect. 2.3). A similar observation was made by Zhang et al. [87] in a different context.

In more detail, $\mathcal{P}$ sends a commitment to $\widetilde{w}(\cdot)$ (i.e., a multilinear extension of its purported witness) to $\mathcal{V}$ *before* the first instance of the sum-check protocol begins using an extractable polynomial commitment scheme for multilinear polynomials. To evaluate $\widetilde{Z}(r_y)$, $\mathcal{V}$ does the following. WLOG, assume $|w| = |io| + 1$. Thus, by the closed form expression of multilinear polynomial evaluations, we have:

$$\widetilde{Z}(r_y) = (1 - r_y[0]) \cdot \widetilde{w}(r_y[1..]) + r_y[0] \cdot \widetilde{(io, 1)}(r_y[1..]),$$

where $r_y[1..]$ refers to a slice of r_y that excludes the the first element.

Putting things together. We assume that there exists an extractable polynomial commitment scheme for multilinear polynomials $\mathsf{PC} = (\mathsf{Setup}, \mathsf{Commit}, \mathsf{Open}, \mathsf{Eval})$.

- $pp \leftarrow \mathsf{Setup}(1^\lambda)$: Invoke $pp \leftarrow \mathsf{PC.Setup}(1^\lambda, \log m)$; output pp.
- $b \leftarrow \langle \mathcal{P}(w), \mathcal{V}(r) \rangle (\mathbb{F}, A, B, C, io, m, n)$:
  1. $\mathcal{P} : (\mathcal{C}, \mathcal{S}) \leftarrow \mathsf{PC.Commit}(pp, \widetilde{w})$ and send $\mathcal{C}$ to $\mathcal{V}$.
  2. $\mathcal{V} : \tau \in_R \mathbb{F}^{\log m}$ and send τ to $\mathcal{P}$.
  3. Let $T_1 = 0$, $\mu_1 = \log m$, $\ell_1 = 3$.
  4. $\mathcal{V}$: Sample $r_x \in_R \mathbb{F}^{\mu_1}$
  5. **Sum-check#1.** $e_x \leftarrow \langle \mathcal{P}_{SC}(\mathcal{G}_{io, \tau}), \mathcal{V}_{SC}(r_x) \rangle (\mu_1, \ell_1, T_1)$
  6. $\mathcal{P}$: Compute $v_A = \widetilde{A}(r_x), v_B = \widetilde{B}(r_x), v_C = \widetilde{C}(r_x)$; send (v_A, v_B, v_C) to $\mathcal{V}$.
  7. $\mathcal{V}$: Abort with $b = 0$ if $e_x \neq (v_A \cdot v_B - v_C) \cdot \widetilde{eq}(r_x, \tau)$.
  8. $\mathcal{V}$: Sample $r_A, r_B, r_C \in_R \mathbb{F}$ and send (r_A, r_B, r_C) to $\mathcal{P}$.
  9. Let $T_2 = r_A \cdot v_A + r_B \cdot v_B + r_C \cdot v_C$, $\mu_2 = \log m$, $\ell_2 = 2$.
  10. $\mathcal{V}$: Sample $r_y \in_R \mathbb{F}^{\mu_2}$
  11. **Sum-check#2.** $e_y \leftarrow \langle \mathcal{P}_{SC}(M_{r_x}), \mathcal{V}_{SC}(r_y) \rangle (\mu_2, \ell_2, T_2)$
  12. $\mathcal{P}$: $v \leftarrow \widetilde{w}(r_y[1..])$ and send v to $\mathcal{V}$.
  13. $b_e \leftarrow \langle \mathcal{P}_{\mathsf{PC.Eval}}(\widetilde{w}, \mathcal{S}), \mathcal{V}_{\mathsf{PC.Eval}}(r) \rangle (pp, \mathcal{C}, r_y, v, \mu_2)$
  14. $\mathcal{V}$: Abort with $b = 0$ if $b_e == 0$.
  15. $\mathcal{V} : v_Z \leftarrow (1 - r_y[0]) \cdot \widetilde{w}(r_y[1..]) + r_y[0] \cdot \widetilde{(io, 1)}(r_y[1..])$
  16. $\mathcal{V} : v_1 \leftarrow \widetilde{A}(r_x, r_y), v_2 \leftarrow \widetilde{B}(r_x, r_y), v_3 \leftarrow \widetilde{C}(r_x, r_y)$
  17. $\mathcal{V}$: Abort with $b = 0$ if $e_y \neq (r_A \cdot v_1 + r_B \cdot v_2 + r_C \cdot v_3) \cdot v_Z$.
  18. $\mathcal{V}$: Output $b = 1$.

Choice of a polynomial commitment scheme. There exist many extractable polynomial commitment schemes for multilinear polynomials [69,84,86,87] that suffice for our purposes. The particular choice impacts the costs of our protocol as well as assumptions, so we review prior commitment schemes' costs and assumptions (Fig. 3). An additional choice here is the scheme of Bünz et al [32] instantiated with class groups, but it requires a modification for our setting where we represent multilinear polynomials using their evaluations over a Boolean hypercube (Sects. 2.2, 2.3).

prior scheme	setup	$\mathcal{P}_{\mathsf{Eval}}$	$|\mathcal{C}|$	communication	$\mathcal{V}_{\mathsf{Eval}}$	assumption
Hyrax-PC [82]	public	$O(\Gamma)$	$O(\sqrt{\Gamma})$	$O(\log \Gamma)$	$O(\sqrt{\Gamma})$	DLOG
vSQL-VPD [87]	private	$O(\Gamma)$	$O(1)$	$O(\log \Gamma)$	$O(\log \Gamma)$	q-PKE
Virgo-VPD [86]	public	$O(\Gamma \log \Gamma)$	$O(1)$	$O(\log^2 \Gamma)$	$O(\log^2 \Gamma)$	CRHF

Fig. 3. A comparison of candidate extractable polynomial commitment schemes for multilinear polynomials. Here, $\Gamma = 2^\mu$ where μ is the number of variables in the multilinear polynomial. Hyrax-PC refers to the scheme of Wahby et al. [84], which also supports shorter commitments at the cost of increasing the verifier's time. vSQL-VPD refers to the zero-knowledge variant [88] of the scheme of Zhang et al. [87]. Virgo-VPD refers to the scheme of Zhang et al. [86]. The communication column refers to the amount of communication required in the interactive argument for PC.Eval.

Analysis of costs. Note that the polynomials over which the sum-check protocol is run in our interactive argument decompose into several multilinear polynomials (four in the first sum-check protocol and two in the second sum-check protocol), so by employing prior ideas [78,82,85] to implement a linear-time prover for the sum-check protocol, the costs of our interactive argument are as follows.

- $\mathcal{P}$ incurs: (1) $O(n)$ costs to participate in the sum-check instances; (2) the cost of PC.Commit and PC.Eval for a $\log m$-variate multilinear polynomial $\widetilde{w}(\cdot)$.
- $\mathcal{V}$ incurs: (1) $O(\log m)$ costs for the sum-check instances; (2) the cost of PC.Eval for a $\log m$-variate multilinear polynomial; and (3) $O(n)$ costs to evaluate $\widetilde{A}(\cdot), \widetilde{B}(\cdot), \widetilde{C}(\cdot)$.
- The amount of communication is: (1) $O(\log m)$ in the sum-check instances; (2) the size of the commitment to $\widetilde{w}(\cdot)$ and the communication in PC.Eval for $\widetilde{w}(\cdot)$.

Proof of Theorem 5.1. The desired completeness of our interactive argument of knowledge follows from the completeness of the sum-check protocol and of the underlying polynomial commitment scheme. Furthermore, in all the four candidate constructions for polynomial commitment schemes, the communication from $\mathcal{P}$ to $\mathcal{V}$ is sub-linear in m (Fig. 4), which satisfies succinctness. Thus, we are left with proving witness-extended emulation, which we prove in the full version of the paper [72].

PC choice	setup	prover	communication	verifier	assumption
Hyrax-PC [82]	public	$O(n)$	$O(\sqrt{m})$	$O(n + \sqrt{m})$	DLOG
vSQL-VPD [87]	private	$O(n)$	$O(\log m)$	$O(n + \log m)$	q-PKE
Virgo-VPD [86]	public	$O(n + m \log m)$	$O(\log^2 m)$	$O(n + \log^2 m)$	CRHF

Fig. 4. Costs of our public-coin succinct interactive argument of knowledge instantiated with different polynomial commitment schemes. The depicted costs are for an R1CS instance $x = (\mathbb{F}, A, B, C, io, m, n)$.

5.2 A Family of NIZKs with Succinct Proofs for R1CS

The interactive argument from the prior subsection is public coin, so we add zero-knowledge using prior techniques [9,40]. There are two compilers that are particularly efficient: (1) the one employed by Hyrax [84], which relies on a zero-knowledge argument protocol for proving dot-product relationships and other relationships in zero-knowledge (e.g., products); and (2) the compiler employed by Libra [85] and Virgo [86], which relies on an extractable polynomial commitment scheme. This transformation does not change asymptotics of $\mathcal{P}$, $\mathcal{V}$, or of the amount of communication (Fig. 4).

Finally, since our protocol is public coin, it can be made non-interactive in the random oracle model using the Fiat-Shamir transform [45], thereby obtaining a family of NIZKs with succinct proofs for R1CS.

6   Computation Commitments: zkSNARKs for R1CS from NIZK

The previous section constructed a family of NIZKs but not zkSNARKs. This is because the verifier incurs costs linear in the size of the R1CS instance to evaluate $\widetilde{A}, \widetilde{B}, \widetilde{C}$ at (r_x, r_y). We now discuss how to achieve sub-linear verification costs. At first blush, this appears impossible: The verifier incurs $O(n)$ costs to evaluate $\widetilde{A}, \widetilde{B}, \widetilde{C}$ at (r_x, r_y) (step 16, Sect. 5.1), which is time-optimal [78,80] if x has no structure (e.g., uniformity). We get around this impossibility by introducing a preprocessing step for $\mathcal{V}$. In an offline phase, $\mathcal{V}$ with access to non-io portions of an R1CS instance $x = (\mathbb{F}, A, B, C, io, m, n)$ executes the following, where $pp_{cc} \leftarrow$ PC.Setup$(1^\lambda, 2 \log m)$ and PC is an extractable polynomial commitment scheme for multilinear polynomials.

Encode$(pp_{cc}, (A, B, C))$:

- $(\mathcal{C}_A, \mathcal{S}_A) \leftarrow$ PC.Commit$(pp_{cc}, \widetilde{A})$
- $(\mathcal{C}_B, \mathcal{S}_B) \leftarrow$ PC.Commit$(pp_{cc}, \widetilde{B})$
- $(\mathcal{C}_C, \mathcal{S}_C) \leftarrow$ PC.Commit$(pp_{cc}, \widetilde{C})$
- Output $(\mathcal{C}_A, \mathcal{C}_B, \mathcal{C}_C)$

$\mathcal{V}$ retains commitments output by Encode (which need not hide the underlying polynomials, so in practice $\mathcal{S}_A = \mathcal{S}_B = \mathcal{S}_C = \bot$). The interactive argument proceeds as in the prior section except that at step 16, instead of $\mathcal{V}$ evaluating $\widetilde{A}, \widetilde{B}, \widetilde{C}$, we have:

- $\mathcal{P} : v_1 \leftarrow \widetilde{A}(r_x, r_y), v_2 \leftarrow \widetilde{B}(r_x, r_y), v_3 \leftarrow \widetilde{C}(r_x, r_y)$. Send (v_1, v_2, v_3) to $\mathcal{V}$.
- $b_1 \leftarrow \langle \mathcal{P}_{\mathsf{PC.Eval}}(\widetilde{A}, \bot), \mathcal{V}_{\mathsf{PC.Eval}}(r) \rangle (pp_{cc}, \mathcal{C}_A, (r_x, r_y), v_1, 2 \log m)$
- $b_2 \leftarrow \langle \mathcal{P}_{\mathsf{PC.Eval}}(\widetilde{B}, \bot), \mathcal{V}_{\mathsf{PC.Eval}}(r) \rangle (pp_{cc}, \mathcal{C}_B, (r_x, r_y), v_2, 2 \log m)$
- $b_3 \leftarrow \langle \mathcal{P}_{\mathsf{PC.Eval}}(\widetilde{C}, \bot), \mathcal{V}_{\mathsf{PC.Eval}}(r) \rangle (pp_{cc}, \mathcal{C}_C, (r_x, r_y), v_3, 2 \log m)$
- $\mathcal{V}$: Abort with $b = 0$ if $b_1 = 0 \vee b_2 = 0 \vee b_3 = 0$.

Lemma 6.1. *The interactive argument from Sect. 5.1 where step 16 is replaced with the above protocol is a public-coin succinct interactive argument of knowledge assuming PC is an extractable polynomial commitment scheme for multilinear polynomials.*

Proof. The result follows from the knowledge soundness property satisfied by PC scheme used in the Encode algorithm. □

If $\mathcal{V}$'s costs to verify the three evaluations and the added communication are sub-linear in $O(n)$, the modified interactive argument leads to a zkSNARK (if we add zero-knowledge and non-interactivity as before).

Unfortunately, existing polynomial commitment schemes do not satisfy the desired efficiency properties: (1) to participate in Eval for any of $\widetilde{A}, \widetilde{B}, \widetilde{C}, \mathcal{P}$ incurs at least quadratic costs i.e., $O(m^2)$; and (2) in some schemes (e.g., Hyrax-PC), the modified interactive argument does not offer improved asymptotics for the verifier.

The next section describes a scheme that meets our efficiency requirements and leads to asymptotics noted in Fig. 2.

7 The SPARK Compiler

This section describes SPARK, a new cryptographic compiler to transform an existing extractable polynomial commitment scheme for dense multilinear polynomials to one that can efficiently handle sparse multilinear polynomials.

For ease of exposition, we focus on describing SPARK that applies to $2 \log m$-variate sparse polynomials $\widetilde{A}, \widetilde{B}, \widetilde{C}$ (where their dense representation is of size $\leq n$) from Sect. 5.1, but our result generalizes to other sparse multilinear polynomials.

7.1 SPARK-naive: A Straw-Man Solution

To present our solution, we describe a straw-man that helps introduce the necessary building blocks as well as articulate difficulties addressed by SPARK. We recall Hyrax [84], a zkSNARK that achieves sub-linear verification costs for uniform circuits, specifically data-parallel circuits. The prover's costs in Hyrax can be made linear in the circuit size using subsequent ideas [85]. Furthermore, the verifier's costs are $O(d \log n + e)$ where d is the depth of the circuit and e is the cost to the verifier to participate in PC.Eval to evaluate a $\log |w|$-variate multilinear polynomial where w is a witness to the circuit.

Details. Let M denote one of $\{A, B, C\}$ and let $s = \log m$, so $\mu = 2s$. Recall the closed-form expression for multilinear polynomial evaluations at $r \in \mathbb{F}^\mu$.

$$\widetilde{M}(r) = \sum_{i \in \{0,1\}^\mu \, :: \, M(i) \neq 0} M(i) \cdot \widetilde{\mathrm{eq}}(i, r) \tag{1}$$

The above sum has at most n terms since $M(i) \neq 0$ for at most n values of i. Also, each entry in the sum can be computed with $O(\mu)$ multiplications. Consider the following circuit to evaluate $\widetilde{M}(r)$.

A $O(\log \mu)$-depth circuit with $O(n \cdot \mu)$ gates that:

- Takes as witness the list of n tuples of the form $(i, M(i)){::}M(i) \neq 0$, where each i is represented with a vector of μ elements of $\mathbb{F}$, so each entry in the list is $\mu + 1$ elements of $\mathbb{F}$ (in other words, the witness is a $\log(n \cdot (\mu + 1))$-variate multilinear polynomial whose dense representation is the above list of tuples);
- Takes as public input $r \in \mathbb{F}^\mu$;
- Asserts that in each of the n tuples, the first μ elements are either 0 or 1.
- Computes $v \leftarrow \widetilde{M}(r)$ using Equation 1;
- Outputs v

Note that the above circuit is uniform: there are n identical copies of a sub-circuit, where each sub-circuit computes $O(\mu)$ multiplications; the outputs of these sub-circuits is fed into a binary tree of addition gates to compute the final sum. Furthermore, there is no sharing of witness elements across data-parallel units, so it truly data-parallel.

Construction. Given an extractable polynomial commitment scheme PC for multilinear polynomials, we build a scheme for sparse multilinear polynomials as follows.

$\mathsf{PC}^{\mathsf{naive}}$:

- $pp \leftarrow \mathsf{Setup}(1^\lambda, \mu, n)$: PC.Setup$(1^\lambda, \log((\mu + 1) \cdot n))$
- $(\mathcal{C}; \mathcal{S}) \leftarrow \mathsf{Commit}(pp, \widetilde{M})$: PC.Commit$(pp, \mathcal{D})$, where $\mathcal{D}$ is the unique $\log((\mu + 1) \cdot n)$-variate multilinear polynomial whose dense representation is the list of tuples $(i, M(i)){::}M(i) \neq 0$ and each entry is $(\mu + 1)$ elements of $\mathbb{F}$.
- $b \leftarrow \mathsf{Open}(pp, \mathcal{C}, \widetilde{M}, \mathcal{S})$: PC.Open$(pp, \mathcal{C}, \mathcal{D}, \mathcal{S})$, where $\mathcal{D}$ is defined as above.
- $b \leftarrow \mathsf{Eval}(pp, \mathcal{C}, r, v, \mu, n; \widetilde{M}, \mathcal{S})$: $\mathcal{P}$ and $\mathcal{V}$ use Hyrax to verify the claim that $\widetilde{M}(r) = v$ using the circuit described above.

Analysis of costs. Recall that computing $\widetilde{M}(r)$ for $M \in \{A, B, C\}$ and $r \in \mathbb{F}^\mu$ takes $O(n)$ costs. The principal downside of $\mathsf{PC}^{\mathsf{naive}}$ is it imposes an asymptotic overhead over its underlying commitment scheme for dense multilinear polynomials.

For example, with Hyrax-PC as the underlying commitment scheme, the prover with $\mathsf{PC}^{\mathsf{naive}}$ incurs $O(n \log n)$ costs to prove an evaluation of a committed sparse multilinear polynomial. This is because the prover must prove the satisfiability of a circuit of size $O(n \cdot \mu)$ as well as prove the evaluations of a constant number of $(\log (n \cdot (\mu + 1)))$-variate multilinear polynomials. This slowdown is also significant in practice (Sect. 8).

Lemma 7.1. $\mathsf{PC}^{\mathsf{naive}}$ *is a polynomial commitment scheme for multilinear polynomials with the costs noted above.*

Proof. Completeness follows from the completeness of PC and Hyrax. Binding follows from the uniqueness of the dense representation of a sparse multilinear polynomial. Knowledge soundness follows from the witness-extended emulation offered by Hyrax and PC.Eval. The claimed prover's slowdown follows from the costs of Hyrax and PC applied to a constant number of $(\log (n \cdot (\mu + 1)))$-variate multilinear polynomials. □

7.2 Eliminating Asymptotic Overheads by Leveraging Memory Checking

We now improve on the straw-man scheme by devising an $O(n)$-sized circuit for sparse polynomial evaluation. Naturally, the size of the witness to the circuit is also of size $O(n)$. This allows SPARK to achieve a linear-time prover if the underlying polynomial commitment scheme offers linear-time costs for the prover [69,84]. More generally, when transforming an existing polynomial commitment scheme that meets our requirements (Sect. 2.3), SPARK does not add asymptotic overheads to the prover for proving the evaluations of committed sparse multilinear polynomials.

Observe that for $M \in \{A, B, C\}$, $M \in \mathbb{F}^{m \times m}$ and any $r \in \mathbb{F}^\mu$, we can rewrite the evaluation of $\widetilde{M}(r)$ as follows. In our context $\mu = 2 \log m$, interpret r as a tuple (r_x, r_y) where $r_x, r_y \in \mathbb{F}^s$ and $s = \log m = \mu/2$. Thus, we can rewrite Eq. 1 as:

$$\widetilde{M}(r_x, r_y) = \sum_{(i,j) \in (\{0,1\}^s, \{0,1\}^s) \, :: \, M(i,j) \neq 0} M(i,j) \cdot \widetilde{\mathsf{eq}}(i, r_x) \cdot \widetilde{\mathsf{eq}}(j, r_y)$$

In our context, the above sum still contains n terms. Also, computing each entry in the sum still requires $(\mu + 1)$ multiplications over $\mathbb{F}$. However, it is possible to compute a table of evaluations of $\widetilde{\mathsf{eq}}(i, r_x)$ for all $i \in \{0,1\}^s$ in $O(2^s) = O(m)$ time. Similarly, it is possible to compute evaluations of $\widetilde{\mathsf{eq}}(j, r_y)$ for all $j \in \{0,1\}^s$ in $O(m)$ time.

Unfortunately, this observation is insufficient: even though these tables can be computed in $O(m)$ time, the sum is taken over the list of $(i, j) \in (\{0,1\}^s, \{0,1\}^s)$

where $M(i, j) \neq 0$ and for an arbitrary $2s$-variate sparse multilinear polynomial, such a list has no structure, so computing the sum requires n random accesses into two tables each with m entries. We could attempt to build a circuit that supports RAM operations. Unfortunately, existing techniques to encode RAM in circuits incur a logarithmic blowup or constants that in practice are larger than a logarithmic blowup.

For m RAM operations over a memory of size m,

- Pantry [31], using Merkle trees, trees [24,67], offers a circuit of size $O(m \log m)$.
- Buffet [83], using permutation networks [13], offers a circuit of size $O(m \log m)$ with constants smaller than the ones in Pantry.
- vRAM [89] offers an $O(m)$-sized circuit with a constant of $\log |\mathbb{F}|$ (to encode consistency checks over a memory transcript), so, in practice, this does not improve on the straw-man. Other downsides: (1) it only supports 32-bit sized memory cells, whereas we need a memory over elements of $\mathbb{F}$; (2) nearly all of the circuit's non-deterministic witness must be committed by $\mathcal{P}$ during circuit evaluation.

Our solution specializes and improves upon a recent implementation of offline memory checking techniques [24] in Spice [73], which builds circuits to encode operations on persistent storage with serializable transactions. The storage abstraction can be used as a memory abstraction where for m operations, the circuit is of size $O(m)$, but the constants are worse than those of VRAM: ≥ 1000 (to encode an elliptic-curve based multiset collision-resistant hash function for each memory operation). We get around this issue by designing an offline memory checking primitive via a new randomized check that only uses public coins. Furthermore, unlike a vRAM-based solution, most of the non-deterministic witness needed by the circuit can be created by PC.Commit (i.e., by the Encode algorithm in the context of computation commitments).

7.2.1   An $O(n)$-sized Circuit for Evaluating $\widetilde{M}$

We now describe an $O(n)$-sized circuit to compute an evaluation of $\widetilde{M}$. We prove that the circuit indeed computes the correct evaluation of the sparse polynomial in Lemma 7.5. In the description of the circuit, we assume hash functions H and $\mathcal{H}$, which are defined below (Eqs. 2 and 3). Before we describe the circuit for polynomial evaluation, we specify an encoding of sparse polynomials that our circuit leverages.

Encoding sparse polynomials. Given a sparse polynomial $\widetilde{M}$ (e.g., $\widetilde{M} \in \{\widetilde{A}, \widetilde{B}, \widetilde{C}\}$), we encode it using three vectors of size n as follows. Since $\widetilde{M}$ is represented by n tuples of the form $(i, j, M(i, j))$, where each tuple has 3 elements of $\mathbb{F}$ such that $M(i, j) \neq 0$. Note that this encoding differs from the encoding in the straw-man where each i and j were encoded using a vector of s elements of $\{0, 1\} \in \mathbb{F}$. The encoding here essentially packs s bits in i (or j) into a single element of $\mathbb{F}$ in the obvious way, which works because $s < \log |\mathbb{F}|$. In some canonical order, let row, col, val be three vectors that encode the above n tuples such that for $k \in [0, n-1]$ $row(k) = i, col(k) = j, val(k) = M(i, j)$.

Encoding metadata for memory checking: "Memory in the head". The circuit below takes as witness additional metadata about $\widetilde{M}$ (besides row, col, val introduced above). This metadata accelerates memory checking during the evaluation of $\widetilde{M}(r)$.

The metadata is in the form of six vectors: $read\text{-}ts_{row} \in \mathbb{F}^n$, $write\text{-}ts_{row} \in \mathbb{F}^n$, $audit\text{-}ts_{row} \in \mathbb{F}^m$, $read\text{-}ts_{col} \in \mathbb{F}^n$, $write\text{-}ts_{col} \in \mathbb{F}^n$, and $audit\text{-}ts_{col} \in \mathbb{F}^m$. We specify how these are computed below with pseudocode. Note that computing this metadata only needs the following parameters: memory size (which is determined by $2^s = m$) and the sequence of addresses at which the memory is accessed (which are provided by row and col). In a nutshell, $read\text{-}ts_{row}$ and $write\text{-}ts_{row}$ denote the timestamps associated with read and write operations, and $audit\text{-}ts_{row}$ denotes the final timestamps of memory cells in the offline memory checking primitive [24, §4.1] for the address sequence specified by row over a memory of size $m = O(2^s)$. Similarly, $read\text{-}ts_{col}, write\text{-}ts_{col}$, and $audit\text{-}ts_{col} \in \mathbb{F}^m$ denote timestamps for the address sequence specified by col. They are computed as follows (*vec!* uses Rust notation).

MemoryInTheHead($m, n, addrs$):

- $read\text{-}ts \leftarrow vec![n; 0]; \quad write\text{-}ts \leftarrow vec![n; 0]; \quad audit\text{-}ts \leftarrow vec![m; 0]; \quad ts \leftarrow 0$
- for i in $(0..addrs.len())$:
  - $addr \leftarrow addrs[i]$
  - $r\text{-}ts \leftarrow audit\text{-}ts[i]$
  - $ts \leftarrow max(ts, r\text{-}ts) + 1$
  - $read\text{-}ts[i] \leftarrow r\text{-}ts$
  - $write\text{-}ts[i] \leftarrow ts$
  - $audit\text{-}ts[addr] \leftarrow ts$
- return $(read\text{-}ts, write\text{-}ts, audit\text{-}ts)$

Circuit description. The circuit below evaluates a sparse polynomial using the encoding and preprocessed metadata described above. It relies multiset hash functions, which we now define. Unlike ECC-based multiset hash functions in Spice [73], we employ a public-coin hash function that verifies the desired multiset relationship. Specifically, we define two hash functions: (1) $h_\gamma : \mathbb{F}^3 \rightarrow \mathbb{F}$; and (2) $\mathcal{H}_\gamma : \mathbb{F}^* \rightarrow \mathbb{F}$, where $\mathbb{F}^*$ denotes a multiset with elements from $\mathbb{F}$ and $\gamma \in_R \mathbb{F}$.

$$h_\gamma(a, v, t) = a \cdot \gamma^2 + v \cdot \gamma + t \tag{2}$$

$$\mathcal{H}_\gamma(\mathcal{M}) = \Pi_{e \in \mathcal{M}}(e - \gamma) \tag{3}$$

Given $(A, V, T) \in (\mathbb{F}^\ell, \mathbb{F}^\ell, \mathbb{F}^\ell)$ for $\ell > 0$, we define a map $H_\gamma : (\mathbb{F}^\ell, \mathbb{F}^\ell, \mathbb{F}^\ell) \rightarrow \mathbb{F}^\ell$:

$$H_\gamma(A, V, T) = [h_\gamma(A[0], V[0], T[0]), \ldots, h_\gamma(A[\ell-1], V[\ell-1], T[\ell-1])]$$

We capture the soundness errors of these hash functions in Lemma 7.2 and Lemma 7.3.

An $O(n)$-sized, $O(\log n)$-depth circuit ($Circuit_{\text{eval-opt}}$).

- Takes as witness the following lists (Hyrax can accept witness in separate lists).
  1. a succinct description of $\widetilde{M}$: three lists row, col, val, where each list has n entries.
  2. two lists e_{row}, e_{col}, where each list contains n elements of $\mathbb{F}$.
  3. six lists: $read\text{-}ts_{row}, read\text{-}ts_{col}, write\text{-}ts_{row}, write\text{-}ts_{col}, audit\text{-}ts_{row}$, and $audit\text{-}ts_{col}$. The first four are of size n and the last two are of size m; each entry is an element of $\mathbb{F}$.
  4. two challenges $\gamma_1, \gamma_2 \in \mathbb{F}$.
- Takes as public input $r = (r_x, r_y) \in \mathbb{F}^\mu$;
- Output $\widetilde{M}(r)$ using $v \leftarrow \sum_{k=0}^{n-1} val[k] \cdot e_{row}[k] \cdot e_{col}[k]$.
- Memory checking for e_{row}:
  - $mem_{row} \leftarrow [\widetilde{\text{eq}}(0, r_x), \ldots, \widetilde{\text{eq}}(m-1, r_x)] \in \mathbb{F}^m$
  - $Init_{row} \leftarrow H_{\gamma_1}([0, \ldots, m-1], mem_{row}, [0, \ldots, 0]) \in \mathbb{F}^m$
  - $RS_{row} \leftarrow H_{\gamma_1}(row, e_{row}, read\text{-}ts_{row}) \in \mathbb{F}^n$
  - $WS_{row} \leftarrow H_{\gamma_1}(row, e_{row}, write\text{-}ts_{row}) \in \mathbb{F}^n$
  - $Audit_{row} \leftarrow H_{\gamma_1}([0, \ldots, m-1], mem_{row}, audit\text{-}ts_{row}) \in \mathbb{F}^m$
  - Assert $\mathcal{H}_{\gamma_2}(Init_{row}) \cdot \mathcal{H}_{\gamma_2}(WS_{row}) = \mathcal{H}_{\gamma_2}(RS_{row}) \cdot \mathcal{H}_{\gamma_2}(Audit_{row})$
- Memory checking for e_{col}:
  - $mem_{col} \leftarrow [\widetilde{\text{eq}}(0, r_y), \ldots, \widetilde{\text{eq}}(m-1, r_y)] \in \mathbb{F}^m$
  - Let $Init_{col} \leftarrow H_{\gamma_1}([0, \ldots, m-1], mem_{col}, [0, \ldots, 0]) \in \mathbb{F}^m$
  - Let $RS_{col} \leftarrow H_{\gamma_1}(col, e_{col}, read\text{-}ts_{col}) \in \mathbb{F}^n$
  - Let $WS_{col} \leftarrow H_{\gamma_1}(col, e_{col}, write\text{-}ts_{col}) \in \mathbb{F}^n$
  - Let $Audit_{col} \leftarrow H_{\gamma_1}([0, \ldots, m-1], mem_{col}, audit\text{-}ts_{col}) \in \mathbb{F}^m$
  - Assert $\mathcal{H}_{\gamma_2}(Init_{col}) \cdot \mathcal{H}_{\gamma_2}(WS_{col}) = \mathcal{H}_{\gamma_2}(RS_{col}) \cdot \mathcal{H}_{\gamma_2}(Audit_{col})$

Lemma 7.2. *For any two pairs* $(a_1, v_1, t_1) \in \mathbb{F}^3$ *and* $(a_2, v_2, t_2) \in \mathbb{F}^3$, $\Pr_\gamma\{h_\gamma(a_1, v_1, t_1) = h_\gamma(a_2, v_2, t_2) | (a_1, v_1, t_1) \neq (a_2, v_2, t_2)\} \leq 3/|\mathbb{F}|$.

Proof. This follows from the Schwartz-Zippel lemma. $\square$

Lemma 7.3. *For any* $\ell > 0$, $(A_1, V_1, T_1) \in (\mathbb{F}^\ell, \mathbb{F}^\ell, \mathbb{F}^\ell)$ *and* $(A_2, V_2, T_2) \in (\mathbb{F}^\ell, \mathbb{F}^\ell, \mathbb{F}^\ell)$ $\Pr_\gamma\{\exists i :: H_\gamma(A_1, V_1, T_1)[i] = H_\gamma(A_2, V_2, T_2)[i] | (A_1, V_1, T_1) \neq (A_2, V_2, T_2)\} \leq 3 \cdot \ell/|\mathbb{F}|$.

Proof. This follows from a standard union bound with the result of the Lemma 7.2. $\square$

Lemma 7.4. *For any two multisets* $\mathcal{M}_1, \mathcal{M}_2$ *of size* ℓ *over* $\mathbb{F}$,

$$\Pr_\gamma\{\mathcal{H}_\gamma(\mathcal{M}_1) = \mathcal{H}_\gamma(\mathcal{M}_2) | \mathcal{M}_1 \neq \mathcal{M}_2\} \leq \ell/|\mathbb{F}|$$

Proof. This follows from the Schwartz-Zippel lemma. $\square$

Lemma 7.5. *Assuming that* $|\mathbb{F}|$ *is exponential in* λ *and* $n = O(\lambda)$, *for any* $2\log m$-*variate multilinear polynomial* $\widetilde{M}$ *whose dense representation is of size at most* n *and for any given* $e_{row}, e_{col} \in \mathbb{F}^n$,

$$\Pr_{\gamma_1,\gamma_2} \{Circuit_{eval\text{-}opt}(w, (\gamma_1, \gamma_2), r) = v | \widetilde{M}(r) \neq v\} \leq \mathtt{negl}(\lambda),$$

where $w = (row, col, val, e_{row}, e_{col}, \mathsf{MemoryInTheHead}(m, n, row), \mathsf{MemoryInTheHead}(m, n, col))$ *and* (row, col, val) *denotes the dense representation of* $\widetilde{M}$.

Proof. This follows from the soundness of the memory checking primitive [24] and the collision-resistance of the underlying hash functions used (Lemmas 7.4 and 7.3). $\qquad\square$

7.2.2 Construction of a Polynomial Commitment Scheme

Given an extractable polynomial commitment scheme PC for multilinear polynomials, we build a scheme for sparse multilinear polynomials as follows.

Note that our focus is on designing a polynomial commitment scheme for efficiently realizing computation commitments (Sect. 6). For this purpose, the Spartan verifier runs the Commit algorithm (of the sparse polynomial commitment scheme) as part of the Encode algorithm, so unlike the general setup of polynomial commitments, the entity creating a commitment is the verifier itself (not an untrusted entity). As a result, the additional memory-checking metadata about the sparse polynomial as part of Commit is created by the verifier, so we do not need to verify that the timestamps are well-formed according to its specification in the MemoryInTheHead procedure as required by Lemma 7.5. This is only an optimization and not a limitation. In the general setting where Commit (of the sparse polynomial commitment scheme) is run by an untrusted entity, we can require it to additionally produce a proof that proves that timestamps are well-formed. In the description below, given our focus on computation commitments, we omit those proofs.

$\mathsf{PC}^{\mathrm{SPARK}}$:

- $pp \leftarrow \mathsf{Setup}(1^\lambda, \mu, n)$: $(\mathsf{PC}.\mathsf{Setup}(1^\lambda, \mu)), \mathsf{PC}.\mathsf{Setup}(1^\lambda, \log(n)))$
- $(\mathcal{C}; \mathcal{S}) \leftarrow \mathsf{Commit}(pp; \widetilde{M})$:
  - Let $(pp_m, pp_n) \leftarrow pp$
  - Let (row, col, val) denote the dense representation of $\widetilde{M}$ as described in text.
    - $(\mathcal{C}_{row}, \mathcal{S}_{row}) \leftarrow \mathsf{PC}.\mathsf{Commit}(pp_n, \widetilde{row})$
    - $(\mathcal{C}_{col}, \mathcal{S}_{col}) \leftarrow \mathsf{PC}.\mathsf{Commit}(pp_n, \widetilde{col})$
    - $(\mathcal{C}_{val}, \mathcal{S}_{val}) \leftarrow \mathsf{PC}.\mathsf{Commit}(pp_n, \widetilde{val})$
  - Let $(read\text{-}ts_{row}, write\text{-}ts_{row}, audit\text{-}ts_{row}) \leftarrow \mathsf{MemoryInTheHead}(2^{\mu/2}, n, row)$
    - $(\mathcal{C}_{read\text{-}ts_{row}}, \mathcal{S}_{read\text{-}ts_{row}}) \leftarrow \mathsf{PC}.\mathsf{Commit}(pp_n, \widetilde{read\text{-}ts_{row}})$
    - $(\mathcal{C}_{write\text{-}ts_{row}}, \mathcal{S}_{write\text{-}ts_{row}}) \leftarrow \mathsf{PC}.\mathsf{Commit}(pp_n, \widetilde{write\text{-}ts_{row}})$
    - $(\mathcal{C}_{audit\text{-}ts_{row}}, \mathcal{S}_{audit\text{-}ts_{row}}) \leftarrow \mathsf{PC}.\mathsf{Commit}(pp_m, \widetilde{audit\text{-}ts_{row}})$
  - Let $(read\text{-}ts_{col}, write\text{-}ts_{col}, audit\text{-}ts_{col}) \leftarrow \mathsf{MemoryInTheHead}(2^{\mu/2}, n, col)$

- $(\mathcal{C}_{read\text{-}ts_{col}}, \mathcal{S}_{read\text{-}ts_{col}}) \leftarrow \mathsf{PC.Commit}(pp_n, \widetilde{read\text{-}ts}_{col})$
- $(\mathcal{C}_{write\text{-}ts_{col}}, \mathcal{S}_{write\text{-}ts_{col}}) \leftarrow \mathsf{PC.Commit}(pp_n, \widetilde{write\text{-}ts}_{col})$
- $(\mathcal{C}_{audit\text{-}ts_{col}}, \mathcal{S}_{audit\text{-}ts_{col}}) \leftarrow \mathsf{PC.Commit}(pp_m, \widetilde{audit\text{-}ts}_{col})$
  - Let $\mathcal{C} \leftarrow (\mathcal{C}_{row}, \mathcal{C}_{col}, \mathcal{C}_{val}, \mathcal{C}_{read\text{-}ts_{row}}, \mathcal{C}_{write\text{-}ts_{row}}, \mathcal{C}_{audit\text{-}ts_{row}}, \mathcal{C}_{read\text{-}ts_{col}}, \mathcal{C}_{write\text{-}ts_{col}}, \mathcal{C}_{audit\text{-}ts_{col}})$
  - Let $\mathcal{S} \leftarrow (\mathcal{S}_{row}, \mathcal{S}_{col}, \mathcal{S}_{val}, \mathcal{S}_{read\text{-}ts_{row}}, \mathcal{S}_{write\text{-}ts_{row}}, \mathcal{S}_{audit\text{-}ts_{row}}, \mathcal{S}_{read\text{-}ts_{col}}, \mathcal{S}_{write\text{-}ts_{col}}, \mathcal{S}_{audit\text{-}ts_{col}})$
  - Output $(\mathcal{C}, \mathcal{S})$
- $b \leftarrow \mathsf{Open}(pp, \mathcal{C}, \widetilde{M}, \mathcal{S})$:
  - Let $(pp_m, pp_n) \leftarrow pp$.
  - Let row, col, val denote dense representation of $\widetilde{M}$ as defined above.
  - Output $\mathsf{PC.Open}(pp_n, \mathcal{C}.\mathcal{C}_{row}, \widetilde{row}, \mathcal{S}.\mathcal{S}_{row}) \wedge \mathsf{PC.Open}(pp_n, \mathcal{C}.\mathcal{C}_{col}, \widetilde{col}, \mathcal{S}.\mathcal{S}_{col}) \wedge \mathsf{PC.Open}(pp_n, \mathcal{C}, \mathcal{C}_{val}, \widetilde{val}, \mathcal{S}.\mathcal{S}_{val})$
- $b \leftarrow \mathsf{Eval}(pp, \mathcal{C}, r, v, \mu, n; \widetilde{M}, \mathcal{S})$:
  - Let $(pp_m, pp_n) \leftarrow pp$ and let $(r_x, r_y) = r$, where $r_x, r_y \in \mathbb{F}^{\mu/2}$.
  - Let row, col, val denote dense representation of $\widetilde{M}$ as defined above.
  - $\mathcal{P}$:
    - Compute e_{row} and e_{col} with $2n$ lookups over a table of size $m = 2^{\mu/2}$. That is, $e_{row} = [\widetilde{eq}(row(0), r_x), \ldots, \widetilde{eq}(row(n-1), r_x)]$; let $e_{col} = [\widetilde{eq}(col(0), r_y), \ldots, \widetilde{eq}(col(n-1), r_y)]$.
    - $(\mathcal{C}_{e_{row}}, \mathcal{S}_{e_{row}}) \leftarrow \mathsf{PC.Commit}(pp_n, \widetilde{e_{row}})$; send $\mathcal{C}_{e_{row}}$ to $\mathcal{V}$.
    - $(\mathcal{C}_{e_{col}}, \mathcal{S}_{e_{col}}) \leftarrow \mathsf{PC.Commit}(pp_n, \widetilde{e_{col}})$; send $\mathcal{C}_{e_{col}}$ to $\mathcal{V}$.
  - $\mathcal{V}$: $(\gamma_1, \gamma_2) \in_R \mathbb{F}^2$. Send (γ_1, γ_2) to $\mathcal{P}$.
  - $\mathcal{P}$ and $\mathcal{V}$ use Hyrax (with PC as the extractable polynomial commitment scheme) to verify the claim that $\widetilde{M}(r) = v$ using $Circuit_{\text{eval-opt}}$.

Analysis of costs. $Circuit_{\text{eval-opt}}$ is uniform because computing $\mathcal{H}$ using a binary tree of multiplications [78] constitutes nearly all of the work in the above circuit. Figure 5 depicts the costs of $\mathsf{PC}^{\text{SPARK}}$ with different choices for PC.

PC choice	setup	$\mathcal{P}_{\mathsf{Eval}}$	$\lvert\mathcal{C}\rvert$	communication	$\mathcal{V}_{\mathsf{Eval}}$
Hyrax-PC [82]	public	$O(n)$	$O(\sqrt{n})$	$O(\log^2 n)$	$O(\sqrt{n})$
vSQL-VPD [87]	private*	$O(n)$	$O(1)$	$O(\log^2 n)$	$O(\log^2 n)$
Virgo-VPD [86]	public	$O(n \log n)$	$O(1)$	$O(\log^2 n)$	$O(\log^2 n)$

Fig. 5. Costs of $\mathsf{PC}^{\text{SPARK}}$ with different choices for PC. Here, n is number of entries in the dense representation of the multilinear polynomial.

Lemma 7.6. *Assuming that $\mathsf{PC}^{\text{SPARK}}.\mathsf{Commit}$ is run by an honest entity, then $\mathsf{PC}^{\text{SPARK}}$ is a polynomial commitment scheme for multilinear polynomials with the costs noted.*

Proof. Completeness follows from the completeness of PC, Hyrax, and $Circuit_{\text{eval-opt}}$. Binding follows from the uniqueness of the dense representation of the sparse multilinear polynomial as (row, col, val). Knowledge soundness follows from the witness-extended emulation offered by Hyrax and PC, and from the negligible soundness error of $Circuit_{\text{eval-opt}}$ (Lemma 7.5). Finally, the claimed costs follow from the cost model of Hyrax and of PC applied to a constant number of $O(\log n)$-variate multilinear polynomials.   □

7.2.3   Optimizations

We now describe many optimizations to SPARK to reduce constants.

1. Instead of using Hyrax as a black box, we tailor it for $Circuit_{\text{eval-opt}}$ using prior ideas [78]. This reduces overall costs significantly. We also do not need Hyrax's zero-knowledge compiler for computation commitments.
2. For computation commitments, we build a single circuit that produces evaluations of $\widetilde{A}, \widetilde{B}, \widetilde{C}$ at (r_x, r_y). This enables reusing parts of the memory checking circuit (related to the state of the memory) across evaluations.
3. In our particular context, we can set $\forall 0 \leq i < n$: $write\text{-}ts_{row}[i] = read\text{-}ts_{row}[i] + 1$ and $write\text{-}ts_{col}[i] = read\text{-}ts_{read}[i] + 1$. This is because unlike the traditional setting of offline memory checking, the read timestamps are not untrusted. This avoids having to commit to $\widetilde{write\text{-}ts}_{row}$ and $\widetilde{write\text{-}ts}_{col}$.
4. During $\mathsf{PC}^{\text{SPARK}}$.Eval, at the witness layer in Hyrax, $\mathcal{V}$ needs to evaluate a number of multilinear polynomials at either $r_{row}, r_{col} \in \mathbb{F}^{\log n}$ or $r_{mem} \in \mathbb{F}^{\log m}$. We avoid having to commit to them by leveraging their succinct representations.
   - $\mathcal{V}$ can compute $\widetilde{mem}_{row}(r_{row})$ and $\widetilde{mem}_{col}(r_{col})$ in $O(\log m)$ as follows:

$$\widetilde{mem}_{row}(r_{row}) \leftarrow \widetilde{eq}(r_{row}, r_x)$$

$$\widetilde{mem}_{col}(r_{col}) \leftarrow \widetilde{eq}(r_{col}, r_y)$$

   - We leverage the following facts: (1) $\widetilde{(0, 1, \ldots, m-1)}(r_{mem}) = \sum_{i=0}^{\log m} 2^i \cdot r_{mem}[i]$; (2) $\widetilde{(0, 0, \ldots, 0)}(r_{mem}) = 0$.
5. It is possible to combine k μ-variate multilinear polynomials into a single multilinear polynomial over $\mu + \log k$ variables. We employ this technique to reduce the number of committed multilinear polynomials from 23 to 3.

8   Implementation and Optimizations

We implement Spartan as a modular library in about 8,000 lines of Rust including optimizations listed throughout the paper as well as optimizations from prior work [78,80,82,84,85]. We find that the prover under SPARK outperforms the prover under SPARK-naive by $>10\times$ for R1CS instances with 2^{20} constraints. We also implement SPARK with and without our optimizations. At 2^{20} constraints, our optimizations reduce proof lengths from 3.1 MB to 138.4 KB, a improvement of $23\times$; our optimizations also improve prover and verification times by about $10\times$.

In the next section, we present results from SPARK instantiated with Hyrax-PC [84] i.e., we evaluate a zkSNARK whose security holds under the discrete logarithm problem. For curve arithmetic, we use `curve25519-dalek` [1], which offers an efficient implementation of a prime-order Ristretto group [2,53] called `ristretto255`. The scalar arithmetic in the library is however slow since it represents the underlying scalar elements as byte strings for fast curve arithmetic. To cope with this, we optimize the underlying scalar arithmetic by $\approx 10\times$ by adapting other code [28].

9   Experimental Evaluation

This section experimentally evaluates our implementation of Spartan and compares it with state-of-the-art zkSNARKs and proof-succinct NIZKs.

9.1   Metrics, Methodology, and Testbed

Our principal evaluation metrics are: (1) $\mathcal{P}$'s costs to produce a proof; (2) $\mathcal{V}$'s costs to preprocess an R1CS instance; (3) $\mathcal{V}$'s costs to verify a proof; and (4) the size of a proof. We measure $\mathcal{P}$'s and $\mathcal{V}$'s costs using a real-time clock and the size of proofs in bytes by serializing proof data structures. For Spartan, we use `cargo bench` to run experiments, and for baselines, we use profilers provided with their code.

We experiment with Spartan and several baselines (listed below) using a Microsoft Surface Laptop 3 on a single CPU core of Intel Core i7-1065G7 with 16 GB RAM running Ubuntu 20.04 atop Windows 10. We report results from a single-threaded configuration since not all our baselines leverage multiple cores. As with prior work [16], we vary the size of the R1CS instance by varying the number of constraints and variables m and maintain the ratio n/m to approximately 1. In all Spartan experiments $|io| = 10$.

Baselines. We compare Spartan with the following zkSNARKs and NIZKs.

1. Groth16 [51], the most efficient zkSNARK with trusted setup based on GGPR [47].
2. Ligero [3], a prior proof-succinct NIZK with a light-weight prover.
3. Hyrax [84], a prior transparent zkSNARK that achieves sub-linear verification costs for data-parallel computations.
4. Aurora [16], a prior proof-succinct NIZK.
5. Fractal [36], a recent transparent zkSNARK that instantiates computation commitments to achieve sub-linear verification costs.

We provide a comparison with additional baselines in an extended report [72].

Methodology and parameters. For Spartan$_{DL}$, we report results from two variants: SpartanSNARK (which incurs sub-linear verification) and SpartanNIZK (which incurs linear-time verification). This is because several baselines offer only a linear-time verifier. Also, for data-parallel workloads, the NIZK variant depicts the performance that SpartanSNARK can achieve for the prover and proof sizes since SpartanSNARK can amortize the costs of computation commitments across data-parallel units.

For Groth16, we benchmark its implementation from `libsnark` with `bn128` curve [64].

For Hyrax, we use its reference implementation with curve25519 [62]. To compare Spartan with Hyrax, we transform R1CS instances to depth-1 arithmetic circuits where the circuit evaluates constraints in the R1CS instance, and outputs a vector of zeros when all constraints are satisfied. For an arbitrary R1CS instance, this circuit has no structure, and hence Hyrax incurs linear-time verification costs.

For Ligero, Aurora, and Fractal, we use their implementations from `libiop` with a prime field of size $\approx 2^{256}$ [63]. The implementations of Aurora and Fractal support two sets of parameters: proven and non-proven (also known as heuristic). The default choice in their code is the heuristic parameters, which rely on non-standard conjectures related to Reed-Solomon codes (e.g., in the FRI protocol) for soundness [10, Appendix B]. Concretely, the heuristic parameters use $\approx 10\times$ fewer query repetitions of FRI compared to the proven parameters. As expected, the heuristic versions achieve $\approx 10\times$ lower verification costs and proof sizes than the corresponding provable versions. Note that very recent work makes progress toward proving some of these heuristics [11].

9.2 Performance Results

Prover. Figure 6 depicts the prover's costs under Spartan and its baselines. Spartan outperforms all its baselines. When compared to the most closely related system, SpartanSNARK is $36\times$ faster than Fractal at 2^{18} constraints.[4] When we compare Ligero, Aurora, and Hyrax with SpartanNIZK (since all of them are proof-succinct NIZKs and incur linear-time verification costs), SpartanNIZK is $24\times$ faster than Ligero, $152\times$ faster than Aurora, and $99\times$ faster than Hyrax at 2^{20} instance sizes. Finally, compared to Groth16, SpartanSNARK is $2\times$ faster and SpartanNIZK is $16\times$ faster for 2^{20} constraints.

Proof sizes. Figure 7 depicts proof sizes under Spartan and its baselines. Although SpartanSNARK's proofs are asymptotically larger than Fractal (Fig. 2), SpartanSNARK offers $\approx 23\times$ shorter proofs at 2^{18} constraints. When we compare the proof-succinct NIZKs, SpartanNIZK offers proofs that are 1.2–416× shorter than its baselines. All transparent zkSNARKs produce orders of magnitude longer proofs than Groth16.

---

[4] Unfortunately, we could not run Fractal at 2^{19} or 2^{20} constraints because it crashes by running out of memory.

	2^{10}	2^{11}	2^{12}	2^{13}	2^{14}	2^{15}	2^{16}	2^{17}	2^{18}	2^{19}	2^{20}
Groth16	0.17	0.26	0.46	0.85	1.5	2.8	5.4	10.1	23.2	44.7	76.2
Hyrax	1.2	1.7	2.8	4.1	7.2	13.9	22.5	44.6	90	181	447
Ligero	0.2	0.3	0.6	1.2	2.3	3.4	6.7	13.7	27.2	56.3	112
Ligero-heuristic	0.16	0.3	0.6	1.3	2.4	3.5	6.6	13	25	51.3	101
Aurora	0.7	1.2	2.5	4.6	9	17.3	36	69	140	282	688
Aurora-heuristic	0.4	0.7	1.4	3.2	5.8	12.2	24.8	52.2	108	224	509
Fractal	1	1.8	3.6	6.7	15	30	61	125	337	–	–
Fractal-heuristic	0.8	1.5	3	6.5	14	29	60	125	342	–	–
SpartanNIZK	0.02	0.03	0.04	0.06	0.1	0.17	0.33	0.57	1.1	2.14	4.5
SpartanSNARK	0.07	0.13	0.21	0.39	0.79	1.3	2.6	4.9	9.2	18.5	36.3

Fig. 6. Prover's performance (in seconds) for varying R1CS instance sizes under different schemes.

	2^{10}	2^{11}	2^{12}	2^{13}	2^{14}	2^{15}	2^{16}	2^{17}	2^{18}	2^{19}	2^{20}
Hyrax	13.7	15.7	16.8	19.9	21	26.3	27.5	37	38.2	56.4	57.5
Ligero	546	628	1M	1.2M	2M	3M	5M	5M	10M	10M	20M
Ligero-heuristic	559	620	1M	1.1M	2M	3M	5M	5M	10M	10M	20M
Aurora	447	510	610	717	810	931	1M	1.1M	1.3M	1.5M	1.6M
Aurora-heuristic	53	58	70	75	82	95	101	111	121	129	141
Fractal	1.1M	1.2M	1.4M	1.5M	1.7M	1.8M	2M	2.1M	2.3M	–	–
Fractal-heuristic	125	136	148	163	177	189	206	219	234	–	–
SpartanNIZK	9.3	10	11.7	12.5	15.2	16	20.7	21.5	30.3	31.1	48
SpartanSNARK	32	37	41.7	48	54	63	71.6	85	98	120	142

Fig. 7. Proof sizes in KBs for various zkSNARKs. Entries with "M" are in megabytes. The proof sizes under Groth16 [51] is 128 bytes for all instance sizes.

Verifier. Figure 8 depicts the verifier times under different schemes. Groth16 offers the fastest verifier, but it requires a trusted setup. Among schemes without trusted setup, Spartan offers the fastest verifier. Specifically, SpartanSNARK's verifier is 3.6× faster than Fractal (at the largest instance size Fractal can run), and at 2^{20} constraints, it is 1326× faster than Aurora, 383× faster than Ligero, and 80× faster than Hyrax. This type of performance is expected because Aurora, Ligero, and Hyrax incur linear costs for the verifier whereas SpartansNARK (and Fractal) incur sub-linear verification costs due to the use of computation commitments, which requires preprocessing the non-*io* component of an R1CS instance (we quantify the costs of that process below). Among proof-succinct NIZKs, SpartanNIZK is 22× faster than Hyrax, 363× faster than Aurora, and 105× faster than Ligero at 2^{20} constraints.

Encoder. Figure 9 depicts the cost to the verifier to preprocess an R1CS instance (without the *io* component) under SpartansNARK, Fractal [36], and Groth16 [51]. We do not depict other baselines because they do not require any preprocessing. SpartansNARK's encoder is up to 52× faster than Fractal's encoder and about 4.7× faster than the trusted setup for Groth16 at the largest instance sizes.

	2^{10}	2^{11}	2^{12}	2^{13}	2^{14}	2^{15}	2^{16}	2^{17}	2^{18}	2^{19}	2^{20}
Hyrax	206	231	253	257	331	473	594	926	1.6s	3.1s	8.1s
Ligero	52	100	183	398	823	1.2s	2.2s	4.8s	9.5s	19s	38.5s
Ligero-heuristic	53	99	176	446	822	1.2s	2.3s	4.3s	8.3s	16.6s	34.6s
Aurora	221	351	694	1.1s	2.1s	4.1s	8.3s	14.7s	30s	56s	133s
Aurora-heuristic	16	25	47	86	166	359	597	1.2s	2.4s	5.3s	10s
Fractal	147	138	165	172	174	195	195	198	204	–	–
Fractal-heuristic	11	8.5	10	13	14	16	14	15	16	–	–
SpartanNIZK	5	6	7.4	9.2	12.4	17.5	28	49	88.4	188.9	366
SpartanSNARK	9.6	11.4	13.9	16.4	21	25	34.3	42	55.9	70.8	100.3

Fig. 8. Verifier's performance (in ms) under different schemes. Entries with "s" are in seconds. The verifier under Groth16 [51] takes ≈ 2 ms at all instance sizes.

	2^{10}	2^{11}	2^{12}	2^{13}	2^{14}	2^{15}	2^{16}	2^{17}	2^{18}	2^{19}	2^{20}
Groth16	0.13	0.23	0.4	0.75	1.5	2.8	5.3	10.9	21.4	48.4	71.9
Fractal	0.3	0.6	1.3	2.6	6	12.7	26.8	56	120	389	–
Fractal-heuristic	0.3	0.6	1.2	2.6	5.9	12.5	26.1	55	119	358	–
SpartanSNARK	0.04	0.06	0.12	0.19	0.4	0.7	1.4	2.2	4.5	7.4	15.1

Fig. 9. Encoder's performance (in seconds) for varying R1CS instance sizes under different schemes.

Acknowledgment. Comments from Sebastian Angel, Melissa Chase, Ben Fisch, Esha Ghosh, Abhiram Kothapalli, Satya Lokam, Bryan Parno, Ioanna Tzialla, Ramarathnam Venkatesan, and the CRYPTO reviewers helped improve this paper. Special thanks to Justin Thaler, Riad Wahby, and Michael Walfish for their detailed attention and thorough comments, which helped clarify several aspects of this work. We thank Jonathan Lee for insightful discussions on various topics covered in this work.

References

1. A pure-Rust implementation of group operations on Ristretto and Curve25519. https://github.com/dalek-cryptography/curve25519-dalek
2. The Ristretto group. https://ristretto.group/
3. Ames, S., Hazay, C., Ishai, Y., Venkitasubramaniam, M.: Ligero: lightweight sublinear arguments without a trusted setup. In: CCS (2017)
4. Arasu, A., et al.: Concerto: a high concurrency key-value store with integrity. In: SIGMOD (2017)
5. Arora, S., Lund, C., Motwani, R., Sudan, M., Szegedy, M.: Proof verification and the hardness of approximation problems. J. ACM **45**(3), 501–555 (1998)
6. Arora, S., Safra, S.: Probabilistic checking of proofs: a new characterization of NP. J. ACM **45**(1), 70–122 (1998)
7. Babai, L., Fortnow, L., Levin, L.A., Szegedy, M.: Checking computations in polylogarithmic time. In: STOC (1991)
8. Babai, L., Fortnow, L., Lund, C.: Non-deterministic exponential time has two-prover interactive protocols. Comput. Complex. **2**(4), 374 (1992)

9. Ben-Or, M., et al.: Everything provable is provable in zero-knowledge. In: Goldwasser, S. (ed.) CRYPTO 1988. LNCS, vol. 403, pp. 37–56. Springer, New York (1990). https://doi.org/10.1007/0-387-34799-2_4

10. Ben-Sasson, E., Bentov, I., Horesh, Y., Riabzev, M.: Scalable, transparent, and post-quantum secure computational integrity. ePrint Report 2018/046 (2018)

11. Ben-Sasson, E., Carmon, D., Ishai, Y., Kopparty, S., Saraf, S.: Proximity gaps for Reed-Solomon codes. Cryptology ePrint Archive, Report 2020/654 (2020)

12. Ben-Sasson, E., et al.: Zerocash: decentralized anonymous payments from Bitcoin. In: S&P (2014)

13. Ben-Sasson, E., Chiesa, A., Genkin, D., Tromer, E.: Fast reductions from RAMs to delegatable succinct constraint satisfaction problems: extended abstract. In: ITCS (2013)

14. Ben-Sasson, E., Chiesa, A., Genkin, D., Tromer, E.: On the concrete efficiency of probabilistically-checkable proofs. In: STOC, pp. 585–594 (2013)

15. Ben-Sasson, E., Chiesa, A., Genkin, D., Tromer, E., Virza, M.: SNARKs for C: verifying program executions succinctly and in zero knowledge. In: Canetti, R., Garay, J.A. (eds.) CRYPTO 2013. LNCS, vol. 8043, pp. 90–108. Springer, Heidelberg (2013). https://doi.org/10.1007/978-3-642-40084-1_6

16. Ben-Sasson, E., Chiesa, A., Riabzev, M., Spooner, N., Virza, M., Ward, N.P.: Aurora: transparent succinct arguments for R1CS. In: Ishai, Y., Rijmen, V. (eds.) EUROCRYPT 2019. LNCS, vol. 11476, pp. 103–128. Springer, Cham (2019). https://doi.org/10.1007/978-3-030-17653-2_4

17. Ben-Sasson, E., Chiesa, A., Spooner, N.: Interactive oracle proofs. In: Hirt, M., Smith, A. (eds.) TCC 2016. LNCS, vol. 9986, pp. 31–60. Springer, Heidelberg (2016). https://doi.org/10.1007/978-3-662-53644-5_2

18. Ben-Sasson, E., Chiesa, A., Tromer, E., Virza, M.: Succinct non-interactive zero knowledge for a von Neumann architecture. In: USENIX Security (2014)

19. Ben-Sasson, E., Goldreich, O., Harsha, P., Sudan, M., Vadhan, S.: Short PCPs verifiable in polylogarithmic time. In: Computational Complexity (2005)

20. Ben-Sasson, E., Sudan, M.: Simple PCPs with poly-log rate and query complexity. In: STOC, pp. 266–275 (2005)

21. Ben-Sasson, E., Sudan, M.: Short PCPs with polylog query complexity. SIAM J. Comput. **38**(2), 551–607 (2008)

22. Bitansky, N., Canetti, R., Chiesa, A., Tromer, E.: From extractable collision resistance to succinct non-interactive arguments of knowledge, and back again. In: ITCS (2012)

23. Bitansky, N., Chiesa, A., Ishai, Y., Paneth, O., Ostrovsky, R.: Succinct non-interactive arguments via linear interactive proofs. In: Sahai, A. (ed.) TCC 2013. LNCS, vol. 7785, pp. 315–333. Springer, Heidelberg (2013). https://doi.org/10.1007/978-3-642-36594-2_18

24. Blum, M., Evans, W., Gemmell, P., Kannan, S., Naor, M.: Checking the correctness of memories. In: FOCS (1991)

25. Blumberg, A.J., Thaler, J., Vu, V., Walfish, M.: Verifiable computation using multiple provers. ePrint Report 2014/846 (2014)

26. Boneh, D., Boyle, E., Corrigan-Gibbs, H., Gilboa, N., Ishai, Y.: Zero-knowledge proofs on secret-shared data via fully linear PCPs. ePrint Report 2019/188 (2019)

27. Bootle, J., Cerulli, A., Chaidos, P., Groth, J., Petit, C.: Efficient zero-knowledge arguments for arithmetic circuits in the discrete log setting. In: Fischlin, M., Coron, J.-S. (eds.) EUROCRYPT 2016. LNCS, vol. 9666, pp. 327–357. Springer, Heidelberg (2016). https://doi.org/10.1007/978-3-662-49896-5_12

28. Bowe, S.: A BLS12-381 implementation. https://github.com/zkcrypto/bls12_381
29. Bowe, S., Chiesa, A., Green, M., Miers, I., Mishra, P., Wu, H.: ZEXE: enabling decentralized private computation. ePrint Report 2018/962 (2018)
30. Brassard, G., Chaum, D., Crépeau, C.: Minimum disclosure proofs of knowledge. J. Comput. Syst. Sci. **37**(2), 156–189 (1988)
31. Braun, B., Feldman, A.J., Ren, Z., Setty, S., Blumberg, A.J., Walfish, M.: Verifying computations with state. In: SOSP (2013)
32. Bunz, B., Fisch, B., Szepieniec, A.: Transparent SNARKs from DARK compilers. ePrint Report 2019/1229 (2019)
33. Bünz, B., Bootle, J., Boneh, D., Poelstra, A., Wuille, P., Maxwell, G.: Bulletproofs: short proofs for confidential transactions and more. In: S&P (2018)
34. Campanelli, M., Fiore, D., Querol, A.: LegoSNARK: modular design and composition of succinct zero-knowledge proofs. ePrint Report 2019/142 (2019)
35. Chiesa, A., Forbes, M.A., Spooner, N.: A zero knowledge sumcheck and its applications. CoRR, abs/1704.02086 (2017)
36. Chiesa, A., Ojha, D., Spooner, N.: Fractal: post-quantum and transparent recursive proofs from holography. ePrint Report 2019/1076 (2019)
37. Clarke, D., Devadas, S., van Dijk, M., Gassend, B., Suh, G.E.: Incremental multiset hash functions and their application to memory integrity checking. In: Laih, C.-S. (ed.) ASIACRYPT 2003. LNCS, vol. 2894, pp. 188–207. Springer, Heidelberg (2003). https://doi.org/10.1007/978-3-540-40061-5_12
38. Cormode, G., Mitzenmacher, M., Thaler, J.: Practical verified computation with streaming interactive proofs. In: ITCS (2012)
39. Costello, C., et al.: Geppetto: versatile verifiable computation. In: S&P, May 2015
40. Cramer, R., Damgård, I.: Zero-knowledge proofs for finite field arithmetic, or: can zero-knowledge be for free? In: Krawczyk, H. (ed.) CRYPTO 1998. LNCS, vol. 1462, pp. 424–441. Springer, Heidelberg (1998). https://doi.org/10.1007/BFb0055745
41. Delignat-Lavaud, A., Fournet, C., Kohlweiss, M., Parno, B.: Cinderella: turning shabby X.509 certificates into elegant anonymous credentials with the magic of verifiable computation. In: S&P (2016)
42. Dinur, I.: The PCP theorem by gap amplification. J. ACM **54**(3) (2007)
43. Dwork, C., Naor, M., Rothblum, G.N., Vaikuntanathan, V.: How efficient can memory checking be? In: Reingold, O. (ed.) TCC 2009. LNCS, vol. 5444, pp. 503–520. Springer, Heidelberg (2009). https://doi.org/10.1007/978-3-642-00457-5_30
44. Feige, U., Goldwasser, S., Lovász, L., Safra, S., Szegedy, M.: Interactive proofs and the hardness of approximating cliques. J. ACM **43**(2), 268–292 (1996)
45. Fiat, A., Shamir, A.: How to prove yourself: practical solutions to identification and signature problems. In: Odlyzko, A.M. (ed.) CRYPTO 1986. LNCS, vol. 263, pp. 186–194. Springer, Heidelberg (1987). https://doi.org/10.1007/3-540-47721-7_12
46. Fiore, D., Fournet, C., Ghosh, E., Kohlweiss, M., Ohrimenko, O., Parno, B.: Hash first, argue later: adaptive verifiable computations on outsourced data. In: CCS (2016)
47. Gennaro, R., Gentry, C., Parno, B., Raykova, M.: Quadratic span programs and succinct NIZKs without PCPs. In: Johansson, T., Nguyen, P.Q. (eds.) EUROCRYPT 2013. LNCS, vol. 7881, pp. 626–645. Springer, Heidelberg (2013). https://doi.org/10.1007/978-3-642-38348-9_37
48. Gentry, C., Wichs, D.: Separating succinct non-interactive arguments from all falsifiable assumptions. In: STOC, pp. 99–108 (2011)
49. Goldwasser, S., Kalai, Y.T., Rothblum, G.N.: Delegating computation: interactive proofs for muggles. In: STOC (2008)

50. Groth, J.: Short pairing-based non-interactive zero-knowledge arguments. In: Abe, M. (ed.) ASIACRYPT 2010. LNCS, vol. 6477, pp. 321–340. Springer, Heidelberg (2010). https://doi.org/10.1007/978-3-642-17373-8_19

51. Groth, J.: On the size of pairing-based non-interactive arguments. In: Fischlin, M., Coron, J.-S. (eds.) EUROCRYPT 2016. LNCS, vol. 9666, pp. 305–326. Springer, Heidelberg (2016). https://doi.org/10.1007/978-3-662-49896-5_11

52. Groth, J., Kohlweiss, M., Maller, M., Meiklejohn, S., Miers, I.: Updatable and universal common reference strings with applications to zk-SNARKs. In: Shacham, H., Boldyreva, A. (eds.) CRYPTO 2018. LNCS, vol. 10993, pp. 698–728. Springer, Cham (2018). https://doi.org/10.1007/978-3-319-96878-0_24

53. Hamburg, M.: Decaf: eliminating cofactors through point compression. In: Gennaro, R., Robshaw, M. (eds.) CRYPTO 2015. LNCS, vol. 9215, pp. 705–723. Springer, Heidelberg (2015). https://doi.org/10.1007/978-3-662-47989-6_34

54. Håstad, J.: Some optimal inapproximability results. In: STOC, pp. 1–10 (1997)

55. Ishai, Y., Kushilevitz, E., Ostrovsky, R.: Efficient arguments without short PCPs. In: Computational Complexity (2007)

56. Ishai, Y., Kushilevitz, E., Ostrovsky, R., Sahai, A.: Zero-knowledge from secure multiparty computation. In: STOC, pp. 21–30 (2007)

57. Kate, A., Zaverucha, G.M., Goldberg, I.: Constant-size commitments to polynomials and their applications. In: Abe, M. (ed.) ASIACRYPT 2010. LNCS, vol. 6477, pp. 177–194. Springer, Heidelberg (2010). https://doi.org/10.1007/978-3-642-17373-8_11

58. Kilian, J.: A note on efficient zero-knowledge proofs and arguments (extended abstract). In: STOC (1992)

59. Kosba, A., Miller, A., Shi, E., Wen, Z., Papamanthou, C.: Hawk: the blockchain model of cryptography and privacy-preserving smart contracts. In: S&P (2016)

60. Kosba, A., Papamanthou, C., Shi, E.: xJsnark: a framework for efficient verifiable computation. In: S&P (2018)

61. Lee, J., Nikitin, K., Setty, S.: Replicated state machines without replicated execution. In: S&P (2020)

62. libfennel. Hyrax reference implementation. https://github.com/hyraxZK/fennel

63. libiop. A C++ library for IOP-based zkSNARK. https://github.com/scipr-lab/libiop

64. libsnark. A C++ library for zkSNARK proofs. https://github.com/scipr-lab/libsnark

65. Lipmaa, H.: Progression-free sets and sublinear pairing-based non-interactive zero-knowledge arguments. In: Cramer, R. (ed.) TCC 2012. LNCS, vol. 7194, pp. 169–189. Springer, Heidelberg (2012). https://doi.org/10.1007/978-3-642-28914-9_10

66. Lund, C., Fortnow, L., Karloff, H., Nisan, N.: Algebraic methods for interactive proof systems. In: FOCS, October 1990

67. Merkle, R.C.: A digital signature based on a conventional encryption function. In: Pomerance, C. (ed.) CRYPTO 1987. LNCS, vol. 293, pp. 369–378. Springer, Heidelberg (1988). https://doi.org/10.1007/3-540-48184-2_32

68. Micali, S.: CS proofs. In: FOCS (1994)

69. Papamanthou, C., Shi, E., Tamassia, R.: Signatures of correct computation. In: Sahai, A. (ed.) TCC 2013. LNCS, vol. 7785, pp. 222–242. Springer, Heidelberg (2013). https://doi.org/10.1007/978-3-642-36594-2_13

70. Parno, B., Gentry, C., Howell, J., Raykova, M.: Pinocchio: nearly practical verifiable computation. In: S&P, May 2013

71. Reingold, O., Rothblum, G.N., Rothblum, R.D.: Constant-round interactive proofs for delegating computation. In: STOC, pp. 49–62 (2016)

72. Setty, S.: Spartan: efficient and general-purpose zkSNARKs without trusted setup. ePrint Report 2019/550 (2019)
73. Setty, S., Angel, S., Gupta, T., Lee, J.: Proving the correct execution of concurrent services in zero-knowledge. In: OSDI, October 2018
74. Setty, S., Blumberg, A.J., Walfish, M.: Toward practical and unconditional verification of remote computations. In: HotOS, May 2011
75. Setty, S., Braun, B., Vu, V., Blumberg, A.J., Parno, B., Walfish, M.: Resolving the conflict between generality and plausibility in verified computation. In: EuroSys, April 2013
76. Setty, S., McPherson, R., Blumberg, A.J., Walfish, M.: Making argument systems for outsourced computation practical (sometimes). In: NDSS, February 2012
77. Setty, S., Vu, V., Panpalia, N., Braun, B., Blumberg, A.J., Walfish, M.: Taking proof-based verified computation a few steps closer to practicality. In: USENIX Security, August 2012
78. Thaler, J.: Time-optimal interactive proofs for circuit evaluation. In: Canetti, R., Garay, J.A. (eds.) CRYPTO 2013. LNCS, vol. 8043, pp. 71–89. Springer, Heidelberg (2013). https://doi.org/10.1007/978-3-642-40084-1_5
79. Thaler, J., Roberts, M., Mitzenmacher, M., Pfister, H.: Verifiable computation with massively parallel interactive proofs. In: HotCloud (2012)
80. Vu, V., Setty, S., Blumberg, A.J., Walfish, M.: A hybrid architecture for verifiable computation. In: S&P (2013)
81. Wahby, R.S., Howald, M., Garg, S., Shelat, A., Walfish, M.: Verifiable ASICs. In: S&P (2016)
82. Wahby, R.S., et al.: Full accounting for verifiable outsourcing. In: CCS (2017)
83. Wahby, R.S., Setty, S., Ren, Z., Blumberg, A.J., Walfish, M.: Efficient RAM and control flow in verifiable outsourced computation. In: NDSS (2015)
84. Wahby, R.S., Tzialla, I., Shelat, A., Thaler, J., Walfish, M.: Doubly-efficient zkSNARKs without trusted setup. In: S&P (2018)
85. Xie, T., Zhang, J., Zhang, Y., Papamanthou, C., Song, D.: Libra: succinct zero-knowledge proofs with optimal prover computation. ePrint Report 2019/317 (2019)
86. Zhang, J., Xie, T., Zhang, Y., Song, D.: Transparent polynomial delegation and its applications to zero knowledge proof. In: S&P (2020)
87. Zhang, Y., Genkin, D., Katz, J., Papadopoulos, D., Papamanthou, C.: vSQL: verifying arbitrary SQL queries over dynamic outsourced databases. In: S&P (2017)
88. Zhang, Y., Genkin, D., Katz, J., Papadopoulos, D., Papamanthou, C.: A zero-knowledge version of vSQL. ePrint Report 2017/1146 (2017)
89. Zhang, Y., Genkin, D., Katz, J., Papadopoulos, D., Papamanthou, C.: vRAM: faster verifiable RAM with program-independent preprocessing. In: S&P (2018)

NIZK from LPN and Trapdoor Hash via Correlation Intractability for Approximable Relations

Zvika Brakerski$^{(\boxtimes)}$, Venkata Koppula, and Tamer Mour

Weizmann Institute of Science, Rehovot, Israel
{zvika.brakerski,venkata.koppula,tamer.mour}@weizmann.ac.il

Abstract. We present new non-interactive zero-knowledge argument systems (NIZK), based on standard assumptions that were previously not known to imply it. In particular, we rely on the hardness of both the learning parity with noise (LPN) assumption, and the existence of *trapdoor hash functions* (TDH, defined by Döttling et al., Crypto 2019). Such TDH can be based on a number of standard assumptions, including DDH, QR, DCR, and LWE.

We revisit the correlation intractability (CI) framework for converting Σ-protocols into NIZK, and present a different strategy for instantiating it by putting together two new components. First, while prior works considered the search-complexity of the relations for which CI is sought, we consider their *probabilistic representation*. Namely, a distribution over lower-complexity functions that bitwise-computes the target function with all but small (constant) probability. The second component is a new perspective for quantifying the class of relations for which CI is achieved. We show that it is instructive to consider *CI for approximable relations* (CI-Apx) which is quantified by a class of relations, but requires CI to hold against *any approximation* of any relation in this class.

We show that CI-Apx for just constant-degree polynomials suffices for NIZK, if the underlying Σ-protocol is implemented using a suitable commitment scheme. We show that such a commitment scheme can be constructed based on low noise LPN. We then show how to construct CI-Apx for constant-degree polynomials from any suitable TDH (with an enhanced correctness property that is satisfied by all existing TDH constructions).

1 Introduction

Zero-Knowledge (ZK) [17] is one of the most celebrated and widely used notions in modern cryptography. A ZK proof is a protocol in which a prover conveys the validity of a statement to a verifier in a way that reveals no additional information. In a non-interactive ZK proof system (NIZK), we wish to construct a singe-message ZK proof system. Common setup is necessary for NIZK, and by default

---

A full version can be found at https://eprint.iacr.org/2020/258.

© International Association for Cryptologic Research 2020
D. Micciancio and T. Ristenpart (Eds.): CRYPTO 2020, LNCS 12172, pp. 738–767, 2020.
https://doi.org/10.1007/978-3-030-56877-1_26

(and always in this work) NIZK is considered in the common random/reference string (CRS) model. In the CRS model, a trusted string is sampled from a pre-scribed distribution (preferably uniform) and made available to both the prover and the verifier. Ideally, we would have liked to construct a NIZK proof system for all NP languages (or equivalently for some NP-complete language).[1] NIZK for NP turns out to be extremely useful for many applications such as CCA secu-rity [13,23], signatures [3,5], and numerous other applications, including recent applications in the regime of cryptocurrencies [4]. From this point and on, we use the term NIZK to refer to "NIZK for NP" unless otherwise stated.

While ZK proofs for all NP languages are known under the minimal assump-tion that one-way functions exist, this is far from being the case for NIZK. We focus our attention on constructions in the standard model and under standard cryptographic assumptions. For many years, NIZK under standard assumptions were only known based on Factoring [7] (or doubly enhanced trapdoor functions, which are only known to exist based on Factoring [15]) or assumptions on groups with bilinear maps [18].

More recently, constructions based on indistinguishability obfuscation were presented as well [25]. Most recently, a new line of works, starting with [10,19,21], focused on obtaining NIZK based on the notion of *correlation intractability* (CI) [11]. In the CI framework, it was shown that in order to construct NIZK, it suffices to construct a family of hash functions $\mathcal{H}$ with the following property. For every efficient f, given a hash function $H \leftarrow \mathcal{H}$ from the family, it is compu-tationally hard to find x s.t. $f(x) = H(x)$. If such correlation intractable hash (CIH) is constructed, then it can be used to securely instantiate the Fiat-Shamir paradigm [16] and derive NIZK from so-called Σ-protocols. This line of works culminated in two remarkable achievements. Canetti et al. [9] constructed NIZK based on the existence of circular secure fully homomorphic encryption. Peikert and Shiehian [24] constructed NIZK based on the hardness of the learning with errors (LWE) problem.[2]

These recent results opened a new avenue in the study of NIZK and raised hope that construction under additional assumptions can be presented. How-ever, it appears that there is an inherent barrier to expanding known techniques beyond LWE-related assumptions. The current approaches for constructing CI hash from standard assumptions use the notion of *somewhere statistical CI*, in which, for any f, it is possible to sample from a distribution $\mathcal{H}_f$ which is indis-tinguishable from the real $\mathcal{H}$, and for which the CI game is *statistically* hard to win. Roughly speaking, this is achieved, in known constructions [9,24] by making $\mathcal{H}_f$ perform some homomorphic evaluation of f on the input x. Thus, it appears that homomorphic evaluation of complex functions f is essential to apply these tools.

---

[1] In this work we only consider ZK/NIZK proof systems where the honest prover is computationally efficient given a witness to the NP language.

[2] To be more accurate, [24] showed how to construct a CI hash function for size s circuits, for any parameter s. This is slightly weaker than a single $\mathcal{H}$ for all functions, but it suffices in order to instantiate the framework.

The starting point of our work is the observation that, under the learning parity with noise (LPN) assumption, we can reduce the complexity of functions for which achieving CIH implies NIZK down to functions with *probabilistic constant-degree representation*. That is, ones that can be approximated by a distribution on constant-degree polynomials.

We substantiate the usefulness of this approach by identifying a general connection between correlation intractability for a function class $\mathcal{F}$, which has probabilistic representation by a class $\mathcal{C}$ (potentially of lower complexity), and CI for relations that are *approximable* by $\mathcal{C}$.

Correlation Intractability for relations approximable by $\mathcal{C}$ (denoted "CI-Apx for $\mathcal{C}$") is a stronger notion than the one studied in prior works, namely CI for relations searchable by $\mathcal{C}$. In CI-Apx, we require that for all $C \in \mathcal{C}$ it is hard not only to find x such that $C(x) = \mathcal{H}(x)$ but, rather, that it is hard to find an x such that $\mathcal{H}(x)$ and $C(x)$ are *close* in Hamming distance.[3] When the probabilistic representation $\mathcal{C}$ of our target class $\mathcal{F}$ is sufficiently simple, e.g. constant-degree polynomials, then the reduction from CI for $\mathcal{F}$ to CI-Apx for $\mathcal{C}$ opens the possibility for new constructions of CIH from standard assumptions. Specifically from assumptions that are not known to apply fully-homomorphic encryption or similarly strong primitives.

In particular, we show that CI-Apx for a function class $\mathcal{C}$ can be constructed based on a *rate-1 trapdoor hash* scheme for $\mathcal{C}$. Trapdoor hash (TDH) is a fairly new cryptographic primitive which was recently introduced by Döttling et al. [14]. They also constructed rate-1 TDH for constant-degree polynomials from a number of standard assumptions, including DDH, QR, and DCR (which are not known to imply fully-homomorphic encryption) and also LWE. Consequently, we obtain CI-Apx for constant-degree polynomials from such assumptions and, therefore, CI for any class of functions with probabilistic constant-degree representation. We note that we require a slightly stronger correctness property from TDH, compared to the definition provided in [14], but it is satisfied by all known constructions.

On an interesting remark, we point out that the construction by Piekert and Shiehian [24] of CI for bounded-size circuits can be shown to satisfy the stronger notion of CI-Apx for the corresponding class of relations.

Consequences. We get non-interactive (computational) zero knowledge argument systems for NP, in the common random string model, based on the existence of any rate-1 trapdoor hash for constant degree and further assuming low-noise LPN. We stress that we can generically abstract the LPN requirement as a requirement for an extractable commitment scheme with very low-complexity approximate-extraction. By instantiating our construction using the rate-1 TDH from [14], we get, in particular, the first NIZK from low-noise LPN and DDH.

---

[3] Note that even non-searchable relations can potentially be approximable by a class of functions. Thus via the notion CI-Apx we can extend our capabilities for constructing CIH even beyond searchable relations. This is not of direct use in this work, but may be useful for future works.

Open Questions. The main open question we leave unanswered is whether it is possible to minimize the required assumptions for constructing NIZK using CI-Apx. One may approach this problem either by constructing CI-Apx for constant degree functions based on the LPN assumption, or by further extending the CI-Apx framework to allow a more general utilization for NIZKs, possibly depending on assumptions already implying CI-Apx.

Another open question is whether we can obtain stronger notions of NIZKs, in particular NIZK proofs or NISZK, from a similar set of standard assumptions. To achieve statistical ZK using our approach simply requires the underlying commitment (with low-degree extraction) to be lossy. Getting statistically sound proof systems via CI-Apx, however, seems to be inherently more difficult, as it requires the resulting CI to be "somewhere statistical" for the approximated class of functions.

Lastly, the new constructions of ZAPs [2,20,22] rely on the CI framework but, unfortunately, we do not know how to extend them since the notion of commitment that is required for the ZAPs is not known to be constructible from LPN (or other assumptions with very low complexity extraction). At a high level, these works requires the public parameters of the commitment scheme to be statistically close to uniform (and this seems hard to achieve with our LPN noise regime).

1.1 Overview of Our Techniques and Results

Our construction of NIZK instantiates the general Correlation Intractability (CI) framework. The approach followed in prior work for constructing CI hash, for relations searchable by a function class $\mathcal{F}$, considers the straight-forward representation of $\mathcal{F}$ as a class of circuits. In this work, we take a different angle, and tackle the CI problem for relations searchable by $\mathcal{F}$ through its probabilistic representation by a much simpler class $\mathcal{C}$. Such an approach allows us to obtain CI hash for classes of relations that are sufficiently rich to imply NIZK, while avoiding the use of FHE or similar heavy machinery.

NIZK from Correlation Intractability. Our starting point for constructing NIZK is similar to the approach in previous works of applying Fiat-Shamir on ZK protocols, in a provably-sound manner, using CI hash. We start with a public-coin trapdoor Σ-protocol that follows the natural "commit-then-open" paradigm, where the prover first sends a set of commitments, then, upon receiving the verifier's challenge bit $e \in \{0,1\}$, he replies by opening some of the commitments. Lastly, the verifier checks that the openings are valid, and then performs an additional check over the opened values. An example of such a protocol is the ZK protocol for Hamiltonicity from [6,15].

An important property of commit-then-open trapdoor-Σ protocols is the *unique bad challenge property*: for any instance x not in the language, if (a, e, z) is an accepting transcript, then e is uniquely determined by the first message a. This connection is characterized by a function denoted by $\mathsf{BadChallenge} : a \mapsto e$.

In the CI paradigm, we apply Fiat-Shamir over sufficiently many repetitions of such a protocol, using a CI hash for the relation searchable by BadChallenge, which is defined as follows. A vector of first messages $\mathbf{a}$ is in a relation with a vector of verifier's challenges $\mathbf{e}$ if on each coordinate, the corresponding $\mathbf{e}$ entry is the unique bad challenge of that coordinate in $\mathbf{a}$. If a cheating prover P^* succeeds in breaking the soundness of the protocol, then he must have found a BadChallenge correlation, i.e. vectors $(\mathbf{a}, \mathbf{e})$ in the relation, implying an attack against the CI of the underlying hash family.

Prior work considered protocols where the bad challenge is efficiently computable and, consequently, focused on constructing CI for all efficiently searchable relations. These contain, in particular, the relations efficiently searchable by BadChallenge. We deviate from this approach. We observe that BadChallenge can be approximated by a distribution over constant-degree polynomials when instantiating this template with an appropriate commitment scheme. This reduces our CI task to achieving CIH for functions with constant-degree *probabilistic representation*. Such CIH is implied by a special notion of correlation intractability against constant-degree functions – CI for *approximable relations*, or CI-Apx for short. Details follow.

Probabilistic Representation, Approximable Relations and CI. Assume that a class of functions $\mathcal{F} : \{0,1\}^n \to \{0,1\}^m$ has a *probabilistic representation* by some simpler class of functions $\mathcal{C}$. Namely, for any $f \in \mathcal{F}$, there exists a distribution $\mathfrak{C}_f$ over $\mathcal{C}$ such that $\Pr[\Delta(C(x), f(x)) \le \epsilon m] > 1 - \mathsf{negl}(\lambda)$ for any x and a random $C \xleftarrow{\$} \mathfrak{C}_f$.

Let $\mathcal{H} : \{0,1\}^n \to \{0,1\}^m$ be a hash family. An adversary $\mathcal{A}$ that is able to find a correlation $\mathcal{H}(x) = f(x)$ for some f is able to find, with overwhelming probability over a random $C \leftarrow \mathfrak{C}_f$, an "approximate correlation" $\Delta(\mathcal{H}(x), C(x)) \le \epsilon m$ for some small ϵ. It follows therefore that by considering probabilistic representation, we can identify a connection between correlation intractability against f and correlation intractability against any relation that is *approximable* (or approximately searchable) by some function $C \in \mathfrak{C}_f$. We denote this class of relations

$$R_C^\epsilon = \{(x, y) \in \{0,1\}^n \times \{0,1\}^m \mid \Delta(y, C(x)) \le \epsilon m\} \ .$$

More formally, an adversary that breaks the CI of $\mathcal{H}$ for a relation searchable by f is able to break the CI of the same hash $\mathcal{H}$ for the relation R_C^ϵ defined by some $C \in \mathfrak{C}_f$. Hence, CI-Apx for $\mathcal{C}$ (i.e. CI for all relations R_C^ϵ) implies CI for $\mathcal{F}$.

Theorem 1.1 (CI through Probabilistic Representation, Informal). *Let $\mathcal{F}$ be a class of functions with probabilistic representation by $\mathcal{C}$. Then, any CI-Apx hash family for $\mathcal{C}$ is a CI hash for $\mathcal{F}$.*

Probabilistic Constant-Degree Representation of the Bad Challenge Function. Recall that in a commit-then-open trapdoor Σ-protocol, the verification is either performed over a subset of commitment openings corresponding to $e = 0$ or a subset of openings corresponding to $e = 1$. From the unique bad challenge property, it is impossible that the verification on both subsets succeed if $x \notin L$. Thus, the BadChallenge function can be computed in two steps: an extraction step, to extract the messages underlying the commitments of one of the aforementioned subsets, say the one corresponding to $e = 1$, followed by an efficient verification (for $e = 1$) over the extracted values. If the verification accepts, then the bad challenge must be $e = 1$ and, otherwise, the bad challenge is either $e = 0$ or does not exist (in which case a is not in the relation and the output may be arbitrary). Hence, we can split the task of probabilistically representing BadChallenge to two sub-tasks: extraction and post-extraction verification.

Post-extraction Verification as a 3-CNF. The post-extraction verification is an arbitrary polynomial computation and, generally, may not have probabilistic constant-degree representation as is. The first step towards a constant-degree approximation of BadChallenge is observing that, by relying on the Cook-Levin approach for expressing the verification procedure as a 3-CNF satisfiability problem, we may reduce the complexity of the verification to 3-CNF as follows. Let Φ_e denote the 3-CNF formula that captures the verification corresponding to challenge e; that is, Φ_e has a satisfying witness w_e if and only if the verifier accepts the prover's second message for challenge bit e. The prover can compute w_e efficiently (using the Cook-Levin approach, this witness simply consists of all intermediate steps of the verification). Therefore, we let the prover also include commitments to w_0, w_1 in his first message. When the verifier sends challenge e, the prover also provides openings for w_e, and the verifier checks decommitments then evaluates Φ_e. By transforming the protocol as described, the bad challenge computation now consists, as before, of extraction, then an evaluation of the 3-CNF formula Φ_1, rather than an arbitrary poly-time verification.

We can then use standard well-known randomization techniques to probabilistically approximate any 3-CNF formula by constant-degree polynomials (see Lemma 3.13).

Extraction via a Randomized Linear Function. For the extraction step, we observe that by adapting the (low-noise) LPN-based PKE scheme of Damgård and Park [12] (which is closely related to the PKE scheme by Alekhnovich [1]) we can construct an extractable commitment scheme whose extraction algorithm can be probabilistically represented by a linear function. The secret extraction key is a matrix $\mathbf{S}$, and the public key consists of a matrix $\mathbf{A}$ together with $\mathbf{B} = \mathbf{A} \cdot \mathbf{S} + \mathbf{E}$. Here, $\mathbf{E}$ is chosen from a noise distribution with suitably low noise rate. To compute a commitment for bit x, the Commit algorithm chooses a low Hamming weight vector $\mathbf{r}$, and outputs $\mathbf{u} = \mathbf{r}\mathbf{A}$ and $\mathbf{c} = \mathbf{r}\mathbf{B} + x^\ell$. The opening for the commitment is the randomness $\mathbf{r}$, and the verification algorithm simply checks that $\mathbf{r}$ has low Hamming weight, and that the Commit algorithm, using $\mathbf{r}$, outputs the correct commitment. Finally, note that using $\mathbf{S}$, one can extract the message underlying a commitment $(\mathbf{u}, \mathbf{c})$: simply compute $\mathbf{u}\mathbf{S} + \mathbf{c} = x^{\ell} + \mathbf{r}\mathbf{E}$. By carefully setting the LPN-parameters (the noise distribution is Bernoulli with parameter $1/n^c$ for some fixed constant $c \in (1/2, 1)$), we ensure that if $(\mathbf{u}, \mathbf{c})$ is a valid commitment (i.e. can be opened with some x and $\mathbf{r}$), then $\mathbf{r}\mathbf{E}$ has sufficiently low Hamming weight. Therefore, by sampling a random column $\mathbf{s}$ in $\mathbf{S}$, we get that $\mathbf{u}\mathbf{s} + \mathbf{c} = x$ with sufficiently high probability.

The Case of Invalid Commitments. We have shown that, using a distribution over linear functions, we can approximate extraction of valid commitments. A cheating prover, however, may chose to send invalid commitments. We claim that, in such a case, we may allow the probabilistic representation to behave arbitrarily.

Fix some $x \notin L$ and a first message a. If there exist no bad challenge for a or if the (unique) bad challenge is $e = 1$, then all commitments in a corresponding to inputs of Φ_1 must be valid (since the prover is able to open them in a way that is accepted by the verifier). Thus, we potentially have a problem only in the case where $e = 0$ is the bad challenge, i.e. the commitments of input bits to Φ_0 are valid and $\Phi_0(w_0) = 1$ on their respective openings w_0. Our concern is that since our bad challenge function only looks at the Φ_1 locations, which may be arbitrary invalid commitments, we have no guarantee on the extraction, and therefore our bad challenge function will output $e = 1$ even though the unique bad challenge is $e = 0$. We show that this is not possible.

Let w_1' be the arbitrary value computed by the approximate extraction algorithm on the possibly invalid commitments in the locations of the Φ_1 inputs. We will see that it still must be the case that $\Phi_1(w_1') = 0$ and therefore the bad challenge function outputs $e = 0$ as required. The reason is that otherwise we can put together *valid commitments of both* w_0 and w_1', so as to create a first message a' which refutes the soundness of the original Σ-protocol, since it can be successfully opened both for $e = 0$ and for $e = 1$.

Constructing CI for Approximable Relations. The main idea behind recent constructions of CI for relations searchable by some function class $\mathcal{C}$ [9,24] is to construct a *somewhere statistical* CI hash family $\mathcal{H}$. That is, one where there exists, for any $C \in \mathcal{C}$, a distribution of hash functions $\mathcal{H}_C$ that are indistinguishable from the real $\mathcal{H}$, and are statistically CI for that specific C. Namely, for any C, there exists no x such that $\mathcal{H}_C(x) = C(x)$ or, equivalently, the image of the "correlation function" $x \mapsto \mathcal{H}_C(x) + C(x) \mod 2$ does not contain 0.

Our Approach for CI-Apx: Sparse Correlations. Our first observation is that if we are able to construct a hash family $\mathcal{H}$ where, for every $C \in \mathcal{C}$, the function $x \mapsto \mathcal{H}_C(x) + C(x)$ actually has exponentially-sparse image (as a fraction of the entire space), then we obtain (somewhere statistical) CI-Apx for $\mathcal{C}$.

To see this, consider the hash function $\hat{\mathcal{H}}(x) = \mathcal{H}(x) + r \mod 2$, where r is a uniformly random string sampled together with the hash key. The task of breaking CI of $\hat{\mathcal{H}}(x)$ for some $C \in \mathcal{C}$ reduces to the task of finding x s.t. $\mathcal{H}_C(x) + C(x) = r \mod 2$. Clearly, with overwhelming probability, such x does not exist when the image of $\mathcal{H}_C(x) + C(x)$ is sufficiently small. We can push our statistical argument even further to claim CI-Apx for $\mathcal{C}$: an adversary that breaks the CI-Apx of $\hat{\mathcal{H}}$ for C finds x s.t. $\mathcal{H}_C(x)$ is in a small Hamming-ball around $C(x)$, i.e $\mathcal{H}_C(x) + C(x) + z = r \mod 2$, where z is a vector with relative Hamming weight at most ϵ. If $x \mapsto \mathcal{H}_C(x) + C(x)$ has exponentially-sparse image, then (for properly set parameters) so does $(x, z) \mapsto \mathcal{H}_C(x) + C(x) + z$, and therefore it is very unlikely that r is in the image.

Our goal is thus reduced to constructing a hash family $\mathcal{H}$, with indistinguishable distributions $\mathcal{H}_C$ as described above, such that, for every $C \in \mathcal{C}$, the function $x \mapsto \mathcal{H}_C(x) + C(x)$ has exponentially-sparse image.

Construction from Trapdoor Hash. Our construction of CI-Apx is based on trapdoor hash (TDH) [14]. At a high level, trapdoor hash allows us to "encrypt" any function $C : x \mapsto y$ to an encoding $\mathsf{E} : x \mapsto \mathsf{e}$ such that C is computationally hidden given a description of E and yet, for any input x, $y = C(x)$ is *almost* information-theoretically determined by $\mathsf{e} = \mathsf{E}(x)$. More accurately, the range of the correlation $\mathsf{e} + y \pmod{2}$ is *sparse*. The idea is then to use such an encoding as the hash function $\mathcal{H}_C$ described above.

More specifically, in a rate-1 TDH for a function class $\mathcal{C}$, we can generate, for any $C \in \mathcal{C}$, an encoding key ek_C that comes with a trapdoor td_C. Using the encoding key ek_C, one can compute a value $\mathsf{e} \leftarrow \mathsf{E}(\mathsf{ek}_C, x)$ which is essentially a rate-1 encoding of $C(x)$ (i.e. $|\mathsf{e}| = |C(x)|$). There exists also a decoding algorithm D which determines the value $C(x)$ as $C(x) = \mathsf{e} + \mathsf{D}(\mathsf{td}_C, \mathsf{h}, \mathsf{e})$, i.e. given e and "little additional information" about x in the form of a hash value $\mathsf{h} = \mathsf{H}(x)$ whose length is independent of the length of x. The security property we are interested in is *function privacy*: for any $C, C' \in \mathcal{C}$, the encoding keys ek_C and $\mathsf{ek}_{C'}$ are indistinguishable.

We use rate-1 TDH to construct, for every $C \in \mathcal{C}$, a hash family $\mathcal{H}_C$ such that: (i) the "correlation function" $x \mapsto \mathcal{H}_C(x) + C(x)$ has exponentially-sparse image for all $C \in \mathcal{C}$, and (ii) $\mathcal{H}_C$ and $\mathcal{H}_{C'}$ are indistinguishable, for all $C \neq C'$. This suffices to construct CI hash for any class of functions $\mathcal{F}$ with probabilistic representation in $\mathcal{C}$, as outlined above.

In the heart of our construction is the following simple observation: from the correctness of the TDH, it holds that $\mathsf{E}(\mathsf{ek}_C, x) + \mathsf{D}(\mathsf{td}_C, \mathsf{H}(x), \mathsf{e}) = C(x)$. Put differently, if we define $\mathcal{H}_C(x) = \mathsf{E}(\mathsf{ek}_C, x)$, then it holds that $\mathcal{H}_C(x) + C(x) = \mathsf{D}(\mathsf{td}_C, \mathsf{H}(x), \mathsf{e})$. This value depends on x only through its hash $\mathsf{H}(x)$. If the hash function H is sufficiently compressing, i.e. the length of the hash is much smaller than $|C(x)|$, then we obtain an exponentially-sparse image for $\mathcal{H}_C(x) + C(x)$ and, essentially, requirement (i) from above. Property (ii) follows from the function privacy of the underlying TDH. Overall, we get the following result.

Theorem 1.2 (CI-Apx from TDH, Informal). *Assume there exists a rate-1 TDH for $\mathcal{C}$. Then, there exists a CI hash for relations approximable by $\mathcal{C}$ (CI-Apx for $\mathcal{C}$).*

We note that the notion of TDH that we require deviates slightly from the one defined in [14]. On one hand, they require properties that we do not, such as input privacy, and they require that the decoding algorithm is efficiently computable, whereas for our purposes inefficient decoding would have sufficed. On the other hand, we require that the underlying TDH satisfies an enhanced notion of correctness, which is satisfied by all known constructions of TDH.

We obtain CI-Apx for constant degree from standard assumptions by instantiating Theorem 1.2 based on the work of Döttling et al. [14]. They construct rate-1 TDH scheme for linear functions from various standard assumptions, including QR, DCR and LWE. Such a scheme can be easily bootstrapped to support polynomials of constant degree $d > 1$. For the DDH assumption, they construct TDH for a stricter class of "index functions". We show in the full version [8] that their construction can be slightly adjusted, based on existing ideas, to capture also constant-degree functions and, hence, get an instantiation also from DDH.

1.2 Paper Organization

In Sect. 2, we provide some essential preliminaries. In Sect. 3, we present the framework which allows using our CI constructions to obtain NIZK, starting with the generic paradigm laid out by prior work. In Sect. 4, we show how to exploit a simple probabilistic representation of a function class for obtaining CI hash and, lastly, in Sect. 5, we show our construction of CI-Apx from TDH.

2   Preliminaries

Notation. For an integer $n \in \mathbb{N}$, $[n]$ denotes the set $\{1, \ldots, n\}$. We use λ for the security parameter and $\mathsf{negl}(\lambda)$ and $\mathsf{poly}(\lambda)$ for a negligible function and, resp., a polynomial in λ. We use $\overset{c}{\equiv}$ and $\overset{s}{\equiv}$ to denote computational and, resp., statistical indistinguishability between two distribution ensembles. For a distribution (or a randomized algorithm) D we use $x \overset{\$}{\leftarrow} D$ to say that x is sampled according to D and use $x \in D$ to say that x is in the support of D. For a set S we overload the notation to use $x \overset{\$}{\leftarrow} S$ to indicate that x is chosen uniformly at random from S.

2.1   Learning Parity with Noise

We hereby define the standard *Decisional Learning Parity with Noise (DLPN)* assumption, which we use in this paper.

Definition 2.1 (Decisional LPN Assumption). *Let $\tau : \mathbb{N} \to \mathbb{R}$ be such that $0 < \tau(\lambda) < 0.5$ for all λ, and let $n := n(\lambda)$ and $m := m(\lambda)$ be polynomials such that $m(\lambda) > n(\lambda)$ for all λ. The (n, m, τ)-Decisional LPN $((n, m, \tau)$-DLPN) assumption states that for any PPT adversary $\mathcal{A}$, there exists a negligible function $\mathsf{negl} : \mathbb{N} \to \mathbb{R}$, such that*

$$|\Pr[\mathcal{A}(\mathbf{A}, \mathbf{As} + \mathbf{e}) = 1] - \Pr[\mathcal{A}(\mathbf{A}, \mathbf{b}) = 1]| < \mathsf{negl}(\lambda)$$

where $\mathbf{A} \overset{\$}{\leftarrow} \mathbb{Z}_2^{m \times n}$, $\mathbf{s} \overset{\$}{\leftarrow} \mathbb{Z}_2^n$, $\mathbf{e} \overset{\$}{\leftarrow} \mathsf{Ber}_\tau^m$ and $\mathbf{b} \overset{\$}{\leftarrow} \mathbb{Z}_2^m$.

It is well-known that DLPN remains secure even given polynomially many samples of independent secrets and error vectors.

Proposition 2.2. *Let τ, n and m be as in Definition 2.1 above, and let $k :=$ $k(\lambda)$ be an aribitrary polynomial in the security parameter. Then, under the (n, m, τ)-DLPN assumption, for any PPT adversary $\mathcal{A}$, there exists a negligible function* negl *such that*

$$|\Pr[\mathcal{A}(\mathbf{A}, \mathbf{AS} + \mathbf{E}) = 1] - \Pr[\mathcal{A}(\mathbf{A}, \mathbf{B}) = 1]| < \mathsf{negl}(\lambda)$$

where $\mathbf{A} \xleftarrow{\$} \mathbb{Z}_2^{m \times n}$, $\mathbf{S} \xleftarrow{\$} \mathbb{Z}_2^{n \times k}$, $\mathbf{E} \xleftarrow{\$} \mathsf{Ber}_\tau^{m \times k}$ *and* $\mathbf{B} \xleftarrow{\$} \mathbb{Z}_2^{m \times k}$.

2.2 Trapdoor Hash

We hereby recall the definition of *trapdoor hash functions* (TDH) from Döttling et al. [14], with few minor modifications. First, we are fine with weakly correct trapdoor hash schemes (as defined in [14]), where we allow the error in correctness to be two-sided. This modification further allows us to simplify the syntax of decoding for rate-1 schemes. Second, to construct correlation intractable hash, we do not require the trapdoor hash scheme to be input-private (i.e. that the hash of an input x hides x) and, consequently, we assume w.l.o.g. that the hash and encoding functions, H and E, are deterministic (in the original definition, H and E share the same randomness - this was necessary for achieving both input privacy and correctness).

Definition 2.3 (Rate-1 Trapdoor Hash). *A* rate-1 trapdoor hash scheme (TDH) *for a function class* $\mathcal{C} = \{\mathcal{C}_n : \{0,1\}^n \to \{0,1\}\}$ *is a tuple of five PPT algorithms* $\mathsf{TDH} = (\mathsf{S}, \mathsf{G}, \mathsf{H}, \mathsf{E}, \mathsf{D})$ *with the following properties.*

- *Syntax:*
    - hk $\leftarrow$ S$(1^\lambda, 1^n)$. *The sampling algorithm takes as input a security parameter λ and an input length n, and outputs a hash key* hk.
    - (ek, td) $\leftarrow$ G(hk, C). *The generating algorithm takes as input a hash key* hk *a function $C \in \mathcal{C}_n$, and outputs a pair of an encoding key* ek *and a trapdoor* td.
    - h $\leftarrow$ H(hk, x). *The hashing algorithm takes as input a hash key* hk *and a string* x $\in \{0,1\}^n$, *and deterministically outputs a hash value* h $\in \{0,1\}^n$.
    - e $\leftarrow$ E(ek, x). *The encoding algorithm takes as input an encoding key* ek *and a string* x $\in \{0,1\}^n$, *and deterministically outputs an encoding* e $\in \{0,1\}$.
    - e$'$ $\leftarrow$ D(td, h). *The decoding algorithm takes as input a trapdoor* td, *a hash value* h $\in \{0,1\}^n$, *and outputs a 0-encoding* e$'$ $\in \{0,1\}$.
- *Correctness:* TDH *is (weakly)* $(1 - \tau)$-*correct (or has two-sided τ error probability), for $\tau := \tau(\lambda) < 1$, if there exists a negligible function* negl(λ) *such that the following holds for any $\lambda, n \in \mathbb{N}$, any* x $\in \{0,1\}^n$ *and any function $C \in \mathcal{C}_n$.*

$$\Pr[\mathsf{e} + \mathsf{e}' = C(x) \mod 2] \geq 1 - \tau - \mathsf{negl}(\lambda)$$

where $\mathsf{hk} \leftarrow \mathsf{S}(1^\lambda, 1^n)$, $(\mathsf{ek}, \mathsf{td}) \leftarrow \mathsf{G}(\mathsf{hk}, C)$, $\mathsf{h} \leftarrow \mathsf{H}(\mathsf{hk}, \mathsf{x})$, $\mathsf{e} \leftarrow \mathsf{E}(\mathsf{ek}, \mathsf{x})$, *and* $\mathsf{e}' \leftarrow \mathsf{D}(\mathsf{td}, \mathsf{h})$. *When* $\tau = 0$ *we say that the scheme is* fully correct.

- **Function Privacy:** TDH *is function-private if for any polynomial-length* $\{1^{n_\lambda}\}_{\lambda \in \mathbb{N}}$ *and any* $\{f_n\}_{n \in \mathbb{N}}$ *and* $\{f'_n\}_{n \in \mathbb{N}}$ *such that* $f_n, f'_n \in \mathcal{F}_n$ *for all* $n \in \mathbb{N}$, *it holds that*

$$\{(\mathsf{hk}_\lambda, \mathsf{ek}_\lambda)\}_{\lambda \in \mathbb{N}} \stackrel{c}{\equiv} \{(\mathsf{hk}_\lambda, \mathsf{ek}'_\lambda)\}_{\lambda \in \mathbb{N}}$$

  where $\mathsf{hk}_\lambda \stackrel{\$}{\leftarrow} \mathsf{S}(1^\lambda, 1^{n_\lambda})$, $(\mathsf{ek}_\lambda, \mathsf{td}_\lambda) \stackrel{\$}{\leftarrow} \mathsf{G}(\mathsf{hk}_\lambda, f_{n_\lambda})$ *and* $(\mathsf{ek}'_\lambda, \mathsf{td}'_\lambda) \stackrel{\$}{\leftarrow} \mathsf{G}(\mathsf{hk}_\lambda, f'_{n_\lambda})$.

- **Compactness:** *we require that the image length of the hash function,* η, *is independent of* n, *and is bounded by some polynomial in the security parameter* λ.

As pointed in [14] (Remark 4.2), we may consider a natural extension of trapdoor hash for a general class of functions $\mathcal{C} = \{\mathcal{C}_n : \{0,1\}^n \to \{0,1\}^m\}$ (where $m := m(\lambda) > 1$ is a fixed polynomial). Further, if any $C \in \mathcal{C}_n$ can be represented as m parallel computations in some class $\mathcal{C}'_n : \{0,1\}^n \to \{0,1\}$, then a trapdoor hash scheme for $\mathcal{C}' = \{\mathcal{C}'_n\}$ directly implies a trapdoor hash scheme for $\mathcal{C}$ with hash length independent in m.

2.3   Extractable Commitments

We hereby provide the definition of an extractable commitment scheme.[4]

Definition 2.4 (Extractable Commitment). *An* extractable (bit) commitment scheme *is a tuple of four PPT algorithms* $\mathsf{Com} = (\mathsf{Gen}, \mathsf{Commit}, \mathsf{Verify}, \mathsf{Extract})$ *with the following properties.*

- **Syntax:**
  - $(\mathsf{pk}, \mathsf{td}) \leftarrow \mathsf{Gen}(1^\lambda)$: *The key generation algorithm takes as input the security parameter* 1^λ *and outputs a pair of a public key* pk *and trapdoor* td.
  - $\mathsf{com} \leftarrow \mathsf{Commit}(\mathsf{pk}, \mathsf{x}; r)$: *The committing algorithm takes as input a public key* pk, *a bit* $\mathsf{x} \in \{0,1\}$ *and randomness* r, *and outputs a commitment* com.
  - $\{0,1\} \leftarrow \mathsf{Verify}(\mathsf{pk}, \mathsf{com}, \mathsf{x}; r)$: *The verification algorithm takes as input a public key* pk, *a commitment* com, *a bit* $\mathsf{x} \in \{0,1\}$ *and randomness* $r \in \{0,1\}^*$, *then either accepts or rejects.*
  - $\mathsf{x}' \leftarrow \mathsf{Extract}(\mathsf{td}, \mathsf{com})$: *The extraction algorithm takes as input a trapdoor* td *and a commitment* com *and outputs a bit* $\mathsf{x}' \in \{0,1\}$ *or* $\perp$.
- **Correctness:** Com *is correct if there exists a negligible function* negl, *such that for any* $\mathsf{x} \in \{0,1\}$,

$$\Pr[\mathsf{Verify}(\mathsf{pk}, \mathsf{Commit}(\mathsf{pk}, \mathsf{x}; r), \mathsf{x}; r)] > 1 - \mathsf{negl}(\lambda)$$

  where $(\mathsf{pk}, \cdot) \stackrel{\$}{\leftarrow} \mathsf{Gen}(1^\lambda)$ *and* $r \stackrel{\$}{\leftarrow} \{0,1\}^*$.

---

[4] The notion of extractable commitment is equivalent to standard public-key encryption. We use the commitment terminology since it is more natural for our setting.

- **Hiding:** Com *is* (computationally) hiding *if it holds that*

$$\{\mathsf{Commit}(\mathsf{pk}, 0; r)\}_\lambda \stackrel{c}{\equiv} \{\mathsf{Commit}(\mathsf{pk}, 1; r)\}_\lambda$$

  where $(\mathsf{pk}, \cdot) \stackrel{\$}{\leftarrow} \mathsf{Gen}(1^\lambda)$ *and* $r \stackrel{\$}{\leftarrow} \{0, 1\}^*$ *for all* $\lambda \in \mathbb{N}$.
- **Binding:** Com *is* (statistically) binding *if there exists a negligible function* negl *such that*

$$\Pr[\exists \mathsf{com}, r_0, r_1 \ \ s.t. \ \ \mathsf{Verify}(\mathsf{pk}, \mathsf{com}, 0, r_0) = \mathsf{Verify}(\mathsf{pk}, \mathsf{com}, 1, r_1) = 1] < \mathsf{negl}(\lambda)$$

  where $(\mathsf{pk}, \cdot) \stackrel{\$}{\leftarrow} \mathsf{Gen}(1^\lambda)$.
- **Extraction:** Com *has* correct extraction *if there exists a negligible function* negl, *such that for any* $\mathsf{x} \in \{0, 1\}$ *and* $r \in \{0, 1\}^*$, *if* $\mathsf{Verify}(\mathsf{pk}, \mathsf{Commit}(\mathsf{pk}, \mathsf{x}; r), \mathsf{x}; r)$

$$\Pr[\mathsf{Verify}(\mathsf{pk}, \mathsf{com}, \mathsf{x}; r) = 1 \wedge \mathsf{Extract}(\mathsf{td}, \mathsf{com}) \neq \mathsf{x}] < \mathsf{negl}(\lambda)$$

  where $(\mathsf{pk}, \mathsf{td}) \stackrel{\$}{\leftarrow} \mathsf{Gen}(1^\lambda)$ *and* $\mathsf{com} = \mathsf{Commit}(\mathsf{pk}, \mathsf{x}; r)$.

Remark 2.5. Throughout the paper, we will implicitly assume that if $\mathsf{Commit}(\mathsf{pk}, \mathsf{x}; r) \neq \mathsf{com}$ then $\mathsf{Verify}(\mathsf{pk}, \mathsf{x}, r) \neq 1$. This is achieved by any commitment scheme with a natural verification function (that possibly performs additional verification). Notice that in such a case correct extraction implies statistical binding.

2.4 Non-interactive Zero-Knowledge Arguments

We formally define non-interactive zero knowledge arguments as follows.

Definition 2.6 (Non-interactive Zero Knowledge). *Let* $n := n(\lambda)$ *be a polynomial in the security parameter. A* non-interactive zero knowledge (NIZK) *argument* Π *for an NP language* L, *with a corresponding instance-witness relation* R, *consists of three PPT algorithms* $\Pi = (\mathsf{Setup}, \mathsf{P}, \mathsf{V})$ *with the following properties.*

- **Syntax:**
    - $\mathsf{crs} \leftarrow \mathsf{Setup}(1^\lambda)$: *the setup algorithm takes a security parameter* 1^λ *and ouputs a common reference string* crs.
    - $\pi \leftarrow \mathsf{P}(\mathsf{crs}, \mathsf{x}, \mathsf{w})$: *the prover takes as input the common reference string* crs, *a statement* $\mathsf{x} \in \{0, 1\}^n$ *and a witness* w *such that* $(\mathsf{x}, \mathsf{w}) \in R$, *and outputs a proof* π.
    - $\{0, 1\} \leftarrow \mathsf{V}(\mathsf{crs}, \mathsf{x}, \pi)$: *the verifier takes as input the common reference string* crs, *a statement* $\mathsf{x} \in \{0, 1\}^n$ *and a proof* π, *and either accepts (outputs 1) or rejects (outputs 0).*
- **Completeness:** Π *is* complete *if for every* $\lambda \in \mathbb{N}$ *and* $(\mathsf{x}, \mathsf{w}) \in R$, *it holds that*

$$\Pr[\mathsf{V}(\mathsf{crs}, \mathsf{x}, \mathsf{P}(\mathsf{crs}, \mathsf{x}, \mathsf{w}))] = 1$$

  where $\mathsf{crs} \stackrel{\$}{\leftarrow} \mathsf{Setup}(1^\lambda)$.

- **Soundness:** Π *is* sound *if for every PPT cheating prover* P^*, *there exists a negligible function* negl, *such that for every* $\{\mathsf{x}_\lambda \notin L\}_\lambda$ *where* $\mathsf{x}_\lambda \in \{0,1\}^n$ *for all* λ, *it holds that*

$$\Pr[\mathsf{V}(\mathsf{crs}, \mathsf{x}_\lambda, \mathsf{P}^*(\mathsf{crs})) = 1] < \mathsf{negl}(\lambda)$$

where $\mathsf{crs} \xleftarrow{\$} \mathsf{Setup}(1^\lambda)$.

- **Zero Knowledge:** Π *is* zero knowledge *if there exists a PPT simulator* Sim *such that for every* $\{(\mathsf{x}_\lambda, \mathsf{w}_\lambda) \in R\}_\lambda$, *where* $\mathsf{x}_\lambda \in \{0,1\}^n$ *for all* $\lambda \in \mathbb{N}$, *it holds that*

$$\{(\mathsf{crs}, \mathsf{P}(\mathsf{crs}, \mathsf{x}_\lambda, \mathsf{w}_\lambda))\}_\lambda \stackrel{c}{\equiv} \{\mathsf{Sim}(1^\lambda, \mathsf{x}_\lambda)\}_\lambda$$

where $\mathsf{crs} \xleftarrow{\$} \mathsf{Setup}(1^\lambda)$.

We further consider few optional stronger properties that a NIZK system can satisfy:

- **Adaptive Soundness:** Π *is* adaptively sound *if for every PPT cheating prover* P^*, *there exists a negligible function* negl, *such that*

$$\Pr[\mathsf{x} \notin L \ \wedge \ \mathsf{V}(\mathsf{crs}, \mathsf{x}, \pi) = 1] < \mathsf{negl}(\lambda)$$

where $\mathsf{crs} \xleftarrow{\$} \mathsf{Setup}(1^\lambda)$ *and* $(\mathsf{x}, \pi) \leftarrow \mathsf{P}^*(\mathsf{crs})$.

- **Adaptive Zero Knowledge:** Π *is* adaptively zero knowledge *if there exist a (stateful) PPT simulator* Sim *such that for every PPT adversary* $\mathcal{A}$, *it holds that*

$$\{\mathsf{Real}_{\mathsf{Sim}, \mathcal{A}}(1^\lambda)\}_\lambda \stackrel{c}{\equiv} \{\mathsf{Ideal}_{\mathsf{Sim}, \mathcal{A}}(1^\lambda)\}_\lambda$$

where $\mathsf{Real}_{\mathsf{Sim}, \mathcal{A}}$ *and* $\mathsf{Ideal}_{\mathsf{Sim}, \mathcal{A}}$ *are as defined in Fig. 1.*

$\mathsf{Real}_{\mathsf{Sim}, \mathcal{A}}(1^\lambda)$:	$\mathsf{Ideal}_{\mathsf{Sim}, \mathcal{A}}(1^\lambda)$:
1. $\mathsf{crs} \leftarrow \mathsf{Setup}(1^\lambda)$	1. $\mathsf{crs} \leftarrow \mathsf{Sim}(1^\lambda)$
2. $(\mathsf{x}, \mathsf{w}) \leftarrow \mathcal{A}(\mathsf{crs})$, s.t. $(\mathsf{x}, \mathsf{w}) \in R$	2. $(\mathsf{x}, \mathsf{w}) \leftarrow \mathcal{A}(\mathsf{crs})$
3. $\pi \leftarrow \mathsf{P}(\mathsf{crs}, \mathsf{x}, \mathsf{w})$	3. $\pi \leftarrow \mathsf{Sim}(\mathsf{crs}, \mathsf{x})$
4. Output $(\mathsf{crs}, \mathsf{x}, \pi)$	4. Output $(\mathsf{crs}, \mathsf{x}, \pi)$

Fig. 1. $\mathsf{Real}_{\mathsf{Sim}, \mathcal{A}}$ and $\mathsf{Ideal}_{\mathsf{Sim}, \mathcal{A}}$

2.5   Correlation Intractability

Correlation intractable hash [11] constitutes one of the main building blocks in our work. We hereby provide a formal definition.

Definition 2.7 (Correlation Intractable Hash). *Let* $\mathcal{R} = \{\mathcal{R}_\lambda\}$ *be a relation class. A hash family* $\mathcal{H} = (\mathsf{Sample}, \mathsf{Hash})$ *is said to be* correlation intractable *for* $\mathcal{R}$ *if for every non-uniform polynomial-time adversary* $\mathcal{A} = \{\mathcal{A}_\lambda\}$*, there exists a negligible function* $\mathsf{negl}(\lambda)$*, such that for every* $R \in \mathcal{R}_\lambda$*, it holds that*

$$\Pr[(x, \mathsf{Hash}(\mathsf{k}, x)) \in R] \leq \mathsf{negl}(\lambda)$$

where $\mathsf{k} \overset{\$}{\leftarrow} \mathsf{Sample}(1^\lambda)$ *and* $x = \mathcal{A}_\lambda(\mathsf{k})$.

We further define an essential property for utilizing CI hash for obtaining NIZK protocols.

Definition 2.8 (Programmable Hash Family). *A hash family* $\mathcal{H} = (\mathsf{Sample}, \mathsf{Hash})$*, with input and output length* $n := n(\lambda)$ *and, resp.,* $m := m(\lambda)$*, is said to be* programmable *if the following two conditions hold:*

– *1-Universality: For every* $\lambda \in \mathbb{N}$*,* $x \in \{0,1\}^n$ *and* $y \in \{0,1\}^m$*,*

$$\Pr[\mathsf{Hash}_\mathsf{k}(x) = y] = 2^{-m}$$

where $\mathsf{k} \overset{\$}{\leftarrow} \mathsf{Sample}(1^\lambda)$.

– *Programmability: There exists a PPT algorithm* $\widetilde{\mathsf{Sample}}(1^\lambda, x, y)$ *that samples from the conditional distribution* $\mathsf{Sample}(1^\lambda) \mid \mathsf{Hash}_\mathsf{k}(x) = y$.

3 Non-interactive Zero Knowledge from Correlation Intractability

In this section, we provide the formal framework for constructing NIZK for NP from the following building blocks:

(i) An extractable commitment scheme where the extraction function can be probabilistically presented by constant-degree polynomials.
(ii) A correlation intractable hash function for relations probabilistically searchable by constant-degree polynomials.

Our framework is essentially a special case of a more general paradigm that was extensively investigated in prior works [9, 10, 21] for constructing NIZKs from general correlation intractability. Our contribution in this part of the paper is relaxing the requirement for correlation intractability, assuming a commitment scheme with the above property exists.

3.1 A Generic Framework

We first recall the generic framework from Canetti et al. [9] for achieving non-interactive zero knowledge systems from correlation intractable hash.

In its most general form, the paradigm applies the Fiat-Shamir transform [16] over Σ-protocols, which are special honest-verifier ZK protocols (possibly in the CRS model), using correlation intractable hash, in a provably-sound manner.

Roughly speaking, in Σ-protocols, for every prover's first message a there exists (if any) a unique verifier's challenge e that may allow a cheating prover to cheat. Thus, if we instantiate Fiat-Shamir using a hash family $\mathcal{H}$ that is CI for the relation between such pairs (a, e), then the soundness of the transform can be reduced to the correlation intractability of $\mathcal{H}$: any prover who finds a first message a where $\mathcal{H}(a)$ is the "bad challenge" e, essentially breaks $\mathcal{H}$.

Therefore, the type of relations we target in the above outline is formally specified as follows.

Definition 3.1 (Unique-Output Relations). *We say that a class of relations $\mathcal{R} \subset \{0,1\}^n \times \{0,1\}^m$ is* unique-output *if for every $x \in \{0,1\}^n$ there exists at most one value $y \in \{0,1\}^m$ such that $(x, y) \in \mathcal{R}$. We sometimes use function notation to describe such an $\mathcal{R}$ where every $R \in \mathcal{R}$ is denoted by a function $R : \{0,1\}^n \to \{0,1\}^m \cup \perp$ with $R(x) = y$ for $(x, y) \in R$ and $R(x) = \perp$ if there exists no such y.*

As observed in [9], we can reduce the class of relations we target in the CI to relations that are efficiently searchable, i.e. unique-output relations where the unique output is efficiently computable. It is not the case, however, that any Σ-protocol defines such a corresponding relation. This leads us to define *trapdoor Σ-protocols* [9], which are Σ-protocol where the relation between a prover's first message and its unique "bad challenge" is efficiently computable given a trapdoor. We formalize below.

Definition 3.2 (Searchable Relations). *Let $\mathcal{R} : \{0,1\}^n \to \{0,1\}^m \cup \perp$ be a unique-output class of relations. We say that $\mathcal{R}$ is* searchable *by a function class $\mathcal{F} : \{0,1\}^n \to \{0,1\}^m \cup \perp$ if for every $R \in \mathcal{R}$, there exists $f_R \in \mathcal{F}$ such that*

$$\forall x \quad s.t. \quad R(x) \neq \perp, \quad (x, f_R(x)) \in R$$

We say that $\mathcal{R}$ is efficiently searchable *if $\mathcal{F}$ is efficiently computable.*

Definition 3.3 (Trapdoor Σ-Protocol [9]). *Let $\Pi = (\mathsf{Setup}, \mathsf{P}, \mathsf{V})$ be a public-coin three-message honest-verifier zero knowledge proof system for a language L in the common reference string model. Define the relation class $\mathcal{R}_\Sigma(\Pi) = \{R_{\mathsf{crs},x} \mid \mathsf{crs} \in \mathsf{Setup}(1^\lambda), x \notin L\}$ where*

$$R_{\mathsf{crs},x} = \{(\mathbf{a}, \mathbf{e}) \mid \exists \mathbf{z} \quad s.t. \quad \mathsf{V}(\mathsf{crs}, x, \mathbf{a}, \mathbf{e}, \mathbf{z}) = 1\}$$

We say that Π for L is a trapdoor Σ-protocol *if $R_{\mathsf{crs},x}$ is a unique-output relation (see Definition 3.1) and there exist two PPT algorithms, $\mathsf{tdSetup}$ and $\mathsf{BadChallenge}$, with the following properties:*

- **Syntax:**
  - $(\mathsf{crs}, \mathsf{td}) \leftarrow \mathsf{tdSetup}(1^\lambda)$: *The trapdoor setup algorithms takes as input a security parameter* 1^λ *and outputs a common reference string* crs *and a trapdoor* td.
  - $e \leftarrow \mathsf{BadChallenge}(\mathsf{crs}, \mathsf{td}, \mathsf{x}, a)$: *The bad challenge algorithm takes as input a common reference string* crs *and its trapdoor* td, *an instance* x, *and a first message* a, *and outputs a second message* e *or* $\bot$.
- **CRS Indistinguishability:** *We require that a common reference string* $\mathsf{crs} \xleftarrow{\$} \mathsf{Setup}(1^\lambda)$ *is computationally indistinguishable from a random reference string* crs' *sampled with a trapdoor by* $(\mathsf{crs}', \mathsf{td}) \xleftarrow{\$} \mathsf{tdSetup}(1^\lambda)$.
- **Correctness:** *We require that for all* $\lambda \in \mathbb{N}$ *and any instance* $\mathsf{x} \notin L$, *first message* a, *and* $(\mathsf{crs}, \mathsf{td})$, *such that* $R_{\mathsf{crs},\mathsf{x}}(a) \neq \bot$, *it holds*

$$\mathsf{BadChallenge}(\mathsf{crs}, \mathsf{td}, \mathsf{x}, a) = R_{\mathsf{crs},x}(a)$$

Equivalently, we require that $\mathcal{R}_\Sigma(\Pi)$ *is searchable by*

$$\mathcal{F}_\Sigma(\Pi) = \{f_{\mathsf{crs},\mathsf{td},x}(a) = \mathsf{BadChallenge}(\mathsf{crs}, \mathsf{td}, x, \cdot) \mid (\mathsf{crs}, \mathsf{td}) \in \mathsf{Setup}(1^\lambda), x \notin L\}$$

We recall the following theorem from [9].

Theorem 3.4 ([9]). *Assume:*

(i) Π *is a trapdoor* Σ-*protocol for* L.
(ii) $\mathcal{H}$ *is a programmable correlation intractable hash family for relation searchable by* $\mathcal{F}_\Sigma(\Pi)$.

Then, the Fiat-Shamir [16] transform over Π *using* $\mathcal{H}$, $\mathsf{FS}(\Pi, \mathcal{H})$, *is an NIZK argument system for* L *with adaptive soundness and adaptive zero-knowledge.*

Canetti et al. [9] show that any correlation intractable hash family for a reasonable class of relations can be easily transformed to a programmable hash family while preserving correlation intractability. We stress, however, that our Construction of correlation intractable hash in Sect. 2.5 directly satisfies programmability.

3.2 Special Case: Commit-then-Open Protocols

Equipped with the generic framework laid by prior work, we may now present a special case that comprises the starting point of our work.

Commit-then-Open Protocols. We consider protocols of a special form called *commit-then-open* Σ-*protocols*. This notion captures a natural approach for constructing ZK protocols. In particular, a variant of the ZK protocol for Graph Hamiltonicity from [6,15] is a commit-then-open Σ-protocol.

Roughly speaking, commit-then-open Σ-protocols are protocols that use a commitment scheme (possibly in the CRS model), where the prover's first message is a commitment on some proof string π, and his second message is always a decommitment on a subset of π, which depends on the verifier's challenge. Upon receiving the decommitments, the verifier checks that they are valid, then runs some verification procedure on the opened values. We hereby provide a formal definition.

Definition 3.5 (Commit-then-Open Σ-Protocols). *A commit-then-open Σ-protocol is a Σ-protocol $\Pi^{\mathsf{Com}} = (\mathsf{Setup}^{\mathsf{Com}}, \mathsf{P}^{\mathsf{Com}}, \mathsf{V}^{\mathsf{Com}})$, with black-box access to a commitment scheme Com (possibly in the CRS model), such that there exist four PPT algorithms:*

- *$\mathsf{crs}' \leftarrow \mathsf{Setup}'(1^\lambda, \mathsf{pk})$: Takes as input a security parameter 1^λ and a commitment key pk, and outputs a common reference string crs'.*
- *$(\pi, \mathsf{state}) \leftarrow \mathsf{P}_1(\mathsf{crs}, \mathsf{x}, \mathsf{w})$: Takes as input a common reference string crs, an instance x and its witness w and outputs a proof $\pi \in \{0,1\}^\ell$ (for some polynomial $\ell := \ell(\lambda)$) and a local state state.*
- *$I \leftarrow \mathsf{P}_2(\mathsf{crs}, \mathsf{x}, \mathsf{w}, e, \mathsf{state})$: Takes as input crs, x, w and state as above, and a verifier's challenge $e \in \{0,1\}^*$, and outputs a subset $I \subseteq [\ell]$.*
- *$\{0,1\} \leftarrow \mathsf{V}'(\mathsf{crs}, \mathsf{x}, e, (I, \pi_I))$: Takes as input crs, x, $e \in \{0,1\}^*$, $I \subseteq [\ell]$ as above, and a substring of the proof $\pi_I \in \{0,1\}^{|I|}$.*

using which Π^{Com} is defined as follows:

- *$\mathsf{Setup}^{\mathsf{Com}}(1^\lambda)$: Sample a commitment key $\mathsf{pk} \leftarrow \mathsf{Com.Gen}(1^\lambda)$ and possibly additional output $\mathsf{crs}' \leftarrow \mathsf{Setup}'(1^\lambda, \mathsf{pk})$, and output*

$$\mathsf{crs} = (\mathsf{crs}', \mathsf{pk})$$

- *$\mathsf{P}^{\mathsf{Com}}(\mathsf{crs}, \mathsf{x}, \mathsf{w})$: The prover computes $(\pi, \mathsf{state}) \leftarrow \mathsf{P}_1(\mathsf{crs}, \mathsf{x}, \mathsf{w})$, keeps the local state state, and sends a commitment on the proof π to the verifier,*

$$a = \mathsf{Com.Commit}(\mathsf{pk}, \pi)$$

- *$\mathsf{P}^{\mathsf{Com}}(\mathsf{crs}, \mathsf{x}, \mathsf{w}, e)$: The prover's second message consists of a decommitment on the proof bits corresponding to locations $I \leftarrow \mathsf{P}_2(\mathsf{crs}, \mathsf{x}, \mathsf{w}, e, \mathsf{state})$,*

$$z = (I, \mathsf{Com.Decommit}(a_I))$$

- *$\mathsf{V}^{\mathsf{Com}}(\mathsf{crs}, \mathsf{x}, a, e, z)$: The verifier verifies that z contains a valid decommitment to π_I and outputs*
$$\mathsf{V}'(\mathsf{crs}, \mathsf{x}, e, (I, \pi_I))$$

We sometimes override notation and denote $\Pi^{\mathsf{Com}} = (\mathsf{Setup}', \mathsf{P}_1, \mathsf{P}_2, \mathsf{V}')$.

Proposition 3.6 ([6,15]). *There exists a commit-then-open Σ-protocol with soundness $1/2$ for an NP-complete language L.*

It turns out that commit-then-open Σ-protocols allow us to relax the CI requirement for a sound Fiat-Shamir to CI for relations that are *probabilistically searchable* by constant-degree polynomials. We elaborate in the following.

3.3   Probabilistically Searchable Relations

We consider a standard notion of approximation, which we refer to as *probabilistic representation*. Roughly speaking, a function f is probabilistically represented by a function class $\mathcal{C}$ if there exists a randomized $C \in \mathcal{C}$ that computes f with high probability, on any input.

Definition 3.7 (Probabilistic Representation). *Let $n, m \in \mathbb{N}$ and $0 < \epsilon < 1$. Let $f : \{0,1\}^n \to \{0,1\}^m \cup \bot$ be a function and denote $f(x) = (f_1(x), \ldots, f_m(x))$ where $f_i : \{0,1\}^n \to \{0,1\} \cup \bot$ for all $i \in [m]$. A (bit-by-bit) ϵ-probabilistic representation of f by a class of functions $\mathcal{C} : \{0,1\}^n \to \{0,1\}$ consists of m distributions $\mathfrak{C}_1, \ldots, \mathfrak{C}_m \subseteq \mathcal{C}$ such that*

$$\forall i \in [m], \ \forall x \ \ s.t. \ \ f(x) \neq \bot, \quad \Pr_{C_i \xleftarrow{\$} \mathfrak{C}_i} [f_i(x) = C_i(x)] > 1 - \epsilon$$

The following simple lemma connects between probabilistic representation and approximation. Its proof follows immediately from Chernoff's tail bound.

Lemma 3.8 (From Probabilistic Representation to Approximation). *Let $n \in \mathbb{N}$, $\epsilon := \epsilon(\lambda) > 0$, and $m := m(\lambda)$ be a sufficiently large polynomial. For any $\lambda \in \mathbb{N}$, let $f : \{0,1\}^n \to \{0,1\}^m \cup \bot$, and let $\mathfrak{C} = (\mathfrak{C}_1, \ldots, \mathfrak{C}_m)$ be an ϵ-probabilistic representation of f by $\mathcal{C} : \{0,1\}^n \to \{0,1\}$. Then, there exists a negligible function negl, such that*

$$\forall x \ \ s.t. \ \ f(x) \neq \bot, \quad \Pr_{C \xleftarrow{\$} \mathfrak{C}} [\Delta(f(x), C(x)) > 2\epsilon m] < \mathsf{negl}(\lambda)$$

If a class of functions $\mathcal{R}$ is searchable by functions with probabilistic representation by $\mathcal{C}$, we say that $\mathcal{R}$ is *probabilistically searchable* by $\mathcal{C}$.

Definition 3.9 (Probabilistically-Searchable Relations). *Let $\mathcal{R} : \{0,1\}^n \to \{0,1\}^m \cup \bot$ be a unique-output class of relations. We say that $\mathcal{R}$ is ϵ-probabilistically searchable by $\mathcal{C} : \{0,1\}^n \to \{0,1\}$ if it is searchable by $\mathcal{F}$ and, for every $R \in \mathcal{R}$, letting $f_R \in \mathcal{F}$ be the corresponding search function (see Definition 3.2), $f_R \in \mathcal{F}$ has an ϵ-probabilistic representation by $\mathcal{C}$.*

Notice that CI for relations searchable by $\mathcal{F}$ is a weaker notion than relation probabilistically searchable by $\mathcal{F}$. Our hope is to be able to probabilistically represent $\mathcal{F}$ by a much simpler class of functions $\mathcal{C}$ such that the CI task is actually simplified.

3.4   CI for Probabilistic Constant-Degree Is Sufficient for NIZK

Lastly, we show that through commit-then-open protocols, we can reduce our task to achieving CI for relations probabilistically searchable by constant-degree polynomials. More specifically, we show that any commit-then-open Σ-protocol Π^{Com} can be transformed to a slightly different commit-then-open Σ-protocol $\widetilde{\Pi}^{\mathsf{Com}}$ such that:

– Assuming Com is extractable, $\widetilde{\Pi}^{\mathsf{Com}}$ is a trapdoor Σ-protocol.
– Assuming, further, that the extraction function $f_{\mathsf{td}}(a) = \mathsf{Com.Extract}(\mathsf{td}, a)$ has probabilistic constant-degree representation, then so does the trapdoor function BadChallenge, corresponding to $\widetilde{\Pi}^{\mathsf{Com}}$ and, therefore $\mathcal{R}_{\Sigma}(\widetilde{\Pi}^{\mathsf{Com}})$ is probabilistically searchable by constant-degree polynomials.

We formalize below.

Theorem 3.10. *Let Π^{Com} be a commit-then-open Σ-protocol for L with soundness $1/2$ where the output of P_1 is of length $\ell := \ell(\lambda)$. Let Com be a statistically-binding extractable commitment scheme where, for any td, the function $f_{\mathsf{td}}(x) = \mathsf{Com.Extract}(\mathsf{td}, x)$ has an ϵ-probabilistic representation by c-degree polynomials, for a constant $c \in \mathbb{N}$ and $0 < \epsilon(\lambda) < 1/\ell$. Then, for any polynomial $m := m(\lambda)$, there exists a trapdoor Σ-protocol $\widetilde{\Pi}^{\mathsf{Com}}$ for L with soundness 2^{-m} such that $\mathcal{R}_{\Sigma}(\widetilde{\Pi}^{\mathsf{Com}})$ (see Definition 3.3) is ϵ'-probabilistically searchable by $6cc'$-degree polynomials, where $c' \in \mathbb{N}$ is an arbitrary constant and $\epsilon' = \ell \cdot \epsilon + 2^{-c'}$.*

Combining Proposition 3.6, Theorem 3.10, and Theorem 3.4, we obtain the following.

Corollary 3.11 (Sufficient Conditions for NIZK for NP). *The following conditions are sufficient to obtain a NIZK argument system for NP (with adaptive soundness and adaptive zero-knowledge):*

(i) *A statistically-binding extractable commitment scheme where, for any td, the function $f_{\mathsf{td}}(x) = \mathsf{Extract}(\mathsf{td}, x)$ has an ϵ-probabilistic representation by c-degree polynomials, for a constant $c \in \mathbb{N}$ and $0 < \epsilon(\lambda) < 1/\ell(\lambda)$ for an arbitrarily large polynomial ℓ.*

(ii) *A programmable correlation intractable hash family for relations ϵ-probabilistically searchable by c'-degree polynomials, for some constant $\epsilon > 0$ and arbitrarily large constant $c' \in \mathbb{N}$.*

For instantiating Corollary 3.11 based on standard assumptions, we may use a variant of the LPN-based PKE scheme of Damgård and Park [12] to construct a suitable extractable commitment scheme as required in (i). We discuss the details of the commitment scheme in the full version [8] and, in the following section, focus on how to obtain CI hash schemes satisfying (ii).

We now proceed and prove Theorem 3.10.

Proof of Theorem 3.10. We start by presenting the transformation from Π^{Com} to $\widetilde{\Pi}^{\mathsf{Com}}$. In fact, for simplicity, we first show how to construct a protocol $\widetilde{\Pi}_1^{\mathsf{Com}}$ which has soundness $\frac{1}{2}$. The final protocol $\widetilde{\Pi}^{\mathsf{Com}}$ with amplified soundness simply consists of m parallel repetitions of $\widetilde{\Pi}_1^{\mathsf{Com}}$. We later show that all required properties are preserved under parallel repetition and, therefore, we now focus on $\widetilde{\Pi}_1^{\mathsf{Com}}$.

Using the Cook-Levin approach, we represent any (poly-size) circuit C as a (poly-size) 3-CNF formula Φ_C such that for any input x, $C(x) = 1$ if and only if there exists an assignment w for which $\Phi_C(x, w) = 1$. We call such an assignment w a *Cook-Levin witness for $C(x)$*.

Construction 3.1. *Let* $\Pi^{\mathsf{Com}} = (\mathsf{Setup}', \mathsf{P}_1, \mathsf{P}_2, \mathsf{V}')$ *be a commit-then-open Σ-protocol with soundness $1/2$, i.e. where the verifier's challenge e consists of a single public coin. We construct a commit-then-open Σ-protocol $\widetilde{\Pi}_1^{\mathsf{Com}} = (\mathsf{Setup}', \widetilde{\mathsf{P}}_1, \widetilde{\mathsf{P}}_2, \widetilde{\mathsf{V}}')$ as follows.*[5]

- $\widetilde{\mathsf{P}}_1(\mathsf{crs}, \mathsf{x}, \mathsf{w})$: *The prover generates a proof $\pi \leftarrow \mathsf{P}_1(\mathsf{crs}, \mathsf{x}, \mathsf{w})$ and computes $I_0 \leftarrow \mathsf{P}_2(\mathsf{crs}, \mathsf{x}, \mathsf{w}, 0)$ and $I_1 \leftarrow \mathsf{P}_2(\mathsf{crs}, \mathsf{x}, \mathsf{w}, 1)$. Without loss of generality, we assume that subsets $I_0, I_1 \subseteq [\ell]$ are represented, in the natural way, as matrices over $\mathbb{Z}_2$ such that $I_e \cdot \pi = \pi_{I_e}$ (for $e \in \{0, 1\}$). It then generates, for every $e \in \{0, 1\}$, a Cook-Levin witness w_e for the computation $C_{\mathsf{crs}, \mathsf{x}, e}(I_e, \pi_{I_e}) = 1$ where*

$$C_{\mathsf{crs}, \mathsf{x}, e}(I_e, \pi_{I_e}) := \mathsf{V}'(\mathsf{crs}, \mathsf{x}, e, I_e, \pi_{I_e})$$

The prover then outputs

$$\tilde{\pi} = (\pi, I_0, I_1, w_0, w_1)$$

- $\widetilde{\mathsf{P}}_2(\mathsf{crs}, \mathsf{x}, \mathsf{w}, e)$: *Outputs the subset $\tilde{I}_e$, which corresponds to the locations of π_{I_e}, I_e, and w_e in z.*
- $\widetilde{\mathsf{V}}'(\mathsf{crs}, \mathsf{x}, e, (\tilde{I}, \tilde{\pi}_{\tilde{I}}))$: *The verifier parses $\tilde{\pi}_{\tilde{I}} = (I_e, \pi_{I_e}, w_e)$ then verifies that*

$$\Phi_{\mathsf{crs}, \mathsf{x}, e}(I_e, \pi_{I_e}, w_e) = 1$$

where $\Phi_{\mathsf{crs}, \mathsf{x}, e}$ is the Cook-Levin 3-CNF formula for $C_{\mathsf{crs}, \mathsf{x}, e}$ verification.

We begin by showing that, if the underlying commitment scheme is extractable, then $\widetilde{\Pi}_1^{\mathsf{Com}}$ is a trapdoor Σ-protocol.

Lemma 3.12. *Let $\mathsf{Com} = (\mathsf{Gen}, \mathsf{Commit}, \mathsf{Verify}, \mathsf{Extract})$ be a statistically binding extractable commitment scheme, and let $\Pi^{\mathsf{Com}} = (\mathsf{Setup}', \mathsf{P}_1, \mathsf{P}_2, \mathsf{V}')$ be commit-then-open Σ-protocol with soundness $1/2$. Then, $\widetilde{\Pi}_1^{\mathsf{Com}}$ from Construction 3.1 is a trapdoor Σ-protocol with:*

- $\mathsf{tdSetup}(1^\lambda)$: *Sample $(\mathsf{pk}, \mathsf{td}) \leftarrow \mathsf{Com}.\mathsf{Gen}(1^\lambda)$ and $\mathsf{crs}' \leftarrow \mathsf{Setup}'(1^\lambda, \mathsf{pk})$, then output*

$$((\mathsf{crs}', \mathsf{pk}), \mathsf{td})$$

- $\mathsf{BadChallenge}(\mathsf{crs}, \mathsf{td}, \mathsf{x}, a)$: *Compute $\tilde{\pi}' \leftarrow \mathsf{Extract}(\mathsf{td}, a)$, and parse $\tilde{\pi}' = (\pi', I_0, I_1, w_0, w_1) \in \{0, 1, \bot\}^*$. For every $e \in \{0, 1\}$, if $I_e \in \{0, 1\}^*$, set $\tilde{\pi}'_e = (I_e, \pi'_{I_e}, w_e)$ and otherwise set $\tilde{\pi}'_e = \bot$.*
  1. *If $\tilde{\pi}'_0 \in \{0, 1\}^*$ and $\Phi_{\mathsf{crs}, \mathsf{x}, 0}(\tilde{\pi}'_0) = 1$, output 0.*
  2. *If $\tilde{\pi}'_1 \in \{0, 1\}^*$ and $\Phi_{\mathsf{crs}, \mathsf{x}, 1}(\tilde{\pi}'_1) = 1$, output 1.*
  3. *Otherwise, output $\bot$.*

---

[5] Recall that the algorithms for the actual setup, prover and verifier, are obtained by combining the algorithms in the construction with the commitment scheme Com, as described in Definition 3.5.

Proof. It is evident that, based on the statistical binding of Com, the transformation preserves the soundness of the protocol and that, based on the computational hiding of Com, it also preserves honest-verifier zero knowledge (the honest-verifier uses the simulator of $\varPi^{\mathsf{Com}}$ in a straight-forward manner and generates random commitments where necessary).

It is also clear that $\mathsf{tdSetup}(1^\lambda)$ outputs a common reference string identical to $\mathsf{crs} \leftarrow \mathsf{Setup}(1^\lambda)$. We therefore focus on proving correctness of $\mathsf{BadChallenge}$.

Let $\mathsf{x} \notin L$, and crs, td and a be such that $R_{\mathsf{crs},\mathsf{x}}(a) = e \neq \bot$ (where $R_{\mathsf{crs},\mathsf{x}} \in \mathcal{R}_\varSigma(\widetilde{\varPi}_1^{\mathsf{Com}})$ as defined in Definition 3.3). From definition of $R_{\mathsf{crs},\mathsf{x}}$, there exists $(\tilde{I}, \tilde{\pi}_{\tilde{I}})$ such that $\tilde{\mathsf{V}}(\mathsf{crs}, \mathsf{x}, a, e, (\tilde{I}, \tilde{\pi}_{\tilde{I}})) = 1$. From the statistical binding and correct extraction of Com, it necessarily holds that $\tilde{\pi}_{\tilde{I}} = \mathsf{Extract}(a_{\tilde{I}}) = \tilde{\pi}'_e$. Further, we have $\mathsf{V}'(\mathsf{crs}, \mathsf{x}, e, (\tilde{I}, \tilde{\pi}_{\tilde{I}})) = 1$ and, therefore, $\varPhi_{\mathsf{crs},\mathsf{x},e}(\tilde{\pi}_{\tilde{I}}) = 1$ implying

$$\varPhi_{\mathsf{crs},\mathsf{x},e}(\tilde{\pi}'_e) = 1 \tag{1}$$

On the other hand, since $R_{\mathsf{crs},\mathsf{x}}$ is a unique-output relation (due to Lemma 3.12 and Definition 3.3), then there exists no $(\tilde{I}, \tilde{\pi}_{\tilde{I}})$ such that $\tilde{\mathsf{V}}(\mathsf{crs}, \mathsf{x}, a, 1 - e, (\tilde{I}, \tilde{\pi}_{\tilde{I}})) = 1$ and, in particular, this holds for $\tilde{\pi}'_{1-e}$. Therefore, if $\tilde{\pi}'_{1-e}$ is a valid opening of $a_{\tilde{I}}$ (with $\tilde{I}$ being the set of locations supposedly corresponding to $(I_{1-e}, \pi'_{I_{1-e}}, w_{1-e})$ in a), i.e. $\tilde{\pi}'_{1-e} = \mathsf{Extract}(a_{\tilde{I}})$, then

$$\varPhi_{\mathsf{crs},\mathsf{x},1-e}(\tilde{\pi}'_{1-e}) = 0 \tag{2}$$

By combining (1) and (2), we obtain that $\mathsf{BadChallenge}(\mathsf{crs}, \mathsf{td}, \mathsf{x}, a) = e = R_{\mathsf{crs},\mathsf{x}}(a)$ and we finish. $\qquad\square$

Having shown that the protocol is a trapdoor $\varSigma$-protocol, our goal now is to show that the trapdoor function $\mathsf{BadChallenge}$, which is specified in Lemma 3.12, has probabilistic representation as constant degree polynomials. Observe that, roughly speaking, $\mathsf{BadChallenge}$ is a composition of the extraction function, which we assume has a probabilistic constant-degree representation, and an evaluation of two CNF formulas. Since the protocol is a $\varSigma$-protocol, we show that, in fact, the randomized polynomials need to (probabilistically) evaluate only one of these formulas on the extracted value.

Thus, as a first step towards constructing efficient probabilistic constant-degree representation for $\mathsf{BadChallenge}$, we seek to evaluate CNF formulas using randomized polynomials. This is done through the following lemma using standard randomization techniques. We refer the reader to the full version [8] for a full proof.

Lemma 3.13 (k-CNF via Probabilistic Polynomials). *Let $\ell, k, c \in \mathbb{N}$. For any k-CNF formula $\varPhi : \{0,1\}^\ell \to \{0,1\}$, there exists a 2^{-c}-probabilistic representation by $c(k+1)$-degree polynomials $\mathfrak{P}_\varPhi$.*

We now use Lemma 3.13, and the assumption that $\mathsf{Extract}$ has probabilistic constant-degree representation, to obtain such a representation for $\mathsf{BadChallenge}$.

Lemma 3.14. *Let $c, c' \in \mathbb{N}$ be arbitrary constants, and let $0 < \epsilon(\lambda) < 1/\ell(\lambda)$. Let* Com *be an extractable commitment scheme where, for any* td, *the extraction function* Extract$(\mathsf{td}, \cdot)$ *has an ϵ-probabilistic representation by c-degree polynomials. Consider the protocol $\widetilde{\Pi}^{\mathsf{Com}}$ from Construction 3.1. Then, the function*

$$f_{\mathsf{crs},\mathsf{td},\mathsf{x}}(a) = \mathsf{BadChallenge}(\mathsf{crs}, \mathsf{td}, \mathsf{x}, a),$$

as defined in Lemma 3.12, has ϵ'-probabilistic representation by $6cc'$-degree polynomials, with $\epsilon' = \ell \cdot \epsilon + 2^{-c'}$.

Proof. Let $\mathfrak{P}_{\mathsf{td}}$ be the efficient ϵ-probabilistic representation of Extract$(\mathsf{td}, \cdot)$ by c-degree polynomials. We now show a probabilistic representation of $f_{\mathsf{crs},\mathsf{td},\mathsf{x}}$ by c'-degree polynomials, denoted by $\mathfrak{P}_{\mathsf{crs},\mathsf{td},\mathsf{x}}$. For simplicity, we describe $\mathfrak{P}_{\mathsf{crs},\mathsf{td},\mathsf{x}}$ as a randomized algorithm.

$\mathfrak{P}_{\mathsf{crs},\mathsf{td},\mathsf{x}}(a)$:

1. Sample $P_{\mathsf{td}} \xleftarrow{\$} \mathfrak{P}_{\mathsf{td}}^{\ell}$, and compute $\tilde{z} = P_{\mathsf{td}}(a)$.
2. Parse $\tilde{z} = (z, I_0, I_1, w_0, w_1)$ and compute $\tilde{z}_1 = (I_1, z_{I_1}, w_1)$.
3. Denote by $\mathfrak{P}_{\Phi}$ the $2^{-c'}$-probabilistic representation of $\Phi_{\mathsf{crs},\mathsf{x},1}$ by $3c'$-degree polynomials (due to Lemma 3.13). Sample $P_{\Phi} \xleftarrow{\$} \mathfrak{P}_{\Phi}$, then output $b = P_{\Phi}(\tilde{z}_e)$.

We know that P_{td} and P_{Φ} are random polynomials of degrees c and $3c'$, respectively. It is also clear that, from the representation of I_1 as a matrix, then the transformation $(I_1, z) \mapsto z_{I_1}$ and, therefore, step 2 of $\mathfrak{P}_{\mathsf{crs},\mathsf{td},\mathsf{x}}$, can be described using a fixed 2-degree polynomial. We conclude that $\mathfrak{P}_{\mathsf{crs},\mathsf{td},\mathsf{x}}$ can be described as a distribution over $6cc'$-degree polynomials.

It remains to show that $\mathfrak{P}$ probabilistically computes $f_{\mathsf{crs},\mathsf{td},\mathsf{x}}$. From the correctness of $\mathfrak{P}_{\mathsf{td}}$ and following Definition 3.7, if $\tilde{\pi}'_1 = \mathsf{Extract}_{\mathsf{td}}(a_{I_1}) \in \{0,1\}^*$, then

$$\forall i \in I_1, \Pr[\tilde{\pi}'_i \neq \tilde{z}_i] \leq \epsilon$$

Applying union bound on the above, we get that $\Pr[\tilde{\pi}' \neq \tilde{z}] \leq |I_1| \cdot \epsilon \leq \ell \cdot \epsilon$.

Now, conditioning on $\tilde{\pi}' = \tilde{z}$, and from the correctness of $\mathfrak{P}_{\Phi}$, we get that $\Pr[b \neq \Phi_{\mathsf{crs},\mathsf{x},1}(\tilde{\pi}'_1)] \leq 2^{-c'}$ and, therefore, overall, we get that

$$\Pr_{P \xleftarrow{\$} \mathfrak{P}_{\mathsf{crs},\mathsf{td},\mathsf{x}}} [P(a) \neq \Phi_{\mathsf{crs},\mathsf{x},1}(\tilde{\pi}'_1)]$$

$$\leq \Pr[\tilde{\pi}' \neq \tilde{z}] + \Pr[P(a) \neq \Phi_{\mathsf{crs},\mathsf{x},1}(\tilde{\pi}'_1) \mid \tilde{\pi}' = \tilde{z}]$$

$$\leq \ell \cdot \epsilon + 2^{-c'} \qquad (3)$$

Now, if $f_{\mathsf{crs},\mathsf{td},\mathsf{x}}(a) = 1$, then it must be the case that $\tilde{\pi}'_1 \in \{0,1\}^*$ and $\Phi_{\mathsf{crs},\mathsf{x},1}(\tilde{\pi}'_1) = 1$, and therefore, from (3), $P(a) = 1$ with the required probability. Otherwise, if $f_{\mathsf{crs},\mathsf{td},\mathsf{x}}(a) = 0$, then $\tilde{\pi}'_0 \in \{0,1\}^*$ and $\Phi_{\mathsf{crs},\mathsf{x},0}(\tilde{\pi}'_0) = 1$. Since $\widetilde{\Pi}^{\mathsf{Com}}$ is a Σ-protocol and $\mathcal{R}_{\Sigma}(\widetilde{\Pi}^{\mathsf{Com}})$ is unique output (Lemma 3.12), then there exist no $\tilde{z}_1 \in \{0,1\}^*$ such that $\Phi_{\mathsf{crs},\mathsf{x},1}(\tilde{z}_1) = 1$ and, therefore, $P(a) = 0$ with the required probability. This completes the proof. $\qquad \square$

Combining Lemmas 3.12 and 3.14, we have so far proven Theorem 3.10 for the special case of $m = 1$. To derive the theorem for the general case, consider the protocol $\widetilde{\Pi}^{\mathsf{Com}}$ that consists of m parallel repetitions of $\widetilde{\Pi}_1^{\mathsf{Com}}$. Parallel repetition preserves honest-verifier zero knowledge and the Σ-protocol property ($\mathcal{R}_\Sigma$ being unique-output) and, consequently, amplifies soundness to 2^{-m}. Further, if $\widetilde{\Pi}_1^{\mathsf{Com}}$ is a trapdoor Σ-protocol with tdSetup and BadChallenge, then $\widetilde{\Pi}^{\mathsf{Com}}$ is a trapdoor Σ-protocol with tdSetup and BadChallenge^m, where BadChallenge^m(crs, td, x, $a_1, \ldots, a_m$) computes $e_i = $ BadChallenge(crs, td, x, a_i) for all $i \in [m]$ then outputs $(e_1, \ldots, e_m)$ if $\forall i\; e_i \in \{0, 1\}$ and outputs $\bot$ otherwise. By Definition 3.7, if BadChallenge has ϵ'-probabilistic $6cc'$-degree representation, then so does BadChallenge^m.

Hence, the proof of Theorem 3.10 is complete.

4   CI Through Probabilistic Representation

In this section, we show that if a function class $\mathcal{F}$ has a probabilistic representation by a potentially simpler class $\mathcal{C}$ (see Definition 3.7) then CI for relations searchable by $\mathcal{F}$ can be reduced to CI for a class of relations that are "approximated" by $\mathcal{C}$. This is the first step we make towards constructing CI hash, as required by Corollary 3.11, from standard assumptions.

4.1   Approximable Relations and CI-Apx

We start by defining the notion of *approximable relations* and a related special case of correlation intractability, CI-Apx.

Definition 4.1 (CI-Apx). *Let* $\mathcal{C} = \{\mathcal{C}_\lambda : \{0, 1\}^{n(\lambda)} \to \{0, 1\}^{m(\lambda)}\}$ *be a function class and let* $0 < \epsilon < 1$. *For every* $C \in \mathcal{C}$, *we define the relation* ϵ-*approximable by* C *as follows*

$$\mathcal{R}_C^\epsilon = \{(x, y) \in \{0, 1\}^n \times \{0, 1\}^m \mid \Delta(y, C(x)) \leq \epsilon m\}$$

A hash family that is CI for all relations $\{\mathcal{R}_C^\epsilon \mid C \in \mathcal{C}\}$ *is said to be* CI-Apx$_\epsilon$ *for* $\mathcal{C}$.

4.2   From CI-Apx for $\mathcal{C}$ to CI for $\mathcal{F}$

We now state and prove the following general theorem.

Theorem 4.2. *Let* $\mathcal{F}$ *be a function class that has an* ϵ-*probabilistic representation by* $\mathcal{C}$. *If* $\mathcal{H}$ *is* CI-Apx$_{2\epsilon}$ *hash for* $\mathcal{C}$, *then* $\mathcal{H}$ *is CI for relations searchable by* $\mathcal{F}$ *(i.e.* ϵ-*probabilistically searchable by* $\mathcal{C}$).

Proof of Theorem 4.2. Suppose $\mathcal{R}$ is searchable by $\mathcal{F} : \{0,1\}^n \to \{0,1\}^m$. Fix some $R \in \mathcal{R}$ and consider its corresponding search function $f \in \mathcal{F}$. Let $\mathfrak{C}_f$ be the ϵ-probabilistic representation of f by $\mathcal{C}$.

We start by defining a game $\mathsf{Game}_0(\mathcal{A})$ against an adversary $\mathcal{A}$ as follows.

$\mathsf{Game}_0(\mathcal{A})$:
1. $\mathsf{k} \xleftarrow{\$} \mathsf{Sample}(1^\lambda)$.
2. $x \leftarrow \mathcal{A}(\mathsf{k})$.
3. Output 1 if and only if $f(x) \neq \bot$ and $\mathsf{Hash}_\mathsf{k}(x) = f(x)$.

It is clear that the probability of an adversary $\mathcal{A}$ to win Game_0 upper bounds the probability he breaks the correlation intractability of $\mathcal{H}$ for R (immediate from Definition 3.2). Our goal, then, is to show that for any PPT adversary $\mathcal{A}$, there exists a negligible function negl such that $\Pr[\mathsf{Game}_0(\mathcal{A}) = 1] < \mathsf{negl}(\lambda)$.

We now reduce Game_0 to Game_1, which is defined below.

$\mathsf{Game}_1(\mathcal{A})$:
1. $C \xleftarrow{\$} \mathfrak{C}_f$.
2. $\mathsf{k} \xleftarrow{\$} \mathsf{Sample}(1^\lambda)$.
3. $x \leftarrow \mathcal{A}(\mathsf{k})$.
4. Output 1 if and only if $\Delta(\mathsf{Hash}_\mathsf{k}(x), C(x)) \leq 2\epsilon m$.

Lemma 4.3. *For any (possibly unbounded) adversary $\mathcal{A}$, there exists a negligible function negl, such that*

$$\Pr[\mathsf{Game}_0(\mathcal{A}) = 1] \leq \Pr[\mathsf{Game}_1(\mathcal{A}) = 1] + \mathsf{negl}(\lambda)$$

Proof. The proof is derived from the fact that C in Game_1 is sampled independently of the adversary's choice x and from Lemma 3.8, as follows.

$$\begin{aligned}
\Pr[\mathsf{Game}_0(\mathcal{A}) = 1] &= \Pr[f(x) \neq \bot \wedge \mathsf{Hash}_\mathsf{k}(x) = f(x)] \\
&\leq \Pr_{C \xleftarrow{\$} \mathfrak{C}_f} [f(x) \neq \bot \wedge \Delta(f(x), C(x)) > 2\epsilon m] \\
&\quad + \Pr_{C \xleftarrow{\$} \mathfrak{C}_f} [f(x) \neq \bot \wedge \Delta(\mathsf{Hash}_\mathsf{k}(x), f(x)) \leq 2\epsilon m] \\
&\leq \Pr[\mathsf{Game}_1(\mathcal{A}) = 1] + \mathsf{negl}(\lambda)
\end{aligned}$$

$\square$

To complete the proof of Theorem 4.2, we show that Game_1 is hard to win with non-negligible probability, based on the correlation intractability of $\mathcal{H}$ for relations 2ϵ-approximable $\mathcal{C}$.

Lemma 4.4. *If $\mathcal{H}$ is CI-Apx$_{2\epsilon}$ for $\mathcal{C}$ then, for any $f \in \mathcal{F}$ and any PPT adversary $\mathcal{A}$, there exists a negligible function such that*

$$\Pr[\mathsf{Game}_1(\mathcal{A}) = 1] < \mathsf{negl}(\lambda)$$

Proof. Assume towards contradiction there exists $f \in \mathcal{F}$ and $\mathcal{A}$ for which the above does not hold, namely $\Pr[\mathsf{Game}_1(\mathcal{A}) = 1] > 1/\mathsf{poly}(\lambda)$. Then, there exists some fixed $C \in \mathfrak{C}_f$ such that $\Pr[\mathsf{Game}_1^C(\mathcal{A}) = 1] > 1/\mathsf{poly}(\lambda)$, where Game_1^C is defined as Game_1 with C being fixed (rather than sampled from $\mathfrak{C}_f$). From definition, such an adversary breaks the CI-Apx$_{2\epsilon}$ of $\mathcal{H}$ for C.   □

We conclude the proof of the theorem by combining Lemmas 4.3 and 4.4.

5 CI-Apx from Trapdoor Hash

Having shown in the previous section that CI-Apx is a useful notion to obtain CI for a function class that has a simple probabilistic representation, we now show how to construct, from rate-1 trapdoor hash for any function class $\mathcal{C}$ [14], an CI-Apx hash for $\mathcal{C}$. In fact, in our proof of CI, we require that the underlying TDH scheme satisfies the following stronger notion of correctness.

Definition 5.1. (Enhanced Correctness for TDH). *We say that a (rate-1) trapdoor hash scheme* TDH *for* $\mathcal{C} = \{\mathcal{C}_n : \{0,1\}^n \to \{0,1\}\}$ *has* enhanced $(1 - \tau)$-correctness *for* $\tau := \tau(\lambda) < 1$ *if it satisfies the following property:*

- **Enhanced Correctness:** *There exists a negligible function* $\mathsf{negl}(\lambda)$ *such that the following holds for any* $\lambda, n, \in \mathbb{N}$, *any* $\mathsf{h} \in \{0,1\}^{\eta(\lambda)}$, *any* $\mathsf{hk} \in \mathsf{S}(1^\lambda, 1^n)$, *and any function* $C \in \mathcal{C}_n$:

$$\Pr[\forall x \in \{0,1\}^n : \mathsf{H}(\mathsf{hk}, x) = \mathsf{h}, \ \mathsf{e} + \mathsf{e}' = C(x) \mod 2] \geq 1 - \tau - \mathsf{negl}(\lambda)$$

where $(\mathsf{ek}, \mathsf{td}) \leftarrow \mathsf{G}(\mathsf{hk}, C)$, $\mathsf{e} = \mathsf{E}(\mathsf{ek}, x)$, $\mathsf{e}' = \mathsf{D}(\mathsf{td}, \mathsf{h})$ *and the probability is over the randomness used by* G.

Theorem 5.2. *Assume there exists rate-1 trapdoor hash scheme* TDH *for* $\mathcal{C} = \{\mathcal{C}_n : \{0,1\}^n \to \{0,1\}^m\}$ *with enhanced* $(1-\tau)$-*correctness where the hash length is* $\eta := \eta(\lambda)$. *Then, for any* ϵ *s.t.* $\epsilon + \tau < \epsilon_0$ *(for some fixed universal constant* ϵ_0*), there exists a polynomial* $m_{\epsilon,\eta,\tau}(\lambda) = O((\eta + \lambda)/\tau + \log(1/\epsilon))$ *such that, for every polynomial* $m > m_\epsilon$, *there exists a CI-Apx$_\epsilon$ hash family for* $\mathcal{C}$ *with output length* $m(\lambda)$.[6]

Recalling Corollary 3.11, and using the result from Section 4, obtaining CI-Apx for constant-degree functions is sufficient for our purpose of constructing NIZK. To instantiate Theorem 5.2 for constant-degree functions from standard assumption, we use the following result of Döttling et al. [14].

Theorem 5.3. (TDH from Standard Assumptions [14]). *For any constant* $c \in \mathbb{N}$ *and arbitrarily small* $\tau := \tau(\lambda) = 1/\mathsf{poly}(\lambda)$, *there exists a rate-1 trapdoor hash scheme, for c-degree polynomials over* $\mathbb{Z}_2$, *with enhanced* $(1-\tau)$-*correctness and function privacy under the DDH/QR/DCR/LWE assumption[7].*

---

[6] In fact, as implicitly implied by the proof of the theorem, our construction satisfies the stronger notion of somewhere statistical CI for the corresponding hamming-ball relations [9]. However, applying Theorem 4.2 on the construction does not preserve this property.

[7] The error probability in the QR, DCR, and LWE constructions is even negligible.

We note some gaps between the result from [14] and the theorem above. First, the aforementioned work considers only linear functions (i.e. degree-1 polynomials) over $\mathbb{Z}_2$. Second, their DDH-based construction supports even a stricter class of functions, namely only "index functions" of the form $f_i(x) = x_i$. Third, all known constructions are not proven to have enhanced correctness. In the full version [8], we show how to close these gaps by simple adjustments to the constructions and proofs from [14]. Combining Theorems 5.2 and 5.3, we obtain.

Corollary 5.4. *Let $c \in \mathbb{N}$. There exists a constant $\epsilon > 0$ such that, for any sufficiently large polynomial $m := m(\lambda)$, there exists a programmable correlation intractable hash family with output length m for all relations ϵ-approximable by c-degree polynomials over $\mathbb{Z}_2$.*

5.1   The Hash Family

We now present our construction of CI-Apx from rate-1 TDH. We note that we do not use the full power of a TDH. Specifically, the decoding algorithm need not be efficient and, further, we do not use input privacy (as defined in [14]).

Construction 5.1 (Correlation Intractability from TDH). *Let $n := n(\lambda)$ and $m := m(\lambda)$ be polynomials in the security parameter, and let $\epsilon := \epsilon(\lambda) < 0.32$. Let $\mathcal{C} : \{0,1\}^n \to \{0,1\}$ be a function class and let $\mathsf{TDH} = (\mathsf{S}, \mathsf{G}, \mathsf{H}, \mathsf{E}, \mathsf{D})$ be a rate-1 trapdoor hash scheme for $\mathcal{C}$. Our construction of CI-Apx$_\epsilon$ hash for $\mathcal{C}$ consists of the following algorithms.*

- $\mathsf{Sample}(1^\lambda)$: *Sample* $\mathsf{hk} \xleftarrow{\$} \mathsf{S}(1^\lambda)$ *and, for all $i \in [m]$, $(\mathsf{ek}_i, \mathsf{td}_i) \xleftarrow{\$} \mathsf{G}(\mathsf{hk}, C_0)$ for an arbitrary fixed $C_0 \in \mathcal{C}$, and a uniform $r \xleftarrow{\$} \{0,1\}^m$, then output*

$$\mathsf{k} = ((\mathsf{ek}_1, \ldots, \mathsf{ek}_m), r)$$

- $\mathsf{Hash}(\mathsf{k}, x)$: *The hash of an input $x \in \{0,1\}^n$ under key $\mathsf{k} = ((\mathsf{ek}_i)_{i \in [m]}, r)$ is computed as follows*

$$\mathsf{h} = \mathsf{E}((\mathsf{ek}_1, \ldots, \mathsf{ek}_m), x) + r \mod 2$$

5.2   Proof of Theorem 5.2

Programmability of the construction is trivial and, thus, we focus on proving CI.
    Fix some $C = (C_1, \ldots, C_m) \in \mathcal{C}^m$ and consider the relation ϵ-probabilistically searchable by C, R_C^ϵ. The advantage of an adversary $\mathcal{A}$ in breaking the CI for R_C^ϵ is demonstrated in his advantage in winning in the following game.

$\mathsf{Game}_0(\mathcal{A})$:
1. $\mathsf{k} \xleftarrow{\$} \mathsf{Sample}(1^\lambda)$.
2. $x \leftarrow \mathcal{A}(\mathsf{k})$.
3. Output 1 if and only if $\Delta(\mathsf{Hash}_\mathsf{k}(x), C(x)) \leq 2\epsilon m$.

To show $\Pr[\mathsf{Game}_0(\mathcal{A}) = 1] < \mathsf{negl}(\lambda)$, we define a different game, Game_1, in which we switch the encoding keys $(\mathsf{ek}_1, \ldots, \mathsf{ek}_m)$ in k to encoding keys corresponding to the functions $C_1, \ldots, C_m$ (rather than C_0).

$\mathsf{Game}_1(\mathcal{A})$:
1. Sample $\mathsf{hk} \leftarrow \mathsf{S}(1^\lambda, 1^n)$ and $(\mathsf{ek}_i', \mathsf{td}_i') \leftarrow \mathsf{G}(\mathsf{hk}, C_i)$ for every $i \in [m]$. Sample a uniform $r \xleftarrow{\$} \{0,1\}^m$, then set $\mathsf{k} = ((\mathsf{ek}_1', \ldots, \mathsf{ek}_m'), r)$.
2. $x \leftarrow \mathcal{A}(\mathsf{k})$.
3. Output 1 if and only if $\Delta(\mathsf{Hash}_\mathsf{k}(x), C(x)) \leq 2\epsilon m$.

We claim that, based on the function privacy of the underlying trapdoor hash, we may reduce Game_0 to Game_1.

Lemma 5.5. *Under the function privacy of* TDH, *for any PPT adversary* $\mathcal{A}$, *there exists a negligible function* negl *such that*

$$\Pr[\mathsf{Game}_0(\mathcal{A}) = 1] \leq \Pr[\mathsf{Game}_1(\mathcal{A}) = 1] + \mathsf{negl}(\lambda)$$

Proof. Assume towards contradiction there exists an adversary $\mathcal{A}$ for which the above does not hold.

We use $\mathcal{A}$ to construct an adversary $\mathcal{A}_{\mathsf{TDH}}$ that distinguishes between $(\mathsf{hk}, (\mathsf{ek}_1, \ldots, \mathsf{ek}_m))$ and $(\mathsf{hk}, (\mathsf{ek}_1', \ldots, \mathsf{ek}_m'))$, where $\mathsf{hk} \leftarrow \mathsf{S}(1^\lambda, 1^n)$, $\mathsf{ek}_i \leftarrow \mathsf{G}(\mathsf{hk}, C_0)$ and $\mathsf{ek}_i' \leftarrow \mathsf{G}(\mathsf{hk}, C_{f_i})$ (for every $i \in [m]$), with non-negligible advantage. Such an adversary breaks the function privacy of TDH via a standard hybrid argument.

On input $(ek_1, \ldots, ek_m, C)$, $\mathcal{A}_{\mathsf{TDH}}$ simply calls $x \leftarrow \mathcal{A}((ek_1, \ldots, ek_m), r))$, and outputs 1 iff $\Delta(\mathsf{Hash}_\mathsf{k}(x), C(x)) \leq 2\epsilon m$. It holds that

$$| \Pr[\mathcal{A}_{\mathsf{TDH}}(\mathsf{hk}, (ek_1, \ldots, ek_m)) = 1] - \Pr[\mathcal{A}_{\mathsf{TDH}}(\mathsf{hk}, (ek_1', \ldots, ek_m')) = 1]|$$
$$= | \Pr[\mathsf{Game}_1(\mathcal{A}) = 1] - \Pr[\mathsf{Game}_2(\mathcal{A}) = 1]| \geq 1/\mathsf{poly}(\lambda)$$

$\square$

Lastly, we show that Game_1 is statistically hard to win. This, together with Lemma 5.6, implies Theorem 5.2.

Lemma 5.6. *For any (possibly unbounded) adversary* $\mathcal{A}$, *there exists a negligible function* negl *s.t.*
$$\Pr[\mathsf{Game}_1(\mathcal{A}) = 1] < \mathsf{negl}(\lambda)$$

Proof. It suffices to show that there exists a negligible function negl such that

$$\Pr_\mathsf{k}[\exists x : \ \Delta(\mathsf{Hash}_\mathsf{k}(x), C(x)) \leq 2\epsilon m] < \mathsf{negl}(\lambda)$$

where k is sampled as in Game_1. We denote the above event by Bad and observe that

$$\Pr[\mathsf{Bad}] = \Pr_\mathsf{k}[\exists x, z \in \{0,1\}^m : \ |z| \leq 2\epsilon m \ \wedge \ C(x) + z = \mathsf{Hash}_\mathsf{k}(x) \mod 2]$$

For any $\mathsf{hk} \in \mathsf{S}(1^\lambda, 1^n)$, let Bad_hk be the event Bad where the hash key is fixed to hk, and the probability space is over random $(\mathsf{ek}_i, \mathsf{td}_i)$ and r. It is sufficient, then, to show that for all $\mathsf{hk} \in \mathsf{S}(1^\lambda, 1^n)$, $\Pr[\mathsf{Bad}_\mathsf{hk}] \leq \mathsf{negl}(\lambda)$.

For any $\mathsf{hk} \in \mathsf{S}(1^\lambda, 1^n)$, let $\mathsf{TDHCor}_{\mathsf{hk}}$ denote the following event:

$$\mathsf{TDHCor}_{\mathsf{hk}} = [\forall x, \Delta(\mathsf{E}(\mathsf{ek}, x) + C(x), \mathsf{D}(\mathsf{td}, h)) \leq 2\tau m].$$

Then $\Pr[\mathsf{Bad}_{\mathsf{hk}}] \leq \Pr[\neg\mathsf{TDHCor}_{\mathsf{hk}}] + \Pr[\mathsf{Bad}_{\mathsf{hk}} \wedge \mathsf{TDHCor}_{\mathsf{hk}}]$. We will separately show that both $\Pr[\neg\mathsf{TDHCor}_{\mathsf{hk}}]$ and $\Pr[\mathsf{Bad}_{\mathsf{hk}} \wedge \mathsf{TDHCor}_{\mathsf{hk}}]$ are negligible in λ.

First, we bound $\Pr[\neg\mathsf{TDHCor}_{\mathsf{hk}}]$ based on the enhanced $(1 - \tau)$-correctness of TDH and Chernoff bound: for every fixed $\mathsf{h} \in \{0,1\}^\eta$ and $\mathsf{hk} \in \mathsf{S}(1^\lambda, 1^n)$,

$$\Pr[\exists x : \mathsf{H}(\mathsf{hk}, x) = \mathsf{h}, \quad \Delta(\mathsf{E}(\mathsf{ek}, x) + C(x), \mathsf{D}(\mathsf{td}, \mathsf{h})) > 2\tau m] \leq e^{-\tau m/3}$$

Applying union bound over all $\mathsf{h} \in \{0,1\}^\eta$ gives

$$\Pr[\neg\mathsf{TDHCor}_{\mathsf{hk}}] = \Pr[\exists x, \quad \Delta(\mathsf{E}(\mathsf{ek}, x) + C(x), \mathsf{D}(\mathsf{td}, \mathsf{H}(\mathsf{hk}, x))) > 2\tau m] < e^{\eta - \tau m} = \mathsf{negl}(\lambda).$$

Second, note that $\Pr[\mathsf{Bad}_{\mathsf{hk}} \wedge \mathsf{TDHCor}_{\mathsf{hk}}] \leq \Pr[\exists x : \Delta(r, \mathsf{D}(\mathsf{td}, \mathsf{H}(\mathsf{hk}, x))) \leq 2(\tau + \epsilon)]$ where the probability is over choice of td and r. Let $\epsilon' = 2(\epsilon + \tau)$ and (for fixed hk, td) let

$$Y = \{\mathsf{D}(\mathsf{td}, \mathsf{h}_x) + z' \mod 2 \mid x \in \{0,1\}^n, \mathsf{h}_x = \mathsf{H}(\mathsf{hk}, x), z' \in \{0,1\}^m \text{ s.t. } |z'| \leq \epsilon' m\}$$

For fixed hk, td, $\Pr_r[\exists x : \Delta(r, \mathsf{D}(\mathsf{td}, \mathsf{h}_x)) < \epsilon' m] = 2^{-m}|Y|$. Thus, it suffices to show that $2^{-m}|Y|$ is negligible. Clearly, $|\{\mathsf{D}(\mathsf{td}, \mathsf{h}_x) : x \in \{0,1\}^n, \mathsf{h}_x = \mathsf{H}(\mathsf{hk}, x)\}| \leq 2^\eta$. Further, we can bound

$$|\{z' \in \{0,1\}^m \mid |z'| \leq \epsilon' m\}| = \sum_{i=1}^{\epsilon' m} \binom{m}{i} \leq \sum_{i=1}^{\epsilon' m} \left(\frac{me}{i}\right)^i \leq (e/\epsilon')^{\epsilon' m + 1}$$

and consequently, $|Y| \leq 2^\eta \cdot (e/\epsilon')^{\epsilon' m + 1}$. If ϵ' is a (universally) sufficiently small constant, and $m \geq (\lambda + \eta + \log(e/\epsilon'))/(1 - \epsilon' \log(e/\epsilon')) = O((\eta + \lambda)/\tau + \log(1/\epsilon))$,

$$2^{-m}|Y| \leq 2^{-m}(e/\epsilon)^{\epsilon' m + 1} 2^\eta < 2^{(\epsilon' \log(e/\epsilon') - 1)m + \log(e/\epsilon') + \eta} < 2^{-\lambda}.$$

$\square$

Acknowledgments. We thank Brent Waters for pointing out an inaccuracy in a proof in a previous version of this work, and for other comments. We thank the anonymous reviewers of CRYPTO 2020 for their helpful feedback and pointers.

Research supported by the Binational Science Foundation (Grant No. 2016726), and by the European Union Horizon 2020 Research and Innovation Program via ERC Project REACT (Grant 756482) and via Project PROMETHEUS (Grant 780701). Venkata Koppula was also supported by the Simons-Berkeley Fellowship. This work was done in part while the author was visiting the Simons Institute for the Theory of Computing.

References

1. Alekhnovich, M.: More on average case vs approximation complexity. In: 44th Symposium on Foundations of Computer Science (FOCS 2003), Proceedings, Cambridge, MA, USA, 11–14 October 2003, pp. 298–307. IEEE Computer Society (2003). https://doi.org/10.1109/SFCS.2003.1238204

2. Badrinarayan, S., Fernando, R., Jain, A., Khurana, D., Sahai, A.: Statistical zap arguments. Cryptology ePrint Archive, Report 2019/780 (2019)

3. Bellare, M., Micciancio, D., Warinschi, B.: Foundations of group signatures: formal definitions, simplified requirements, and a construction based on general assumptions. In: Biham, E. (ed.) EUROCRYPT 2003. LNCS, vol. 2656, pp. 614–629. Springer, Heidelberg (2003). https://doi.org/10.1007/3-540-39200-9_38

4. Ben-Sasson, E., et al.: Zerocash: decentralized anonymous payments from bitcoin. In: 2014 IEEE Symposium on Security and Privacy, pp. 459–474, May 2014

5. Bender, A., Katz, J., Morselli, R.: Ring signatures: stronger definitions, and constructions without random oracles. In: Halevi, S., Rabin, T. (eds.) TCC 2006. LNCS, vol. 3876, pp. 60–79. Springer, Heidelberg (2006). https://doi.org/10.1007/11681878_4

6. Blum, M.: How to prove a theorem so no one else can claim it. In: Proceedings of the International Congress of Mathematicians, pp. 1444–1451 (1987)

7. Blum, M., Feldman, P., Micali, S.: Non-interactive zero-knowledge and its applications (extended abstract). In: 20th Annual ACM Symposium on Theory of Computing, 2–4 May 1988, pp. 103–112. ACM Press, Chicago (1988)

8. Brakerski, Z., Koppula, V., Mour, T.: NIZK from LPN and trapdoor hash via correlation intractability for approximable relations. Cryptology ePrint Archive, Report 2020/258 (2020). https://eprint.iacr.org/2020/258

9. Canetti, R., et al.: Fiat-Shamir: from practice to theory. In: Proceedings of the 51st Annual ACM SIGACT Symposium on Theory of Computing, STOC 2019, pp. 1082–1090. Association for Computing Machinery, New York (2019). https://doi.org/10.1145/3313276.3316380

10. Canetti, R., Chen, Y., Reyzin, L., Rothblum, R.D.: Fiat-Shamir and correlation intractability from strong KDM-secure encryption. In: Nielsen, J.B., Rijmen, V. (eds.) EUROCRYPT 2018, Part I. LNCS, vol. 10820, pp. 91–122. Springer, Cham (2018). https://doi.org/10.1007/978-3-319-78381-9_4

11. Canetti, R., Goldreich, O., Halevi, S.: The random oracle methodology, revisited. J. ACM **51**(4), 557–594 (2004). https://doi.org/10.1145/1008731.1008734

12. Damgård, I., Park, S.: How practical is public-key encryption based on LPN and ring-LPN? Cryptology ePrint Archive, Report 2012/699 (2012). http://eprint.iacr.org/2012/699

13. Dolev, D., Dwork, C., Naor, M.: Non-malleable cryptography (extended abstract). In: 23rd Annual ACM Symposium on Theory of Computing, 6–8 May 1991, pp. 542–552. ACM Press, New Orleans (1991)

14. Döttling, N., Garg, S., Ishai, Y., Malavolta, G., Mour, T., Ostrovsky, R.: Trapdoor hash functions and their applications. In: Boldyreva, A., Micciancio, D. (eds.) CRYPTO 2019. LNCS, vol. 11694, pp. 3–32. Springer, Cham (2019). https://doi.org/10.1007/978-3-030-26954-8_1

15. Feige, U., Lapidot, D., Shamir, A.: Multiple noninteractive zero knowledge proofs under general assumptions. SIAM J. Comput. **29**(1), 1–28 (1999). https://doi.org/10.1137/S0097539792230010

16. Fiat, A., Shamir, A.: How to prove yourself: practical solutions to identification and signature problems. In: Odlyzko, A.M. (ed.) CRYPTO 1986. LNCS, vol. 263, pp. 186–194. Springer, Heidelberg (1987). https://doi.org/10.1007/3-540-47721-7_12

17. Goldwasser, S., Micali, S., Rackoff, C.: The knowledge complexity of interactive proof-systems (extended abstract). In: 17th Annual ACM Symposium on Theory of Computing, pp. 291–304, 6–8 May 1985. ACM Press, Providence (1995)

18. Groth, J., Ostrovsky, R., Sahai, A.: New techniques for noninteractive zero-knowledge. J. ACM **59**(3) (2012). https://doi.org/10.1145/2220357.2220358

19. Holmgren, J., Lombardi, A.: Cryptographic hashing from strong one-way functions (or: one-way product functions and their applications), pp. 850–858, October 2018. https://doi.org/10.1109/FOCS.2018.00085

20. Jain, A., Jin, Z.: Statistical zap arguments from quasi-polynomial LWE. Cryptology ePrint Archive, Report 2019/839 (2019)

21. Kalai, Y.T., Rothblum, G.N., Rothblum, R.D.: From obfuscation to the security of Fiat-Shamir for proofs. In: Katz, J., Shacham, H. (eds.) CRYPTO 2017, Part II. LNCS, vol. 10402, pp. 224–251. Springer, Cham (2017). https://doi.org/10.1007/978-3-319-63715-0_8

22. Lombardi, A., Vaikuntanathan, V., Wichs, D.: 2-message publicly verifiable WI from (subexponential) LWE. Cryptology ePrint Archive, Report 2019/808 (2019). https://eprint.iacr.org/2019/808

23. Naor, M., Yung, M.: Public-key cryptosystems provably secure against chosen ciphertext attacks. In: 22nd Annual ACM Symposium on Theory of Computing, 14–16 May 1990, pp. 427–437. ACM Press, Baltimore (1990)

24. Peikert, C., Shiehian, S.: Noninteractive zero knowledge for NP from (plain) learning with errors. In: Boldyreva, A., Micciancio, D. (eds.) CRYPTO 2019. LNCS, vol. 11692, pp. 89–114. Springer, Cham (2019). https://doi.org/10.1007/978-3-030-26948-7_4

25. Sahai, A., Waters, B.: How to use indistinguishability obfuscation: deniable encryption, and more. In: Shmoys, D.B. (ed.) 46th Annual ACM Symposium on Theory of Computing, 31 May – 3 June 2014, pp. 475–484. ACM Press, New York (2014)

Shorter Non-interactive Zero-Knowledge Arguments and ZAPs for Algebraic Languages

Geoffroy Couteau[1]([⊠]) and Dominik Hartmann[2]

[1] CNRS, IRIF, Université de Paris, Paris, France
couteau@irif.fr
[2] Ruhr-University Bochum, Bochum, Germany
Dominik.Hartmann@rub.de

Abstract. We put forth a new framework for building pairing-based non-interactive zero-knowledge (NIZK) arguments for a wide class of algebraic languages, which are an extension of linear languages, containing disjunctions of linear languages and more. Our approach differs from the Groth-Sahai methodology, in that we rely on pairings to compile a Σ-protocol into a NIZK. Our framework enjoys a number of interesting features:

- conceptual simplicity, parameters derive from the Σ-protocol;
- proofs as short as resulting from the Fiat-Shamir heuristic applied to the underlying Σ-protocol;
- fully adaptive soundness and perfect zero-knowledge in the common random string model with a single random group element as CRS;
- yields simple and efficient two-round, public coin, publicly-verifiable perfect witness-indistinguishable (WI) arguments(ZAPs) in the plain model. To our knowledge, this is the *first* construction of two-rounds *statistical* witness-indistinguishable arguments from pairing assumptions.

Our proof system relies on a new (static, falsifiable) assumption over pairing groups which generalizes the standard kernel Diffie-Hellman assumption in a natural way and holds in the generic group model (GGM) and in the algebraic group model (AGM).

Replacing Groth-Sahai NIZKs with our new proof system allows to improve several important cryptographic primitives. In particular, we obtain the shortest tightly-secure structure-preserving signature scheme (which are a core component in anonymous credentials), the shortest tightly-secure quasi-adaptive NIZK with unbounded simulation soundness (which in turns implies the shortest tightly-mCCA-secure cryptosystem), and shorter ring signatures.

Keywords: Zero-knowledge arguments · Non-interactive zero-knowledge arguments · Satistical witness-indistinguishability · Pairing-based cryptography · Tight security · Structure-preserving signatures

© International Association for Cryptologic Research 2020
D. Micciancio and T. Ristenpart (Eds.): CRYPTO 2020, LNCS 12172, pp. 768–798, 2020.
https://doi.org/10.1007/978-3-030-56877-1_27

1   Introduction

Zero-knowledge proof systems, introduced in the seminal paper of Goldwasser, Micali, and Rackoff [38], allow a prover to convince a verifier of the truth of a statement, without revealing anything beyond this. Zero-knowledge proofs are among the most fundamental cryptographic primitives, and enjoy a tremendous number of applications. A particularly useful kind of zero-knowledge proof systems are *non-interactive zero-knowledge proofs* (NIZKs) [13], which consist of a single flow from the prover to the verifier. NIZKs have found a wide variety of applications in cryptography, ranging from low-interactions secure computation protocols to the design of advanced cryptographic primitives and protocols such as verifiable encryption, group signatures, structure-preserving signatures, anonymous credentials, KDM-CCA2 and identity-based CCA2 encryption, among many others.

Early feasibility results for NIZKs were established in the 90's, under standard assumptions such as factorization, or the existence of (doubly-enhanced) trapdoor permutations [29]. While these results demonstrated the possibility of building NIZKs under standard assumption for all NP languages (in the common reference string model), they were typically built upon a reduction to an NP-complete language such as graph hamiltonicity, and were concretely inefficient.

The Fiat-Shamir (FS) transform [30], which relies on a hash function to compile an interactive ZK proof into a NIZK, provides a practical alternative to the above, leading to efficient NIZK arguments; however, it only offers heuristic security guarantees and any security proof for the FS transform must overcome several barriers [7,37][1]. Hence, for two decades after their introduction, essentially two types of NIZKs coexisted: inefficient NIZKs provably secure in the standard (common reference string) model, and heuristically secure practical NIZKs.

1.1   Pairing-Based NIZKs

With the advent of pairing-based cryptography, this somewhat unsatisfying situation changed. Starting with the celebrated work of Groth and Sahai [44], a variety of pairing-based NIZK proof systems have been introduced. These proof systems have in common that they handle directly a large class of languages over abelian groups, avoiding the need for expensive reductions to NP-complete problems. Due to its practical significance, the Groth-Sahai proof system (and its follow-ups) initiated a wide variety of cryptographic applications. As of today, all known practically efficient (publicly verifiable) NIZKs in the standard model rely on pairing-based cryptography. Existing pairing-based NIZK proof systems can be divided in two categories:

NIZKs Based on the Groth-Sahai (GS) Methodology. These NIZKs directly rely on the techniques developed in [44], and enhance the seminal

---

[1] Alternatively, the Fiat-Shamir transform offers provable security in the random oracle model; we note that there have been recent developments regarding instantiating Fiat-Shamir in the standard model under strong assumptions [16,55].

construction in various ways [12,25,27,66]. Unfortunately, in spite of these optimizations, Groth-Sahai proofs remain often unsatisfyingly inefficient, and are in particular notably less efficient than (heuristic) NIZKs obtained with the Fiat-Shamir transform. Furthermore, the design and analysis of a suitable NIZK, taking into account all existing optimizations, is often a tedious and error-prone task.

Quasi-Adaptive NIZKs for Linear Languages. In light of the above, an alternative line of research, starting with the work of [51] and culminating with [57], has investigated a different strategy for building pairing-based NIZKs. Roughly, the approach relies on a hash proof system [22] (HPS) for the target language over some abelian group $\mathbb{G}_1$, which can be seen as a kind of designated-verifier NIZK proof, and makes it publicly verifiable by embedding the secret hashing key in the group $\mathbb{G}_2$. Verifying the proof is done with the help of a pairing operation between $\mathbb{G}_1$ and $\mathbb{G}_2$. The HPS-based approach leads to conceptually simple and very efficient proofs (e.g. a membership proof for the DDH language can be made as short as a single group element in [57]). However, this efficiency comes with strong limitations: this approach can only handle linear languages, and only provides a quasi-adaptive type of soundness, where the common reference string is allowed to depend on the language.

1.2 Our Contribution

In this work, we introduce a new approach for building efficient, pairing-based non-interactive zero-knowledge arguments for a large class of languages, where soundness relies on a new (but plausible, static, and falsifiable) assumption, which extends the kernel Diffie-Hellman assumption [63] in a natural way. Our approach is very simple and natural; yet it has to our knowledge never been investigated. It leads to proofs which are shorter and conceptually much simpler than proofs obtained with the GS methodology. At the same time and unlike the HPS-based methodology, our proof system is not limited to linear languages, but handles a more general class of *witness samplable* languages where, roughly, the language parameters can be sampled together with a trapdoor which can be used to decide membership in the language (in particular, this captures the important case of disjunctions of linear languages, from which one can build linear-size NIZKs for circuit satisfiability using the GOS methodology [42]) and achieves fully adaptive soundness with very short common random strings.

Statistical ZAPs and NIWIs. An additional benefit of our NIZK proof system is that it works in the common *random* string model, where the CRS is just a random bit string. Furthermore, we show that if we let the verifier pick the CRS himself, our proof system still satisfies *statistical witness-indistinguishability*. Therefore, we obtain the shortest two-round publicly-verifiable witness-indistinguishable argument system in the plain model (i.e., a ZAP [26]) for witness-samplable algebraic languages. Our ZAPs can be turned into fully non-interactive witness-indistinguishable arguments in the plain model, using the derandomization method of [8]. We emphasize that the ZAPs obtained with our method are *statistically* witness-indistinguishable; to our knowledge, our construction is the first pairing-based statistical ZAP (it is in addition publicly verifiable, and public coin). Existing constructions of statistical ZAPs rely on the quasipolynomial hardness of LWE [6, 49], or rely on subexponential variants of standard assumptions and are not public coin [54]. While our result comes at the cost of basing soundness on a new pairing-based assumption, we believe that it represents a significant contribution to the important and long standing open question of building statistical ZAPs.

High Level Overview. At a high level, our approach consists in compiling a three-move public coin zero-knowledge protocol (so called Σ-protocol) with linear answers over an abelian group $\mathbb{G}_1$ into a non-interactive zero-knowledge argument, by embedding the challenge e into a group $\mathbb{G}_2$ such that there is an asymmetric pairing between $\mathbb{G}_1 \times \mathbb{G}_2$ and a target group $\mathbb{G}_T$, and adding the embedded challenge to the common reference string. Intuitively, correctness is preserved because the pairing can be used to perform the verification procedure, zero-knowledge is perfect, and soundness follows from the fact that a cheating adversary must compute a value in $\mathbb{G}_1$ which has a non-trivial relation to e, which is conjectured to be intractable. An important part of our work is devoted to the analysis of the soundness property of our proof system, and the underlying assumption.

In addition to the efficiency improvements it provides, an important conceptual advantage of our approach over the Groth-Sahai methodology is that it gives a very simple and natural way to construct NIZKs. The construction of optimized Groth-Sahai proofs is generally cumbersome, and a significant amount of expertise is often required for the design of the best-possible GS proof in a given context. In contrast, Σ-protocols are typically straightforward to construct, and require considerably less expertise to optimize. Building a NIZK with our approach requires only to design an algebraic Σ-protocol for the target language distribution, and compiling it into a NIZK (which essentially amounts to adding a single group element to the CRS). Computation, communication and the underlying assumption can be obtained in a straightforward way from the parameters of the underlying Σ-protocol. We believe that this conceptual simplicity is an important feature toward making the use of pairing-based NIZKs accessible to a wider spectrum of researchers and industrials.

1.3 Technical Overview

The starting point of our approach is a (somewhat folklore) Σ-protocol for algebraic languages [10, 17]. A Σ-protocol is a three-move public-coin honest-verifier zero-knowledge proof system (i.e., the message of the verifier is a random string, and the zero-knowledge property holds against verifiers that do not deviate from the specifications of the protocol). In the following, we use the implicit notations introduced in [28]: given a group $\mathbb{G}$ in additive form, we fix a generator g and write $[x]$ for $x \cdot g$. Most, if not all, algebraic languages over abelian groups considered in the literature can be written as

$\mathcal{L}_{\mathbf{M},\Theta} := \{\mathbf{x} \in \mathbb{G}^l | \exists \mathbf{w} \in \mathbb{Z}_p^t : \mathbf{M}(\mathbf{x}) \cdot \mathbf{w} = \Theta(\mathbf{x})\}$, where $\mathbf{M} : \mathbb{G}^l \mapsto \mathbb{G}^{n \times t}$ and $\Theta : \mathbb{G}^l \mapsto \mathbb{G}^n$ are linear maps sampled according to a distribution $\mathcal{D}_{par}$. This captures all algebraic languages defined by systems of polynomial equations between secret exponents. Most Σ-protocols for algebraic languages can then be seen as particular instantiations of the generic Σ-protocol represented on Fig. 1.

To compile this Σ-protocol into a NIZK, we assume that all computations take place in a group $\mathbb{G}_1$, such that there exists another group $\mathbb{G}_2$ together with an asymmetric pairing $\bullet : \mathbb{G}_1 \times \mathbb{G}_2 \mapsto \mathbb{G}_T$. We use the standard brackets with subscripts $[\cdot]_1, [\cdot]_2, [\cdot]_T$ to extend the implicit notation to the three groups $\mathbb{G}_1, \mathbb{G}_2, \mathbb{G}_T$. The setup algorithm of our proof system picks a random $e \in \mathbb{Z}_p$ and sets the common reference string to $[e]_2$. The prover computes $[\mathbf{a}]_1$ as in the Σ-protocol, and obtains the value $\mathbf{d}$ embedded in $\mathbb{G}_2$ by computing $[\mathbf{d}]_2 := \mathbf{w} \cdot [e]_2 + \mathbf{r} \cdot [1]_2$. Checking the verification equation can still be done, with the help of the pairing: the verifier checks that $[\mathbf{M}(\mathbf{x})]_1 \bullet [\mathbf{d}]_2 \overset{?}{=} [\Theta(\mathbf{x})]_1 \bullet [e]_2 + [\mathbf{a}]_1 \bullet [1]_2$. While this construction is relatively simple, the bulk of our technical contribution is the detailed analysis of the security guarantees it provides.

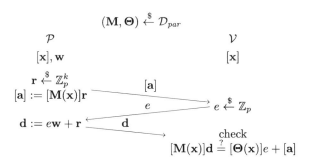

Fig. 1. Generic Σ-protocol for algebraic languages $\mathcal{L}_{\mathbf{M},\Theta}$ from a distribution $\mathcal{D}_{par}$

The Extended-Kernel Matrix Diffie-Hellman Assumption. To prove the soundness of our NIZK, we introduce a new family of assumptions, which we call the *extended-kernel Matrix Diffie-Hellman* assumption (extKerMDH). The regular KerMDH assumption with respect to a distribution Dist over an asymmetric pairing group states that, given a matrix $[\mathbf{A}]_2$ sampled from Dist, it is infeasible to find a vector $[\mathbf{v}]_1$ where $\mathbf{v}$ is in the kernel of $\mathbf{A}$. It is a natural computational analogue of the decisional Matrix Diffie-Hellman assumption (which it implies), and was introduced in [63]. Our new assumption further generalizes the KerMDH assumption as follows: it states that it should be infeasible, given $[\mathbf{A}]_2$, to find another matrix $[\mathbf{A}']_2$ and a matrix $[\mathbf{B}]_1$ such that $\mathbf{B}$ spans the entire kernel of $\mathbf{A}||\mathbf{A}'$. Intuitively, the adversary is allowed to extend the matrix $[\mathbf{A}]_2$, which facilitates finding $\mathbb{G}_1$-vectors in its kernel; but each time the adversary extends $\mathbf{A}$ by one column, he must provide an additional $\mathbb{G}_1$-vector (linearly independent of the previous vectors) in the kernel of the extended matrix.

The extKerMDH assumption is a static, non-interactive assumption, which generalizes the KerMDH assumption in a natural way. To provide further evidence for the security of our assumption, we prove that it is unconditionally secure in the generic group model [70] (GGM), and that it reduces to the discrete logarithm assumption in the algebraic group model [31] (AGM). On the downside, the extKerMDH assumption might not in general be a falsifiable assumption [36,64]: it states that it is infeasible to output $[\mathbf{A}']_2$ and a *basis* $[\mathbf{B}]_1$ of the kernel of $\mathbf{A}||\mathbf{A}'$, but verifying whether the $\mathbb{G}_1$-matrix $[\mathbf{B}]_1$ is full rank is not efficiently feasible in general (indeed, the hardness of deciding whether a matrix given in a group $\mathbb{G}$ is full rank is exactly the decisional matrix Diffie-Hellman assumption). However, we show that for all *witness-sampleable languages*, there is a language trapdoor which does allow to efficiently check whether $\mathbf{B}$ is full rank (intuitively, the trapdoor allows to put $[\mathbf{B}]_1$ in triangular form, from which the rank can be easily checked), turning our new assumption into a falsifiable assumption.

Witness Samplable Languages. We give an intuition of the class of algebraic languages which satisfy our requirements. Intuitively, an algebraic language $\mathcal{L}$ admits a NIZK (using our compiler) where soundness reduces to a falsifiable assumption if the parameters of $\mathcal{L}$ can be sampled together with a trapdoor which allows to efficiently check language membership. For example, this captures the DDH language $\mathcal{L}_{\mathsf{DDH}}$: given language parameters $([1]_1, [s]_1)$, the words in $\mathcal{L}_{\mathsf{DDH}}$ are of the form $([x]_1, [x \cdot s]_1)$, and the trapdoor s allows to verify that a word (c_1, c_2) belongs to $\mathcal{L}_{\mathsf{DDH}}$ by checking whether $s \cdot c_1 - c_2 = [0]_1$. Witness samplable languages need not be linear languages: for example, the language of ElGamal encryptions (in the exponent) of a plaintext $m \in \{0, 1\}$ is not a linear language, yet the ElGamal secret key allows to efficiently check wether a pair of group elements indeed encrypts a bit, hence it is also captured by our methods. More generally, the conjunctions and disjunctions of witness samplable languages are still witness samplable. On the other hand, some natural algebraic languages are not witness-samplable; for example, the language of triples of the form $([1]_1, [x]_1, [x^2]_1)$ does not seem to be witness samplable (since it is not clear how one could generate a word-independent trapdoor allowing to check membership to this language).

Witness-sampleable languages were originally introduced in [51], but were restricted to linear languages. We extend this notion of witness-sampleability to arbitrary algebraic languages, and will show that many languages of interest are actually witness sampleable. For these languages, we therefore obtain shorter NIZKs under a natural, static, *falsifiable* assumption. We note that for the case of linear languages (such as the language of DDH tuple), our generalized notion of witness-samplability is the same as the notion of [51], and applying our compiler to witness-samplable linear languages leads to NIZKs which are actually secure under the standard KerMDH assumption (while still being shorter than GS proofs).

1.4   Applications

Our new NIZKs have several attractive features and can be used to improve the efficiency of many NIZK-based primitives. We provide a non-exhaustive list of some applications below. All applications we describe rely on witness-sampleable algebraic languages, making the underlying extKerMDH assumption falsifiable.

Adaptive NIZKs for Linear Languages. We achieve the shortest and most efficient adaptive NIZKs for (witness-sampleable) linear languages, with perfect zero-knowledge and computational soundness under the kernel Diffie-Hellman assumption: a Groth-Sahai proof for the language of DDH tuples consists of four group elements, while our NIZK requires only three group elements, and considerably less pairings. We note that in the quasi-adaptive setting, where the common reference string is allowed to depend on the language, the work of [57] gives NIZKs with two group elements (for non witness-sampleable languages), or even a single group element (for witness-sampleable languages). Therefore, our work can be seen as filling a remaining gap, providing a more complete picture of the size of NIZKs for linear languages, depending on whether we allow quasi-adaptive soundness, and rely on witness-sampleability. In addition to providing a stronger soundness guarantee, full adaptivity also leads to increased efficiency when many proofs are run in some high level application: it allows to rely on a single CRS (which, in our case, consists of a *single* group element), even when executing many linear subspace proofs for different languages. In contrast, QA-NIZKs have a language-dependent CRS; hence, a different CRS must be generated for each language. The comparison is summarised in Table 1.

Table 1. Comparison of existing NIZKs for the DDH language (linear languages described by an $n \times t$ matrix). CRS/Proof size denotes the number of group elements in the common reference string/a proof. Pairings denotes the number of pairing operations in proof verification. "WS" indicates whether the proof system is restricted to witness sampleable languages.

Scheme	Assumption	CRS	Proof size	Pairings	WS	Fully Adaptive
GS [44]	SXDH	4	$4(n+2t)$	$24(n(4t+8))$	✗	✓
KW [57]	KerMDH	$6(n+2t+2)$	$2(2)$	$3(n+1)$	✗	✗
KW [57]	KerMDH	$4(n+t+1)$	$1(1)$	$2(n)$	✓	✗
Ours	KerMDH	1	$3(n+t)$	$6(n+nt+2)$	✓	✓

Adaptive NIZKs for Disjunctions. Since our NIZKs are built by compiling a Σ-protocol, they are compatible with the OR-trick of [21]. The OR-trick provides a general method to construct Σ-protocols of partial satisfiability, such as "k of those n words belong to the language $\mathcal{L}$", from a Σ-protocol for proving membership to $\mathcal{L}$. Building upon this observation, we obtain shorter NIZKs for disjunctions of statements. The state-of-the-art NIZK for partial satisfiability of equations is the one in [66]. For the important case of the disjunction between two (resp. n) DDH languages, it gives proofs of size 10 group elements under the SXDH assumption (resp. $4n + 2$ group elements for 1-out-of-n proofs). For the same language, our approach leads to proofs of size 7 (resp. $3n + 1$ group elements for 1-out-of-n proofs). This is detailed in Table 2. NIZKs for disjunctions of languages are a core component in several applications; we outline some applications below.

Table 2. Comparison of existing NIZKs for the OR of two DDH languages (two linear languages described by $n_i \times t_i$ matrices for $i \in \{1, 2\}$). CRS denotes the number of group elements in the common reference string. "WS" indicates whether the proof system deals only with witness sampleable languages. Note that our scheme can in fact handle non-witness sampleable languages; however, this comes at the cost of making the underlying extKerMDH assumption non-falsifiable.

Scheme	Assumption	CRS	Proof size	Pairings	WS
[43,66]	SXDH	4	$10(\sum_{i=1}^{2} n_i + 2t_i + 2)$	$24(\sum_{i=1}^{2} 4n_i + 2n_i t_i)$	✗
Ours	extKerMDH	1	$7(\sum_{i=1}^{2} n_i + t_i + 1)$	$12(\sum_{i=1}^{2} n_i + n_i t_i + 4)$	✓

Ring Signatures. Ring signatures [67] allow a signer to anonymously sign on behalf of an ad-hoc group to which it belongs. They are a core component in some e-voting and e-cash schemes [71] and anonymous cryptocurrencies such as Monero [65]. A $O(\sqrt{N})$-size proof of membership in a ring of size N was designed by Chandran, Groth and Sahai [18] and subsequently improved in [66]; it relies at its core on a NIZK for $(\ell - 1)$-out-of-ℓ disjunction of DDH languages. Using our improved NIZK for disjunction, we reduce the ring signature size by $\sqrt{N} - 1$ group elements, for rings of size N.

We observe that a $O(\log N)$-size ring signature scheme was recently introduced in [5]. The authors do not provide a concrete efficiency analysis and use generic tools which would likely render concrete instantiations inefficient for reasonable group sizes. We note, though, that our proof system can be used to instantiate the non-interactive witness indistinguishable proof system they rely upon, and would likely lead to efficiency improvements comparable to what we get over the ring signature of [66], for concrete instantiations of their building blocks.

Tightly-Secure QA-NIZKs with Unbounded Simulation Soundness. In several applications in cryptography, the constructions require a NIZK for linear languages which satisfies a stronger soundness guarantee: soundness should hold even if the adversary is allowed to see an arbitrary number of simulated proofs. This stronger notion is known as *unbounded simulation-soundness*. The recent work of [3] introduced the first unbounded simulation-sound quasi-adaptive NIZK (USS-QA-NIZK) which achieves simultaneously compact CRS, compact proof size, and a tight security reduction. At the core of their construction is the disjunction NIZK of [66], which has 10 group elements; this accounts for most of the size of their USS-QA-NIZK, which has 14 group elements. By replacing the disjunction proof by our new NIZK, we reduce the size of their USS-QA-NIZK to only 11 group elements, and also reduce the CRS size, at the cost of requiring our new assumption. We provide a comparison to existing USS-QA-NIZKs for linear languages on Table 3. In particular, our result allows to further reduce the size of the tightly-secure IND-mCCA-secure public-key encryption scheme of [4] (IND-mCCA refers to indistinguishability against chosen ciphertext attacks in the multi-user, multi-challenge setting), with a security reduction independent of the number of decryption-oracle requests of the CCA2 adversary, from 17 group elements to 14 group elements.

Table 3. Comparison of existing unbounded simulation-sound NIZKs for linear languages. The notation (x_1, x_2) denotes x_1 elements in $\mathbb{G}_1$ and x_2 elements in $\mathbb{G}_2$. Q denotes the number of simulation queries, λ is the security parameter. (n, t) are the parameters of the underlying linear language, defined by a matrix $\mathbf{M} \in \mathbb{Z}_p^{n \times t}$, with $n > t$.

	CRS Size	Proof Size	Pairings	Sec. Loss	Assumption
[58]	$2n + 3(t + \lambda) + 10$	20	$2n + 30$	$O(Q)$	DLIN
[57]	$(2t + 6, n + 6)$	$(4, 0)$	$t(n + t + 2)$	$O(Q)$	SXDH
[59]	$2n + 3t + 24\lambda + 55$	42	$2n + 10$	$3\lambda + 7$	DLIN
[33]	$(t + 6\lambda + 1, n + 2)$	$(3, 0)$	$n + 4$	$4\lambda + 1$	SXDH
[4]	$(3t + 14, n + 12)$	$(n + 16, 2t + 5)$	$7n + 5t + 3nt + 121$	$36 \log(Q)$	SXDH
[3]	$(4t + 4, 2n + 8)$	$(8, 6)$	$n + 30$	$6 \log(Q)$	SXDH
Ours	$(4t + 8, 2n + 3)$	$(8, 3)$	$n + 18$	$6 \log Q$	SXDH, extKerMDH

Tightly-Secure Structure-Preserving Signatures. The notion of structure-preserving cryptography gives a paradigm for building modular protocols designed to be naturally expressed as systems of pairing-product equations, which makes them compatible with the Groth-Sahai methodology. Structure-Preserving Signatures (SPS) are one of the most fundamental primitives in structure-preserving cryptography. They are the core component in a variety of important applications, such as anonymous credentials (see e.g. [9,14,15,19, 23,32,46,61], to name just a few), mixnets and voting systems [41], or simulation-sound NIZKs [40,59].

A cryptographic scheme is tightly secure if its security loss is independent of the number of users of the scheme. A tight security reduction gives guarantees that do not degrade with the size of the setting in which the system is used. Tight security is especially important in structure-preserving cryptography, where many components rely on the same cyclic group: if a non-tightly-secure scheme is used and the number of users increases, this might require increasing the group size to compensate for the security loss, degrading the performance of all other schemes relying on the same cyclic group. There has been a long sequence of works that seeked to obtain increasingly shorter structure preserving signatures with tight security reductions; we summarize them in Table 4.

The work of [34] provides a tightly-secure SPS with 14 group elements, which combines an algebraic MAC scheme with the proof of [66] for the disjunction of two DDH languages. The latter has proof size of 10 group elements. Replacing the OR-NIZK in their work by the shorter proof which we introduce leads to a tightly-secure SPS with 11 group elements, matching the size of the best known tightly-secure SPS [3]. The work of [3] improves over [34] by replacing the underlying OR-NIZK by a *designated-prover* OR-NIZK, which suffices in this context. They show that in the designated-prover setting, the size of the OR-NIZK can be reduced to 7 group elements. We observe that their technique is actually compatible with our improved OR-NIZK, and leads to a quasi-adaptive designated-prover OR-NIZK with only 5 group elements (which can be of independent interest). Overall, this leads to a tightly-secure SPS with only 9 group elements under (a falsifiable flavor of) the extKerMDH assumption, significantly improving over the efficiency of the state-of-the-art. Considering a setting with security parameter $\lambda = 80$, a large possible number of signing queries $Q = 2^{30}$, and choosing a group $\mathbb{G}$ of order $p \approx 2^{2(\lambda + \log L)}$ to account for the security loss of $L(Q)$ (assuming that the best attack on the group is the generic $\sqrt{p}$-time attack), our scheme is actually computationally more efficient than the state-of-the-art non-tightly-secure SPS of [52], and produces signatures which are only slightly larger: 241 Bytes versus 201 Bytes.

Table 4. Comparison of existing structure-preserving signatures for message space $\mathbb{G}_1^n$, in their most efficient variant. For [4], n and t are defined as in Table 3. The notation (x_1, x_2) denotes x_1 elements in $\mathbb{G}_1$ and x_2 elements in $\mathbb{G}_2$. Q denotes the number of signing queries, λ is the security parameter. In the tree-based scheme of [47], ℓ denotes the depth of the tree (which limits the number of signing queries to 2^ℓ).

Scheme	Sig. Size	PK Size	Pairings	Sec. Loss	Assumption
[47]	$10\ell + 6$	13	$81l + 1$	$O(1)$	DLIN
[1]	$(7, 4)$	$(5, n + 12)$	16	Q	SXDH, XDLIN
[60]	$(10, 1)$	$(16, 2n + 5)$	$17 + 2n$	$O(Q)$	SXDH, XDLINX
[56]	$(6, 1)$	$(0, n + 6)$	$3n + 4$	$2Q^2$	SXDH
[52]	$(5, 1)$	$(0, n + 6)$	$n + 3$	$Q \log Q$	SXDH
[2]	$(13, 12)$	$(18, n + 11)$	$n + 16$	80λ	SXDH
[50]	$(11, 6)$	$(7, n + 16)$	$n + 22$	116λ	SXDH
[34]	$(8, 6)$	$(2, n + 9)$	$n + 11$	$6 \log Q$	SXDH
[4]	$(6, 6)$	$(2, n + 5)$	$7n + 5t + 3nt + 121$	$36 \log Q$	SXDH
[3]	$(7, 4)$	$(2, n + 11)$	$n + 31$	$6 \log Q$	SXDH
Ours	$(7, 2)$	$(7, n + 8)$	$n + 23$	$6 \log Q$	SXDH, extKerMDH

1.5 Related Work

We already mentioned related works on NIZKs and SPS. Our work was partly inspired by a line of work initiated in [17,24], which compiles Σ-protocols into *designated-verifier* NIZKs, by encrypting the challenge with a malleable cryptosystem, and putting the ciphertext in the CRS. The idea of hiding the challenge of an interactive protocol in a CRS was also used in different contexts; for example, it bears similarity with methods used in [35,53].

1.6 Organization

In Sect. 2, we recall necessary preliminaries. Section 3 introduces our new NIZK argument system. Section 4 is devoted to the security analysis of the new proof system; to this end, it introduces the notion of algebraic witness sampleability and the extKerMDH assumption. Section 5 extends our construction to disjunctions of algebraic languages. We outline several applications of our results in Sect. 6. The full version of this paper [20] introduces some missing preliminaries for completeness, together with examples to illustrate some of the notions we introduce, and includes a proof of security of our new assumption in the generic group model and in the algebraic group model. It also describes a variant of our compiler which yields (dual-mode) NIZK *proofs* based on the SXDH assumption for arbitrary algebraic languages, shows how disjunctions of languages are in fact directly captured by the framework of algebraic languages without going through the OR-trick of [21], and gives an application of our compiler to the designated-prover QA-NIZK from [3].

2 Preliminaries

Let $\mathbb{P}$ denote the set of all primes and $\lambda \in \mathbb{N}$ denote the security parameter. A probabilistic polynomial time algorithm (PPT, also denoted *efficient* algorithm) runs in time polynomial in the (implicit) security parameter λ. A function f is *negligible* if for any positive polynomial p there exists a bound $B > 0$ such that, for any integer $k \geq B$, $|f(k)| \leq 1/|p(k)|$. We will write $f(\lambda) \approx 0$ to indicate that f is a negligible function of λ; we also write $f(\lambda) \approx g(\lambda)$ for $|f(\lambda) - g(\lambda)| \approx 0$. For sampling an element according to a distribution or selecting it uniformly random from a (finite) set, we write $p \xleftarrow{\$} S$. We use the same notation for the output of a probabilistic algorithm. For output y of a deterministic algorithm A on input x, we will also use $y := A(x)$. Matrices will always be bold, upper-case letters and vectors will be bold, lower-case letters. For a matrix $\mathbf{A}$ let $\mathrm{span}(\mathbf{A}) := \{\mathbf{x}|\exists \mathbf{r} : \mathbf{x} = \mathbf{Ar}\}$ and $ker(\mathbf{A}) := \{\mathbf{x}|\mathbf{x}^T\mathbf{A} = 0\}$ the *left* kernel of $\mathbf{A}$. All interactive protocols will be performed between a prover $\mathcal{P}$ and a verifier $\mathcal{V}$. If one party can deviate from the protocol, we will denote this by $\hat{\mathcal{P}}$ and $\hat{\mathcal{V}}$ respectively. Additionally, a simulator will be called $\mathcal{S}$. For language parameters ρ sampled from a language distribution $\mathcal{D}$, let $\mathcal{L}_\rho$ denote the language defined by ρ and let R_ρ denote its witness relation. Finally, for a distribution $\mathcal{D}$, we write $\mathsf{Supp}(\mathcal{D})$ for the support of the distribution.

2.1   Groups and Pairings

Throughout this work, let $p \in \mathbb{P}$ denote a prime with bit length polynomial in the security parameter λ. Let $\mathbb{G}_1$, $\mathbb{G}_2$, $\mathbb{G}_T$ be finite groups of prime order p with generators g_1, g_2 respectively and $e : \mathbb{G}_1 \times \mathbb{G}_2 \to \mathbb{G}_T$ a bilinear map. We set $g_T := e(g_1, g_2)$, which is a generator of $\mathbb{G}_T$. $\mathcal{PG} = (p, \mathbb{G}_1, \mathbb{G}_2, \mathbb{G}_T, g_1, g_2, e)$ is called a pairing group setting, if the following properties hold: $e(g_1, g_2) \neq 0_T$ (non-degenerate); $e(ag_1, bg_2) = ab \cdot e(g_1, g_2)$ (bilinearity); and e is efficiently computable. Furthermore, we require the existence of a probabilistic algorithm $PGGen$, which on input 1^λ generates pairing parameters as above with a group order close to 2^λ, i.e. $\mathcal{PG} \xleftarrow{\$} PGGen(1^\lambda)$.

Throughout this work, we will write all groups in implicit notation, i.e. for an additive pairing group setting $\mathcal{PG} = (p, \mathbb{G}_1, \mathbb{G}_2, \mathbb{G}_T, g_1, g_2, e)$, we write $[1]_i := g_i$ and $[x]_i := x \cdot g_i$ for all $x \in \mathbb{Z}_p$ and $i \in \{1, 2, T\}$. If the group is clear from context, we will omit the index. We write $[x]_1 \bullet [y]_2 := e([x]_1, [y]_2) = [xy]_T$ for pairings. The implicit notation also extends to matrices and vectors. For $\mathbf{A} \in \mathbb{Z}_p^{n \times t}$, $\mathbf{A} = (a_{ij})$, let $[\mathbf{A}]_k = ([a_{ij}]_k) \in \mathbb{G}_k^{n \times t}$ for $k \in \{1, 2, T\}$ and we also extend the pairing notation from above to $[\mathbf{A}]_1 \bullet [\mathbf{B}]_2 := e([\mathbf{A}]_1, [\mathbf{B}]_2) = [\mathbf{AB}]_T$ for matrices $\mathbf{A} \in \mathbb{Z}_p^{n \times t}, \mathbf{B} \in \mathbb{Z}_p^{t \times m}$. Furthermore, we extend the implicit notation to linear (multivariate) polynomials. Let $\mathcal{P}_l := \{[a_0] + \sum_{i=0}^{l} a_i X_i | a_i \in \mathbb{Z}_p$ for $i \in \{0, \dots, l\}\} \subset \mathbb{G}[\mathbf{x} = (X_1, \dots, X_l)]$ be the set of linear multivariate polynomials over $\mathbb{G}$ in l variables. For $f \in \mathcal{P}_l$ and $\mathbf{y} = (y_1, \dots, y_l) \in \mathbb{Z}_p^l$, we define the evaluation of f in $\mathbf{y}$ as applying the group operation in the exponent, i.e.

$$f([\mathbf{y}]) := f(\mathbf{y}) = [a_0] + \sum_{i=1}^{l} a_i [y_i] = [a_0] + \sum_{i=0}^{l} [a_i y_i]$$

This allows us (in a slight abuse of notation) to use polynomials from $\mathcal{P}_l$ inside of matrices and equations in implicit notation without changing variable names, i.e. $[a_0] X_0 = [a_0 X_0]$, since the evaluation of the polynomial is defined exactly that way. For a matrix $\mathbf{A} = (a_{i,j}) \in \mathcal{P}_l^{n \times t}$, the evaluation of the matrix (or vector) over $\mathcal{P}_l$ in a vector $\mathbf{y} \in \mathbb{G}^l$ denotes the evaluation of all entries in the given vector, i.e. $\mathbf{A}(\mathbf{y}) := (a_{i,j}(\mathbf{y})) \in \mathbb{G}^{n \times t}$.

The assumptions used in this work are parametrised over matrix distributions. These are defined as follows.

Definition 1 (Matrix Distribution). *Let $k, l \in \mathbb{N}$ with $k < l$. We call $\mathcal{D}_{k,l}$ a matrix distribution, if it outputs matrices over $\mathbb{G}^{l \times k}$ of full rank k in polynomial time. If $l = k + 1$, we write $\mathcal{D}_k$ instead. Without loss of generality, we assume that the first k rows of a matrix $\mathbf{A} \in \mathsf{Supp}(\mathcal{D}_{k,l})$ form an invertible matrix.*

An example for a matrix distribution for which the KerMDH and MDDH assumptions hold in the AGM is the following:

$$
\mathcal{L}_k : \mathbf{M} = \begin{bmatrix}
1 & 1 & 1 & \cdots & 1 \\
e_1 & 0 & 0 & \cdots & 0 \\
0 & e_2 & 0 & & 0 \\
0 & 0 & e_3 & \ddots & 0 \\
\vdots & & \ddots & \ddots & \vdots \\
0 & \cdots & & 0 & e_k
\end{bmatrix}
$$

For $k = 1$, this distribution generates Diffie-Hellman matrices and for $k \geq 2$ these matrices correspond to the k-Lin assumption [48]. We will only consider the distribution $\mathcal{L}_k$ in this work as it is sufficient for all of our applications.

2.2 Σ-Protocols

A Σ-protocol for an NP language $L = \{x : \exists w, |w| = \mathsf{poly}(|x|) \wedge (x, w) \in R\}$ (where R is a polytime checkable relation) is a public-coin, three-move interactive proof between a prover $\mathcal{P}$ with witness w and a verifier $\mathcal{V}$, where the prover sends an initial message $a = P_1(x, w)$, the verifier responds with a random $e \xleftarrow{\$} \{0,1\}^\lambda$ and the prover concludes with a message $d = P_2(x, w, a, e)$. Lastly, the verifier outputs 1, if it accepts and 0 otherwise.

Three properties are required for a Σ-protocol: completeness, special soundness and special honest-verifier zero-knowledge.

Definition 2 (Completeness). *A three-move protocol Π_R for a relation R with prover $\mathcal{P}$ and verifier $\mathcal{V}$ is complete, if*

$$
Pr\left[\mathsf{out}(V(x, a, e, d)) = 1 \,\middle|\, \begin{array}{l} (x, w) \in R, a \xleftarrow{\$} P_1(x, w), \\ e \xleftarrow{\$} \{0,1\}^\lambda, d \xleftarrow{\$} P_2(x, w, a, e) \end{array}\right] = 1
$$

Definition 3 (Special soundness). *A three-move protocol Π_R for a relation R has the* special soundness *property, if a polynomial time algorithm E exists, which for a statement x and two accepting transcripts $(a, e, d), (a, e', d')$ of Π_R with $e \neq e'$ outputs a witness w, s.t. $(x, w) \in R$ with overwhelming probability.*

Definition 4 (Special honest-verifier zero-knowledge). *A three-move protocol Π_R for a relation R is* special honest-verifier zero-knowledge, *if there exists a polynomial-time simulator $\mathcal{S}$ such that the distributions of $\mathcal{S}(x, e)$ and the transcript of an honest protocol execution between $\mathcal{P}$ and $\mathcal{V}$ are identical for $(x, w) \in R, e \in \{0,1\}^\lambda$.*

2.3   Non-interactive Zero-Knowledge Arguments

An adaptive NIZK Π for a family of language distribution $\{\mathcal{D}_{par}\}_{par}$ consists of four probabilistic algorithms:

- CRSGen(1^λ). On input 1^λ generates public parameters *par* (such as group parameters), a CRS and a trapdoor $\mathcal{T}$. For simplicity of notation, we assume that any group parameters are implicitly included in the CRS.
- Prove(CRS, ρ, x, w). On input of a CRS, a language description $\rho \in \mathcal{D}_{par}$ and a statement x with witness w, outputs a proof π for $x \in \mathcal{L}_\rho$.
- Verify(CRS, ρ, x, π). On input of a CRS, a language description $\rho \in \mathcal{D}_{par}$, a statement and a proof, accepts or rejects the proof.
- SimProve(CRS, $\mathcal{T}, \rho, x$). Given a CRS, the trapdoor $\mathcal{T}$, a language description $\rho \in \mathcal{D}_{par}$ and a statement x, outputs a simulated proof for the statement $x \in \mathcal{L}_\rho$.

Note that the CRS does not depend on the language distribution or language parameters, i.e. we define fully adaptive NIZKs for language distributions.

The following properties need to hold for a NIZK argument (see e.g. [44]).

Definition 5 (Perfect Completeness:). *A proof system Π for a family of language distributions $\{\mathcal{D}_{par}\}_{par}$ is perfectly complete, if*

$$
Pr\left[\text{Verify}(\text{CRS}, \rho, x, \pi) = 1 \,\middle|\,
\begin{array}{l}
(par, \text{CRS}, \mathcal{T}) \xleftarrow{\$} \text{CRSGen}(1^\lambda); \rho \in \text{Supp}(\mathcal{D}_{par}); \\
(x, w) \in R_\rho; \pi \xleftarrow{\$} \text{Prove}(\text{CRS}, \rho, x, w)
\end{array}\right] = 1
$$

A proof system is sound, if it is hard to find proofs of incorrect statements. This is captured in the following definition.

Definition 6 (Computational Soundness). *A NIZK proof system Π for a family of language distributions $\{\mathcal{D}_{par}\}_{par}$ is computationally sound, if for every efficient adversary $\mathcal{A}$*

$$
\Pr\left[
\begin{array}{c}
\text{Verify}(\text{CRS}, \rho, x, \pi) = 1 \\
\wedge x \notin \mathcal{L}_\rho
\end{array}
\,\middle|\,
\begin{array}{l}
(par, \text{CRS}, \mathcal{T}) \xleftarrow{\$} \text{CRSGen}(1^\lambda); \\
\rho \in \text{Supp}(\mathcal{D}_{par}); (\pi, x) \xleftarrow{\$} \mathcal{A}(\text{CRS}, \rho)
\end{array}
\right] \approx 0
$$

with the probability taken over CRSGen.

A proof system is zero knowledge, if it is impossible to distinguish between the output of SimProve and Prove. This is formalised as follows.

Definition 7 (Perfect Zero Knowledge). *A NIZK proof system Π for a family of language distributions $\{\mathcal{D}_{par}\}_{par}$ is called perfectly zero-knowledge, if for all λ, all $(par, \text{CRS}, \mathcal{T}) \in \text{Supp}(\text{CRSGen}(1^\lambda))$, all $\rho \in \text{Supp}(\mathcal{D}_{par})$ and all $(x, w) \in R_\rho$, the distributions*

$$\text{Prove}(\text{CRS}, \rho, x, w) \text{ and } \text{SimProve}(\text{CRS}, \mathcal{T}, \rho, x)$$

are identical.

We can relax the security of a NIZK argument to a Non-Interactive Witness Indistinguishable (NIWI) argument by replacing the zero-knowledge property with the following witness indistinguishability property. Note that unlike NIZKs, which can only exist in the CRS model, NIWIs are possible in the plain model.

Definition 8 (Statistical Witness Indistinguishability). *A proof system* $\Pi = (\mathsf{CRSGen}, \mathsf{Prove}, \mathsf{SimProve}, \mathsf{Verify})$ *for a family of language distributions* $\{\mathcal{D}_{par}\}_{par}$ *is* statistically witness indistinguishable, *if for every adversary* $\mathcal{A}$, *every* λ, *every* $(par, \mathsf{CRS}, \mathcal{T}) \in \mathsf{Supp}(\mathsf{CRSGen}(1^\lambda))$, *all* $\rho \in \mathsf{Supp}(\mathcal{D}_{par})$ *and all* $x \in \mathcal{L}_\rho$ *with witnesses* w_1, w_2, *we have*

$$|\Pr[\mathcal{A}(\mathsf{CRS}, \rho, x, \pi) = 1 | \pi \xleftarrow{\$} \mathsf{Prove}(\mathsf{CRS}, \rho, x, w_1)]$$
$$- \Pr[\mathcal{A}(\mathsf{CRS}, \rho, x, \pi) = 1 | \pi \xleftarrow{\$} \mathsf{Prove}(\mathsf{CRS}, \rho, x, w_2)]| \approx 0$$

The property adapts to interactive protocols in a natural way.

3   A Pairing-Based Compiler for NIZKs from Σ-Protocols

In this section, we will describe our new approach to pairing-based non-interactive zero-knowledge arguments. Our starting point is a natural Σ-protocol for algebraic languages over abelian groups, which was used (implicitly or explicitly) in previous works [11,17,45]. Before describing the protocol and our NIZK construction, we formally introduce algebraic languages.

3.1   Algebraic Languages

We focus on languages that can be described by a set of algebraic equations over an abelian group. More precisely, we will consider languages of the form $\{\mathbf{x} \in \mathbb{G}^l | \exists \mathbf{w} \in \mathbb{Z}_p^t : \mathbf{M}(\mathbf{x}) \cdot \mathbf{w} = \mathbf{\Theta}(\mathbf{x})\}$, where $\mathbf{M} : \mathbb{G}^l \mapsto \mathbb{G}^{n \times t}$ and $\mathbf{\Theta} : \mathbb{G}^l \mapsto \mathbb{G}^n$ are linear maps, which can be sampled efficiently according to a language distribution $\mathcal{D}_{par}$. These languages have been used previously in several works on zero-knowledge proofs and hash proof systems over abelian groups [11,17,45], and are quite expressive: they capture a wide variety of languages, including but not limited to, linear and polynomial relations between committed values and the plaintexts of ElGamal-style ciphertexts, or polynomial relations between exponents. We call these languages *algebraic languages*.

It will prove convenient in this work to view the linear maps $\mathbf{M}$ and $\mathbf{\Theta}$ as matrices and vectors over $\mathcal{P}_l$, where $\mathcal{P}_l$ is the set of linear multivariate polynomial in l variables, via the natural extension.

Definition 9 (Algebraic Languages). *Let* $t, l, n \in \mathbb{N}, n > t$ *and* $\mathcal{P}_l := \{[a_0] + \sum_{i=1}^l a_i X_i\} \subset \mathbb{G}[\mathbf{X} = (X_1, \dots, X_l)]$ *the set of linear multivariate polynomials of degree at most 1. Let* $\mathcal{D}_{par}$ *be a distribution that outputs pairs* $(\mathbf{M}, \mathbf{\Theta}) \in \mathcal{P}_l^{n \times t} \times \mathcal{P}_l^n$. *We define the algebraic language* $\mathcal{L}_{\mathbf{M}, \mathbf{\Theta}} \subset \mathbb{G}^n$:

$$\mathcal{L}_{\mathbf{M}, \mathbf{\Theta}} := \{\mathbf{x} \in \mathbb{G}^l | \exists \mathbf{w} \in \mathbb{Z}_p^t : \mathbf{M}(\mathbf{x}) \cdot \mathbf{w} = \mathbf{\Theta}(\mathbf{x})\}$$

where $\mathbf{M}(\mathbf{x})$ *(resp.* $\mathbf{\Theta}(\mathbf{x})$*) denotes the matrix(resp. vector) received by evaluating every entry of* $\mathbf{M}$*(resp.* $\mathbf{\Theta}$*) in the points of* $\mathbf{x}$.

Example: Linear Languages. Linear languages, capturing e.g. DDH relations, are obtained as a special case of algebraic languages by restricting $\mathbf{M}(\mathbf{x})$ to be a constant matrix, independent of $\mathbf{x}$ and Θ to being the identity. NIZKs for linear languages have been widely studied, see e.g. [51,57].

Definition 10 (Linear subspace languages). *Let $\mathcal{D}_{par}$ be a parameter distribution that outputs matrices from $\mathbb{G}^{n \times t}$. For $\mathbf{A} \in \mathsf{Supp}(\mathcal{D}_{par})$, we define the language $\mathcal{L}_{\mathbf{A}} := \{\mathbf{x} | \exists \mathbf{w} : \mathbf{A}\mathbf{w} = \mathbf{x}\}$. Specifically, the relation $R_{\mathbf{A}}$ is defined such that $(\mathbf{x}, \mathbf{w}) \in R_{\mathbf{A}} \Leftrightarrow \mathbf{x} = \mathbf{A}\mathbf{w}$. We call $\mathcal{D}_{par}$ witness samplable, if there is a distribution $\mathcal{D}'_{par}$ which outputs matrices from $\mathbb{Z}_p^{n \times t}$ s.t. the distributions of $\mathbf{A} \overset{\$}{\leftarrow} \mathcal{D}_{par}$ and $[\mathbf{B}] \overset{\$}{\leftarrow} \mathcal{D}'_{par}$ are indistinguishable.*

Effectively, witness-samplability states that the language parameters can be sampled together with a trapdoor matrix $\mathbf{T}$ which allows to check whether $\mathbf{x} \in L$. For linear languages, this trapdoor matrix is simply the exponents of all matrix entries, so the original matrix can be computed from the trapdoor, hence we only sample the latter in the distribution $\mathcal{D}'_{par}$.

Σ-Protocol for Algebraic Languages. We introduce a generic Σ-protocol Π_{Σ} for algebraic languages on Fig. 2.

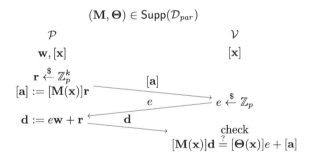

Fig. 2. Σ-protocol Π_{Σ} for the generic language $\mathcal{L}_{\mathbf{M},\Theta}$

Theorem 11. *The Σ-protocol Π_{Σ} is complete, special honest-verifier zero-knowledge and special sound.*

For the proof of Theorem 11 refer to e.g. [62]. We will however recall the special honest-verifier zero-knowledge simulation algorithm $\mathcal{S}_{\Pi}$, since we need it in our construction. The simulator receives as input $([\mathbf{x}], e)$ and samples $\mathbf{d} \overset{\$}{\leftarrow} \mathbb{Z}_p^t$. Then it sets $[\mathbf{a}] := \mathbf{M}(\mathbf{x})\mathbf{d} - e[\Theta(\mathbf{x})]$ and returns $([\mathbf{a}], \mathbf{d})$.

3.2 Compiling Π_{Σ} into a NIZK

The main idea of our construction is to keep the Σ-protocol in group $\mathbb{G}_1$ while moving the challenge e to a group $\mathbb{G}_2$, which admits a bilinear pairing $e : \mathbb{G}_1 \times$

$\mathbb{G}_2 \to \mathbb{G}_T$. This keeps the challenge hidden while allowing verification due to the pairing. For protocol Π_Σ, the compiled NIZK Π_Σ^C is described in Fig. 3. We present a detailed security analysis in Sect. 4.

CRSGen (1^λ):

$par := \mathcal{PG} \overset{\$}{\leftarrow} PGGen(1^\lambda)$

$e \overset{\$}{\leftarrow} \mathbb{Z}_p$

$\mathsf{CRS} := (\mathcal{PG}, [e]_2), \mathcal{T} := e$

return $(par, \mathsf{CRS}, \mathcal{T})$

Prove $(\mathsf{CRS}, ([\mathbf{M}]_1, [\mathbf{\Theta}]_1), [\mathbf{x}]_1 \in \mathbb{G}_1^l, \mathbf{w} \in \mathbb{Z}_p^t)$:

$\mathbf{r} \overset{\$}{\leftarrow} \mathbb{Z}_p^t$

$[\mathbf{a}]_1 := [\mathbf{M}(\mathbf{x})]_1 \mathbf{r}$

$[\mathbf{d}]_2 := [e]_2 \mathbf{w} + [\mathbf{r}]_2$

return $\sigma := ([\mathbf{a}]_1, [\mathbf{d}]_2)$

SimProve $(\mathsf{CRS}, e, ([\mathbf{M}]_1, [\mathbf{\Theta}]_1), [\mathbf{x}]_1)$:

$([\mathbf{a}]_1, \mathbf{d}) := \mathcal{S}_\Pi([\mathbf{x}]_1, e)$

return $\sigma := ([\mathbf{a}]_1, [\mathbf{d}]_2)$

Verify $(\mathsf{CRS}, ([\mathbf{M}]_1, [\mathbf{\Theta}]_1), [\mathbf{x}]_1, \sigma = ([\mathbf{a}]_1, [\mathbf{d}]_2))$:

check

$[\mathbf{M}(\mathbf{x})]_1 \bullet [\mathbf{d}]_2 \overset{?}{=} [\mathbf{\Theta}(\mathbf{x})]_1 \bullet [e]_2 + [\mathbf{a}]_1 \bullet [1]_2$

Fig. 3. Compiled protocol Π_Σ^C, where $\mathcal{S}_\Pi$ denotes the special honest-verifier simulator of Π_Σ and $([\mathbf{M}]_1, [\mathbf{\Theta}]_1) \in \mathcal{P}_l^{n \times t} \times \mathcal{P}_l^n$ is sampled from $\mathcal{D}_{par}$.

3.3   Compiled **NIZK** as a **ZAP**

The CRS in our compiled NIZK consists of just one (random) group element from $\mathbb{G}_2$; therefore, our protocol actually works in the common *random* string model. Furthermore, we observe that by allowing the verifier to choose the CRS himself and send it as its first flow, we can transform the NIZK into a statistical ZAP in the *plain model* (*i.e.*, a two-round publicly-verifiable statistical witness-indistinguishable argument system, where the first flow can be reused for an arbitrary (polynomial) number of proofs). We stress that this provides the first known construction of statistical ZAPs from pairing-based assumptions; to our knowledge, the only existing constructions rely on the quasipolynomial hardness of LWE [6,49]. We can apply the derandomisation technique from [8] to obtain a NIWI argument in the plain model. Since correctness and soundness carry over directly from the NIZK case, it remains to show that our 2-round proof system is witness-indistinguishable. This is shown in Lemma 12.

Lemma 12. *The ZAP resulting from the protocol Π_Σ^C for a family of language distributions $\{\mathcal{D}_{par}\}_{par}$ as described above is perfectly witness indistinguishable.*

Proof. Let $\rho := (\mathbf{M}, \mathbf{\Theta}) \in \mathsf{Supp}(\mathcal{D}_{par})$ and $\mathbf{x} \in \mathcal{L}_\rho$ with two witnesses $\mathbf{w}_1, \mathbf{w}_2$ and let $\hat{\mathcal{V}}$ be a (potentially misbehaving) verifier. Let $[e]_2$ be the CRS (*i.e.*, first flow) chosen by $\hat{\mathcal{V}}$. We have to show that the distributions $\mathsf{Prove}([e]_2, \rho, \mathbf{x}, \mathbf{w}_1)$ and $\mathsf{Prove}([e]_2, \rho, \mathbf{x}, \mathbf{w}_2)$ are indistinguishable. A proof consists of the two vectors $[\mathbf{a}_i]_1 = [\mathbf{M}(\mathbf{x})]_1 \mathbf{r}_i$ and $[\mathbf{d}_i]_2 = [e]_2 \mathbf{w}_i + [\mathbf{r}_i]_2$ for random vectors $\mathbf{r}_i$, witnesses $\mathbf{w}_i$ and e chosen by the verifier. Let $\mathbf{w} := \mathbf{w}_1 - \mathbf{w}_2$. Note that $\mathbf{M}(\mathbf{x})\mathbf{w} = 0$, since $\mathbf{M}(\mathbf{x})\mathbf{w} = \mathbf{M}(\mathbf{x})(\mathbf{w}_1 - \mathbf{w}_2) = \mathbf{\Theta}(\mathbf{x}) - \mathbf{\Theta}(\mathbf{x}) = 0$. For $i = 1$, we have $\pi_1 = ([\mathbf{a}_1]_1 = [\mathbf{M}(\mathbf{x})\mathbf{r}_1]_1, [\mathbf{d}_1]_2 = [e]_2 \mathbf{w}_1 + [\mathbf{r}_1]_2)$. For $i = 2$ and by replacing $\mathbf{w}_2$

with $\mathbf{w}_1 - \mathbf{w}$, we get $\pi_2 = ([\mathbf{a}_2]_1 = [\mathbf{M}(\mathbf{x})]_1 \mathbf{r}_2, [\mathbf{d}_2]_2 = [e]_2 \mathbf{w}_1 + ([\mathbf{r}_2 - e\mathbf{w}]_2))$. Let $\mathbf{r}' := -e\mathbf{w} + \mathbf{r}_2$ and consider a proof using witness $\mathbf{w}_1$ and random vector $\mathbf{r}'$. We get $[\mathbf{a}']_1 = [\mathbf{M}(\mathbf{x})]_1 \mathbf{r}' = [\mathbf{M}(\mathbf{x})]_1 (-e\mathbf{w} + \mathbf{r}_2) = -e [\mathbf{M}(\mathbf{x})]_1 \mathbf{w} + [\mathbf{M}(\mathbf{x})]_1 \mathbf{r}_2 = [\mathbf{M}(\mathbf{x})]_1 \mathbf{r}_2 = [\mathbf{a}_2]_1$ and $[\mathbf{d}']_2 = [e]_2 \mathbf{w}_1 + [\mathbf{r}']_2 = [\mathbf{d}_2]_2$. This is identical to the proof using $\mathbf{w}_2$ and randomness $\mathbf{r}_2$. $\mathbf{r}_1, \mathbf{r}_2$, and $\mathbf{r}'$ are distributed identically (i.e. uniformly random), hence the proof distributions for witness $\mathbf{w}_1$ and $\mathbf{w}_2$ are identical.

4 Security Analysis

4.1 Generalised Witness Samplablility

The definition of witness samplability for linear languages does not carry over to the case of algebraic languages, since only linear languages can be in the span of the kernel of their language trapdoor. To handle this issue, we adapt the witness samplability by requiring the samplability of a language trapdoor $\mathbf{T}$, sampled together with the parameters of the language, which allows to efficiently check the *rank* of $(\mathbf{M}\|\mathbf{\Theta})(\mathbf{x})$, which will be full for words *not* in the language, and lower otherwise. We formally define our new notion of algebraic witness samplability in Definition 13.

Definition 13 (Algebraic Witness Samplability).   *Let* $t, l, n \in \mathbb{N}$ *with* $n > t$. *An algebraic language distribution* $\mathcal{D}_{par}$, *outputting pairs* $\rho = (\mathbf{M}, \mathbf{\Theta}) \in \mathcal{P}_l^{n \times t} \times \mathcal{P}_l^n$ *is called witness samplable, if there exists a second distribution* $\mathcal{D}'_{par}$ *outputting pairs* $(\rho' = (\mathbf{M}', \mathbf{\Theta}'), \mathbf{T}_{\rho'} \in \mathbb{Z}_p^{n \times n})$, *with* $\mathcal{D}'_{par}(1)$ *denoting the distribution of* $\mathcal{D}'_{par}$ *restricted to the first component, such that the following properties hold.*

1. *The distributions* $(\mathcal{D}_{par})$ *and* $(\mathcal{D}'_{par}(1))$ *are identical.*
2. $\mathsf{rank}(\mathbf{T}_{\rho'} \cdot (\mathbf{M}'\|\mathbf{\Theta}')(\mathbf{x})) = \begin{cases} t+1 & \mathbf{x} \notin \mathcal{L}_{\rho'} \\ l' < t+1 & \mathbf{x} \in \mathcal{L}_{\rho'} \end{cases}$
3. $\exists \mathbf{R}, \mathbf{S}$ *permutation matrices such that* $(\mathbf{R} \cdot \mathbf{T}_{\rho'} \cdot (\mathbf{M}'\|\mathbf{\Theta}') \cdot \mathbf{S})(\mathbf{x})$ *is an upper triangular matrix*

A family of language distributions $\{\mathcal{D}_{par}\}_{par}$ *is witness samplable, if* $\mathcal{D}_{par}$ *is witness samplable for all possible par.*

Note that $\mathbf{R}, \mathbf{S}$ are efficiently computable from $\mathbf{T}_{\rho'} \cdot (\mathbf{M}\|\mathbf{\Theta})(\mathbf{x})$ (even without knowledge of $\mathbf{T}_{\rho'}$), as they only rearrange the rows and columns of $\mathbf{T}_{\rho'} \cdot (\mathbf{M}'\|\mathbf{\Theta}')(\mathbf{x})$ to a specific form.

The first property states that we can sample a distribution with or without a trapdoor without altering the distribution. The second property is the rank condition itself, which shows language membership. The last property guarantees that the second condition can always be verified in polynomial time. To provide a better intuition of this property, we illustrate it on the language of ElGamal encryptions of a bit (which is a special case of the OR-language for DDH tuples) in the full version of this paper [20].

Definition 14 (Trapdoor Reducibility). *Let $t, l, m, n \in \mathbb{N}$ with $n > t$ and $\mathcal{D}_{par}$ be an algebraic language distribution which outputs pairs $\rho = (\mathbf{M}, \mathbf{\Theta}) \in \mathcal{P}_l^{n \times t} \times \mathcal{P}_l^n$.*

*$\mathcal{D}_{par}$ is m-**trapdoor reducible**, if it is witness samplable with trapdoor distribution $\mathcal{D}'_{par}$ and for every language $(\rho', \mathbf{T}_{\rho'}) \in \mathsf{Supp}(\mathcal{D}'_{par})$, we can instead sample a reducibility trapdoor $\mathbf{T}'_{\rho'} \in \mathbb{Z}_p^{(n-m) \times n}$ such that the following properties hold.*

- *$\mathbf{T}'_{\rho'} \subset \mathbf{T}_{\rho'}$, i.e. the rows of $\mathbf{T}'_{\rho'}$ are a subset of the rows of $\mathbf{T}_{\rho'}$.*
- *$\mathsf{rank}(\mathbf{T}'_{\rho'} \cdot (\mathbf{M}||\mathbf{\Theta})(\mathbf{x})) = \begin{cases} n - m & \mathbf{x} \notin \mathcal{L}_{\rho'} \\ m' < n - m & \mathbf{x} \in \mathcal{L}_{\rho'} \end{cases}$*
- *m columns of $\mathbf{T}'_{\rho'} \cdot (\mathbf{M}||\mathbf{\Theta})$ are zero-columns and the last column is a non-zero column.*

A family of language distributions $\{\mathcal{D}_{par}\}_{par}$ is trapdoor reducible, if $\mathcal{D}_{par}$ is trapdoor reducible for all possible par.

Trapdoor reducibility captures a stronger notion of witness samplability where in addition to checking the rank of the matrix, we can also reduce the size of the check. Although this is not a necessary property, it allows us to perform reductions to weaker-parametrised assumptions and therefore to strengthen the security guarantees of our constructions for specific language distributions. We illustrate it as well in the full version of this paper [20].

4.2 Extended-Kernel Matrix Diffie-Hellman Assumption

For the linear case, the security of our compiled NIZKs can be reduced to the KerMDH assumption. However for OR-proofs or general algebraic languages, it seems to be insufficient. Hence we propose a generalisation of the KerMDH assumption, which we will call the extKerMDH assumption, and to which we can reduce the soundness of our compiler for all algebraic languages.

Inadequacy of the KerMDH. Before we introduce our new assumption, we want to argue why the existing KerMDH assumption is not sufficient for our application. To do so we give an (informal) example.

For a linear language (described by matrix $\mathbf{A}$), we can reduce soundness to the $\mathcal{L}_1$-KerMDH assumption for matrix distribution $\mathcal{L}_1$ as follows. Suppose that a verifier in the Σ-protocol for a linear language (Fig. 2) sends e as its challenge. Then the verification equation is $[\mathbf{A}d] = [\mathbf{x}]e + [\mathbf{a}]$. If $\mathbf{A}$ is from a witness samplable distribution, we can use the trapdoor to find a vector $\mathbf{t}$ in the kernel of $\mathbf{A}$, i.e. $\mathbf{t} \cdot \mathbf{A} = 0$. Multiplying the above equation with $\mathbf{t}$ then yields $0 = [\mathbf{tx}]e + [\mathbf{ta}]$ and if $\mathbf{x}$ and $\mathbf{a}$ are not in the span of $\mathbf{A}$, we have a non-zero vector in the kernel of $[\begin{smallmatrix} 1 \\ e \end{smallmatrix}]_2$, namely $\begin{pmatrix} \mathbf{ta} \\ \mathbf{tx} \end{pmatrix}^T$ and therefore a solution to the KerMDH problem for $[\begin{smallmatrix} 1 \\ e \end{smallmatrix}]_2 \in \mathsf{Supp}(\mathcal{L}_1)$. However for the simple binary OR proof from [21] (see Fig. 4 for more details), this approach already fails. Instead of one such equation, we get two equations of the form $0 = [\mathbf{t}_i \mathbf{x}_i]e_i + [\mathbf{t}_i \mathbf{a}_i]$ for $i \in \{0, 1\}$ and with $e = e_0 + e_1$.

Since the two vectors consist of group elements, we can't combine them to a single solution for the matrix $[\begin{smallmatrix}1\\e\end{smallmatrix}]_2$. However, what we obtain are two linearly independent vectors in the kernel of $[1, e, e_0]_2^\intercal$, namely $v_1 = [\mathbf{t_0 a_0}, 0, \mathbf{t_0 x_0}]^\intercal$ and $v_2 = [\mathbf{t_1 a_1}, \mathbf{t_1 x_1}, -\mathbf{t_1 x_1}]^\intercal$. We assume that such a relation is also hard to compute and we formalise it as the extKerMDH assumption.

The extKerMDH Assumption.

Definition 15 ($\mathcal{D}_k$-l-extended Kernel Diffie-Hellman Assumption ($\mathcal{D}_k$-l-extKerMDH)). *Let $l, k \in \mathbb{N}$, $\mathcal{PG} = (p, \mathbb{G}_1, \mathbb{G}_2, \mathbb{G}_T, g_1, g_2, e) \xleftarrow{\$} \mathrm{PGGen}(1^\lambda)$ and $\mathcal{D}_k$ be a matrix distribution. The $\mathcal{D}_k$-l-extKerMDH assumption holds in $\mathbb{G}_s$ relative to PGGen, if for all efficient adversaries $\mathcal{A}$, the following probability is negligible.*

$$\Pr\left[\begin{array}{c} [\mathbf{C}]_{3-s} \in \mathbb{G}_{3-s}^{l+1\times k+l+1} \wedge [\mathbf{B}]_s \in \mathbb{G}_s^{l\times k} \\ \wedge [\mathbf{C}]_{3-s} \bullet [\mathbf{D}']_s = 0 \\ \wedge \mathsf{rank}(\mathbf{C}) \geq l+1 \end{array} \middle| \begin{array}{c} \mathcal{PG} \xleftarrow{\$} \mathrm{PGGen}(1^\lambda), \mathbf{D} \xleftarrow{\$} \mathcal{D}_k \\ ([\mathbf{C}]_{3-s}, [\mathbf{B}]_s) \xleftarrow{\$} \mathcal{A}(\mathcal{PG}, [\mathbf{D}]_s) \\ [\mathbf{D}']_s := [\begin{smallmatrix}\mathbf{D}\\\mathbf{B}\end{smallmatrix}]_s \end{array}\right]$$

The probability is taken over then randomness of $\mathcal{A}$, $\mathcal{D}_k$ and PGGen.

If in addition to the rank condition, $\mathbf{C}$ is also required to be an upper triangular matrix (in which case the bound on the rank can be verified in polynomial time), the assumption is called falsifiable $\mathcal{D}_k$-l-extKerMDH.

This assumption is to the best of our knowledge new and so we want to give an intuition on why we deem it reasonable. First, it is a natural extension of the KerMDH assumption. We give the adversary more freedom by allowing it to extend the given matrix but require it to output multiple, linearly independent vectors in the kernel. As long as the number of linearly independent vectors is strictly larger than the number of vectors the adversary gets to add, breaking the assumption requires finding vectors in $\mathbb{G}_1$ which depend on $[\mathbf{M}]_2$ in a non-trivial way. Second, it is a static family of assumptions (as opposed to Q-type assumptions; once $[\mathbf{M}]_2$ is fixed, our proof system will rely on an extKerMDH assumption with fixed parameters). Third, we consider the issue of falsifiability. It turns out that the extKerMDH assumption is not always falsifiable: to check the given matrix $\mathbf{C}$ for being a basis, one must break a DDH-like problem. However in many concrete cases of interest (formally, each time we will consider *witness samplable* languages), the matrix $\mathbf{C}$ can be brought in an upper triangular form where the rank will be visible and we can instead reduce the security to the *falsifiable* variant. Eventually, the assumption is unconditionally secure in the Generic Group Model (GGM) and can be reduced to the discrete logarithm problem in the Algebraic Group Model (AGM). For the proofs, refer to the full version of this paper [20].

4.3 Security Proof

With the two definitions and the new extKerMDH assumption, we can now finally prove the security of our construction.

Theorem 16. *1. The protocol Π_Σ^C described in Fig. 3 is a NIZK argument for any algebraic language distribution $\mathcal{D}_{par}$ outputting pairs $\rho = (\mathbf{M}, \mathbf{\Theta}) \in \mathcal{P}_l^{n \times t} \times \mathcal{P}_l^n$, if the $\mathcal{L}_1$-t-extKerMDH assumption holds in $\mathbb{G}_2$ relative to PGGen.*
2. If the language distribution is witness samplable with trapdoors $\mathbf{T}_\rho \in \mathbb{Z}_p^{n \times n}$, then it is a NIZK argument if the falsifiable $\mathcal{L}_1$-t-extKerMDH holds in $\mathbb{G}_2$ relative to PGGen.
3. If the language distribution is m-trapdoor reducible, then it is a NIZK argument if the falsifiable $\mathcal{L}_1$-$(t-m)$-extKerMDH holds in $\mathbb{G}_2$ relative to PGGen.

Proof. To prove theorem 16, we have to show *completeness, perfect zero knowledge* and *computational soundness*. The first two properties are identical for all parts of the theorem. For the second and third part, the witness samplability and the trapdoor reducibility directly imply the soundness statements, if soundness holds in the first part.

Perfect Completeness: Let $\rho = (\mathbf{M}, \mathbf{\Theta}) \in \mathsf{Supp}(\mathcal{D}_{par})$. If $\mathbf{\Theta}(\mathbf{x}) = \mathbf{M}(\mathbf{x}) \cdot \mathbf{w}$ and $\mathbf{a} = \mathbf{M}(\mathbf{x}) \cdot \mathbf{r}$, we get

$$
\begin{aligned}
[\mathbf{M}(\mathbf{x})]_1 \bullet [\mathbf{d}]_2 = \quad & [\mathbf{M}(\mathbf{x}) \cdot \mathbf{d}]_T \\
= \quad & [\mathbf{M}(\mathbf{x}) \cdot (e \cdot \mathbf{w} + \mathbf{r})]_T \\
= \quad & [\mathbf{M}(\mathbf{x}) \cdot \mathbf{w} \cdot e]_T + [\mathbf{M}(\mathbf{x})\mathbf{r} \cdot 1]_T \\
= \quad & [\mathbf{\Theta}(\mathbf{x}) \cdot e]_T + [\mathbf{a} \cdot 1]_T \quad (\text{since } \mathbf{\Theta}(\mathbf{x}) = \mathbf{M}(\mathbf{x}) \cdot \mathbf{w}) \\
= \quad & [\mathbf{\Theta}(\mathbf{x})]_1 \bullet [e]_2 + [\mathbf{a}]_1 \bullet [1]_2
\end{aligned}
$$

Perfect Zero Knowledge: We have to show that the distributions Prove and SimProve are identical. This directly follows from the perfect honest-verifier zero-knowledge property of the Σ-protocol, since we use its simulator in SimProve.

Computational Soundness: We will show that Π_Σ^C is computationally sound, if the $\mathcal{L}_1$-t-extKerMDH holds in $\mathbb{G}_2$ relative to $PGGen$. Assume an adversary $\mathcal{A}$ which forges a proof for Π_Σ^C with non-negligible probability. We will construct an adversary $\mathcal{B}$ against the $\mathcal{L}_1$-t-extKerMDH assumption, that uses adversary $\mathcal{A}$ and has the same success probability. $\mathcal{B}$ receives a challenge $[\begin{smallmatrix}1\\e\end{smallmatrix}]_2$ from its challenger. $\mathcal{B}$ then sets $[e]_2$ as the CRS and samples language parameters $\rho \xleftarrow{\$} \mathcal{D}_{par}$. Now $\mathcal{B}$ runs $\mathcal{A}(\mathsf{CRS}, \rho)$ and receives a statement $\mathbf{x}$ and a proof $\pi = ([\mathbf{a}]_1, [\mathbf{d}]_2)$ which are accepting with non-negligible probability, i.e.

$$
\begin{aligned}
[\mathbf{M}(\mathbf{x})]_1 \bullet [\mathbf{d}]_2 &= [\mathbf{\Theta}(\mathbf{x})]_1 \bullet [e]_2 + [\mathbf{a}]_1 \bullet [1]_2 \\
0 &= [\mathbf{a}]_1 \bullet [1]_2 + [\mathbf{\Theta}(\mathbf{x})]_1 \bullet [e]_2 - [\mathbf{M}(\mathbf{x})]_1 \bullet [\mathbf{d}]_2 \\
0 &= [\mathbf{a}||\mathbf{\Theta}(\mathbf{x})|| - \mathbf{M}(\mathbf{x})]_1 \bullet [1\ e\ \mathbf{d}]_2^\mathsf{T}
\end{aligned}
$$

If $\mathbf{C} := (\mathbf{a}||\mathbf{\Theta}(\mathbf{x})|| - \mathbf{M}(\mathbf{x}))$ has at least $\mathsf{rank}(\mathbf{C}) = t + 1$, then $([\mathbf{C}]_1, [\mathbf{d}]_2)$ is a solution for the assumption, since $\mathbf{d}$ has length t. This can be seen with simple linear algebra.

We know that $\mathbf{M}(\mathbf{x})$ has full rank t. By adding the two columns $\mathbf{a}$ and $\mathbf{\Theta}(\mathbf{x})$, the rank cannot decrease. Assume $\mathbf{\Theta}(\mathbf{x})$ and $\mathbf{a}$ are not in the span of $\mathbf{M}$, i.e.

$\mathcal{A}$ did produce a forgery. Then $\mathbf{a}$ and $\mathbf{\Theta}(\mathbf{x})$ are completely independent of $\mathbf{M}$ and therefore the rank of the matrix will be increased by at least 1 and $\mathcal{B}$ has a solution. For a regular proof however, $\mathbf{a}$ and $\mathbf{\Theta}(\mathbf{x})$ are in the span of $\mathbf{M}(\mathbf{x})$ and therefore linearly dependant on the columns of $\mathbf{M}(\mathbf{x})$, therefore the rank can not increase. This shows that $\mathbf{C}$ is full rank if and only if $\mathcal{A}$ outputs a valid forgery and $\mathcal{B}$ wins in this exact case.

For the second part of the theorem, $\mathcal{B}$ samples $(\rho, \mathbf{T}_\rho)$ from the trapdoor distribution $\mathcal{D}'_{par}$, which is by definition indistinguishable from sampling ρ regularly. The statement is seen exactly as the first one except for a multiplication with the trapdoor matrix, which yields a full rank matrix in upper triangular form if and only if the given word is not in the language and we get a falsifiable solution. For the third part, $\mathcal{B}$ samples $(\rho, \mathbf{T}'_\rho)$ from the trapdoor reducibility distribution (which is again indistinguishable from regular sampling) and $\mathcal{B}$ takes the matrix received by the multiplication with the reducibility trapdoor. By removing the zero columns and removing the corresponding elements from $\mathbf{d}$, $\mathcal{B}$ can reduce $\mathbf{d}$'s size by exactly m and therefore gets a solution to the $\mathcal{L}_1$-$(t - m)$-extKerMDH.

5   Extension to Disjunctions of Languages

In this section, we will show how to obtain efficient OR-proofs by applying our compiler to the generic Σ-protocols for k-out-of-n disjunctions of [21].

We briefly recall the method of [21] (for concreteness, we focus on 1-out-of-2 proofs; the general case is similar). It starts from two Σ-protocols for memberships into languages $\mathcal{L}_{\rho_0}, \mathcal{L}_{\rho_1}$, and produces a Σ-protocol for the language $\mathcal{L}_{\rho_0 \vee \rho_1}$. Consider a prover knowing a witness w for $\mathbf{x}_i \in \mathcal{L}_{\rho_i}$ but not for $\mathbf{x}_{1-i} \in \mathcal{L}_{\rho_{(1-i)}}$. The prover chooses a random $e_{1-i} \xleftarrow{\$} \mathbb{Z}_p$ and uses the special honest-verifier zero-knowledge simulation algorithm to generate $[a_{1-i}], d_{1-i}$ which form an accepting proof for $\mathbf{x}_{1-i} \in \mathcal{L}_{\rho_{(1-i)}}$. Additionally it computes an honest commitment $[a_i]$ for the Σ-protocol for $\mathcal{L}_{\rho_i}$ and sends $[a_0], [a_1]$ to the verifier, which returns a challenge e. The prover now sets $e_i := e - e_{1-i}$ and continues the honest protocol for $\mathbf{x}_i \in \mathcal{L}_{\rho_i}$, calculating d_i and concludes the protocol by sending d_0, d_1 and e_0. The verifier can then calculate $e_1 := e - e_0$ and check both proofs. This protocol can be seen in Fig. 4. While this does not immediately fit into the framework of Sect. 3, our approach is still applicable: The prover again chooses a challenge $e_{1-i} \xleftarrow{\$} \mathbb{Z}_p$ and simulates the first proof as in the interactive variant and gets the second challenge for the honest proof part only in $\mathbb{G}_2$ as $[e_i]_2 = [e]_2 - ([1]_2 e_{1-i})$. In addition to the two regular proofs, we have to include $[e_0]_2$ in the proof. This is illustrated in Fig. 5. We get the following new, efficient OR-proof.

Theorem 17. *Let $\mathcal{D}^{(0)}_{par}, \mathcal{D}^{(1)}_{par}$ be two algebraic language distributions outputting matrices of dimension $n_0 \times t_0$ and $n_1 \times t_1$ respectively. Applying the construction from Fig. 5 yields a fully adaptive NIZK argument for the OR-language of $\rho_0 \in$ Supp$(\mathcal{D}^{(0)}_{par}), \rho_1 \in$ Supp$(\mathcal{D}^{(1)}_{par})$ of size $n_0 + n_1 + t_0 + t_1 + 1$, if the $\mathcal{L}_1 - (n_0 + n_1 + 1) - $extKerMDH assumption holds in $\mathbb{G}_2$.*

If both language distributions are witness samplable, the above holds for the falsifiable $\mathcal{L}_1 - (n_0 + n_1 + 1) - extKerMDH$ assumption.

If $\mathcal{D}_{par}^{(0)}$ resp. $\mathcal{D}_{par}^{(1)}$ is m_0- resp. m_1-trapdoor reducible, the above holds for the $\mathcal{L}_1 - (n_0 - m_0 + n_1 - m_1 + 1) - extKerMDH$ assumption.

The proof for Theorem 17 is almost identical to one for Theorem 16. The only difference lies in the soundness proof, where we apply the witness samplability (trapdoor reducibility) trapdoors of each language to the respective proofs separately and then combine the results by expressing e_1 as $e - e_0$.

The construction naturally extends to the 1 out of n setting by letting the prover choose $n - 1$ challenges itself and setting the last as the difference of e

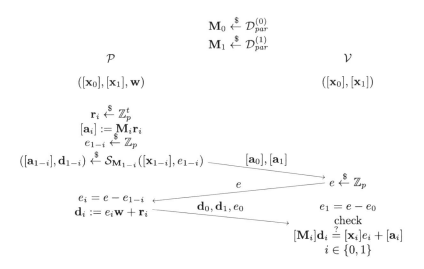

Fig. 4. Sigma protocol $\Pi_{\mathbf{M}_0 \vee \mathbf{M}_1}$ for the or language $\mathcal{L}_{\mathbf{M}_0 \vee \mathbf{M}_1}$ from [21]

CRSGen (1^λ):

$par := \mathcal{PG} \overset{\$}{\leftarrow} PGGen(1^\lambda)$
$e \overset{\$}{\leftarrow} \mathbb{Z}_p$
CRS $:= (\mathcal{PG}, [e]_2)$, $\mathcal{T} := e$
return $(par, \text{CRS}, \mathcal{T})$

Prove (CRS, $([\mathbf{M}_i]_1)_{i\in\{0,1\}}, [\mathbf{x}_0]_1, [\mathbf{x}_1]_1, \mathbf{w}$):

$//\ \mathbf{x}_i = \mathbf{M}_i \mathbf{w}$
$\mathbf{r}_i \overset{\$}{\leftarrow} \mathbb{Z}_p^{t_i}, e_{1-i} \overset{\$}{\leftarrow} \mathbb{Z}_p$
$[e_i]_2 = [e]_2 - [e_{1-i}]_2$
$([\mathbf{a}_i]_1, [\mathbf{d}_i]_2) := ([\mathbf{M}_i]_1 \mathbf{r}_i, [e_i]_2 \mathbf{w} + [\mathbf{r}_i]_2)$
$([\mathbf{a}_{1-i}]_1, \mathbf{d}_{1-i}) \overset{\$}{\leftarrow} \mathcal{S}_{\mathbf{M}_{1-i}}([\mathbf{x}_{1-i}]_1, e_{1-i})$
return $\pi := ([\mathbf{a}_0]_1, [\mathbf{a}_1]_1, [\mathbf{d}_0]_2, [\mathbf{d}_1]_2, [e_0]_2)$

SimProve (CRS, $\mathcal{T} = e, ([\mathbf{M}_i]_1)_{i\in\{0,1\}}, [\mathbf{x}_0]_1, [\mathbf{x}_1]_1$):

$e_0 \overset{\$}{\leftarrow} \mathbb{Z}_p$
$e_1 = e - e_0$
$([\mathbf{a}_j]_1, \mathbf{d}_j) \overset{\$}{\leftarrow} \mathcal{S}_{\mathbf{M}_j}([\mathbf{x}_j]_1, e_j)$ for $j \in \{0,1\}$
return $\pi := ([\mathbf{a}_0]_1, [\mathbf{a}_1]_1, [\mathbf{d}_0]_2, [\mathbf{d}_1]_2, [e_0]_2)$

Verify (CRS, $([\mathbf{M}_i]_1)_{i\in\{0,1\}}, [\mathbf{x}_0]_1, [\mathbf{x}_1]_1, \pi$):

parse $\pi = ([e_0]_2, ([\mathbf{a}_i]_1, [\mathbf{d}_i]_2)_{i\in\{0,1\}})$
$[e_1]_2 = [e]_2 - [e_0]_2$
for $j \in \{0,1\}$ check
$[\mathbf{M}_j]_1 \bullet [\mathbf{d}_j]_2 \overset{?}{=} [\mathbf{x}_j]_1 \bullet [e_j]_2 + [\mathbf{a}_j]_1 \bullet [1]_2$

Fig. 5. Compiled protocol $\Pi^c_{\mathbf{M}_0 \vee \mathbf{M}_1}$. $\mathcal{S}_{(\cdot)}$ denotes the SHVZK-simulator for the respective language.

and the sum of all chosen challenges. With n matrices $\mathbf{M}_i$, we get the following size, as the prover has to send $n - 1$ challenges to uniquely determine the last challenge: $\sum_{i=1}^{n}(n_i + t_i) + n - 1$. In the special case of the disjunction of two DDH languages (as needed in e.g [34]), the compiled OR-trick yields a proof with 7 group elements. The construction can easily be adapted to the setting of k-out-of-n disjunctions, by using a threshold secret sharing (e.g. [69]) to force the adversary to choose at most $n - k$ challenges by itself. Our compiler can be applied in the same way as for the 1 out of n setting and yields NIZK arguments of size $\sum_{i=1}^{n}(n_i + t_i) + n - k$.

6   Applications

6.1   NIZK for Linear Languages

Let $\mathbb{G}$ be a finite group of prime order p and $\mathcal{D}_{k,n}$ be a matrix distribution. We apply our compiler to the standard Σ-protocol for membership to the linear language generated by $\mathbf{A}$, for $\mathbf{A} \in \mathsf{Supp}(\mathcal{D}_{k,n})$. This protocol was formally analyzed in [62]. Applying our compiler yields the protocol $\Pi_{\mathbf{A}}^{C}$ shown in Fig. 6.

CRSGen (1^λ):

$par := \mathcal{PG} \stackrel{\$}{\leftarrow} PGGen(1^\lambda)$

$[e]_2 \stackrel{\$}{\leftarrow} \mathbb{Z}_p$
CRS $:= (\mathcal{PG}, [e]_2),\ \mathcal{T} := e$
return $(par, \text{CRS}, \mathcal{T})$

Prove(CRS, $[\mathbf{A}]_1, [\mathbf{x}]_1, \mathbf{w}$):

$\mathbf{r} \stackrel{\$}{\leftarrow} \mathbb{Z}_p^k$

$[\mathbf{a}]_1 := [\mathbf{A}]_1\, \mathbf{r}$
$[\mathbf{d}]_2 := [e]_2\, \mathbf{w} + [\mathbf{r}]_2$
return $\pi := ([\mathbf{a}]_1, [\mathbf{d}]_2)$

SimProve(CRS, $\mathcal{T} = e, [\mathbf{A}]_1, [\mathbf{x}]_1$):

$\mathbf{d} \stackrel{\$}{\leftarrow} \mathbb{Z}_p^k$
$[\mathbf{a}]_1 := [\mathbf{A}]_1\, \mathbf{d} - [\mathbf{x}]_1\, e$
return $\pi := ([\mathbf{a}]_1, [\mathbf{d}]_2)$

Verify(CRS, $[\mathbf{A}]_1, [\mathbf{x}]_1, \pi = ([\mathbf{a}]_1, [\mathbf{d}]_2)$):

check $[\mathbf{A}]_1 \bullet [\mathbf{d}]_2 \stackrel{?}{=} [\mathbf{x}]_1 \bullet [e]_2 + [\mathbf{a}]_1 \bullet [1]_2$

Fig. 6. Compiled protocol $\Pi_{\mathbf{A}}^{c}$.

Theorem 18. *Protocol $\Pi_{\mathbf{A}}^{c}$ is a NIZK for the language $\mathcal{L}_{\mathbf{A}}$, if $\mathcal{D}_{k,n}$ is witness samplable and the $\mathcal{L}_1$-kerMDH (= $\mathcal{L}_1$-0-extKerMDH) assumption holds in $\mathbb{G}_2$ relative to $\mathcal{PG}$.*

Proof. If we show that $\mathbf{A}$ is k-trapdoor reducible, then the proof follows from Theorem 16. It is easy to see that all witness samplable matrix distributions $\mathcal{D}_{k,n}$ are k-trapdoor reducible. We sample $\mathbf{A} \in \mathbb{Z}_p^{n \times k}$ and compute an element in the kernel of $\mathbf{A}$, which is exactly the reducibility trapdoor.

The construction above includes proofs for DDH tuples, the Schnorr protocol [68], and general linear subspace membership. We compare our construction instantiated for the DDH language (and asymptotic) with the Groth-Sahai framework [44] and the Kiltz-Wee proofs [57] on Table 1 from Sect. 1. Our construction is more efficient than Groth-Sahai both in terms of proof size as well as CRS size. For the verification, we also need less pairings (6 versus 24 for Groth-Sahai). Of course this comes at the (mild) cost of assuming witness sampleability of the language (Note that the security is based on the standard kerMDH assumption). On the other hand, our proofs are longer than the proofs from [57] (linear versus constant size). However our construction yields fully adaptive zero-knowledge arguments, while theirs yields quasi-adaptive zero-knowledge arguments and our CRS size is constant while theirs is linear. Our construction closes a gap in characterizing the efficiency of NIZKs for linear languages (with or without witness sampleability, with or without full adaptivity).

6.2 Disjunction of DDH Languages and Tight USS-QA-NIZKs

Using the construction of Sect. 5, we obtain a NIZK for the disjunction of two DDH languages with only 7 group elements. This is three group elements less than the best previously known NIZK for this language [66]. We provide a self-contained description of the resulting proof system in Fig. 5. As discussed in the introduction, combining this proof with the result of [3], we obtain shorter tightly-secure QA-NIZKs with unbounded simulation-soundness (11 versus 14 group elements) and shorter IND-mCCA-secure PKE with tight security reduction (14 versus 17 group elements).

6.3 Tightly-Secure Structure-Preserving Signatures

NIZKs arguments are an important building block in structure-preserving signatures (SPS). Since our constructions yield shorter NIZK arguments for OR-proofs and (in the fully adaptive case) for linear subspaces, substituting existing proofs with our constructions directly improves various SPS schemes. For example, Gay et al. [34] use an Or-proof for two DDH languages in their construction; using our OR-proof reduces the size of their tightly-secure SPS from 14 group elements to 11.

The same size was achieved recently by Abe et al. [3]. They use a new approach in describing the used OR-language as a conjunction statement and build a designated-prover quasi-adaptive NIZK from this formalization, which is shorter than the (publicly-verifiable) OR-proof of [66] (7 versus 10 group elements). We notice that their OR-proof is compatible with our compiler, which allows us to reduce its size down to 5 group elements. This in turn reduces the size of the SPS by 2, resulting in a size of 9 group elements per signature. The exact construction is shown in the full version of this paper [20] and yields the following lemma:

Lemma 19. *There exists a structure-preserving signature scheme which reduces to the SXDH assumption and the $\mathcal{L}_1$-1-extKerMDH assumption with security loss $6 \log Q$, where Q is the number of signing queries, with a signature size is 9 group elements and a public key size of $n + 15$ elements (for length-n messages).*

A comparison of the resulting SPS to existing schemes can be found in Table 4. We note that our tight SPS can be converted into a bilateral tight SPS (where messages can be from both $\mathbb{G}_1$ and $\mathbb{G}_2$) using the generic transform of [56], leading to a bilateral tightly-secure SPS of size 12 group elements (versus 14 for the best known bilateral tight SPS [3]).

6.4 Ring Signatures

An example of the use of k-out-of-n OR-proofs is the construction of sublinear ring signatures in the standard model [18,66]. The two constructions produce signatures of size $\mathcal{O}(\sqrt{N})$, where N is the size of the ring. The previous works reduce the size of the signature by rearranging the list of potential signers in the ring into a square matrix, and commit to two bit vectors of weight one, where one denotes the row and the other the column of the used key. Then, a NIZK is used to show that the signature was produce with the key at the corresponding (committed) coordinates in the matrix. This NIZK requires at its core a proof that the two vectors are actually bit vectors and sum to 1. This can be rephrased as an $(n-1)$-out-of-n proof of opening of the commitments to 0, together with a proof that their sum opens to one. The proof given in [66] requires $4 \cdot \sqrt{N}$ group elements, while our proof from Sect. 5 only requires $3 \cdot \sqrt{N} + 1$ group elements.

We note that there are also constructions achieving sizes of $\sqrt[3]{N}$ [39], however these constructions are not compatible with our NIZK arguments, as they require proofs of knowledge, which our construction does not provide. Furthermore, the constant factors of the construction are quite large, so improving $\sqrt{N}$ constructions might still be useful.

Acknowledgements. We would like to thank Dennis Hofheinz for discussions and contributions to early stages of this work, Eike Kiltz for helpful comments and Carla Ràfols for discussion and pointers.

The first author was supported by ERC Project PREP-CRYPTO (724307), and the second author was funded by the Deutsche Forschungsgemeinschaft (DFG, German Research Foundation) under German's Excellence Strategy – EXC 2092 CASA – 390781972, and the German Federal Ministry of Education and Research (BMBF) iBlockchain project.

References

1. Abe, M., Chase, M., David, B., Kohlweiss, M., Nishimaki, R., Ohkubo, M.: Constant-size structure-preserving signatures: generic constructions and simple assumptions. In: Wang, X., Sako, K. (eds.) ASIACRYPT 2012. LNCS, vol. 7658, pp. 4–24. Springer, Heidelberg (2012). https://doi.org/10.1007/978-3-642-34961-4_3

2. Abe, M., Hofheinz, D., Nishimaki, R., Ohkubo, M., Pan, J.: Compact structure-preserving signatures with almost tight security. In: Katz, J., Shacham, H. (eds.) CRYPTO 2017, Part II. LNCS, vol. 10402, pp. 548–580. Springer, Cham (2017). https://doi.org/10.1007/978-3-319-63715-0_19

3. Abe, M., Jutla, C.S., Ohkubo, M., Pan, J., Roy, A., Wang, Y.: Shorter QA-NIZK and SPS with tighter security. In: Galbraith, S.D., Moriai, S. (eds.) ASIACRYPT 2019, Part III. LNCS, vol. 11923, pp. 669–699. Springer, Cham (2019). https://doi.org/10.1007/978-3-030-34618-8_23

4. Abe, M., Jutla, C.S., Ohkubo, M., Roy, A.: Improved (almost) tightly-secure simulation-sound QA-NIZK with applications. In: Peyrin, T., Galbraith, S. (eds.) ASIACRYPT 2018, Part I. LNCS, vol. 11272, pp. 627–656. Springer, Cham (2018). https://doi.org/10.1007/978-3-030-03326-2_21

5. Backes, M., Döttling, N., Hanzlik, L., Kluczniak, K., Schneider, J.: Ring signatures: logarithmic-size, no setup—from standard assumptions. In: Ishai, Y., Rijmen, V. (eds.) EUROCRYPT 2019, Part III. LNCS, vol. 11478, pp. 281–311. Springer, Cham (2019). https://doi.org/10.1007/978-3-030-17659-4_10

6. Badrinarayanan, S., Fernando, R., Jain, A., Khurana, D., Sahai, A.: Statistical ZAP arguments. In: Canteaut, A., Ishai, Y. (eds.) EUROCRYPT 2020, Part III. LNCS, vol. 12107, pp. 642–667. Springer, Cham (2020). https://doi.org/10.1007/978-3-030-45727-3_22

7. Barak, B.: How to go beyond the black-box simulation barrier. In: 42nd FOCS, pp. 106–115. IEEE Computer Society Press, October 2001

8. Barak, B., Ong, S.J., Vadhan, S.P.: Derandomization in cryptography. In: Boneh, D. (ed.) CRYPTO 2003. LNCS, vol. 2729, pp. 299–315. Springer, Heidelberg (2003). https://doi.org/10.1007/978-3-540-45146-4_18

9. Belenkiy, M., Chase, M., Kohlweiss, M., Lysyanskaya, A.: P-signatures and non-interactive anonymous credentials. In: Canetti, R. (ed.) TCC 2008. LNCS, vol. 4948, pp. 356–374. Springer, Heidelberg (2008). https://doi.org/10.1007/978-3-540-78524-8_20

10. Ben Hamouda, F., Blazy, O., Chevalier, C., Pointcheval, D., Vergnaud, D.: Efficient UC-secure authenticated key-exchange for algebraic languages. In: Kurosawa, K., Hanaoka, G. (eds.) PKC 2013. LNCS, vol. 7778, pp. 272–291. Springer, Heidelberg (2013). https://doi.org/10.1007/978-3-642-36362-7_18

11. Benhamouda, F., Couteau, G., Pointcheval, D., Wee, H.: Implicit zero-knowledge arguments and applications to the malicious setting. In: Gennaro, R., Robshaw, M.J.B. (eds.) CRYPTO 2015, Part II. LNCS, vol. 9216, pp. 107–129. Springer, Heidelberg (2015). https://doi.org/10.1007/978-3-662-48000-7_6

12. Blazy, O., Fuchsbauer, G., Izabachène, M., Jambert, A., Sibert, H., Vergnaud, D.: Batch Groth-Sahai. In: Zhou, J., Yung, M. (eds.) ACNS 2010. LNCS, vol. 6123, pp. 218–235. Springer, Heidelberg (2010). https://doi.org/10.1007/978-3-642-13708-2_14

13. Blum, M., Feldman, P., Micali, S.: Non-interactive zero-knowledge and its applications (extended abstract). In: 20th ACM STOC, pp. 103–112. ACM Press, May 1988

14. Camenisch, J., Kohlweiss, M., Soriente, C.: An accumulator based on bilinear maps and efficient revocation for anonymous credentials. In: Jarecki, S., Tsudik, G. (eds.) PKC 2009. LNCS, vol. 5443, pp. 481–500. Springer, Heidelberg (2009). https://doi.org/10.1007/978-3-642-00468-1_27

15. Camenisch, J., Lysyanskaya, A.: Signature schemes and anonymous credentials from bilinear maps. In: Franklin, M. (ed.) CRYPTO 2004. LNCS, vol. 3152, pp. 56–72. Springer, Heidelberg (2004). https://doi.org/10.1007/978-3-540-28628-8_4

16. Canetti, R., Chen, Y., Reyzin, L., Rothblum, R.D.: Fiat-Shamir and correlation intractability from strong KDM-secure encryption. In: Nielsen, J.B., Rijmen, V. (eds.) EUROCRYPT 2018, Part I. LNCS, vol. 10820, pp. 91–122. Springer, Cham (2018). https://doi.org/10.1007/978-3-319-78381-9_4

17. Chaidos, P., Couteau, G.: Efficient designated-verifier non-interactive zero-knowledge proofs of knowledge. In: Nielsen, J.B., Rijmen, V. (eds.) EUROCRYPT 2018, Part III. LNCS, vol. 10822, pp. 193–221. Springer, Cham (2018). https://doi.org/10.1007/978-3-319-78372-7_7

18. Chandran, N., Groth, J., Sahai, A.: Ring signatures of sub-linear size without random oracles. In: Arge, L., Cachin, C., Jurdziński, T., Tarlecki, A. (eds.) ICALP 2007. LNCS, vol. 4596, pp. 423–434. Springer, Heidelberg (2007). https://doi.org/10.1007/978-3-540-73420-8_38

19. Chase, M., Meiklejohn, S., Zaverucha, G.: Algebraic MACs and keyed-verification anonymous credentials. In: Ahn, G.J., Yung, M., Li, N. (eds.) ACM CCS 14, pp. 1205–1216. ACM Press, November 2014

20. Couteau, G., Hartmann, D.: Shorter non-interactive zero-knowledge arguments and zaps for algebraic languages. IACR Cryptology ePrint Archive 2020, 286 (2020)

21. Cramer, R., Damgård, I., Schoenmakers, B.: Proofs of partial knowledge and simplified design of witness hiding protocols. In: Desmedt, Y.G. (ed.) CRYPTO 1994. LNCS, vol. 839, pp. 174–187. Springer, Heidelberg (1994). https://doi.org/10.1007/3-540-48658-5_19

22. Cramer, R., Shoup, V.: Universal hash proofs and a paradigm for adaptive chosen ciphertext secure public-key encryption. In: Knudsen, L.R. (ed.) EUROCRYPT 2002. LNCS, vol. 2332, pp. 45–64. Springer, Heidelberg (2002). https://doi.org/10.1007/3-540-46035-7_4

23. Damgård, I.B.: Payment systems and credential mechanisms with provable security against abuse by individuals. In: Goldwasser, S. (ed.) CRYPTO 1988. LNCS, vol. 403, pp. 328–335. Springer, New York (1990). https://doi.org/10.1007/0-387-34799-2_26

24. Damgård, I., Fazio, N., Nicolosi, A.: Non-interactive zero-knowledge from homomorphic encryption. In: Halevi, S., Rabin, T. (eds.) TCC 2006. LNCS, vol. 3876, pp. 41–59. Springer, Heidelberg (2006). https://doi.org/10.1007/11681878_3

25. Daza, V., González, A., Pindado, Z., Ràfols, C., Silva, J.: Shorter quadratic QA-NIZK proofs. In: Lin, D., Sako, K. (eds.) PKC 2019, Part I. LNCS, vol. 11442, pp. 314–343. Springer, Cham (2019). https://doi.org/10.1007/978-3-030-17253-4_11

26. Dwork, C., Naor, M.: Zaps and their applications. In: 41st FOCS, pp. 283–293. IEEE Computer Society Press, November 2000

27. Escala, A., Groth, J.: Fine-tuning Groth-Sahai proofs. In: Krawczyk, H. (ed.) PKC 2014. LNCS, vol. 8383, pp. 630–649. Springer, Heidelberg (2014). https://doi.org/10.1007/978-3-642-54631-0_36

28. Escala, A., Herold, G., Kiltz, E., Ràfols, C., Villar, J.L.: An algebraic framework for Diffie-Hellman assumptions. J. Cryptol. **30**(1), 242–288 (2017). https://doi.org/10.1007/s00145-015-9220-6

29. Feige, U., Lapidot, D., Shamir, A.: Multiple non-interactive zero knowledge proofs based on a single random string (extended abstract). In: 31st FOCS, pp. 308–317. IEEE Computer Society Press, October 1990

30. Fiat, A., Shamir, A.: How to prove yourself: practical solutions to identification and signature problems. In: Odlyzko, A.M. (ed.) CRYPTO 1986. LNCS, vol. 263, pp. 186–194. Springer, Heidelberg (1987). https://doi.org/10.1007/3-540-47721-7_12

31. Fuchsbauer, G., Kiltz, E., Loss, J.: The algebraic group model and its applications. In: Shacham, H., Boldyreva, A. (eds.) CRYPTO 2018, Part II. LNCS, vol. 10992, pp. 33–62. Springer, Cham (2018). https://doi.org/10.1007/978-3-319-96881-0_2

32. Garman, C., Green, M., Miers, I.: Decentralized anonymous credentials. In: NDSS 2014. The Internet Society, February 2014

33. Gay, R., Hofheinz, D., Kiltz, E., Wee, H.: Tightly CCA-secure encryption without pairings. In: Fischlin, M., Coron, J.S. (eds.) EUROCRYPT 2016, Part I. LNCS, vol. 9665, pp. 1–27. Springer, Heidelberg (2016). https://doi.org/10.1007/978-3-662-49890-3_1

34. Gay, R., Hofheinz, D., Kohl, L., Pan, J.: More efficient (almost) tightly secure structure-preserving signatures. In: Nielsen, J.B., Rijmen, V. (eds.) EUROCRYPT 2018, Part II. LNCS, vol. 10821, pp. 230–258. Springer, Cham (2018). https://doi.org/10.1007/978-3-319-78375-8_8

35. Gennaro, R., Gentry, C., Parno, B., Raykova, M.: Quadratic span programs and succinct NIZKs without PCPs. Cryptology ePrint Archive, Report 2012/215 (2012). http://eprint.iacr.org/2012/215

36. Gentry, C., Wichs, D.: Separating succinct non-interactive arguments from all falsifiable assumptions. In: Fortnow, L., Vadhan, S.P. (eds.) 43rd ACM STOC, pp. 99–108. ACM Press, June 2011

37. Goldwasser, S., Kalai, Y.T.: On the (in)security of the Fiat-Shamir paradigm. In: 44th FOCS, pp. 102–115. IEEE Computer Society Press, October 2003

38. Goldwasser, S., Micali, S., Rackoff, C.: The knowledge complexity of interactive proof systems. SIAM J. Comput. **18**(1), 186–208 (1989)

39. González, A.: Shorter ring signatures from standard assumptions. In: Lin, D., Sako, K. (eds.) PKC 2019, Part I. LNCS, vol. 11442, pp. 99–126. Springer, Cham (2019). https://doi.org/10.1007/978-3-030-17253-4_4

40. Groth, J.: Simulation-sound NIZK proofs for a practical language and constant size group signatures. In: Lai, X., Chen, K. (eds.) ASIACRYPT 2006. LNCS, vol. 4284, pp. 444–459. Springer, Heidelberg (2006). https://doi.org/10.1007/11935230_29

41. Groth, J., Lu, S.: A non-interactive shuffle with pairing based verifiability. In: Kurosawa, K. (ed.) ASIACRYPT 2007. LNCS, vol. 4833, pp. 51–67. Springer, Heidelberg (2007). https://doi.org/10.1007/978-3-540-76900-2_4

42. Groth, J., Ostrovsky, R., Sahai, A.: Non-interactive zaps and new techniques for NIZK. In: Dwork, C. (ed.) CRYPTO 2006. LNCS, vol. 4117, pp. 97–111. Springer, Heidelberg (2006). https://doi.org/10.1007/11818175_6

43. Groth, J., Ostrovsky, R., Sahai, A.: New techniques for noninteractive zero-knowledge. J. ACM (JACM) **59**(3), 11 (2012)

44. Groth, J., Sahai, A.: Efficient non-interactive proof systems for bilinear groups. In: Smart, N.P. (ed.) EUROCRYPT 2008. LNCS, vol. 4965, pp. 415–432. Springer, Heidelberg (2008). https://doi.org/10.1007/978-3-540-78967-3_24

45. Hamouda, F.B., Blazy, O., Chevalier, C., Pointcheval, D., Vergnaud, D.: Efficient UC-Secure authenticated key-exchange for algebraic languages. Cryptology ePrint Archive, Report 2012/284 (2012). http://eprint.iacr.org/2012/284

46. Hanser, C., Slamanig, D.: Structure-preserving signatures on equivalence classes and their application to anonymous credentials. In: Sarkar, P., Iwata, T. (eds.) ASIACRYPT 2014, Part I. LNCS, vol. 8873, pp. 491–511. Springer, Heidelberg (2014). https://doi.org/10.1007/978-3-662-45611-8_26

47. Hofheinz, D., Jager, T.: Tightly secure signatures and public-key encryption. In: Safavi-Naini, R., Canetti, R. (eds.) CRYPTO 2012. LNCS, vol. 7417, pp. 590–607. Springer, Heidelberg (2012). https://doi.org/10.1007/978-3-642-32009-5_35

48. Hofheinz, D., Kiltz, E.: Secure hybrid encryption from weakened key encapsulation. Cryptology ePrint Archive, Report 2007/288 (2007). http://eprint.iacr.org/2007/288

49. Jain, A., Jin, Z.: Statistical zap arguments from quasi-polynomial LWE. Technical report, Cryptology ePrint Archive, Report 2019/839 (2019). https://eprint.iacr.org

50. Jutla, C.S., Ohkubo, M., Roy, A.: Improved (almost) tightly-secure structure-preserving signatures. In: Abdalla, M., Dahab, R. (eds.) PKC 2018, Part II. LNCS, vol. 10770, pp. 123–152. Springer, Cham (2018). https://doi.org/10.1007/978-3-319-76581-5_5

51. Jutla, C.S., Roy, A.: Shorter quasi-adaptive NIZK proofs for linear subspaces. In: Sako, K., Sarkar, P. (eds.) ASIACRYPT 2013, Part I. LNCS, vol. 8269, pp. 1–20. Springer, Heidelberg (2013). https://doi.org/10.1007/978-3-642-42033-7_1

52. Jutla, C.S., Roy, A.: Improved structure preserving signatures under standard bilinear assumptions. In: Fehr, S. (ed.) PKC 2017, Part II. LNCS, vol. 10175, pp. 183–209. Springer, Heidelberg (2017). https://doi.org/10.1007/978-3-662-54388-7_7

53. Kalai, Y., Paneth, O., Yang, L.: On publicly verifiable delegation from standard assumptions. Cryptology ePrint Archive, Report 2018/776 (2018). https://eprint.iacr.org/2018/776

54. Kalai, Y.T., Khurana, D., Sahai, A.: Statistical witness indistinguishability (and more) in two messages. In: Nielsen, J.B., Rijmen, V. (eds.) EUROCRYPT 2018, Part III. LNCS, vol. 10822, pp. 34–65. Springer, Cham (2018). https://doi.org/10.1007/978-3-319-78372-7_2

55. Kalai, Y.T., Rothblum, G.N., Rothblum, R.D.: From obfuscation to the security of Fiat-Shamir for proofs. In: Katz, J., Shacham, H. (eds.) CRYPTO 2017, Part II. LNCS, vol. 10402, pp. 224–251. Springer, Cham (2017). https://doi.org/10.1007/978-3-319-63715-0_8

56. Kiltz, E., Pan, J., Wee, H.: Structure-preserving signatures from standard assumptions, revisited. In: Gennaro, R., Robshaw, M.J.B. (eds.) CRYPTO 2015, Part II. LNCS, vol. 9216, pp. 275–295. Springer, Heidelberg (2015). https://doi.org/10.1007/978-3-662-48000-7_14

57. Kiltz, E., Wee, H.: Quasi-adaptive NIZK for linear subspaces revisited. In: Oswald, E., Fischlin, M. (eds.) EUROCRYPT 2015, Part II. LNCS, vol. 9057, pp. 101–128. Springer, Heidelberg (2015). https://doi.org/10.1007/978-3-662-46803-6_4

58. Libert, B., Peters, T., Joye, M., Yung, M.: Non-malleability from malleability: simulation-sound quasi-adaptive NIZK proofs and CCA2-secure encryption from homomorphic signatures. In: Nguyen, P.Q., Oswald, E. (eds.) EUROCRYPT 2014. LNCS, vol. 8441, pp. 514–532. Springer, Heidelberg (2014). https://doi.org/10.1007/978-3-642-55220-5_29

59. Libert, B., Peters, T., Joye, M., Yung, M.: Compactly hiding linear spans-tightly secure constant-size simulation-sound QA-NIZK proofs and applications. In: Iwata, T., Cheon, J.H. (eds.) ASIACRYPT 2015, Part I. LNCS, vol. 9452, pp. 681–707. Springer, Heidelberg (2015). https://doi.org/10.1007/978-3-662-48797-6_28

60. Libert, B., Peters, T., Yung, M.: Short group signatures via structure-preserving signatures: standard model security from simple assumptions. In: Gennaro, R., Robshaw, M.J.B. (eds.) CRYPTO 2015, Part II. LNCS, vol. 9216, pp. 296–316. Springer, Heidelberg (2015). https://doi.org/10.1007/978-3-662-48000-7_15

61. Lysyanskaya, A., Rivest, R.L., Sahai, A., Wolf, S.: Pseudonym systems. In: Heys, H.M., Adams, C.M. (eds.) SAC 1999. LNCS, vol. 1758, pp. 184–199. Springer, Heidelberg (2000). https://doi.org/10.1007/3-540-46513-8_14

62. Maurer, U.M.: Unifying zero-knowledge proofs of knowledge. In: Preneel, B. (ed.) AFRICACRYPT 2009. LNCS, vol. 5580, pp. 272–286. Springer, Heidelberg (2009). https://doi.org/10.1007/978-3-642-02384-2_17

63. Morillo, P., Ràfols, C., Villar, J.L.: The kernel matrix Diffie-Hellman assumption. In: Cheon, J.H., Takagi, T. (eds.) ASIACRYPT 2016, Part I. LNCS, vol. 10031, pp. 729–758. Springer, Heidelberg (2016). https://doi.org/10.1007/978-3-662-53887-6_27

64. Naor, M.: On cryptographic assumptions and challenges (invited talk). In: Boneh, D. (ed.) CRYPTO 2003. LNCS, vol. 2729, pp. 96–109. Springer, Heidelberg (2003). https://doi.org/10.1007/978-3-540-45146-4_6

65. Noether, S.: Ring signature confidential transactions for monero. Cryptology ePrint Archive, Report 2015/1098 (2015). http://eprint.iacr.org/2015/1098

66. Ràfols, C.: Stretching Groth-Sahai: NIZK proofs of partial satisfiability. In: Dodis, Y., Nielsen, J.B. (eds.) TCC 2015, Part II. LNCS, vol. 9015, pp. 247–276. Springer, Heidelberg (2015). https://doi.org/10.1007/978-3-662-46497-7_10

67. Rivest, R.L., Shamir, A., Tauman, Y.: How to leak a secret. In: Boyd, C. (ed.) ASIACRYPT 2001. LNCS, vol. 2248, pp. 552–565. Springer, Heidelberg (2001). https://doi.org/10.1007/3-540-45682-1_32

68. Schnorr, C.P.: Efficient identification and signatures for smart cards (abstract) (rump session). In: Quisquater, J.J., Vandewalle, J. (eds.) EUROCRYPT 1989. LNCS, vol. 434, pp. 688–689. Springer, Heidelberg (1990). https://doi.org/10.1007/3-540-46885-4_68

69. Shamir, A.: How to share a secret. Commun. Assoc. Comput. Mach. **22**(11), 612–613 (1979)

70. Shoup, V.: Lower bounds for discrete logarithms and related problems. In: Fumy, W. (ed.) EUROCRYPT 1997. LNCS, vol. 1233, pp. 256–266. Springer, Heidelberg (1997). https://doi.org/10.1007/3-540-69053-0_18

71. Tsang, P.P., Wei, V.K.: Short linkable ring signatures for e-voting, e-cash and attestation. In: Deng, R.H., Bao, F., Pang, H.H., Zhou, J. (eds.) ISPEC 2005. LNCS, vol. 3439, pp. 48–60. Springer, Heidelberg (2005). https://doi.org/10.1007/978-3-540-31979-5_5

Non-interactive Zero-Knowledge Arguments for QMA, with Preprocessing

Andrea Coladangelo$^{(\boxtimes)}$, Thomas Vidick, and Tina Zhang

Computing and Mathematical Sciences, Caltech, Pasadena, USA
`acoladan@caltech.edu`

Abstract. A non-interactive zero-knowledge (NIZK) proof system for a language $L \in$ NP allows a prover (who is provided with an instance $x \in L$, and a witness w for x) to compute a *classical certificate* π for the claim that $x \in L$ such that π has the following properties: 1) π can be verified efficiently, and 2) π does not reveal any information about w, besides the fact that it exists (i.e. that $x \in L$). NIZK proof systems have recently been shown to exist for all languages in NP in the common reference string (CRS) model and under the learning with errors (LWE) assumption.

We initiate the study of NIZK *arguments* for languages in QMA. An argument system differs from a proof system in that the honest prover must be efficient, and that it is only sound against (quantum) polynomial-time provers. Our first main result is the following: if LWE is hard for quantum computers, then any language in QMA has an *NIZK argument with preprocessing*. The preprocessing in our argument system consists of (i) the generation of a CRS and (ii) a *single (instance-independent) quantum message* from verifier to prover. The instance-dependent phase of our argument system, meanwhile, involves only a single *classical* message from prover to verifier. Importantly, verification in our protocol is entirely classical, and the verifier needs not have quantum memory; its only quantum actions are in the preprocessing phase. NIZK proofs of (classical) knowledge are widely used in the construction of more advanced cryptographic protocols, and we expect the quantum analogue to likewise find a broad range of applications. In this respect, the fact that our protocol has an entirely classical verification phase is particularly appealing.

Our second contribution is to extend the notion of a classical *proof of knowledge* to the quantum setting. We introduce the notions of *arguments* and *proofs of quantum knowledge* (AoQK/PoQK), and we show that our non-interactive argument system satisfies the definition of an AoQK, which extends its domain of usefulness with respect to cryptographic applications. In particular, we explicitly construct an extractor which can recover a quantum witness from any prover who is successful in our protocol. We also show that any language in QMA has an (interactive) *proof of quantum knowledge*, again by exhibiting a particular proof system for all languages in QMA and constructing an extractor for it.

Electronic supplementary material The online version of this chapter (https://doi.org/10.1007/978-3-030-56877-1_28) contains supplementary material, which is available to authorized users.

D. Micciancio and T. Ristenpart (Eds.): CRYPTO 2020, LNCS 12172, pp. 799–828, 2020.
https://doi.org/10.1007/978-3-030-56877-1_28

Keywords: Zero-knowledge · Non-interactive proof · Argument systems · QMA

1   Introduction

The paradigm of the interactive proof system is commonly studied in cryptography and in complexity theory. Intuitively speaking, an interactive proof system is a protocol in which an *unbounded* prover attempts to convince an *efficient* verifier that some problem instance x is in some language L. The verifier represents an entity less computationally powerful or less informed than the prover; the prover holds some knowledge that the verifier does not (namely, that $x \in L$), and the prover attempts to convince the verifier of this knowledge. We say that there is an interactive proof system *for a language L* if the following two conditions are satisfied. Firstly, for any $x \in L$, there must exist a prover (the 'honest' prover) which causes the (honest) verifier to accept in the protocol with high probability; and secondly, for any $x \notin L$, there is no prover which can cause the honest verifier to accept, except with some small probability. These two conditions are commonly referred to as the 'completeness' and 'soundness' conditions. We can also consider a relaxed soundness condition where, when $x \notin L$, we require only that it be computationally intractable (rather than impossible) to cause the verifier to accept. A protocol satisfying this relaxed soundness condition, and which has an efficient honest prover, is known as an interactive *argument* system.

Some interactive proof and argument systems satisfy a third property known as *zero-knowledge* [GMR85], which captures the informal notion that the verifier (even a dishonest verifier) 'learns no new information' from an interaction with the honest prover, except for the information that $x \in L$. This idea is formalised through a *simulator*, which has the same computational powers as the verifier V does, and can output transcripts that (for x such that $x \in L$) are indistinguishable from transcripts arising from interactions between V and the honest prover. As such, V intuitively 'learns nothing', because whatever it might have learned from a transcript it could equally have generated by itself. The property of zero-knowledge can be *perfect* (PZK), *statistical* (SZK) or *computational* (CZK). The difference between these three definitions is the extent to which simulated transcripts are indistinguishable from real ones. In a PZK protocol, the simulator's output distribution is *identical* to the distribution of transcripts that the honest prover and (potentially dishonest) verifier generate when $x \in L$. In SZK, the two distributions have negligible statistical distance, and in CZK, they are computationally indistinguishable. In this work we will primarily be concerned with CZK.

A *non-interactive* proof system (or argument system) is a protocol in which the prover and the verifier exchange only a single message that depends on the problem instance x. (In general, an instance-independent setup phase may be allowed in which the prover and verifier communicate, with each other or with a trusted third party, in order to establish shared state that is used during the protocol execution proper. We discuss this setup phase in more detail in the following paragraph.) Non-interactive zero-knowledge (NIZK) proofs and arguments have seen widespread application in classical cryptography, often in venues where their interactive counterparts would be impracticable—including, notably, in CCA-secure public-key cryptosystems [NY90, Sah99], digital signature schemes [BG90, CP92, BMW03], verifiable delegated computation [PHGR13] and, recently, a number of blockchain constructions [GGPR13, Com14, Lab17]. A particularly attractive feature of classical NIZK systems is that they can be amplified *in parallel* to achieve better security parameters [BDSMP91], which is in general not true of their interactive (private-coin) counterparts.

It is known [GO94] that NIZK proofs and arguments in the *standard model* (namely, the model where the only assumption is that adversarial entities are computationally efficient) exist only for languages in BPP. As such, in order to construct NIZK protocols for more interesting languages, it is customary to consider *extended* cryptographic models. Examples of these include the *common reference string* (CRS) model, in which the verifier and the prover are assumed to begin the protocol sharing access to a common string sampled from a specified distribution; and the *random oracle* (RO) model, in which prover and verifier have access to an efficiently evaluable function that behaves like a function sampled uniformly at random from the set of possible functions with some specified, and finite, domain and range. In these extended models, and under certain computational hardness assumptions, non-interactive computational zero-knowledge proof systems for all languages in NP are known. For instance, Blum, Santis, Micali and Persiano [BDSMP91] showed in 1990 that NIZK proofs for all languages in NP exist in the CRS model, assuming that the problem of quadratic residuosity is computationally intractable.

At this point, a natural question arises: what happens in the *quantum* setting? Ever since Shor's algorithm for factoring [Sho95] was published in 1995, it has been understood that the introduction of quantum computers would render a wide range of cryptographic protocols insecure. For example, quadratic residuosity is known to be solvable in polynomial time by quantum computers. Given that this is so, it is natural to ask the following question: in the presence of quantum adversaries, is it still possible to obtain proof systems for all languages in NP that are complete and sound, and if it is, in which extended models is it feasible? This question has been studied in recent years. For example, Unruh showed in [Unr15] that quantum-resistant NIZK proof systems for all languages in NP exist in the quantum random oracle (QRO) model, a quantum generalisation of the random oracle model. More recently, Peikert and Shiehian [PS19] achieved a more direct analogue of Blum et al.'s result, by showing that NIZK proofs for all languages in NP exist in the CRS model, assuming that learning with errors (LWE)—a problem believed to be difficult for quantum computers—is computationally intractable.[1]

However, the advent of large-scale quantum computers would not only render some cryptosystems insecure; it would also provide us with computational powers that extend those of our current classical machines, and give rise to new cryptographic tasks that were never considered in the classical literature. A second natural question which arises in the presence of quantum computers is the following: in which models is it possible to obtain a NIZK proof or argument system not only for all languages in NP, but for all languages in 'quantum NP' (i.e. QMA)? Loosely speaking, NIZK protocols for NP languages allow the prover to prove any statement that can be checked efficiently by a classical verifier who is given a classical witness. A NIZK protocol for QMA languages would, analogously, allow the prover to prove to the verifier (in a non-interactive, zero-knowledge way) the veracity of statements that require a quantum witness and quantum computing power to check. To our knowledge, the question of achieving NIZK protocols for QMA has not yet been studied. In 2016, Broadbent, Ji, Song and Watrous [BJSW16] exhibited a zero-knowledge proof system for QMA with an efficient honest prover, but their protocol requires both quantum and classical interaction.

In this work, our first contribution is to propose a non-interactive (computational) zero-knowledge argument system for all languages in QMA, based on the hardness of LWE, in which both verifier and prover are quantum polynomial time. The model we consider is the CRS (common reference string) model, augmented by a single message of (quantum) preprocessing. (The preprocessing consists of an instance-independent quantum message from the verifier to the prover.) The post-setup single message that the prover sends to the verifier, after it receives the witness, is classical; the post-setup verifier is also entirely classical; and, if we allow the prover and verifier to share EPR pairs *a priori*, as in a model previously considered by Kobayashi [Kob02], we can also make the verifier's preprocessing message classical. Like classical NIZK protocols, our protocol shows itself to be receptive to parallel repetition (see Sect. 2.3 of the supplementary material), which allows us to amplify soundness concurrently without affecting zero-knowledge. Our model and our assumptions are relatively standard ones which can be fruitfully compared with those which have been studied in the classical setting. As such, this result provides an early benchmark of the kinds of assumptions under which NIZK can be achieved for languages in QMA.

An example of an application in which the unique properties of our protocol might be useful is the setting of *verifiable delegated computation*, in which a prover (who is generally a server to whom a client, the verifier, has delegated

---

[1] Peikert and Shiehan construct, based on LWE, a NI(C)ZK proof system in the common *reference* string model, and a NI(S)ZK argument system in the common *random* string model. They do not explicitly consider the applications of either result to the quantum setting. We show, however, for our own purposes, that the latter of these results generalises to quantum adversaries. In other words, we show (in Sect. 1.3 of the Supplementary Material) that the Peikert-Shiehan NIZK *argument* system in the common *random* string model is adaptively sound against quantum adversaries and adaptively (quantum computational) zero-knowledge.

a quantum task) wishes to prove to the verifier a statement about a history state representing a certain computation. Suppose that the prover and the verifier complete the setup phase of our protocol when the delegation occurs. After the setup phase is complete, *the verifier does not need to preserve any quantum information*, meaning that it could perform the setup phase using borrowed quantum resources, and thereafter return to the classical world. When it receives the prover's single-message zero-knowledge proof, the verifier can verify its delegated computation without performing any additional quantum operations—a property that our protocol shares with protocols that have purely classical verification, such as Mahadev's classical-verifier argument system for QMA [Mah18]. An additional advantage of our protocol, however, is that the server can free the quantum memory associated with the verifier's computation *immediately* after the computation terminates, rather than holding the history state until the verifier is available to perform the verification.

Our second contribution is to show that our protocol also satisfies a notion of *argument of quantum knowledge*. In the classical setting, some proof systems and argument systems for NP languages satisfy a stronger notion of soundness wherein a witness can be *extracted* from any prover P who convinces the verifier to accept with high probability. More formally, in such a setting, there is an *extractor* machine which—given black-box access to any P who convinces the verifier to accept with high probability (on the input x)—is able to efficiently compute a witness w that testifies that the problem instance x is in the language L. Such protocols are known as *proofs* and *arguments of knowledge* (PoK and AoK). Intuitively speaking, the notion of PoK/AoK is a framework for describing situations where the prover is not necessarily more powerful, but only *better informed*, than the verifier. In these situations, the prover possesses knowledge (the witness w, which could represent a password or some other form of private information) that the verifier does not; and the prover wishes to convince the verifier, possibly in a zero-knowledge way (i.e. without revealing sensitive information), that it indeed 'knows' or 'possesses' the witness w (so that it might, for example, be granted access to its password-protected files, or cash a quantum cheque). The idea of a machine 'knowing' some witness w is formalised by the existence of the extractor.

Until now, the witness w has always been classical, and the notion of a proof of *quantum* knowledge (PoQK) has not been formally defined or studied. In this paper, we formulate a definition for a PoQK that is analogous to the classical definition of a PoK,[2] and we exhibit a protocol that is an (interactive) PoQK for any language in QMA.[3] We also introduce the notion of an *argument of quantum knowledge* (AoQK), and we prove that our NIZK protocol for QMA is (under this definition) a zero-knowledge argument of quantum knowledge. We present our definitions of PoQK and AoQK in Sect. 2.4.

There are two main difficulties in extending the classical notion of a PoK to the quantum setting. The first is that we must precisely specify how the extractor

---

[2] This definition is joint work with Broadbent and Grilo.

[3] This result is also obtained in independent and concurrent work by Broadbent and Grilo [BG19].

should be permitted to interact with the successful (quantum) prover. For this, we borrow the formalism of quantum interactive machines that Unruh [Unr12] uses in defining quantum proofs of *classical* knowledge. The second difficulty is to give an appropriate definition of success for the extractor. In the classical setting, the NP relation R which defines the set of witnesses w for a problem instance x is binary: a string w is either a witness or it is not. In the quantum setting, on the other hand—unlike in the classical case, in which any witness is as good as any other—different witnesses might be accepted with different probabilities by some verification circuit Q under consideration. In other words, some witnesses may be of better 'quality' than others. In addition, because QMA is a probabilistic class, the choice of Q (which is analogous to the choice of the NP relation R) is more obviously ambiguous than it is in the classical case. Different (and equally valid) choices of verifiers Q for a particular language $L \in$ QMA might have different probabilities of accepting a candidate witness ρ on a particular instance x. In our definition, we define a 'QMA relation' with respect to a fixed choice of verifying circuit (family) Q; we define the 'quality' of a candidate witness ρ for x to be the probability that Q accepts (x, ρ); and we require that the successful extractor returns a witness whose quality lies strictly above the soundness parameter for the QMA relation.

The Interactive Protocol from [BJSW16]

Our protocol is inspired by the protocol exhibited in [BJSW16], which gives a zero-knowledge (interactive) proof system for any language in QMA. The [BJSW16] protocol can be summarized as follows. (For a more detailed exposition, see Sect. 2.2.)

1. The verifier and the prover begin with an instance x of some interesting problem, the latter of which is represented by a (promise) language $L = (L_{yes}, L_{no}) \in$ QMA. The prover wishes to prove to the verifier that $x \in L_{yes}$. The first step is to map x to an instance H of the QMA-complete *local Clifford Hamiltonian problem*. In the case that x is a yes instance, i.e. $x \in L_{yes}$, the prover, who receives a witness state $|\Phi\rangle$ for x as auxiliary input, performs the efficient transformation that turns the witness $|\Phi\rangle$ for x into a witness $|\Psi\rangle$ for H. (The chief property that witnesses $|\Psi\rangle$ for H have is that $\langle\Psi|H|\Psi\rangle$ is *small*—smaller than a certain threshold—which, rephrased in physics terminology, means that $|\Psi\rangle$ has *low energy with respect to H*.) The prover then sends an *encoding* of $|\Psi\rangle$ to the verifier (under a specified quantum authentication code which doubly functions as an encryption scheme). The prover also *commits* to the secret key of the authentication code.

2. The Clifford Hamiltonian H to which x has been mapped can be written as a sum of polynomially many terms of the form $C^* |0^k\rangle \langle 0^k| C$, where C is a Clifford unitary. (This is the origin of the name 'Clifford Hamiltonian'.) The verifier chooses a string r uniformly at random. r plays a role analogous to that of the verifier's choice of edge to check in the 3-colouring zero-knowledge protocol introduced by [GMR85]: intuitively, r determines the verifier's challenge to the prover. Each r corresponds to one of the terms $C_r^* |0^k\rangle \langle 0^k| C_r$ of the Clifford Hamiltonian.

The verifier then measures the term $C_r^* |0^k\rangle \langle 0^k| C_r$ on the encoded witness (this can be done 'homomorphically' through the encoding). The outcome z obtained by the verifier can be thought of as an encoding of the true measurement outcome, the latter of which should be *small* (i.e. correspond to low energy) if $|\Psi\rangle$ is a true witness. The verifier sends z (its measurement outcomes) and r (its choice of Hamiltonian term) back the prover.

3. Finally, using a zero-knowledge NP proof system,[4] the prover provides an (interactive) ZK proof for the following NP statement: there *exists* an opening to its earlier (perfectly binding) commitment such that, if the verifier had the opened encoding keys, it *would* accept. This is an NP statement because the witness string is the encoding keys. Proving that the verifier 'would accept' amounts to proving that the verifier's measurement outcomes z, decoded under the keys which were committed to earlier, would correspond to a low-energy outcome. Because the proof that the prover provides is zero-knowledge, the verifier learns nothing substantial from this exchange, but it becomes convinced that it should accept.

In the protocol from [BJSW16], it is critical to soundness that the prover sends the encoding of the witness to the verifier *before* the verifier chooses r. The zero-knowledge property holds because the encoding that the prover applies to the witness state functions like an authenticated encryption scheme: its encryption-like properties prevent the verifier from learning anything substantial about the witness while handling the encoded state, and its authentication code–like properties ensure that the verifier cannot deviate very far from its honest behaviour.

Our Non-interactive Protocol

We wish to make the protocol from [BJSW16] *non-interactive*. To start with, we can replace the prover's proof in step 3 with a NIZK proof in the CRS model. NIZK proofs for all languages in NP have recently been shown to exist [CLW19, PS19] based on the hardness of LWE only, and we prove that the Peikert-Shiehian construction from [PS19] remains secure (i.e. quantum computationally sound and zero-knowledge) against quantum adversaries, assuming that LWE is quantum computationally intractable. However, the more substantial obstacle to making the [BJSW16] protocol non-interactive is the following: in order to do away with the verifier's message in step 2, it seems that the prover would have to somehow *predict* z (the verifier's measurement outcomes) and send a NIZK proof corresponding to this z. Unfortunately, in order for the authentication code to work, the number of possible outcomes z has to be exponentially large (and thus the prover cannot provide a NIZK proof of consistency for each possible outcome). Even allowing for an instance-independent preprocessing step between the verifier and the prover, it is unclear how this impasse could be resolved.

Our first main idea is to use *quantum teleportation*. We add an instance-independent preprocessing step in which the verifier creates a number of EPR

---

[4] It is known that there are quantumly sound and quantumly zero-knowledge proof systems for NP: see [Wat09].

pairs and sends half of each to the prover. We then have the verifier (prematurely) make her measurement from step 2 *during the preprocessing step* (and hence *independently of the instance!*), and send the measurement outcomes z to the prover. Once x is revealed, the prover *teleports* the encoded witness to the verifier, and sends the verifier the teleportation outcomes d, along with a commitment to his encoding keys. The prover then provides an NIZK proof of an opening to the committed keys such that d, z and the encoding keys are consistent with a low-energy outcome. The hope is that, because the prover's and the verifier's actions commute (at least when the prover is honest), this protocol will be, in some sense, equivalent to one where the prover firstly teleports the witness, *then* the verifier makes the measurements, and finally the prover sends an NIZK proof. This latter protocol would be essentially equivalent to the [BJSW16] protocol.

There are three main issues with this strategy:

1. In the preprocessing step, the verifier does not yet know what the instance x (and hence what the Clifford Hamiltonian) is. Thus, she cannot measure the term $C_r^* |0^k\rangle \langle 0^k| C_r$, as she would have done in what we have called step 2 of the protocol from [BJSW16].
2. The second issue is that the verifier cannot communicate her choice of r in the preprocessing step in the clear. If she does, the prover will easily be able to cheat by teleporting a state that passes the check for the rth Hamiltonian term, but that would not pass the check for any other term.
3. The third issue is a bit more subtle. If the prover knows the verifier's measurement outcomes z before he teleports the witness state to the verifier, he can misreport the teleportation outcomes d, and make a clever choice of d such that d, z and the committed keys are consistent with a low-energy outcome even when he does not possess a genuine witness.

The first issue is resolved by considering the (instance-independent) verifying circuit Q *for the* QMA *language* L (recall that Q takes as input both an instance x and a witness state), and mapping Q itself to a Clifford Hamiltonian $H(Q)$. (For comparison, in the protocol from [BJSW16], it is the circuit $Q(x, \cdot)$ which is mapped to a Clifford Hamiltonian.) In the instance-dependent step, the prover will be asked to teleport a "history state" corresponding to the execution of the circuit Q on input $(x, |\Psi\rangle)$, where $|\Psi\rangle$ is a witness for the instance x. In the preprocessing step, the verifier will measure a uniformly random term from $H(Q)$, and will also perform a special measurement (with some probability) which is meant to certify that the prover put the correct instance x into Q when it was creating the history state. Of course, the verifier does not know x at the time of this measurement, but she will know x at the point where she needs to verify the prover's NIZK proof.

Our second main idea, which addresses the second and the third issues above (at the price of downgrading our proof system to an argument system), is to have the prover *compute his NIZK proof homomorphically*. During the preprocessing step, we have the verifier send the prover a (computationally hiding) commitment σ to her choice of r; and, in addition, we ask the verifier to send the prover a *homomorphic encryption* of r, of the randomness s used to commit to σ, and of her measurement outcomes z. At the beginning of the instance-dependent step, the prover receives a witness $|\Psi\rangle$ for the instance x. During the instance-dependent step, and after having received the verifier's ciphertexts in the preprocessing step, we ask the prover firstly to commit to some choice of encoding keys, and then to teleport to the verifier (an encoding of) the history state corresponding to the execution of Q on input $(x, |\Psi\rangle)$. Let d be the outcome of the teleportation measurements. After the prover has committed to his encoding keys, we ask the prover to homomorphically encrypt d and his encoding keys, and homomorphically run the following circuit: check that r, s is a valid opening to σ, and (using the properties of the authentication code) check also that the verifier performed the honest measurement during preprocessing. If all the checks pass, then the prover *homomorphically* computes an NIZK proof that there exist encoding keys consistent with his commitment such that these keys, together with r, z, d, indicate that the verifier's measurement result was a low-energy outcome. The homomorphic encryption safeguards the verifier against a malicious prover who may attempt to take advantage of knowing r, or of the freedom to cleverly choose d, in order to pass in the protocol without holding a genuine witness.

In summary, the structure of our protocol is as follows. Let Q be a QMA verification circuit, and let $H(Q)$ be the Clifford Hamiltonian obtained from Q by performing a circuit-to-Clifford-Hamiltonian reduction.

1. *(preprocessing step)* The verifier creates a (sufficiently large) number of EPR pairs, and divides them into 'her halves' and 'the prover's halves'. She interprets her halves as the qubits making up (an encoding of) a history state generated from an evaluation of the circuit Q. Then, the verifier samples r (her 'challenge') uniformly at random, and according to its value, does one of two things: either she measures a uniformly random term of $H(Q)$ on 'her halves' of the EPR pairs, or she makes a special measurement (on her halves of the EPR pairs) whose results will allow her later to verify that the circuit Q was evaluated on the correct instance x. Following this, the verifier samples a public-key, secret-key pair (pk, sk) for a homomorphic encryption scheme. She sends the prover:
   (a) pk;
   (b) the 'prover's halves' of the EPR pairs;
   (c) a commitment to her choice of challenge r;
   (d) homomorphic encryptions of
       i. r,
       ii. the randomness s used in the commitment, and
       iii. the measurement outcomes z.
2. *(instance-dependent step)* Upon receiving x, and a witness $|\Psi\rangle$, the prover computes the appropriate history state, and samples encoding keys. Then, he teleports an encoding of the history state to the verifier using the half EPR pairs that he previously received from her. Notice that the verifier has already measured the other half of the EPR pairs on her side during the

preprocessing step: hence the encoded history state is not being physically teleported. Nonetheless, because the measurements of the verifier and the prover commute, the net effect in terms of measurement outcome statistics is the same. Let d be the teleportation measurement outcomes. The prover sends to the verifier:

(a) d;
(b) a commitment σ to his encoding keys;
(c) a homomorphic encryption of a NIZK proof (homomorphically computed) of the existence of an opening to σ such that the opened keys, together with d, z, r, are consistent with a low-energy outcome.

Upon receiving d, σ, and an encrypted proof $\tilde{\pi}$ from the prover, the verifier decrypts $\tilde{\pi}$ to obtain π, and checks that π is a valid proof and that it is consistent with d and σ (i.e the d and σ from steps (a) and (b) are the same that appear in the statement being proven).

Analysis

Our protocol is a non-interactive, zero-knowledge argument system in the CRS model with a one-message preprocessing step. It is straightforward to see that the protocol satisfies completeness.

Intuitively, soundness follows from the fact that the encryptions the prover receives in the preprocessing step should be indistinguishable (assuming the prover is computationally bounded) from encryptions of the zero string. As such, the encryptions of z, r, s (and the commitment to r) cannot possibly be helping the prover in guessing r or in selecting a false teleportation measurement outcome d' which makes z, r, d' and the authentication keys consistent with a low-energy outcome. Soundness then essentially reduces to soundness of the protocol in [BJSW16].

The zero-knowledge property follows largely from the properties of the protocol in [BJSW16] that allowed Broadbent, Ji, Song and Watrous to achieve zero-knowledge. One key difference is that, in order to avoid rewinding the (quantum) verifier, the authors of [BJSW16] use the properties of an *interactive coin-flipping protocol* to allow the efficient simulator to recover the string r (recall that r determines the verifier's challenge) with probability 1. (The traditional alternative to this strategy is to have the simulator guess r, and rewind the verifier if it guessed incorrectly in order to guess again. This is typical in classical proofs of zero-knowledge [GMR85]. However, because quantum rewinding [Wat09] is more delicate, the authors of [BJSW16] avoid it for simplicity.) As our protocol is non-interactive, we are unable to take the same approach. Instead, we ask the verifier to choose r and commit to it using a commitment scheme with a property we call *extractability*. Intuitively, extractability means that the commitment scheme *takes a public key determined by the CRS*. We then show that the simulator can efficiently recover r from the verifier's commitment by taking advantage of the CRS. For an LWE-based extractable commitment scheme, see Sect. 1.2 of the Supplementary Material.

Another subtlety, unique to homomorphic encryption, is that the verifier may learn something about the homomorphic computations performed by the prover (and hence possibly about the encoding keys) by looking at the *encryption randomness* in the encryption (of an NIZK proof) that the prover sends the verifier. (Recall that the verifier possesses the decryption key sk for the homomorphic encryption scheme.) This leads us to require the use of a fully homomorphic encryption scheme which satisfies the property of *circuit privacy*. For a definition of this property, see Sect. 1.2 of the Supplementary Material.

Remark 1. The technique we proposed to remove interaction from the protocol of [BJSW16] is based on two main ingredients: the use of quantum teleportation, which allows the verifier to *anticipate* her measurements of the state she receives from the prover in the instance-dependent step, and the use of classical homomorphic encryption to allow the prover to demonstrate (homomorphically) that he has performed a certain computation correctly. These two ingredients work in tandem to ensure that the soundness and the zero-knowledge property of the [BJSW16] protocol are preserved. We believe that this technique could find use more broadly. In particular, it may be applicable as a general (soundness and zero-knowledge preserving) transformation to any interactive proof system for QMA with an efficient honest prover. We leave a more thorough investigation of this as a direction for future work.

A Non-interactive Argument of Quantum Knowledge

One desirable feature of our non-interactive argument system is that it is also an *argument of quantum knowledge*. As we mentioned earlier, one of our contributions is to generalize the definitions of PoKs and AoKs for NP-relations to definitions of PoKs and AoKs for *QMA relations*. In the latter setting, the prover wishes to convince the verifier that he 'knows' or 'possesses' the quantum witness for an instance of a QMA problem. In order to show that our protocol satisfies this additional property, we need to exhibit an extractor that, for any yes instance x, and given quantum oracle access to any prover that is accepted with high probability in our protocol, outputs a quantum state which is a witness for x. In Sect. 6, we explicitly construct such an extractor K for our non-interactive protocol. The intuition is the following. K (the extractor) has oracle access to a prover P^*, and it simulates an execution of the protocol between P^* and the honest verifier V. We show that, if P^* is accepted in our protocol with sufficiently high probability, then it must teleport to V (and hence to K) the *encoding* $\tilde{\rho}$ of a witness state, and a commitment σ to the encoding keys. If K knew the encoding keys, it would be able to decode $\tilde{\rho}$, but it is not clear *a priori* how K could obtain such keys. Crucially, the same feature of our protocol that allows the *zero-knowledge* simulator to extract r from the verifier's commitment to r also plays in K's favour: when K simulates an execution of the protocol, it samples a common reference string which is given to both V and P^*, and in our protocol, the CRS contains a public key which P^* uses to make his commitment. As such, in order to extract a witness from P^*, the extractor samples a CRS containing a public key pk for which it knows the corresponding secret key sk, and provides this particular CRS as input to P^*. Then, when K receives $\tilde{\rho}$ and σ from P^*, it is able to extract the committed keys from σ, and use these to decode $\tilde{\rho}$.

An Interactive Proof of Quantum Knowledge

Our non-interactive protocol is an *argument system*, which means that it is sound only against computationally bounded provers. In Sect. 7, we introduce a separate but complementary result to our NIZK argument (of knowledge) for QMA by showing that the zero-knowledge proof system for QMA exhibited in [BJSW16] (with some minor modifications) is also a *proof of quantum knowledge*.

2   Preliminaries

2.1   Notation

For an integer $\ell \geq 1$, $[\ell]$ denotes the set $\{1, \ldots, \ell\}$. We use $\mathrm{poly}(n)$ and $\mathrm{negl}(n)$ to denote an arbitrary polynomial and negligible function of n respectively (a negligible function f is any computable function such that $f(n)q(n) \to_{n \to \infty} 0$ for all polynomials q). For an integer $d \geq 1$, $\mathrm{D}(\mathbb{C}^d)$ denotes the set of density matrices on $\mathbb{C}^d$, i.e. positive semidefinite ρ on $\mathbb{C}^d$ such that $\mathrm{Tr}(\rho) = 1$. For a set S and an element $s \in S$, we write $s \xleftarrow{\$} S$ to mean that s is sampled uniformly at random from S. For an integer l, we denote by $\{0,1\}^{\leq l}$ the set of binary strings of length at most l. We use the notation S_N to denote the set of all permutations of a set of N elements.

We use the terminology PPT for *probabilistic polynomial time* and QPT for *quantum polynomial time* to describe algorithms.

2.2   The [BJSW16] Protocol

The following exposition is taken from [VZ19]. For an introduction to the Local Hamiltonian problem, and the associated notation, we refer the reader to the Supplementary Material.

In [BJSW16], Broadbent, Ji, Song and Watrous describe a protocol involving a quantum polynomial-time verifier and an unbounded prover, interacting quantumly, which constitutes a zero-knowledge proof system for languages in QMA. (Although it is sound against arbitrary provers, the system in fact only requires an honest prover who is provided with a single witness state to perform quantum polynomial-time computations.) We summarise the steps of their protocol below. For details and fuller explanations, we refer the reader to [BJSW16, Section 3].

Notation. Let L be any language in QMA. For a definition of the *k-local Clifford Hamiltonian problem*, see [BJSW16, Section 2] (this is the defined analogously to the k-local Hamiltonian problem, except that the Hamiltonian instance consists of Clifford terms, as introduced in the previous subsection). The k-local Clifford Hamiltonian problem (with exponentially small ground state energy) is QMA-complete for $k = 5$; therefore, for all possible inputs x, there exists a 5-local Clifford Hamiltonian H (which can be computed efficiently from x) whose terms are all operators of the form $C^* |0^k\rangle \langle 0^k| C$ for some Clifford operator C, and such that

- if $x \in L$, the ground energy of H is $\leq 2^{-p}$,
- if $x \notin L$, the ground energy of H is $\geq \frac{1}{q}$,

for some positive integers p and q which are bounded above by polynomials in $|x|$.

Parties. The proof system involves a *verifier*, who implements a quantum polynomial-time procedure; a *prover*, who is unbounded, but who is only required by the protocol to implement a quantum polynomial-time procedure. The verifier and the prover communicate quantumly.

Inputs
1. Input to the verifier: (a) The Hamiltonian H. (b) A quantum computationally concealing, perfectly binding (classical) commitment protocol. In this section, we refer to the commitment algorithm from this protocol as commit; $\mathrm{commit}(\mu, s)$ takes as input a message μ and a random string s and produces

---

Auth.Enc:
Parameters: $N(\cdot)$, a polynomially bounded function in $|x|$. (N functions as a security parameter.)
Input: An m-qubit state ρ.
The prover firstly applies a concatenated Steane code (which maps every one qubit to $N(|x|)$ qubits) to each qubit in ρ. (For details on the concatenated Steane code, see [BJSW16, Appendix A.6]. It will be important to Broadbent et al.'s purposes, and ours, that this code admits transversal applications of Clifford operations.) It then executes the following steps:

(a) Concatenate N trap qubits to the end of each logical qubit (alternatively, to the end of each N-qubit block) in the result of applying the concatenated Steane code to ρ. Each trap qubit is initialised uniformly at random to one of $|0\rangle, |+\rangle, |+_y\rangle$. ($|+_y\rangle$ here refers to the state $\frac{1}{\sqrt{2}}(|0\rangle + i|1\rangle)$.) Denote the string that records the choices of trap qubits for all m logical qubits by $t = t_1, \ldots, t_N \in \{|0\rangle, |+\rangle, |+_y\rangle\}^{mN}$.
(b) Permute each $2N$-tuple of qubits in the result of (a) according to a uniformly random permutation $\pi \in S_{2N}$. (Note that the same permutation π is applied to every $2N$-tuple.)
(c) Apply a Pauli one-time pad $X^a Z^b$, for uniformly random $a, b \in \{0, 1\}^{2mN}$, to the entire $2mN$-qubit state.

Fig. 1. The authentication code

a commitment string z. (c) A proof system for NP sound against arbitrary quantum provers.
2. Input to the prover: (a) The Hamiltonian H. (b) The n-qubit quantum state ρ, where ρ is a ground state of the Hamiltonian H. (c) A quantum computationally concealing, perfectly binding (classical) commitment protocol. (d) A proof system for NP sound against arbitrary quantum provers.

Protocol
1. *The prover's encoding step.* The prover applies the following encoding to the witness state ρ.
   We refer to t, π, a, b as 'the authentication keys' or 'the encoding keys'.
   The prover's encoding applied to ρ is denoted by $E(\rho)$, and the procedure E is fully determined by the encoding key (t, π, a, b) which the prover chose to use. At this point, the prover sends the state $E(\rho)$ to the verifier, along with a commitment (using some perfectly binding, computationally concealing classical commitment protocol) to the tuple (π, a, b). (A commitment to the sequence of trap qubits t is unnecessary because, in a sense, the trap qubits exist only to check the verifier.) Let the prover's commitment string be denoted z.
2. *Coin-flipping protocol.* The prover and the verifier execute a coin-flipping protocol, choosing a string r of fixed length uniformly at random. This random string r determines a local Hamiltonian term $H_r = C_r^* |0^k\rangle \langle 0^k| C_r$ that is to be tested. (This step can be implemented [DL09] using the same classical commitment protocol that the prover employed in the previous step.)
3. *Verifier's challenge.* The verifier applies the Clifford C_r transversally to the qubits on which the k-local Hamiltonian term H_r acts nontrivially, and measures them in the standard basis. It then sends the measurement results $u_{i_1}, \ldots, u_{i_k}$ which it obtained to the prover. (Each u_i is a $2N$-bit string, and $i_1, \ldots, i_k$ are the indices of the logical qubits on which the term H_r acts nontrivially.)
4. *Prover's response.* The prover receives the verifier's measurement results u, and firstly checks whether they cause a predicate $\tilde{Q}(t, \pi, a, b, r, u)$ to be satisfied. (We will explain the predicate $\tilde{Q}$ in more detail shortly. Intuitively, $\tilde{Q}$ is satisfied if and only if both verifier *and* prover behaved honestly. Note that we have used the notation $\tilde{Q}$ to represent this predicate, while the authors of [BJSW16] simply call it Q. We add the tilde in order to differentiate their predicate from our predicate Q, the latter of which we define in Definition 13.) If $\tilde{Q}$ is not satisfied, the prover aborts, causing the verifier to reject. If $\tilde{Q}$ is satisfied, then the prover proves to the verifier, using an NP zero-knowledge protocol, that there exists randomness s_P and an encoding key (t, π, a, b) such that $z = \mathsf{commit}((\pi, a, b), s_P)$ and $\tilde{Q}(t, \pi, a, b, r, u) = 1$.

Here $\tilde{Q}$ represents the prover's check after it has update the one-time pad keys based on the Clifford C_r, and reversed the effects of the one-time pad keys. We refer the reader to [BJSW16] for a formal definition of $\tilde{Q}$.

2.3   Argument Systems

Interactive Quantum Machines. The definitions of *interactive quantum machines*, their *executions* and *oracle access* to an interactive quantum machine are taken from [Unr12], and are omitted from this version due to space constraints.

Oracle Access to an Interactive Quantum Machine. We say that a quantum algorithm A has oracle access to an interactive quantum machine M (and we write this as A^M, or sometimes $A^{|M\rangle}$ to emphasize that M is a quantum machine and that oracle access includes the ability to apply the inverse of M) to mean the following. Besides the security parameter and its own classical input x, we allow A to execute the quantum circuit $M_{\mu x}$ specifying M, and its inverse (these act on the an "internal" register S and on a "network" register N of M). Moreover, we allow A to provide and read messages from M (formally, we allow A to act freely on the network register N). We do not allow A to act on the internal register S of M, except via $M_{\mu x}$ or its inverse.

Argument Systems with Setup. First we define the kinds of relations that underlie our argument systems. Classically, a relation over finite sets $\mathcal{X} \times \mathcal{Y}$ is a subset $R \subseteq \mathcal{X} \times \mathcal{Y}$. An NP relation $R = \{(x, w) : V_{|x|}(x, w) = 1\}$ has the additional property that given any $x \in \mathcal{X}$ and $w \in \mathcal{Y}$, the claim that $(x, w) \in R$ can be verified by a uniformly generated family of circuits $V = \{V_n\}$ (the "verifier").

In the quantum case the "input" x (the first argument to the relation) remains classical, but the "witness" w (the second argument) can be a quantum state $|\psi\rangle$. Before we give our definition of a QMA relation we introduce some notation. Fix a uniformly generated family of polynomial-size quantum circuits $Q = \{Q_n\}_{n \in \mathbb{N}}$ such that for every n, Q_n takes as input a string $x \in \{0, 1\}^n$ and a quantum state σ on $p(n)$ qubits (for some polynomial $p(n)$) and returns a single bit as output. For any $0 \leq \gamma \leq 1$ define

$$R_{Q,\gamma} = \bigcup_{n \in \mathbb{N}} \left\{ (x, \sigma) \in \{0, 1\}^n \times D(\mathbb{C}^{p(n)}) \,\middle|\, \Pr(Q_n(x, \sigma) = 1) \geq \gamma \right\}$$

and

$$N_{Q,\gamma} = \bigcup_{n \in \mathbb{N}} \left\{ x \in \{0, 1\}^n \,\middle|\, \forall \sigma \in D(\mathbb{C}^{p(n)}),\ \Pr(Q_n(x, \sigma) = 1) < \gamma \right\}.$$

Note the presence of the parameter γ, that quantifies the expected success probability for the verifier; γ can be thought of as a measure of the "quality" of a witness $|\psi\rangle$ (or mixture thereof, as represented by the density matrix σ) that is sufficient for the witness to be acceptable with respect to the relation R.

Definition 1 (QMA relation). *A QMA relation is specified by triple (Q, α, β) where $Q = \{Q_n\}_{n \in \mathbb{N}}$ is a uniformly generated family of quantum circuits such* *that for every n, Q_n takes as input a string $x \in \{0,1\}^n$ and a quantum state $|\psi\rangle$ on $p(n)$ qubits and returns a single bit, and $\alpha, \beta : \mathbb{N} \to [0,1]$ are such that $\alpha(n) - \beta(n) \geq 1/p(n)$ for some polynomial p and all $n \in \mathbb{N}$. The QMA relation associated with (Q, α, β) is the pair of sets $R_{Q,\alpha}$ and $N_{Q,\beta}$.*

We say that a language $L = (L_{yes}, L_{no})$ *is specified by a QMA relation (Q, α, β) if*

$$L_{yes} \subseteq \bigcup_{n \in \mathbb{N}} \{x \in \{0,1\}^n | \exists \sigma \in \mathrm{D}(\mathbb{C}^{p(n)}) \ s.t. \ (x, \sigma) \in R_{Q,\alpha}\}, \qquad (1)$$

and $L_{no} \subseteq N_{Q,\beta}$.

Note that in contrast to an NP relation, we define a QMA relation using two sets: the first set, $R_{Q,\alpha}$, is the set of (instance, witness) pairs that are deemed to form part of the relation. The second set, $N_{Q,\beta}$, is the set of instances that are deemed to be such that they are in relation to no witness. Some instances may lie in neither (the projection of) $R_{Q,\alpha}$ or $N_{Q,\beta}$; this is analogous to the necessity for a "promise" between the completeness and soundness parameters α and β in the definition of the class QMA, that do not appear in the definition of NP. In particular, note that, whenever $\alpha - \beta > 1/\mathrm{poly}(n)$, a language L that is specified by (Q, α, β) lies in QMA. Conversely, any language in QMA is specified by some QMA relation (of course such relation is not unique).

Definition 2 (protocol with setup). *A* protocol with setup *is a triple of interactive machines (S, P, V) with the following properties:*

1. *$S = \{S_{\mu n}\}_{\mu \in \mathbb{N}}$ depends on the security parameter μ and an instance size n, takes no input and returns a classical output in the message registers N_{SP} and N_{SV}. When the output in both registers is the same, we refer to it as "common reference string".*
2. *Each of P and V has two phases: $P = (P_1, P_2)$ and $V = (V_1, V_2)$. $P_1 = \{P_{1,\mu n}\}$ and $V_1 = \{V_{1,\mu n}\}$ are interactive machines that depend on the security parameter μ and an instance size parameter n, take a classical message input in register N_{SP} and N_{SV} respectively and return a quantum message as output in registers $\mathsf{N}_{P_1 P_2}$ and $\mathsf{N}_{V_1 V_2}$ respectively. $P_2 = \{P_{2,\mu n}\}$ and $V_2 = \{V_{2,\mu n}\}$ are interactive machines that depend on the security parameter μ and an input size n. V_2 takes as input the output of V_1, in register $\mathsf{N}_{V_1 V_2}$, as well as an instance x such that $|x| = n$. P_2 takes as input the output of P_1, in register $\mathsf{N}_{P_1 P_2}$, an instance x such that $|x| = n$, and a quantum state ρ. V_2 returns a single bit $b \in \{0,1\}$ as output, and P_2 returns no output. If $b = 1$ then we say that V accepts, and otherwise we say that it rejects.*

We refer to the first phase of P and V as the *preprocessing phase*, and to the second phase as the *instance-dependent phase*.

Definition 3 (argument system with completeness c and soundness s). *Let (Q, α, β) be a QMA relation and $s, c : \mathbb{N} \to [0,1]$. An* argument system *(with setup) for (Q, α, β), with completeness c and soundness s, is a protocol with setup (S, P, V) such that S, P, V are quantum polynomial-time and, in addition, the following hold:*

1. *(Completeness) For all $(x, \rho) \in R_{Q,\alpha}$, for all integer μ, the execution $(S, P(x, \rho), V(x))$ returns 1 with probability at least $c(\mu)$.*
2. *(Soundness) For all $x \in N_{Q,\beta}$, all integer μ and all polynomial-time P^* the execution $(S, P^*(x), V(x))$ returns 1 with probability at most $s(\mu) + negl(\mu)$.*

When the second phase of a protocol with setup (S, P, V) consists of a single message from P to V we refer to it as a *non-interactive* protocol with setup. If it is a an argument system with setup, we refer to it as a *non-interactive* argument system with setup. When the first phase involves some communication between P and V, we specify that it is a non-interactive argument system with setup *and preprocessing*. When S outputs a common reference string (as defined in 2), we refer to it as an argument system *with CRS setup* (possibly with preprocessing).

Note that Definition 3 requires that the execution $(S, P(x, \rho), V(x))$ returns 1 with probability at least $c(\mu)$. In the case of sequential or parallel repetition of a protocol, it may not be possible for the prover to succeed with a single copy of the witness ρ as input. In this case we may considering relaxing the definition as follows.

Definition 4 (Completeness of argument system with setup—alternative definition). *Let Q^q be the circuit that runs Q on q registers, and accepts if all executions accept. There exists a polynomial $q > 0$, such that for all $(x, \rho) \in R_{Q^q, \alpha}$, for all integers μ, the execution $(S, P(x, \rho), V(x))$ returns 1 with probability at least $c(\mu)$.*

We will clarify, whenever we refer to an argument system with setup, which definition we refer to.

Finally, we define the notion of *adaptive soundness*, which captures security against adversaries that are allowed to choose the common instance x *after* having carried out the preprocessing phase.

Definition 5 (Adaptive soundness). *An argument with setup (S, P, V) for a QMA relation (Q, α, β) has adaptive soundness $s(\mu)$ if for every QPT algorithm $P^* = \{(P^*_{1,\mu n}, P^*_{2,\mu n})\}$, for all μ,*

$$\Pr_{\substack{(\sigma_{PV}) \leftarrow (S_{\mu n}, P^*_{1,\mu n}, V_{1,\mu n}), \\ (x, \tau) \leftarrow P^*_{2,\mu n}(\sigma_P)}} \left(x \in N_{Q,\beta} \wedge (P^*_{2,\mu n}(x, \tau), V_{2,\mu n}(x, \sigma_V)) = 1 \right) \leq s(\mu) + negl(\mu).$$

The terminology that follows Definition 3 is modified in the natural way in the case of adaptive soundness.

2.4   Proofs and Arguments of Quantum Knowledge

The content of this subsection, as it pertains to *proofs of quantum knowledge*, was written in collaboration with Broadbent and Grilo, and appears with slight differences in [BG19].

A *Proof of Knowledge (PoK)* is an interactive proof system for some relation R such that if the verifier accepts some input x with high enough probability, then she is "convinced" that the prover "knows" some witness w such that $(x, w) \in R$. This notion is formalized by requiring the existence of an efficient *extractor* K that is able to return a witness for x when given oracle access to the prover (including the ability to rewind its actions, in the classical case).

Definition 6 (Classical Proof of Knowledge). *Let $R \subseteq \mathcal{X} \times \mathcal{Y}$ be a relation. A proof system (P, V) for R is a Proof of Knowledge for R with knowledge error κ if there exists a polynomial $p > 0$ and a polynomial-time machine K such that for any classical interactive machine P^*, any $\mu \in \mathbb{N}$, any polynomial $l > 0$, any instance $x \in \{0,1\}^n$ for $n = \text{poly}(\mu)$ and any string y: if the execution $(P^*(x, y), V(x))$ returns 1 with probability $\varepsilon > \kappa(\mu)$, we have*

$$\Pr\left(\left(x, K^{P^*(x,y)}(x)\right) \in R\right) \geq p\left(\varepsilon - \kappa(\mu), \frac{1}{\mu}\right) - negl(\mu)$$

In this definition, y corresponds to the side information that P^* has, possibly including some w such that $(x, w) \in R$.

PoKs were originally defined only considering classical adversaries, and this notion was first studied in the quantum setting by Unruh [Unr12]. The first issue that arises in the quantum setting is to formalize the type of query that the extractor K is able to make. In order to do so, we assume that P^* always performs a fixed unitary operation U when invoked. Notice that this can be assumed without loss of generality since (i) we can always consider a purification of P^*, (ii) all measurements can be performed coherently, and (iii) P^* can keep track of the round of communication in some internal register and U can implicitly control on this value. Then, the quantum extractor K has oracle access to P^* in the sense that it may perform U and $U^\dagger$ on the message register and private register of P^*, but has no direct access to the latter. We denote the extractor K with such oracle access to P^* by $K^{|P^*(x,\rho)\rangle}$, where ρ is some (quantum) side information held by P^*.

Definition 7 (Quantum Proof of (Classical) Knowledge). *Let $R \subseteq \mathcal{X} \times \mathcal{Y}$ be a relation. A proof system (P, V) for R is a Quantum Proof of Knowledge for R with knowledge error κ if there exists a polynomial $p > 0$ and a quantum polynomial-time machine K such that for any quantum interactive machine P^*, any $\mu \in \mathbb{N}$, any polynomial $l > 0$, any instance $x \in \{0,1\}^n$ for $n = \text{poly}(\mu)$ and any state ρ: if the execution $(P^*(x, \rho), V(x))$ returns 1 with probability $\varepsilon > \kappa(\mu)$, we have*

$$\Pr\left(\left(x, K^{|P^*(x,\rho)\rangle}(x)\right) \in R\right) \geq p\left(\varepsilon - \kappa(\mu), \frac{1}{\mu}\right).$$

Remark 2. In the fully classical case of 6, the extractor could repeat the procedure in sequence polynomially many times in order to increase the probability of a successful extraction (which, in Definitions 6 and 7, is allowed to be inverse-polynomially small in the security parameter). This is not known to be possible for a general quantum P^*, since the final measurement to extract the witness could possibly disturb the internal state of P^*, making it impossible to simulate the side information that P^* had originally in the subsequent simulations.

We finally move on to the full quantum setting, where we want a *Proof of Quantum Knowledge* (PoQK). Intuitively, at the end of the protocol, we would like the verifier to be 'convinced' that the prover 'has' a *quantum witness* for the input x. The main difference from Quantum Proofs of (classical) Knowledge is that in the case of QMA relations, as defined in Sect. 2.3, the notion of a witness is not as unambiguous as in the case of NP relations. We introduce a parameter q which quantifies the probability that the witness returned by the extractor makes the verifying circuit accept. We refer to this parameter as the "quality" of the PoQK. We also allow the extractor K to return a special symbol "$\perp$" in a designated portion of the output register, and we require that either the extractor returns "$\perp$" or it returns a witness of a certain quality. Formally, we assume that the output of the extractor is measured according to $\{|\perp\rangle\langle\perp|, I-|\perp\rangle\langle\perp|\}$. We ask that the outcome of this measurement be the latter with at least inverse-polynomial probability, and that, conditioned on the latter outcome, the post-measurement state be a witness (of a certain quality).

Definition 8 (Proof of Quantum Knowledge). *Let (Q, α, β) be a QMA relation. A proof system (P, V) is a Proof of Quantum Knowledge for (Q, α, β) with knowledge error κ and quality $q > \beta$, if there exists a polynomial $p > 0$ and a quantum polynomial-time machine K such that for any quantum interactive machine P^*, any $\mu \in \mathbb{N}$, any polynomial $l > 0$, any instance $x \in \{0, 1\}^n$ for $n = \mathrm{poly}(\mu)$ and any state ρ: if the execution $(P^*(x, \rho), V(x))$ returns 1 with probability $\varepsilon > \kappa(\mu)$, we have, letting $\sigma = \frac{(I-|\perp\rangle\langle\perp|)K^{|P^*(x,\rho)\rangle}(x)(I-|\perp\rangle\langle\perp|)}{\mathrm{Tr}[(I-|\perp\rangle\langle\perp|)K^{|P^*(x,\rho)\rangle}(x)]},$*

$$\mathrm{Tr}[(I-|\perp\rangle\langle\perp|)K^{|P^*(x,\rho)\rangle}(x)] > p\left(\varepsilon - \kappa(\mu), \frac{1}{\mu}\right) - negl(\mu), \text{ and } (x, \sigma) \in R_{Q, q(|x|, \varepsilon)}.$$

The intuition behind the last equation is that we want the probability that the extractor K does not output '$\perp$' to be at least p, and we want the state conditioned on not outputting $\perp$ to be a good enough witness.

Remark 3. Note that quality of the witness returned by the extractor K in Definition 8 may be lower than the quality of the witness used by the prover to produce the proof. We suspect that this loss is inherent. Consider the following simple example. Suppose the prover is given a witness ρ that has quality $0 < c < 1$ with respect to some QMA verification procedure. The prover uses ρ in a protocol that executes one of two tests, each with probability $1/2$: (i) an "energy test" that is designed to check ρ, and (ii) a "structure test" that is designed to check some property of the prover's strategy.

Now consider two provers, P_1 and P_2, each of which succeeds in this protocol with probability $c' = (1+c)/2$. P_1 is given a witness of quality c and plays optimally in the structure test. P_2 is given a witness of quality 1 and purposefully succeeds in the structure test with probability c only. Then because of the existence of P_1, it would be unreasonable to expect that the extractor can extract witnesses of quality $> c$ from provers that succeed with probability $\leq c'$. This means that running P_2 on a witness returned by the extractor will succeed with probability $c < c'$ only.

We also define *arguments* of quantum knowledge (with a setup). The main difference is that the proof system is replaced by an argument system with setup. Moreover, the extractor is allowed to create the setup as they wish (they can "impersonate" the setup procedure S).

Definition 9 (Quantum Argument of (Classical) Knowledge). *Let $R \subseteq \mathcal{X} \times \mathcal{Y}$ be a relation. An argument system with setup $\Pi = (S, P, V)$ for R is a Quantum Argument of Knowledge with setup for R with knowledge error κ if there exists a polynomial $p > 0$ and a quantum polynomial-time machine K such that for any quantum polynomial-time interactive machine P^*, any $\mu \in \mathbb{N}$, any polynomial $l > 0$, any instance $x \in \{0,1\}^n$ for $n = \text{poly}(\mu)$ and any state ρ: if the execution $(S, P^*(x, \rho), V(x))$ returns 1 with probability $\varepsilon > \kappa(\mu)$, we have*

$$\Pr\left(\left(x, K^{|P^*(x,\rho)\rangle}(x)\right) \in R\right) \geq p\left(\varepsilon - \kappa(\mu), \frac{1}{\mu}\right) - negl(\mu).$$

Definition 10 (Argument of Quantum Knowledge). *Let (Q, α, β) be a QMA relation. An argument system with setup $\Pi = (S, P, V)$ is an Argument of Quantum Knowledge with setup for (Q, α, β) with knowledge error κ and quality $q > \beta$ if there exists a polynomial $p > 0$ and a quantum polynomial-time interactive machine K such that for any quantum polynomial-time interactive machine P^*, any $\mu \in \mathbb{N}$, any polynomial $l > 0$, any instance $x \in \{0,1\}^n$ for $n = \text{poly}(\mu)$ and any state ρ: if the execution $(S, P^*(x, \rho), V(x))$ returns 1 with probability $\varepsilon > \kappa(\mu)$, we have, letting $\sigma = \frac{(I - |\perp\rangle\langle\perp|) K^{|P^*(x,\rho)\rangle}(x)(I - |\perp\rangle\langle\perp|)}{\text{Tr}[(I - |\perp\rangle\langle\perp|) K^{|P^*(x,\rho)\rangle}(x)]},$*

$$\text{Tr}[(I - |\perp\rangle\langle\perp|) K^{|P^*(x,\rho)\rangle}(x)] > p\left(\varepsilon - \kappa(\mu), \frac{1}{\mu}\right) - negl(\mu), \text{ and } (x, \sigma) \in R_{Q, q(|x|, \varepsilon)}.$$

As for the several possible specializations to the definition of Argument of Quantum Knowledge with setup based on the properties of the underlying argument system (NIZK, CRS setup, preprocessing etc.), we naturally apply the terminology introduced in Sect. 2.3, and in Sect. 1.3 of the Supplementary Material.

Reducing the Knowledge Error Sequentially. One of the most natural properties of Proofs of Knowledge that one investigates in the classical setting is reducing the knowledge error by sequential repetition. Classically, it is well-known that the knowledge error drops exponentially fast in the number of sequential repetitions [BG92]. Just like in the classical case, sequential repetition of a proof of quantum knowledge reduces the knowledge error exponentially fast. This is an immediate consequence of the proof of a lemma from Unruh [Unr12] for the case of quantum Proofs of (classical) Knowledge. We refer the reader to the Supplementary Material for a formal statement.

3   The Protocol

3.1   Notation and Predicates

For a circuit Q_n, we denote by $H(Q_n)$ the local Clifford Hamiltonian obtained by performing the circuit-to-Clifford-Hamiltonian reduction from [BJSW16, Section 2]. In the rest of this section, Q_n will always be taken from a family $Q = \{Q_n\}_{n \in \mathbb{N}}$, where Q specifies a QMA relation (Q, α, β), and we will let the r-th term of the Clifford Hamiltonian $H(Q_n)$ be $C_r^* |0^k\rangle \langle 0^k| C_r$. So,

$$H(Q_n) = \sum_{r=1}^{m} C_r^* |0^k\rangle \langle 0^k| C_r, \tag{2}$$

where each C_r is a k-local Clifford unitary. (Following [BJSW16], we use the short-hand $|0^k\rangle\langle 0^k|$ to denote a projector which is $|0\rangle\langle 0|$ on at most k qubits and identity everywhere else. As shown in [BJSW16], we can take $k = 5$ without loss of generality.)

We denote by $\mathcal{H}_{\text{clock}} \otimes \mathcal{H}_{\text{instance}} \otimes \mathcal{H}_{\text{witness}}$ the Hilbert space that $H(Q_n)$ acts on. For notational convenience, we assume in the rest of this section that $\mathcal{H}_{\text{instance}}$ is n qubits, that is, $\mathcal{H}_{\text{instance}} = \mathbb{C}^{2^n}$.

For clarity and notational convenience, we define predicates R_r and Q below, which we will refer to in our description of our protocol.

Remark 4. Predicates Q and R_r are defined with respect to a fixed problem instance x and a fixed Clifford Hamiltonian H, where

$$H = \sum_{r=1}^{m} C_r^* |0^k\rangle \langle 0^k| C_r$$

for some m that is polynomial in n.

Definition 11 (Definition of R_r). *As in Sect. 2.2, we write $\mathcal{D}_N$ to represent the set of all valid (classical) N-bit codewords of a particular error-correcting code. We will generally refer to this error-correcting code as 'the concatenated Steane code'. (This code is the same concatenated Steane code which is outlined in [BJSW16, Appendix A.6].) We may write $\mathcal{D}_N = \mathcal{D}_N^0 \cup \mathcal{D}_N^1$, where $\mathcal{D}_N^0$ is the set of all codewords that encode 0, and $\mathcal{D}_N^1$ is defined analogously.*

We assume that r takes values in $[m + 1]$, where m is the number of terms in the Clifford Hamiltonian H. Our R_r is defined differently when $r \in [m]$ and when $r = m + 1$.

1. *If $r \in [m]$: Let $u_{i_1}, \ldots, u_{i_k} \in \{0,1\}^{2N}$, $\pi \in S_{2N}$, and $t_{i_1}, \ldots, t_{i_k} \in \{0, +, +_y\}^N$. For each $i \in \{i_1, \ldots, i_k\}$, define strings p_i, q_i in $\{0,1\}^N$ such that $\pi(p_i \| q_i) = u_i$ (alternatively: $\pi^{-1}(u_i) = p_i \| q_i$). We define a predicate $\tilde{R}_r(t, \pi, u)$ that takes value 1 if and only if the following two conditions are met:*

(a) $p_i \in \mathcal{D}_N$ for every $i \in \{i_1, \ldots, i_k\}$, and $p_i \in \mathcal{D}_N^1$ for at least one index $i \in \{i_1, \ldots, i_k\}$. ($\mathcal{D}_N = \mathcal{D}_N^0 \cup \mathcal{D}_N^1$ is the set of all valid classical N-bit codewords of the concatenated Steane code).

(b) $\langle q_{i_1} \cdots q_{i_k} | C_r^{\otimes n} | t_{i_1} \cdots t_{i_k} \rangle \neq 0$.

Here $|t_{i_1} \cdots t_{i_k}\rangle$ is the state of kN qubits obtained by tensoring $|0\rangle, |+\rangle$ and $|+_y\rangle$ in the natural way. Then, we define $R_r(t, \pi, u) = \tilde{R}_r(t, \pi, u)$.

2. If $r = m + 1$, then we set $R_r = R_{m+1}$, where R_{m+1} is defined below (Definition 12).

Definition 12 (Definition of R_{m+1}). Let $u = u_{clock_1}, u_{instance_1}, \ldots, u_{instance_n}$ be a string in $\{0, 1\}^{2N(n+1)}$.

Remark 5. Each u_{label}, for $label \in \{clock_1, instance_1, \ldots, instance_n\}$, is a $2N$-bit string, and intuitively represents the result of measuring the logical qubit with an index specified by $label$. (For notational convenience in the exposition below, we replace the iterator $label$ by the iterator i.) For example, u_{clock_1} is the string that results from measuring the first logical qubit of the clock register. The logical clock register consists of many logical qubits, and each logical qubit is encoded in $2N$ physical qubits as a result of applying the authentication code described in Fig. 1.

For $\pi \in S_{2N}$, and for each $i \in \{clock_1, instance_1, \ldots, instance_n\}$, define strings p_i, q_i in $\{0, 1\}^N$ such that $\pi(p_i \| q_i) = u_i$ (alternatively: $\pi^{-1}(u_i) = p_i \| q_i$). The predicate $R_{m+1}(t, \pi, u)$ takes the value 1 if and only if the following two conditions (1. and 2.) are met:

1. Either

$p_{clock_1} \in \mathcal{D}_N^1$ (this corresponds to the first qubit of the clock register, expressed in unary, being in state 1, i.e. the clock register is not at time 0),

or

For every $i \in \{instance_1, \ldots, instance_n\}$, $p_i \in \mathcal{D}_N^{x_i}$.

2. $\langle q_{clock_1} q_{instance_1} \cdots q_{instance_n} | t_{clock_1} t_{instance_1} \cdots t_{instance_n} \rangle \neq 0$.

We now define our predicate Q in terms of the R_r defined in Definition 11.

Definition 13 (Definition of Q). Let $d = (x_1, \ldots, x_{2Np(n)}, y_1, \ldots, y_{2Np(n)})$ be a string in $\{0, 1\}^{4Np(n)}$, for some polynomial $p(n)$ of n. Define

$$\mathbb{P}_{m+1} = |0\rangle \langle 0|_{clock_1} \otimes \left(I - |x\rangle \langle x| \right)_{instance} \otimes I_{witness}$$
$$+ (I - |0\rangle \langle 0|)_{clock_1} \otimes I_{instance} \otimes I_{witness}$$

where $|x\rangle \langle x|$ is a shorthand for the projector onto the standard-basis bitstring $\langle x \rangle$, and

$$C_{m+1} = I_{clock} \otimes I_{instance} \otimes I_{witness}.$$

For $r \in [m + 1]$, define

$$\mathbb{P}_r = \begin{cases} C_r^* |0^k\rangle \langle 0^k| C_r & r \in [m] \\ \mathbb{P}_{m+1} & r = m + 1 \end{cases}$$

Let $i_1, .., i_k$ be the indices of the qubits on which $\mathbb{P}_r$ acts non-trivially. Let

$$
\begin{aligned}
d' &= (a', b') \\
&= (a'_{i_1}, \ldots, a'_{i_k}, b'_{i_1}, \ldots, b'_{i_k}) \\
&= (x_{2Ni_1+1}, \ldots, x_{2Ni_1+2N}, \ldots, x_{2Ni_k+1}, \ldots, x_{2Ni_k+2N}, \\
&\quad\; y_{2Ni_1+1}, \ldots, y_{2Ni_1+2N}, \ldots, y_{2Ni_k+1}, \ldots, y_{2Ni_k+2N})
\end{aligned}
$$

be a string in $\{0, 1\}^{4Nk}$. (The example below, wherein $k = 2, N = 2, i_1 = 1, i_2 = 3$, and $d' = (a', b') = 01001000$, may clarify the notation.)

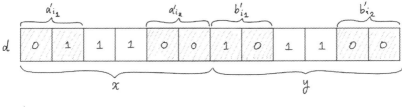

$k = 2 \qquad N = 2 \qquad i_1 = 1, \; i_2 = 3$

$d' = a' \parallel b' = 0100\,1000$

Let $e_{i_1}, \ldots, e_{i_k}$ be the unique strings such that

$$
\begin{aligned}
C_r^{\otimes 2N}(X^{(a \oplus a')_{i_1}} Z^{(b \oplus b')_{i_1}} &\otimes \cdots \otimes X^{(a \oplus a')_{i_k}} Z^{(b \oplus b')_{i_k}}) \\
&= \alpha(X^{e_{i_1}} Z^{f_{i_1}} \otimes \cdots \otimes X^{e_{i_k}} Z^{f_{i_k}}) C_r^{\otimes 2N}
\end{aligned}
\tag{3}
$$

for some $\alpha \in \{1, i, -1, -i\}$ and some $f_{i_1}, \ldots, f_{i_k} \in \{0, 1\}^{2N}$. (It is possible to efficiently compute $e = e_{i_1}, \ldots, e_{i_k}$ and $f = f_{i_1}, \ldots, f_{i_k}$ given a, b and C_r.) Predicate Q is defined as follows:

$$
Q(t, \pi, a, b, r, z, d) = R_r(t, \pi, z \oplus e_{i_1} \cdots e_{i_k}).
$$

3.2   The Protocol

Parties. The argument system involves

1. A (QPT) *verifier* V,
2. A (QPT) *prover* P, and
3. A (classical PPT) *setup machine* S.

The verifier sends a single quantum message to the prover in the preprocessing phase of the protocol, and the prover sends the verifier a single classical message in the instance-dependent phase of the protocol. S sends an identical classical message to both the prover and the verifier during the preprocessing phase.

Inputs. (Unless otherwise stated, all inputs are common to all three parties.)

1. Preprocessing stage:
   (a) An instance size parameter n and a security parameter μ.

(b) A QMA relation (Q, α, β).

(c) The Clifford Hamiltonian $H(Q_n)$ (see Eq. (2)).

(d) Other parameters:
  i. $c(n)$, an upper bound on the number of qubits in a witness state;
  ii. $p(n)$, an upper bound on the number of qubits in a history state corresponding to an execution of Q_n on a witness state of length $c(n)$ and an instance of size n;
  iii. $m = \text{poly}(n)$, the number of terms in the Clifford Hamiltonian (Eq. (2));
  iv. $N = \text{poly}(n)$, the number of physical qubits per logical qubit in the Steane code introduced in Sect. 2.2.

(e) A perfectly binding, quantum computationally concealing (classical) commitment scheme Com = (Com.gen, Com.commit, Com.reveal, Com.verify, Com.recover), of the form described in Sect. 1.2 of the Supplementary Material.

(f) A NIZK argument system with setup for NP, such as the one described in Sect. 1.3 of the Supplementary Material. We denote this argument system by a triple (NIZK.S, NIZK.P, NIZK.V).

(g) A levelled fully homomorphic encryption scheme with circuit privacy, FHE = (FHE.Gen, FHE.Enc, FHE.Dec, FHE.Eval, FHE.Refresh).

2. Instance-dependent stage:
  (a) The instance x.
  (b) Auxiliary (private) input to the prover: a witness ρ for the claim that $x \in R_{Q,\alpha}$.

Protocol

Refer to Fig. 2 for a diagram charting the essential structure of the protocol below.

3.3   Preprocessing Step

(S) S samples $\gamma \leftarrow$ NIZK.$S(1^{q(n)}, 1^\mu)$, for a sufficiently large polynomial $q > 0$, in addition to $(pk_P, sk_P), (pk_V, sk_V) \leftarrow$ Com.gen(1^μ) (the two pairs are sampled independently). S then outputs (γ, pk_P, pk_V).

(i) V samples $r' \overset{\$}{\leftarrow} [m + n]$. Sets $r = r'$ if $r \leq m$, and $r = m + 1$ otherwise. Computes $\sigma \leftarrow$ Com.commit$(pk_V; r)$. Let s_V be the randomness used.

(ii) V creates $2Np(n)$ EPR pairs ($2N$ for each qubit of the history state). The second qubit of each EPR pair will be sent to P in step (iv). We refer to the remaining qubits (i.e. the first qubit in each EPR pair) as "V's qubits".

(iii) V interprets her $2Np(n)$ qubits as the encoding (according to the authentication code of Fig. 1) of a history state for $H(Q_n)$.
  – If $r \in [m]$: V applies C_r transversally to the subset of her $2Np(n)$ qubits which encode the k logical qubits on which C_r acts. Measures those qubits in the computational basis, obtaining an outcome string z.
  – If $r = m+1$: V measures the subset of the $2Np(n)$ qubits corresponding to the first qubit of $\mathcal{H}_{\text{clock}}$ and all the qubits of $\mathcal{H}_{\text{instance}}$ in the computational basis, obtaining an outcome string z.

(iv) V samples $(pk_E, sk_E) \leftarrow$ FHE.Gen(1^n). V sends to P:
  - $\alpha \leftarrow$ FHE.Enc$(pk_E, (r, s_V, z))$.
  - pk_E and σ.

3.4 Instance-Dependent Step

- **Prover's message:**
  1. P computes the history state corresponding to an evaluation of the circuit Q_n on the input $|x\rangle \otimes |\psi\rangle$. This is the state $|\Psi\rangle = \sum_{t=0}^{T} |t\rangle_{\text{clock}} \otimes \Pi_{j=1}^{t} U_j\big(|x\rangle \otimes |\psi\rangle \otimes |0\rangle^{\otimes n}\big)$ for some unitary U_j, which can be computed efficiently. P computes $|\tilde{\Psi}\rangle \leftarrow$ Auth.Enc$(|\Psi\rangle)$ according to the authentication scheme of Fig. 1. Let the sampled authentication keys be:
     (a) $a = a_1, .., a_{p(n)}$, $b = b_1, .., b_{p(n)}$ for $a_1, .., a_{p(n)}, b_1, .., b_{p(n)} \in \{0,1\}^{2N}$,
     (b) $\pi \in S_{2N}$,
     (c) $t = t_1, .., t_{p(n)}$ where $t_1, .., t_{p(n)} \in \{0, +, +_y\}^N$.
     P samples commitment randomness s_P, and computes
     $\sigma_{\text{keys}} \leftarrow$ Com.commit$(pk, (t, \pi, a, b), s_P)$.
  2. P teleports the state ρ to V using his halves of the $2Np(n)$ shared EPR pairs received in step (iv) of the preprocessing step. Let $d = (x_1, \ldots, x_{2Np(n)}, y_1, \ldots, y_{2Np(n)}) \in \{0,1\}^{4Np(n)}$ be the Bell basis measurement outcomes obtained during the teleportation.
  3. P computes $\beta \leftarrow$ FHE.Enc$\big(pk_E, (d, \sigma, \sigma_{\text{keys}}, (t, \pi, a, b), s_P)\big)$, where σ is the commitment received in step (iv) of the preprocessing step. P homomorphically evaluates the following circuit C using β and the ciphertext α that it received from the verifier. (Recall that α is an encryption of (r, s_V, z).)
        C takes as input $d, \sigma, r, s_V, z, \sigma_{\text{keys}}, t, \pi, a, b, s_P$. It checks that (r, s_V) is a valid opening for σ, and that $Q(t, \pi, a, b, r, z, d) = 1$, where Q is defined in Definition 13. If its checks pass, using γ it computes an NIZK argument for the existence of an opening to σ_{keys} such that the opened value (t, π, a, b) satisfies $Q(t, \pi, a, b, r, z, d) = 1$. If its checks do not pass, it outputs "$\perp$".
  4. Let $\tilde{\pi}$ be the encrypted proof that P obtains in step 4. P computes $\tilde{\pi}' \leftarrow$ FHE.Refresh$(\tilde{\pi})$. Sends d, σ_{keys} and $\tilde{\pi}'$ to V.
- **Verifier's check:** V decrypts $\tilde{\pi}'$, and executes NIZK.V to check the decrypted proof. It checks that the d received from P is the same d that appears in the statement being proven.

Theorem 1. *Assuming that LWE is intractable for quantum polynomial-time (QPT) adversaries, every language in* QMA *has an adaptively zero-knowledge non-interactive argument system with CRS setup and preprocessing (where completeness is according to Definition 4) with* negl *adaptive soundness. Moreover, the preprocessing phase consists of a single quantum message from the verifier to the prover.*

We refer to the combination of the protocols of Sects. 3.3 and 3.4 as "the protocol".

To show Theorem 1 we start with an arbitrary language $L \in$ QMA. Using standard amplification techniques, for any polynomial t there is a family of polynomial-size verification circuits Q such that L is the language associated with the QMA relation $(Q, 1 - 2^{-t}, 2^{-t})$ as in Definition 1. We show that the protocol associated to this relation is an NIZK argument with setup for $(Q, 1 - 2^{-t}, 2^{-t})$. Completeness is easy to verify, as for any $(x, \rho) \in R_{Q,1-2^{-t}}$ the prover described in Sect. 3.4 is accepted with probability negligibly close to 1, given access to ρ. In Sect. 4 we prove soundness inverse polynomially close to 1, and in Sect. 2.3 of the Supplementary Material we show how soundness can be amplified in parallel to any 2^{-p} for polynomial p (provided t is taken large enough compared to p). After parallel amplification, completeness holds only if we allow the prover to receive polynomially many copies of the witness (as in Definition 4). Finally, in Sect. 5 we prove the zero-knowledge property.

4   Soundness

In this section we prove soundness of our protocol from Sect. 3.2. This is captured by the following lemma.

Lemma 2. *Assume that LWE is intractable for quantum polynomial-time (QPT) adversaries. Let (Q, α, β) be a QMA relation. Then the non-interactive protocol with setup and preprocessing for (Q, α, β) described in Sect. 3.2 has negligible adaptive soundness.*

We give an overview of the proof of Lemma 2 in the next subsection.

4.1   Overview

The structure of the proof is as follows. We show through a sequence of hybrids that it is possible to transform an execution of our protocol on some instance x, into an execution of the protocol from [BJSW16] on a specific local Clifford Hamiltonian derived from x. We show that this transformation can at most negligibly decrease the optimal acceptance probability of the prover. Thus, soundness of our protocol reduces to soundness of the protocol from [BJSW16]. The main steps in our sequence of hybrids are the following:

- Remove the encryption of V's choice of r, randomness s_V and measurement outcomes z sent in step (iv) of the preprocessing step.
- Replace the step where P teleports the encoded witness to V through shared EPR pairs (step 2 in Sect. 3.4) with one where P directly sends the qubits of the encoded witness to V.
- Remove the portion of the CRS corresponding to the NIZK argument, and replace the NIZK argument sent by the prover in step 4 of Sect. 3.4 with a ZK proof.

In Sect. 2.3 of the Supplementary Material, we amplify soundness by repeating the protocol in parallel. One can check that our proof goes through unchanged for the case of adaptive soundness as well. In particular, the key is that the NIZK proof system for NP employed in our protocol is adaptively sound.

5   Zero-Knowledge Property

Lemma 3. *Assume that LWE is intractable for quantum polynomial-time (QPT) adversaries. Let L be a language in QMA, let $x \in \{0,1\}^*$ be a problem instance, and let $V^* = \{V^*_{\mu n}\}$ be an arbitrary QPT verifier for the protocol of Sect. 3. There exists a QPT simulator $S = \{S_{\mu n}\}$ such that, for any μ, n and yes-instance $x \in L$ with $|x| = n$, and for any auxiliary quantum input Z_0 to the verifier, the distribution of V^*'s final output after its interaction with the honest prover P in the protocol is quantum computationally indistinguishable from S's output distribution on auxiliary input Z_0.*

Furthermore, the simulator S only requires knowledge of the instance x after the preprocessing phase has been executed (simulated) with V^*. As such, the zero-knowledge property holds in the adaptive setting.

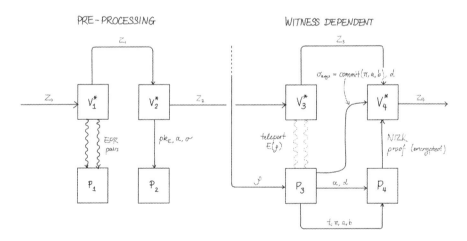

Fig. 2. Diagram representing the original protocol execution between the honest prover P and a cheating verifier V^*. For visual clarity, the prover and the (cheating) verifier have been split into parts $\{P_i\}$ and $\{V^*_i\}$ with $i \in \{1, 2, 3, 4\}$, respectively, where parts 1 and 2 execute the preprocessing phase of the protocol, and parts 3 and 4 execute the instance-dependent phase of the protocol. Communications between verifier and prover are labelled in orange; internal communications on either side are labelled in grey. In the two subsequent diagrams, we will omit the auxiliary input Z_0 that the cheating verifier receives, as well as the internal communications Z_1, Z_2, Z_3 between the different parts of the cheating verifier.

Due to space constraints, we provide the proof of Lemma 3 in Sect. 3 of our supplementary material. In order to show that our protocol is (adaptively) zero-knowledge, we proceed through the following hybrid argument, in which we make a series of replacements, and show at each stage that the verifier's final output after the replacement is made is (computationally or statistically) indistinguishable from its output before. Figure 2 is a diagram that numbers the stages of the prover and the verifier in the original protocol. For convenience, we use the numbering scheme presented in that figure.

1. In the original protocol, P_4 offers an encryption (under a homomorphic encryption scheme FHE) of a non-interactive NP proof π, which has been computed homomorphically, to the last component of the potentially cheating verifier, V_4^*. We replace the encryption of the genuine proof π with the encryption of a *simulated* proof π'. π' is indistinguishable from π because the proof system is zero-knowledge. We use the circuit privacy property of FHE to show that the encryption of π' is also indistinguishable from the encryption of π.

2. Step 1 allows us (details of how are provided in supplementary material) to replace the commitment to encoding keys that P_3 sends to V_4^* with a commitment to a fixed string, which the verifier could generate by itself.

3. After the replacement in step 2 has been made, we are then able to replace the genuine witness ρ which the honest P_3 receives with a *simulated* witness that can be efficiently prepared without knowledge of the real witness. Arguing that the verifier's final output after this replacement is (statistically) indistinguishable from its output before is perhaps the most involved step in the proof, and involves in particular making use of the *extractability* property of the commitment scheme (see Sect. 1.2 of the supplementary material) that the verifier uses to commit to its challenge r in order to argue that the simulator can efficiently recover r and then construct a simulated witness which passes only the challenge determined by r.

6   NIZK Argument of Quantum Knowledge with Preprocessing for QMA

In this section we show that for any QMA relation the NIZK argument system with CRS setup and preprocessing described in Sect. 3 is also a NIZK Argument of Quantum Knowledge with CRS setup and preprocessing (as defined in Sect. 2.4). The intuition for this is simple. From the proof of soundness of the protocol from [BJSW16], to which soundness of our argument system reduces, we are able to infer that any prover which is accepted in our protocol with high probability must be teleporting to the verifier *an encoding* of a low-energy witness state for the given instance of the 5-local Clifford Hamiltonian problem. Then, all that an extractor (given oracle access to such a prover) has to do in order to output a good witness is:

– Simulate an honest verifier so as to receive (by teleportation) such an encoded witness from the prover,

– Find a way to recover the committed encoding keys and use them to decode the received state.

We formalize this sketch in Sect. 4 of the Supplementary Material.

7   Proofs of Quantum Knowledge for QMA

The interactive protocol that we show is a proof of quantum knowledge for languages in QMA is identical to the protocol from [BJSW16], as recalled in Sect. 2.2, except for one modification: at the same time as the prover sends the encoded state $E(\rho)$ and the commitment σ to the verifier (end of step 1 of the protocol), the prover also sends a classical zero-knowledge PoK of an opening to the commitment. More precisely, define a relation R such that $R(\sigma, z) = 1$ if z is a valid opening for the commitment σ. V and P engage in a ZK PoK protocol for the relation R on common input σ, as defined in Definition 6. If the verifier rejects in this protocol, then the verifier outputs "reject" for the whole protocol; otherwise the verifier proceeds to the next phase.

Informally, the extractor K first takes the quantum state ρ^* sent by P^* in the first message. It then executes an extractor K' for an opening to the commitment sent in the first message, that must exist by the quantum proof of knowledge property for the sub-protocol. If K' succeeds in recovering the committed keys, K decodes the state received in the first message using these keys and returns the decoded state. Otherwise, K returns an abort symbol "$\perp$". We formalize this sketch in Sect. 5 of the Supplementary Material.

References

[BDSMP91] Blum, M., De Santis, A., Micali, S., Persiano, G.: Noninteractive zero-knowledge. SIAM J. Comput. **20**(6), 1084–1118 (1991)

[BG90] Bellare, M., Goldwasser, S.: New paradigms for digital signatures and message authentication based on non-interactive zero knowledge proofs. In: Brassard, G. (ed.) CRYPTO 1989. LNCS, vol. 435, pp. 194–211. Springer, New York (1990). https://doi.org/10.1007/0-387-34805-0_19

[BG92] Bellare, M., Goldreich, O.: On defining proofs of knowledge. In: Brickell, E.F. (ed.) CRYPTO 1992. LNCS, vol. 740, pp. 390–420. Springer, Heidelberg (1993). https://doi.org/10.1007/3-540-48071-4_28

[BG19] Broadbent, A., Grilo, A.B.: Zero-knowledge for QMA from locally simulatable proofs (2019)

[BJSW16] Broadbent, A., Ji, Z., Song, F., Watrous, J.: Zero-knowledge proof systems for QMA. In: 2016 IEEE 57th Annual Symposium on Foundations of Computer Science (FOCS), pp. 31–40. IEEE (2016)

[BMW03] Bellare, M., Micciancio, D., Warinschi, B.: Foundations of group signatures: formal definitions, simplified requirements, and a construction based on general assumptions. In: Biham, E. (ed.) EUROCRYPT 2003. LNCS, vol. 2656, pp. 614–629. Springer, Heidelberg (2003). https://doi.org/10.1007/3-540-39200-9_38

[CLW19] Canetti, R., Lombardi, A., Wichs, D.: Fiat-Shamir: from practice to theory, part II (2019)

[Com14] Electric Coin Company. Zcash Cryptocurrency (2014)

[CP92] Chaum, D., Pedersen, T.P.: Wallet databases with observers. In: Brickell, E.F. (ed.) CRYPTO 1992. LNCS, vol. 740, pp. 89–105. Springer, Heidelberg (1993). https://doi.org/10.1007/3-540-48071-4_7

[DL09] Damgaard, I., Lunemann, C.: Quantum-secure coin-flipping and applications. arXiv e-prints, arXiv:0903.3118, March 2009

[GGPR13] Gennaro, R., Gentry, C., Parno, B., Raykova, M.: Quadratic span programs and succinct NIZKs without PCPs. In: Johansson, T., Nguyen, P.Q. (eds.) EUROCRYPT 2013. LNCS, vol. 7881, pp. 626–645. Springer, Heidelberg (2013). https://doi.org/10.1007/978-3-642-38348-9_37

[GMR85] Goldwasser, S., Micali, S., Rackoff, C.: The knowledge complexity of interactive proof-systems. In: Proceedings of the Seventeenth Annual ACM Symposium on Theory of Computing, STOC 1985, pp. 291–304. ACM, New York (1985)

[GO94] Goldreich, O., Oren, Y.: Definitions and properties of zero-knowledge proof systems. J. Cryptol. **7**(1), 1–32 (1994). https://doi.org/10.1007/BF00195207

[Kob02] Kobayashi, H.: Non-interactive quantum statistical and perfect zero-knowledge. arXiv e-prints, quant-ph/0207158, July 2002

[Lab17] O(1) Labs. Coda Cryptocurrency (2017)

[Mah18] Mahadev, U.: Classical verification of quantum computations. In: 2018 IEEE 59th Annual Symposium on Foundations of Computer Science (FOCS), pp. 259–267. IEEE (2018)

[NY90] Naor, M., Yung, M.: Public-key cryptosystems provably secure against chosen ciphertext attacks. In: Proceedings of the Twenty-second Annual ACM Symposium on Theory of Computing, STOC 1990, pp. 427–437. ACM, New York (1990)

[PHGR13] Parno, B., Howell, J., Gentry, C., Raykova, M.: Pinocchio: nearly practical verifiable computation. In: 2013 IEEE Symposium on Security and Privacy, pp. 238–252. IEEE (2013)

[PS19] Peikert, C., Shiehian, S.: Noninteractive zero knowledge for NP from (plain) learning with errors. IACR Cryptology ePrint Archive 2019:158 (2019)

[Sah99] Sahai, A.: Non-malleable non-interactive zero knowledge and adaptive chosen-ciphertext security. In: Proceedings of the 40th Annual Symposium on Foundations of Computer Science, FOCS 1999, p. 543. IEEE Computer Society, Washington, DC (1999)

[Sho95] Shor, P.W.: Polynomial-time algorithms for prime factorization and discrete logarithms on a quantum computer. arXiv e-prints, quant-ph/9508027, August 1995

[Unr12] Unruh, D.: Quantum proofs of knowledge. In: Pointcheval, D., Johansson, T. (eds.) EUROCRYPT 2012. LNCS, vol. 7237, pp. 135–152. Springer, Heidelberg (2012). https://doi.org/10.1007/978-3-642-29011-4_10

[Unr15] Unruh, D.: Non-interactive zero-knowledge proofs in the quantum random oracle model. In: Oswald, E., Fischlin, M. (eds.) EUROCRYPT 2015. LNCS, vol. 9057, pp. 755–784. Springer, Heidelberg (2015). https://doi.org/10.1007/978-3-662-46803-6_25

[VZ19] Vidick, T., Zhang, T.: Classical zero-knowledge arguments for quantum computations. arXiv e-prints, arXiv:1902.05217, February 2019

[Wat09] Watrous, J.: Zero-knowledge against quantum attacks. SIAM J. Comput. **39**(1), 25–58 (2009)

Author Index

Printed in the United States
By Bookmasters